THE GRANTS REGISTER
1983-1985

Editors
Craig Alan Lerner
Roland Turner

M

ISBN 978-1-349-04975-2   ISBN 978-1-349-04973-8 (eBook)
DOI 10.1007/978-1-349-04973-8

Copyright © by Macmillan Publishers Ltd., 1982
Softcover reprint of the hardcover 1st edition 1982
All rights reserved. No part of this publication may be reproduced or transmitted in any form or by any means, without permission.

First published by MACMILLAN PUBLISHERS LTD.
(Journals Division) 1982

Editor's Note

The Grants Register is primarily intended for students at or above the graduate level and for all who require further professional or advanced vocational training. The following kinds of assistance—from government agencies, and international, national or private organizations—are listed:

1. Scholarships, Fellowships and Research Grants.

2. Exchange Opportunities, Vacation Study Awards and Travel Grants.

3. Grants-in-Aid—including equipment, publication and translation grants, and funds for attending seminars, courses, conferences, etc.

4. Grants for all kinds of artistic or scientific projects.

5. Competitions, Prizes and Honoraria—including awards in recognition or support of creative work.

6. Professional and Vocational Awards—including opportunities for academic and administrative staff of educational institutions.

7. Special Awards—for refugees, minority groups, etc., and funds for students in unexpected financial difficulties.

No attempt is made to list awards that are solely sponsored by a particular university or college as such awards are already well-publicized.

The Grants Register aims to provide full, current information on awards for nationals of the United States and Canada, the United Kingdom and Ireland, Australia and New Zealand, South Africa and the developing countries. However, as many of the awards listed are international in scope, the book is also useful to students from other countries who are seeking exchange opportunities or international scholarships.

In this eighth edition, the Subject Index has been further refined so that users may more quickly locate all the awards for which they may be eligible. All other sections of the book have been fully revised.

A new edition of *The Grants Register* appears every two years. The ninth edition will be available in Autumn 1984.

We are extremely grateful to all the organizations listed in *The Grants Register* and to the many agencies, embassies, colleges and universities that have so readily offered information and advice. The generous cooperation we have received has greatly assisted us in our aim to provide a detailed and comprehensive survey of awards.

—Craig Alan Lerner
—Roland Turner

TABLE OF CONTENTS

How to Use *The Grants Register* ix

Subject Index xi

    1: All Subjects xi

    2: Creative & Applied Arts xi

    3: Humanities & Social Sciences xiv

    4: Natural & Mathematical Sciences xx

    5: Applied Sciences, Technology & Engineering xxiii

    6: Medical & Health Sciences xxvi

    7: Agriculture & Veterinary Science xxix

    8: Natural Resources & Environment Protection xxx

    9: Education & Teaching xxx

    10: Social Development & Welfare xxxi

    11: Professions & Occupations xxxiii

The Awards 1

Index of Awards and Awarding Bodies 827

Bibliography 865

How to Use the Grants Register

All awards may be located through the Subject Index (page xi). Numbers listed in the Subject Index refer to the code numbers at the head of each entry in the main text.

To ascertain which numbers are applicable, readers should consult the Index Codes below, and then turn to the Subject Index and make a note of all relevant numbers under Section 1 (All Subjects) and under other appropriate Sections. It is necessary to note the numbers under *General* (which appears directly after the heading of each Section) *as well as* the numbers of specific subjects applicable to the reader.

Readers who wish to locate an award by name, or the awards of a particular organization by its name, should refer to the Index of Awards and Awarding Bodies, page 827.

Index Codes

AA	Australasia	ME	Middle East
AC	American Continent	MX	Mexico
AF	Africa	NA	North Africa
AFS	Southern Africa	NE	Near East
AR	Arab countries	NI	Northern Ireland
AS	Asia	NZ	New Zealand
AU	Australia	PC	Pacific
CA	Canada	PH	Philippines
CB	Caribbean	PN	Pakistan
CW	Commonwealth	REF	Refugees
DC	Developing countries (and Third World)	SA	South Africa
		SAM	South America
EA	East Africa	SC	Scotland
EE	Eastern Europe	SEA	Southeast Asia
EN	England	SPC	South Pacific
ES	English-speaking	UK	United Kingdom
EU	Europe	US	United States
FE	Far East	WA	Wales
IN	India	WAF	West Africa
IR	Ireland (Eire)	WE	Western Europe
IS	Israel	WH	Western Hemisphere
JE	Jews	ZB	Zimbabwe
LA	Latin America		

m—men only   w—women only

Please note:

Numbers listed in bold are for nationals of all countries.

AUSTRALIAN citizens/residents should note relevant bold numbers and those with the suffix AU or CW

CANADIAN citizens/residents should note relevant bold numbers and those with the suffix CA or CW

IRISH citizens/residents should note relevant bold numbers and those with the suffix IR or EU or WE

NEW ZEALAND citizens/residents should note relevant bold numbers and those with the suffix NZ or CW

SOUTH AFRICAN citizens/residents should note relevant bold numbers and those with the suffix SA

UNITED KINGDOM citizens/residents should note relevant bold numbers and those with the suffix UK or CW or EN (English only) or NI (Northern Ireland citizens only) or SC (Scots only) or WA (Welsh only)

UNITED STATES citizens/residents should note relevant bold numbers and those with the suffix US

Nationals of DEVELOPING COUNTRIES should note relevant bold numbers and those with the suffix DC

SUBJECT INDEX

ALL SUBJECTS and CREATIVE & APPLIED ARTS

See How to Use The Grants Register, page ix

Section 1

ALL SUBJECTS: 9-DC, 11-AF, 15-AF-AS-DC, **62**-w, 94-IS-US, 112-US (Am-Indian), 153, 168 + 169-US, 210 + 211-UK, 213-UK, 214-JE, 215-UK, **248**, 249-AS, 256-AF, 266-CW, 267 + 268-SEA, 278-CA, 280-286-CA, 288-295-CA, 309-AU, 310-AU, 314 + 315-AU, **323-326**-w, 339-AU, 361-AF-ZB, 362-US, **393** excl. UK, 394-UK, **395**, 396-EE-UK, 397-UK-China, 398-UK, 401-IR-UK, **403**-w, **440**, **442**-w, 443-w-US, 448-w-LA, **449**-w, 467-CA, 469-CW, 477-CA, 492-DC, 509-CA, 532 + 533-DC, **539**, 559-AU, **560**, 561-UK, 578-AS-DC, 587-CW, 588-AU-NZ-UK, 592 + 593-DC (CW), 614-EU-IR-UK, 621-US, **622**, 651-AU-CA-DC-EU-IN-IR-IS-UK, **652**, 664-EU, 665-667-AU, 668-AU-NZ, 669 + 670-CA-NZ-UK, 671-CW excl. AU, 673-EU, 674-NI, 675-EN-WA, 686-AF-PC, 689-NZ, 701-SA, 712-AU, 745-DC, 750-SA, **754** excl. US, 758 + 765-UK, 767 + 768-AU, 769-US, **794**, 795-EU-IR-UK, **801**, **802**, 803-CW, 812-EU-UK, **813**-w, **852**, 853-SA, 857-NZ, **858**, 866-AU, 872-AF-AS-EU-IR-UK, 878-EU-IR-PH-UK, 879-CA-US, 896-EU-IR-UK, 902-UK, 903-US, 934-UK, 937-EU-IR-UK-US, 954-US, **986**, **1063** + **1064** excl. US, 1065-US, **1066** excl. US, 1068-1070-US, **1073**excl. US, 1118 + 1119-US, **1134** excl. US, 1142-DC, 1145-CA, 1152-UK, 1153-EU-IR-UK, 1159-WA, 1172-US, 1189-UK, 1191-CA, 1194-AU-NZ-SPC, 1195-AU, 1199-CA-US, 1201-US, **1203**, 1215-AU, 1221-1224-UK, 1242-US, **1258**, 1259-US, 1310-CA, **1313**, 1314-DC, 1315-US, 1313-AU-CA-EU-IN-IR-IS-UK-US, **1318**, 1320 + 1321-US, **1323**, **1327**, 1329-EU-UK-US, 1332-AU-EU-IN-NZ-PN-UK-US, **1333**, **1334**, 1335-US, 1338-CW, **1341**, **1342**, 1343-IR-UK, **1345**, 1346 + 1352 + 1353-DC, **1354**, 1355 + 1357-US, **1359**, 1360-AU-CA-EU-IS-SA-UK-US, **1362**, 1365-EU-IN-IR-MX-SA-UK-US, **1366**, **1367**, 1380, **1406**, 1442-US (Blacks), 1443-AU-CA-EU-NZ-UK, 1529-UK, 1530-FE-IN, 1531-UK, 1534-SEA, 1560-SA, 1571 + 1573-CW, 1575-w-NZ, 1607-w-UK, 1614-SA-ZB, 1618-LA-US, **1633**-w-excl. US + CA, 1676 + 1691-UK, 1710-w-UK, 1721-AU-CA-CB-IN-NZ-PN-SA-US-ZB, 1727-US, **1728**, **1730**, 1820-UK, **1828**, 1834-EN-SC, **1837**, 1838-IR, 1839-US, 1862 + 1865-SC, 1885-CW-UK, 1889-SC, 1892-UK, 1928-CA, 1948-IR, **1960**-w, 1961-w-SA, **1962**-w, 1963 + 1964-w-SA, 1967 + 1970-SA, **1986**, 1998-UK, 2009-SA, 2014-CA-EU-UK, 2015-IR-UK-WE, **2016**, 2038-UK, 2058-US, 2073-Namibia-SA, 2076-AS-PC, **2082** (Refugees), 2085-CA, **2093** (Refugees), **2094**, 2097 + 2101-NZ, **2108**, **2111**, 2113-SA, **2114**-w, 2123-US, **2135**, 2182-DC (Refugees), 2202 + 2203-w-AU

Section 2

CREATIVE & APPLIED ARTS

General: 27-US, 35-IS, 39-US, 45-US, 212 + 213-UK, 244-IR, 245-UK, 247-NI, 250-AS-US, 310-AU, **442**-w, **453**, 454-456-CA, 597-DC (CW), 880-CW-IR-UK, **921**, **1045**, 1151-IS, 1172-US, 1193-US, 1196-UK, 1221-UK, 1247-US, 1260-AU, **1302**, 1322-CW, **1334**, 1337-DC, **1347**, **1364**, 1375-w-US, 1435-US, 1691-UK, 1699-NZ, **1720**, 1780-WA, 1783-CW-NZ-SA-UK, 1786 + 1859 + 1860-SC, 1871-AU, 1884-FE-UK, **1986**, 2113-SA, 2148-WA, **2190**

Applied arts (general): 244-IR, 245-UK, **638**, **921**, 1720

Architecture
  General: 45-US, **62**-w, 114 + 115-US, 116 + 117-CA-US, 227-UK, **228**, 232-AU, 250-AS-US, **262**, 279-CA, 412-NI-UK, 427-CW-UK, 445 + 446-US, 587-CW, **638**, 780-UK, 795-EU-IR-UK, 815-CA-US, **1116**, 1193-US, 1260-AU, 1465 + 1466 + 1729-US, 1745 + 1746-AU, **1773**, 1780-WA, 1785 + 1786-SC, 1884-FE-UK, 2021-CA-EU-UK-US
  Chinese: 806
  Health care facilities: 117-CA-US
  Landscape: 45-US, 795-EU-IR-UK
  Restoration: **941**, 1956-UK
  Also see related subjects in sections 5, 10 & 11.

Ballet: *See* Dance-Ballet.
Cartoon/caricature art: **2012**
Ceramics: **638**, **888**, **1720**
Cinema arts
  General: 3, 4-US, 35-IS, 92-US, 244-IR, 245-UK, 250-AS-US, 327-AU, 386-US, 880-CW-IR-US, 1247-US, 1699-NZ, 1859-SC, 2148-WA

SUBJECT INDEX   *See How to Use The Grants Register, page ix*

Experimental: 245-UK
Film making: 92-US, 245-UK, 327-AU, 455-CA, 749-US, 1859-SC, 2148-WA
Video: 92-US, 245-UK, 455-CA, 880-CW-IR-UK
Creative writing: *See* Writing.
Crafts
  General: 250-AS-US, **453**, **888**, 1780 + 2148-WA
  Blacksmithing: **888**
  Fabric: **638**, **888**
  Glass: **888**, **1720**
  Jewelry: **888**, **1720**
  Metalsmithing: **638**, **888**, **1720**
  Papermaking: **888**
  Pottery: 355-NZ
  Quiltmaking: **888**
  Printing/printmaking: 355-NZ, 412-NI-UK, 427-CW-UK, **638**, 1247-US, **1647** excl. US, 1692-US
  Weaving: **638**, **888**
  Wood: **888**, **1720**
Dance
  General: **3**, 35-IS, 244-IR, 245-UK, 250-AS-US, 386-US, 455 + 456-CA, **545**, 565-AU, **1158**, **1561**, 1699-NZ, 1859-SC, **2011**, 2148-WA
  Ballet: 231-UK, 565-AU, **1044**, 1260-AU, **1561**, 1699-NZ
Design
  General: 45-US, 245-UK, 250-AS-US, **638**, 716-UK, 1151-IS, 1196-UK, 1430-CA, 1464-US, **1720**
  Ceramic: 1430-CA
  Furniture: 1430-CA, **1720**
  Graphic: *See* Graphic arts.
  Industrial: *See section 5.*
  Interior: 1464-US
  Lighting: 245-UK
  Lyric theatre: 245-UK
  Textile: 1430-CA, 2033-UK
  Theatre: 245-UK, 455-CA
  Also see Design subjects in sections 5 & 11.
Drama: *See* Theatre arts.
Drawing: 864, 1672, 1995-US, **2012**
Film arts: *See* Cinema arts.
Fine arts (general): 244-IR, 245-UK, 279-CA, 287-CA, 307-AU, 386-US, **453**, 455 + 456 + 509-CA, **545**, **638**, 815-CA-US, 864, 921, 1193 + 1247-US, **1302**, 1319-EU-IN-IS-UK, **1364**, 1859-SC, 1981-SEA, 2086-US, **2111**
Graphic arts: 746 + 747-US, **888**, 1430-CA, 1467 excl. US, 2032-US
Holography: 880-CW-IR-UK
Illustration
  Book: 381-US, 454-CA, 1577-NZ, **1672**, 2041-CW-UK
  Cartoon: **1672**, 2087-US

Mime: 245-UK, 1859-SC
Mosaic: **1056**
Music
  General: **3**, 8-IS, 35-IS, 39-US, 183-US, 231-UK, 244-IR, 245 + 246-UK, 250-AS-US, 254-AF-CW-FE-IN-NZ-SA-ZB, 279 + 287-CA, 307-AU, **451**, **517**, **570**, 637-CW-UK, **642**, **653**, **740**, 815-CA-US, **1046**, **1055**, 1110, 1193-US, **1251**, **1260**-AU, **1393**, 1646-US, 1699-NZ, 1783-CW-NZ-SA-UK, **1784**, **1827**, **1836**, 1859-SC, **1883**, 1884-FE-UK, 1890 + 1891-SC, 1982-AFS-SA-ZB, 2086-US, **2111**, 2148-WA, 2188-UK
  Chamber: 569-UK
  Church: **1564** excl. US
  Composition: 45-US, **46**, 77-US, 244-IR, 245 + 246-UK, **365**, 432-CA-LA-US-WH, **451**, **529**, **550**, 569-UK, 602-CA, **653**, 815-CA-US, **909**, **1076**, **1078**, **1239**, 1247-US, 1295-IR-UK, 1299-UK, 1612 + 1646-US, **1687**, **1690**, 1694-US, **1697**, **1700**, **1831**, 1859-SC, 1863-UK, 1881-AC, 1982-AFS-SA-ZB, **1983**, **2008**, **2110**, **2127**, **2129**, **2130**, 2148-WA, **2159**, 2188-UK, **2192**
  Conducting: **365**, **550**, **1077**, 1646-US, 2188-UK
  Contemporary: 880-CW-IR-UK, **909**
  History: *See Section 3.*
  Instrumental: 77-US, 245 + 246-UK, 337-AU, **351**, **365**, 376-IR-UK, **450**, **517**, **528**, **529**, **545**, **550**, **556**, **563**, **603**, **641**, 649-US, **740**, **775**, **814**, 815-CA-US, **868**, 904-UK, **935**, **1036**, **1074**, **1078**, **1091**, **1092**, **1109**, **1111**, **1131**, 1200-US, **1214**, **1234**, **1237**, **1239**, **1250**, **1251**, 1261-UK, **1377**, **1379**, **1381**, 1383-UK, **1392**, **1393**, 1439-UK, **1487**, **1557**, **1565**, **1620**, **1634**, 1646-US, **1685**, **1697**, 1780-WA, 1813-CW-UK, **1840**, **1878**, **1880**, 1979-SA, **1993**, **2022**, **2030**, **2031**, **2045**, 2086-US, **2107**, **2117**, **2120**, **2129**, 2148-WA, **2159**, 2188-UK, 2199 + 2200-US, **2201**
  Jazz/folk/ethnic: 77-US, 245-UK
  Musicology: *See Section 3.*
  Performance: 245 + 246-UK, 376-IR-UK, **528**, **603**, **641**, **775**, **909**, **935**, **1074**, **1075**, **1078**, **1109**, **1112**, **1131**, **1234**, **1250**, **1379**, 1383-UK, **1393**, **1557**, **1620**, 1646-US, 1783-CW-NZ-SA-UK, **1836**, **1878**, **1880**, 1891-SC, 1982-AFS-SA-ZB, **1993**, **2022**, **2034**-w-UK, **2045**, **2117**, **2120**, **2128**, **2134**, 2188-UK, 2199 + 2200-US, **2201**
  Teaching: **570**
  Violin-making: **2159**
  Vocal: 77-US, 209-UK, 245 + 246-UK, 337-AU, **351**, **365**, 376-IR-UK, **517**, **545**, **550**, 565-AU-NZ, **603**, 649-US, **837**, **1036**, **1079**, **1109**, **1111**, **1112**, **1126**, **1127**, 1200-US, **1239**, 1260-AU, **1377**, 1383-UK, **1392**, **1393**, 1439-UK,

xii

SUBJECT INDEX   *See How to Use The Grants Register, page ix*

1640, 1646-US, 1780-WA, 1783-CW-NZ-SA-UK, **1784**, 1813-CW-UK, **1840**, 1864-SC, **2031**, 2034-w-UK, **2128**, **2129**, **2134**, 2148-WA, 2199-US
Opera: 231-UK, 244-IR, 245-UK, **550**, **1079**, 1303, 1486 + 1612-US, 1864-SC, 2154-US, **2201**
Also see **Opera administration** *in Section 11*.
Painting
  General: 32-US, 45-US, 232-AU, 245-UK, 250-AS-US, 412-NI-UK, 427-CW-UK, **436**, 455 + 456 + 509-CA, **638**, 811-US, **864**, 873, 1247-US, 1260-AU, **1302**, 1400-US, **1647** excl. US, **1720**, 1783-CW-NZ-SA-UK, 1785 + 1786 + 1859-SC, 1995-US, 2040-US, 2110-NZ, **2130**, 2148-WA, **2190**
  Portrait: 847-w-AU
Performing arts: 245-UK, 880-CW-IR-UK, **921**, 1201-US, 1260-AU, 1859-SC
Also see **Theatre arts**.
Photography: 3, 245-UK, 250-AS-US, 455-CA, **638**, **888**, 1151-IS, 1197-UK, **1672**, 1692-US, 1720, 1780-WA, 1786-SC, **2130**
Plastic arts (general): 35-IS
Poetry: *See* **Writing—Poetry**.
Puppetry: 3
Sculpture: 32-US, 45-US, 232-AU, 245-UK, 250-AS-US, 355-NZ, 412-NI-UK, 427-CW-UK, **436**, 455 + 456-CA, **638**, 811-US, **873**, 1247-US, 1260-AU, **1302**, **1647** excl. US, **1720**, 1785 + 1786 + 1859-SC, 2040-US, 2110-NZ, **2130**, 2148-WA, **2192**
Television arts: 3, 35-IS
Also see **Broadcasting** *in Section 11*.
Theatre arts
  General: 3, 35-IS, 73-US, 231-UK, 245-UK, 250-AS-US, 386-US, 650-US, 880-CW, IR-UK, 1486 + 1731-US, 1859-SC, 2148-WA
  Costumes/wigmaking: 245-UK
  Musical theatre: 245-UK, 1612-US
  Scenery/properties: 245-UK
  Stage management: 245-UK
  Theatre technician work: 245-UK
Also see **Performing arts** *and* **Writing—Plays**.
Visual arts (general): 244-IR, 245-UK, **864**, **1449**, 1699-NZ, **2192**
Writing
  General: 8-IS, 39-US, 45-US, **203**, 217-AU-NZ, 244-IR, 245-UK, 308-AU, 354-IR, 374-JE, **387**, **437**, 442-w, 454-AU-CA, 455 + 456-CA, 464-CA, 523-US, 542-SA, **612**, 690-692-NZ, **731**, 761-ES-SA-ZB, 886-US, 887-UK, 912-UK, 1149-IR, **1157**, **1167**, 1190-UK, **1210**, 1247-US, 1253-NZ, 1260-AU, **1410**, **1563**, 1630-US, 1632-ZB, **1672**, **1722**, 1859-SC, 1942-UK, **2130**, 2142-NZ, 2148-WA, **2190**, **2192**

Autobiography: 379-IR-UK, 1176-CA-JE-US, 1694-US, **1722**, 2148-WA
Biography: 184-CA-US, 308-AU, **371**, 379-IR-UK, 542-SA, 609-UK, **1241**, 1463-US, 1694-US, **1722**, 1937-US, 1942-UK, 2148-WA
Children's books: 379-IR-UK, 381-US, **387**, 454-AU-CA, 460-CA, 552-UK, 629-NZ, 874-CW-UK, **1117**, 1176-CA-JE-US, 1568-US, 1577-NZ, 2041-CW-UK
Cookbooks: 833-US
Creative: 220-US, 245-UK, 308-AU, **437**, 454-AU-CA, **723**, 761-ES-SA-ZB, **762**, 871-UK, 887-UK, **1210**, 1254-NZ, 1631-NZ, **1722**, 1815-CA, 1859-SC, 1898-CW-UK, 2096-UK, 2110-NZ
Criticism: 184-CA-US, **1252**, 1373-US, **1449**, 1942-UK, 2087-US, 2121-EU, 2148-WA
Also see **Art criticism**, **Literature—Dramatic criticism**, *and* **Literature—Literary criticism**, *Section 3*.
Essays: 106-US, 184-CA-US, 1176-CA-JE-US, 2087-US, 2121-EU, 2148-WA, 2153-US.
Fiction: 245-UK, 308-AU, **387**, 454-AU-CA, 460-CA, 691-NZ, 761-ES-SA-ZB, 796-CW-IR-SA-UK, 884-US, **920**, 1147-US, 1176-CA-JE-US, **1210**, 1288-US, **1410**, 1630-US, **1722**, 1859-SC, 1942-UK, 1985-US, 2025-AU, **2177**, **2198**
Journalism: *See Section 11*.
Libretto: 1612-US
Literature: 39-US, 244-IR, 308-AU, 454-AU-CA, 690-692-NZ, **731**, 1148 + 1149-IR, 1185-EA, 1241-US, **1252**, **1410**, **1592**, 1780-WA, 1815-CA, 1821-CW-IR-UK, 1859-SC, 1898-CW-UK, 2025-AU, 2110 + 2142-NZ, **2177**
Non-fiction: **387**, 454-AU-CA, 460-CA, 542-SA, 691-NZ, **731**, 761-ES-SA-ZB, 886-US, **908**, **920**, 1176-CA-JE-US, 1288-US, **1391**, **1410**, 1463-US, **1621**, 1694-US, **1696**, 1708-NZ, **1711**, 1815-CA, 1942-UK, 1958 + 1985-US, 2025-AU, 2041-CW-UK, **2189**, **2198**
Novels: 245-UK, 308-AU, **371**, 379-IR-UK, 542-SA, **723**, 826-AU, 874-CW-UK, 1115-SC, 1374-AFS, **1410**, 1630-US, 1821-CW-IR-UK, 1859-SC, 2148-WA
Plays: 73-US, 245-UK, 308-AU, 460-CA, 542-SA, 691-NZ, **1210**, 1288 + 1562 + 1611-US, **1711**, **1722**, 1780-WA, 1859-SC, 1867-US, **2035**, **2169**, **2177**
Poetry: 1 + 2-US, 245-UK, 308-AU, 377-US, **387**, 454-AU-CA, 460-CA, 542-SA, 609-UK, 691-NZ, 796-CW-IR-SA-UK, 1176-CA-JE-US, **1210**, 1260-AU, 1288-US, **1410**, 1440 + 1630-US, 1631-NZ, **1641**, 1673-US, **1674**, 1675-US, 1694-US, **1711**, **1722**, 1780-WA, 1942-UK, 2131-US, 2148-WA, **2177**, **2189**, 2194-US

Prose: 245-UK, 460-CA, 691-NZ, 796-CW-IR-SA-UK, 811-US, 838-US, 1185-EA, **1210**, 1260-AU, 1631-NZ
Short stories: 245-UK, **302**, 308-AU, 356-w-NZ, 460-CA, 542-SA, 763-CW-IR-SA-UK, 1147-US, **1210**, 1374-AFS, **1410**, 1630-US, **1641**, 1859-SC, 2131-US, 2148-WA, **2189**
Travel: 1410

Section 3

HUMANITIES & SOCIAL SCIENCES

Humanities (general): 10-SA, 33-DC-w, 45-US, 79-US, 81-83-US, 85-US, 123-US, 145-CA-US, 212-UK, 250-AS-US, 274-CA, 308-AU, 310-312-AU, **357**, 366-UK, 388-UK, 389-EU-UK, 390-UK, 454-CA, 476 + 477 + 479-CA, 492-DC, **535**, **539**, 587-CW, 597-DC (CW), **652**, 658-US, 662-AU, 676-EN-WA, 680 + 681-EN-WA, **801**, **921**, 926-932-SA, 946-CA, **961**, 964-US, 999-US, **1045**, 1065-US, **1083**, **1089** + **1090**-w, 1118-1120 + 1122 + 1123-US, **1160**, **1161**, **1164**, **1165**, 1166-AS, 1170-US, 1172-US, 1196-UK, 1201-US, 1221-UK, 1242 + 1243-US, **1258**, 1322-CW, **1323**, **1325**, **1328**, **1334**, 1334-DC, 1351-IN-IR-IS-UK, **1363**, 1435-1438-US, 1441 + 1442-US (Blacks), 1527-US, **1556**, **1581**, **1582**, 1583-US, 1585-w-US, **1603**, 1694-US, 1677-CA, 1691-UK, 1693-CA, 1721-AU-CA-CB-IN-NZ-PN-SA-US-ZB, **1725**, 1779-IR, 1814 + 1815-CA, 1837-US, 1860-SC, 1869 + 1870-CA, 1871-AU, **1879**, 1913-1921-CA-US, **1922**, 1923-CA-US, 1924-AF (North)-ME, 1925-CA-US, **1926**, 1928-1936-CA, **1986**, **2064**, **2077**, **2078**, 2098-NZ, **2115**-w, **2162**
Also see **Cultural/ethnic studies.**

Social sciences (general): 10-SA, 33-DC-w, 45-US, 79-US, 81-83-US, 85-US, 122 + 123-US, 212-UK, 250-AS-US, 274-CA, 308-AU, 310-312-AU, 357, 388-UK, 389-EU-UK, 390-UK, 454-CA, 476 + 477 + 479-CA, 492 + 493-DC, **539**, 587-CW, 597-DC (CW), 619-EU-IR-UK, **652**, 654-UK, 658-US, 662-AU, 674-NI, 682-CA, 712-AU, 736-US, 744-IR, 792-EU-IR-UK, 798-US, **801**, 831-w-CA, 854-US, **877**, **921**, 926-932-SA, 946-CA, **962**, 964-US, 1000-US, **1031**, **1045**, 1065-US, **1089** + **1090**-w, 1104-DC, 1118-1120 + 1122 + 1123-US, **1144**, 1150-CA-US, **1160**, **1161**, **1164**, **1165**, 1166-AS, 1170-US, 1172-US, 1182-UK, 1201-US, **1205**, 1221-UK, 1242 + 1243-US, **1258**, 1269-NZ, 1322-CW, 1323, 1328, 1337-DC, 1351-IN-IR-IS-UK, **1363**, 1437-US, 1441 + 1442-US (Blacks), 1497 + 1520 + 1521-US, **1581**, **1582**, 1583-US, 1585-w-US, 1586 + 1587-US, **1603**, 1605-UK, 1610-US, 1628-UK, **1671**, **1678**, 1691-UK, 1693-CA, 1721-AU-CA-CB-IN-NZ-PN-SA-US-ZB, 1779-IR, 1814 + 1815-CA, 1837-US, 1848 + 1857-UK, 1869 + 1870-CA, 1871-AU, **1879**, **1882**, 1905-1911-UK, 1912-US, 1913-1921-CA-US, **1922**, 1923-CA-US, 1924-AF (North)-ME, 1925-CA-US, **1926**, 1928-1936-CA, 1958-US, 1968-SA, **1986**, 1999-US, 2042-CA-LA-US, **2064**, **2077**, **2078**, 2084-DC, 2100 + 2104-NZ, **2115**-w, **2162**
Also see Section 10.

Humanities & Social Sciences (area studies)— including Cultural/ethnic studies by area.
  Aboriginal: 328, 662-AU
  African: 13, **1006**, 1442-US (Blacks), **1621**, 1900, 1913 + 1918-CA-US, 2113-SA
  African (North): 1916 + 1923-CA-US
  Albanian: 84-US
  American: **50**, 52-US, 250-AS-US, **452**, 588-AU-NZ-UK, 829 + 975 + 976-US, **1066** + **1134** excl. US, **1900**, **1901**, **1903**, **2162**
  American Indian: 1580-US
  American Jewish: 2195 + 2197-US
  Asian: 250-AU-US, 738-AS-PC-US, 1242-US, 1914-CA-US
  Asian (East): **2162**
  Asian (South): 1925-CA-US
  Asian (Southeast): 1001-AS-AU-SEA-UK, 1003-SEA, **1926**
  Australian: 310-AU
  Balkan: 965-UK
  Belgian: 278-CA
  Bolivian: 1336-US
  British: 1959-UK
  Bulgarian: 84-US, 1118-US
  Canadian: 713-CA, 1485-CA, 1815-CA
  Canadian Eskimo: 688-CA
  Canadian (Northern): 991-CA
  Caribbean: **1031**, 1715-US, 1915-CA-US, **1922**
  Celtic: **727**, 1265-SC
  Chinese: 80-CA-US, 279-CA, 307-AU, 312-AU, 919-CA-US
  Chinese (Taiwan): **555**, **1331**
  Czechoslovakian: 84-US, 1118-US
  Eastern (Middle): 203, 1442-US (Blacks), 1916 + 1923-CA-US
  Eastern (Near): 172 + 173-US, 1916 + 1923-CA-US
  European: 574, 784 + 795-EU-IR-UK, 964-US, 1684-IR-EU-UK
  European (East): 1118 + 1122 + 1123-US

SUBJECT INDEX *See How to Use The Grants Register, page ix*

European (West): 1917-CA-US
European Jewish: 2195-US
French: 409-CW-IR-UK, 830-CA-US, 834-US
Finnish: 1317
German: 896-EU-IR-UK
German (East): 84-US, 1118-US
Greek: 872-AF-AS-EU-IR-UK, 965-UK, 1319-EU-IN-IS-UK
Hungarian: 84 + 936-US, 1118-US
Ibero American: 2042-CA-LA-US
Icelandic: 1311
Indian: 951-AF-AS-IN, 1869 + 1870-CA, 1914 + 1925-CA-US
Iranian: 410-CW-UK
Israeli: 203, 213-UK, 758-UK, 1176-CA-JE-US
Italian: 45-US, 425-CW-UK, 1347
Italian-American: 130-US
Japanese: 248, 310-AU, 974, 1160, 1161, 1920-CA-US
Jewish: 374-JE, 894, 1176-CA-JE-US, 1293 + 1294-JE
Korean: 1921-CA-US
Latin America: 722-US, 1031, 1915-CA-US, 1922, 2162
Maori: 1699-NZ
Mediterranean: 720
Mexican: 1325
Norwegian: 288-CA, 1132, 1351-IN-IR-IS-UK
Oriental: 172 + 173-US, 1258
Pakistani: 1696, 1914 + 1925-CA-US
Persian: 410-CW-UK
Polish: 84-US, 1118-US, 1172-US, 1198-US, 1199-CA-US, 1201-US, 1676-UK
Polish American: 1198 + 1201-US
Portuguese: 997
Romanian: 84-US, 1118-US
Saudi Arabian: 1188
Scandinavian: 1132
South African/Jewish: 1246-JE-SA
South Pacific: 1699-NZ
Soviet: 1122 + 1123-US, 2162
Spanish: 216-UK, 1170-US
Turkish: 166, 1334
Yugoslavian: 84-US, 801, 1118-US
Anthropology
  General: 536, 953, 1170-US, 1233-UK, 1368, 1678, 1738-CW-IR-UK, 1740, 1823, 1901, 1903, 2088-IS-US, 2112-US, 2149, 2150
  Aboriginal: 328, 662-AU
  African: 13, 1006, 2028
  Biological: 1739
  Caribbean: 1715-US
  European (East): 1120-US
  European (West): 1917-CA-US
  Oriental: 172 + 173-US
  Prehistoric: 172 + 173-US

Social: 328, 1905-1911-UK, 2113-SA
Soviet: 1120-US
Spanish: 1170-US
Antiquities: 392-UK, 425 + 426-CW-UK, 1155, 1939-UK
Applied social sciences: *See* General & Section 10.
Archaeology
  General: 45-US, 171-IS-US, 250-AS-US, 279-CA, 307-AU, 390-UK, 392-UK, 536, 613-UK, 961, 1437-US, 1779-IR, 1903, 1939-UK, 1981-SEA
  African: 408, 1006, 1670
  American: 250-AS-US
  Anatolian: 407-CW-UK
  Asian: 250-AS-US
  Bolivian: 1336-US
  Byzantine: 732, 1302
  Canadian: 1485-CA
  Classical: 170-CA-US, 171-IS-US, 2122-CA-US
  Eastern (Middle): 423 + 424-CW-UK, 1151, 1635-UK
  Eastern (Near): 172-174-US, 423 + 424-CW-UK, 1648-UK
  Etruscan: 1155, 1248
  European (East): 1120-US
  Excavation/prospection: 1635-UK, 1216-EU-IR-NA-NE-UK, 1686 + 1939-UK
  Finnish: 1317
  Greek: 170-CA-US, 171-IS-US, 1302, 1319-EU-IN-IS-UK, 1665-w, 2122-CA-US
  Iranian: 410-CW-UK
  Iraqi: 422-CW-UK
  Israeli: 423 + 424-CW-UK, 1151
  Italian: 1302, 2122-CA-US
  Mediterranean: 720
  Oriental: 172-174-US, 1648-UK
  Palestinian: 423 + 424-CW-UK, 1151
  Persian: 410-CW-UK
  Prehistoric: 1686-UK
  Soviet: 1120-US
  Turkish: 406 + 407-CW-UK
  Venetian: 658-US
Art/architecture/historic preservation: 941, 1302, 1527-US, 1903, 1956-UK, 2077, 2078
Art criticism: 1151-IS, 1449, 1859-SC
Arts studies: *See* Humanities (general)
Behavioral science: 201 + 202-US, 272-CA, 535, 730, 877, 1047, 1060, 1205, 1297 + 1298-UK, 1401 + 1497 + 1520-US, 1855-UK, 1992-US
Also see Psychology
Bibliography
  General: 415-UK, 1106, 1437-US
  Early American: 49 + 51
Christianity: *See* Religion.

SUBJECT INDEX *See How to Use The Grants Register, page ix*

Civics: 568-US, 2113-SA
Civilization
  General: **782**, 792-EU-IR-UK, 1886-UK, **2064**
  Aboriginal: 662-AU
  African: 13, **1900**, 2113-SA
  American: **1071** excl. US, **1900**, **1900**, 1903
  Ancient: 425-CW-UK
  Byzantine: 45-US, **732**
  Canadian: 1485-CA
  Caribbean: 1715-US
  Chinese: 80-US, 83-US
  Classical: 170-CA-US
  Contemporary: **1725**
  Etruscan: **1155**, **1248**
  French: 409-CW-IR-UK
  German: 862-CA-EU-IR-UK-US
  Greek: 170-CA-US
  Indian: 1869 + 1870-CA
  Islam: 1916 + 1923-CA-US
  Italian: 425-CW-UK
  Japanese: 248
  Mediaeval: 45-US, 425-CW-UK, 1677-CA
  Mexican: 1325
  Norwegian: 1132
  Pakistani: **1696**
  Pre-Columbian: **732**
  Saudi Arabian: 1188
  Scandinavian: 1132
  Spanish: 216-UK
  Turkish: **166**
Classics: 170 + 2122-CA-US
Also see Civilization, History of art *and* Literature
Criminology: 616-EU-IR-UK, **639**, 1905-1911-UK, 2059-2061-US
Cultural/ethnic studies: **536**, 1437-US, **1725**, 1879
Also see Humanities & Social Sciences (area studies)
Defence studies: 270-CA
Demography/population studies: 738-AS-PC-US, 1099-AS-PC, 1120-US, **1141**, 1183-US, 1326-UK, **1678**, 1709-AF, 1905-1911-UK, 1915-CA-US, 2063-DC
Divinity: *See* Religion.
Economics
  General: 10-SA, **16**, 121-US, 212-UK, 279-CA, 389-EU-IR-UK, 435-US, 479-CA, 525 + 526-SC, 567-US, 568-US, 654-UK, 736-US, 744-IR, **782**, 792-EU-IR-UK, 818, 831-w-CA, 914-US, **966**, **1039**, 1150-CA-US, 1170-US, 1206-CB-LA, 1221 + 1326-UK, 1497-US, 1666-w-CA-US, **1678**, 1698-DC, 1871-AU, 1893-CA-US, 1905-1911-UK, 1927-IS-US-WE, 1978-SA, **2077**, **2078**, 2084-DC, 2088-IS-US
  Business (teaching): 1150-CA-US

Economics education: 568-US, 1169-US
  International: 16, 279-CA, **438**, **647**, **782**, 848-DC, 854-US, **1007**, **1108**, 1192-CA, 1927-IS-US-WE, 2084-DC, 2088-IS-US, 2100-NZ
  Petroleum: 606-UK-US
  Transport: 2111
  Women's employment: 447-US
  Also see related subjects in other sections.
Economics (area studies)
  Aboriginal: 662-AU
  African: 13, **1621**, 1913-CA-US, 2075-AF, 2113-SA
  American: 914-US
  Australian: 1716 + 1717-AU, **1718**
  Belgian: 278-CA
  Canadian: 1485-CA
  Caribbean: 1915-CA-US
  Chinese: 307-AU, 1648-UK, 1920-CA-US
  Developing countries: **882**, **974**, 1348-DC, 1627-UK, 1698 + 2072 + 2084-DC
  European: 574, **782**, 964-US
  European (East): 1120-US
  European (West): 1917-CA-US
  German: 856-US
  Latin American: 1206-CB-LA, 1915-CA-US
  Norwegian: 288-CA, **1132**, 1351-IN-IR-IS-UK
  Scandinavian: 1132
  Soviet: 1120-US
  Spanish: 1170-US
Epigraphy
  General: 172 + 173-US
  Israeli: 424-CW-UK
  Palestinian: 424-CW-UK
Ergonomics: 1855-UK
Ethics: *See* Philosophy—Ethics.
Ethnic studies: *See* Cultural/ethnic studies.
Ethnology: 1905-1911-UK
Also see Humanities & Social Sciences (area studies) *and* Cultural/ethnic studies.
Etruscology: 1155, 1248
Folklore
  General: **536**, **953**
  Aboriginal: 662-AU
  Balkan: 1319-EU-IN-IS-UK
  Bolivian: 1336-US
  Canadian: 1485-CA
  Finnish: 1317
  Jewish: 2195-US
  Norwegian: 288-CA, 1351-IN-IR-IS-UK
Geography: *See* Section 4 *and* Human Geography *(this section)*.
Government: *See* Political science/government.
History
  General: 45-US, 105-CA-LA-UK-US, 106-US, 364-w-CA-US, 380-w-UK, 390-UK, **430**,

xvi

SUBJECT INDEX *See How to Use The Grants Register, page ix*

525 + 526-SC, 568-US, 609-UK, 655-US, 736-US, 792-EU-IR-UK, 914-US, 921, 953, 961, 962, 1192-CA, 1437 + 1570-US, 1664-US, 1722, 1823, 2051-UK, 2077, 2078, 2108-AU, 2162, 2166
Ancient: 425 + 426-CW-UK, 537-US, 2122-CA-US
Catholic: 67-CA-US
Christian: 177-US, 721-EN-WA, 827-UK
Classical: 1319-EU-IN-IS-UK, 2122-CA-US
Diplomatic: 353, 647, 1949-US
Ecclesiastical: 67-CA-US, 177-US
Economics: 585-US, 757, 1905-1911-UK
Eighteenth-century: 184-CA-US
Industrial: 1588-US
Mediaeval: 425 + 426-CW-UK, 1287-CA-US, 1677-CA
Military: 271-CA, 344-AU
Modern: 389-EU-UK, 914-US, 2113-SA
Political: 914-US, 1582
Prehistory: 328
Reformation: 538-US, 981, 982
Social: 1437-US, 1582, 1905-1911-UK
History (area studies)
African: 13, 1900, 1901
African (East): 408, 1006
American: 50, 52-US, 105-CA-LA-UK-US, 107-US, 353, 756, 757, 914-US, 939, 975 + 976 + 1463 + 1617 + 1694-US, 1900, 1903, 1937-US, 2001-w-US, 2138-US, 2162
American Indian: 1580-US
American Jewish: 2195 + 2197-US
American (Southern): 1241 + 1984 + 2069-US
American (Truman administration): 2049
Asian: 105-CA-LA-UK-US
Asian (East): 2162
Australian: 344 + 2002-AU
Australian Aboriginal: 328
Balkan: 965-UK
Belgian: 278-CA
British: 105-CA-LA-UK-US
Byzantine: 732, 1319-EU-IN-IS-UK
Canadian: 477 + 1485 + 1815-CA
Caribbean: 1922
Chinese: 105-CA-LA-UK-US, 279-CA, 307-AU, 1648-UK, 1919-CA-US
Eastern (Near): 172-174-US
English: 939
Etruscan: 1155, 1248
European: 105-CA-LA-UK-US, 784-EU-IR-UK, 964-US, 981, 982
European Jewish: 2195-US
Finnish: 1317
French: 757, 830-CA-US, 834-US, 959-US
French colonial: 832
German: 856-US

Greek (Ancient): 537-US, 1665-w, 2122-CA-US
Greek (Modern): 965-UK, 1319-EU-IN-IS-UK, 1665-w
Icelandic: 1311
Indian: 105-CA-LA-UK-US
Indo-Muslem: 1696
Iranian: 410-CW-UK
Iraqi: 422-CW-UK
Italian: 45-US, 105-CA-LA-UK-US, 425 + 426-CW-UK, 1154, 1155, 1951 + 2122-CA-US
Italian American: 130-US, 605-LA-US
Jewish: 374-JE, 1176-CA-JE-US
Latin American: 105-CA-LA-UK-US, 1922, 2162
Mexican: 1325, 1326-UK
New Zealand: 910-NZ
North American (West): 2153-US
Norwegian: 1132, 1351-IN-IR-IS-UK
Oriental: 172-174-US
Pakistani: 1696
Persian: 410-CW-UK
Polish: 1201-US
Saudi Arabian: 1188
Scottish: 1772
Soviet: 2162
Turkish: 166, 1334
History of architecture
General: 1193 + 1527-US, 1773
Chinese: 806
Mediterranean: 720
Venetian: 658-US
History of art
General: 45-US, 250-AS-US, 279-CA, 307-AU, 390-UK, 392-UK, 856-US, 941, 1302, 1448-US, 1449, 1527-US, 1900, 1901, 1903
African: 1900
American: 250-AS-US
Ancient: 426-CW-UK, 1302
Asian: 250-AS-US
British: 2193
Byzantine: 732, 1302
Caribbean: 1915-CA-US
Chinese: 149 + 150-US, 279-CA, 307-AU, 1920-CA-US
Classical: 2122-CA-US
Dutch: 1448-US
Etruscan: 1155, 1248
Flemish: 1448-US
German: 856-US
Greek: 1302, 2122-CA-US
Italian: 425 + 426-CW-UK, 1155, 1238, 1302, 2122-CA-US
Latin American: 1915-CA-US
Mediaeval: 426-CW-UK
Oriental ceramics: 1619-UK

SUBJECT INDEX *See How to Use The Grants Register, page ix*

Rock art: 328
History of astronomy: 301-AFS
History of aviation: 1899-US
History of business: 1588-US
History of cartography: 1582
History of costume: 1302
History of ideas: 390-UK, **1556**
History of landscape architecture: 732
History of law: 64-US
History of medicine: 2105-CA-US
History of music: 451, 1055, 1646-US, **1883**
History/philosophy of education: **1613**
History/philosophy of science: 390-UK, 911-CA-US, 1498-US, **1900, 1901, 1903, 1905-1911-UK**
History of printing and publishing: 49 + 51
History of technology: 757, **1900, 1901, 1903, 1950**
History of typography: 1106
Human geography: 1815-CA, **1905-1911-UK**
Human relations: *See Section 10.*
International affairs/relations
  General: 161-US, 329-AU, 378-EU-IR-UK-US, 620-US, 736-US, **794**, 854-US, 896-EU-IR-UK, 914-US, 949, **971** excl. IN, 973, 993, 1007, 1144, 1168, 1192-CA, 1221 + **1386**-UK, **1387, 1496, 1576**-NZ, **1610**-US, **1725, 1726** (esp. w-DC-minorities), **1879**, **1905-1911-UK**, 1995-US, 2084-DC, **2092**, 2100-NZ, **2162**
  Agriculture: **1726** (esp. w-DC-minorities)
  Arab-Israeli: 203, 993
  Arms control: 1007
  Australian-foreign: 310-AU, 329-AU
  Australian-Japanese: 310-AU
  Australian-Southeast Asian: 1004-SEA
  Conflicts: **1726** (esp. w-DC-minorities)
  Cultural: 949, **1879, 2077, 2078**
  Diplomacy: 949, 2084-DC
  East Germany: 973
  Eastern Mediterranean: 973
  Energy: **1726** (esp. w-DC-minorities)
  European: 854-US, **1059**
  European integration: 782, 783, 784 + 790 + 795-EU-IR-UK, **1059**, 1348-EU
  Food: **1726** (esp. w-DC-minorities)
  Ibero-American: 2041-CA-LA-US
  Indian: **971** excl. IN
  Industrial: **1905-1911-UK**
  Korean: 973
  Latin American: 1326-UK
  NATO: 1593-CA-UK-US-WE
  Norwegian: 1132
  Ocean territories: 2171
  Peace: 203, 522, 949, **1059**, 1132, **1592**
  Security: **1726** (esp. w-DC-minorities), **2162**
  United States: 435 + 620 + 854 + 914 + 1949-US
  USA-European: 854-US, 914-US
Jurisprudence: *See* **Law—General.**
Language
  General: 385-UK, 390-UK, 849-US, **921, 961, 986**, 1236-UK, 1373-US, 1886-UK, **2077, 2078,** 2108-AU
  Ancient: 828-UK, 2108-AU
  Modern: 525 + 526-SC, 2108-AU
Languages (by area)
  African: 2113-SA
  Arabic: 257-AF
  Bulgarian: 1121-US
  Canadian Eskimo: 688-CA
  Chinese: 80-CA-US, 279-CA, 307-AU, **1331**, 1648-UK
  English: **206** (excl. Eng.-speaking), 257-AF, 713-CA, 753-SA, **794**, 1373-US, 1981-SEA, 2023-SA
  English (teaching): **986**, 1373 + 1428-US
  Esperanto: 2089
  European: 964-US
  Finnish: 1317
  French: 257-AF, 409-CW-IR-UK, 713-CA, **794**, 1665-w
  Gaelic: 1265-SC
  German: 348-US, 856-US, 862-CA-EU-IR-UK-US, **987, 1996**
  Greek (Ancient): **1665**-w
  Greek (Modern): 965-UK, **1665**-w
  Hebrew: 2187-CA-US
  Icelandic: 1311
  Iraqi: 422-CW-UK
  Italian: 1155, 1347
  Japanese: 309-AU, **1323**
  Mediterranean: 720
  Norwegian: 288-CA, 1132
  Polish: 1201 + 1676-UK
  Portugese: 997
  Slavonic: 1121-US, 1676-UK
  Spanish: **794**
  Turkish: 166, **1334**
  Yiddish: 2195 + 2196-US
Language teaching: 1373-US
Language translation: 309-AU, 454-CA, 1437-US, 2047-UK
Law
  General: 62-w, 274-CA, 389-EU-UK, 445 + 446-US, 461-CA, 479-CA, 581-SA, 624-US, 694-697-CA, 792-EU-IR-UK, 914-US, 984-US, 1170-US, 1183-US, 1209 + 1304-US, 1322-CW, 1351-IN-IR-IS-UK, **1380, 1386**-UK, 1436 + 1644-US, 1698-DC, 1871-AU, 1884-FE-UK, 1968 + 1971-SA, 2059-2061-US, 2084-DC, **2094, 2098**+2104-NZ, 2124-AU, 2139-US
  Comparative: 64-US, 617-EU-IR-UK, 696-

SUBJECT INDEX *See How to Use The Grants Register, page ix*

CA, 914-US
Copywriting/licensing: 1080
Enforcement: 445 + 446-US
International: 856-US, **881**, 914-US, **1007**, 1144, 1192-CA, **1387**, **1726** (esp. w-DC-minorities), 2084-DC
Juvenile justice: 2062-US
Legal processes: 158-US
Legislative drafting: 693-CA
Preventive: 439-US
Social: 1905-1911-UK, 1924-AF (North)-ME
Welfare: 2111
Law (area studies)
African (North): 1924-CA-US
American: 64-US
Belgian: 278-CA
British: 64-US
Canadian: 693 + 695-697-CA
Chinese: 1920-CA-US
Eastern (Middle & Near): 1924-CA-US
European: **574**, 617-EU-IR-UK
South African: **2094**
Linguistics
General: **328**, 390-UK, 849-US, **961**, **1232**, 1373-US, 1409 + 1779-IR, 1905-1911-UK
African: **1006**
Iranian: 410-CW-UK
Spanish: 1326-UK
Literature
General: 386-US, 390-UK, **921**, **961**, 1330-AF-AS, 1373-US, **1592**, 1664-US, 1886-UK, **2077**, **2078**, 2102-NZ
Ancient: 426-CW-UK, 537-US
Classical: 45-US, 2122-CA-US
Comparative: 1373-US
Dramatic criticism: 1399-US
Literary criticism: **1252**, 1373-US, 1664-US
Mediaeval: 426-CW-UK
Old Testament: 828-UK
Renaissance: 1584-US
Strindberg: **2017**
Teaching: 1373-US
Literature (by language/area)
African: **13**, **1006**
American: **939**, 1373-US
Austrian: 348-US
Canadian: **612**
Canadian Eskimo: 688-CA
Caribbean: 1915-CA-US
Chinese: 279-CA, 307-AU, 1648-UK
Eastern (Middle): **203**
English: 380-w-UK, 390-UK, **391**, **430**, 525 + 526-SC, 753-SA, **939**, 1149-IR, 1373-US, 2023-SA
English teaching: 1373-US
Esperanto: **1604**, 2089

European: 964-US
Finnish: **1317**
French: 409-CW-IR-UK, 830-CA-US, 959 + 1584-US, **1665**-w
German: 856-US, 862-CA-EU-IR-UK-US, **987**
Greek (Ancient): 537-US, **1665**-w, 2122-CA-US
Greek (Modern): **1665**-w
Icelandic: **1311**
Iranian: 410-CW-UK
Irish: 1148 + 1149-IR
Israeli: **203**
Italian: 425 + 426-CW-UK, **1155**, 1373-US, 2122-CA-US
Latin American: 1326-UK, 1915-CA-US
Norwegian: 288-CA, **1132**, 1351-IN-IR-IS-UK
Persian: 410-CW-UK
Polish: 1201-US
Portugese: **997**
Swedish: **2017**
Turkish: **166**
Yiddish: 1176-CA-JE-US, 2195 + 2196-US
Literature translation: 1176-CA-JE-US, 1630 + 1675-US, 2047-UK
Museology: **1302**, 1570-US
Musicology: 142-US, **328**, **451**, **536**, **909**, 1120-US, **1883**, 2188-UK
Numismatics: 144 + 145-CA-US, **363**
Palaeography (16th century): 538-US
Philology
General: 170-CA-US
Belgian: 278-CA
Byzantine: **732**
Greek: 170-CA-US
Polish: 1676-UK
Philosophy
General: **153**, 390-UK, 736-US, **961**, **1083**, **1258**, **1556**, 1664-US, **1725**, 2108-AU
Ethics: 1000 + 1183-US, **1725**
Mediaeval: 1677-CA
Marxist thought: **717**
Political: 279-CA, 307-AU, 984-US
Philosophy (by area)
Belgian: 278-CA
Chinese: 307-AU, 1648-UK
European: 964-US
German: 856-US
Greek (Ancient): 537-US
Italian: **1155**
Jewish: 374-JE, 1176-CA-JE-US
Political science/government
General: 158-161-US, 340-AU, 389-EU-UK, 435-US, 445 + 446-US, 508-CA, 568-US, 609-UK, **647**, 654-UK, 736-US, 792-EU-IR-UK, 798-US, 854-US, **867**, 914-US, **971** excl. IN, **973**, 984-US, **1007**, 1144, 1168, 1170-US,

SUBJECT INDEX *See How to Use The Grants Register, page ix*

1182-UK, 1192-CA, 1221-UK, 1610-US, **1678**, 1698-DC, **1726** (esp. w-DC-minorities), 1905-1911-UK, 2084-DC, **2162**
Constitutional government: **971** excl. IN
European integration: **583**
Free enterprise: 567-US
Local government: *See section 10.*
Teaching: 2026-US
Political science/government (by area)
  African: 13, 2113-SA
  American: 158 + 160 + 161-US, 435-US, 914-US, **1168**, 2026 + 2156-US, **2162**
  American-European: 854-US
  Asian (East): **2162**
  Asian (Southeast): 1001-AS-AU-SEA-US
  Australian: 340-AU
  Belgian: 278-CA
  Canadian: 508-CA
  Developing countries: 741
  European: 574, **582**, **583**, 782, 783, 784 + 790-EU-IR-UK, 964-US
  European (East): 1120-US
  Finnish: 1317
  Indian: **971** excl. IN
  Latin American: **2162**
  Palestinian: 993
  Soviet: 1120-US, **2162**
  Spanish: 1170-US
Population studies: *See* Demography/population studies.
Psychology
  General: 165-US, **328**, 534-CA-US, **730**, 736 + 778 + 798-US, **877**, 964-US, 1120-US, 1170-US, **1258**, 1297 + 1298 + 1855 + 1905-1911-UK, 1920-CA-US, 1957 + 1992-US
  Child: **1060**, 1187-AU
  Clinical: 1296-US, **2111**
  Developmental: 2088-IS-US
  Experimental: 1183-US, 1544-CA
  Parapsychology: 200-US, **1638**
  Psychical research: 200-US, 1649-UK
  Social: 54-US, 1815-CA, 1917-CA-US, 1957-US, 2088-IS-US
Public affairs: *See Section 10.*
Race relations: *See Section 10.*
Religion
  General: 390-UK, **557** excl. UK, 721-EN-WA, 779-US, 1159-WA, 1213-UK, **1245**, 1288-US, **1370**, 1664-US, **1711**, 1884-FE-UK, 2067 + 2070 + 2071-US
  Biblical studies: 358-IR-UK, 510-CA, 640-IR-UK, 828-UK
  Christian history: *See* History—Christian.
  Christianity: 177-US, 577-CW-IR-SA-UK, 842 + 843-CA-US, 844-US
  Church/ecclesiastical history: 67-CA-US, 177-US, 827-UK
  Church leadership: *See* **Christian/church leadership** *in Section 10.*
  Comparative: 375-UK, 410-CW-UK, **1258**, 1987
  Divinity: 274-CA, 1196-UK, 1971-SA
  Jewish: 374-JE, 1290-1294-JE, 2187-CA-US
  Ministry: 779-US, 842 + 843-CA-US, 844 + 2067 + 2070 + 2071-US
  Missiology: **1370**
  Orthodox church: 2116-IR-ME-UK
  Religious education: 30-UK, 573-UK, 1884-FE-UK
Semantics: 849-US
Sociology
  General: 201-US, 212-UK, **536**, 877, 914-US, **1007**, 1297 + 1298 + 1326 + 1605-UK, **1725**, 1879, 1905-1911 + 1959-UK
  Applied: 202-US
  Comparative: 914-US, **1007**
Sociology (by area)
  Aboriginal: 662-AU
  African: **1006**, 1913-CA-US, 2113-SA
  American: 914-US
  Chinese: 1920-CA-US
  European: 964-US, 1684-EU-IR-UK
  European (East): 1120-US
  Greek: 1319-EU-IN-IS-UK
  Rural: 798-US
  Soviet: 1120-US
  Women's studies: 447-US, 1348-DC, 1585-w-US, 2163-US
Theology: 358-IR-UK, 445 + 446-US, 721-EN-WA, 779-US, 842 + 843-CA-US, 844-US, 859-SC, 1213-UK, **1245**, **2066**, 2067-US
Topography: 172 + 173-US
Translation: *See* Language translation *and* Literature translation.
Urban studies: 333-AU
Visual arts theory: 1449

Section 4

NATURAL & MATHEMATICAL SCIENCES

General: 5-US, 7-AF-AR, 10-SA, 11-AF, 33-DC-w, 54-US, 122-US, **203**, 213-UK, 249-AS, 273 + 274-CA, **357**, 366-UK, **434**, 454-CA, 479-CA, 492 + 493-DC, 525 + 526-SC, **539**, 558-US, 578-AS-DC, 587-CW, 597-DC (CW), 626-633-SA, **652**, **672**, 674-NI, 712-AU, 750-SA, 907-UK, 946-CA, **962**, 991-CA, 994-CA-US, **1045**, 1104-DC, 1118 + 1119-US, **1164**, **1165**, 1166-AS, 1172-US, 1196-UK, 1201-US, 1312-UK,

SUBJECT INDEX *See How to Use The Grants Register, page ix*

1322-CW, **1323**, **1328**, 1330-AF-AS, **1347**, **1364**, **1369**, **1391**, 1401-US, **1407**, **1424**, 1442-US (Blacks), 1491-NZ, **1492**, 1493, 1516-US, 1517-DC-US, 1518 + 1520 + 1525-US, 1543 + 1544-CA, **1546**, 1547-1550-CA, 1551-CA-EU-UK-US, 1552-1555-CA, 1594 + 1595 + 1598 + 1599-CA-UK-US-WE, 1600-US, **1603**, 1664-US, **1671**, 1691-UK, 1698-DC, 1721-AU-CA-CB-IN-NZ-PN-SA-US-ZB, 1779-IR, **1782**, 1801-UK, 1814 + 1815-CA, 1837-US, 1841-1845 + 1848-1854 + 1856 + 1857-UK, **1858**, 1872-AU, **1882**, 1884-FE-UK, 1888-SC, 1981-SEA, **1986**, **2019**, 2021-CA-EU-UK-US, 2027-UK, **2053**, **2054**, 2057-US, 2075-AF, **2077**, **2078**, 2088-IS-US, 2098 + 2102 + 2104-NZ, 2113-SA, 2115-w, 2204-DC

Major areas

Biological sciences: **86**, 123-US, **194**, 255-AF, **313**, **328**, 343-AU-SEA, 515 + 516-CA, **527**, **535**, **536**, 562-IR-UK, 598-AU, 610-US, 710-AU-UK, **730**, 786-EU-IR-UK, **791**, **835**, **877**, 893-IS-US, **1089**-w, **1090**-w, **1156**, 1233-UK, **1240**, 1269-NZ, 1286-US, 1441-US (Blacks), 1497-US, 1520-US, 1537-1542 + 1606-UK, **1639**, 1712-CA-US, 1767-IR-PN-SA-CW-excl. UK, 1768-CW-IR-PN-SA-UK, **1789**, 1803-UK, 1806-IR-UK-WE, 1807-EE-UK, 1808-UK, 1809-IS-UK, 1810-UK, 1811-LA-UK, **1900**, **1901**, **1903**, 2152-AU, 2157-CA-US

Chemical sciences: 10-SA, 55-US, 123-US, 148-US, **154**, **194**, 404-UK, **527**, 546-CA, 547-CA-US, 562-IR-UK, 581-SA, 606-UK-US, 610-US, 725-US, 764-UK, 860-CA-EU-IR-UK-US, **1089**-w, **1090**-w, 1146-US, **1240**, 1269-NZ, 1409-IR, **1472**, 1498 + 1500 + 1588-US, **1592**, 1606-UK, **1639**, 1705 + 1706-CW-UK, 1712-CA-US, 1742-AU, 1775-UK, **1781**, **1789**, **1794**, **1797**, 1803-UK, 1806-IR-UK-WE, 1807-EE-UK, 1808-UK, 1809-IS-UK, 1810-UK, 1811-LA-UK, 1816 + 1817-UK, 1893-CA-US, 1966-SA, 2010-CA, 2043-DC, 2052-US, 2108-AU, **2143**

Mathematical sciences: 10-SA, 34-CA, 125-US, **137**, **154**, 255-AF, 512-CA, 581 + 750-SA, 764-UK, **1057**, **1372**, 1409-IR, 1494-SA, 1498 + 1588-US, 1693-CA, 1893-CA-US, 2108-AU, **2143**

Physical sciences: 10-SA, 34-CA, 59-US, **86**, 122-US, 123-US, 125-US, 126-US, **154**, **313**, 512-CA, 581-SA, 598-AU, 682-CA, 710-AU-UK, 764 + 805-UK, 860-CA-EU-IR-UK-US, **996**, **1089**-w, **1090**-w, 1409-IR, 1441-US (Blacks), 1472, 1498-US, 1537-1542-UK, 1588-US, **1592**, 1606-UK, 1707-US, 1712-CA-US, 1767-IR-PN-SA-CW-excl. UK, 1768-CW-IR-PN-SA-UK, 1775-UK, **1789**, **1794**, 1802 + 1803-UK, 1804-CW-UK, 1806-IR-UK-WE, 1807-EE-UK, 1808-UK, 1809-IS-UK, 1810-UK, 1811-LA-UK, 1893-CA-US, **1903**, 1966-SA, 2010-CA, 2052-US, 2108-AU, **2143**

Specific subjects

Aeronautics: *See Section 5.*
Aeronomy: 1505-US, **1506**, 1511-US, 1512
Aerospace sciences: 875 + 876-CA-US, 1525-US, **2205**
Analytical chemistry: 264-CA-US, **1639**
Animal science: *See* **Mammalian science** *and Section 7.*
Arctic/Antarctic studies: **229**, **230**, 1515-US, 2046-AU-NZ-SA-UK
Astronomy
 General: 126-US, **300**, **524**, **728**, 734-US, 764-UK, **1040**, **1364**, **1489**, 1505-US, **1506**, **1507**, 1508-LA-US, **1509**, **1510**, 1511-US, **1512**, 1544 + 1553 + 1815-CA, **1818**, 1855-UK, **1903**
 Infra-red: 1505 + 1511-US, 1512
 Radar: 1505-US, **1506**
 Radio: **1489**, 1505-US, **1506**, **1509**, **1903**
 Also see **History of astronomy**, *Section 3.*
Astrophysics: **524**, 1893-CA-US, **1903**
Atmospheric sciences: 683-CA, 1422-US, **1423**, **1493**, 1511 + 1520-US, **1902**, 2088-IS-US
Also see **Environmental sciences.**
Atomic energy: 304-CW, **818**, 1042 + 1043-DC
Atomic physics: **524**, **996**, **1903**
Atomic spectroscopy: 1941-US
Biochemistry: **101**, 102-US, **313**, 368-UK, 369-EU-UK, 463-CA, 546-CA, 725-US, **895**, **1101**, **1102**, 1124-DC, 1146-US, 1289-SA, 1535-UK, 1742-AU, 1855-UK, 1966-SA, **2143**
Biology: *See* **Major areas.**
Biophysics: **154**, **895**, **996**, 1289-SA, **2143**
Botany: **328**, 382-CA-US, 383-SA, **536**, 607-US, **1368**, 1622-UK, **1797**, 1965-w-SA, **2094**
Cell research: **730**, 1497-US
Chemical physics: **154**
Chemistry: *See* **Major areas.**
Climatology: 1422-US, **1423**
Computer science: *See Section 5.*
Cosmic physics: **996**, 1336-US
Cosmic rays: **728**
Crystallography: **86**
Cybernetics: 1855-UK
Earth sciences: **1493**, 1513 + 1520-US, 1537 + 1542-UK, 1815-CA, **1900**, **1901**, **1903**, 1947, 2088-IS-US

xxi

SUBJECT INDEX *See How to Use The Grants Register, page ix*

Ecology: 709, 742-US, 989-DC, 1537 + 1542-UK, 2152-AU
Also see Section 8.
Electronics: 1472, 1499, 1707-US, 2010-CA
Embryology: 524
Energy: 434, 682-CA, 699-AU, 980-UK, 985-DC, 1002-PH-SEA, **1202**, 1409-IR, 1600-US, 2088-IS-US
Also see Atomic energy.
Engineering sciences: *See Section 5.*
Entomology: 322-AU, 861-US, **1101, 1102,** 1124-DC, 1535-UK
Environmental biology: 1497-US
Environmental sciences: 263-US, 320-AU, **434, 527,** 658-US, 674-NI, 683-CA, **709,** 840, 1348-DC, **1493,** 1536-CA-MX-US, 1537-1542-UK, 1597-CA-UK-US-WE, 1848-UK, 2088-IS-US, 2111
Also see Atmospheric sciences *and* Earth sciences.
Experimental chemistry: 1817-UK
Experimental physics: 154, **996,** 1804-CW-UK
Experimental science: 2143
Field science: 122-US
Fluid dynamics: 154, **1423,** 2136
Freshwater biology: 1537-1542-UK
Gas research: 404-UK, 1408-IR
Geochemistry: 524, 944-UK, 1513-US, 1537-1542-UK, 1893-CA-US
Geography
  General: 258-US, **536,** 587-CW, 682-CA, 798-US, **1334, 1450,** 1544 + 1553-CA, 1771-CW, **1823**
  Agricultural: 258-US
  Applied: *See Section 5.*
  Human: *See Section 3.*
  Physical: *See* General *above.*
Geography (by area)
  African: **1620**
  European (East): 1120-US
  Norwegian: 288-CA, 1351-IN-IR-IS-UK
  Poland: 1676-UK
  Saudi Arabia: **1188**
  Soviet: 1120-US
  United States: 258-US
Geology
  General: 5-US, 6, 512-CA, **536,** 709, 764-UK, 850-CA-US, 1233-UK, 1351-IN-IR-IS-UK, 1472, 1513-US, 1537-1542-UK, 1544 + 1553-CA, 1815-CA, **1823,** 1875 + 1876-UK, **1877,** 1966-SA
  Hydrogeology: 850-CA-US
  Mining: 1026-AU-CA-NZ-SA-UK, 1028-UK
Geomorphology: 850-CA-US
Geophysics: 512-CA, **524,** 581-SA, **728,** 764-UK, 944-UK, **996,** 1513-US, 1537-1542-UK, 1553-CA, 1689-SA, **1770,** 1815-CA, **1823,** 1875 + 1876-UK, **1877, 1947,** 2113-SA
Geothermics: 1097
History/philosophy of science: *See Section 3.*
Human factors in science: 1597-CA-UK-US-WE
Hydraulics: *See Section 5.*
Hydrology: 938 + 1054 + 1348-DC, 1537-1542-UK
Information science: *See Section 5.*
Ionospheric science: **1505,** 1511-US, **1512**
Life sciences: *See* Biological sciences (Major areas) *and life science subjects in this Section and Section 6.*
Limnology: 346-DC, 1553-CA, 1799-UK, 2088-IS-US
Lipid chemistry: 148-US
Lunar science: **1244**
Mammalian science: **1156, 1249,** 1800-UK
Also see Section 7.
Marine biology: 140, 893-IS-US, **1041,** 1409-IR, 1537-1541-UK, 1894-US
Marine science: **536, 711,** 1514-US, 1537-1541-UK, 1597-CA-UK-US-WE, 2041-CA-LA-US, 2171
Materials science: **791,** 1498-US, 1597-CA-UK-US-WE, 1855-UK, **1903,** 1966 + 2007-SA, 2088-IS-US
Mathematical physics: 154
Mathematics: *See* Major areas.
Mathematics education: 1521-US
Metallurgy: 10-SA, 31-US, 490 + 514-CA, 860-CA-EU-IR-UK-US, 944 + 1025-UK, 1026-AU-CA-NZ-SA-UK, 1027 + 1028-UK, **1082, 1472,** 1553-CA, **1787, 1794,** 1855-UK, 1966 + 2007-SA, 2109-DC
Meteorology: 138-US, **536,** 581-SA, 1301-DC, **1423,** 1511-US, **1512,** 1537-1542-UK, 1553-CA, 2178
Metrology: *See Section 5.*
Microbiology: 192 + 822-US, **895,** 950-IN, 989-DC, **1639,** 1966-SA
Mineralogy: 944 + 945 + 1025-UK, 1026-AU-CA-NZ-SA-UK, 1027 + 1028-UK, 1409-IR, 1472, 1537-1542-UK
Molecular biology: 463-CA, **730,** 786-EU-IR-UK, 1497-US
Molecular physics: **996, 1902**
Mycology: 1396-CA-US
Natural history
  General: 1351-IN-IR-IS-UK, 1537-1542-UK
  Australia: **1371**
  Aquatic: 1537-1542-UK
  Fauna: **139,** 141-US, 515 + 516-CA, **940, 956,** 2099-NZ
  Flora: 383-SA, **940, 2094**
  Norway: 288-CA

SUBJECT INDEX *See How to Use The Grants Register, page ix*

Nematology: 1101, 1102
Nuclear physics: **154**, 524, 787, 788 + 789-EU-UK, **996**, 1855-UK
Nuclear science: **154**, 330-332, 787, 788 + 789-EU-UK, **1474**
Oceanographic sciences: 709, **1033**, 1422-US, **1423**, 1514 + 1520-US, 1537-1542-UK, 1544 + 1553-CA, 1601-DC, **1609**, 1799-UK, **1823**, 2088-IS-US, **2170-2172**
Also see Environmental sciences.
Oil/petroleum research: 836-EU-IR-UK, 944-UK, 1408-IR, 1650-US
Ornithology: 139, **536**, 2099-NZ, 2164 + 2165-US
Paleobotany: 382-CA-US
Paleontology: 5-US
Parasitology: *See Section 6.*
Petroleum research: *See* **Oil/petroleum research**.
Petrology: 1513-US
Photosynthesis: 198-CA-US
Physical chemistry: **154**, 1797, **2143**
Physics: *See* Major areas.
Physics education: **996**
Physiology: *See Section 6.*
Phytochemistry: 382-CA-US
Planetary physics: 524
Planetary science: 25-SA, **524**, **1244**, 1505 + 1511-US, **1512**, 1899-US, **1902**
Plant sciences
  General: 359-AU, 382-CA-US, **524**, **527**, 607-US, **818**, 861-US, **895**, **958**, 1348-DC, 1535 + 1622-UK, **1793**
  Breeding: 1101, 1102, 1124-DC, 1427-US
  Ecology: 1537-1542-UK
  Genetics: 1427-US, 1535-UK
  Morphology: 607-US
  Pathology: 359-AU, **1101**, **1102**, 1124-DC, 1535-UK
  Physiology: 198-CA-US, 336 + 359-AU, 989-DC, **1101**, **1102**, 1124-DC, 1535-UK
Polar research: *See* **Arctic/Antarctic studies**.
Polymer science: **154**, 1855-UK
Pteridology: 382-CA-US
Radiation: 1422-US
Radiology: 1497-US
Also see Section 6.
Science education: 1519 + 1522-US
Science teaching: **2143**
Seismology: 1100-AF-AS-LA-ME
Soil science: **527**, **1101**, **1102**, 1124 + 1348-DC, **1493**, 1535-UK, 1601-DC, 1622-UK
Solar energy: **1902**
Solar physics: **1423**, 1505 + 1511-US, **1512**
Solar studies: 1505-US, **1507**, **1510**, 1511-US, **1512**, **1902**, **1903**
Solid-state physics: **154**

Space science: 791, **1244**, 1525-US, 1553-CA, 1855-UK, **1903**
Spectroscopy: **154**, 313, 1941-US
Speleology: 1526-US
Starch science: 55-US
Statistics: *See Section 5.*
Stellar studies: **1903**
Subnuclear physics: 787, 788 + 789-EU-UK, **996**
Surface physics: **154**
Theoretical physics: **154**, **539**, **729**, 787, **996**, **1057**
Theoretical science: **2143**
Thermodynamics: 1500-US
Vacuum science: 1143
Wildlife biology: 515 + 516-CA, 1537-1542-UK
Zoology: 1233-UK
Also see **Veterinary medicine** *Section 7.*

Section 5

APPLIED SCIENCES, TECHNOLOGY & ENGINEERING

General: 7-AF-AR, 10-SA, 11-AF, 33-DC-w, 185-US, **205**, 249-AS, 273-CA, **357**, 454-CA, 578-AS-DC, 587-CW, 598-AU, 626-633-SA, **652**, 712-AU, 750-SA, **921**, 946-CA, 955-US, 957-UK, 985-DC, **1037**, 1104 + 1107-DC, 1118 + 1119-US, 1312-UK, **1327**, 1348 + 1352 + 1353-DC, **1356**, 1361d-DC, **1407**, 1409-IR, 1491-NZ, **1492**, **1493**, 1499 + 1504 + 1521 + 1525-US, 1533-SEA, 1543-CA, **1546**, 1547-1550-CA,-1551-CA-EU-UK-US, 1552 + 1554-CA, 1594 + 1595 + 1598 + 1599-CA-UK-US-WE, **1603**, 1606-UK, **1671**, 1695-CA, 1775-UK, 1779-IR, **1782**, **1789**, 1801 + 1803-UK, 1807-EE-UK, 1808-UK, 1809-IS-UK, 1810-UK, 1811-LA-UK, 1815-CA, 1841-1857-UK, 1872-AU, **1882**, 1888-SC, **1986**, 2032-US, **2053**, **2054**, 2063-DC, 2075-AF, **2077**, **2078**, 2102-NZ, 2113-SA, 2204-DC
Aeronautical engineering: 985-DC, 1525-US, 1855-UK, 1943-AU-NZ
Aeronautics: 113-US, 876-CA-US, 1732 +- 1733-CW-UK, 1734-UK, 1735 + 1736-CW-UK, 1737-UK
Aerospace engineering: 185 + 925-US, 1124-DC, 2044-SA, **2205**
Agricultural chemistry: 1622-UK
Agricultural engineering: 175, 251-AS, 359-AU, 804-SA, **1101**, **1102**, 1308-UK
Aids for handicapped: 1499-US
Air conditioning: 187
Air safety: 224-US, 1736-CW-UK
Aircraft design: 1734-UK

SUBJECT INDEX *See How to Use The Grants Register, page ix*

Aircraft engineering/technology: 925-US, 1734-UK, **2205**
Applied biology: 343-AU-SEA, 1767-IR-PN-SA-CW-excl. UK, 1768-CW-IR-PN-SA-UK
Applied chemistry: **154, 1781**
Applied geography: 587-CW, 1771-CW
Applied geophysics: 1408-IR
Applied mathematics: 10-SA, 34-CA, **137, 154,** 581-SA, 925-US, **2143**
Applied mechanics: 1502-US
Applied nuclear science: **154,** 787, 788-EU-UK
Applied physics: 34-CA, 125-US, **154, 434,** 787, 788-EU-UK, **996,** 1767-IR-PN-SA-CW-excl. UK, 1768-CW-IR-PN-SA-UK, **2143**
Applied protein science: 413
Applied science (general): 1841-1845 + 1848-1854 + 1856-UK
Applied spectroscopy: 1941-US
Arc welding: 1231-US
Architectural engineering: 128-US, 1337-DC, 1465-US, 1745 + 1746-AU, **1773**
Architecture: *See Section 2. Also see related subjects in this Section and Sections 10 & 11.*
Astronautics: 113 + 1525-US
Automatic control: 63-US
Automation: 1499-US
Automobile engineering: 1023-UK, 1943-AU-NZ, 1944-US
Balloon technology: 1512
Bioengineering: 1499-US
Biomedical engineering: 185-US
Biostatistics: 1454-AU
Biotechnology: 1857-UK
Building/construction: 384-DC, 634-SA, 944-UK
Cartography: *See Section 11.*
Cereal chemistry: 55-US, 1124-DC
Chemical engineering: 10-SA, 120-US, 547-CA-US, 562-IR-UK, 606-UK-US, 994-CA-US, 1472, 1503 + 1504-US, **1639,** 1742-AU, 1817 + 1855-UK, 2007-SA, 2043-DC, 2113-SA
Chemical technology: **154,** 562-IR-UK, 1742-AU
Civil aviation: 1061-DC
Civil engineering: 10-SA, 128 + 129-US, **178,** 179-181-US, 725-US, 1008-1010-UK, 1054-DC, 1500-1504-US, 1855 + 1873-UK, 2007-SA
Clothing technology: 572-UK
Communications sciences: 252
Communications technology: 252, 1257-US
Computer engineering: 1499-US
Computer sciences: 10-SA, **221,** 251-AS, 255-AF, 261-US, 925-US, 1494-SA, 1498 + 1503 + 1504-US, 1553-CA, 1855-UK, 1895-DC, 2052-US, **2143**
Also see Computer industry *in Section 11.*
Construction: *See* Building/construction.

Construction engineering: **178,** 1008-UK
Copper research: 1082
Cosmetic sciences: 1946-US
Defence sciences: 1312-UK, 1593-1599-CA-UK-US-WE
Defence technology: **2053, 2054**
Diffraction: 86
Domestic science: *See* Home economics, Section 10.
Earthquake engineering: 1100-AF-AS-LA-ME, 1501-US
Electric/hydro power: 1601-DC
Electrical engineering: 10-SA, 185-US, **527,** 755-w-US, 925-US, **977-979,** 1011-1016-UK, **1433,** 1472, 1499 + 1503 + 1504-US, 1529-UK, 1707-US, 1802 + 1855-UK, 2007 + 2113-SA
Electrical/optical communications: 1499-US
Electricity (uses): 755-w-US
Electronics: *See Section 4.*
Electronics engineering: 925-US, **978, 979,** 1011-1016-UK, 1499-US, 1529-UK, **1667,** 1824-UK
Energy engineering: 699-AU, 980-UK
Energy systems: 251-AS, 699-AU, 1002-PH-SEA, 1855-UK
Engineering (general): 10-SA, 185-US, 251-AS, 255-AF, 262, 274-CA, 307-AU, 445 + 466-US, 493-DC, 512-CA, 558-US, 581-SA, 604-CW-DC, 626-633-SA, **672,** 682-CA, 750-SA, 760-CA-US, 764-UK, 795-EU-IR-UK, 804-SA, 805-UK, 836-EU-IR-UK, 876-CA-US, 1009 + 1010 + 1196-UK, 1201-US, 1322-CW, 1337 + 1348-DC, **1364,** 1401-US, **1402, 1407,** 1493, 1499-1504 + 1521 + 1525-US, 1529-UK, 1543 + 1544-CA, 1551-CA-EU-UK-US, 1552-1555-CA, 1594 + 1595-CA-UK-US-WE, 1622-UK, **1639, 1782, 1794,** 1815-CA, 1819-SC, 1841-1857-UK, **1858,** 1872-AU, 1873-UK, 1885-CW-UK, 1972-SA, **1986,** 2021-CA-EU-UK-US, 2029-US, 2036-SA, 2052-US, 2075-AF, **2077, 2078,** 2081-DC, 2098-NZ, 2113-SA, **2115**-w, 2204-DC
Engineering design: 185-US
Engineering education: 185-US
Engineering energetics: 1500-US
Engineering geology: 512-CA, 850-CA-US
Engineering mathematics: 1857-UK
Engineering physics: 1707-US
Engineering technology: 185-US
Environmental engineering: 251-AS, 263 + 1501-US
Environmental technology: 263-US
Fire engineering: 1017-CW-UK
Fish technology: 1601-DC
Flight structures: 875-CA-US
Fluid mechanics: 1502-US
Food science: 55-US, 124-CA-US, **175,** 486-

xxiv

CA, **527**, 610-US, **816**, **818**, 983-CA-US, 1002-PH-SEA, **1060**, 1704-US, 2118-UK
Food technology: **175**, 610-US, 797-AS-SEA, 983-CA-US, 1002-PH-SEA
Frost combating: 2044-SA
Fuel preparation/utilization: 980-UK
Fuel technology: 980 + 1817-UK
Gas engineering/technology: 404-UK, 1018-UK, 1408-IR
Geodesy: 76-US
Geotechnical engineering: 1501-US
Geotechnics: 251-AS, 1501-US
Graphics: *See Section 2.*
Heating engineering: **187**
Highway sciences: **1125** excl. US, 1672-UK, 1723-CA
Histochemistry: 618-EU-IR-UK
Home economics: *See Section 10.*
Hydraulic engineering: 179 + 180-US, 1622-UK
Hydraulics: 180-US, 1054-DC
Hydrodynamics: 1778-UK
Industrial design: 514-CA, 716-UK, 1430-CA, 1464-US, **1720**, 1812-UK
Industrial engineering: 251-AS
Industrial science/technology: 598-AU, 604-CW-DC, **652**, **820**, 994-CA-US, 1537-1539-UK, **1639**, 1841-1857-UK, 1888-SC, 2083-DC
Information science technology: 131-CA-US, **252**, 985-DC, **1060**, 1087-DC, 1497-US, 1553-CA, 1989-1991-CA-US
Instrumentation: 10-SA, 1802-UK
Jet propulsion: 876-CA-US
Lead/zinc—processes/applications: **1105**
Library science: *See Section 11.*
Manufacturing: **1639**, 1855 + 1857-UK
Marine engineering/technology: 1107-DC, 1855 + 1857-UK, 1953-CA
Materials engineering processing: 1500-US
Materials science: *See Section 4.*
Mechanical engineering: 185-US, **190**, **527**, 876-CA-US, 925-US, 985-DC, 1019-1023-UK, 1502-US, 1847 + 1855 + 1873-UK, 2007-SA
Mechanics: 876-CA-US, 1502-US
Metallurgical engineering: 944-UK, 1503 + 1504-US
Metallurgy: *See Section 4.*
Metrology: **1048**
Microstructures engineering: 1499-US
Military science: *See Defence science.*
Mineral processing: 1025-UK, 1026-AU-CA-NZ-SA-UK, 1027-UK, 1500-US
Mining
  General: 490-CA, 944 + 945-UK, 1026-AU-CA-NZ-SA-UK, 1028-UK, 2109-DC
  Metal: 490-CA, 944 + 945 + 1025 + 1027 + 1028-UK
  Mineral: 944 + 945-UK, 2109-DC
Mining engineering: 606-UK-US, 1024 + 1025-UK, 1026-AU-CA-NZ-SA-UK, 1027 + 1028-UK, 2113-SA
Motor combustion engineering: 836-EU-IR-UK
Naval architecture: 1107-DC, 1777 + 1778-UK, 1953-CA
Navigation: **990**, 1107-DC
Nuclear/atomic energy—peaceful uses: 1042 + 1043-DC
Nuclear engineering/technology: 143-US, **154**, 330-332, **527**, 1029-UK, **1474**
Offshore engineering: **709**, 1408-IR, 1601-DC, 1873-UK
Oil/petroleum exploration: 1408-IR, 1601-DC, 1875 + 1876-UK, **1877**
Operational research: 1855-UK
Optical engineering: 944-UK, 1954-US
Packaging technology: 1669-UK
Paper science: 994-CA-US, 1669-UK
Parenteral technology: **1639**
Petroleum engineering: 207-UK, 606-UK-US, 836-EU-IR-UK, 1408-IR, 1650-US, 1874-UK
Petroleum geology: 58 + 1650-US, 1874-1876-UK, **1877**
Petroleum refining: 995-DC, 1650-US
Petroleum technology: 273-CA, 836-EU-IR-UK, 944-UK, 1872-AU, 1873-UK
Photogrammetry: 76-US, 195-197-US, **1129**
Photo-optical instrumentation: 1954-US
Plant engineering: 985-DC, 1030-UK
Plastics engineering/technology: **1955**
Plastics sciences: **1955**
Polymer engineering: **154**, 1857-UK
Printing technology: 1669-UK
Process engineering: 1500-1504-US
Production research: 1502-US
Pulp/paper technology: 994-CA-US, 1398-NZ, 1601-DC, 1669-UK, 1695-CA
Quantum electronics: 1499-US
Radiation technology: 143-US
Radio astronomy: *See Section 4.*
Radio science: **252**, **1702**
Refrigeration engineering: **187**
Road design/engineering: *See* **Highway sciences.**
Satellite communication technology: **252**
Ship technology: 985-DC, 1777 + 1778-UK
Solid mechanics: 1502-US
Solid state engineering: 1499-US
Space technology: **791**, 1525-US
Statistics: 599-DC (CW), 744-IR, **1130**, 1337-DC, 1553-CA, 1698-DC, 1855-UK
Steam utilization: 1588-US
Steel/iron construction: 128 + 129-US, 985-DC
Strategic studies: *See* **Defence science.**

SUBJECT INDEX

See How to Use The Grants Register, page ix

Structural engineering: 251-AS
Structural mechanics: 1501-US
Structural steel: 514-CA, 1008-UK
Systems engineering: **178**, 925 + 1499 + 1503 + 1504-US
Technical studies/training (general): 249-AS, 347-DC, 492-DC, 578-AS-DC, **1037**, 1104-DC, **1328**, 1340-CW (DC), 1344-DC, **1347**, 1352-DC, **1356**, 1361d-DC, **1407**, **1986**, 2126-AU
Technology (general): 11-AF, 14-AF, 212-UK, 251-AS, 347-DC, 525-SC, 597-DC (CW), 626-633-SA, **672**, 957-UK, **1037**, 1052-DC, 1499 + 1500 + 1504-US, 1803-UK, 1807-EE-UK, 1808-UK, 1809-IS-UK, 1810-UK, 1811-LA-UK, 1841-1857-UK, **1858**, 1872-AU, 1899-US, **1986**, 2021-CA-EU-UK-US, 2052-US, 2075-AF, **2077**, **2078**, 2083-DC, 2088-IS-US, 2204-DC
Technology innovation: 1502-US
Telecommunications: **252**, 277-CA, 985-DC, **1133**, **1702**, 1707-US
Television technology: 1824 + 1855-UK, 2037-DC
Textile engineering: 1884-FE-UK
Transportation technology: 251-AS, 944-UK, 985-DC, **1125** excl. US, 1723-CA, 1980-AU, 2048-CA
Vacuum techniques/applications: 1143
Water supply: 205-US, 251-AS, 2141-AU
Wine research/analysis: 1952
Wood science/technology: 820

Section 6

MEDICAL & HEALTH SCIENCES

General: **28 + 29**, 33-DC-w, **62**-w, 70 + 71-CA-US, 193-US, 241-CA, 255-AF, 274-CA, 279-CA, **305**, **306**, 307-AU, 341 + 342-AU, 360-IN-IR-PN-UK, 366-UK, **370**, 417 + 418-UK, **434**, 444-US, 454 + 495 + 501-CA, 525 + 526-SC, **536**, 576-US, 578-AS-DC, 581-SA, 587-CW, 589-US, 594-597-DC (CW), 599-DC (CW), 618-EU-IR-UK, **636**, **652**, 656-US, 687-UK, **702**, **748** excl. US, **793**, **835**, 889-891-UK, 892-CA, **933**, 950-IN, 952-US, **1045**, **1088**, 1118 + 1119-US, **1156**, 1159-WA, **1173**, **1180**, 1196-UK, 1199-CA-US, 1201-US, **1230** excl. US, 1233-UK, **1240**, 1266 + 1267-SC, **1271**, 1272-1275-UK, 1276-1282-CA, 1283-IR, 1284 + 1285-NZ, 1286 + 1306-US, 1322-CW, **1328**, 1330-AF-AS, 1337 + 1348-DC, **1358**, **1380**, 1401-US, **1407**, 1409-IR, 1436-US, 1451-1455-AU, **1469**, 1480-US, 1491-NZ, **1492**, 1533-SEA, **1563**, **1592**, **1603**, 1636-CA-LA-US, **1643**, **1671**, 1719-US, **1724**, 1743-AU, 1750 + 1751-UK, 1753 + 1754 + 1756-CA, 1758-UK, 1761-CW-UK, **1789-1791**, 1795 + 1796-UK, **1798**, 1801-UK, 1815-CA, 1822-UK, **1823**, 1837-US, 1848-UK, **1882**, 1884-FE-UK, 1885-CW-UK, 1973-1975-SA, **1986**, 2024-SA, 2027-UK, 2050-WAF (CW)-UK, 2057-US, 2075-AF, 2088-IS-US, **2094**, 2102-NZ, 2106-UK, 2108-AU, **2115**-w, 2141-NZ, 2145-UK, 2146-DC-UK, **2147**, 2151-WAF, 2157-CA-US, **2167**-w, **2176**
Academic medicine: *See* Teaching of medicine.
Aging: 99 + 1616-US
Also see related subjects in this section and Section 10.
Alcoholism: 718-US
Allergy: 296-US, 1454-AU
Anatomy: 1173
Anesthesiology: 176-US, 259-IR-UK, 1822-UK
Antibiotics: **1994**
Arthritis: 233-UK, 234-236-US, 237-239-UK, 240-243-CA, **845**
Asthma: 296-US, 297 + 298-AU, 299-UK, 416-UK
Also see Bronchial asthma.
Audiology: 1431-US, 2068-CA-US
Autism: 226-AU
Back pain: 352
Bacteriology: 1173, 1815-CA
Behavioral science: *See Section 3.*
Biomedicine: 338-AU, **730**, **793**, 950-IN, 1273-UK, 1284-NZ, **1679**, **1724**, 1800-UK, **2039**, 2057-US, 2088-IS-US, 2157-CA-US
Birth defects: 1255-US
Blindness: 417-UK, 1523-US, 1769-CW (DC)
Blood transfusion: 618-EU-IR-UK
Brain research/diseases: 1047
Bronchial asthma: 298-AU, 416-UK
Cancer: 65 + 66-US, 222-AU, 223-S. Aust., 318-AU, 341 + 342-AU, 417-UK, 465 + 466-CA, 518-UK, **519**, 520-NZ, **554**, **636**, 839-US, **845**, 942-UK, **943** excl. UK, 950-IN, 967 + 968-UK, **1034**, **1135-1138**, **1204**, 1411-1415-SA, 1416-1421-CA, **1558**, **1559**, 1566 + 1567-AU, **1749**, 1750-UK, **1829**, **1830**, 1887-AU, **2013**, **2094**
Cardiology/cardiovascular diseases: 68-US, 100-US, **101**, 102 + 103-US, **104**, 405-UK, 417-UK, 481-485-CA, 521-AU-NZ, 656-US, **730**, **845**, 950-IN, 1225-1228-AU-NZ, 1456-1460-AU, 1461-NZ, **1467**, **1558**, **1559**, **1994**, **2018**
Cerebral diseases: 36, 1047, 1988-UK, 2068-CA-US
Chest diseases: 68-US, **2018**
Child care: *See* Mother/child care, *Section 10.*
Child health and development: *See* Paediatrics.
Childhood diseases: 553-AU, 643-US, 918-CA, 1060, **2039**
Chinese medicine/pharmacology: 279-CA
Chiropractic medicine: 821-US
Circulatory/vascular diseases: 75-US

SUBJECT INDEX *See How to Use The Grants Register, page ix*

Clinical medicine/science: 61-US, **101**, 102-US, 182-US, 191-193-US, **194**, 495 + 501 + 511-CA, **571**, 643-US, 656-US, 687-UK, **835**, 870-US, **1088**, **1180**, **1262**, 1279-1282-CA, 1296-US, **1300** excl. US, 1306-US, 1418-CA, 1445 + 1446-US, 1454-AU, **1639**, **1724**, 1754-1756-CA, **1829**, 2057-US, 2145-UK, **2167**-w
Clinical pharmacology: 444-US, 918-CA
Communicative disorders: **1473**
Community medicine: 890-UK, 950-IN, 1454-AU, 2057-US
Contraception: *See* Family planning, Section 10.
Crippling diseases: 1447-UK, 1904-CA
Cystic fibrosis: 470-474-CA, 643-645-US, 646-UK
Deafness: **1701**
Dentistry
  General: **62**-w, 97-US, 274-CA, 399-UK, 400-NI-UK, 475 + 479-CA, 480-CA, 594-597-DC (CW), 660 + 661-SA, 687-UK, **739**, **1084**, 1274-UK, 1284-NZ, **1328**, **1380**, **1407**, 1451 + 1452 + 1455-AU, 1760-UK, 1973-1975 + 2113-SA
  Laboratory technology: 98-US, **1639**, 2113-SA
  Periodontology: 44-US
  Teaching: 95-US, 399-UK, 480-CA
Dermatology: 950-IN, 1454-AU, 1616-US, 1822-UK, **1994**
Developmental medicine: **36**, 2057-US
Diabetes: 87-US, 401-IR-UK, 781-EU-IR-UK, 1174 + 1175-US
Dietetics: 88 + 89-US, **1060**, 1468-US, 1973-SA
Digestion: 402-UK
Disease prevention: 2039
Drugs: **194**, **1639**, 1656-US, **1994**
Electroencephalography: 870-US
Endocrinology: 71 + 759-CA-US, 855-EU-IR-UK
Epidemiology: **101**, 102-US, 416-UK, 495-CA, 730, **963**, 1306-US, 1418-CA, 1454-AU
Epilepsy: **194**, 776-778-US
Experimental medicine: **1798**, **2147**
Family planning: *See Section 10.*
Family practice: 38-US, **1060**
Forensic medicine: 417-UK
Fungal diseases: **1994**
Gastroenterology: 643 + 645-US
General practice: 417-UK, 576-US, 1743-AU
Genetics: **1156**, 1454-AU
Geriatrics: *See* Aging.
Gynaecology: 57 + 540-US, **1749**, 1822-UK
Headache/migraine: 61-US, **1305**
Health development: **203**, 599-DC (CW), **702**, 1454-AU, **1469**, **2039**, 2057-US, 2088-IS-US, **2176**
Health education: **203**, **265**, 889-891-UK, 952-US, 1436 + 1446-US, 1475-CA-US, 1636-CA-LA-US, 2057-US, **2176**
Health care services: 99-US, **203**, 890-UK, 892-CA, 1446-US, 1454-AU, 1762-UK, 2057-US, **2176**
Hearing: *See* Audiology.
Heart disease: *See* Cardiology.
Hematology/coagulation: 192 + 1462-US, 2145-UK
Hemophilia: 1462-US
Hepatic disease: 402-UK, 496-498-CA
History of medicine: *See Section 3.*
Hospital practice: 417-UK
Human reproduction: **1679**
Humane research: 26-UK, **719**, **933**, **2091**
Immunology: 192-US, 296 + 822-US
Industrial health/medicine: 606-UK-US, 2057-US
Internal medicine: 70-CA-US, 950-IN, **1230** excl. US, 1751-UK, **1897**
Kidney diseases: 334-AU, 1186-CA, **1477**, 1478-SA
Laboratory science/technology: **194**, 513-CA, **1180**, 1445 + 2057-US
Labour medicine: **1434**
Laryngology: 416-UK, **549**
Legal and insurance medicine: **1434**
Leprosy: 414-UK, **800**, **897-899**, 950-IN
Leukemia: **1204**, 1217-UK, **1218-1220**, **1479**
Lung diseases: 133-135-CA-US, 136-US, 499 + 500-CA, 643 + 645-US, 1275-UK
Malignant diseases: **1204**
Medical care: 495-CA
Medical chemistry: **1639**
Medical education: 1753-CA
Medical electronics/technology: **1639**
Medical jurisprudence: 417-UK
Medical missionary: **1271**
Medical statistics: 1418-CA, 1454-AU
Medical technology: 191-193-US, 513-CA
Medicinal chemistry: 93-US
Mental health: **164**, 417-UK, 635-US, **730**, 1297 + 1298-UK, 1481 + 2057-US, **2175**
Mental retardation: **164**, 225-AU, **265**, 918 + 1470 + 1471-CA, 1615-US, **2175**
Microbiology: *See Section 4.*
Midwifery: **1264**
Migraine: *See* Headache/migraine.
Morphology: 1654-US
Mother/child care: *See Section 10.*
Multiple sclerosis: 1384-CA, **1385**, **1482-1484**
Muscular dystrophy: **1388**, **1389**, **1394**, **1395**
Neurology: 40-CA, 541-US, 576-US, **730**, 777 + 778 + 870-US, **901**, 1183-US, 1378-CA, **1473**, 1788, 1893-CA-US, **2020**
Neuromuscular disease: **1388**, **1389**
Neuropharmacology: 1629-UK

Neurophysiology: 730, 869, 870-US
Neurosurgery: See Surgery.
Nursing: 133-CA-US, 146-US, 366-UK, 483 + 505-CA, 89-UK, **1264**, 1453-AU, 1608-US, 1884-FE-UK, 1885-CW-UK-1973 + 1977-SA, 2125-CA
Nutrition: 42-CA-US, 88-US, 108-CA-US, 124-CA-US, **527**, 726-CW, **817, 818**, 918-CA, 950-IN, 1002-PH-SEA, **1060, 1256, 1382-DC, 1429-US, 1454-AU, 1601-DC, 1622** + 1762-UK, **2039**, 2118 + 2119-UK
Also see Food science *in Section 5.*
Obstetrics: 57 + 540-US, **1749**, 1822-UK
Occupational therapy: See Therapy *and Section 11.*
Oncology: 466 + 1418 + 1421-CA
Ophthalmology: 417-UK, 502-CA, **549**, 807-810, 947-CA, 950-IN, **1086**, 1113, 1275-UK, 1495, 1523-US, **1744**-AU, 1763-UK, 1769-CW (DC), 1822-UK, 1826-AU, 2133-UK
Orthopaedics: 419-CA-UK-US
Osteopathy: 349-CA-US, 506-CA, 1488-US
Otolaryngology: 37-US
Otology: 416-UK, 1275-UK
Otosclerosis: 152
Paediatrics: 41-AC-CA-SAM-US, 43-CA-US, 319-AU, 420-CW-UK, 551 + 553-AU, 918-CA, 992-UK, **1060, 1747, 1748, 2039**, 2068-CA-US
Pain research/studies: 61-US
Paralysis
  General: **1637**
  Assistive devices: **1637**
Paramedical services: 618-EU-IR-UK, 1453-AU
Parasitology: 989-DC
Parenteral drugs: **1639**
Parkinsons disease: 1642-UK
Pathology
  General: 101, 102-US, 730, 1173, 1233-UK, **1643**, 1940-UK, 2145-UK, **2179**
  Clinical: 182-US, 2145-UK
Perinatal medicine: 917
Periodontics: See Dentistry.
Pharmaceutical chemistry: **1639**
Pharmaceutical education: 93-US
Pharmacology: 93-US, **194**, 279-CA, 730, **1240, 1262, 1300** excl. US, **1558, 1559, 1639**, 1652-1658-US, 1661-UK, 1662-SA, 1663-CA, 1752-IR-UK, **1792**, 1994
Pharmacy
  General: 93-US, 255-AF, 478 + 479 + 507-CA, 905-SA, **1407, 1639, 1651**, 1659-1661-UK, 1662-SA, **1994**, 2021-CA-EU-UK-US, 2137-CA
  Hospital: 188 + 189-US, 478-CA, **1651**
  Industrial: 93-US, 478-CA
Physical education: 1475-CA-US
Physical medicine: 75-US, 900-NZ

Physical therapy: 155-US
Physiology: 101, 102-US, 989-DC, 1173, 1233-UK, **1592, 1668**-UK, **1791, 1792**
Also see Section 4.
Physiopathology: 823
Pneumology: 2018
Podiatry: 157-US
Pregnancy/childbearing health risks: 417-UK
Psychiatry
  General: 164, 541-US, 576-US, 1297 + 1298-UK, **1376**, 1454-AU
  Biological: **1376**
  Forensic: 164
  Schizophrenia: 72, **1994**
  Teaching: 164
Psychology: See Section 3.
Psychopharmacology: 1629-UK
Psychology (applied): See Section 10.
Public health: 274-CA, 417-UK, **527**, 618-EU-IR-UK, 778-US, 892-CA, **1060**, 1196-UK, 1453-AU, 1636-CA-LA-US, 1885-CW-UK, 1971-SA, 1981-SEA, 2057-US, **2176**
Radioassay: 192-US
Radiology: 411-UK, 1741-AU-NZ-UK, 1757-UK
Rehabilitation medicine: 75-US
Also see Disabled rehabilitation *and* Vocational rehabilitation *in Section 10.*
Reproduction: See Human reproduction.
Respiratory diseases: 133-135-CA-US, 136-US, 297 + 298-AU, 299-UK, 417-UK, 499 + 500-CA, 548-UK
Retinitis pigmentosa: 1495
Rheumatology/rheumatic diseases: 233-UK, 234-US, 237-239-UK, 240-243-CA, **845**, 900-NZ, 1750-UK
Spastic paralysis: 1988-UK
Speech pathology: 1431-US, 2068-CA-US
Spinal cord injury: **1637**
Spinal studies: 352
Sports medicine: 1005-UK
Sterile medication: **1639**
Stroke: 100-US, 101, 102 + 103-US, **1473**
Surgery
  General: 1062-US, 1754-1756-CA, **1897**, 2106 + 2145-UK
  Neurosurgery: 40-CA, 541 + 870-US, 1378-CA
  Orthopaedic: 419-CA-UK-US, 992 + 1759-UK
  Paediatric: **1747, 1748**
  Pathology: 1421-CA
  Plastic: 37-US, 199-US, 1764-UK
  Reconstructive: 199-US
  Tropical: 1761-CW-UK
Teaching of medicine: 241-CA, 1445 + 1446-US
Therapeutics: **194**, 1233-UK, **1262**, 1752-IR-UK
Thoracic medicine: 499 + 500-CA
Thyroidology: 855-EU-IR-UK

SUBJECT INDEX *See How to Use The Grants Register, page ix*

Tobacco and health: 342-AU, **636**
Toxicology: 1655 + 1656-US
Trachoma: 549, 1113
Traumatology: 1434
Tropical medicine: **963**, 1113, 1361bc-CW (Tropical), 1624-1626-CW, 1750-UK, 1761-CW-UK, 1981-SEA
Tuberculosis: 499 + 500-CA
Urology: 204-US, 334-AU, 1186-CA
Veterinary medicine: *See Section 7.*
Virology: 822-US, **1173**

Section 7

AGRICULTURE & VETERINARY SCIENCES

Agriculture (general): 15-AF-AS-DC, 18-IR, 19-CA-CW-DC, 22-UK, **23 + 24**, 25-SA, 255-AF, 343-AU, 359-AU, **457**, 479-CA, **527**, 578-AS-DC, 581-SA, 587-CW, 597-DC (CW), 598-AU, 599-DC (CW), 610-US, **652**, 663-SC, 798-US, 799-AU, 804-SA, **816, 817, 1035**, 1053, 1085, 1101, 1102, 1104-DC, 1118 + 1119-US, 1124-DC, 1159-WA, 1263-UK, 1307 + 1308-UK, 1322-CW, **1334**, 1348-DC, 1361a-UK, **1402**, 1491-NZ, **1492**, 1553-CA, 1602-EU-UK, 1622-UK, 1805-CW-UK, 1848-UK, **1882**, 1981-SEA, **1986**, 1997-DC, 2021-CA-EU-UK-US, 2057-US, 2063-DC, 2075-AF, **2077, 2078**, 2098 + 2102 + 2104-NZ, 2168-w-US
Agricultural cooperatives: 1622-UK
Agricultural development/planning: 15-AF-AS-DC, 17-AS, 18-IR, 19-CA-CW-DC, 1051-EU-IR-UK, 1263-UK
Agricultural economics: 17-AS, 48-US, **175**, 336-AU, 345-AU, 359-AU, 459-CA, 586-DC (CW), 798-US, 816-818, 1101, 1102, 1124-DC, 1307 + 1308-UK, **1402**, 1622-UK, 1698-DC
Agricultural economics teaching: 48-US, 1050-EU-IR-UK
Agricultural education: 1053
Agricultural engineering: *See Section 5.*
Agricultural extension: 1124-DC, 1308-UK
Agricultural meteorology: 1101, 1102, 1301-DC, 2044-SA
Agricultural statistics: 816-818, 1124-DC, **1270**, 1308-UK
Agroclimatology: *See* Agricultural meteorology.
Agronomy: 307-AU, 359-AU, 1049-1051-EU-IR-UK, **1101, 1102, 1402**, 1622-UK, 1997-DC
Animal health: *See* Veterinary medicine.
Animal production: 336-AU, **1270**
Animal science: 336-AU, **527**, 601-CW, 1269-NZ, **1270**

Also see Veterinary medicine *(below) and related subjects in Section 4.*
Arboriculture: 1128
Barley industry: 359-AU
Breeding: 336-AU
Cattle industry: 335 + 336-AU, 1269-NZ, **1270**
Crop cultivation: 610-US, **1101, 1102**, 1124-DC, 1680-1682-UK
Dairy industry: 648-AU, 1307-UK, 1429-US
Egg marketing: 708-AU, 752-UK
Estate management: 1308-UK, 1536-CA-MX-US
Farm management: 1308-UK
Farm mechanization: 1101, 1102, 1308-UK
Farming: *See* Agriculture (general).
Fisheries: *See Section 8.*
Floriculture: 861-US, 2168-w-US
Forestry: *See Section 8.*
Grazing: 335 + 336-AU
History of agriculture: *See Section 3.*
Honey industry: 707-AU
Horticulture: 737-UK, 916-US, **1085**, 1159-WA, 1308 + 1896-UK
Husbandry: 1051-EU-IR-UK, **1085**, 1308-UK, 1601-DC
Landscaping/gardening: 916-US, 2168-w-US
Livestock management: 1703-CA-US
Marketing/distribution of products: 708-AU, 752-UK, **1270**, 1307 + 1308-UK, 2103-NZ
Meat/carcase studies: 335 + 336-AU, 1269-NZ, **1270**
Park administration: *See Section 8.*
Pasture: 335 + 336 + 922-AU
Pig husbandry: 705-AU
Plant marketing: 916-US
Plant production: 916-US
Plant science: *See Section 4.*
Potatoes: 1680-1682-UK
Poultry husbandry: 1703-CA-US
Poultry science: 708-AU, 1528-US, 1703-CA-US
Range management: *See Section 8.*
Rice: 1124-DC
Rural studies: *See Section 8.*
Sheep farming: 345-AU, 2161-NZ
Soil science: *See Section 4.*
Tillage: 359-AU
Timber: *See* Forestry, *Section 8.*
Tropical agriculture: 1058-DC (Tropics), **1101, 1102**
Vegetables: 1535-UK
Veterinary medicine
 General: 20 + 21-UK, 25-SA, **62**-w, 218 + 219-UK, 255-AF, 336-AU, 343-AU, 428-IR-UK, 431-IR-UK, **527**, 587-CW, 597-DC-CW, 601-CW, **652**, 663-SC, 915-UK, **1156, 1469**, 1622-UK, **1643**, 1765-UK, 1766-CW-IR-UK, **1790,**

1973-1975-SA, **1986**, **2091**, 2102-NZ, 2146-DC-UK, **2147**
Also see Medicine—General.
Animal health: 218-UK, 336-AU
Clinical medicine: 428-IR-UK
Immunology: 1103
Infectious diseases: 336-AU
Parasitology: 336-AU, 1103
Pathology: 74-US, 336-AU, **1643**
Physiology: 336-AU
Protozoology: 336-AU
Small animal: 428-IR-CW
Viticulture: 186-US
Weed control: 1535-UK
Wheat industry: 359-AU
Wool production: 345-AU, 1579 + 2161-NZ

Section 8

NATURAL RESOURCES & ENVIRONMENT PROTECTION

General: 320-AU, 503 + 504-CA, 674-NI, 683-CA, **709**, 738-AS-PC-US, 742-US, 771-US, **940**, 991-CA, **1007**, **1132**, 1322-CW, 1348-DC, 1361a-UK, **1402**, 1491-NZ, **1492**, 1535-UK, 1536-CA-MX-US, 1537-1542-UK, 1596-CA-UK-US-WE, 1805-CW-UK, 1833-AFS-SA, **1986**, 2140-CA-US, 2152-AU, **2183**, **2184**, 2185-AU
Also see related subjects in Sections, 4, 5 & 7.
Air pollution: 771-US
Conservation: **313**, 320-AU, 503 + 504-CA, **536**, 607-US, 819-CA, **840**, 1041, 1536-CA-MX-US, 1537-1542-UK, 1833-AFS-SA, 1866-US, 2152-AU, 2168-w-US, **2183**, **2184**, 2185-AU
Conservation education: 1536-CA-MX-US
Drainage: *See* Irrigation/land drainage.
Energy resources: 682 + 683-CA, 980-UK, 1002-PH-SEA, 1536-CA-MX-US
Environmental protection: 263-US, 503 + 504-CA, 771-US, **840**, 2152-AU
Environmental sciences: *See Section 4.*
Fisheries: **303**, 599-DC (CW), 683-CA, **684**, 685-IR, 706-AU, **816-818**, 1041, 1361a-UK, 1601-DC, 1622-UK, 1805-CW-UK
Fisheries industry: 706-AU
Forestry: 255-AF, 445 + 446-US, 581-SA, 597-DC (CW), 599-DC (CW), 683-CA, 704-AU, **816-818**, 819-CA, **973**, **1128**, **1139**, 1159-WA, 1309-CW-ZB, 1361a-UK, 1397-NZ, 1536-CA-MX-US, 1537-1542-UK, 1544-CA, 1622-UK, 1805-CW-UK, 1835-CA-US, 2021-CA-EU-UK-US, **2077**, **2078**

Industrial waste treatment: 263-US
Irrigation/land drainage: **1035**, 1049-EU-IR-UK, 1124-DC
Land/water development: 818, 1537-1542-UK
Marine policy: **1033**, 2171
Marine resources: **1033**
Monument preservation: *See* Art/architecture/historic preservation *in Section 3.*
Natural resources: 320-AU, 578-AS-DC, 599-DC (CW), 682-CA, 738-AS-PC-US, 1537-1542 + 1622-UK, 1805-CW-UK, 2152-AU
Nature protection: 320-AU, 383-SA, 503 + 504-CA, 865-AU, **940**, 1537-1542-UK, 1833-AFS-SA, 2152-AU, **2183-2184**, 2185-AU
Ocean management: **1033**, 2171
Park administration: 1536-CA-MX-US
Pasture: *See Section 7.*
Pesticides control: 771-US
Petroleum conservation: 273-CA, 1536-CA-MX-US
Pollution control: 15-AF-AS-DC, 1107-DC, 1536-CA-MX-US
Reservoirs: 1601-DC
Rural extension: **1035**
Soil conservation: 1536-CA-MX-US
Solid waste disposal: 263-US, 771 + 772-US
Toxic substance control: 771-US
Waste water treatment: 263-US
Water conservation: 205-US, 263-AS, 2141-AU, 2191-CA
Water management: 1124-DC
Water pollution: 205-US, 771 + 773 + 774-US, 1536-CA-MX-US, 2191-CA
Water resources: 205-US, 683-CA, 700-AU, 938-DC, 1002-PH-SEA, 1536-CA-MX-US, 1601-DC, 2141-AU
Wildlife management: 503 + 504 + 515 + 516-CA, 865-AU, 1536-CA-MX-US, 2144 + 2160-US
Wildlife preservation: 320-AU, 503 + 504-CA, 865-AU, **940**, **956**, 1536-CA-MX-US, 1833-AFS-SA, 2144-US, 2152-AU, **2183**, **2184**, 2185-AU

Section 9

EDUCATION & TEACHING

General: 30-UK, 33-DC-w, 90-US, 269-CA-DC, 274-CA, 276-CA, 310-AU, 316-AU, **328**, 468-CA, **527**, 568-US, 578-AS-DC, 581-SA, 599-DC-CW, 651-EU-IR-UK, 659-CA-EU-MX-UR-US, 664-EU, 665-AU, 669-CA-NZ-

SUBJECT INDEX *See How to Use The Grants Register, page ix*

UK, 675-EN-WA, 738-AS-PC-US, 751-US, **794**, 948-UK, **1060**, 1065-US, **1066** excl. US, **1067** excl. US, **1071** excl. US, **1095**, **1096**, 1170-US, 1181-US, 1196-UK, 1221-UK, **1258**, **1325**, 1337-DC, 1339-CW, 136le-UK, **1432**, 1522-US, 1574-NZ, **1613**, 1622-UK, 1646-US, 1698-DC, 1727-US, 1837-US, 1969-SA, 1981-SEA, **1986**, 2055-US, 2063-DC, 2075-AF, **2077-2079**, **2111**, 2113-SA, 2158-US

NB: *Teachers should also refer to their special subjects in other sections.*

Education (by area)
  American: **206**, 253-UK, 316-AU, 766-UK, **1066** excl. US, **1067** excl. US, 1532-UK, 2055 + 2158-US
  Australian: 343-AU, 664-EU, 669-CA-NZ-UK, **2111**
  Canadian: 468-CA
  Caribbean: 1208-CB-LA
  European: 615-EU-IR-UK
  Indian: 1339-CW
  Jewish: 374-JE, 1294-JE
  Latin American: 1208-CB-LA
  Maori: 1574-NZ
  Norwegian: **1132**
Administration
  General: 78-US, 316 + 343-AU, 398-UK, 445 + 446-US, 587-CW, 599-DC (CW), 798-US, **1066** + **1071** excl. US, 1339-CW, 1361e-UK, **1613**, 2055-US
  University/college: 78-US, 260-CW, 343-AU, 398-UK, 587-CW, 1208-CB-LA, 1339 + 1572 + 1573-CW
Adult: **1613**, **2079**
Behavioral science in education
  Applied psychology: **1613**
  Research: 1992 + 2055-US
Broadcasting: 948-UK
Career counseling/placement: 575-US
College students: 90-US
Comparative education: 468-CA, 615-EU-IR-UK
Conditions: 2055-US
Cooperative education: **2079**
Curriculum education: 59-US, 1361e-UK, 1574-NZ, **1613**, 2055-US
Disadvantaged: 1615 + 2055-US
Dyslexia: 735-AU
Early childhood: 321-AU, **1060**, 1574-NZ
Education of the blind: 1769-CW (DC)
Education of the mentally retarded: **2175**
Education policy: 78 + 751 + 2055-US
Educational improvement: 59-US, 1117, 1169-US, 1208-CB-LA, 2055-US
Educational measurement: **1613**
Educational research: 1208-CB-LA, 1371,
1373-US, 1574-NZ, **1613**, 2055-US
Educational technology: **1613**, 1981-SEA
Elementary education: 733-CA, **1060**
Handicapped: 733-CA, 1615-US, **1701**, 2055-US
History/philosophy of education: *See Section 3.*
Informal settings: 2055-US
Kindergarten: **1060**, 1187-AU, 1382-DC
Learning disabilities: 735-AU, 1117, 1615 + 2055-US, **2175**
Literacy: 1117, 2055-US
Planning: 599-DC (CW), **1095**, **1096**, 1361e-UK, **1613**, 2055-US
Pre-school education: 715-AU, **1060**, 1187-AU
Primary education: 316-AU
Reading education: 1117
Secondary education: 59-US, 316-AU, 1971-SA
Sociology in education: **1613**
Special education: 568-US, **623**, 733-CA, 788 + 1183-US, **1613**, 1615-US, **2111**, **2175**
Teacher exchange: **206**, 1065-US, **1066** excl. US, **1067** excl. US, **1071** excl. US, 1072-US, 1211-UK, 2055-US
Teacher sabbatical studies: 863-UK, **1095**, 1339-CW, **1432**, 1532-UK
Teacher training: 30-UK, **206**, 599-DC (CW), 675-EN-WA, **794**, **1066** excl. US, 1208-CB-LA, 1337-DC, 1361e-UK, **1720**, 1861-SC, 1969-SA
Television: 948-UK
Vocational subjects teaching: 568 + 2055-US
Worker's education: **2079**

Section 10

SOCIAL DEVELOPMENT & WELFARE—including human rights and relations, public and social administration and services, planning, special problem areas, and applied social sciences.

General: 11 + 12-AF, 14-AF, 15-AF-AS-DC, 33-DC-w, 91-US, 249-AS, 578-AS-DC, 587-CW, 599-DC (CW), 635-US, **657**, 703, 738-AS-PC-US, 854-US, **913**, **1098**, 1104 + 1337 + 1348 + 1382-DC, **1496**, 1607-w-UK, 1837-US, 1884-FE-UK, 1905-1911-UK, 1912-US, **1986**, 2063 + 2072-DC, **2077**, **2078**, 2113-SA, 2158-US
Accident prevention: 551-AU
Addiction: *See Section 6* and **Drug/alcohol abuses**, *this Section.*
Aging: 2056 + 2057-US
Aging—services: 99 + 110 + 854-US, 1976-SA,

SUBJECT INDEX *See How to Use The Grants Register, page ix*

2056 + 2057-US
Also see Section 6.
Animal rights/welfare: 1938-US, **2091**
Autistic care: 226-AU
Blind welfare/rehabilitation: 1769-CW (DC)
Broadcasting: *See Section 11.*
Child welfare: 551 + 715-AU, **1060**
Also see Mother/child care.
Christian/church leadership: 2070 + 2071-US
Citizen participation: 714-CA, 854 + 2026 + 2158-US
Citizen's rights: **657**, 714-CA, 854 + 1209-US
Civil liberties: **657**, 854-US, **908**, 1209 + 1569-US
Community services: 310-AU, 854 + 1181-US, 1382-DC, **1496**, 2158-US, **2186**-w
Development: *See* Planning & development
Disabled care: 1426-SA
Disabled rehabilitation: 1426-SA, 1490 + 2181-US
Domestic science: *See* Home economics.
Drug/alcohol abuses: 2057-US
Economic welfare: 12-AF, **16**, 2158-US
Education: *See Section 9.*
Emergency planning: 272-CA
Employment: 854 + 1912-US
Family planning: **1060**, 2063-DC
Food problems: **1060**
Foreign service: 2084-DC
Government service: 2156-US
Health education: *See Section 6.*
Home economics: 108-US, **109** excl. US, 110-US, **111**, 486-489-CA, 1382-DC, 1688-w-SA, 2115-w, 2118-UK
Also see Dietetics *and* Nutrition *in Section 6.*
Housing: 384-DC, 458-CA, 854-US, **1116**, 2063-DC, 2158-US
Human relations: 2113-SA
Human rights
 General: **657**, 714-CA, **1007**, **1167**, 1209-US, **1696**, **1725**, 2072-DC, 2158-US
 Gay community: **846**
Industrial relations: **16**, 854-US, 1221-UK, 1707-US
Jewish community work: 1246-JE-SA, 1291 + 1292-JE, 1476-CA-US, 2187-CA-US
Juvenile delinquency: 2057-US
Labour studies: 854-US, **1098**
Law enforcement: 854 + 2059-2061-US
Living conditions: 1181-US
Local government: 564-US, **1140**, **1496**
Mother/child care: 715-AU, **1060**, 1688-w-SA
Narcotics: 2072-DC
Nursing: *See Section 6.*
Occupational therapy: 147-US
Organizations/institutions
 General: 1081-DC, 1184

 Caribbean: 1922
 Cooperative: 1081 + 2095-DC
 European: 784-EU-IR-UK
 European community: 582, 782, 784-EU-IR—UK
 International: 794, 1184, 2084-DC
 Labour movement: 1052-DC, 1094-AF-AS-CB
 Latin American: 1922
 NATO: 1593-CA-UK-US-WE
 Red Cross: 1212
 Rural: 816, 818
 Trade unions: 445 + 446-US, 1052-DC, 1094—AF-AS-CB
 Unesco: **2079**
 United Nations: **2074**, 2084-DC
 YMCA: **2173**
 Youth: **2080**
 YWCA: **2186**-w, 2202-w-AU
Outdoor recreation: 1536-CA-MX-US
Peace: *See* International affairs/relations, *Section 3.*
Planning & development
 General: 12-AF, 14-AF, 156-CA-US, 212-UK, 491-CA, 599-DC-CW, 738-AS-PC-US, 1094-AF-AS-CB, 1104 + 1348-DC, 1596-CA-UK-US-WE, 1627-UK, 1868-DC, 1905-1911-UK, 2072-DC, 2075-AF, 2083-DC
 City: 156-CA-US
 Communications: 14-AF, 738-AS-PC-US
 Community: 156-CA-US, 1382 + 2063-DC, 2158-US
 Cooperation: 738-AS-PC-US, 1094-AF-AS-CB, 1166-AS, 2158-US
 Cultural: 738-AS-PC-US
 Economic: 12-AF, 14-AF, 212-UK, **438**, **743**, **1007**, **1130**, 1207-CB-LA, 1344 + 1348 + 1350 + 1623 + 1698 + 1868-DC, 1905-1911-UK, 2072-DC, 2075-AF, 2083-DC
 Environmental: 1596-CA-UK-US-WE
 Housing: 384-DC
 Industrial: 1714-DC, 2075-AF, 2083-DC
 Regional/rural/urban: 14-AF, 156-CA-US, 333-AU, 458-CA, 564-US, 578-AS-DC, 1002-PH-SEA, 1326-UK, 1348 + 1382-DC, 1776-UK, **1825**, 1868-DC, 1917 + 1920-CA-US, 2075-AF, 2158-US
 Social: **741**, 1207-CB-LA, 1344 + 1348-DC, 1596-CA-UK-US-WE, 1623 + 1713 + 1714 + 1868-DC, 1905-1911-UK, 2072-DC, 2075-AF, 2204-DC
 Technical cooperation: 578-AS-DC, 1166-AS, 1361d-DC
Planning & development (by area)
 African: 12 + 14 + 255-AF, 1913-CA-US, 2075-AF
 American: 2158-US

xxxii

SUBJECT INDEX   *See How to Use The Grants Register, page ix*

American Indian: 112-US
Asian: 578-AS-DC, 738-AS-PC-US, 1001-AS-AU-SEA-US, 1002-PH-SEA, 1914-CA-US
Australian Aboriginal: 662-AU
Caribbean: 1915-CA-US
Chinese: 1920-CA-US
Developing countries: 491-CA, 599-DC (CW), 686-AF-PC, 741, 743, 848-DC, **882**, 974, 1104-DC, 1221-UK, 1344 + 1348 + 1350 + 1601 + 1623-DC, 1627-UK, 1698 + 1868 + 2072 + 2083 + 2204-DC
Eastern (Near & Middle): 1916-CA-US
European (West): 1917-CA-US
Indian: 1914-CA-US
Latin American: 1326-UK, 1915-CA-US
Norwegian: **1132**
Pakistani: 1914-CA-US
Scandinavian: **1132**
Public administration/services: 14-AF, 274-CA, 546-US, 581-SA, 854-US, 906-SA, **1140**, 1184, 1196-UK, 1348-DC, **1496**, 1678, 1774-CW, 1905-1911-UK, 1971-SA, 2003-NZ, 2063-DC, 2075-AF, **2077**, **2078**, 2113-SA
Public affairs: 568-US, 611-US, 854 + 856-US, **1496**, 1596-CA-UK-US-WE, 1995-US
Public health: *See Section 6.*
Public information: 818, 854-US, **1177**, **1391**
Public opinion: 60-US
Race relations: 220-US, **543**, 584-UK, **657**, **908**, 1246-JE-SA, 2113-SA
Racial affairs: 584-UK, 1968-SA
Rehabilitation: *See* **Disabled rehabilitation** *and* **Vocational rehabilitation** *in this section, and* **Rehabilitation medicine** *in Section 6.*
Rehabilitation counseling: 1490-US
Rural services: 816, 818, 1382-DC
Social education: 1361e-UK
Social conditions: 854 + 1181-US
Social policy: **657**, 854-US, **1098**, 1181-US, 1905-1911-UK
Social services: 619-EU-IR-UK, **623**, **1060**, **1496**, 2065-w-SA
Social welfare: 91-US, 599-DC (CW), 619-EU-IR-UK, **703**, **908**, **1358**, 1884-FE-UK, 1905-1911-UK, 2158-US
Social work. 445 + 446-US, 635 + 778-US, **1060**, 1861-SC, 1976-SA, **2186**-w
Therapy: *See* **Occupational therapy** *in this section, and* **Therapy** *in Section 6.*
Urban planning: 333-AU, 564-US, 795-EU-IR-UK, 1698-DC, **1825**
Vocational rehabilitation: 1490-US
Welfare: *See* **Social welfare**.
Youth services: 310-AU, 600-CW, **623**, 1181-US, 1382-DC, 1443-AU-CA-EU-NZ-UK, 1861-SC, 2006-CA, **2080**, 2158-US

Section 11

PROFESSIONS, INDUSTRIES & OCCUPATIONS—Study and/or training.

General: 33-DC-w, 249-AS, **442**-w, **449**-w, 477-CA, **557** excl. UK, 559-AU, **560**, 561-UK, 578-AS-DC, 587-CW, 599-DC (CW), 665-AU, 686-AF-PC, 745-DC, **754** excl. US, 769-US, **1160**, 1170-US, 1337 + 1348 + 1352 + 1353-DC, 1861-SC, 1895-DC, 1912 + 1957-US, **1960**-w, **1986**, 2113-SA, 2126-AU
NB: *Readers should also refer to their specialist subjects in other areas.*
Accountancy: 47-US, 119-US, 208-US, 970-UK, **972**, 1578-NZ, 1905-1911-UK, **1945**
Actuarial sciences: 960-UK, **1945**
Administration/administrative sciences: 69-US, 255-AF, 445 + 446-US, 998-CA, **1093**, **1140**, **1496**, 1572-CW, **2174**
Aerial photography: *See Section 5.*
Agroindustry: 985-DC
Aircraft industry: 1734-UK
Architecture: *See Section 2 and related subjects in Sections 5 & 10.*
Art administration: 245-UK, 445 + 446-US, 1859-SC, 2148-WA
Art restoration: *See* **Art/architecture/historic preservation** *in Section 3.*
Baking industry: 118-US, 1895-DC
Banking
  General: 121-US, 919-UK, 985-DC, 1201-US, 1206-CB-LA, 1978-SA
  International: **438**, **1108**
Bookselling: 415-UK, 1898-CW-UK
Broadcasting
  General: 317-AF-PC-SEA, 1178 + 1257 + 1403 + 1683 + 1707 + 1866-US
  Radio: 317-AF-PC-SEA, 1257-US
  Television: 1257-US, 2037 + 2132-DC
  Also see **Media (general)**.
Building industry: 634-SA, 1745 + 1746-AU
Building restoration: 1956-UK
Business
  General: 10-SA, **16**, 33-w-DC, 433-CA, **438**, 599-DC (CW), 750-SA, **770**, 919-UK, 1150-CA-US, 1221-UK, **1380**, 1707-US, 2191-CA
  Administration/management: **16**, 53-US, 162 + 163-US, 255-AF, 274 + 275-CA, 445 + 446-US, 599-DC (CW), 606-UK-US, 608-US, 625-US, 785-EU-IR-UK, 834-US, **966**, **969**, 1120 + 1201-US, 1666-w-CA-US, 1707-US, 1713 + 1714-DC, 1841-1845 + 1848-1854 + 1856 + 1857-UK, 1895-DC, **1945**, 1971 + 2007-SA, 2075-AF, 2083-DC, 2113-SA, 2191-CA
  Education: 1268-US

SUBJECT INDEX *See How to Use The Grants Register, page ix*

Teaching: 433 + 2191-CA
Cartography: 76-US, 258-US, **536**
Civil aviation industry: 1061-DC
Civil service: *See* Government service, Section 10.
Coalmining industry: 1024-UK
Commerce (general): 212-UK, 581-SA, 848-DC, **1039**, 1235-US, 1236-UK, 1871-AU, 2098 + 2104-NZ
Communications (general): **252**, 599-DC (CW), 1178 + 1183-US, 2063-DC, **2077, 2078**
Computer industry: 261-US
Consumer affairs: 487-CA, 1425-US
Culinary study/training: 1468-US
Documentation: 1437 + 1438-US, 1895-DC, 1939-UK
Education: *See* Section 9.
Engineering industry: 2007-SA
Estate management: *See* Section 7.
Exports: 385-UK
Finance
　General: 599-DC (CW), **770**, 919-UK, 1201-US, 1713 + 1714 + 1895-DC, **1945**, 1971 + 1978-SA
　International: **438**, 1108
Fire administration: **1038**
Fire fighting: 1017-CW-UK
Food services/administration: **175**, 487-CA, 1468-US
Forest products industry: **818, 820**, 1397-NZ
Gas industry: 404-UK, 1018-UK
Graphic arts industry: 746 + 747-US
Health/hospital administration: 69-US, 96-US, 99-US, 445 + 446-US, 890-UK, 2057-US
Hotel/restaurant management: 1468-US
Industry
　General: **16, 770**, 1052-DC, 1549-CA, 1714-DC, 1841-1845 + 1848-1854 + 1856 + 1857-UK, 2063 + 2083-DC
　Small: 599-DC (CW), 1895 + 2083-DC
Institutional management: 1468-US
Insurance: **167,** ·923 + 924-CA-US, 1229-CA, 2000-US
Inventory control: 162 + 163-US
Journalism
　General: 255-AF, 421-UK, 445 + 446-US, 587-CW, 591-CW-UK, 841-US, 1032-CA-LA-US, **1114**, 1117, **1171**, 1178 + 1179 + 1201 + 1257 + 1436 + 1589 + 1590-US, **1591**, 1683 + 1694 + 1707-US, **1726** (esp. w-DC-minorities), 1866-US, 1942-w-UK, 2037-DC, **2077, 2078**, 2155-US
　American affairs: 367-US, 580-CA-LA-US, 841 + 1694 + 1866-US, 2087-US, **2180** excl. US
　Aviation: 350-US
　British affairs: 421-UK

Business/Finance: 579-US, 883 + 1235-US
Cartoon: 421-UK
Conservation: 1536-CA-MX-US
Electronic: 1257-US
Engineering: 1524-US
Environment/natural resources: 2140-CA-US
European affairs: 1171
International affairs: 421-UK, 1114, **1171**
Investigative: 841-US
Legal: 462-CA
Medical: 151-US, 644-US, **1563**
News reporting: 1163-PH-SEA
Photographic: 421-UK, **1591**, 1694-US
Print: 1257 + 1645-US
Scientific: 54 + 126-US, **1114**, 1177, 2140-CA-US
Social: 367 + 578-US, **908**, 1590 + 2087-US
Space: 350-US
Teaching: 1589-US
Television: 2132-DC
Also see Media (general).
Labour/manpower/personnel: 698-CA, 1698 + 2063-DC
Leather industry: **413**
Librarianship
　General: 131-CA-US, 132-US, 372-AU-NZ, 373-UK, 415-UK, 479-CA, 494-CA, **531**, 590-CW, 677-EN-WA, 678 + 679-UK, **724**, 851-US, 1087-DC, 1577-NZ, 1861-SC, 1989-1991-CA-US
　Bibliographical: 132-US, 1577-NZ
　Children's: 131-CA-US, 530-US, 885-US
　Current affairs: 132-US
　History: 132-US
　Law: 56-US
　School: 132-US
　Science: 1545-CA
　Special: 1989-1991-CA-US
　University: 398-UK
Management (general): 69-US, 599-DC (CW), 608-US, 625-US, 785-EU-IR-UK, **966, 969**, 988-UK, 1052-DC, 1713 + 1714-DC, 1861-SC, 1895-DC, 1905-1911-UK, 2075-AF, 2083-DC, **2174**
Manpower: *See* Labour/manpower/personnel.
Maritime affairs: 1107-DC
Marketing: 1707-US, 1713 + 1714 + 1895-DC
Mass communication: 1178 + 1866-US
Materials management: 1404 + 1707-US
Meat & livestock industry: 1269-NZ, **1270**
Media (general): 310-AU, **908**, 1866-US
Milling industry: 610-US
Nursing: *See* Section 6.
Opera administration: 1486-US
Packaging industry: 1669-UK
Paper industry: 1669 + 2004 + 2005-UK
Personnel: *See* Labour/manpower/personnel.

Petrochemical industry: 995-DC
Petroleum industry: 273-CA, 606-UK-US, 1873-1876-UK, **1877**
Pharmaceutical industry: 1752-IR-UK
Postal services: 2090-DC
Printing: 746+747-US, 1257-US, 1669+2004+2005-UK, 2032-US
Production management: 162+163-US
Productivity: 988-UK
Public administration: See **Administration/administrative sciences**.
Public relations: 824-US
Public relations teaching: 825-US
Publishing
  General: 415-UK, 746+747-US, 2004+2005-UK
  Editing: 1437-US
  Production: 1437+2032-US
Purchasing and supply: 1404-US
Railways: 544-UK
Real estate: 127-US
Risk management: **167**
Road transport: 544-UK, 1723-CA
Science administration: 445+446-US
Shipping industry: 985+1601-DC
Shoe industry: 572-UK
Sports: 310-AU
Steel industry: 2007-AU
Surveying
  General: 76-US, 1776-UK
  Land: 586-DC (CW)
  Quantity: 586-DC (CW)
Teaching: See Section 9.
Technical/vocational studies or training: 1052-DC, 1340-CW (DC)
Also see **Technical studies** in Section 5.
Textile industry: 2033-UK
Tourist industry: 429-UK
Trade
  General: 599-DC (CW), 1698-DC
  International: 848-DC, 1698-DC
Transportation
  General: 544-UK, 599-DC (CW), 1980-AU, 2048-CA, 2063-DC
  Air/sea: 985-DC
Vocational training: See **General** and **Technical/vocational studies or training**.
Watchmaking: **441** excl. US
Wine and grape industry: 186-US

A

See *How to Use The Grants Register*, page ix

[1]

ACADEMY OF AMERICAN POETS, INC.

Fellowship

Purpose: To reward distinguished poetic achievement.

No. offered: One Fellowship annually.

Value: US$10,000.

Tenable for one year.

Eligibility: Open to United States citizens.

Note: All nominations are made by the Board of Chancellors of the Academy. Fellows are elected by majority vote in confidential mail ballots.

Address:
Academy of American Poets, Inc.
177 East 87th Street
New York, New York 10028
U.S.A.

[2]

ACADEMY OF AMERICAN POETS, INC.

Lamont Poetry Selection is awarded annually. Publishers, who may obtain entry forms from the Academy, are invited to submit their best poetry manuscripts by United States poets who have already had one book of poetry published. The Academy contracts to buy 1,000 copies of the winning book for distribution to its members. Applications from individuals are not accepted.

Harold Morton Landon Translation Award of US$1,000 is offered in even-numbered years for a published translation into English of poetry from any language. The translated work may be a book-length poem, a collection of poems, or a translation of drama into verse. Translators should be U.S. citizens. Publications should be submitted by 1st January of the Award year.

Walt Whitman Award is given annually for the publication of an American poet's first book. The cash value is US$1,000. The Academy distributes 1,250 copies of the winning book to its members. Manuscripts must be submitted between 15th September and 16th November for consideration. The required entry form may be obtained from the Academy.

Further information from:
Academy of American Poets, Inc.
177 East 87th Street
New York, New York 10028
U.S.A.

[3]

ACADEMY OF ARTS *(Czechoslovakia)*

Exchange Scholarships

Subjects: Music, dance, drama, puppetry, cinema, photography and television.

Value: Cost of tuition and certain expenses.

Tenable at the Academy in Prague for a maximum of four or five years.

Eligibility: Open to nationals of countries with which the Academy or Czechoslovakia has an exchange agreement. Candidates should possess a bachelor's degree.

Closing date: End of December.

Not confirmed for 1983.

Further information from:
Academy of Arts
Smetanovo Nabr. 2
Prague 1
Czechoslovakia

[4]

ACADEMY OF MOTION PICTURE ARTS AND SCIENCES (U.S.A.)

Student Film Awards

In addition to the Academy Awards, or Oscars, which carry no prize money, the Academy and the Academy Foundation, in cooperation with the American Telephone and Telegraph Company, offers up to thirteen Student Film Awards annually.

Four top Achievement Awards of US$1,000; up to eight Merit Awards of US$500, and at the Academy's discretion, one Honorary Award of US$750 may be granted. Any student having completed a film at an accredited college or university after 1st April is eligible. Award winners are flown to Los Angeles, California to accept their prizes at a public ceremony.

Further information from:
Elaine Richard
Academy of Motion Picture Arts and Sciences
8949 Wilshire Boulevard
Beverly Hills, California 90211
U.S.A.

[5]

ACADEMY OF NATURAL SCIENCES OF PHILADELPHIA

Hayden Memorial Geological Award of US$300 and a bronze medal is given every three years for the best publication, exploration, discovery or research in the sciences of geology and paleontology.

Leidy Medal of US$500 and a bronze medal is given every three years for the best publication, exploration, discovery or research in the natural sciences.

Note: The Academy also awards the *Richard Hopper Day Memorial Medal* and the *Gold Medal*, which have monetary value.

Further information from:
Academy of Natural Sciences of Philadelphia
Nineteenth and the Parkway
Philadelphia, Pennsylvania 19103
U.S.A.

[6]

ACADEMY OF SCIENCES OF THE USSR (Moscow)

International Geological L.A. Speniarov Prize

Purpose: To encourage the development of geological sciences and to help strengthen international scientific cooperation.

No. offered: One Prize every four years.

Value: The equivalent of 500 roubles, to be paid in the national currency of the Prize winner.

Eligibility: Open to geoscientists of any nationality who have proven their ability and cooperation through their work.

Note: The award is traditionally given to a citizen of the country which is hosting the current International Geological Congress. The last Prize was given in Paris during 1980.

Further information from:
USSR National Committee of Geologists
Pyzhevsky 7
109017 Moscow Zh-17
U.S.S.R.

[7]

ACADEMY OF SCIENTIFIC RESEARCH AND TECHNOLOGY (Cairo)

Research facilities, for periods from six months to three years, are offered through the Ministry of Higher Education, to students particularly from Arab and African countries. Students may conduct research in scientific or technical fields or undertake further training in those fields or in the repair and maintenance of scientific instruments. Candidates undertaking research must have at least a B.Sc. degree or its equivalent. For technical training, a high school certificate or equivalent is required.

Further information from:
Academy of Scientific Research and Technology
101 Kasr el Aini Street
Cairo
Arab Republic of Egypt

[8]

ACUM LTD. *(Tel-Aviv)*

Prizes

Up to 20 Prizes, ranging in value from IS2,500 to IS7,000 are awarded annually for musical and literary works of all kinds. The Prizes are awarded to Israeli citizens only.

Closing date: 31st May of each year.

Further information from:
  Acum Ltd.
  Acum House
  188 Rothschild Boulevard
  Tel Aviv 61110
  Israel

[9]

KONRAD ADENAUER FOUNDATION *(West Germany)*
Institute for the Sponsorship of Talented Students *(West Germany)*

Scholarships

Purpose: To give exceptionally intelligent young people the opportunity to have a good university education in preparation for positions in public life, science, industry, business and international organizations.

Subjects: Any university studies, including education and the arts.

Value: From DM780 to DM1,300 per month.

Tenable at universities in the Federal Republic.

Eligibility: Open to German and foreign students and graduates who are at universities in the Federal Republic, and to graduate students from the developing counties. Candidates should be not more than 32 years of age.

Further information from:
  Institute for the Sponsorship of Talented
    Students
  Konrad Adenauer Foundation
  Rathausallee 12
  D-5205 St. Augustin 1
  West Germany

[10]

AECI LTD. *(South Africa)*

Research Fellowships

Subjects: Chemistry, physics and metallurgy; chemical, civil, mechanical, electrical and instrument engineering; accounting, business science and economics; pure, applied and statistical mathematics; computer science; social sciences.

Value: R6,000 per annum paid to candidate; R1,200 per annum paid to university department in which study is being carried out.

Tenable at any recognized university in South Africa for two years; renewable for up to one further year subject to satisfactory progress.

Eligibility: Open to graduates on academic merit; candidates must hold at least a four-year degree in an appropriate subject.

Note: Fellows are not permitted to accept lectureships or any other bursaries, and must not be tied in any way to an organization other than AECI Ltd. There are, however, no obligations as to employment after the successful completion of studies.

Closing date: 31st July.

Further information from:
  Personnel Manager
  AECI Ltd.
  P.O. Box 1122
  Johannesburg 2000
  South Africa

[11]

AFRICAN—AMERICAN INSTITUTE

African Graduate Fellowship Program (AFGRAD): A varying number of Fellowships are offered to sub-Saharan African students for study in priority fields directly related to participating African countries development plans and needs. The Fellowships are tenable in the United States for one academic year and are renewable subject to satisfactory progress until the required degree is obtained. Open to those students who have achieved superior undergraduate academic records and who are nominated by their government. The financial provisions include tuition and fees, round trip travel, and an allowance for maintenance, books, etc. There are no allowances for dependents of Fellows. English language training is provided if necessary. On completion of the study, Fellows are expected to return to their home country. Applications are generally considered in October and November for commencement the following year.

Development Training for Portuguese-Speaking Africans Program (DTPSA): Grants are awarded to government nominated candidates from the Portuguese-speaking countries of Africa. Awards are tenable for technical and university level study programs at institutions in Africa, the U.S., and Portugal. Fields of study will be the priority development areas specified by the governments. English language training will be provided where necessary. Awards include round-trip travel, tuition, maintenance and books.

Southern African Refugee Education Project (SAREP): Grants are available to qualified candidates who are refugees from the minority-ruled countries of southern Africa for study at post-secondary schools, vocational institutions, and universities in Africa. Priority will be given to individuals wishing to study manpower fields relevant to the economic developmental needs of their home countries. Awards provide for transportation, tuition, insurance, maintenance and books.

Southern African Student Program (SASP): Awards for a maximum of two years to pursue specialized training or a masters degree in the United States are offered to qualified candidates from Zimbabwe, South Africa or Namibia. Awards vary according to individuals financial needs. Preference is given to candidates who seek training in fields directly related to the manpower developmental needs of Africa, and who plan to return to Africa to seek employment upon completion of the program.

Southern African Training Program (SATP): In anticipation of black majority rule in southern Africa, training Awards are offered to nationals of Zimbabwe, South Africa and Namibia. Awards are available for post-secondary school study programs in technical institutions and universities in the U.S. and Africa. Awards cover travel, tuition, maintenance, books and related expenses. Students who are accepted for study in the U.S. are expected to return to Africa upon completion of their program.

Special Nigerian Assistance Program: Graduate degree training programs are administered for Nigerian students through agreements with the Nigerian Centre for Management Development or with individual Nigerian universities. Candidates are nominated by the participating institution, and are generally expected to meet AFGRAD academic standards and to be eligible for tuition wavers from participating U.S. graduate schools. Maintenance, books, special fees and other allowances are provided as stipulated by the nominating Nigerian institution.

Not confirmed for 1983.

Further information from:
African-American Institute
833 United Nations Plaza
New York, New York 10017
U.S.A.

[12]

AFRICAN INSTITUTE FOR ECONOMIC DEVELOPMENT AND PLANNING *(Dakar)*

Fellowships and Grants

The Institute offers a limited number of Fellowships and Grants for studies at the Institute on economic development and planning to nationals of African member and associate member countries of the Economic Commission for Africa: Algeria, Benin, Botswana, Burundi, Cameroon, Cape-Verde, Central African Republic, Chad, Republic of Congo, Arab Republic of Egypt, Ethiopia, Gabon, Gambia, Ghana, Guinea, Ivory Coast, Kenya, Lesotho, Liberia, Libya, Malagasy Republic, Malawi, Mali, Mauritania, Morocco, Niger, Nigeria, Rwanda, Senegal, Sierra Leone, Somalia, Sudan, United Republic of Tanzania, Togo, Tunisia, Uganda, Republic of Zaïre, Zambia and Zimbabwe.

The Fellowships are offered to persons holding a B.A. degree or its equivalent in economics and are tenable for 9 to 18 months (for the nine-month programme on economic development and planning the three-month specialized programme and the six-month research programme). Each Fellowship carries a stipend of *CFA*130,000 per month, plus the cost of transportation and books. Candidates should, preferably, have had some experience in working with a planning organization and must have the support of their governments or be formally nominated by them.

Further information from:
Director
African Institute for Economic Development and Planning
B.P. 3186
Dakar
Senegal

[13]

AFRICAN STUDIES ASSOCIATION *(U.S.A.)*

Herskovits Award

The Award of US$500 is given annually to the author of a distinguished work on Africa published or distributed in the United States during the preceding year. The work must be an original scholarly publication. Edited collections, symposia, new editions of previously published books, bibliographies and dictionaries are not eligible.

Publishers may submit works by 1st April for consideration by the Committee.

Further information from:
African Studies Association
255 Kingsley Hall
University of California at Los Angeles
Los Angeles, California 90024
U.S.A.

[14]

AFRICAN TRAINING AND RESEARCH CENTRE IN ADMINISTRATION FOR DEVELOPMENT (CAFRAD) *(Tangier)*

Assistance for Participation in CAFRAD's Activities

CAFRAD organises scientific meetings, seminars and in-service training courses for high-ranking officals from the public and private sectors in African countries who play a significant role in development. This includes: a regular programme of courses for trainers in public administration schools and institutes; seminars for senior administrators; applied research activities, documentation and publication services; a programme of specialized senior staff development activities covering problems of human resources, rural and urban development, top management, and training of trainers; etc.

Member states: Algeria, Botswana, Burundi, Cameroon, Central African Republic, Chad, Egypt, Gabon, Gambia, Ghana, Guinea-Bissau, Ivory Coast, Kenya, Lesotho, Liberia, Libya, Mauritania, Mauritius, Morocco, Niger, Nigeria, Senegal, Sierra Leone, Somalia, Sudan, Swaziland, Tanzania, Togo, Tunisia, Uganda, Upper Volta, Zaïre, and Zambia.

Not confirmed for 1983.

Further information from:
CAFRAD
B.P. 310
Tangier
Morocco

[15]

AFRO-ASIAN INSTITUTE IN VIENNA

Scholarships

Purpose: To promote cultural exchange and development aid.

Subjects: Unrestricted

No. offered: 5 to 10 Scholarships annually, including extensions.

Value: Individually varying amounts for trainees, students and lecturers; paid in monthly instalments.

Tenable at a university, vocational school, or similar institution in Austria.

Eligibility: Open to nationals of developing countries in Africa and Asia who are between 21 and 35 years of age, and have had adequate previous study or vocational practice in the specific field for which the Scholarship is applied. It is preferred that candidates be able to speak German. Only those in financial need will be considered, and applicability of the special branch of study or training in the applicant's home country is essential. Preference will be given to university assistants and collaborators in social, sanitary and agricultural projects.

Note: Applicant must verify by document his intended employment upon completion of the Scholarship.

Closing date: 15th May for the following academic year.

Further information from:
Afro-Asian Institute in Vienna
Student Division
Türkenstrasse 3
A-1090 Vienna
Austria

[16]

AGENCY FOR TECHNICAL, INDUSTRIAL AND ECONOMIC COOPERATION *(France)*

Purpose: To enable specialists of advanced level (engineers, company executives and managers, economists, financiers and senior government officials) to follow training programmes which will give them opportunities for contact with French companies, special departments and experts.

Subject: Any field related to industrial or economic matters.

No. offered: Approximately 1,600 Awards annually.

Value: Monthly basic allowance of FF2,280. Monthly housing allowance of FF1,720.

Tenable at all French firms interested in specialized cooperation with foreign specialists and engineers, for a period between one and four months.

Eligibility: Open to persons with a university level education who have had several years of professional practice and hold, or hope to obtain, a position of responsibility in the firm to which they belong.

Note: Details of programmes may be obtained from the French Commercial Counsellor in the applicant's country of birth; the Commercial Counsellor will also handle applications.

Address
Agence pour la Cooperation Technique, Industrielle et Economique
64-66 rue Pierre Charron
75008 Paris
France

[17]

AGRICULTURAL DEVELOPMENT COUNCIL, INC. *(U.S.A.)*

Fellowships and Research Grants

The Council offers the following support to selected Asian social sceintists, in an effort to help them increase their competence in dealing with the human and economic problems of agricultural and rural development, primarily in Asia.

Fellowships: For graduate study at the M.S. level in rural social science fields. Tenable at universities in Asia and Australia, and cover maintenance, tuition, travel and book expenses.

Research Grants: For study on selected policy-related questions with a bearing on agricultural and rural development. Tenable in Asia, and usually cover direct research expenses only.

Further information from:
Agricultrual Development Council, Inc.
1290 Avenue of the Americas
New York, New York, 10019
U.S.A.

[18]

AGRICULTURAL INSTITUTE *(Ireland)*

Agricultural Research Scholarships

Scholarships of £1,600 to £1,850 (subject to annual review) plus fees and certain expenses, are offered annually to the children of persons born or normally resident in Ireland. Candidates must be first or second class honours graduates of a recognised university. The Scholarships, for study appropriate to agricultural research needs in Ireland (specific subjects decided each year by the Council of the Institute), are tenable at university departments in Ireland or abroad, a research centre of the institute, or at other research institutes, for up to three years.

Further information from:
   Head, Manpower Development Unit
   Agricultrual Institute
   19 Sandymount Avenue
   Ballsbridge
   Dublin 4
   Ireland

[19]

AGRICULTURAL INSTITUTE OF CANADA
Commonwealth Foundation *(U.K.)*
Canadian International Development Agency

CIDA-Commonwealth Foundation Exchange Program

Purpose: To finance exchange visits between Canadian agrologists and those of developing Commonwealth countries, so that the two-way flow of information is enhanced.

No. offered: Seven Exchanges annually.

Value: Can$2,000 to Can$2,500.

Tenable in Commonwealth developing countries and Canada for up to two months.

Eligibility: Open to scientists, economists, agricultural engineers and extension workers who have demonstrable ability and potential in their chosen field. Preference will be given to younger applicants and those who have not had previous experience in developing countries. Canadian participants must be either AIC members or members of a scientific society affiliated to the AIC.

Closing date: Six months prior to departure.

Further information from:
   Agricultural Institute of Canada
   Suite 907, 151 Slater Street
   Ottawa, Ontario
   Canada K1P 5H4

[20]

AGRICULTURAL RESEARCH COUNCIL *(U.K.)*

Veterinary Fellowships

Purpose: To enable outstanding young veterinary graduates to devote their full time to original and independent research.

Subject: Original work in any field of veterinary medicine applicable to farm animals.

No. offered: Six Awards annually.

Value: The United Kingdom universities non-clinical academic salary is used and is related to age.

Tenable at any of the six veterinary schools in the United Kingdom for up to three years.

Eligibility: Open to British subjects normally resident in the United Kingdom who hold an acceptable degree in veterinary science.

Closing date: 31st May.

Note: Applications should be made to the ARC through the host veterinary school and contain a recommendation from the candidate's current supervisor or head of department.

Further information from:
   Secretary
   Agricultural Research Council
   160 Great Portland Street
   London
   England W1N 6DT

[21]

AGRICULTURAL RESEARCH COUNCIL *(U.K.)*

Veterinary Training Grants

Purpose: To enable veterinary graduates to undertake a formal course of instruction in a specific scientific discipline before embarking on a career in research on farm animals.

Subject: Any project of relevance to agricultural research.

No. offered: Up to four Awards annually.

Value: A maintenance allowance, reimbursement of compulsory fees, travelling expenses and, where appropriate, dependants and post-graduate experience allowances.

Eligibility: Open to candidates who have

been resident in the United Kingdom, Channel Isles or the Isle of Man for three years immediately preceding the date of application, and have graduated with a first or upper second class honours degree. Students who are ordinarily resident in Northern Ireland, the Channel Isles or the Isle of Man should apply to their respective Education Authorities.

Closing date: 31st March.

Further information from:
Secretary
Agricultural Research Council
160 Great Portland Street
London
England W1N 6DT

[22]

AGRICULTURAL RESEARCH COUNCIL (U.K.)

Postgraduate Research Studentships

Purpose: To enable science graduates to study for a higher degree at one of the Council's research institutes.

Subject: Any project of relevance to agricultural research.

No. offered: 30 Studentships annually.

Value: A maintenance allowance, reimbursement of compulsory fees, travelling expenses and, where appropriate, dependants' and postgraduate experience allowances.

Tenable at one of the Council's research institutes in the United Kingdom for up to three years.

Eligibility: Open to candidates who have been resident in the United Kingdom, Channel Isles or the Isle of Man for three years immediately preceding the date of application, and have graduated with a first or upper second class honours degree. Students who are ordinarily resident in Northern Ireland, the Channel Isles or the Isle of Man should apply to their respective Education Authorities.

Closing date: 31st March.

Further information from:
Secretary
Agricultural Research Council
160 Great Portland Street
London
England W1N 6DT

[23]

AGRICULTURAL RESEARCH COUNCIL OF NORWAY

Postdoctorate Fellowship

Subject: Agriculture.

Value: An annual stipend of 60,000 Norwegian kroner for single Fellows, 76,000 kroner for married Fellows accompanied by their spouse; plus an additional 4,000 kroner for each accompanying dependant child. ARCN may pay travel expenses for the Fellow.

Tenable at a research institution in Norway for one year; often renewable for a second year.

Eligibility: Open to nationals of all countries wishing to undertake agricultural research in Norway. Candidates should hold qualifications equivalent at least to a British or American Ph.D.

Note: Application should be made to the institution where the Fellow intends to work. If the institution is interested in having a Postdoctorate Fellow, application will then be made to the Council.

Closing date: 1st April and 1st October.

Further information from:
Agricultural Research Council of Norway
P.O. Box 8154 Dep.
Oslo 1
Norway

[24]

AGRICULTURAL RESEARCH COUNCIL OR NORWAY

Senior Scientist Visiting Program

Subject: Agriculture.

No. offered: Usually 2 or 3, annually.

Value: 12,000 Norwegian kroner per month; ARCN may pay travel expenses.

Tenable at a research institution in Norway for three months.

Eligibility: Open to senior scientists of all countries who are of interest to Norwegian institutions. Candidates should intend to undertake research on a specific subject.

Closing date: 1st April and 1st October.

Further information from:
Agricultural Research Council of Norway
P.O. Box 8154 Dep.
Oslo 1
Norway

[25]

AGRICURA LTD. *(South Africa)*

Bursaries

Two Bursaries are awarded annually for postgraduate research: one for research in the veterinary sciences; one for research in plant entomology, plant pathology or herbicide science.

Value: R1,000 each, paid in a lump sum.

Tenable in South Africa or overseas; renewable, depending upon progress of holder and number of applicants.

Eligibility: Open to South African residents holding a Bachelor's degree.

Closing date: 31st December.

Further information from:
Director or Research and Development
Agricura Ltd.
P.O. Box 55
Silverton 0127
South Africa

[26]

AIR CHIEF MARSHAL THE LORD DOWDING FUND FOR HUMANE RESEARCH *(U.K.)*

Awards are available to suitably qualified people for projects concerned with the development of alternative techniques to replace the use of live animals in medical and scientific research.

Further information from:
Air Chief Marshal the Lord Dowding Fund for Humane Research
51 Harley Street
London W1N 1DD
England

[27]

EDWARD F. ALBEE FOUNDATION, INC. *(U.S.A.)*

The Foundation maintains the William Flanagan Memorial Creative Persons Center (known as the "Barn") in Montauk, Long Island as a residence for writers and painters.

The Center is open 1st May to 15th October and can accommodate six persons at a time. The standards for admission are talent and need. The environment is communal and residents are expected to do their share in maintaining the condition of the Center.

Applicants should submit recommendations and a biography. Painters and sculptors should include photographs or slides; writers should include samples of work.

Application materials must be accompanied by a pre-paid return envelope.

Further information from:
Edward F. Albee Foundation, Inc.
14 Harrison Street
New York, New York 10013
U.S.A.

[28]

ALFRED HOSPITAL *(Melbourne)*

Edward Wilson Memorial Fellowship

Subject: Medical research.

No. offered: One Fellowship every one or two years.

Value: Stipend between A$10,000 and A$25,000 appropriate to qualifications and experience. Assistance to secure appropriate accommodation, and the equivalent of one return economy air fare in the case of an overseas appointee, will be given.

Tenable for one or two years at Alfred Hospital (including Monash University and Baker Medical Research Unit).

Eligibility: Open to medical practitioners or science graduates with senior qualifications.

Note: Applications should be made on the prescribed form.

Closing date: Early September.

Further information from:
Chief Executive Officer
Alfred Hospital
Commercial Road
Prahran, Victoria
Australia 3181

[29]

ALFRED HOSPITAL *(Melbourne)*

Medical Research and Travelling Scholarships

Purpose: To enable university graduates to undertake projects in medical research at Alfred Hospital or kindred institutions.

No. offered: Varies according to value of individual awards.

Tenable at Alfred Hospital (including Monash University and Baker Medical Research Institute) for one year with the possibility of extensions.

Value: Determined by the standing of the applicant, the quality of the proposed research project and the time to be devoted to the study. Usually the Scholarships will range from A$2,000 to A$20,000, for one year.

Eligibility: Open to medical and science graduates.

Closing date: Early September.

Further information from:
Chief Executive Officer
Alfred Hospital
Commercial Road
Prahran, Victoria
Australia 3181

[30]

ALL SAINTS EDUCATIONAL TRUST *(U.K.)*

Grants

The object of the Trust is the advancement of higher and further education by making Grants to persons who are, or intend to become, teachers especially of religious education or home economics or in the field of multicultural education, to enable them to become qualified or better qualified. Grants are also available to individuals or corporate bodies for research, particularly in these fields. In the application of income, the Trustees seek to advance education in accordance with the doctrines of the Church of England or of a Church in communion with it.

Closing date: 31st January.

Further information from:
Secretary
All Saints Educational Trust
122 White Hart Lane
Tottenham, London
England N17 8HP

[31]

ALLEGHENY INTERNATIONAL *(U.S.A.)*

Graduate Fellowships

Purpose: To increase the number of academically qualified personnel in the field of metallurgy.

No. offered: Three Fellowships annually; one at each of the following institutions: Carnegie-Mellon University, Massachusetts Institute of Technology and Rensselaer Polytechnic Institute.

Value: US$5,000 each, to Fellows at Carnegie-Mellon and RPI; US$5,800 to Fellow at MIT.

Tenable for one year; renewable for a maximum of three years.

Eligibility: Open to graduate students who have selected the subject of doctoral research and who are nominated by department heads of participating institutions.

Note: Application procedures are carried out through appropriate department heads and deadlines are set by the participating institutions.

Further information from:
Allegheny International
Two Oliver Plaza
Pittsburgh, Pennsylvania 15222
U.S.A.

[32]

ALLIED ARTISTS OF AMERICA, INC.

Awards

Forty or more Awards, with values ranging from US$100 to US$600 are given annually to encourage American painters and sculptors. The competitions are open to all U.S. citizens and are based solely on the quality of the work submitted.

Further information from:
Allied Artists of America, Inc.
c/o National Arts Club
15 Gramercy Park South
New York, New York 10003
U.S.A.

[33]

ALTRUSA INTERNATIONAL FOUNDATION, INC. *(U.S.A.)*

Grants-In-Aid

Purpose: To provide emergency funds for the completion of graduate work.

Subject: Sciences, social welfare, medicine, education and business fields.

No. offered: Variable.

Value: Based on need and merit, from US$250 to US$1,000. Local Altrusans extend hospitality and offer personal assistance to recipients.

Tenable in accredited graduate schools outside the recipient's home country (and in a country where Altrusa is established) for the remaining period of the studies. There are Altrusa Clubs in Australia, Bermuda, Canada, Dominican Republic, England, Guatemala, India, Ireland, Mexico, New Zealand, the Philippines, Puerto Rico, Scotland and the United States.

Eligibility: Open to women from Africa, Latin America, Asia, the Middle East, Polynesia and Melanesia who have completed at least one-half of their graduate study program in a foreign accredited school. Grant recipients must return to their home country upon completion of studies.

Note: Applicants should complete the official forms and submit a letter of purpose and photographs.

Further information from:
Chairman, Grants-in-Aid Committee
Altrusa International Foundation, Inc.
8 South Michigan Avenue
Chicago, Illinois 60603
U.S.A.

[34]

ALUMINIUM COMPANY OF CANADA, LTD.

Alcan Fellowships

Purpose: To foster increased academic/industrial interaction.

Subjects: Pure and applied mathematical and physical sciences.

No. offered: Seven Fellowships annually.

Value: Can$7,500 per annum.

Tenable for one year at one of seven institutions—listed with their respective preferred fields: University of British Columbia; metallurgy; Laval University, chemical engineering; McGill University, metallurgy; Queen's University, chemistry; Universty of Toronto, metallurgy; University of Montreal, chemistry; and McMaster University, material science.

One Fellowship is tenable at each institution. Fellowships may be renewed annually.

Eligibility: Open to persons who have been accepted for postgraduate work at one of the institutions concerned.

Note: Enquiries should be directed to the relevant departments at the institutions concerned.

Address:
Aluminum Company of Canada, Ltd.
P.O. Box 8400
Kingston, Ontario
Canada K7L 4Z4

[35]

AMERICA-ISRAEL CULTURAL FOUNDATION *(Israel)*

Shareet Scholarships and Short-term Fellowships

Purpose: To enable the recipient to cover part of his tuition fees and additional expenses while studying in Israel and to enable those who have exhausted their possibilities for study in Israel to continue abroad.

Subjects: Various fields of art, including music, dance, theatre, plastic arts, film and television.

No. offered: Usually one or two in each field annually, depending upon qualifications of applicants and the Foundation's budget.

Value: Varies according to individual need and the Foundation's budget.

Tenable in Israel and abroad. Scholarships for one year; Fellowships for up to six months.

Eligibility: Open to Israeli citizens. Age limits for Scholarships vary according to the field, up to 30 years of age. Applicants for Fellowships should be artists or teachers with wide professional experience. No age limits are set for Fellowships.

Closing dates: Vary annually. October-November for Scholarships abroad and short-term Fellowships; February-March for Scholarships in Israel.

Not confirmed for 1983.

Further information from:
American-Israel Cultural Foundation
32 Allenby Road
Tel-Aviv
Israel

[36]

AMERICAN ACADEMY FOR CEREBRAL PALSY AND DEVELOPMENTAL MEDICINE

Research Support Program

To encourage clinical and basic research in developmental medicine, the Academy offers annual Grants of up to US$5,000. Additional funding may be available under special circumstances. The number offered is determined by monies available. Payment is made in a lump sum and Grants may be renewed for up to two years, if approved.

There are no specific requirements in regard to age, sex, citizenship or residency. Applicants should submit an informal proposal with complete information.

Closing date: 1st July.

Further information from:
American Academy for Cerebral Palsy and Developmental Medicine
2405 Westwood Avenue, P.O. Box 11083
Richmond, Virginia 23230
U.S.A.

[37]

AMERICAN ACADEMY OF FACIAL PLASTIC AND RECONSTRUCTIVE SURGERY

Awards

Benjamin Shuster Memorial Award: One annual Prize of US$250 is given to the top paper based on clinical or research study in the field of plastic and reconstructive surgery of the head and neck. The competition is open to residents or fellows in otolaryngology who are the sole or senior author of the paper. Studies prepared during the first year after completion of residency training will be considered provided that the research was conducted during the author's residency training program. *Closing dates:* end of November for notification of intent to participate; end of January for submission of the paper.

Ira J. Tresley Research Award: An annual Prize of US$500 is awarded for the best paper based on any research study in the field of plastic and reconstructive surgery of the head and neck. The competition is open to any physician who has been board certified for at least three years. *Closing dates:* end of November for notification of intent to participate; end of January for submission of the paper.

Further information from:
American Academy of Facial Plastic and Reconstructive Surgery
70 West Hubbard Street
Suite 202
Chicago, Illinois 60610
U.S.A.

[38]

AMERICAN ACADEMY OF FAMILY PHYSICIANS

Mead Johnson Awards for Graduate Education in Family Practice

Purpose: To provide financial assistance for outstanding young physicians planning careers in the family practice of medicine in the United States.

Subject: Residency training in family practice.

No. offered: 20 Awards annually.

Value: US$1,500 per annum; paid monthly.

Tenable for 12 months in hospital training programs approved by the American Medical Association; not renewable.

Eligibility: Open to United States physicians who are second-year residents in an approved family practice residency program. They must express the intention to enter the family practice of medicine in the United States.

Closing date: 1st December.

Address for application:
Chairman,
Mead Johnson Awards Committee
American Academy of Family Physicians
1740 West 92nd Street
Kansas City, Missouri 64114
U.S.A.

[39]

AMERICAN ACADEMY AND INSTITUTE OF ARTS AND LETTERS

Arts and Letters Awards: 17 Awards of US$5,000 each are given annually to honor and encourage distinguished artists, composers and writers who are not Institute members and to help them continue their creative work.

Note: The Academy/Institute also offers a number of special awards in art, literature and music, as well as scholarships and fellowships in music. None of these may be applied for, with the exception of the *Richard Rodgers Production Award.* Applications for this may be obtained by sending a self-addressed stamped envelope to the address below.

Further information from:
American Academy and Institute of Arts and Letters
633 West 155th Street
New York, New York 10032
U.S.A.

[40]

AMERICAN ACADEMY OF NEUROLOGICAL SURGERY

An annual Award of US$100, an engraved certificate and travel expenses to the Academy's annual meeting is given for the best presentation reporting original clinical or laboratory research pertaining to the nervous system. Material should not have been published in any journal prior to the date of the Academy meeting, nor previously presented at any other national meeting. Candidates are restricted to doctors of medicine currently in training in neurological surgery in North America or to those who will complete their training on or after 30th June of the Award year. Persons with equivalent certification from other organizations are not eligible.

Closing date: 1st August of the Award year.

Further information from:
Dr. John T. Garner, Secretary
American Academy of Neurological Surgery
1127 East Green Street
Pasadena, California 91106
U.S.A.

[41]

AMERICAN ACADEMY OF PEDIATRICS

E. Mead Johnson Awards for Research in Pediatrics

Purpose: For research work which has been published during recent years.

No. offered: 2 Awards annually.

Value: US$3,000 each, plus a certificate and travel expenses for the recipient and head of the department at which the Award work was accomplished, to and from the annual meeting of the Academy, where the Award will be presented.

Eligibility: Open to physicians in North and South America who have graduated from a medical school no more than 17 years prior to the year in which the award was made.

Note: Nominations may be made by pediatric department heads and should be submitted to the Academy no later than 15th January of the year of the Award. Selection will be made prior to 1st April.

Further information from:
Jean D. Lockhart, M.D.
Director, Department of Committees
American Academy of Pediatrics
1801 Hinman Avenue
Evanston, Illinois 60204
U.S.A.

[42]

AMERICAN ACADEMY OF PEDIATRICS

Nutrition Award

Purpose: For outstanding achievements in research relating to nutrition of infants and children.

No. offered: One Award, annually.

Value: US$3,000.

Eligibility: Open to residents of the United States or Canada whose research has been completed and publicly reported during the seven years preceding that in which the award is given. There are no age restrictions for the Award; however, it is hoped that younger persons will be considered.

Note: The Award is made to an individual, or for one project.
No more than ten separate nominations may be submitted by an individual. Nominations should be sent to *Jean D. Lockhart, M.D., Director, Department of Health Care and Pediatric Practice, American Academy of Pediatrics, P.O. Box 1034, Evanston, Illinois 60204.*
This Award is made possible by a grant from the General Mills Foundation.

Closing date: 15th December.

Further information from:
Director, Department of Committees
American Academy of Pediatrics
1801 Hinman Avenue
Evanston, Illinois 60204
U.S.A.

[43]

AMERICAN ACADEMY OF PEDIATRICS

Residency Fellowships

Purpose: To enable young physicians to complete their pediatric training.

Value: According to individual circumstances normally from US$500 to US$3,000 each.

Tenable for one year at institutions acceptable to the American Board of Pediatrics.

Eligibility: Open to legal residents of the United States and Canada who have completed, or will have completed by 1st July, a qualifying approved internship (PL-0) or have completed a PL-1 program, and have made a definite commitment for a first year pediatric residency (PL-1 or PL-2) acceptable to the American Board of Pediatrics; or pediatric residents (PL-1, PL-2 or PL-3) in a training program who have made a definite commitment for a second year of residency in a program acceptable to the American Board of Pediatrics; and have need of financial assistance.

Note: Up to twenty-five percent of the Fellowships may be awarded to physicians desiring a third or fourth year of pediatric residency.

Applications should include a letter from the Chief of Service substantiating the above requirements. If a change in residency programs is contemplated, a letter certifying acceptance in the new program is required.

These Fellowships are provided through grants made by Mead Johnson Laboratories, Gerber Products Company, and the McNeil Consumer Products Company.

Closing date: 1st March.

Further information from:
Jean D. Lockhart, M.D.
Director, Department of Health Services and Government Affairs
American Academy of Pediatrics
P.O. Box 1034
Evanston, Illinois 60204
U.S.A.

[44]

AMERICAN ACADEMY OF PERIODONTOLOGY

Balint Orban Prize

Purpose: To recognize and acknowledge an excellent research paper related to periodontology presented by a graduate student.

No. offered: One Prize annually; two in the case of a tie.

Value: US$200, divided in the case of a tie.

Eligibility: Open to graduate students in periodontics, or those who have completed their graduate training within the eighteen months prior to submission.

Note: The Academy also annually selects one winner for its Gold Medal Award. The Gold Medal and a cash prize of US$1,000 are given to honor men of dental science who have made outstanding contributions to the understanding and treatment of periodontal disease.

Further information from:
Executive Secretary
American Academy of Periodontology
211 East Chicago Avenue, Room 924
Chicago, Illinois 60611
U.S.A.

[45]

AMERICAN ACADEMY IN ROME

Rome Prize Fellowships

Purpose: To provide the facilities and program within which a small number of individuals of exceptional promise or achievement have the opportunity to pursue their creative work and research in favorable surroundings. The variety of disciplines included in the Academy community provides the possibility of creative interaction. There is no course of instruction and no formal teaching staff.

Subject: Architecture; landscape architecture; design; musical composition; painting; sculpture; writing; classical literature; history and archeology; postclassical humanistic studies; history of art; modern Italian studies; Byzantine and Medieval Studies.

No. offered: Approximately 30 Fellowships annually.

Value: Each Fellow receives a stipend and allowances for travel and working supplies which amount to US$6,400-US$8,000. In addition, each Fellow receives free housing, a study or studio and full access to the library and other facilities.

Tenable at the American Academy in Rome, for six months or one year.

Eligibility: Open only to citizens of the United States who possess a Bachelor's or Ph.D. degree, depending upon the field of application. However, there are some vacancies for scholarly work for predoctoral candidates. Some Fellowships are awarded only to candidates who have completed their formal training, and others to those with a licensure and/or five years' professional experience.

Note: Recipients are advised to begin their study of Italian before leaving the United States and to continue immediately upon arrival in Italy.

Closing date: 15th November.

Further information from:
American Academy in Rome
41 East 65th Street
New York, New York 10021
U.S.A.

[46]

AMERICAN ACCORDION MUSICOLOGICAL SOCIETY

Music Competition Contest

Purpose: To encourage composers to write classical accordion music.

Subject: Original accordion composition.

No. offered: Two Awards annually.

Value: Amateur Award of US$100 and Professional Award of US$500; paid in a lump sum.

Eligibility: Open to any composer acquainted with the various types of accordion. There are no restrictions in regard to age or nationality.

Note: Applicants competing for the Professional Award should have at least one composition already published.

Closing date: 30th September.

Further information from:
American Accordion Musicological Society
334 South Broadway
Pitman, New Jersey 08071
U.S.A.

[47]

AMERICAN ACCOUNTING ASSOCIATION

Fellowships

Purpose: To increase the supply of qualified teachers of accounting in the United States and Canada.

Subject: Accountancy, or another area suited to preparing the applicant for teaching accounting.

No. offered: Variable number of Fellowships annually.

Value: US$1,000 per annum.

Tenable at United States universities with programs accredited by the American Association of Collegiate Schools of Business for one academic year plus, in some cases, the summer term; renewable for a second year.

Eligibility: Open to United States citizens who have completed at least one year of graduate study in accountancy and have been accepted in a doctoral program at a qualified university or business school.

Closing date: 1st March.

Not confirmed for 1983.

Further information from:
Administrative Secretary
American Accounting Association
5717 Bessie Drive
Sarasota, Florida 33583
U.S.A.

[48]

AMERICAN AGRICULTURAL ECONOMICS ASSOCIATION

Excellence in a Doctoral Program Awards: Three Awards of US$250 each are offered for outstanding Ph.D. dissertations in agricultural economics.

Excellence in a Master's Program Awards: Three Awards of US$250 each are offered for outstanding master's theses.

Distinguished Extension Programs Awards: Two Awards are offered to encourage the development of excellence in extension economics teaching; one to an individual and one to a group.

Distinguished Undergraduate Teaching Awards: Two Awards are offered to recognize and encourage meritorious performance in undergraduate teaching in agricultural economics, one for teachers with at least ten years' experience and one for a teacher with under ten years' experience.

Distinguished Policy Contributions Awards: Awards are offered to recognize outstanding contributions to policy decisions, or advancement of public and human welfare on a national or international level.

Research and Outstanding Publications Awards: Four major Awards are offered to recognize and encourage meritorious research and publication in agricultural economics. Selection for these Awards will be made from published research, textbooks, extension publications, and articles in the *American Journal of Agricultural Economics.*

Further information from:
Dr. Sydney C. James, Secretary
American Agricultural Economics
    Association
Department of Economics
Iowa State University
Ames, Iowa 50011
U.S.A.

[49]

AMERICAN ANTIQUARIAN SOCIETY
(Worcester, Massachusetts)

Albert Boni Fellowship

Purpose: To enable a qualified scholar to work at the Society in the general field of American bibliography and printing and publishing history through 1876.

No. offered: One Fellowship annually.

Value: Up to US$1,250, paid in monthly installments.

Tenable for a period of one to two months at the Society; not renewable.

Eligibility: Open to all scholars in the field of early American bibliography and printing and publising history, including foreign nationals and persons at work on their doctoral dissertations.

Note: Award will be given on the basis of scholarly qualifications, general interest of the proposed project, and on the appropriateness of the inquiry to the Society's holdings.

Closing date: 1st February for application and three letters of recommendation.

Further information from:
John B. Hench, Assistant Director for
    Research and Publication
American Antiquarian Society
185 Salisbury Street
Worcester, Massachusetts 01609
U.S.A.

[50]

AMERICAN ANTIQUARIAN SOCIETY
(Worcester, Massachusetts)

Samuel Foster Haven Fellowships

Purpose: To enable persons who might not otherwise be able to do so, to travel to the Society to make use of its research facilities in early American history and culture.

Value: Variable according to a Fellow's needs, to a maximum of US$1,800.

Tenable at the Society for one to three months.

Eligibility: Open to individuals engaged in scholarly research and writing including foreign nationals and persons at work on doctoral theses who reside more than 50 miles from Worcester, Massachusetts.

Closing date: 1st February.

Further information from:
John B. Hench, Assistant Director for
    Research and Publication
American Antiquarian Society
185 Salisbury Street
Worcester, Massachusetts 01609
U.S.A.

[51]

AMERICAN ANTIQUARIAN SOCIETY
(Worcester, Massachusetts)

Frances Hiatt Fellowship

Subjects: The general field of American bibliography and printing and publishing history through 1876.

Purpose: To provide the opportunity to a qualified individual to work in the above mentioned field at the Society.

No. offered: One Fellowship annually.

Value: Up to US$1,200; paid in monthly installments.

Tenable at the Society for a minimum of six weeks.

Eligibility: Open to graduate students of any nationality who are engaged in the general field of early American bibliography and printing and publishing history.

Note: Candidates are judged on the basis of scholarly qualifications, general interest of the proposed project and on the appropriateness of the inquiry to the Society's holdings.

Closing date: 1st February.

Further information from:
John B. Hench, Assistant Director for Research and Publication
American Antiquarian Society
185 Salisbury Street
Worcester, Massachusetts 01609
U.S.A.

[52]

AMERICAN ANTIQUARIAN SOCIETY
(Worcester, Massachusetts)

National Endowment for the Humanities Visiting Fellowships

Purpose: To make the Society's research facilities in early American history and culture more readily available.

No. offered: Two or more Fellowships annually.

Value: Negotiable up to US$1,833 per month.

Tenable at the Society's library in Worcester, Massachusetts, for six to twelve months.

Eligibility: Fellowships may not be awarded to degree candidates or for study leading to advanced degrees; nor may they be granted to foreign nationals unless they have been resident in the United States for at least three years immediately prior to receiving the award.

Note: Fellows may not accept teaching assignments or undertake any other major activities during the tenure of the award. Other major fellowships, except sabbaticals or grants from the Fellow's own institution, may not be held concurrently with a Fellowship.

Closing date: 1st February.

Further information from:
John B. Hench, Assistant Director for Research and Publication
American Antiquarian Society
185 Salisbury Street
Worcester, Massachusetts 01609
U.S.A.

[53]

AMERICAN ASSEMBLY OF COLLEGIATE SCHOOLS OF BUSINESS

Doctoral Fellowships

R.J. Reynolds Doctoral Fellowships

Purpose: To assist qualified students to devote their full time toward the completion of a doctoral dissertation in business administration.

No. offered: Two Fellowships annually.

Value: US$1,000 paid monthly.

Tenable for one year; not renewable.

Eligibility: Open to graduates at accredited Schools of the Assembly. A School without a doctoral program may nominate one of its graduates enrolled in the doctoral program of another accredited School provided the nominee is endorsed by the dean of the School which he is attending. Nominees should be reasonably sure that the dissertation will be completed during the period of the Fellowship.

Closing date: 20th January.

Further information from:
American Assembly of Collegiate Schools of Business
11500 Olive Boulevard
Suite 142
St. Louis, Missouri 63141
U.S.A.

[54]

AMERICAN ASSOCIATION FOR THE ADVANCEMENT OF SCIENCE

Prizes and Awards

A.A.A.S.-Newcomb Cleveland Prize: Awarded annually to the author of an outstanding paper, published from August through July in the Articles or Reports sections of *Science* magazine. *Value*—US$5,000 and a bronze medal.

To be eligible, a paper must be a first time publication of the author's own research.

Throughout the year, readers are invited to nominate papers appearing in the Reports section.

A.A.A.S.-Scientific Freedom and Responsibility Award: US$1,000 and a plaque are awarded annually to a scientist or engineer whose exemplary actions, often taken at significant personal cost, have served to foster scientific freedom and responsibility. Nominations are invited.

A.A.A.S. Socio-Psychological Prize: Awarded for a meritorious essay in socio-psychological inquiry that furthers understanding of the psychological-social-cultural behavior of human beings. *Value*—US$1,000.

Entries, of not more than 120 pages, should present a completed analysis of a problem, the relevant data, and an interpretation of the data in terms of the postulates with which the study began.

Purely empirical studies and purely theoretical formulations are not eligible.

Closing date for receipt of entries is 1st July.

A.A.A.S.-Westinghouse Science Journalism Awards: Five annual Awards of US$1,000 each are offered in recognition of outstanding reporting on the natural sciences and their engineering and technological applications, in newspapers and general circulation magazines, and on television and radio within the United States.

Further information from:
American Association for the Advancement of Science
1515 Massachusetts Avenue, N.W.
Washington, D.C. 20005
U.S.A.

[55]

AMERICAN ASSOCIATION OF CEREAL CHEMISTS, INC.

Alsberg-Schoch Memorial Lectureship

US$1,000 is awarded on an irregular basis to recognize starch chemists who have made notable contributions to fundamental starch science.

Further information from:
Prof. J. Zaborszky, President
American Association of Cereal Chemists, Inc.
c/o Department of Systems Science and Mathematics
Washington University
St. Louis, Missouri 63130
U.S.A.

[56]

AMERICAN ASSOCIATION OF LAW LIBRARIES

Scholarship Program

Four types of Scholarships are offered annually: *Type 1: Library Degree Scholarship for Law Graduates:* Up to US$2,000 for tuition and school-related expenses are offered to law graduates who are degree candidates at accredited library schools.

Type 2: Final Year of Law School for Library School Graduates: Up to US$2,000 for tuition and school-related expenses are offered to library school graduates who have successfully completed two years, or the equivalent, in accredited law schools and have law library experience.

Type 3: Library Degree Scholarships for Non-Law Graduates: Up to US$2,000 for tuition and school-related expenses are offered to college graduates with meaningful law library experience who are degree candidates in accredited library schools.

Type 4: Special Course in Law Librarianship: Up to US$150 for tuition, plus US$25 for incidentals are awarded to persons registering for special courses in law librarianship, which are taken for credit at accredited library schools.

Closing date: 1st April.

Further information from:
American Association of Law Libraries Scholarship Committee
53 West Jackson Boulevard
Chicago, Illinois 60604
U.S.A.

[57]

AMERICAN ASSOCIATION OF OBSTETRICIANS AND GYNECOLOGISTS FOUNDATION, INC.

Foundation Prize Thesis

Purpose: To promote research in obstetrics and gynecology.

No. offered: One Prize annually.

Value: US$1,500, paid in a lump sum.

Eligibility: Open to interns, residents and graduate students in obstetrics and gynecology, as well as any persons holding an M.D. or scientific degree approved by the Award Committee.

Not confirmed for 1983.

Further information from:
American Association of Obstetricians and Gynecologists Foundation, Inc.
University of Colorado
Medical Center
4200 East Ninth Avenue
Denver, Colorado 80262
U.S.A.

[58]

AMERICAN ASSOCIATION OF PETROLEUM GEOLOGISTS

President's Award

An Award of US$250 is made annually to recognize the author of an original article published by the Association. The article, which should deal with petroleum geology, need not be written by an Association member. Articles previously published elsewhere must have substantive additonal material in the Association publication. Nominations are welcomed from anyone, and should be submitted to the editor of the *Bulletin* no later than 1st March following the year of publication.

Not confirmed for 1983.

Further information from:
American Association of Petroleum Geologists
Post Office Box 979
Tulsa, Oklahoma 74101
U.S.A.

[59]

AMERICAN ASSOCIATION OF PHYSICS TEACHERS

Awards

Innovative High School Teacher Awards: High School teachers are invited to compete for small grants intended to support the operation of innovative physics teaching programs or activities that seek to increase student enrollment or to enhance student achievement in physics. Awards range from US$100 to US$400. Recipients are given one year to complete their projects and submit a final report. *Closing date:* 31st October for proposals.

Millikan Lecture Award: US$1,500 from a contribution by *Prentice-Hall Publishing Company*, a medal and citation are given annually to an outstanding college or university teacher for creative work in the teaching of physics. The winner is also afforded the opportunity to lecture on a topic related to physics teaching at the annual summer meeting of the Association. A printed version of the lecture will appear in the *AAPT News* and *The Physics Teacher* publications.

Oersted Medal Award: US$2,000, a medal and certificate are given annually in recognition of notable contributions to the teaching of physics. Recipients must be college or university teachers, and contributions usually include works published in AAPT journals as well as the development of instructional materials.

Richtmyer Memorial Lecture Award: US$1,000 is awarded annually to a physicist of distinction who has been chosen by the awards committee. In addition to the monetary prize, the lecture is published in the *AAPT News* publication.

Further information from:
American Association of Physics Teachers
Executive Office
Graduate Physics Building
SUNY at Stony Brook
Stony Brook, New York 11794
U.S.A.

[60]

AMERICAN ASSOCIATION FOR PUBLIC OPINION RESEARCH

Paper Competition

Purpose: To encourage the study of public opinion and related areas.

Subjects: Substantive or methodological issues in public opinion or public opinion research.

No. offered: Two Awards annually.

Value: First prize, US$200; Second prize, US$100.

Eligibility: Open to registered students of graduate or undergraduate status.

Note: Recipients will present their papers at the Association's annual meeting. Free accommodation will be provided. The paper will be abstracted and may be published in the *Public Opinion Quarterly*.
The Competition is sponsored by the Helen S. Dinerman Memorial Fund.

Closing date: 31st January.

Further information from:
American Association for Public Opinion Research
c/o Professor Kurt Lang
Department of Sociology
State University of New York at Stony Brook
Stony Brook, New York 11794
U.S.A.

[61]

AMERICAN ASSOCIATION FOR THE STUDY OF HEADACHE

Harold G. Wolff, M.C. Lecture Award

A Prize of US$1,000 is awarded annually for the best original paper on headache, head pain or the nature of pain itself. The recipient will be invited to present his paper at the Association's annual meeting. Papers may be concerned with basic research, clinical studies or both.

Closing date: 1st February.

Further information from:
Donald J. Dalessio, M.D.
Editor, *HEADACHE*
10666 North Torrey Pines Road
La Jolla, California 92037
U.S.A.

[62]

AMERICAN ASSOCIATION OF UNIVERSITY WOMEN (EDUCATIONAL FOUNDATION)

Graduate Fellowships for Women

Dissertation Fellowships for Women of the United States: Approximately 70 Awards are offered to women who have completed all the course work and examinations for a doctorate, except the dissertation, by 2nd January of the Fellowship year. The awards carry a stipend of US$3,500 to US$7,000 per annum.
Several awards of up to US$9,000 per annum for postdoctoral research are made to women holding doctorates at the time of application. Preference is given to applicants holding the doctorate for at least three years.
In addition, one *Founders Fellowship* of US$12,000 is awarded to a woman of outstanding scholarly achievement.
Closing date: 15th April.

Graduate Fellowships for Women of the United States for Advanced Training in the Selected Professions: Fellowships are offered to assist women in the final year of professional training in the fields of law, dentistry, medicine, veterinary medicine, and architecture. Awards may also be used toward completion of an M.B.A. degree. Awards range from US$3,500 to US$7,000 per for completion of professional training, and US$5,000 for completion of an M.B.A. *Closing date:* 15th April.

Graduate Fellowships for Women of Countries other than the United States: Approximately 40-50 awards are offered annually, with stipends ranging from US$2,500 to US$9,000 per annum, for graduate study or advanced research at approved institutions in the United States.

Six awards are offered for advanced research in any country other than the Fellow's own, to women who are members in their own country of national associations/federations affiliated with the International Federation of University Women.

Closing date: 1st December.

Further information from:
American Association of University Women
Educational Foundation Programs Office
2401 Virginia Avenue, N.W.
Washington, D.C. 20037
U.S.A.

[63]

AMERICAN AUTOMATIC CONTROL COUNCIL

Awards

Eckman Award: US$300 and a certificate are awarded annually to an outstanding young contributor in the field of automatic control. Nominees are to be less than 30 years of age as of 1st July of the year of the Award. Contributions may include technical or scientific publications, theses, patents, inventions or a combination of these in the field of automatic control. Candidates must have been resident in the United States at the time the contributions were made. *Closing date:* 1st March for nominations.

Education Award: US$200 and a certificate are awarded in recognition of oustanding contributions and distinguished leadership in automatic control education. Nominees may be from U.S. industries, universities or government. *Closing date:* 1st March for nominations.

Schuck Award: US$100 and a certificate is awarded for the best paper presented at the meeting of the Council. The award is based on the following criteria: written and oral presentation, technical contribution, timeliness and practicality. *Closing date:* 1st March for nominations.

Further information from:
Professor G.F. Franklin, Chairman
Awards Committee
American Automatic Control Council
Department of Electrical Engineering
Stanford University
Stanford, California 94305
U.S.A.

[64]

AMERICAN BAR FOUNDATION

Fellowships in Legal History

Purpose: To encourage and assist scholars engaged in legal historical studies to produce original research in English and American legal history.

No. offered: Approximately five to eight awards, annually.

Value: Up to a maximum of US$6,000; usually paid quarterly.

Tenable for three to nine months.

Eligibility: Open to individuals who hold the LL.B. or J.D. degree, or the Ph.D. degree in history or a related subject, and to those who have passed qualifying examinations for the Ph.D. degree and have made substantial progress toward completion of the doctoral dissertation.

Note: Preference is normally given to younger scholars who show promise of original contribution to knowledge.

Closing date: 1st January.

Further information from:
Program in Legal History
American Bar Foundation
1155 East 60th Street
Chicago, Illinois 60637
U.S.A.

[65]

AMERICAN CANCER SOCIETY, INC.

Postdoctoral Fellowships

Purpose: To enable a young investigator to qualify for an independent career in cancer research.

Value: The amount of a grant is determined on an individual basis and will provide an annual stipend of US$15,000, paid monthly in advance, travel expenses to and from the institution of training for the fellow only; an institutional allowance of up to US$1,000 per year may be requested.

Tenable for one or two years at suitable institutions in the United States or abroad; renewable for an additional year only in exceptional circumstances.

Eligibility: Applicants should be, or have legally declared their intent to become, United States Citizens. Candidates shall have been awarded a doctoral degree prior to the activation date of the Fellowship.

Note: Grants are awarded with the understanding that the recipient will not accept funds for the same purpose from any other fund granting agency. When necessary, the institution may supplement the Society's stipend, providing that the supplemental funds are not from an American Cancer Society grant.

A plan of training (didactic, teaching, research, etc.) must be formulated and agreed upon by the mentor and the applicant, and described in detail in the application.

The Society also offers the following Grants in support of personnel for research not-for-profit located within the U.S., its territories, and the Commonwealth of Puerto Rico: *Junior Faculty Research Awards; Faculty Research Awards; Scholars in Cancer Research;* and *Research Professorships.* Support is also provided through *Research and Clinical Investigation Grants; Institutional Research Grants*; and the *American Cancer Society-Eleanor Roosevelt International Cancer Fellowships* [see entry for International Union Against Cancer].

Closing dates: 1st October for commencement 1st July; 1st March for commencement 1st January.

Further information from:
Research Department
American Cancer Society, Inc.
777 Third Avenue
New York, New York 10017
U.S.A.

[66]

AMERICAN CANCER SOCIETY, INC.

Physician's Research Training Fellowships

Purpose: To prepare qualified physicians in research training necessary to bring them to the level of competence of recent Ph.D. graduates.

Subjects: Full time basic or clinical research in cancer.

Value: The amount of a grant is determined on an individual basis and will provide an annual stipend of US$15,000, paid monthly in advance, travel expenses to and from the institution of training for the Fellow only; an institutional allowance of up to US$1,000 per year may be requested.

Tenable for one or two years at suitable institutions in the United States or abroad.

Eligibility: Applicants should be qualified physicians who are, or have legally declared their intent to become, United States citizens.

Note: Grants are awarded with the understanding that the recipient will not accept funds for the same purpose from any other fund granting agency. When necessary, the institution may supplement the Society's stipend, providing that the supplemental funds are not from an American Cancer Society grant.

A plan of training (didactic, research, etc.) must be formulated and agreed upon by the mentor and the applicant, and described in detail in the application.

Closing dates: 1st October for commencement 1st July; 1st March for commencement 1st January.

Further information from:
  Research Department
  American Cancer Society, Inc.
  777 Third Avenue
  New York, New York 10017
  U.S.A.

[67]

AMERICAN CATHOLIC HISTORICAL ASSOCIATION

Peter Guilday Prize: To stimulate interest in the history of the Catholic Church among younger scholars, the Prize of *US*$100 is offered annually to the author of an article on the history of the Catholic Church, broadly considered, which must be his first scholarly publication and which is judged to be the best of those in that category accepted for publication in a given year by the editors of the *Catholic Historical Review*. Manuscripts must not exceed thirty double-spaced typewritten pages (footnotes included), and must be submitted by 1st October.

Howard R. Marraro Prize: The Prize of *US*$500 for a book, or a smaller amount for an article, is offered each year for a work on Italian history, or Italo-American history or relations, published within the year prior to the deadline. Candidates must be citizens or permanent residents of the United States or Canada and must apply by 1st September.

John Gilmary Shea Prize: The Prize of *US*$300 is offered to a United States or Canadian citizen or resident for a book on church history, published in English during the twelve months preceding the closing date. Although works of broad significance are preferred, consideration will be given to books on a highly specific topic or of a narrow compass, especially when such publications have made a notable contribution to ecclesiastical history. Works must be submitted by 15th October.

Further information from:
  American Catholic Historical Association
  Catholic University of America
  Mullen Library/305
  Washington, D.C. 20064
  U.S.A.

[68]

AMERICAN COLLEGE OF CHEST PHYSICIANS

Cecile Lehman Mayer Research Awards

Purpose: To encourage original investigations by young physicians in the disciplines of cardiovascular and pulmonary medicine.

No. offered: Two Awards annually: one for cardiovascular study and one for pulmonary study.

Value: US$1,000.

Eligibility: Open to physicians of residency or fellowship status, and to physicians under the age of 35. Competition is open and takes place at the College's Annual Meeting.

Closing date: 15th April.

Further information from:
  Chairman, Research Forum
  American College of Chest Physicians
  911 Busse Highway
  Park Ridge, Illinois 60068
  U.S.A.

[69]

AMERICAN COLLEGE OF HOSPITAL ADMINISTRATORS

James A. Hamilton Hospital Administrators' Book Award

Purpose: To recognize the author of an outstanding book which contributes to literature on management and deals with some facet of the administrative process.

Subject: The broad fields of management and administration.

No. offered: One Award annually.

Value: US$500, a certificate and medallion.

Eligibility: Open to authors of books published two years prior to the date of the Award presentation.

Note: The Award is sponsored by the *Alumni*

Association of the Graduate Program in Hospital and Health Care Administration, University of Minnesota.

Closing date: Spring of the Award year.

Not confirmed for 1983.

Further information from:
Book Award Committee
American College of Hospital
  Administrators
840 North Lake Shore Drive
Chicago, Illinois 60611
U.S.A.

[70]

AMERICAN COLLEGE OF PHYSICIANS

Teaching and Research Scholarships

Purpose: Intended for support of young physicians who may not have decided upon an academic career, or who have not attained a tenured position on a medical school faculty.

Subjects: Medical education and research.

No. offered: Five Scholarships in the general field of internal medicine or related specialities.

Value: US$12,000 in the first year, increasing to US$13,000 in the second year, and US$14,000 in the third year.

Tenable at suitable institutions in the United States or Canada, for three years.

Eligibility: Open to candidates proposed by the chairperson of the department of medicine in any institution in the United States or Canada having a recognized program of medical education and research, and endorsed by the appropriate official of the university or college concerned. Scholarships may be made only on behalf of physicians who are citizens of the United States or Canada, or non-citizens who can show intent to become a citizen by virtue of a permanent visa status or its equivalent. At the time of the appointment, which begins in July of each year, the candidate should have no less than four years of professional training nor have been graduated from medical school more than eight years, inclusive of time spent in obligatory military service.

Closing date: 1st July.

Further information from:
Secretary, Fellowship and Scholarships
  Committee
American College of Physicians
4200 Pine Street
Philadelphia, Pennsylvania 19104
U.S.A.

[71]

AMERICAN COLLEGE OF PHYSICIANS

Traveling Scholarships

Six Scholarships are offered annually to enable young physicians to spend a month, more or less, as visiting fellows at some institution, or institutions, for observation and postgraduate study. These are the *A. Blaine Brower Traveling Scholarships* (two, unrestricted), the *Alfred Stengel Traveling Scholarship* (unrestricted), the *George C. Griffith Traveling Scholarship* (unrestricted), as well as the *Willard O. Thompson Memorial Traveling Scholarship* and the *Dorothy S. Hutton Scholarship* (both restricted to endocrinology).

Applicants who must be citizens of the United States or Canada, and Members or Fellows of the College, are chosen and institutions delegated by the Fellowships and Scholarships Committee, approved by the Board of Regents of the College. The stipend of US$1,000 is used for payment of travel or other expenses, in whole or in part. Application closing date is 1st July; notification of awards takes place after mid-November, to take effect after 1st January.

Further information from:
Secretary, Fellowships and Scholarships
  Committee
American College of Physicians
4200 Pine Street
Philadelphia, Pennsylvania 19104
U.S.A.

[72]

AMERICAN COLLEGE OF PSYCHIATRISTS

Stanley R. Dean Award

The Award of US$3,500 is offered for research which has been undertaken in schizophrenia. The recipient is selected during the summer by a committee of the College which receives recommendations from College members. A presentation of the winner's work is made in February at the Annual Meeting of the College, at which time the Award is given.

Further information from:
American College of Psychiatrists
1700 18th Street, N.W.
Washington, D.C. 20009
U.S.A.

[73]

AMERICAN COLLEGE THEATRE FESTIVAL

Playwriting Awards

The following Awards are open to the author of an original work who is either an undergraduate enrolled for at least twelve credit hours of work during the year of the production or during the two years preceding the production, or to a graduate of no more than two years preceding the year of the production.

David Library of the American Revolution Awards: First Prize of US$2,000 and a second Prize of US$1,000 to the author of a play, which is to be full-length and on the broad subject of American freedom.

Lorraine Hansberry Award: First Prize of US$2,500 to the author and US$750 to the college or university theatre department producing the play, and a second Prize of US$1,000 to the author and US$500 to the college or university theatre department producing the play, which is to be on the Black experience in America.

Norman Lear Award: One Award of US$3,200 plus fee-paid membership in the Writers Guild of America to the author of the best written teleplay of a Norman Lear comedy television series.

National Playwriting Award: One Award of US$2,500 to the author, presented by the William Morris Agency, plus the offer of an agency management contract, publication and distribution of the play for stock and amateur production by Samuel French, Inc., full membership in the Dramatists Guild, and production of the play in Washington, D.C. as part of the ACTF National Festival. In addition, the college or university theatre department which produces the play will be awarded US$1,000 by the University/College Theatre Association.

Further information from:
American College Theatre Festival
John F. Kennedy Center for the
    Performing Arts
Washington, D.C. 20566
U.S.A.

[74]

AMERICAN COLLEGE OF VETERINARY PATHOLOGISTS

Burroughs Wellcome Resident Fellowship in Veterinary Pathology

One Fellowship of US$50,000, tenable for three years, is offered for advanced training in veterinary pathology. The program seeks to help satisfy the unmet and expanding need for qualified veterinary pathologists in academic and industrial research, in regulatory and diagnostic veterinary medicine, and in teaching.

Closing date: 15th October.

Further information from:
Paul K. Hildebrandt, D.V.M.
Secretary-Treasurer
American College of Veterinary
    Pathologists
P.O. Box 2108
Rockville, Maryland 20852
U.S.A.

[75]

AMERICAN CONGRESS OF REHABILITATION MEDICINE

Bernard M. Baruch Essay Contest for Medical Students: A first prize of US$200 and a copy of the Baruch Medal, a second prize of US$100 and a third prize of US$50 are given annually for essays on any subject relating to physical medicine or rehabilitation. The competition is open to medical students who submit an original manuscript, not to exceed 3,000 words. Essays must not have been previously published. The winning essay becomes the exclusive property of the *Congress* and will be published, along with any other exceptional essays submitted to the competition, in the *Archives of Physical Medicine and Rehabilitation. Closing date:* 20th June.

Essay Contest for Interns, Residents and Graduate Students: An Award of US$200 is given annually for an outstanding review, article or presentation of a scientific investigation in any field of interest in physical medicine and rehabilitation. The Contest is open to interns, residents, graduate students and fellows in physical medicine and rehabilitation. Manuscripts should not exceed 5,000 words and should not have been previously published. The winning entry, along with any other exceptional essays submitted to the competition, will be published in the *Archives of Physical Medicine and Rehabilitation. Closing date:* 20th June.

Conrad Jobst Foundation Award: An Award of US$250 and a plaque are given annually for the best scientific paper, presented at the Annual Session of the *American Congress of Rehabilitation Medicine*, pertaining to the field of peripheral vascular disease or circulation in the extremities. All physicians and members of the allied health professions are eligible. Manuscripts should reflect original work, not exceed 5,000 words, and must not have been published or submitted for publication in any other journal. All manuscripts become the property of the *Congress* and will be considered for publication in the *Archives of Physical Medicine and Rehabilitation. Closing date:* 20th June.

Further information from:
American Congress of Rehabilitation
  Medicine
30 North Michigan Avenue
Chicago, Illinois 60602
U.S.A.

[76]

AMERICAN CONGRESS ON SURVEYING AND MAPPING

Keuffel & Esser Fellowship in Surveying and Cartography: One award of US$2,500 is offered as an encouragement to both students and former students in civil engineering, surveying and cartography to do graduate work in advanced fields of surveying and/or cartography at an appropriate school, under faculty guidance.

Wild Heerbrugg Geodetic Fellowship Award: One Fellowship of US$4,000 is given annually to encourage qualified graduates to further their education in geodesy and to promote the development of geodetic science. Applicants should have completed at least one undergraduate course in surveying or photogrammetry and must be either members of the Congress or regular students of an accredited school who are sponsored by a member. The award is renewable.

Closing date: 15th January.

Further information from:
Executive Director
American Congress on Surveying and
  Mapping
210 Little Falls St.
Falls Church, Virginia 22046
U.S.A.

[77]

AMERICAN CONSERVATORY OF MUSIC

Scholarships

Subjects: Piano, flute, violin, organ, and other orchestral instruments, voice, composition and jazz studies.

Value: US$100 to US$1,000.

Tenable at the American Conservatory of Music, Chicago.

Eligibility: Open to graduate students and undergraduates in the United States.

Further information from:
Dean
American Conservatory of Music
116 South Michigan Avenue
Chicago, Illinois 60603
U.S.A.

[78]

AMERICAN COUNCIL ON EDUCATION

ACE Fellows Program in Academic Administration

Purpose: To strengthen leadership in American higher education by identifying and training individuals who have shown promise for responsible positions in academic administration.

Subjects: Academic administration in higher education; problems and policies in higher education; management of colleges and universities.

No. offered: 35-40 Fellowships annually.

Value: The nominating institution supports the salaries of the ACE Fellows and the Council provides support for programmatic costs.

Tenable at the nominating institution or at a host college or university for one academic year.

Eligibility: Open to members of a college faculty or junior staff with a minimum of five years teaching or administrative experience, and who show evidence of potential for academic administration. Persons lacking some of the above qualifications may be chosen if they show other strong supporting evidence of potential.

Note: Candidates must be nominated by the president or vice-president of an ACE member institution. ACE Fellows work with a mentor, normally a president or chief academic officer, at policy and routine levels. The Fellowship experience is supplemented with national and regional seminars and meetings.

Closing date: Late November.

Further information from:
Dr. Madeleine F. Green
ACE Fellows Program in Academic
  Administration
American Council on Education
One Dupont Circle
Washington, D.C. 20036
U.S.A.

[79]

AMERICAN COUNCIL OF LEARNED SOCIETIES (ACLS)

Fellowships

Purpose: To provide opportunities for scholars to engage in research in the fields listed below.

Subject: Humanities—philosophy (including philosophy of law and science); aesthetics; philology; languages; literature and linguistics; archaeology; art history and musicology; history (including history of science, law and religions); cultural anthropology; folklore. Programs with a predominantly humanistic emphasis in economics, geography, political science, psychology, sociology and the natural sciences will also be considered.

Value: Maximum of US$13,500 including travel expenses, purchase of materials, and research assistance.

Tenable for six uninterrupted months of full-time research; maximum tenure of twelve months.

Eligibility: Open to citizens or permanent residents of the United States who hold a doctoral degree or are able to demonstrate scholarly maturity by professional experience and publications, and are usually no more than 50 years of age. Fellowships are not restricted to members of academic faculties.

Note: Recipients may use their Fellowships at any time within a period of 18 months beginning 1st July following award notification.

The conditions of these Fellowships should make them of particular interest to scholars whose teaching loads restrict time for research, or whose normal places of work are remote from repository or research materials.

Closing date: 39th September.

Further information from:
Office of Fellowships and Grants
American Council of Learned Societies
800 Third Avenue
New York, New York 10022
U.S.A.

[80]

AMERICAN COUNCIL OF LEARNED SOCIETIES (ACLS)

Mellon Fellowships for Chinese Studies

Purpose: To provide scholars in Chinese studies, who are at the early stage of their professional careers, with the opportunity for research, advanced substantive or methodological study, and language training.

Value: Up to a maximum of US$17,000.

Tenable at major university centers of Chinese studies in the United States or East Asia for a minimum of one semester.

Eligibility: Open to citizens or permanent residents of the United States or Canada who are trained in the area of historical or contemporary Chinese studies.

Note: These Grants are sponsored jointly with the Social Science Research Council [q.v.], and funded by the Andrew W. Mellon Foundation.

Closing date: 1st December.

Further information from:
 Office of Fellowships and Grants
 American Council of Learned Societies
 800 Third Avenue
 New York, New York 10022
 U.S.A.

[81]

AMERICAN COUNCIL OF LEARNED SOCIETIES (ACLS)

Research Fellowships for Recent Ph.D. Recipients

Subjects: Philosophy (including the philosophy of law and science), aesthetics, philology, languages, literature, linguistics, archaeology, art history, musicology, history (including the history of science, law and religions), cultural anthropology, folklore.

Value: Up to a maximum of US$8,500.

Tenable for at least six months.

Eligibility: Open to citizens or permanent residents of the United States who have held a Ph.D. for two years (including the competition year).

Closing date: 30th September.

Further information from:
 Office of Fellowships and Grants
 American Council of Learned Societies
 800 Third Avenue
 New York, New York 10022
 U.S.A.

[82]

AMERICAN COUNCIL OF LEARNED SOCIETIES (ACLS)

Grants-in-Aid

Purpose: Grants are intended to be used exclusively to advance specific programs of research in progress by contributing to the scholar's essential personal expenses for that purpose.

Subjects: Humanities [see entry for ACLS Fellowships].

Value: Maximum of US$3,000.

Eligibility: Open to citizens or permanent residents of the United States who hold a doctoral degree or are able to demonstrate scholarly maturity by professional experience and publications.

Note: A Grant-in-Aid is tenable immediately following acceptance of an award, and should be expended within one year.

Closing date: 15th December.

Further information from:
 Office of Fellowships and Grants
 American Council of Learned Societies
 800 Third Avenue
 New York, New York 10022
 U.S.A.

[83]

AMERICAN COUNCIL OF LEARNED SOCIETIES (ACLS)

Grants for Research on Chinese Civilization

Subjects: Humanities and social sciences relating to pre-1911 China.

Value: Maximum of US$25,000.

Tenable for at least six months.

Eligibility: Open to citizens or permanent residents of the United States who hold a doctoral degree or who are able to demonstrate scholarly maturity by professional experience and publications. Preference will be given to scholars who have not had substantial research support during the previous three years.

Note: Grants are awarded for research-related domestic or foreign travel, research assistance and maintenance.

Application may be made for funds to supplement sabbatical salaries or awards from other sources provided that these funds would intensify or extend the contemplated research.

Closing date: 1st December.

Further information from:
Office of Fellowships and Grants
American Council of Learned Societies
800 Third Avenue
New York, New York 10022
U.S.A.

[84]

AMERICAN COUNCIL OF LEARNED SOCIETIES (ACLS)

Grants for Postdoctoral Research in East European Studies

Purpose: To provide opportunities for scholars to engage in research on the countries listed below.

Subject: Humanities and social sciences relating to Albania, Bulgaria, Czechoslovakia, Hungary, Poland, Romania, Yugoslavia, East Germany since 1945, and modern Greece.

Value: Up to a maximum of US$15,000.

Tenable in the United States or abroad for a maximum period of one year.

Eligibility: Open to citizens or permanent residents of the United States who hold a doctoral degree or are able to demonstrate scholarly maturity by professional experience and publications.

Note: The above-mentioned Grant is sponsored jointly with the Social Science Research Council [q.v.].

Closing date: 1st December.

Further information from:
Office of Fellowships and Grants
American Council of Learned Societies
800 Third Avenue
New York, New York 10022
U.S.A.

[85]

AMERICAN COUNCIL OF LEARNED SOCIETIES (ACLS)

Travel Grants for Humanists to International Meetings Abroad

Travel Grants are available to enable humanists who are citizens or permanent residents of the U.S. to participate in international conferences held outside North America and the Caribbean. Grants are also offered to social scientists having a strong humanistic orientation, attending meetings concerned with the humanistic aspects of their discipline. Only those taking active official part in the meeting are eligible for Grants.

Closing date: 1st March, July and November for meetings taking place three to six months later.

Further information from:
Travel Grant Program
American Council of Learned Societies
800 Third Avenue
New York, New York 10022
U.S.A.

[86]

AMERICAN CRYSTALLOGRAPHIC ASSOCIATION

Awards

Fankuchen Award: This award is made every three years (next awarded in 1983) to an outstanding crystallographer or X-ray diffractionist of any nationality who has made significant contributions to the teaching of the subject, though he need not be a teacher by profession. The Award of US$1,500, a certificate, and an additional sum of money to cover expenses will be presented at the meeting of the Association at the Polytechnic Institute of Brooklyn. The recipient will present the Fankuchen Memorial Lecture at this time, as well as at two additional institutions.

A.L. Patterson Award: This triennial Award, to be first given in 1981, is offered to recognize and encourage research in the structure of matter by diffraction methods. These include significant contributions to the methodology of structure determination, innovative application of diffraction methods, and the elucidation of biological, chemical, geological or physical phenomena using structural information. The Award is open to anyone, regardless of age, nationality or Association membership.

Bertram E. Warren Award: This triennial Award, next given in 1982, is made for an important recent contribution to the physics of solids or liquids using X-ray, neutron, or electron diffraction techniques. The Award is not meant to include crystal structure determinations. US$1,000 and a certificate are given for the work, which should be published within a six-year period ending 30th June of the year preceding the Award.

Not confirmed for 1983.

Further information from:
American Crystallographic Association
335 East 45th Street
New York, New York 10017
U.S.A.

[87]

AMERICAN DIABETES ASSOCIATION, INC.

Research and Development Awards

Purpose: To assist exceptionally promising young investigators in their transition to the level of established investigators.

Value: US$25,000, paid monthly.

Tenable at an appropriate institution for one academic year; renewable.

Eligibility: Open to members of university-affiliated institutions within the United States and its possessions who have had at least three years research experience in a relevant field; residency training is not considered the equivalent of research experience. Preference will be given to applicants who intend to pursue an academic career and who can produce tangible evidence of research experience.

Note: A sponsoring institution must submit an application on behalf of a candidate.

Further information from:
Research Coordinator
American Diabetes Association, Inc.
2 Park Avenue
New York, New York 10016
U.S.A.

[88]

AMERICAN DIETETIC ASSOCIATION

The following award categories are offered in the field of dietetics to U.S. citizens, and are based on the candidate's scholarship, professional potential and financial need. Applicants may apply for only one category of awards in a particular year. Application forms may be obtained from the address below.

Graduate Scholarships: A varying number of Scholarships are awarded annually. Values range from US$500 to US$2,500, paid in two installments. Candidates should intend to practice in the field of dietetics, have or obtain membership in the American Dietetic Association prior to the granting of the Scholarship, and be a dietetic intern or a senior in a coordinated undergraduate program, or be admitted to or present pursuit of a program of graduate study in the field.

Internships: A varying number of Internship awards are given annually. Values range from US$500 to US$750, paid in two installments. Candidates must confirm acceptance to an accredited dietetic internship program prior to May of the awarding year.

Dietetic Technicians: A varying number of Dietetic Technician awards are given annually. Values range from US$500 to US$600, paid in two installments. Candidates should show evidence of leadership and academic ability, and be first year students in a dietetic technician program approved by the Association.

Mary C. Zahasky Memorial Awards for short-term educational programs (seminars, workshops, etc.). Candidates should be registered dietitians wishing to widen, renew and elaborate their professional development. Applicants should inquire to the President, at the address below.

Closing date: 15th February of the awarding year for all categories. Requests for applications will be accepted up until 15th January of the awarding year.

Further information from:
Awards, Scholarships, and Loan Fund Committee
American Dietetic Association
430 North Michigan Avenue
Chicago, Illinois 60611
U.S.A.

[89]

AMERICAN DIETETIC ASSOCIATION

Sunkist Growers Essay Competition

Prizes are annually offered for worthy case studies or effective dietary care of patients with special emphasis on the role of diet in the patients' progress. First prize—US$150; two second prizes of US$100 each. The Competition is open to members of the Association, dietetic interns enrolled in an approved internship, seniors in a coordinated undergraduate program, and to graduate students of nutrition in an accredited university.

Closing date: 1st May.

Further information from:
Awards, Scholarships, and Loan Fund Committee
American Dietetic Association
430 North Michigan Avenue
Chicago, Illinois 60611
U.S.A.

[90]

AMERICAN EDUCATIONAL RESEARCH ASSOCIATION
AMERICAN COLLEGE TESTING PROGRAM

AERA/ACT Award

Purpose: To encourage sophisticated research on substantive issues of college student growth and development, to facilitate the impact of research on improved college programs for students, and to recognize a research scholar who has made an important contribution towards better understanding of college students through a completed research article, book or project.

Subject: College student growth and development.

No. offered: One Award annually.

Value: US$1,500 paid in a lump sum, and a framed certificate.

Tenable for one year.

Eligibility: Requirements are only that the recipient of the Award be an eminent scholar in the field.

Note: If appropriate, the research may be published as part of the ACT Research Report or monograph series.

Not confirmed for 1983.

Further information from:
American Educational Research Association
1230 17th Street, N.W.
Washington, D.C.
U.S.A.

[91]

AMERICAN FEDERATION OF LABOR AND CONGRESS OF INDUSTRIAL ORGANIZATIONS

Murray Green Award

The Award of US$5,000 and an appropriately inscribed medallion is offered annually to any individual or organization that has made outstanding contributions to the improvement of health, welfare and recreation of people all over the world.

Nominations are invited from all AFL-CIO affiliates and their members as well as from persons engaged in the social welfare field. Nominations should be submitted during the first four months of each year.

Not confirmed for 1983.

Further information from:
AFL/CIO Department of Community Services
815 16th Street, N.W.
Washington, D.C. 20006
U.S.A.

[92]

AMERICAN FILM INSTITUTE

Independent Filmmaker Program Grant

Purpose: To encourage the creative development of filmmakers and to advance the art of filmmaking.

Value: From US$500 to US12,000. Payment is made at each of the following four stages: beginning photography; beginning post-production; completion of rough cut; and delivery of three release prints.

Tenable films may be made anywhere within the United States.

Duration: Films must be started within three months of receiving a grant and must be completed within 18 months. Grants are not renewable and are limited one per individual.

Eligibility: Open to any United States citizen or permanent resident in possession of a Green Card. The candidate should have completed a film or video work for which he or she has had primary creative responsibility.

Note: Film may be 16mm or 35mm. Video projects are also accepted.
    Applicants may not be enrolled as students, either at the time of application, three months prior to that time, or during the period of the Grant.

Closing date: For January cycle, 15th September of the previous year for applications; 15th October of the previous year for supporting materials.

Further information from:
    Independent Filmmaker Program
    American Film Institute
    2021 North Western Avenue
    Los Angeles, California 90027
    U.S.A.

[93]

AMERICAN FOUNDATION FOR PHARMACEUTICAL EDUCATION

Graduate Fellowships

Purpose: To offer Fellowship support leading to a Ph.D. degree.

Subjects: Any of the pharmaceutical sciences, including pharmaceutics, pharmacology, manufacturing pharmacy and medicinal chemistry.

No. offered: Approximately 45 Fellowships annually.

Value: US$6,000 each, for ten Fellowships; US$4,200 each for the remainder of the available Fellowships. Payments are made to the university for the selected student in twelve monthly installments.

Tenable at appropriate universities for twelve months; renewable for two additional years.

Eligibility: Open to U.S. citizens who are currently enrolled in a graduate program and have received a B.S. degree in pharmacy or in another scientifically oriented course of study.

Closing date: 15th March for Fellowships to begin in September.

Further information from:
    American Foundation for Pharmaceutical Education
    Radburn Plaza Building
    14-25 Plaza Road
    Fair Lawn, New Jersey 07410
    U.S.A.

[94]

AMERICAN FRIENDS OF THE HEBREW UNIVERSITY

Grants

Purpose: To enable students to participate in a degree program, or the One Year program at the Hebrew University of Jerusalem.

Value: Varies according to circumstances.

Tenable at the Hebrew University for one year; renewal is based on financial need and academic performance.

Eligibility: Open to students who qualify for enrollment at the Hebrew University.

Closing date: 15th April.

Further information from:
American Friends of the Hebrew University
1140 Avenue of the Americas
New York, New York 10036
U.S.A.

[95]

AMERICAN FUND FOR DENTAL HEALTH

Dental Teacher Training Fellowships

Purpose: To strengthen dental faculties through the establishment of graduate study Fellowships for the training of dental school teachers.

No. offered: 12 Fellowships annually.

Value: A stipend of US$6,000 plus tuition costs and an allowance of US$500 for spouse and each dependent under 19 years of age. Maximum award is US$10,000 per year.

Tenable for one year. Upon reapplication the Fellowship may be renewed for a second year of study.

Eligibility: Open to resident citizens of the United States who are graduates of dental schools approved by the Council on Dental Education of the American Dental Association and who are eligible for admission to a graduate dental education center in the United States.

Note: The recipient of an award may not hold any other fellowship or scholarship.
  Recipients, upon completion of their studies, must teach full-time, as determined by the institution where employed, for five consecutive years at a dental school accredited by the ADA.

Closing date: 1st February.

Further information from:
American Fund for Dental Health
211 East Chicago Avenue, Suite 1630
Chicago, Illinois 60611
U.S.A.

[96]

AMERICAN FUND FOR DENTAL HEALTH

Hillenbrand Fellowship in Dental Administration

Purpose: To provide an opportunity for involvement and study in dental administration, combining academic work and actual staff assignment in dental organizations.

No. offered: One Fellowship, every other year.

Value: A stipend of US$1,250 per month, plus an adequate budget for subsistence, travel and any related course work.

Tenable for one year; six month training program and a six month internship.

Eligibility: Open to U.S. citizens giving evidence of strong interest in pursuing a career in dental administration who are graduates of an accredited dental school, possess an M.B.A. degree, or have a Bachelor's degree with experience in business management.

Note: Candidates must agree, at the time of application, to apply for and accept a position in dental administration. Personal interviews may be required.
  The Fellowship recipient is expected to attend the Association's Administrative Orientation Program, prior to the June starting date of the award.

Closing date: 1st December for applications; selection to be announced the following February.

Further information from:
Director of Programs
American Fund for Dental Health
211 East Chicago Avenue, Suite 1630
Chicago, Illinois 60611
U.S.A.

[97]

AMERICAN FUND FOR DENTAL HEALTH

Dental Scholarships for Minority Students

Purpose: To attract students who may not

have previously considered or felt that they could aspire to a dental career.

No. offered: Approximately 40 Scholarships annually.

Value: US$2,000 for first year dental school expenses. A maximum of US$4,000 may be paid over a two year period.

Tenable at dental schools in the United States accredited by the American Dental Association, for one year; renewable for a second year.

Eligibility: Open to United States citizens from minority groups which are currently under-represented in the dental profession, such as Blacks, Mexican-Americans, American Indians, and Puerto Ricans. Scholarships are awarded only to those students who have been accepted at a dental school.

Closing date: 1st May.

Further information from:
American Fund for Dental Health
211 East Chicago Avenue, Suite 1630
Chicago, Illinois 60611
U.S.A.

[98]

AMERICAN FUND FOR DENTAL HEALTH

Scholarships in Dental Laboratory Technology

Purpose: To help overcome the shortage of dental laboratory technicians.

No. offered: Approximately 20 Scholarships annually.

Value: From US$500 to US$600.

Tenable for one year; renewable for a second year.

Eligibility: Open to resident citizens of the United States who have a high school diploma and who are enrolled, or plan to do so, in a dental laboratory technology program accredited by the American Dental Association.

Note: Application forms are available from dental laboratory technology schools.

Closing date: 1st June.

Further information from:
American Fund for Dental Health
211 East Chicago Avenue, Suite 1630
Chicago, Illinois 60611
U.S.A.

[99]

AMERICAN GERIATRICS SOCIETY, INC.

Awards

Edward B. Allen Award of US$1,000 and a scroll is given every three years to a scientist for an important contribution to the field of geriatric psychiatry. The next Award will be given in 1983.

Henderson Lectureship Award of US$1,000 and a scroll is given annually to a scientist for eminent and exceptional contributions to a better understanding of the problems of health care for the aging and aged, through research and published works in the field of life sciences relating to the aging of man.

Willard O. Thompson Award of US$1,000 and a scroll is given every three years to a scientist for distinguished contributions to the field of geriatric medicine. The next Award will be given in 1984.

Note: The Society also gives the *Malford W. Thewlis Award* which is eligible to members of the Society only.

Further information from:
American Geriatrics Society, Inc.
10 Columbus Circle
New York, New York 10019
U.S.A.

[100]

AMERICAN HEART ASSOCIATION, INC.

Clinician-Scientist Award

Purpose: To encourage talented young physicians to undertake careers in investigation.

Subjects: Any field broadly related to cardiovascular function and disease including stroke or related fundamental problems.

No. offered: Varies annually.

Value: US$30,000 per annum, paid in monthly installments, up to US$3,000 per annum for laboratory expenses, and moving expenses of up to US$2,500 each way. In addition, if the award is extended for the full five years, start-up funds of up to US$20,000 will be provided at the time the awardee returns to the sponsoring department.

Tenable at a sponsoring institution department within the U.S. and at a preceptor's laboratory, either within the U.S. or abroad, for three years, with a possible extension of two additional years; not renewable.

Eligibility: Open to U.S. citizens and permanent residents, or persons furnishing a notarized statement as to proof of legal right to stay and work permanently in the U.S. Applicants should be holders of an M.D. or equivalent medical degree who will ordinarily be under age 35 at the time the award is activated, have completed at least three years training and will have usually qualified for specialty board certification upon award activation. Holders of M.D./Ph.D. degrees without substantial appropriate postdoctoral training will also be considered.

Note: Applicants should submit a specific plan for the development of a career in investigative science. Statements and commitments are required from the applicant, a sponsor in a clinical department (usually a department chairman or division chief), and a research preceptor who need not be in the sponsor's institution.
Grants may be supplemented by the sponsoring institution in consultation with the American Heart Association, but not by income directly through private practice of fees for service.

Closing date: 1st July.

Further information from:
Division of Research Awards
American Heart Association, Inc.
7320 Greenville Avenue
Dallas, Texas 75231
U.S.A.

[101]

AMERICAN HEART ASSOCIATION, INC.

Grants-in-Aid

Purpose: To support research activities broadly related to cardiovascular function and disease or to related fundamental problems.

Subjects: All basic disciplines, such as physiology, biochemistry, pathology, as well as epidemiological and clinical investigation which bear on cardiovascular problems, including stroke. Limited funds are available for support of research in the basic sciences irrespective of apparent direct application to the field of cardiovascular disease.

Value: Approximately US$25,000 per annum.

Tenable at accredited institutions in the United States or abroad for one to three years.

Eligibility: Open to United States citizens or foreign nationals with an exchange visitor or permanent residence visa, who hold an M.D., Ph.D., D.Sc., D.V.M. or equivalent domestic or foreign degree and will be engaged in essentially full-time research.

Closing date: 1st October.

Further information from:
Division of Research Awards
American Heart Association, Inc.
7320 Greenville Avenue
Dallas, Texas 75231
U.S.A.

[102]

AMERICAN HEART ASSOCIATION, INC.

Established Investigatorships

Purpose: To assist talented young physicians and scientists to develop in careers of research in academic medicine and biology.

Subjects: Cardiovascular field and related studies in the basic sciences such as physiology, biochemistry, pathology as well as epidemiological and clinical investigations which bear on cardiovascular problems, including stroke: full-time program of research

Value: Minimum of US$16,000 per annum plus fringe benefits, and an annual increment of US$1,000; maximum of US$30,000 per annum.

Tenable in the United States (only occasionally elsewhere) for five years, subject to annual review.

Eligibility: Open to citizens or permanent residents of the United States who are under 40 years of age, have an M.D., Ph.D., D.Sc., D.D.S., D.V.M. or equivalent domestic or foreign degree, and have had three years postdoctoral research experience.

Closing date: 1st July.

Further information from:
Division of Research Awards
American Heart Association, Inc.
7320 Greenville Avenue
Dallas, Texas 75231
U.S.A.

[103]

AMERICAN HEART ASSOCIATION, INC. BRITISH HEART FOUNDATION

British-American Research Fellowships

Purpose: To offer additional postdoctoral training in research in the broad field of cardiovascular function and disease, including stroke, or related fundamental problems, to promising individuals who are perhaps not yet clearly qualified to conduct independent research.

No. offered: Three Fellowships annually.

Value: US$16,000 per annum plus US$600 for each dependent to a maximum of four dependents, plus benefits, including retirement. A grant of US$750 is made to the department where a Fellow is engaged in research.

Tenable in an accredited institution in the United Kingdom for one year.

Eligibility: Open to United States citizens who hold an M.D., Ph.D., D.Sc., D.D.S., D.V.M. or equivalent domestic or foreign degree and are under 35 years old.

Closing date: 1st July.

Further information from:
Division of Research Awards
American Heart Association, Inc.
7320 Greenville Avenue
Dallas, Texas 75231
U.S.A.

[104]

AMERICAN HEART ASSOCIATION NEW YORK STATE AFFILIATE, INC.

Research Grant-In-Aid; Research Fellowship

Purpose: To support scientific investigation in the field of health or disease designed to furnish new knowledge or to provide further support for existing knowledge relating to the cardiovascular system.

No. offered: Varies annually.

Value: Ranges from US$7,500 to US$25,000; median range is US$12,000.

Tenable in New York State, usually for a term of two years.

Eligibility: Applicants should hold an M.D., Ph.D. or equivalent degree. Awards are given to New York State investigators. Research Fellowships are open to noncitizens and are awarded on a competitive basis.

Closing date: 1st October.

Further information from:
American Heart Association
New York State Affiliate, Inc.
214 South Warren Street
Syracuse, New York 13202
U.S.A.

[105]

AMERICAN HISTORICAL ASSOCIATION

Herbert Baxter Adams Prize of US$300 is awarded annually on a two-year cycle for a distinguished book by an American author on either ancient, medieval or early modern European history, or nineteenth and twentieth century European history.

Troyer Steele Anderson Prize is awarded every ten years to the person whom the Council of the Association consideres to have made the most outstanding contribution to the advancement of the purposes of the Association during the preceding ten years.

George Louis Beer Prize of US$300 is awarded annually for the best work by a young scholar (first or second book) in the field of European international history since 1895.

Albert J. Beveridge Award of US$1,000 is given annually for the best book in English on American history (history of the United States, Canada and Latin America) from 1492 to the present.

Albert B. Corey Prize in Canadian-American Relations of US$2,000 is awarded in even-numbered years for the best book on the history of Canadian-United States relations, or on the history of both countries, and is awarded in conjunction with the Canadian Historical Association.

John H. Dunning Prize of US$300 is awarded in even-numbered years for a scholarly book on any subject relating to American history. Entries must be an author's first or second book and must have been published or completed in the two years preceding the award.

John K. Fairbank Prize in East Asian History of US$500 is given in odd-numbered years for an outstanding book on the history of China proper, Vietnam, Chinese Cultural Asia, Mongolia, Manchuria, Korea or Japan, since 1800.

Leo Gershoy Award of US$1,000 is awarded in odd-numbered years for the most outstanding work in seventeenth- or eighteenth-century European history.

Clarence H. Haring Prize of US$500 is awarded every five years to a Latin American who, in the opinion of the Committee, has published the most outstanding book on Latin American history during the preceding five years. The Prize will next be awarded in 1986.

Howard R. Marraro Prize in Italian History of US$500 is given annually for the best book or article by an American or Canadian citizen on Italian history in any epoch, of Italian cultural history, or of Italian-American relations.

Robert Livingston Schuyler Prize of US$500 is awarded every five years by the Taraknath Das Foundation for the best work by an American scholar on any period of British history since 1485. It will next be awarded in 1986.

Watumull Prize of US$1,000 is awarded in even-numbered years for the best scholarly work on the history of India originally published in the United States.

Further information from:
American Historical Association
400 A Street, S.E.
Washington, D.C. 20003
U.S.A.

[106]

AMERICAN HISTORICAL ASSOCIATION— PACIFIC COAST BRANCH

Louis Knott Koontz Memorial Award

The Board of Editors of the *Pacific Historical Review* annually awards US$200 for the best published article appearing in the review during the past year. Criteria for selection are based on literary ability, originality and soundness of research.

Further information from:
John A. Schutz, Secretary-Treasurer
American Historical Association—Pacific Coast Branch
c/o University of Southern California
ADM203, University Park
Los Angeles, California 90007
U.S.A.

[107]

AMERICAN HISTORICAL ASSOCIATION LIBRARY OF CONGRESS

J. Franklin Jameson Fellowship in American History

Purpose: To support scholarly research in the collections of the Library of Congress by young historians.

Subject: American history.

No. offered: One Fellowship annually.

Value: Variable.

Tenable for three to nine months, at least three of which are to be spent at the Library of

Congress where working space will be provided.

Eligibility: Open to young historians who have received a Ph.D. or equivalent degree within the past five years and have not published or had accepted for publication a book-length historical work.

Note: Fellowships are not awarded to permit completion of doctoral dissertations.

Note: Prior to the conclusion of the fellowship, the Jameson Fellow will be required to summarize the results of his or her research at a professional gathering arranged by the Library of Congress and the Association. Fellows are not required to complete their project during tenure of the Fellowship, nor are they required to publish the results of their research.

Closing date for applications: Postmarked no later than 1st March and received by 15th March.

Further information from:
J. Franklin Jameson Fellowship
American Historical Association
400 A Street, S.E.
Washington, D.C. 20003
U.S.A.

[108]

AMERICAN HOME ECONOMICS ASSOCIATION FOUNDATION

Awards and Grants

American Council of Life Insurance Project Grant: US$2,500 is awarded for research or demonstration projects in family economics. Proposals should address the basic elements of family economic behavior. *Closing date:* 20th November of the year preceding that in which the award is given.

Borden Award: US$1,000 and a gold medal are presented to an individual for significant research in nutrition and/or experimental foods. Open to any home economist in the U.S. or Canada who has published research. Preference is given to AHEA members. *Closing date for nominations:* Nominations must be received by 1st February of the award year.

Kraft, Inc. Nutrition Grant: US$2,500 is awarded to a home economist with a degree in home economics for an innovative program or project in nutrition related to current consumer concerns. Candidates should be pursuing or intend to pursue a career in nutrition in the business community. *Closing date:* 20th November of the year preceding that in which the award is given.

Ruth O'Brian Project Grant: US$3,000 is awarded to one or more individuals concerned with the research and development of home economics. *Closing date:* 20th November of the year preceding that in which the award is given.

Virginia HEA Project Grants: Grants of US$100 to US$1,000 are available to AHEA members for projects concerned with problems of aging related to food, clothing and shelter.

Teacher of the Year Award: This cash Award aims to: identify outstanding education programs, working methods and techniques; activities that can provide stimulus to other teachers and give visibility to home economics teachers who improve individual and family living and contribute to healthier communities. One national award of US$1,000, and three merit awards of US$500 each are conferred annually. Individuals wishing to participate should contact their state Teacher of the Year chairman for details. *Closing date for nominations:* 26th March of the award year.

Further information from:
Fellowships Committee Staff Liaison
American Home Economics Association Foundation
2010 Massachusetts Avenue, N.W.
Washington, D.C. 20036
U.S.A.

[109]

AMERICAN HOME ECONOMICS ASSOCIATION FOUNDATION

International Fellowships

The following Fellowships are offered annually to non-U.S. citizens for study, primarily at the graduate level, of home economics in the U.S.

AHEAF Fellowship: US$2,000, plus US$500

in fees and/or tuition from the cooperating college.

Ethel L. Parker Fellowship: US$3,000, plus US$500 in fees and/or tuition from the cooperating college, is offered to foreign students desiring to study home economics in the U.S.

Marion K. Piper Fellowship: US$2,000, plus US$500 in fees and/or tuition from the cooperating college.

D. Elizabeth Williams Fellowship: US$2,000, plus US$500 in fees and/or tuition from the cooperating college.

Note: Although the International Fellowships are intended for graduate level study, exceptions may be made for applicants whose home country offers little or no training in home economics.

International students residing in the U.S. at the time of application must submit a US$10 fee. Six copies of the completed application form should be submitted. Those students residing outside the U.S. are not required to submit an application fee, and need complete only one copy of the application form.

Application forms may be obtained by writing to the address below.

Closing date: 15th January.

Further information from:
American Home Economics Association Foundation
2010 Massachusetts Avenue, N.W.
Washington, D.C. 20036
U.S.A.

[110]

AMERICAN HOME ECONOMICS ASSOCIATION FOUNDATION

National Fellowships

The following Fellowships are offered to U.S. citizens or permanent residents of the U.S. who are members of AHEA.

AHEAF General Fellowship: US$2,500 offered annually for graduate study in home economics.

Freda A. DeKnight Memorial Fellowship: US$1,000 to a Black American graduate student for study in home economics communication or cooperative extension.

Marie Dye Memorial Fellowship: US$2,000 to a doctoral candidate studying home economics.

Kappa Omicron Phi—Hettie Margaret Anthony Fellowship: US$2,000 to a master's or doctoral student who is also a member of Kappa Omicron Phi.

Kappa Omicron Phi—Mabel Cook Fellowship: US$1,500 to a master's or doctoral student who is also a member of Kappa Omicron Phi.

Kappa Omicron Phi—Presidents Fellowship: US$2,000 to a master's or doctoral student who is also a member of Kappa Omicron Phi.

Ella H. McNaughton Fellowship: US$1,500 to provide for graduate study in the area of aging.

National Porketts Fellowship: US$5,000 to a home economics doctoral student to support study and research in an area related to pork.

Inez Eleanor Radell Memorial Fellowship: US$1,000 for graduate study in the design, construction, and/or marketing of clothing for the aging and/or handicapped adult.

Ellen H. Richards Fellowship: US$3,000 awarded bi-annually to a home economics graduate who plans to pursue advanced study with emphasis on administration. Applicants should have had work experience in an administrative area such as supervision, college or university administration, cooperative extension work, or business.

Note: Applicants must have completed at least one year of professional home economics experience by the beginning of the academic year for which the award is made.

Application forms may be obtained by writing to the address below and enclosing an application fee of US$10. Six copies of the completed forms should be submitted.

Closing date: 15th January.

Further information from:
American Home Economics Association
  Foundation
2010 Massachusetts Avenue, N.W.
Washington, D.C. 20036
U.S.A.

[111]

AMERICAN HOME ECONOMICS ASSOCIATION FOUNDATION

Special Fellowships

Carley-Canoyer-Cutler Fellowship in Consumer Studies: US$1,000 is awarded to a member of a minority group or an international student for consumer studies at the graduate level.

Flemmie P. Kittrell Fellowship for Minorities: US$3,000 is offered annually for graduate study to a member of a minority group in the U.S. or a student from a developing country. Recipients from developing countries receive an additional US$500 by the cooperating college for fees and/or tuition.

Note: Application forms may be obtained by writing to the address below. A US$10 application fee must accompany any request from U.S. citizens and those international students who may be currently residing in the U.S.

Closing date: 15th January.

Further information from:
American Home Economics Association
  Foundation
2010 Massachusetts Avenue, N.W.
Washington, D.C. 20036
U.S.A.

[112]

AMERICAN INDIAN SCHOLARSHIPS, INC.

Indian Graduate Student Support: Awards are available to American Indian graduate students in need of financial assistance for studies in any discipline directed towards the upgrading of Indian education, health and standard of living. The number and value of awards vary according to the number of applicants and individual need. Payments are usually made in monthly installments. Awards are made for periods up to one year and are renewable upon approval.

Candidates should be of certified 1/4 or more Indian blood, be enrolled in a graduate school, and obtain two academic and two personal recommendations to qualify.

Note: Written acceptance of Awards is required.

Closing date: Two months prior to the beginning of the course of study for which the applicant requests assistance.

Further information from:
American Indian Scholarships, Inc.
P.O. Box 1106
Taos, New Mexico 87571
U.S.A.

[113]

AMERICAN INSTITUTE OF AERONAUTICS AND ASTRONAUTICS
(New York City)

Awards

The Institute offers various awards within the fields of aeronautics and astronautics. Awards are presented at meetings of the Institute throughout the year.

Further information from:
Miss Roberta Shapiro
Honors and Awards
American Institute of Aeronautics and
  Astronautics
1290 Avenue of the Americas
New York, New York 10104
U.S.A.

[114]

AMERICAN INSTITUTE OF ARCHITECTS

AIA Research Communications Fellowship

Purpose: To provide greater understanding of the cause, scope and nature of the communication problem between the research community and practising architects, and to make a significant contribution toward devising creative methods of overcoming the problem.

No. offered: One Fellowship annually.

Value: US$3,000.

Tenable in a graduate-level architectural program of the applicant's choice for one year.

Eligibility: Enrollment in a graduate-level architectural program during the year of the Fellowship. Students who are currently enrolled in undergraduate programs in architecture, or graduates of accredited programs in architecture who are in an intern-architect status or a professional status, or students with non-environmental design backgrounds who will be enrolled in a graduate level architectural program during the year of the Fellowship, are eligible to apply.

Note: Applicants should prepare and submit a detailed proposal describing the subject to be investigated, the objectives of the study and the proposed procedure for the investigation.

The Fellowship is awarded conditionally and is confirmed upon the Fellow's acceptance into the graduate program of his or her choice.

Closing date: 15th March.

Further information from:
Director, Education Programs
American Institute of Architects
1735 New York Avenue, N.W.
Washington, D.C. 20006
U.S.A.

[115]

AMERICAN INSTITUTE OF ARCHITECTS

William H. Scheick Research Fellowship

Purpose: To assist a graduate student in architecture to pursue an original investigation.

Subject: Human needs and requirements in low-income housing of the multi-family type.

No. offered: One Fellowship annually.

Value: US$2,500.

Tenable in a graduate-level architectural program of the applicant's choice for one year.

Eligibility: Enrollment in a graduate-level architectural program during the year of the Fellowship. Students who are currently enrolled in undergraduate programs in architecture, or graduates of accredited programs in architecture who are in an intern-architect status or a professional status, or students with non-environmental design backgrounds who will be enrolled in a graduate level architectural program during the year of the Fellowship, are eligible to apply.

Note: Applicants should prepare and submit a detailed proposal describing the subject to be investigated, the objectives of the study and the proposed procedure for the investigation.

The Fellowship is awarded conditionally and is confirmed upon the Fellow's acceptance into the graduate program of his or her choice.

Closing date: 15th March.

Further information from:
Director, Education Programs
American Institute of Architects
1735 New York Avenue, N.W.
Washington, D.C. 20006
U.S.A.

[116]

AMERICAN INSTITUTE OF ARCHITECTS

AIA-AIAF Scholarship Program

Subject: Architecture.

Value: Awards range from US$200 to US$2,000.

Tenable for a full academic year at schools accredited by the National Architecture Accrediting Board or recognized by the Royal Architectural Institute of Canada.

Eligibility: First professional degree Scholarships are open to students who are in their third or fourth year of a five year program leading to a B.Arch. or equivalent, or in their fourth or fifth year of a six year program leading to a M.Arch or equivalent; also open to students who are in their second or third year of a three to four-year program which results in a M.Arch. and whose undergraduate degrees are in a discipline other than architecture.

Scholarships for study or research beyond the first professional degree are open to candidates who are currently students in the final year of a first professional degree program resulting in a B.Arch. or equivalent and to practitioners, interns, educators or others who have received the first professional degree in architecture.

Note: All first profesional degree candidates must apply through the office of the head of an accredited school of architecture or through its scholarship committee. Professional candidates (practitioners, educators and interns) may apply by writing to the address below.

Closing date: 15th January.

Further information from:
  Scholarship Programs
  American Institute of Architects
  1735 New York Avenue, N.W.
  Washington, D.C. 20006
  U.S.A.

[117]

AMERICAN INSTITUTE OF ARCHITECTS AMERICAN HOSPITAL ASSOCIATION

AIA—AHA Fellowship in Health Facilities Design: One or more graduate Fellowships in a total amount of up to US$6,000, for study in one of the following settings: *(i)* Graduate study of one academic year in any accredited school of architecture linked with a school of hospital administration and/or adequate area hospital resources to supplement prescribed graduate architectural courses in health facilities design. *(ii)* Independent graduate-level study, research or design in the health facilities field, to be completed in one calendar year. *(iii)* Travel with in-residence research in selected health care facilities in a predetermined area, to be completed within one calendar year.

Eligibility: Open to citizens of the U.S. and Canada who have either earned and received a professional degree from an accredited school of architecture or who are in the final year of undergraduate work leading to such a degree.

Closing date: 15th March.

Further information from:
  American Hospital Association
  Department of Health Facilities and
    Standards
  840 North Lake Shore Drive
  Chicago, Illinois 60611
  U.S.A.

[118]

AMERICAN INSTITUTE OF BAKING

Scholarships for Advanced Study in Baking Science and Technology

Purpose: To enable Scholars to advance rapidly in the baking and allied industries.

Subjects: Comprehensive instruction in the scientific basis of baking and the technology of modern bakery production.

No. offered: At least 14 Scholarships annually.

Value: US$1,000.

Tenable for 19 weeks at the Institute.

Eligibility: Candidates must meet entrance requirements for baking science and technology class.

Note: Scholarships are offered twice annually, in February and August.

Closing dates: 1st June and 1st December.

Further information from:
  Registrar
  American Institute of Baking
  1213 Bakers Way
  Manhattan, Kansas 66502
  U.S.A.

[119]

AMERICAN INSTITUTE OF CERTIFIED PUBLIC ACCOUNTANTS

Grants-in-Aid for Doctoral Dissertations in Accounting

Purpose: To encourage research in accounting, to enable recipients to concentrate on their dissertations and to encourage candidates to consider careers in teaching.

No. offered: Several Grants, awarded twice annually.

Value: US$600 per month for persons with no dependent children; US$700 per month for persons with dependent children.

Tenable at a school that is a member of the

American Assembly of Collegiate Schools of Business, for a maximum of one year.

Eligibility: Applicants should be working for the doctorate degree at a school that is a member of the American Assembly of Collegiate Schools of Business, and should express an interest in becoing a teacher of accounting.

Before payments are made grantees should have completed all requirements for the degree except the dissertation and the examinations that follow its completion. Candidates must have an approved dissertation topic. The selection committee will also consider applicants who have progress on dissertations and who may need assistance to complete them.

Closing dates: 1st March and 1st September.

Further information from:
Subcommittee on Relations with
   Educational Institutions
American Institute of Certified Public
   Accountants
1211 Avenue of the Americas
New York, New York 10036
U.S.A.

[120]

AMERICAN INSTITUTE OF CHEMICAL ENGINEERS

Awards

Alpha Chi Sigma Award for Chemical Engineering Research: The Award of US$2,000 and a certificate is given to recognize outstanding recent accomplishments by an individual in fundamental or applied research in the field of chemical engineering. The research, normally conducted in North America, should have been carried out during the ten year period preceding the presentation of the Award. Awards are given at the discretion of the Awards Committee, but not more than one Award per calendar year. The Award is sponsored by the *Alpha Chi Sigma Fraternity.*

Warren K. Lewis Award for Contributions to Chemical Engineering Education: *US$2,000* and a scroll is give for important and continuing contributions to chemical engineering education as judged by one or more of the following criteria: success as a teacher; contributions of lasting educational influence such as superior textbooks, lectures, laboratory techinques or models; impact on education through creative ability evidenced by contributions to literature, by inventions, by developments in the industry, through consulting or government service; or through key leadership in administrating a department or similar group which has made outstanding contributions. Awards are given at the discretion of the Awards Committee, but not more than one Award per calendar year. This Award is jointly sponsored by *Exxon International, Inc. and Exxon Research and Engineering Company.*

Professional Progress Award for Outstanding Progress in Chemical Engineering: The Award of US$2,000 and a certificate is offered to a scientist who has not yet reached his 45th birthday at the time of the Award, and has made a significant contribution to the science of chemical engineering through one of the following: A theoretical discovery or development of a new principle; an invention or development of new equipment; or some distinguished service rendered to the profession of chemical engineering. Awards are given at the discretion of the Awards Committee, but not more than one Award per calendar year. The Awards are sponsored by the *Celanese Corporation of America.*

R.H. Willhelm Award in Chemical Reaction Engineering: US$2,000 and a scroll is awarded to recognize significant and new contributions in chemical reaction engineering. Candidates shall be judged as advancing the frontiers of the field with an emphasis on originality, creativity and novelty of concept and application. Awards are given at the discretion of the Awards Committee, but not more than one Award per calendar year. This Award is sponsored by the *Mobil Oil Corporation.*

Further information from:
American Institute of Chemical Engineers
345 East 47th Street
New York, New York 10017
U.S.A.

[121]

AMERICAN INSTITUTE FOR ECONOMIC RESEARCH *(Great Barrington, Mass.)*

Graduate, Summer and In-Absentia Fellowships

Purpose: To enable those persons who are

interested primarily in scientific research on money and banking, special privilege, or human effort problems, to spend at least one summer at the American Institute for Economic Research to demonstrate their potential for development as economic scientists. Those who demonstrate sufficient potential may apply for Institute Fellowships in-absentia for graduate work in economics elsewhere, with tuition paid.

Value: Graduate Fellowships—Tuition costs, plus *US*$300 per month and dependents' allowance of *US*$75 per month each.

Tenable at the Institute for a minimum of three months, and subsequently for two or more years elsewhere.

Eligibility: Open to the United States citizens who hold a bachelor's degree in economics or a closely related field. Undergraduates who are majoring in economics or finance and who have completed their junior year may apply.

Further information from:
Director of Education
American Institute for Economic Research
Great Barrington, Massachusetts 01230
U.S.A.

[122]

AMERICAN INSTITUTE FOR EXPLORATION

Fellowships

Purpose: To encourage and support original field research in natural, physical or social sciences.

Subject: Field research in Alaska or Japan.

No. offered: Two Fellowships annually.

Value: US$500 to US$1,000 paid as partial defrayment of transportation.

Tenable in Alaska or Japan for two to six months, renewable.

Eligibility: Open to college graduates with at least a B.S. or B.A. degree and a strong interest in pursuing graduate work in a field science. Candidates should have an acceptable research plan and the training and experience to carry it out.

Note: Two reports are required of the recipient; one half-way through and a second at the completion of the research.

Not confirmed for 1983.

Further information from:
Aleuthian-Bering Sea Expedition
American Institute for Exploration
1809 Nichols Road
Kalamazoo, Michigan 49007
U.S.A.

[123]

AMERICAN INSTITUTE OF INDIAN STUDIES

The following awards are open to American citizens who are studying the humanities, social sciences or natural sciences. In some cases resident aliens may also be eligible. Selection will be made regardless of race, color, sex or religion.

Junior Fellowships: These are awarded to graduate students specializing in Indian aspects of academic disciplines for dissertation research. Fellows are required to affiliate themselves with an Indian university for the period of their work in India.

Library Service Fellowships: These are offered to librarians with a specialization in South Asia.

Post-Doctoral Study Tour Awards: Awards are available to persons whose primary field of interest is South Asia but who have never been to India. Applicants should be recent Ph.D. candidates wishing to make a visit to India for a period of up to three months in order to visit persons and institutions in India that are of interest to them. The awards may not be used for research purposes. Only applicants who have received their Ph. D. from a member institution or who are on the staff of a member institution are eligible.

Professional Developmental Awards: Applications for these Awards will be accepted from scholars in the fields of medicine, biological sciences, physical sciences, business administration, law, and journalism to work with their counterparts in India on problems of mutual interest.

Note: Because of the current shortage of funds the AIIS is compelled to charge administrative overheads to grantees from non-member institutions: Junior Fellows *US$400*; Senior Fellows *US$750*. The institution with which the Fellow is associated is responsible for payment of these fees.

Closing date: 1st July for all awards.

Further information from:
American Institute of Indian Studies
Foster Hall, University of Chicago
1130 East 59th Street
Chicago, Illinois 60637
U.S.A.

[124]

AMERICAN INSTITUTE OF NUTRITION

Bio-Serve Award in Experimental Animal Nutrition of *US$1,000* is given annually for meritorious research in nutrition by an investigator who has received the doctoral degree within the last ten years. A primary requirement is that the work deals with nutrition of experimental animals used as models. Nominations are maintained in an active file until each has been considered by three successive juries of award.

Borden Award in Nutrition of *US$1,000* and an engraved plaque is given annually in recognition of distinctive research by investigators in the United States and Canada, which has emphasized the nutritional significance of any food or food component. The Award, primarily made for the publication of specific papers during the previous two years, may be given for important contributions made over a more extended period of time. There are no restrictions as to age; however it is intended that the Award be a stimulus to professionally active nutrition scientists. Nominations are maintained in an active file until each has been considered by two successive juries of award.

Conrad A. Elvehjem Award for Public Service in Nutrition of *US$1,500* and an inscribed scroll is given annually for recognition of specific and distinguished service to the public through the science of nutrition. Contributions of an investigative nature would not necessarily be excluded. There are no age restrictions for the Award. Nominations are maintained in an active file until each has been considered by three successive juries of award. This Award is made available by the *Ralston Purina Company*.

Lederle Award in Human Nutrition of *US$1,500*, an inscribed scroll and a contribution toward travel is given annually in recognition of recent investigative contributions of contemporary significance to the basic understanding of human nutrition. Contributions need not be restricted to investigative work in humans, insofar as the contributions may have relevance to human nutrition and health. There are no restrictions as to age. Preference will be given to scientists in the Western Hemisphere. Nominations are maintained in an active file until each has been considered by three successive juries of award.

Mead Johnson Award for Research in Nutrition of *US$1,000* and an inscribed scroll is offered annually for recent research in nutrition. Investigators should not have reached their 40th birthday before the presentation of the Award. Nominations are maintained in an active file until each has been considered by three successive juries of award.

Osborne and Mendel Award of *US$1,000* and an inscribed scroll is awarded annually for the recognition of outstanding recent basic research accomplishments in the general field of nutrition. The accomplishment may be in the form of a series of papers of outstanding significance. Preference will normally be given to investigators working in the United States or Canada; however investigators in other countries, especially those sojourning in the United States or Canada for a period of time, are eligible. There are no age restrictions; however it is intended that the Award be a stimulus to professionally active nutritional scientists. Nominations are maintained in an active file until each has been considered by three successive juries of award.

Note: Nominations for all awards may be made by anyone, and should be sent to the current chairperson of the nominating committee (name and address available from the address below).

Closing date: 30th September for all awards, for consideration in the following year.

Further information from:
American Institute of Nutrition
9650 Rockville Pike
Bethesda, Maryland 20014
U.S.A.

[125]

AMERICAN INSTITUTE OF PHYSICS

Karl Taylor Compton Medal recognizes the outstanding statesmanship in science of distinguished physicists.

Dannie N. Heinemann Prize for Mathematical Physics, awarded by the American Physical Society and the American Institute of Physics, serves to recognize outstanding publication in the field of mathematical physics.

Prize for Industrial Applications of Physics recognizes outstanding contributions by individual(s) in this field. Offered once every two years. Value: US$5,000 and a certificate, plus travel allowance up to US$500 to receive the prize.

John T. Tate International Medal recognizes distinguished service to physics on an international level.

Further information from:
American Institute of Physics
335 East 45th Street
New York, New York 10017
U.S.A.

[126]

AMERICAN INSTITUTE OF PHYSICS UNITED STATES STEEL FOUNDATION

Science Writing Awards in Physics and Astronomy

Purpose: To stimulate distinguished reporting and writing of advances in physics and astronomy by either (a) physicists, astronomers and members of A.I.P. member societies, or (b) journalists.

No. offered: One Award in each of the above categories annually.

Value: US$1,500 together with a certificate.

Note: Entries must represent the work of individuals who are permanent residents of the United States, Mexico or Canada, and have been printed in any recognized international, national or local medium of communication, such as newspapers, magazines or books. The media should normally be available to and intended for the general public; purely scientific, technical, and trade publications are excluded.

Entries must have been published in the United States or its territories, Mexico or Canada during the period one year immediately prior to the application deadline date.

No more than three entries may be submitted by one individual (persons other than the author may submit entries on behalf of the author in accordance with the rules).

An author may submit a series or articles as one entry; he may also use one or two separate individual articles from the series, clearly labelled, as his one or two other entries, thus submitting a total of three.

Closing dates: Scientist Award—31st May; Journalist Award—31st December.

Further information from:
Public Information Division
American Institute of Physics
335 East 45th Street
New York, New York 10017
U.S.A.

[127]

AMERICAN INSTITUTE OF REAL ESTATE APPRAISERS

Research and Educational Trust Fund

Scholarships: Five graduate Scholarships of US$1,500 each are offered to students enrolled in graduate programs in land economics, real estate, real estate appraising, or allied fields at accredited member schools of the American Assembly of Collegiate Schools of Business, Inc. Applications, on the prescribed forms, should be submitted by mid-February.

AIREA Course Grants: The Grants are offered to professionals to attend any of the Institute's nine real estate appraisal courses. Enrollment fees are provided and required textbooks are free of charge.

Further information from:
American lushtuke of Real Estate
 Appraisers
430 North Michigan Avenue
Chicago, Illinois 60611
U.S.A.

[128]

AMERICAN INSTITUTE OF STEEL CONSTRUCTION, INC.

AISC Fellowships

Purpose: To encourage expertise in the creative use of fabricated structural steel.

Subject: Civil or architectural engineering course related to fabricated steel structures.

No. offered: Up to eight Fellowships annually.

Value: US$4,750: US$4,000 for Fellow and US$750 for department chairman's use in administering the award.

Tenable at an approved ABET college or university for one year; not renewable.

Eligibility: Open to United States citizens who are senior or graduate civil or architectural engineering students majoring in structural engineering. Candidates should be attending or accepted by an accredited ABET college or university offering a graduate engineering degree program and must be recommended by the college or university. Master's degree candidates will be given preference over Ph.D. candidates.

Note: Application kits may be obtained from the department chairman and from the AISC Education Foundation.

Closing date: Early February.

Further information from:
Education Foundation
American Institute of Steel Construction,
 Inc.
400 North Michigan Avenue
Chicago, Illinois 60611
U.S.A.

[129]

AMERICAN INSTITUTE OF STEEL CONSTRUCTION, INC.

T.R. Higgins Lectureship Award

Purpose: To recognize the author of the technical paper or papers judged to be the most significant contribution to engineering literature on fabricated structural steel.

No. offered: One Award annually.

Value: An engraved certificate and US$2,000.

The winner will be expecting to present an oral review of the prizewinning paper at AISC's annual National Engineering Conference and, upon invitation by AISC, at five other locations during the year.

Eligibility: The author must be a permanent resident of the United States. The paper or papers must have been published in a professional journal which provides for a discussion of papers by the engineering profession, within a period of five years prior to 1st January of the current year. The paper or papers will be judged on originality, contribution to engineering knowledge, projected future significance, clarity of presentation, and value to the fabricated structural steel industry.

Closing date: Usually early January.

Further information from:
Education Foundation
American Institute of Steel Construction,
 Inc.
400 North Michigan Avenue
Chicago, Illinois 60611
U.S.A.

[130]

AMERICAN-ITALIAN HISTORICAL ASSOCIATION *(U.S.A.)*

Leonard Covello Award

A Prize of US$200 is given to the author of the best article-length manuscript submitted on any aspect of the Italian-American experience. Essays resulting from original research, or those of synthesis or new interpretations are sought by the judges. The Competition is open to graduate students and recipients of the doctorate degree within the past three years. Contestants with no previous publication record are especially encouraged to submit their work.

Not confirmed for 1983.

Further information from:
American-Italian Historical Association
209 Flagg Place
Staten Island, New York 10304
U.S.A.

[131]

AMERICAN LIBRARY ASSOCIATION

Scholarships and Grants

ALA scholarship Program-David H. Clift Scholarship: Given annually in the amount of US$3,000 to a worthy student to begin his or her library education at the graduate level without regard to race, creed, color, national origin or sex. The recipient should be a U.S. or Canadian citizen and must enter a formal program of graduate study leading to a master's degree at an ALA-accredited school. Number of awards depends on available funds. Applications, to be postmarked no later than 4th January, may be obtained from *Margaret Myers, Staff Liaison, ALA.*

AlA Scholarship Program-Frederick Winthrop Faxon Scholarship: One annual Scholarship of US$3,000 plus an expense-paid ten week internship at F.W. Faxon Company, Westwood, Massachusetts, is given to a worthy student beginning an ALA accredited master's level program in library or information sciences. Candidates should have a specific interest in the field of serials management and control. Applications, to be postmarked no later than 4th January, may be obtained from *Margaret Myers, Staff Liaison, ALA.*

ALA Scholarship Program-Louise Giles Minority Scholarship: Given in the amount of US$3,000 to a worthy student who is a U.S. or Canadian citizen and is also a member of a principal minority group (American Indian or Alaskan native, Asian or Pacific Islander, Black, or Hispanic). The recipient must enter a formal program of graduate study leading to a master's degree at an ALA-accredited library school. Number of awards depends on available funds. Applications, to be postmarked no later than 4th January, may be obtained from *Margaret Myers, Staff Liaison, ALA.*

JMRT Professional Development Grant: Cash Awards presented to librarians to attend the annual conference of the ALA. Recipients must be members of the ALA and the Junior Members Round Table. Nominations should be submitted before 15th November. Further information from JMRT Professional Development Grant, c/o ALA.

Frederic G. Melcher Scholarship: Two annual Awards of US$4,000 to encourage and assist young people who wish to enter the field of library service to children. Presented to a qualified candidate who has been accepted for admission to an ALA-accredited library school. Applications, to be submitted before 1st March, from *Mary Jane Anderson, Staff Liaison, ALA.*

Shirley Olofson Memorial Award: An annual cash Award made to individuals to attend their second annual conference of the ALA. Recipients must be members of the ALA and be potential or current members of the Junior Members Round Table. Applications should be submitted before 1st January to *Shirley Olofson Memorial Award, c/o ALA.*

Herbert W. Putnam Award: Presented as a Grant-in-aid in the amount of US$500 to an American librarian of outstanding ability, for travel, writing, or other use that might improve his or her service to the library profession or to society. The Award is presented when the Putnam Fund accumulates US$500. Inquiries should be sent to *Peggy Barber, Interim Staff Liaison, ALA.*

Charles Scribner's Sons Award: Four annual cash Awards in the amount of US$325 each, presented to two school librarians and two public library children's librarians, to enable them to attend ALA's annual conference. Recipients must be members of the Association for Library Service to Children, have one to ten years experience, and never have attended on ALA annual conference. Applications, to be submitted before 1st January, from *Mary Jane Anderson, Staff Liaison, ALA.*

Further information from:
Awards Committee
American Library Association
50 East Huron Street
Chicago, Illinois 60611
U.S.A.

[132]

AMERICAN LIBRARY ASSOCIATION

Awards

AASL President's Award is given annually in the amount of US$2,000 to an individual who has demonstrated excellence and provided an outstanding national or international contribution to school librarianship and school library development. Nominations should be submitted before 4th December to *AASL President's Award, c/o ALA.*

ACRL Academic or Research Librarian of the Year Award of US$2,000 is presented annually to an individual for an outstanding national or international contribution to academic and research librarianship and development. Nominations should be submitted before 1st January to ACRL Award, c/o ALA.

Beta Phi Mu Award, consisting of US$500 and a citation, is presented annually to a library school faculty member or to an individual for distinguished service to education for librarianship. Nominations should be sent no later than 15th December to *Beta Phi Mu Award, c/o ALA.*

CIS/GODORT/ALA "Documents to the People" Award, consisting of a citation and a cash stipend of US$1,000, is given annually to promote professional advancement in the field of librarianship. The Award is presented to the individual and/or library, organization, or other appropriate noncommercial group that has most effectively encouraged the use of federal documents in support of library services. Nominations should be submitted before 15th December to *Documents to the People Award, c/o ALA.*

Facts on File Award: An annual award of US$1,000 is presented to a librarian who has made current affairs more meaningful to adult audiences. Programs, bibliographies, pamphlets, and innovative approaches of all types and in all media will apply. Nominations should be submitted by 15th December to *Facts on File Award, c/o ALA.*

Grolier Foundation Award of US$1,000 and a citation is presented annually to a librarian in a community or in a school who has made an unusual contribution to the stimulation and guidance of reading by children and young people. The Award is given for outstanding work with children and young people through high school age, for continuing service, or in recognition of one particular contribution of lasting value. Nominations and five copies of the statement should be submitted before 15th December to *Grolier Award, c/o ALA.*

John Philip Immroth Award for Intellectual Freedom in the amount of US$500 and a plaque is given annually to an intellectual freedom fighter who has made a notable contribution to intellectual freedom and has demonstrated remarkable personal courage. Nominations should be submitted before 1st December to *JPIM Award for Intellectual Freedom, c/o ALA.*

Library Research Round Table Research Award: Up to two Awards of US$500 each are presented annually to encourage excellence in library research. Papers submitted are not to exceed 75 pages in length. Entries are judged on the following points: definition of the research problem; application of research methods; clarity of reporting; significance of conclusions. Research papers completed in pursuit of an academic degree are not eligible. Entries must be submitted by 1st April to *LRRT Research Award, c/o ALA.*

Joseph Lippincott Award, consisting of US$1,000, an engraved medal, and a citation, is presented annually to a librarian for distinguished service in the profession of librarianship, such service to include outstanding participation in the activities of professional library associations, notable published professional writing, or other significant activity on behalf of the profession and its aims. Nominations should be submitted before 15th December to *Lippincott Award, c/o ALA.*

Eunice Rockwell Oberly Memorial Award is given in odd-numbered years to an American citizen who compiles the best bibliography in the field of agriculture or one of the related sciences in the two-year period preceding the award. A citation and a cash prize are given. Nominations should be submitted before 1st January to *Oberly Award, c/o ALA*.

PLA Allie Beth Martin Award of US$2,000 and certificate to a librarian who, in a public library setting, has demonstrated an extraordinary range and depth of knowledge about books or other library materials and has exhibited a distinguished ability to share that knowledge. Nominations should be submitted by 1st January to *PLA Allie Beth Martin Award, c/o ALA*.

RTSD Resources Scholarship Award consisting of a citation and a scholarship grant of US$1,000 is presented to the author or authors of an outstanding monograph, published article, or original paper on acquisitions pertaining to college or university libraries. The scholarship grant is given to the library school of the winner's choice. Entries should be submitted before 15th December to *RTSD Resources Scholarship Award, c/o ALA*.

John R. Rowe Memorial Award: An annual award of US$500 is made to an individual or group to aid or improve some particular aspect of librarianship or library service on the basis of need in the profession or in the operation of professional library associations. Applications should be submitted before 1st April to *Rowe Award, c/o ALA*.

Ralph R. Shaw Award for Library Literature consisting of US$500 and a citation is presented to an American librarian to recognize an outstanding contribution to library literature issued during the three years preceding the presentation. Nominations should be made before 15th January to *RRS Award for Library Literature, c/o ALA*.

Judson Winsor Prize Essay of US$200 is presented to the author of an essay which demonstrates excellence in research in library history. Entries, which should not exceed twenty-five type-written pages, should be in manuscript form and not previously published nor currently under consideration for publication. Essays should combine original and historical research on a significant subject of library history. The winner will be offered the privilege of having the essay published in *The Journal of Library History*. Entries should be submitted no later than 1st April to *Winsor Prize Essay, c/o ALA*.

Note: The ALA offers the following medals to individuals, with no cash prizes: *Randolph Caldecott Medal; James Bennet Childs Award; Dartmouth Medal; Melvil Dewey Medal; John Newberry Medal;* and the *Laura Ingalls Wilder Medal*.

Also offered by the ALA to individuals (cash prizes) are the following citations: *ALTA Honor Award; ASCLA Exceptional Service Award; Armed Forces Librarians Achievement Citation; Francis Joseph Campbell Citation; Margaret Mann Citation; Isadore Gilbert Mudge Citation; Ester J. Piercy Award; Distinguished Library Service Award for School Administrators;* and the *Trustees Citations*.

Further information from:
Awards Committee
American Library Association
50 East Huron Street
Chicago, Illinois 60611
U.S.A.

[133]

AMERICAN LUNG ASSOCIATION

Nursing Fellowships in Respiratory Disease

Purpose: To prepare nursing graduates with a current R.N. license as respiratory clinical nurse specialists, teachers or researchers.

Value: Up to US$9,000.

Tenable at United States institutions, for a maximum of two years.

Eligibility: Open to United States or Canadian citizens or holders of permanent visas for training in United States institutions.

Closing date: 1st April.

Further information from:
Director of Medical Affairs
American Lung Association
1740 Broadway
New York, New York 10019
U.S.A.

[134]

AMERICAN LUNG ASSOCIATION

Training Fellowships

Purpose: To stimulate the training of clinicians, teachers and scientific investigators in the prevention and control of lung disease.

Value: Up to US$14,000.

Tenable in the United States for three years.

Eligibility: Open to physicians entering their second or later years of residency training in internal medicine, pediatrics, thoracic surgery or other specialty relevant to lung disease; individuals holding a M.D., Ph.D., or Sc.D. for further training as scientific investigators in this field. Awards are limited to United States and Canadian citizens or holders of U.S. permanent visas working in U.S. institutions. Priority will be given to candidates interested in academic careers.

Note: The third year of the Fellowship is limited to research only.

Closing date: 1st October.

Further information from:
Director of Medical Affairs
American Lung Association
1740 Broadway
New York, New York 10019
U.S.A.

[135]

AMERICAN LUNG ASSOCIATION

Edward Livingston Trudeau Fellowships

Purpose: To give promising young physicians in medical schools an opportunity to stay in academic medicine and to prove themselves as teachers, investigators and coordinators of teaching in the field of the lung and its disorders.

Value: Up to US$15,000. The award is intended to supplement the salary paid by the medical school.

Tenable at United States and Canadian medical schools. Awards are made on a yearly basis, and are renewable.

Eligibility: Open to United States citizens in United States or Canadian medical schools and to Canadian citizens in United States medical schools.

Closing date: 1st October.

Further information from:
Director of Medical Affairs
American Lung Association
1740 Broadway
New York, New York 10019
U.S.A.

[136]

AMERICAN LUNG ASSOCIATION

Research Grants

Purpose: To assist young, not yet established investigators in carrying out research into the prevention and control of lung diseases.

Subjects: Research may be laboratory, clinical, epidemiologic or social.

No. offered: Approximately 44 Grants annually.

Value: US$10,000-US$15,000.

Tenable for a period of one or two years.

Eligibility: Applicants should be United States citizens, or hold a permanent visa for working in a United States institution.

Closing date: 1st November.

Further information from:
Director of Medical Affairs
American Lung Association
1740 Broadway
New York, New York 10019
U.S.A.

[137]

AMERICAN MATHEMATICAL SOCIETY

Prizes

Bôcher Memorial Prize: US$1,450 is awarded every five years for a notable research memoir in analysis, which has been pulbished in a recognized North American journal during the five year peiod preceding the presentation of the Prize. Next awarded in 1984.

Frank Nelson Cole Prizes in Algebra and in Number Theory: US$2,250 is awarded in each category at five year intervals. Contributions in these fields must have been published in a recognized North American journal during the five year period preceding the presentation of the Prize. Next awarded in 1985 (Algebra).

LeRoy P. Steele Prizes: Up to three Prizes are awarded annually in the following categories: (1) for the cumulative influence of the total mathematical work of the recipient, high level of research over a period of time, particular influence on the development of a field, and influence on mathematics through Ph.D. students; (2) for a book or substantial survey or expository research paper; (3) for a paper, whether recent or not, which has proved to be of fundamental or lasting importance in its field, or a model of important research.

Oswald Veblen Prize in Geometry: Two Prizes normally awarded every five years for research in geometry of topology. Contributions in these fields must have been published in a recognized North American journal during the five year period preceding the presentation of the Prize. Next awarded in 1986.

Note: In addition, the Society sponsors a number of funds which make awards of varying amounts from time to time. These awards may be in the form of fellowships, prizes, or grants for publication of important mathematical books, memoirs and periodicals.

Further information from:
American Mathematical Society
P.O. Box 6248
Providence, Rhode Island 02940
U.S.A.

[138]

AMERICAN METEOROLOGICAL SOCIETY

Max A. Eaton Prize of US$400 and a certificate is given for the best student paper presented at each Technical Conference on Hurricanes and Tropical Meteorology. Entrants should be currently enrolled in high school, college or graduate school, or be recent degree graduates who have not begun regular employment at the time of the conference.

Banner I Miller Award of US$300 is presented annually to an individual for the best contribution to the science of hurricane and tropical weather forecasting published in a journal with international circulation, within the 24 months preceding the presentation of the Award.

Second Half Century Award, consisting of a medallion and a nominal stipend, is presented annually to no more than three members for excellence in their contributions to the geofluid sciences. Recipients should be fifty years of age or less at the time of presentation.

Note: The Society also makes the following awards to individuals: *Cleveland Abbe Award; Charles Franklin Brooks Award; Editor's Award; Father James B. Macelwane Awards in Meteorology; Howard H. Hanks, Jr. Scholarship in Meteorology; Meisinger Award; Howard T. Orville Scholarship in Meteorology; Award for Outstanding Achievement in Bioclimatology; Award for Outstanding Contribution to the Advance of Applied Meteorology; Award for Outstanding Service by a Broadcast Meteorologist; Award for Outstanding Service by a Weather Forecaster; Carl-Gustaf Rossby Research Medal; Sverdrup Gold Medal;* and Special Awards and Citations.

Further information from:
American Meteorological Society
45 Beacon Street
Boston, Massachusetts 02108
U.S.A.

[139]

AMERICAN MUSEUM OF NATURAL HISTORY
FRANK M. CHAPMAN MEMORIAL FUND

Grants are intended to support and foster research in ornithology from a broad and international point of view. Grants are primarily designed to encourage and aid less experienced scientists, especially graduate students and individuals with recent graduate degrees, although there are no restrictions as to age, the formal qualifications of applicants or the locality in which research is to be conducted. In this regard, Grant proposals are encouraged from graduate students and visiting scientists from outside the United States, to enable them to work for a period at the American Museum of Natural History or one of its field stations. The average Grant is approximately US$500. Proposals for museum, field and laboratory investigations are invited. Consideration is seldom given to projects which foster research more indirectly, such as publication subsidies, travel expenses to attend important ornithological meetings, and temporary field assistance.

Chapman and Naumburg Fellowships are intended to enable postgraduate scholars and distinguished ornithologists to carry out a year of research at the American Museum of Natural History or one of its field stations. One or two Fellowships are awarded annually and support includes a stipend and possible contributions toward research expenses. One of these Fellowships, to be called the *Elsie Binger Naumburg Fellowship*, will be restricted to the general field of tropical American ornithology.

Closing dates: 15th February and 15th September; in exceptional ciricumstaces, applications will be considered at other times or the year.

Further information from:
Frank M. Chapman Memorial Fund
American Museum of Natural History
Central Park West at 79th Street
New York, New York 10024
U.S.A.

[140]

AMERICAN MUSEUM OF NATURAL HISTORY
LERNER-GRAY FUND FOR MARINE RESEARCH

Grants

Modest financial assistance in the form of Grants is available to scientists beginning careers in marine biology. The support is normally offered when funding from large foundations and granting agencies is unavailable.

The Grants, averaging US$590 per award, are usually tenable for one year and may be used for field work in marine biological research anywhere in the world. Support may be applied to costs of transportation, living expenses, expendable equipment and supplies. It may not be applied to salaries or for the purchase of non-expendable equipment.

There are no restrictions as to eligibility other than candidates should be at the graduate or postdoctoral level. Application forms may be obtained by writing to the address below.

Closing date: 15th March of each year.

Further information from:
Lerner-Grey Fund for Marine Research
American Museum of Natural History
Central Park West at 79th Street
New York, New York 10024
U.S.A.

[141]

AMERICAN MUSEUM OF NATURAL HISTORY
THEODORE ROOSEVELT MEMORIAL FUND

Fellowships: Open to doctoral candidates or postdoctoral scholars for research in any field of natural history related to the fauna of North America, except ornithology. Support for up to one year will include a modest stipend and contributions toward research needs.

Applicants should include the candidate's educational and scientific backgrounds, a detailed project description including estimated costs, two letters of approval and recommendation for the project candidate from faculty advisors or colleagues, and a statement from the chairman of the department of the museum at which the proposed work will be done.

Grants: Intended primarily for less experienced scientists, especially graduate students and individuals with recent graduate degrees, to meet modest financial needs not usually available from large foundations or granting agencies. Grants for no more than several hundred dollars are made in support of field work, including transportation, subsistence, expendable supplies and equipment, and may be obtained for investigations anywhere on the North American continent.

Grants are expected to submit a project report and statement of expenses at the end of the project period (report may be waived if results are to be published within one year).

Applications should be accompanied by a project description, itemized budget for the proposed project, two letters of recommendation, and information on the applicant's relevant training, experience and publications.

Closing date: 15th February, for both Awards.

Further information from:
Theodore Roosevelt Memorial Fund
American Museum of Natural History
Central Park West at 79th Street
New York, New York 10024
U.S.A.

[142]

AMERICAN MUSICOLOGICAL SOCIETY, INC.

Alfred Einstein Award: One Award of US$400 is given annually to a scholar under the age of 36 who has written the best article on a musicological subject.

Noah Greenberg Award: One Award of up to US$1,000 is given annually for a distinguished contribution to the study and performance of early music, up to the end of the seventeenth century.

Otto Kinkeldey Award: One Award of US$400 is given annually to any member of the Society, regardless of age, who has written the best book in the field of musicology.

The recipients of the above Awards are selected by two committees appointed each year by the president of the Society. Scholars who might be eligible for Awards may call attention to their books and articles by contacting any member of the committees, preferably before May.

Note: In addition to these Awards, very few grants for travel to participate in international congresses are awarded by the Society in collaboration with the American Council of Learned Societies. These grants are awarded for travel only to officially sanctioned meetings. Inquiries should be addressed to *Prof. Frank Traficante, Music Department, Claremont Graduate School, Claremont, California 91711.*

Further information from:
Professor Alvin H. Johnson, Executive Director
American Musicological Society, Inc.
201 South 34th Street
Philadelphia, Pennsylvania 19104
U.S.A.

[143]

AMERICAN NUCLEAR SOCIETY

ANS Special Award: One award of US$1,000 is given at the annual meeting for outstanding work in an area specified each year by the Board of Directors.

Arthur Holly Compton Award: One award of US$1,000 is given at the annual meeting to a person who has made an outstanding contribution to nuclear science and/or engineering education.

Samuel Glasstone Award: One award of US$500 is given to the student branch(es) of the ANS which accomplished the most notable achievements in public service and the advancement of nuclear engineering.

Mark Mills Award: One award of US$500 is given at the annual winter meeting to a graduate student who submits the best original technical paper which contributes to the advancement of science and/or engineering relating to the atomic nucleus.

Radiation Industry Award: One award of US$1,000 is conferred at the winter meeting on a scientist or engineer who has made a significant contribution to the application of radiation technology to industry.

Note: The Society also offers *Distinguished Service Awards, Fellow Awards* and the *Young Engineers Award* to selected members, and together with the Atomic Industrial Forum, confers the *Henry DeWolf Nuclear Statesman Award.*

Further information from:
American Nuclear Society
555 North Kensington Avenue
La Grange Park, Illinois 60525
U.S.A.

[144]

AMERICAN NUMISMATIC SOCIETY

ANS Graduate Fellowship

Purpose: To further the study of numismatics as an ancillary discipline.

Subject: A dissertation topic in which the use of numismatics plays a significant part.

No. offered: One Fellowship annually.

Value: US$3,500

Tenable at a university in the United States or Canada.

Eligibility: Open to persons enrolled at universities in the United States or Canada who have completed the general examinations (or the equivalent) for the doctoral degree, and have attended one of the Society's Summer Seminars [see next entry].

Closing date: 1st March.

Further information from:
Chief Curator
American Numismatic Society
Broadway at 155th Street
New York, New York 10032
U.S.A.

[145]

AMERICAN NUMISMATIC SOCIETY

Grants for ANS Summer Seminar in Numismatics

Purpose: To provide a selected number of graduate students with a deeper understanding of the contribution numismatics makes to other fields of study.

No. offered: Approximately ten Awards annually.

Value: US$900.

Tenable at the American Numismatic Society for nine weeks during the summer.

Eligibility: Open to persons who have had at least one year's graduate study at a university in the United States or Canada, and are students of classical studies, history, Near Eastern studies or other humanistic fields.

Closing date: 1st March.

Further information from:
Chief Curator
American Numismatic Society
Broadway at 155th Street
New York, New York 10032
U.S.A.

[146]

AMERICAN NURSES' FOUNDATION, INC.

Research Award

One Award of less than US$2,500 is made annually in support of research on clinical aspects of patient care. Awards are held for one year; not renewable. Candidates should be registered nurses who are U.S. residents.

Further information from:
American Nurses' Foundation
2420 Pershing Road
Kansas City, Missouri 64108
U.S.A.

[147]

AMERICAN OCCUPATIONAL THERAPY FOUNDATION, INC.

AOTF Scholarships

Ten Scholarships in the amount of US$750 each are available annually to full-time undergraduate and graduate students in the field of occupational therapy. Grants are awarded on the basis of financial need and scholastic ability. Candidates should be enrolled or accepted for enrollment in an occupational curriculum.

Not confirmed for 1983.

Further information from:
American Occupational Therapy
Foundation, Inc.
6000 Executive Boulevard
Rockville, Maryland 20852
U.S.A.

[148]

AMERICAN OIL CHEMISTS' SOCIETY

AOCS Award in Lipid Chemistry

Purpose: Lipid chemistry.

No. offered: One Award annually.

Value: US$2,500 and a plaque.

Eligibility: Open to individuals who are actively associated with research in lipid chemistry and who have made fundamental discoveries that affect a large segment of the field.

Note: Recipients must deliver an address at the Society's national meeting, at which time the Award presentation will be made.
Nominations are solicited each summer.

Closing date: 1st November.

Further information from:
American Oil Chemists' Society
508 South Sixth Street
Champaign, Illinois 61820
U.S.A.

[149]

AMERICAN ORIENTAL SOCIETY

Fellowship in the Study of the History of Chinese Painting

Purpose: To assist a student in further pursuit of his interest in Chinese painting.

No. offered: One Fellowship annually.

Value: US$5,000.

Tenable for one year, wherever the subject may be suitably studied; usually the student should be associated with a musuem where Chinese paintings are available to him.

Eligibility: Open to US citizens who are students, have completed three years of Chinese language study or the equivalent, and have met all requirements for the Ph.D. in Chinese painting studies, except for travel, the written dissertation and its defense; need should be demonstrated.

Closing date: 1st February.

Further information from:
Secretary American Oriental Society
329 Sterling Memorial Library
Yale Station
New Haven, Connecticut 06520
U.S.A.

[150]

AMERICAN ORIENTAL SOCIETY

Louise Wallace Hackney Scholarship

Subject: Chinese art, with special relation to painting, and the translation into English of works on the subject.

Value: US$5,000.

Tenable in an American museum where paintings and adequate language guidance are available.

Eligibility: Open to United States citizens who are graduate students and have successfully completed at least three years of Chinese language study at a recognized university and have some knowledge or training in art. Applicants should have the sponsorship of recognized scholars in the fields of Chinese language and culture. Duplicate *curriculum vitae*, academic records, proposed plans of study and three passport-sized photographs should be submitted to the Secretary by 1st February.

Further information from:
Secretary American Oriental Society
329 Sterling Memorial Library
Yale Station
New Haven, Connecticut 06520
U.S.A.

[151]

AMERICAN OSTEOPATHIC ASSOCIATION

Journalism Awards

Purpose: To recognize journalists who report and interpret osteopathic medicine to the scientific community and to the general public.

Subject: Any aspect of osteopathic medicine, including scientific advances, college and hospital programs, or activities of individual osteopathic physicians.

No. offered: Three Awards annually.

Value: One Award of US$1,000 and two Awards of US$500 each; paid in a lump sum.

Eligibility: Open to writers for newspapers, wire services, magazines or other regularly published periodicals of general circulation, or by members of the broadcast media. Entries must be submitted by the writer/broadcaster or editor/director, and not by a third party. Entries should have been published or broadcast during the previous year.

Members of the osteopathic profession, their spouses and employees, as well as the Association's employees, are ineligible.

Note: Award winners may apply with new entries for future competitions.

Articles should be mounted on white paper; original articles are required. Broadcasts should be submitted in tape or videocassette form, plus script if available.

Closing date: 1st March.

Further information from:
Journalism Awards Competition
American Osteopathic Association
212 East Ohio Street
Chicago, Illinois 60611
U.S.A.

[152]

AMERICAN OTOLOGICAL SOCIETY

Research Grants

Subjects: All aspects of otosclerosis.

No. offered: varies annually.

Value: Up to US$15,000.

Tenable at any suitable institution or laboratory for one year, renewable.

Eligibility: Open to any individual who can supply evidence of capability of research in the field of otosclerosis and related problems.

Closing date: 31st January.

Further information from:
Robert J. Ruben, M.D.,
Secretary-Treasurer
Research Fund of the American
Otological Society
Department of Otolaryngology
Albert Einstein College of Medicine
1300 Morris Park Avenue
Bronx, New York 10461
U.S.A

[153]

AMERICAN PHILOSOPHICAL SOCIETY

Research Grants

Purpose: To assist with the costs of basic research in all fields of learning.

Subjects: All fields (not restricted to philosophy): postdoctoral research.

No. offered: Approximately 300 Grants annually.

Value: Averages US$1,250 for full professors. Grants seldom exceed US$2,500.

Tenable anywhere in the world for varying periods of time.

Eligibility: Open to persons with a doctoral degree or equivalent experience who are able to demonstrate through publications their competence for research.

A few Grants are also made to non-United States citizens or residents for studies related to U.S. topics.

Note: Grants are for research in the strictest sense, at the postdoctoral level only.

Applications must be made on the appropriate forms, available from the address below.

Closing dates: Eight weeks before the first Friday in February, April, June, October, or December.

Further information from:
Research Committee American
Philosophical Society
104 South Fifth Street
Philadelphia, Pennsylvania 19106
U.S.A.

[154]

AMERICAN PHYSICAL SOCIETY (*New York City*)

Prizes

Nominations for the following Prizes are made by members of the Society. All awards are conferred at the Society's general meeting.

Biological Physics Prize of US$3,000, a certificate, and travel expenses to the Society's general meeting is awarded annually to recognize and encourage outstanding achievement in biological physics research. Nominations are open to scientists of all nationalities regardless of the geographical site at which the work was done. The Prize may be awarded to more than one investigator on a shared basis.

Tom W. Bonner Prize in Nuclear Physics of US$1,000 and a certificate is awarded to recognize outstanding experimental research, including development of a method, technique, or device that significantly contributes in a general way to nuclear physics research. Nominees should be involved primarily with experimental physics; however, a particularly outstanding piece of theoretical work will take precedence over experimental research. There are no time limitations on the work involved.

Herbert P. Broida Prize in Atomic and Molecular Spectroscopy or Chemical Physics of US$5,000, a certificate and travel expenses to the Society's general meeting is given in odd-numbered years to recognize outstanding experimental advancements in the fields of atomic and molecular spectroscopy or chemical physics. Nominees should have made an important contribution in one of the above-mentioned fields, especially to that done in the five year period preceding the award. Preference will be given to an individual whose contributions have displayed a high degree of breadth, originality and creativity. This Prize is sponsored by the *Office of Naval Research*.

Oliver E. Buckley Solid-State Physics Prize of US$5,000 and a certificate is awarded to recognize outstanding theoretical or experimental contributions to solid-state physics. This Prize is sponsored by *Bell Laboratories*.

Davisson-Germer Prize of US$2,500 and a certificate is given annually for outstanding work in surface physics, in odd-numbered years and for atomic physics in even-numbered years. The work should have been conducted in the U.S. This Prize is sponsored by *Bell Laboratories*.

Dannie Heineman Prize for Mathematical Physics of US$5,000 and a certificate is awarded annually for outstanding publication in the field of mathematical physics. There are no restrictions as to a candidate's citizenship or place of residence. This Prize is jointly administered by the *American Institute of Physics* and the *American Physical Society*.

High-Polymer Physics Prize of US$3,000 and a certificate is awarded annually to recognize outstanding accomplishment and excellence of contributions in high-polymer physics research. Nominees may be scientists of any nationality, regardless of the geographical site at which the work was carried out. This Prize is sponsored by the *Ford Motor Company*.

International Prize for New Materials of US$5,000, a certificate and travel expenses to the Society's general meeting is given to recognize outstanding achievement in the science and application of new materials, including theoretical and experimental work contributing significantly to the understanding of such materials. Nominees may be scientists of any nationality regardless of the geographical site at which the work was carried out. This Prize is sponsored by the *International Business Machines Corporation*.

Frank Isakson Prize for Optical Effects in Solids of US$3,000, a certificate and travel expenses to the Society's general meeting is given in even-numbered years to recognize outstanding contributions to the field of optical effects in solids. Nominees may be scientists of any nationality regardless of the geographical site at which the work was carried out.

Irving Langmuir Prize in Chemical Physics of US$5,000 and a certificate is awarded annually to recognize outstanding interdisciplinary research in chemistry and physics. Contributions to these fields should have been made during the ten years preceding the award. Nominees must be residents of the U.S. at the time of selection, and Prize funds are to be used within the U.S. or its possessions. This Prize is administered in alternating years by the *American Physical Society* and the *American Chemical Society*. It is sponsored by the *General Electric Foundation*.

James Clerk Maxwell Prize or Plasma Physics of US$3,500 and a certificate is given annually to recognize outstanding contributions to the field of plasma physics. Nominees should be US residents who have made important contributions to the advancement and diffusion of the knowledge of properties of highly ionized gases of natural or laboratory origin. Work must have been carried out primarily in

U.S. This Prize is sponsored by *Maxwell Laboratories, Inc.*

Earle K. Plyer Prize of US$1,000 and a certificate is given annually to recognize notable contributions to molecular spectroscopy, either mental or theoretical. The nominations are open to scientists in North America. This Prize is sponsored by the *George E. Crouch Foundation.*

Prize in Fluid Dynamics of US$3,000, a certificate and travel expenses to the Society's general meeting is given for major contributions to fundamental fluid dynamics during a career of outstanding work in the United States. This Prize is sponsored by the *Office of Naval Research.*

Further information from:
Dr. W.W. Havens, Jr.
The American Physical Society
335 East 45th Street
New York, New York 10017.
U.S.A.

[155]

AMERICAN PHYSICAL THERAPY

McMillan Scholarship Program

Purpose: To honor and provide financial assistance to outstanding students enrolled in their final year of study in an approved educational program accredited by an agency recognized by either the U.S. Commissioner of Education or the Council on Postsecondary Accreditation.

Subject: Physical therapy.

No. offered: Appoximately three Scholarships annually.

Value: For each award, US$500 to the student and US$500 to the program in which the student is enrolled.

Eligibility: Candidates must be enrolled in the final years of study in an approved professional program of physical therapy, as described above. Each program may nominate one student per year.

Note: Students should apply for further information from the director of the program in which they are enrolled.

Closing date: 1st February.

Further information from:
Department of Educational Affairs
American Physical Terapy Association
1156 15th Street, N.W.
Washington, D.C. 20005
U.S.A.

[156]

AMERICAN PLANNING ASSOCIATION

APA Planning Fellowships

Purpose: To provide financial assistance to racial groups that are under-represented in the planning profession.

No. offered: Four Fellowships annually.

Value: US$4,000 to be paid to the university and divided in equal sums per term or semester. Monies will be disbursed by the university to the student, contingent on continued good standing as a full-time student.

Tenable for one year only in a planning program leading to a master's degree recognized by the National Education Development Committee of the American Planning Association.

Eligibility: Candidates must be full-time students enrolled in an APA recognized master's degree program, nominated by the school; be a citizen of the U.S. or Canada; and be black, Mexican-American, American Indian, or Puerto Rican. Students must document a need for financial assistance to enable them to pursue a graduate education.

Closing date: 31st May.

Note: The Society also administers the *Charles Abrams Memorial Scholarship* in cooperation with planning departments of certain universities, and the APA Student Awards which have no monetary value.

Further information from:
APA Planning Fellowship Program
American Planning Association
1776 Massachusetts Avenue, N.W.
Washington, D.C. 20036
U.S.A.

[157]

AMERICAN PODIATRY ASSOCIATION

Fellowships

Subjects: Advanced work in a field related to podiatry, such as public health; education; the basic sciences.

No. offered: Three Fellowships annually.

Value: US$7,500 each (US$3,750 per semester).

Eligibility: Fellowships are limited to graduates of colleges of podiatric medicine, or to those individuals affiliated with a college of podiatric medicine at the time of application.

Closing date: 30th April.

Further information from:
Committee on Fellowships
American Podiatry Association
20 Chevy Chase Circle, N.W.
Washington, D.C. 20015
U.S.A.

[158]

AMERICAN POLITICAL SCIENCE ASSOCIATION

Congressional Fellowships

Purpose: To equip outstanding young political scientists and journalists with a better understanding of the United States legislative process.

No. offered: Varies annually.

Value: US$14,000 per annum, plus travel allowance.

Tenable in the Senate and House offices, Washington, D.C., for one year.

Eligibility: Open to (a) political scientists who have completed the doctorate within the last fifteen years, or are nearing completion (b) journalists with a bachelor's degree and between two and ten year's professional experience in newspaper, magazine, radio or television work.

Note: The program consists of a month-long orientation period followed by nine months working as a full-time aide to members of the House or Senate, or on the staff of a congressional committee.

Closing date: 1st December.

Further information from:
American Political Science Association
1527 New Hampshire Avenue, N.W.
Washington, D.C. 20036
U.S.A.

[159]

AMERICAN POLITICAL SCIENCE ASSOCIATION

Graduate Fellowships for Black Students

Purpose: To identify and aid prospective black graduate students.

Subject: Political Science.

No. offered: Three Fellowships carrying stipends, plus a number of other Fellowships having no monetary value, annually.

Value: Approximately US$4,700 each.

Tenable at any accredited university in the United States.

Eligibility: Open to Black Americans who qualify for acceptance at accredited institutions of higher learning. Priority will be given to those candidates about to enter graduate school.

Note: Where all other criteria for meeting Fellowship requirements are equal, the candidate with the greatest financial need will be chosen.
  Graduate schools are encouraged to support Fellows during their remaining years of study.
  Fellows who are designated without stipends are recommended to graduate departments of political science as deserving of consideration for fellowships at the departmental level.

Closing date: 31st December.

Further information from:
American Political Science Association
1527 New Hampshire Avenue, N.W.
Washington, D.C. 20036
U.S.A.

[160]

AMERICAN POLITICAL SCIENCE ASSOCIATION

Travel Grant Program for Foreign Graduate Students

The Association provides Travel Grants on an annual basis to advanced, foreign graduate students who are enrolled, full-time, in American universities. These awards enable the recipients to attend the Association's Annual Meeting. Eligible candidates may not receive any United States funding toward academic or travel expenses, or full financial assistance from any organization, corporation, foundation or foreign government. Graduate students having refugee, immigrant or tourist visa status are ineligible. Application forms are available from the address below.

Note: These Travel Grants are made possible through funds provided by the Asia Foundation and the International Communications Agency via the Institute of International Education.

Closing date: 15th July.

Further information from:
American Political Science Association
1527 New Hampshire Avenue, N.W.
Washington, D.C. 20036
U.S.A.

[161]

AMERICAN POLITICAL SCIENCE ASSOCIATION
WOODROW WILSON FOUNDATION

Woodrow Wilson Award

An annual cash Award of US$1,000 and a medal are given to perpetuate the spirit of Woodrow Wilson's writing and to encourage significant research and reflection in the fields of politics, government and international relations. If more than one book is chosen in any year, the winners share the cash Award. Both authors and publishers may submit works for consideration.

Further information from:
American Political Science Association
Woodrow Wilson Foundation
1527 New Hampshire Avenue, N.W.
Washington, D.C. 20036
U.S.A.

[162]

AMERICAN PRODUCTION AND INVENTORY CONTROL SOCIETY, INC.

Graduate Student Awards Program

Purpose: To increase student awareness of production management problems and to encourage them to enter the field.

Subjects: Any discipline related to operations management, production management, industrial management, logistics management, operations research/management science, or business administration.

No. offered: Six Awards (three national and three regional) annually.

Value: National Awards—1st Prize of US$500, 2nd Prize of US$300, 3rd Prize of US$200; Regional Awards—1st Prize of US$150, 2nd Prize of US$100, 3rd Prize of US$50.

Eligibility: Open to full-time graduate students taking six or more hours per semester or quarter.

Closing date: Papers should be submitted to local APICS Chapters no later than 1st June.

Further information from:
Vice-President of Education and Research
American Production and Inventory Control Society, Inc.
Suite 504, Watergate Building
2600 Virginia Avenue, N.W.
Washington, D.C. 20037
U.S.A.

[163]

AMERICAN PRODUCTION AND INVENTORY CONTROL SOCIETY, INC.

Research Grants

Purpose: To advance the professionalism of production and inventory control practitioners through a continuing program of support to education and research in this field.

Subjects: Inventory planning; forecasting; material requirements planning; shop floor controls; capacity planning and control.

Value is determined by the Board of Directors.

Eligibility: All funds must be applied within the United States. All requests for Grants must be approved by the National APICS Education and Research Committee with funding approval required from the Educational and Research Foundation.

Further information from:
Vice-President of Education and Research
American Production and Inventory Control Society, Inc.
Suite 504, Watergate Building
2600 Virginia Avenue, N.W.
Washington, D.C. 20037
U.S.A.

[164]

AMERICAN PSYCHIATRIC ASSOCIATION

The following, with the exception of the *Blanche F. Ittleson Award* and *Foundation's Fund Prize*, are open to nationals of all countries.

Administrative Psychiatry Award: One Award of US$200-US$300 is given to a distinguished member of the APA who has achieved national prominence in the practice and teaching of psychiatric administration.

Marie H. Eldredge Award: One Award of US$1,000 to be given to APA members or residents of Hawaii, Pennsylvania or New Jersey, for research work in the cause and treatment of the various neuroses and mental retardation in all age groups. Applicants must work in one of the above mentioned states and be under 40 years of age.

Manfred S. Gutmacher Award: One Award of US$500 is given annually for the most significant paper in the field of forensic psychiatry, with first priority to an author under 35 years of age and second priority to an author under 55 years of age who submits his paper to the Award Board prior to 1st April.

Samuel G. Hibbs Award: One Award of US$1,500 is presented for the best unpublished paper on a clinical psychiatric subject. A lecture by the winner will be presented at the APA Annual Meeting. Candidates must be members of the APA.

Blanche F. Ittleson Research Award: One Award of US$2,000 to a U.S. or Canadian psychiatrist or group of investigators for the published results of research pertaining to the mental health of children. Six copies of the work, published within the last three years, should be submitted no later than 1st November.

Oskar Pfister Award: One Award of US$500 is given for outstanding contributions to the fields of psychiatry and religion.

Agnes Purcell McGavin Award: US$500 is given for an outstanding contribution to the prevention of emotional disorders in children.

Robert T. Morse Writers Award: One Award of US$500 is given to a lay writer as a gesture of appreciation for his or her outstanding contributions to furthering the public understanding of psychiatry.

Isaac Ray Award: One Award of US$1,500 is given biennially to a psychiatrist or jurist who has made outstanding contributions to furthering understanding between psychiatry and the law.

Benjamin Rush Lectureship on the History of Psychiatry: US$500, plus expenses, is given to a person who has achieved renown in the history of psychiatry field.

Seymour Vestermark Memorial Lectureship: A lecture on teaching psychiatry will be given annually in the Washington, D.C. area, and will concentrate on the teaching of psychiatry in its broadest aspects with special emphasis upon teaching teachers and improved techniques of teaching. The Lectureship carries a stipend of US$1,000.

Adolf Meyer Lectureship: US$1,500 is given to an outstanding investigator for a lecture at the APA annual meeting to advance psychiatric research.

Foundation's Fund Prize for Research in Psychiatry: One Award of US$1,500 is given for distinguished research accomplishment in psychiatry and mental hygiene. Applicants must be United States or Canadian citizens. Six copies of investigative results must be submitted by 1st November for the following year's Awards.

Further information from:
American Psychiatric Association
1700 18th Street, N.W.
Washington, D.C. 20009
U.S.A.

[165]

AMERICAN PSYCHOLOGICAL ASSOCIATION

National Media Awards

The purpose of the *National Media Awards* is to recognize and encourage outstanding, accurate reporting which increases the public's knowledge and understanding of psychology. Winners are chosen in five categories: newspaper; magazine writing; radio; television and film; books and monographs. All winners will receive US$1,000, a citation and a trip to the Annual Convention of the American Psychological Association.

Articles or programs must be about psychology or draw on psychological studies, and must have been produced during the year prior to the closing date. Entrants in the television/film and radio categories must send review copies by 5th May. Only 3/4 inch videotape cassettes and 16mm film will be accepted. Newspaper and books/monographs must be submitted in triplicate.

Further information from:
Jacci Conley
American Psychological Association
1200 Seventeenth Street, N.W.
Washington, D.C. 20036
U.S.A.

[166]

AMERICAN RESEARCH INSTITUTE IN TURKEY, INC.

Fellowships

Purpose: To encourage research on Turkey in ancient, medieval and modern times, in all fields of the humanities and social sciences.

Subjects: Those suitable for study and research in Turkey.

No. offered: 6-10 Fellowships annually.

Value: Variable, depending on the length of study period.

Tenable in Turkey for one to twelve months; renewable only in exceptional cases.

Eligibility: Open to nationals of all countries. Candidates must be graduates who have passed their Ph.D. orals or who already hold a Ph.D. degree, and are members of educational or research institutions in the United States or Canada.

Closing date: 15th November.

Further information from:
American Research Institute in Turkey, Inc.
University Museum
33rd and Spruce Streets
Philadelphia, Pennsylvania 19104
U.S.A.

[167]

AMERICAN RISK AND INSURANCE ASSOCIATION, INC.

Elizur Wright Award and Clarence A. Kulp Memorial Award: The Wright and Kulp Awards, each in the amount of US$1,000, are presented annually to the authors of the two most outstanding contributions to the literature of risk and insurance. All works considered should have a publication date two years prior to the year of the Award. Publishers or authors may submit works to the Wright-Kulp Awards Committee.

Journal of Risk and Insurance Awards: $1,000 is distributed annually by the Association to the authors of the feature articles and other contributed items which are judged to be most outstanding in the quarterly issues of each yearly volume of the Journal.

Further information from:
Dr. Richard E. Johnson, Executive Director
American Risk and Insurance Association, Inc.
c/o Department of Risk Management and Insurance
Brooks Hall, University of Georgia
Athens, Georgia 30602
U.S.A.

[168]

AMERICAN-SCANDINAVIAN FOUNDATION

Fellowships and Grants-in-Aid

Purpose: To increase understanding between the United States and Scandinavia.

Subjects: Usually unrestricted.

No. offered: Varies each year.

Value: From US$500 to US$6,000.

Tenable in Denmark, Finland, Iceland, Norway, Sweden; for up to 12 months.
Eligibility: Open to United States residents who have completed undergraduate studies. Outstanding proposals from all sources are encouraged and will be carefully considered, including those from beginning graduate students who plan programs emphasizing participation in university lectures and courses in Scandinavia, which are to be an integral part of an advanced U.S. degree.
Candidates are expected to have undertaken appropriate correspondence with institutions and scholars in Scandinavia. Competence in the necessary language is expected.

Note: Awards are also available to Scandinavians wishing to undertake study or research programs in the United States; candidates are recommended by agencies cooperating with ASF.

Closing date: 1st November.

Further information from:
Exchange Division
American-Scandinavian Foundation
127 East 73rd Street
New York, New York 10021
U.S.A.

[169]

AMERICAN-SCANDINAVIAN FOUNDATION

George C. Marshall Fellowships for Study in Denmark

The Fellowships are awarded to U.S. citizens for short-term professional observation or for a year of academic research, usually at the graduate level. Preference is given to younger and unestablished American scholars. Maximum age: forty. Language competency is desirable. Awards are up to US$6,000 for full academic year programs. *Closing date:* 1st November.

Further information from:
Exchange Division
American-Scandinavian Foundation
127 East 73rd Street
New York, New York 10021
U.S.A.

[170]

AMERICAN SCHOOL OF CLASSICAL STUDIES AT ATHENS

Fellowships (Thomas Day Seymour; John Williams White; James Rignall Wheeler; and Heinrich Schliemann)

Subjects: Classical philology and archaeology; post-classical Greek studies.

No. offered: Four Fellowships annually.

Value: US$4,500 per annum and an dependency allowance.

Tenable at the American School of Classical Studies at Athens, for one academic year.

Eligibility: Open to United States or Canadian citizens who have a B.A. degree with a major in classics or classical archaeology.
Non-United States and Canadian citizens may apply if they have received an appropriate degree from one of the 105 United

States and Canadian colleges and universities which support the School.

Applications are judged on the basis of examinations and credentials.

The one post-classical Fellowship is awarded to an appropriately prepared graduate student or postdoctoral candidate without examination.

Further information from:
American School of Classical Studies at Athens
41 East 72nd Street
New York, New York 10021
U.S.A.

[171]

AMERICAN SCHOOL OF CLASSICAL STUDIES AT ATHENS

Jacob Hirsh Fellowship

Subjects: Pre-classical, classical, or post-classical archaeology.

No. offered: One annually.

Value: Up to US$5,000, determined by need and qualifications.

Tenable in Greece for one academic year, not renewable.

Eligibility: Open to a United States or Israeli graduate student writing a dissertation, or to a recent Ph.D. completing a project, such as a dissertation, for publication.

Applications will be awarded on the basis of appropriate credentials, including references.

Closing date: 31st January.

Further information from:
American School of Classical Studies at Athens
41 East 72nd Street
New York, New York 10021
U.S.A.

[172]

AMERICAN SCHOOLS OF ORIENTAL RESEARCH

Fellowships

Subjects: Near-Eastern studies: archaeology, epigraphy, topography, prehistoric anthropology, history, and other types of study best suited to field work.

George A. Barton Fellowship provides a stipend of US$2,000 and a living allowance of US$3,000. The living allowance may be used in cash to provide room and board in Jerusalem, or may be used to purchase room and board at the Albright Institute in Jerusalem, where a reduced rate for Fellows is available.

William Foxwell Albright Fellowship provides US$5,000 to assist with the cost of travel, plus room and board for the academic year. It may be used, under the supervision of the Committee, in any country of the Middle East, for research in fields for which the applicant has the necessary qualifications.

The Schools also offer the *Nelson Glueck* and *Edward Robinson Fellowships*, details of which are available from the address below.

Eligibility: Open to graduate students and to junior faculty members of institutions which belong to the Corporation of the American Schools of Oriental Research.

Closing date: 15th November.

Further information from:
American Schools of Oriental Research
126 Inman Street
Cambridge, Massachusetts 02139
U.S.A.

[173]

AMERICAN SCHOOLS OF ORIENTAL RESEARCH

Research Associates

Subjects: Near-Eastern studies: archaeology, epigraphy, topography, prehistoric anthropology, history, etc. Each year a limited number of appointments for resident research will be made without stipend. These are open to younger scholars who have a research project needing the facilities and help of the staff of the Albright Institute. Applicants should send a description of their proposed research, the assistance needed, and the length of residence at the Institute which is requested, to the address below.

Professors and students of member institutions may reside at the Institute in Jerusalem, where there is space available, in order to carry out their own research. Applications should be made in writing to the *Director of the Albright Institute, P.O. Box 19096, Jerusalem, Israel 97200.*

All those who spend time in residence at the Institute, excepting appointees, may participate in the program of the Institute (seminars, field trips, etc.) at the discretion of the Director.

Further information from:
American Schools of Oriental Research
126 Inman Street
Cambridge, Massachusetts 02139
U.S.A.

[174]

AMERICAN SCHOOLS OF ORIENTAL RESEARCH
NATIONAL ENDOWMENT FOR THE HUMANITIES

Post-doctoral Fellowships

Purpose: To promote research at overseas centers for advanced study.

Subjects: Archaeology and ancient Near Eastern studies.

No. offered: Four Fellowships.

Value: Up to US$22,000 each, paid in quarterly instalments.

Tenable Two Fellowships at the Albright Institute of Archaeological Research, Jerusalem, Israel, and two Fellowships at the American Center of Oriental Studies, Amman, Jordan. All awards are for up to one year and are not renewable.

Eligibility: Open to U.S. citizens who have received their Ph.D. before 15th January of the year of the award.

Closing date: 1st January.

Further information from:
American Schools of Oriental Research
126 Inman Street
Cambridge, Massachusetts 02139
U.S.A.

[175]

AMERICAN SOCIETY OF AGRICULTURAL ENGINEERS

Dairy and Food Industries Supply Association, Inc.—ASAE Food Engineering Award: US$2,000, a gold medal and a certificate is presented in odd-numbered years, for original contributors in research, development or design or in the management of food processing equipment or techniques of significant economic value to the food industry and the consumer. Candidates must be nominated.

Kishida International Award: An engraved diploma and US$1,000 is presented annually to recognize outstanding contributions to engineering-mechanization-technological related programs of education, research, development, consultation, or technology transfer that have resulted in significant improvement of food production, living conditions and/or education for people living outside the United States. Candidates must be Society members in good standing, and be nominated. Eligibility is not restricted to U.S. citizens and residents. *Closing date:* 1st November for nominations.

Note: Information regarding nomination procedures for both Awards may be obtained by writing to the address below.

The Society also makes a number of other awards which have no monetary value.

Further information from:
Executive Vice-President
American Society of Agricultural
 Engineers
P.O. Box 410
St. Joseph, Michigan 49085
U.S.A.

[176]

AMERICAN SOCIETY OF ANESTHESIOLOGISTS

Medical Student Preceptorships

A number of awards of US$800 are offered to medical students between their second and third year of training. These Preceptorships are tenable for an eight-week period, for work with a practicing clinical anesthesiologist.

Note: The Society also administers a one-year postdoctoral research fellowship in anesthesiology, sponsored by the *Burroughs Wellcome Fund.*

Further information from:
American Society of Anesthesiologists
515 Busse Highway Park Ridge
Chicago, Illinois
U.S.A.

[177]

AMERICAN SOCIETY OF CHURCH HISTORY

Prizes

Brewer Prize: One Award of US$2,000 is given annually for a book-length manuscript on church history, in order to assist the author in the publication of the manuscript in a manner acceptable to the Society. In the case of a tie, preference will be given to entries having topics relating to the history of Congregationalism. *Closing date:* 15th December.

Philip Schaff Prize: One Award of US$1,000 to the author of the best book published in English, originating in the North American scholarly community, and presenting original research or interpretation in the history of Christianity or any period thereof. Books nominated should be published during the year for which the award is given. Nominations should be received no later than 1st March of the following year.

Further information from:
American Society of Church History
305 East Country Club Lane
Wallingford, Pennsylvania 19086
U.S.A.

[178]

AMERICAN SOCIETY OF CIVIL ENGINEERS

O.H. Ammann Research Fellowship in Structural Engineering

Purpose: To create new knowledge in the field of structural design and construction.

No. offered: One Fellowship every two years.

Value: US$4,000.

Tenable at approved institutions in any country.

Eligibility: Open to members of the Society in any grade and to applicants for membership. Non-United States citizens may apply if they are eligible under the Society's rules.
Selection for the Fellowship is made on the basis of transcripts of scholastic records; evidence indicating ability to conceive and explore original ideas in the field of structural engineering; description of proposed research and its objectives, including a statement from the institution at which the research is to be done that the applicant and proposed research are acceptable to the institution.

Note: During tenure, the Fellow may not work on research projects other than that for which the award has been granted, but Fellows may accept other awards if their conditions are the same as those for this Fellowship.
Each application must include a statement in general terms of the purpose for which the funds are expected to be used. The Fellow must submit a full report on his completed research.

Closing date: 1st December in odd-numbered years.

Further information from:
American Society of Civil Engineers
United Engineering Center
345 East 47th Street
New York, New York 10017
U.S.A.

[179]

AMERICAN SOCIETY OF CIVIL ENGINEERS

Freeman Fellowship

Purpose: For research in the science or art of hydraulic construction.

Subjects: Grants are made towards expenses for visits, experiments, observations and compilations to discover new and accurate data that will be useful in engineering; assistance in the translation or publication in English of papers or books in foreign languages pertaining to hydraulics.

Value: US$3,000.

Eligibility: Open to members of the American Society of Civil Engineers and the American Society of Mechanical Engineers. Preference is given to young engineers.

Note: The Fellowship is offered in odd-numbered years. (In even-numbered years a similar grant is offered by the American Society of Mechanical Engineers [q.v.].
Each application must include a statement, in general terms, of the purpose for which funds are expected to be used.

Closing date: 1st December of the year preceding that in which the award is available.

Further information from:
American Society of Civil Engineers
United Engineering Center
345 East 47th Street
New York, New York 10017
U.S.A.

[180]

AMERICAN SOCIETY OF CIVIL ENGINEERS

J. Waldo Smith Hydraulic Fellowship

Purpose: Research in experimental hydraulics to advance knowledge of the laws of hydraulic flow.

Value: US$2,000 per annum, plus an additional amount not in excess of US$1,000 as may be required for physical equipment connected with the research.

Tenable at approved institutions in any country for one academic year.

Eligibility: The Fellow will be selected on the basis of the quality of his application. He should be a graduate student at the time the award is made and preferably an associate member of the Society.

Note: The Fellowship is offered every third year. Applications for the Fellowship come through the various institutions applying.

Closing date: 1st December.

Further information from:
American Society of Civil Engineers
United Engineering Center
345 East 47th Street
New York, New York 10017
U.S.A.

[181]

AMERICAN SOCIETY OF CIVIL ENGINEERS

ASCE Student Chapter Scholarships

Purpose: To assist students to continue their formal education at the undergraduate or graduate level.

Subject: Civil engineering.

No. offered: Twelve Scholarships annually.

Value: US$500.

Tenable at approved institutions in the United States.

Eligibility: Open to members of ASCE student chapters in ECPD accredited programs.

Closing date: 1st December.

Further information from:
American Society of Civil Engineers
United Engineering Center
345 East 47th Street
New York, New York 10017
U.S.A.

[182]

AMERICAN SOCIETY OF CLINICAL PATHOLOGISTS

Sheard-Sanford Awards: Awards are made annually to medical students who have conducted original, undergraduate research in clinical pathology. Value: Two all-expense paid trips to present papers at the ASCP National Meeting held in the spring; certificate for meritorious original student research in pathology; and the Bausch and Lomb medal. Applications are submitted to the Society in the spring and summer.

Further information from:
Sheard-Sanford Award
American Society of Clinical Pathologists
2100 West Harrison Street
Chicago, Illinois 60612
U.S.A.

[183]

AMERICAN SOCIETY OF COMPOSERS, AUTHORS AND PUBLISHERS

ASCAP-Deems Taylor Awards

Purpose: To encourage excellence in American writing about music and/or its creators.

Subjects: (i) Awards for the best books; and (ii) Awards for the best newspaper or magazine articles.
Subject matter may be biographical or critical, reportorial or historical.

No. offered: Varies annually.

Value: US$500 each for (i) books, and US$250 each for (ii) newspaper and magazine articles.

Eligibility: Open to any works published in the U.S. in English during the previous calendar year.

Note: Works may be submitted by writers, publishers or editors. Four copies of each entry are required.
Entries may be in any form of non-fictional prose. Works of fiction and instructional textbooks are not eligible.

Closing date: 1st March.

Further information from:
ASCAP-Deems Taylor Awards
American Society of Composers, Authors and Publishers
One Lincoln Plaza
New York, New York 10023
U.S.A.

[184]

AMERICAN SOCIETY FOR EIGHTEENTH-CENTURY STUDIES

Prizes

James L. Clifford Prize of US$300 is awarded annually for the best submitted article appearing in a journal, festschrift, or other serial publication in a given academic year. Articles should be outstanding studies of some aspect of eighteenth-century culture, interesting to any eighteenth-century specialist, regardless of the discipline, and no longer than 7500 words. Articles may be nominated by any Society member, or by its author. Nominations must be accompanied by an offprint or copy of the article. At the time of the award presentation, the recipient should be a member of the Society in good standing.

Closing date: 15th February.

Louis Gottschalk Prize of US$500 is awarded annually for an outstanding historical or critical study on a subject of eighteenth-century interest. Books, which may be commentaries, critical studies, biographies or critical editions, can be written in any modern language. Books which are primarily translations are not eligible. All works should be published during the year for which the Prize is made, and be submitted to the Society by the publisher. Authors should be North American scholars, and be either U.S. or Canadian citizens or permanent residents. At the time of the award presentation, the recipient should be a member of the Society in good standing.

Closing date: 15th March of the year following that for which the Prize will be given.

Further information from:
Professor R.C. Rosbottom, Executive Secretary
American Society for Eighteenth-Century Studies
421 Denney Hall
Ohio State University
Columbus, Ohio 43210
U.S.A.

[185]

AMERICAN SOCIETY FOR ENGINEERING EDUCATION

Aerospace Division/AIAA Educational Achievement Award is given to a distinguished contributor to aerospace engineering education to recognize a recent outstanding educational achievement and to encourage original, innovative improvements in aerospace engineering. The Award of US$1,000, a certificate, and a suitably engraved medal is not renewable.

Vincent Bendix Minorities in Engineering Award of US$1,000 a US$500 reimbursement grant for ASEE Annual Conference travel expenses, and a certificate is given to honor an engineering educator for exceptional achievement in increasing participation and retention of minority and/or women students in engineering curricula.

Biomedical Engineering Division Outstanding Biomedical Engineering Educator Award is given for significant contributions to the biomedical engineering and education professions. The Award consists of US$300 and a plaque.

Chester F. Carlson Award of US$1,000 and a plaque is presented by the Xerox Corporation, and given annually to an individual innovator who has made a significant contribution to engineering education. The recipient will have demonstrated an ability to recognize the influence of a changing sociological and technological environment on academic customs and will have responded by applying creative talents in the design and implementation of new instructional technique, methodology or concept. Innovators in engineering education without geographical or institutional constraint are eligible.

Chemical Engineering Division Lectureship Award of US$1,000, a US$500 honorarium for completion of the lecture series, reimbursement of travel expenses, and an engraved certificate is given annually to a distinguished engineering educator to recognize and encourage outstanding achievement in an important field of fundamental chemical engineering theory or practice. The recipient delivers the Annual Lecture of the Chemical Engineering Division at ASEE's Annual Conference and at a few departments of chemical engineering selected by the recipient in consultation with the Award Committee. The Award is sponsored by the 3M Corporation.

Dow Outstanding Young Faculty Award is given to send one young faculty member of each of twelve ASEE sections to the Annual Conference. Recipients receive round-trip fare, living expenses, registration fees and an Award certificate.

Experimental and Laboratory-Oriented Studies Division Award for Excellence in Laboratory-Oriented Studies is given to recognize outstanding contributions of an individual who provided and promotes excellence in experimentation and laboratory instruction. The Award consists of US$1,000 provided by the Tektronix Foundation and a certificate.

Clement J. Freund Award of US$2,000, a certificate, plaque, and reimbursement of travel expenses to attend the Annual Conference, is given to honor an individual in business, government or education who has made a positive impact on cooperative education programs in engineering and engineering technology.

Eugene L. Grant Award of US$250 is awarded annually to the author of the best paper published in the *Engineering Economist* quarterly publication of the Engineering Economy Division of the Society.

Curtis W. McGraw Research Award of US$1,000 and a certificate, awarded annually by the Engineering Research Council with the assistance of the McGraw-Hill Book Company, to recognize outstanding early achievements by young engineering college research workers and to encourage the continuance of such productivity. Nominees must be under 40 years of age on 30th June of the year in which the awardee selection is made.

James H McGraw Award of US$1,000 and a certificate is given in recognition of outstanding service in engineering technology education. Awarded to a teacher, author or administrator who is, or has been, affiliated with an institution which provides engineering technology education. The Award, funded by the McGraw-Hill Book Company, is not renewable.

Fred Merryfield Design Award of US$1,000, a US$500 travel stipend to attend the ASEE Annual Conference and a plaque, and US$500 to the Awardee's institutional department is given to recognize an engineering educator for excellence in the teaching of engineering design as well as acknowledging other significant contributions related to engineering design teaching.

Frank Oppenheimer Award—Engineering Design Graphics Division: An honorarium of US$100 is given by the division to the author of the best paper presented at its midyear conference.

Ralph Coats Roe Award of US$1,000, a plaque, and reimbursement of travel expenses to attend the ASEE Annual Conference is given annually by Kenneth A. Roe of Burns and Roe, Inc. and sponsored by the Mechanical Engineering Division, to recognize a mechanical engineering educator who is an outstanding teacher and who has made a notable professional contribution.

Frederick Emmons Terman Award is given annually to an outstading young electrical engineering educator in recognition of his or her contributions to the profession. The Award of US$2,000, a gold-plated medal and bronze replica, a presentation scroll and reimbursement of travel expenses to attend the ASEE Annual Conference is sponsored by the Hewlett-Packard Company.

Western Electric Fund Awards of US$1,500 and a certificate are given for excellence in the instruction of engineering students. Two Awards in each ASEE section with more than 1,000 members. Closing dates for nominations are 1st February for sections holding a meeting during the spring semester, and 1st May for sections holding a meeting during the fall semester.

George Westinghouse Award of US$1,000, US$500 travel grant to the ASEE Annual Conference, a certificate, and US$500 to the awardee's academic department is presented by the Westinghouse Education Foundation to encourage young educators whose past accomplishments give evidence of excellence and effective innovation in the teaching of engineering. Candidates should be under 45 years of age on 1st July of the year in which the awardee selection is made.

William Elgin Wickenden Award of US$1,000 and a certificate is given to encourage excellence in writing by recognizing the author of the best paper published in *Engineering Education*, the journal of the Society, during the preceding year.

Note: The Society also makes a number of other awards which do not carry a monetary value.

Closing date: 1st February for all award nominations other than the Western Electric Fund Awards.

Further information from:
 Marge White
 Office of Executive Director
 American Society for Engineering
  Education
 Suite 200, Eleven Dupont Circle, N.W.
 Washington, D.C. 20036
 U.S.A.

[186]

AMERICAN SOCIETY OF ENOLOGISTS

Scholarships

At least two Scholarships, in the amount of US$1,500 each, are offered annually to high school seniors, undergraduate and graduate students who are U.S. citizens enrolled or planning to be enrolled in enology or viticulture studies, or in a curriculum which emphasizes a science basic to the wine and grape industry, and can demonstrate a scholastic achievement of no less than a 3.2 grade point average. Candidates are also required to submit transcripts of previous education, information on financial need and a written statement of intention to pursue a career in the wine or grape industry.

Awards are for one academic year, payable in equal installments upon proof of registration for each quarter or semester. Previous recipients are eligible each year in open competition with all other applicants.

Closing date: 15th March.

Further information from:
  Secretary-Treasurer
  American Society of Enologists
  P.O. Box 411
  Davis, California 95616
  U.S.A.

[187]

AMERICAN SOCIETY OF HEATING, REFRIGERATING AND AIR CONDITIONING ENGINEERS, INC.

Grants-In-Aid

Purpose: To stimulate interest in the areas of heating, refrigeration, air conditioning and ventilation through the encouragement of original research in those fields.

Value: Dependent upon the needs and nature of the request. Normally awards do not exceed US$5,000.

Tenable at the grantee's institution, usually for one year or less.

Eligibility: Open to graduate engineering students capable of undertaking appropriate and scholarly research. Grants are not restricted to United States citizens.

Note: Prospective applicants should submit a letter containing the following information: (i) significance of proposed research; (ii) outline of plan of procedure; (iii) approximate budget and extent to which the applicant's institution will support the work; (iv) plans for seeking other funds for this or related work; (v) anticipated plans for publication of research results; (vi) student's transcript; (vii) student's need for assistance; (viii) recommendations from faculty advisor.

Closing date: Before the first of February for consideration at a meeting during March.

Further information from:
  Director of Technology
  American Society of Heating,
    Refrigerating and Air Conditioning
    Engineers, Inc.
  1791 Tullie Circle, N.E.
  Atlanta, Georgia 30329
  U.S.A.

[188]

AMERICAN SOCIETY OF HOSPTIAL PHARMACISTS RESEARCH AND EDUCATION FOUNDATION

Research Publication Awards

Three Awards of US$1,00 each, plus travel expenses to attend the Awards presentation, are offered annually to reward publication efforts of hospital pharmacists. Hospital pharmacy practitioners, teachers and students are eligible. A separate Student Award of US$500, plus travel expenses to attend the Awards presentation, is also offered. *Closing date for applications:* 1st July.

Further information from:
  Assistant to the Executive Vice-President
  American Society of Hospital
    Pharmacists Research and Education
    Foundation
  4630 Montgomery Avenue
  Washington, D.C. 20814
  U.S.A.

[189]

AMERICAN SOCIETY OF HOSPITAL PHARMACISTS RESEARCH AND EDUCATION FOUNDATION

Research Grants Program

Four Awards of US$2,500, paid in a lump sum, are presented annually for one year; not renewable. The Awards are given to encourage research in hospital pharmacy and candidates must submit a proposal, including budget, of no more than 10 pages by 15th August.

Further information from:
  Assistant to the Executive Vice-President
  American Society of Hospital
    Pharmacists Research and Education
    Foundation
  4630 Montgomery Avenue
  Washington, D.C. 20814
  U.S.A.

[190]

AMERICAN SOCIETY OF MECHANICAL ENGINEERS

Blackall Machine Tool and Gage Award is

given annually for the best paper or papers concerned with or relating to the design or application of machine tools, gages or dimensional measuring instruments. The Award of US$100 and a plaque is open to anyone submitting a paper to ASME for presentation and publication before 1st February.

Henry Hess Award of US$250, a certificate and an expense supplement to enable the winner to attend the presentation, is given to an author under 31 years of age for an original technical paper. Closing date for nominations is 1st March.

James N. Landis Award of US$1,000, bronze medal, certificate, and travel expenses to attend the presentation meeting is given annually for outstanding personal performance in nuclear or fossil fuel stations coupled with humanitarian pursuits. Closing date for nominations is 1st February.

Gustus L. Larson Award of US$1,000, an engraved certificate, and expenses to attend the presentation meeting is given annually to an engineering graduate who has demonstrated outstanding achievement in mechanical engineering within ten to twenty years following graduation from a regular engineering course of a recognized college or university. Closing date for nominations is 1st February.

Charles Russ Richards Award of US$1,000, an engraved certificate, and expenses to attend the presentation meeting is given annually to an engineering graduate who has demonstrated outstanding achievement in mechanical engineering twenty years or more following graduation from a regular engineering course of a recognized college or university. Closing date for nominations is 1st February.

Henry R. Worthington Award of US$1,000, a bronze medal and certificate is given for achievement in the field of pumping machinery. Closing date for nominations is 1st February.

ASME Medal of US$1,000, a gold medal and a certificate is awarded annually for "eminently distinguished engineering achievement." Closing date for nominations is 1st March.

Edwin F. Church Medal is given annually to an individual who has rendered eminent service in increasing the value, importance and attractiveness of mechanical engineering education. The Award is in the amount of US$1,000 and a bronze medal. Nomination forms and detailed information on this award may be obtained from the address below. Closing date for nominations is 1st March.

Melville Medal is given annually for the best current original paper submitted. It consists of US$1,000, a bronze medal and a certificate. The author must be a corporate member of the Society. Closing date for nominations is 1st March.

Pi Tau Sigma Gold Medal is awarded to the young engineering graduate who has demonstrated outstanding achievement in mechanical engineering within ten years after graduation from a regular engineering course of a recognized college or university. The recipient receives US$1,000, a gold medal, an engraved certificate and an expense supplement to the presentation meeting. Closing date for nominations is 1st February.

James Henry Potter Gold Medal is awarded in recognition of eminent achievement or distinguished service in the science of thermodynamics in mechanical engineering. The award consists of US$1,000, medal and certificate. Closing date for nominations is 1st February.

Ralph Coats Roe Medal is presented annually to an individual selected by the Society for a significant contribution to a better public understanding and appreciation of the engineer's worth to contemporary society. The recipient receives US$1,000, a bronze medal, a certificate, and travel expenses to attend the presentation meeting. Closing date for nominations is 1st February.

Worcester Reed Warner Medal is given annually for an outstanding contribution to the permanent literature of engineering. The gold medal is accompanied by US$1,000 and a certificate. Closing date for nominations is 1st March.

Arthur L. Williston Medal is given to a student member or associate member for the best paper or thesis by an undergraduate or junior engineer setting forth ideas fostering a spirit of civic service. The bronze medal is accompanied by a US$500 honorarium, a certificate and an expense supplement to enable the winner to attend the presentation. Closing date for nomination is 1st March.

"Old Guard" Prize is given to a student member for the best paper presentation in the Student Member National Contest at the Winter Annual Meeting. The US$500 honorarium is accompanied by a certificate and expense supplement to enable the winner to attend the presentation.

Freeman Scholarship in fluids engineering, details of which vary for each offering, is presented in even numbered years and consists of US$3,000 and travel expenses to the award presentation.

Note: A number of other awards, medals and prizes which have no monetary value are given by the Society for achievements in various relevant fields. Other literature awards are given in specialized areas of mechanical engineering.

Further information from:
Honors Office
American Society of Mechanical Engineers
United Engineering Center
345 East 47th Street
New York, New York 10017
U.S.A.

[191]

AMERICAN SOCIETY FOR MEDICAL TECHNOLOGY EDUCATION AND RESEARCH FUND, INC.

Research Grants Program

Clay Adams Grant: Up to US$1,000 is offered to facilitate research directly related to medical technology. The project may be either developmental or evaluative research in education or applied scientific research in education or applied scientific research, including instrumentation and methodology studies. The work shall culminate in a document suitable for publication, to be submitted for consideration to the American Journal of Medical Technology. The project should be completed within 24 months. Open to all clinical laboratory practitioners or educators who are permanent residents and citizens of the U.S.

Further information from:
Scholarships and Grants Program
ASMT Education and Research Fund, Inc.
330 Meadowfern
Houston, Texas 77067
U.S.A.

[192]

AMERICAN SOCIETY FOR MEDICAL TECHNOLOGY EDUCATION AND RESEARCH FUND, INC.

Continuing Education and Advanced Speciality Study Scholarships

Dade Scholarship in Clinical Chemistry: US$1,000 is offered to assist clinical laboratory practitioners or educators in clinical chemistry in pursuing advanced degree or continuing programs to enhance their expertise in clinical chemistry. Open to all clinical laboratory practitioners or educators who fulfill requirements for admission into the program or course(s) proposed in the application, have been engaged in clinical laboratory performance for at least one year.

Dade Scholarship in Hematology/Coagulation: US$1,000 is offered to assist clinical laboratory practitioners or educators in hematology/coagulation in pursuing advanced degrees or continuing education programs to enhance their expertise in hematology/coagulation. Open to all clinical laboratory practitioners or educators who fulfill requirements for admission into the program or course(s) proposed in the application, have been engaged in clinical laboratory performance in hematology/coagulation for at least one year.

Dade Scholarship in Immunohematology: US$1,000 is offered to assist clinical laboratory practitioners or educators in immunohematology in pursuing a program of study leading to BB(ASCP) certification or an advanced degree in a program of study relevant to immunohematology. Open to all laboratory practitioners or educators who fulfill the requirements for admission to a center which conducts a program leading to BB(ASCP) certification or for admission into a program leading to a master's or doctorate degree in an area of study relevant to immunohematology, have been engaged in clinical laboratory performance for at least one year.

Difco Scholarship in Microbiology: US$1,000 is offered to assist clinical laboratory practitioners or educators in clinical microbiology in pursuing advanced degrees or continuing education program to enhance their expertise in clinical microbiology. Open to all clinical laboratory practitioners or educators who fulfill requirements for admission into the program or course(s) proposed in the application, have been engaged in clinical laboratory performance in microbiology for at least one year and are current members of ASMT.

Ortho Diagnostics Scholarship in Immunohematology: US$1,000 is offered to assist clinical laboratory practitioners or educators in immunohematology in pursuing a program of study leading to BB(ASCP) certification or an advanced degree in a program of study relevant to immunohematology. Open to any clinical laboratory practitioners or educators who fulfill the requirements for admission to a center which conducts a program leading to BB(ASCP) certification or for admission into a program leading to a master's or doctorate degree in an area of study relevant to immunohematology, have been engaged in clinical laboratory performance in immunohematology for at least one year.

Further information from:
  Scholarships and Grants Program
  ASMT Education and Research Fund, Inc.
  330 Meadowfern
  Houston, Texas 77067
  U.S.A.

[193]

AMERICAN SOCIETY FOR MEDICAL TECHNOLOGY EDUCATION AND RESEARCH FUND, INC.

Graduate and Advanced Study Scholarships

Ames Company Advanced Study Scholarships: Two Scholarships of US$500 each, plus travel and hotel expenses for the annual ASMT meeting, are offered to assist individuals within the profession of medical technology in pursuing advanced study (degree or non-degree) in the clinical laboratory or related sciences. Open to all clinical laboratory practitioners or educators who fulfill requirements for admission to the program or course(s) proposed in the application, have been engaged in clinical laboratory performance for at least one year.

General Diagnostics Teaching Scholarships: US$1,500, plus travel and hotel expenses for the annual ASMT meeting, are offered to assist individuals within the profession of medical technology in developing or improving their abilities to teach in medical technology through pursuit of an advanced degree in the field of medical technology education, or one of the clinical laboratory sciences or other areas of study relevant to improving teaching in medical technology. Open to all medical technologists who fulfill requirements for admission or are currently enrolled in a program leading to a master's or doctoral degree in medical technology or medical technology education or one of its clinical laboratory or related sciences.

ASMT Education and Research Fund Graduate Scholarship: US$1,000 is offered to assist individuals within the profession of medical technology in pursuing an advanced degree in medical technology or one of its clinical laboratory specialties. Open to all clinical laboratory practitioners or educators who fulfill requirements for admission or are currently enrolled in a program leading to a master's or doctorate degree in medical technology or one of its clinical laboratory related sciences, have been engaged in clinical laboratory performance for at least one year, and are permanent residents and citizens of the U.S.

Scientific Products Foundation Graduate Scholarship: US$1,000 is offered to assist individuals within the profession of medical technology in pursuing an advanced degree in medical technology or medical technology education or one of its clinical laboratory specialties. Open to all clinical laboratory practitioners or educators who fulfill requirements for admission or are currently enrolled in a program leading to a master's or doctorate degree in medical technology or one of its clinical laboratory or related sciences, are permanent residents and citizens of the U.S., have been engaged in clinical laboratory performance for at least one year.

Further information from:
  Scholarships and Grants Program
  ASMT Education and Research Fund, Inc.
  330 Meadowfern
  Houston, Texas 77067
  U.S.A.

[194]
AMERICAN SOCIETY FOR PHARMACOLOGY AND EXPERIMENTAL THERAPEUTICS, INC.

John J. Abel Award Pharmacology: US$2,500 and a bronze medal is awarded for the purpose of stimulating original and outstanding fundamental research in pharmacology and experimental therapeutics by young investigators. Candidates may not have reached their thirty-sixth birthday as of 30th April of the year of the award, and must not have previously received any other award sponsored by *Eli Lilly and Company*, the sponsors of this award, for the same technical accomplishment. Candidates need not be members of the Society; however nominations must be made by ASPET members. *Closing date:* 15th October.

ASPET Award for Experimental Therapeutics: US$2,500 and a bronze medal is awarded to recognize outstanding research in pharmacology and experimental therapeutics; either basic laboratory or clinical research which has had or potentially will have a major impact on the pharmacological treatment of disease. Candidates are not restricted as to age or institutional affiliation, and membership in the Society is not required; however nominations must be made by ASPET members. This Award is sponsored by *Hoffmann-La Roche, Inc. Closing date:* 15th October.

Epilepsy Research Award: US$1,000 is given annually in recognition of outstanding research leading to better clinical control of epileptic seizures. This may include basic screening and testing of new therapeutic agents, mechanism of action studies, metabolic disposition, pharmacokinetics, and clinical pharmacology studies. There are no restrictions as to age, sex, nationality or institutional affiliation. Candidates may be nominated by members of any recognized scientific association, domestic or foreign. This Award is sponsored by *The International League Against Epilepsy. Closing date:* 1st November.

Harry Gold Award: US$1,000 and a certificate is given biennially to honor excellence in research and/or teaching in clinical pharmacology. There are no restrictions as to age, institutional affiliation or membership in ASPET; however nominations must be made by ASPET members. *Closing date:* 15th February.

Goodman and Gilman Award in Drug Receptor Pharmacology: US$2,500 and a plaque is awarded in even-numbered years to recognize and stimulate outstanding research in the pharmacology of biological receptors. Such research might provide a better understanding of the mechanism of biological processes and potentially provide the basis for the discovery of drugs useful in the treatment of diseases. There are no restrictions as to age, sex, nationality or institutional affiliation of the candidate, and membership in ASPET is not required; however nominations must be made by ASPET members. *Closing date:* 1st November of the year preceding the year in which the award is made.

Torald Sollmann Award in Pharmacology: US$2,500 and a medal is given every third year (next award in 1984) for significant contributions over many years to the advancement and extension of knowledge in the field of pharmacology. Candidates are not restricted as to age or institutional affiliation, and they need not be members of ASPET. Nominations, however, must be made by ASPET members. *Closing date:* 1st February of the year in which the Award is to be made.

Theodore Wicker Memorial Award: US$10,000 and a certificate is given annually to an active investigator who has made sustained, distinguished contributions in pharmacology. Research may involve work leading to new concepts or knowledge in pharmacology or the development of drugs useful in the treatment of human disease. Studies concerned with means of improving drug therapy or decreasing toxicity of drugs or other chemical substances are also acceptable. There are no restrictions as to age or institutional affiliation of the candidate, and membership in ASPET is not required. However, nominations must be made by ASPET members. *Closing date:* 15th September.

Note: The *Bernard B. Brodie Award* is restricted to ASPET members.

Further information from:
  Executive Officer
  American Society for Pharmacology and
    Experimental Therapeutics, Inc.
  9650 Rockville Pike
  Bethesda, Maryland 20014
  U.S.A.

[195]

AMERICAN SOCIETY OF PHOTOGRAMMETRY

Alan Gordon Memorial Award: US$100, a trophy and certificate is given annually to an individual, not necessarily a Society member, to encourage and commend contributions of significant achievement in remote sensing and photographic interpretation.

Practical Papers Award: Three prizes of US$500, US$300, and US$200, plus a certificate and trophy each, are given to individuals, not necessarily members of the Society, for papers of practical or applied value which have been published in Photogrammetric Engineering and Remote Sensing.

Further information from:
American Society of Photogrammetry
105 North Virginia Avenue
Falls Church, Virginia 22046
U.S.A.

[196]

AMERICAN SOCIETY OF PHOTOGRAMMETRY

Bausch & Lomb Photogrammetric Award

Purpose: To stimulate an interest in photogrammetry in college and graduate students in the United States and to recognize the meritorious students who display outstanding ability and interest in photogrammetry.

No. offered: One undergraduate and one graduate Award annually.

Value: US$250 and a three-year membership of the Society, plus an all-expenses-paid trip to the Society's annual meeting for each recipient.

Eligibility: Open to regular students in the United States. Awards are made on the basis of papers of not more than 4,000 words submitted by the contestants. Such papers should describe a new use of photogrammetry or of photogrammetric equipment, or an adaptation or improvement in the use of photogrammetry or of photogrammetric equipment to any field of study.

Closing date: 15th January.

Further information from:
American Society of Photogrammetry
105 North Virginia Avenue
Falls Church, Virginia 22046
U.S.A.

[197]

AMERICAN SOCIETY OF PHOTOGRAMMETRY

Wild Heebrugg Photogrammetric Fellowship

Purpose: To encourage qualified candidates to pursue graduate education in photogrammetry and thereby to promote the development of photogrammetric science.

No. offered: One Fellowship annually.

Value: US$4,000

Tenable for one year of graduate study at an accredited school; if the grantee elects to study overseas, his choice of study center must be ratified by the donor. Successful applicants may reapply for an extension of the Fellowship in succeeding years.

Eligibility: Open to any regular or student member of the Society; as part of his undergraduate course of study, an applicant must have completed at least one undergraduate course in surveying or photogrammetry.

Note: Applications are judged on previous academic record, applicant's statement of his study objectives, applicability of previous courses to graduate work in photogrammetry, recommendation of faculty member, and financial need. Grantees are expected to submit a report to the Society in June on their academic accomplishments during the year of Fellowship.

Closing date: 15th January

Further information from:
American Society of Photogrammetry
105 North Virginia Avenue
Falls Church, Virginia 22046
U.S.A.

[198]

AMERICAN SOCIETY OF PLANT PHYSIOLOGISTS

Awards

Stephen Hales Prize Award of US$1,000 and a certificate is given biennially to a resident of North America who has served the science of plant physiology in some noteworthy manner. Candidates need not be members of the Society.

Charles F. Kettering Award of US$1,000 and a certificate is made biennially for recognized excellence in the field of photosynthesis.

Charles Albert Shull Award of US$1,000 and a certificate is given biennially to a scientist in recognition of outstanding investigations in the field of plant physiology. Candidates should be North American residents who are under forty years of age.

Further information from:
American Society of Plant Physiologists
P.O. Box 1688
Rockville, Maryland 20850
U.S.A.

[199]

AMERICAN SOCIETY OF PLASTIC AND RECONSTRUCTIVE SURGEONS, INC.
Educational Foundation

Scholarship Contest

Annual Scholarship Prizes for essays resulting from original work in the field of plastic and reconstructive surgery are awarded in three classifications. Works which have previously been published in their entirety are not acceptable. The criteria are: originality, value to plastic surgery, depth and completeness of investigation, and organization (clarity, neatness, caliber of illustrations and conciseness). Closing date for all submission: 15th March. Manuscripts should be sent to: *J. Latane Ware, M.D., 5855 Bremo Road, Richmond, Virginia 23226, U.S.A.*

Junior Classification—Prizes offered in two separate categories: basic science and clinical research. First Prize—US$1,000 and US$1,000 travel allowance (to be used within three years of award date); Second Prize—US$750; Third Prize—US$500. Open to residents and plastic surgeons who have been in practice no longer than five years.

Senior Classification—US$750 for winning essay. Open to plastic surgeons with more than five years' experience.

Investigators Award—US$750 for winning essay. Open to investigators and research workers who are not included in the Junior and Senior Classifications.

Not confirmed for 1983.

Further information from:
Victoria M. Doretti, Administrative Director
American Society of Plastic and Reconstructive Surgeons, Inc.
Educational Foundation
29 East Madison Street, Suite 800
Chicago, Illinois 60602
U.S.A.

[200]

AMERICAN SOCIETY FOR PSYCHICAL RESEARCH, INC.

Scholarship

One Scholarship of US$2,000 is awarded annually to a doctoral candidate studying parapsychology. The award is not ordinarily renewable. Closing date for applications varies from year to year.

Further information from:
Scholarship Committee
American Society for Psychical Research Inc.
5 West 73rd Street
New York, New York 10023
U.S.A.

[201]

AMERICAN SOCIOLOGICAL ASSOCATION

Minority Fellowship Program—Doctoral Fellowships in Sociology

Purpose: To contribute to the development of sociology by recruiting persons who will add differing orientations and creativity to the field.

Subject: Sociological research on mental health.

No. offered: Approximately ten Fellowships annually.

Value: Up to US$5,040 per academic year for each Fellowship, plus tuition.

Tenable at accredited institutions of higher learning for one year, renewable for two additional years.

Eligibility: Open to students beginning or continuing study in sociology, who express a commitment to sociological research on mental health. Candidates must be U.S. citizens or permanent visa residents, including, but not limited to, Blacks, American Indians, Asian Americans, and Spanish-speaking Americans.

Note: Upon completion of the Fellowship, the recipient is expected to engage in behavioral research or teaching, or a combination thereof, for a period equal to the period of support.

A limited number of awards to support dissertation research will also be made.

Closing date: 1st February.

Further information from:
Minority Fellowship Program
American Sociological Association
1722 N Street, N.W.
Washington, D.C. 20036
U.S.A.

[202]

AMERICAN SOCIOLOGICAL ASSOCIATION

Minority Fellowship Program—Doctoral Fellowships in Applied Sociology

Purpose: To assist in the preparation of persons from minority backgrounds for careers as researchers and applied sociologists.

Subject: Sociological research with an emphasis on the application of sociological knowledge to the identification, analysis, and reduction of group mental health problems.

No. offered: Approximately ten Fellowships annually.

Value: Up to US$5,040 per academic year for each Fellowship, plus tuition.

Tenable at accredited institutions of higher learning.

Eligibility: Open to students beginning or continuing study in sociology departments that offer training in applied sociology or in areas of the discipline that can be readily applied. Persons not enrolled in applied sociology programs may also be eligible if their dissertations reflect an applied orientation or they express a clear intent to approach sociology from an applied perspective. Candidates must be U.S. citizens or permanent visa residents, including, but not limited to, Blacks, American Indians, Asian Americans, and Spanish-speaking Americans.

Note: Upon completion of the Fellowship, the recipient is expected to engage in behavioral research or teaching, or a combination thereof, for a period equal to the period of support.

A limited number of awards to support dissertation research will also be made.

Closing date: 1st February; recipients to be chosen by 15th April.

Further information from:
Minority Fellowship Program
American Sociological Association
1722 N Street, N.W.
Washington, D.C. 20036
U.S.A.

[203]

AMERICAN TECHNION SOCIETY *(New York City)*
TECHNION-ISRAEL INSTITUTE OF TECHNOLOGY, INC. *(Haifa)*

Harvey Prize

Two Prizes of US$35,000 each are awarded to outstanding personalities whose achievements in one of the following fields have served as a source of inspiration to many others: science and technology; human health; advancement of peace in the Mid-East; literature of profound insight about the mores and life of the Mid-East people. The Prize is awarded without regard to race, religion, nationality or sex. Recipients are invited to Israel where they will remain as guests of the Technion, and spend time at the Institute teaching their subject. Nominations may be made by anyone; however candidates may not nominate themselves. Persons making nominations are requested not to inform the proposed candidate.

Not confirmed for 1983.

Further information from:
American Technion Society
271 Madison Avenue
New York, New York 10016
U.S.A.

[204]

AMERICAN UROLOGICAL ASSOCIATION

Scholars Program

Fellowships of US$15,00 are awarded to urologists to pursue research studies in the field of urology. The Fellowship is tenable for two years.

Note: Scholarships must be matched by the sponsoring institution.

Further information from:
American Urological Association
E. Darracott Vaughan, Jr., M.D.
Chairman, Research Committee
Box 94, Department of Urology
New York Hospital
525 East 68th Street
New York, New York 10021
U.S.A.

[205]

AMERICAN WATER WORKS ASSOCIATION

Academic Achievement Awards on Water Supply Subjects

A First Prize of US$1,000 and a Second Prize of US$500 are offered for master's or doctoral theses or dissertations, in any area of study from agriculture to zoology, including engineering and physical sciences, economics, business and public administration, and the social sciences. The judging committee will determine whether the subject matter is of significant value to the public water supply field. Prizes are not restricted to United States citizens.

Not confirmed for 1983.

Further information from:
Academic Achievement Award Committee
American Water Works Association
6666 West Quincy Avenue
Denver, Colorado 80235
U.S.A.

[206]

AMITY INSTITUTE *(U.S.A.)*

Amity Scholarships

Subjects: American education, American civilization, conversational English, and intern teaching of candidate's native language

No. offered: About 100 Scholarships annually.

Value: Approximately US$1,000 per week to cover intern teaching and program of study. Scholars reside with a host family. Some transportation costs within the United States may be paid.

Tenable at elementary and secondary schools, colleges and universities in the United States for 18, 27 or 36 weeks, with the possibility of renewal.

Eligibility: Open to students between the ages of 20 to 30 whose native tongue is Spanish, French or German and who have a good command of the English language. Occasionally, candidates with another language are accepted. Applicants should have an excellent academic background, some experience of university studies or teacher training, and an interest in language learning and teaching. They should demonstrate interest in American education and the furtherance of international understanding.

Note: Candidates should obtain a copy of *Amity Highlights* brochure before making their application.

Closing date: 31st January.

Further information from:
Amity Institute
Box 118
Del Mar, California 92014
U.S.A

[207]

**AMOCO (UK) EXPLORATION COMPANY
British Gas
Imperial College of Science and Technology** *(London)*

Scholarship in Petroleum Engineering

Purpose: To prepare graduates for careers in petroleum engineering in the oil industry.

No. offered: One Scholarship annually.

Value: Award will not normally be less than a basic Research Council Award plus fees and approved fieldwork expenses.

Tenable for one academic year in the postgraduate course in petroleum engineering at the Imperial College of Science and Technology, London, including a vacation assignment with the sponsoring company.

Eligibility: Open to candidates who hold or expect to obtain a good honours degree in some appropriate branch of engineering, basic physical sciences, or geology. Good academic references are essential.

Closing date: 15th March.

Further information from:
 Registrar
 Imperial College of Science and
  Technology
 London
 England SW7 2AZ

[208]

ARTHUR ANDERSEN & CO. FOUNDATION *(U.S.A.)*

Fellowships for Doctoral Candidates at the Dissertation Stage

Purpose: To aid in the development of more and better university professors in the field of accounting.

Value: Tuition plus US$750 per month.

Tenable for the period required to write the doctoral dissertation, up to a maximum of twelve months.

Eligibility: Open to doctoral candidates at a member school of the American Assembly of Collegiate Schools of Business or any other American association of corresponding stature as an accrediting body, if all doctoral requirements have been met except the writing of the dissertation. Recipients must agree not to enroll in any college or university courses during the anticipated period of Fellowship support.

Note: Recipients must accept a moral obligation to teach accounting at university level for at least three of the first five years following termination of the Fellowship award.

Closing date: 1st March.

Further information from:
 Arthur Andersen & Co. Foundation
 69 West Washington Street
 Chicago, Illinois 60602
 U.S.A.

[209]

ANGLO-AUSTRIAN MUSIC SOCIETY

Richard Tauber Prize

Purpose: To enable a British or Austrian singer to travel and study in order to broaden his or her musical experience.

No. offered: One Prize in even numbered years.

Value: A travel bursary of £800 and a study grant of £250 to enable the recipient to prepare for a public recital in London.

Tenable for a minimum of two months in Austria (for British singers) or in Britain (for Austrian singers).

Eligibility: Open to British and Austrian singers who are between the ages of 21 and 32 for men, and 21 and 30 for women.

Note: Preliminary auditions are held in London and Vienna in March. A public final audition is held in London in April or May. Applicants attend the preliminary auditions at their own expense.

Closing date: 29th January.

Further information from:
Richard Tauber Memorial Scholarship
   Committee
Anglo-Austrian Music Society
46 Queen Anne's Gate
London
England SW1H 9AU

[210]

ANGLO-DANISH SOCIETY

Anglo-Danish Society's (London) Scholarships

Purpose: To promote Anglo-Danish friendship.

Subjects: Unrestricted.

No. offered: Normally one Scholarship annually.

Value: £120 per month, plus £60 travelling expenses.

Tenable at the universities of Copenhagen, Odense or Aarhus in Denmark for a period of up to six months from the beginning of the academic year or such other date as might be approved.

Eligibility: Open to graduate or advanced students who are citizens of the United Kingdom.

Note: Successful applicants will be required to submit a report on work undertaken to the Society at the end of the study period.
The Scholarships also provide for a Danish student to attend a British university.

Closing date: 15th January.

Further information from:
Secretary
Anglo-Danish Society
7 St. Helen's Place
London
England EC3A 6BH

[211]

ANGLO-DANISH SOCIETY

Rentokil Foundation Scholarships

Purpose: To encourage citizens of the United Kingdom to further their studies in Denmark.

Subjects: Unrestricted.

No. offered: Two or more Scholarships annually.

Value: £120 per month, plus £60 for travelling expenses.

Tenable at Danish educational establishments for three to six months; not renewable.

Eligibility: Open to citizens of the United Kingdom.

Note: Successful applicants will be required to submit a report on the work undertaken to the Foundation at the end of the period of study.
These Scholarships also provide for Danish students to study in Great Britain.

Closing date: 15th January.

Further information from:
Secretary
Anglo-Danish Society
7 St. Helen's Place
London
England EC3A 6BH

[212]

ANGLO-GERMAN FOUNDATION FOR THE STUDY OF INDUSTRIAL SOCIETY

The Foundation has the following objectives: (a) to promote the study and to deepen the understanding of modern industrial society and to advance the knowledge of the British and German people about that society and about the ways and means of resolving problems which arise in it; (b) to advance and foster education and knowledge in the two States in the fields of science, technology, commerce, economics, sociology and the arts with a view to stimulating the development of industrial society in a manner most beneficial to the community.

In furtherance of these aims the Foundation is prepared to award research grants, or to support conferences, seminars, workshops and exchange visits. Applications for project support which involve amounts greater than £2,000 must be submitted in final form three months before the meeting at which they are to be considered. The Foundation generally meets in February, June and October.

Further information from:
  Secretariat
  Anglo-German Foundation for the Study of Industrial Society
  St. Stephen's House
  Victoria Embankment
  London
  England SW1A 2LA

[213]

ANGLO-ISRAEL ASSOCIATION

Wyndham Deedes Travel Scholarships to Israel

Subjects: Intensive study of some aspect of life in Israel (sociological, scientific, cultural, economic, etc.) in the area in which the recipient is specially qualified.

No. offered: Two Scholarships annually.

Value: £400 to contribute towards the cost of direct travel to and from Israel and residence.

Tenable in Israel for a minimum period of four to six weeks.

Eligibility: Open to British citizens under 35 years of age, who have graduated from a British university or institute of higher education, and who intend to reside permanently in the United Kingdom. Recipients must undertake to submit a 5,000 word report on their project within six months of their return. The Association has a right to publish these reports.

Closing date: 1st March.

Further information from:
  Secretary
  Anglo-Israel Assocation
  9 Bentinck Street
  London
  England W1M 5RP

[214]

ANGLO-JEWISH ASSOCIATION

Educational Trust Funds Grants

Purpose: To help Jewish students from overseas to study in the United Kingdom. Occasionally Jewish students of British nationality are given awards.

Subjects: Unrestricted.

No. offered: Approximately 30 new Grants annually.

Value: £100 to £400 annually payable in three installments.

Tenable at universities and polytechnics in the United Kingdom for the duration of the university course. Grants may occasionally be renewed for a further postgraduate course.

Eligibility: Open to Jewish students from outside the United Kingdom. Grants are normally given to those students over 18 years of age who wish to study at a university.

Closing date: 1st May.

Further information from:
  Anglo-Jewish Association
  Woburn House, 5th Floor
  Upper Woburn Place
  London
  England WC1H 0EP

[215]

ANGLO-SOVIET CULTURAL AGREEMENT

Postgraduate Exchange Studentships for United Kingdom Citizens

Subjects: Unrestricted, including up to four Studentships for studies in the theory of arts and in the performing arts.

No. offered: Approximately 50 Studentships annually (this figure includes short-term and undergraduate Studentships).

Value: Cost of maintenance and tuition, and return fares at surface rates.

Tenable at universities and other educational institutions in the U.S.S.R. Duration—ten months for full Studentships; between two and six months for short-term Studentships.

Eligibility: Open to United Kingdom graduates who are under 35 years of age and are currently engaged in teaching, study or research at a university or similar institution in the United Kingdom. Candidates must have a working knowledge of Russian.

Note: Candidates may at the same time apply for full or short-term Studentships. [Also see Soviet Government Awards entry].

Further information from:
Regional Officer (Soviet Union)
East Europe and North Asia Department
British Council
10 Spring Gardens
London
England SW1A 2BN

[216]

ANGLO-SPANISH CULTURAL FOUNDATION *(London)*

Vicénte Canada Blanch Fellowships

Purpose: To enable citizens of the United Kingdom to study the culture and civilization of Spain.

No. offered: One Junior and one Senior Fellowship annually.

Value: Junior—approximately £2,500; Senior—approximately £3,500. Travel expenses not exceeding £200 may be paid.

Tenable for one year in Spain.

Eligibility: Open to university graduates who are citizens of the United Kingdom.

Note: The Foundation also offers awards to Spanish graduates to enable them to study scientific and engineering subjects in the United Kingdom.

Further information from:
Secretary, Scholarships Committee
University of London
Senate House, Malet Street
London
England WC1E 7HU

[217]

ANGUS AND ROBERTSON PTY. LTD. *(Australia)*

Writers' Fellowship

A contract with an advance of A$2,000 is offered for a manuscript or a project of outstanding originality, preferably from a new writer who is either a permanent resident of Australia or New Zealand or an Australian or New Zealand national living abroad. Submissions may be fiction, non-fiction or poetry, but not play texts; they may be completed or partly completed manuscripts or writing projects; only in the latter case they must be supported by some evidence of literary skill or a testimonial to the writer's capacity to complete the project. Closing date is 31st December.

Further information from:
Writers' Fellowship
Angus and Robertson Publishers
Unit 4, Eden Park
31 Waterloo Road
North Ryde, N.S.W.
Australia 2113

[218]

ANIMAL HEALTH TRUST *(UK)*

Wooldridge Farm Livestock Research Fellowships

Purpose: To promote research into the health problems of farm animals in the United Kingdom.

Subjects: Studies of the major factors, including epidemiology, influencing the health and productivity of cattle, sheep or pigs.

No. offered: Varies according to size of stipends given each year.

Value: Stipends, depending on age and experience, range from £5,000 per annum, plus a reasonable sum for approved expenditure.

Tenable for up to three years at an agreed place of work.

Eligibility: Open to veterinarians and scientists with postgraduate research experience who design an approved programme of study, together with its budget.

Further information from:
Animal Health Trust
Lanwades Hall, Kennett
Newmarket, Suffolk
England CB8 7PN

[219]

ANIMAL HEALTH TRUST *(U.K.)*

Research Training Scholarships

Subject: Veterinary or allied sciences.

No. offered: At least one Scholarship annually.

Value: £1,250 per annum, plus a reasonable grant towards essential fees.

Tenable at appropriate institutions in the United Kingdom for up to three years.

Eligibility: Open to British citizens under 30 years of age who are veterinary surgeons or graduates in allied subjects, and wish to pursue a career in veterinary science. Candidates should have secured a place in a United Kingdom university or recognized laboratory.

Closing date: 30th April.

Further information from:
Animal Health Trust
Lanwades Hall, Kennett
Newmarket, Suffolk
England CB8 7PN

[220]

ANISFIELD-WOLF AWARD IN RACE RELATIONS *(U.S.A.)*
Cleveland Foundation

Each year two Awards are offered for published works which in any way contribute to the betterment of race relations. The first Award is for a scholarly book published in the field of race relations. The second is for a book concerned with racial problems in the field of creative literature. Works of fiction, drama, poetry, biography or autobiography are eligible. The value of each Award is US$1,500. Closing date is 31st January of the year following that for which the Awards are to be made.

Further information from:
Ashley Montagu
Chairman of Committee
Anisfield-Wolf Award in Race Relations
321 Cherry Hill Road
Princeton, New Jersey 08540
U.S.A.

[221]

ANNUAL SIMULATION SYMPOSIUM

Ira Kay Memorial Research Grant in Computer Simulation

One Grant of US$4,000 to US$10,000 is given annually for research intended to help improve the quality of computer simulations work by making possible the demonstration of new techniques, the development of new tools, the application of the techniques of digital simulation to new problems, and the dissemination of information concerning these tools, techniques and applications.

Research undertaken must deal with simulation by digital computer. The application of simulation can be to any area of inquiry. Originality, potential contribution to the art and science of digital simulation and evidence that this Grant would be of major significance in furthering the research, are principal considerations in judging the award.

Anyone working in the field of simulation is eligible. Candidates may be employed by a firm, research organization, government agency, or be employees or students at an institution of higher education.

Further information from:
Dr. W.M. Bunker
General Electric Company
P.O. Box 2500
Daytona Beach, Florida 32015
U.S.A.

[222]

ANTI-CANCER COUNCIL OF VICTORIA *(Australia)*

Research Grants

Financial support to promote and subsidise research into the cause, prevention and treatment of cancer may be given in the form of *Annual Grants; Triennial Grants;* and *Travel Grants.* Individuals desiring support must first arrange with the head of a university department or director of an institute or other approved establishment to sponsor their research by providing the necessary facilities and by making an application for a Grant on their behalf. Preference is given to full-time research workers.

Further information from:
   Secretary
   Anti-Cancer Council of Victoria
   90 Jolimont Street
   East Melbourne, Victoria
   Australia 3002

[223]

ANTI-CANCER FOUNDATION OF THE UNIVERSITIES OF SOUTH AUSTRALIA

Research Grants

Subjects: Any scientific or medical field directly concerned with the cause, diagnosis, prevention or treatment of cancer.

No. offered: Approximately ten Grants annually.

Value: Varies according to the needs of the proposed research project and available funds.

Tenable at an appropriate establishment in South Australia for up to three years.

Eligibility: Open to postgraduate research workers who have established themselves in the field of cancer research or show promise of doing so, who are residents of South Australia.

Closing date: Mid-September.

Further information from:
   Executive Secretary
   Anti-Cancer Foundation of the
      Universities of South Australia
   G.P.O. Box 498
   Adelaide, South Australia
   Australia 5001

[224]

AOPA AIR SAFETY FOUNDATION
(U.S.A.)

Grants, Fellowships, Scholarships

Purpose: To improve safety in every manner in all phases of aviation and to promote research into the scientific aspects of aviation and related subjects.

Value: Variable, depending on the needs and nature of the request, but generally determined by the urgency of the proposed project.

Eligibility: Open to qualified individuals and organizatons with appropriate interests.

Not confirmed for 1983.

Further information from:
   Executive Vice-President
   AOPA Air Safety Foundation
   7315 Wisconsin Avenue
   Washington, D.C. 20014
   U.S.A.

[225]

APEX FOUNDATION FOR RESEARCH INTO MENTAL RETARDATION LTD.
(Australia)

Research Grants

Subject: Mental retardation: its causes and forms.

No. offered: Approximately two Grants annually.

Value: By individual assessment; Grants in a given year total about A$10,000.

Tenable at any recognised university, hospital, or other institution for twelve months.

Eligibility: Open to reputable and qualified persons who work in the general field of mental retardation (e.g. doctors, teachers, etc.).

Further information from:
  K. Morrish, Honorary Secretary
  Apex Foundation for Research into
    Mental Retardation Ltd.
  G.P.O. Box 1695P
  Melbourne, Victoria
  Australia 3001

[226]

APEX TRUST FOR AUTISM *(Australia)*

Grants

Grants, ranging between A$8,000 and A12,000 are made available for work in any discipline concerned with the cause, diagnosis, prevention, care or treatment of autism.

Further information from:
  Chairman
  Apex Trust for Autism
  P.O. Box 421
  Milsons Point, N.S.W.
  Australia 2601

[227]

ARCHITECTS REGISTRATION COUNCIL OF THE UNITED KINGDOM

Education Fund Awards

The Fund provides for grants for the assistance of British students training for architectural registration in Britain and intending to practice in Britain, whose means appear to the Council to be insufficient to enable them to pursue their studies.

Further information from:
  Architects Registration Council of the
    United Kingdom
  73 Hallam Street
  London
  England W1N 6EE

[228]

ARCHITECTURAL ASSOCIATION *(U.K.)*

Anthony Pott Memorial Fund Award of approximately £800 is awarded biennially to United Kingdom architects, and students of architecture and related subjects. The Award may be used for research or the publication of studies. *Closing date:* 31st December, 1984.

Michael Ventris Memorial Fund Award of approximately £500 is offered in odd-numbered years to architects or students of any nationality who have gained RIBA intermediate status, or other comparable level of achievement. The Award should support a specific project rather than a continuing programme of study. *Note:* In alternate years the Award is offered to promote the study of Mycenaean civilization through the Institute of Classical Studies, University of London. *Closing date:* 31st December.

Further information from:
  Secretary
  Architectural Association
  34/36 Bedford Square
  London
  England WC1B 3ES

[229]

ARCTIC INSTITUTE OF NORTH AMERICA

Grants-in-Aid

Purpose: To support field research in problems relating to the Arctic Ocean and the adjacent land area.

Subjects: Relating to the natural or social sciences (e.g. biological oceanography, cold weather physiology, community planning and development, geophysics, permafrost, physical and chemical oceanography, potable water supplies and pollution, resource development and the environment) in the Arctic and Subarctic, and in other areas where similar conditions prevail.

Eligibility: Open to candidates holding a Ph.D. degree or equivalent (or to be supervised by someone holding such a degree). There are no citizenship or residency restrictions.

Closing date: 1st January; applications, however, may be reviewed throughout the year.

Note: Special opportunities for research exist in arctic North America at the Devon Island Research Station in the Queen Elizabeth Islands, the Icefield Rangers Research Project in the St. Elias Mountains, Yukon Territory, and the Inuvik Research Laboratory.
  The Institute also maintains a polar research and reference library at its offices in Calgary, Canada.

Small Grants are also available to provide support for the individual investigator who wishes to accomplish a small-scale study on a modest budget. The maximum award is approximately US$2,000. If the investigator is a student he must present evidence of his supervisor's approval.

Further information from:
Secretary of the Research Committee
Arctic Institute of North America
University of Calgary
University Library Tower
2500 University Drive, N.W.
Calgary, Alberta
Canada T2N 1N4

[230]

ARCTIC INSTITUTE OF NORTH AMERICA

Research Grants in the Social Sciences

Subjects: Fields associated with the human and/or social sciences (e.g. anthropology, sociology, archaeology, linguistics, folklore, curriculum development); studies leading to advanced degrees.

No. offered: Three of four Grants annually.

Value: Up to US$2,500 each.

Eligibility: Open to students of any nationality whose proposed studies relate to, or will be accomplished, in the Arctic or Middle North.

Note: Applications must be endorsed by the student's academic supervisor prior to submission. Proposals should reach the Institute by the end of the calendar year for consideration during the following field season.

Further information from:
Secretary of the Research Committee
Arctic Institute of North America
University of Calgary
2500 University Drive, N.W.
Calgary, Alberta
Canada T2N 1N4

[231]

STEPHEN ARLEN MEMORIAL FUND
(U.K.)

Stephen Arlen Bursary

An award of up to £1,500 is made periodically at the discretion of the Trustees for the further artistic development of a person aged between 20 and 30 who is resident in the United Kingdom and is following a career in any branch of opera, music, drama or ballet. It is awarded to the person who submits the most imaginative programme of further study (in the widest sense of the word), and subsequently satisfies a Board of Adjudicators of his or her professional ability at an interview and audition. The Award is intended for support of a programme or project away from the more routine extension of academy or university training. The Trustees will require a formal report on the result of the project for which the Award is made.

Closing date: 31st March.

Further information from:
Secretary
Stephen Arlen Memorial Fund
London Coliseum, St. Martin's Lane
London
England WC2N 4ES

[232]

ART GALLERY OF NEW SOUTH WALES
Dyason Bequest

Supplementary Financial Assistance

Grants are made to Australian art students who have won travelling art scholarships, in order that they may further their studies in architecture, sculpture, or painting in countries outside Australia and New Zealand.

Applicants should have held their travelling scholarships for at least nine months before applying. They may apply at home or from overseas.

Further information from:
The Trustees
Art Gallery of New South Wales
Art Gallery Road
Sydney, N.S.W.
Australia 2000

[233]

ARTHRITIS CARE *(U.K.)*

Sociological Research Award

Purpose: To encourage research into any form of aid, device or social welfare problem connected with rheumatism and arthritis.

Value: Dependent upon requirements.

Eligibility: Open to any British subject over 21 years of age.

Further information from:
Arthritis Care
6 Grosvenor Crescent
London
England SW1X 7ER

[234]

ARTHRITIS FOUNDATION *(U.S.A.)* (National Office)

Postdoctoral Fellowships
Arthritis Investigator Awards
Senior Fellowships Awards

Postdoctoral Fellowships in the amount of US$14,000 to US$16,000 per annum (based on postdoctoral experience) with a yearly increment of US$500, are awarded to holders of a Doctor of Medicine, Philosophy, Osteopathy, or an equivalent doctoral degree, who intend to pursue a program of study in the rheumatic diseases. The support is awarded for two years and may be renewed for an additional year. A grant of US$500 will be awarded to the sponsoring institution for each year of the fellowship, to be applied to the costs of annuity programs, laboratory expenses, travel, etc. Fellows are expected to devote 90% of their professional time in activities related to the fellowship.

Arthritis Investigator Awards in the amount of US$20,000 to US$24,000 per annum (based on postdoctoral experience) with a yearly increment of US$1,000 are awarded to holders of a Doctor of Medicine, Philosophy or equivalent degree, who have a minimum of 3 to 7 years postdoctoral training, and show distinct promise and evidence of productivity in arthritis-related research. Awards are for two years, with a possible third year renewal on a competitive basis. The sponsoring institution will receive a grant of US$1,000 for each year of the fellowship. Awardees are expected to devote 80% of their professional time to activities related to the award program.

Senior Fellowship Awards in the amount of US$30,000 per annum, are awarded to support individuals who have demonstrated outstanding competence in academic medicine. The Fellowships are tenable for five years and are open to applicants holding a doctoral degree. A Doctor of Medicine is required of candidates who plan to work directly with patients. Applicants must be sponsored by an institution (usually academic) in the United States, which will receive a grant of US$1,000 for each year of the fellowship. Fellows are expected to devote 80% of their professional time in activities related to the fellowship.

Closing date for applications: 1st September for Fellowships to commence 1st July of the following year.

Further information from:
Research Department
Arthritis Foundation
3400 Peachtree Road, N.E.
Atlanta, Georgia 30326
U.S.A.

[235]

ARTHRITIS FOUNDATION *(U.S.A.)* (National Office)

Allied Health Professionals Fellowships

Purpose: To involve nurses and other health professionals in arthritis research, teaching, and implementation of creative patient care services.

Value: US$14,000 per annum, with an increment of US$500 for the second year, paid monthly to the sponsoring institution. A grant of US$1,000 is paid annually to the sponsoring institution to defray costs of annuity programs, research expenses, travel, etc.

Tenable for two years, with a progress report required for continuation of the second year.

Eligibility: Open to applicants who have relevant professional expertise; a Master of Science or Arts, or other equivalent degree; or who intend to earn such a degree through the Fellowship. Candidates should plan to pursue a program of study in the rheumatic diseases.

Note: Fellows are expected to devote full time to clinical investigation, field studies or training. Up to twenty percent of the total professional time may be spent in teaching, providing it significantly contributes to the Fellow's own education and development.

Doctors of Medicine and Philosophy are ineligible for these fellowships.

Closing date for applications: 1st November for Fellowships to commence 1st July of the following year.

Further information from:
Research Department
Arthritis Foundation
3400 Peachtree Road, N.E.
Atlanta, Georgia 30326
U.S.A.

[236]

ARTHRITIS FOUNDATION *(U.S.A.)* (National Office)

Allied Health Professionals Research Grants

Grants of up to US$1,500 are awarded for up to two years to enable health professionals to design and carry out innovative research projects related to rheumatic diseases in an area of arthritis management and/or comprehensive patient care. The Grants are paid quarterly to the investigator's institution and earmarked for his or her work. Grants may be renewed for a third year on a competitive basis. Open to applicants with relevant professional experience who work directly with the rheumatic diseases.

Closing date for applications: 1st November for grants to commence 1st July of the following year.

Further information from:
Research Department
Arthritis Foundation
3400 Peachtree Road, N.E.
Atlanta, Georgia 30326
U.S.A.

[237]

ARTHRITIS AND RHEUMATISM COUNCIL FOR RESEARCH *(U.K.)*

Copeman Travelling Fellowship

Purpose: To provide training and experience in rheumatology for doctors up to and including senior registrar status.

Tenable for one year at a centre of the Fellow's choice, subject to the Council's approval.

Further information from:
General Secretary
Arthritis and Rheumatism Council
41 Eagle Street
London
England WC1R 4AR

[238]

ARTHRITIS AND RHEUMATISM COUNCIL FOR RESEARCH *(U.K.)*

Research Fellowships

Purpose: To further research into the rheumatic diseases.

Value: Amount of the Fellowship is dependent upon the recipient's previous experience and qualifications.

Tenable at any suitable centre in the United Kingdom for a maximum of three years.

Eligibility: Open to citizens of the United Kingdom and Commonwealth with previous experience of investigation and research. Preference is given to individuals wishing to take part in an existing programme of research.

Note: A programme of proposed work must be submitted. Papers resulting from the work carried out should be offered for publication to *Annals of Rheumatic Diseases.*

Closing dates: 1st March; 15th May; 1st September; 1st December.

Further information from:
General Secretary
Arthritis and Rheumatism Council
41 Eagle Street
London
England WC1R 4AR

[239]

ARTHRITIS AND RHEUMATISM COUNCIL FOR RESEARCH *(U.K.)*

Project Grants

Purpose: To further research into the rheumatic diseases.

Value: Variable.

Tenable at any suitable centre for up to a maximum of three years.

Eligibility: Open to citizens of the United Kingdom and Commonwealth with previous experience of investigation and research.

Note: Grants are made in support of specific research projects.
A programme of proposed work must be submitted. Papers resulting from the work carried out should be offered for publication to *Annals of Rheumatic Diseases*.

Closing dates: 1st March; 15th May; 1st September; 1st December.

Further information from:
General Secretary
Arthritis and Rheumatism Council
41 Eagle Street
London
England WC1R 4AR

[240]

ARTHRITIS SOCIETY *(Canada)*

Assistantships

Purpose: To provide partial salary support for fully-trained rheumatologists taking up new faculty appointments.

Subject: Rheumatology.

Value: The Society will match salary funds made available to the Assistant through faculty budgets or practice earnings pools until the Society's share reaches a maximum of Can$10,000 per annum, plus a pro-rated portion of the employer's share of staff benefits to which the Assistant is entitled. Stipends are paid monthly, in advance.

Tenable at Canadian medical schools for a maximum of two years.

Eligibility: Open to Canadian rheumatologists taking up new faculty appointments.

Note: Assistantships are awarded by the Society on the advice of its Medical and Scientific Committee, and it reserves the right to approve or decline any application without stating reasons.

Applications on behalf of candidates should be made by the chairman of the department of medicine of the concerned school, and countersigned by the dean. They should outline the candidate's qualifications, duties to be performed, professional, scientific, financial and administrative amenities he will enjoy and the manner in which the proposed Assistantship will contribute to the attainment of the objectives of the program of the rheumatic disease unit to which he will be appointed. Assistants must report to the Society annually on their professional activities.

Closing date: 15th October.

Further information from:
Arthritis Society
Suite 420, 920 Yonge Street
Toronto, Ontario
Canada M4W 3J7

[241]

ARTHRITIS SOCIETY *(Canada)*

Associateships in Basic Science

Purpose: To provide support for trained persons with a major interest in teaching or research.

Subjects: The basic sciences, Rheumatology and other areas of academic medicine.

Value: Stipends, paid monthly in advance, are determined by the medical school, and are in accordance with the scale in effect at that school. If an Associateship is renewed, during the second term, a total of 90% of the stipend will be paid by the Society while the remaining 10% is to be paid by the school. The society will also pay 90% of the employer's share of the staff benefits to which the Associate would otherwise be entitled.

Tenable at Canadian medical schools for five years, renewable for an additional five years.

Eligibility: Open to Canadian personnel with a major interest in teaching or research, who are engaged in full-time careers in academic medicine and have demonstrated aptitude in research by a substantial record of publication in leading peer reviewed journals. Applicants should at least hold the rank of assistant professor to be considered.

Note: Associateships are awarded by the Society on the advice of its Medical and Scientific Committee, and it reserves the right to approve or decline any application without stating reasons.

Applications on behalf of the candidates should be made by the chairman of the department of medicine of the concerned school, and then countersigned by the dean. They should outline the candidate's qualifications, working conditions, and professional, scientific, financial and administrative amenities he will enjoy and the manner in which the proposed Associateship will contribute to the attainment of the objectives of the program of the rheumatic disease unit to which he will be appointed.

It is expected that Associates will spend at least 75% of their time in the prosecution of research in laboratories formally assigned to the Rheumatic Disease Unit.

Associates in basic science should expect to obtain Research Grants from the Medical Research Council of Canada and other research fund granting bodies, not the Arthritis Society.

Associates may receive additional emolument from teaching and consulting practice at the discretion of the Chairman of the department.

Associates must report to the Society annually on their research and other professional activities.

Closing date: 15th October.

Further information from:
Arthritis Society
Suite 420, 920 Yonge Street
Toronto, Ontario
Canada M4W 3J7

[242]

ARTHRITIS SOCIETY *(Canada)*

M.D. and Ph.D. Fellowships

Purpose: To augment residency training programs in rheumatology, and to enhance the training of rheumatologists likely to embark on careers in academic medicine.

Subjects: Rheumatology and, in special circumstances, other fields of medicine and the medical sciences.

Value: Payments are made monthly in advance, except when a Fellowship is taken outside of Canada.

Fellows training in Canada who possess the M.D. degree will be paid at the same rates and in the same manner, and will enjoy the same fringe benefits as residents at the medical school concerned.

Fellows training abroad who possess the M.D. degree will receive stipends in accordance to those paid by the Medical Research Council of Canada to Fellows of the same training and experience: *Can*$23,000 (fourth year graduate training); *Can*$24,000 (fifth year); *Can*$26,000 (sixth year); *Can*$27,500 (seventh and subsequent years). Payments are made quarterly, in advance. Fringe benefits are not paid to M.D. Fellows abroad.

Fellows training in Canada who hold the Ph.D. degree receive the following stipends: *Can*$17,000 (first year of post-doctoral training); *Can*$18,200 (second year); *Can*$19,400 (third year). Fellows will enjoy the same fringe benefits as other Ph.D.s at the same institution who have similar stipends.

Tenable for one year, usually commencing 1st July, at Canadian medical schools. Fellowships may be held outside Canada provided the candidate will have completed at least one year of training in rheumatology in Canada. Fellowships may be renewed for a second year.

Eligibility: Open to Canadians or landed immigrants who have completed at least three years of graduate training in medicine approved by the Royal College of Physicians and Surgeons (Canada) or the Corporation of Physicians and Surgeons of Quebec, and should have completed one year of training in rheumatology in Canada prior to the commencement of the year of training in rheumatology for which the Fellowship is sought.

Fellowships for research training may be granted to candidates who have completed the prerequisites of the Royal College of Physicians and Surgeons (Canada) or the Corporation of Physicians and Surgeons of Quebec in internal medicine or rheumatology, or both, and are likely to embark on careers in academic medicine in Canada.

Note: Fellowships are awarded by the Society on the advice of its Medical and Scientific Committee, and it reserves the right to approve or decline any application without stating reasons.

A candidate should arrange to furnish the Society with a certified transcript of his undergraduate record; a statement from either the Royal College of Physicians and Surgeons (Canada) or the Corporation of Physicians and Surgeons of Quebec providing an assessment of his training in relation to the pertaining prerequisites; two letters of recommendation (one from his most recent or current supervisor), and a letter of acceptance from his future supervisor at the institution in which he has arranged his training. Letters should be sent directly to the Society by those individuals, and not by the applicant along with the application.

Closing date: 15th October. Applications received after that date will be considered only after all timely applications have been dealt with.

Further information from:
  Arthritis Society
  Suite 420, 920 Yonge Street
  Toronto, Ontario
  Canada M4W 3J7

[243]

ARTHRITIS SOCIETY *(Canada)*

Research Grants

Purpose: To assist in defraying costs of research.

Subject: Basic and clinical research relevant to the rheumatic diseases.

Value: Varies, based on approval, in whole or in part, of the applicant's estimate of his research expenditure under various items—personnel, equipment, supplies and other expenses. Payment made in advance in monthly installments.

Tenable for twelve months only at Canadian universities or other recognized Canadian institutions. Grants may be continued for an additional twelve month period by reapplication.

Eligibility: Open to investigators holding staff appointments at Canadian universities or other recognized institutions.

Note: Grants are awarded by the Society on the advice of its Medical and Scientific Committee, and it reserves the right to make or decline awards without stating reasons. Preference will be given to projects making significant contributions to the development of well-trained clinical personnel capable of academic leadership. Grants are not intended to cover total costs of research, and are not to be used for the remuneration of the grantee or other principal investigators. Space and basic facilities at the institution concerned are prerequisite to an application. Applications should be countersigned by the director of the rheumatic disease unit concerned.

Further information from:
  Arthritis Society
  Suite 420, 920 Yonge Street
  Toronto, Ontario
  Canada M4W 3J7

[244]

ARTS COUNCIL *(Ireland)*

Early each year the Arts Council announces details of bursaries, scholarships and other awards it intends to give to individuals working in the following fields: literature, drama, cinema, dance, music, opera, visual arts, actors, musicians, and art education. In 1981 the total amount available was IR£140,000. Those of Irish birth or residence may apply and in most cases applications must be received by March or April.

Macaulay Fellowships and Marten Toonder Awards: These awards, value £2,000-£2,500 each are given annually to creative artists, writers, composers and visual artists. In the case of the Macaulay Fellowship, applicants must be under 30 years of age (or exceptionally, under 35 years) and be of Irish birth. Two awards are offered each year and the rotation is as follows: 1980—music composition and literature; 1981—literature and visual arts; 1982—visual arts and music composition.

Further information from:
Secretary
Arts Council/An Chomhairle Ealaton
70 Merrion Square
Dublin 2
Ireland

[245]

ARTS COUNCIL OF GREAT BRITAIN

The Council aims to develop and improve the knowledge, understanding and practice of the arts and to increase their accessibility to the public. Awards are available to artists through a multiplicity of schemes which are intended, in many cases, to enable the individual to buy time to further his or her art. The schemes are usually open to professional creative artists of British nationality and generally tenable in Britain only.

Art for Public Sites: Grants of up to 50% can be made towards the cost of commissioning or purchasing work by living British artists for display on public sites.

Artists-in-Residence: Grants can be made to organisations wishing to establish residencies for artists on a short or longer term basis.

Assisted Purchase: Grants can be made to supplement the purchasing of budgets of organisations (excluding museums).

Exhibition Subsidy: Grants and guarantees can be made towards the cost of organising temporary art exhibitions, particularly those which are concerned with contemporary art and those which will tour to one or more galleries.

Art Publishing Grants: Applications are considered from artists, writers and publishers for financial support for books by artists and books on art, especially 20th Century British art.

Purchases of Works of Art: Paintings, sculptures and drawings by British artists, and prints by British and foreign artists are purchased for inclusion in Arts Council touring exhibitions and for long-term loan to museums, galleries and other public buildings. Further information is available from the Curator of the Arts Council Collection.

Studios for Artists: Grants are made towards the conversion costs of premises serving as communal studios for a number of artists and for the provision of equipment to establish print workshops and other non-commercial resource centers for the use of professional artists. Applications for grants towards the cost of conversion of studios in individual occupation should be made to Regional Arts Association.

Artists' Films and Video Awards: Financial aid, on a materials only basis, is available for avant-garde experimental films/video by means of awards for specific film/video projects, expanded cinema gallery installations, festivals, prints for distribution, and for work in progress.

Arts Documentaries: Awards will be granted for professionally made documentary films on the arts. Animation projects are also considered where the subject falls within the terms of reference.

Drama Training Grants and Bursaries

Theatre Performers: Bursaries are available to give professional refreshment to an individual's career by enabling him/her to learn new skills, carry out a period of research, or pursue a line of relevant interest. Bursaries cover performers with at least three years of experience in any type of theatre, including dance, drama, music theatre and opera.

Theatre Performers' Group Training: Grants are available to existing companies or for groups who come together specifically to enable them to engage specialists to teach them particular skills.

Theatre Designers: (1) The Council offers selected young designers attachments of approximately ten months as additional members of a theatre's design staff, to enable them to gain both training and practical experience in a working theatre. The award may be extended to enable designers to widen their experience by visiting other theatres in Great Britain. Selected designers are paid in bursary in addition to a small wage paid by the theatre company. (2) Bursaries are offered to experienced designers to provide a period of refreshment, allied to a specific project of the applicant's choosing, and to enable the designer to extend his or her professional worth. This includes lighting designers.

Directors: Bursaries are available for (1) young directors to enable them to study all aspects of directing and the artistic direction of a theatre company for a period of one year with possibilities of extension; (2) directors with experience wishing to extend their knowledge and experience in a specific area of work for periods of up to six months; (3) a director with experience who has not been responsible for the artistic direction of a theatre to be appointed as an associate director of a theatre company for up to one year.

Theatre Technicians and Stage Management: The Association of British Theatre Technicians administers on behalf of the *Arts Council* a number of in-service, day-release and full-time courses for theatre technicians. Further information is available from the *Technical Officer, ABTT, 4—7 Great Pulteney Street, London W1R 3DF.* There is also an *Arts Council* bursary scheme for stage managers and technicians working in stage department, sound, electrics, scenic construction, scene painting and properties, costume and wig making. This scheme is intended to help the above eligible stage managers and technicians to undertake projects which will enhance their professional worth, and further their careers. Before applications are submitted under any of these schemes, full particulars should be obtained by writing to the Training Officer.

Playwrights: (1) Bursaries are available to help writers who are working in temporary isolation from the theatre; (2) the *Contract Writers' Scheme* enable theatres to offer realistic sums to writers working for them on a wage, fee or commission basis; (3) *Royalty Supplement Guarantees* ensure that writers who might otherwise be paid low royalties on the production of a new play receive a supplement to ensure fair payment for their work; (4) *Resident Dramatist Attachments* are available to enable theatres to apply for considerable financial help in employing a resident dramatist for a long-term period of nine to twelve months; (5) small sums are available to assist towards the costs of writers' workshops.

Writers' Bursaries

A small number of Bursaries are available for writers of outstanding literary achievement who need financial assistance for the research or writing of their next book. The Bursaries are open to British writers resident in England and to non-British subjects normally resident in England. Applicants may be writers of fiction, poetry, or non-fiction of literary value, including that non-fiction which is a support to literature. The amount of each award will vary according to the individual circumstances of the recipient and the length of time for which financial support is needed. Application forms, which, when completed, must be endorsed by a sponsor (e.g. publisher, editor, literary agent), are available from the Literature Department. The closing date for applications will be in May or June of each year.

Music, Dance and Mime Projects and Awards

Music and Dance Awards are made to individual creative artists such as composers, choreographers and lyric theatre designers, either as bursaries to "buy time" or to assist in specific projects, e.g. payment of fees for commissions from promoting organizations. Special information about commission fees for composers is available from the Music Director. Applications for commission fees for composers of up to £1,250 should be submitted to the Regional Arts Association in whose area the first performance is to take place. A few bursaries for composers are also available. In the case of jazz composers, provisions have sometimes been made for subsidising recordings since they constitute a more satisfactory demonstration of finished works than written scores. Commission fees for choreography may be recommended in response to applications from recognized promoting organizations (generally holding charitable status). Information compiled for the benefit of musicians and music students seeking financial assistance for further training or advanced studies is available from the Music Director.

Dance and Mime Projects and Awards: Fees are offered for the encouragement of young choreographers who have already given evidence of potential talent. Major dance companies are not eligible to apply for commission fees. Applications can be considered from smaller professional dance and mime groups for aid towards particular performance projects. Commission fees for the composition of scores to accompany dance works, and design commission fees for the decor and costumes are considered in response to application from recognized organizations not in receipt of annual subsidy. Funds are not available for dance and mime training, but applications may be considered for other specialized advanced training or research projects that are not eligible for help from other sources

Application forms (where applicable) for assistance under any of the foregoing schemes may be obtained from the Music and Dance Directors respectively, to whom any enquiries should be sent.

Photography

The overall aim of the Council's subsidy program in photography is to assist in the contribution it makes to our culture. Individuals, groups, researchers, museums, galleries, publishers, universities, colleges, public institutions and other non-profit-distributing organizations may apply. Undergraduate or postgraduate students who are eligible for grants from other government departments or agencies are not eligible for these awards.

Exhibition Research Grants: A limited number of grants are available to individuals to fund research on work suitable for eventual exhibition. Themes dealing primarily with British photography may be given preference.

Publication Research Grants: Authors may apply for research grants to enable them to undertake or complete research into, or writing on, subjects concerning the theory or social and aesthetic history of photography for eventual publication. Themes dealing primarily with British Photography may be given preference.

Training Grants: Photographers may apply for training grants to contribute toward the costs of attending specific training workshops, courses, conferences or other events that will extend the applicant's experience, knowledge and skills as a photographer. Administrators, editors and others may also apply for training grants to contribute towards the costs of attending specific training workshops, courses, conferences or other events, including the costs of undertaking personal research or investigation into topics that will extend the applicant's knowledge, experience and skills in the fields of the support and promotion of photography. Grants are not available for full- or part-time courses at universities, polytechnics or other colleges.

Training in Arts Administration

A limited number of bursaries are available to students attending the two full-time courses which are run in conjunction with the Council. Overseas nationals who are not resident and working in Britain are not eligible.

In-service Bursaries: (1) To enable working administrators to extend their knowledge and experience by short training periods away from their work. (2) Bursaries are available for a major piece of training research to be carried out by an established administrator. Further details and application forms are available from the Training Officer.

Note: Applicants are advised that all awards and bursaries may be taxable in the hands of the recipients.

The award schemes listed in this entry are liable to change from time to time. Applicants should contact the Council to ascertain those schemes in operation in a particular field of interest. The Council publishes a booklet entitled *A Guide to Awards and Schemes* which sets out the extent of awards and bursaries in operation. Separate information sheets giving particulars on each award are usually available free of charge from the various departments of the Council.

The awards set out in this entry generally relate to England only. For assistance available in Scotland, see entry for Scottish Arts Council and in Wales, see Welsh Arts Council. Candidates from Northern Ireland should refer to the entry for the Arts Council of Northern Ireland. In addition, Regional Arts Associations offer awards.

Further information from:
Arts Council of Great Britain
105 Piccadilly
London
England W1V OAU

[246]

ARTS COUNCIL OF GREAT BRITAIN

The following private trust funds are administered by the Music Department of the Arts Council.

Dio Fund: An annual award of not less than £50 is offered to a young composer as commission fee for an intrumental and/or vocal work. Composers are invited to submit an example of recent work for consideration by a panel. The successful applicant will be able to claim the award on securing a commission for a new piece for public performance by an approved commissioning body or individual. Preference will be given to a composer still seeking recognition for creative ability, who so far has succeeded in publishing few works, if any. Experimental works are eligible, though proof of conventional musical literacy will be required. The closing date for the receipt of applications and scores is 31st December. There is no application form.

Guilhermina Suggia Gift for the 'Cello: The Advisers will consider applications requesting financial assistance towards the cost of 'cello studies and technical training "from exceptionally talented 'cello students of any nationality who", in the written opinion of their referees and of the adjudicating panel at the annual summer auditions, "may be judged to possess the potential qualities of a first-class solo performer." Applicants must be under 21 years of age. A printed leaflet (with application form attached) giving full particulars, is available upon request.

H.A. Thew Fund: This Fund is for the benefit of music students and musical organizations in Liverpool and Merseyside. Modest awards are made for the purpose of furthering and encouraging the practice of music in Liverpool, and for the benefit of young musicians in the city. Auditions are held as required. A printed leaflet (with accompanying application form) giving further particulars, is available upon request.

Henry and Lily Davis Fund: This Fund is restricted to fully trained young professional performers (not conductors or composers) wishing to pursue specialist, short-term projects requiring specific coaching, not at a formal training institution, which will lead towards a public appearance already scheduled. Awards are not made for continuing basic or postgraduate tuition. Auditions are held in the spring and late autumn of each year. Applicants should be between the ages of 21 and 30 years, and must complete the appropriate form; they may be required to attend preliminary interviews.

Miriam Licette Scholarship: A substantial scholarship(s) is offered annually by competition to a female singer to finance further study in Paris during the academic year following the competition. Applicants must be under the age of 30, and be either British born or normally domiciled in Great Britain. An application form with further particulars is available upon request.

Further information from:
  Music Department
  Arts Council of Great Britain
  9 Long Acre
  London
  England WC2E 9LH

[247]

ARTS COUNCIL OF NORTHERN IRELAND

Awards and Bursaries

A number of Bursaries and Awards, including the *Alice Berger Hammerschlag Trust Award* and the *Bass Charrington Arts Award*, are given annually, normally to residents of Northern Ireland, for accomplishments and proposed projects in all aspects of the creative arts. The Awards and Bursaries vary in value, and are made June each year.

Note: At the time of going to press, this information had not been confirmed.

Further information from:
  Awards Secretary
  Arts Council of Northern Ireland
  181a Stranmillis Road
  Belfast BT9 5DU
  Northern Ireland.

[248]

ASAHI SHIMBUN PUBLISHING COMPANY *(Japan)*

Asahi Prize

An annual Prize of one million yen is offered in recognition of an outstanding contribution to the advancement of Japanese culture or society. The Prize may be awarded for contributions in any field. No restrictions are placed on applicants as to nationality, age or sex.

Further information from:
Asahi Shimbun Publishing Company
5-3-2 Tsukiji
Chuo-ku
Tokyo
Japan

[249]

ASIA FOUNDATION

The Asia Foundation occasionally awards scholarships, fellowships, and special training grants to persons in countries in which it is represented (Bangladesh, Indonesia, Japan, Korea, Malaysia, Pakistan, the Philippines, Republic of China, Singapore, Sri Lanka, Thailand) as well as Nepal and the Pacific Islands. Grants are available to persons nominated by Asian institutions in fields of interest to the Foundation. Awards are usually related to Foundation projects and are given for study within the individual's own country, in another Asian country, or in America. Under the same conditions, travel grants may be awarded to enable Asians to accept scholarships and fellowships in other countries. Research grants may also be awarded to qualified Asian scholars to study in their native countries.

Further information from:
Asia Foundation
550 Kearny Street
San Francisco, California 94119
U.S.A.

[250]

ASIAN CULTURAL COUNCIL *(U.S.A.)*

Fellowship Grants Program

Purpose: To provide training or experience which will be of value to the recipients in fulfilling professional responsibilities in their home countries, and to promote direct contact between Asians and Americans in order for each to gain a fuller appreciation of the other's traditions, values, and beliefs.

Subjects: Asian culture in the United States and American culture in Asia. Fields of award include archaeology, architecture, art history, crafts, dance, design, film, museology, music, painting, photography, sculpture and theater; research, graduate study; specialized training; professional observation tours; creative activities. Artists seeking aid for personal exhibitions or performances, and students enrolled in undergraduate degree programs cannot be considered.

Value: Varies according to type and duration of project.

Tenable for the duration of the project in the United States for Asian candidates and in Asia (eastward from Afghanistan through Japan) for United States candidates.

Eligibility: Open to suitably qualified Asians and Americans engaged in cultural/artistic studies or activities who will return to their countries of origin at the conclusion of the Fellowship period.

Note: Interested individuals and institutions should send a brief project description to the Council. If the proposal falls within the Council's guidelines, application forms will be forwarded to individual candidates or more detailed information will be requested from institutional applicants.

Closing date: Completed applications should be submitted at least six months prior to planned commencement of the project.

Further information from:
Asian Cultural Council
280 Madison Avenue
New York, New York 10016
U.S.A.

[251]

ASIAN INSTITUTE OF TECHNOLOGY *(Bangkok)*

Scholarships

Subjects: Engineering: agricultural, environmental, structural, transportation, geotechnical, industrial, water resources, human settlements development: Computer applications technology, energy technology, study toward graduate diploma, or master's or doctoral degree.

No. offered: Approximately 350 Scholarships are available from various sources.

Value: US$750 per month to cover tuition and fee costs, travel and maintenance expenses.

Tenable at the Institute for eight months (for

graduate diploma), for 20 months (for master's degree), or for 24 months (for doctoral degree).

Eligibility: Open to nationals of all Asian countries. Candidates studying for the graduate diploma or master's degree must have a good bachelor's degree; candidates for the doctoral degree must have a master's degree. Instruction is in English.

Closing dates: 15th January, 15th May, and 15th September.

Further information from:
Administrative Officer (Admissions)
Asian Institute of Technology
P.O. Box 2754
Bangkok
Thailand

[252]

ASPEN INSTITUTE FOR HUMANISTIC STUDIES

Marconi International Fellowship

Purpose: To recognize achievement in the fields of communications science and technology for the betterment of mankind, and to commission a work in the recipient's field, of his own choosing; to be completed within a two year period.

Subjects: Communications science and technology.

Value: US$35,000, to be paid as determined by the Fellow.

Eligibility: Open to persons who have made outstanding contributions in the above mentioned fields, irrespective of age, nationality or other restrictions. Nominations are welcome from colleges, universities, learned societies and academies of all countries, as well as from individuals in science, industry and public life.

Further information from:
Marconi International Fellowship Council
Aspen Institute for Humanistic Studies
Academy Conservatory
970 Aurora, Campus Box 64
Boulder, Colorado 80309
U.S.A.

[253]

ASSISTANT MASTERS AND MISTRESSES ASSOCIATION *(U.K.)*

Walter Hines Page Scholarships

Two Scholarships in the amount of £450 each, plus full hospitality, are offered annually to British teachers who wish to visit the United States. Scholarships are tenable for four weeks. These awards are given in conjunction with the English-Speaking Union of the Commonwealth.

Closing date: 30th November.

Further information from:
Assistant Masters and Mistresses
   Association
29 Gordon Square
London
England WC1H OPX

[254]

ASSOCIATED BOARD OF THE ROYAL SCHOOLS OF MUSIC *(U.K.)*

Music Scholarships

No. offered: Seven or eight Scholarships annually.

Value: £12,500 per annum, which includes tuition fees and a £700 grant for living expenses and a contribution towards travel from the United Kingdom to the home country upon completion of studies.

Tenable at one of the four Royal Schools of Music in the United Kingdom for three years.

Eligibility: Open to students, preferably between the ages of 16 and 22, from Bermuda, Cyprus, Ghana, Gibraltar, Guyana, Hong Kong, India, Indonesia, Kenya, Malaysia, Malta, Mauritius, New Zealand, Singapore, South Africa, Sri Lanka, West Indies, Zambia, Zimbabwe, and other African countries. Candidates must have a good standard of general education and must have qualified by passing, with distinction, Grade VIII in a practical examination of the Board's, or the L.R.S.M. Diploma, plus one other practical examination of the Board's above Grade V.

Note: Candidates should apply to the Board's

resident secretary in their own country, or to:
Associated Board of the Royal Schools
of Music
14 Bedford Square
London
England WC1B 3JG

[255]

ASSOCIATION OF AFRICAN UNIVERSITIES

AAU Graduate Scholarships

Purpose: To contribute to the pool of university trained manpower in the fields of study improvement for the development of African countries, and to promote contact and co-operation between African Universities.

Subjects: Agriculture, forestry, biological and physical sciences, medicine, veterinary medicine, pharmacy, engineering, computer science, management/business administration, and journalism.

No. offered: 10 Scholarships annually.

Value: Variable, depending on the nature of Scholarship and the university at which study is taken.

Tenable at an African University for one year; renewable once.

Eligibility: Open to staff of member universities possessing at least a very good first degree.

Note: Candidates sould be nominated by the vice-chancellors of their universities.

Further information from:
Association of African Universities
P.O. Box 5744
Accra-North
Ghana

[256]

ASSOCIATION OF AFRICAN UNIVERSITIES

Staff Exchange Programme

Purpose: To enable university staff to visit selected universities in Africa in order to exchange ideas with their counterparts in those universities.

No. offered: Varies annually according to availability of funds.

Value: Covers travel and subsistence allowance and does not extend over 14 days. The per diem offered varies from country to country.

Tenable at any African member university.

Eligibility: Applicants should be members of an African university staff.

Note: Candidates are required to choose the universities (universities in Africa only) they wish to visit. Applications, enclosing the approval of their vice-chancellors, should be addressed to the Secretary General of the Association.

Further information from:
Association of African Universities
P.O. Box 5744
Accra-North
Ghana

[257]

ASSOCIATION OF AFRICAN UNIVERSITIES

Language Training Program

In order to break down the barrier of communication between linguistic groups in Africa and to promote cooperation among African Universities, the Association organizes from time to time an intensive Language Training Program (French, English and Arabic) for both staff and students of member universities who possess a working knowledge of either of the languages. Applications for awards under this programme are sent direct to the Association. One francophone and one anglophone university host and train the students. Travel costs and per diem allowances are paid by the Association.

Further information from:
Association of African Universities
P.O. Box 5744
Accra-North
Ghana

[258]

ASSOCIATION OF AMERICAN GEOGRAPHERS

AAG Research Grants and Funds

Wallace W. Atwood Research Fund is intended to encourage field studies in physical geography.

L.P. Denoyer/O.E. Geppert Fund is intended to support geographic research and cartographic development.

Gibson Fund offers annual Grants of approximately US$500 for support of research on the agricultural geography of an area within the United States, preferably the South. Graduate students are ordinarily ineligible.

Warren Nystrom Fund offers awards to young geographers for papers presented at the annual meeting of the Association. Applicants should have received their doctorate within the last two years, and the paper submitted should be based on their dissertation.

Note: The Association also offers the *Robert H. Hodgson Ph.D. Dissertation Research Grant* which is awarded to AAG members only.
  Guidelines for individuals wishing to apply for research grants are printed in the *AAG Newsletter*.

Further information from:
  Patricia J. McWethy, Executive Director
  Association of American Geographers
  1710 Sixteenth Street, N.W.
  Washington, D.C. 20009
  U.S.A.

[259]

ASSOCIATION OF ANAESTHETISTS OF GREAT BRITAIN AND IRELAND

Research Grants, Travel Grants

Subject: Research or education in anaesthesia or related fields.

No. offered: Varies according to funds available.

Value: Research Grants to a maximum of £5,000 each; Travel Grants to a maximum of approximately £250 each.

Tenable anywhere in the world for an unspecified duration.

Eligibility: Open to members in any category of the Association.

Note: Travel Grants are not awarded for attendance at a meeting of a learned society, but may be considered for extensions of such a journey. They may be given for study or for assistance in undertaking an approved teaching tour.

Further information from:
  Honorary Secretary
  Association of Anaesthetists of Great
    Britain and Ireland
  Room 475/478, Tavistock House South
  Tavistock Square
  London
  England WC1H 9LG

[260]

ASSOCIATION OF COMMONWEALTH UNIVERSITIES

Administrative Travelling Fellowships

Purpose: To enable Commonwealth university administrative staff to visit a university or universities in other Commonwealth countries to study aspects of university administration of relevance to the Fellow and his university.

No. offered: Fourteen to twenty Fellowships annually; normally at least one to each region of the Commonwealth.

Value: Varies according to the project; not more than three will be offered on a scale intended to provide complete support, both travel and subsistence. The value of these will rarely exceed £1,750.

Tenable in Commonwealth country/countries for one to three months.

Eligibility: Open to administrative or executive officers of Commonwealth universities in grades equivalent to lecturer or above. Candidates must have held permanent full-time administrative posts for five years.

Note: Applications should be made through the employing authorities of candidates' universities. Recipients must submit a report on their Fellowship to the Association after their return.

The Association also offers assistance to academic and administrative staff through the *Third World Academic Exchange Scheme*, and the *Times Higher Education Supplement Third World Academic Exchange Scheme*.

Further information from:
Secretary General
Association of Commonwealth
  Universities
36 Gordon Square
London
England WC1H OPF

[261]

ASSOCIATION FOR COMPUTING MACHINERY *(New York City)*

Awards

Eckert-Mauchly Award of US$1,000 and a certificate is given for technical contributions to hardware/software design and the analysis of computing and of digital systems.

Grace Murray Hopper Award of US$1,000 and a certificate is presented annually to an outstanding young computer professional on the basis of a single recent major technical or service contribution which is clearly outstanding in its own right. Candidates should be less than 30 years of age at the time the contribution was made.

Programming Systems and Languages Paper Award of US$500 and a certificate is presented annually for the best paper submitted in this area.

A.M. Turing Award of US$2,000, a gift of appreciation and a certificate is presented annually for a contribution of a technical nature to the computer community. The recipient will present a lecture at the Association's annual meeting, at which time the Award will be made. The lecture will subsequently be published in one of the Association periodicals.

Further information from:
Nina Toberoff
Association for Computing Machinery
11 West 42nd Street
New York, New York 10036
U.S.A.

[262]

ASSOCIATION OF ENGINEERS AND ARCHITECTS IN ISRAEL

Arnan Price Award of an unspecified monetary value is given for an original book or research in some aspects of architecture or engineering which has been published within the previous two years.

Zeev Rechter Award of approximately US$300 is given every two years to encourage the advancement of architecture in Israel and to bring architectural achievements to public awareness. The Award is made for a completed building which has been erected within the ten year period preceding the presentation of the Award. Any person or institution may propose a candidate, who may be anyone worthy of the Award, regardless of nationality.

Further information from:
Association of Engineers and Architects
  in Israel
200 Dizengoff Street
Tel Aviv
Israel

[263]

ASSOCIATION OF ENVIRONMENTAL ENGINEERING PROFESSORS *(U.S.A.)*

Awards

Engineering-Science, Inc./AEEP Award: One Award of US$2,000, to be divided equally between student and professor, is given annually for the best doctoral thesis contributing to the advancement of environmental engineering and science. Applicants should submit their theses to *Engineering-Science, Inc., 150 North Santa Anna Avenue, Arcadia, California 91006* no later than 30th June. Further information may be obtained by writing to the Association at the address below.

Nalco/AEEP Awards: Two Awards in chemical research, one in water and wastewater treatment, and the other in industrial and combined waste treatment, are given annually for the best doctoral thesis submitted in each of the two areas. Each Award carries a value of US$2,500, divided equally between student and professor. Applicants should submit their theses to the Association at the address below no later than 1st March (for water and wastewater treatment) and 30th June (for industrial and combined waste treatment).

Further information from:
John T. Novack, Awards Committee
Association of Environmental Engineering
Virginia Polytechnic Institute and State University
Blacksburg, Virginia 24061
U.S.A.

[264]

ASSOCIATION OF OFFICIAL ANALYTICAL CHEMISTS *(U.S.A.)*

Harvey W. Wiley Award

Purpose: To recognize a scientist, or group of scientists, who have made outstanding contributions to the development and establishment of methods of analysis of those materials for which provision is made in the Association's *Official Methods of Analysis.*

Subjects: Foods, vitamins, food additives, color additives, pesticides, drugs, cosmetics, plants, feeds, fertilizers, and contaminants of food, water, air, or soil.

No. offered: One Award annually.

Value: US$750, plus a plaque and expenses incident to attending the meeting at which the Award will be presented.

Tenable for one year.

Eligibility: Nominees should be scientists who, except in unusual cases, are residents of North America.

Note: Any interested person may submit one nomination for the Award on forms available from the address below. Nominations should include age, list of publications, work on which the nomination is based, and an appraisal of the nominee's accomplishments, particularly the work to be recognized by the proposed Award.

Closing date: 1st April.

Further information from:
A.O.A.C.
1111 North 19th Street, Suite 210
Arlington, Virginia 22209
U.S.A.

[265]

ASSOCIATION FOR RETARDED CITIZENS *(U.S.A.)*

Rosemary F. Dybwad International Awards

Purpose: To encourage an exchange of information and ideas among voluntary associations for the mentally retarded throughout the world.

Value: Up to US$2,000.

Tenable for one year; not renewable.

Eligibility: Open to professionals or volunteers actively engaged in the field of mental retardation who (a) would travel to other countries to study in depth a particular aspect of mental retardation, or (b) would attend conferences concerned with the retarded, to which they could bring information and knowledge about developments affecting the retarded in their own countries.

Closing date: 1st November; announcement of award winners is normally made about 15th February.

Further information from:
International Relations Resource Panel
Association for Retarded Citizens
National Headquarters
2501 Avenue "J"
Arlington, Texas 76011
U.S.A.

[266]

ASSOCIATION OF RHODES SCHOLARS IN AUSTRALIA

Postgraduate Scholarship

Purpose: To enable an overseas Commonwealth student to undertake postgraduate study at an Australian university.

Subjects: Unrestricted.

No. offered: One Scholarship awarded periodically, depending on available funds.

Value: A$4,200 per annum, plus compulsory university fees and an approved return economy air fare. A contribution is also paid towards travelling expenses to enable the Scholar to visit other Australian universities besides that at which he or she is based.

Tenable at an Australian university for one or two years; renewable for a further period depending on the study undertaken.

Eligibility: Open to graduates of a Commonwealth university approved by the Committee administering the Scholarship.

Further information from:
 Secretary, Research and Graduate Studies
 University of Melbourne
 Melbourne
 Australia

[267]

ASSOCIATION OF SOUTHEAST ASIAN INSTITUTIONS OF HIGHER LEARNING

ASAIHL Academic Exchange Scheme

Purpose: To encourage an interchange of distinguished scholars for longer periods of time than allowed under the Fellowship scheme.

Subject: Unrestricted.

Value: An amount to cover air fare for the scholar (and wife, if the visit exceeds six months), and an allowance of US$200 per month; the receiving institution will provide accommodation, local transportation and medical care; the recipient's own institution will continue regular salary and where the receiving university operates a higher salary schedule, it will pay the difference.

Tenable for a minimum of one term or semester at a member university other than the scholar's own.

Eligibility: Open to distinguished scholars from member universities.

Note: ASAIHL provides a clearing house service supplying lists of persons available for study visits; arrangements are made on a bilateral basis. Member institutions are found in the following countries: Hong Kong, Indonesia, Malaysia, Philippines, Singapore, Thailand and Vietnam.

Not confirmed for 1983.

Further information from:
 Executive Secretary, ASAIHL
 Ratasastra Building
 Chulalongkorn University
 Henri Dunant Road
 Bangkok 5
 Thailand

[268]

ASSOCIATION OF SOUTHEAST ASIAN INSTITUTIONS OF HIGHER LEARNING

ASAIHL Fellowships

Purpose: To enable distinguished scholars, not necessarily professors, to undertake lecture tours and short visits to other member universities.

Subject: Unrestricted.

Value: Travel expenses plus a US$12 per diem allowance; accommodation and local transportation and medical care are provided by the receiving universities; the recipient's own university will continue regular salary.

Tenable for periods from two to six weeks at each of at least two member universities in a country other than the Fellow's own.

Eligibility: Open to senior staff members of member universities (see Note, preceding entry).

Not confirmed for 1983.

Further information from:
 Executive Secretary, ASAIHL
 Ratasastra Building
 Chulalongkorn University
 Henri Dunant Road
 Bangkok 5
 Thailand

[269]

ASSOCIATION OF UNIVERSITIES AND COLLEGES OF CANADA

CADESS Trust Fund Grants

Purpose: To encourage exchange between university adult educators in Canada and other countries. Programmes are organized in association with CADESS (Canadian Association of Departments of Extension and Summer Schools).

Value: Limited travel and assistance to enable adult educators to extend their stay in the country being visited. Applicants should have the means to visit the country of their choice as the Fund cannot provide travel fare to the country.

Eligibility: Open to Canadian adult educators who wish to broaden their observations and study while visiting abroad and to adult educators from developing countries who wish to extend their knowledge of university adult education in Canada.

Note: Applicants must complete an application form giving their curriculum vitae, the amount of financial aid needed and the purpose for which the money is required.

Further information from:
 Director of Awards
 CADESS Trust Fund Grants
 Association of Universities and Colleges
  of Canada
 151 Slater Street
 Ottawa, Ontario
 Canada K1P 5N1

[270]

ASSOCIATION OF UNIVERSITIES AND COLLEGES OF CANADA

Department of National Defence Scholarship and Fellowship Program

Subjects: A wide range of disciplines having bearing on military and strategic studies of interest to Canada, including work on the national and international aspects of security, studies of strategic theory, alliances and United Nations, and civil-military relations.

No. offered: Varies annually.

Value: Scholarships—*Can*$8,000; Fellowships—*Can*$16,000 per annum. These sums are intended to cover tuition fees and all other expenses related to the award.

Tenable usually in Canada, and occasionally elsewhere, for one year; renewable for an additional year at the M.A. level, and for two additional years at the doctoral level.

Eligibility: Scholarships are open to Canadian citizens who hold an honours B.A. degree or its equivalent. Fellowships are open to Canadian citizens who before taking up the award, hold a doctoral degree or equivalent qualification.

Note: Award recipients may not concurrently hold any other awards whose cumulative value exceeds two-thirds of the value of the Scholarship or Fellowship accepted under this program.
 Upon completion of award, a thesis or detailed account of the research done should be submitted to the Awards Officer.

Closing date: 1st February.

Further information from:
 Awards Officer
 Canadian Awards Section
 Department of National Defence
 Scholarship and Fellowship Program
 Association of Universities and Colleges
  of Canada
 151 Slater Street
 Ottawa, Ontario
 Canada K1P 5N1

[271]

ASSOCIATION OF UNIVERSITIES AND COLLEGES OF CANADA

Department of National Defence Postdoctoral Fellowships in Military History

Subjects: History, with special relevance to the Canadian Armed Forces. Studies may relate to any aspect of military history or related fields, including operations, policy, technology, and the economic and social dimensions of armed forces national security.

No. offered: One or two Fellowships annually.

Value: Can$10,500 plus research expenses up to *Can*$1,500.

Tenable in Canada for one year. Permission may be granted to undertake research outside Canada.

Eligibility: Applicants must be Canadian citizens who hold or will hold, prior to closing date of competition, a Ph.D. degree or equivalent level of knowledge or experience in the field considered adequate by the Selection Committee.

Note: Fellows may not hold concurrently any other major award.

Upon completion of the Fellowship, a manuscript resulting from research done should be submitted to the Awards Officer. 10% of the total Award will be withheld until receipt of these results.

Closing date: 1st February.

Further information from:
Awards Officer
Canadian Awards Division
Association of Universities and Colleges
  of Canada
151 Slater Street
Ottawa, Ontario
Canada K1P 5N1

[272]

ASSOCIATION OF UNIVERSITIES AND COLLEGES OF CANADA

Emergency Planning Canada Research Fellowship

Subjects: Human behavior under stress, focusing on reactions of groups and organizations in natural, technological, industrial and other disasters, and the delivery of emergency services to victims in the community-wide emergencies.

No. offered: One Fellowship annually.

Value: Can$7,000 per annum if held in Canada, or US$6,000 per annum if held in the United States; plus tuition and compulsory fees, plus Can$2,000 for a married fellow when accompanied by a spouse.

Tenable at the Institute of Environmental Studies, University of Toronto, and at the Disaster Research Center, Ohio University, Columbus, for up to four years, depending on the length of time required to complete the graduate degree for which the award is made.

Eligibility: Open to Canadian citizens. Preference is given to students who hold a master's degree in sociology, geography, political science, or urban or regional planning. However, candidates with a first degree major in one of the above mentioned fields, will also be considered. Acceptance into a doctoral program is normally, but not essentially, a prerequisite.

Closing date: 1st February.

Further information from:
Awards Officer
Canadian Awards Division
Association of Universities and Colleges
  of Canada
151 Slater Street
Ottawa, Canada
Canada K1P 5N1

[273]

ASSOCIATION OF UNIVERSITIES AND COLLEGES OF CANADA

Gulf Canada Limited Graduate Fellowships

Subjects: Business and management studies, computer sciences, mathematics, geology, geophysics, engineering, physics, chemistry, ecologically-oriented studies and other sciences directly related to the petroleum industry.

No. offered: Ten Fellowships annually.

Value: Can$9,000 per annum: Can$8,000 to successful candidate and Can$1,000 to the relevant department of the receiving university in which the Fellow is registered.

Tenable at any university or college which is a member, or affiliated to a member, of AUCC, for one academic year. Fellows may, on the recommendation of their supervisors, reapply in the competition the following year.

Eligibility: Open to Canadian citizens and persons who have held landed immigrant status for one year prior to submitting application. Applicants must be graduates of a Canadian university or college which is a member, or affiliated to a member, of AUCC.

Note: Fellows may not concurrently hold any other award in excess of a total value of Can$3,000, nor may they undertake paid employment at any university unless approval is given by the supervisor of studies and does not exceed four hours a week including preparation time.

Upon completion of the Fellowship, a thesis or detailed account of work done should be forwarded to the Awards Officer.

Closing date: 1st February.

Further information from:
Awards Officer
Canadian Awards Division
Gulf Canada Limited Graduate
  Fellowships
Association of Universities and Colleges
  of Canada
151 Slater Street
Ottawa, Ontario
Canada K1P 5N1

Closing date: 1st December.

Further information from:
Awards Officer
Canadian Awards Section
Frank Knox Memorial Fellowships
Association of Universities and Colleges
  of Canada
151 Slater Street
Ottawa, Ontario
Canada K1P 5N1

[274]

ASSOCIATION OF UNIVERSITIES AND COLLEGES OF CANADA

Frank Knox Memorial Fellowships—Harvard University

Subjects: Arts and sciences (including engineering), business administration, dental medicine, design, divinity, education, law, medicine, public administration, and public health.

No. offered: Two Fellowships annually.

Value: Can$5,000, tuition, and student health insurance.

Tenable at Harvard University, Cambridge, Massachusetts, for one academic year; renewable for a maximum of two years in order to complete a degree programme of more than one year's duration.

Eligibility: Open to Canadian citizens who have graduated or are about to graduate from a university or college in Canada which is a member, or affiliated to a member, of the AUCC. No application is considered from a student already in the United States. Acceptance by a school is a prior condition to the award of a Fellowship.

Note: Each candidate must apply directly to the graduate school of his choice at the earliest possible date.
  Candidates applying to the School of Business Administration are required to take the Admissions Test for Graduate Study in Business in October or January. This is arranged by contacting *Educational Testing Service, Box 966, Princeton, New Jersey 08540.* Normally two months notice should be given to ETS.

[275]

ASSOCIATION OF UNIVERSITIES AND COLLEGES OF CANADA

Lever Brothers Limited Bilingual Exchange Fellowship in Business Administration

Subject: Business administration leading to an M.B.A. or M.Sc. degree.

No. offered: One or two Fellowships annually.

Value: Can$10,000 paid over a period of two years, plus summer employment.

Tenable for two years at any Canadian university which is a member or affiliated to a member of the AUCC. French language winners will be required to attend a Canadian English-language institute and English language winners will attend a Canadian French-language institute.

Eligibility: Candidates must be Canadian citizens. Preference will be given to those under 30 years of age who have clearly demonstrated a proficiency in the language of the institution they wish to attend.
  Preference is shown to candidates entering their first year of the master degree program, however consideration is given to those having completed one year of the program in the second language.

Note: Employment for one summer is guaranteed, and will normally be taken between the first and second year of tenure.

Closing date: 1st February.

Further information from:
  Awards Officer
  Canadian Awards Division
  Association of Universities and Colleges
   of Canada
  151 Slater Street
  Ottawa, Ontario
  Canada K1P 5N1

[276]

ASSOCIATION OF UNIVERSITIES AND COLLEGES OF CANADA

Nuffield Travel Grants

Travel Grants for Teachers in Canadian Community Colleges

Information concerning these awards is given under the Nuffield Foundation [q.v.].

[277]

ASSOCIATION OF UNIVERSITIES AND COLLEGES OF CANADA

Teleglobe Canada Fellowship

Subjects: Engineering, chemistry, computer science, social sciences, law, administration, etc.—related to international telecommunications.

No. offered: One Fellowship annually. The Fellow may re-apply in the competition the following year.

Value: Can$7,500: Can$6,500 to the Fellow and Can$1,000 to the department of the university in which the Fellow is registered.

Tenable at any Canadian university or college which is a member, or affiliated to a member, of the AUCC.

Eligibility: Open to candidates who are Canadian citizens or have held landed immigrant status for one year prior to submitting application and are graduates of a Canadian university or college which is a member, or affiliated to a member, of the AUCC.

Note: The Fellowship will only be awarded to a candidate whose field of study is directly related to international telecommunications.
Upon completion of the Fellowship, a thesis or reasonably detailed account of work done should be sent to the Awards Officer.
The Fellow may not hold concurrently any other awards in excess of a total value of Can$3,500.

Closing date: 1st February.

Further information from:
  Awards Officer
  Canadian Awards Division
  Association of Universities and Colleges
   of Canada
  151 Slater Street
  Ottawa, Ontario
  Canada K1P 5N1

[278]

ASSOCIATION OF UNIVERSITIES AND COLLEGES OF CANADA

Belgian Government Fellowships

Subjects: Study and research in the fine arts including music and architecture, art education, mathematics, chemistry, biology, zoology, botany, geology, physical geography, applied sciences, medicine, veterinary medicine, pharmacy, agronomy, social sciences including political science and economics, law, philology, history, philosophy, psychology, teaching.

No. offered: Five Scholarships annually.

Value: Study awards—14,000 Belgian francs to 17,000 Belgian francs monthly; Research awards—17,000 Belgian francs monthly. In addition, all Fellows receive return economy air fare; reimbursement of course and examination fees; up to 6,000 Belgian francs reimbursement for books and materials; support toward cost of printing a thesis; accident and health insurance for the Fellow and his or her family.

Tenable at certain universities and institutions in Belgium for one academic year, renewable (for study awards); for one to six months (for research awards).

Eligibility: Open to Canadian citizens who are graduates of a Canadian university or college which is a member or affiliated to a member of the AUCC. Candidates must have a good knowledge of French or Dutch for specialized work and either of these or English for other work. There is no age restriction for research awards; applicants for study awards must be under 35 years of age by 20th April in the year of application.

Note: Applicants in fine arts, music and architecture are required to submit certain materials. Addition information is available from the address below.

Closing date: 31st October.

Further information from:
Director, International Programs
Association of Universities and Colleges
  of Canada
151 Slater Street
Ottawa, Ontario
Canada K1P 5N1

[279]

ASSOCIATION OF UNIVERSITIES AND COLLEGES OF CANADA

Canada-People's Republic of China Exchange Scholarships

Subjects: Studies in Chinese language, literature, history, as well as philosophy, political economy, archaeology, music, art, art history, architecture, pharmacology, Chinese pharmacology, Chinese pharmacology, medicine and Chinese medicine.

No. offered: Approximately seven or eight Scholarships annually.

Value: Tuition, accommodation, medical and internal travel expenses are provided by the Chinese authorities; a supplemental allowance of *Can*$100 per month and return economy air fare to the People's Republic of China are provided by the Canadian Department of External Affairs.

Tenable in the People's Republic of China for one academic year; renewable for a further year.

Eligibility: Open to Canadian citizens with a first degree from a university recognized by the AUCC. Preference will be given to candidates under age 35. Applicants for studies in medicine are expected to have completed a major portion of their medical studies before arriving in China.

Note: These Awards are not normally intended for research purposes; however, if applications for research are received from eligible candidates who already have an M.A. degree and are working towards a Ph.D. degree, they will be considered.

Married Scholars are not permitted to be accompanied by their spouses.

Closing date: 31st October.

Further information from:
Director, International Programs
Association of Universities and Colleges
  of Canada
151 Slater Street
Ottawa, Ontario
Canada K1P 5N1

[280]

ASSOCIATION OF UNIVERSITIES AND COLLEGES OF CANADA

Danish Government Scholarships

Subjects: Postgraduate studies and research in all subjects.

No. offered: One Scholarship annually.

Value: Approximately 2,470 Danish kroners per month for postgraduate studies and approximately 2,850 Danish kroners per month for research. In addition Scholars receive tuition costs. The Canadian government provides return economy air fare for the Scholar.

Tenable in Denmark for eight months.

Eligibility: Open to Canadian citizens who have obtained the equivalent of a first degree from a Canadian university as of the effective date of the Scholarship. Research Scholarship candidates must hold at least a master's degree. Preference is given to applicants who are under 35 years of age.

Note: As lectures are conducted in Danish, some knowledge of the language desirable. Language courses are available to Scholars during the period of the award at the Scholars own expense.
Candidates for awards in the fine arts must submit samples of original work.
Scholarships may not be held concurrently with other awards.

Closing date: 31st October.

Further information from:
Director, International Programs
Association of Universities and Colleges
of Canada
151 Slater Street
Ottawa, Ontario
Canada K1P 5N1

[281]

ASSOCIATION OF UNIVERSITIES AND COLLEGES OF CANADA

Government of Finland Scholarships

Subjects: Unrestricted.

No. offered: Three Scholarships annually.

Value: 1,100 to 1,200 Finnish marks per month, plus free accommodation, tuition and travel expenses connected to the study program. In addition, the Canadian government will pay return economy air fare to Finland.

Tenable at any Finnish university up to nine months with the possibility of renewal.

Eligibility: Open to Canadian citizens under 35 years old with a first degree from a Canadian university. Applicants who have followed a professional career for several years after the termination of their studies will not be considered. Candidates must have a working knowledge of English, German, Finnish or Swedish.

Note: Scholars must submit a report on their studies to the Finnish Ministry of Education at the conclusion of the scholarship period.
Other awards may not be held concurrently.

Closing date: 31st October.

Further information from:
Director, International Programs
Association of Universities and Colleges
of Canada
151 Slater Street
Ottawa, Ontario
Canada K1P 5N1

[282]

ASSOCIATION OF UNIVERSITIES AND COLLEGES OF CANADA

France-Canada Cultural Agreement University Scholarships

Subjects: All cultural and scientific disciplines.

No. offered: Varies annually.

Value: FF 1,700 per month, plus round-trip travel expenses, university registration fees, medical and hospital coverage, access to university facilities. Various allowances for housing, travel, thesis costs, etc. may also be given if required.

Tenable in France; for nine months for a master's degree, and for up to thirty-three months for a doctoral degree.

Eligibility: Open to Canadian citizens who hold an honours degree, have a sound knowledge of the French language, and are not more than thirty-five years of age by 1st October of the year preceding the award.

Note: Scholarships cover only a partial contribution toward payment of the awardess maintenance costs, and are strictly for the use of the Scholar. Other awards or remuneration may not be held concurrently with ths Scholarship.
Where appropriate, a special supplementary scholarship in language training may be granted for a period of two to three months. This must be specifically applied for.

Closing date: 31st October.

Further information from:
Director, International Programs
Association of Universities and Colleges
of Canada
151 Slater Street
Ottawa, Ontario
Canada K1P 5N1

[283]

ASSOCIATION OF UNIVERSITIES AND COLLEGES OF CANADA

German Academic Exchange Service Fellowships

Subjects: Unrestricted, except for pharmacy,

medicine, and dentistry.

No. offered: Seventeen Fellowships annually.

Value: DM870 to DM1,300 per month, depending upon candidate's level of previous training; return fare; baggage allowance; tuition; course fees; university and examination fees; social fees; a book allowance of DM100 per semester; and an additional expenses allowance at the beginning of the Fellowship of DM200. A separate allowance of DM300 per month will be awarded to married Fellows accompanied by their spouse.

Tenable for ten months at certain universities, institutions and academies of art and music in West Germany.

Eligibility: Open to Canadian citizens who have at least a Canadian bachelor's degree and are not more than 32 years of age by 1st October of the year the Fellowship becomes effective. Applicants must also be able to provide a Germany language proficiency certificate from a recognized teacher of the German language.

Note: Candidates may not hold any other awards concurrently with the Fellowship.
[Also see entry for *German Academic Exchange Service (DAAD)*].

Closing date: 31st October.

Further information from:
Director, International Programs
Association of Universities and Colleges
  of Canada
151 Slater Street
Ottawa, Ontario
Canada K1P 5N1

[284]

ASSOCIATION OF UNIVERSITIES AND COLLEGES OF CANADA

Canada-Hungary Exchange Scholarships

Subjects: Postgraduate studies or research in all subjects.

No. offered: Two Scholarships annually.

Value: 3,500 forints per month for postgraduate studies and 5,000 forints per month for research. In addition all Scholars will receive from the Canadian government return economy air fare and two-thirds cost of that transportation for the Scholar's spouse, provided the spouse remains in Hungary for at least six months.

Tenable in Hungary for ten to twelve months, beginning in September. Postgraduate studies candidates only may be eligible for renewal of the Scholarship.

Eligibility: Open to Canadian citizens who have obtained at least the equivalent of a first Canadian university degree as of the effective date of the Scholarship. Preference is given to candidates who are under 35 years of age.

Note: Knowledge of the Hungarian language is only essential for specific fields of study, such as Hungarian literature or linguistics.
Scholarships may not be held concurrently with other awards.

Closing date: 31st October.

Further information from:
Director, International Programs
Association of Universities and Colleges
  of Canada
151 Slater Street
Ottawa, Ontario
Canada K1P 5N1

[285]

ASSOCIATION OF UNIVERSITIES AND COLLEGES OF CANADA

Mexican Government Scholarships

Subjects: All areas, except medicine.

No. offered: Five Scholarships annually.

Value: 8,000 pesos per month living expenses, book allowance of 2,500 pesos, pesos for thesis expenses, and 2,000 pesos for travel in investigation and working programs. In addition, the Scholarship covers free tuition. The Mexican Government pays the recipient's round-trip ticket and the Mexican Ministry of Education covers medical and pharmaceutical expenses, plus life and accident insurance.
The value of the award is sufficient to meet the needs of one person only.

Tenable in Mexico for one academic year.

Eligibility: Open to Canadian citizens with a first degree from a Canadian university. Applicants who are either over 35 years of age or who have followed a professional career for several years after finishing their studies are not eligible. Candidates must have a good knowledge of Spanish.

Note: Candidates may not hold concurrently any other awards.

Closing date: 31st October.

Further information from:
   Director, International Programs
   Association of Universities and Colleges
      of Canada
   151 Slater Street
   Ottawa, Ontario
   Canada K1P 5N1

[286]

ASSOCIATION OF UNIVERSITIES AND COLLEGES OF CANADA

Netherlands Government Scholarships

Subjects: Unrestricted.

No. offered: Seven Scholarships annually.

Value: 1,000 Dutch guilders per month; 300 Dutch guilders book allowance; 300 Dutch guilders relocation costs; one-way economy air fare from the Netherlands to Canada, to be paid upon completion of the Scholarship; emergency medical treatment while in the Netherlands. Scholars enrolled in a regular program of a university or institute at university level will receive free tuition; those enrolled in international courses may, in exceptional circumstances, receive a partial or total tuition waver.

Tenable in the Netherlands for ten months.

Eligibility: Open to Canadian citizens who hold a bachelor's degree or its equivalent, and are not more than thirty-five years of age.

Note: Awards are granted subject to the candidate's acceptance by a university or a qualified tutor.
   It is recommended that applicants have some knowledge of the Dutch language. International courses are given in English or French.
   Accommodation is not provided.

Further information may be obtained from the address below, or by writing to the *Royal Netherlands Embassy, 275 Slater Street, Ottawa, Ontario K1P 5N1.*

Closing date: 31st October.

Further information from:
   Director, International Programs
   Association of Universities and Colleges
      of Canada
   151 Slater Street
   Ottawa, Ontario
   Canada K1P 5N1

[287]

ASSOCIATION OF UNIVERSITIES AND COLLEGES OF CANADA

Netherlands Government Fellowships

Subjects: Fine arts and music.

No. offered: Two Fellowships annually.

Value: 1,200 Dutch guilders per month; tuition if enrolled in a regular program of study at art academies or conservatories of music; 300 Dutch guilders for relocation costs; 300 Dutch guilders book and study material allowance; medical coverage; one way economy air fare from the Netherlands to Canada, to be paid after completion of the course; travel expenses in Canada.

Tenable in the Netherlands for ten months.

Eligibility: Open to Canadian citizens. Artists and musicians should have passed passed final examinations at art schools or conservatories of music, and have had a few years experience in their profession.

Note: Fellowships are granted subject to the candidate's acceptance by an appropriate institution in the Netherlands or by a qualified tutor.
   No additional allowances are given for married students.
   The Netherlands Ministry of Culture will aid in finding suitable accommodation for candidates.
   Upon completion of the Fellowship, a written report on the studies undertaken should be submitted to the Ministry of Culture, Recreation and Social Work through the Netherlands Embassy in Ottawa.

Additional information on study programs may be obtained from the address below, or by writing to the *Royal Netherlands Embassy, 275 Slater Street, Ottawa, Ontario K1P 5H9*.

Closing date: 31st October.

Further information from:
Director, International Programs
Association of Universities and Colleges
  of Canada
151 Slater Street
Ottawa, Ontario
Canada K1P 5N1

[288]

ASSOCIATION OF UNIVERSITIES AND COLLEGES OF CANADA

Norwegian Government Scholarships

Subjects: Unrestricted; special preference given to Norwegian related areas of study, such as Norwegian language, literature, history, law, folklore, natural history, geography and economics.

No. offered: Undetermined.

Value: 2,300 Norwegian kroner per month; relocation allowance of 500 Norwegian kroner; travel expenses in Norway related to study; tuition.

Tenable for nine months at the universities of Oslo, Bergen, Trondheim, Tromso, the Norwegian Institute of Technology, College of Art and Science of the University of Trondheim.

Eligibility: Open to Canadian citizens who have a first degree from a recognized university as of the effective date of the Scholarship. Candidates must have a good command of English or of a Scandinavian language. Preference is given to applicants who are no more than 35 years of age at the time of application.

Note: No provisions are made for support of the Scholar's family.

Closing date: 31st October.

Further information from:
Director, International Programs
Association of Universities and Colleges
  of Canada
151 Slater Street
Ottawa, Ontario
Canada K1P 5N1

[289]

ASSOCIATION OF UNIVERSITIES AND COLLEGES OF CANADA

Canada-Poland Exchange Scholarships

Subjects: Postgraduate studies or research in all subjects.

No. offered: Three Scholarships annually.

Value: 2,400 zlotys per month for postgraduate studies and 3,400 zlotys per month for research. In addition all Scholars will receive a housing allowance of up to a maximum of 2,000 zlotys per month, study or research-related travel within Poland, tuition, medical, dental and hospital services. The Canadian government will provide return economy air fare and two-thirds cost of that transportation for the Scholar's spouse, provided the spouse remains in Poland for at least six months.

Tenable in Poland for ten to twelve months, beginning in September; renewable through reapplication only.

Eligibility: Open to Canadian citizens who have obtained at least the equivalent of a first Canadian university degree as of the effective date of the Scholarship. Candidates for research Scholarships must hold a Ph.D. Preference is given to applicants under 35 years of age.

Note: Language courses are available in Poland for Scholars who require them.
  Scholarships may not be held concurrently with other awards.

Closing date: 31st October.

Further information from:
Director, International Programs
Association of Universities and Colleges
  of Canada
151 Slater Street
Ottawa, Ontario
Canada K1P 5N1

[290]

ASSOCIATION OF UNIVERSITIES AND COLLEGES OF CANADA

Portugese Government Fellowships and Scholarships

Subjects: Any field of the arts or Portugese culture (Fellowship); unrestricted (Scholarships).

No. offered: Three awards annually; One Fellowship and two Scholarships.

Value: 11,000 Portugese escudos per month.

Tenable in Portugal for three to six months (Fellowships) and for six to ten months (Scholarships).

Eligibility: Open to Canadian citizens who have obtained the equivalent of a first Canadian university degree as of the effective date of the award.

Closing date: 31st October.

Further information from:
Foreign Government Awards
Association of Universities and Colleges
 of Canada
151 Slater Street
Ottawa, Ontario
Canada K1P 5N1

[291]

ASSOCIATION OF UNIVERSITIES AND COLLEGES OF CANADA

Canada-Spain Exchange Scholarships

Subjects: Unrestricted.

No. offered: Two Scholarships annually.

Value: 25,000 pesetas upon arrival in Spain, plus a monthly allowance of 25,000 pesetas for the duration of the Scholarship. Scholars also receive free registration in Spanish official centres as well as medical insurance, excluding drugs.

Tenable in Spain for one academic year, beginning in October.

Eligibility: Open to Canadian citizens who have obtained the equivalent of a first Canadian university degree and are proficient in the Spanish language. Preference is given to applicants who are under 35 years of age.

Closing date: 31st October.

Further information from:
Director, International Programs
Association of Universities and Colleges
 of Canada
151 Slater Street
Ottawa, Ontario
Canada K1P 5N1

[292]

ASSOCIATION OF UNIVERSITIES AND COLLEGES OF CANADA

Swiss University Scholarships

Subjects: All subjects.

No. offered: Three Scholarships annually.

Value: 900 Swiss francs per month for first degree holders, and 1,100 Swiss francs per month for postgraduate degree holders; tuition fees; health and accident insurance; book allowance; and air fare from Switzerland to Canada at the conclusion of the Scholarship.

Tenable in Switzerland for nine months with the possibility of renewal for twelve months.

Eligibility: Open to Canadian citizens having at least a first degree from a recognized university as of the effective date of the Scholarship. Candidates should have a good knowledge of either French or German, depending upon the university they will be attending. Persons who have been engaged in a professional career for several years after completion of their studies, as well as those who are more than thirty-five years of age are not eligible.

Note: Candidates judged to have insufficient knowledge of French or German will be required to take a two and one-half month language trainig course in Fribourg. An extra allowance of 2,000 Swiss francs will be added to the Scholarship of those candidates.

Closing date: 31st October.

Further information from:
   Director, International Programs
   Association of Universities and Colleges
      of Canada
   151 Slater Street
   Ottawa, Ontario
   Canada K1P 5N1

[293]

ASSOCIATION OF UNIVERSITIES AND COLLEGES OF CANADA
Unesco

Thailand Fellowships

Subjects: Unrestricted.

No. offered: Varies.

Value: 20,000 bahts per annum. This is sufficient for the maintenance of the Fellow only, and does not cover travel expenses.

Tenable in Thailand for one year at the Behavioral Science Research Institute and the following universities: at Chulalongkorn, Kasetsart, Mahidol, Silpakorn, and Thammasat.

Eligibility: Open to Canadian citizens who have obtained at least a Bachelor's degree, except in the case of research into the fine arts when a recommendation from an art school or institution recognized by the AUCC is needed. There is no age limit, but preference will be given to mature persons who are of scholarly or professional status in a given field. Candidates must have a good knowledge of either English or Thai languages.

Closing date: 31st January.

Further information from:
   Director, International Programs
   Association of Universities and Colleges
      of Canada
   151 Slater Street
   Ottawa, Ontario
   Canada K1P 5N1

[294]

ASSOCIATION OF UNIVERSITIES AND COLLEGES OF CANADA

Canada-USSR Exchange Scholarships

Subjects: Unrestricted.

No. offered: Eight Scholarships annually.

Value: 180 roubles per month, plus an additional supplemental allowance of *Can*$70 per month for single Scholars, *Can*$120 for married Scholars accompanied by their spouses. Tuition, accommodation, travel and medical expenses are all paid.

Tenable at any institution of higher learning in the USSR for ten months.

Eligibility: Open to Canadian citizens holding a first degree from a university recognized by the AUCC. Preference will be given to candidates under the age of 35. Candidates should have a working knowledge of one of the languages of the USSR.

Note: Also see Soviet government awards, 1962.

Closing date: 30th November.

Further information from:
   Director, International Programs
   Association of Universities and Colleges
      of Canada
   151 Slater Street
   Ottawa, Ontario
   Canada K1P 5N1

[295]

ASSOCIATION OF UNIVERSITIES AND COLLEGES OF CANADA

Canada-Yugoslavia Exchange Scholarships

Subjects: Postgraduate studies and research in all subjects.

No. offered: Three Scholarships annually.

Value: 4,300 dinars to 5,000 dinars per month for postgraduate studies and 4,600 dinars to 5,200 dinars per month for research. In addition, all Scholars receive a book allowance of 1,150 dinars to 1,650 dinars, tuition, study or research related travel within Yugoslavia, medical, dental and hospital services. The Canadian government provides the Scholar with return economy air fare to Yugoslavia and two-thirds cost of that transportation for the Scholar's spouse, provided the spouse remain in Yugoslavia for at least six months.

Tenable in Yugoslavia for ten to twelve months

beginning in October; only postgraduate Scholarships may be renewed.

Eligibility: Open to Canadian citizens who have obtained at least the equivalent of a first Canadian university degree as of the effective date of the Scholarship. Preference is given to candidates under 35 years of age.

Note: Scholars are not encouraged to bring their families, due to the difficulty of finding suitable accommodation.

Scholarships cannot be held concurrently with other awards.

Closing date: 31st October.

Further information from:
Director, International Programs
Association of Universities and Colleges of Canada
151 Slater Street
Ottawa, Ontario
Canada K1P 5N1

[296]

ASTHMA & ALLERGY FOUNDATION OF AMERICA

Fellowships

Purpose: Research and training to combat asthma and allergic diseases.

Subjects: Allergy and/or immunology: clinical study and research.

No. offered: Varies annually.

Value: By individual assessment, depending upon available funds. Two year Fellows are paid quarterly; one year Fellows are paid in one lump sum.

Eligibility: Open to United States and Canadian citizens or permanent residents holding an M.D. degree.

Note: Fellows must be nominated by the dean of their medical school and by the preceptor in charge of their research.

Following completion of the Fellowship, it is expected that recipients will teach and/or conduct research in the field of study.

Closing date: 1st November, for commencement 1st July.

Further information from:
Asthma & Allergy Foundation of America
1707 N Street, N.W.
Washington, D.C. 20036
U.S.A.

[297]

ASTHMA FOUNDATION OF VICTORIA
(Australia)

Grants-in-Aid for Medical Research

Purpose: To promote and assist a specified research programme broadly related to asthma problems.

No. offered: Varies annually.

Value: Up to a maximum of A$12,000 per annum.

Tenable in an approved Australian, nonprofit making institution for up to two years.

Eligibility: Open to a responsible investigator with the approval of his head of department or institution.

Note: The investigator's salary will not normally be provided by the Grant and must be reasonably assured for the duration of the proposed study.

Closing date: 31st August.

Further information from:
Chairman
Medical and Scientific Committee
Asthma Foundation of Victoria
2 Highfield Grove
Kew, Victoria
Australia 3101

[298]

ASTHMA FOUNDATION OF VICTORIA
(Australia)

Lillian Roxon Asthma Research Travel Grant

Subjects: The causes, prevention and treatment of bronchial asthma.

No. offered: One Grant annually.

Value: Up to A$2,000.

Tenable overseas; not renewable.

Eligibility: Open to a suitably qualified person currently engaged in research into bronchial asthma wishing to take up a study leave appointment or to participate in a recognized international meeting.

Closing date: 31st August.

Further information from:
Trustees
Lillian Roxon Asthma Research Trust
c/o Asthma Foundation of Victoria
2 Highfield Grove
Kew, Victoria
Australia 3101

[299]

ASTHMA RESEARCH COUNCIL *(U.K.)*

Research Awards

Purpose: To support research into the causes and cure of asthma.

No. offered: Approximately 10 Awards annually.

Value: Variable, according to the nature and extent of the research project being undertaken.

Tenable for between one year and three years at hospitals, universities and other research institutions in the United Kingdom.

Eligibility: Open to suitably qualified research workers resident in the United Kingdom.

Note: Awards are normally given to a university professor or hospital specialist who can supervise the nominated research worker after approval by the Council's Medical Advisory Committee and the Council itself.

Further information from:
Asthma Research Council
12 Pembridge Square
London
England W2 4EH

[300]

ASTRONOMICAL SOCIETY OF THE PACIFIC *(San Francisco)*

Awards

Amateur Achievement Award of *US$250* and a plaque is given annually for outstanding contributions to astronomy by an amateur. Nominations may be submitted by any individual or group.

Dorothea Klumpe-Roberts Award of *US$500* and a plaque is given annually for outstanding contributions to public understanding and appreciation of astronomy. Nominations are made by a special committee of the Society.

Robert J. Trumpler Award of *US$500* and a plaque is given annually for a Ph.D. thesis in the field of astronomy. Candidates should have received their Ph.D. from an institution in North America. Nominations may be made by chairpersons of the astronomy and physics departments of these institutions.

Note: The Society also awards the *Catherine Wolfe Bruce Gold Medal* which carries no monetary value.

Further information from:
Andrew Fraknoi, Executive Officer
Astronomical Society of the Pacific
1290 24th Avenue
San Francisco, California 94122
U.S.A.

[301]

ASTRONOMICAL SOCIETY OF SOUTHERN AFRICA

McIntyre Award

From time to time the Society offers the McIntyre Award for work in the field of history of astronomy. The monetary value of the award is normally not less than R200.

Nominations in respect of a work, which must have been published in book form or in a journal of recognized standing within the previous five years, may be made to the Honorary Secretary by any council member or alternate member of the Society. Direct applications are not acceptable.

Further information from:
Astronomical Society of Southern Africa
P.O. Box 9
Observatory 7935, Cape
South Africa

[302]

ATLANTIC MONTHLY *(Boston, Mass.)*

Atlantic "Firsts" Awards

Prizes of US$750 and US$250 are awarded periodically to recognize outstanding short stories by unestablished authors who are making their first appearance in a major publication. Both prizes are in addition to payment for the story at regular rates. Manuscripts may run from 2,000 to 6,000 words. The Prizes are not restricted to United States citizens.

Further information from:
Atlantic Monthly
8 Arlington Street
Boston, Massachusetts 02116
U.S.A.

[303]

ATLANTIC SALMON TRUST LTD. *(U.K.)*

Awards

Purpose: To support projects, studentships or fellowships aimed at conserving, improving and expanding stocks of Atlantic salmon (salmo salar L) and of seatrout (salmo trutta L).

Subjects: All factors affecting the above species, particularly general ecology, migration, practices and techniques in the management of hatcheries, fisheries and salmon fish farms.

Value: Not pre-determined; payments are made to suit the particular circumstances of each Award.

Tenable as circumstances of each particular Award may require.

Eligibility: Open to nationals of any country.

Note: Applications should be forwarded through academic institutions or professional organisations.

Further information from:
Director
Atlantic Salmon Trust Ltd.
14 Downing Street
Farnham, Surrey
England

[304]

ATOMIC ENERGY RESEARCH ESTABLISHMENT, HARWELL *(U.K.)*

Fellowships: A very limited number of Fellowships are available from time to time in the Establishment's various divisions. Experienced Commonwealth citizens (and very rarely, others) who are faculty members of academic institutions or on the staff of Commonwealth research centres may apply. Fellows spend up to three years at Harwell; stipends match those of permanent scientific staff. Opportunities also exist for senior staff of suitable institutions to visit Harwell for a few months.

Vacation Associateships: These are open to teaching and research staff of universities and research laboratories who possess qualifications relevant to the programmes of the Establishment. Associates (most are over 30) spend up to 48 days at Harwell; they may re-visit in subsequent years. A daily fee is paid and a subsistence allowance may be available for weekends.

Note: Prior to application, candidates should obtain latest details regarding availability of award programmes.

Further information from:
Personnel Department A
AERE, Harwell
Didcot, Oxfordshire
England OX11 ORA

[305]

AUCKLAND MEDICAL RESEARCH FOUNDATION *(N.Z.)*

Medical Research Project Grant

Purpose: To promote medical research with a preference for work in the Auckland province.

Note: Grants are made biannually on the recommendations of the Medical Committee of the Board of the Foundation which assesses applications for their professional competence.

Preference is given to supporting research workers by the payment of salaries rather than by the provision of equipment. The number of awards, the value of each award and the place and duration of tenancy depend on applications received and the Medical Committee's assessment of the applications. Renewal of Grants for limited periods of up to two years is considered. There are no requirements with regard to age, sex, citizenship or residency.

Applications are to be made on the prescribed form obtainable from the Foundation, and should be submitted by 30th April or 31st October.

Further information from:
  Secretary
  Auckland Medical Research Foundation
  Box 7151
  Auckland
  New Zealand

[306]

AUCKLAND MEDICAL RESEARCH FOUNDATION *(N.Z.)*

Travel Grant

Purpose: To allow staff engaged in or associated with medical research projects to travel for a specific purpose.

No. offered, Value and Tenancy: Dependent on application.

Eligibility: Open normally, but not exclusively, to staff associated with the Auckland Hospital Board, the School of Medicine in the University of Auckland, or to recipients of other grants from the Foundation. There are no requirements as to age, sex, citizenship or residency.

Further information from:
  Secretary
  Auckland Medical Research Foundation
  Box 7151
  Auckland
  New Zealand

[307]

AUSTRALIA/CHINA STUDENT EXCHANGE SCHEME

Scholarships

Subjects: Chinese language, philosophy, literature, history, archeology, music, fine arts, history of fine arts, political economy, engineering, agronomy and medicine.

No. offered: Eight Scholarships annually.

Value: Return economy air fare; living and study allowance; accommodations; contributions to cost of internal travel in China and medical and dental expenses.

Tenable usually for a total of two years at the Peking Languages Institute and any Chinese university open to foreign students.

Eligibility: Open to Australian citizens under 35 years of age who hold a Higher School Certificate or equivalent degree, and who have studied at a university. Candidates are expected to have achieved a reasonably high level of proficiency in the Chinese language. Successful applicants must undergo a strict medical examination.

Note: In exceptional cases, applicants with no knowledge of the language but who can demonstrate a serious commitment to other areas of Chinese Studies will also be considered.

Closing date: Usually January of the academic year (beginning September) in which the award will be taken up.

Further information from:
  Secretary
  Department of Education
  Australia/China Student Exchange
    Scheme
  P.O. Box 826
  Woden, A.C.T.
  Australia 2606

[308]

AUSTRALIA COUNCIL
Literature Board

The Literature Board's aim is the support of all forms of creative literature—novels, short stories, plays, poetry, biographies, histories and writing on the humanities in general.

This is done in the first instance by a program of direct grants to writers: (a) to allow them extensive writing periods in which they can give their full attention to writing (Fellowships); (b) to help them to meet living expenses while writing a particular literary work (General Writing Grants); or (c) to underwrite expenses associated with particular projects (Special Purpose Grants).

To enable creative writing to reach the public, the Board has developed a publishing subsidies scheme which aims to assist Australian book publishers with the costs of producing literary works at a marketable price. It also subsidises the publication of literary magazines and periodicals.

Projects of many kinds which are designed to promote Australian literature and Australian writers both within the country and abroad are also initiated and supported by the Board.

Note: Applicants should obtain a copy of the Literature Board's prospectus which gives a full account of the programs of support. Write to:
Secretary, Literature Board
Australia Council
P.O. Box 302
North Sydney, N.S.W.
Australia 2060

[309]

AUSTRALIA/JAPAN BUSINESS CO-OPERATION COMMITTEE

Scholarships and Travel Grants Exchange Scheme

Subjects: Scholarships—unrestricted; Travel Grants—Japanese language.

No. offered: Two Scholarships and two Travel Grants annually.

Value: Scholarships—A$12,080 per annum; Grants—A2,000 per annum.

Tenable for 12 months.

Eligibility: Scholarships are open to Australian graduates; Travel Grants are open to Australian teachers of Japanese and Japanese-speaking graduates to learn simultaneous interpretation skills in Japan.

Note: AJBCC and the Australian Government share the cost of Scholarships and Travel Grants.

Closing date: July.

Further information from:
Australian/Japan Business Co-operation Committee
G.P.O. Box 14
Canberra, A.C.T.
Australia 2600

[310]

AUSTRALIA-JAPAN FOUNDATION (*Sydney*)

Awards

The Foundation offers numerous awards of varying amounts to Australian and Japanese residents, as well as to institutions of these countries. Most awards fall under one of the following programs: community liaison, education, media, publication and library, research, sports, travel, and youth. The Foundation is also responsive to individual applications submitted for projects which do not lie within the aims of the above mentioned schemes.

Further information from:
Australia-Japan Foundation
P.O. Box H260
Australia Square
Sydney, N.S.W.
Australia 2000

[311]

AUSTRALIAN ACADEMY OF THE HUMANITIES (*Canberra*)
Meyer Foundation

Grants-In-Aid

Four Grants-in-Aid of A$800 each are normally made on an annual basis to Australian scholars who are engaged in research overseas. The awards are to be used as a contribution towards the cost of one return air-fare between the applicant's place of employment in Australia and the research centre overseas. Research projects should be near a state of completion. Applications for periods abroad of less than six weeks will not be accepted. Eligible candidates should be engaged in full-time teaching or other full time employment.

Applications may be obtained through the Academy between February and June of each year.

Closing date: 30th June.

Further information from:
Secretary
Australian Academy of the Humanities
P.O. Box 93
Canberra, A.C.T.
Australia 2600

[312]

AUSTRALIAN ACADEMY OF THE HUMANITIES
ACADEMY OF THE SOCIAL SCIENCES IN AUSTRALIA

Australia-China Exchange in the Humanities and Social Sciences

Up to five exchange fellowships are awarded annually to Australian scholars wishing to study the humanities and social sciences in China. The joint committee assists with cost of fares from Australia to Peking and expenses in China are paid by the Chinese Academy. The fellowships are tenable for periods of three weeks to three months at institutions under the control of the Chinese Academy. Applications may be obtained from the address below.

Closing date: 1st August.

Further information from:
Secretary
Academy of the Social Sciences in Australia
2nd Floor, National Library of Australia
Parkes, A.C.T.
Australia 2600

[313]

AUSTRALIAN ACADEMY OF SCIENCE

Fellowships

Geoffrey Frew Fellowship: One Fellowship is offered every two years to enable distinguished overseas scientists to participate in the Australian Spectroscopy Conferences and to visit scientific centres in Australia. The Fellowship is not open to application.

Rudi Lemberg Travelling Fellowships: A varying number of Fellowships are offered annually in any field of biology, but especially biochemistry, conservation and the Australian flora, to enable overseas scientists of standing to visit scientific centres in Australia, and to enable Australian scientists of standing to visit scientific centres in Australia other than their own. The Fellowship is tenable for two to twelve weeks, and covers costs for return air fare for overseas Fellows, air fares within Australia, a daily allowance at a rate determined by the Academy Council, and expenses determined by the Council to be incidental to the award. There are no restrictions as to age, sex or nationality. Nominations should be accompanied by a publications list, a detailed curriculum vitae, and a proposed itinerary.

Closing date: 30th September.

Selby Fellowship: One Fellowship is awarded annually to bring a senior scientist to Australia for a short visit. The Fellowship is not open to application.

Further information from:
Executive Secretary
Australian Academy of Science
P.O. Box 783
Canberra City, A.C.T.
Australia 2601

[314]

AUSTRALIAN-AMERICAN EDUCATIONAL FOUNDATION

Postdoctoral Fellow and Junior Researcher/Lecturer Awards (Fulbright-Hays Program)

Purpose: To increase understanding between the peoples of Australia and the United States.

Subjects: Unrestricted.

Value: One economy class air fare to and from the United States, baggage allowance and A$6,000 per calendar year.

Tenable in the United States for up to twelve months; recommended grant period is nine months (most of which should be spent at the host institution). May be renewable in some circumstances.

Eligibility: Australian citizens who are less than four years post-Ph.D. and who wish to accept a postdoctoral appointment in the United States, or Australian citizens who have completed their postdoctoral years (or have reached a similar advanced standing in disciplines where a Ph.D. is not part of the normal academic progression) and who are still in the early stages of their academic careers. Awards are for postdoctoral research, further professional training, or lecturing at a tertiary institution.

Note: Before grants can be awarded, it is essential that applicants produce evidence of affiliation with an American institution of higher education and of adequate financial support for the duration of their projects. It is emphasised that an applicant may apply in anticipation of fulfilling these conditions.

Applications must be obtained from and returned to the *Department of Education, P.O. Box 826, Woden, A.C.T. 2606, Australia,* between 1st July and 30th September.

Further information from:
Australian-American Educational Foundation
Box 1559
Canberra City, A.C.T.
Australia 2601

[315]

AUSTRALIAN-AMERICAN EDUCATIONAL FOUNDATION

Travel Grants for Postgraduate Students, and Senior Scholars (Fulbright-Hays Program)

Purpose: To increase understanding between the peoples of Australia and the United States.

Subjects: Unrestricted.

Value: One economy-class air fare to and from the United States, and baggage allowance.

Tenable in the United States for three to twelve months (most of which should be at the host institution); renewable for postgraduate students.

Eligibility: (a) Postgraduate Students (including medical candidates) must already hold a university degree or its equivalent, and should undertake an approved course of study for an American higher degree or equivalent, engage in research applicable to an Australian higher degree, or undertake advanced professional training. Preference is given to persons who have not previously studied in the United States. Australian citizenship is required.

(b) Senior Scholars should already have held a senior degree for more than four years, possess equivalent research or professional experience and have achieved professional distinction in their fields. Australian citizenship is required.

Note: Before Travel Grants can be awarded, it is essential that applicants produce evidence of affiliation with an American institution of higher education and of adequate financial support for the duration of their projects. It is emphasised that an applicant may apply in anticipation of fulfilling these conditions.

Although the Foundation has no scholarships at its disposal, postgraduate students with very good academic records can make a personal application to universities in the United States for scholarships or assistantships with reasonable hope of success.

Applications must be obtained from and returned to the *Department of Education, P.O. Box 826, Woden, A.C.T. Australia 2606* between 1st July and 30th September.

Further information from:
Australian-American Educational Foundation
Box 1559
Canberra City, A.C.T.
Australia 2601

[316]

AUSTRALIAN-AMERICAN EDUCATIONAL FOUNDATION

Educational Development Program (Fulbright-Hays Program)

Purpose: To enable Australian-qualified educators to gain a knowledge of educational systems in the United States through study, observation, and travel in the United States.

Subjects: Any subjects related to primary and secondary education including administration, supervision, program or curriculum development, innovative techniques and special education programs.

Value: Transportation to and from the east coast of the United States, travel allowance for internal United States, travel not covered by the international ticket, baggage and incidentals allowances, and a per diem of US$35.

It is hoped that participating institutions, from whose staffs the applicants may be recruited, will retain them on the payroll at full or partial salaries during the terms of their awards in order to meet the needs of dependents during their absence.

Tenable in the United States for a period of three months.

Eligibility: Open to Australian citizens who are teachers or officials of state education departments or non-government schools or secondary colleges and have had at least three continuous years of successful full-time teaching experience. Preference is given to persons who have not previously visited the United States.

Note: Candidates must be willing to return to Australia to continue in the same positions or related work on termination of their awards.

Applications may be obtained from and returned to the *Department of Education, P.O. Box 826, Woden, A.C.T. 2606 Australia* between 1st August and 30th November.

Further information from:
 Australian-American Educational
  Foundation
 Box 1559
 Canberra City, A.C.T.
 Australia 2601

[317]

AUSTRALIAN BROADCASTING COMMISSION

Training Courses in Radio

Subjects: Rural broadcasting; educational radio broadcasting.

Tenable in Australia for approximately twelve weeks.

Eligibility: Open to nationals of all countries participating in the Colombo Plan, the Special Commonwealth African Assistance Plan and the Australian South Pacific Technical Assistance Plan. Participants must have a reasonable fluency in English and the necessary experience in the subject of the course undertaken.

The course in rural braodcasting is intended for broadcasters with an agricultural background or extension workers whose efficiency would be increased by the use of radio; the course in educational radio broadcasting (in alternate years) for administrators of educational broadcasting and producers of radio educational broadcasts.

Note: Apart from formal courses, the ABC (in collaboration with the Australian government) also provides observation and attachments for officers from overseas organisations: in radio and television education, journalism, rural broadcasting, drama, films, production facilities, engineering, administration and financial control.

Applications will be considered only when submitted by the candidate's employer through the official government channels to the Australian government representatives in the country concerned.

Further information from:
 Head of Training
 Australian Broadcasting Commission
 Broadcast House
 145-149 Elizabeth Street
 Sydney, N.S.W.
 Australia 2001

[318]

AUSTRALIAN CANCER SOCIETY

Research Grants: Approximately A$10,000 is available for interstate investigational programs of cancer research. Funds may be provided for programs providing access to an adequate number of patients and which are supported by host institutions. Grants are made for one year and may be renewed on submission of satisfactory reports. Salaries, equipment, maintenance, computer costs and travel are all eligible for funding. Applications should be submitted by 1st August for the following calendar year.

Technology Transfers: Travel and accomodation expenses for a maximum of six weeks is provided to enable applicants to undertake visits to selected research institutions for consultations and comparisons on study progress. Applicants must be engaged in cancer research and may be recommended by their institutions. Applications may be submitted at any time.

Further information from:
 Executive Director
 Australian Cancer Society
 Box 4708 G.P.O.
 Sydney, N.S.W.
 Australia 2001

[319]
AUSTRALIAN COLLEGE OF PAEDIATRICS

Nestlé Paediatric Travelling Fellowships

Purpose: (a) To provide travel expenses for a person taking up a post in a hospital abroad and who is then returning to Australia; (b) to enable a person to attend paediatric meetings or to spend a short period at some overseas centre or centres to study a particular problem.

No. offered: One to three Fellowships annually.

Value: Variable, paid in a lump sum.

Eligibility: Open to young Australian paediatricians, paediatric surgeons and paediatric specialists.

Closing date: the end of August.

Further information from:
 Registrar
 Australian College of Paediatrics
 P.O. Box 34
 Parkville, Victoria
 Australia 3052

[320]
AUSTRALIAN CONSERVATION FOUNDATION, INC.

Research Grants

The special projects of the Foundation, outlined in their annual brochure, are concerned with research into the conservation of natural resources of air, land and water of Australia and its territories.
 Grants are offered to suitably qualified staff of academic institutions and to postgraduate students.

Further information from:
 Director
 Australian Conservation Foundation, Inc.
 672B Glenferrie Road
 Hawthorn, Victoria
 Australia 3122

[321]
AUSTRALIAN EARLY CHILDHOOD ASSOCIATION, INC.

Alice Creswick Scholarship

Purpose: To encourage overseas study in the field of early childhood education. More recently, the scope of the Scholarship has been widened, and its purpose is now to provide opportunity for travel, observation, and/or study in the early childhood field.

No. offered: One Scholarship periodically, as funds are available.

Value: Variable, depending upon available funds. Recent Scholarships have been in the A$1,000—A$4,000 range.

Tenable for up to 90 days, but this could be extended under special circumstances.

Eligibility: Open to Australian citizens actively involved in early childhood services.

Note: The Scholarship is available within Australia, or overseas. Projects submitted may include observation tours. The Award may also be used as partial subsidy for longer courses or studies.

Further information from:
 Australian Early Childhood
  Association, Inc.
 Knox Street
 Watson, A.C.T.
 Australia 2602

[322]
AUSTRALIAN ENTOMOLOGICAL SOCIETY INC.

Student Research Award

Purpose: To encourage interest in entomology by Australian students.

No. offered: One Award at intervals of approximately 12-18 months.

Value: A$25 plus registration and accommodation at a general scientific meeting of the Society, and return air fare from the student's home in Australia to the meeting.

Eligibility: Open to persons under 25 years of age on 1st January of the year of the Award.

The Award is offered for the best paper reporting original entomological research conducted by the entrant. The winner is expected to read his paper and receive the Award in person at the scientific meeting held in that year.

Further information from:
Dr. K.R. Brown, Secretary
Australian Entomological Society
Biology FO7
University of Sydney
Sydney, N.S.W.
Australia 2006

[323]

AUSTRALIAN FEDERATION OF UNIVERSITY WOMEN

Georgina Sweet Fellowship

Subjects: Unrestricted: advanced study or research.

No. offered: One Fellowships every two years (one available in 1983 for tenancy in 1984.

Value: A$5,000.

Tenable in Australia for up to one year.

Eligibility: Open to women graduates who are not normally resident in Australia, and who are members of their National Federation of University Women.

Further information from:
Fellowships Convener
Australian Federation of University
  Women
c/o Ursula College
P.O. Box 702
Canberra City, A.C.T.
Australia 2601

[324]

AUSTRALIAN FEDERATION OF UNIVERSITY WOMEN—QUEENSLAND

AFVW—Queensland Freda Bage Fellowship

Subjects: Unrestricted.

No. offered: One Fellowship annually.

Value: A$6,000, paid in two installments.

Tenable at any Australian university or approved institution of higher learning other than that from which the applicant graduated. Not renewable. If an Australian receives the Fellowship it may be taken up at an overseas university.

Eligibility: Open to all members of the international Federation of University Women wishing to undertake postgraduate research.

Closing date: 30th August.

Further information from:
Mrs. Audrey N. Jorss, Hon. Secretary
Australian Federation of University
  Women Fellowship Committee
19 Cawmore Road
Galloways Hill
Brisbane, Queensland
Australia 4171

[325]

AUSTRALIAN FEDERATION OF UNIVERSITY WOMEN—SOUTH AUSTRALIA

Jean Gilmore Bursary

Purpose: To enable the recipient to proceed to a higher degree, to complete a research project, or to engage in a short-term project.

Subjects: Unrestricted.

No. offered: One Bursary in odd-numbered years.

Value: A$2,000.

Tenable for one year; not renewable.

Eligibility: Open to women graduates who

have research experience and who are members of the Australian Federation of University Women.

Closing date: 28th February.

Further information from:
  Fellowships Convener
  Australian Federation of University
    Women
  Box 16, University of Adelaide
  Adelaide, South Australia
  Australia 5000

[326]

AUSTRALIAN FEDERATION OF UNIVERSITY WOMEN—VICTORIA

Scholarships

Subjects: Unrestricted: advanced study or research.

No. offered: One Scholarship annually.

Value: A$2,500.

Tenable in any country for one year.

Eligibility: Open to women graduates who are members of the Australian Federation of University Women.

Closing date: 31st January.

Further information from:
  Mrs. R. Fincher
  Australian Federation of University
    Women—Victoria
  55 Molesworth Street
  Kew, Victoria
  Australia 3101

[327]

AUSTRALIAN FILM INSTITUTE

Film Awards

To recognize the latest achievements of the nation's film industry, the Australian Film Institute makes several awards of varying amounts in all aspects of film and film-making. Films which are eligible should be produced substantially in Australia using Australian facilities, and made by persons permanently resident in Australia.

Closing date: April of each year.

Further information from:
  Australian Film Institute
  P.O. Box 165
  Carlton South, Victoria
  Australia 3053

[328]

AUSTRALIAN INSTITUTE OF ABORIGINAL STUDIES (Canberra City)

Research Assistance

The Institute provides funds for projects concerned with Australian Aborigines and Torres Strait Islanders in fields such as human biology, social anthropology, linguistics, ethnomusicology, material culture, rock art, prehistory, ethnobotany, psychology education and Aboriginal history including oral history. Nationals of any country are eligible for assistance. Applicants for assistance from the Institute should submit an application form by 31st May for a period to be commenced on or after 1st November in any year. Decisions will be announced in October.

Further information from:
  Australian Institute of Aboriginal Studies
  P.O. Box 553
  Canberra City, A.C.T.
  Australia 2601

[329]

AUSTRALIAN INSTITUTE OF INTERNATIONAL AFFAIRS

Research Grants

Purpose: To assist with expenses of research on manuscripts for publication by the institute in its research programme.

Subjects: Generally within the field of international affairs and foreign policy, especially in subjects relevant to Australian concerns.

No. offered: A few awards annually on an ad hoc basis.

Value: Variable according to requirement and funds available.

Tenancy: Unrestricted.

Eligibility: Awards are normally restricted to qualified persons resident in Australia, and are made on the basis of a judgment by the Research Committee of the capacity of the applicant and the significance of the proposed research.

Note: Applicants should include a synopsis of the proposal, a curriculum vitae, names of three referees, and details of financial assistance sought. Applications are usually considered in February and August each year.

Further information from:
Secretary
Australian Institute of International Affairs
G.P.O. Box E181
Canberra, A.C.T.
Australia 2600

[330]

AUSTRALIAN INSTITUTE OF NUCLEAR SCIENCE AND ENGINEERING

AINSE Research Fellowships

Subjects: Nuclear science and engineering.

No. offered: Up to four Fellowships annually.

Value: A$6,000 to A$22,000 per annum. Fares to and from Australia for Fellow and his dependents may be offered.

Tenable at any university in Australia or directly with AINSE at Lucas Heights, New South Wales, for two years.

Eligibility: Open to scientists and engineers, who hold a Ph.D. or equivalent qualification, and are at a relatively early stage of an independent research career.

Note: Candidates for Fellowships may be nominated only by an Australian University or by the Australian Atomic Energy Commission.

Closing dates: 28th February; 31st August.

Further information from:
Executive Officer
Australian Institute of Nuclear Science
  and Engineering
Private Mail Bag
P.O. Sutherland, N.S.W.
Australia 2232

[331]

AUSTRALIAN INSTITUTE OF NUCLEAR SCIENCE AND ENGINEERING

AINSE Grants

Grants are periodically awarded for one year in support of projects undertaken by member organizations of AINSE in fields associated with nuclear science and engineering.

Further information from:
Executive Officer
Australian Institute of Nuclear Science
  and Engineering
Private Mail Bag
P.O. Sutherland, N.S.W.
Australia 2232

[332]

AUSTRALIAN INSTITUTE OF NUCLEAR SCIENCE AND ENGINEERING

AINSE Research Studentships

Subjects: Nuclear science and engineering.

Value: A$5,105 per annum for single Students; A$7,325.40 for married Students, plus A$520 in respect of each dependent child. In addition all compulsory university fees, with the exception of graduation fees, will be paid along with aid for equipment and the cost of preparing the thesis.

Tenable at any Australian University, initially for one year; renewable up to a maximum of four years. At least one quarter of the total period of tenure must be spent at the A.A.E.C. research establishment at Lucas Heights, New South Wales.

Eligibility: Open to individuals who have completed, or who hope to complete within six months of nomination, the requirements for a B.E. or B.Sc. degree (or their equivalent) at a recognised university, and who are enrolled, or expect to enroll within six months, as a postgraduate at an Australian University.

Note: Candidates for Studentships must be nominated by the Australian University at which they wish to hold tenure of the award.

Further information from:
  Executive Officer
  Australian Institute of Nuclear Science
    and Engineering
  Private Mail Bag
  P.O. Sutherland, N.S.W.
  Australia 2232

[333]
AUSTRALIAN INSTITUTE OF URBAN STUDIES

Grants

Grants are offered for urban studies. Researchers for the Institute's various projects may be selected by direct aproach. The Institute also places advertisements for positions and welcomes proposals from individuals. Prior to application, candidates should enquire as to the present interests of the Institute.

Further information from:
  Director
  Australian Institute of Urban Studies
  P.O. Box 809
  Canberra City, A.C.T.
  Australia 2601

[334]
AUSTRALIAN KIDNEY FOUNDATION

Grants-in-Aid
Research Scholarships

Purpose: To promote research into the functions or diseases of the kidney, urinary tract and related organs, or relevant problems.

No. offered: 20-25 Grants-in-Aid annually; up to two Scholarships annually.

Value: Up to A$7,000 per annum for Grants-in-Aid; A$10,145 to A$11,598 per annum for Scholarships.

Tenable at any Australian medical centre for up to a total of three years.

Eligibility: Available to Australian citizens connected with Australian universities or medical centres with requisite research facilities.

Closing dates: 15th June for Grants-in-Aid; 1st September for Scholarships.

Further information from:
  Medical Director
  Australian Kidney Foundation
  P.O. Box 1850
  Canberra City, A.C.T.
  Australia 2601

[335]
AUSTRALIAN MEAT RESEARCH COMMITTEE

Overseas Study Awards

Purpose: To provide an opportunity for overseas study so that, on return to Australia, the recipient will be equipped to make an improved contribution to the Australian grazing industry.

Subjects: Grazing pastoral industry.

Value: Maximum of US$19,250 per annum in the United States or Canada; £4,500 per annum in Europe. In addition, transportation and tuition is provided, plus supplementary allowances for dependent wife and family.

Tenable outside Australia for one year.

Eligibility: Open to senior Australian scientists or extension workers who have made a noteworthy contribution to the sheep and/or cattle industries. Preference will be given to candidates who have limited opportunities for overseas study.

Closing date: Late July.

Further information from:
  Executive Officer
  Australian Meat Research Committee
  Box 4129, G.P.O.
  Sydney, N.S.W.
  Australia 2001

[336]
AUSTRALIAN MEAT RESEARCH COMMITTEE

Postgraduate Studentships

Subjects: Research into agricultural economics, agricultural extension, agronomy, animal breeding, meat and carcase studies, plant ecology, plant physiology, reproductive physiology, ruminant nutrition, veterinary parasitology and protozoology, veterinary pathology and infectious diseases.

Value: A$4,620 per annum, plus fees and dependents' allowances, for research in Australian institutions. Overseas awards carry £2,650 for study in Europe and US$7,400 for study in the United States, plus return fares, fees and dependents' allowances.

Tenable at universities or institutions in Australia or overseas for two years (except those awarded for postgraduate diploma courses of one year's duration), with the possibility of extension up to a maximum of four years where necessary for the completion of a Ph.D. degree.

Eligibility: Open to individuals residing in Australia who have had experience in research of interest to the AMRC since graduation.

Overseas Studentships are awarded to Australian residents, specifically for studies towards a Ph.D. degree. Applicants must demonstrate a special reason for overseas training.

Closing date: Late July.

Further information from:
Executive Officer
Australian Meat Research Committee
Box 4129, G.P.O.
Sydney, N.S.W.
Australia 2001

[337]

AUSTRALIAN MUSIC FOUNDATION IN LONDON

Award

A major Award of £6,000 is offered to an Australian musician under 30 years of age—singer or instrumentalist—payable at the rate of £3,000 per annum for 2 years. The second installment is subject to re-assessment. Applications are considered in the first instance by the Foundation Committee with a panel of adjudicators making the final choice. The award is for study in Europe. At the time of applying candidates may be resident in Australia or the United Kingdom. Upon receipt of the Award in London, the winner undertakes a course of musical study in his or her chosen aspect of the art. It is stressed that this award is intended for musicians of merit and ability.

The Foundation will also take into account how applicants—in the event of winning—propose to use the award to further their careers. Closing date is 1st February for announcement of Award winner in June.

Further information from:
Australian Music Foundation in London
Peat, Marwick, Mitchell & Co.
1 Puddle Dock, Blackfriars
London
England ECHV 3PD

[338]

AUSTRALIAN NATIONAL UNIVERSITY

Florey Fellowship

Subjects: Biomedical sciences: postdoctoral research and training.

No. offered: One Fellowship biennially.

Value: £9,210 per annum, plus return economy air fare for Fellow and dependents. Under certain conditions, an additional London allowance of £740 may be awarded.

Tenable at any university research establishment in the United Kingdom for two years.

Eligibility: Open to persons holding a Ph.D. or equivalent qualification in the biomedical sciences who are identified with Australia by reason of residence, citizenship, or some other relation deemed appropriate by the Committee.

Note: Preference may be given to applicants who have not had the opportunity to study overseas and to persons who are working in the fields of mammalian physiology, biochemistry, and pathology or pharmacology.

A similar award is made in the United Kingdom by the Royal Society for study in Australia (see the Society's entries).

Closing date: As advertised.

Further information from:
Secretary
Florey Fellowship Committee
Australian National University
P.O. Box 4
Canberra, A.C.T.
Australia 2600

[339]

AUSTRALIAN NATIONAL UNIVERSITY

Robert Gordon Menzies Scholarship to Harvard University

Subjects: Unrestricted.

No. offered: One Scholarship annually.

Value: Up to US$5,000 per annum.

Tenable at Harvard University, Cambridge, Massachusetts, for one year.

Eligibility: Open to a graduate of any Australian university who is a resident of Australia and who has been accepted for admission to a graduate school at Harvard. Candidates should intend to return to Australia to work in a field of benefit to Australia.

Closing date: 31st December.

Further information from:
Registrar
Australian National University
P.O. Box 4
Canberra, A.C.T.
Australia 2600

[340]

AUSTRALIAN PARLIAMENT

Parliamentary Political Science Fellowship

Purpose: To provide an opportunity for young political scientists with a higher degree to serve Parliament for a year, and in so doing to gain a better understanding of the practical aspects of the national legislative processes. The Fellow is required to write papers in response to requests from members of parliament, and also to undertake a research project related to the Parliament.

No. offered: One Fellowship annually.

Value: Salary approximately A$18,708 per annum, paid fortnightly.

Tenable in the Legislative Research Service of the Parliamentary Library, Parliament House, Canberra, for two years, commencing 1st January; not renewable.

Eligibility: Open to Australians who possess at least a master's degree, with appropriate qualifications in political science. Applicants are required to provide references.

Note: The Fellow is required to work as a full time member of the Legislative Research Service of the Parliamentary Library.

Closing date: Approximately mid-August.

Further information from:
Parliamentary Librarian
Parliament House
Canberra, A.C.T.
Australia 2600

[341]

AUSTRALIAN POSTGRADUATE FEDERATION IN MEDICINE

Fellowships of the Mayo Graduate School of Medicine: The Federation annually invites applications and submits nominations for two Fellowships to the Mayo Graduate School of Medicine, Rochester, Minnesota.

The Fellowships are designed to afford opportunity to Australian graduates who intend to work or practise in Australia, to obtain training and experience at the Mayo Clinic and in the Graduate School of Medicine, University of Minnesota. The Fellowships, normally tenable for three or four years, carry a stipend of US$12,600—US$16,400.

Further information from:
Australian Postgraduate Federation in Medicine
22 Lascelles Avenue
Toorak, Victoria
Australia 3142

[342]

AUSTRALIAN TOBACCO RESEARCH FOUNDATION

The following awards are provided for research into the relationship in Australia between tobacco smoking and health and disease in its widest context. Applications should be submittd by 30th June for research commencing the following January.

Postgraduate Scholarships: Scholarships may be awarded to medical graduates, who will be studying full time for a higher degree, to enable them to carry out, or participate in, relevant research projects under the full time supervision and tuition of a responsible investigator in an approved Australian Institution. They are awarded initially for one year but may be renewed for one or more years. Stipends will be paid according to relevant National Health and Medical Research Council scales. Family allowances are payable.

Research Grants: Grants, to be awarded to non-profit institutions in Australia equipped with the basic facilities for research may be used to provide salaries for graduate, technical and other assistants, and for the purchase of equipment and supplies. They will be made initially for one to three years to support a specific programme of basic medical or clinical research under the direction of an experienced full-time investigator.

Further information from:
  Medical Secretary
  Australian Tobacco Research Foundation
  c/o Department of Medicine
  University of Sydney
  Sydney, N.S.W.
  Australia 2006

[343]

AUSTRALIAN VICE-CHANCELLORS' COMMITTEE
Australian-Asian Universities' Cooperation Scheme

AAUCS Visiting Fellowships of up to A$4,000 are offered in the fields of librarianship, applied biology, agriculture and veterinary medicine. They are tenable for a study leave of 90 days or more at Nanyang University, Universiti Pertanian Malaysia, National University of Singapore and at Indonesian universities. The Fellowships are open to the academic staff of Australian universities as well as those of the universities of Nanyang, Pertanian Malaysia and Singapore. Fellows are expected to teach and/or conduct research. Application should be made through the home institution by 30th June or 31st December.

AAUCS Visitors Program: Senior academic staff and educational administrators from Indonesian universities, the Universiti Pertanian Malaysia or the National University of Singapore are offered 3 to 4 week visits to study university education and administration in Australia. The awards are made by invitation only; applications are not accepted and information is not given to individuals.

Address:
  Director, AAUCS
  Australian Vice-Chancellors' Committee
  P.O. Box 1142
  Canberra City, A.C.T.
  Australia 2601

[344]

AUSTRALIAN WAR MEMORIAL
Research Grants Scheme

Grants, for work in the field of Australian military history and related subjects such as biography, weapons, equipment and art, are awarded as follows: (a) one post-graduate scholarship to a candidate undertaking supervised research at a tertiary institution under terms similar to Australian Commonwealth Postgraduate Scholarships; (b) a number of grants-in-aid of up to A$3,000 and tenable for one year; renewable for an additional year. *Closing date:* mid-June for both awards.

Further information from:
  Director
  Australian War Memorial
  P.O. Box 345
  Canberra City, A.C.T.
  Australia 2601

[345]

AUSTRALIAN WOOL CORPORATION
Postgraduate Scholarships

Subjects: Any field of research relevant to wool production, harvesting, distribution and processing, including wool economics.

No. offered: Up to ten Scholarships annually.

Value: A$4,620 per annum, plus allowances for spouse and dependents where applicable. Additional allowances are available to assist with project expenses and fees. All allowances are subject to change from time to time.

Tenable at any Australian university for up to three years, with a possible extension of one additional year.

Eligibility: Open to persons holding at least an upper second class honours or master's degree who intend to reside permanently in Australia in employment applicable to the Australian sheep and wool industry. Preference is given to candidates who are not in receipt of any other award.

Applications must be sponsored and submitted to the Corporation by an Australian organization.

Closing date: Normally early September or late January.

Further information from:
 Australian Wool Corporation
 Research and Development Department
 261 George Street
 Sydney, N.S.W.
 Australia 2000

[346]

AUSTRIAN ACADEMY OF SCIENCES INSTITUTE OF LIMNOLOGY *(Vienna)*

Postgraduate Training Fellowships

Purpose: To give Fellows an overall insight into the various problems of limnology so that they may be better equipped to implement necessary research in their home countries in order to find solutions to their practical problems.

Subject: All aspects of limnology.

No. offered: 10 Fellowships annually.

Value: 5,500 schillings paid monthly to cover lodging, food and personal expenses, free tuition, health insurance, study material and equipment for laboratory and field work, plus traveling expenses to and from training sites within Austria.

Tenable in Austria for nine months.

Eligibility: Open to candidates from developing countries who are between the ages of 25 and 35, have a good working knowledge of English, have been recommended by the appropriate authorities in the applicant's own country, and have a master's or similar degree in science, agriculture or veterinary medicine from a university or other recognized institution of higher education. Applicants should have practical experience within at least one special subject of their field of professional training.

Note: No provisions are provided for dependants. It is strongly advised that dependents do not accompany Fellows due to frequent moves during the course.

Fellows must provide their own transportation to and from Austria. A partial refund of these expenses will be made from a grant provided by *Unesco.* Participants originating from certain developing countries will be further assisted by the Austrian Government so that travel expenses will be fully covered.

Application forms and further information may be obtained from the Austrian Diplomatic Mission, Cultural Attaché or Cultural Institute in the applicant's home country, or from the Institute.

Closing date: 15th October.

Further information from:
 Institute of Limnology
 Berggasse 18/19
 A-1090 Vienna
 Austria

[347]

AUSTRIAN FEDERAL ECONOMIC CHAMBER

Study Scholarships are available annually to not more than 20 nationals of developing countries for study at Austrian technical or economic universities, the University of Mining in Leoben, or at the University of Agriculture in Vienna. Candidates should be between 19 and 30 years of age and must be enrolled as regular students. Scholarships are tenable for one academic year and renewable if good progress in study is achieved. The value is 4,300 schillings per month. Application should reach the Austrian Federal Economic Chamber by May at the latest.

Further information from:
 Internationales Studentenheim
 Der Bundeskammer der Gew. Wirtschaft
 Starkfriedgasse 15
 A1180 Vienna
 Austria

[348]

AUSTRIAN INSTITUTE *(New York City)*

Purpose: To enable American teachers and students to further their research projects or schooling in Austria.

Subject: German language and Austrian literature.

Value: Nine monthly installments each of 5,000 Austrian schillings for undergraduates; 5,500 schillings for doctoral candidates; and 6,500 schillings for professors. Grants also cover free tuition at universities, health and accident insurance, and a travel allowance of 2,500 schillings for trips within Austria.

Tenable for nine months at Austrian universities and other institutions.

Eligibility: Candidates should be American teachers or students of German who are between the ages of 20 and 35 years.

Note: Candidates should have an excellent command of the German language. Students must have completed at least two years of satisfactory study at a college or university.
  A resumé in German, copies of transcripts, at least two letters of recommendation, and a detailed description of any study project to be undertaken should be submitted prior to closing date to the address below.

Closing date: 15th January.

Further information from:
  Austrian Institute
  11 East 52nd Street
  New York, New York 10022
  U.S.A.

[349]

AUXILIARY TO THE AMERICAN OSTEOPATHIC ASSOCIATION

National Osteopathic College Scholarships

The Association awards Scholarships annually to U.S. or Canadian citizens who have been accepted to an approved college of osteopathic medicine. Scholarships are for one year and may be renewed for a second year. One award of US$4,000 is paid to the school in which the awardee has matriculated US$1,000 per semester. Approximately 25 awards of US$2,000 are paid to the school in which the awardee has matriculated US$500 per semester. Applicants must have high scholastic standing (minimum 3.0 grade point average on the 4.0 scale), be of good moral character, and demonstrate financial need. Applications may be obtained from the Financial Aid Office of the approved college, or from the address below. *Closing date:* 1st May.

Further information from:
  Auxiliary to the American Osteopathic
    Association
  212 East Ohio Street
  Chicago, Illinois 60611
  U.S.A.

[350]

AVIATION/SPACE WRITERS ASSOCIATION *(U.S.A.)*

Journalism Awards

The Association offers an honorarium of US$100 plus a scroll for aviation or space writing during the calendar year. There are nine entry categories: newspapers with under 200,000 circulation; newspapers with over 200,000 circulation; magazine—special interest/trade; magazine—general interest; books—non-fiction; books—technical/training; television/radio—documentary (locally produced); and photo journalism—still photography. Both members and non-members of the Association may apply. *Closing date:* 5th January.
  The Association also offers the following awards for entries in the categories listed above, but no entries are to be submitted for them: *Robert S. Ball Memorial Award* (US$500) for space writing in any media; *Earl D. Osborn award* (US$500) for writing or reporting in any media on the subject of general aviation; *James J. Strebig Memorial Award* (US$500) for aviation writing or reporting in any media.

Further information from:
  Aviation/Space Writers Association
  c/o William F. Kaiser, Executive
    Secretary
  Cliffwood Road
  Chester, New Jersey 07930
  U.S.A.

B

See *How to Use The Grants Register*, page ix

[351]

JOHANN SEBASTIAN BACH INTERNATIONAL COMPETITION
(Leipzig)

Various monetary prizes, medals and certificates are offered in the Competition which is held from time to time. Sections—piano, organ, vocal music, violin and harpsichord (1984). Musicians from all countries who are under 32 years of age may apply.

Further information from:
Secretariat, Bach-Competition
Grassistrasse 8
DDR-701 Leipzig
German Democratic Republic

[352]

BACK PAIN ASSOCIATION, LTD. *(U.K.)*

The following awards are for work in any area of knowledge that may contribute to improvements in the prevention, diagnosis or treatment of pain in the region of the spine. The value of awards is individually assessed.

Research Fellowships are open to suitably qualified and experienced scientists or clinicians. Fellows conduct research for 12 months (renewable for a further year) in an agreed United Kingdom research centre. Fellowships are not provided for work toward a higher degree.

Travelling Fellowships are offered for suitably qualified United Kingdom residents to spend up to 12 months in an agreed institution outside the United Kingdom, and for residents of foreign countries to spend up to 12 months in United Kingdom institutions. The value of each Fellowship includes return travel costs, institutional fees and a subsistence allowance.

Research Grants are offered for both individual and group projects and are tenable in the United Kingdom at suitable establishments for 12 months, renewable for up to two years. Candidates should be appropriately qualified and experienced, but medical qualifications are not necessarily required. Applications should be received by 15th April for commencement on 1st October.

Further information from:
Back Pain Association, Ltd.
Grundy House, Somerset Road
Teddington
England TW11 8TD

[353]

BANCROFT PRIZES *(U.S.A.)*
Columbia University

Two prizes of US$4,000 each are given annually to authors of distinguished works in the following categories: American history (including biography); American diplomacy. The competition is open to all, regardless of citizenship. The word "American" is interpreted to include all the Americas, North, South and Central; however, the award is confined to works originally written in English or of which there is a published translation in English. Books to be considered should be first published during the year preceding that of the award.

Published works should be submitted to the address below no later than 1st November; page-proof copy may be submitted later, provided the work is published before 31st December.

Further information from:
Bancroft Prize Committee
202A Low Library
Columbia University
New York, New York 10027
U.S.A.

[354]

BANK OF IRELAND

Geore Russel A E Memorial Fund Award

One Award of £100 is made every five years in recognition of published or unpublished work, creative or scholarly, which is of high standard.

Further information from:
    Trustee Department, Head Office
    Bank of Ireland
    Lower Baggot Street
    Dublin 2
    Ireland

[355]

BANK OF NEW ZEALAND
New Zealand Academy of Fine Arts

BNZ Art Awards

Two Awards of NZ$500 each are given annually to New Zealanders for works in pottery, sculpture and print which have not previously been exhibited in Wellington, New Zealand. Applicants may exhibit in more than one medium; up to six works in any one category and not more than eight works in total.

Closing date: May/June.

Further information from:
    Director
    New Zealand Academy of Fine Arts
    Private Bag
    Wellington
    New Zealand

[356]

BANK OF NEW ZEALAND
New Zealand Women Writers' Society

BNZ Writers' Awards

Competitors for the following Awards should be New Zealanders by birth or naturalisation, or resident in New Zealand for 5 years continuously before the date of the Award. Entries must be submitted under a pen name by August of the year of the Award. Application forms are available.

B.N.Z. Katherine Mansfield Awards of NZ$500—first prize and NZ$250—second prize are offered in odd-numbered years for an unpublished short story with a maximum length of 7,000 words.

B.N.Z. Novice Writers' Award of NZ$250 is offered biennially for unpublished short stories with maximum lengths of 5,000 words. Candidates should be amateur writers who have not had works previously published.

Further information from:
    Administering Committee
    Katherine Mansfield Memorial/Young
        Writers' Awards
    c/o Bank of New Zealand
    P.O. Box 2392
    Wellington 1
    New Zealand

[357]

BANK OF SWEDEN TERCENTENARY FOUNDATION

Bank of Sweden Tercentenary Fund

Fellowships are available through the Fund for the purpose of promotion and support of research connected with Sweden. The areas of research are unrestricted and priority is given to new research activities which require rapid and substantial aid, and to fields of research whose requirements are not adequately provided from other sources. The Fund seeks to promote relations with international research and concerns itself in particular with support of large and long-term research projects.

There are no formal application forms. Applications should include a detailed description of the project, time required, expected results and methods the applicant will use in order to achieve them, and a detailed calculation of the costs involved.

Closing date: 1st February and 1st September.

Further information from:
    Bank of Sweden Tercentenary Fund
    Box 1649
    S-11186 Stockholm
    Sweden

[358]

BAPTIST UNION OF GREAT BRITAIN AND IRELAND

Scholarship

Purpose: To promote biblical and theological learning.

No. offered: One Scholarship annually.

Value: £450 per annum.

Tenable at a college affiliated to the Baptist Union for one or two years.

Eligibility: Open to candidates who are studying for a theology degree in colleges affiliated to the Baptist Union and plan to engage in postgraduate study; graduates wishing to read for an advanced theology degree at a college affiliated to the Baptist Union.
Applicants should be members of a church in membership with the Baptist Union and must intend to serve in the home ministry as Accredited Ministers to the Baptist Union.

Closing date: 31st March.

Further information from:
Head of Department of Ministry
Baptist Union of Great Britain and Ireland
4 Southampton Row
London
England WC1B 4AB

[359]

BARLEY INDUSTRY RESEARCH COUNCIL *(Australia)*
WHEAT INDUSTRY RESEARCH COUNCIL *(Australia)*

Research Grants

Subjects: Scientific, technical or economic research in connection with the Australian barley and wheat industries—includes breeding, agronomy, physiology, diseases, tillage, engineering, and economics.

No. offered: Approximately 20 barley Grants and 160 wheat Grants annually.

Value: Allocations are based on individual merit within availability of funds.

Eligibility: Open to those who can satisfy the relevant Council regarding their ability to undertake the proposed research.

Closing date: 1st March for following financial year. Interested persons should obtain additional application instructions in time to finalize applications by the due date.

Further information from the Secretary of the Barley Industry Research Council or the Secretary of the Wheat Industry Research Council at:
Department of Primary Industry
Canberra, A.C.T.
Australia 2600

[360]

BEIT MEMORIAL FELLOWSHIPS *(U.K.)*

Junior Fellowships
Senior Fellowships

Subjects: Research in medicine, and allied sciences in relation to medicine.

No. offered: Approximately five Fellowships annually.

Value: £6,880 to £8,515 per annum, plus £967 London allowance.

Tenable at an approved college, hospital or medical school in the United Kingdom for three years.

Eligibility: Open to graduates of any faculty from an approved university in the United Kingdom, British Dominions, Protectorates, Mandated Territories, India, Pakistan, and Ireland. Occasionally, a medical diploma registerable in the United Kingdom will be accepted as qualification.

Closing date: 3rd week of March.

Further information from:
Professor W.G. Spector, Secretary
Beit Memorial Fellowships
Histopathology Department
St. Bartholomew's Hospital
London
England EC1A 7BE

[361]

BEIT TRUST (Zimbabwe)

Postgraduate Fellowships

Subjects: Unrestricted.

No. offered: Four Fellowships annually to persons domiciled in Zimbabwe; three Fellowships annually to persons domiciled in Zambia.

Value: £2,500 per annum personal allowance, plus tuition and additional fees if held overseas; Z$3,200 per annum if held in Southern Africa.

Tenable at approved universities and other institutions in the United Kingdom, Ireland, Finland and Southern Africa for two years, with possibility of extension for a further year.

Eligibility: Open to persons under 30 years of age (35 in the case of doctors) who are university graduates domiciled in Zambia or Zimbabwe.

Closing date: 31st October.

Further information from:
Secretary to the Advisory Board
Beit Trust Fellowships
18 Samora Machel Avenue
Salisbury C.1
Zimbabwe

[362]

BELGIAN AMERICAN EDUCATIONAL FOUNDATION, INC.

C.R.B. Advanced Fellowships for Study in Belgium

Purpose: To promote independent study and research on projects for which Belgium provides special advantages.

Subjects: Unrestricted.

No. offered: Six or seven Fellowships annually.

Value: US$8,000. Additional funds must be provided by married Fellows for dependents.

Tenable in Belgium for ten months; not renewable.

Eligibility: Open to American citizens, preferably under 30 years of age who have a master's degree or are working towards a Ph.D. or equivalent degree. A speaking and reading knowledge of either French or Dutch is required.

Note: Candidates must be nominated by the dean of their graduate school.

Closing date: (for nominations) 31st December.

Further information from:
Belgian American Educational
 Foundation
420 Lexington Avenue
New York, New York 10017
U.S.A.

[363]

BELGIAN ROYAL SOCIETY OF NUMISMATICS

Prize

Purpose: To promote the study of scientific numismatics.

Subjects: Numismatics and any studies directly related to it.

No. offered: One Prize every four years. Next awarded in 1985.

Value: Approximately 30,000 Belgian francs, paid in one lump sum.

Eligibility: Open to anyone, regardless of citizenship, age, sex, or academic titles. Studies should be at least 100 typewritten pages.

Note: Members of the bureau of the Society are not eligible to apply.
 In the event of publication, the Society must be acknowledged.

Closing date: 15th December, 1984.

Further information from:
Professor Tony Hackens, Secretary
28a Avenue Leopold
B 1330 Rixensart
Belgium

[364]

BERKSHIRE CONFERENCE OF WOMEN HISTORIANS

Awards

Purpose: To promote historical scholarship by women.

Subjects: All fields of history.

No. offered: One annual Award in each category—books and articles.

Value: US$100 each.

Eligibility: Open to any woman historian who is a citizen or resident of the United States or Canada.

Closing date: 15th February of each year.

Further information from:
Berkshire Conference of Women
  Historians
University of Maryland
Department of History
College Park, Maryland 20742
U.S.A.

[365]

BERKSHIRE MUSIC CENTER *(Lenox, Massachusetts)*

Fellowships

Purpose: To meet the needs of young musicians (instrumentalists, singers, composers and conductors) who have completed their formal training and are active performers wishing to undertake intensive work on performance.

No. offered: Approximately 140 Fellowships annually.

Value: Fellowship underwrites complete tuition, with additional aid for housing and travel where necessary.

Tenable at the Berkshire Music Center, Tanglewood, Lenox, Massachusetts, for eight weeks (July and August).

Eligibility: Open to persons between 18 and 30 years of age. No particular academic qualifications are necessary.

Note: An audition is required; tapes are acceptable under certain circumstances.

Closing date: 1st March.

Further information from:
Berkshire Music Center Fellowships
Boston Symphony Orchestra, Inc.
Symphony Hall
Boston, Massachusetts 02115
U.S.A.

[366]

ANEURIN BEVAN MEMORIAL FOUNDATION *(U.K.)*

Indian Government Fellowship

Subjects: Humanities, medicine, nursing, science.

Value: Maintenance allowance of 200 rupees per day, local transport costs and incidental expenses, actual medical expenses, plus tourist class return air passage to India from the United Kingdom and back.

Tenable in India for three months.

Eligibility: Open to citizens of the United Kingdom holding senior status in the fields of study.

Further information from:
Educational/Scientific Adviser
India House, Aldwych
London
England WC2B 4NA

[367]

WORTH BINGHAM MEMORIAL FUND *(Washington, D.C.)*

Bingham Prize

The Prize of US$1,000 is designed to honor newspaper or magazine reporting that investigates and analyses situations of national significance in the Washington political community where the public interest is being ill-served. Situations may involve the congress, executive or judiciary branches of government, lobbyists or the press itself. Judges will be guided by such factors as the reporting enterprize, obstacles overcome in getting information, accuracy, clarity of analysis and writing style, magnitude of the situation, and impact on the public, including any reforms that may have resulted.

Entries may be single stories, a series of related articles or up to three unrelated articles. Columns and editorials are also eligible. Single entries and at least half the articles in a series should have been published during the year prior to that in which the Prize is given. Individuals are encouraged to submit their own work.

Closing date: 15th February.

Further information from:
Worth Bingham Memorial Fund
1321 31st Street, N.W.
Washington, D.C. 20007
U.S.A.

[368]

BIOCHEMICAL SOCIETY *(U.K.)*

Boehringer Mannheim Travelling Fellowships

Purpose: To enable research students and other young biochemists to spend short periods of research or training outside their own country.

No. offered: Up to three Fellowships annually.

Value: A total sum of £400.

Eligibility: Open to members of the Society who are under the age of 30.

Closing date: 31st January.

Further information from:
Executive Secretary
Biochemial Society
7 Warwick Court
London
England WC1R 5DP

[369]

BIOCHEMICAL SOCIETY *(U.K.)*

Unilever European Fellowships

Purpose: To enable biochemists to undertake research in any field of biochemistry in a laboratory outside their own country.

No. offered: One Fellowship annually.

Value: Variable within U.K. university lecturer scale, plus approved travelling expenses.

Tenable at any laboratory or institute, including Unilever research laboratories in (a) continental Europe, or (b) the United Kingdom, for one year.

Eligibility: Open to (a)·United Kingdom citizens and (b) European nationals with a Ph.D. degree or equivalent qualification.

Closing date: 15th February.

Further information from:
Executive Secretary
Biochemical Society
7 Warwick Court
London
England WC1R 5DP

[370]

R.D. BIRLA SMARAK KOSH *(India)*
Bombay Hospital Trust

An endowment in the memory of Shri Rameshwardasji Birla provides funds for assistance through the Medical Research Centre (MRC) of Bombay Hospital Trust and directly through the Bombay Hospital Trust (BHT).

Annual Award (MRC) of 100,000 rupees is awarded each year for outstanding work in medical and related fields carried out by an Indian in India.

Triennial Award (MRC) of 500,000 rupees is awarded every three years for an outstanding contribution in the field of medicine or related fields. This Award is not restricted to Indians.

Research Fellowships (MRC) with stipends of up to 1,000 rupees a month in India, or US$500 a month abroad, are offered to Indians for research or training in medical or related fields.

Scholarships (BHT) of 3,000 rupees per annum in India, or 20,000 rupees per annum abroad, are offered to Indians engaged in the study of medicine or related fields.

R.D. Birla Memorial Lectures (BHT): Eminent Indians or foreigners are invited to deliver lectures on a subject of public, academic or humanitarian interest. Monographs of the lectures are published.

Note: The Trust also provides assistance to charity hospitals and medical institutions, preferably in rural areas.

Further information from:
 N. Nanjundiah, Director
 R.D. Birla Smarak Kosh
 Bombay Hospital Trust
 Bombay Hospital Avenue
 Bombay 400 020
 India

[371]

JAMES TAIT BLACK MEMORIAL PRIZES
(U.K.)
University of Edinburgh
Scottish Arts Council

Two prizes of about £1,000 each are given each spring for the best novel and the best biographical work published in the previous calendar year. The choice is made by the Regius Professor of Rhetoric and English Literature at the University of Edinburgh. The Prizes are not restricted to United Kingdom citizens.

Publishers should submit works for consideration on publication.

Further information from:
 James Tait Black Memorial Prizes
 Secretary to the University
 University of Edinburgh
 Old College, South Bridge
 Edinburgh
 Scotland EH8 9YL

[372]

BLACKWELL'S BOOKSHOP *(Oxford, U.K.)*

James Cook Bicentenary Scholarship

Purpose: To provide an opportunity for middle-ranking librarians in Australia and New Zealand to further their professional interests and to study specialized aspects of librarianship.

No. offered: One Scholarship in even-numbered years.

Value: Approximately £9,000, plus supplement for married Scholars; paid in two installments.

Tenable for an academic year in the United Kingdom in a work situation or at an approved institution of higher education.

Eligibility: Open to Australian or New Zealand citizens of at least five years standing who are graduates of a recognized university and hold professional qualifications that entitle them to be on the professional register of the LAA or NZLA. Applicants must be under 35 years of age, in good health and must give an undertaking to return to their home country on completion of their research.

Further information from:
 Harrison Bryan, Convener
 James Cook Bicentenary Scholarship
 National Library of Australia
 Canberra, A.C.T.
 Australia 2600

[373]

BLACKWELL'S BOOKSHOP *(Oxford, U.K.)*

Nancy Stirling Lambert Scholarship

Purpose: To enable librarians to carry out research into matters of common concern to libraries and the book trade.

No. offered: One Scholarship annually.

Value: Approximately £5,500, to cover travelling and other expenses necessarily incurred in the course of research and personal maintenance.

Tenable at the College of Librarianship, Aberystwyth, Wales, for twelve months; not renewable.

Eligibility: Open to graduates with professional qualifications in librarianship residing in a specific region announced each time the award is advertised. Candidates are required to register for the University of Wales degree of Master of Librarianship.

Closing date: As advertised.

Further information from:
 Registrar
 College of Librarianship
 Aberystwyth
 Wales SY23 3AS

[374]

B'NAI B'RITH INTERNATIONAL Commission on Adult Jewish Education

B'nai B'rith International Literary Award

One Award of US$1,000 is offered annually in recognition of a body of work which has advanced scholarship in Jewish studies or supported Jewish values.

Not confirmed for 1983.

Further information from:
 Rabbi Irwin M. Blank, Director
 Commission on Adult Jewish Education
  of B'nai B'rith International
 1640 Rhode Island Avenue, N.W.
 Washington, D.C. 20036
 U.S.A.

[375]

BOARD FOR MISSION AND UNITY OF THE GENERAL SYNOD OF THE CHURCH OF ENGLAND

Anglican Studentships for Priests/Ordinands

Purpose: To promote postgraduate study of Roman Catholic, Old Catholic or Orthodox Churches at their institutes or universities, as part of the growing ecumenism between the Anglican and other churches.

No. offered: Varies at each centre.

Value: Supplementary grants are provided in accordance with finance and facilities offered by the host church.

Tenable at Old Catholic Faculty of Theology, University of Berne, Switzerland; Orthodox Theological Institute, Bucharest, Romania; Orthodox Theological Academy, Belgrade, Yugoslavia; and Faculties of Theology, Universities of Louvain, Belgium, or elsewhere by arrangement. Duration dependent upon nature of study-visit or scholarship. Maximum one academic year.

Eligibility: Open to ministers (usually postgraduates) or accepted ordinands of the Church of England, sponsored by their bishop and/or college principal. The accommodation and finance available normally require that applicants be unmarried. A working knowledge of the language concerned as well as previous study of theology is also required.

Closing date: 31st January.

Further information from:
 Ecumenical Scholarships Secretary
 Board for Mission and Unity
 Church House
 Dean's Yard
 London
 England SW1P 3NZ

[376]

BOISE FOUNDATION *(U.K.)*

Two Boise Scholarships, one of up to £1,000 and one of a smaller amount, are awarded annually to enable vocalists, or performing artists on any musical instrument, to further their musical education either in the United Kingdom or by travel and/or tuition abroad. Awards are made on the basis of a competitive audition held annually, for which candidates must be nominated; names of nominators are available on request from the Foundation Secretary. Musical students of any nationality, under the age of 30, ordinarily resident in Britain or Ireland, or students from the British Commonwealth temporarily resident in Britain for their musical education or foreign nationals who have been resident in the United Kingdom for at least three years prior to commencing musical training, are eligible for the awards, at the discretion of the Foundation Committee. Awards are held at musical centres either in the United Kingdom or abroad, subject to the approval of the Scholar's plan of study by the Chairman of the Committee.

Further information from:
Honorary Secretary
Boise Foundation
14 Bedford Square
London
England WC1B 3JG

[377]

BOLLINGEN PRIZE IN POETRY OF THE YALE UNIVERSITY LIBRARY *(New Haven, Connecticut)*

The Prize is awarded in odd-numbered years to the American poet whose work, in the opinion of the Committee, represents the highest achievement in the field of American poetry during the two years under review. The Prize, in the amount of US$5,000, is based upon published work during the review period, although prior achievement may be taken into consideration. Individuals who are citizens of the United States and have not won the Prize previously are eligible. Because the Committee automatically considers all eligible books, authors and publishers are not encouraged to submit work.

Further information from:
Bollingen Prize in Poetry
Collection of American Literature
Box 1603 A, Yale Station
New Haven, Connecticut 06520
U.S.A.

[378]

BOLOGNA CENTER OF THE JOHNS HOPKINS UNIVERSITY

Bologna Center Fellowships

Subject: International affairs.

No. offered: Varies annually, depending on the number of qualified candidates seeking support.

Value: Fellowships vary in amount, and include tuition and a maintenance allowance. Non-American students may receive a maintenance allowance of up to 200,000 lire per month.

Tenable at the Bologna Center, Italy, for one academic year. Non-American students have the option of spending a second year at the Center to study for an M.A. degree.

Eligibility: Open to American and European college or university graduates with adequate preparation in the social sciences. They should have background knowledge of economics, history and political science and also a good command of English, since classes are conducted in that language.

Note: The Bologna Center is an integral part of the School of Advanced International Studies of the Johns Hopkins University. However, American students who wish to take the M.A. degree in international relations must spend one year at the school in Washington, either before or after their year at the Center.

Second-year Fellowships will be awarded for a year at the SAIS in Washington for those seeking an M.A. degree. At least six of these are available to European candidates. Similar Fellowships are offered by the Johns Hopkins University of Baltimore, Maryland and Carleton University, Ottawa, Canada.

Applicants must obtain official application forms and will have to attend an interview before selection. American students should apply to the *Admissions Office of the School of Advanced International Studies, 1740 Massachusetts Avenue, N.W., Washington, D.C. 20036*. European students should apply to the address below.

Closing dates: Bologna—1st April; Washington, D.C.—1st February.

Address:
Registrar
Bologna Center
Via Belmeloro 11
40 126 Bologna
Italy

[379]

BOOKSELLERS ASSOCIATION OF GREAT BRITAIN AND IRELAND
Whitbread and Company Ltd.

Whitbread Literary Awards

Three Awards of £3,000 each are offered annually for a novel, a biography or autobiography and a children's book—suitable for children aged seven or over. The Awards are made to authors who are domiciled in the United Kingdom or Ireland for at least five years prior to the year in which the Award is given. Works for consideration may only be submitted by publishers and books must have been published, or be about to be published, in the year of the Award. *Closing date:* 1st September.

Note: In addition, a further Award of £1,000 is offered for a special fiction category to be chosen by a poll of leading literary editors. No submissions are necessary for this Award.

Further information from:
  Whitbread Literary Awards
  Booksellers Association of Great Britain and
    Ireland
  154 Buckingham Palace Road
  London
  England SW1W 9TZ

[380]

THEODORA BOSANQUET BURSARY FUND *(U.K.)*

Theordora Bosanquet Bursary

The Bursary is intended to provide residence and board for up to four weeks at Crosby Hall, Chelsea, London for women students or women postgraduate students who are researching in English literature or history and require the use of reference libraries or other sources of information in London.

Closing date: 23rd November.

Further information from:
  Trustees
  Theordora Bosanquet Bursary
  c/o Crosby Hall
  Cheyne Walk London
  England SW3 5AZ

[381]

BOSTON GLOBE *(U.S.A.)*

Boston Globe-Horn Book Awards
Children's Book Awards Competition

Three Awards, in the amount of US$200 each, will be given annually for a book of original fiction or poetry, for illustration, and for non-fiction prose. Entries should have been published in the U.S. between 1st July and 30th June of the year of the Competition. Books should be submitted to judges by April 1st. Textbooks and new or revised editions are not eligible.

Further information from:
  Mrs. Stephanie Loer
  Children's Book Editor
  Boston Globe
  Boston, Massachusetts 02107
  U.S.A.

[382]

BOTANICAL SOCIETY OF AMERICA, INC.

Darbaker Award of approximately US$425 is given annually for meritorious work in the study of microscipical algae; it is restricted to residents of North American and based upon papers, in the English language, published within two yers of the closing date which is 1st January.

Paleobotanical Section Award of US$100 is given annually to the author of the most outstanding paper presented at the Annual Paleobotanical Section Meeting of the Society.

Jeanette Siron Pelton Award of US$1,000 is given periodically to a scientist for sustained and imaginative productivity in the field of experimental plant morphology. Closing date: January.

Phytochemical Section Award of US$100 is given annually to the author of the most outstanding paper presented at the Annual Phytochemical Section Meeting of the Society.

Pteridological Section Award of US$100 is given annually to the author of the most outstanding paper presented at the Annual Pteridologial Section Meeting of the Society.

Note: The Society also gives one or more *Merit Awards* annually to a person or persons judged to have made outstanding contributions in any area of the botanical sciences. The Award consists of a certificate, and there are no restrictions as to residence, age, sex or citizenship.

Further information from:
  Office of the Secretary
  Botanical Society of America
  c/o Dr. Carol C. Baskin
  School of Biological Sciences
  University of Kentucky
  Lexington, Kentucky 40506
  U.S.A.

[383]

BOTANICAL SOCIETY OF SOUTH AFRICA

Flora Conservation Scholarship

Purpose: To promote research in plant ecology in connection with any aspect of conservation of South African indigenous flora.

Value: R500, annually. Payments are made in six-monthly instalments upon receipt of satisfactory progress reports.

Tenable for two years, with a possible one year extension.

Eligibility: Open to South Africans who hold an honours degree in botany and are proceeding to a higher degree.

Note: The Society also awards the *Bolus Medal* from time to time to non-professional botanists who have contributed significantly to botanical science in South Africa.

Closing date: 31st October.

Further information from:
  Secretary
  Botanical Society of South Africa
  Kirstenbosch
  Claremont, Cape Province 7735
  South Africa

[384]

BOUWCENTRUM INTERNATIONAL EDUCATION *(Rotterdam)*

Fellowships for Courses

Courses: International Course on Housing Planning and Building.

Value: Variable.

Tenable at Bouwcentrum, usually for five months.

Eligibility: Open to graduates of any Third World country who possess a bachelor's degree from a recognized university of similar institution and who are engaged in work directly related to the field of the course concerned. Candidates must have a working knowledge of English.

Note: Applications should be initiated at national government level. Technical assistance agencies include: United Nations (details of Fellowships and procedure to be followed from: Resident Representative, U.N. Development Programme in the applicant's home country); European Economic Community (Citizens of countries associated with the EEC through the Lomë Convention may be recommedned for Fellowships by their national governments. Applications to: Commission of the European Communities, Directorate General for Development, Education and Training Division, 200 rue de la Loi, 1049 Brussels, Belgium); Netherlands Government (applications to: Netherlands Embassy in the applicant's home country); for Latin America only: Applications to: Office of the local O.A.S. or Pan American Union Representative.

Further information from:
  Bouwcentrum International Education
  P.O. Box 299
  Rotterdam
  Netherlands

[385]

BRADFORD CHAMBER OF COMMERCE

John Speak Trust Scholarships

Purpose: To promote British trade abroad by assisting people to perfect a basic knowledge of a foreign language.

No. offered: Approximately four Scholarships annually.

Value: Approximately £1,050.

Tenable abroad for six months, or three months if a candidate's knowledge of a language is advanced; not renewable.

Eligibility: Open to British-born nationals intending to follow a careeer connected with the export trade of the United Kingdom who are over 18 years of age. A sound, basic knowledge of a language is required.

Closing dates: 28th February, 31st May, 31st October.

Further information from:
Miss W.M. Walker
Bradford Chamber of Commerce
Cheapside, Bradford
England BD1 4JZ

[386]

BRANDEIS UNIVERSITY CREATIVE ARTS AWARDS *(Waltham, Mass.)*

Purpose: To recognize the achievements of artists beyond the scope of university life, and to encourage and develop artistic and cultural life in America.

No. offered: One Award each in music, theatre arts, fine arts, literature, dance, and film.

Value: US$2,500 each.

Note: All selections are made by juries and no applications are accepted.

Awards are presented to established American artists for recognition of a lifetime achievement or for recognition of a talented American artist actively engaged and/or in mid-career.

Further information from:
Mrs. Marcia S. Isaacs
Creative Arts Commissions of Brandeis University
Brandeis House, 12 East 77th Street
New York, New York 10021
U.S.A.

[387]

BREAD LOAF WRITERS' CONFERENCE *(Middlebury, Vermont)*

Fellowships and Scholarships

Purpose: To provide both recognition for established writers and writers who show unusual promise, and an atmosphere in which writing can be discussed and criticized intensively.

Subjects: Fiction, non-fiction, poetry and children's literature.

No. offered: Varies.

Value: Fellowships carry no cash value but all regular charges at the Conference are paid for. Scholarships cover full or partial tuition.

Tenable at the Bread Loaf campus, Middlebury College, Vermont, for the last two weeks of August.

Eligibility: Open to persons nominated by a publisher, editor, agent, established writer, or teacher of writing. Candidates for Fellowships are assumed to have published a book or to have had a book-length manuscript accepted for publication. Candidates for Scholarship assistance usually have had articles published in periodicals. There are no restrictions regarding nationality or citizenship.

Closing date: 1st March.

Further information from:
Bread Loaf Writers' Conference
Middlebury College
Middlebury, Vermont 05753
U.S.A.

[388]

BRITISH ACADEMY

Research Awards

The Academy makes a number of Research Awards to support research in any branch of the humanities and social sciences. Applicants must normally be resident in the United Kingdom and may apply on their own behalf or on behalf of some British body.

Awards are intended for the following purposes: (a) travel and maintenance expenses in connection with an approved programme of research; (b) fieldwork, whether historical, philogical, archaeological or anthropological; (c) provision of mechanical or photographic aids for research; (d) costs of preparation of research for publication; (e) in special cases aid with the publication of research.

Closing dates: The end of February, April, September and December.

Note: The Academy Awards are never available for degree work and are tenable on a yearly basis.

Further information from:
Secretary
British Academy
Burlington House, Piccadilly
London
England W1V ONS

[389]

BRITISH ACADEMY

Fellowships

British Academy/Wolfson Visiting Fellowships: These Fellowships are available for the following purposes: (a) to enable British scholars to study in France, West Germany, Italy, the Netherlands, Belgium and Scandinavia; (b) to bring to the United Kingdom scholars from these Western European countries. Suitable subjects for study are: history, law, economics and political studies, particularly with regard to the history and understanding of the modern world. Preference is given to younger scholars.

Thank-Offering to Britain Research Fellowships: Fellowships of up to £3,750 are available for study in any European country.

Note: The Academy awards are never available for degree work and are tenable on a yearly basis.

Further information from:
Secretary
British Academy
Burlington House, Piccadilly
London
England W1V ONS

[390]

BRITISH ACADEMY

Small Grants Research Fund in the Humanities

The University Grants Committee, the Department of Education and Science, the Scottish Education Department and the Department of Education for Northern Ireland have made available funds, to be administered on the recommendation of the Nominating Committee of the British Academy, to support research by individual scholars in the humanities. Applicants should be serving members of the staff of universities or other institutions of higher education in the United Kingdom. Preference may be given to applications from younger scholars. Awards are intended to cover expenses incurred in research in specified subject areas not already covered by existing schemes, and will be made only to individuals. Awards will not be made to cover general institutional expenses nor for unspecified work. No grant will normally exceed £2,000 nor will it normally be renewable.

Subject areas are: language and literature (including the history of language and linguistic studies); philosophy; religious studies; history (in its widest sense, including the history of art, music, ideas, science, etc.); law; and archaeology (excluding excavations, field work and laboratory analysis). Grants for research in the last two named areas will have regard to other sources of support.

Awards are intended for the following purposes; (a) travel and maintenance expenses in the United Kingdom or overseas in connection with an approved programme of research; (b) outside part-time secretarial assistance; (c) research costs, e.g. computer time, microfilm, reprography, photographic materials; (d) the cost of preparation of research for publication (but excluding aid with publication itself).

Closing dates for the receipt of applications are the end of September, December, February and April.

Note: Applicants will be notified of decisions within three months of the relevant closing date.

Further information from:
Secretary
British Academy
Burlington House, Piccadilly
London
England W1V ONS

[391]

BRITISH ACADEMY

Rose Mary Crawshay Prizes

Annual Prizes are awarded by the Academy to

a woman of any nationality who, in the judgement of the Council of the British Academy, has written or published an historical or critical work of sufficient value on any subject connected with English literature, preference being given to a work regarding Byron, Shelley or Keats. The work submitted must have been written or published within three years immediately preceding the year of the Award.

Further information from:
  Secretary
  British Academy
  Burlington House, Piccadilly
  London
  England W1V ONS

[392]

BRITISH ARCHAEOLOGICAL ASSOCIATION

Reginald Taylor Prize

The Prize of £100 is awarded annually for the best unpublished essay, not exceeding 7,500 words, on any subject of archaeological, art historical or antiquarian interest within the period from the Roman era to AD 1830.

The successful candidate may be invited to read his essay before the Association, and the essay will go before the editorial committee for consideration for publication in the Journal.

Competitors are advised to notify the Hon. Editor in advance of the intended subject of their work and the completed essay should reach the Editor not later than 31st December.

Further information from:
  Hon. Editor, Paul Everson
  British Archaeological Association
  c/o County Offices
  Newland, Lincoln
  England

[393]

BRITISH COUNCIL

British Council Scholarships

Subjects: Unrestricted: research or advanced study, but not necessarily toward a higher degree.

No. offered: Approximately 500 Scholarships are anticipated annually for the period 1982 to 1984 (approximately to Commonwealth countries and the remainder to the Middle East, Africa, Southeast Asia, Far East, Latin America, and Europe—including the Soviet Union).

Value: To cover tuition fees, personal maintenance grant, a grant for books and equipment, and approved travelling expenses in Britain, and in some cases fares to and from Britain. No financial help or other assistance can be provided for wives and children.

Tenable in Britain, normally for one academic year.

Eligibility: Open to persons, preferably between 25 and 35 years of age, who have already successfully completed a first degree course at a university, or who have equivalent academic or professional qualifications, and have already had some experience in original research or in their profession. Candidates must have a good knowledge of written and spoken English.

Unless a period of three years has elapsed, aplications cannot normally be considered from anyone who has previously visited Britain with financial aid either from the British Council, or from any other scheme whose funds are provided by the British government.

Preference is given to candidates likely to take a full part in the social and economic life of the community after their return to their home country.

Note: Applications should be made through the British Council's representatives overseas (or the British embassy or other duly appointed agent in countries where there is no representative) from whom aplication forms and other information may be obtained. Applications should not be forwarded to British Council offices in Britain.

No Scholar may be attached to his embassy, legation of high commissioner's office during tenure of his Scholarship, and he may not take paid employment without the consent of the Council; neither may he change his course of study without the Council's consent.

A Scholar is expected to return to his own country on completion of the Scholarship.

Closing date: Usually November/December for the academic year beginning the following October.

Address:
British Council
10 Spring Gardens
London
SW1A 2BN
England

[394]

BRITISH COUNCIL

Foreign Government Scholarships

Subjects: Variable; in most cases unrestricted.

No. offered: Approximately 300 Scholarships annually.

Value: Variable.

Tenable in most European countries and some in Asia and South America.

Eligibility: Candidates should normally be British citizens who qualify for postgraduate study or research.

Note: The Scholarships are offered by foreign governments and universities, and are mainly intended for postgraduate study and research.

Information concerning many foreign government awards is given in entries for foreign governments, ministries, etc. (see *Index of Awards and Awarding Bodies* and *Subject Index*).

Candidates are also advised to see the booklet *Scholarships Abroad* available from the British Council.

Closing date: Usually between November and March in the academic year preceding the year of award.

Further information from:
Overseas Educational Appointments Department
British Council
10 Spring Gardens
London
England SW1A 2BN

[395]

BRITISH COUNCIL

Academic Links and Interchange Scheme (ALIS)

Purpose: To promote direct contact between departments in universities, polytechnics and other institutions of higher education in Britain and equivalent institutions overseas with mutual scientific and academic interests and to encourage the development of longer term cooperation and research.

The following activities can be funded: joint research: joint publication; curriculum/course development; student exchange/mobility (exploratory visits by staff only); academic/professional/administrative staff exchange and development. Conference attendance not eligible for support but the design and planning of international seminars/workshops is.

Priority is given to visits which form part of, or might lead to a programme of collaboration in research, publication or teaching. Funding will normally be provided for exploratory visits or for visits during the formative stages of a link.

Subjects: Unrestricted.

No. offered: Varies annually.

Value: Normally a contribution towards travel expenses of visits either to or from Britain. Where travel expenses are not required a fixed per diem subsistence allowance may be paid. This is intended to cover meals, internal travel and other incidentals but not accommodation.

Eligibility: Awards are open to academic and research staff for visits throughout the world, with the exception of Eastern Europe and China, for which other arrangements appply.

Note: Applications should be made on standard application forms which are available from any British Council office and should be submitted along with relevant supporting documentation and letters of invitation to (overseas applicants) the local British Council Representative; UK applicants apply to address below.

All arrangements for outgoing and incoming visits should be made directly between the institutions concerned and are not the responsibility of the British Council.

Closing date: None, but applicants are advised to submit forms at least three months before the proposed visit.

Further information from:
Schemes Unit
Higher Education Division
British Council
10 Spring Gardens
London
England SW1A 2BN

[396]

BRITISH COUNCIL

Academic Links with Eastern Europe Scheme (ALEES)

Purpose: To facilitate exchange visits of staff and research workers in universities, polytechnics and other institutions of higher education in Britain and equivalent institutions in Eastern Europe with mutual scientific and academic interests and to encourage the development of longer term cooperation and research.

The following activities can be funded: joint research; joint publication; curriculum-/course development; student exchange/mobility (exploratory visits by staff only); academic/professional/administrative staff exchanges and development. Conference attendance is not eligible for support but the design and planning of international seminars/workshops is.

Priority is given to visits which form part of, or might lead to a programme of collaboration in research, publication or teaching. Funding will normally be provided for exploratory visits or for visits during the formative stage of a link, after which the link is expected to be self-supporting.

Subjects: Unrestricted.

No. offered: Varies annually.

Value: For visits from Britain a contribution is made towards travel expenses. It is expected that the host institution in Eastern Europe will meet subsistence and accommodation expenses. For visitors to Britain a contribution is made towards subsistence expenses.

Eligibility: Awards are open to academic and research staff for visits to or from Bulgaria, Czechoslovakia, the German Democratic Republic, Hungary, Romania and the Soviet Union.

Note: Applications should be made on standard application forms which are available from any British Council office and should be submitted along with relevant supporting documentation and letters of invitation to (overseas applicants) the Cultural Section of the British Embassy; UK applicants apply to the address below.

All arrangements for outgoing and incoming visits should be made directly between the institutions concerned and are not the responsibility of the British Council.

Closing date: None, but applicants are advised to submit forms at least three months before the proposed visit.

Further information from:
Schemes Unit
Higher Education Division
British Council
10 Spring Gardens
London
England SW1A 2BN

[397]

BRITISH COUNCIL

Academic Links with China Scheme (ALSC)

Terms and conditions are similar to those of the Academic Links with Eastern Europe Scheme, described in the preceding entry.

Further information from:
Schemes Unit
Higher Education Division
British Council
10 Spring Gardens
London
England SW1A 2BN

[398]

BRITISH COUNCIL

The Inter-University Council for Higher Education Overseas was merged with the British Council in 1981.

Latest information on the programmes of the former Inter-University Council may be obtained from the British Council. These programmes include: Appointments in Overseas Universities (recruitment of U.K. academic staff); Librarian Training Awards (periods in the U.K. for overseas university library administrators); Resettlement Fellowships (re-employment in the U.K. of expatriate university staff); Senior Fellowships (periods in the U.K. for senior staff members of university institutions); University Interview Fund (interviews in U.K. institutions for expatriate staff wishing to return); Training Scheme for University Administrators (short visits for senior and experienced administrators); Technician Training Scheme (periods in the U.K. for university technicians); and Staff Development Scholarships (periods in the U.K. for junior staff members of overseas universities).

Further information from:
British Council
Committee for International Cooperation
  in Higher Education
Higher Education Division
10 Spring Gardens
London
England SW1A 2BN

[399]

BRITISH DENTAL ASSOCIATION

Amalgamated Dental Company Scholarships

Purpose: To provide assistance to undergraduate and postgraduate dental students.

Tenable in dental schools in the United Kingdom, for one year.

Eligibility: Open to students who are studying at, or have been accepted for admission to, one of the recognised dental schools in the United Kingdom. Character, academic record, standard of scholarship, all-round ability, and financial circumstances will be taken into account. Other things being equal, preference is given to applicants who are related to practising or decreased dentists.

Closing date: 31st May.

Further information from:
  Amalgamated Dental Company
    Scholarship Fund
  c/o British Dental Association
  64 Wimpole Street
  London
  England W1M 8AL

[400]

BRITISH DENTAL ASSOCIATION

L.S. Farrar Dental Scholarship

Purpose: To give financial assistance to prospective dental surgeons.

No. offered and value: According to funds available.

Tenable at dental schools in the United Kingdom and Northern Ireland for one year; may be renewed.

Eligibility: Open to dental technicians in the United Kingdom and Northern Ireland who, through lack of financial means, would not other wise be in a position to qualify as dental surgeons. Students who are preparing for examinations to qualify themselves as dental technicians may also apply.

Closing date: 30th June.

Further information from:
  Secretary
  British Dental Association
  64 Wimpole Street
  London
  England W1M 8AL

[401]

BRITISH DIABETIC ASSOCIATION

Hermon Whittaker Memorial Bursaries: Ten Bursaries are awarded annually to assist diabetic medical students in the United Kingdom and Ireland with their studies. Bursaries, in the amount of £100 per annum, are tenable at any recognised medical school in the United Kingdom or Ireland for one year; renewable on reciept of satisfactory annual progress reports.
Closing date: 31st October.

Lawrence Research Fellowships: Fellowships are offered as advertised, for research in diabetes mellitus. The Fellowship is tenable in the United Kingdom for two years and open to suitably qualified members of the medical or scientific professions, who are resident in the United Kingdom.

Eli Lilly Fellowship: One Fellowship is offered every two years, as advertised for research in diabetes mellitus in children and adolescents. The Fellowship is tenable in the United Kingdom for two years and open to suitably qualified members of the medical or scientific professions, who are resident in the United Kingdom.

Further information from:
 British Diabetic Association
 10 Queen Anne Street
 London W1M 0BD
 England

[402]

BRITISH DIGESTIVE FOUNDATION

Fellowships and Grants

Purpose: To provide for gastro-enterological research into the prevention and treatment of alimentary and liver disorders.

No. offered: Ten or more Fellowships annually, vacancies occur; usually in June.

Value: A sum, in accordance with the status of the applicant, to be paid quarterly.

Tenable at recognised and established research centres in the United Kingdom for a period of one year, renewable.

Eligibility: Open to younger research workers wishing to conduct research in established centres under supervision.

Note: The above awards are offered in the following names: *Derek Crouch Research Fellowship; M. Cussins Research Fellowship; Thomas Hunt Memorial Grant; Hurst Research Travel Grant; W.E.C. Knott Research Fellowship; Markland Research Fellowship; S.K.F. Research Fellowship; Amelie Waring Fellowship; C.P. Zochonis Fellowship. If funds are available, the Foundation will make some smaller grants in addition to these awards.*

Closing date: As advertised in *Gut*, and *The Lancet*.

Further information from:
 British Digestive Foundation
 Room D, 7 Chandos Street
 Cavendish Square
 London
 England W1A 2LN

[403]

BRITISH FEDERATION OF UNIVERSITY WOMEN, LTD.

Awards

A small number of Awards are made each year for postgraduate study and research. These are open to members of any national affiliate of the International Federation of University Women.

Further information from:
 Secretary
 British Federation of University Women
 Crosby Hall, Cheyne Walk
 London
 England SW3 5BA

[404]

BRITISH GAS CORPORATION

Research Scholarships

Subjects: The subject proposed for research, which will normally lead to a Ph.D. or D. Phil degree, must afford scope for original work and be of a scientific character aproved by British Gas. It could be in one of the suggested fields—heat or mass transfer, flame and combustion, fluid mechanics, acoustics, physical metallurgy, corrosion, stress analysis, fracture mechanics, control engineering, surface chemistry and catalysis, and computing science. Proposals in other relevant fields will also be considered.

No. offered: Up to ten Scholarships annually.

Value: £3,320 per annum in London; £2,795 per annum elsewhere; £2,190 per annum for Scholars living at home. In addition, allowances for dependents, tuition, travel and additional experience will be paid.

Tenable at a United Kingdom university for three years.

Eligibility: Open normally to citizens of the United Kingdom who hold a good honours (1st or upper 2nd class) degree in a suitable discipline (usually in science or technology) from a British university. The head of department wil be required to submit in writing an estimate of the research potential of his candidate.

Note: The Scholarships will be distributed through the heads of departments or research schools. Applications will not be accepted directly from individual students.

Closing date: 15th December.

Further information from:
  Director of Research
  British Gas Corporation
  326 High Holborn
  London
  England WC1V 7PT

[405]

BRITISH HEART FOUNDATION

British American Research Fellowships, British Heart Foundation European Travelling Scholarships, British Heart Foundation Fellowships, Cardiac Care Equipment Grants, Research Awards.

Purpose: To encourage research into the causes, diagnosis, prevention and advances of cardiovascular disease; to inform doctors throughout the country of advances in the diagnosis, cure and treatment of heart diseases; and to improve facilities for treatment of heart patients where the National Health Service is unable to help.

No. offered: Approximately 100 to 120 Awards annually.

Value: £5,000 to £50,000 paid quarterly.

Tenable at any recognised research institutions for two to three years, renewable for up to five years.

Eligibility: Open to any graduate student of any age and either sex, who is resident in the United Kingdom.

Note: Research Funds Committee meet four times a year; Education Funds Committee meet four times a year; Cardiac Care Committee meet four times a year.

At the time of going to press, the information had not been confirmed.

Further information from:
  Medical Administrator
  British Heart Foundation
  102 Gloucester Place
  London
  England W1H 4DH

[406]

BRITISH INSTITUTE OF ARCHAEOLOGY AT ANKARA

Grants

Research Grants for studying the archaeology of Turkey-of all periods-are awarded for work at the Ankara Institute or at other centres in Turkey. Value and duration of the award is determined individually in regard to the level of work involved, qualifications and seniority of the applicant, and any other relevant factors. Preference is given for research projects in areas in which the Institute is already interested. Applicants should be a citizen of the United Kingdom or other British Commonwealth, and be qualified to undertake advanced research.

Travel Grants: Three or four Grants of up to £400, paid in one lump sum, are offered annually for travel to Turkey related to the study of its archaelology of any period. Open to graduates or undergraduates who are nationals of a British Commonwealth country.

Closing date for both Grants: 18th January.

Further information from:
  British Institute of Archaeology at Ankara
  c/o London Secretary
  69 Arlington Road
  London
  England NW1 7ES

[407]

BRITISH INSTITUTE OF ARCHAEOLOGY AT ANKARA

Michael Gough Memorial Prize

The Prize of approximately £200 is awarded every two or three years (last Prize given for 1983) for the best essay on a subject within the field of the archaeology of the Late Roman or Byzantine periods in Antolia. Open to United Kingdom or other British Commonwealth citizens who are less than thirty years of age as of 1st December of the year prior to that in which the award is made. Essays should be typescript, written in English, and not more than 10,000 words in length.

Closing date: 1st December.

Further information from:
British Institute of Archaeology at Ankara
c/o The British Academy
Burlington House
London
England W1V 0NS

[408]

BRITISH INSTITUTE IN EASTERN AFRICA

Grants-in-Aid
Research Studentships

Subject: Pre-Colonial history and archaeology in Eastern Africa: field research.

Value: Varies.

Tenable in Kenya, Tanzania or Uganda for one or two years, but may be extended.

Eligibility: Grants-in-Aid—open to nationals of all countries; Studentships—open to citizens of East African countries, the United Kingdom and the Commonwealth who are over 21 years of age. Candidates must have a B.A. or equivalent degree and graduate or undergraduate training in African studies, archaeology or social anthropology. Archaeological students may be required to assist in excavation carried out by the Institute's staff.

Further information from:
Director
British Institute in Eastern Africa
P.O. Box 30710
Nairobi
Kenya

[409]

BRITISH INSTITUTE IN PARIS

Quinn Scholarship
Nathan Scholarship
Esmond Scholarship

Subjects: Postgraduate research in the field of French studies.

No. offered: Quinn and Nathan Scholarships offered annually; Esmond Scholarship offered from time to time, according to availability of funds.

Value: Quinn and Nathan Scholarships up to £2,000 each; Esmond Scholarship up to £100 when available.

Tenable in Paris.

Eligibility: Open to United Kingdom, Irish or Commonwealth citizens, under 28 years of age, who are graduates or undergraduates in their final year, and possess sufficient knowledge of French to pursue their proposed studies.

Applications should be accompanied by a written recommendation from the candidate's professor or tutor. The names of two other academic referees must be given.

Closing date: Early March.

Further information from:
Miss J. Fenton, Secretary
British Institute in Paris
University of London
Senate House, Malet Street
London
England WC1E 7HU

[410]

BRITISH INSTITUTE OF PERSIAN STUDIES

Research Fellowship and Bursaries

Subjects: Iranian art, archaeology, history, literature, linguistics, religion, philosophy.

No. offered: Two or more Fellowships and two Bursaries; annually.

Tenable for one academic year.

Eligibility: Open to postgraduate students of the United Kingdom and the Commonwealth. Preference is given to recent graduates.

Note: Award holders may work on original Iranian material outside of Iran, so long as access to that country remains restricted.

The Selectors reserve the right to vary the amount of the awards in the event of there being two or more candidates of equal merit.

Closing date: 1st May.

Further information from:
  Mrs. M.E. Gueritz, Assistant Secretary
  British Institute of Persian Studies
  13 Cambrian Road
  Richmond, Surrey
  England TW10 6JQ

[411]

BRITISH INSTITUTE OF RADIOLOGY

Stanley Melville Memorial Award

Purpose: To enable a member of the Institute to visit clinics and institutions abroad.

Subject: Radiology.

No. offered: One Award every three years; next in 1984.

Value: Approximately £150.

Eligibility: Open to members of the Institute who are under 35 years of age.

Note: While the successful applicant will not be obliged to write a formal report on his visit, it is hoped that he will submit a description of the work he has seen during the visit in a form suitable for publication in the Journal.
The Institute annually offers the *Barclay Prize* and the *Rönigen Prize* for contributions to the Institute's publication, *British Journal of Radiology*. These two Prizes are not open to application.

Closing date: 31st December of the year preceding the year of the Award.

Further information from:
  General Secretary
  British Institute of Radiology
  36 Portland Place
  London
  England W1N 3DG

[412]

BRITISH INSTITUTION FUND
Royal Academy of Arts

Scholarship Prizes

The Institution gives Prizes in four categories of competition: painting, sculpture, architecture and printmaking. The awards may be made in the form of Scholarships of £100 a year, tenable in Great Britain, extending over a two year period; or Travelling Scholarships or Prizes, usually of up to £200, according to the circumstances of the successful candidate. The examination takes place in December.
Applicants should submit with their works a certified statement of their previous study of art, either whole or part-time, for a period of not less than one year in a recognized school of art in Great Britain or Northern Ireland, and their current attendance at such a school.

Further information from:
  Secretary
  British Institution Fund
  Royal Academy of Arts
  Piccadilly, London
  England W1V ODS

[413]

BRITISH LEATHER MANUFACTURERS' RESEARCH ASSOCIATION
Dr. Dorothy Jordan Lloyd Memorial Trust

Fellowship Award

Purpose: To permit international exchange of young scientists interested in the leather industry.

Subject: Postgraduate research in applied protein science with direct relevance to leather manufacture.

No. offered: Approximately one Fellowship every five years.

Value: Variable.

Tenable for one to three years, normally at the Association's headquarters.

Eligibility: Open to graduates who are fluent in English. Candidates must intend to return to their home country to work in the leather industry. The Fellowship may not be offered to an applicant resident in, or citizen of, a country which has in force legislation which restricts free trade in hides, skins, or leather.

Further information from:
  British Leather Manufacturers' Research Association
  Kings Park Road, Northampton
  England NN3 1JD

[414]

BRITISH LEPROSY RELIEF ASSOCIATION (LEPRA)

Grants

Purpose: To encourage an interest in leprosy among doctors and research workers.

Eligibility: For research, the applicant must submit a programme considered useful by the Medical Board; for training, the applicant must submit a course deemed useful by the Board and will be expected to undertake leprosy control work.

Note: Value, tenancy and number of awards offered are dependent on the nature of the research or training and the funds available. Arrangements are made for, and financial help given, to enable interested medical students to spend their elective period in India, working on specific research projects.
 Annual awards are also given to registered medical students in the U.K. for the best essay or essays on a specific subject.

Further information from:
 Director, LEPRA
 Fairfax House, Causton Road
 Colchester
 England CO1 1PU

[415]

BRITISH LIBRARY

BNB Research Fund

The Fund exists to support research into book trade and related library activities in the United Kingdom. The two areas of particular interest are the study of the relations between bookseller, librarian and publisher, and the general theme of books and their use within the community. The fund has limited resources and directs its efforts towards areas which do not qualify for research funding from other sources. Money cannot be allocated, however, for the preparation of historical bibiliographies. The Fund is administered by a committee whose members represent the Library Association, Publishers' Association, Booksellers' Association, National Book League, British Council, Royal Security, Aslib and the Joint Committee of the Four Copyright Libraries. Applications from any source are welcomed by the Research Fund Committee.

Further information from:
 BNB Research Fund Secretariat
 British Library, Research and Development Department
 Sheraton Street
 London
 England W1V 4BH

[416]

BRITISH MEDICAL ASSOCIATION

Fellowship and Prizes

T.V. James Research Fellowship: Up to £7,200 is awarded annually to a member of the Association to assist research into the nature, causation, prevention or treatment of bronichial asthma. The Fellowship is tenable for one year; renewable for an additional year. Candidates must be members of the BMA.

Walter Jobson Horne Prize: The Prize, consisting of a certificate and £200, is awarded by recommendation every year to a member of the Association who has advanced the science and practice of laryngology and otolgy particularly in reference to general medicine. Applicants are not invited.

H.C. Roscde Fellowship: One Fellowship of £12,000 is offered annually to promote research into the elimination of the common cold. It is open to members of BMA and to non-medical scientists working in association with a BMA member.

Stewart Prize: The Prize, consisting of a certificate and £75, is awarded by recommendation every two years in recognition of important work done on the origin and spread of epidemic disease. Alternatively, a practitioner may be asked to investigate any aspect of epidemic disease which seems likely to yield important results. Applications are not involved.

Further information from:
 Secretary
 Board of Science and Education
 British Medical Association
 Tavistock Square
 London
 England WC1H 9JP

[417]

BRITISH MEDICAL ASSOCIATION

Research Awards

Brackenbury Award: One Award of £500 is awarded trienally to assist one year of research of immediate practical importance to public health, to a medico-political or medico-sociological problem, or to an educational question whether general, medical or postgraduate. Candidates must be members of the BMA.

John William Clark Award: One Award of £2,500 (renewable) is offered annually to assist research into the causes of blindness. It is open to members of BMA.

T.P. Gunton Award: One Award of £3,500 is offered annually to assist research into health education with special regard to the earlier diagnosis and treatment of cancer. It is open to both medical and non-medical scientists.

Katherine Bishop Harman Award: One Award of £500 is awarded biennially to assist research into the diminution and avoidance of risks to health and life in pregnancy and childbearing for one year. Candidates must be medical practitioners registered in the United Kingdom or any country at any time forming part of the British Empire.

Nathaniel Bishop Harman Award: One Award of £500 is awarded biennially to assist research in hospital practice for one year. Candidates must be registered medical practitioners on staff of a hospital in Great Britain or Northern Ireland who are not members of the staff of a recognised undergraduate of postgraduate medical school.

Sir Charles Hastings and Charles Oliver Hawthorne Award: £1,000 for the Hastings Award, and £250 for the Hawthorn Award, awarded biennially to assist observation, research and record in general practice for one year. Candidates must be members of the BMA engaged in general practice.

Geoffrey Holt and Edith Walsh Awards: The two Awards of £1,000 each, are awarded annually to assist research into cardiovascular and respiratory disease for one year. Candidates must be members of BMA.

Insole Award: One Award of £250 is awarded biennially to assist research into the causation, prevention or treatment of disease for one year. Candidates must be members of BMA.

Middlemore Award: One Award of £500 is awarded triennially to assist research in any branch of opthalmic medicine or surgery for one year. Open to all opthalmic practitioners.

C.H. Milburn Award: One Award of £500 is awarded biennially to assist research in medical jurisprudence and/or forensic medicine for one year. Candidates must be registered medical practitioners.

Doris Odlum Award: One Award of £500 is awarded biennially to assist research in mental health for one year. Candidates must be medical practitioners registered in the British Commonwealth or the Republic of Ireland.

Helen Tomkinson Award: One Award of £2,200 is offered annually to assist research into cancer. It is open to members of BMA.

Further information from:
  Secretary
  Board of Science and Education
  British Medical Association
  Tavistock Square
  London
  England WC1H 9JP

[418]

BRITISH MEDICAL STUDENTS' TRUST

Scholarships and Travel Grants

Subject: Medicine: study and travel outside the United Kingdom.

No. offered: Approximately 60 Scholarships and Travel Grants annually.

Tenable for periods from two weeks to three months.

Eligibility: Open to students (pre-clinical or clinical) from British medical schools and hospitals.

Further information from:
Secretary
British Medical Students' Trust
British Medical Association House
Tavistock Square
London
England WC1H 9JP

[419]

BRITISH ORTHOPAEDIC ASSOCIATION

American, British and Canadian Travelling Fellowship
United Kingdom Traveling Scholarship
Robert Jones Prize Essay

Purpose: To advance the art and science of orthopaedic surgery.

No. offered: Six Fellowships biennially; three Scholarships annually; one Prize annually.

Value: Fellowships—six to eight week visit to orthopaedic centres in the United States and Canada, with all expenses paid; Scholarships-£4,000 each; Prize—£250.

Eligibility: Scholarships and Fellowships are open to members of the Association and are designed for orthopaedic surgeons or senior registrars below the age of 40 years; Prizes are open to members of the Association.

Closing dates: Scholarship and Fellowship—end of September; Essay—end of December.

Further information from:
Honorary Secretary
British Orthopaedic Association
Royal College of Surgeons
35-43 Lincoln's Inn Fields
London
England WC2A 3PN

[420]

BRITISH PAEDIATRIC ASSOCIATION

Heinz Fellowships

Subject: Paediatrics.

Fellowship A: Two or three Fellowships annually are open to paediatricians from any part of the British Commonwealth who will benefit from spending six to eight weeks in the United Kingdom meeting British paediatricians and seeing something of their work. Preference is given to those recently established in an academic career who will arrange their visit to allow attendance at the meeting of the British Paediatric Association (April or May).

The Fellowship provides a subsistence allowance plus a travel allowance of £210 and return air fare.

Fellowship B: Up to three Fellowships annually are open to paediatricians from the United Kingdom of senior registrar or consultant status, but in the early years of professional life, who wish to make a short working visit (up to three months) to a centre in a developing country to teach or conduct research which will benefit both Fellow and hosts. The applicant should submit a brief programme and indicate the benefits likely to accrue.

The Fellowship comprises expenses allowance and return air fare.

Closing dates: 31st December for Fellowship A, and 31st January for Fellowship B.

Further information from:
British Paediatric Association
23 Queen Square
London
England WC1N 3AZ

[421]

BRITISH PRESS AWARDS

Annual Awards are given in the following categories: Journalists—Journalist of the Year; Reporter of the Year; International Reporter of the Year; Provincial Journalist of the Year; Young Journalist of the Year; General Feature Writer of the Year; Sports-Journalist of the Year; Columnist of the Year; Critic of the Year; Campaigning Journalist of the Year; David Holden Award for contribution to international understanding; Photographers—Photographer of the Year; News Photographer of the Year; Cartoonist of the Year. All Awards are in the amount of £250, with the exception of the Journalist of the Year which carries a prize value of £1,000. Entries selected for commendation will receive prizes of £100.

Awards are open to British professional journalists and photographers whose work has appeared in any morning, evening, Sunday or weekly newspaper in England, Scotland, Wales or Northern Ireland during the year for which the Awards are made. Entries should consist of up to six examples of published work bearing the name of the newspaper and publication date. Journalists' entries should be for material which has been published with a by-line. News Photographer of the Year entries should consist of a single photograph only.

Closing date: 14th January of the Year following that for which the Awards will be made.

Further information from:
David Tyler, Secretary
British Press Awards
Room 302, Orbit House
9 New Fetter Lane
London
England, EC4A 1AR

[422]

BRITISH SCHOOL OF ARCHAEOLOGY IN IRAQ

Grants and Travel Grants

Subjects: Archaeology, history, and language of Iraq from the earliest times to A.D. 1700.

Value: Usually between £300 and £1500, depending on the nature of the research and circumstances of the applicant.

Tenable for an academic year, some of which must be spent in Iraq.

Eligibility: Open to United Kingdom or Commonwealth citizens, over 21 years of age, who are postgraduates with a knowledge of Western-Asiatic archaeology. Two references are required.

Closing date: 31st March.

Further information from:
Honorary Secretary
British School of Archaeology in Iraq
31-34 Gordon Square
London
England WC1H OPY

[423]

BRITISH SCHOOL OF ARCHAEOLOGY IN JERUSALEM

Travel Grant

Purpose: To enable a student to participate in archaeological excavation or to gain experience in a related field.

No. offered: One or more Grants annually.

Value: Up to £2,000 each.

Tenable in Jordan, Syria, Lebanon, Saudi Arabia or Israel for periods of two to three months.

Eligibility: Open to bona-fide students of archaeology who are citizens of the United Kingdom or of a British Commonwealth country.

Closing date: Mid-February.

Further information from:
Assistant Secretary
British School of Archaeology in Jerusalem
2 Hinde Mews, Marylebone Lane
London
England W1M 5RH

[424]

BRITISH SCHOOL OF ARCHAEOLOGY IN JERUSALEM

Jerusalem Research Scholarship

Subjects: Archaeology, including history, epigraphy and architecture of Palestine and surrounding countries from prehistoric to Islamic period.

No. offered: One Scholarship annually.

Value: £2,750.

Tenable in Jordan, Syria, Lebanon, Saudi Arabia or Israel. At least eight months must be spent in the Middle East.

Eligibility: Open to British Commonwealth citizens who are graduates of a British Commonwealth university.

Note: The Scholar must undertake full-time approved research within the subjects listed.

Closing date: Mid-February.

Further information from:
  Assistant Secretary
  British School of Archaeology in
    Jerusalem
  2 Hinde Mews, Marylebone Lane
  London
  England W1M 5RH

[425]

BRITISH SCHOOL AT ROME

Grants in Aid of Research

Purpose: To enable persons engaged in research either for a higher degree or at the postdoctoral level to spend a period of one to four months in the furtherance of their studies.

Subjects: Research in ancient, medieval and later Italian studies: history, art history, antiquities or literature.

Value: Up to £975.

Tenable in Italy.

Eligibility: Candidates, of either sex, must be citizens of the United Kingdom or Commonwealth. There is no age limit.

Closing date: Mid-April.

Further information from:
  Secretary
  Faculty of Archaeology, History and
    Letters
  British School at Rome
  1 Lowther Gardens, Exhibition Road
  London
  England SW7 2AA

[426]

BRITISH SCHOOL AT ROME

Rome Scholarships

Purpose: To give a few students of distinction the opportunity of devoting their whole time for a period of one year to the furtherance of their studies.

Subject: Research in the history, art history, antiquities or literature of some period before AD 500, and since AD 300.

No. offered: Usually not more than three Scholarships annually.

Value: £100 per annum, payable in two installments, increased to £1,840 per annum payable in ten installments where the Scholar does not hold a State Studentship or other similar award.

Tenable at the British School at Rome.

Eligibility: Candidates, of either sex, must be citizens of the United Kingdom or Commonwealth. Preference may be given to graduates. There is no age limit.

Closing date: Early December.

Further information from:
  Secretary
  Faculty of Archaeology, History and
    Letters
  British School at Rome
  1 Lowther Gardens, Exhibition Road
  London
  England SW7 2AA

[427]

BRITISH SCHOOL AT ROME

(a) Rome Scholarships (Art)
(b) Abbey Major Scholarship
(c) Gulbenkian Rome Scholarship

Purpose: To give a few students of distinction and exceptional promise the opportunity of devoting their whole time to the furtherance of their studies.

Subjects: (a) Painting, printmaking, sculpture, and architecture; (b) painting; (c) sculpture.

No. offered: (a) One Scholarship in each subject annually; (b) one Scholarship annually; (c) one Scholarship every other year.

Value: £1,840 per annum, paid monthly, with additional grants for materials and travel.

Tenable at the British School at Rome for one or two years.

Eligibility: Candidates, of either sex, must be citizens of the United Kingdom or Commonwealth and under 35 years of age (30 for the Rome Scholarship in architecture). Candidates for the architecture Scholarship must have passed the RIBA final examination or its recognized equivalent, or must be currently sitting for finals and will be eligible only if they pass.

Closing dates: Mid-March for the sculpture Scholarships; mid-February for the printmaking Scholarship; early December for the painting Scholarships; and late January for the architecture Scholarship.

Further information from:
Hon. General Secretary
British School at Rome
1 Lowther Gardens, Exhibition Road
London
England SW7 2AA

[428]

BRITISH SMALL ANIMAL VETERINARY ASSOCIATION
Clinical Studies Trust Fund, Ltd.

Research Grants

Subject: Veterinary medicine—research of benefit in treating, or leading to a better understanding of aetiology, of a clinical condition.

Value: Varies according to the nature of the proposed project.

Tenable at approved institutions for the agreed duration of the project.

Eligibility: Open to residents of the United Kingdom and Ireland who hold appropriate veterinary qualifications or who plan to work with a qualified researcher.

Further information from:
Chairman
Clinical Studies Trust Fund, Ltd.
British Small Animal Veterinary Association
c/o British Veterinary Association
7 Mansfield Street
London
England W1M OAT

[429]

BRITISH TRAVEL EDUCATIONAL TRUST

Grants are given for short-term research projects on some aspects of tourism in the United Kingdom. Grants are not normally offered to full-time students undertaking a regular course of study. The type of awards are decided on by the Trustees, and vary annually.

Applications are solicited through the travel trade press and other organizations involved in travel and tourism.

Further information from:
Hon. Secretary
c/o British Tourist Authority
Queen's House
64 St. James's Street
London
England SW1A 1NF

[430]

BRITISH UNIVERSITIES SUMMER SCHOOLS JOINT COMMITTEE

Bursaries

Subjects: Within the scope of the subjects of the summer schools, which are usually, but not invariably, English literature or history.

Value: A limited number of Bursaries are offered to cover part of the costs of board, residence and tuition at the summer school.

Tenable for six, and less often, three weeks at the Summer Schools at Stratford-upon-Avon (University of Birmingham), London (University of London), or Oxford (University of Oxford).

Eligibility: Preference in the awarding of Bursaries is given to graduate students and those about to graduate. Applicants may be nationals of any country.

Closing dates: 15th March for United States candidates; 31st March for candidates from all other countries.

Note: Candidates should apply to the local representative of the British Council, usually in the capital city. United States candidates apply to the *Institute of International Education, 809 United Nations Plaza, New York, New York 10017,* and Canadians apply to *Awards Officer, AUCC, 151 Slater Street, Ottawa, Ontario K1P 5N1.*

United Kingdom address:
  Secretary
  British Universities Summer Schools Joint
    Committee
  Department of Extra-Mural Studies
  University of London
  26 Russell Square
  London
  England WC1B 5DP

[431]

BRITISH VETERINARY ASSOCIATION

Harry Steele-Bodger Memorial Travelling Scholarship

One Scholarship of approximately £300, which may be split between two people, is awarded at least once every four years, for travel to any overseas country for studies in veterinary science. Members of the Royal College of Veterinary Surgeons and final year students at veterinary colleges in the United Kingdom and Ireland may apply. Recipients must be prepared to submit a record of their study abroad. Application should be made by the end of June each year.

Further information from:
  British Veterinary Association
  7 Mansfield Street
  London
  England W1M OAT

[432]

BROADCAST MUSIC, INC. *(U.S.A.)*

BMI Awards to Student Composers

Purpose: Awards are made for vocal or instrumental compositions to encourage the creation of concert music.

Value: Prizes totaling US$15,000 and ranging from US$500 to US$2,500 will be awarded at the discretion of the judges.

Eligibility: Open to citizens or permanent residents of countries within the Western Hemisphere who are either enrolled in an accredited public, private or parochial secondary school, an accredited college or conservatory of music, or engaged in the private study of music with recognized and established teachers. Candidates must not have reached their 26th birthday by 31st December.

Compositions must be original works which have never been published or awarded any prize. No specific style is demanded, nor are there any limitations as to instrumentation or length of manuscript. Electronic music and tapes of work which cannot adequately be presented in score may be submitted.

Compositions will be judged on evidence of true creative talent. Academic finesse, while not disregarded, will be considered secondary to the vital musicality of the composer's work.

Note: A composer may enter no more than one composition, which need not have been composed during the year of entry.

Jointly written works will be considered as single entries.

Closing date: 15th February.

Further information from:
  Mr. James G. Roy, Jr., Director
  BMI Awards to Student Composers
  Broadcast Music, Inc.
  320 West 57th Street
  New York, New York 10019
  U.S.A.

[433]

SAMUEL BRONFMAN FOUNDATION
(Canada)

Seagram Business Faculty Awards

Purpose: To stimulate advanced scholarship and research in business by university faculty members and to increase the supply of qualified university teachers of business in Canada.

Value: Doctoral Fellowships—*Can*$6,000 each; Senior Research Awards—average *Can*$3,000 each.

Tenable at Canadian universities for one year, with the possibility of renewal.

Eligibility: Doctoral Fellowships are intended for persons having significant teaching experience in a Canadian university, who plan to work toward the doctoral degree in business in a recognized formal Ph.D. or D.B.A. program. Senior Research Awards are intended for faculty members who plan to engage in worthwhile research not directed toward a doctoral degree. No distinction is made regarding possession of a doctoral degree.

Candidates must be nominated by members of Canadian universities offering the bachelor's degree in business.

Note: Nomination forms are obtainable only from the deans or directors of eligible Canadian universities where there are no separate business schools. Each eligible school or department may nominate a maximum of five candidates for each of the Awards.

Closing date: 15th March in the year preceding the academic year for which the Award is intended.

Further information from:
Prof. Basil Kalymon
Awards Chairman
Canadian Association of Administrative Sciences
Faculty of Management Studies
University of Toronto
246 Bloor Street West
Toronto, Ontario
Canada M5S 1V4

[434]

BROOKHAVEN NATIONAL LABORATORY *(U.S.A.)*

Postdoctoral Research Associateships

Purpose: To provide postdoctoral fellows the opportunity for supplementing and broadening research experience.

Subjects: Physics, including accelerator physics; chemistry; biology; medicine; mathematics.

No. offered: Approximately 50 new appointments each year.

Value: Varies; minimum US$15,000 per annum, payable in monthly installments.

Tenable at Brookhaven National Laboratory for up to three years.

Eligibility: Open to unaffiliated scientists and engineers of any nationality who must have completed the requirements for a doctoral degree.

Further information from:
Office of Scientific Personnel
Brookhaven National Laboratory
Associated Universities, Inc.
Upton, Long Island, New York 11973
U.S.A.

[435]

BROOKINGS INSTITUTION *(U.S.A.)*

Research Fellowships

Purpose: To support policy-oriented predoctoral research in economics, government and foreign policy.

Value: US$7,500 payable on a twelve-month basis, for eleven months of research at the Brookings Institution and one month of vacation. Up to US$500 will be provided for typing and other essential research requirements, plus access to computer facilities.

Tenable at the Institution for twelve months; not renewable.

Eligibility: Open to doctoral candidates whose dissertation topics are directly related to public policy issues and thus to the major interests of the Institution. The recipients are scholars whose research will benefit from access to the data, opportunities for interviewing, and consultation with senior staff members afforded by the Institution and by residence in Washington, D.C. Only candidates nominated by graduate departments of universities are considered. Candidates must have completed their preliminary examinations for the doctorate and be prepared to submit research plans leading to completion of their dissertations for the nominating university. Essential criteria are relevance of the topic to the appropriate Brookings research program and evidence that the research will be facilitated by access to the Institution's resources or to federal government agencies.

Closing date: Late February.

Further information from:
Director of Economic/Governmental/ Foreign Policy Studies
Brookings Institution
1775 Massachusetts Avenue, N.W.
Washington, D.C. 20036
U.S.A.

[436]

BROOKLYN MUSEUM ART SCHOOL
(New York)

Max Beckmann Memorial Scholarships in Painting
Robert Smithson Memorial Scholarships in Sculpture

No. offered: Up to 22 Beckmann Scholarships and up to 5 Smithson Scholarships awarded annually.

Value: Free tuition.

Tenable at the Brooklyn Museum Art School, for one academic year; not renewable.

Eligibility: Open to nationals of all countries.

Note: Candidates must submit a portfolio of 12 slides and two letters of recommendation, one from the former school, and one from an instructor or well-known professional artist, and a college transcript in English.

Closing date: 30th April.

Further information from:
 Registrar
 Brooklyn Museum Art School
 188 Eastern Parkway
 Brooklyn, New York 11238
 U.S.A.

[437]

BROOME AGENCY, INC. *(Sarasota, Florida)*

Broome Literary Awards

A book Award of US$1,250 and a short story Award of US$750 is given annually to encourage creative writing. The unpublished manuscripts, which may be submitted by anyone, should be no less than 50,000 words in length for books and no more than 5,000 words in length for short stories.

Closing date: 31st December of each year.

Further information from:
 Broome Agency, Inc.
 3080 North Washington Boulevard
 Sarasota, Florida 33580
 U.S.A.

[438]

TORE BROWALDH FOUNDATION FOR SOCIAL SCIENCE RESEARCH AND EDUCATION *(Stockholm)*
JAN WALLANDER FOUNDATION FOR SOCIAL SCIENCE RESEARCH *(Stockholm)*

Social Science Research Grants

Subjects: Business and economic research, preferably concerning international payments and capital movements, internal payments system, monetary and capital market problems, and economic planning.

Value: To cover approved expenses connected with the research work.

Tenable for up to one year; renewable subject to new application and satisfactory progress. Non-Swedish students are only eligible if they have planned their studies within a Swedish research institute or university where they intend to work, and can therefore present good Swedish references; such candidates should therefore first contact the centre where they intend to study.

Eligibility: Open to postgraduate students who are qualified for a Grant. Foreign students are requested to do their research in Sweden in co-operation with a Swedish research institute. The students must be established in Sweden before applying.

Closing date: 1st March.

Further information from:
 Secretary of the Board
 Tore Browaldh and Jan Wallander
  Foundations
 S-103 28 Stockholm
 Sweden

[439]

EMIL BROWN FUND *(Los Angeles, California)*

Preventive Law Prize Awards

An annual Award of US$1,000 will be made for a praiseworthy leading article or book, and US$500 for a student work in the field of preventive law published in a law review, bar journal or other professional publication.

No entries need be submitted; however, the Fund welcomes the advising of any writings which may come within the scope of the Awards.

Further information from:
Louis M. Brown, Administrator
Emil Brown Fund
Preventive Law Prize Awards
1901 Avenue of the Stars, Suite 850
Los Angeles, California 90067
U.S.A.

[440]

BULGARIAN INSTITUTE FOR FOREIGN STUDENTS

Bulgarian Government Scholarships
Exchange Scholarships

Subjects: Unrestricted.

No. offered: (a) ten Scholarships annually; (b) approximately 2,300 Scholarships annually.

Value: A monthly allowance to cover maintenance, lodging and tuition fees; grants for book purchase and personal expenses; return fares at surface rates and necessary travel expenses within Bulgaria.

Tenable at a Bulgarian university or other institution of higher education and research for two to ten months.

Eligibility: (a) Open to students from developing countries; (b) open to citizens of countries with whom Bulgaria has exchange agreements and certain other countries, who have finished their secondary education. Applicants should have a good knowledge of Bulgarian; a one year course for those who lack this is available.

Note: Candidates should seek further information from their government's agency for foreign awards. United Kingdom candidates should apply to *Higher Education Department, British Council, 10 Spring Gardens, London SW1A 2BN*, by 20th November.

Address:
Bulgarian Institute for Foreign Students
125 Lenin Street
Sofia
Bulgaria

[441]

JOSEPH BULOVA SCHOOL OF WATCHMAKING *(Woodside, N.Y.)*

Arde Bulova Memorial Fellowship

The Fellowship is offered for training in watch repair and precision technology to disabled applicants with the potential to become instructors. There must be a plan for the graduate to return to his country to teach other disabled. Tenable for two years at the School of Watchmaking. Fellowship includes tuition charges, some medical services and room and board; it does not include transportation or any medical services requiring hospitalization. Open to disabled nationals of all countries outside the United States within the ages of 18 and 35, with the following qualifications: reading comprehension of English at minimum of United States fifth grade level; superior intellectual capacity; 20/20 eyesight, corrected; fine finger dexterity; good eye-hand coordination, mechanical aptitude and insight.

Further information from:
Joseph Bulova School of Watchmaking
40-24 62nd Street
Woodside, New York 11377
U.S.A.

[442]

MARY INGRAHAM BUNTING INSTITUTE
(Cambridge, Massachusetts)
Radcliffe College

Bunting Fellowships

Purpose: To provide opportunity and support to professional women who wish to complete substantial projects in their chosen fields, and thus advance their careers.

Subjects: Independent study in any academic or professional field, creative writing and the arts.

No. offered: Ten Fellowships annually.

Value: Approximately US$13,500, paid in monthly installments. In addition, the Fellow receives an office or studio space, auditing privileges, and access to libraries and other resources and facilities of Radcliffe College and Harvard University.

Tenable at the Institute for one year. Fellows must reside in the Boston area during the appointment.

Eligibility: Open to women candidates of any race, color, age, national or ethnic origin, who are at any stage of their career, from early postdoctoral, or its equivalent, to senior professional ranks, who have received their doctorate not later than 30th June of the year preceding the academic year for which the Fellowship is granted.

Note: Fellows are expected to give a colloquium on their current work during their appointment.

Closing date: 15th October of the year preceding the academic year for which the Fellowship is made.

Further information from:
 Bunting Fellowship Program
 Bunting Institute
 Radcliffe College
 10 Garden Street
 Cambridge, Massachusetts 02138
 U.S.A.

[443]

MARY INGRAHAM BUNTING INSTITUTE
(Cambridge, Massachusetts)
Radcliffe College

Non-Tenured Women Faculty Fellowships

Purpose: To provide opportunity for junior faculty women at major research universities throughout the country to work in projects that promise to make significant contributions to their fields, and to enhance their opportunities for tenure.

Subjects: All fields of academic research.

No. offered: An unspecified number of Fellowships annually.

Value: Approximately US$15,000, research expenses of US$3,000, and up to US$1,000 for travel between the Fellows home and Cambridge during each year of her appointment. Fellows also receive office space, auditing privileges, and access to the libraries and other resources and facilities of Radcliffe College and Harvard University.

Tenable for two years. Fellows must reside in the Boston area during the appointment, and spend one full year or one semester of each year at the Institute.

Eligibility: All non-tenured faculty women of major research universities in the United States may apply. Applicants may be nominated by their institutions, or apply directly to the Institute themselves.

Note: Fellows are expected to give a colloquium on their work in progress each year.

Closing date: 15th October of the year preceding the academic Award period.

At the time of going to press, these Fellowships were being reviewed.

Further information from:
 Bunting Institute
 Radcliffe College
 3 James Street
 Cambridge, Massachusetts 02138
 U.S.A.

[444]

BURROUGHS WELLCOME FUND *(U.S.A.)*

William N. Creasy Visiting Professorships of Clinical Pharmacology: A number of Professorships are offered annually in order to stimulate interest in clinical pharmacology and support for its development in the nation's medical schools. Open to U.S. medical schools which serve as the host institution for a distinguished visiting professor whose scientific interests relate to clinical pharmacology. The professor may be a U.S. resident or from abroad. The Award is comprised of a US$2,500 honorarium plus travel expenses for the visiting professor and accompanying spouse. In addition, each host institution receives US$250 for expenses. Eight copies of each application should be submitted. Closing date: 5th May.

Wellcome Research Travel Grant Program: The Fund sponsors travel grants to Great Britain and Ireland for U.S. research workers in the field of health sciences; tenable for periods of two to twelve weeks. Full-time, established research workers in institutions in the field of health sciences who are citizens or permanent residents of the United States are eligible. The Grants are not awarded to predoctoral fellows or medical students or in support of sabbatical leaves. Applications for these grants are accepted on a continuous basis.

Further information from:
Executive Director
Burroughs Wellcome Fund
3030 Cornwallis Road
Research Triangle Park, North Carolina 27709
U.S.A.

[445]

BUSH FOUNDATION *(U.S.A.)*

Bush Leadership Fellowships

Purpose: To enrich, through academic or internship periods or both, the experience of highly motivated individuals in mid-career and to prepare them for high-level responsibility.

Subjects: Architecture, business, engineering, forestry, government, journalism, law and law enforcement, social work, theology, trade unionism, and administration of arts, education, health or scientific organizations.

No. offered: Approximately 20 Fellowships annually.

Value: US$2,000 monthly, plus half of tuition and US$700 travel allowance.

Tenable in the U.S. at approved institutions for periods of up to 18 months.

Eligibility: Open to candidates who are between the ages of 28 and 50, have five years of work experience, are U.S. citizens and resident of Minnesota, North or South Dakota, or the 26 counties of Wisconsin which lie within the Ninth Federal Reserve District.

Closing date: Early January.

Further information from:
Bush Leadership Fellows Program
P.O. Box 15125
Minneapolis, Minnesota 55415
U.S.A.

[446]

BUSH FOUNDATION *(U.S.A.)*

Bush Summer Fellowships

Purpose: To enrich, through academic or internship periods or both, the experience of highly motivated individuals in mid-career and to prepare them for high-level responsibility.

Subjects: Architecture, business, engineering, forestry, government, journalism, law and law enforcement, social work, theology, trade unionism, and administration of arts, education, health or scientific organizations.

No. offered: Approximately 30 Summer Fellowships annually.

Value: US$420 weekly, plus half of tuition and US$500 travel allowance.

Tenable in the U.S. at approved institutions for periods of up to 10 weeks.

Eligibility: Open to candidates who are between the ages of 28 and 50, have three years of work experience, are U.S. citizens and resident of Minnesota, North or South Dakota, or the 26 counties of Wisconsin which lie within the Ninth Federal Reserve District.

Closing date: Early March.

Further information from:
Bush Leadership Fellows Program
P.O. Box 15125
Minneapolis, Minnesota 55415
U.S.A.

[447]

BUSINESS AND PROFESSIONAL WOMEN'S FOUNDATION *(U.S.A.)*

Lena Lake Forrest Fellowship

Purpose: To promote research on women's employment issues.

Subjects: Contemporary and historical studies which provide historical perspectives on economic issues affecting the business or professional woman.

No. offered: Two to four Fellowships annually.

Value: US$500 and US$3,000, depending upon budget sumbitted.

Tenable for one year; not renewable.

Eligibility: Open to United States citizens who are either pre-doctoral candidates, post-doctoral scholars, or persons able to demonstrate that the proposed research will be conducted under standards of scholarship recognized at the doctoral level.

Note: Those interested in receiving application materials should send a brief description of the proposed research project and information on academic background to the address below.

Closing dates: 15th December for application materials requests; 1st January for completed applications.

Further information from:
Mary Rubin, Research and Information Services
Business and Professional Women's Foundation
2012 Massachusetts Avenue, N.W.
Washington, D.C. 20036
U.S.A.

[448]

BUSINESS AND PROFESSIONAL WOMEN'S FOUNDATION *(U.S.A.)*

Sally Butler International Scholarship Program

Two to four Scholarships, ranging between US$500 and US$3,000 each, are given annually for research in any field at the predoctoral or advanced level. Eligible candidates are Latin American women (as defined by descent or citizenship) including those from North, Central and South America, and from the Caribbean. Candidates must write a preliminary letter stating academic background and research topic. Application materials may be requested between September and 15th December of each year.

Closing date: 1st January for completed applications.

Further information from:
Sally Butler International Scholarship Program
Business and Professional Women's Foundation
2012 Massachusetts Avenue, N.W.
Washington, D.C. 20036
U.S.A.

[449]

BUSINESS AND PROFESSIONAL WOMEN'S FOUNDATION *(U.S.A.)*

Career Advancement Scholarships Clairol Loving Care Scholarships

Purpose: To assist mature women in need of financial assistance to upgrade skills or complete their education for career advancement.

Subjects: Awards may be used for either full-time or part-time study in academic (undergraduate and masters level), or vocational/paraprofessional/office skills training.

No. offered: Approximately 550 Scholarships annually.

Value: Range from US$100 to US$1,000; average Scholarship is between US$200 and US$500.

Tenable for twelve months at an accredited vocational or academic school in the United States; renewable.

Eligibility: Any woman who is a United States citizen and at least 25 years of age may apply. There are no specific academic or professional requirements, but the applicant must show that she has a reasonabe chance of success in her planned program of study and has the prospect of being able to use the desired training in a practical and immediate way. These scholarships are designed primarily for continuing education to assist mature women who wish to return to school after a break in education due to professional or family responsibilities.

Note: Emphasis is on technical training and study in fields which are not already overcrowded or those where opportunities for women are increasing.
   Awards for study in a foreign country, correspondence courses, or study at the doctoral level will not be given.

Further information from:
　Scholarships Department
　Business and Professional Women's
　　Foundation
　2012 Massachusettss Avenue, N.W.
　Washington, D.C. 20036
　U.S.A.

[450]

F. BUSONI INTERNATIONAL PIANO COMPETITION

A Prize of 5,000,000 lire plus several important concert contracts is offered to the winner of the annual competition, 2nd Prize—2,500,000 lire; 3rd Prize—1,500,000 lire; 4th Prize—1,000,000 lire; 5th Prize—900,000 lire; and 6th Prize—800,000 lire. Pianists of any nationality who are under 32 years of age may apply.

The Competition is held in Bolzano in August and September each year.

Further information from:
　La Segretaria
　Concorso Pianistico Internazionale "F.
　　Busoni"
　Conservatorio Statale di Musica "C.
　　Monteverdi"
　Piazzq Domenicani 19
　39100 Bolzano
　Italy

[451]

BUXTEHUDE PRIZE *(Lübeck)*

One Prize of DM5,000 is offered every three years to reward outstanding artistic and creative achievement, and meritorious service in the research and publication of the works of Dietrich Buxtehude.

Further information from:
　Buxtehude Prize
　Der Senat der Hansestadt Lübeck
　Amt für Kultur, Rathaushof
　D 2400 Lübeck 1
　West Germany

[452]

HUGH FULTON BYAS MEMORIAL FOUNDATION *(U.S.A.)*

Awards

Purpose: To enable students from England to pursue degree work (required) in the United States while engaging in a piece of research required by the course of study, the objective of which is to promote friendship and good will between England and the United States. Research requirement may be waived in certain areas of study.

Subjects: Areas which will promote the aims of the Foundation are considered; e.g., research into the common origins of England and the United States; the United States civil service system (based on the United Kingdom system); English architecture adapted in the United States; industrial or other skills brought by Englishmen to the United States. No racial, political, or religious topics are acceptable.

No. offered: Varies according to the amounts awarded to individuals.

Value: Very liberal; dependent on the individual's requirements. Payments are usually made monthly through the university.

Tenable in the United States for whatever period is required to complete the degree or degrees and the paper if required.

Eligibility: Open to students and older persons with an English background and parentage, who are over 21 years of age. Candidates must be currently-active members of one of the orthodox religious denominations (Catholic, Jewish or Protestant), and must furnish from their clergyman a certification to this effect. Students may be required to submit a paper related to their course work and research. Candidates must guarantee to return to England for permanent residence after completing study.

Under the terms of the Award, students from Scotland, Wales and Northern Ireland are not eligible.

Further information from:
　Hugh Fulton Byas Memorial Foundation
　937-A Summit Avenue
　Jersey City, New Jersey 07307
　U.S.A.

C

See *How to Use The Grants Register*, page ix

[453]

CALIFORNIA COLLEGE OF ARTS AND CRAFTS *(Oakland)*

Graduate Scholarships

Three to eight Scholarship units per student are offered annually to U.S. and foreign nationals who possess a bachelor or fine arts degree, or its equivalent. Candidate should have a good knowledge of the English language. Awards are *US*$450 to *US*$1,200, granted on the basis of need and merit.

Not confirmed for 1983.

Further information from:
Graduate Department
California College of Arts and Crafts
5212 Broadway
Oakland, California 94618
U.S.A.

[454]

CANADA COUNCIL

Governor General's Literary and Drama Awards: Eight prizes are awarded annually to those judged to be the best books published during the year by Canadian authors. Four are given for books in English and four for books in French. The four categories are drama, poetry, fiction and non-fiction. The cash value of the Award is *Can*$5,000 each. All literary works published by Canadians during the previous year are automatically considered by the selection committee.

Research Fellowships are offered in any of the following broad fields: humanities, social sciences, natural sciences, medicine, engineering.

Canada-Australia Literary Prize: A Prize of *Can*$2,500 is awarded in alternate years to an Australian or Canadian writer. The winner is announced in the spring and the Prize is presented in the country making the award. The Prize is administered by the Council in collaboration with the Department of External Affairs.

Children's Literature Prizes: Two Prizes of *Can*$5,000 are awarded annually to Canadian writers and illustrators for the best Canadian children's books in English and French published during the previous calendar year. Formal applications are not required. Prize-winning titles are announced in the spring.

I.W. Killam Memorial Prize of *Can*$50,000 is given annually to honor an eminent Canadian scholar in recognition of a distinguished career and general contribution to one of the fields of natural sciences, medicine, or engineering.

Molson Prizes: Three Prizes are given annually in recognition of outstanding achievement in the arts, humanities and social sciences. The cash value of the Prize is *Can*$20,000 each. Prizes are awarded to Canadian citizens whose contribution is deemed to have enriched the cultural or intellectual heritage of Canada, or to have contributed to national unity. Applications are not entertained.

Translation Prizes: Two annual Prizes of *Can*$5,000 each are awarded for the best translation of a Canadian work from English into French, and from French into English. The books must be written and translated by Canadian citizens and have been published in the previous calendar year. No formal applications are required.

Further information from:
Canada Council
255 Albert Street
P.O. Box 1047
Ottawa, Ontario
Canada K1P 5V8

[455]

CANADA COUNCIL

Grants

Project Cost Grants of up to *Can*$2,700 are intended to cover the cost of goods and services necessary to the completion of a specific project. They may also include a travel allowance but not a living allowance for the artist. Visual artists, photographers, theatre designers, filmmakers and video artists may receive up to *Can*$4,000 for extraordinary costs. The Grants are tenable for an indefinite period of time.

Short-Term Grants of *Can*$800 per month, plus travel expenses are offered to enable artists to work on a specific short-term project for a maximum of three months, not necessarily consecutive. Recipients may receive, if warranted by the project and justified by a detailed budget, an additional project cost allowance of up to *Can*$1,000.

Travel Grants are given to enable artists to travel on occasions important to their professional career. Awards cover travel expenses and may include an allowance of *Can*$20 per day for up to five days to help defray living expenses.

Video Grants are given to artists who wish to pursue professional activity other than a specific production. Applicants should have several noncommercial video productions to their credit to be otherwise recognized as professionals in the field.

Eligibility: All grants are open to Canadian citizens or landed immigrants who have resided in Canada for at least five years and have finishd basic training or have the necessary competence to be considered professional artists.

Note: For all categories of grants, artists must submit at least 20 slides illustrating their work, especially over the last three years. Applicants for Video Grants must submit at least one videotape and, if their project differs markedly from previous work, a demo-tape.

Further information from:
Arts Awards Service
Canada Council
255 Albert Street
P.O. Box 1047
Ottawa, Ontario
Canada K1P 5V8

[456]

CANADA COUNCIL

Arts Grants

Arts Grants "A": Provide free time for personal creative activity for senior artists who have made significant contribution over a number of years and are still active in their profession. The Grants of up to *Can* $19,000 cover living expenses and project costs; travel costs necessary to their program may also be provided. Visual artists may receive up to *Can*$28,000 if they can show that they will incur extraordinary materials costs. Recipients may apply for renewal in regular competition. Only in unusual circumstances will an artist be awarded more than two consecutive grants.

Arts Grants "B": Artists who have completed basic training or are recognized as professionals are eligible for these grants of up to *Can*$11,600 for living expenses and project costs. Travel allowances may be awarded in addition. The grants are tenable for four to twelve months in Canada or elsewhere if required. Grants may be renewed by re-applying.

Eligibility: Candidates for either Grant should be a Canadian citizen or a landed immigrant who has resided in Canada for at least five years, and have finished basic training or have the necessary competence to be considered a professional artist.

Note: Artists must submit at least 20 slides illustrating their work, especially over the last three years.

Recipients must devote the major part of their time to their program.

Further information from:
Arts Awards Service
Canada Council
255 Albert Street
P.O. Box 1047
Ottawa, Ontario
Canada K1P 5V8

[457]

CANADA DEPARTMENT OF AGRICULTURE
NATIONAL RESEARCH COUNCIL

Visiting Fellowships

Purpose: To stimulate the research effort of the Department of Agriculture by bringing into the laboratories high quality young scientists from institutes of higher learning all over the world, and to give young promising scientists the opportunity to work with distinguished researchers in their respective fields before embarking on careers in scientific research.

No. offered: 20 Fellowships annually.

Value: Annual stipend is approximately Can$22,000 per annum, paid in monthly installments, plus travel expenses to and from location where the Fellowship is tenable.

Tenable in research institutes and stations of the Department for one year; renewable for a second year upon the recommendation of the Fellow's director, with a maximum tenure of 27 months.

Eligibility: Applicants should possess a Ph.D. degree from a recognized university, or expect to obtain such a degree before taking up an award. Candidates having equivalent research experience may also be considered. Applicants should have normally received their Ph.D. degree or equivalent experience within the past five years. There are no restrictions regarding nationality of applicants, but successful candidates must meet all Canadian immigration requirements.

Closing date: 15th January.

Note: Applicants are advised to confirm that these particulars are correct.

Further information from:
   Awards Administrative Officer
   Canada Department of Agriculture
   Research Program Service
   Ottawa, Ontario
   Canada K1A OC6

[458]

CANADA MORTGAGE AND HOUSING CORPORATION

Graduate Scholarship Program

Subjects: Areas related to housing in its urban and regional context.

Value: Currently up to Can$7,500 per annum, travel expenses from place of residence to place of study, tuition fees and an allowance of Can$960 for each dependent. These values may be increased.

Tenable for one year, renewable.

Eligibility: Open to candidates who are Canadian citizens or who have been landed immigrants for not less than 18 months. Awards are made to candidates of demonstrated ability and high academic promise.

Note: Applications must be made through the university at which the candidate proposes to enroll.

Closing date: 15th March.

Further information from:
   Administrative Officer
   Graduate Scholarship Program
   Canada Mortgage and Housing
     Corporation
   Montreal Road
   Ottawa, Ontario
   Canada K1A OP7

[459]

CANADIAN AGRICULTURAL ECONOMICS SOCIETY

Master's Thesis Awards

The Society gives two annual Awards of Can$175 and Can$100 for theses written for a course of study in agricultural economics at the master's level, at a Canadian university. Nominations should be made by the faculty committee at the Department of Agricultural Economics located at the university.

Note: Two annual student Essay Awards of Can$100 and Can$50 are also offered to undergraduate students with an interest in agricultural economics.

Closing date: 28th February.

Further information from:
Secretary-Treasurer
Canadian Agricultural Economics Society
Suite 907, 151 Slater Street
Ottawa, Ontario
Canada K1P 5H4

[460]

CANADIAN AUTHORS ASSOCIATION

Association Awards: An annual Award of Can$500 plus a silver medal is given in each of the following four categories: prose fiction, prose non-fiction, poetry, and drama (for any medium).

Applicants should be Canadian writers whose work has been published, or in the case of drama, produced during the calendar year prior to that in which the Award is made. Authors may win in a particular category only once. These Awards are funded by *Harlequin Enterprises Ltd. Closing date:* 31st January of the year following publication of production.

Vicky Metcalf Award: A Prize of Can$1,000 is given annually to a Canadian author for a number of children's books. The books may be fiction, non-fiction or picture books. *Closing date:* 31st March.

Vicky Metcalf Short Story Award: A Prize of Can$500 is given annually for the best short story for children published in a Canadian magazine during the previous year.

Further information from:
Headquarters Chairman
Canadian Authors Association
24 Ryerson Avenue
Toronto, Ontario
Canada M5T 2P3

[461]

CANADIAN BAR ASSOCIATION

Viscount Bennett Fellowship

Purpose: To encourage a high standard of legal education, training and ethics.

No. offered: Two Fellowships annually.

Value: Can$7,500 or Can$12,000 paid in two equal installments.

Tenable at an institution of higher learning in Canada, the United Kingdom, France, or the United States, for one year; renewable only in exceptional circumstances.

Eligibility: Open to Canadians who have graduated from an approved law school in Canada, or who, at the time of application, are pursuing final-year studies as undergraduate students at an approved law school.

Note: The Can$12,000 Fellowship must be held exclusively.

Closing date: 15th December.

Further information from:
Director of Coummunications
Canadian Bar Association
Suite 1700
130 Albert Street
Ottawa, Ontario
Canada K1P 5G4

[462]

CANADIAN BAR ASSOCIATION

Louis S. St. Laurent Fellowship in Legal Journalism

Purpose: To give competent professionals in the press, radio and television, familiarity with the institutions and processes of the judicial systems in Canada.

No. offered: Two Awards annually.

Value: Award in the amount of the Fellow's regular salary during the university session up to the equivalent of Can$2,000 per month payable in eight monthly installments; all university fees; and reasonable costs of transportation for the Fellow and his family.

Tenable at Queens University, Kingston, or Laval University, Quebec, for one year.

Eligibility: There are no specific academic requirements. Applicants should be working journalists with at least five years experience in newspaper, magazine or radio/TV, and should have the consent of their employer for a leave of absence for one university year. The candidate should undertake to rejoin his employer for a minimum of one year after the Fellowship is concluded.

Note: Selection of candidates is on the basis of professional competence and potential as specialists in legal reporting.

Closing date: 1st February.

Further information from:
 Canadian Bar Association
 Suite 1700
 130 Albert Street
 Ottawa, Ontario
 Canada K1P 5G4

[463]

CANADIAN BIOCHEMICAL SOCIETY

Ayerst Award: Can$1,000 is offered annually to recognize meritorious research in biochemistry in Canada and to stimulate fundamental research by younger biochemists in Canada.

Nominations may be made by any member of the Society, but nominees need not be members. A nominee should not have passed his 40th birthday by 30th April in the year in which the Award is made and should have accomplished outstanding research in biochemistry in the early part of his career. Closing date for nominations is 1st January.

Boehringer-Mannheim Canada Prize: Can$1,000 is offered every two years to a Canadian citizen, for recognition of outstanding research in biochemistry and molecular biology in Canada. Nominations may be made by any member of the Society, but nominees need not be members. Self nominations are not accepted. Closing date: 1st February.

Further information from:
 Secretary
 Canadian Biochemical Society
 c/o Department of Biochemistry
 University of Saskatchewan
 Saskatoon, Saskatchewan
 Canada S7N OWO

[464]

CANADIAN BOOKSELLERS ASSOCIATION

CBA Author of the Year Award

The Award of *Can*$1,000 is offered annually to a Canadian author who in the opinion of the Association's directors, has written the most outstanding work published during the year. Applications are not accepted.

Further information from:
 Canadian Booksellers Association
 Suite 400, 56 the Esplanade
 Toronto, Ontario
 Canada M5E 1A7

[465]

CANADIAN CANCER SOCIETY

Blair Awards (Travelling Fellowships)

Purpose: To enable members of the medical staff of approved hospitals or members of the teaching staffs of medical schools to follow a course of training oriented towards the diagnosis or treatment of cancer.

Value: Fellowships are calculated on a basis of *Can*$55 per day, and travel expenses may be supported up to a maximum of *Can*$1,200; payable in advance. The Society has sole discretion, however, as to the amount of the award.

Tenable at an approved institution for any length of time up to a maximum of six months.

Eligibility: Open to graduates in medicine of an approved faculty or school of medicine who have been (a) a member of the teaching staff of a faculty or school of medicine in Canada, or (b) a member of the staff of a Canadian hospital approved for residency training for not less than two years.

Note: The training sought must not be available in the institution where the applicant holds an appointment. Endorsement will be required from the Dean of the school of medicine or from the head of the hospital department concerned with the field of cancer in which training is sought.

For further information, consult the manual *Support for Research and Training* available from the address below.

Closing date: At least six months in advance of the proposed starting date.

Further information from:
 Canadian Cancer Society
 130 Bloor Street West, Suite 1001
 Toronto, Ontario
 Canada M5S 2V7

[466]

CANADIAN CANCER SOCIETY

McEachern Awards (Fellowships)

Purpose: To provide opportunity for special training in oncology for physicians with a particular interest in clinical care, research and teaching in the field of cancer.

Value: Can$21,500 for twelve months of training for Fellows having three years postgraduate training; increments based on additional acceptable postgraduate study. If tuition fees are payable, a further allowance of up to Can$750 is available upon application. Other costs of training will be the responsibility of the Fellow.

Tenable in Canada or abroad for a period of 12 months, renewable. A tenure of only six months may be considered in special circumstances. Fellowships may be renewable. Special training or study should be pursued in a centre other than the one at which the Fellow has received his prior training.

Eligibility: Open to graduates in medicine of an approved faculty or school of medicine in Canada. Candidates should have completed not less than three years of postgraduate training after receipt of the M.D. degree. Preference will be given to those candidates who have fulfilled the training requirements in their chosen specialty.

Endorsement will be required from the dean of the school of medicine or from the head of the hospital department in the field in which the candidate intends to pursue his studies. The sponsors must establish that needs from the proposed knowledge and skills exist within the geographic region serviced by the university or the hospital, and must indicate the appointment which will be given to the candidate upon successful completion of the training.

If the study is to be followed abroad, the candidate must undertake to return to Canada to practice upon completion of the Fellowship.

Note: Sitting for examinations which lead to qualification as a Medical Specialist is expressly prohibited during the tenure of the Fellowship, except with prior permission from the National Advisory Committee on Fellowships.

For further details and conditions of application, consult the manual *Support for Research and Training* available from the address below.

Closing date: 1st December, for Awards to commence the following 1st July.

Further information from:
Canadian Cancer Society
130 Bloor Street West, Suite 1001
Toronto, Ontario
Canada M5S 2V7

[467]

CANADIAN COMMONWEALTH SCHOLARSHIP AND FELLOWSHIP COMMITTEE

Commonwealth Research Fellowships

Purpose: To enable scholars from Commonwealth countries to visit Canadian universities thus benefiting themselves, their country and the receiving institution. Fellows may undertake personal studies and build up contacts with Canadian colleagues. The Fellowships are provided by the Canadian government and fall within the framework of the Commonwealth Scholarship and Fellowship Plan [q.v.].

Subjects: Unrestricted.

No. offered: Up to three Fellowships annually.

Value: A maintenance allowance of Can$1,500 per month, plus air transportation to and from Canada for Fellow, wife and dependent children. Cost of authorized travel within Canada and approved medical and hospitalization services are also provided.

Tenable at Canadian universities for one year, or exceptionally, for one term; not renewable. The programme may include short visits to other institutions. Permission may be granted for two weeks' travel outside Canada, but funds will not be provided for this.

Eligibility: Open to scholars of established reputation from universities and research centres in Commonwealth countries other than Canada.

Note: Fellowships are made by direct invitation, and are not open for personal application.

Address:
Secretary
Canadian Commonwealth Scholarship
  and Fellowship Committee
c/o Association of Universities and
  Colleges of Canada
151 Slater Street
Ottawa, Ontario
Canada K1P 5N1

Address:
Secretary
Canadian Commonwealth Scholarship
  and Fellowship Committee
c/o Association of Universities and
  Colleges of Canada
151 Slater Street
Ottawa, Ontario
Canada K1P 5N1

[468]

CANADIAN COMMONWEALTH SCHOLARSHIP AND FELLOWSHIP COMMITTEE

Commonwealth Visiting Fellowships

Purpose: To enable educators from Commonwealth countries to visit Canada to discuss educational matters with Canadian colleagues and to advise on techniques and problems in their field, thus benefiting the Fellow, his country and the host institution. The Fellowships are provided by the Canadian government and fall within the framework of the Commonwealth Scholarship and Fellowship Plan [q.v.].

No. offered: Up to five Fellowships annually.

Value: A maintenance allowance of *Can*$1,500 per month plus air transportation to and from Canada for the Fellow only. Costs of authorized travel within Canada and approved medical and hospitalization services are also provided.

Tenable at an educational institution or agency in Canada, usually for two to four months; not renewable.

Eligibility: Open to citizens of Commonwealth countries who are prominent in various fields of education, including universities, colleges, schools and technical institutions.

Note: Fellowships are made by direct invitation, and are not open for personal application. They are not intended to cover research projects.

[469]

CANADIAN COMMONWEALTH SCHOLARSHIP AND FELLOWSHIP COMMITTEE

Commonwealth Scholarships

Purpose: To enable citizens of Commonwealth countries to visit Canada to undertake advanced study or research leading towards a university degree or similar qualification. The Scholarships are provided by the Canadian government and fall within the framework of the Commonwealth Scholarship and Fellowship Plan (see 574).

Subjects: Any university studies excluding clinical training and work towards medical or dental degrees.

Value: Return economy air passage to Canada; approved tuition and other university fees (excluding board and residence); personal maintenance allowance of *Can*$400 to *Can*$475 per month; approved medical and hospital expenses; an allowance of *Can*$200 for books, supplies, photocopies, etc.; a clothing allowance of *Can*$350 during the first year of study and *Can*$250 per year in subsequent years; in special cases provision for travel within Canada up to a total of *Can*$800 if it is an essential part of the Scholar's academic programme; under certain conditions a marriage allowance of *Can*$150 per month while the spouse resides with the Scholar in Canada, plus two-thirds of the cost of the spouse's return fare to Canada.

Tenable in Canadian universities. Graduate awards are made for two academic years and the intervening summer, except in cases where a shorter period is required to complete the programme for which the award was granted. Extensions may be granted if required. Undergraduate awards are normally made for the period the programme of studies requires.

Eligibility: Open to men and women of high intellectual promise who are citizens of a Commonwealth country and are normally resident in any part of the Commonwealth other than Canada, but students already in Canada may apply. Usually, candidates should not have reached their 35th birthday by 1st October of the year of the award. Before taking up a Scholarship, students must hold a bachelor's or master's degree from a recognized university, or some equivalent qualification. In exceptional cases an award may be made for undergraduate study, or to a graduate who wishes to study for another undergraduate degree if the programme of studies he wishes to follow is not available in his own country. A candidate must have an adequate knowledge of English or French, and may be required to demonstrate this by taking a test.

Note: Scholars may not hold any other major awards during tenure, but may accept minor awards not exceeding *Can*$1,000 per annum. Part-time teaching or research assignments at the prevailing rate of pay at the institution, not exceeding four hours a week or 100 hours per calendar year, may be undertaken if approved by the Committee.

Scholars must undertake to return to their homeland immediately following termination of their awards.

Applications must be submitted through the appropriate agency in the candidate's country.

Further information from:
Secretary
Canadian Commonwealth Scholarship
  and Fellowship Committee
c/o Association of Universities and
  Colleges of Canada
151 Slater Street
Ottawa, Ontario
Canada K1P 5N1

[470]

CANADIAN CYSTIC FIBROSIS FOUNDATION

CCFF Fellowships

Subjects: Research or advanced training in areas of medical science pertinent to cystic fibrosis, such as: molecular genetics, tissue culture, physiology or biochemistry of the exocrine glands, membrane transport, pulmonary physiology, gastroenterology and nutrition.

No. offered: A limited number of Fellowships annually.

Value: The stipends are at levels similar to those of the Medical Research Council.

Tenable in any aproved university, hospital or research institute in Canada, the United States or abroad, for 12 months, renewable for up to two subsequent years.

Eligibility: Open to graduates of both medical or non-medical programs. Preference is given to candidates who will be in a structural program that will lead to a career in exemplary care for cystic fibrosis, research or training. Fellowships are only very rarely offered to persons not normally resident in Canada.

Closing date: 1st October.

Further information from:
Canadian Cystic Fibrosis Foundation
161 Eglinton Avenue East
Suite 503
Toronto, Ontario
Canada M4P 1J5

[471]

CANADIAN CYSTIC FIBROSIS FOUNDATION

Grants-in-Aid of Research: Investigators may apply, singly or in groups, for funds for projects that will have immediate or long-term relevance to cystic fibrosis. Applications, which must be received by 1st October, should state the objectives and specific aims of the research, the background of the problem, methods of procedure and the significance of the research to the problem of cystic fibrosis. Grants are payable quarterly.

Summer Student Research Program: Students engaged in summer research projects in the field of cystic fibrosis may apply for support through clinic directors or investigators. Students will be paid at a level similar to that of the Medical Research Council. Until adequate funds become available, Foundation support will be limited to one student per institution. Applications must be received by 15th February. *William J. Skelly Kinsmen Award* of *Can*$500 is given annually to the student engaged in the most worthwhile summer research project.

Travel Grants for Attendance at Scientific Meetings: The Foundation encourages CCFF-supported investigators and fellows to participate in cystic fibrosis sessions at scientific meetings, and subject to the availability of funds, awards Travel Grants. Grants may not exceed the equivalent of the prevailing return economy air fare, plus maintenance up to Can$40 per day for a maximum of two days.

Further information from:
Canadian Cystic Fibrosis Foundation
161 Eglinton Avenue East
Suite 503
Toronto, Ontario
Canada M4P 1J5

[472]

CANADIAN CYSTIC FIBROSIS FOUNDATION

Term Grants in Aid of Research

Purpose: To continue high quality and long range research programs which have reached a relatively stable level of expenditure.

Subjects: Priority is given to those applications advancing new conceptual approaches to the basic defect in cystic fibrosis, which require continued support over several years for their fruition.

Clinical research proposals which require interdisciplinary and multidisciplinary efforts will also be considered, especially those aimed at: the development of a specific genetic marker for prenatal and heterozygote detection; improvement of therapeutic approaches (including multicentre).

No. offered: A limited number of three-year Term Grants, awarded annually.

Value: Continued support for a period up to three years. The grant will be paid automatically during the term of the award without annual submission of an application or progress report.

Eligibility: Candidates must be currently working in areas that have immediate or long term relevance to cystic fibrosis and have made significant contributions to the field.

Closing date: 1st October.

Further information from:
Canadian Cystic Fibrosis Foundation
161 Eglinton Avenue East
Suite 503
Toronto, Ontario
Canada M4P 1J5

[473]

CANADIAN CYSTIC FIBROSIS FOUNDATION

Scholarships for Research in Cystic Fibrosis

Purpose: To provide salary support for an investigator to undertake research into the basic defect of cystic fibrosis.

Value: The initial salary will depend on the qualifications and experience of the successful candidate.

The salary of the Scholar may be supplemented by the institution to which he is appointed or by clinical earnings up to 25% of the salary paid by the Foundation.

Tenable at a medical school upon the sponsorship of the chairman of the department and the dean of the faculty.

A young investigator is appointed for three years, renewable for two years. An experienced investigator is appointed for five years. In no case will the appointment exceed five years.

Eligibility: The candidate should hold an M.D. of Ph.D. (or equivalent), show evidence of scholarly activity and have a scientific background that would enable the undertaking of research relevant to the basic defect of cystic fibrosis.

Note: Applications will be considered by the Medical Advisory Committee at intervals to be announced in advance by the Foundation.

The application, which should outline the research to be undertaken during the intial years of the Scholarship, should be accompanied by a complete post-secondary academic record and four copies of publications or reprints. Three letters from individuals familiar with the candidates work should be sent directly to the Foundation.

The Scholar is expected to devote 75% of his time for research and the remaining 25% in teaching or clinical activities. He is also expected to hold an academic appointment in the department commensurate with his experience. The Scholar would be allowed to participate in Departmental activities.

Further information from:
Canadian Cystic Fibrosis Foundation
161 Eglinton Avenue East
Suite 503
Toronto, Ontario
Canada M4P 1J5

[474]

CANADIAN CYSTIC FIBROSIS FOUNDATION

CCFF Studentships

Subjects: Full-time training in research in the health sciences relevant to cystic fibrosis.

No. offered: A limited number of Studentships annually.

Value: The stipends are at levels similar to those of the Medical Research Council.

Tenable under supervision of department members of approved schools, universities and provincial government laboratories in Canada which offer relevant training in the applicant's field of study. Studentships are renewable.

Eligibility: Open to applicants having a high academic standing who hold or are about to receive an honours B.Sc. degree or its equivalent; or who have completed or expect to complete sufficient academic work to be admitted in full standing to a graduate school as of the effective date of the Studentship; or are already engaged in an M.Sc. or Ph.D. program.

Note: Individuals planning to proceed towards an M.D., D.D.S., or D.V.M. degree are ineligible.

Closing date: 1st December.

Further information from:
Canadian Cystic Fibrosis Foundation
161 Eglinton Avenue East
Suite 503
Toronto, Ontario
Canada M4P 1J5

[475]

CANADIAN DENTAL RESEARCH FOUNDATION

Graduate Dental Research Award

Purpose: To encourage research related to dentistry by graduate or postgraduate students in Canada.

No. offered: One Award annually.

Value: Can$1,000, a plaque, and Can$200 travel expenses are presented to the student who submits the best report on a research project.

Eligibility: Open to students who have conducted research in question in association with the dental faculty of a Canadian university.

Note: One double-spaced typewritten copy should be submitted in the form of a paper, together with four extra copies of any photographs and illustrations. Equally acceptable is a previously published paper on the candidate's graduate work either in press or already published in a scientific journal, provided the candidate for the competition is the senior author. Such manuscripts or publications must be submitted within two years of completion of the graduate program.

Closing date: 1st December.

Further information from:
Canadian Dental Research Foundation
c/o Executive Director
Canadian Dental Association
1815 Alta Vista Drive
Ottawa, Ontario
Canada K1G 3Y6

[476]

CANADIAN FEDERATION FOR THE HUMANITIES
SOCIAL SCIENCE FEDERATION OF CANADA

Aid to Scholarly Publications Programmes

Purpose: To assist the publication of works of advanced scholarly research, which make an important contribution to the advancement of knowledge in the humanities and social sciences, but which are unlikely ever to be self-supporting.

Subjects: Humanities—languages and literatures (ancient and modern), history, philosophy, fine arts, musicology, archaeology and religious studies; social sciences—anthropology, economics, political science, geography, history, law, sociology, education, psychology.

Value: Grant in aid of publication based on an estimate of costs submitted by a prospective publisher.

Eligibility: Open to persons who are normally resident in Canada, whose works of advanced scholarships in one of the fields listed above are to be published by a reputable Canadian publisher. (Exceptions may be made for works by non-Canadians dealing with Canadian topics, or, in unusual cases, for works by Canadians being published outside Canada).

Note: In general, only book-length manuscripts are eligible; these may be submitted to the appropriate Committee on Aid to Publication either by the author or a publisher. At least two specialists in the field will evaluate each manuscript. Unrevised theses will not be considered.

The Aid to Scholarly Publications Programmes are funded by the Social Science and Humanities Research Council of Canada.

Further information from:
Philip J. Cercone, Director
Aid to Scholarly Publications Programmes
Canadian Federation for the Humanities
  or Social Science Federation of
  Canada
151 Slater Street, Suite 410
Ottawa, Ontario
Canada K1P 5H3

[477]

CANADIAN FEDERATION OF UNIVERSITY WOMEN

Margaret Dale Philp Award: Can$600 is given annually to a woman who is a Canadian citizen or has held landed immigrant status for at least one year prior to submission of application. Candidates should hold a bachelor's degree or its equivalent from a recognized Canadian university, reside in Canada, and wish to embark on, or continue, a programme leading to an advanced degree in the humanities or social sciences. Special consideration will be given to candidates who wish to specialize in Canadian history.

Margaret McWilliams Pre-Doctoral Fellowship: Can$5,000 paid in two half yearly installments, is awarded annually to a woman who is a Canadian citizen or has held landed immigrant status for at least one year prior to submission of application. A candidate should hold a master's degree or its equivalent from a recognized university, not necessarily in Canada, and be at an advanced stage in her doctoral programme. Candidates need not be studying in Canada at time of application. The Fellowship is not renewable.

Professional Fellowship: One Fellowship of *Can*$3,500, paid in two half yearly installments, is awarded annually to a woman who is a Canadian citizen or has held landed immigrant status for at least one year prior to submitting application. Candidates should hold a bachelor's degree or its equivalent from a recognized Canadian university, and wish to pursue graduate work at a recognized professional school, either in or outside of Canada. The Fellowship is not renewable.

Alice E. Wilson Grants: At least six Grants of *Can*$600 each are awarded to women who are Canadian citizens or have held landed immigrant status for at least one year prior to submitting application. Candidates should have a bachelor's degree or its equivalent from a recognized university, not necessarily in Canada, and wish to do refresher work in their chosen field, to do specialized study, or to retrain in new techniques applicable to their fields. Grants are tenable in or outside of Canada, and may be renewable.

Closing date: 15th December of each year.

Further information from:
Margery Trenholme, Fellowships
  Chairman
Canadian Federation of University
  Women
4990 Clanranald Avenue, No. 5
Montreal, Quebec
Canada H3X 2S2

[478]

CANADIAN FOUNDATION FOR THE ADVANCEMENT OF PHARMACY

Fellowships in Hospital Pharmacy: Four Fellowships, with a value of *Can*$500 each, are awarded annually on a national competition basis, and are intended to assist the recipient on a one-year residency in hospital pharmacy. *Closing date:* 1st June.

Fellowships in Professional Practice: Four Fellowships, with a value of *Can*$500 each, are offered annually to candidates selected from Canadian universities which have a school of pharmacy. The Study Fellowship will enable the recipient to carry on postgraduate work at the university. *Closing date:* 1st June.

Fellowships in Industrial Pharmacy: Four Fellowships, with a lump sum value of *Can*$250 are offered on a competition basis to students registered in Canadian schools of pharmacy who have completed an Industrial Pharmacy Summer Studentship Program. Fellowships are offered annually and are not renewable. *Closing date:* 1st September.

Past Presidents' Award: An Award of *Can*$250 is annually made to the most outstanding student in a Canadian school of pharmacy.

Note: For further information apply to the dean of the particular school of pharmacy, or to:
   Canadian Foundation for the
      Advancement of Pharmacy
   123 Edward Street, Suite 303
   Toronto, Ontario
   Canada M5G 1E2

[479]

CANADIAN FRIENDS OF THE HEBREW UNIVERSITY

Grants for Canadians

Subjects: Law, dentistry, social science and economics, humanities (arts), science, agriculture, pharmacy and library science.

Value: Between *Can*$250 and *Can*$1,500 at the discretion of the Academic Affairs Committee.

Tenable at the Hebrew University in Jerusalem, for one year of undergraduate or postgraduate study.

Eligibility: Open to Canadian citizens or residents of Canada who are able to fulfil the entrance requirements of the Hebrew University in their chosen fields of study. The Committee gives special encouragement to candidates with at least a second-class academic average in the arts and a high second-class in the sciences.

Closing date: 31st March.

Further information from:
   Academic Affairs Committee
   Canadian Friends of the Hebrew
      University
   Suite 208, Yorkdale Place
   1 Yorkdale Road
   Toronto, Ontario
   Canada M6A 3A1

[480]

CANADIAN FUND FOR DENTAL EDUCATION

C.F.D.E. Teacher/Researcher Training Fellowships

Purpose: To provide teachers and researchers for Canadian dental schools.

Value: Variable.

Tenable for one year at an approved institution; renewable.

Eligibility: Open to Canadian citizens or landed immigrants who have completed an undergraduate course in dentistry or a program in science and are eligible for admission to a graduate school. Candidates must be able to prove their intention to serve at least half-time in a Canadian faculty of dentistry.

Closing date: 1st March.

Further information from:
   Canadian Fund for Dental Education
   Suite 205
   44 Eglinton Avenue West
   Toronto, Ontario
   Canada M4R 1A1

[481]

CANADIAN HEART FOUNDATION

Medical Scientist Fellowship

Purpose: To bring scientifically trained people and those with potential for independent research into a medical programme in order to produce outstanding cardiovascular scientists.

Subjects: Research related to the cardiovascular field.

Value: The Fellowship's stipend will be related to the recipient's qualifications at entry.

Eligibility: Open to individuals under the age of 35 who have conducted independent research. Selection will be based on background, experience, dedication and the validity of extending the recipient's research interests to include clinical studies.

Note: Arrangements must be made with the institution for an appropriate training or research programme; this institution must be fully aware of its responsibilities.

Further information from:
 Canadian Heart Foundation
 Suite 1200, One Nicholas Street
 Ottawa, Ontario
 Canada K1N 7B7

[482]

CANADIAN HEART FOUNDATION

Research Fellowships

Subjects: Cardiovascular research.

Value: Can$8,900 to Can$27,500 per annum, depending on candidate's qualifications, plus an allowance for travel expenses incurred in connection with the research.

Tenable at approved institutions in Canada, on an annual basis, for a maximum of four years.

Eligibility: Open to qualified investigators working in Canada, with an interest in research, training or development in the cardiovascular field, who have at least a first degree.

Note: Applicants must arrange for their own admission to an approved institution, and submit a statement of acceptance from the department.

Senior Research Fellowships and Research Association Awards are offered by the *Ontario Heart Foundation, 310 Davenport Road, Toronto, Ontario M5R 3K2.*

Closing date: 1st October.

Further information from:
 Canadian Heart Foundation
 Suite 1200, One Nicholas Street
 Ottawa, Ontario
 Canada K1N 7B7

[483]

CANADIAN HEART FOUNDATION

Nursing Research Fellowship

Purpose: To attract and encourage nurses to train in a chosen area of the cardiovascular and stroke field to the level of a master's or Ph.D. degree.

Value: Can$17,000 per annum depending on qualifications. In addition, Can$500 per annum is available for travel purposes.

Tenable at an appropriate institution for up to four years, renewable annually.

Eligibility: Open to suitably qualified nurses with some research experience who are Canadian citizens. Each application will be considered as a joint effort of the candidate and the institution at which he/she will be working.

Further information from:
 Canadian Heart Foundation
 Suite 1200, One Nicholas Street
 Ottawa, Ontario
 Canada K1N 7B7

[484]

CANADIAN HEART FOUNDATION

Grants-in-Aid

Purpose: For the support of projects of an experimental nature.

Subject: Cardiovascular research or development.

No. offered: Approximately 250 Grants-in-Aid annually.

Value: To cover research expenses only, and not the recipient's personal support.

Tenable at recognized institutions in Canada, either on an annual renewable basis, or for a three-year term.

Eligibility: Open to graduates of recognized institutions and, in the case of three-year term Grants, qualified scientists with well-developed programs of research which have a relatively stable level of expenditure.

Note: Term Grants are available to scientists with well-developed programs in their particular fields of research which have a relatively stable level of expenditure. Grants are available for three years.

Closing date: 1st October.

Further information from:
 Canadian Heart Foundation
 Suite 1200, One Nicholas Street
 Ottawa, Ontario
 Canada K1N 7B7

[485]

CANADIAN HEART FOUNDATION

Research Scholarship

Subject: Cardiovascular research.

Value: Can$18,500 to *Can*$33,500 per annum, plus up to *Can*$750 travel allowance for scientific purposes.

Tenable at suitable institutions in Canada, initially for a period of three years.

Eligibility: Open to persons with an M.D. or Ph.D. degree, or equivalent qualifications, who have recently completed a period of supervised research and show promise of ability to initiate and carry out independent research.

Note: Applications must be made on behalf of an individual by a university or affiliated institute which must guarantee the applicant an appropriate rank if awarded the Scholarship.

Closing date: 1st October.

Further information from:
 Canadian Heart Foundation
 Suite 1200, One Nicholas Street
 Ottawa, Ontario
 Canada K1N 7B7

[486]

CANADIAN HOME ECONOMICS ASSOCIATION

Carnation Company Incentive Award

Purpose: To assist a student undertaking postgraduate study leading to an advanced degree.

Subjects: Home economics, especially foods and food sciences.

No. offered: One Award annually.

Value: Can$500.

Tenable for one year at any suitable location.

Eligibility: Open to students who have received a degree in home economics or a closely allied discipline at a Canadian university and who intend to undertake postgraduate study leading to an advanced degree.
 Special consideration will be given to a student undertaking postgraduate study in foods or food sciences.

Closing date: 15th January.

Further information from:
 Chairman
 Awards Selection Committee
 Canadian Home Economics Association
 151 Slater Street, Suite 805
 Ottawa, Ontario
 Canada K1P 5H3

[487]

CANADIAN HOME ECONOMICS ASSOCIATION

Robin Hood Multifoods Limited Award

One Award of *Can*$1,000 is given to a graduate in Home Economics from a Canadian University for graduate study leading to an advanced degree. The Award is based on academic achievement, personal qualities, and past and/or potential contribution to the Home Economics profession. Preference is given to candidates planning a career in business, the consumer service (foods) field or food service management.

Closing date: 15th January.

Further information from:
Chairman
Awards Selection Committee
Canadian Home Economics Association
151 Slater Street, Suite 805
Ottawa, Ontario
Canada K1P 5H3

[488]

CANADIAN HOME ECONOMICS ASSOCIATION

Ruth Binnie Scholarship

Two Scholarships, in the amount of *Can*$3,000 each, are given for full-time graduate study from a Canadian university in the field of home economics or home economics education. Applicants should be holders of a professional teaching certificate who are residents of Canada. First consideration will be given to applicants proceeding towards a Masters in Education on a full-time basis. Second consideration will go to part-time students and Scholarship monies will be prorated. Third consideration will go to Ph.D. applicants planning to return to university teaching in Home Economics Education.

All candidates should have a high commitment to the teaching profession and Home Economics education.

The awards are based on scholarship, personal qualities, contributions toward Home Economics education in junior or senior high school, and potential in the education field.

Closing date for application is: 15th January.

Further information from:
Chairman
Awards Selection Committee
Canadian Home Economics Association
151 Slater Street, Suite 805
Ottawa, Ontario
Canada K1P 5H3

[489]

CANADIAN HOME ECONOMICS ASSOCIATION

Mary A. Clarke Memorial Scholarship
Silver Jubilee Scholarship

Purpose: To promote skilled and imaginative inquiry in the field of home economics.

No. offered: One Mary A. Clarke Memorial Scholarship and one Silver Jubilee Scholarship annually.

Value: Can$2,000 each.

Tenable for one year at any suitable location.

Eligibility: Open to graduates in home economics from a Canadian university who are resident in Canada and are planning to undertake, or are currently engaged in, graduate study leading to a higher academic degree.

The awards will be based on scholarship, personal qualities, past and/or potential contribution to the profession of home economics, and financial considerations.

Closing date: 15th January, for both Scholarships.

Further information from:
Chairman
Awards Selection Committee
Canadian Home Economics Association
151 Slater Street, Suite 203
Ottawa, Ontario
Canada K1P 5H3

[490]

CANADIAN INSTITUTE OF MINING AND METALLURGY
Technical Divisions/Societies

Student Essay Prizes

Undergraduate Prizes: Two Prizes of *Can*$400 and *Can*$200 are awarded for the first and second best essays in each of the following technical divisions of the Institute: Canadian Mineral Processors Division; Coal Division; Geology Division; Industrial Minerals Division; Mechanical/Electrical Division; Metallurgical Society; Metal Mining Division; Petroleum Society.

Open to undergraduate students at Canadian universities including students who received a bachelor's degree in engineering or science in the year preceding that of the competition, providing the essay is submitted to the Institute Secretary within one month following the date of graduation. *Closing date:* 15th January.

Graduate Prizes: Two General Prizes of *Can*$1,000 and *Can*$500 are awarded for the first and second best essays on any subject pertaining to the mineral industry.

Open to Institute Members or Student Members currently or recently enrolled as graduate students at a Canadian university, including students who received a master's or doctoral degree in engineering or science in the year preceding that of the competition, providing the essay is submitted to the Institute Secretary within one month following conferment of the degree. *Closing date:* 15th January.

President's Gold Medal: This Medal may be awarded either singly or in duplicate, for the best essay submitted either by an undergraduate student or by a graduate student, or by both.

Note: The Technical Divisions/Societies of the Institute also sponsor Prizes for essays by undergraduate students at colleges of technology in Canada. First and second Prizes of *Can*$300 and *Can*$200 are awarded for essays in each of the following study areas: mining technology, metallurgical technology; geoscience technology; petroleum technology.

Open to undergraduate students at colleges of technology in Canada, including students who received an appropriate diploma in the year preceding that of the competition and submitted their essays to the Institute Secretary within one month following the date of graduation. *Closing date:* 15th January.

Further information from:
Secretary-Treasurer
Canadian Institute of Mining and
  Metallurgy
400-1130 Sherbrooke West
Montreal, Quebec
Canada H3A 2M8

[491]

CANADIAN INTERNATIONAL DEVELOPMENT AGENCY

Development Awards for Canadians

Purpose: To provide opportunities for further studies for Canadians wishing to develop or further their careers in the field of development assistance.

Subjects: Advanced study programs in any area or discipline, related to some specific developmental need or problem. While participation in a formal academic program is not required, some portion of the study must provide for related practical experience, field observation or research in a developing country.

No. offered: Up to 25 Awards annually.

Value: Up to a maximum of *Can*$15,000 per annum.

Tenable for up to two years in Canada and/or in a developing country; continuation of the Award will be dependent on satisfactory review.

Eligibility: Applicants must be Canadian citizens who have completed a provincially recognized post-secondary course of studies, and whose proposed study programs are accompanied by the consent of a supervisor. Candidates will be expected to provide indication of their intention to pursue a career in international development activities, and some preference will be accorded to those who have completed a tour of duty with a development agency, public or private.

Note: Research programs must have a practical orientation and should not be used exclusively for academic or theoretical studies. Ph.D. programs will not be considered.

Closing date: 31st January.

Further information from:
Human Resources Division
Canadian International Development
  Agency
200 Promenade du Portage
Hull, Quebec
Canada K1A OGH

[492]

CANADIAN INTERNATIONAL DEVELOPMENT AGENCY

Technical Assistance Scholarships and Fellowships

Purpose: To assist developing nations in Asia, Africa, the Caribbean and Latin America to meet their needs by training their nationals in academic, technical and practical fields.

Subjects: Unrestricted.

Value: Approximately Can$10,000 per annum. Travel, living allowances, tuition, books, clothing and other related expenses are covered by the award.

Tenable at universities, colleges, technical institutions and commercial or industrial enterprises in Canada or in other developing countries.

Eligibility: Open to students from developing countries whose governments have a cooperation agreement with Canada and who are suitably qualified to undertake the proposed training program. Priority is given to postgraduate and specialist training. Candidates must have been accepted by a training institution and be capable of communicating either in English or French.

Note: Direct applications by individuals will not be considered. Applications should be made to the appropriate ministry of local government which selects and then nominates candidates to CIDA through the Canadian high commission or embassy in, or accredited to, the country concerned.

Address:
Human Resources Division
Canadian International Development
 Agency
200 Promenade du Portage
Hull, Quebec
Canada K1A OGH

[493]

CANADIAN INTERNATIONAL DEVELOPMENT AGENCY
NATURAL SCIENCES AND ENGINEERING RESEARCH COUNCIL

CIDA-NSERC Research Associateships for Scientists from Developing Countries

The Program is intended to permit scientists from developing countries to utilize training they receive in Canada to carry out research projects which will benefit certain needs of their home countries. Associates may spend annually in Canada a period of up to three months during which they will be associated with Canadian scientists who will guide and assist them with their research programs.

Scientists may be eligible under one of the following CIDA-supported programs, namely: Commonwealth Caribbean Assistance Program; Special Commonwealth Africa Assistance Plan; Colombo Plan; French-Speaking African States Program; and Latin American Program.

Further information from:
 CIDA-NSERC Research Associateships
  Program
 Natural Sciences and Engineering
  Research Council
 Ottawa, Ontario
 Canada K1A OR6

[494]

CANADIAN LIBRARY ASSOCIATION

The following awards are open to Canadian citizens and landed immigrants. The awards are tenable for one year. Consideration is given to both academic standing and financial need.

CLA Dafoe Scholarship: One Scholarship of Can$1,750 is given for entrance to an accredited library school in Canada; a program of study or series of courses leading to a further, not an initial, library degree.

Howard V. Phalin-World Book Graduate Scholarship in Library Science: One Scholarship with a maximum value of Can$2,500 is given for a program of study or series of courses either leading to a further library degree or related to library work in which the candidate is currently engaged, or to library work which will be undertaken upon completion of the studies. This Scholarship is also tenable at an accredited library school in the United States. Candidates should hold a B.L.S. or M.L.S. degree but in exceptional circumstances consideration will be given to an outstanding candidate with a degree in another discipline who wishes to obtain a B.L.S. or M.L.S. degree.

H.W. Wilson Foundation Award: Value: One Scholarship of Can$2,000 is given for entrance to an accredited library school in Canada.

Closing date: 1st March.

Further information from:
Scholarships and Awards Committee
Canadian Library Association
151 Sparks Street
Ottawa, Ontario
Canada K1P 5E3

[495]

CANADIAN LIFE AND HEALTH INSURANCE ASSOCIATION

Medical Awards; Research Awards

Purpose: To assist Canadian medical schools in developing and retaining clinical teaching and research staff.

Subjects: Clinical and epidemiological medical research and teaching, including research in health services administration and medical care.

No. offered: Two Awards annually.

Value: Can$75,000 over a three year period will be given to the medical school as a contribution to the recipient's total salary.

Tenable at Canadian medical schools for three years.

Eligibility: Open to individuals who are suitably qualified, have a full-time appointment to the staff of a medical school, demonstrate both interest and ability in clinical teaching and research, show primary interest in academic medicine in Canada rather than private practice, and are nominated by the dean of a medical school of a Canadian university.

Note: Each Canadian medical school may nominate one candidate annually.

Closing date: 15th December.

Further information from:
Director
Educational Division
Canadian Life and Health Insurance Association
200 Queen Street West, Suite 2500
Toronto, Ontario
Canada M5H 3S2

[496]

CANADIAN LIVER FOUNDATION

Fellowship Program

Subject: Hepatic physiology and disease.

No. offered: Limited number of Fellowships annually.

Value: The value of each Fellowship will be equivalent to current scales of other national agencies.

Tenable in any recognized institution for one year; renewable by re-application.

Eligibility: Open to Canadian citizens or landed immigrants resident in Canada who hold an M.D. or Ph.D. and are under 32 years of age.

Note: Applications must be sponsored by a Canadian faculty of medicine or health sciences and accompanied by a letter of support from the dean, or his designate.

Closing date: 15th November.

Further information from:
Valerie M. Price, Executive Director
Canadian Liver Foundation
Suite 510, 42 Charles Street East
Toronto, Ontario
Canada M4Y 1T4

[497]

CANADIAN LIVER FOUNDATION

Research Grants Program

A limited number of Grants are available to help support the research projects of Canadian investigators studying the liver and its diseases. The awards, not to exceed *Can*$10,000 per year, are for operating costs or special equipment.

Address: See next entry.

[498]

CANADIAN LIVER FOUNDATION

Scholarship Program

Subjects: Hepatic physiology and disease.

No. offered: One Scholarship annually.

Value: Comparable to the scale of other national agencies.

Tenable at any Canadian medical school, normally for three years; extendable to a maximum of five years.

Eligibility: Open to Canadians holding an M.D. or Ph.D. who are under 35 years of age.

Note: Summer Studentships are available for up to three months to encourage Canadian undergraduate students to develop an interest in the liver and its diseases. *Closing date:* 28th February.

Further information from:
Valerie M. Price, Executive Director
Canadian Liver Foundation
Suite 510, 42 Charles Street East
Toronto, Ontario
Canada M4Y 1T4

[499]

CANADIAN LUNG ASSOCIATION

Fellowships

Purpose: To permit physicians and those holding doctoral degrees in the health sciences to be funded for a period of research training so that they may be better able to contribute to Canadian work in the field of respiratory disease.

Subjects: Lung disease including tuberculosis: teaching or research project.

Value: To be decided annually.

Tenable at a university medical or research centre or hospital in Canada for a period of one to three years; applications that involve a period of work outside Canada will be considered.

Eligibility: Open to medical graduates who have completed one or more years of residency.

Note: The teaching or research project should be outlined in the application and must be approved by the head of the department in which the candidate expects to work.

Address: See next entry.

[500]

CANADIAN LUNG ASSOCIATION

Research Grants

Purpose: To promote research into any field of acute or chronic lung disease.

Subjects: May include clinical investigation, pathology, immunology, pulmonary physiology and function, and the sociological aspects of lung disease prevention.

Value: Varies according to project; two payments are ordinarily made, the first in July and the second in January.

Tenable at a specific Canadian institute with concurrence of the institution's executive head; normally for one year only, from 1st July to 30th June, but reapplication may be made for continued support.

Eligibility: Grants are awarded towards the cost of research proposed by individual investigators holding, or otherwise enjoying the privileges of staff appointments at Canadian universities or other recognized institutions.

Closing date: 15th December.

Further information from:
Executive Director
Canadian Lung Association
75 Albert Street, Suite 908
Ottawa, Ontario
Canada K1P 5E7

[501]

CANADIAN MEDICAL ASSOCIATION

Osler Scholarship

Purpose: To improve through the pursuit of studies the teaching of clinical medicine.

No. offered: One Scholarship annually.

Value: Can$2,000, paid in a lump sum.

Tenable at any Canadian university school of medicine; not renewable.

Eligibility: Open to all graduates of Canadian faculties of medicine within the past ten years who have received a recent appointment to a Canadian university faculty of medicine and who wish to pursue studies relative to improving the teaching of clinical medicine.

Note: A written report, suitable for publication, must be submitted following completion of the scholarship period.

Closing date: 31st October.

Further information from:
 Joseph L. Chouinard, Coordinator
 Council on Medical Education
 Canadian Medical Association
 P.O. Box 8650
 Ottawa, Ontario
 Canada K1G OG8

[502]

CANADIAN NATIONAL INSTITUTE FOR THE BLIND
E.A. Baker Foundation for Prevention of Blindness

Fellowships, Research Grants and Miscellaneous Awards

Purpose: To further the prevention of blindness in Canada.

No. offered: Varies, depending on available funds.

Value: Based on individual request and need; paid quarterly.

Tenable in Canada or other parts of the world for one year; renewable for up to two additional years.

Subject: Ophthalmology.

Eligibility: Fellowships are open to Canadian citizens.

Note: On application, a second grant may be awarded to candidates for additional studies.
 The grantee must submit to the Committee a brief report or summary of the work done not more than two months after the termination of the grant, and yearly for long-term grants. Progress reports are necessary when specially requested.

Closing date: 15th December for commencement 1st July.

Further information from:
 Administrative Secretary
 E.A. Baker Foundation
 Professional Advisory Committee
 Canadian National Institute for the Blind
 1929 Bayview Avenue
 Toronto, Ontario
 Canada M4G 3E8

[503]

CANADIAN NATIONAL SPORTSMEN'S FUND

Conservation Scholarships

Subjects: Doctoral level study directed towards improving understanding and better management of Canadian wildlife and its habitat.

No. offered: Three Scholarships per year; normally one new and two continuing.

Value: At least Can$11,000, paid quarterly; normally starting in September.

Tenable at any Canadian university for one year; renewable up to a total of three years subject to satisfactory performance.

Eligibility: Open to Canadian citizens or landed immigrants who can provide confirmation of acceptance as a full-time student in a relevant programme.

Note: Applicants must be willing to appear for

a personal, expenses paid, interview if requested.

Closing date: Normally 1st November.

Further information from:
Canadian National Sportsmen's Fund
P.O. Box 168
Toronto Dominion Centre
Toronto, Ontario
Canada M5K 1H8

[504]

CANADIAN NATIONAL SPORTSMEN'S FUND

Postdoctoral Fellowship

Subjects: Postdoctoral research directed towards improved understanding and better management of Canadian wildlife and its habitat.

No. offered: One Fellowship annually; selection is made by March 31st.

Value: At least *Can*$18,700 paid in three equal installments. An additional sum equal to half of the value of the Fellowship is paid to the department to support the holder's research.

Tenable at any Canadian university for twelve months; renewal is considered in competition with new applicants.

Eligibility: Open to Canadian citizens or landed immigrants. Candidates must be reasonably assured of completing all of the requirements of the Ph.D., including defence of the thesis, by December 31st of the year following application. Ordinarily a recipient is expected to undertake postdoctoral work at an institution other than the one at which the Ph.D. is obtained.

Note: Applicants must be willing to appear for a personal, expenses paid, interview if requested.

Closing date: 1st December.

Further information from:
Canadian National Sportsmen's Fund
P.O. Box 168
Toronto Dominion Centre
Toronto, Ontario
Canada M5K 1H8

[505]

CANADIAN NURSES' FOUNDATION

CNF Fellowships
Eleanor Jean Martin Nursing Award
Agnes Campbell Neill Memorial Award
Katherine E. MacLaggan Fellowship
Helen McArthur Fellowship for Graduate Studies
Virginia A. Lindabury Scholarship

Purpose: To assist nurses in Canada who wish to prepare themselves academically for leadership positions in nursing.

Subjects: Nursing and other subjects which can be shown to be relevant to nursing.

No. offered: Varies annually.

Value: *Can*$3,000 for a master's program; *Can*$4,500 for a doctoral program.

Eligibility: Open to members of the Canadian Nurses' Association.

Note: In accepting an award from the Foundation, a recipient agrees to serve in a nursing position in Canada for a period of one year for each year of financial assistance, and to submit to the library of the CNA a copy of any thesis, study or major paper undertaken as part of the course.
When a recipient of a Foundation award receives financial assistance from another source, the amount of the Foundation award will be reduced by the amount that the award from other resources exceeds *Can*$2,000.

Closing date: 31st March.

Further information from:
Ginette Rodger
Secretary-Treasurer
Canadian Nurses' Foundation
50 The Driveway
Ottawa, Ontario
Canada K2P 1E2

[506]

CANADIAN OSTEOPATHIC EDUCATIONAL TRUST FUND

Scholarship

Purpose: To guarantee the continuance of

osteopathic health care in Canada.

No. offered: One Scholarship annually.

Value: Can$12,000 per year to cover tuition plus a monthly stipend.

Tenable for four years at any accredited college of osteopathic medicine in Canada.

Eligibility: Open to interested persons with a strong motivation to practise osteopathic medicine.

Note: Scholars are required to practise in Canada for five years upon completion of study.

Not confirmed for 1983.

Further information from:
Patricia Roper, Secretary-Treasurer
Canadian Osteopathic Educational Trust Fund
575 Waterloo Street
London, Ontario
Canada N6B 2R2

[507]

CANADIAN PHARMACEUTICAL ASSOCIATION

C.Ph.A. Canada Centennial Award

Purpose: To encourage good student citizenship and student-body leadership and to provide students with the opportunity to visit top manufacturing research and control facilities in principal Canadian cities and government locations, and to participate in the Annual Canadian Pharmaceutical Conference.

No. offered: Nine Awards annually.

Value: Can$400 each plus air fare.

Tenable at each of the nine university faculties of pharmacy in Canada.

Eligibility: Open to students at Canadian university faculties of pharmacy with satisfactory standing during the first three years of their pharmacy course, who show active leadership in student activities.

Note: Awardees are selected each February by their respective faculties of pharmacy. The award is activated in May for a duration of two weeks, ending with the Annual Pharmaceutical Conference.

Further information from:
Canadian Pharmaceutical Association
1815 Alta Vista Drive
Ottawa, Ontario
Canada K1G 3Y6

[508]

CANADIAN POLITICAL SCIENCE ASSOCIATION

Parliamentary Internships

Purpose: To give university graduates an opportunity to supplement their theoretical knowledge of Parliament with practical experience of the day to day work of the Members of Parliament, and to provide back-bench Members with highly qualified assistants.

No. offered: Ten Internships annually.

Value: Can$8,000.

Tenable in Ottawa for the ten-month period from 1st September to 30th June; not renewable.

Eligibility: Open to men and women 21 to 35 years of age who have recently graduated from a Canadian university, preferably with degrees in political science, law, journalism, history, economics, business administration, or other social sciences. Candidates should be Canadian citizens.

Note: Interns will be assigned specific responsibilities with Members of the House of Commons, and will be required to attend seminars and prepare a paper analyzing an aspect of parliamentary government in Canada.

Closing date: Mid-January.

Further information from:
Robert J. Jackson, Director
Parliamentary Internships Programme
Canadian Political Science Association
c/o Arts Tower
Carleton University
Ottawa, Ontario
Canada K1S 5B6

[509]

CANADIAN-SCANDINAVIAN FOUNDATION

Awards

Brucebo Scholarship is available to a young Canadian painter or other person in the field of fine arts for a two month stay at Brucebo, the Island of Gotland.

CSF Special Purpose Grants are available to qualified Canadians wishing to spend a short period in Scandinavia.

Scandinavian Airlines Systems Travel Grant is available to cover the transatlantic air fare to a capital city in Scandinavia served by the airline during off-season and for a period of approximately two months.

Swedish Institute Bursaries are available to qualified Canadian students wishing to pursue academic studies at a postgraduate level, or other advanced studies or research. The recipient must spend four or eight months in Sweden.

Sylvia Weldon Travel Scholarship is given annually to a Canadian wishing to make a study visit to Norway. The grant will cover round trip travel costs plus a maintenance allowance for a few weeks.

Closing date: 20th February.

Further information from:
Dr. Jan Ludgren
Canadian-Scandinavian Foundation
c/o Department of Geography
McGill University
805 Sherbrooke Street West
Montreal, Quebec
Canada H3A 2K6

[510]

CANADIAN SOCIETY OF BIBLICAL STUDIES

Essay Prize

Purpose: To promote biblical scholarship among Canadian postgraduate students.

No. offered: Two Prizes annually.

Value: Can$50, plus cost of travel to the annual meeting of the Society, where the winner shall read his or her paper.

Eligibility: Open to postgraduate students at Canadian universities.

Note: Essays may be written in French or English.

Closing date: 1st January.

Further information from:
Dr. G.P. Richardson, Executive Secretary
University College
University of Toronto
Toronto, Ontario
Canada M5S 1A1

[511]

CANADIAN SOCIETY FOR CLINICAL INVESTIGATION

Schering Travelling Fellowships

Fellowships of up to *Can*$2,000 are offered to clinical investigators who are members of the Society for a 4-week or more visit to appropriate centres outside Canada or for an invited visit to a medical faculty in Canada. Applications should be submitted by 1st December for visits in the following year.

Further information from:
Dr. Jean-Gil Joly, Secretary-Treasurer
Canadian Society for Clinical Investigation
Hôpital Saint-Luc, 1058 St-Denis
Montreal, Quebec
Canada

[512]

CANADIAN SOCIETY OF EXPLORATION GEOPHYSICISTS

Scholarships

Purpose: To promote the study of geophysics.

Subject: Geophysics, or a closely related field, such as geology, physics, mathematics or engineering.

No. offered: At least fifteen Scholarships annually.

Value: Approximately *Can*$750 each; two Awards of *Can*$250 each.

Tenable at any Canadian university. The two Awards of *US*$250 are tenable only at SAIT at Calgary and NAIT at Edmonton. All Awards are initially for one year, and are intended to be re-awarded to deserving students through receipt of a degree.

Eligibility: Open to students intending to pursue a career in geophysics or a closely related field. Financial need is taken into consideration.

Not confirmed for 1983.

Further information from:
Canadian Society of Exploration
   Geophysicists
Scholarship Trust Fund
612 604 1 St., S.W.
Calgary, Alberta
Canada

[513]

CANADIAN SOCIETY OF LABORATORY TECHNOLOGISTS

Founder's Fund

Harold Amy Memorial Award: A Book prize of approximately *Can*$50 plus an allocation of *Can*$200, to be payable in support of continuing education within the subsequent two-year period, is awarded annually to the candidate having the highest markes in hemotology in the C.S.L.T. General Certificate examinations. In the event of a tie, the Award is given to the candidate with the highest aggregate mark. Nominees should have been enrolled with the C.S.L.T. AS Associate (Trainee) members and have received training in an approved Canadian program.

Continuing Education Award: One or more Awards in the amount of *Can*$250 or less may be granted annually for continuing education of members in need of financial support. Awards may be offered for refresher or advanced training.

F.J. Elliot Memorial Award: One or more Awards may be granted annually in the amount of *Can*$250 or less, for advancing the general academic education of the individual technologist, and may only be used for advanced training courses in medical technology.

Note: Applicants for any of the above awards should be registered at the time of application. All applications should be sponsored and submitted through an officer of C.S.L.T., a provincial branch and/or affiliated society or local chapter, or a supervisor at laboratory where employed.

Closing date: 1st March and 1st September.

Further information from:
Canadian Society of Laboratory
   Technologists
P.O. Box 830
Hamilton, Ontario
Canada L8N 3N8

[514]

CANADIAN STEEL CONSTRUCTION COUNCIL
Research Grants

Purpose: To support research at Canadian universities aimed at improving the efficiency and economy of the use of steel in construction.

Subject: Analysis, design and behaviour of structural steel.

No. offered: Varies annually.

Value: Maximum of *Can*$50,000 is available from funds for Grants.

Tenable at any Canadian university for one year; renewable.

Eligibility: Open to members of engineering faculties at Canadian universities.

Note: A priority list of possible research topics is sent to each Canadian university. Applicants need not confine their applications to subjects on the priority list. Certain conditions regarding reports and payment must be accepted.

Closing date: Usually 1st February.

Further information from:
Canadian Steel Construction Council
Suite 300, 201 Consumers Road
Willowdale, Ontario
Canada M2J 4G8

[515]

CANADIAN WILDLIFE SERVICE

Environment Canada
University Research Support Fund

Purpose: To provide financial assistance for graduate research.

Subject: Wildlife (excluding fishery resources).

No. offered: Ten to fifteen awards annually.

Value: Up to Can$2,500.

Tenable at any Canadian university for one year. May be renewed for a second year upon re-application.

Eligibility: Open to any Canadian university professor who is performing research in Canada and is the supervisor of a student with Canadian citizenship and the principal supervisor of a student registered for postgraduate work.

Note: Although project proposals should deal with research in the field of wildlife, they need not be directly related to Canadian Wildlife Service activities or programs.
   Selected applicants will be offered a contract between the Canadian Wildlife Service and the university's graduate school or other designated agency or department, to include requirements for a research project report and a financial statement. Any required administration charges will also be included.

Closing date: 15th February.

Further information from:
   Director General
   Canadian Wildlife Service
   Environment Canada
   Ottawa, Ontario
   Canada K1A 0E7

[516]

CANADIAN WILDLIFE SERVICE

Environment Canada
Wildlife Biology Scholarships

Subject: Wildlife biology (excluding fishery resources).

No. offered: Four Scholarships annually.

Value: Can$2,500.

Tenable at any Canadian university for one academic year. May be renewed for one additional year.

Eligibility: Open to Canadian postgraduates studying wildlife biology at a Canadian University who are engaged in a program of research related to the Canadian Wildlife Service, and are not the recipients of another Scholarship exceeding Can$2,000 in value.

Note: An award will not be made to a successful candidate until confirmation of his registration at a Canadian university for the following academic year has been received.

Closing date: 1st March.

Further information from:
   Director General
   Canadian Wildlife Service
   Environment Canada
   Ottawa, Ontario
   Canada K1A 0E7

[517]

MARIA CANALS
INTERNATIONAL MUSIC CONTEST
(Barcelona)

Monetary prizes totalling 1,300,000 pesetas, engagements, medals and diplomas are offered in the music Competition, held each spring. Scholarships providing bed and breakfast are given to the first 40 competitors who enroll. Instrumentalists should be aged between 18 and 32; singers between 18 and 35. The closing date for entry is January.

Further information from:
   Maria Canals International
      Music Contest
   Gran Via 654 Pral
   Barcelona 10
   Spain

[518]

CANCER RESEARCH CAMPAIGN *(U.K.)*

Research Grant

Scope: Any project which is relevant to cancer

and which shows promise of increasing existing knowledge of the disease without unnecessarily duplicating work already being carried out.

Value: Salary, paid monthly, appropriate to qualifications; research expenses paid quarterly or half-yearly.

Tenable at any recognized research centre, normally for one year in the first instance; renewable annually, usually for a minimum duration of three years.

Eligibility: Open to persons who possess suitable academic qualifications and have the support of the head of the department in the proposed place of work. Grants are normally offered to United Kingdom citizens.

Note: Limited funds are also available for cancer education projects.

The Campaign also awards a limited number of fellowships providing security of tenure for senior research workers who have already proved their worth in cancer research. These Fellowships are not open to application.

Closing date: Mid-April for the academic year commencing 1st October.

Further information from:
Secretary General
Cancer Research Campaign
2 Carlton House Terrace
London
England SW1Y 5AR

[519]

CANCER RESEARCH SOCIETY, INC.
(Quebec, Canada)

International Fellowships and Grants

The Society awards individual Fellowships and Grants to researchers who will be working in cancer research centres in Canada. Recipients are selected annually by the Society's medical advisory board on the basis of the scientific value of the research projects submitted.

Further information from:
Ora Benjacob, Comptroller
Cancer Research Society, Inc.
C.P./P.O. Box 183
19 Esterel, Place Bonaventure
Montreal, Quebec
Canada H5A 1A9

[520]

CANCER SOCIETY OF NEW ZEALAND

Travelling Fellowships

Purpose: To enable senior medical graduates to travel outside New Zealand for up to six weeks to concentrate on a particular aspect of cancer. This may be either in the research or clinical field; the latter may concern diagnosis or treatment.

No. offered: One or more Fellowships annually.

Value: Return fares plus a living allowance of up to NZ$45 per day and expenses incurred in travelling to New Zealand centres.

Note: On return to New Zealand, the Fellow is required to visit appropriate centres to present a review of the particular aspect of cancer he or she has been studying. The Fellowship is to be taken up within one year of confirmation of tenure.

Closing date: 31st July.

Further information from:
Secretary
Cancer Society of New Zealand
P.O. Box 10-340
Wellington
New Zealand

[521]

CARDIAC SOCIETY OF AUSTRALIA AND NEW ZEALAND

R.T. Hall Prize in Cardiology

Purpose: To encourage research of a fundamental or clinical nature into cardiovascular function or disease.

No. offered: One Prize annually.

Value: A$1,000, plus an inscribed book.

Eligibility: Open to qualified medical practitioners under 35 years of age as of the closing date. Applicants should submit either a previously unpublished manuscript or a manuscript accepted for publication within twelve months of the closing date.

Note: If the submitted manuscript has joint authorship, the entry should include evidence that the majority of the work has originated from, and been performed by the applicant.

Closing date: 31st August.

Further information from:
Honorary Secretary
Cardiac Society of Australia and New Zealand
145 Macquarie Street
Sydney, N.S.W.
Australia 2000

[522]

CARNEGIE FOUNDATION *(Netherlands)*

Wateler Peace Prize

An annual Prize of approximately 40,000 Dutch florins is awarded in alternating years to a Dutchman and a foreigner for valuable service in the cause of peace or for contributions to finding the means of combating war.

Further information from:
Carnegie Foundation
Wateler Peace Prize
Peace Palace
The Hague
Netherlands

[523]

CARNEGIE FUND FOR AUTHORS *(U.S.A.)*

The Fund awards emergency grants to authors who have had one or more reasonable length books published commercially and who have suffered a financial emergency resulting from illness or injury to self or dependent family or some other misfortune.

Further information from:
Chairman
Carnegie Fund for Authors
330 Sunrise Highway
Rockville Centre, New York 11570
U.S.A.

[524]

CARNEGIE INSTITUTION OF WASHINGTON

Predoctoral Fellowships are awarded to Ph.D. candidates to undertake their thesis research in the Institution's laboratories and observatories.

Postdoctoral Fellowships: Each year the Institution appoints about 45 to 55 Postdoctoral Fellows to its five departments. The Fellowships are usually tenable for one to two years and provide financial support and, in some cases, travel allowances. Candidates should apply directly to the department concerned.

The following is a list of the departments and their areas of work: *Mount Wilson and Las Campanas Observatories, Pasadena, California* (astronomical study on the struture and dimensions of the universe, and the physical nature, chemical composition and evolution of celestial bodies); *Geophysical Laboratory, Washington, D.C.* (physicochemical studies of geological problems); *Department of Terrestrial Magnetism, Washington, D.C.* (a wide range of studies in physics and related science including astrophysics, geophysics, geochemistry, planetary physics, and nuclear and atomic physics); *Department of Plant Biology, Stanford, California* (study of photosynthesis and the evolutionary mechanisms by which plants have reached their variation in form); *Department of Embryology, Baltimore, Maryland* (study of the mechanisms of differentiation, growth, and morphogenesis, and the manner in which these processes are coordinated in a number of developing systems, both normal and abnormal).

Subjects: Candidates need not be United States citizens.

Further information from:
Editor
Carnegie Institution of Washington
1530 P Street, N.W.
Washington, D.C. 20005
U.S.A.

[525]

CARNEGIE TRUST FOR THE UNIVERSITIES OF SCOTLAND

Carnegie Grants

Purpose: To support research projects or aid in the publication of books in certain fields, where likely to benefit the Universities of Scotland.

Subjects: Science, medicine, history, economics, English literature, modern languages; other subjects cognate to a technical or commercial education which have been brought within the scope of the university curriculum.

Value: Varies according to requests; candidates must provide a detailed estimate of anticipated costs.

Eligibility: Applicants must be graduates of a Scottish university, or full-time members of staff of a Scottish university.

Closing date: 1st January, February, March, June or November, prior to Executive Committee meetings in those months.

Further information from:
 Secretary
 Carnegie Trust for the Universities of
  Scotland
 Merchants' Hall, 22 Hanover Street
 Edinburgh
 Scotland EH2 2EN

[526]

CARNEGIE TRUST FOR THE UNIVERSITIES OF SCOTLAND

Carnegie Scholarships

Subjects: Science, medicine, history, economics, modern languages, and English literature.

Value: £2,376.

Tenable for a maximum of three years subject to annual renewal. There are no restrictions as to place of tenancy.

Eligibility: Open to persons possessing a first-class honours degree from a Scottish university. Candidates should be nominated by a senior member of the staff of a Scottish university.

Closing date: 15th March.

Further information from:
 Secretary
 Carnegie Trust for the Universities of
  Scotland
 Merchants' Hall, 22 Hanover Street
 Edinburgh
 Scotland EH2 2EN

[527]

CARVER RESEARCH FOUNDATION
Tuskegee Institute *(Alabama)*

Graduate Research Fellowships and Assistantships

Purpose: To assist qualified graduate students to pursue their graduate program at Tuskegee Institute.

Subjects: Agriculture sciences; animal, plant and soil sciences; biology; chemistry; environmental science; nutritional science; food science; public health nutrition; electrical, mechanical or nuclear engineering; veterinary sciences; education (adult, elementary, special, mathematics and science, student personnel services, agricultural, language arts, guidance and counseling, science, early childhood, social science, home economics, supervision and administration).

No. offered: 35 Fellowships; 25 Teaching Assistantships; 10 Graduate Assistantships— offered as vacancies occur.

Value: Varies; minimum US$3,600 for Fellowships; minimum of US$5,500 for Assistantships.

Tenable at Tuskegee Institute, Alabama, for one year; renewable for one year.

Eligibility: Open to graduates of any nationality with a major in the field of interest, who wish to enter Tuskegee Institute's graduate program leading to an M.S. or M.Ed. degree.

Note: Applicants should indicate their specific field of study and area of research interest in making initial inquiry.

Closing date: Applications received by 15th

March will receive first preference. Applications received at later dates will be reviewed at monthly intervals.

Further information from:
  Director
  Carver Research Foundation of
    Tuskegee Institute
  Tuskegee Institute, Alabama 36088
  U.S.A.

[528]

ALESSANDRO CASAGRANDE INTERNATIONAL PIANO COMPETITION
(Terni, Italy)

Prizes of 2,000,000 lire, 1,000,000 lire, and 500,000 lire are offered in the competition which is held every two years (next in 1984). Pianists of any nationality who are not more than 32 years of age, may apply.

Further information from:
  Secretariat
  Alessandro Casagrande International
    Piano Competition
  Comune di Terni
  I-05100 Terni
  Italy

[529]

ALFREDO CASELLA INTERNATIONAL COMPETITION OF THE MUSIC ACADEMY OF NAPLES

Various monetary prizes are offered in the Competition which is held each year in the summer. Pianists between 18 and 32 years of age and composers of any age may apply. There are no restrictions on citizenship. The closing date for entry is 15th April.

Further information from:
  Secretariat
  Alfredo Casella International Competition
  Music Academy of Naples
  c/o Circolo della Stampa
  Villa Communale
  I-80121 Naples
  Italy

[530]

CATHOLIC LIBRARY ASSOCIATION
(U.S.A.)

Worldbook-Childcraft Award

Purpose: To foster added proficiency in library work with children or in school libraries.

No. offered: One to four Awards annually.

Value: US$1,000 which can be divided among four participants.

Tenable at continuing education workshops, institutes, etc., for one year.

Eligibility: Open to members of the Catholic Library Association

Note: Awards are intended primarily for continuing education, and cannot be used for programs leading to a graduate degree.
  Applicants are to submit program proposals along with projected costs.

Closing date: 1st February.

Further information from:
  Scholarship Committee
  Catholic Library Association
  461 West Lancaster Avenue
  Haverford, Pennsylvania 19041
  U.S.A.

[531]

CATHOLIC LIBRARY ASSOCIATION
(U.S.A.)

Rev. Andrew L. Bouwhuis Scholarship

Subject: Library science.

No. offered: One Scholarship annually.

Value: US$1,500.

Tenable at any graduate school of library science in the United States, for one year.

Eligibility: Open to graduates of approved colleges, of any nationality, who have a good scholastic record and show evidence of a need for financial help.
  Candidates must have been accepted by a graduate school of library science.

Closing date: 1st February.

Further information from:
Scholarship Committee
Catholic Libary Association
461 West Lancaster Avenue
Haverford, Pennsylvania 19041
U.S.A.

[532]

CATHOLIC WOMEN'S LEAGUE OF AUSTRIA

Study Aid Grants

A number of Grants are awarded, as vacancies occur, to assist students from non-European developing countries to complete their studies. Grants are in varying amounts and tenable for one year at institutions of higher learning in the applicant's home country or in Austria. Candidates must be no more than 35 years of age, recommended by academic or church authorities, have reached the final stage of their studies, and demonstrate financial need.
Closing date: for application is first April of each year.

Further information from:
Catholic Women's League of Austria
Department of Development Aid
Spiegelgasse 3/2
A-1010 Vienna
Austria

[533]

CATHOLIC WOMEN'S LEAGUE OF AUSTRIA

Scholarships

Subjects: Unrestricted.

No. offered: 30 Scholarships annually; as vacancies occur.

Value: 4,000 Austrian schillings per month, plus four semester grants of 1,000 schillings each.

Tenable at institutions of higher learning in Scholar's home country or in Austria for two to three years; may be extended in special cases.

Eligibility: Open to nationals of non-European developing countries who are not more than 35 years of age, have at least a master's degree, and have sufficient knowledge of the German language.
Financial need must be demonstrated.

Note: It is expected that Scholars will return to their home countries at the conclusion of their studies.

Closing date: 1st April

Further information from:
Catholic Women's League of Austria
Department for Devlopment Aid
Spiegelgasse 3/2
A-1010 Vienna
Austria

[534]

JAMES McKEEN CATTELL FUND *(U.S.A.)*

Supplemental Sabbatical Awards for Psychologists

Purpose: By supplementing sabbatical allowances, to encourage research and scholarly endeavor on the part of psychologists at colleges and universities, especially research likely to lead to useful applications in the field of psychology.

No. offered: Five or six Awards annually.

Value: The Award is intended to supplement the regular sabbatical allowance provided by the applicant's institution; the Award will be limited to half salary for an academic year and to an amount that will bring the total of university allowance plus Award up to the individual's normal academic year salary. Modest supplemental grants are sometimes made for travel or specific research projects included in the sabbatical plan. Maximum award is US$18,000.

Tenable for one year of sabbatical leave to be spent in full-time scholarly activity, including study, research or writing. Leave for a single semester will usually not be supported.

Eligibility: Candidates should be psychologists who are tenured members of college and university faculties in North America and who are eligible, according to the regulations of their institutions, for sabbatical leave.

Note: Awardees should not teach during the

period of the Award, nor engage in gainful work except as specified in their applications.

Closing date: 1st December.

Further information from:
Dr. Robert L Thorndike
Secretary-Treasurer
James McKeen Cattell Fund
Box 219, 525 West 120th Street
New York, New York 10027
U.S.A.

[535]

CENTER FOR ADVANCED STUDY IN THE BEHAVORIAL SCIENCES *(Stanford, California)*

Postdoctoral Fellowships

Subjects: Behavioral sciences, biological sciences, and the humanities.

No. offered: 40 to 50 Fellowships annually.

Value: Equal to a university salary, plus travel allowance to and from the Center for recipient and his family.

Tenable at the Center, for nine to twelve months.

Eligibility: Candidates should be nominated by academic officers or distinguished scholars. There are no restrictions with regard to citizenship.

Note: Applicants are expected to seek additional sources of support to share in Fellowship costs.
All names submitted will be kept for periodic reviews at two-year intervals.
Persons authorized for Fellowships are invited to indicate the year which would best suit their program.

Further information from:
Gardner Lindzey, Director
Center for Advanced Study in the
 Behavioral Sciences
202 Junipero Serra Boulevard
Stanford, California 94305
U.S.A.

[536]

CENTER FOR FIELD RESEARCH *(U.S.A.)*

Grants for Field Research

Purpose: To provide grants for field research projects that can constructively utilize teams of non-specialists in accomplishing their research goals.

Subjects: Disciplines include, but are not limited to: anthropology, archaeology, biology, botany, cartography, conservation, ethology, folklore, geography, geology, marine sciences, medicine, meteorology, musicology, ornithology, restoration, and sociology.

No. offered: Approximately 75 Awards annually.

Value: Varies; Grants awarded on a per capita basis, depending upon the number of participants. Normal range of support is US$4,000 to US$15,000. Greater support may be arranged through additional teams.

Tenable at research sites around the world. Approximately one-half of the research currently funded takes place within the U.S. Teams are in the field for two to three weeks; longer term support is available through additional teams. Renewals are encouraged.

Eligibility: There are no residency requirements or nomination process. Preference is given to applicants who hold a Ph.D. and have both field and teaching experience.

Note: Projects approved by the Center are funded and managed by their affiliate, *Earthwatch.*

Closing date: 1st April for winter/spring of the following year; 1st October for summer/fall of the following year.

Further information from:
Center for Field Research
10 Juniper Road, Box 127G
Belmont, Massachusetts 02178
U.S.A.

[537]

CENTER FOR HELLENIC STUDIES
(Washington, D.C.)

Junior Fellowships

Subjects: Ancient Greek literature, philosophy, history.

No. offered: Eight Junior Fellowships annually.

Value: Negotiable; up to US$9,000 plus living quarters and a study at the Center building.

Tenable at the Center for Hellenic Studies, for approximately nine months (September-June), not renewable.

Eligibility: Open to scholars and teachers of Ancient Greek with a Ph.D. degree or equivalent qualification.

Note: Residence at the Center is required.

Closing date: 31st October.

Further information from:
Bernard M.W. Knox, Director
Center for Hellenic Studies
3100 Whitehaven Street, N.W.
Washington, D.C. 20008
U.S.A.

[538]

CENTER FOR REFORMATION RESEARCH *(U.S.A.)*

Summer Institute Fellowships

Purpose: To improve research skills of students interested in the Reformation, to enable them to do research in the field, to provide access to the Center's resources, and to bring them into contact with other scholars through seminars and lectures.

Subject: Paleography.

No. offered: Eight Fellowships, offered in odd-numbered years.

Value: US$750 plus travel expenses, paid in one lump sum.

Tenable at the Center and at libraries and archives in the St. Louis area for six weeks during the months of June and July in odd-numbered years; non-renewable.

Eligibility: Open to graduate and postdoctoral students of Reformation history.

Note: Those eligible may apply directly to the Center. Selections are made by a committee of established scholars in the field.

Closing date: 1st April.

Further information from:
Center for Reformation Research
6477 San Bonita Avenue
St. Louis, Missouri 63105
U.S.A.

[539]

CENTER FOR THEORETICAL STUDIES
(Coral Gables, Florida)

University of Miami

Objectives: The Center is dedicated to bringing together under conditions of compatibility scientists and other thinkers interested in the fundamental questions of science, culture, and society. Besides basic theoretical research in physics, biology, chemistry, mathematics, and the history and philosophy of science, one of the Center's principal purposes is to foster the development of younger scientists and to help broaden the scope of their interests. These aims of the Center are served by including in its membership senior scientists of great distinction (Fellows of the Center) and recent doctoral graduates (postdoctoral residents) who show exceptional promise.

Programs: Fellows have no assigned duties; they are free to engage in research in their primary areas of interest, as well as in other fields, to prepare manuscripts for publication, or to confer with their colleagues. A Fellow may lecture if he or she chooses, both informally and at graduate and postgraduate seminars, if requested by the various departments.
   The Center accepts applications from recent doctoral graduates. Positions are generally tenured for a period of one year and may be renewed. Established scientists are invited or may apply to the Center for short residencies or for stays of one to several semesters, depending on their schedules, and Fellows and Visiting Members on leave of absence or sabbatical leave may bring with them gradu-

ate students or associates from their parent institutions. Scientists from industrial laboratories and governmental institutions who are engaged in fundamental and applied research are traditionally welcomed at the Center as Industrial Research Participants.

Much of the research at the Center has been in theoretical physics (fundamental interactions, generalized theory of gravitation, relativistic astrophysics, atomic and molecular physics, many body phenomena), theoretical chemistry (protonic semi-conductors, quantum chemistry, transport phenomena) and theoretical biology (neurosciences, physics of biological membranes). Recent programs have been initiated on the theory of laser fusion, global energy balance, and a study of the dynamics of international terrorism. There are, however, no limits placed on the range of subjects covered in published papers of the Center.

J. Robert Oppenheimer Memorial Prize is awarded each January to recognize outstanding contributions to the theoretical natural sciences (physics, chemistry, biology), mathematics, and the philosophy of science. The work for which a person is nominated must have been done in the decade preceding the award of the Prize, although it may be extended to research done previously whose importance is only recognized during this period. The contribution may be a theory, original idea, prediction or explanation of a natural phenomenon, or work which is crucial to further theoretical progress.

There are no stipulations as to the age of the recipient, but it is intended that particular attention be paid to original research done by people young enough to continue to pursue their inquiries and perhaps to exceed the contribution for which they are rewarded.

Further information from:
Center for Theoretical Studies
University of Miami
P.O. Box 249055
Coral Gables, Florida 33124
U.S.A.

[540]

CENTRAL ASSOCIATION OF OBSTETRICIANS AND GYNECOLOGISTS
(U.S.A.)

Annual Prize Award
Certificate of Merit Award
Community Hospital Award

Awards are offered annually for original unpublished papers on investigative or clinical work in the field of obstetrics or gynecology.

Value: Prize—US$1,000; Certificate—US$500; Hospital Award—US$250.

Eligibility: Open to accredited physicians, teachers, research workers and medical students whose work was undertaken in the geographic area of the Association: Alabama, Arizona, Arkansas, Colorado, Idaho, Illinois, Indiana, Iowa, Kansas, Kentucky, Louisiana, Michigan, Minnesota, Mississippi, Missouri, Montana, Nebraska, New Mexico, North Dakota, Ohio, Oklahoma, South Dakota, Tennessee, Texas, Utah, West Virginia, Wisconsin and Wyoming.

Note: Papers must be written expressly for the competition.

Manuscripts, in quadruplicate, must be submitted to the Secretary by 15th April. The author's identity should not be shown on any of the four copies, the only identification being a covering letter and an abstract not to exceed 150 words on which the author's name should appear.

Further information from:
G.D. Malkasian, M.D.
Central Association of Obstetricians and Gynecologists
Mayo Clinic
200 1st Street, S.W.
University of Michigan Medical Center
Rochester, Minnesota 55901
U.S.A.

[541]

CENTRAL NEUROPSYCHIATRIC ASSOCIATION

William C. Menninger Award

An Award of *US*$300, and two honorable mention Awards of *US*$50 each are presented annually for an original unpublished essay or paper. Candidates are restricted to residents in the field of neurology, psychiatry or neurosurgery. The essay or research study must be completed during the candidate's residency and submitted before or within three years after completion of his residency education.

Closing date: 30th May.

Further information from:
Claresa F.M. Armstrong, M.D.,
  Secretary-Treasurer
Central Neuropsychiatric Association
1301 Astor Street
Chicago, Illinois 60610
U.S.A.

[542]

CENTRAL NEWS AGENCY LTD. *(South Africa)*

CNA Literary Award

Two Awards, for English and Afrikaans respectively, of R3,500 each, are given annually for the best book published during the year in the following categories: novels or short stories; poetry; biography; drama; history; and travel. The books submitted must be original works published in South Africa. Poetry or short story collections are eligible even though they may have been previously published in journals, magazines or anthologies. Anthologies, translations and reprints are not acceptable except translations made wholly and solely by the author. Translations of any books which have previously won the CNA Award in the other qualifying language are not accepted. Authors must be South African citizens or registered permanent residents of South Africa.

Books may be submitted only by the publishers, who are asked to send four copies of a book, together with brief biographical details of the author. Where possible, books should be submitted on or before publication date; proof copies are acceptable. Results are announced in the press about mid-March of the year following the closing date. A function will be held shortly after the announcement and Award winners are expected to attend and make a short speech on a theme relating to writing in South Africa.

Closing date: 31st December.

Further information from:
Secretary, Literary Award
Central News Agency Ltd.
P.O. Box 9380
Johannesburg
South Africa

[543]

CENTRE FOR INTERGROUP STUDIES
University of Cape Town

Research Fellowships and Assistantships

Purpose: To promote research concerned with intergroup relations in Southern Africa (especially between race and language groups).

Value: Based on university salary scales.

Tenable at the Centre. Duration is flexible.

Eligibility: Research Fellows must have postgraduate qualifications and experience in research.
There are no restrictions with regard to age, sex, citizenship or residency.

Further information from:
Centre for Intergroup Studies
c/o University of Cape Town
Rondebosch 7700
South Africa

[544]

CHARTERED INSTITUTE OF TRANSPORT *(U.K.)*

The following awards are offered to residents of the United Kingdom.

Henry Spurrier Awards: The Awards are offered to encourage study and research in subjects connected with road transport. The amount available annually is about £750 and this can be awarded to one person or divided between more than one according to the merit of the applications. The following purposes have been acceptable: full-time study (fees, books, subsistence) at a university or other recognised college by persons employed in, or in connection with road transport; travel at home or abroad in order to study some aspects of goods or passenger road transport (administration, operation, engineering, staff, traffic, etc.), or of subjects connected with road transport, including traffic engineering; part-time study (fees, books, non-local travelling expenses) at a recognised college or with an approved correspondence college by persons employed in or in connection with road transport; research into any subject connected with road transport (subsistence, clerical assistance and other expenses).

Application forms are available in April from the Institute and should be returned before 31st May.

Sir William Chamberlain Awards: The Awards are offered to encourage study and research in subjects connected with road transport from persons engaged, or intending to be engaged, in road transport in the North West (defined as Cheshire, Cumbria, Greater Manchester, Merseyside or Lancashire). Other details are the same as for the *Henry Spurrier Awards* listed above, except that the total amount available is £200.

C.M.U.A. Road Transport Research Fellowship: Up to £750 is offered to enable a British subject, over 30 years of age and engaged in road transport in the United Kingdom, to examine and report upon road transport arrangements abroad.

Robert Bell Travelling Scholarship: Up to £300 is offered to assist a candidate (engaged in railway transport in the United Kingdom) to travel abroad for the purpose of observing overseas railway practice.

British Ports Association Studentship: One Studentship not exceeding £200 is offered for the best paper on a dock, harbour or conservancy subject submitted to the Institute. The competition is limited to employees of dock, harbour and conservancy authorities in Great Britain and Ireland who are not more than 40 years old.

Road Haulage Association Travelling Scholarship: One Scholarship of £300 is offered to assist a candidate engaged in public road haulage in the United Kingdom to meet expenses for travel abroad to observe overseas road haulage practice.

Note: The Council of the Institute also awards a number of prizes for papers in the various fields of transport. These include the *BET Road Passenger Transport Award* of £1,000, the *London Transport Award* of £200 and the *Canal Association Award*. Closing date for applications is 31st May; in some cases candidates must be members of the Institute.

Further information from:
 Chartered Institute of Transport
 80 Portland Place
 London
 England W1N 4DP

[545]

CHAUTAUQUA INSTITUTION

Pre-Season Awards

Courses given in instrumental and vocal music, art, and dance are held for six to eight weeks in July and August for young children and adults. Awards are annual and paid in lump sum at registration. Value ranges between *US*$250 and *US*$400. Awards are not renewable. Recipients must register for a full course of study.

Note: There are no sex, citizenship or age requirements. Most Scholarships are given in music. No travel grants are provided.

Closing date for applications: 15th February.

Further information from:
 Chautauqua Institution
 Box 1098 Schools Office
 Chautauqua, New York 14722
 U.S.A.

[546]

CHEMICAL INSTITUTE OF CANADA

Ogilvie Flour Mills—Kenneth Armstrong Memorial Fellowship

Subjects: Physical biochemistry, colloidal chemistry of biological materials or natural product chemistry.

No. offered: One Fellowship annually.

Value: Can$5,000 per annum.

Tenable at a Canadian university or institution accredited for postgraduate work for one year; renewable up to a maximum of three years.

Eligibility: Open to graduates in chemistry, biochemistry or chemical engineering from a

Canadian university who are proceeding to a master's or doctor's degree.

Closing date: 15th November.

Further information from:
Executive Director
Chemical Institute of Canada
151 Slater Street, Suite 906
Ottawa, Ontario
Canada K1P 5H3

[547]

CHEMICAL MANUFACTURERS ASSOCIATION *(U.S.A.)*

CMA National and Regional Catalyst Awards

National Awards (US$1,500 each) and Regional Awards (US$500 each) are given to honor high school teachers and two-year and four-year college professors for excellence in teaching chemistry or chemical engineering, dedication to science instruction, and motivating students toward careers in science, in the United States and Canada.

Four National Awards for four-year college professors, one National Award and four Regional Awards for two-year college professors, and one National Award and eight Regional Awards for high school teachers, are offered annually.

Completion of ten years' full-time teaching is required for National Awards, which are not renewable. Regional Awards are eligible for National Awards after an interval of five years.

Further information from:
Ms. Carolyn Shipe Teneyck
Awards Coordinator
Chemical Manufacturers Association
2501 M Street, N.W.
Washington, D.C. 20037
U.S.A.

[548]

CHEST, HEART AND STROKE ASSOCIATION *(U.K.)*

Research Awards

Subject: Respiratory diseases.

Value: Variable.

Tenable at appropriate United Kingdom research centres for the duration of the approved research. Occasionally awards may be made for research, or a study visit, outside the United Kingdom.

Eligibility: Open to suitably qualified researchers normally resident in the United Kingdom.

Note: Awards are offered about twice a year as vacancies occur. The programme is under review; candidates should acquire latest information before making an application.

Address:
Director-General
Chest, Heart and Stroke Association
Tavistock House North
Tavistock Square
London
England WC1H 9JE

[549]

M.S.D. CHIBRET LABORATORIES
(Clermont-Ferrand, France)

Prize for a Thesis in Ophthalmology: A Prize of FF10,000 is awarded annually for the best original work on any subject connected with ophthalmology. The thesis should be written in French and be of no more than two years standing. Closing date: 1st February.

Prize for a Thesis in Otorhinolaryngology: A Prize of FF10,000 is awarded annually for the best thesis on any aspect of otorhinolaryngology. The thesis should have been written in French and should be of no more than two years standing.

Trachoma Gold Medal: One award of FF7,500 is given annually for outstanding work or research on trachoma. There are no restrictions regarding age, citizenship or residency.

Closing date: 1st July.

Further information from:
Laboratories M.S.D. Chibret
200 boulevard Et. Clémentel
630 18 Clermont-Ferrand Cédex
France

[550]

CHIGIANA MUSICAL ACADEMY *(Siena)*

Summer Course Scholarships

Purpose: To enable students to attend the annual Courses in composition, conducting, voice and various instruments.

No. offered: A number of Scholarships annually. Ten Scholarships are available to Latin American students wishing to attend the courses.

Value: 3,500 lire per day, paid fortnightly, plus tuition fees.

Tenable for the duration of the Course during the months of July and August at the Academy.

Eligibility: Open to students who pass the entrance examination with particular merit.

Note: To obtain a Scholarship from the Italian Ministry of Foreign Affairs, students must apply to the Italian embassy or other Italian cultural institutions in their own country.

Further information from:
Segreteria
Accademia Musicale Chigiana
Via de Citta n. 89
53100 Siena
Italy

[551]

CHILD ACCIDENT PREVENTION FOUNDATION OF AUSTRALIA

Research Grants

Subjects: Causes of accidental injury to children and the development of preventative methods, including environmental design.

Value: Variable.

Tenable in Australia for the full period of the proposed research.

Eligibility: Open to residents of Australia. Applicants must be qualified to conduct the proposed research.

Note: Monthly progress reports are required.

Applications may be submitted at any time on forms provided.

Further information from:
R.L. Due, Executive Officer
Child Accident Prevention Foundation of Australia
College of Surgeons Gardens
Spring Street
Melbourne, Victoria
Australia 3000

[552]

CHILDREN'S BOOK CIRCLE *(U.K.)*

Eleanor Farjeon Award

The annual Award of £100 is given to a librarian, teacher, author, artist, publisher, reviewer, television producer or anyone working with or for children through books who, in the judgement of the Committee, has made a distinguished contribution to the field of children's books. Nominations may be made by Children's Book Circle members only.

Further information from:
Martin West
Penguin Books Ltd.
536 Kings Road
London SW10
England

[553]

CHILDREN'S MEDICAL RESEARCH FOUNDATION *(Australia)*
Royal Alexandra Hospital for Children
University of Sydney

Research Fellowships

Purpose: To promote research into the causation, prevention and treatment of childhood diseases.

Subjects: Human lymphocyte metabolism; teratology/embryology; neurosciences.

No. offered: Approximately ten Fellowships, as vacancies occur.

Value: A regular salary.

Tenable within the organization for up to five years; renewable depending upon seniority.

Eligibility: Open to Australian residents with suitable qualifications in science or medicine.

Further information from:
Director
Children's Medical Research Foundation
P.O. Box 61
Camperdown, N.S.W.
Australia 2050

[554]

JANE COFFIN CHILDS MEMORIAL FUND FOR MEDICAL RESEARCH (U.S.A.)

Fellowships

Subjects: Medical and related sciences relevant to the causes, origins and treatment of cancer; research.

No. offered: 15 to 20 Fellowships each year.

Value: US$15,000 per annum plus dependent child allowance of US$750 each, and usually US$1,000 per annum departmental grant.

Tenable at laboratories and other institutions where the candidate's proposed research is acceptable and where adequate facilities for work exist, for one to three years.

Fellowships for non-United States citizens are only tenable at institutions in the United States.

Eligibility: Open to persons under 30 years of age who possess an M.D. or Ph.D. degree in the field in which they propose work.

Closing date: 1st January.

Address for application:
Office of the Director
Jane Coffin Childs Memorial Fund for Medical Research
333 Cedar Street
New Haven, Connecticut 06510
U.S.A.

[555]

CHINESE CULTURE UNIVERSITY
(Taipei)

Scholarships, Exchange Scholarships, and Teaching Assistantships

No. offered: Scholarships—nine annually; Exchange Scholarships—variable; Teaching Assistantships—many available in various fields.

Eligibility: Open to nationals of all countries who have a Bachelor of Arts degree from an accredited school.

Closing date: 30th June.

Further information from:
Registrar
Chinese Culture University
Hwa Kang, Yang Ming Shan
Taipei, Taiwan
Republic of China

[556]

FREDERIC CHOPIN INTERNATIONAL PIANO CONTEST *(Warsaw)*

The Competition takes place in Warsaw every five years, and is open to pianists of any nationality, between the ages of 17 and 30. The next Competition will be held in October, 1985. Prizes: 1st—100,000 zlotys and gold medal; 2nd—75,000 zlotys and silver medal; 3rd—50,000 zlotys and bronze medal; 4th—40,000 zlotys; 5th—35,000 zlotys; 6th—30,000 zlotys; and six Prizes of 20,000 zlotys.

Further information from:
Frederic Chopin International Piano Contest
c/o Société Frederic Chopin
Zamek Ostrogskich, Okolnik 1
Warsaw
Poland

[557]

CHRISTIAN AID
British Council of Churches

Scholarships

Purpose: To provide opportunities for the training of men and women in order to help people (including providing training for refugees) groups, churches and/or institutions in the search for and development of forms of Christian living relevant to particular contexts.

No. offered: 65 Scholarships annually.

Value: Variable, according to individual requirements.

Tenable for one to four academic years in the United Kingdom or the Republic of Ireland.

Eligibility: Open to students from overseas countries.

Further information from:
  Scholarships Secretary
  Christian Aid
  P.O. Box 1
  London
  England SW9 8BH

[558]

WINSTON CHURCHILL FOUNDATION OF THE UNITED STATES

Churchill Scholarships

Subjects: Sciences, engineering and mathematics.

No. offered: Ten Scholarships annually.

Value: Tuition, fees and a travel grant of US$500 travel allowance. A living allowance of US$2,000 for a one-year grant, US$2,500 for a three-year grant.

Tenable at Churchill College, University of Cambridge, England for either one or three years.

Eligibility: Open to citizens of the United States between the ages of 19 and 26 who hold a bachelor's degree from a participating university or college in the United States.

Note: Candidates should ascertain whether the educational institution at which they are enrolled participates in the program. If so, candidates should contact the Foundation representative at the institution for application.

Not confirmed for 1983.

Further information from:
  Winston Churchill Foundation of the
    United States
  Box 1248
  Gracie Station
  New York, New York 10028
  U.S.A.

[559]

WINSTON CHURCHILL MEMORIAL TRUST *(Australia)*

Churchill Fellowships

Subjects: Unrestricted—study and/or research in all vocations, including primary industry, secondary industry and commerce, professional and academic occupations, education, public service, the arts, community service, etc.

No. offered: Between 50 and 60 Fellowships annually.

Value: The average is approximately A$5,000 —to cover return overseas air fare, personal maintenance allowance, tuition fees, incidental travel expenses, dependents' allowance, and other incidental expenses.

Tenable for up to six months outside Australia, except for Fellows who are indigenous inhabitants of Australian territories, in which case Fellowships are tenable inside Australia.

Eligibility: Open to all Australian citizens who are not less than 18 years of age and who show promise of future achievement, or whose achievements are already substantial in their chosen field of work. The value of the candidate's work in the community and the extent to which it will be enhanced by overseas study and experience are important considerations in relation to awards of Fellowships.
  Academic qualifications are not essential.

Closing date: Last day of February for tenure to begin the following calendar year.

Note: Preference will be given to candidates who have not had previous oversease experience.
  Recipients must undertake to return to Australia, or to the Australian territory concerned, at the conclusion of tenure of a Fellowship.

Further information from:
   Chief Executive Officer
   Winston Churchill Memorial Trust (B)
   P.O. Box 478
   Canberra City, A.C.T.
   Australia 2601

[560]

WINSTON CHURCHILL MEMORIAL TRUST *(N.Z.)*

Awards

Purpose: To help provide assistance to some investigation or activity which will contribute to the advancement of the awardee's vocation, or will in some way be of general benefit to New Zealand or will aid the maintenance of the British Commonwealth as a beneficial influence in world affairs.

Subjects: Unrestricted; however, Awards are not normally made to assist purely academic study.

No. offered: Varies, depending upon available funds.

Value: Varies according to the needs of the successful applicants and their projects.

Tenable in New Zealand and abroad. Not renewable.

Eligibility: Open to New Zealand citizens or persons restricted outside New Zealand whose visit will benefit New Zealand. Applicants must have sufficient ability and experience to be regarded as likely to make a contribution to New Zealand through their careers.

Note: Applicants must be able to contribute a portion of the actual costs.

Further information from:
   Secretary
   Winston Churchill Memorial Trust
   P.O. Box 12-347
   Wellington North
   New Zealand

[561]

WINSTON CHURCHILL MEMORIAL TRUST *(U.K.)*

Fellowships

Purpose: To enable men and women from all walks of life and all ages to travel abroad in pursuit of a worthwhile purpose and so to contribute more to their trade or profession, their community and their country.

Subjects: Approximately twelve categories of occupation, which vary annually, and are representative of culture, social and public service, commerce and industry, agriculture and nature, recreation and adventure.

No. offered: Approximately 100 Fellowships annually.

Value: By individual assessment, to cover all travel, living and equipment expenses. Average award is £1,700.

Tenable in any country or countries outside the United Kingdom for one to three months; Grants are not normally given for formal or academic studies.

Eligibility: Open to citizens of the United Kingdom whose purposes must be covered by one of the categories chosen for the year.

Note: Fellows must undertake to disseminate the information they gain and to remain officially resident in the United Kingdom for three years following the termination of their Fellowship.
   Applications are accepted in September and October of every year, and awards are announced at the beginning of February.
   Travel expenses of short-listed candidates will be paid within the United Kingdom only.

Closing date: 1st November.

Further information from:
   Director General
   Winston Churchill Memorial Trust
   15 Queen's Gate Terrace
   London
   England SW7 5PR

[562]

CIBA-GEIGY FELLOWSHIP TRUST *(U.K.)*

CIBA-GEIGY Senior Fellowships

Purpose: To improve and increase the interchange of ideas between scientists in the United Kingdom and Europe by providing opportunities for staff members of United Kingdom and Irish universities, polytechnics, or comparable teaching institutions to work on the European continent.

Subjects: Chemistry, biochemistry, biology, chemical technology, and chemical engineering.

No. offered: Varies from four to six Fellowships annually.

Value: £8,000 per annum plus travel allowance.

Tenable at universities on the continent of Europe for a minimum period of six months and a maximum of two years.

Eligibility: Open to lecturers, senior lecturers, readers, or persons having similar teaching positions for a period of at least five years, at universities polytechnics or comparable teaching institutions of the United Kingdom or the Republic of Ireland.

Note: Applicants are advised to confirm that these Fellowships are being offered.

Further information from:
 Secretary
 CIBA-GEIGY Fellowship Trust
 30 Buckingham Gate
 London
 England SW1E 6LH

[563]

CITY OF MONTEVIDEO INTERNATIONAL PIANO COMPETITION

Eliane Richepin Association

US$5,000, medals and concert engagements are offered in the Competition which is held every four years. The next Competition will be held in August 1986. Pianists of any nationality, between the ages of 15 and 32 years, may apply.

Closing date: 15th June, 1986.

Further information from:
 Secretariat
 City of Montevideo International Piano Competition
 Enrique Muñoz 815
 Montevideo
 Uruguay

[564]

CITY OF NEW YORK URBAN FELLOWS PROGRAM *(New York City)*

Purpose: To provide the opportunity and challenge of intensive field work experience in urban government.

Subject: The workings and problems of local government.

No. offered: Twenty Fellowships annually.

Value: Fellows receive a stipend, a choice of paid health insurance plans, and reimbursement of travel expenses to New York City. In addition, it is expected that the Fellow will receive a tuition waiver and supplementary grant from their college or university.

Tenable in New York City for one academic year, running from mid-September to mid-June.

Eligibility: Open to students in the United States who are in their senior year of college or have been accepted to or enrolled in graduate school. A candidate should have the academic endorsement of his or her college or university and be prepared to participate in the program on a full time basis. All students who are interested in an involvement in urban government are encouraged to apply, regardless of their previous field of training.

Note: Approximately fifty finalists are invited to an expense paid interview in New York City, on the basis of which, the twenty Fellows will be selected.

Applications and additional information may be obtained through the financial aid or fellowship officers of their school, or by writing to the address below.

Closing date: 15th March for Fellowships to begin mid-September of the same year.

Address:
  Director
  Urban Fellows Program
  220 Church Street
  New York, New York 10013
  U.S.A.

[565]

CITY OF SYDNEY CULTURAL COUNCIL

'Sun' Aria Contest

Prizes and Scholarships: The Contest is open to both amateur and professional singers who are born in Australia or New Zealand, or are citizens of the British Commonwealth by birth or naturalisation and have been domiciled in Australia or New Zealand for at least six years prior to the Contest. Contestants should not be more than thirty-two years of age as of the opening day of the Eisteddfod.

Value: 1st Prize, A$2,000 and Scholarship, A$3,500; 2nd Prize, A$500; 3rd Prize, A$300; 4th—6th Prizes, A$150 each.

Note: The Scholarship will only be awarded if the winner undertakes to study music and/or singing overseas for a minimum of two years.

Closing date: 30th June.

Further information from:
  Executive Officer
  City of Sydney Cultural Council
  161 Clarence Street
  Sydney, N.S.W.
  Australia 2000

[566]

CITY OF SYDNEY CULTURAL COUNCIL

Peter Stuyvesant Cultural Foundation Ballet Scholarship

One Scholarship of A$4,500 is awarded annually to enable a person to pursue his/her studies overseas. The contest is open to professional or amateur dancers who have at least reached their 16th birthday as of 31st December, but have not yet reached their 21st birthday as of that date.
  A second Scholarship of A$500 is awarded for study within Australia.

Closing date: 30th June.

Further information from:
  Executive Officer
  City of Sydney Cultural Council
  161 Clarence Street
  Sydney, N.S.W.
  Australia 2000

[567]

CIVITAN INTERNATIONAL FOUNDATION *(U.S.A.)*

Roy M. Abagnale Memorial Fellowship Award

One award in the amount of US$3,000 is presented annually for an original research paper promoting understanding of the free enterprise system. Graduate students in an accredited university program or internship in the areas of economics, political science, business or marketing are eligible. The payment will be made in two installments; the first upon notification and the final payment upon completion of the research paper. The Award, intended to assist in completion of the winner's scholastic program, will be aid directly to the recipient's university or as determined by the Foundation Trustees. Outlines should be submitted with the application form available from the address below.

Closing date: 1st March.

Further information from:
  Civitan International Foundation
  P.O. Box 2102
  Birmingham, Alabama 35201
  U.S.A.

[568]

CIVITAN INTERNATIONAL FOUNDATION *(U.S.A.)*

Dr. Courtney W. Shropshire Memorial Scholarship Grants

Subjects: History, political science, civics, economics, vocational or special education.

Value: US$500 to US$2,000 for tuition and other approved purposes.

Tenable for one year at any accredited college or university in the United States; not renewable.

Eligibility: Open to deserving students striving to complete the final year of undergraduate work or obtaining a master's degree who are planning on a career in teaching in one or more of the above subjects. Proof of admission to a college or university must be provided by the dean of admissions of the school the applicant will be attending.

Note: Applicants must apply to their local club for an interview.

Further information from:
  Civitan International Foundation
  P.O. Box 2102
  Birmingham, Alabama 35201
  U.S.A.

[569]

CLEMENTS MEMORIAL PRIZE *(U.K.)*
South Place Concert Society *(U.K.)*

Chamber Music Competition

Three Prizes of £150 each are offered biennially in odd-numbered years to British subjects for chamber works composed for unmodified musical instruments without electronic assistance. Entries must have been composed within the three year period prior to the application deadline. Works may previously have been performed in public, but may not have won a prize in any other competition. The winning composition will remain the copyright of its author and will be broadcast by the British Broadcasting Corporation.

Closing date: 1st October.

Further information from:
  Honorary Secretary
  Clements Memorial Prize
  Conway Hall, Red Lion Square
  London
  England WC1R 4RL

[570]

CLEVELAND INSTITUTE OF MUSIC
(U.S.A.)

Scholarships (approximately 150 annually) of US$500 to US$3,000 each, tenable at the Institute for one year (renewable), are offered to United States and foreign nationals.

Teaching Fellowships (between three and ten annually) of US$864 to US$1,296 each, tenable at the Institute from August to the following June, are offered to United States and foreign nationals. Candidates should have a bachelor of music degree or equivalent and must be proficient in English.

Note: No travel grants are provided.

Further information from:
  Dean
  Cleveland Institute of Music
  11021 East Boulevard
  Cleveland, Ohio 44106
  U.S.A.

[571]

CLINICAL RESEARCH INSTITUTE OF MONTREAL

Research Fellowships

Subjects: Clinical research in areas for which the Institute has facilities, which include molecular biology, bioengineering, bioethics, reproduction, neurobiology, hypertension, Parkinsonism and research in the fields of hormones, carbohydrates, metabolism, the nervous system, radioimmunoessays and rednin and tonin systems.

No. offered: Varies. About 40 are current at any one time.

Tenable at the Institute for up to three years.

Eligibility: Open to persons possessing an M.D. or Ph.D. degree.

Note: Value of the Fellowships varies.
Fellows may register for M.Sc. or Ph.D. degree programs at the University of Montreal or at McGill University.

Further information from:
  Scientific Director
  Clinical Research Institute of Montreal
  110 avenue des Pins ouest
  Montreal, Quebec
  Canada H2W 1R7

[572]

CLOTHING AND FOOTWEAR INSTITUTE *(U.K.)*

Bursaries and Travel Scholarships

Industrial Art Bursaries: Open to young designers who are full or part-time students between the ages of 17 and 30, and are or intend to be engaged in the shoe industry. These Bursaries are sponsored by the Institute and administered by the *Royal Society of Arts*.

Travel Scholarships: Up to £500 each are available for one or two annual Scholarships in the field of clothing technology, with special reference to aspects of production and design. The Scholarships, tenable outside the United Kingdom for one to three months, are open to fellows or associates of the Institute who are over 25 years of age, have passed the examinations of the Institute or of the City and Guilds of London Institute.

Closing date: 1st October.

Further information from:
 Director
 Clothing and Footwear Institute
 Albert Road
 London
 England NW4 2JS

[573]

CLOTHWORKERS' COMPANY *(U.K.)*

Walter Pothecary Scholarship

Purpose: To promote research in religious education.

No. offered: One Scholarship annually.

Value: £100.

Tenable at the University of London Institute of Education.

Eligibility: Applicants should be registered for a higher degree or other advanced study in education with special reference to religious education.

Further information from:
 Head, Religious Education Department
 University of London Institute of
  Education
 20 Bedford Way
 London
 England WC1H OAL

[574]

COLLEGE OF EUROPE *(Bruges)*

Scholarships

Subject: European studies.

No. offered: Varying number of Scholarships annually by the applicants' respective governments, the Belgian government under the agreements on cultural cooperation between Belgium and other countries, and by various foundations.

Value: 150,000 Belgian francs.

Tenable at the College of Europe, Bruges, for one academic year.

Eligibility: Open to individuals holding a university degree in law, economics, political science, public administration, or international relations, who possess a good knowledge of both English and French. There are no restrictions as to citizenship.

Note: The course of study leads to the Diploma of Advanced European Studies. Holders of the Certificate may receive the Degree of Master in Advanced European Studies upon presentation of a reserach dissertation.

Applicants from Ireland should apply to *Irish Council of the European Movement, 32 Nassau Street, Dublin 2*; applicants from Great Britain to *British Committee for the College of Europe, Europe House, 1a Whitehall Place, London SW1A 2HA*; and applicants from the United States and other non-European countries should apply directly to the College.

Address:
 Rectorate
 College of Europe
 Dyver 11
 B-8000 Bruges
 Belgium

[575]

COLLEGE PLACEMENT SERVICES, INC. *(U.S.A.)*

Julius A. Thomas Fellowships: One or two Fellowships in the amount of US$2,500 are offered annually to persons from ethnic minority backgrounds who are graduate students at the master's degree level. Fellowships are intended to afford the Fellow the opportunity to prepare for service in career counseling and placement at colleges and universities. Fellowships include an internship in a college career counseling and placement center and possible summer placement in a business organization. Interested persons should contact the placement officer at their college or university, or write to the address below.

Closing date: 1st May.

Further information from:
 College Placement Services, Inc.
 62 Highland Avenue
 Bethlehem, Pennsylvania 18017
 U.S.A.

[576]

JOSEPH COLLINS FOUNDATION *(U.S.A.)*

Grants

Purpose: To aid needy medical students with broad cultural interests, who wish to receive an adequate medical education without sacrificing other interests.

Subject: Medicine.

No. offered: Varies annually. 172 awarded in 1980.

Value: Varies up to a maximum of US$2,000 annually. Average grants are usually substantially less than the maximum amount.

Tenable at any accredited medical school for one year, renewable at the discretion of the foundation.

Eligibility: Open to anyone attending an accredited medical school in the United States who intends to specialize in neurology, psychiatry or general practice.

Note: Consideration for all applicants will be based on financial need, scholastic record and demonstrated interest in arts and letters or other cultural pursuits outside the field of medicine. Preference will be given to advanced students who commenced medical training before reaching age 30, are unmarried, and reside within 200 miles of the medical school they attend.

Applications should be obtained through medical school authorities.

Awards are not made to pre-medical or postgraduate medical students.

Closing date: 1st March.

Further information from:
 Joseph Collins Foundation
 Citicorp Center Building
 153 East 53rd Street
 New York, New York 10022
 U.S.A.

[577]

COLLINS PUBLISHERS *(U.K.)*

Collins Biennial Religious Book Award

An Award of £1,000 is given biennially to the author of a book which, in the opinion of the judges, has made the most distinguished contribution to the relevance of Christianity in the modern world, in one of the following subjects: science, ethics, sociology, philosophy, psychology and other religions. The competition is open to living citizens of the United Kingdom, the Commonwealth, the Republic of Ireland and South Africa. Entries should have been published within the two-year period beginning 1st July, two years prior to the year in which the Award is offered, and 30th June of the Award year. Entries should be submitted by the publisher to the address below.

Further information from:
 Robin Baird-Smith
 Collins Publishers
 14 St. James's Place
 London
 England SW1A 1PS

[578]

COLOMBO PLAN

Scholarships, Fellowships, and Training Awards

Colombo Plan Scholarships, etc., are awarded bilaterally after direct negotiation between two Colombo Plan member countries (donor and recipient). A request for an Award usually originates from a recipient developing country on the basis of its priority needs, and the donor country to which the request is directed may grant it if training facilities and resources in the requested field are available. In some cases, however, offers of training originate from the donor countries themselves.

Many member countries of the Colombo Plan act as both donor and recipients; however, the majority of the Awards are donated by member countries outside the Asian area—Australia, Canada, Japan, New Zealand, United Kingdom, and United States.

The Asian member countries are as follows: Afghanistan, Bangladesh, Bhutan, Burma, Fiji, India, Indonesia, Papua New Guinea, Republic of Korea, Malaysia, Republic of Maldive, Nepal, Pakistan, Philippines, Singapore, Sri Lanka, and Thailand.

Individuals wishing to apply for Colombo Plan Scholarships, etc., must be sponsored by their own governments. The appropriate government department or agency to which applications must be made are listed below, along with a brief description of the type of Colombo Plan Awards donated by these governments to nationals of other Colombo Plan member countries.

Australia—*Department of Foreign Affairs, Canberra, A.C.T.* (International Training Courses for study in Australia).

Burma—*Ministry of National Planning, Rangoon* (Colombo Plan Scholarships and Training Awards for study in Burma).

Canada—*Canadian International Development Agency, Ottawa, Ontario K1A 9G40* (Technical Assistance Fellowships and Scholarships for study in Canada, see CIDA entry).

India—*Department of Economic Affairs, Ministry of Finance, New Delhi 1* (Colombo Plan Scholarships for study in India).

Indonesia—*Chief of Foreign Aid Division, State Secretariat, Djalan Segara 20, Djakarta* (Colombo Plan Scholarships for study in Indonesia).

Japan—*First Technical Cooperation Section, Bureau of Economic Cooperation, Ministry of Foreign Affairs, Tokyo* (Technical Cooperation Fellowships for study in Japan).

Malaysia—*Economic Secretariat, Prime Minister's Department, Brockman Road, Kuala Lumpur* (Colombo Plan Scholarships and Training Awards for study in Malaysia).

New Zealand—*Ministry of Foreign Affairs, Wellington* (Colombo Plan Training Awards for study in New Zealand, see Ministry's entry).

Pakistan—*President's Secretariat, Economic Affairs Division, Islamabad* (Colombo Plan Scholarships and Training Awards for study in Pakistan).

Philippines—*Department of Foreign Affairs, Manila* (Colombo Plan Scholarships and Training Awards for study in the Philippines).

Singapore—*National Development Division, Ministry of Law and National Development, 21st Floor, National Development Building, Maxwell Road* (Colombo Plan Scholarships and Fellowships for study in Singapore, see Ministry's entry).

Sri Lanka—*Division of External Resources, Ministry of Planning, Second Floor, Ceylinco House, Colombo 1* (Colombo Plan Scholarships in Mechanical, Civil, and Electrical Engineering Technology).

Thailand—*Technical Cooperation Bureau, Department of Technical and Economic Cooperation, Krung Kasem Road, Bangkok* (Colombo Plan Scholarships and Training Awards for study in Thailand).

United Kingdom—*Ministry of Overseas Development, Eland House, Stag Place, London SW1 E5DH* (Colombo Plan Scholarships and Training Awards for study in the United Kingdom).

United States—*Agency for International Development, Department of State, Washington, D.C. 20523* (Participant Training Program for study in the United States, see AID entry).

[579]

COLUMBIA UNIVERSITY *(New York)*
Graduate School of Journalism

Walter Bagehot Fellowship in Economics and Business Journalism

Purpose: To improve the quality of economics and business journalism through instruction to mid-career journalists.

No. offered: Ten Fellowships annually.

Value: US$14,000, paid in two installments, plus free tuition for the full academic year.

Eligibility: Fellows must be professional journalists with at least four years of experience.

Closing date: First week of April.

Further information from:
 Chris Welles, Director
 Walter Bagehot Fellowship Program
 Graduate School of Journalism
 Columbia University
 New York, New York 10027
 U.S.A.

[580]

COLUMBIA UNIVERSITY *(New York)*

Graduate School of Journalism—Office of Special Programs

Paul Tobenkian Memorial Award: A Prize of US$250 and a certificate from Columbia University is awarded annually to recognize outstanding reporting in the fight against racial and religious bigotry. The Award is open to all newspaper reporters in the United States. Entries must be submitted by the reporter, his/her editor, or an interested third party, and must be accompanied by a letter from the editor summarizing the work, a brief biographical resume of the reporter and no more than ten clippings. Four complete sets of each entry are required. *Closing date:* 15th February.

Maria Moors Cabot Prizes: Usually two or three Prizes are awarded annually to journalists who have made distinguished contributions in the field of inter-American understanding and freedom of information. Each recipient is awarded an honorarium of US$1,000, a Cabot gold medal, plus round trip air fare to the University campus for the award ceremonies. The recipient's organization usually receives a silver plaque on ebony. There are no restrictions as to nationality; at least one award is made to a Latin American journalist and at least one to a United States or Canadian journalist. Awards are often based on work done over a period of years, but emphasis is placed on work accomplished during the preceding calendar year, and awards may be based on a single article or broadcast or a series of articles or broadcasts.

Nomination forms are sent to approximately 500 persons each January and will be sent to others on request. *Closing date:* 15th March.

Further information from:
 Columbia University
 Graduate School of Journalism
 Office of Special Programs
 Room 706, Journalism Building
 New York, New York 10027
 U.S.A.

[581]

COMMISSION FOR ADMINISTRATION
(South Africa)

Public Service Bursary Scheme

Purpose: To enable suitable candidates to qualify for positions in the South Africa Public Service by assisting them to obtain degrees in agriculture, commerce, forestry, physics, mathematics, applied mathematics, chemistry, engineering, geohydrology, geophysics, geology, public administration or qualifications in various other directions, such as law, medicine, meteorology and education.

Value: R2,400 per annum for full-time university study; R1,500 per annum for full-time study at colleges and technicons; R700 per annum for part-time study (only for officers in the Public Service).

Tenable at an approved university in South Africa for the minimum prescribed duration of the course or remaining prescribed minimum duration.

Eligibility: Open to South African citizens who are prepared to enter into an agreement with the Commission to serve the Public Service after the completion of their studies, for a period equal to the number of years the Bursary was tenable.

Closing date: 31st October of the year preceding the academic year which commences in January/February.

Further information from:
  Secretary
  Commission for Administration
  Transvaal House
  Vermeulen and Van der Walt Streets
  Private Bag X121
  Pretoria 0001
  South Africa

[582]

COMMISSION OF THE EUROPEAN COMMUNITIES

Grants for In-Service Training

Subjects: Activities and working methods of the European Communities.

No. offered: Varies depending on availability of funds.

Value: 6,500 Belgian francs per month. In addition, married award holders, whose spouses have no lucrative employment, receive a monthly supplement of 3,400 Belgian francs. Travel expenses, equivalent to second class train fares, are reimbursed for the journey to and from Brussels.

Tenable twice yearly in Brussels for periods of 3 to 5 months.

Eligibility: Open to persons under 30 years of age, who have a university degree or have completed at least four years of university study. Candidates may be public or private sector employees, provided they have a University degree or its equivalent, or have been engaged in advisory duties for at least three years. Trainees are in principle selected from among nationals of the Member States of the European Communities, however, a limited number of nationals of non-member countries may be accepted.
  Applicants from member countries must have a thorough knowledge of one community language and a satisfactory knowledge of one other. Applicants of non-member countries need have a good knowledge of only one Community language.

Note: The practical part of the Course is intended for information purposes only, and is in no way a probationary period and does not entitle an award holder to subsequent employment.

Closing dates: 30th April for tenure beginning 16th September; 30th September for tenure beginning 16th February.

Further information from:
  Commissions of the European
    Communities
  200 rue de la Loi
  1040 Brussels
  Belgium

[583]

COMMISSION OF THE EUROPEAN COMMUNITIES

Grants for Research Into European Integration

Purpose: To enable young university teachers at the start of their careers to conduct research on European integration and write a report on their findings.

No. offered: 20 Grants annually.

Value: Up to a maximum of 180,000 Belgian francs each paid in two installments, the first at the beginning of tenure, the second after the award holder has submitted the final report on his research. The Commission reserves the right to assist in the publication of work by awarding up to a maximum of 30,000 Belgian francs.

Tenable at a research institute or university faculty for one year; not renewable.

Eligibility: There are no restrictions of nationality. Staff of the institutions of the European Communities, their spouses and children are not eligible.
  Candidates should be postgraduate researchers, assistants or teachers at the start of their career who are studying European integration, either individually or in a group, at a research institute or university faculty.

Note: Applications should be accompanied by a typed research proposal, an estimate of expenses, a curriculum vitae and evidence of university qualifications.

The report on the work must be written in one of the official languages of the European Communities (German, French, Italian, Danish, Dutch, or English). Two copies of the text, typed, must be submitted not later than twelve months following tenure.

Closing date: 31st March.

Further information from:
University Information
Commissions of the European Communities
200 rue de la Loi
1049 Brussels
Belgium

[584]

COMMISSION FOR RACIAL EQUALITY *(U.K.)*

Community Relations Bursary Scheme

Purpose: To enable those young people working closely with immigrant communities in the United Kingdom to visit the country of origin of the ethnic group with which they are particularly concerned, in order to obtain a better understanding of community problems, conditions and customs.

No. offered: Six to twelve Bursaries annually.

Value: Air fares plus subsistence allowance.

Tenable for about 45 days. Recipients will be expected to spend their time in a few places rather than visit many places.

Eligibility: Applicants should be of reasonable seniority in their profession but young enough to be able to look forward to a number of years' further service. No specific professional qualifications are required. Applicants' employers must agree to pay their salaries etc. during their absence.

Note: Bursaries are not awarded to persons wishing to visit countries with which they are already familiar.

Further information from:
Pamela Bhalla
Commission for Racial Equality
Elliot House
10/12 Allington Street
London
England SW1E 5EH

[585]

COMMITTEE ON RESEARCH IN ECONOMIC HISTORY *(U.S.A.)*

Economic History Association
Arthur H. Cole Grants-in-Aid

Purpose: To support individual research in economic history.

Subjects: Unrestricted.

Value: Up to a maximum of *US*$1,200 for one year.

Eligibility: Preference is given to recent Ph.D. recipients, but predoctoral candidates may also apply.

Note: These Grants are intended to supplement other awards or income.

Closing date: 1st April.

Further information from:
R.D. Williams, Secretary-Treasurer
Economic History Association
Eleutherian Mills Historical Library
Wilmington, Delaware 19807
U.S.A.

[586]

COMMONWEALTH ASSOCIATION OF SURVEYING AND LAND ECONOMY *(U.K.)*

Aubrey Barker Awards

Purpose: To promote the study of and the acquisition and dissemination of skill and knowledge in the disciplines of land surveying, quantity surveying and land economy, and in particular to promote the same in developing countries in order to benefit the community.

No. offered: One or two Awards annually.

Value: Variable.

Tenable in a Commonwealth country with facilities for furthering the relevant studies, for six to twelve months.

Eligibility: Open to nationals who are residents of any of the developing Commonwealth countries (exclusive of Australia, Canada, Hong Kong, New Zealand and the United Kingdom). Applicants must be qualified and have at least two years' experience in land surveying, quantity surveying or land economy.

Note: Each candidate must undertake to return to his own country on completion of the course.

Further information from:
 Honorary Secretary
 Aubrey Barker Fund
 Commonwealth Association of Surveying
  and Land Economy
 12 Great George Street
 London
 England SW1P 3AD

[587]

COMMONWEALTH FOUNDATION *(U.K.)*

Awards for short-term study, refresher and advisory visits, and training attachments are available to professional men and women throughout the Commonwealth, tenable for periods not exceeding three months in a Commonwealth country other than the applicant's own. Applications, accompanied by details of career, evidence of support from an employer and of facilities or programmes offered in the country to be visited, should be addressed directly to the Commonwealth Foundation.

Awards for attendance at conferences are available to Commonwealth citizens for attendance at professional conferences within the Commonwealth. Application should be made to the organisers of the particular conference; individual cases will be judged by the backing they receive from the host organisation and/or their own immediate employers and by the benefit they and their communities and others attending the conference are likely to derive in the short-term from their presence, with preference being given to younger professional men and women.

Commonwealth Foundation lectureships are awarded annually to eminent professionals who travel to other regions of the Commonwealth to lecture in their specialties and to discuss professional problems with their counterpart in government service, private practice, and on the faculties and rosters of universities.

Short term bursary, interchange, and medical elective schemes are financed through the Association of Commonwealth Universities (for university administrators); through the Agricultural Institute of Canada (for exchanges between younger agronomists in the developing Commonwealth and their Canadian counterparts); through the Ontario Veterinary College, Canada (to the benefit of practising veterinarians); through the Royal Society (for scientists); through the Royal Geographical Society (for research workers in the field of applied geography); and through the Royal Architectural Institute of Canada (for young architects). Short term fellowships are also awarded on occasion through the Commonwealth Press Union to journalists from the newer Commonwealth.

Special awards are also made for specific projects promoting professional growth and cooperation throughout the Commonwealth, upon application from individuals and groups.

Note: No awards are made to students.
 Preference is given to projects involving movement to or from Third World countries. Grants are not made in support of theoretical research, and rarely provide for travel allowances within countries outside the Commonwealth. In most cases grants cover 75% return economy air fare plus a daily subsistance allowance.
 All awards are subject to close "follow through" procedures, and individual grantees are required to present reports at the close of their assignments.

Further information from:
 Commonwealth Foundation
 Marlborough House, Pall Mall
 London
 England SW1Y 5HU

[588]

COMMONWEALTH FUND *(New York)*

Harkness Fellowships

Purpose: To promote international understanding by providing opportunities for rigorously selected young potential leaders from various countries to become familiar with the American people and culture.

Subjects: Unrestricted.

No. offered: 26 Fellowships annually as follows: Twenty Fellowships for candidates from the United Kingdom; four Fellowships for Australians; two Fellowships for New Zealanders.

Value: Variable, including travel to and from the United States for the recipient, spouse and up to two children, university and research fees, basic and family allowances, books and equipment, medical insurance and United States travel.

Tenable at any United States university or comparable institution for two academic years.

Eligibility: Varies for each of the three countries. Candidates from the United Kingdom should enquire details from *Miss Sheila Widra, Assistant Director, Harkness Fellowships, 38 Upper Brook Street London W1Y 1PE, England*; candidates from Australia should enquire details from *Mr. L.T. Hinde, Australian Representative, Harkness Fellowships, Reserve Bank of Australia, Box 3947, G.P.O., Sydney, N.S.W. Australia 2001*; candidates from New Zealand should enquire details from *Mr. Ian Baumgart, Q.S.O.. New Zealand Representative, Harkness Fellowships, 27 Onehuka Road, Lower Hutt, New Zealand.*

Closing dates: United Kingdom—first week in October; Australia—early August; New Zealand—early August.

Further information from:
  Commonwealth Fund
  Harkness House
  1 East 75th Street
  New York, New York 10021
  U.S.A.

[589]

COMMONWEALTH FUND (*New York*)

Book Program

Purpose: To assist able medical scholars to prepare and publish book-length monographs on major aspects of their thought and work.

Publication Subsidies: The Program is carried out under a cooperative arrangement with Harvard University Press. To qualify for a subsidy, the manuscript must be accepted not only by the Scholarly Review Board of the Press, but also by the Fund which, with the help of expert consultants, reviews and approves each work to be selected for publication by the Press as a Commonwealth Fund book.

Grants-in-Aid: The Program is designed to help meet on a selective basis the needs of authors who are preparing scholarly monographs in medicine and related fields. Awards are tailored to meet the individual needs of each awardee and may include, for example, bibliographic assistance, assistance for the preparation of illustrations and tabular material, secretarial help, or travel essential for the completion of a monograph. Each applicant must prepare a detailed prospectus on his proposed monograph, including a definitive work program, together with documentation of his ability to undertake and complete the project. In making awards, the Fund regularly invokes a process of peer review by qualified experts in the appropriate scholarly field.

Note: Book Program grants are awarded to senior scholars and are rarely, if ever, made outside the United States.

At the time of going to press, this program was under review.

Further information from:
  Commonwealth Fund Book Program
  Harkness House
  1 East 75th Street
  New York, New York 10021
  U.S.A.

[590]

COMMONWEALTH LIBRARY ASSOCIATION (*Jamaica*)

Attachments and Internships Scheme

Purpose: To enable library staff from Commonwealth countries to gain work experience in another country.

Subject: Any aspect of librarianship.

No. offered: Varies, depending upon available funds.

Value: J$1,600 per Award.

Tenable at various locations within the Commonwealth.

Eligibility: Open to Commonwealth citizens who are members of library staff. Preferably, candidates should be under 40 years of age and professionally qualified.

Note: Applications must be channelled through the COMLA Councillor of the candidate's home country.

Not confirmed for 1983.

Further information from:
Executive Secretary
Commonwealth Literary Association
P.O. Box 534
Kingston 10
Jamaica, West Indies

[591]

COMMONWEALTH PRESS UNION *(U.K.)*

Harry Brittain Memorial Fellowships: Approximately ten Fellowships are awarded annually to journalists from overseas Commonwealth countries employed by newspapers, news agencies or periodicals who are members of the CPU. Nominations must be submitted by employing editors in December of each year.

Travelling Scholarships: Usually only one or two Scholarships are awarded each year to British journalists to visit overseas Commonwealth countries. Applicants should be employed by members of the CPU and be nominated by their editors.

Further information from:
Commonwealth Press Union
Studio House, 184 Fleet Street
London
England EC4A 2DU

[592]

COMMONWEALTH SCHOLARSHIP COMMISSION IN THE UNITED KINGDOM

Commonwealth Academic Staff Fellowships

Purpose: To help universities in the developing countries of the Commonwealth build up the numbers and enhance the experience of their locally born staff. The Fellowships are provided by the United Kingdom government and fall within the framework of the Commonwealth Scholarship and Fellowship Plan (see   ). They are intended to enable promising staff members from universities and similar institutions in the developing Commonwealth to obtain experience in a university or other appropriate institution in the United Kingdom. The Fellow's programme is devised by the Commission in conjunction with the candidate's own university and receiving institution (not necessarily the one proposed by the candidate) and will be related as closely as possible to the employment to which the Fellow will return. Fellowships are not given for study for higher degrees.

Subjects: Any academic discipline other than medicine.

No. offered: Maximum of 45 Fellowships annually.

Value: £372 per month plus approved air fares to and from the United Kingdom and in certain circumstances a marriage and child allowance. A grant for approved travel within the United Kingdom, and a book grant are also paid, and where recommended an initial clothing allowance is offered. The emoluments are not subject to United Kingdom income tax.

Tenable at a university or comparable institution in the United Kingdom, for one academic year; not renewable. The Fellowship may not be held concurrently with other awards or with paid employment.

Eligibility: Open to citizens of the Commonwealth and to British projected persons permanently resident in a developing Commonwealth country. Preference is given to candidates between 28 and 40 years of age. Candidates should normally hold a doctorate or other equivalent postgraduate qualification and should have had at least two years' experience as a staff member of a university or similar institution in their own country. Candidates may be required to provide evidence of competence in English and satisfactory health.

Note: Fellows are required to sign an undertaking to return to resume their academic post in their own country on completion of the Fellowships.

Candidates must be nominated by one of the following: (a) the vice-chancellor of a British university; (b) the vice-chancellor of the university on whose permanent staff the applicant serves or is to serve (heads of Indian universities should send their nominations to the University Grants Commission in New Delhi and heads of Bangladesh universities to the University Grants Commission in Dacca); (c) the Commonwealth Scholarship agency in the candidate's own country (for address see   ); (d) the heads of autonomous non-university institutions in the Commonwealth.

Closing date: 31st January for awards beginning October. For Fellowships starting after the academic year has already commenced, nominations should be made at least eight months before the proposed commencement date.

Address:
Joint Secretary
Commonwealth Scholarship Commission
 in the United Kingdom
c/o Association of Commonwealth
 Universities
36 Gordon Square
London
England WC1H 0PF

[593]

COMMONWEALTH SCHOLARSHIP COMMISSION IN THE UNITED KINGDOM

Commonwealth Academic Staff Scholarships

Purpose: As for Commonwealth Academic Staff Fellowships (see   ). Scholarships are intended for those preparing for a postgraduate qualification.

Subjects: Unrestricted.

Value: To cover cost of return fare to the United Kingdom, approved tuition, laboratory and examination fees, personal maintenance allowance at the rate of £269 per month, grant for books and apparatus and for typing of thesis where applicable, grant for approved travel within the United Kingdom, an initial clothing grant in special cases, and in certain circumstances a marriage and child allowance. The emoluments are not subject to United Kingdom income tax.

Tenable at a university or comparable institution in the United Kingdom, normally for two years; renewable for a further year.

Eligibility: Open to Commonwealth citizens or British protected persons permanently resident in a developing country of the Commonwealth. A candidate should hold, or be about to obtain, a degree or an equivalent qualification, and should already hold a teaching appointment in a university or similar institution or have the assurance of such an appointment on his return. Candidates should be under 35 years of age at the time the award is taken up; preference will be given to persons between 22 and 28 years of age. All candidates must have sufficient competence in English to profit by the proposed study.

Note: See *Note* section for further requirements and nomination procedure.

Address
Joint Secretary
Commonwealth Scholarship Commission
 in the United Kingdom
c/o Association of Commonwealth
 Universities
36 Gordon Square
London
England WC1H 0PF

[594]

COMMONWEALTH SCHOLARSHIP COMMISSION IN THE UNITED KINGDOM

Commonwealth Medical Fellowships

Purpose: To assist in the creation or expansion of facilities for medical education in the Commonwealth. The Fellowships are provided by the United Kingdom government and fall within the framework of the Commonwealth Scholarship and Fellowship Plan. They are primarily intended for established medical and dental teachers who require a programme of study in depth to enable them to enhance their experience. Fellowships are not given for study for formal qualifications.

Subjects: Medicine, surgery, dentistry, and in certain circumstances basis medical sciences.

No. offered: Up to 60 Fellowships annually.

Value: £385 per month maintenance allowance plus approved return air fare to the United Kingdom; book and study travel expenses; clothing grant; marriage allowance where appropriate. Emoluments are not subject to United Kingdom income tax.

Tenable at a university, medical school, or comparable institution in the United Kingdom for one year; not renewable. The Fellowships may not be held concurrently with other awards or with paid employment.

Eligibility: Open to citizens of the Commonwealth and to British protected persons permanently resident in a Commonwealth country outside the United Kingdom. Preference is given to candidates between 30 and 40 years of age. Candidates should possess suitable postgraduate degrees, and except for teachers of basic medical sciences, must hold qualifications registrable in the United Kingdom. Candidates may be required to provide evidence of competence in English and of satisfactory health.

Note: Fellows are required to sign an undertaking to return to their own country on completion of the Fellowship.

Candidates must be nominated by (a) their own university vice-chancellor or medical school principal; (b) responsible authorities of universities or medical schools in the United Kingdom; or (c) the Commonwealth Scholarship agency in their own country (for addresses see   ). Candidates who are permanent residents of India may be nominated only by the Commonwealth Scholarship agency in India. Nominations are considered twice yearly.

Address
   Administrator for Commonwealth Medical Awards
   Associations of Commonwealth Universities
   36 Gordon Square
   London
   England WC1H 0PF

[595]

COMMONWEALTH SCHOLARSHIP COMMISSION IN THE UNITED KINGDOM

Commonwealth Senior Medical Fellowships

Purpose: To assist in the creation or expansion of facilities for medical education in the Commonwealth. The Fellowships are provided by the United Kingdom government and fall within the framework of the Commonwealth Scholarship and Fellowship Plan (see). Senior Felowships are primarily intended to enable senior teachers to acquaint themselves at first hand with the facilities available in Britain for the intensive training of their senior teaching staff. They are suitable for deans and principals of educational institutions. Full time professorial department heads may also be considered.

Subjects: Medicine, surgery, dentistry.

No. offered: Up to 15 Senior Fellowships annually.

Value: £36 per day and approved air fares to and from the United Kingdom. The fellowships are not subject to United Kingdom income tax.

Tenable at a university, medical school or comparable institution in the United Kingdom for three months; not renewable. The Fellowships may not be held concurrently with other awards or paid employment.

Eligibility: Open to citizens of the Commonwealth and to British protected persons permanently resident in Commonwealth countries outside the United Kingdom who suit the terms of the Fellowships (see *Purpose*).

Note: Fellows are required to sign an undertaking to return to their own country on completion of the Fellowships.

Candidates must be nominated by the responsible authorities of universities or medical schools in the United Kingdom or by the Commonwealth Scholarship agency in their own country (for addresses see). Nomination of candidates permanently resident in India will be made solely by the Commonwealth Scholarship agency in India. Nominations are considered twice yearly.

Further information from:
   Administrator for Commonwealth Medical Awards
   Association of Commonwealth Universities
   36 Gordon Square
   London
   England WC1H 0PF

[596]

COMMONWEALTH SCHOLARSHIP COMMISSION IN THE UNITED KINGDOM

Commonwealth Medical Scholarships

Commonwealth Scholarships are awarded for training in the United Kingdom in medicine, surgery and dentistry among other academic disciplines. The medical and dental awards are intended primarily but not exclusively for preparation for postgraduate qualifications of universities or the Royal Colleges in Britain. For conditions see Entry.

Address
  Administrator for Commonwealth Medical Awards
  Association of Commonwealth Universities
  36 Gordon Square
  London
  England WC1H 0PF

[597]

COMMONWEALTH SCHOLARSHIP AND FELLOWSHIP PLAN

Commonwealth Scholarships and Commonwealth Visiting Professorships (or Fellowships)

Purpose: To enable Commonwealth students of high intellectual promise to pursue studies in Commonwealth countries other than their own so that on their return home they could make a distinctive contribution to life in their own countries and to mutual understanding in the Commonwealth.

The following Commonwealth countries are offering Commonwealth Scholarships under the Plan: United Kingdom, Canada, Australia, New Zealand, India, Sri Lanka, Ghana, Malaysia, Nigeria, Jamaica, Hong Kong, Malta, and Trinidad and Tobago. Professorships, Fellowships or awards for senior scholars and educational administrators have so far been instituted by the United Kingdom, Canada, Australia, New Zealand and India.

Subjects: In general—arts, social studies, pure science, technology, medicine (largely tenable in the United Kingdom), dentistry, agriculture and forestry, and veterinary science.

No. offered: Over 1,000 Commonwealth Scholarships; relatively few Commonwealth Visiting Professorships or Fellowships.

Value: Determined by each awarding country (i.e., the country in which the award is tenable). Generally, the emoluments for Scholarships include fares to and from the awarding country, payment of tuition fees, allowances for books, special clothing and local travel, and a personal maintenance allowance. In some countries a marriage allowance is paid.

Visiting Fellows will receive fares to and from the awarding country, a per diem expenses allowance, medical and hospital services and an allowance for travel within the awarding country.

Tenable at universities, colleges and other educational institutions in Commonwealth countries for one to three academic years (Scholarships), or for three months to one academic year (Fellowships).

Eligibility: (a) *Commonwealth Scholarships* are open to persons under 35 years of age (preferably between 22 and 28) who are citizens of a Commonwealth country and are normally resident in some part of the Commonwealth other than the particular awarding country. Scholarships are intended for young graduates of high intellectual promise who may be expected to make a significant contribution to their own countries on their return from postgraduate study overseas. (Scholarships may also be awarded for undergraduate study in special circumstances).

(b) *Commonwealth Visiting Professorships (or Fellowships)* are intended for a few senior scholars of established reputation and achievement. The main emphasis is on awards in the academic (including technological) fields, but the possibility is not excluded of some awards being made to persons outside these fields who play important roles in the life of their country.

Note: Scholarship holders must undertake to return to their own countries on competition of their studies overseas.

Applications for Scholarships should be made to the appropriate Scholarship agency in the candidate's country of normal residence. These agencies distribute prospectuses and application forms for the various awards and will, generally speaking, be the best local centres for information about the Plan.

Visiting Professorships, Fellowships and other awards for senior scholars are usually

awarded by invitation only or through nomination by an individual's own university.

Local Agency Addresses:

Antigua—Permanent Secretary, Ministry of Education, Church Street, St. John's, Antigua, Leeward Islands, West Indies.

Australia—Secretary, Department of Education, P.O. 826, Woden, A.C.T. 2606.

Bahamas—Permanent Secretary, Ministry of Education, P.O. Box N3913/14, Nassau.

Bangladesh—Permanent Secretary, Ministry of Education, Government of Bangladesh, Bangladesh Secretariat, Dacca.

Barbados—Permanent Secretary, Ministry of Education, Jemmott's Lane, Bridgetown.

Belize—Permanent Secretary, Ministry of Education, Belmopan.

Bermuda—Chief Education Officer, Department of Education, P.O. Box 1185, Hamilton 5.

Botswana—Chief Education Officer, Ministry of Education, Private Bag 005, Gaborone.

British Virgin Islands—Secretary, B.V.I. Scholarships Committee, Government of the B.V.I., Tortola.

Brunei—H.E. the High Commissioner for Brunei, British High Commission, Bandar Seri Begawan, Brunei.

Canada—Secretary, Canadian Commonwealth Scholarship and Fellowship Committee, 151 Slater Street, Ottawa, Ontario K1P 5N1.

Cayman Islands—Chief Education Officer, Education Council, P.O. Box 910, Government Administration Building, Grand Cayman.

Cyprus—Director General, Ministry of Foreign Affairs, Nicosia.

Dominica—Permanent Secretary, Ministry of Education, Government Headquarters, Roseau, Dominica, West Indies.

Falkland Islands—Chief Secretary, Secretariat, Stanley, Falkland Islands, South Atlantic.

Fiji—Secretary, Government Scholarships Unit, Public Service Commission, Box 2211, Government Buildings, Suva.

Gambia—Secretary, Scholarship Advisory Committee, Ministry of Education, Bedford Place Building, Banjul.

Ghana—Registrar of Scholarships, Scholarships Secretariat, P.O. Box M75, Ministry Branch Post Office, Accra.

Gibraltar—Director of Education, Department of Education, 277 Main Street, Gibraltar.

Grenada—Permanent Secretary, Training Division, Prime Minister's Office, St. George's.

Guyana—Permanent Secretary, Public Service Training Centre, 65-67 High Street, Kingston, Georgetown.

Hong Kong—Director of Education, Overseas Students and Scholarships Section, Education Department Branch Office, Leighton Centre, 15th Floor, 77 Leighton Road, Hong Kong.

India—(for general Commonwealth Scholarships) Deputy Education Adviser (ES), Department of Education, New Delhi-110001; (for Commonwealth Academic Staff Fellowships and Scholarships) Additional Secretary, University Grants Commission, Bahadur Shah Zafar Marg, New Delhi-110002.

Jamaica—Permanent Secretary, Ministry of Education, Scholarships Section, 97A Church Street, Kingston.

Kenya—Permanent Secretary, Ministry of Education, Jogoo House, Harambee Avenue, P.O. Box 30040, Nairobi.

Kiribati—Secretary, Ministry of Education, P.O. Box 263, Bikenibeu, Tarawa, Kiribati, Central Pacific.

Lesotho—Permanent Secretary for Education, Ministry of Education, P.O. Box 47, Maseru.

Malawi—Secretary, Office of the President, Personnel Division, P.O. Box 30227, Capital City, Lilongwe 3.

Malaysia—Secretary, Malaysian Liaison Committee, Commonwealth Education Scheme, Ministry of Education, Federal House, Kuala Lumpur.

Malta—Director of Education, Education Department, Lascaris, Valletta.

Mauritius—Permanent Secretary, Ministry of Education, Government House, Port Louis.

Montserrat—Permanent Secretary, Manpower and Administration, Governor's Office, Plymouth, Montserrat, West Indies.

Nauru—Secretary, Department of Education, Republic of Nauru, Nauru Island, Central Pacific.

New Zealand—Secretary, New Zealand Commonwealth Scholarships and Fellowships Committee, University Grants Committee, P.O. Box 12-348, Wellington North.

Nigeria—Permanent Secretary, Federal Ministry of Education, Scholarships Section, P.M.B. 12573, Lagos.

Papua New Guinea—Principal Private Secretary, Office of the Prime Minister, Waigani.

St. Christopher, Nevis & Anguilla—Permanent Secretary, Establishment Division, Government Headquarters, P.O. Box 186, St. Kitts, West Indies.

St. Helena—Education Officer, Education Department, Jamestown.

St. Lucia—Permanent Secretary, Establishment Division, Premier's Office, Government Buildings, Castries, St. Lucia, West Indies.

St. Vincent and the Grenadines—Chief Personnel Officer, Service Commissions Department, Kingstown, St. Vincent, West Indies.

Seychelles—Permanent Secretary, Ministry of Education, P.O. Box 48, Mahe.

Sierra Leone—Permanent Secretary, Ministry of Education, New England, Freetown.

Singapore—Secretary, Public Service Commission, 2nd Floor, City Hall, St. Andrew's Road, Singapore 0617.

Solomon Islands—Permanent Secretary, Ministry of Education and Training, P.O. Box 584, Honiara.

Sri Lanka—Permanent Secretary, Ministry of Higher Education, 18 Ward Place, Colombo 7.

Swaziland—Permanent Secretary, Swaziland Government, Department of Establishments and Training, P.O. Box 170, Mbabane.

Tanzania—Principal Secretary, Ministry of National Education, P.O. Box 9121, Dar es Salaam.

Tonga—Director of Education, Ministry of Education, P.O. Box 61, Nuku'alofa.

Trinidad and Tobago—Chief Personnel Officer, Training Division, 30 Queen's Park West, Port-of-Spain, Trinidad.

Turks & Caicos Islands—Secretary, Ministry of Education, Grand Turk, Turks & Caicos Islands, West Indies.

Tuvalu—Senior Education Officer, Vaiaku, Funafuti, Tuvalu, West Pacific.

Uganda—Permanent Secretary, Ministry of Education, Crested Towers, P.O. Box 7063, Kampala.

United Kingdom—Joint Secretaries, Commonwealth Scholarship Commission in the United Kingdom, 36 Gordon Square, London WC1H OPF.

Vanuatu—Director of Scholarships, Scholarships and Training Department, Ministry of Education, Vila.

Western Samoa—Scholarship Committee, c/o Prime Minister's Department, P.O. Box 193, Apia.

Zambia—Secretary, Bursaries Committee, P.O. Box 50093, Lusaka.

Zimbabwe—Permanent Secretary, Ministry of Education and Culture, P.O. Box 8022, Causeway, Salisbury.

[598]

COMMONWEALTH SCIENTIFIC AND INDUSTRIAL RESEARCH ORGANIZATION (*Australia*)

CSIRO Postdoctoral Award Scheme

Purpose: To provide opportunities for recently

graduated Ph.D. degree holders to gain post-doctoral experience.

Subjects: Physical, industrial, biological and agricultural sciences.

No. offered: Approximately 10 Postdoctoral Awards annually.

Value: The current annual rate for stipends is £5,500 in Britain or US$19,250 in the U.S., plus transportation and tuition, up to A$800 for approved visits, equipment and certain maintenance expenses, and an allowance for dependants.

Tenable for the first year at any suitable laboratory in Australia or overseas; for the second year at a CSIRO Division; or in a university, industry or government department in Australia for work on an approved joint research project with the CSIRO.

Eligibility: Open to those who are normally Australian residents who possess a Ph.D. degree or its equivalent, or who are nearing completion of the degree or its equivalent, and have not previously had the opportunity to carry out postgraduate research overseas.

Note: At the time of going to press, Award values were under review.

Closing date: March.

Further information from:
Secretary
CSIRO Postdoctoral Awards Committee
P.O. Box 225
Dickson, A.C.T.
Australia 2602

[599]

COMMONWEALTH SECRETARIAT

Commonwealth Fund for Technical Cooperation—Education Training Programme

Purpose: To finance the education and training of personnel from one developing Commonwealth country in another. The programme is flexible, responding to requests by individual governments, and may include short-term fellowships or extended training periods, teaching assignments, study visits, or travel grants for senior professional personnel who wish to observe developments in their own fields in other developing countries.

Subjects: Priority is given to studies within the programmes which will materially contribute to a country's economic and social development, especially in: agricultural development, including forestry and fisheries; education, including teacher training, teaching/learning techniques, educational planning and administration; industrial development, including the construction industry and small scale industries; monetary and fiscal development; exploitation and assessment of natural resources; public and business administration; social development, including health and social welfare; trade development; transport and communications; development planning; statistics.

Note: Agencies have been established in participating Commonwealth countries which select and nominate candidates for training in other developing countries. Applications should be forwarded to the appropriate agency in the candidate's own country and will be screened to ensure suitability and language proficiency, medical fitnesss and vertification of qualifications for the particular project planned. The value of each award will be based on covering the costs of approved fees, books and apparatus, special clothing where necessary, travel, and personal maintenance allowance.

Further information from:
Managing Director, CFTC
Commonwealth Secretariat
Marlborough House, Pall Mall
London
England SW1Y 5HX

[600]

COMMONWEALTH YOUTH PROGRAMME
(U.K.)

Bursaries and Fellowships

Purpose: To provide support for the training (both formal and informal) of key officials in youth programmes of both governmental and non-governmental agencies.

Value: Bursaries—travel, tuition, field study expenses, books, board and lodging; Fellowships—economy air travel to and from the host country, local travel costs and board and lodging.

Tenure: Bursaries—tenable solely at the Programme's Regional Centres and at the University of the South Pacific, Fiji, for participation in the diploma courses in Youth and Development; Fellowships—tenable for periods of up to 28 days.

Eligibility: Open to persons who are citizens of or normally resident in a Commonwealth country, actively engaged in youth work (either full-or part-time, paid or voluntary), and in a position to make a significant contribution to youth work or to convey some benefit to young people on their return home. All candidates must be supported by the relevant ministry, department or organisation in their own countries.

Note: All applications should be accompanied by government endorsement of the application and, where appropriate, must also be approved to the department or organisation for which the applicant works.

Further information from:
Commonwealth Youth Programme
Marlborough House, Pall Mall
London
England SW1Y 5HX

[601]

COMMONWEALTH VETERINARY INTERCHANGE FUND

Travel Grants

The Commonwealth Foundation in London and the Canadian International Development Agency in Ottawa have combined to establish the Commonwealth Veterinary Interchange Fund so that veterinarians in Commonwealth countries may acquire new knowledge and expertise in their own field of interest which they will apply for the benefit of their home institutions.

Funds are offered to enable veterinarians in the member countries of the Commonwealth to undertake short periods of specialized study in other Commonwealth countries, and to provide grants for veterinarians in these countries, who are involved in veterinary education, regulatory work research or practice to spend, normally, up to six weeks (extended to ten weeks in exceptional cases), of study in their special field of interest at an approved institution in another Commonwealth country.

Normally, travel grants cover economy class air fare, surface travel, and room and meals at *Can*$40 per day for a period of six weeks.

Applicants are required to make their own arrangements for study visits with prospective sponsors.

Note: Grants are provided primarily for veterinarians to pursue a period of concentrated study and are not intended to underwrite a tour of visits to a number of institutions. However, this does not preclude brief excursions to achieve the purposes of the grant, if this is thought necessary by the host institution.

Grantees are expected to give one or two lectures or seminars at the host institution on an aspect of veterinary activities in their home countries. This and the discussion of topics of mutual interest with the host staff contribute greatly to the objectives of the CVIF.

To assess the success of the CVIF program, grantees and their hosts are expected to report to the Executive Director of the Fund, on the outcome of visits.

Further information from:
Dr. T. Lloyd Jones, Executive Director
Commonwealth Veterinary Interchange Fund
Room 205
Ontarion Veterinary College
University of Guelph
Guelph, Ontario
Canada N1G 2W1

[602]

COMPOSERS, AUTHORS AND PUBLISHERS ASSOCIATION OF CANADA LTD.

William St. Clair Low, Sir Ernest MacMillan and Hugh Le Caine Awards for Young Composers

Purpose: The Awards are intended as incentives to young composers who wish to embark upon musical careers.

No. offered: Seven prizes annually.

Value: A total of *Can*$7,000 annually to be disbursed as follows: electronic music category—one Award of *Can*$1,000; Chamber and orchestral music categories—one Award each of *Can*$1,500; *Can*$1,000; and *Can*$500.

Eligibility: Open to Canadian citizens who are under 30 years of age as of the closing date of the competition. Candidates should be members of CAPAC, or not members of any other performing rights society. Membership in CAPAC is not mandatory.

Note: Awards are given on the basis of evaluation by a jury, of compositions submitted by the applicant.

Closing date: 30th September.

Further information from:
   Composers, Authors and Publishers
      Association of Canada, Ltd.
   1240 Bay Street
   Toronto, Ontario
   England M5R 2C2

[603]

CONCERT ARTISTS GUILD, INC *(U.S.A.)*

Debut Recital Awards

Purpose: To promote the career development of musical artists through a New York debut recital, radio appearances, and other professional engagements.

No. offered: Up to ten Awards annually.

Value: US$1,000 to cover all recital expenses.

Eligibility: Open to instrumentalists up to 32 years of age, vocalists up to 35 years of age, and ensembles whose combined ages average 32 years or under as of 15th January of the Award year. Entrants are not restricted to United States citizens.

Note: Artists must submit a preliminary tape recording to be selected for the live auditions held in New York City in April. Award winners are presented in their debut recitals at the Carnegie Recital Hall in the following concert season.

Closing date: 15th January.

Further information from:
   Concert Artists Guild, Inc.
   154 West 57th Street
   New York, New York 10019
   U.S.A.

[604]

CONFEDERATION OF BRITISH INDUSTRY

Overseas Scholarships

No. offered: Approximately 80 to 100 scholarships are offered annually to participating countries for industrial training in Britain, the number depending upon the size and commercial importance of the countries.

Scholarships are offered to citizens of the British Commonwealth, and certain developing countries, in two categories:

Type A: These are for recently-graduated engineers with one to four years' industrial experience who require general practical training in engineering. They provide an allowance of £269 per month for 12 to 18 months to cover basic cost of living, plus fares to and from Britain.

Type B: These are for more experienced applicants, normally under 35 years old, who have been following their careers for a minimum of five years since graduation and now desire advanced training in more limited and specialised fields. They offer from four to twelve months' training, which might include such items as project work, design office, the more advanced phases of industry, and new techniques. They provide an allowance of £336 per month, but scholars are required to pay the cost of travel to and from their own countries. Allowances are reviewed annually in September.

Eligibility: Open to graduates holding a degree or diploma in engineering issued by a recognised university faculty, institute or school; applicants should be able to profit from training in industrial—as distinct from academic—surroundings; be medically fit; speak and write English well; possess good character, initiative and sense of responsibility; and undertake to return and follow their profession in their own country.

Note: Applications should be sent to the British Embassy, British High Commission, or British Council in the candidate's home country.
   Candidates are required to return to their own country upon completion of the scholarship.

Closing date: End of March.

United Kingdom address:
Manager, Overseas Scholarships
Confederation of British Industry
Centre Point
103 New Oxford Street
London
England WC1A 1DU

Further information from:
Conference on Latin American History
Secretariat: Center for Latin America
San Diego State University
San Diego, California 92182
U.S.A.

[606]

CONOCO, INC. *(U.S.A.)*

Scholarships and Fellowships

Purpose: To encourage widespread and enlightened higher education, fundamental research, and the continued existence of private colleges and universities.

[605]

CONFERENCE ON LATIN AMERICAN HISTORY *(U.S.A.)*

Herbert E. Bolton Memorial Prize of US$500 is awarded annually for the best English language book on any aspect of Latin American history published during the year preceding that of the Award.

Howard F. Cline Memorial Prize of US$200 is awarded annually for the best article in the general field of ethnohistory published during the year preceding that of the Award.

Conference on Latin American History Prize of US$200 is awarded annually for the best article on Latin American history published in a journal other than the *Hispanic American Historical Review* during the year preceding that of the Award.

Distinguished Service Award of US$500 is awarded at the discretion of the General Committee, not more than every second year, to a Conference member whose career in scholarship, teaching, publishing, librarianship, institutional development or other fields evidences significant contributions to the advancement of the study of Latin American history in the U.S.

Clarence H. Haring Memorial Prize is awarded once every five years for the best historical study published by a Latin American during the preceding five year period. Nominations are made by a committee of Conference members. Stipends vary.

James A. Robertson Memorial Prize of US$200 is awarded annually for the best article appearing in the *Hispanic American Historical Review* the year the Award is given.

Subjects: Chemistry, chemical engineering, mining engineering, petroleum engineering, business administration, petroleum economics, and industrial hygiene.

Value: Approximately US$2,000-US$5,000 depending on need, requirements and funds available.

Tenable at colleges and universities in the United States and the United Kingdom where Scholarships and Fellowships have been established.

Note: Recipients are selected by the various colleges and universities, from whom eligibility and application information must be obtained.
A list of colleges and universities in the United States and the United Kingdom having Conoco that have Scholarships and Fellowships may be obtained from:
Conoco Inc.
University Relations and Corporate
  Contributions
High Ridge Park
Stamford, Connecticut 06904
U.S.A.

[607]

CONSERVATION AND RESEARCH FOUNDATION, INC. *(U.S.A.)*

Jeanette Siron Pelton Award

Purpose: To recognize sustained and imaginative productivity in the field of experimental plant morphology.

No. offered: One Award every two or three years.

Value: US$1,000, paid in a lump sum.

Tenable anywhere without restriction.

Eligibility: Candidates are nominated by the Pelton Award Committee of the Botanical Society of America, which welcomes suggestions. Candidates must have published research within the last five years, and be forty years of age or less.

Further information from:
Conservation and Research Foundation
Box 1445
Connecticut College
New London, Connecticut 06320
U.S.A.

[608]

CONSORTIUM FOR GRADUATE STUDY IN MANAGEMENT *(U.S.A.)*

Fellowships in Minorities

Purpose: To hasten the entry of minority men and women into management positions in business by enabling them to obtain a master's degree in business administration.

No. offered: 100 to 125 Fellowships annually.

Value: US$3,000 plus tuition (paid directly to the university) for the first year; US$1,500 plus tuition for the second year after successful completion of the first; cash stipend paid monthly.

Tenable for two years at graduate schools of management at the following universities: Indiana University; University of North Carolina; University of Rochester; University of Southern California; Washington University; University of Wisconsin.

Eligibility: Open to United States citizens who are Black, Chicano, Puerto Rican, Cuban or American Indian. Applicants must hold a baccalaureate degree and must have taken the Graduate Management Admission Test (GMAT) in Business (Educational Testing Service).

Further information from:
Dr. Wallace L. Jones, Director
Consortium for Graduate Study in Management
101 North Skinker Boulevard, Box 1132
St. Louis, Missouri 63130
U.S.A.

[609]

DUFF COOPER MEMORIAL TRUST FUND *(U.K.)*

Duff Cooper Memorial Prize

The annual Prize is given for a literary work in the field of biography, history, politics, or poetry published in English or French during the previous 24 months.

Further information from:
Duff Cooper Memorial Trust Fund
c/o The Warden
New College
Oxford
England

[610]

CORN INDUSTRIES RESEARCH FOUNDATION *(U.S.A.)*
CORN REFINERS ASSOCIATION, INC. *(U.S.A.)*

A number of Fellowships are awarded annually to support research projects relating to the products, process or raw materials associated with the corn wet milling industry. This support is tenable on a one-year basis, and may be renewed.

Closing date: 30th April for applications to be considered for funding the following January.

Further information from:
Corn Industries Research Foundation
Corn Refiners Association, Inc.
1001 Connecticut Avenue, N.W.
Washington, D.C. 20036
U.S.A.

[611]

CORO FOUNDATION *(U.S.A.)*

Fellowships

Purpose: To prepare men and women for effective participation in public affairs.

No. offered: 36 Fellowships annually.

Value: According to individual needs, up to US$5,000.

Tenable for nine months, from September to June at each of the three Foundation Centers in San Francisco, Los Angeles and St. Louis.

Eligibility: Open to United States citizens who hold a bachelor's degree (no specific major required) and an interest in the government-political field, demonstrated through student leadership positions, professional preparation, work experience or community activities.

Closing date: 15th January.

Further information from:
  Coro Foundation
  Northern California Center
  1370 Mission Street
  San Francisco, California 94103
  U.S.A.

[612]

CORPORATION OF THE CITY OF TORONTO

City of Toronto Book Award

One or more Awards, totaling not more than Can$5,000, are presented annually for books based on or concerned with the City of Toronto. Eligibility is open to anyone whose work has been published during the year preceding the Award.

Closing date: December of the year of the Award.

Further information from:
  Corporation of the City of Toronto
  Toronto Book Award
  Department of the City Clerk
  City Hall
  Toronto, Ontario
  Canada M5H 2N2

[613]

COUNCIL FOR BRITISH ARCHAEOLOGY

British Archaeological Research Trust Grants

Purpose: To support personal archaeological research, particularly that which breaks new ground and extends the range of techniques available to archaeologists.

No. offered: Two to three Grants in even-numbered years.

Value: Approximately £1,000.

Tenable at an approved place in the United Kingdom; may be held concurrently with other income.

Eligibility: Open to United Kingdom residents; academic qualifications are not required.

Further information from:
  Director
  Council for British Archaeology
  112 Kennington Road
  London
  England SE11 6RE

[614]

COUNCIL OF EUROPE

CCC Higher Education Scholarship Scheme

Under this Scheme the following member states of the Council for Cultural Cooperation (CCC) offer Scholarships annually to graduates from other member countries to enable them to engage in study or research in the territory: Austria, France, Federal Republic of Germany, Greece, Italy, Sweden, Switzerland, and Turkey.

To be eligible for one of these Scholarships, candidates must be a national of a member state of the CCC who holds a first degree in higher education (French candidates must be students in the "troisième cycle"). The Scholarships are awarded for one to three years and are administered by the national authorities concerned.

Further information from:
Division for Higher Education and Research
Council of Europe
F-67006 Strasbourg Cedex
France

[615]

COUNCIL OF EUROPE

CCC Teacher Bursaries Scheme

This scheme enables educationalists (inspectors, head teachers and teachers) from member states of the Council for Cultural Cooperation (CCC) to attend short national in-service training courses organized in Austria, Belgium, Denmark, France, Federal Republic of Germany, Greece, Ireland, Italy, Liechtenstein, Netherlands, Norway, Portugal, Spain, Sweden, Switzerland, Turkey and the United Kingdom. Subsistence expenses and enrollment fees are borne by the host countries. Austria, Federal Republic of Germany, the Netherlands, Spain, and the United Kingdom also pay the travel expenses of foreign participants. Travel expenses are also covered by the Cultural Fund of the Council of Europe which grants approximately 135 travel scholarships.

Course programmes covering all subjects related to general, technical and vocational education, as well as application forms, are distributed by the Council of Europe. Secretariat to a network of national liaison officers of ministries of education in the CCC member states.

Good knowledge of the working language of the course is required.

Further information from:
School Education Division
Council of Europe
Secretariat General
67006 Strasbourg Cedex
France

[616]

COUNCIL OF EUROPE

Criminological Fellowship Programme

Individual Criminological Fellowships are offered to enable research workers to increase their knowledge of objectives and methods concerning criminological research adopted in the member countries of the Council of Europe. The Fellowships are tenable for up to one year (usually between three and six months).

Note: The Fellowships are normally offered to nationals of member countries of the Council of Europe (see preceding entry).

Address:
Division of Crime Problems
Council of Europe, Secretariat General
67006 Strasbourg Cedex
France

[617]

COUNCIL OF EUROPE

Fellowship for European Legal Studies and Research

Fellowships for studies and research in European legal studies and research are available to persons who have completed a course of studies in law at university level for studies relating to: (a) comparative law of European states; (b) law governing European organisations and institutions; or (c) law emanating from conventions and other instruments of such organisations and institutions. Applicants must normally be nationals of member states of the Council of Europe (see 597) or of Finland. Grants, consist of a lump sum fixed in each case by the selection committee, and must be used within one calendar year.

Further information from:
Division II, Directorate of Legal Affairs
Council of Europe, Secretariat General
67006 Strasbourg Cedex
France

[618]

COUNCIL OF EUROPE

Medical Fellowship Programme

Individual Medical Fellowships (approximately 130) are offered to enable health personnel to become conversant with different techniques used in European countries. The Fellowships are tenable for periods from fifteen days to one year (preference is given to shorter-term Fellowships) and provide FF3,726 per month for resident Fellows or FF4,740 per month for travelling Fellows (rates in 1982), plus travel costs. Candidates must be able to demonstrate high competence in the field and should possess a working knowledge of the language(s) of the host country/countries concerned.

Coordinated Medical Research Fellowships and *Coordinated Blood Transfusion Research Fellowships* are offered to enable three specialists of different nationalities to study a subject of common European medical interest under a study director appointed by the European Health Committee. The Fellowships are tenable for up to 25 days plus three meetings of a total duration of up to 9 days, and provide FF356 per day plus travel expenses.

Fellowships for Blood Transfusion Courses and for *Courses on Histocompatability* are offered to suitably qualified individuals for participation in the biennal Courses which are of one to two weeks duration and provide FF138 per day plus travel costs.

Note: The Fellowships are offered to nationals of member countries of the Council of Europe (see 597), and to nationals of Finland.
Irish candidates should apply to the *Department of Health, Custom House, Dublin 1*, and United Kingdom candidates to *International Health Division, Department of Health and Social Security, Alexander Fleming House, London SE1 6BY*.

Address:
Health Division
Council of Europe, Secretariat General
BP431 R6
67006 Strasbourg Cedex
France

[619]

COUNCIL OF EUROPE

Social Fellowship Programme

Individual Social Fellowships (approximately 90) are offered to enable personnel in administration or services responsible for social welfare, social security and problems related to employment and labour to increase their technical knowledge and experience through study in member countries of the Council of Europe and in Finland. The Fellowships are usually tenable for periods from two weeks to one month and provide FF4,140 per month or FF138 per day for shorter periods (rates in 1982), plus travel costs, registration fees and compulsory insurance charges. Candidates must be able to demonstrate high competence in their field and should possess a working knowledge of the language(s) required by the host country or countries concerned.

Coordinated Social Research Fellowships (four) are offered to enable specialists in the social field to take part in study and research projects. Study trips may last for up to 25 days plus three meetings of a total duration of nine days, and are undertaken by a team of four research workers and a director of studies. The theme is chosen each year by the Council's Secretary-General on the recommendation of the Steering Committee for Social Affairs.

Note: The Fellowships are offered to nationals of member countries of the Council of Europe: Austria, Belgium, Cyprus, Denmark, France, Federal Republic of Germany, Greece, Iceland, Ireland, Italy, Liechtenstein, Luxembourg, Malta, Netherlands, Norway, Portugal, Spain, Sweden, Switzerland, Turkey and the United Kingdom; and to nationals of Finland.
Irish candidates should apply to the *Department of Labour, Council of Europe Section, Mespil Road, Dublin 4*, and United Kingdom candidates to *Higher Education Division, British Council, 10 Spring Gardens, London SW1A 2BN*.

Address:
Division of Social Affairs
Council of Europe, Secretariat General
67006 Strasbourg Cedex
France

[620]

COUNCIL OF FOREIGN RELATIONS, INC. *(U.S.A.*

International Affairs Fellowships

Purpose: To bridge the gap between theory and practice in international relations and to encourage the better use of scholarly reflective wisdom in the making of decisions on international problems.

Subjects: Important problems in international affairs and their implications for the interests and policies of the United States, foreign states or international organizations.

No. offered: 10 to 15 Fellowships annually.

Value: Variable according to need, with a maximum of US$25,000 per annum. The Fellowship stipend does not normally exceed the salary relinquished during the Fellowship period.

Tenable normally for a period not to exceed twelve months. The Fellow may find it advantageous to be in residence at the Council for all or part of the Fellowship period, but is not required to do so. Usually the Fellow is not permitted to remain at his home institution during the Fellowship period.

Eligibility: Open to American citizens (or permanent residents who have applied to become citizens), normally between the ages of 27 and 35, with demonstrated intellectual ability and promise who come from the academic, government, business and professional communities. The Ph.D. degree or its equivalent is not a firm requirement.

Note: Application is primarily by invitation. However, people who apply directly and who meet preliminary requirements may also be invited to apply without formal nomination.

Fellowships will not be awarded to support writing or dissertations or research toward the Ph.D., and the program is not intended to support research of which the results will be of primary interest only to scholars or theoreticians.

While the Fellow is not required to produce a book, article or report, it is hoped that some written output will result.

Further information from:
Council on Foreign Relations, Inc.
58 East 68th Street
New York, New York 10021
U.S.A.

[621]

COUNCIL FOR INTERNATIONAL EXCHANGE OF SCHOLARS *(U.S.A.)*

Senior Fulbright Program Advanced Research Grants and Lecturing Appointments

The Council publicizes and conducts the competition and screening of applications for Grants for advanced research and university lectureships abroad, provided by the United States government and supplemented by various foreign governments to citizens of the United States.

The United States government Grants are provided as a part of the educational exchange program administered by the International Communication Agency under the Fulbright-Hays Act (see Agency's entries).

Note: Grants for predoctoral study, research or professional training offered by the United States Government or various foreign governments are administered by the Institute of International Education (see Institute entry). Fulbright grants for scholars of other countries are administered by local Fulbright offices or a local office of the International Communication Agency.

Further information from:
Council for International Exchange of Scholars
11 Dupont Circle, N.W., Suite 300
Washington, D.C. 20036
U.S.A.

[622]

COUNCIL FOR INTERNATIONAL EXCHANGE OF SCHOLARS *(U.S.A.)*

Senior Fulbright Program and Similar Awards, University Lecturing and Advanced Research

Purpose: To offer a variety of programs for international exchange of scholars for university lecturing and advanced research.

Subjects: Unrestricted.

No. offered: At least 500 Awards for U.S. scholars annually, and a similar number of Awards to scholars from abroad.

Value: Varies considerably depending upon program and country involved.

Tenable in more than 100 countries for U.S. scholars, and in the U.S. for scholars from abroad.

Eligibility: Open to citizens of the country from which they are applying, who in most cases, have achieved a postdoctoral or equivalent professional status.

Note: Most of the Awards which the Council helps to administer are a part of the Mutual

Educational and Cultural Exchange Program, conducted under the Fulbright-Hays Act (see *Index of Awards and Awarding Bodies*.

Non-U.S. scholars should contact their respective national agencies for closing dates, application forms and further information. U.S. scholars may obtain application forms by writing the address below.

Closing date: Usually June and July for U.S. scholars.

Further information from:
Council for International Exchange of Scholars
11 Dupont Circle, N.W., Suite 300
Washington, D.C. 20036
U.S.A.

[623]

COUNCIL OF INTERNATIONAL PROGRAMS FOR YOUTH LEADERS AND SOCIAL WORKERS, INC. *(U.S.A.)*

Scholarships are offered to approximately 200 nationals from any country for four to thirteen month program study and field work in the United States. Candidates should be between 23 and 40 years of age and actively engaged as professional or voluntary workers in youth leadership, social work or special education at high school graduate level. Tuition, maintenance and a small weekly allowance are paid. Candidates should apply by September of the preceding year.

Exchange Scholarships: Approximately 25 United States citizens who are social workers or youth leaders may participate in 3-monthly summer exchanges organized with France, the Federal Republic of Germany, Sweden, Turkey, and the United Kingdom. All necessary expenses are paid, plus transportation for the German Scholars only.

Further information from:
Council of International Programs for Youth Leaders and Social Workers
1001 Huron Road
Cleveland, Ohio 44115
U.S.A.

[624]

COUNCIL ON LEGAL EDUCATION OPPORTUNITY *(U.S.A.)*

Stipends

Purpose: To assist educationally and economically disadvantaged students to enter and matriculate in law school.

Subject: Law school preparatory program.

No. offered: 200 Stipends annually.

Value: US$1,000 yearly, for three years.

Tenable for three years at an ABA-accredited law school.

Eligibility: Open to U.S. citizens or permanent residents who are from economically disadvantaged backgrounds and meet federal poverty income guidelines. Candidates should have completed an undergraduate degree program and have taken the LSAT examination.

Not confirmed for 1983.

Further information from:
Ms. G.G. Wessel, Admissions Analyst
Council on Legal Education Opportunity
818 18th Street, N.W.
Suite 940
Washington, D.C. 20007
U.S.A.

[625]

COUNCIL FOR OPPORTUNITY IN GRADUATE MANAGEMENT EDUCATION *(U.S.A.)*

COGME Fellowships

Purpose: To increase the flow of minority group members into positions of managerial responsibility by enabling them to obtain master's degrees in management.

No. offered: Varies according to funds available.

Value: 80% of financial need (tuition fees and living expenses) for the first year of graduate management school.

Tenable at the Universities of California at

Berkeley, Chicago, Pennsylvania, Carnegie-Mellon University, Columbia University, Cornell University, Stanford University, Harvard University, Dartmouth College and Massachusetts Institute of Technology, for the first year of a two year M.B.A. program.

Eligibility: Open to Afro-Americans, American Indians, Asian-Americans and Hispanic Americans who are accepted for admission at one of the member schools. Applicants must possess an undergraduate degree and should be citizens of the United States and legal residents in one of the 50 states or the District of Columbia.

Note: Support for the second year of graduate study will be provided through the financial aid programs of the member schools in the form of fellowships and/or loans.

Further information from:
Council for Opportunity in Graduate Management Education
675 Massachusetts Avenue
Cambridge, Massachusetts 02139
U.S.A.

[626]

COUNCIL FOR SCIENTIFIC AND INDUSTRIAL RESEARCH *(South Africa)*

Post-B.Sc. Bursary for Fourth Study Year

Subjects: Pure and applied sciences.

Value: R1,800 or R2,000 per annum, depending on merit. Bursaries may be increased, subject to review.

Tenable at residential South African universities for full-time study for one year; not renewable.

Eligibility: Open to South African citizens and registered permanent residents who possess a B.Sc. degree. Science candidates should have obtained an aggregate of 60% in their major subjects at the end of their third year of study.

Note: The awarding of a Bursary does not bind the certificate to enter the Council's service. Awards may be supplemented from other sources.

Closing date: 31st March.

Further information from:
University Research Division
Council for Scientific and Industrial Research
P.O. Box 395
Pretoria 0001
South Africa

[627]

COUNCIL FOR SCIENTIFIC AND INDUSTRIAL RESEARCH *(South Africa)*

Post-B.Sc. (Hons.) Bursaries for Fifth and Sixth Study Year

Subjects: Pure and applied sciences.

Value: Either R2,250 or R2,500 per annum depending on merit. Bursaries may be increased, subject to review.

Tenable at residential South African universities for full-time study for one year; renewable.

Eligibility: Open to South African citizens and registered permanent residents who possess a B.Sc. degree. Science candidates should have obtained an aggregate of 60% in their major subjects at the end of their fourth study year. Engineering candidates should have obtained an aggregate of 55% in their final year subjects.

Note: The awarding of a Bursary does not bind the candidate to enter the Council's service. Awards may be supplemented from other sources.

Closing date: 31st March.

Further information from:
University Research Division
Council for Scientific and Industrial Research
P.O. Box 395
Pretoria 0001
South Africa

[628]

COUNCIL FOR SCIENTIFIC AND INDUSTRIAL RESEARCH *(South Africa)*

Post-M.Sc. Bursaries

Subjects: Pure and applied sciences.

Value: R4,000 per annum. Bursaries may be increased, subject to review.

Tenable at residential South African universities for one year; renewable.

Eligibility: Open to South African citizens and registered permanent residents who possess an M.Sc. Post-M.Sc. students from overseas may also be considered if they are registered at a South African university for full-time Ph.D. study.

Note: The awarding of a Bursary does not bind the candidate to enter the Council's service. Awards may be supplemented from other sources.

Closing date: 15th August.

Further information from:
  University Research Division
  Council for Scientific and Industrial
    Research
  P.O. Box 395
  Pretoria 0001
  South Africa

[629]

COUNCIL FOR SCIENTIFIC AND INDUSTRIAL RESEARCH *(South Africa)*

Postdoctoral Bursaries

Subjects: Pure and applied sciences: postdoctoral research.

Value: R5,000 per annum. Bursaries may be increased, subject to review.

Tenable at South African universities or research institutions for one year; not renewable.

Eligibility: Open to South African graduates with a Ph.D. or D.Sc. degree. Overseas candidates may also be considered if they have been accepted by a South African university or research institution.

Note: Applications should be submitted through the sponsoring institution. Recipients are not bound to enter the service of the Council. Awards may be supplemented from other sources.

Closing date: 15th August.

Further information from:
  University Research Division
  Council for Scientific and Industrial
    Research
  P.O. Box 395
  Pretoria 0001
  South Africa

[630]

COUNCIL FOR SCIENTIFIC AND INDUSTRIAL RESEARCH *(South Africa)*

Overseas Bursaries

Subjects: Pure and applied sciences.

Value: Post-M.Sc.—R4,500 per annum, plus class fees up to a maximum of R2,000 per annum and travel; Postdoctorate—R5,500 per annum, plus travel. Bursaries may be increased, subject to review.

Tenable at approved institutions outside South Africa for one to three years. Post-M.Sc. Bursaries are renewable for up to three years depending upon progress. Postdoctorate Bursaries are not renewable.

Eligibility: Open to South African residents possessing an M.Sc., Ph.D. or D.Sc. degree. Candidates must undertake to return to South Africa on completion of studies overseas.

Note: Bursaries are awarded to M.Sc. graduates only if they can prove that facilities for the projects they wish to undertake are not available in South Africa, or are inadequate. Awards may be supplemented from other sources.

Closing dates: 15th March for candidates under the age of 35; 15th August for candidates over the age of 35.

Further information from:
  University Research Division
  Council for Scientific and Industrial
    Research
  P.O. Box 395
  Pretoria 0001
  South Africa

[631]

COUNCIL FOR SCIENTIFIC AND INDUSTRIAL RESEARCH (South Africa)

Special Merit Bursaries

Subjects: Pure and applied sciences.

No. offered: Ten Bursaries annually; more may be awarded if applications merit the increase.

Value: R4,250 for the first year of study, R4,500 for the second, R4,750 for the third. Bursaries may be increased, subject to review.

Tenable for full-time doctoral study at South African institutions.

Eligibility: Open to South African citizens under the age of 30 with M.Sc. degrees or equivalent qualifications, and with outstanding academic records.

Note: Recipients are not bound to enter the service of the Council.

Closing date: 15th August.

Further information from:
University Research Division
Council for Scientific and Industrial Research
P.O. Box 395
Pretoria 0001
South Africa

[632]

COUNCIL FOR SCIENTIFIC AND INDUSTRIAL RESEARCH (South Africa)

Attendance of International Scientific Conferences

Subjects: Pure and applied sciences.

Value: The Council's contributions are currently limited to R850, R1,100, or R1,200 depending upon the country to be visited (the amounts may be increased, subject to review). The sponsoring organization should guarantee a further contribution of at least 30% of the costs.

Tenable at international scientific conferences for up to ten days.

Eligibility: Open to South African university or museum staff members possessing a Ph.D. or D.Sc. degree, who are willing to present a paper at the conference, return to South Africa, and also submit a report.

Note: Applications should be submitted through the university or museum sponsoring the candidate.

Closing dates: 15th March; 15th September.

Further information from:
University Research Division
Council for Scientific and Industrial Research
P.O. Box 395
Pretoria 0001
South Africa

[633]

COUNCIL FOR SCIENTIFIC AND INDUSTRIAL RESEARCH (South Africa)

Equipment Grants, Assistantships, Travel Grants, Running Expenses

Subjects: Pure and applied sciences.

Value: Dependent upon requirements.

Tenable at South African universities and museums.

Eligibility: Open to South African university and museum staff members who have a degree in science.

Note: Applications should be submitted through the institution where the research will be undertaken. Progress reports and copies of publications have to be submitted.

Closing date: 15th August.

Further information from:
University Research Division
Council for Scientific and Industrial Research
P.O. Box 395
Pretoria 0001
South Africa

[634]

COUNCIL FOR SCIENTIFIC AND INDUSTRIAL RESEARCH *(South Africa)*

**National Development Fund for the Building Industry
Institute of South African Architects
Association of South African Quantity Surveyors**

Norman Hanson Awards

These Awards are for research in fields relating to building, viz., building design, construction, materials research, labour, training, or in other fields of interest to the building industry. They are open to graduates in a profession relating to building, including university staff members and other suitably qualified persons in the building and construction industry in South Africa.

Project Grant: This Grant of R2,000 per annum may be awarded to an established research worker at a South African university or other appropriate South African research organization to enable him to undertake a research project of his own choice related to the building and construction industry in South Africa.

Applicants are required to state how the Grant will be used and whether the facilities at their disposal are adequate for research of the nature proposed.

Note: Award values may be increased, subject to review.

Closing date: 31st March.

Further information from:
University Research Division
Council for Scientific and Industrial Research
P.O. Box 395
Pretoria 0001
South Africa

[635]

COUNCIL ON SOCIAL WORK EDUCATION *(U.S.A.)*

Minority Fellowship Program

An unspecified number of doctoral Fellowships are offered in preparation for leadership roles in the field of mental health, and for specialization in research relevant to ethnic minorities.

Awards include tuition, required fees and a monthly stipend. Fellowships are for one year, and may be renewed upon reapplication. Applicants should be American citizens or hold a permanent visa, and be a member of an ethnic minority group, under-represented in social work. Priority will be given to the applicant who has demonstrated financial need, a potential for assuming leadership roles and for success in doctoral studies, an interest in indigenous research, and a commitment to a career in providing services to ethnic minority clients and communities.

Closing date: 15th February.

Further information from:
CSWE Minority Fellowship Program
Council on Social Work Education
111 Eighth Avenue, Suite 501
New York, New York 10011
U.S.A.

[636]

COUNCIL FOR TOBACCO RESEARCH—U.S.A., INC.

Grants

The Council supports investigation of fundamental matters relating to a connection between tobacco use and human health. The importance of independent research by competent investigators is recognized by the Council and Grants are made after consideration of the merits of proposals and of the qualifications of the investigator and his/her institution undertaking the work.

Unless otherwise requested, payments are made quarterly in advance to the institutions at which research is being conducted.

Grantees are required to furnish semi-annual reports on activities. With the consent of the Grantee, the Council may recommend the exchange of interim information between investigators working on different projects of the interim results indicate a relationship between projects.

The Council approves the publication of research results only in accepted medical and scientific journals or before accepted medical or scientific societies. It has no objection to dissemination to the public of conclusions from projects.

Further information from:
  Secretary
  Council for Tobacco Research—
  U.S.A., Inc.
  110 East 59th Street
  New York, New York 10022
  U.S.A.

[637]

COUNTESS OF MUNSTER MUSICAL TRUST *(U.K.)*

Awards

Purpose: To enable students, selected after interview and audition, to pursue a course of specialist or advanced musical studies either in the United Kingdom or abroad.

No. offered: Approximately 60 Awards annually.

Value: By individual assessment to meet tuition fees and maintenance according to need.

Tenable for one year, with possibility of renewal.

Eligibility: Open to United Kingdom or Commonwealth citizens under 30 years of age, who show outstanding musical ability and potential.

Closing date: 31st January.

Further information from:
  Secretary
  Countess of Munster Musical Trust
  Wormley Hill, Godalming
  Surrey
  England GU8 5SG

[638]

CRANBROOK ACADEMY OF ART
(Bloomfield Hills, Michigan)

Tuition Grants

Subjects: Fine and applied arts—specifically, architecture, ceramics, design, fiber, metalsmithing, photography, printmaking, painting and sculpture.

No. offered: Varies.

Value: Up to maximum of US$3,000 per annum.

Tenable at Cranbrook Academy of Art for on-campus education only.

Eligibility: Open to students from most countries in competition with students from the United States, who would qualify for a course of study leading to a M.F.A. or M.Arch. degree. Candidates must demonstrate, through the submission of photographs or slides of their work, significant achievement in the field of art they intend to pursue while attending the Academy.

Note: Scholarships will help defray only a part of the expense of study at the Academy.

The minimum cost of one year's study, exclusive of travelling expenses to and from the Academy is approximately US$8,000 per annum.

Current Academy catalogs are available throughout the world from the offices of the United States Information Service.

Closing date: 1st March.

Further information from:
  Registrar
  Cranbrook Academy of Art
  500 Lone Pine Road, Box 801
  Bloomfield Hills, Michigan 48013
  U.S.A.

[639]

CRIMINOLOGY RESEARCH COUNCIL
(Australia)

Approximately twelve awards are made each year to encourage and assist criminological research in Australia. The awards average A$10,500, are paid in installments in accordance to needs, and are generally tenable for twelve months. Awards may be extended for periods of up to three years.

There are no basic requirements as to citizenship, academic qualifications, age or sex. Applicants need only to be Australian residents or visitors (actual or intending) who are pursuing or intend to pursue studies of consequence to the furtherance of criminological research in Australia.

Note: The Council does not ordinarily entertain applications involving travelling expenses outside of Australia. Applications are considered four of five times yearly.

Further information from:
  Assistant Secretary
  Criminological Research Council
  P.O. Box 28
  Woden, A.C.T.
  Australia 2606

[640]

CROMBIE SCHOLARSHIP *(U.K.)*

Crombie Scholarship in Biblical Criticism

No. offered: One Scholarship annually.

Value: £100.

Tenable at an approved Scottish university for one year.

Eligibility: Open to persons possessing a first- or second-class honours degree from a university in the United Kingdom or Ireland.

Note: The Scholarship is made through a competitive written examination held at St. Mary's College, St. Andrews University, Scotland, in September.

Closing date: 1st August.

Further information from:
  Crombie Scholarship
  c/o Messrs. J. and F. Anderson
  48 Castle Street
  Edinburgh
  Scotland EH2 3LX

[641]

ALBERTO CURCI FOUNDATION *(Italy)*

International Violin Competition

One Prize each of 3,000,000 lire, 1,500,000 lire, and 750,000 lire, and five Prizes of 200,000 lire each, are awarded to violinists of any nationality who are less than 32 years of age on 31st October of the Competition year. The annual Competition takes place during the month of November in Naples.

Closing date: 30th June.

Further information from:
  Competition Secretary
  Alberto Curci Foundation
  Via Nardones, 8
  80132 Naples
  Italy

[642]

CURTIS INSTITUTE OF MUSIC
(Philadelphia)

Curtis Institute Scholarships

Subject: Music.

No. offered: As vacancies occur.

Value: US$6,500 per school year, per award.

Tenable at the Institute for the duration of approved study.

Eligibility: Open to U.S. and foreign nationals who are under 21 years of age. All students at the Institute are admitted on a Scholarship basis. Admission is limited to those whose musical ability shows promise of development to a high quality. Acceptability is based on talent and not degree of attainment.

Note: The Institute offers its students full tuition Scholarships. Fees are required, however, for application, audition and annual registration. The Institute does not provide travel assistance.

Closing date: 15th January.

Further information from:
  Curtis Institute of Music
  Admissions Officer
  1726 Locust Street
  Philadelphia, Pennsylvania 19103
  U.S.A.

[643]

CYSTIC FIBROSIS FOUNDATION *(U.S.A.)*

Awards and Grants

New Investigator Awards of up to US$40,000 per annum for two years are available to provide initial research support to basic scientists at the beginning of their careers. Applicants should have two years of postdoctoral experience in an area related to Cystic Fibrosis research and be able to commit themselves, during the award period, to such research for at least 70% of the time. Applicants cannot have been the recipient of a National Institute of Health Research Career Development Award. *Closing dates:* 1st April and 1st September.

Research Scholar Award is intended to encourage a sustained commitment to Cystic Fibrosis and related diseases on the part of an individual already engaged in an independent, creative, research career. Awards are tenable for up to three years with a maximum value of US$75,000 per annum, up to US$30,000 of which per year may be used as a stipend. *Closing date:* 1st September.

Research Grants of up to US$50,000 per annum, for up to two years are offered in support of high-quality research in basic laboratory investigation and clinical management of Cystic Fibrosis and related pulmonary and G.I. diseases of children and young adults. The Grants are intended to be used as "seed money" to help the investigator obtain preliminary data in order to be more competitive in applying for support through other funding agencies. *Closing dates:* 1st April and 1st September.

Further information from:
Cystic Fibrosis Foundation
Medical Department
Office of Grants Management
6000 Executive Boulevard
Suite 309
Rockville, Maryland 20852
U.S.A.

[644]

CYSTIC FIBROSIS FOUNDATION *(U.S.A.)*

CFF Communications Award: Two Awards, one in the category of print and one for broadcast, are offered annually to recognize and encourage outstanding news feature reporting about Cystic Fibrosis and the consequences of this disease. The Awards of US$1,000 each are made for the winning entries which have been published or broadcast in the United States during the period from 1st January of the previous year through 30th June of the year in which the Awards are given. Entries may be submitted by writers, reporters, editors, producers, and publishers, as well as by Cystic Fibrosis chapters on behalf of and with the permission of the author. Applications may be obtained from local Cystic Fibrosis chapters or by writing to the address below.

Closing date: 15th July.

Further information from:
Cystic Fibrosis Foundation
6000 Executive Boulevard
Suite 309
Rockville, Maryland 20852
U.S.A.

[645]

CYSTIC FIBROSIS FOUNDATION *(U.S.A.)*

Fellowships and Traineeships

Clinical Fellowships of up to US$15,400 for the first year and up to US$16,400 for the second year are awarded to prepare eligible physicians for careers in academic pulmonology or gastroenterology. Applicants should be U.S. citizens or have permanent resident visas, and be physicians with at least two years of training in pediatrics (PL1, PL2) or board eligibility in internal medicine. *Closing date:* 1st October.

Research Fellowships are offered for postdoctoral training in basic research. Fellowships are awarded annually and may be renewed for a second year. The basic Fellowship is US$15,000 per annum plus US$500 for each year of relevant postdoctoral experience, up to a maximum of three years. A supplement of US$500 is given for each dependent, up to a maximum of three. *Closing date:* 1st September.

Student Traineeships are offered twice yearly to introduce students at the undergraduate or graduate level who may still be uncommitted to a career goal, to Cystic Fibrosis research. Traineeships are for a minimum period of ten weeks, and are in the amount of US$1,500. A maximum of US$300 of the stipend may be used toward laboratory expenses. *Closing dates:* 1st February and 1st October.

Further information from:
  Cystic Fibrosis Foundation
  Office of Grants Management
  Medical Department
  6000 Executive Boulevard
  Suite 309
  Rockville, Maryland 20852
  U.S.A.

[646]

CYSTIC FIBROSIS RESEARCH TRUST
(U.K.)

Research Grants

Approximately £650,000 is available each year for clinical and fundamental research strictly related to cystic fibrosis. Grants, for up to three years but subject to annual renewal, are made to individuals to cover such matters as: personal salaries; graduate and technical assistance; supplies and equipment, including special apparatus.

Applications must be made through heads of department or consultants in charge. In the first instance, a letter sending out the details and purposes of the research should be sent to the Executive Director. If, after consideration, the research is thought appropriate to cystic fibrosis an application form will be forwarded for completion. The Research Committee meets four times a year at irregular intervals to consider applications.

Further information from:
  Executive Director
  Cystic Fibrosis Research Trust
  5 Blyth Road
  Bromley, Kent
  England BR1 3RS

D

See *How to Use The Grants Register*, page ix

[647]

J.W. DAFOE FOUNDATION *(Canada)*

Dafoe Fellowships

Purpose: To assist in the development of a greater flow of 'laborers' in the international field, to work for the creation of healthy, hospitable climates for international cooperation.

Subjects: Political science, economics, diplomatic and other history.

No. offered: Two Fellowships annually.

Value: Can$5,000 per annum.

Tenable at the University of Manitoba, Winnipeg, or the University of British Columbia, Vancouver.

Eligibility: Open to graduate stdents from universities in Canada, the United States, and overseas.

Note: Candidates should file initial enquiries and final applications with the registrar of the university where graduate studies are to be undertaken.
   The universities are then responsible for the nomination of candidates to the Dafoe Foundation prior to its annual meeting in May.
   Each university determines the conditions of application.

Not confirmed for 1983.

Further information from:
   J.W. Dafoe Foundation
   c/o Department of History
   University of Manitoba
   Winnipeg, Manitoba
   Canada R3T 2N2

[648]

DAIRYING RESEARCH COMMITTEE *(Australia)*

Dairy Education Scheme

The Dairy Education Scheme is a comprehensive program comprising Dairy Industry Bursaries, Postgraduate Studentships and Overseas Postgraduate Travel Grants. This program was developed to serve the needs of the dairy industry from the factory operative level through to the technologist, engineer, factory manager, agricultural extension worker and more mature research scientists engaged in dairy research in Australia.

Dairy Industry Bursaries: These awards provide for tertiary training and are designed to attract qualified personnel to the dairy industry and orient training towards the need of industry and relevant organisations.

Overseas Postgraduate Travel Grants: These are normally awarded to graduate personnel working on dairy research projects to facilitate study tours of research institutions involved in related work.

Postgraduate Studentships: Assistance and incentive is provided through these awards for persons already engaged in dairy research to further develop their skills. These are available to mature graduates currently involved in dairy research projects, requiring assistance to undertake additional studies which would materially enhance the effectiveness of their future research; or to postgraduate students engaged in high priority dairy research projects.

Study Grants: These awards are intended to provide financial assistance to research workers, extension officers and factory technologists wishing to visit other research groups within Australia, to seek and study new techniques or investigate the application of findings for adoption by industry.

Not confirmed for 1983.

Further information from:
Dairying Research Committee
576 St. Kilda Road
Melbourne, Victoria
Australia 3004

[649]

DALLAS MORNING NEWS *(U.S.A.)*

Dallas News G.B. Dealey Awards

Competitions in piano and strings, and in voice are held annually to assist young artists toward a professional career. Three Prizes are awarded in each category: piano and strings—1st Prize of *US*$1,500, a bronze medal and appearances with the Dallas Symphony Orchestra for one season as soloist, 2nd Prize of *US*$750, 3rd Prize of *US*$500; voice—1st Prize of *US*$1,000, a bronze medal and a contract for a featured role with the Dallas Civic Opera, 2nd Prize of *US*$500, 3rd Prize of *US*$350. Finalists of both categories will receive engraved certificates.

Open to all serious students of piano, violin, cello and voice who are studying in the U.S. and are between the ages of 17 and 28 for the instrumental competition, and the ages of 20 and 30 for the vocal competition, as of 10th June of the year in which the Awards are given.

Not confirmed for 1983.

Further information from:
Dallas Morning News
G.B. Dealey Awards
P.O. Box 2977
Dallas, Texas 75221
U.S.A.

[650]

DALLAS THEATER CENTER *(Texas)*
Graduate Drama School of Trinity University

Scholarships

Subjects: MFA degree program in theater, with emphasis on practical application.

No. offered: Approximately 30 Scholarships annually.

Value: Up to a maximum of *US*$1,600 per semester which is deducted from tuition.

Tenable at the Center, renewable for a second year.

Eligibility: Candidates must have a B.A. or B.F.A. degree in theater and must be of high academic standing. A resumé of the applicant's total theater training and experience must be provided along with references. Candidates must be accepted by Trinity University, San Antonio, Texas.

Closing date: 15th February.

Further information from:
Graduate Registrar
Dallas Theater Center
3636 Turtle Creek Boulevard
Dallas, Texas 75219
U.S.A.

[651]

MINISTRY OF EDUCATION

Danish Government Scholarships

Purpose: To enable non-Danish persons to study at Danish universities or other institutions of higher learning.

Subjects: Unrestricted.

Value: Annual Scholarships are as follows: for undergraduates: 2,660 Danish kroner per month. For research workers: 3,065 Danish kroner per month. Candidates from developing countries will furthermore receive a contribution towards travel expenses.

Tenable at institutions of higher learning in Denmark. Scholarships are normally of eight months' duration (one academic year).

Eligibility: Open to undergraduates and graduates from the following countries: Australia, Austria, Belgium, Bulgaria, Canada, China, Czechoslovakia, Egypt, Finland, France, East Germany, West Germany, Greece, Hungary, Iceland, India, Iran, Ireland, Israel, Italy, Japan, Republic of Korea, Netherlands, Poland, Portugal, Romania, Spain, Sweden, Switzerland, Thailand, Turkey, U.S.S.R., United Kingdom and Yugoslavia. Candidates must have a knowledge of Danish, English or German.

Note: Ten Scholarships are earmarked annually for graduate applicants from developing countries.

Candidates should apply through the appropriate government agency in their own country (usually the Ministry of Education or the Ministry of Foreign Affairs). United Kingdom candidates should apply by 8th February, to the *British Council, 10 Spring Gardens, London SW1A 2BN*. Each candidate must be approved by the Danish Ministry of Education, and approval is subject to acceptance by the institution concerned. However, when a candidate has been notified of acceptance by the Ministry, this condition can be regarded as having been fulfilled.

Closing dates: 1st April each year. Applications for Scholarships in theoretical physics and in fine arts should be received by the Danish Ministry of Education before 1st March.

Further information from:
   International Relations Division,
     Scholarship Section
   Danish Ministry of Education
   Frederiksholms Kanal 27 F
   1220 Copenhagen K
   Denmark

[652]

DANISH RESEARCH COUNCILS

Grants

Purpose: To strengthen research in Denmark by making it possible for Danish research workers to study inside or outside Denmark, and (if it is important for Danish research) for persons from other countries who are sponsored by suitably qualified Danish citizens to work within a Danish institute for a period of time.

Subjects: Natural sciences, medical sciences, agricultural and veterinary sciences, social sciences, art and humanities, applied science and industrial research.

No. offered: About 50 Grants twice a year.

Value: According to Danish wages for persons of corresponding academic training.

Tenable in Danish or foreign institutes normally for periods of not more than one year; renewable once or twice.

Eligibility: Open to Danish graduate research workers and to foreign research workers at a postdoctoral level sponsored by a Danish institute. For renewal, the award-holder must show satisfactory progress, and, in the case of a foreign Grantee, must satisfy the Council in question that it is important for Danish research that his stay be extended.

Note: Foreign applicants must submit their applications through a Danish sponsor.

These awards are offered by the Danish Natural Science Research Council, the Danish Medical Science Research Council, the Danish Agricultural and Veterinary Research Council, the Danish Social Science Research Council, the Danish Research Council for the Humanities, and the Danish Council for Scientific and Industrial Research.

Closing dates: 15th March; 1st October.

Further information from:
   Forskningssekretariatet
   Holmens Kanal 7
   1060 Copenhagen K
   Denmark

[653]

DARMSTADT INTERNATIONAL MUSIC INSTITUTE *(West Germany)*

Scholarships for Vacation Courses

International Vacation Courses in new music are held for two weeks in the summer of even-numbered years. The programme includes lectures on composition and interpretation, concerts, work-studies, etc. The Course is open to professionals in the field of music who are at least 18 years of age. Instruction is in Germany, English and French. A limited number of Scholarships are available to participants of all countries. As well, the *Kranichsteiner Music Prize* is awarded to a Course participant. Closing date for Course application is 1st May.

Further information from:
   Internationales Musikinstitut Darmstadt
   Nieder-Ramstädter Strasse 190
   D-6100 Darmstadt
   West Germany

[654]

DARTMOUTH STREET TRUST *(U.K.)*

Research Grants

Grants are awarded for research in social, economic and political fields. Grants are not made for course work.

Further information from:
Dartmouth Street Trust
11 Dartmouth Street
London
England SW1H 9BN

[655]

SHELBY CULLOM DAVIS CENTER FOR HISTORICAL STUDIES *(Princeton, New Jersey)*

Research Fellowships

A limited number of Fellowships are offered annually for one or two semesters of research. Open to highly recommended younger scholars and senior scholars with established reputations. Candidates should have completed their dissertation and have a full-time, paid position to return to upon completion of the Fellowship teaching experience.

Note: Fellows are expected to live in Princeton in order to take an active part in the intellectual interchange with other Seminar members.

Closing date: 1st December.

Further information from:
Shelby Cullom Davis Center for Historical Studies
Princeton University
129 Dickson Hall
Princeton, New Jersey 08544
U.S.A.

[656]

DeBAKEY MEDICAL FOUNDATION *(U.S.A.)*

Awards

Subjects: Fellowships and scholarships for medical study or research, grants for institutional research and funds for hospital care projects. Support is given to all areas of medical research with emphasis on investigations that have direct clinical application, particularly in the field of cardiovascular disease. Preference is given to projects with potential for new and expanded knowledge or technological advancement.

Value: Assistance varies in amount, depending on the needs and nature of the request.

Eligibility: Open to qualified individuals with appropriate interests.

Closing date: Applications may be submitted at any time and are considered on an individual basis.

Further information from:
DeBakey Medical Foundation
1200 Moursund Avenue
Houston, Texas 77030
U.S.A.

[657]

EUGENE V. DEBS FOUNDATION *(U.S.A.)*

Bryant Spann Memorial Prize

The Prize of US$750 (or US$375 if divided) is offered annually for an article on the theme of social justice in the tradition of Eugene V. Debs, an active protester against social injustice.

Articles, which should be submitted by April 30th, may be published (since 1976) or unpublished. If unpublished, the entry should be typed, double space, on manuscript paper.

Announcement of the Prize-winning work(s) will be made in the Fall.

Further information from:
Bryant Spann Memorial Prize Committee
Eugene V. Debs Foundation
c/o Department of History
Indiana State University
Terre Haute, Indiana 47809
U.S.A.

[658]

GLADYS KRIEBLE DELMAS FOUNDATION *(U.S.A.)*

Fellowships

Subjects: The history of Venice and the former Venetian empire in its various aspects—art, architecture, archaeology, theatre, music, literature, natural science, political science, economics, the law; also studies related to the contemporary Venetian environment such as ecology, oceanography, urban planning and rehabilitation.

No. offered: Usually between 15 and 25 Fellowships annually.

Value: From US$500 up to a maximum of US$10,000 for a full academic year. At the discretion of the trustees and advisory board of the Foundation, funds may be made available for aid in publication of results.

Tenable in Venice for up to one academic year.

Eligibility: Open to United States citizens who have some experience in advance research, and, if graduate students, have fulfilled all doctoral requirements except for completion of the dissertation.

Note: Candidates should obtain the Foundation's instruction sheet for applications.

Closing date: 15th January.

Further information from:
Gladys Krieble Delmas Foundation
40 Wall Street
New York, New York 10005
U.S.A.

[659]

DELTA KAPPA GAMMA SOCIETY INTERNATIONAL *(U.S.A.)*

Educator's Award

One Award of US$5,000 is offered annually for a book recognized as a substantive contribution to education which may influence future directions in the profession. Women in the United States, Puerto Rico, Canada, Norway, El Salvador, Finland, Guatemala, Iceland, the Netherlands, Great Britain, Mexico and Sweden whose books have been copyrighted in their first edition during the year preceding the Award, may apply. Methods and skills books, textbooks, unpublished manuscripts and books written specifically for children are not considered. In the case of dual authorship, the prize is divided in the same manner as royalties are divided by the Awardees' publisher.

Note: The winning book must be published or translated into English within a prescribed one-year period.

Closing date: 1st February.

Further information from:
Executive Secretary
Delta Kappa Gamma Society
International
P.O. Box 1589
Austin, Texas 78767
U.S.A.

[660]

DENTAL ASSOCIATION OF SOUTH AFRICA

Elida-Gibbs Postgraduate Fellowship

Purpose: To promote dental research and ensure its continuation in South Africa.

Subjects: Any biological field related to dentistry.

No. offered: One Fellowship annually.

Value: Up to a maximum of R4,000.

Tenable in South Africa, unless facilities are not available, for one year; renewable in special circumstances.

Eligibility: Open to South African nationals, normally resident in South Africa, who are either (a) dentists registered with the South African Medical and Dental Council, wishing to qualify themselves further or to equip themselves for research by taking an additional degree, or (b) suitably qualified persons wishing to concentrate on dental research.

Note: Applications must be made on an official application form and must be supported by and submitted through a university or another such institution.
 An award may be made for research overseas, provided that the application is accompanied by a statement from the sponsoring institution that the proposed project can best be carried out in another country. A Fellow working overseas must undertake to return to South Africa for a minimum period of three

years after completing his project under the award, or refund to the Fellowship Fund any money he has received.

Closing date: 30th September.

Further information from:
Executive Secretary
Dental Association of South Africa
Private Bag 1
2041 Houghton
South Africa

[661]

DENTAL ASSOCIATION OF SOUTH AFRICA

J.C. Middleton-Shaw Postgraduate Fellowship

Purpose: To provide support for individuals wishing to pursue dental education at a postgraduate level.

Subjects: Any aspect of dentistry, including the study of teaching methods or dental administration. The award is specifically not meant to support research or the study of research techniques.

No. offered: One Fellowship annually.

Value: Approximately R4,000.

Tenable in South Africa, unless facilities are not available.

Eligibility: Open to graduates of a South African dental school or to dentists practising in South Africa.
Applicants must be sponsored by a South African dental school.

Closing date: 30th September.

Further information from:
Executive Secretary
Dental Association of South Africa
Private Bag 1
2041 Houghton
South Africa

[662]

DEPARTMENT OF ABORIGINAL AFFAIRS *(Australia)*

Research Grants

Purpose: To collect data which will help in determining government policy on Aboriginal advancement; to assist Aboriginal communities to tackle recognised problems hampering Aboriginal advancement; and to improve the economic and social situation of Australia's Aboriginal population.

No. offered: Approximately six Grants annually.

Value: Up to A$30,000 per annum, paid in quarterly installments.

Tenable in Australia for one year; renewable subject to satisfactory progress.

Criteria: The Aboriginals concerned must be consulted and support the research being undertaken in their community; Aboriginal communities must be the main beneficiaries of the research; and wherever possible Aboriginals should be employed in conducting the research.
Additional, specific conditions may be applied to particular projects.
Upon selection, researchers will be expected to submit a research plan which should incorporate a work plan to show estimated dates for reaching specific objectives. Progress reports will also be required.

Closing date: October each year.

Further information from:
Assistant Secretary, Evaluating Branch
Department of Aboriginal Affairs
P.O. Box 17
Woden, A.C.T.
Australia 2606

[663]

DEPARTMENT OF AGRICULTURE AND FISHERIES FOR SCOTLAND

Postgraduate Agricultural Studentships

Subjects: Agriculture—husbandry, farm management, economics, statistics, marketing, engineering, estate management, agricultural science, and agricultural extension.

Value: A maintenance allowance, compulsory fees, certain travel and other allowances—in accordance with official rates and conditions for U.K. government Studentships. This is a special allowance for overseas work.

Tenable at approved United Kingdom universities or other institutions, and preferably not at the university where the Student's first degree has been undertaken. When necessary, Students may study abroad.

Eligibility: Open to citizens of the United Kingdom and Colonies or Commonwealth citizens who have been ordinarily resident in Scotland throughout the period of three years preceding the date of application. The standard normally required is first or upper second class in an honours degree, but a lower class of honours degree may be acceptable in the case of applicants wishing to take an advanced course of instruction. Candidates should be under 27 years of age on 1st October in the year of application, but occasionally applications are considered on behalf of older candidates.

Note: Application should be made in duplicate on the prescribed form obtainable from the Department. English and Welsh applicants should apply to the Ministry of Agriculture, Fisheries and Food in London [q.v.]. Northern Irish applicants should apply to the Department of Agriculture for Northern Ireland in Belfast.

Closing date: End of February.

Further information from:
Department of Agriculture and Fisheries for Scotland
Room 619, Chesser House
500 Gorgie Road
Edinburgh
Scotland EH11 3AW

[664]

DEPARTMENT OF EDUCATION *(Australia)*

Australian-European Awards Program

Visiting Fellowships: Four Fellowships are awarded annually to enable eminent overseas scholars and educationalists to visit Australia for the purposes of viewing recent developments in the Fellow's particular field of interest, and to participate in discussions with senior academics and personnel in relevant organizations on subjects of mutual interest. The Fellowships, which may be held concurrently with other awards, are open to distinguished academics from any European country and are tenable for one to three months. The award value is in the amount of A$53 per day, an establishment allowance of A$100 paid on arrival, plus economy class to and from Australia as well as within the country, as required by the program. Fellowships are not subject to Australian income tax. These awards, provided by the Australian government, are not open to personal application and are made by direct invitation only.

Scholarships: Sixteen Scholarships are awarded annually to enable graduates to undertake programs of postgraduate study or research at suitable Australian institutions of literary studies. Tenable for one academic year (9 months), with the possibility of extension for three additional months. The Scholarships have a value of A$4,200 per annum. An allowance of A$1,632.80 per annum is given for accompanying dependent wives, and A$390 per annum for each accompanying dependent child. Allowances are paid fortnightly. In addition, an establishment allowance of A$162 is paid on arrival and there is a A$200 per annum equipment allowance as well as a A$100 vacation travel allowance. All fares and travelling within Australia, essential to the Scholar's study, are paid. The Australian government pays all compulsory fees. Candidates should usually be no more than twenty-eight years of age and should be a graduate of one of the following European countries: Austria, Belgium, Denmark, the Federal Republic of Germany, Finland, France, Greece, Hungary, Ireland, Italy, the Netherlands, Switzerland, or Yugoslavia.

Further information on the Program and how to apply may be obtained from the Australian embassy in the candidate's home country, or by writing to the Department.

Closing date: 31st May of the year preceding commencement of tenure.

Not confirmed for 1983.

Further information from:
Secretary
Australian European Awards Program
Department of Education
P.O. Box 826
Woden, A.C.T.
Australia 2606

[665]

DEPARTMENT OF EDUCATION *(Australia)*

Postgraduate Awards at Colleges of Advanced Education

Purpose: To provide opportunities for students who have gained a first degree or diploma, been in employment for some years, and who wish to improve their professional competence in their fields.

Subjects: Unrestricted, although the course must be approved.

Value: A$4,200 per annum living allowance, paid fortnightly, plus dependents, establishment, thesis and travel allowances.

Tenable at advanced education institutions in Australia for full-time study in approved courses leading to the master's degree by either research or course work. A limited period of supervised study overseas of up to twelve months, may be approved for those studying for a degree by research.

Eligibility: Open to Australian citizens or persons with permanent resident status preferably with some work experience. People without employment experience may also apply.

Note: Applications are to be made to the institution concerned, which in turn nominates applicants for consideration by a selection committee.

Not confirmed for 1983.

Further information from:
Assistant Secretary
Tertiary Student Assistance Branch
Department of Education
P.O. Box 826
Woden, A.C.T.
Australia 2606

[666]

DEPARTMENT OF EDUCATION *(Australia)*

Postgraduate Course Awards

Purpose: To provide opportunities for further study to individuals who have gained a first degree, been in employment for some years, and who wish to improve their professional competence in their fields.

Subjects: Unrestricted, although the course must be approved by the Minister.

No. offered: Varies. 125 Awards in 1980.

Value: A$4,200 per annum living allowance, plus dependents', travel, establishment and thesis allowances. Allowances are subject to Australian income tax.

Tenable in universities in Australia for full-time study in approved courses leading to the master's degree by course work.

Eligibility: Open to Australian citizens or persons with permanent resident status. Preference is given to applicants with employment experience although individuals without this are eligible to be considered.

Note: Nominations are to be made to the university concerned which in turn nominates applicants for consideration by a central selection committee.

Not confirmed for 1983.

Further information from:
Assistant Secretary
Tertiary Student Assistance Branch
Department of Education
P.O. Box 826
Woden, A.C.T.
Australia 2606

[667]

DEPARTMENT OF EDUCATION *(Australia)*

Postgraduate Research Awards

Subjects: Unrestricted; full-time research normally leading to a master's or Ph.D. degree.

No. offered: Varies. 555 Awards in 1980.

Value: A living allowance at the rate of A$4,200 per annum; dependents' allowances; a travel allowance plus an establishment allowance in certain cases; and a thesis allowance. Allowances are subject to Australian income tax.

Tenable at universities in Australia, and in certain cases, abroad (approval must be obtained for study overseas and is available for up to twelve months). A candidate for a master's degree may hold an award for a period not in excess of two years; a Ph.D. candidate may hold an award for three years, and an extension for a fourth year may be granted.

Eligibility: Open to citizens of Australia or persons with permanent resident status who are suitably qualified to undertake full-time research. Applicants should hold, or expect to obtain, at least an upper second class honours degree or its equivalent. A person with a master's degree may apply to undertake research towards a Ph.D.

Note: Award holders may, with the approval of their supervisors, engage in a limited amount of paid part-time employment, provided that such employment does not interfere with their study programme, nor exceed six hours in any one week, or a total of 180 hours in a year.

Candidates should apply to the university concerned.

Closing date: 31st October.

Not confirmed for 1983.

Further information from:
 Assistant Secretary
 Tertiary Students Assistance Branch
 Department of Education
 P.O. Box 826
 Woden, A.C.T.
 Australia 2606

[668]

DEPARTMENT OF EDUCATION *(Australia)*

ANZAC Fellowships

Purpose: To enable Australian citizens who have achieved distinction or have shown potential in the professions, trade, business, public service, or the arts, to train, study or further their professional experience in New Zealand.

Subjects: Unrestricted; programs may include practical experience, investigation and research and are not restricted to academics.

Value: Maintenance allowance plus allowance for spouse and dependent children, return air fares, approved travel costs, tuition and fees, and medical insurance.

Tenable in New Zealand for one year, or where appropriate, for shorter periods of not less than three months.

Eligibility: Open to Australian citizens, preferably under 45 years of age. Fellows should return to Australia on completion of their studies.

Note: These ANZAC Fellowships are offered by the New Zealand Government. The New Zealand Government also participates in the scheme by making similar awards available annually to New Zealanders [see Department of Internal Affairs, New Zealand].

Senior Anzac Fellowships are made available for Australians and New Zealanders who have achieved eminence in their fields, academics being considered equally with other citizens. These Fellowships are usually tenable for up to three months, but may be extended. They are intended to encourage dissemination of knowledge through personal contact, lecture tours, etc. in New Zealand (for Australians) and in Australia (for New Zealanders). Senior Fellowships are by invitation only.

Closing date: Normally early in August.

Further information from:
 Secretary
 ANZAC Fellowships
 Department of Education
 P.O. Box 826
 Woden, A.C.T.
 Australia 2606

[669]

DEPARTMENT OF EDUCATION *(Australia)*
Commonwealth Scholarship and Fellowship Plan—In Australia

Visiting Fellowships

Purpose: To enable eminent overseas scholars and educationists to visit Australia for discussion with senior academics and personnel in relevant organisations on subjects of mutual interest in the field of education or educational administration, and to see something of recent developments in the Fellow's particular field of interest. The Fellowships are provided by the Australian government and fall within the framework of the Commonwealth Scholarship and Fellowship Plan [q.v.].

No. offered: Four Fellowships annually.

Value: A maintenance allowance of A$53 per day, economy class international travel and travel within Australia as required by the program, establishment allowance of A$100 paid on arrival. The Fellowships are not subject to Australian income tax.

Tenable for periods of from one to three months. Program of visits arranged by the Department of Education in consultation with the Fellow and his nominator. The Fellowships may be held concurrently with other awards or income.

Eligibility: Open to citizens of the United Kingdom, Canada, and New Zealand who are distinguished in an academic field of study.

Note: Awards are made by direct invitation, and are not open for personal application.

Further information from:
  Secretary
  Commonwealth Scholarship and
    Fellowship Plan
  Department of Education
  P.O. Box 826
  Woden, A.C.T.
  Australia 2606

[670]

DEPARTMENT OF EDUCATION *(Australia)*
Commonwealth Scholarship and Fellowship Plan—in Australia

Visiting Professorships

Purpose: To enable Commonwealth professors to visit Australia to teach or undertake personal research. The Professorships are provided by the Australian government and fall within the framework of the Commonwealth Scholarship and Fellowship Plan [q.v.].

Subjects: Unrestricted.

No. offered: Three Professorships annually.

Value: Cost of economy class air travel to and from Australia. Other expenses are paid by the receiving institution.

Tenable at a university in Australia for one academic year; not renewable. The Professorships may be held concurrently with other awards.

Eligibility: Open to distinguished professors from the United Kingdom, Canada and New Zealand.

Note: Awards are made by direct invitation, and are not open for personal application. Nominations are made by Australian universities on a rotational basis.

Further information from:
  Secretary
  Commonwealth Scholarship and
    Fellowship Plan
  Department of Education
  P.O. Box 826
  Woden, A.C.T.
  Australia 2606

[671]

DEPARTMENT OF EDUCATION *(Australia)*
Commonwealth Scholarship and Fellowship Plan—in Australia

Scholarships

Purpose: To enable young graduates of high intellectual promise who may be expected to make a signifiant contribution to life in their own countries, to undertake postgraduate studies in Australia. The Scholarships are provided by the Australian government and fall within the scope of the Commonwealth Scholarship and Fellowship Plan [q.v.].

Subjects: All tertiary studies.

No. offered: Up to 70 new Scholarships offered annually. At any one time, up to 150 award-holders may be in Australia.

Value: A living allowance of A$4,200 per annum; marriage allowance of A$1,632.80 per annum for accompanying dependent wife; allowance of A$390 per annum for each dependent child; all the above paid fortnightly. Establishment allowance of A$162 paid on arrival; all compulsory fees paid by the Australian government, equipment allowance of A$200 per annum; A$100 vacation travel allowance for duration of award; fares and travelling allowance for travel within Australia essential to the Scholar's study program.

Tenable at tertiary institutions in Australia for two or three academic years, with possibility of extension if required and justified by the Scholar's record.

Eligibility: Open to Commonwealth citizens or British protected persons resident in countries of the Commonwealth other than Australia. Usually, candidates should be no more than 28 years of age.

Applications must be made through the appropriate agency in the country of the candidate's normal residence. [See entry for Commonwealth Scholarship and Fellowship Plan].

Closing date for receipt of applications is 30th July of the year preceding commencement of tenure.

Not confirmed for 1983.

Further information from:
 Secretary
 Commonwealth Scholarship and
   Fellowship Plan
 Department of Education
 P.O. Box 826
 Woden, A.C.T.
 Australia 2606

[672]

DEPARTMENT OF EDUCATION *(Ireland)*

Postdoctoral Research Fellowships

Subjects: Science and engineering.

No. offered: Up to 10 Fellowships annually.

Value: £5,392—£6,081 per annum; in the case of engineers or technologists whose industrial experience and special circumstances warrant it, £7,056 per annum.

Tenable at University College, Dublin; University College, Cork; University College, Galway; Trinity College, Dublin; the Agricultural Institute; Institute for Industrial Research and Standards; or St. Patrick's College, Maynooth.

Duration: Subject to satisfactory performance, for two years in the first instance, with possibility of extension to three years.

Eligibility: Open to nationals of all countries under 30 years of age, and preferably under 28 years of age, who hold a Ph.D. degree, or have equivalent research experience.

Applications will be considered from engineers and technologists with suitable industrial experience. Preference will be given to candidates proposing to work in institutions other than those in which they are working at the time of application.

Closing date: 20th March.

Further information from:
 Secretary
 Department of Education
 Marlborough Street
 Dublin 1
 Ireland

[673]

DEPARTMENT OF EDUCATION *(Ireland)*

Exchange Scholarships

Scholarships are offered by the Government of Ireland to enable students of the following countries to study in Ireland: Austria, Belgium, Denmark, Finland, France, West Germany, Italy, Japan, Netherlands, Norway, Spain, and Switzerland. Scholarships for all countries are for one academic year and carry a stipend of £1,050 plus fees. In addition, summer school scholarships are offered to students of Spain and Italy, each having a value of £170; a 4-month scholarship of £525 plus fees is also offered to a Norwegian student. Under bilateral arrangements these countries offer similar scholarships to Irish students.

See also Scholarship Exchange Board.

Further information from:
 Secretary
 Department of Education
 Marlborough Street
 Dublin 1
 Ireland

[674]

DEPARTMENT OF EDUCATION *(Northern Ireland)*

Postgraduate Studentships and Bursaries

The Department awards on a competitive basis, postgraduate studentships and bursaries corresponding to the research, advanced course and diploma awards made by the department of Education and Science (England and Wales), the Science and Engineering Research Council, the Social Science Research Council, and the Natural Environment Research Council.

The rules under which awards are made are adapted from the Department of Education and Science or appropriate Research Council rules. The provisions in Northern Ireland, including details of the value per award, duration of award and terms of eligibility, are kept as far as possible in line with those pertaining in other parts of the United Kingdom. However, candidates should be ordinarily resident in Northrn Ireland and the closing date each year for the receipt of completed applications for these awards, i.e. awards tenable at institutions in Great Britain and the Republic of Ireland is 1st May (forms available in March from the Department of Education), and for quota awards, i.e. awards tenable at institutions in Northern Ireland (forms available from the institution concerned), is 1st August of each year. The number of awards available each year is in proportion to the number available in Great Britain.

Further information from:
   Department of Education
   Rathgael House, Balloo Road
   Bangor, County Down
   Norther Ireland

[675]

DEPARTMENT OF EDUCATION AND SCIENCE *(England and Wales)*

Financial Aid to Teachers for Long Courses: Serving teachers employed by local education authorities may be secondary on salary for the duration of a full-time course, provided they have completed five years teaching service. Teachers with shorter length of experience may be seconded to one of the courses for teachers of handicapped children. Authorities may provide additional assistance in paying tuition fees and necessary travelling expenses.

Serving teachers whose employers are not local education authorities may also be granted aid for the full-time duration of courses.

Teachers employed by local education authorities who are not seconded on salary to attend full-time courses may apply to their local education authority for financial assistance. Any aid, whether by secondment on salary or by payment to or on behalf of a teacher is entirely at the local authority's discretion.

Note: A description of the courses offered and details of application, both for a course and for financial aid, are given in the Department's brochure *Long Courses for Teachers*, available from the address below.

Teacher Training Grants: Mandatory grants are given to students on initial teacher-training courses, provided they meet the requirements of the Awards Regulations and have been ordinarily resident in the United Kingdom for the three year period immediately preceding the year in which the grant is made. Similar arrangements apply for post-graduate certificates in education. Applications for grants should be made to the applicant's local education authority. Students ineligible for these grants may receive discretionary awards, made by the local authorities as they consider appropriate.

Further information from:
   Department of Education and Science
   Elizabeth House
   York Road
   London
   England SE1 7PH

[676]

DEPARTMENT OF EDUCATION AND SCIENCE *(England and Wales)*

State Bursaries

Purpose: To enable students to obtain a first postgraduate qualification by full-time study.

Subjects: Humanities.

Value: Provides for the payment of approved fees, a grant to the student for his maintenance and in certain circumstances a grant towards the maintenance of his dependents, and travel and other expenses. Standard maintenance rates are: £1,535 for a student living in college or lodging (£1,825 for students resident in London colleges); £1,180 for students living in the parental home.

Tenable at United Kingdom universities and other institutions for courses which have been designated for the purpose of the Bursary scheme.

Eligibility: A candidate for a Bursary should (i) normally be under 40 years of age on 1st September of the year of taking up the Bursary, (ii) have been ordinarily resident in England or Wales for at least three years, or would have been so resident had he or either of his parents not been employed for the time being abroad, (iii) hold a degree or qualification equivalent to a degree. Candidates with other qualifications will be considered exceptionally.

A candidate who has previously been assisted from public funds for postgraduate study will be considered only exceptionally.

Note: Bursaries are offered on a quota basis. They are the only source of grant from United Kingdom public funds for students following these courses; grants are no longer available from local education authorities.

A candidate should consult the authorities of the institution where he proposes to undertake his studies as early as possible. He will be required to complete an application form obtainable from institution authorities, who will forward their nominations for Bursaries to the Department. The Department will inform the candidate whether his nomination has been successful and if so, will ask him to complete a statement of financial circumstances so that the value of his Bursary may be assessed. In no circumstances should a student apply directly to the Department.

Further information is given in *Postgraduate Awards 1*, published by the Department.

Scottish candidates should refer to details listed under Scottish Education Department, and candidates from Northern Ireland should refer to details under Department of Education (Northern Ireland).

Further information from:
Department of Education and Science
Honeypot Lane
Stanmore, Middlesex
England HA7 1AZ

[677]

DEPARTMENT OF EDUCATION AND SCIENCE *(England and Wales)*

State Bursaries in Librarianship

No. offered: Approximately 225 Bursaries annually.

Value: As for the Department's ordinary State Bursaries. See.

Tenable in the United Kingdom at library schools in universities, polytechnics and technical colleges for one year of full-time postgraduate study.

Eligibility: Open to students ordinarily resident in England and Wales. Candidates should first apply for a course place at the academic institution of their choice. The institution selects those candidates it wishes to nominate for a Bursary from its quota.

All candidates should realise that the offer of a course place by an institution does not automatically mean that they will be nominated for a Department Bursary. It is essential that all students should obtain a clear statement from the institution concerned as to whether they are being offered (a) a firm nomination for a Bursary, (b) inclusion on a reserve list for a Bursary, or (c) simply a course place without the possibility of a Bursary.

Note: In no circumstances should a student apply directly to the Department, but Northern Ireland candidates should apply to the Department of Education, Northern Ireland.

Further information from:
Department of Education and Science
Honeypot Lane
Stanmore, Middlesex
England HA7 1AZ

[678]

DEPARTMENT OF EDUCATION AND SCIENCE *(England and Wales)*

Library Studentships

No. offered: A small, limited number annually.

Value: As for the Department's State Studentships. See.

Tenable for a one-year course of study leading to an M.A. degree. Awards are currently available for only two courses, i.e. at Sheffield University and at University College London.

Eligibility: Open to students resident in England, Scotland or Wales who possess at least a lower second class honours degree and who have been offered a place in one of the two courses for which Studentships are available. The institution sends a list of nominated candidates to the Department.

Note: In no circumstances should a student apply directly to the Department, but Northern Ireland candidates should apply to the Department of Education, Northern Ireland, and residents of the Channel Islands and the Isle of Man should consult their respective education authorities.

Address:
Department of Education and Science
Honeypot Lane
Stanmore, Middlesex
England HA7 1AZ

[679]

DEPARTMENT OF EDUCATION AND SCIENCE *(England and Wales)*

Two-Year Research Library Studentships

Purpose: To enable candidates to undertake research leading to a higher degree in librarianship or a closely related subject.

No. offered: Two Studentships annually.

Value: £2,245 for a student living in college or lodgings (£2,770 for London); £1,640 for a student living in the parental home.

Eligibility: Open to candidates normally resident in England, Scotland or Wales who possess a good upper (or equivalent undivided) second class honours degree. In the case of those with librarianship qualifications, applications will be considered on their merits. Applicants should have not had more than one year's previous support from central government funds for postgraduate training of any sort.

Note: Nominations should be made by the head of the department in which the student wishes to carry out research as soon as possible and not later than 1st May. Applications are available from the address below.

Applicants should obtain a copy of the Department's *Postgraduate Awards for Librarianship and Information Science and Postgraduate Awards 2.*

Further information from:
Department of Education and Science
Honeypot Lane
Stanmore, Middlesex
England HA7 1AZ

[680]

DEPARTMENT OF EDUCATION AND SCIENCE *(England and Wales)*

State Studentships

Purpose: To enable the Student to take a postgraduate course leading to a qualification which can normally be obtained after one year's full-time study and which the holder is expected to complete in one year. (State Studentships cannot be held by a student who has already commenced the postgraduate course for which he seeks an award or by a student taking the first year of a course which is unlikely to lead to a qualification until after more than one year of full-time study.)

The Studentships are available, on a competitive basis, for (i) certain courses of study or research leading to a higher degree; (ii) certain certificate or diploma courses designated by the Secretary of State to be postgraduate or comparable to postgraduate, but excluding courses mainly professional or vocational in character.

Subjects: Humanities.

Value: £2,245 (£2,770 for London) per annum for students living in college, hostel or lodgings; £1,640 per annum for students living at home. In addition, tuition, examination and other approved fees will be paid. Reductions are made for courses of less than a year.

Tenable at any university or similar institution in the United Kingdom and, exceptionally, elsewhere, for one year. In no circumstances will the tenure of a State Studentships for a one-year course be extended but a holder of a State Studentsship will not be precluded from applying in a subsequent year for a Major State Studentship (see) for a further qualification.

Eligibility: Open to graduates from United Kingdom universities and students at United Kingdom universities in their final year of undergraduate study who are normaly resident in England or Wales. Applicants should normally be under 35 years old.

Note: Applications should be submitted through the university or college authorities and in no circumstances should they be made directly to the Department. The majority of applicants will find it convenient to apply through the university of their first degree, but an aplication may be submitted through the university where the postgraduate study is to be undertaken.

Before application, candidates are advised to obtain a copy of *Postgraduate Awards 2*, published by the Department.

Scottish candidates should refer to details listed under Scottish Education Department [q.v.] and candidates from Northern Ireland should refer to details under Department of Education (Northern Ireland) [q.v.].

Closing date: 1st May for the receipt of applications from university and college authorities, but candidates should apply through their university or college well before that date.

Further information from:
Department of Education and Science
Honeypot Lane
Stanmore, Middlesex
England HA7 1AZ

[681]

DEPARTMENT OF EDUCATION AND SCIENCE *(England and Wales)*

Major State Studentships

Purpose: To enable the student to take an approved programme of postgraduate study for up to three years.

The Studentships are available, on a competitive basis, for (i) certain courses of study or research leading to a higher degree; (ii) certain certificate or diploma courses designated by the Secretary of State to be postgraduate or comparable to postgraduate, but excluding courses mainly professional or vocational in character.

Subjects: Humanities.

Value: £2,245 (£2,770 for London) per annum for students living in college, hostel or lodgings; £1,640 per annum for students living at home. In addition, tuition, examination and other aproved fees will be paid. Reductions are made for courses of less than a year.

Tenable at any university or similar institution in the United Kingdom and, exceptionally, elsewhere, for periods up to three years. Where, however, a student has already undertaken any other course of postgratuate study while supported by a central government department (e.g., by a State Studentship or by a research council), the maximum three year tenure will be reduced by the period of such attendance.

Eligibility: Open to graduates from United Kingdom universities and students at United Kingdom universities in their final year of undergraduate study who are normally resident in England or Wales. Applicants should normally be under 35 years old.

Note: Applications hould be made through the university or college authorities and in no circumstances directly to the Department. The majority of applicants will find it convenient to apply through the university of their first degree, but an application may be submitted through the university where the postgraduate study is to be undertaken.

Before application, candidates are advised to obtain a copy of *Postgraduate Awards 2*, published by the Department.

Scottish candidates should refer to details listed under Scottish Education Department [q.v.], and candidates from Northern Ireland should refer to details under Department of Education (Northern Ireland) [q.v].

Closing date: 1st May for the receipt of applications from university and college authorities, but candidates should apply through their university or college well before that date.

Further information from:
Department of Education and Science
Honeypot Lane
Stanmore, Middlesex
England HA7 1AZ

[682]

DEPARTMENT OF ENERGY, MINES AND RESOURCES *(Canada)*

Research Agreement

Purpose: To facilitate better use of Canadian minerals and energy resources and to provide information on Canada's land mass.

Subjects: Natural, physical and social sciences; engineering.

Value: Grants will be awarded for expenses that can be directly attributed to a research project: payment of assistants; travel expenses; purchase of materials and special apparatus essential for the investigation.

Tenable for one year; renewable.

Eligibility: Open to members of Canadian research organizations which are not directly managed by the Canadian government who wish to undertake research projects related to the Department's objectives.

Closing date: 15th November.

Further information from:
Co-ordinator
External Research Programs
Department of Energy, Mines and Resources
580 Booth Street
Ottawa, Ontario
Canada K1A OE4

[683]

DEPARTMENT OF THE ENVIRONMENT *(Canada)*

Science Subvention Program

Programs of subventions for research by non-government scientists have been instituted by the Department to encourage investigations into environmental and renewable resource problems of interest to the Department, and to establish an effective dialogue between non-government scientific institutions and the Department in areas of mutual concern. The program is meant to facilitate the supplort of uni-, multi-, or interdisciplinary studies involving physical, biological, engineering and social sciences and the humanities, and will stress research which requires a significant component of concept development and exploration of novel approaches. There are currently four Subvention Programs in the Department.

Forestry Program aims to promote the preservation, enhancement and wise use of a healthy, attractive and bountiful forest resource for the economic and social benefit of all Canadians.

Water Resources Research Suport Program aims to promote the planning and implementation of water resource development and water quantity and quality research.

Fisheries and Marine Service—Fisheries Program aims to manage the conservation and development of the fisheries and their associated environmental and economic considerations.

Atmospheric Research Program encourages atmospheric and ice research in the fields of atmospheric processes, air quality, environmental problems and observing and forecasting systems, to contribute to the long term improvement of national economic, environmental and social conditions and to promote Canada's national atmospheric interests in the international dimension.

Note: The number of awards made in a given year depends upon prior commitment, funds available, and applications received; the value of each award varies according to the particular proposal. Funds are awarded only for expenses that can be directly attributed to the research activity, such as salaries, limited travel, services, and the purchase of supplies, materials and other special essential apparatus. Both an annual report and a comprehensive report are required, and due acknowledgement must be made in publications resulting from the work.

Especially in the case of complex proposals, applicants are advised firsst to submit a brief outline for consideration; if the problem is of interest, the applicant will be encouraged to develop a more comprehensive proposal.

Not confirmed for 1983.

Further information from:
Department of the Environment
Fontaine Building
Ottawa, Ontario
Canada K1A 0H3

[684]

DEPARTMENT OF FISHERIES AND FORESTRY *(Ireland)*

Junior Fellowships

Subject: Fishery science.

No. offered: One or two Fellowships at irregular intervals.

Value: £3,100 to £4,100 per annum.

Tenable for three years; renewable only in exceptional circumstances.

Eligibility: Open to graduates possessing an M.Sc. or equivalent higher degree who are studying for a Ph.D. Preference is given to graduates of Irish universities, but graduates from other universities may apply.

Closing date: Mid-June.

Further information from:
Department of Fisheries and Forestry
Sixth Floor, East Block
Agriculture House, Kildare Street
Dublin 2
Ireland

[685]

DEPARTMENT OF FISHERIES AND FORESTRY *(Ireland)*

Studentships

Subjects: Fishery science and related areas.

No. offered: Three Studentships annually.

Value: £640—first year; £700—second year; £700—third year. In addition, travelling and subsistence expenses will be paid.

Tenable in association with one of the Irish universities for two years; renewable for a further year.

Eligibility: Open to graduates of Irish Universities who possess at least an upper second honours degree in a science subject.

Closing date: Mid-June.

Further information from:
Department of Fisheries and Forestry
Sixth Floor, East Block
Agriculture House, Kildare Street
Dublin 2
Ireland

[686]

DEPARTMENT OF FOREIGN AFFAIRS *(Australia)*

International Training Courses

Purpose: To provide professional and technical training for the developing countries of Asia, Africa and the South Pacific participating in Australian technical cooperation arrangements, under th Colombo Plan, the Special Commonwealth African Assistance Plan, the Australia-Papua New Guinea Education and Training Scheme, Australian Universities International Development Program, Commonwealth Cooperation in Education Scheme and the Commonwealth Scholarship and Fellowship Plan.

Subjects: Any subjects related to the economic and social development of developing countries, excluding fine arts and military training.

Value: Scholarship—A$3,551 per annum; Fellowship—A$4,944 per annum; plus return air fare and allowances for travel in Australia, for clothes and for the initial few weeks in Australia.

Tenable at appropriate institutions in Australia for variable periods of time.

Eligibility: Open to persons nominated by the governments of countries in Asia, Africa and the South Pacific participating in Australian technical cooperation arrangements, who can meet the qualifications set by the training institutions.
Recipients of technical assistance: (a) under the *Colombo Plan*—Bangladesh, Bhutan, Burma, India, Indonesia, Korea, Laos, Malaysia, Maldives, Nepal, Pakistan, Philippines, Singapore, Sri Lanka, Thailand; (b) under the *Special Commonwealth African Assistance Plan (S.C.A.A.P.)*—Botswana, Gambia, Ghana, Kenya, Lesotho, Malawi, Mauritius, Namibia, Nigeria, Seychelles, Sierra Leone, Sudan, Swaziland, Tanzania, Uganda, Zambia, Zimbabwe; (c) under the *South Pacific Aid Programme (S.P.A.P.)*—Fiji, Western Samoa, Tonga, Kir-

ibati, Tuvalu, Niue, Cook Islands, Solomon Islands, Vanuatu.

Note: Developing countries other than those listed above may submit nominations for Australian development Haining awards. Whether awards are granted will depend on the type of training sought and the availability of funds.

Commonwealth countries which are approaching or have recently attained independence, especially those not provided for under other aid programmess, may nominate under the Commonwealth Co-operation in Education Scheme, which incorporates the Commonwealth Scholarship and Fellowship Plan.

Applications should be submitted to the central external aid authority of the candidate's own government which in turn may submit nominations to the Australian Development Assistance Bureau in Australia at the address below. Applications cannot be received from private persons or directly from other government departments or agencies.

Further information may be obtained from the nearest Australian diplomatic mission, or from:
Assistant Secretary
Training Development Branch
Australian Development Assistance Bureau
P.O. Box 887
Canberra City, A.C.T.
Australia 2601

[687]

DEPARTMENT OF HEALTH AND SOCIAL SERVICES, NORTHERN IRELAND

Fellowships and Grants in Clinical Research

Subjects: Unrestricted within the fields of medicine, dentistry or the basic medical sciences.

No. offered: Usually six Fellowships and 20 to 25 Grants annually.

Value: Grants within the range of £50 to £9,400 per annum for a maximum of three years have been awarded in past years. The awards have not involved the purchase of equipment exceeding £7,000 in total. Fellows who are graduates in medicine or dentistry are remunerated on the scale £7,100 to £8,070 per annum, £8,070 to £9,840 per annum or £9,330 to £11,900 per annum and other graduates on the scale £6,072 to £11,900 per annum— Amounts are in accordance with official rates and conditions for U.K. government Fellowships.

Tenable in Northern Ireland for one year; renewable for up to three years.

Eligibility: Research Grants are open to suitably qualified persons employed in the health field who are carrying out research in addition to their service work and want financial assistance with miscellaneous expenses, to purchase equipment, or to employ technicians or scientific officers or clerical staff on their research projects.

Fellowships are open to suitably qualified graduates in medicine, dentistry or in the basic medical sciences.

Closing date: December each year.

Further information from:
Research and Intelligence Unit
Annese 2, Castle Buildings
Stormont Estate
Upper Newtonards Road
Belfast
Northern Ireland BT4 3UD

[688]

DEPARTMENT OF INDIAN AND NORTHERN AFFAIRS *(Canada)*

Cultural Grants

Approximately 15 Grants are made annually for the promotion and preservation of Eskimo culture and language. The awards in the fields of literature, music and art, cross cultural workshops and cultural exchange travel are available to Canadian Inuit whose applications meet the purpose of the program. The Grants, averaging *Can*$2,000 and not to exceed *Can*$5,000 per award, are tenable anywhere and for any suitable period of time. They are not, however, renewable. Applications are accepted throughout the year.

Further information from:
Department of Indian and Northern Affairs
Social and Cultural Development
9th Floor, North Tower
Les Terraces de la Chaudiere
Ottawa, Ontario
Canada K1A 0H4

[689]

DEPARTMENT OF INTERNAL AFFAIRS
(N.Z.)

ANZAC Fellowships

Purpose: To enable New Zealanders who have shown outstanding ability and achievement in such fields as primary and secondary industry, commerce, education, the arts or public service, to spend up to one year studying or gaining practical experience in Australia.

The Fellowships will be directed towards persons who are likely to benefit both themselves and the New Zealand community by a period in Australia.

No. offered: Two or three Fellowships annually.

Value: A daily allowance of A$29 (A$10,585 per annum), a marriage allowance of A$830 per annum, and a dependent child allowance at the rate of A$330 per annum (currently under review). Fellowships include provision for return air fares to Australia, approved internal travel costs and approved tuition or other fees.

Tenable in Australia for periods of three to twelve months; not renewable.

Eligibility: Open to New Zealand citizens under the age of 45, and preferably under the age of 35, who are of high standing in their occupation.

Note: The New Zealand Selection Committee will make nominations to the Australian Selection Committee which in turn will make appropriate arrangements with the institutions or organisations concerned and will make the final selection of candidates.

These ANZAC Fellowships are offered by the Australian government. The New Zealand government also participates in the scheme by amking similar awards available annually to Australians [see Department of Education, Australia].

Closing date: 1st September.

Further information from:
   Secretary, New Zealand ANZAC
   Fellowship Selection Committee
   c/o Department of Internal Affairs
   Private Bag
   Wellington
   New Zealand

[690]

DEPARTMENT OF INTERNAL AFFAIRS
(N.Z.)

New Zealand Literary Fund Scholarships in Letters

Purpose: To enable a writer of recognised merit to stand out of employment and work on an approved literary project.

No. offered: One Scholarship annually.

Value: NZ$9,000.

Tenable for one year. To date, the Scholarship has not been awarded to the same person for two years in succession, although it is possible for the same person to receive it for two non-consecutive years.

Eligibility: Open to men and women who are published writers of recognised merit and are normally resident in New Zealand.

Note: The writer must submit details of the project he intends to pursue together with some of his work that has already been published. He must be prepared to give up any form of employment to work on his proposed project.

Closing date: Variable, but usually in mid-October. The Scholarship is advertised each year in the main metropolitan newspapers.

Further information from:
   Secretary, New Zealand Literary
   Fund Advisory Committee
   Department of Internal Affairs
   Private Bag
   Wellington
   New Zealand

[691]

DEPARTMENT OF INTERNAL AFFAIRS (N.Z.)

New Zealand Literary Fund

Awards

Award for Achievement: An annual Award of NZ$500 is given in recognition of one person's contribution to literature. Applications are not accepted.

New Zealand Book Awards: The New Zealand Literary Fund in conjunction with the Queen Elizabeth II Arts Council of New Zealand annually awards two prizes of NZ$2,000 each: (a) for the best book published each year in the categories of poetry, fiction and non-fiction by a citizen or resident of New Zealand, but not necessarily published in that country; (b) for the best produced book, published in New Zealand by a citizen or resident of that country. The books must have been published in the year preceding the one in which the Awards are made.

Publishers are required to send three copies of any books they wish to be considered for these Awards to the Secretary of the Literary Fund. All books must be in the hands of the Secretary by 1st May. The Awards are announced in the following July by the Minister for the Arts.

Note: The Fund also makes a number of small awards throughout the year, usually in small amounts which rarely exceed NZ$2,000. This assistance is given to writers, usually undertaking work in the fields of prose, drama and poetry.

Further information from:
 Secretary, New Zealand Literary
 Fund Advisory Committee
 Department of Internal Affairs
 Private Bag
 Wellington
 New Zealand

[692]

DEPARTMENT OF INTERNAL AFFAIRS (N.Z.)

New Zealand Literary Fund

Bursaries

Choya Bursary for Children's Writers: An annual Bursary of NZ$5,000 is jointly funded by the New Zealand Literary Fund and by Quality Packers Limited to enable an author of imaginative literature for children to work full-time for a period of up to one year on an approved project. Open to any writer normally resident in New Zealand. *Closing date:* 1st August.

ICI Writer's Bursary: The annual Bursary is intended to grant substantial financial help to an author with potential, whose reputation is not yet well established, by enabling him/her to work full-time on an approved programme for a period of up to one year. Co-sponsored by the Fund and by ICI New Zealand Ltd., the award is open to authors of any kind of original writing who are normally resident in New Zealand. The Bursary is for NZ$5,000. Should the standard of applications merit, the New Zealand Literary Fund will provide a second Bursary of NZ$4,000. *Closing date:* 1st May.

Further information from:
 Secretary, New Zealand Literary
 Fund Advisory Committee
 Department of Internal Affairs
 Private Bag
 Wellington
 New Zealand

[693]

DEPARTMENT OF JUSTICE (Canada)

Fellowships in Legislative Drafting

Purpose: To encourage lawyers to enter the field of drafting statutes, subordinate legislation and legal instruments.

Subjects: English and French language programs in legislative drafting; comprehension of legislation; legislative process; and advanced courses in public law.

No. offered: Eight Fellowships annually.

Value: Can$9,900 plus tuition fees.

Tenable at the University of Ottawa Faculty of Law for one academic year.

Eligibility: Open to Canadian residents with superior academic qualifications who (a) are members of the bar of one of the provinces or territories of Canada, or (b) hold a law degree from a recognized Canadian law school granted upon completion of courses of instruction directed toward admission to the practice of law in Canada.

Closing date: 30th April.

Further information from:
  Secretary of the Selection Committee
  Department of Justice
  Ottawa, Ontario
  Canada K1A 0H8

[694]

DEPARTMENT OF JUSTICE *(Canada)*

Native Law Students Programme

Purpose: To encourage students of native ancestry to enter the legal profession.

Subjects: Pre-law orientation and LL.B programmes.

No. offered: Up to five new Fellowships, as vacancies occur. Partial Fellowships are available to students already enrolled in an LL.B. programme when vacancies occur.

Value: Tuition, monthly stipend, textbook allowance and moving and travel expenses where applicable.

Tenable for the duration of an eight week Programme of Legal Studies for Native People offered by the University of Saskatchewan Native Law Centre, Saskatoon; or an LL.B. programme at a Canadian law school.

Note: Similar funding for status Indians is provided by the Canadian Department of Indian Affairs.

Closing date: Spring of each year.

Further information from:
  Chief of Native Programs
  Department of Justice
  Justice Building
  Kent and Wellington Streets
  Ottawa, Ontario
  Canada K1A 0H8

[695]

DEPARTMENT OF JUSTICE *(Canada)*

Consultation and Development Fund

Purpose: To assist individuals and organizations interested in undertaking activities in one or more of the following areas: legal research and the publication of material directed toward professionals in the legal area; the development and/or publication of legal information materials for the layman; consultation in relation to reports and recommendations of the Law Reform Commission in the Civil and Administrative Law areas; and non-governmental conferences of specific interest to the Department.

No. offered: Varies annually.

Value: Maximum single award of Can$5,000; total annual budget of Can$50,000.

Eligibility: Open to Canadian citizens or residents engaged in legal research, and to Canadian organizations and associations engaged in innovative legal developments.

Note: Applications may be submitted throughout the year. Awards are made in the spring and fall.

Further information from:
  General Counsel
  Programmes and Law Information
    Development Section
  Department of Justice
  Justice Building
  Ottawa, Ontario
  Canada K1A 0H8

[696]

DEPARTMENT OF JUSTICE *(Canada)*

Civil Law/Common Law Student Exchange Programme

Purpose: To foster a better knowledge of both legal systems among future Canadian lawyers, while promoting bilingualism and biculturalism at the same time.

Subjects: Introduction to comparative law and selected areas of Canadian constitutional law to all students. Introduction to common law, property-trusts, contracts and torts to civil law students; and introduction to civil law, obligations, property and régimes matrimoniaux to common law students.

No. offered: Thirty Scholarships in each legal system.

Value: Can$1,400 plus meals, accommodation and transportation.

Tenable for ten weeks during the summer.

Eligibility: Open to students in an LL.B. programme in a Canadian law school who rank within the top half of their group and possess a good written comprehension of the other official language.

Note: Common law will be taught in English, while civil law will be taught in French. The host faculties will set up a language programme designed to improve the students' oral comprehension of the lectures.

Closing date: 28th February.

Further information from any Canadian faculty or law, or:
General Councel
Programmes and Law Information
  Development Section
Department of Justice
Justice Building
Ottawa, Ontario
Canada K1A 0H8

[697]

DEPARTMENT OF JUSTICE *(Canada)*

Duff-Rinfret Scholarship

Purpose: To promote legal research in Canadian law schools at the master's level.

Subjects: Various areas of the law falling within federal jurisdiction.

No. offered: Seven Scholarships annually.

Value: Varies; Can$9,300 paid in 1982-83, plus tuition fees and necessary travel expenses.

Tenable for one academic year in a master's programme offered by a Canadian law school.

Eligibility: Open to any person who is in the final year of an LL.B. programme at a Canadian law school or who already has obtained an LL.B. degree granted by a Canadian university, provided that he or she intends to follow a course of studies or research in an area of law under federal jurisdiction, and enrolls in a master's programme offered by a Canadian law school.

Note: The applicant should establish that he or she has been rated as a superior student in the class at law school.

Closing date: Mid-January.

Further information from:
General Councel
Programmes and Law Information
  Development Section
Department of Justice
Justice Building
Ottawa, Ontario
Canada K1A 0H8

[698]

DEPARTMENT OF LABOUR *(Canada)*

University Research Program: Grants-in-Aid

Purpose: To increase the body of knowledge on labour matters and to stimulate greater interest in this field in Canada among established scholars and graduate students.

Subjects: The economics, industrial relations,

social and other aspects of labour, including wages, incomes, productivity, technological change, collective bargaining, labour law and labour history.

Value: Up to Can$5,000 per annum for individuals; appropriately more for research groups or teams.

Grants are normally awarded as contributions towards such expenses as travel, research assistance, clerical and stenographic help, and computer work; under some circumstances, however, Grants to graduate students may also include a living allowance.

Eligibility: Open to graduate students, university faculty members, and others possessing research qualifications, provided that they are Canadian citizens or can demonstrate that they will be residing in Canada on a continuing basis. Evidence is required of ability to carry out research in the social sciences without close supervision. Research groups or teams working on a single subject are also eligible.

Graduate students are required to have a faculty member act as a consultant on their research projects.

Note: Applicants should submit a clear and concise outline of their proposed research project.

Closing date: 15th February.

Further information from:
Secretary
University Research Committee
Department of Labour
Ottawa, Ontario
Canada K1A 0J2

[699]

DEPARTMENT OF NATIONAL DEVELOPMENT AND ENERGY (Australia)
National Energy Office

Project Support Grants

Subjects: Energy research, development and demonstration projects.

Value: All costs except for administrative overheads and salaries for existing staff are usually provided. The National Energy Office welcomes projects for which joint funding with private industry is proposed.

Grants are awarded to the organisation in which the work is being carried out, not to the project leader.

Tenable at institutions within Australia for up to three years; renewable subject to satisfactory progress. In certain circumstances approval is given to the transfer of projects between organisations where the project leader changes his/her place of employment.

Eligibility: The project leader should have adequate training and a proven record of expertise in the field. The applicant organisation is expected to have the necessary technical support and facilities to fully execute the project.

Note: Applicants are assessed on a comparative basis against the defined priorities, given in the booklet "Priorities for R, D & D Support Grants." This, and application forms, will be sent upon request.

Coal Research Grants previously administered by the National Coal Research Advisory Committee are now incorporated with this program.

Further information from:
Assistant Secretary
Research Policy and Programs Branch
National Energy Office
Department of National Development and Energy
P.O. Box 5
Canberra, A.C.T.
Australia 2600

[700]

DEPARTMENT OF NATIONAL DEVELOPMENT AND ENERGY (Australia)
Australian Water Resources Council

Water Research Fund

Purpose: To foster and support fundamental and applied research into all aspects of water resources with the aim of providing a better basis for the assessment, development and management of Australia's water resources.

No. offered: Approximately 30 Awards every three years.

Value: Varies, depending upon project.

Awards usually range between A$10,000 to A$100,000.

Tenable normally within Australia, usually for one to three years.

Eligibility: Open to Australian research workers wishing to carry out research projects within Australia.

Note: Research projects are approved on the basis of advice provided by the Council's Research and Development Committee.
Priorities for the research projects change, and are prepared by the Department every three years.

Further information from:
Secretary
Australian Water Resources Council
c/o Department of National Development and Energy
P.O. Box 5
Canberra, A.C.T.
Australia 2600

[701]

DEPARTMENT OF NATIONAL EDUCATION *(South Africa)*

Exchange Awards

The Department administers the South African part of various scholarship exchange programmes: *German Academic Exchange Service*-South African Scholarships [q.v.]; *South African-Swiss Scholarship Exchange Programme* [q.v.]; *South African Union of the University of Edinburgh; South African-French Scholarship Exchange Programme* [q.v.]; *South African-Austrian Scholarship Exchange Programme* [q.v.]; *South African-British Exchange Programme; South African-Italian Exchange Programme.*

Further information from:
Secretary
Department of National Education
Private Bag X122
Pretoria
South Africa

[702]

DEPARTMENT OF NATIONAL HEALTH AND WELFARE *(Canada)*
Extramural Research Programs Directorate

Visiting National Health Scientist Awards

Subjects: Independent or collaborative health research.

No. offered: Not predetermined.

Value: A stipend (under review) plus travel and other expenses related to the research. Other awards of under *Can*$5,000 may be held concurrently.

Tenable in Canada (for non-Canadians) or in Canada or elsewhere (for Canadians), for periods from 6 months to two years; not renewable.

Eligibility: Open to Canadians and to foreign nationals who can demonstrate high aptitude for the proposed research. Candidates should seek nomination by Canadian universities or research institutions.

Further information from:
Extramural Research Programs Directorate
Department of National Health and Welfare
Ottawa, Ontario
Canada K1A 1B4

[703]

DEPARTMENT OF NATIONAL HEALTH AND WELFARE *(Canada)*
National Welfare Grants Directorate

Senior Welfare Research Fellowships

Subjects: Social welfare—independent research not for research leading to a degree).

No. offered: Up to two Fellowships annually.

Value: Not to exceed the basic annual income of the Fellow, plus up to A$5,000 for travel and other expenses necessitated by the research.

Tenable at any approved institution for up to 12 months; not renewable. The Fellowship may be held concurrently with other awards but all income is taken into account when assessing value.

Eligibility: Open to residents of Canada who can demonstrate high aptitude for the proposed research.

Closing dates: 15th April, September and December.

Further information from:
Welfare Grants Directorate
Department of National Health and Welfare
Ottawa, Ontario
Canada K1A 1B3

[704]

DEPARTMENT OF PRIMARY INDUSTRY
(Australia)

Commonwealth Forestry Postgraduate Research Award

Purpose: To provide assistance, leading to a Ph.D. degree, in research of specific projects nominated by the Australian Forestry Council.

No. offered: A maximum of three Awards annually.

Value: Up to A$10,000, paid fortnightly. Awards are not subject to Australian income tax.

Tenable for a maximum of four years at any Australian University having adequate research facilities.

Eligibility: Open to Australian citizens or those seeking citizenship who are under 45 years of age as of 1st January of the year of application.

Closing date: 31st December of each year.

Further information from:
Assistant Secretary Forestry Branch
Department of Primary Industry
Canberra, A.C.T.
Australia 2600

[705]

DEPARTMENT OF PRIMARY INDUSTRY
(Australia)
Australian Pig Industry Research Committee

Postgraduate Students

Purpose: To promote research relating to the pig industry through the financing of postgraduate research.

No. offered: Two to four Studentships annually.

Value: Salary and allowances will be on a similar scale as those set by the Australian Commonwealth Department of Education.

Tenable at any Australian university for one year; renewable for up to three years.

Eligibility: Open to Australian citizens who are graduates of Australian universities; priority is given to persons already employed or associated with the pig industry.

Closing date: Mid-September.

Further information from:
Secretary
Australian Pig Industry Research
 Committee
c/o Department of Primary Industry
Canberra, A.C.T.
Australia 2600

[706]

DEPARTMENT OF PRIMARY INDUSTRY
(Australia)
Fishing Industry Research Committee

Grants

Grants are offered for scientific, economic or technical research related to the Australian fishing industry. They generally cover salaries and approved travel and equipment expenses.

Further information from:
Secretary
Fishing Industry Research Committee
Fisheries Division
Department of Primary Industry
Canberra, A.C.T.
Australia 2650

[707]

DEPARTMENT OF PRIMARY INDUSTRY
(Australia)
Honey Research Committee

Grants

Grants are offered for research into problems of importance to the honey industry. They are made for a single year from funds made available by honey producers and from matching government funds.

Further information from:
Secretary
Honey Research Committee
Department of Primary Industry
Edmund Bouton Building
Barton, A.C.T.
Australia 2600

[708]

DEPARTMENT OF PRIMARY INDUSTRY
(Australia)
**Poultry Research Advisory Committee
Council of Egg Marketing Authorities of Australia**

Research Grants

Grants varying between A$4,000 and A$20,000 are offered annually for research in aspects of the Australian egg industry, including poultry health, egg quality, product development and marketing.

Further information from:
Secretary
Poultry Research Advisory Committee
Barton, A.C.T.
Australia 2600

[709]

DEPARTMENT OF SCIENCE AND TECHNOLOGY *(Australia)*
Queen's Fellowships and Marine Research Allocations Advisory Committee

Marine Sciences and Technologies Grants

The Australian Government, on the advice of QFMRAAC, offers a number of Grants to stimulate research in the following fields: oceanography, marine biology, geology, ecology, coastal and ocean engineering, and environmental studies. Research is to be carried out in the Great Barrier Reef, the North-West Shelf, the Gulf of Carpentaria, Bass Strait and the adjacent waters of Tasmania, Victoria and South Australia.

There are no specific eligibility requirements.

Further information from:
Executive Officer
Marine Science Grants
Department of Science and Technology
P.O. Box 65
Belconnen, A.C.T.
Australia 2616

[710]

DEPARTMENT OF SCIENCE AND TECHNOLOGY *(Australia)*

Queen Elizabeth II Fellowships and Australian Research Grants Committee

Subjects: Physical and biological sciences—to include mathematics and the scientific aspects of statics, engineering, metallurgy, agriculture, and medicine.

No. offered: Up to ten Fellowships annually.

Value: A$21,509 per annum, increasing to A$23,107 per annum at the age of 28 years. Allowances are payable in respect of a Fellow's dependent spouse (A$500 per annum), each dependent child under 16 years (A$200), superannuation payments (up to 10% of the stipend), appropriate insurance coverage and necessary travel expenses.

Tenable at an Australian university or approved research institution, normally for two years.

Eligibility: Open to Australian or United Kingdom citizens possessing a Ph.D. or equivalent qualification in one of the physical or biological sciences or who are in their final year of doctoral study, and who have exceptional promise and proven capacity for original work. Awards are usually restricted to applicants who are not more than 30 years of age on the date when applications close.

Note: Application forms and a statement of the conditions of the Fellowship may be obtained from the Department, or from

Minister (Scientific), Australia House, The Strand, London WC2B 4LA, England or Counsellor (Scientific), Australian Embassy, 1601 Massachusetts Avenue, Washington, D.C. 20036, U.S.A.

Address:
Secretary
Queen Elizabeth II Fellowships and
  Australian Research Grants Committee
Department of Science and Technology
P.O. Box 65
Belconnen, A.C.T.
Australia 2616

[711]

DEPARTMENT OF SCIENCE AND TECHNOLOGY *(Australia)*

Queen's Fellowships and Marine Research Allocations Advisory Committee

Purpose: To support research projects in marine science nominated by the applicant and approved by the Fellowship Committee.

No. offered: Up to five Fellowships annually.

Value: A$21,509 per annum to the age of 28 years; A$23,107 at age 28; A$500 allowance in respect of a Fellow's dependent spouse and A$200 for each dependent child under 16 years of age.

Tenable at an approved Australian university or institution normally for two years.

Eligibility: Open to nationals of any country who possess a Ph.D. degree or equivalent qualifications or equivalent research or professional experience, in a discipline applicable to marine science in their final year. Awards are not usually granted to applicants over 30 years of age. A knowledge of English is required.

Note: Further information may be obtained from *Minister (Scientific), Australia House, The Strand, London WC2B 4LA, England; Counsellor Scientific, Australian Embassy, 1601 Massachusetts Avenue, Washington, D.C. 20036, U.S.A.;* the registrars of Australian universities; or from
  Executive Officer
  Marine Science Grants
Department of Science and Technology
P.O. BOx 65
Belconnen, A.C.T.
Australia 2616

[712]

DEPARTMENT OF SCIENCE AND TECHNOLOGY *(Australia)*
Australian Research Grants Scheme

Research Grants

Grants are available to individuals or research teams for assistance in research projects in any discipline except medical and dental sciences. Projects must be based in Australia. Applications for support are judged on the quality of the project and the investigator and the appropriateness of it to the general facilities available to the applicant. Projects to be carried out solely in an Australian government or state government authority will not be eligible for consideration.

Closing date: Early April.

Further information from:
Secretary
Australian Research Grants Scheme
Department of Science and Technology
P.O. Box 65
Belconnen, A.C.T.
Australia 2616

[713]

DEPARTMENT OF THE SECRETARY OF STATE *(Canada)*

Grant Programs

Promotion of Official Languages Directorate provides Grants and technical assistance to promote the acquisition and use of the two official languages in the private and non-federal public sectors.

Official Language Minority Groups Program is designed to foster the linguistic and cultural development of official language minorities and to promote a better understanding between the country's two main language groups. The Program offers a number of services to English-speaking Canadians in Quebec, and to French-speaking Canadians in provinces other than Quebec.

Multiculturalism Program is designed to provide individuals and groups with an equal opportunity to develop and express their cultural identity and to share it with other Canadians.

Cultural Integration Program aims to increase the participation of immigrants in all aspects of national life, assisting them to acquire at least one of the official languages through direct programs, grants and contributions to provincial governments, service agencies and citizens' groups.

Native Citizens Program is designed to help native people define and achieve their place in Canadian society by providing them with resources to identify their needs and actively undertake their own development as Canadians. *Address: Native Citizens Program, Department of the Secretary of State, Ottawa, Ontario K1A 0M5.*

Women's Program provides Grants and other resources to women's groups to develop projects and organizations designed to increase their ability to participate in all aspects of society. *Address: Women's Program, Department of the Secretary of State, Ottawa, Ontario K1A 0M5.*

Further information from:
 Communications Directorate
 Department of the Secretary of State
 Ottawa, Ontario
 Canada K1A 0M5

[714]

DEPARTMENT OF THE SECRETARY OF STATE *(Canada)*

Citizens' Participation Program

Assistance to Community Groups Program aims to promote effective participation of Canadian citizens in the decisions that affect the quality of their community life through strengthening the voluntary sector. Grants and advisory services are available to voluntary groups for projects to strengthen Canadian identity and to train and orient citizens for community organizations and voluntary action.

Group Understanding and Human Rights Program aims at promoting and assisting intergroup understanding and enjoyment of human rights and fundamental freedoms. Grants are provided to voluntary organizations that contribute to the progress of group understanding and human rights in Canada and that develop projects to help reduce intergroup tensions, prejudice and discrimination.

Further information from:
 Communications Directorate
 Department of the Secretary of State
 Ottawa, Ontario
 Canada K1A 0M5

[715]

DEPARTMENT OF SOCIAL SECURITY
(Australia)
Office of Child Care

Children's Services Program: Financial grants, value and tenure of which are at the discretion of the Minister, are given to encourage innovative projects in child care at the state, local government or community level. Program functions include pre-school age child education, assistance to parents, and care of the child outside the home (other than in educational institutions). Grants are for research, initiation and development of methods, or evaluation in the above functions, and may be awarded to individuals or organizations.

Note: Special emphasis is given to the needs of children who are handicapped or geographically isolated, from low income families, ethnic minorities, or of single parents.

Further information from:
 Director, Office of Child Care
 Department of Social Security
 P.O. Box 1
 Woden, A.C.T.
 Australia 2606

[716]

DESIGN AND INDUSTRIES ASSOCIATION TRUST *(U.K.)*

DIA Melchett Memorial Award: One Award in the amount of £2,500 is given annually to encourage research into socially responsible design. Projects should show promise of real benefit for people; the criteria being basic human needs, economy and innovation. There are no eligibility requirements. Entrants should state the stage their project has reached, relate its purpose to the requirements of the Award and outline the research it is proposed to undertake. Written statements to the above nature are required, and should be 500 words or less and illustrated if so desired. Statements should be accompanied by a recommendation from the college principal or department head and submitted no later than 4th March to the address below.

Further information from:
Design and Industries Association Trust
Secretary, Mrs. Nell Chamberlain
17 Lawn Crescent
Kew Gardens, Surrey
England TW9 3NR

[717]

ISAAC DEUTSCHER MEMORIAL PRIZE *(U.K.)*

The Prize of £100 is offered annually to the author of a work judged to contribute to the development of Marxist thought. There are no eligibility requirements. Works published or submitted in typescript by 1st May in most European languages will be considered.

Further information from:
Isaac Deutscher Memorial Prize
c/o Lloyd's Bank
68 Warwick Square
London
England SW1V 2AS

[718]

DISTILLED SPIRITS COUNCIL OF THE UNITED STATES, INC. [DISCUS]

Grants-In-Aid

Purpose: To stimulate new ideas and concepts and seek new knowledge, techniques and methods of dealing more effectively with the illness of alcoholism.

Subjects: The causes, nature, extent, treatment and understanding of the various problems related to the excessive use of beverage alcohol.

Value: Grants vary in amount, depending on the needs and the nature of the request. Normally, awards have a maximum of US$15,000.

Eligibility: Open to researchers in the biological, medical and behavioral sciences who have promising ideas or hypotheses and wish to undertake preliminary or pilot studies.

Further information from:
Scientific Advisory Council
DISCUS
1300 Pennsylvania Building
Washington, D.C. 20004
U.S.A.

[719]

DR. HADWEN TRUST FOR HUMANE RESEARCH *(U.K.)*

A number of grants, depending upon the availability of funds, are made to scientists to promote the development of humane alternatives to the use of living animals in biomedical research. There are no fixed values for the awards, which vary in amount according to need. Payments are usually made quarterly, and may be used as salary for the researcher, for technical assistance, for expenses incurred during the research, purchase of equipment, or for attendance at meetings. Grants are tenable for a maximum of three years; interim progress reports are required. Renewal past three years is awarded only in exceptional circumstances. Applications may be made by any postgraduate in a university, medical school, hospital or other scientific institution. Exceptionally, applications may be considered from postgraduates not attached to an institution, or from more junior scientists. Recipients are required to sign an agreement not to use trust funds for any procedure using living animals. Applications must be signed by the candidate's head of department and administrative authority. Applications may be submitted at any time.

Further information from:
Dr. G. Langley
Dr. Hadwen Trust for Humane Research
46 Kings Road
Hitchin, Hertfordshire
England SG5 1RD

[720]

DR. M. AYLWIN COTTON FOUNDATION *(Italy)*

Cotton Research Fellowship

The annual Research Fellowship of £1,500,

paid quarterly, is awarded to promote the study of archaeology, architecture, history, language and arts of the Mediterranean. The Fellowships is tenable for one year, and is not normally renewable. It is open to senior scholars engaged in research work pertaining to the above subjects. The results of the work will be published. There are no restrictions as to age, sex, citizenship or residency. The Fellow may not engage in political activities while holding the Fellowship.

The Foundation also provides annually one or two *Grants Towards Publication* £500 each, paid as a lump sum, to finance the publication costs of work already finished or due for publication in the immediate future.

Closing date: 31st March.

Further information from:
Honorary Secretary
Dr. M. Aylwin Cotton Foundation
Via Tevere Residence
Vie Isonzo, 32
00198 Rome
Italy

[721]

DR. WILLIAMS'S TRUST *(U.K.)*

Glasgow Bursary

Subject: Religious studies, i.e., theology, Christian history, etc.

No. offered: Usually one Award annually.

Value: Normally £4,000 per annum, paid each term.

Tenable at the University of Glasgow Faculty of Divinity for one year; renewable for a second year.

Eligibility: Open to: Protestant Dissenting ministers wishing to take refresher courses; graduate Protestant Dissenting ministers for a course toward the degree of M.Th. and mature students intending to enter the Protestant Dissenting ministry. Applicants must be South Britons (i.e. from England or Wales).

Closing date: 1st January.

Further information from:
Secretary
Dr. Williams's Trust
14 Gordon Square
London
England WC1H 0AG

[722]

HENRY L. AND GRACE DOHERTY CHARITABLE FOUNDATION, INC.
Princeton University *(New Jersey)*

Doherty Fellowships

Subjects: Social Studies in the Latin America area (Spanish- and Portuguese-speaking republics).

Value: To cover the cost of return travel, and provide an allowance for living expenses and minimal research needs.

Tenable in Latin America for one year.

Eligibility: Open to United States advanced graduate students or scholars whose primary interest is Latin American Studies, and who can supply evidence of training and preparation which give promise of an ability to carry out a project successfully.

Applications from persons over 40 years of age and from persons who have already spent as much as one year in Latin America will be considered only in exceptional cases.

Closing date: 1st February.

Further information from:
Doherty Fellowship Committee
Program in Latin American Studies
240 East Pyne, Princeton University
Princeton, New Jersey 08540
U.S.A.

[723]

DOUBLEDAY AND COMPANY, INC. *(U.S.A.)*

Doubleday-Columbia University Fellowship is awarded to a writer who has completed a published or unpublished novel, and is preparing to begin another. The Fellowship provides tuition for one semester of a workshop in creative writing at Columbia University's School of General Studies. Complete or partial manuscripts should be sent to the address below.

Further information from:
Doubleday and Company, Inc.
245 Park Avenue
New York, New York 10167
U.S.A.

[724]

ROBERT B. DOWNS AWARDS *(U.S.A.)*
University of Illinois

One Award is given annually to honor a person or group which has made an outstanding contribution to the cause of intellectual freedom in libraries. Any person or group is eligible, although preference is given to acceptable candidates within the United States.

Closing date: 15th April.

Further information from:
Robert B. Downs Award
Graduate School of Library and
  Information Science
410 David Kinley Hall
1407 West Gregory Drive
University of Illinois
Urbana, Illinois 61801
U.S.A.

[725]

CAMILLE AND HENRY DREYFUS FOUNDATION, INC. *(U.S.A.)*

Teacher-Scholar Grants: Each year, 15 Grants in chemistry, biochemistry, or chemical engineering are offered to young faculty members. Successful applicants are allocated US$37,000 of the US$40,000 paid to their institutions. Grants are provided to give young faculty members maximum freedom to develop their potentials both as teachers and scholars by providing unstructured support that will supplement, but not substitute for, the funds normally available.
  The Dreyfus Grants may be used for trying out and developing a new educational program or new teaching material, as seed money for evaluating new research, for the support of teaching or research assistants for the young faculty member, and for necessary travel expenses. In a broad sense, the Grants are to be used by the institution for the benefit of the young faculty member in imaginative ways that will contribute to his/her personal development as a teacher and as a scholar.

Grants for Newly Appointed Faculty in Chemistry: Each year, ten Grants of US$25,000 each are paid to institutions in time for use by young faculty members embarking on their first year of teaching. The Grant funds are primarily for research purposes, particularly as seed money for new ideas and concepts and not for salary during the regular academic year. The funds may also be used for student research stipends, for scientific equipment and for other needs related to research. Except for US$500 which may be retained by the administration, the Grant money should be made available as requested by the young faculty member. Funds may be expended over a period not to exceed five years and are not transferable to another academic institution.

Note: Candidates must be nominated by academic research institutions in the United States. Nominations should be submitted after an academic appointment has been made.

Further information from:
William L. Evers, Executive Director
Camille and Henry Dreyfus Foundation, Inc.
445 Park Avenue
New York, New York 10022
U.S.A.

[726]

DRUMMOND TRUST *(U.K.)*
University College London

Drummond Fellowships for Research in Nutrition

Subjects: Nutrition and allied studies.

Value: In accordance with current academic scales, plus £50 expenses and superannuation.

Tenable at any approved university, college or institution either in the United Kingdom or abroad, normally for two years.

Eligibility: Open to science graduates of distinction from Commonwealth universities and to others of similar standing.

Note: Fellowships are awarded for original research, not for pre-doctoral training; they can only be offered when funds are sufficient and therefore no surplus is available for any other form of grant.

Further information from:
  Honorary Secretary
  Drummond Trust
  University College London
  Gower Street
  London
  England WC1E 6BT

[727]

DUBLIN INSTITUTE FOR ADVANCED STUDIES
School of Celtic Studies

Research Scholarships

Subjects: Celtic studies.

No. offered: Up to six Scholarships annually.

Value: Determined by the Council of the Institute. Stipends are payable monthly.

Tenable at the Institute, normally for one year with the possibility of extension to a maximum of two years.

Eligibility: Open to persons of any nationality possessing a Ph.D. or honours degree in Celtic studies, who can provide evidence of capacity for original research.

Note: The Institute is purely a research body and no set course of instruction is provided.

Closing date: 31st March.

Further information from:
  Lt. Col. John P. Duggan, Registrar
  Dublin Institute for Advanced Studies
  10 Burlington Road
  Dublin 4
  Ireland

[728]

DUBLIN INSTITUTE FOR ADVANCED STUDIES
School of Cosmic Physics

Research Scholarships

Subjects: Astronomy, cosmic rays and geophysics.

No. offered: Up to six Scholarships annually.

Value: Determined by the Council of the Institute. Stipends are payable monthly.

Tenable at the Institute, normally for one year with the possibility of extension to a maximum of three years.

Eligibility: Open to nationals of all countries, possessing an honours degree in astronomy, geology, mathematics or physics.

Note: The Institute is purely a research body and no set course of instruction is provided.

Further information from:
  Lt. Col. John P. Duggan, Registrar
  Dublin Institute for Advanced Studies
  10 Burlington Road
  Dublin 4
  Ireland

[729]

DUBLIN INSTITUTE FOR ADVANCED STUDIES
School of Theoretical Physics

Research Scholarships

Subject: Theoretical physics.

No. offered: Up to six Scholarships annually.

Value: Determined by the Council of the Institute. Stipends are payable monthly.

Tenable at the Institute, normally for one year with the possibility of extension to a maximum of three years.

Eligibility: Open to nationals of all countries, possessing a Ph.D. or honours degree in mathematics or theoretical physics.

Note: The Institute is purely a research body and no set course of instruction is provided.

Closing date: 31st March.

Further information from:
  Lt. Col. John P. Duggan, Registrar
  Dublin Institute for Advanced Studies
  10 Burlington Road
  Dublin 4
  Ireland

[730]

SIMONE AND CINO del DUCA FOUNDATION

Grants

The Foundation offers a number of maintenance and traveling Grants to foreign scientists who wish to work in a French laboratory. Candidates, who may be at any stage of their career, should be devoted to biomedical research in the following areas: cardiovascular system, nervous system, behavior and mental health (molecular and cellular biology, pathology, pharmacology and epidemiology).

Traveling Grants cover return travel expenses between the applicant's home laboratory and the host facility. Applicants must satisfy the Foundation that they have sufficient means to cover the stay's expenses. Maintenance Grants cover all maintenance expenses for periods of eight days to one year. The value is determined in accordance with the scale of salaries of other research workers in the host laboratory, and in consideration to the Grantee's titles, age, and personal situation. Only under very exceptional circumstances are traveling and maintenance Grants offered together, and neither one may be held with similar grants given by other organizations. Applications may be requested from the address below.

Closing date: 14th March, for notification by June.

Further information from:
Simone and Cino del Duca Foundation
10, rue Alfred de Vigny
75008 Paris
France

[731]

SIMONE AND CINO del DUCA FOUNDATION

Cino del Duca World Prize

A Prize of FF200,000 is awarded in June of each year to encourage and promote a writer of any nationality whose work constitutes a message of humanity. The author's work should be of a scientific or literary nature. Applications for this Prize are not solicited.

Further information from:
Simone and Cino del Duca Foundation
10, rue Alfred de Vigny
75008 Paris
France

[732]

DUMBARTON OAKS: TRUSTEES FOR HARVARD UNIVERSITY

Dumbarton Oaks Fellowships and Junior Fellowships

Subject: Byzantine civilization in all its aspects including the Late Roman and Early Christian period, and the Middle Ages generally; studies of Byzantine cultural exchanges with the Late West, Slavic and New Eastern countries; pre-Columbian studies; history of landscape architecture.

No. offered: Ten to twelve in Byzantine studies and two or three in each of the other fields, annually.

Value: Junior Fellowships—A stipend of US$6,000 per annum; *Fellowships*—A basic stipend of US$8,000. Both Junior and regular Fellows receive furnished accommodation or a housing allowance; an additional living allowance of US$1,000 for each accompanying dependent; and an expense account of US$400 for approved research expenditure during the academic year. Fellows who reside outside of North America may be provided with travel assistance.

Tenable for full-time resident work at the Center for up to one academic year; not renewable.

Eligibility: Junior Fellowships—Open to persons of any nationality who have passed all preliminary examinations for a higher degree and are writing a dissertation (or the equivalent) under the direction of a faculty member at their own university. Candidates must have a working knowledge of any languages required for research. *Fellowships*—Open to scholars of any nationality holding a Ph.D. or relevant advanced degree and wishing to pursue research on a project of their own or one sponsored by the Center.

Note: The Center also awards a limited number of *Summer Fellowships* for Scholars at any level of advancement, for periods of four to ten weeks. These awards are intended to cover basic expenses only.

Closing date: On or before 15th November of the academic year preceding that for which the Fellowship is required.

Further information from:
Assistant Director
Dumbarton Oaks
1703 Thirty-second Street, N.W.
Washington, D.C. 20007
U.S.A.

[733]

FLORENCE S. DUNLOP MEMORIAL FELLOWSHIP FUND *(Canada)*

Florence S. Dunlop Memorial Fellowship Award

Purpose: To provide help and inspiration to those who have chosen the field of elementary education for their career.

Subjects: Any field of elementary education for which the applicant has shown evidence of special aptitude or interest, with some preference to the education of the handicapped and the gifted.

No. offered: At least one Fellowship annually.

Value: Can$3,000 per annum minimum.

Tenable at a university of the recipient's choice, subject to the approval of the Trustees, for one year; not renewable.

Eligibility: Open to Canadian citizens who are qualified elementary school teachers, have had three years of successful teaching experience, and hold at least a bachelor's degree from an approved university.

Closing date: 1st March.

Further information from:
M.A. O'Leary, Secretary
Florence S. Dunlop Memorial Fellowship Fund
c/o Alta Vista School
1349 Randall Avenue
Ottawa, Ontario
Canada K1H 7R2

[734]

A.J. DYER OBSERVATORY *(Nashville)* Vanderbilt University

Research Assistantship

Purpose: To provide assistance in research programs of the Dyer Observatory in the field of observational optical astronomy.

No. offered: One Assistantship annually.

Value: US$5,300, paid monthly.

Tenable at the Dyer Observatory, Vanderbilt University, for one year; not ordinarily renewable.

Eligibility: Open to persons holding a bachelor's degree who are acceptable to the Graduate School of Vanderbilt University.

Closing date: 1st February.

Further information from:
Director
A.J. Dyer Observatory
Box 1803 B, Vanderbilt University
Nashville, Tennessee 37235
U.S.A.

[735]

DYSLEXIA RESEARCH FOUNDATION, INC. *(Australia)*

Research Grants

Subject: Projects relate to diagnosis, prevention and/or remediation of dyslexia.

Tenable for the duration of the project, usually between one and three years.

Value: Varies according to nature of project and availability of funds.

Eligibility: Open to professionals in the field of dyslexia research, including classroom teachers.

Further information from:
Secretary
Dyslexia Research Foundation
50a Colin Street
West Perth, W.A.
Australia 6005

E

See *How to Use The Grants Register*, page ix

[736]

EARHART FOUNDATION *(U.S.A.)*

H.B. Earhart Fellowships are awarded to move talented individuals through graduate study in optimum time to embark upon careers in college or university teaching or in research. Awards are made to graduate students nominated by faculty sponsors whose participation is invited annually. The sponsors also monitor performance. Direct applications from candidates or from non-invited sponsors are not accepted.

For the academic year 1980-81, 69 sponsors in 34 U.S. colleges or universities nominated 86 Fellows for graduate work at 36 institutions. The stipends ranged from US$500 to US$4,000 and 58 Fellows also received tuition. Economics and political science were the disciplines primarily represented.

Fellowship Research Grants are awarded upon direct application to individuals who have established themselves professionally. Such persons should be associated with educational and research institutions and the effort supported should lead to the advancement of knowledge through teaching, lecturing and publication. The applications evaluated must include: a personal history statement; a full description of the proposed research; an abstract of approximately one page or 250 words; the intended end use or publication; a budget and time schedule; a list of referees; and a statement about applications pending elsewhere. Proposals should be submitted at least 90-120 days before commencement of the projected work period. Each award is for a specific purpose and progress is monitored.

There were 53 Research Grants in 1980. The maximum was US$21,000, and the minimum US$350, with an average of US$7,250. By field of interest political science numbered 27, international affairs 5, economics 10, history 6, philosophy 4, and psychology 1.

Grants are made upon application to publicly supported educational and research organizations qualified for private foundation support. Specific projects or activities are identified for support and in some instances the Grant also will designate a person named in the application to execute or monitor the activity. Requests for general operating grants and meritorious proposals of a broader scope than the regular program occasionally are considered. Written inquiries are preferable before a formal submission.

In 1980 Grants to organizations numbered 77 with a range of US$700 to US$50,000.

Further information from:
  Earhart Foundation
  Plymouth Building, Suite 204
  2929 Plymouth Road
  Ann Arbor, Michigan 48105
  U.S.A.

[737]

EAST MALLING RESEARCH STATION
Kent Incorporated Society for Promoting Experiments in Horticulture

Blackman Studentships

Purpose: To assist postgraduate students in a field relating to horticulture.

No. offered: One studentship, periodically.

Value: A basic tax free maintenance allowance similar in amount to government studentships; paid monthly.

Tenable for three years at East Malling Research Station.

Eligibility: Open to British subjects who are normally resident in the United Kingdom and who have a first or upper second class honours degree in a relevant scientific subject from a British Commonwealth university.

Further information from:
  Secretary
  East Malling Research Station
  Maidstone, Kent
  England ME19 6BJ

[738]

EAST-WEST CENTER *(Honolulu)*

Scholarships and Fellowships

Purpose: To promote better relations and understanding between the United States and the nations of Asia and the Pacific through cooperative study, training and research.

Subjects: Disciplines encompassed by the activities of the Center's Institutes of Communication, Culture Learning, Environment and Policy, Population, and Resource Systems.

Value: Return travel, tuition and room and board in the Center's residence halls.

Tenable at the University of Hawaii, for 17 to 24 months for the M.A. degree program, up to 36 months for the Ph.D. degree and for visiting researchers and, depending on activity, one week to twelve months for all professional development awards.

Eligibility: Open to senior and mid-career scholars and authorities, mid- and upper-echelon managers of government, business and education and to promising researchers and potential leaders needing managerial experience in education, research or development activities. Candidates must give strong evidence of professional interest in the programs of their choice and at the same time demonstrate interest and potential for contributing to intercultural communication.

Note: Degree study applications should be made through the Center's program representative, if one exists, in the country of the applicant's citizenship. All Americans should apply directly to the address below.

Closing date: All degree program applications should reach the Center by 1st December; all other awards have varying deadlines.

Further information from:
Award Services Officer
East-West Center
1777 East-West Road
Honolulu, Hawaii 96848
U.S.A.

[739]

EASTMAN DENTAL CENTER *(Rochester, New York)*

Clinical Dental Fellowships

Purpose: To enable suitably qualified dental graduates to undertake training and/or research at the Center.

No. offered: Approximately 25 Fellowships annually.

Value: Approximately US$6,500 per annum.

Tenable at the Center, for one academic year; renewable.

Eligibility: Open to recent dental graduates who have a D.D.S. degree or equivalent qualification.
Candidates from overseas must show evidence of high academic achievement and of their intention to follow and academic or research career.

Closing date: Applications must be returned before 30th November for programs starting the following year.

Further information from:
Director
Eastman Dental Center
625 Elmwood Avenue
Rochester, New York 14620
U.S.A.

[740]

EASTMAN SCHOOL OF MUSIC *(Rochester, New York)*

Graduate Awards in Music

No. offered: Approximately 125 Awards annually.

Value: Up to US$9,700.

Tenable at the School for one academic year; renewable.

Eligibility: Open to nationals of all countries. Candidates should have the qualifications necessary for admission to a United States school of music. Non-United States citizens are usually offered service scholarships in ensemble work at the graduate level.

Note: The School also offers the *Cleveland Quartet Competition*, to string quartets from any nation whose members are eligible for admission to the School.

Closing date: 20th February.

Further information from:
Director of Admissions
Eastman School of Music
University of Rochester
26 Gibbs Street
Rochester, New York 14604
U.S.A.

[741]

FRIEDRICH EBERT FOUNDATION *(West Germany)*

Grants

The purpose of the Foundation is to further adult education all over the world and to encourage international cooperation, through its primary interest in the political and socio-economic infrastructures of developing countries. DM750 per month, a book allowance of DM100 per semester and DM200 per year, to cover social insurance payments and obligatory contributions for health insurance, are given to provide highly qualified students and young scientists the oppurtunity to undertake training in the Foundation's institutes for social and political education in Germany or in developing countries, or to further their academic training.

Further information from:
Friedrich Ebert Foundation
Godesberger Allee 149
Bonn 2
West Germany

[742]

ECOLOGICAL SOCIETY OF AMERICA

Buell Award

One Award of US$250 is given for the best paper on basic or applied research in ecology. Candidates should be undergraduate or graduate students and must present their paper at the annual meeting of the Society, usually held in August.

Further information from:
Dr. Paul G. Risser, Secretary
Ecological Society of America
Illinois Natural History Survey
607 Peabody Drive
Champaign, Illinois 61820
U.S.A.

[743]

ECONOMIC DEVELOPMENT INSTITUTE WORLD BANK

Awards for Training Courses

Purpose: To train senior officials of the developing member countries of the World Bank in economic development, and identification, preparation and evaluation of public investment projects.

No. offered: Approximately 300 Awards annually.

Value: Transportation, housing and subsistence allowances.

Tenable in Washington, D.C., for one to three months; not renewable.

Eligibility: Open to senior officials who are responsible for the formulation and administration of policies, programs and projects related to the economic development of its developing member countries. Applicants, preferably between 30 and 45 years of age, should possess a university degree. They must be officially nominated by their government or appropriate agency. Faculty members of universities and other training institutions are considered if they are in a position to pass their training on to others, including teaching in organized training programs.

Note: Approximately eleven Courses are given each year in Washington, D.C. Courses are offered in English, French and Spanish. Announcements of each Course are sent to appropriate agencies about seven months before commencement of the Course.

The EDI is becoming increasingly involved in working with agencies in developing countries to initiate course programs with similar objectives. The EDI provides varying degrees of financial, administrative and teaching support for these courses depending on the circumstances.

Closing date: Approximately five months before commencement of each Course.

Further information from:
Economic Development Institute
World Bank
1818 H Street, N.W.
Washington, D.C. 20433
U.S.A.

[744]

ECONOMIC AND SOCIAL RESEARCH INSTITUTE *(Dublin)*

Postgraduate Fellowships

Purpose: To enable young Irish graduates to proceed to doctorates.

Subjects: Social sciences, economics and statistics.

No. offered: Approximately seven Fellowships annually.

Value: Variable, depending on country of tenure.

Tenable in the United States, Canada or the United Kingdom.

Eligibility: Open to Irish nationals who possess a good honours bachelor's degree and have been accepted by a university which is approved by the Institute.

Note: The Institute is also interested in exchange or sabbatical year arrangements.

Closing date: 31st March.

Further information from:
Secretary
Economic and Social Research Institute
4 Burlington Road
Dublin 4
Ireland

[745]

ECUMENICAL SCHOLARSHIPS PROGRAMME *(West Germany)*

Scholarships

The purpose of the Scholarships is to promote the training of young Christians and non-Christians from developing countries in Asia, Africa and Latin America. Scholarships are granted for vocational, university and/or extension training. Priority is given to project or programme-oriented training.

There are no restrictions as to the field in which the training is to be undertaken. Preference is given to courses in the candidate's own country, or in his home continent if suitable opportunities are lacking in his own country.

Applications should be submitted by the ecumenical parter organizations. Individual applications cannot be accepted.

Closing dates: 30th April, 30th September.

Further information from:
Scholarships Secretary
Ecumenical Scholarships Programme
Postfach 476
7000 Stuttgart 1
West Germany

[746]

EDUCATION COUNCIL OF THE GRAPHIC ARTS INDUSTRY *(U.S.A.)*
National Scholarship Trust Fund

Fellowships in Printing, Publishing and Packaging

Purpose: To promote the progress of science in the printing, publishing and packaging industry.

Subjects: Study areas that have potential application in the industry, such as mathematics, chemistry, physics, industrial education, engineering, and business technology.

No. offered: Several Fellowships, as vacancies occur.

Value: US$1,000 to US$3,000. A portion of the amount is usually made available to the department, and the balance to the Fellow for tuition, fees and expenses.

Tenable at a United States graduate school for one academic year; renewable.

Eligibility: Open to college seniors in the United States who expect to receive the baccalaureate degree during the year for which the award is made, and to graduate students with not less than one year remaining in their program.

Closing date: 1st February.

Note: Fellowships currently offered include: 3M Company Fellowship; Technical Association of the Graphic Arts Fellowship; Western Publishing Company Fellowship; Hallmark Educational Foundation Fellowship; Madeline Gegenheimer McClure Fellowship; Raise/Printing Industries Association, Inc. of Southern California Fellowship; Xerox Corporation Fellowship.

Further information from:
   National Scholarship Trust Fund
   Education Council of the Graphic Arts Industry
   4615 Forbes Avenue
   Pittsburgh, Pennsylvania 15213
   U.S.A.

[747]

EDUCATION COUNCIL OF THE GRAPHIC ARTS INDUSTRY *(U.S.A.)*
National Scholarship Trust Fund

Scholarships in Printing, Publishing and Packaging

Subjects: Graphic arts; printing technology, printing management, graphic arts education and related areas.

No. offered: Approximately 35 Scholarships annually.

Value: From US$100 to US$1,000 per annum.

Tenable for four years at United States colleges and universities with established two- and four-year programs leading to a degree recognized by the graphic communications industries.

Eligibility: Open to United States citizens who have graduated from high school within the previous four years and who are interested in a career in the graphic arts.

Note: A number of Scholarships are also available to students already enrolled at a college or university, and to graduate students wishing to pursue advanced training.

Closing date: 31st January; 31st March for college students.

Further information from:
   National Scholarship Trust Fund
   Education Council of the Graphic Arts Industry
   4615 Forbes Avenue
   Pittsburgh, Pennsylvania 15213
   U.S.A.

[748]

EDUCATIONAL COMMISSION FOR FOREIGN MEDICAL GRADUATES [ECFMG] *(U.S.A.)*

Residencies and Fellowships

Program: Medical education training.

Value: Regular salary.

Tenable at medical institutions in the United States for one year; renewable.

Eligibility: Open to holders of approved medical degrees from institutions listed in the World Directory of Medical Schools. Candidates must be licenced to practise medicine in their own country and must first apply for ECFMG certfiication.

Further information from:
   Education Commission for Foreign Medical Graduates
   3634 Market Street
   Philadelphia, Pennsylvania 19104
   U.S.A.

[749]

EDUCATIONAL FILM LIBRARY ASSOCIATION *(U.S.A.)*
American Film Festival

John Grierson Award

A cash Award is presented annually to a new filmmaker who shows outstanding talent in the social documentary field. Entries must be the first or second professional production of the filmmaker, and should have been released during the two-year period preceding the Award year.

Closing date: 15th January of the Award year.

Further information from:
Educational Film Library Association
43 West 61st Street
New York, New York 10023
U.S.A.

[750]

EDUCATIONAL OPPORTUNITIES COUNCIL *(South Africa)*

Ford Foundation Fellowships are offered to members of staff of the African, coloured or Indian universities for postgraduate study in Europe or the United States. Applicants must possess an honours degree.

S.A. Education Program: Awards are available to black South Africans for study leading to the master's degree in the fields of science, mathematics, engineering and business administration. Candidates must possess an honours degree.

Note: These Programs were previously administered by the South African Institute of Race Relations. The Council may offer other awards as well.

Further information from:
Dr. Mokgethi Motlhabi, Director
Educational Opportunities Council
P.O. Box 31190
Braamfontein
South Africa

[751]

EDUCATIONAL POLICY FELLOWSHIP PROGRAM
INSTITUTE FOR EDUCATION LEADERSHIP, INC.

Education Policy Fellowships

Purpose: To provide policy level experience in education for highly qualified mid-career adults interested in improving the quality of education.

Subject: Education policy at the federal, state, and local levels.

No. offered: Approximately 200 Fellowships annually.

Value: Salaries are paid by the sponsoring agency selected by EPFP.

Tenable for one year at the EPFP. Headquarters are in Washington, D.C., and there are currently fourteen state sites.

Eligibility: Open to candidates who hold a bachelor's degree and have significant professional experience in education and human services.

Closing date: Varies, usually April.

Further information from:
Education Policy Fellowship Program
Institute for Educational Leadership
1001 Connecticut Avenue, N.W.
Suite 310
Washington, D.C. 20036
U.S.A.

[752]

EGGS AUTHORITY *(U.K.)*

Postgraduate Scholarships

Purpose: To promote greater interest and potential in agricultural marketing in the United Kingdom, particularly in the egg sector.

No. offered: One or more Scholarships annually.

Value: £2,200 per annum, plus fees. In addition, a grant of up to £500 per annum is available as an allowance for books and travelling.

Tenable normally for two years—first year at one of the following centres: University of Aberdeen; University of Manchester Institute of Science and Technology; University of Newcastle; University College of Wales; Wye College (University of London); University of Reading; second year at the Authority's headquarters at Tunbridge Wells.

Eligibility: Open to graduates who hold a first class or good second class degree from a United Kingdom university.

Note: These Scholarships are intended to lead to the degrees of M.Sc. or M.Phil., to be taken either as a result of a taught course or by means of a specific research investigation. The successful candidates are expected to undertake research into some substantial aspect of egg marketing.

Closing date: 20th March.

Further information from:
Chief Executive
Eggs Authority
Union House, Eridge Road
Tunbridge Wells, Kent
England TN4 8HF

[753]

1820 FOUNDATION *(South Africa)*

Old Mutual 1820 Settlers Scholarship
Gerald Wright Scholarship

Subject: English language or literature.

No. offered: One Scholarship annually.

Value: R1,500 per annum.

Tenable at any South African university for one year; may be extended for a second year.

Eligibility: Open to full-time South African students. Preference is given to those who propose to read for an honours degree in English.

Closing date: 30th October.

Note: A Scholar may not hold any other scholarship, bursary or paid appointment concurrently, except with the permission of the Council of the Foundation.

The Foundation also offers the *Gerald Wright Scholarships* in the amount of R600 per annum, available to students registering at a recognized South African university or teacher training college for the first time to read a degree in English literature or language. *Closing date:* 30th September.

Further information from:
Director
1820 Foundation
P.O. Box 304
Grahamstown 6140
South Africa

[754]

EISENHOWER EXCHANGE FELLOWSHIPS, INC. *(U.S.A.)*

Exchange Fellowships

Purpose: To enable non-United States citizens who are potential leaders in their professions to undertake a period of training and observation in the United States which will benefit their country on return.

Subjects: Unrestricted.

Value: Variable; the stipend normally covers maintenance and travel expenses.

Tenable for two to four months.

Eligibility: Open to non-U.S. citizens who are between 30 and 50 years of age, and who have already achieved considerable success in their fields.

Note: A bi-national committee, in the country in which the Fellowship is made, nominates the candidates. Further information may be obtained from United States embassies abroad or from:
Eisenhower Exchange Fellowships, Inc.
256 South Sixteenth Street
Philadelphia, Pennsylvania 19102
U.S.A.

[755]

ELECTRICAL WOMEN'S ROUND TABLE, INC. *(U.S.A.)*

Julia Kiene Fellowship

Purpose: To promote electrical living by encouraging high caliber college graduates to study toward advanced degrees.

Subjects: Advertising, education, electrical utilities, electrical engineering, electrical home equipment manufacturing, journalism, radio-television, housing and research.

No. offered: One Fellowship annually.

Value: US$2,000 in two payments.

Tenable for one year at an accredited college or university.

Eligibility: Open to a woman who is a graduating senior or has a degree from an accredited institution. Current EWRT members are not eligible.

Closing date: 1st March.

Further information from:
Marjory L. Joseph, Chairwoman
Department of Home Economics
California State University at Northridge
Northridge, California 91330
U.S.A.

Further information from:
Coordinator, Hagley Program
Eleutherian Mills-Hagley Foundation
P.O. Box 3630
Greenville
Wilmington, Delaware 19807
U.S.A.

[756]

ELEUTHERIAN MILLS-HAGLEY FOUNDATION
University of Delaware

Hagley Fellowships

Purpose: To provide a program of graduate study leading to an M.A. or Ph.D. degree in United States history for students who plan careers as college teachers or researchers in business, economic, labor, and technological history, or who plan careers as administrators of historical agencies such as museums, historical societies, libraries, and restorations.

No. offered: Approximately six Fellowships annually.

Value: US$4,200 for the first two years and US$4,600 for the second two years; an additional US$100 per month to Fellows with dependent children; a small travel allowance and all tuition fees for university courses are paid.

Tenable at the University of Delaware, Newark, for one year; renewable once for those seeking a terminal master's degree and up to three times for those seeking a doctorate.

Eligibility: Open to graduate students of any nationality seeking degrees in United States history. Fellows are selected upon Graduate Record. Examination scores, recommendations, and personal interviews.

Closing date: 7th February.

[757]

ELEUTERIAN MILLS-HAGLEY FOUNDATION

Grants-in-Aid of Research

Subjects: American economic and technological history; French 18th-century history.

No. offered: Approximately three Grants-in-Aid annually.

Value: Up to US$750 per month.

Tenable at the Eleutherian Mills Historical Library, Greenville, and environs, for a minimum period of one month.

Eligibility: Open to graduates of any nationality who hold a Ph.D. degree or equivalent, and to a limited number of Ph.D. candidates. Criteria for selection include the usefulness of the total resources of the library to the candidate's project, the significance of the scholar's project, the significance of the scholar's work to his general field of study, and the stage of development of the candidate's project. Preference will be given to those whose books and articles are near completion.

Note: The resources of the 125 libraries in the greater Philadelphia area will be at the disposal of the visiting scholar.

Further information from:
Director
Eleutherian Mills Historical Library
Eleutherian Mills-Hagley Foundation
P.O. Box 3630
Greenville
Wilmington, Delaware 19807
U.S.A.

[758]

BESSY EMANUEL EDUCATION TRUST
(U.K.)

Bessy Emanuel Travel Scholarships

One, occasionally two, Scholarships of £250 to £300 are provided annually for a small independent research project to be carried out in Israel over a period of 4 to 6 weeks.

Any student in a British institution of higher education is eligible; some preference may be given to applicants from the county of Sussex. Closing date for applications is March for awards announced in May.

Further information may be obtained from *Dr. Julius Carlebach, School of African and Asian Studies, University of Sussex, Falmer, Brighton, Sussex BN1 9QN*. When full details have been received, applications should be sent to:

Ralph N. Emanuel
61 Redington Road
London
England NW3 7RP

[759]

ENDOCRINE SOCIETY

Awards

The following Awards are presented annually to endocrinologists, either Society members or nonmembers, whose major work has been carried out in the United States or Canada. Nominations must be made and seconded by Society members. Additional information on all Awards may be obtained by writing to the address below.

Edwin B. Astwood Lecture Award of US$2,000 plus travel expenses to the Society's annual meeting is granted for scientific achievement in endocrinology. This Award is sponsored by the Nichols Institute.

Ayerst Award of US$2,000 and a certificate is given in recognition of distinguished service in the field of endocrinology. In addition, *Ayerst Travel Fellowships* are made available every fourth year to young endocrinologists to help defray part of the cost of travel to International Congress of Endocrinology.

Fred Conrad Koch Award of US$5,000 and a certificate is presented to a person or persons for work of special distinction in endocrinology.

Ernst Oppenheimer Memorial Award of US$3,000 and a certificate is given in recognition of the meritorious accomplishments of an investigator in the field of basic or clinical endocrinology who has not reached his or her forty-first birthday before 1st July of the year of the Award. This Award is sponsored by the Ciba-Geigy Corporation.

Note: The Society also administers the *Robert H. Williams Distinguished Leadership Award in Endocrinology.*

Address:
Endocrine Society
9650 Rockville Pike
Bethesda, Maryland 20814
U.S.A.

[760]

ENGINEERING FOUNDATION *(U.S.A.)*

Engineering Research Grants

Purpose: To advance the engineering profession for the good of mankind through the promotion of research in engineering and related scientific areas.

Subjects: Engineering—projects are encouraged in (a) innovative approaches to the solution of major national problems (conservation of natural resources; improvements in quality of the environment; improvements in housing, transportation and communications systems; more effective utilization of materials, by increased efficiency, lowered requirements, or recycling) and (b) the development of engineering techniques for the future (for example, new interdisciplinary approaches such as engineering in medicine and in solid waste disposal; the role of engineering in evolving sociological patterns; long-range economic and social implications of engineering solutions to problems; improved methods of teaching engineers).

Value: Variable according to needs and the nature of the request. The total grant expenditure is approximately US$100,000 annually.

Tenable for one year in the United States or Canada; extensions are possible.

Eligibility: Open to qualified United States and Canadian investigators as well as organizations and technical societies.

Note: Proposals are accepted on a continuous basis.

Further information from:
Engineering Foundation
United Engineering Center
345 East 47th Street
New York, New York 10017
U.S.A.

[761]

ENGLISH ACADEMY OF SOUTHERN AFRICA

Thomas Pringle Award: Up to three Awards, each consisting of R100 and a hand-drawn certificate, are given annually for material written in English, eminating from Southern Africa, and published in a Southern African newspaper or periodical. Categories include reviews, literary and educational articles, short-stories, one-act plays and poetry, as well as general essays.

Olive Schreiner Prize: An annual Prize of R250 is awarded to a citizen of South Africa or the territories administered (or formerly administered) by South Africa. The Prize is given, on an annually rotating basis, for drama, prose, and poetry. Writers should not, as yet, be regarded as 'established' authors in the particular catagory for which the Prize is offered.

Further information from:
English Academy of Southern Africa
Ballater House
35 Melle Street
Braamfontein
Johannesburg 2001
South Africa

[762]

ENGLISH AMERICAN INSTITUTE
University of Vienna *(Austria)*

Woursell Stipend

The University of Vienna awards the Stipend at various times to persons of exceptional literary talent who have done promising work in creative writing. Open to individuals within the ages of 22 and 35 who are citizens of any non-Communist country.

Further information from:
English-American Institute
University of Vienna
Universitätsstrasse 7
1010 Vienna
Austria

[763]

ENGLISH CENTRE OF INTERNATIONAL P.E.N.

Katherine Mansfield-Menton Short Story: A triennial Prize of £200 is given by the city of Menton, France, to commemorate Katherine Mansfield's residence in the city. The Prize is awarded for a story printed in English in the United Kingdom, Ireland, the Commonwealth or South Africa during the three years prior to the year of the award, and was last given in 1981. American writers are not eligible. Stories should not be submitted by authors, but by editors, publishers or literary agents. Entries should not exceed 10,000 words.

A corresponding Prize is offered for stories in French. Enquiries should be sent to, *Maison Internationale des P.E.N. Clubs, 6 rue François Miron, Paris 75004.*

Joe Ackerley Prize for autobiography is awarded annually for an outstanding autobiography (personal rather than official) published within the current year.

Note: The Centre also gives the *Silver Pen Award* annually for the most outstanding book in the opinion of the Judges published during the previous year, ending 31st December. Books must be written in English and initially published in the United Kingdom.

Further information from:
Menton Prize
English Centre of International P.E.N.
7 Dike Street
Chelsea, London
England SW3 4JE

[764]

ENGLISH-SPEAKING UNION OF THE COMMONWEALTH *(U.K.)*

Lindemann Trust Fellowships

Subjects: Astronomy, chemistry, engineering, geology, geophysics, mathematics and physics.

No. offered: Two Fellowships annually.

Value: A stipend of at least US$16,000 per annum; round-trip travel expenses; and where appropriate, dependents allowance.

Tenable for one year at a United States university.

Eligibility: Open to United Kingdom and Commonwealth citizens who are less than 35 years of age on 1st September of the Fellowship year, and who are graduates of a United Kingdom university. Candidates must hold an honours degree, have had postgraduate research experience, and be resident in the United Kingdom. Confirmation of Fellowship awards is conditional upon the grant of an exchange-visitor visa by the United States consular authorities.

Note: Fellows are not required to work for an American degree but are expected to be attached to a university, college or seat of advanced learning and technical repute in the United States. The place of study and research programme must be approved by the Committee. A limited amount of teaching as an adjunct to research activities is not excluded.

Closing date: 10th November.

Further information from:
 Secretary
 Lindemann Trust Fund Fellowship
 English-Speaking Union of the
  Commonwealth
 Dartmouth House, 37 Charles Street
 London
 England W1X 8AB

[765]

ENGLISH-SPEAKING UNION OF THE COMMONWEALTH *(U.K.)*

Chautauqua Scholarships; Rebecca Richmond Memorial Scholarships

Purpose: To enable British teachers to study at the Chautauqua Summer School organized by the University of Syracuse (see Chautauqua Institution).

Subjects: Art (painting, ceramics and sculpture), music education, literature and international relations.

No. offered: Two Scholarships annually.

Value: US$250 to cover lectures, board, room, tuition and certain incidental expenses, plus a travel grant of £250.

Tenable for six weeks at Chautauqua Institution's Summer School, Chautauqua, New York, and for three weeks as the guest of the English-Speaking Union of the United States.

Eligibility: Open to British teachers who are prepared to leave the country during the last week of June.

Further information from:
 Director of Education
 English-Speaking Union of the
  Commonwealth
 Dartmouth House, 37 Charles Street
 London
 England W1X 8AB

[766]

ENGLISH-SPEAKING UNION OF THE COMMONWEALTH *(U.K.)*

Senior Page Scholarship

Purpose: To enable British teachers to visit the United States to study a particular aspect of American education in which they are interested.

No. offered: One Scholarship annually.

Value: £600 plus US$250 and full hospitality.

Tenable for eight weeks in the United States, during which a visit to the West Coast must be included. Hospitality is provided by the American members of the English-Speaking Union.

Eligibility: Open to British teachers normally between the ages of 25 and 55. Scholarships must be taken up during the American academic year while educational institutions are in session.

Further information from:
   Director of Education
   English-Speaking Union of the
      Commonwealth
   Dartmouth House, 37 Charles Street
   London
   England W1X 8AB

[767]

ENGLISH-SPEAKING UNION LTD. *(N.S.W. Branch)*

Scholarship

Purpose: To assist Australian graduates who wish to undertake further studies abroad.

Subjects: Unrestricted.

No. offered: One Scholarship annually.

Value: Approximately A$5,000.

Tenable outside Australia; the period is determined by the study project to be undertaken; not renewable.

Eligibility: Open to Australian graduates in the State of New South Wales and the Australian Capital Territory.

Further information from:
   English-Speaking Union (N.S.W. Branch)
   P.O. Box E.156
   St. James, N.S.W.
   Australia 2000

[768]

ENGLISH-SPEAKING UNION LTD. *(Victoria Branch, Australia)*

Travelling Scholarship

Purpose: To promote understanding between English-speaking peoples.

Subjects: Unrestricted.

No. offered: One Scholarship annually.

Value: A$1,000.

Tenable in member countries of the E-SU.

Eligibility: Open to Australian citizens who are residents of Australia, between 21 and 35 years old, wishing to gain experience outside Australia to further their careers.

Note: The Scholarship represents a travel grant to assist a person who has already made arrangements to study overseas and who is regarded as a good ambassador for Australia.

Closing date: 30th June.

Further information from:
   Honorary Secretary
   Travelling Scholarship Committee
   English-Speaking Union (Victoria Branch)
   146 West Toorak Road
   South Yarra, Victoria
   Australia 3141

[769]

ENGLISH-SPEAKING UNION OF THE UNITED STATES

Winston Churchill Traveling Fellowships

Purpose: To enable young Americans to broaden their experience in their fields by exchanging ideas with Commonwealth people and observing techniques in Commonwealth countries.

No. offered: One or two Fellowships annually.

Value: Up to US$4,000 to cover living expenses and travel to, from and within the host countries.

Eligibility: Open to United States citizens between 25 and 45 years of age who have marked ability or promise in their fields. Candidates must be working full-time in a field which falls under the category designated for the year in which they apply.

Note: Fellowships are not intended to finance graduate or post-graduate studies.
   Separate competitions are held by national

and branch organizations of the English-Speaking Union.

Further information from:
Winston Churchill Traveling Fellowships
English-Speaking Union of the United States
16 East 69th Street
New York, New York 10021
U.S.A.

[770]

ENI: ENRICO MATTEI INSTITUTE *(Milan)*

Postgraduate Scholarships

Subjects: Advanced studies concerned with energy economics, business organizations in the field of industry, and the economic environment in which a firm operates.

No. offered: 35 Scholarships plus 20 grants of other Institutions annually.

Value: 500,000 lire per month.

Tenable in Italy for one academic year.

Eligibility: Open to nationals of all countries who have at least a Master's degree in economics, social and political sciences, law, engineering, mathematics, statistics, informatics, chemistry, or natural sciences, and are not more than 32 years of age.

Note: An information booklet is available in Italian and English.

Closing date: 30th June for foreign students; 30th September for Italian students.

Further information from:
ENI: Enrico Mattei Institute (Scuola Superiore Enrico Mattei—ENI)
Metanopoli
20097 San Donato Milanese
Milan
Italy

[771]

ENVIRONMENTAL PROTECTION AGENCY *(U.S.A.)*
Office of Research and Development

Air Pollution Control Research Grants: Purpose—to promote and encourage research and development projects relating to the causes, effects, extent, prevention and control of air pollution. Eligibility—open to individuals of unusually high demonstrated scientific ability, and to non-profit institutions such as universities and colleges, hosptials, laboratories, state and local health departments, etc.

Environmental Protection—Consolidated Research Grants: Purpose—to support research to explore and develop strategies and mechanisms for those in the economic, social, governmental and environmental systems to use in environmental management. Eligibility—open to individuals and public and private non-profit institutions.

Pesticides Control Research Grants: Purpose—to expand research activities on pesticides as related to human and environmental effects from pesticides, pesticide degradation products, and alternatives to pesticides. Eligibility—open to individuals and public and private non-profit institutions and agencies.

Solid Waste Disposal Research Grants: Purpose—to provide Grants for research in all scientific aspects of solid waste collection, storage, utilization, processing, salvage, or final disposal. Eligibility—open to any individual, public or private non-profit institution or agency involved in conducting research germane to solid waste management.

Water Pollution Control Research Development and Demonstration Grants: Purpose—to support and promote the coordination of research, development, and demonstration projects relating to causes, control and prevention of water pollution. Eligibility—open to individuals and public and private agencies, etc.

Safe Drinking Water Research and Demonstration Grants: Purpose—to support research aimed at establishing health criteria for organic, inorganic and microbiological contaminants of drinking water and to establish safe recreational water quality standards. Eligibility—open to individuals, universities, hospitals, laboratories and other public or private institutions.

Toxic Substances Research Grants: Purpose—to support and promote the coordination of research projects relating to the effects, extent, prevention, and control of toxic chemical substances or mixtures. Eligibility—open to individuals who have demonstrated unusually high scientific ability, and to various public and private institutions and agencies.

Not confirmed for 1983.

Further information from:
  Office of Research Program
    Management
  Office of Research and Development
    (RD-674)
  Environmental Protection Agency
  Washington, D.C. 20460
  U.S.A.

[772]

ENVIRONMENTAL PROTECTION AGENCY *(U.S.A.)*
Office of Water and Waste Management

Solid Waste Management Training Grants are offered to assist in and better inform state and local appointed and elected officials and private citizens about solid waste management problems and solutions, and to train solid waste management personnel. Grants are available to federal, state, interstate or local authorities, agencies and U.S. citizens. Each application shall be evaluated in relation to grant regulations and to determine the merit and relevancy of the project or program in question. Grants range from *US$4,000* to *US$100,000* and are tenable for a maximum of three years.

Solid Waste Management Demonstration Grants are offered to promote the demonstration and application of solid waste management and resource recovery technologies and systems which preserve and enhance the quality of the environment and conserve resources, and to conduct solid waste management and resource recovery studies, investigations and surveys. Grants are available to state, interstate, municipal, intermunicipal or other public authorities and agencies; public and private state colleges and universities; private nonprofit agencies and institutions, and U.S. citizens. Each application shall be evaluated in relation to grant regulations and to determine the merit and relevance of the project or program. Potential applicants are urged to contact their EPA Regional Administrator prior to applying. Grants range from *US$100,000* to *US$500,000*, are tenable for a period of one year, and are renewable for up to five years.

Not confirmed for 1983.

Further information from:
  Office of Water and Waste Management
  Environmental Protection Agency
  Washington, D.C. 20460
  U.S.A.

[773]

ENVIRONMENTAL PROTECTION AGENCY *(U.S.A.)*
Office of Water and Waste Management

Water Pollution Control Fellowships

Purpose: To augment the capability of state and local water pollution control agencies through support for upgrading their personnel in professional training at qualified institutions.

Subjects: Water pollution abatement and control.

No. offered: Varies.

Value: Full-time Fellows who are employees of regional, state or local agencies may receive a stipend up to a maximum of *US$6,000*. Part-time Fellows may receive a small stipend when justified by extraordinary needs related to the purpose of the Fellowships. In addition, tuition, fees and a book allowance of up to *US$250* are provided.

Tenable at an accredited educational institution for full- or part-time study.

Eligibility: Open to United States citizens who are present or prospective employees of a regional, state or local environmental pollution control or regulatory agency.

Not confirmed for 1983.

Further information from:
  State Programs Section
  Manpower Planning and Training Branch
    (WH-596)
  Environmental Protection Agency
  Washington, D.C. 20460
  U.S.A.

[774]

ENVIRONMENTAL PROTECTION AGENCY *(U.S.A.)*
Office of Water and Waste Management

Water Pollution Control Training Grants

Traineeships: Available to train and educate technical personnel in the design, operation and maintenance of waste treatment works. The number of awards vary annually.

Traineeships are available as a result of *Technical Training Grants* offered by the Agency to appropriate institutions of higher learning.

Professional Training Grants: Grants are available to United States citizens to improve the training and education of professionals in scientific water environmental programs and to increase the number of adequately trained water pollution control and abatement personnel. These cover tuition and fees and may carry a stipend in the range of US$1,000 to US$3,000.

Not confirmed for 1983.

Further information from:
Manpower Planning and Training Branch (WH-596)
Office of Water Programs Operations
Environmental Protection Agency
Washington, D.C. 20460
U.S.A.

[775]

EPINAL INTERNATIONAL PIANO COMPETITION *(France)*

Prizes of 15,000, 5,000, 3,000 and 2,000 French francs are awarded in the Competition which is held in Epinal. Pianists of any nationality who are under 30 years of age may enter.

Further information from:
Secretariat
Epinal International Piano Competition
3 avenue Victor-Hugo
F-88000 Epinal
France

[776]

EPILEPSY FOUNDATION OF AMERICA
Mary Litty Memorial Fellowships

Subjects: Epilopsy and related problems.

Value: US$300 per month, up to a maximum of US$900.

Tenable at an institution where there is an on-going program of epilepsy service, training or research in the field of vocational rehabilitation.

Eligibility: Open to graduate or undergraduate students of vocational rehabilitation.

Closing date: 1st April.

Note: A supervisor or preceptor must accept responsibility for supervision of the program.

Further information from:
Mary Litty Memorial Fellowships
Research and Training Institute
Epilepsy Foundation of America
4351 Garden City Drive, Suite 406
Landover, Maryland 20903
U.S.A.

[777]

EPILEPSY FOUNDATION OF AMERICA
Medical Student Fellowships

Purpose: To encourage young medical students to specialize in the neurological sciences, especially as they relate to epilepsy.

Value: US$300 per month up to a maximum of US$1,500.

Tenable at clinics and laboratories in the United States for eight to twelve weeks.

Eligibility: Open to United States medical students interested in epilepsy.

Note: Work must be conducted under the supervision of a specific preceptor. Each applicant should submit (a) a letter giving a brief statement about his background, interests, and his reasons for applying for the Fellowship; (b) a brief outline of his proposal for an eight to twelve week period; and (c) a letter from a preceptor who will be responsible for his program, indicating the preceptor's acceptance of the candidate and his program.

Closing date: 1st March.

Further information from:
Fellowship Program
Research and Training Institute
Epilepsy Foundation of America
4351 Garden City Drive, Suite 406
Landover, Maryland 20903
U.S.A.

[778]

EPILEPSY FOUNDATION OF AMERICA

Research Grants

Purpose: To support basic and clinical research to advance the understanding, treatment and prevention of epilepsy.

Subjects: Neurology and neurosciences, psychology, vocational rehabilitation, special education, social casework and public health administration.

Value: Up to US$12,000 per annum. Funds are provided mainly for personnel and consumable supplies.

Tenable at research centers in the United States for periods of one year; renewable.

Eligibility: Open to persons with a demonstrated competence for research in any of the above subjects.

Closing date: 1st September.

Further information from:
Research Grants Program
Research and Training Institute
Epilepsy Foundation of America
4351 Garden City Drive, Suite 406
Landover, Maryland 20903
U.S.A.

[779]

EPISCOPAL CHURCH FOUNDATION
(U.S.A.)

Fellowships

Purpose: To encourage doctoral study by recent seminary graduates to qualify themselves for the teaching ministry of the Episcopal Church.

No. offered: Varies according to funds available.

Value: Depends on individual circumstances. Payments are made in two equal installments in September and in January.

Tenable at accredited institutions in the United States and abroad. Fellowships are renewable for a second and third year.

Eligibility: Applicants should have graduates from an accredited seminary of the Episcopal Church or from another recognized seminary as an Episcopal candidate within the past ten years, or be a member of the senior class. Applicants must be recommended by the deans of their theological seminaries.

Closing date: November.

Further information from:
Episcopal Church Foundation
815 Second Avenue
New York, New York 10017
U.S.A.

[780]

ETERNIT INTERNATIONAL PRIZE FOR ARCHITECTURE
INTERNATIONAL UNION OF ARCHITECTS

Four Prizes of 250,000 Belgian francs each, and five honourable mention Prizes of 50,000 Belgian francs each are made every two years to select and draw attention to architectural works which are outstanding for their human, functional, aesthetic or technical qualities and their relationship with their surroundings. Qualified architects of the United Kingdom, Belgium, the Grand-Duchy of Luxembourg, West Germany, the Netherlands and Italy are eligible to compete. The Prize categories are as follows: (a) single family dwellings; (b) grouped housing developments, dwellings and/or flats; (c) sport complexes, theatres, holiday centres, social centres, etc.; and (d) work in categories (a), (b), or (c) which is judged to have made the most interesting use of materials produced by the Eternit Group. The next Competition will take place in 1982.

Not confirmed for 1983.

Further information from:
Eternit Building Products Ltd.
Whaddon Road
Meldreth, near Royston
Hertfordshire
England SG8 5RL

[781]

EUROPEAN ASSOCIATION FOR THE STUDY OF DIABETES

Minkowski Prize

An annual Prize of DM10,000, a certificate and travel expenses to the Association's annual meeting, are given for publications, based on research conducted in Europe, which contributes to the advancement of knowledge concerning diabetes mellitus. Candidates, who must be nominated by a member of the Association, should be normally resident in Europe and be less than 40 years of age on 1st January of the Prize year. The winner is expected to give a lecture on the research at the Association meeting, as well as write an account of the research for publication in *Diabetologia*, the Association journal.

Closing date: 31st January of the Prize year.

Further information from:
Dr. J.G.L. Jackson, Executive Director
European Association for the Study of
  Diabetes
10 Queen Anne Street
London
England W1M 0BD

[782]

EUROPEAN CENTRE
University of Nancy

CEU Grants

Subjects: Civilization (man in his cultural environment); economics (the theory of economic integration and its application to Europe); politics and law (study of the institutions of the EEC and other European organizations; economic laws of the Community).

No. offered: 45 Grants annually.

Value: FF200 per month.

Tenable at the European Centre, University of Nancy for seven months (October to May).

Eligibility: Open to graduates of all nationalities who are not more than 30 years of age and who have a good working knowledge of French.

Closing date: 1st June.

Further information from:
Centre Européen Universitaire
15 Place Carnot
54042 Nancy Cedex
France

[783]

EUROPEAN COLLEGE FOUNDATION
(Hamburg)

Scholarships are available to foreign postgraduate students wishing to address themselves to various questions relating to European integration. Specific study projects may alter from year to year. Scholarships are tenable at the Foundation's Institute in Hamburg.

Further information from:
European College Foundation
Windmuehlenweg 27
2 Hamburg 52
West Germany

[784]

EUROPEAN CULTURAL FOUNDATION

Project Grants

Grants are awarded for projects aiming to promote cultural, scientific and educational activities of a multinational character and European inspiration. Projects should contribute to European unity. Preference is given to study in the following areas: ecology, education, social strutures, manpower problems, culture, urbanization and European history and institutions. Projects should be of a multidisciplinary nature and must involve collaboration from at least three countries.

Grants will only normally cover part of the sum necessary for the completion of the project and proof must be provided that the organisers can furnish the rest. Grants are generally given for one year. Projects of a longer duration are subject to a new application each year.

Further information from:
European Cultural Foundation
5 Jan van Goyenkade
1075 HN Amsterdam
Netherlands

[785]

EUROPEAN INSTITUTE FOR BUSINESS ADMINISTRATION

Postgraduate Scholarships

Purpose: To enable graduate students to participate in the International MBA Programme.

Subject: Business administration.

No. offered: Approximately 50 Scholarships annually which are offered by specific organisations in different countries.

Value: Up to the equivalent of £2,500 per annum.

Tenable for one academic year at the European Institute for Business Administration, Fontainebleau, France.

Eligibility: Open to nationals of the 30 participating countries who: hold a university degree, have some experience in business or other organizations, and are between 24 and 30 years of age. Candidates should be fluent in English and French, and should strive to improve their knowledge of German before completion of the course.

Further information from:
European Institute for Business
   Administration
Admissions Department
Boulevard de Constance
F-77305 Fontainebleau
France

[786]

EUROPEAN MOLECULAR BIOLOGY ORGANISATION

Short- and Long-Term Fellowships

Short-Term Fellowships: Intended to support visits of one week to twelve weeks to other laboratories for the purpose of carrying out experiments with special techniques or other forms of scientific collaboration or advanced training, and especially to support development arising at short notice.

Long-Term Fellowships: Awarded on individual application for a period of one year, but Fellowships may be renewed for a second year, and in cases of exceptional scientific merit, for a third year. Their purpose is to allow scientists at the postdoctoral level to pursue collaborative research projects for prolonged periods at foreign laboratories.

Eligibility: Open to postdoctoral scientists in the field of molecular biology working in laboratories within the European area.

Note: A limited number of *Senior Fellowships* are available to enable distinguished senior scientists to bring their special expertise to European laboratories.

Closing date: Applications for Short-Term Fellowships may be made at any time. Applications for Long-Term Fellowships should be made by 15th February for a decision by the end of April, and by 15th August for a decision by the end of October.

Further information from:
Dr. J. Tooze, Executive Secretary
European Molecular Biology Organisation
Postfach 1022.40
69 Heidelberg 1
West Germany

[787]

EUROPEAN ORGANISATION FOR NUCLEAR RESEARCH [CERN]

Scientific Associateships

Purpose: To enable scientists from both member states and nonmember states of CERN to collaborate in the work of the CERN laboratories.

Subjects: Experimental and theoretical subnuclear physics and relevant branches of applied physics.

No. offered: Variable.

Value: Approximately 37,000 Swiss francs to 100,000 Swiss francs per annum if fully paid by CERN. The amount paid is calculated according to the status of the individual concerned and other financial support which he may receive.

Tenable at the CERN laboratories in Geneva, for periods of up to one year.

Eligibility: Priority is given to applicants who can make a definite contribution to the work of CERN, or to those who cannot obtain adequate scientific facilities in their own countries.

This scheme is open to nationals of all countries.

Closing date: Papers should be received six weeks before the meeting at which they are to be considered. Meetings are held in April, September and December.

Further information from:
Fellows and Associates Service
Personnel Division
CERN
CH-1211 Geneva 23
Switzerland

[788]

EUROPEAN ORGANISATION FOR NUCLEAR RESEARCH [CERN]

Fellowships

Purpose: To enable young scientists to gain experience by working in a research or development group at CERN.

Subjects: Experimental and theoretical subnuclear physics and relevant branches of applied physics.

No. offered: 55 Fellowships annually.

Value: 37,000 Swiss francs to 67,000 Swiss francs per annum according to age, plus additional allowances.

Tenable at CERN, Geneva, for one year initially; renewable for a second year.

Eligibility: Open to nationals of CERN member states (Austria, Belgium, Denmark, France, West Germany, Greece, Italy, Netherlands, Norway, Sweden, Switzerland, United Kingdom).

Candidates for Fellowships must be young scientists who have obtained at least their first degree, and preferably have had some years of research experience.

Closing date: Applications should be made at least six months before the proposed starting date, and two months before the meeting at which they are to be considered. Meetings are held in January and June.

Applications should be addressed to the national delegation in the candidate's own country. Candidates of United Kingdom nationality should apply to: *Mr. J. Walsh, Science and Engineering Research Council, P.O. Box 18, Swindon, Wiltshire SN2 1ET.*

Further information from:
Fellows and Associates Service
Personnel Division
CERN
CH-1211 Geneva 23
Switzerland

[789]

EUROPEAN ORGANISATION FOR NUCLEAR RESEARCH [CERN]

Travelling Fellowships

Subject: Subnuclear research.

Value: CERN pays travel expenses and a subsistence allowance. The home institute is expected to continue normal salary payments.

Tenable at the Joint Institute for Nuclear Research, Dubna, U.S.S.R., and in certain cases at other institutes in the U.S.S.R., for periods of three to twelve months.

Eligibility: Open to scientists from institutes in CERN member states (Austria, Belgium, Denmark, France, West Germany, Greece, Italy, Netherlands, Norway, Sweden, Switzerland, United Kingdom).

Further information from:
Fellows and Associates Service
Personnel Division
CERN
CH-1211 Geneva 23
Switzerland

[790]

EUROPEAN PARLIAMENT

Robert Schuman Scholarships

Purpose: To promote studies on European integration.

Subjects: Research in subjects relating to the EEC and to European integration.

No. offered: Approximately seven Scholarships annually.

Value: 23,000 Belgian francs per month, plus travel expenses.

Tenable at the European Parliament in Luxembourg, for three months.

Eligibility: Open to nationals of member countries of the EEC who have completed a degree course at a university or have attended an institute of higher education for at least three years (nine academic terms). Applications are not normally considered from employees of EEC institutions or members of their families.

Further information from:
  Secretariat-General
  European Parliament
  P.O. Box 1601
  Luxembourg

[791]

EUROPEAN SPACE AGENCY

Internal Research Fellowships
External Research Fellowships

Purpose: To provide opportunities for research in a field directly related to the programmes of the Agency.

Subjects: Practical and theoretical research in space technology, space science, space applications, material and life sciences.

Value: Up to US$15,000, plus travel expenses.

Tenable (for Internal Fellowships) at an ESA establishment in Paris, France; Darmstadt, Germany; Frascati, Italy; or Noordwijk, Netherlands; (for External Fellowships) at a university or research institute in Europe or the United States. Fellowships are awarded for one year and may be extended for up to one additional year.

Eligibility: Open to nationals of the ESA member states and to nationals of nonmember states in exceptional cases. Candidates should hold a doctorate degree, or be about to receive one.

Further information from:
  Personnel Department
  European Space Agency
  8-10 rue Mario-Nikis
  75738 Paris Cedex 15
  France

[792]

EUROPEAN UNIVERSITY INSTITUTE
(Florence)

The governments of nine European Community member states grant Scholarships to nationals of their own countries for research work at the Institute in Florence. Study, leading to the doctorate degree from the Institute, may be in history and civlization, economics, law, or political and social sciences. The number of annual awards per participating country is as follows: France, the United Kingdom, Italy and the Federal Republic of Germany—22 each; Belgium—12; Netherlands—10; Denmark—7; Ireland—6; Luxemburg—1.

Awards are subject to national regulations concerning grants for study abroad, and therefore vary in amount (awards varied between 420,000 lire and 600,000 lire in 1981). Scholarships are normally tenable for twelve months and renewable for up to an additional two years. Candidates must possess a good honours degree or its equivalent, and have full written and spoken command of at least two of the Institute's official languages. Applications are available from the address below.

Note: Under certain conditions, nationals of countries other than the EEC may also be admitted to the Institute and be eligible for a Scholarship.

Closing date: 15th March.

Further information from:
Academic Service
European University Institute
Badia Fiesolana
Via Badia dei Roccettini 5
500 16 San Domenico di Fiesole
Florence
Italy

[793]

EXCERPTA MEDICA FOUNDATION
(Netherlands)

Excerpta Medica Travel Award

Purpose: To enable a member of the international biomedical community to establish new contacts and strengthen existing contacts with fellow-members of his or her own and related branches of medicine throughout the world.

No. offered: One Award biennially, in odd-numbered years.

Value: The Award covers all travel and accommodation expenses, plus an extra allowance to cover day-to-day expenditure. The recipient may travel with a companion whose expenses are also fully covered.

Tenable for a total period of three months.

Note: Candidates are nominated by the members of the international editorial boards of the various journals published by Excerpta Medica. The final decision is made by the Foundation's trustees and directorial staff.

Not confirmed for 1983.

Further information from:
Travel Award Office
Excerpta Medica Foundation
P.O. Box 1126
1000 BC Amsterdam
Netherlands

[794]

EXPERIMENT IN INTERNATIONAL LIVING *(U.S.A.)*

Community Scholarships: Community Scholarships in the Untied States are available to selected Experiment Ambassadors from all countries who are interested in promoting international understanding. Participants may not remain in the United States after conclusion of these short-term programs. Scholarships cover program expenses in New York City and Washington, D.C. (one week), homestay with United States families (eight weeks), and program travel within the United States. Enquiries and applications should be addressed to the Experiment representative in the candidate's country or to the Department of Incoming Programs at the address below.

International Programs: Some Scholarships are available for participants in Programs offered at the School for International Training. They are: (a) intensive English training at all levels including work in social studies and an introduction to the United States; (b) master of arts in teaching, open to those preparing to be teachers of French, Spanish or English as a second language, including a period of student teaching and homestay; (c) master of intercultural/international administration program designed to prepare students for employment with international/intercultural service and educational organizations, including overseas working experience with an international organization. Applications and enquiries for (a) should be addressed to Director, English Language Programs. *Closing date:* three months prior to commencement of study. Applications and enquiries for (b) and (c) should be addressed to Director, SIT Admissions Office at the address below. *Closing date:* 1st August.

Further information from:
Experiment in International Living
Brattleboro, Vermont 05301
U.S.A.

F

See *How to Use The Grants Register*, page ix

[795]

F.V.S. FOUNDATION *(West Germany)*

Prizes, Scholarships and Grants

The main effort of the F.V.S. Foundation, in compliance with its statutes, is directed mainly towards nature conservancy, preservation of historic monuments and promotion of European unity. In addition, the Foundation, with the help of independent juries or selection committees, awards a number of Prizes and Scholarships to encourage and promote achievements in the above mentioned fields as well as in the fine arts and science. The most important of these Prizes, the majority of which are coupled with Grants for promising young scholars, are the *Hanseatic Goethe Prize*, the *Freiherr vom Stein Prize*, the *Fritz Schumacher Prize* (for town planning, architecture, engineering and landscape architecture), the *European Prizes of Statesmanship, for the Preservation of Historic Monuments and for Folklore*, the *Robert Schuman* and the *Joseph Bech* prizes for achievements in the field of European unification, the *Strasbourg Prize* for services by the younger generation in the cause of Franco-German co-operation, and Prizes for outstanding contributions to European culture as a whole, e.g., the *Shakespeare Prize* (British Isles), the *Steffens Prize* (Scandinavian countries), the *Herder Prize* (East and Southeast European countries) and the *Montaigne Prize* (the Romance-language-speaking countries of Europe).

Further information from:
F.V.S. Foundation
Georgsplatz 10
2 Hamburg 1
West Germany

[796]

FABER & FABER LTD. *(U.K.)*

Geoffrey Faber Memorial Prize

The annual Prize of £500 is awarded in alternate years for a volume of verse and for a volume of prose fiction, on the basis of literary merit. Citizens of the United Kingdom and its colonies, other Commonwealth states, the Republic of Ireland and the Republic of South Africa, who are not more than 40 years of age at the time of publication, are eligible to be nominated by the editors or literary editors of newspapers and magazines which regularly publish poetry or fiction reviews. No submissions will be considered. Works nominated must originally have been published in the United Kingdom during the two years preceding the year of the Prize.

Further information from:
Faber & Faber Ltd.
3 Queen Square
London
England WC1N 3AU

[797]

FAO INTERNATIONAL FOOD TECHNOLOGY TRAINING CENTRE *(Mysore, India)*

Scholarships

Subject: Food technology leading to the M.Sc. (food technology) degree of Mysore University.

No. offered: Variable.

Value: 1,000 rupees per month.

Tenable for two academic years at the Centre.

Eligibility: Open to candidates from countries in South and Southeast Asia and Africa who hold a second class or equivalent degree in science, agriculture, engineering or technology with adequate coverage of chemistry and mathematics at the collegiate level. Instruction is given in English.

Note: The Scholarships are offered through the T.C.S. Colombo Plan and Special Commonwealth African Assistance Programme,

Government of India. Nominations for Scholarships must be made through the Indian diplomatic representative in the candidate's own country.

Closing date: Last week of May.

Further information from:
 Director, FAO International Food Technology Training Centre
 Central Food Technology Research Institute
 Mysore 570013, Karnataka
 India

[798]

FARM FOUNDATION *(U.S.A.)*

Extension Graduate Training Fellowships

Purpose: To stimulate further training in study courses of value in extension work.

Subjects: Social sciences, educational administration and methodology, with emphasis on agricultural economics, rural sociology, psychology, political science and agricultural geography.

No. offered: Six to ten Fellowships annually.

Value: Varies according to need and to the period of study. Maximum, US$4,000 for nine months, paid in monthly installments.

Tenable at selected United States universities for one quarter, one semester or nine months. Recipients may renew by resubmitting applications which will be considered with new applications.

Eligibility: Open only to United States resident agricultural extension workers, with priority given to administrators and supervisory personnel. Applicants should be recommended by their extension directors and accepted by the university selected as the training center.

Further information from:
 Managing Director
 Farm Foundation
 1211 West 22nd Street
 Oak Brook, Illinois 60521
 U.S.A.

[799]

FARRER MEMORIAL TRUST DEPARTMENT OF AGRICULTURE *(N.S.W.)*

Farrer Memorial Research Scholarship

Purpose: To aid study or research into problems of an agricultural nature.

No. offered: One Scholarship at irregular intervals.

Value: A$5,000 per annum, plus payment of certain family allowances, compulsory university fees, medical/hospital fund contributions.

Tenable for twelve months at any appropriate educational establishment approved by the Trustees; renewable for a second and possibly a third year at the discretion of the Trustees.

Eligibility: The Scholarship is traditionally awarded to a graduate who has demonstrated a high level of ability after graduation, but there are no restrictions.

Note: The Scholar must devote his full time to the work for which the Scholarship was granted and may not hold concurrently a scholarship or like appointment from any other source without the approval of the Trustees. Progress reports are required at six-monthly intervals. Conditions may vary from year to year.

Further information from:
 Secretary, Farrer Memorial Trust
 N.S.W. Department of Agriculture
 P.O. Box K220
 Haymarket, N.S.W.
 Australia 2000

[800]

FATHER DAMIAN FOUNDATION FOR THE CAMPAIGN AGAINST LEPROSY *(Belgium)*

Grants and Scholarships are awarded periodically to fight leprosy and improve the conditions of lepers, particularly in Central Africa, although the Foundation's sphere of activities is international.

Closing date: 15th April.

Further information from:
Father Damian Foundation for the Campaign against Leprosy
16 rue Stévin
1040 Brussels
Belgium

[801]

FEDERAL ADMINISTRATION FOR INTERNATIONAL SCIENTIFIC, EDUCATIONAL, CULTURAL AND TECHNICAL COOPERATION *(Yugoslavia)*

Specialization Fellowships

Subjects: Unrestricted, but usually in the broad areas of culture, humanities, and the social sciences.

Value: 6,200 dinars per month if accommodation is provided in student hostels, and 7,300 dinars per month for private accommodations. Fellows who are senior lecturers or university professors receive 6,000 dinars per month and 7,400 dinars per month, respectively.

Tenable at universities and other educational establishments in Yugoslavia for three to nine months; may not be held during the summer vacation.

Eligibility: Open to nationals of foreign countries who possess a university diploma, are less than forty years of age, and have a good knowledge of French, English, Russian, or one of the Yugoslav languages.

Note: Candidates should specify the professor they would like to work with, or name the institution in which they would like to work. They should also possess a letter of recommendation from their supervisory professor in their home country.

Closing date: 31st January.

Further information from:
Federal Administration for International Scientific, Educational, Cultural and Technical Coooperation
Kosančićev venac 29
Belgrade
Yugoslavia

[802]

FEDERAL COMMISSION FOR SCHOLARSHIPS FOR FOREIGN STUDENTS *(Switzerland)*

Scholarships

Subjects: Unrestricted.

No. offered: Approximately 70 Scholarships annually.

Value: 8,000 Swiss francs to 12,000 Swiss francs, to cover tuition fees, study materials and maintenance. The Swiss government undertakes to pay the Scholar's return fare if he comes from a non-European country.

Tenable at any institution of higher education in Switzerland for one academic year (nine months) for Scholars from European countries; (supplementary) for twelve months for Scholars from Australia, Canada, China, Israel, New Zealand, South Africa and the United States; and for the duration of a degree course of Scholars from developing areas.

Eligibility: Candidates must have a good knowledge of French or German which is tested at a preliminary language examination at a Swiss embassy. If a candidate's knowledge is considered inadequate an award is given on the condition that the person follows a preparatory language course at Fribourg.

Note: Candidates should apply to the Ministry of Education in their country. Further information can be obtained from the Swiss diplomatic representative or from the Commission.

Address:
Federal Commission for Scholarships
Route du Jura 1
1700 Fribourg
Switzerland

[803]

FEDERAL MINISTRY OF EDUCATION *(Nigeria)*

Commonwealth Scholarship and Fellowship Plan—in Nigeria

Purpose: To enable persons of high intellectual promise and attainment to pursue advanced courses of study or to undertake research at suitable centres in Nigeria.

Subjects: Unrestricted.

No. offered: Varies annually.

Value: Round trip 1st class sea or tourist air passage to Nigeria; a personal allowance of N2,184 per annum; a book and apparatus allowance of N364 per annum; an allowance for approved travel in Nigeria for the purpose of study or research,, not to exceed N280 per annum; and a one time clothing allowance of N140 for Scholars from temperate countries.

Tenable in Nigerian universities, normally for a period of two years, with the possibility of extension for a third year. Scholarships begin in October of each year.

Eligibility: Open to Commonwealth citizens or British protected persons who are, or will be college or university graduates by the beginning of the Scholarship period. Candidates should normally be resident in a Commonwealth country other than Nigeria and be not more than 35 years of age by 1st October of the Scholarship year. The age limit may, in certain circumstances, be raised.

Note: Scholars will be expected to possess a good knowledge of written and spoken English, to reside in Nigeria for the duration of the Scholarship period and give prior notification of any proposed visits abroad, and to return to his own country upon completion of the study or research. Scholars will not be allowed, except under special circumstances, to take up paid appointments or to hold any other scholarship award. Applications should be made through an appropriate agency in the candidate's country of residence.

Not confirmed for 1983.

Address:
  Commonwealth Scholarship and Fellowship Plan
  Federal Ministry of Education
  Scholarship Division
  Lagos
  Nigeria

[804]

FEDMECH FOUNDATION FOR ADVANCED EDUCATION AND RESEARCH *(South Africa)*

Research Project Awards

Subjects: Agriculture and engineering.

Value: Varies according to the nature of the research project.

Tenable preferably in South Africa, for one year, or until research project is completed.

Eligibility: Open to residents of South Africa who hold a suitable bachelor's degree.

Note: Preference is given to postgraduate research in agricultural mechanization or related fields.
  The Foundation also supports research in fields that contribute to agricultural, industrial, and construction mechanization and manufacturing, to the benefit of the South African economy.

Closing date: 31st August.

Further information from:
  The Secretary
  Fedmech Foundation for Advanced Education and Research
  P.O. Box 677
  Vereeniging, Transvaal 1930
  South Africa

[805]

FELLOWSHIP OF ENGINEERING *(U.K.)*

MacRobert Award

One Award of £25,000 and a gold medal is made annually to an individual, independent team, or team working for a firm, organization or laboratory, who has made an outstanding contribution by way of innovation in the fields of engineering or the other physical sciences. The contribution should be such that has or will enhance the national prestige and prosperity of the United Kingdom.

Closing date: 30th April.

Further information from:
   MacRobert Award Office
   Fellowship of Engineering
   2 Little Smith Street
   London
   England SW1P 3DL

[806]

FENG CHIA UNIVERSITY
(Taichung, Taiwan)

Courses on Chinese Architecture: International Scholarships

Subject: Chinese architecture (construction methods and history).

No. offered: Four Scholarships annually.

Value: To cover tuition, board and lodging.

Tenable at the College for one academic year (September-June).

Eligibility: Open to university graduates of high academic standing who are under 45 years of age and have a good working knowledge of Chinese.

Closing date: 31st March.

Further information from:
   Office of Academic Affairs
   Feng Chia University
   100 Wenhwa Road, Sitwen District
   Taichung
   Taiwan

[807]

FIGHT FOR SIGHT, INC. *(U.S.A.)*

Student Fellowships

Subjects: Ophthalmology and related sciences.

No. offered: 12 to 15 Fellowships annually.

Value: US$300-US$350 per month; US$350-US$400 per month for renewable awards. Recipients may supplement this stipend with funds from another source.

Tenable at approved institutions for periods of two to three months—full-time work during vacation periods.

Eligibility: Open to selected students of medicine and the basic sciences who have demonstrated a special interest in research and have given reasonable assurance of their intention to enter ophthalmology. Applications from foreign nationals for work outside the United States must be deemed particularly significant, or where the circumstances are such to provide unusual opportunities for the proposed research study. Foreign investigators seeking Fellowships at U.S. institutions must show that they will be able to continue to apply their research interests in their home countries and that the tenure within the U.S. may contribute significantly to the total research effort. The candidate's knowledge of the English language will also be a consideration. Student Fellowships are not offered to Americans who wish to study abroad, unless the circumstances are extraordinary. These conditions also apply to Fight for Sight's Postdoctoral Fellowships and Grants-in-Aid.

Note: It is the responsibility of candidates to make arrangements with the institutions of their choice. Applications should then be sent through the head of the department of ophthalmology at that institution.

Closing date: 1st March.

Further information from:
   Secretary
   Fight for Sight, Inc.
   139 East 57th Street
   New York, N.Y. 10022
   U.S.A.

[808]

FIGHT FOR SIGHT, INC. *(U.S.A.)*

Postdoctoral Research Fellowships

Subject: Ophthalmology and its related sciences: fundamental or clinical research.

No. offered: 15 Fellowships annually.

Value: US$4,000 to US$10,000 per annum; US$4,500 to US$10,500 per annum for renewable awards. Recipients may supplement this stipend with funds from another source.

Tenable at any approved institution for one year, with the possibility of renewal.

Eligibility: Open to physicians and other scientists with doctoral degrees who are interested in academic careers, whose proposed projects are original, and whose background and interests are likely to contribute to the project undertaken. See policy regarding foreign applications in.

Note: It is the responsibility of candidates to make arrangements with the institutions of their choice. Applications should then be sent through the head of the department of ophthalmology at that institution.

Closing date: 1st March.

Further information from:
Secretary
Fight for Sight, Inc.
139 East 57th Street
New York, New York 10022
U.S.A.

[809]

FIGHT FOR SIGHT, INC. *(U.S.A.)*

Grants-in-Aid

Purpose: To encourage the younger investigator who has not yet had the opportunity to demonstrate fully his proficiency in ophthalmic research, and therefore finds it especially difficult to enlist assistance in support of his work from other sources.

No. offered: 30 to 50 Grants annually.

Value: By individual assessment from US$1,000 to US$10,000 maximum—to help defray the cost of personnel, equipment and supplies needed for a specific research investigation.

Tenable at any institution in the United States or abroad, which offers research facilities suitable to the research project in question; support may be renewed.

Eligibility: Open to young or mature investigators. See policy regarding foreign applications in.

Note: It is the responsibility of candidates to make arrangements with the institutions of their choice. Applications should then be sent through the head of the department of ophthalmology at that institution.

Applications for support of pilot projects are welcome.

Closing date: 1st March.

Further information from:
Secretary
Fight for Sight, Inc.
139 East 57th Street
New York, N.Y. 10022
U.S.A.

[810]

FIGHT FOR SIGHT, INC. ASSOCIATION FOR RESEARCH IN VISION AND OPHTHALMOLOGY, INC. *(U.S.A.)*

Citation Awards

Two Citations are given annually to recognize investigators who have made significant contributions in the field of vision. One Award is offered for achievement in basic research and the other for achievement in clinical research.

Value: US$500 honorarium and a hand-lettered scroll.

Occasionally, an Award for an extraordinary breakthrough is considered. An honorarium of US$1,000 and a hand-lettered scroll are awarded.

Preference is given to the younger investigator for the first two Awards. There is no age consideration for the third Award.

Further information from:
Secretary
Fight for Sight, Inc.
139 East 57th Street
New York, N.Y. 10022
U.S.A.

[811]

FINE ARTS WORK CENTER IN PROVINCETOWN, INC. *(U.S.A.)*

Fellowships

Purpose: To give young professional writers and visual artists the opportunity to work at the Center in a congenial and stimulating environment and to devote most of their time to their art. The Center is a workshop community, not a school.

Subjects: Painting, sculpture, prose and poetry writing.

No. offered: 20 Fellowships annually.

Value: Between US$270 and US$450 per month.

Tenable in Provincetown, Massachusetts, for about seven months.

Eligibility: Preference is given to young candidates of outstanding promise. Applicants are accepted on the basis of work submitted.

Closing date: 1st February.

Further information from:
Fine Arts Work Center
Box 565
Provincetown, Massachusetts 02657
U.S.A.

[812]

PAUL FINET FOUNDATION *(Luxembourg)*

Grants

Purpose: To grant financial aid to orphans of workers in the coal mines, iron ore mines and steel industry of the European Coal and Steel Community who have died as a consequence of an industrial accident or occupational illness, with a view to permitting or facilitating studies or vocational training corresponding to their aptitudes.

Subjects: Unrestricted.

Value: The amount depends upon available funds, the needs of the applicant, and the nature of studies or vocational training. Aid shall be in the currency of the candidate's own country.

Tenable for one academic year at secondary schools or special teaching establishments leading to a diploma for completed secondary or technical studies; full-time attendance at a professional school leading to a recognized diploma or completion of studies at universities or university-level establishments. Grants are renewable.

Eligibility: Open to orphans of workers who were employed in an undertaking of the coal mining industry, the iron ore mines or the steel industry of the European Coal and Steel Community, and who died after 30th June, 1965 (1st January, 1973 for British, Danish, and Irish nationals). In the case of orphans who are not nationals of a Community country, the Directors of the Foundation shall reach decisions on an individual basis. Candidates should be (a) between 14 and 21 years of age and (b) following a course of studies or vocational training. The age limits may be raised or lowered in special cases.

Further information from:
Secretariat
Paul Finet Foundation
Jean-Monnet-Building-C4
Rue Alcide de Gasperi
Luxembourg/Kircheberg

[813]

FINNISH FEDERATION OF UNIVERSITY WOMEN

International Award

One Award is given periodically to a member of the International Federation of University Women for full-time study in Finland. The value of the Award varies with fluctuations in the cost of living.

Further information from:
Katri Lauste
Tuolukkatie 11dD
02160 ESP00 16
Finland

[814]

CARL FLESCH INTERNATIONAL VIOLIN COMPETITION

City of London Festival—City Arts Trust

The following awards are made in even-numbered years to provide talented violinists with a springboard for a career in Western Europe: *Lloyds Bank Prize/Carl Flesch Medal* of £4,500; *Baker Harris Saunders Prize* of £3,000; *Emily Anderson Prize* of £2,000, in arrangement with the Royal Philharmonic Society; *Finlay Robertson Prize* of £1,000; *Worshipful Company of Musicians Prize* of £750; *W.H. Smith Prize* of £750 to a finalist under 23 years of age; *John and Arthur Beare Prize* of £500; *Audience Prize* of £500, donated by British Reserve Insurance Company; *Albert*

Frost Sonata Prize of £400; *Carl F. Flesch Outstanding Merit Prize* of £300. In addition a list of concert engagements will be offered to one or more of the winners. The Competition is open to violinists of all nationalities who will be under the age of 28 on 1st June of the year of the Competition.

Closing date: 31st March.

Note: The above information applies to the 1982 Competition. Applicants are advised to confirm these details for future Competitions.

Further information from:
Miss V. Harding, Administrator
City Arts Trust
P.O. Box 270
Guildhall, London
England EC2P 2EJ

[815]

FONTAINEBLEAU FINE ARTS AND MUSIC SCHOOLS ASSOCIATION, INC.
(U.S.A.)

Summer School Scholarships

Summer school in music and fine arts are held for eight weeks in July and August at the Palace of Fontainebleau, France. Sessions are held in English or in French with interpretation. The following Scholarships are available annually in variable amounts to participants from the United States and Canada who have been accepted for graduate study by the admissions committee and are less than 30 years of age: *Damrosch Memorial Fine Arts and Music Scholarships; Klumpke Memorial Music Scholarship* (violin or composition); *Palache Memorial Music Scholarships; Gerald Watland Architectural Scholarship;* and the *Edward Maverick Architectural Scholarship* (a full award, including round trip fare).

Participants, except for the Maverick Scholar, are expected to pay their own travel expenses.

Closing date: 31st March for fine arts Scholarships; all others to be announced.

Further information from:
Fontainebleau Fine Arts and Music
  Schools Association, Inc.
47 Fifth Avenue
New York, New York 10003
U.S.A.

[816]

FOOD AND AGRICULTURE ORGANIZATION OF THE UNITED NATIONS [FAO]

Fellowships and Scholarships

Subjects: Agriculture, fisheries, forestry, nutrition, agricultural economics and statistics, rural institutions and services, and related areas.

Value: US$700 to US$1,000 per month, plus training fees, costs of approved travel to, from and within the country of study, and a book allowance.

Tenable for two months to two years.

Eligibility: Open to nationals of countries in which FAO carries out projects of technical assistance provided they are working or destined to work on these projects. Candidates must have adequate basic and technical education and practical experience in the field of study.

Note: Applications must be made to the relevant government department in the candidate's own country. Individual requests are not considered.

These Fellowships and Scholarships are offered under projects within the United Nations Development Programme, and projects jointly operated by FAO and other United Nations agencies, individual governments or foundations under funds in trust arrangements.

Address:
Food and Agriculture Organization of the
  United Nations
Via delle Terme di Caracalla
00100-Rome
Italy

[817]

FOOD AND AGRICULTURE ORGANIZATION OF THE UNITED NATIONS [FAO]

Andre Mayer FAO Research Fellowships

Purpose: To carry out research projects of interest to FAO member-states in institutes selected by FAO. Fellowships are offered to enable very experienced and highly qualified research workers to carry out individual research (original or concerned with the collection and analysis of existing data) as announced by FAO.

Subjects: Agriculture, fisheries, forestry, nutrition, agricultural economics and statistics and related fields.

No. offered: Six Fellowships biennially.

Value: US$700 to US$1,000 per month, plus training fees, transportation and report allowance.

Tenable in any country for a maximum of 30 months.

Eligibility: Open to nationals of all FAO member-states.

Note: Applications must be made to the FAO National Committee, c/o the Ministry of Agriculture or Foreign Affairs in the candidate's own country.

Address:
Food and Agriculture Organization of the United Nations
Via delle Terme di Caracalla
00100-Rome
Italy

[818]

FOOD AND AGRICULTURE ORGANIZATION OF THE UNITED NATIONS [FAO]

Group Training Activities

Subjects: Animal production and health, atomic energy, economic analysis, fisheries, forestry and forest products, land and water development, nutrition, plant production and protection, public information, rural institutions and services, and statistics.

Value: To cover the cost of the Course.

Tenable in FAO member-states for periods of between two weeks and six months.

Eligibility: Open to high-level government officials, technical officers and intermediate-level personnel, from FAO member-states.

Note: Courses are organized under the United Nations Development Programme, government cooperative programmes, and others.
Applications must be made to the relevant government department in the candidate's own country.

Further information from:
Food and Agriculture Organization of the United Nations
Via delle Terme di Caracalla
00100-Rome
Italy

[819]

FOREST HISTORY SOCIETY *(U.S.A.)*

The Society offers three Awards to promote quality writing in the field of North American forest and conservation history.

Theodore C. Blegen Award of US$150 is given annually to the author of the best article published in the preceding calendar year, in journals other than that of the Society, on the subject of North American forest and conservation history. *Closing date:* 1st May.

Forest History Society Book Award of US$500 is given biennially, in odd-numbered years to the author of the best book in the field of North American forest and conservation history published during the previous two-year period. Publishers must nominate and submit four copies of the book. *Closing date:* 1st February in odd-numbered years.

Frederick K. Weyerhaeuser Award of US$150 is given annually to the author of the best article published in the preceding calendar year in *Journal of Forest History* on North American forest and conservation history. Nomination is automatic upon publication.

Further information from:
Harold K. Steen
Forest History Society, Inc.
109 Coral Street
Santa Cruz, California 95060
U.S.A.

[820]

FOREST PRODUCTS RESEARCH SOCIETY *(U.S.A.)*

The Society offers the following Awards annually: (1) *Wood Award*, given to a student enrolled in any graduate school in North America who submits a paper on wood science and technology (1st prize, US$1,000; 2nd prize, US$500); (2) *Borden Chemical Award*, to encourage research providing practical solutions to the problem of off-gassing of formaldehyde from wood-based products used in the construction and furnishing of buildings in which formaldehyde-based resins are utilized (1st prize, US$5,000; 2nd prize, US$3,000; 3rd prize, US$2,000). Closing date: 15th March. (3) *L.J. Markwardt Engineering Award* of US$1,000, a certificate and an engraved plaque, for the author of the most outstanding paper in the field of wood engineering published in the *Forest Products Journal* or *Wood Science* during the two calendar years prior to that of the Award. (4) *Bark Award*, consisting of an engraved plaque, is given to members of the Society or of the wood industry.

Note: Candidates are not restricted to United States citizens.

Further information from:
Forest Products Research Society
2801 Marshall Court
Madison, Wisconsin 53705
U.S.A.

[821]

FOUNDATION FOR CHIROPRACTIC EDUCATION AND RESEARCH

A number of Grants are made at the postdoctoral level to qualified individuals pursuing chiropractic education, training and research. Awards vary according to individual circumstances, and are given on the basis of merit. Grants are normally paid quarterly, and are usually renewable.

Closing dates: 1st March and 1st October.

Further information from:
Research Director
Foundation for Chiropractic Education and Research
3209 Ingersoll
Des Moines, Iowa 50312
U.S.A.

[822]

FOUNDATION FOR MICROBIOLOGY
(U.S.A.)

Grants

The Foundation awards Grants in microbiology, immunology and virology. These Awards are made to both individuals and institutions, and vary in support from a few hundred dollars to several thousand. In particular, the Foundation supports lectureships, meetings, symposia, prizes, unusual publications costs, courses and other projects related to its area of interest. Conventional research projects, travel grants and fellowships are not considered. Project duration is usually less than three years. Application is by letter to the President.

Further information from:
Dr. Byron H. Waksman, President
c/o National Multiple Sclerosis Society
205 East 42nd Street
New York, New York 10017
U.S.A.

[823]

FOUNDATION OF PHYSIOPATHOLOGY-LUCIEN DAUTREBANDE

An international Prize of 1,500,000 Belgian francs is awarded every three years to an author, or group of authors having a long-term association, for a work on human or animal clinical physiopathology, preferably involving therapeutic implications. The aim of the Prize is to assist the recipient in continuing the investigations, which should be at an advanced state.

Applications must be presented by two persons who are university professors, former Prize recipients, or ordinary or associate members of national academies. Summaries of the work must be written in a major language. The Prize may not be granted to recipients of important awards during the previous five year period. The next Prize will be made in 1985.

Closing date: 31st December preceding the year in which the Prize is made.

Further information from:
Dr. J. Stalport
Foundation of Physiopathology-Lucien Dautrebande
35, chausse de Liege
5200 Huy
Belgium

[824]

FOUNDATION FOR PUBLIC RELATIONS RESEARCH AND EDUCATION *(U.S.A.)*

Graduate Scholarships

Subject: Public relations.

No. offered: One scholarship annually.

Value: US$3,000.

Eligibility: Open to senior students at a college or university in the United States who are either majoring in public relations or journalism or in business administration with a major sequence in public relations. Applicants should have achieved an average of at least B in courses in public relations and a cumulative average of B- to B+ during their undergraduate career.

Note: Application forms must be accompanied by the endorsements of three teachers—one of public relations and two of related subjects—of the institution the candidate is attending.

Closing date: 15th May.

Further information from:
Foundation for Public Relations Research and Education
415 Lexington Avenue, Suite 1305
New York, New York 10017
U.S.A.

[825]

FOUNDATION FOR PUBLIC RELATIONS RESEARCH AND EDUCATION *(U.S.A.)*

Fellowships

Purpose: To provide teachers in public relations and related fields with opportunities for first-hand experience of value to their teaching, by enabling them to carry out practical training summer assignments with sponsoring public relations counselling firms or public relations departments.

Value: US$1,000, plus a US$200 travel allowance for transportation to and from the sponsor's place of business.

Tenable for four weeks during the summer.

Eligibility: Open to full-time college or university faculty members in the United States, who are currently teaching courses in public relations.

Further information from:
Foundation for Public Relations Research and Education
415 Lexington Avenue, Suite 1305
New York, New York 10017
U.S.A.

[826]

MILES FRANKLIN LITERARY AWARD

One Award of A$3,000, paid in a lump sum, is made annually for a new novel, presenting some phase of Australian life, and judged to be of the highest literary merit. Entries may be submitted by the author or publisher (with the author's permission). The Permanent Trustee Company must be notified of all titles to be submitted within 28 days of their publication.

Closing dates: 31st January for entries published in December, and within two months of publication for all other books.

Further information from:
Miles Franklin Literary Award
Permanent Trustee Company Ltd.
G.P.O. Box 4270
Sydney, N.S.W.
Australia 2001

[827]

FREE CHURCH FEDERAL COUNCIL *(U.K.)*

Paton Essay Prize

Prizes for essays on the constitution, worship and doctrine of the Early Church, written by United Kingdom ministries or theological students of the Free Churches. The Competitions are held as funds become available.

Further information from:
General Secretary
Free Church Federal Council
27 Tavistock Square
London
England WC1H 9HH

[828]

FREE CHURCH FEDERAL COUNCIL
(U.K.)

Elmslie Memorial Scholarships

Subjects: Studies on the language and literature of the Old Testament.

No. offered: Usually two Scholarships per annum when available.

Value: Maximum of £200 per annum. Each Scholarship is assessed individually.

Eligibility: Open to final year theological students who are United Kingdom citizens, have competence in Hebrew, and are preparing for the Free Church ministry as ministers or theological teachers.

Note: Applications are accepted at any time.
Candidates are asked to write 8,000 words on the language, literature, history or theology of the Old Testament; or a linguistic exercise.

Further information from:
General Secretary
Free Church Federal Council
27 Tavistock Square
London
England WC1H 9HH

[829]

FREEDOMS FOUNDATION AT VALLEY FORGE *(U.S.A.)*

Awards ranging from US$50 to US$5,000 are offered to encourage Americans to propagate and demonstrate faith in the American way of life.

Not confirmed for 1983.

Further information from:
Awards Administration
Freedoms Foundation at Valley Forge
Valley Forge, Pennsylvania 19481
U.S.A.

[830]

FRENCH-AMERICAN FOUNDATION

Tocqueville Grant Program: The Foundation offers up to three research fellowships annually for doctoral candidates in the social sciences who are preparing dissertations on 19th and 20th century France. Candidates should have completed their general examinations.

Each fellowship of US$8,000 is for support of one academic year's full-time doctoral research in France. Applications should be filed by 15th February.

Saint-John Perse Research Fellowships: The Fellowships of US$4,000 are offered for support of full-time graduate or postgraduate research for a six-month period at the Centre Saint-John Perse of the University of Provence (Aix-Marseille I). The awards are open to candidates from universities in the United States and Canada who are preparing studies of the French poet, diplomat and Nobel laureate Saint-John Perse.

Applications should be filed by 1st April.

Further information from:
Cynthia K. April
French-American Foundation
680 Park Avenue
New York, New York 10021
U.S.A.

[831]

FRENCH ASSOCIATION OF UNIVERSITY WOMEN

M.L. Puech Milhaud Award

One Award of FF2,000 is offered in odd-numbered years to a member of the Canadian Federation of University Women or a member of the Association Française des femmes diplômées des Universities to enable the awardee to study in a foreign country. Applications must be received by 15th April.

Further information from:
Association française des femmes
  diplomées des universités
4 rue de Chevreuse
75006 Paris
France

[832]

FRENCH COLONIAL HISTORICAL SOCIETY

Book Award

An annual Award of UA$500 is given in recognition of the most outstanding work in French Colonial history which has been published during the calendar year preceding that in which the Award is made. There are no eligibility restrictions.

Closing date: 15th February.

Further information from:
J. Dean O'Donnell, Secretary
French Colonial Historical Society
Department of History
Virginia Polytechnic Institute
Blacksburg, Virginia 24061
U.S.A.

[833]

R.T. FRENCH COMPANY *(Rochester, New York)*

Tastemaker Award

An Award of US$500, plus several category awards, are given annually for outstanding cookbooks published in the United States during the preceding year. Entries must contain at least 50% recipes and be comprised of new, previously unpublished material.

Not confirmed for 1983.

Further information from:
Laura Weill
R.T. French—Tastemaker Award
Harshe-Rotman and Druck, Inc.
300 East 44th Street
New York, New York 10018
U.S.A.

[834]

FRENCH EMBASSY IN THE UNITED STATES
French Government

Bourses Chateaubriand

Subjects: Social sciences, including business administration—some aspect of contemporary France: doctoral research.

No. offered: Ten awards annually.

Value: 40,000 francs, paid in France in ten monthly installments.

Tenable in France for one academic year.

Eligibility: Open to United States citizens who are doctoral students in the social sciences or business administration. Candidates should have completed their comprehensive and/or general examinations by the time the award commences (upon arrival in France), and should be fluent in spoken and written French.

Closing date: 1st March.

Further information from:
French Embassy
Services Culturels
972 Fifth Avenue
New York, New York 10021
U.S.A.

[835]

FRENCH FOUNDATION FOR MEDICAL RESEARCH

Grants

Grants are awarded to institutions, research teams and individuals, for research, travel and the purchase of scientific materials. The purpose of the Foundation is to promote and coordinate all forms of scientific medical research, especially clinical research and research concerned with the basic biological sciences directly or indirectly related to medicine.

Foreign applicants must first be accepted by a suitable French laboratory. The applicant must also provide assurance that he will return to his own country upon completion of the research period.

Further information from:
French Foundation for Medical Research
10, rue de Lisbonne
75008 Paris
France

[836]

FRENCH PETROLEUM INSTITUTE

Scholarships

Purpose: To enable successful candidates either to obtain a higher degree in engineering, or to work on a research project relevant to the petrol, chemical, and motor combustion industries.

No. offered: Ten Scholarships annually.

Value: FF3,100 per month plus free tuition.

Tenable at the Ecole Nationale Superieure du Petrole et des Moteurs, or at its laboratories or experimental stations, for 11 to 20 months according to specialists.

Eligibility: Open to nationals of any Common Market Country other than France, who hold a B.Sc. or equivalent degree in engineering (other foreign candidates must be holders of a scholarship given by their government or by the French government).

Closing dates: 1st March for non-French-speaking candidates; 15th June for all other candidates.

Further information from:
 Ecole National Superieure de Petrole et
  des Moteurs
 4 avenue de Bois Preau
 BP 311
 92506 Rueil Malmaison Cedex
 France

[837]

FRIDAY MORNING MUSIC CLUB FOUNDATION, INC. *(U.S.A.)*

Washington International Competition

Category: Voice (1983).

No. offered: Four awards in voice.

Value: 1st prizes of US$1,500; 2nd prize—US$750; 3rd prize—US$500. In addition, 1st prize winners are given a paid solo performance in Washington, D.C.

Eligibility: Open to persons from any country who are preparing for a professional career and are not currently under professional management.

Further information from:
 Jan Goetz Lea, Competition Chairman
 Friday Morning Music Club Foundation
 3310-35th Street, N.W.
 Washington, D.C. 20016
 U.S.A.

[838]

FRIENDS OF AMERICAN WRITERS

A first Prize of US$1,000, plus a second Prize of US$750 are awarded annually to encourage and promote high literary standards among new authors who are natives or residents of the mid-western region of the United States, or whose works use that region as the locale. Recipients should not have previously published more than four books, nor have received a major monetary award of US$1,000 or more. Prose works must be submitted by the publisher. Prizes are usually awarded in April.

Further information from:
 Friends of American Writers
 c/o Mrs. Gene Lederer
 755 North Merrill
 Park Ridge, Illinois 60068
 U.S.A.

[839]

ANNA FULLER FUND *(U.S.A.)*

Fellowships and Research Grants

Purpose: To promote research into the cause, treatment and cure of cancer.

Fellowships are awarded in the amount of US15,000 for the first year and US$15,500 for the second year, with an allowance for travel to the host institution for the applicant and a dependent. In general, applications are not favorably reviewed if they are for continued postdoctoral experience in the same institution or if the applicant has already had two years of postdoctoral training. Under special circumstances an institutional award can be arranged to cover minimal costs of supplies during the period of the Fellowship. Fellowships are awarded for a period of two years. In general, preference will be shown for applicants whose training plans reflect the development of an original research program, based on his or her previous training as well as the opportunities in the proposed host laboratory.

Research Grants will be awarded primarily to young investigators who are establishing independent laboratories and need interim funding. Grants are rarely awarded in excess of US$10,000 per annum, and are for one year only.

Further information from:
 Anna Fuller Fund
 333 Cedar Street
 New Haven, Connecticut 06510
 U.S.A.

[840]

FUND FOR ENVIRONMENTAL STUDIES
(West Germany)

Fellowships

Purpose: To provide support for the study of selected problems of environmental conservation.

Subjects: Selected topics in environmental conservation of interest to West German legislators.

No. offered: Variable, depending on the number of projects selected by the Fund.

Value: Variable, depending upon the nature of the project.

Eligibility: Fellows must be qualified researchers. After the Board of the Fund has decided upon the kind of project to be financed, a suitably qualified Fellow is recruited. Individual applications are therefore not accepted.

Further information from:
 Fund for Environmental Studies
 Adenaueralle 214
 5300 Bonn
 West Germany

[841]

FUND FOR INVESTIGATIVE JOURNALISM *(U.S.A.)*

Grants

The Fund aims to increase public knowledge about the concealed, obscure or complex aspects of matters significantly affecting the public. Grants are made to writers to enable them to probe abuses of authority or the malfunctioning of institutions and systems which harm the public. Their reports—factual as distinguished from ideological or philosophical—are published in newspapers, magazines, as books or broadcast. The subjects of Fund Grants have covered a broad spectrum including environmental hazards, political corruption, invasion of privacy, organized crime, threats to civil rights, and abuses of corporate and union authority.

The application should be in the form of a letter to the Executive Director describing the subject of the proposed investigation, its significance, the proof in hand, further evidence needed and the approach that will be used to complete the project. An itemized budget and resumé should be included along with samples of the applicant's published work. The Fund encourages aspirants to investigative journalism so persons without a "track record" should not hesitate to apply. Applications are treated confidentially.

A statement of intent is also required from a suitable outlet that the report will be published if the finished product meets expectations. The writer must be paid the publication's regular compensation for free-lance articles. While the writer keeps the fee, the Fund must know what it is in order to judge the size of the Grant.

Applications for Book Grants are similar. A chapter-by-chapter outline is required. The applicant and a publisher must have a completed contract, the terms of which are to be submitted with the application. Unlike support of articles, the applicant must agree that if the book makes money over the advance, the Grant will be repaid.

Note: The Fund is not endowed and depends for its support entirely on private donations, which are tax exempt.

Further information from:
 Fund for Investigative Journalism, Inc.
 1346 Connecticut Avenue, N.W.
 Washington, D.C. 20036
 U.S.A.

[842]

FUND FOR THEOLOGICAL EDUCATION INC. *(U.S.A.)*

Benjamin E. Mays Fellowships for Ministry

Purpose: To provide financial assistance to outstanding Black North American men and women who are committed vocationally to one of the ordained ministries of the Christian Church. Funds are provided to assist with expenses for study toward the receipt of the master of divinity degree or its equivalent.

Tenable at any theological school which is fully accredited by the Association of Theological Schools in the United States and Canada for one academic year, renewable for up to an additional three years.

Eligibility: Open to Black citizens of the United States or Canada who are no older than 30 years of age at the time of nomination and are at least graduating seniors from a college or university. Persons already attending a fully accredited seminary are also eligible.

Candidates must be nominated by a member of the clergy, faculty or former fellow of programs administered by the Fund. Direct applications are not accepted.

Not confirmed for 1983.

Further information from:
Fund for Theological Education, Inc.
909 State Road
Princeton, New Jersey 08540
U.S.A.

[843]

FUND FOR THEOLOGICAL EDUCATION, INC. *(U.S.A.)*

North American Ministerial Fellowships

Purpose: To provide financial assistance to outstanding men and women who are willing to give serious vocational consideration to the ordained ministries of the Christian Church, and to provide assistance to those who are already candidates for the ministry.

Tenable at any seminary fully accredited with the Association of Theological Schools in the United States and Canada for one academic year, renewable for an additional two years.

Eligibility: Open to men and women who are no older than 30 years of age at the time of nomination, who are at least graduating seniors from colleges or universities or who already hold at least a bachelor's degree and who are citizens of the United States or Canada. Persons already attending a theological school are not eligible.

Candidates must be nominated by a member of the clergy, faculty or former fellow of programs administered by the Fund. Direct applications are not accepted.

Note: Candidates should be prepared to enroll in a theological school the autumn following receipt of their award. No mid-year grants are made.

Not confirmed for 1983.

Further information from:
Fund for Theological Education, Inc.
909 State Road
Princeton, New Jersey 08540
U.S.A.

[844]

FUND FOR THEOLOGICAL EDUCATION, INC. *(U.S.A.)*

Special Opportunity Fellowships to Hispanic-Americans for the Preparation for Ordained Ministries

Purpose: To provide financial assistance to outstanding Hispanic-Americans who are committed vocationally to one of the ordained ministries of the Christian Church. Funds are available to assist with the expenses for the final year of college/university study as well as for the years of study necessary to receive the degree of master of divinity or its equivalent.

Tenable at any theological school which is fully accredited by the Association of Theological Schools in the United States and Canada for one academic year, renewable for up to an additional three years.

Eligibility: Open to Hispanic citizens of the United States who are no older than 35 years of age at the time of nomination and are at least juniors in an accredited college or university. Persons already attending a fully accredited seminary are also eligible.

Candidates must be nominated by a member of the clergy, faculty or former fellow of programs administered by the Fund. Direct applications are not accepted.

Not confirmed for 1983.

Further information from:
Fund for Theological Education, Inc.
909 State Road
Princeton, New Jersey 08540
U.S.A.

G

See *How to Use The Grants Register*, page ix

[845]

GAIRDNER FOUNDATION (Canada)

The Foundation makes International Awards annually, in two classes, to confer recognition upon individuals whose recent work or discoveries constitute tangible achievement in the fields of arthritic, rheumatic and cardiovascular diseases, with emphasis on the fields of allergic, auto-immune and other tissue reactions as being fundamentally important to an improved understanding of the cardiovascular, arthritic and rheumatic diseases and the field of cancer. Awards are given without restriction as to nationality, and are prizes for achievement, not grants for the support of future research. The Awards are presented at an annual formal dinner in Toronto, and the Foundation provides travel and living expenses to the winners, who are expected to accept their Awards in person.

The International awards are made solely at the discretion of the Foundation and are not open to application.

Gairdner Foundation Award of Merit in the amount of Can$25,000 is given to an individual or group of individuals who have made the most outstanding discovery or contribution consistent with the purposes of the Foundation.

Gairdner Foundation Wightman Award of Can$25,000 is given from time to time to a Canadian who, in the Foundation's opinion, has demonstrated outstanding leadership in medicine and medical science consistent with the purposes of the Foundation.

Gairdner Foundation Annual Awards of Can$15,000 each are given to individuals or groups who have also made outstanding contributions or discoveries.

Note: Gairdner Foundation Lectures are held in Toronto, and winners are invited to present brief papers covering their prize-winning work. Lectures are open to the medical profession and to senior undergraduate medical students.

Further information from:
T.V. Kenney, Executive Director
Gairdner Foundation
255 Yorkland Boulevard
Willowdale, Ontario
Canada M2J 1S3

[846]

GAY NEWS (U.K.)

Book Award

A certificate and cash Award is presented annually to the author of a book, published within the last twelve months, which in the opinion of the editor and literary editor of *Gay News* is of most value to the gay community. Open to authors of any nationality without restriction. Those wishing to enter the competition or nominate a book may write to the address below.

Not confirmed for 1983.

Further information from:
Gay News
1A Normand Gardens
Greyhound Road
London
England W14 9SB

[847]

PORTIA GEACH MEMORIAL FUND

Portia Geach Memorial Award

An Award of A$3,750 is given annually for the best portrait, painted from life, of a man or woman distinguished in art, letters or sciences. The competition is open to female Australian residents who are either Australian born or naturalized, or British born. Paintings must have been completed during the twelve month period preceding the closing date (31st May). All entries are to be accompanied by a statutory declaration.

Further information from:
Portia Geach Memorial Fund
c/o Permanent Trustee Company Limited
23-25 O'Connell Street
Sydney, N.S.W.
Australia 2000

[848]

GENERAL AGREEMENT ON TARIFFS AND TRADE [GATT]

Fellowships for Courses

Courses: Commerical policy (study of GATT, multilateral trade negotiations, current issues in international economic relations and their influence on international trade problems and needs of developing countries).

No. offered: 20 Fellowships for each Course.

Value: 2,520 Swiss francs first month, then 1,920 francs per month, plus travel expenses.

Tenable in Geneva from February to June (English-speaking), and from August to December (French-speaking).

Eligibility: Open to civil servants primarily from developing countries which are members of GATT, the United Nations or its specialized agencies. Staff members from regional economic organizations grouping developing countries may also be admitted. Candidates should have a minimum of three years experience in government service in a field compatible with the syllabus of the Course, and should have completed a university education in economics or a related field or equivalent practical experience. A language proficiency certificate is required where the language of the Course is not the candidate's mother language.

Note: Applications for the GATT Fellowships should be submitted by the candidates government in three copies through the offices of the Resident Representative, United Nations Development Programme, which will forward two copies to the Director-General of GATT, Geneva, and retain one copy for his file.

Closing date: Five months prior to the commencement of the Course.

Address:
General Agreement on Tariffs and Trade
Centre William Rappard
154 rue de Lausanne
1211 Geneva 21
Switzerland

[849]

GENERAL SEMANTICS FOUNDATION

Project Grants

Grants, ranging from US$300 to US$4,500, are made available to individuals and organizations for projects specifically in the field of general semantics, or projects explicitly related to it. Support may include graduate studies leading to an M.A. or Ph.D. in general semantics. Applicants must be knowledgeable in this field and be able to show evidence to that fact. The duration of support varies, depending upon the individual project, and may continue for as long as needed to complete the study undertaken. There are no official application forms or closing dates.

Further information from:
Harry E. Maynard
General Semantics Foundation
14 Charcoal Hill
Westport, Connecticut 06880
U.S.A.

[850]

GEOLOGICAL SOCIETY OF AMERICA

Penrose Research Grants

Subjects: Geology (coal geology, engineering geology, geomorphology and hydrogeology) and other closely related fields.

Value: Between US$50 and US$1,800 per annum. Grants are awarded to individuals as an aid to a research project and not to sustain the entire costs. Grants may cover the cost of travel, room, board and travel in the field, materials, supplies and other expenses directly related to the fulfillment of the research contract. Funds may also be awarded for analyses, but may not be used for the purchase of ordinary field equipment, the maintenance of families of Grantees, the employment of persons, other than in some cases the services of a technician, or as reimbursement for work already accomplished and paid for.

Tenable in North America and occasionally abroad, for one year. Applicants should be prepared to re-apply for a Grant for research that extends beyond one year.

Eligibility: Open to citizens of countries within North America. Candidates need not necessarily be members of the Geological Society of America.

Grants are awarded on the basis of the scientific merits of the problem, the capability of the investigator, and reasonableness of the budget, and may be used in support of research on thesis projects. Research projects at the undergraduate level are not eligible.

Preference is given to smaller projects, particularly those that will permit promising candidates for advanced degrees to do worthwhile field or laboratory work. There is no prohibition against applications for larger projects nor those from senior investigators, but it is believed that most established research workers will look for financial aid from those agencies that can more easily support the more elaborate projects.

Closing date: 15th February.

Note: The Society also offers the following: Penrose Medal; Arthur L. Day Medal; Kirk Bryan Award; O.E. Meinzer Award; E.B. Burwell, Jr. Memorial Award; Gilbert H. Cady Award.

Further information from:
Executive Director
Geological Society of America
P.O. Box 9140
Boulder, Colorado 80301
U.S.A.

[851]

GEORGIA LIBRARY ASSOCIATION

Hubbard Scholarship

Purpose: To provide financial aid to a qualified candidate completing a master's degree or higher.

Subject: Library science.

No. offered: One Scholarship biennially.

Value: US$2,000, paid in equal installments at the beginning of each term, semester or quarter.

Tenable at an American Library Association accredited school for one year.

Eligibility: Open to U.S. citizens accepted for admission to a master's program at an ALA accredited library school, who intend to complete the course of study within one year.

Note: The Scholar is required to work in a library, or a library-related capacity in Georgia for one year following completion of the program, or agree to pay back a prorated amount of the Scholarship plus 6% interest within a two-year period.

Closing date: 1st June.

Further information from:
Georgia Library Association
P.O. Box 833
Atlanta, Georgia 30084
U.S.A.

[852]

GERMAN ACADEMIC EXCHANGE SERVICE [DAAD]

Scholarships for Study in West Germany

Subjects: Unrestricted.

Value: DM770, DM870, or DM1,300 per month, according to age, qualifications and experience. Also a book allowance of DM100 per semester, a family allowance of DM300 per month for married Scholars whose spouses also reside in West Germany, a lump sum for a social insurance policy, a single allowance of DM200 at the commencement of the Scholarship, and supplementary health and accident insurance. Return travel expenses are paid for Scholars from non-European countries, and a lump sum towards travel expenses for European Scholars. Scholars from certain non-European countries (the exceptions are Australia, Japan, Canada, New Zealand and the United States) also receive a single clothing allowance of DM400.

Tenable at any university, technical college, music or art academy in West Germany, including West Berlin, for ten months (Scholars from European countries) and twelve months (Scholars from non-European countries). Extensions may be granted to Scholars from non-European countries in cases where the country of origin does not have the same further training opportunities as West Germany.

Eligibility: Open to nationals of all countries (excluding West Germany) who are senior undergraduates or graduate students at a university or college of university standing, are between 18 and 32 years of age, and have a working knowledge of German. (A language course is included in the Scholarship for students from countries with no facilities for German language study).

Note: Applications must be submitted on official DAAD forms, obtainable from diplomatic missions or from:
Deutscher Akademischer
Austauschdienst—DAAD
Kennedyallee 50
D-53 Bonn 2
West Germany

[853]

GERMAN ACADEMIC EXCHANGE SERVICE [DAAD]

Postgraduate Scholarships for South Africans

Purpose: To allow postgraduate students and young academics to study at a university in West Germany.

Subjects: All academic fields, except pharmacy, chemical engineering, music and fine arts.

No. offered: Approximately eleven Scholarships annually.

Value: A monthly allowance of DM850, or DM1,200.

Tenable at any university in West Germany, including West Berlin. Scholarships are normally held for one year and may be renewed for an additional year.

Eligibility: Open to South African citizens who are no more than 32 years of age and have a minimum requirement of a bachelor's honours degree.

Note: Scholars having no adequate knowledge of German will take courses in West Germany for periods of two to six months.

Closing date: 15th October.

Further information from:
German Academic Exchange Service
Embassy of the Federal Republic
  of Germany
P.O. Box 2023
Pretoria, 0001
South Africa

[854]

GERMAN MARSHALL FUND OF THE UNITED STATES

German Marshall Fund Fellowships

Purpose: To support scholars whose work is designed to contribute to the better understanding and resolution of significant contemporary and emerging problems common to industrial societies, domestic and international, particularly their comparative, political, economic and social aspects. Such problems will involve the interests of the United States and both Western and Eastern Europe in all cases but may also be concerned with other societies.

Subjects: Employment and the nature of jobs: programs for the hard-to-employ and disadvantaged; health, safety, and other working conditions; labor force participation by women, youth, and the elderly; and effect of new technologies on jobs. Innovations and alternatives in service delivery: private/public partnerships; deinstitutionalization, decentralization and innovative arrangements for the delivery to families, women, youth and the elderly of such social and public services as housing, transportation, and community development; innovations and alternatives in criminal and juvenile justice administration. Public participation in decision-making; the involvement of clients, consumers, and voluntary organizations in the planning and implementation of policies concerning environment, energy, growth management, community development, and other public sectors. Foreign workers and migrant populations in industrialized countries: issues of employment, education, welfare, and civil rights. International interdependence: trade, monetary, and related questions, (excluding military, security, and defense matters). The Fund attaches priority to the foregoing issue areas, but will consider projects focused on other problems common to industrial societies.

No. offered: Fifteen Fellowships per annum.

Value: A total amount of US$400,000 was awarded in 1980-81. To maximize the Fund's resources, each applicant for financial assistance will be expected to apply any available leave, sabbatical or other funding from his or her home institution, for the Fellow's support during the period of appointment, and then, when feasible, to explore other possible outside sources of funding. Thereafter it is the Fund's policy to attempt to meet—but not exceed—his or her current income. Certain travel expenses necessary to the proposed work may also be available, although the Fellow may also be asked to explore first other sources of travel funding.

Tenable for a period of time from an academic term to a calendar year or longer. There is no restriction on place of tenure.

Eligibility: Fellows may come from careers in any academic field or profession, but most will be established scholars with advanced degrees., There are no arbitrary age limits. Awards will be made only to applicants who will devote themselves full-time to the proposed projects during the appointment periods.

Closing date: 30th November.

Further information from:
Peter R. Weitz, Program Coordinator
Germany Marshall Fund of the United States
11 Dupont Circle, N.W.
Washington, D.C. 20036
U.S.A.

[855]

GERMAN SOCIETY OF ENDOCRINOLOGY

Basedow Research Prizes, totaling DM15,000 are awarded annually to young scientists for outstanding papers in the field of experimental and clinical thyroidology. The competition is open to permanent residents of Europe who are less than 40 years of age. Entries should not exceed 40 type-written pages of 30 lines each, and the portion of illustrations and tables should not comprise more than one-third of the total work. Competition announcements will be made in medical journals throughout Europe.

Marius-Tausk Career Development Award of DM15,000 is given annually for a manuscript, written in English and previously unpublished, dealing with clinical or clinical-experimental endocrinology. The work may deal with any of the various fields of study associated with clinical endocrinology, except that concerning diabetes mellitus and the thyroid gland. Scientists residing in Europe and less than 34 years of age are eligible to apply. Entries should not exceed forty type-written pages of 30 lines each, and the portion of illustrations and tables should not comprise more than one-third or the total work. Competition announcements will be made in medical journals throughout Europe.

Schoeller-Junkmann Prizes are awarded annually to young scientists for outstanding papers in the field of endocrinology. The Prizes, totalling DM15,000, are given in competition to scientists who are permanently resident in Europe and less than forty years of age. Papers may be on any field of endocrinology, clinical or experimental, with the exceptions of those dealing with diabetes mellitus and the thyroid gland. Entries should not exceed forty type-written pages of 30 lines each, and the portion of illustrations and tables should not comprise more than one-third of the total work. Competition announcements will be made in medical journals throughout Europe.

Further information from:
German Society for Endocrinology
c/o Secretary
Institut für Physiologische Chemie II
Moorenstrabe 5
4000 Düseldorf 1
West Germany

[856]

GERMANISTIC SOCIETY OF AMERICA

Fellowships

Subjects: Primarily in the fields of German language, literature, philosophy, history, art history, economics, international law, and public affairs.

No. offered: Usually three or four Fellowships annually.

Value: US$6,000 per annum.

Tenable in Germany for one academic year (nine months).

Eligibility: Open to United States citizens who have a good academic record, capacity for independent study, and preferably a master's degree. Preference is given to prospective teachers of German.

Closing date: 31st October.

Further information from:
  Germanistic Society Fellowships
  Institute of International Education
  809 United Nations Plaza
  New York, New York 10017
  U.S.A.

[857]

ROBERT GIBSON METHODIST TRUST BOARD *(N.Z.)*

Grants

Subjects: Unrestricted.

Value: Each Grant is assessed individually.

Tenable at any university or educational institution in New Zealand or overseas, on an annual basis.

Eligibility: Open to residents of New Zealand. Special preference is given to orphans and to persons whose parents are Methodists or Presbyterians.

Closing date: 30th November.

Further information from:
  Secretary-Administrator
  Public Trust Office
  Robert Gibson Methodist Trust Board
  Box 445, Hawera
  New Zealand

[858]

GILCHRIST EDUCATIONAL TRUST *(U.K.)*

The purpose of the Trust is to assist educational projects of an international character by helping students going to or coming from different parts of the world in their courses of study. Grants are usually made during the last year of the course, and are in very limited amounts. The bulk of the funds are offered to recognised British university expeditions; a small proportion goes to help students of good ability in the United Kingdom to travel abroad for study, and to help students coming to the United Kingdom to study for a degree.

Further information from:
  Gilchrist Educational Trust
  1 York Street, Baker Street
  London
  England W1H 1PZ

[859]

WILLIAM HONYMAN GILLESPIE SCHOLARSHIP TRUST *(Scotland)*

Scholarships

Subjects: Theological studies or research.

No. offered: One Scholarship annually.

Value: Not less than £1,000 per annum.

Tenable at any university or similar institution for two years, or in special circumstances for a period not exceeding four years.

Eligibility: Open to graduates in theology of any Scottish university.

Note: Applications should be submitted through the principal of the theological college of the Scottish university of which the applicant is a graduate, by 15th May.

Address:
  Gillespie Scholarship Trust
  Messrs. Tods, Murray and Jamieson, W.S.
  66 Queen Street
  Edinburgh
  Scotland EH2 4NE

[860]

GILLETTE COMPANY *(U.K.)*

Gillette International Postdoctoral Fellowships

Subjects: Chemistry, metallurgy, physics and related sciences.

No. offered: One or two Fellowships annually.

Value: £6,000 per annum, plus return travel costs.

Tenable at a number of universities in the United Kingdom or Western Europe for one year, renewable by agreement for a second year. The Fellowship will be tenable in a country other than the native country of the Fellow.

Eligibility: Open to citizens of Western Europe, the United States or Canada who are not more than 35 years of age and hold postgraduate qualifications equivalent to the Ph.D. of a United Kingdom university.

Note: University departments are invited to take on a Fellowship and then make their own arrangements for obtaining a suitable Fellow.

Further information from:
Secretary, Gillette International
 Fellowships
Gillette Research Laboratory
454 Basingstoke Road
Reading, Berkshire
England RG2 0QE

[861]

FRED C. GLOECKNER FOUNDATION

Foundation Fellowships

A number of Fellowships are awarded to students at the graduate level, to provide financial aid for research in floriculture and the supporting and allied fields, such as plant physiology, plant pathology, genetics and entomology. Fellowships are also available to qualified students wishing to obtain an M.S. or Ph.D. in these fields. The awards are made annually, and may be continued for additional periods of time, as merited by the work undertaken. Application forms, available from the Foundation, should be submitted by 1st May or 1st November.

Further information from:
Fred C. Gloeckner Foundation
15 East 26th Street
New York, New York 10010
U.S.A.

[862]

GOETHE INSTITUTE *(Munich)*

Training Course Bursaries

Purpose: To give foreign school and university teachers of German the opportunity to attend training courses on a subject of their choice within the field of German literature, civilization, methodics or language-training.

Value: Accommodation, board (at about DM1,200 to DM1,800) and one four-day excursion to Berlin with all expenses paid (DM700).

Tenable in Augsburg, Nuremberg, Hamburg, Rothenburg, Munich, Freiburg, Schwäbisch Hall, Göttingen or Berlin for two or three weeks.

Eligibility: Open to nationals of any European or North American country except Germany, who are qualified teachers with at least four years of professional experience in teaching German language and/or literature. Applicants should be not more than 5 years of age and should speak German fluently; those whose main subject is German take preference.

Note: Candidates are chosen after consultation with local government authorities, the German embassy and the Institute in the applicant's country. German embassies and cultural institutes will provide detailed information and will accept applications.

Closing date: 1st February.

Address:
Goethe-Institut
Referat 32
Externe Fortbuildung
Kaulbachstrasse 91
D-8000 Munich 40
West Germany

[863]

GOLDSMITHS' COMPANY *(U.K.)*

Travelling Grants for Schoolmasters and Schoolmistresses

Purpose: To enable assistant schoolmasters and schoolmistresses to undertake refreshment study during periods of sabbatical leave from their schools.

Value: A contribution, which will not normally exceed £1,500, to the school towards the salary of a substitute for the candidate granted leave, who is expected to receive his or her normal salary during absence; a payment direct to the individual towards travel and incidental expenses that will not normally exceed £1,500 although the Company will take into account the candidate's salary, financial commitments and other estimated expenses.

Tenable for about six months at a university or other appropriate centre in the United Kingdom, although the Company gives higher priority to programmes involving travel overseas. Programmes that involve teaching at another school, however, are unlikely to be approved.

Eligibility: Candidates teaching in schools whose heads are members of the Secondary Heads Association/Head Masters' Conference or National Association of Head Teachers are eligible. They should have had not less than seven years teaching experience and should not normally be over 50 years of age.

Note: Applications must be made through the head of the candidate's school, and should include a letter from the candidate setting out the plan for the period of leave; a statement in tabular form of the candidate's previous career and qualifications, date of birth, education, and experience to date; a letter of recommendation from the head.

Closing date: 1st April.

Further information from:
Clerk of the Goldsmiths' Company
Goldsmiths' Hall, Foster Lane
London
England EC2V 6BN

[864]

ADOLPH AND ESTHER GOTTLIEB FOUNDATION *(U.S.A.)*

Grants for Visual Artists

A few Grants in varying amounts are offered annually to visual artists of any nationality who can demonstrate a 20-year professional commitment to their own art work and who are in need of financial assistance in order to continue their work. United States residency is not required.

Artists who have been awarded a Grant must allow one year to elapse before reapplication. Closing date for application is 31st December.

Further information from:
Adolph and Esther Gottlieb Foundation
380 West Broadway
New York, New York 10012
U.S.A.

[865]

GOULD LEAGUE OF NEW SOUTH WALES

Cayley Memorial Scholarships

Scholarships of A$500 each are offered annually for work designed to promote wildlife management, particularly in relation to bird life. The work must be done in New South Wales.

Closing date: 30th November.

Further information from:
Secretary
Gould League of New South Wales
Public School, Mary Street
Beecroft, N.S.W.
Australia 2119

[866]

GOWRIE SCHOLARSHIP TRUST FUND *(Australia)*

Research Scholarships

Subjects: Unrestricted.

No. offered: Normally two Scholarships annually.

Value: Usually A$3,500 per annum; may be higher under special circumstances.

Tenable for up to two years at universities or other recognized research establishments either in Australia or overseas.

Eligibility: Open to graduates of Australian universities or to persons who have completed a course at other recognised institutions in Australia. The Scholarships are available only to members of the Australian armed forces who served in a combat area during the war of 1939-45, or to their direct descendants. Educational attainments, character, financial means and other activities are considered, and special consideration is shown to descendants of members of the armed forces who were killed on active service.

Note: Applications may be made via the registrar of the university of graduation.

Closing date: 31st October.

Further information from:
Gowrie Scholarship Trust Fund
47 Cherry Street
Warrawee, N.S.W.
Australia 2074

[867]

GRADUATE INSTITUTE OF INTERNATIONAL STUDIES *(Geneva)*

Scholarships

Subjects: Political science: intensive research and study towards a doctorate.

No. offered: Approximately fifteen Scholarships annually.

Value: 700 Swiss francs per month.

Tenable at the Graduate Institute of International Studies, Geneva, for one year, with the possibility of renewal.

Eligibility: Open to any person who can give evidence of a sound knowledge of the French language and of sufficient prior study in political science, economics, law or modern history, by the presentation of a college or university degree.

Note: Scholarships are normally awarded to more advanced students of the Institute. Scholars are expected to assist professors in their research or in their seminars, and to advise and direct less advanced students.

Scholars are exempted from Institute fees, but not from the obligatory fees of the University of Geneva which confers the doctorate (Doctorat ès sciences politiques).

Closing date: 15th April.

Address:
Secretary General
Graduate Institute of International Studies
132 rue de Lausanne
CH-1211 Geneva 21
Switzerland

[868]

GRAND PRIX DE CHARTRES INTERNATIONAL ORGAN CONTEST

Organists from all countries who are not more than 35 years of age may apply to take part in the Contest which is held in even-numbered years. There are two major prizes of FF20,000 each, one for interpretation and one for improvisation, and the same candidate among the finalists may win the two prizes and thus accumulate the combined sum of the two awards. In addition, the winners receive medals, diplomas and concert engagements.

Further information from:
Secretariat
Grand Prix de Chartres
75 rue de Grenelle
75007 Paris
France

[869]

GRASS FOUNDATION *(U.S.A.)*

Fellowships in Neurophysiology

Subjects: Neurophysiology: research.

No. offered: Variable depending upon funds and space available.

Value: To cover travelling and reasonable living expenses while at the Marine Biological Laboratory, plus certain laboratory costs and a modest drawing account for personal expenses; married Fellows receive living expenses for spouse and family.

Tenable at the Marine Biological Laboratory, Woods Hole, Massachusetts, for summer research, normally up to a maximum of fourteen weeks.

Eligibility: Open to persons of any nationality at the predoctoral or early postdoctoral stage. Only those with no prior research experience at the Laboratory will be considered. Candidates are judged on their ability to organize and present pertinent information as witnessed by their applications.

Note: Applicants should write for *Bulletin FA283* which give information essential in preparing an application. The application will request information as to the proposed research program; summary of previous investigations; educational background; age, marital status, etc; estimates of travel expenses, laboratory space requirements, laboratory equipment needs and costs. The recommendation of a senior investigator familiar with the work of the applicant is also required.

Closing date: Beginning of January.

Further information from:
Grass Foundation
77 Reservoir Road
Quincy, Massachusetts 02170
U.S.A.

[870]

GRASS FOUNDATION *(U.S.A.)*

R.S. Morison Fellowships

Morison A Fellowships are for a program combining training in clinical electroencephalography with research training in neurophysiology, especially as related to experimental epilepsy and/or electroencephalography. Applicants should be M.D.'s who have completed a minimum of one year of an approved residencey training program in either of the above specialities.

Morison B Fellowships are for a program in mammalian neurophysiology, and are meant to provide research training to prepare for an academic career as a clinical investigator. Applicants should be M.D.'s who have been accepted to, or are currently enrolled in an approved residency training program of either neurology or neurological surgery.

Value: Both *A* and *B* consist of a stipend of *US*$17,000 for the first year, paid in monthly installments, plus *US*$700 for each dependent, and up to *US*$3,000 for expenses including research costs, tuition, travel, etc.

Tenable within North America for two years; renewable for a third year.

Closing date: 1st April for both *A* and *B*, tenure to begin the following year.

Further information from:
Grass Foundation
77 Reservoir Road
Quincy, Massachusetts 02170
U.S.A.

[871]

GREATER LONDON ARTS ASSOCIATION

C. Day Lewis Fellowships

Purpose: To enable established creative writers to build contact with the public by working with students.

No. offered: Varying number of Fellowships annually.

Value: Approximately £4,500.

Tenable at different universities, colleges, schools, libraries and other institutions within Greater London, normally for one academic year or the equivalent.

Eligibility: Open to United Kingdom residents who are published creative writers. Other qualifications are dependent on the nature of the institution at which the Fellowship is tenable.

Note: The Fellow is required to attend two days per week at the institution concerned, under the direction of its governing authorities during the duration of the Fellowship.

Further information from:
Literature Officer
Greater London Arts Association
25/31 Tavistock Place
London
England WC1H 9SF

[872]

GREEK STATE SCHOLARSHIPS FOUNDATION

Postgraduate Scholarships

Subjects: Graduates from member-states of the Council of Europe or from African or Asian countries may study any discipline of their own choice, in order to compose a doctoral thesis in Greek.

No. offered: Five Scholarships annually for European graduates, five for African graduates, five for Asian graduates.

Value: Approximately US$280 per month plus the cost of travel to and from Greece and up to US$650 for thesis publication.

Tenable from one to four years for Asian and African Scholars and for three years for European Scholars at any institution of higher education in Greece.

Eligibility: Open to graduates from member-states of the Council of Europe or countries of Africa or Asia who are not more than 40 years of age and hold an M.A. or M.Sc. degree or equivalent qualification.

Note: Candidates should apply through the Greek diplomatic mission in their own country.

Closing dates: 30th April (European candidates); 15th June (African and Asian candidates).

Further information from:
Greek State Scholarships Foundation
14 Lysicratus Street
GR 119 Athens
Greece

[873]

ELIZABETH GREENSHIELDS FOUNDATION *(Canada)*

Grants

Approximately 50 awards are made annually to assist young students for a year's study of painting and/or sculpture who wish to develop their careers along traditional lines. Applicants may be nationals of any country, and should have a good knowledge of the fundamentals of craft.

Further information from:
Elizabeth Greenshields Foundation
1814 Sherbrooke Street West
Montreal, Quebec
Canada H3H 1E4

[874]

THE GUARDIAN *(U.K.)*

Guardian Fiction Prize £500 is given annually in November for a novel published during the previous twelve months by a British or Commonwealth writer. The winning novel is chosen by the Guardian's literary editor in conjunction with the Guardian's regular reviewers of new fiction.

Guardian Award for Children's Fiction of £200 is given each spring for the best novel for children, written by a British or Commonwealth author, and published during the previous twelve months.

Note: Publishers of authors may submit works for consideration, although normally choice is made from books considered by the Guardian's editors and reviewers throughout the year.

Not confirmed for 1983.

Further information from:
W.L. Webb, Literary Editor
The Guardian
119-141 Farringdon Road
London EC1
England

[875]

DANIEL AND FLORENCE GUGGENHEIM FOUNDATION *(U.S.A.)*

Flight Structures Fellowships

Purpose: To provide graduate training and research experience for potential leaders in the future development of the aerospace sciences.

Subjects: Flight structures and related subjects: research and training.

Numbered offered: Three or more Fellowships annually.

Value: Up to US$2,400 per annum, plus full tuition.

Tenable at the Daniel and Florence Guggenheim Institute of Flight Structures, Columbia University, New York City, for one year.

Eligibility: Open to United States or Canadian residents who have a bachelor's degree in aeronautical, civil or mechanical engineering, or physics, applied physics, applied mathematics or engineering sciences, and are preferably under 30 years of age.

Closing date: 1st February.

Further information from:
Professor R. Vaicaitis
School of Engineering and Applied Science
Columbia University
610 Mudd Building
New York, New York 10027
U.S.A.

[876]

DANIEL AND FLORENCE GUGGENHEIM FOUNDATION *(U.S.A.)*

Jet Propulsion Fellowships

Purpose: To provide graduate training and research experience for potential leaders in the future development of the aerospace sciences.

Subjects: Jet propulsion and related sciences.

No. offered: Four or more Fellowships annually.

Value: Up to US$4,000 stipend per annum, plus full tuition.

Tenable at the Daniel and Florence Guggenheim Laboratories for the Aerospace Propulsion Sciences, Princeton University, New Jersey, for one year.

Eligibility: Open to United States or Canadian residents who have a bachelor's degree in any physical science or engineering field, and are preferably under 30 years of age.

Closing date: 15th January.

Further information from:
Dean of the Graduate School
Princeton University, Box 255
Princeton, New Jersey 08544
U.S.A.

[877]

HARRY FRANK GUGGENHEIM FOUNDATION *(U.S.A.)*

Research Program

The Foundation operates a program of specific and innovative study and research to promote understanding of human social problems related to dominance, aggreseion and violence. Support is provided mainly for basic research in the social, behavioral and biological sciences, but research which is related to the Foundation's program will be considered regardless of the disciplines involved. Proposals should be for a specific project and should describe well defined aims and methods; they should not be for general institutional support.

Grants may be made to either institutions or individuals in any country. Although they are customarily given for a one-year term, two-year projects may be considered. The average amount of a grant has been approximately $20,000 per annum, but applications for a greater or lesser sum will be judged on their merits.

Grants will be considered for salaries, employee benefits, research assistantships, computer time, supplies and equipment, field work, reasonable secretarial and technical help, and other items necessary to the successful completion of a project. The Foundation cannot supply funds for overhead costs of institutions, travel to professional meetings, summer salaries, publication subsidies, self-education, elaborate fixed equipment or predoctoral support while completing Ph.D. theses (apart from that indirectly involved in research assistantships).

Further information from:
Harry Frank Guggenheim Foundation
120 Broadway
New York, New York 10271
U.S.A.

[878]

JOHN SIMON GUGGENHEIM MEMORIAL FOUNDATION *(U.S.A.)*

Guggenheim Fellowships to Assist Research and Artistic Creation *(Western Hemisphere and The Philippines)*

Subjects: All fields of science, scholarship and

the creative (but not performing) arts.

No. offered: Approximately 30 Fellowships annually.

Value: By individual assessment.

Tenable usually for a period of six months to one year. A period of residence or consultation in the United States is required, otherwise there is no restriction on place of tenure.

Eligibility: Open to citizens and permanent residents of countries and territories of the Western Hemisphere (exclusive of the United States and Canada) and the Philippines who have demonstrated an unusual capacity for productive scholarship or unusual creative ability in the fine arts, including music. Candidates will normally be between the ages of 30 and 45.

Note: Members of the teaching profession receiving sabbatical leave on full or part salary are eligible for appointment, but Guggenheim Fellowships may not be held concurrently with other United States fellowships.

Fellowships in music are awarded only to composers of music or to scholars who propose research into the history or theory of music.

The Fellowships are awarded by the Trustees upon nominations made by a Committee of Selection.

Closing date: 1st December.

Further information from:
John Simon Guggenheim Memorial
   Foundation
90 Park Avenue
New York, New York 10016
U.S.A.

[879]

JOHN SIMON GUGGENHEIM MEMORIAL FOUNDATION *(U.S.A.)*

Guggenheim Fellowships to Assist Research and Artistic Creation *(U.S.A. and Canada)*

Subjects: All fields of science, scholarship and the creative (but not performing) arts.

No. offered: Approximately 300 Fellowships annually.

Value: By individual assessment.

Tenable for a period of six months to one year. There is no restriction on place of tenure.

Eligibility: Open to citizens or permanent residents of the United States or Canada who have demonstrated unusual capacity for productive scholarship or unusual creative ability in the fine arts. Candidates will normally be between the ages of 30 and 45.

Note: Members of the teaching profession receiving sabbatical leave on full or part salary are eligible for appointment, but Guggenheim Fellowships may not be held concurrently with other fellowships.

Fellowships in music are awarded only to composers of music or to scholars who propose research into the history or theory of music.

Fellowships are awarded by the Trustees upon nominations made by a Committee of Selection.

Closing date: 1st October.

Further information from:
John Simon Guggenheim Memorial
   Foundation
90 Park Avenue
New York, New York 10016
U.S.A.

[880]

CALOUSTE GULBENKIAN FOUNDATION *(U.K. Branch)*

The current priorities in the United Kingdom, Commonwealth and the Republic of Ireland are:

Self-Help in the Arts: To help artists and arts organisations survive the present financial climate through the encouragement and support of improved production and administrative methods. The Foundation investigates arts funding patterns and particular initiatives.

Individual Artists Program: Support is concentrated on disciplines which are labour or equipment intensive: areas include video, holography, print-making, film and contemporary music. A Performance Arts Commissioning Fund primarily offers grants for commissions to artists from abroad, especially from the Commonwealth.

Arts for All encourages the integration of arts practice with work and leisure as well as supporting projects which involve professional and amateur practitioners working together creatively.

Note: In the United Kingdom, Commonwealth and Republic of Ireland, the Foundation does not make any kind of retrospective grant; nor does it provide individual education and travel grants (except to further Commonwealth policies). It does not provide research grants to individual research workers (except for its own projects) and direct production, exhibition or performance costs are not supported.

Artists seeking assistance should apply through the artistic organisations to which they belong. An "Information and Advice" pamphlet is available from:

Calouste Gulbenkian Foundation
U.K. Branch
98 Portland Place
London
England W1N 4ET

H

See *How to Use The Grants Register*, page ix

[881]

HAGUE ACADEMY OF INTERNATIONAL LAW

Scholarships

Subject: International law.

No. offered: Variable.

Value: 55 Dutch florins per diem to cover expenses for the period of tenure. Scholars are exempt from registration and examination fees. Travelling expenses are not refunded.

Tenable at summer courses of the Hague Academy of International Law for three weeks in July and August.

Note: Applications should be made by the applicant himself and submitted with a curriculum vitae, a photograph and a statement of the evidence which the applicant considers to be of value in support of his candidature. Every application must be typewritten and accompanied by a recommendation from a professor of international law. Candidates should, if possible, attach copies of any scientific publications. As documents forwarded by applicants in support of their candidature are not returned, university certificates or other diplomas must be submitted in the form of copies duly verified by a competent authority. The teaching period for which the candidate wants to be registered should be clearly stated. Admission to the course does not automatically entitle the student to a Scholarship.

Closing date: 1st March.

Further information from:
Secretariat
Hague Academy of International Law
Peace Palace, Carnegieplein 2
2517 KJ The Hague
Netherlands

[882]

DAG HAMMARSKOLD FOUNDATION
(Sweden)

Awards

The purpose of the Foundation is to organize seminars, conferences and courses on the social and economic problems of the developing countries. It should be emphasized that the Foundation is an operating and not a grant-making body and that its work programmes are carried out under its own auspices. Participants are proposed by the governments concerned, as well as by certain international organizations and academic institutions, on receipt of a special invitation from the Foundation. Individual applications are not accepted.

Further information from:
Dag Hammarskjöld Foundation
Dag Hammarskjöld Centre
Övre Slottsgatan 2
S-752 20 Uppsala
Sweden

[883]

JOHN HANCOCK MUTUAL LIFE INSURANCE COMPANY *(U.S.A.)*

Awards for Excellence in Business and Financial Journalism

Purpose: To recognize writers who have contributed significantly to consumer understanding of business and finance.

No. offered: One Award annually, in each of six categories.

Value: US$2,000 plus expenses to attend an Awards presentation at a leading American university.

Tenable for one year and may be renewed in competition for up to three times, after which the winner will receive a permanent trophy and be ineligible for any future competitions.

Eligibility: Open to any staff reporter or editor whose article, or series of articles, has appeared in a U.S. publication during the year prior to that of the Award.

Note: Applicants may submit more than one entry per competition. Six unmounted copies of each entry should be submitted along with an official entry blank which may be obtained by writing to the address below.

Closing date: 15th January.

Further information from:
Awards for Excellence: T-54
John Hancock Mutual Life Insurance Company
John Hancock Place, P.O. Box 111
Boston, Massachusetts 02117
U.S.A.

[884]

HARTFORD JEWISH COMMUNITY CENTER *(Connecticut)*

Edward Lewis Wallant Memorial Book Award

An annual Award of US$100 and a scroll is given for a fiction work of significance to the American Jew.

Further information from:
Hartford Jewish Community Center
335 Bloomfield Avenue
West Hartford, Connecticut 06117
U.S.A.

[885]

HARTFORD PUBLIC LIBRARY *(Connecticut)*

Caroline M. Hewins Scholarship

Subject: Children's librarianship: study leading to a master's degree.

No. offered: One Scholarship annually.

Value: US$1,400.

Tenable at a school of library science accredited by the American Library Association, for one year.

Eligibility: Open to persons who have, or are about to obtain, the A.B. or B.S. degree, who plan to specialize in library work with children, and who have applied for admission to a library school. Preference is given to candidates who plan a career in public library service.

Closing date: 1st February.

Further information from:
Caroline M. Hewins Scholarship
c/o Librarian, Hartford Public Library
500 Main Street
Hartford, Connecticut 06103
U.S.A.

[886]

HARVARD UNIVERSITY PRESS *(Cambridge, Massachusetts)*

Robert Troup Prize: An award of US$3,000 is made every four years for the best manuscript, on some pre-designated subject in the fields of the natural or social sciences, which has been accepted for publication by the Press. Eligible manuscripts must be original, book-length, and previously unpublished. The current topic is "Agriculture in Theory and Practice". *Closing date:* 31st December 1981.

Thomas J. Wilson Prize: An award of US$500 is presented annually for an author's first book, accepted for publication by the Press, and selected by the Board of Syndics of the Press as outstanding in content, style and mode of presentation.

Further information from:
Patricia K. Abe, Publicity
Harvard University Press
79 Garden Street
Cambridge, Massachusetts 02138
U.S.A.

[887]

HAWTHORNDEN PRIZE *(U.K.)*

The Prize of £100 is given annually to a British writer under 41 years of age for the best work of imaginative literature published during the preceding calendar year. The word "imaginative" is given a broad interpretation. Biographies are not necessarily excluded. Books do not have to be submitted for the Prize; it is awarded without competition.

[888]

HAYSTACK MOUNTAIN SCHOOL OF CRAFTS *(Deer Isle, Maine)*

Short-term Scholarships in Summer Workshops

Subjects: Ceramics, graphics, fabric, wood, weaving, quiltmaking, papermaking, metalsmithing, blacksmithing, jewelry, glass, photography.

No. offered: Approximately thirty-two Scholarships annually.

Value: Tuition, board and room. Foreign nationals are not assisted with travel expenses.

Tenable at the School for one or two three-week summer sessions.

Eligibility: Open to United States and foreign nationals who are capable of graduate level work and are at least 18 years of age.

Closing date: 15th March.

Further information from:
Haystack Mountain School of Crafts
Deer Isle, Maine 04627
U.S.A.

[889]

HEALTH EDUCATION COUNCIL *(U.K.)*

Fellowships (London University)

Purpose: To provide study grants to enable students to read for the degree of master of science (health education) in the Faculty of Education of London University.

Subjects: Health education in the community and in working environments, as well as in educational institutions.

No. offered: Four Fellowships annually.

Value: According to age, qualifications and experience.

Tenable for one year in the Centre of Science Education, Chelsea College, University of London.

Eligibility: Candidates should be residents of England, Wales or Northern Ireland, and possess an honours deree in biological, behavioral, medical, nursing or allied studies plus some teaching experience. Normally, candidates should have prior experience in health education. Selection is by competition. Once nominated, Fellows must be accepted as students by the University.

Note: The course has been designed to meet the anticipated need of the reorganised National Health Service for a new and critical generation of health educational specialists.

Closing date: As notified annually in the press, usually January/February.

Further information from:
Director of Education and Training
Health Education Council
78 New Oxford Street
London
England WC1A 1AH

[890]

HEALTH EDUCATION COUNCIL *(U.K.)*

Fellowships (Manchester University)

Purpose: To provide study grants to enable students to read for the degree of master of science in the Faculty of Medicine at the University of Manchester.

Subjects: Community medicine, health education, health service administration, nursing and research or education in various health fields.

No. offered: Four Fellowships annually.

Value: According to age, qualifications and experience.

Tenable for two years in the Department of Community Medicine, University of Manchester.

Eligibility: Candidates should be residents of England, Wales or Northern Ireland, with a good degree, or equivalent professional qualification, in medicine, nursing, dentistry, physiology, social sciences or statistics. Selection is by competition. Once nominated, Fellows must be accepted as students by the University.

Note: The course is designed to meet the anticipated need of the reorganised National Health Service for a new and critical generation of health education specialists.

Closing date: As notified annually in the press, usually January/February.

Further information from:
Director of Education and Training
Health Education Council
78 New Oxford Street
London
England WC1A 1AH

[891]

HEALTH EDUCATION COUNCIL *(U.K.)*

Dr. A.J. Dalzell-Ward Memorial Research Fellowship

Purpose: To assist the Fellow in working towards a higher degree in association with a research group concerned with health education.

Subject: Research into a topic that contributes to the furthering of the development of health education. The topic must be chosen by the Fellow and approved by the appropriate research group and Health Education Council.

No. offered: Two Fellowships annually.

Value: £3,000 per annum.

Tenable for one or two years at any university or polytechnic in England, Wales or Northern Ireland with health education interests.

Eligibility: Candidates should be graduates in medicine, dentistry, nursing, education, the biological sciences or the social sciences; they should be citizens of the United Kingdom and should intend to carry out research based at a university or polytechnic in England, Wales or Northern Ireland.

Closing date: As notified annually in the press.

Further information from:
Director, Medical Division
Health Education Council
78 New Oxford Street
London
England WC1A 1AH

[892]

HEALTH AND WELFARE CANADA
National Health Research and Development Program

Short-Term Studentships: A limited number of Studentships are offered to support outstanding undergraduate and graduate students and, in special circumstances, postgraduate and postdoctoral students, to gain research training or research experience in areas closely related to public health or health services research. Tenure of Short-Term Studentships may not exceed a period of six months.

M.Sc. Fellowships and Ph.D. Fellowships are offered to provide support for highly qualified students who wish to undertake full-time training leading to an M.Sc. degree (or equivalent) or a Ph.D. degree (or equivalent) in one of a variety of research fields closely related to health care or public health, such as health economics, medical sociology, epidemiology, biostatistics and biomedical engineering, as applied to the promotion of health, the prevention of disease, disability or death or the organization of health services.

Note: Prior to application, candidates should obtain a copy of the agency's "Guide for Research Personnel Training Awards," available from:
Director, Grants and Contributions Division
Extramural Research Programs Directorate
Health Services and Promotion Branch
Health and Welfare Canada
Ottawa, Ontario
Canada K1A 1B4

[893]

HEBREW UNIVERSITY OF JERUSALEM

Tobias Landau Fellowships in Marine Biology

One or more Fellowships are offered annually in the amount of US$5,000 each, paid in a lump sum. The Fellowship is open to American and Israeli citizens for post-doctoral research. Americans will hold their Fellowships at the Heinz Steinetz Marine Laboratory, Elat, Israel. Israelis will hold their Fellowships at an appropriate U.S. laboratory. Tenable for up to one year.

Closing date: 31st December.

Further information from:
 Office of Academic Affairs
 American Friends of the Hebrew
  University
 Graduate Division
 1140 Avenue of Americas
 New York, New York 10036

[894]

HEBREW UNIVERSITY OF JERUSALEM
Institute of Jewish Studies

Moritz and Charlotte Warburg Prizes

Approximately 15 Warburg Prizes of US$3,500 to US$4,000 per annum are offered for graduate or postgraduate study at the Institute of Jewish Studies. The Prizes, tenable for one year (renewable) are open to nationals of all countries. Candidates for Ph.D. degrees should be 30 years of age or younger; postdoctoral fellows may be up to age 35. Applications are due by the end of November.

Further information from:
 Secretary
 Hebrew University
 Institute of Jewish Studies
 Jerusalem
 Israel

[895]

HEINEKEN FOUNDATION *(Netherlands)*

Dr. H.P. Heineken Award

The Award of 200,000 Dutch guilders is given every three years to stimulate work in sciences, and is made to a person, or group of persons, regardless of nationality, having achieved a feat of exceptional importance in the fields of biochemistry, biophysics, microbiology and the germination physiology of seeds. The Awardee receives a symbolic crystal in addition to the monetary Award. Applications will not be considered.

Further information from:
 Heineken Foundation
 2e Weteringplantsoen 21
 Post Box 28
 Amsterdam
 Netherlands

[896]

HEINZ-SCHWARZKOPF-FOUNDATION YOUNG EUROPE *(West Germany)*

Scholarships are awarded to grammar school and university students as well as young trainees between 18 and 26 for summer trips in the Federal Republic of Germany. The amount of the Scholarships is at present DM800. The trip should last at least four weeks and should be undertaken alone. The applicant is required to explore one special aspect of the country and prepare a report.

International Meetings of European youth are held with the purpose of contributing to the creation of a European community, and day meetings are conducted with Germans to discuss vocational matters.

Not confirmed for 1983.

Further information from:
 Secretary
 Heinz-Schwarzkopf-Foundation Young
  Europe
 Rissener Landstrasse 195
 D2000 Hamburg 56
 West Germany

[897]

HEISER FELLOWSHIP PROGRAM *(New York City)*

Postdoctoral Research Fellowships

Purpose: To provide beginning postdoctoral training in areas related to leprosy.

Subjects: Cultivation of fastidious organisms; immunology of mycobacterial infection; experimental transmission of leprosy; pharmacology of anti-leprosy drugs.

No. offered: The Program provides support for approximately 18 Awards, Fellowships and Grants annually.

Value: Between US$14,500 and US$16,500

per annum according to previous postdoctoral experience, cost of living in the location of training and the number of dependents, plus air fare to training location for the Fellow and his dependents and up to US$500 per annum for health insurance. Host institutions will receive a training allowance of US$2,000 per annum.

Tenable for one year at an appropriate institution; renewable for a further year.

Eligibility: Open to young scientists who have M.D. or Ph.D. degrees or equivalent qualifications. There are no citizenship requirements or age limits, but candidates should be at an early stage of postdoctoral research training.

Note: Application may be by an individual seeking assistance or by the head of a laboratory seeking authorization to appoint a Fellow.

Closing date: 1st February.

Further information from:
Heiser Program
450 East 63rd Street
New York, New York 10021
U.S.A.

[898]

HEISER FELLOWSHIP PROGRAM *(New York City)*

Visiting Research Awards

Purpose: To promote collaborative research in studies of leprosy and to encourage clinical experience with leprosy by facilitating access to centers in which clinical manifestations of the disease are being correlated with laboratory findings.

No. offered: The Program provides support for approximately 18 Awards, Fellowships and Grants annually.

Value: Travel and subsistence expenses. Awards do not generally cover salary support.

Tenable for up to six months in a foreign institution.

Eligibility: Candidates should be established investigators in leprosy who wish to carry out specific research objectives in a foreign institution. There are no citizenship requirements.

Closing date: 1st February.

Further information from:
Heiser Program
450 East 63rd Street
New York, New York 10021
U.S.A.

[899]

HEISER FELLOWSHIP PROGRAM *(New York City)*

Research Grants

Purpose: To provide limited support to laboratories involved in leprosy research training.

Subjects: Proposals of high scientific caliber clearly related to leprosy.
Initial funding may be requested for new projects or facilities contributing to leprosy research which show promise of becoming self-supporting within one year.

No. offered: The Program provides support for approximately 18 Awards, Fellowships and Grants annually.

Value: Not to exceed US$15,000.

Tenable for one year.

Eligibility: Applicants should be senior investigators, experienced in leprosy research and associated with a laboratory providing training opportunities in this field. There are no citizenship requirements.

Note: A budget is required as part of the application. Grants will not be made for clinical trials or salaries of personnel, and use for institutional overhead is limited to 10% of total awarded.

Closing date: 1st February.

Further information from:
Heiser Program
450 East 63rd Street
New York, New York 10021
U.S.A.

[900]

ROSE HELLABY MEDICAL SCHOLARSHIPS TRUST *(N.Z.)*

Scholarships

Purpose: To enable the Scholar to pursue and undertake research or postgraduate training and experience in the fields of rheumatic disease, physical medicine, manipulative treatment, and the rehabilitation of musculo-skeletal diseases overseas.

No. offered: One Scholarship periodically, depending on available funds and applications from candidates of sufficient merit.

Value: NZ$5,000 per annum, with provision for additional assistance if necessary; a contribution towards travel expenses may be paid in special cases.

Tenable for up to two years at an approved medical school or other institution overseas; may be extended in special cases. The programme of study to be followed must be one that is approved by the Trust's board of Governors.

Eligibility: Open to persons who are normally resident in New Zealand and are registered or eligible to be registered as medical practitioners.

Note: The Scholar must undertake to return to New Zealand upon the termination of the Scholarship and to engage in the practice of his or her profession in New Zealand for a period of at least three years.

Closing date: February.

Further information from:
  Secretary
  Rose Hellaby Medical Scholarships Trust
  P.O. Box 634
  Auckland 1
  New Zealand

[901]

WILLIAM RAMSAY HENDERSON TRUST *(U.K.)*

Grants

About three or four Grants of up to £500 each are offered annually to established researchers interested in the central nervous system. The Grants, which are not usually renewable, enable recipients to undertake short visit to learn new techniques. All qualified researchers may apply; the Grants are not restricted to university staff. Applications for Grants after 1st April must be received by 31st January.

Further information from:
  Chairman
  William Ramsay Henderson Trust
  Anatomy Department
  Teviot Place
  Edinburgh
  Scotland EH8 9AG

[902]

CHARLES AND JULIA HENRY FUND *(U.K.)*

Henry Fellowships *(Harvard)*

Purpose: To strengthen bonds between Britain and the United States.

Subjects: Unrestricted, but subject to approval and feasibility.

No. offered: One Fellowship annually.

Value: US$6,000 per annum, plus tuition fees.

Tenable at Harvard University, Cambridge, Massachusetts, or Yale University, New Haven, Connecticut, for one year only.

Eligibility: Open to citizens of the United Kingdom and colonies who are unmarried and under 26 years of age, and either (a) undergraduates of a university in the United Kingdom who have completed six terms of residence by 1st January, or (b) graduates of a university in the United Kingdom who are in their first year postgraduate study at a United Kingdom university.

Note: Applicants must produce evidence of intellectual ability and must also submit a scheme of study or research not consisting of a degree course. The Fellowships are not awarded in conjunction with other awards to finance a continuing course of study and are not tenable for degree courses.
  Fellows must undertake to return to the British Isles or some other part of the British

Commonwealth on the expiration of their term of tenure.

The Fellowship must be vacated if the Fellow marries.

Closing date: late November.

Further information from:
Secretary, Henry Fund
c/o University Registry
The Old Schools
Cambridge
England CB2 9TN

[903]

CHARLES AND JULIA HENRY FUND *(U.S.A.)*

Henry Fellowships (Oxford or Cambridge)

Purpose: To strengthen bonds between Britain and the United States.

Subjects: Unrestricted, but subject to approval and feasibility; a definite scheme of study or research.

Value: £2,615 plus a travel grant and approved fees.

Tenable at the universities of Oxford or Cambridge, England, for one year.

Eligibility: Open to single United States citizens who have obtained a bachelor's degree in the five years preceding application, and who show promise of high performance in postgraduate studies. Preference will be given to students in their last year of undergraduate work.

Note: Applications should be sent to *The Office of the Secretary, Yale University, New Haven, Connecticut 06520,* or *Secretary to the Corporation of Harvard University, Cambridge, Massachusetts 02138.*

The Fellowships have been temporarily restricted to Harvard and Yale students in alternate years, with the hope that they will be restored to open competition.

Fellowships must be vacated on marriage.

Closing date: 12th December.

Address:
Charles and Julia Henry Fund
17 Quincy Street
Cambridge, Massachusetts 02138
U.S.A.

[904]

MYRA HESS TRUST *(U.K.)*

Awards for Instrumentalists

The Trust makes Awards to outstanding young instrumentalists between 18 and 30 years of age. Preference is given to those entering upon a professional career. Assistance is given for the purchase of instruments, for tuition and maintenance, and towards the cost of first recitals. Funds are limited and Awards are therefore modest. Selected applicants are asked to audition in January or June/July.

Further information from:
Secretary
Myra Hess Trust
16 Ogle Street
London
England W1P 7LG

[905]

B.G. HEYDENRYCH TRUST FUND *(South Africa)*

B.G. Heydenrych Pharmaceutical Scholarships

Purpose: To enable young men to qualify as pharmaceutical chemists.

Value: R600 per annum.

Tenable at an approved South African institution for one academic year; renewable up to a maximum period of three years.

Eligibility: Open to young South African men of the Protestant faith who hold a first class matriculation certificate and have successfully completed at least one year of academic study. Postgraduate Scholarships may be granted to students with outstanding academic records.

Closing date: 1st January.

Further information from:
   Board of Executors
   B.G. Heydenrych Trust Fund
   4 Wale Street
   Cape Town
   South Africa

[906]

B.G. HEYDENRYCH TRUST FUND *(South Africa)*

B.G. Heydenrych Public Service Scholarships

Purpose: To support young men training in law, administration or technical subjects acceptable to the Public Service Commission in South Africa.

Value: R1,200 per annum.

Tenable for one academic year; renewable up to a maximum period of three years.

Eligibility: Open to young South African men of the Protestant faith who hold a first class matriculation certificate and have successfully completed a first year of higher study. Applicants for postgraduate study should have an exceptional academic record.

Note: Candidates must undertake to serve in a state or provincial department of the Public Service for a period of up to five years after qualifying, depending on the extent of the grant.

Closing date: 1st January.

Further information from:
   Board of Executors
   B.G. Heydenrych Trust Fund
   4 Wale Street
   Cape Town
   South Africa

[907]

HIGHER COUNCIL FOR SCIENTIFIC RESEARCH *(Spain)*

Research Scholarships

Subjects: Most scientific fields—research.

No. offered: Two Scholarships annually.

Value: 45,000 pesetas per month, plus cost of tuition and approved travel in Spain. Fares to and from Spain will be paid, the cost of the outward journey being met by the British Council and that of the return journey by the Council. Board and lodgings will probably be available upon request at the Council's residence, but cheaper student accommodation is also available in Madrid.

Tenable in Spain for ten months, i.e., one month longer than the academic year. In exceptional circumstances, Scholarships for short periods will be considered.

Eligibility: Open to British nationals who have obtained, or expect to obtain before taking up the Scholarship, a good honours degree. A working knowledge of Spanish is essential.

Note: Application forms are available from the *Minister for Cultural Affairs, Spanish Embassy, 24 Belgrave Square, London SW1X 8QA.* Applicants should send a stamped addressed foolscap envelope.
   The Council operates similar exchange schemes with Argentina, Belgium, France, the Federal Republic of Germany, Italy, Netherlands, Portugal, and Switzerland.

Address:
   Consejo Superior de Investigaciones
      Cientificas
   Serrano 17
   Madrid-6
   Spain

[908]

SIDNEY HILLMAN FOUNDATION, INC. *(U.S.A.)*

Awards

The Awards of US$750 each are offered annually for outstanding contributions on such themes as civil liberties, race relations, the labor movement, the advancement of social welfare and economic security, greater world understanding, and related problems. Contributions must be in the fields of daily or periodical journalism, non-fiction, radio and television. The Awards are open to anyone but submission must have been published or produced under professional auspices during the year for which an Award is sought. No unpublished manuscripts are considered.

Closing date: 15th January.

Further information from:
Sidney Hillman Foundation, Inc.
15 Union Square
New York, New York 10003
U.S.A.

[909]

HINRICHSEN FOUNDATION *(U.K.)*

A number of Awards, depending upon available funds, are offered to financially assist contemporary music composition, performance and research. There is no fixed value per Award, and U.K. applicants will be shown preference.

Further information from:
Hinrichsen Foundation
10—12 Baches Street
London N1 6DN
England

[910]

HISTORICAL ASSOCIATION *(Christchurch, N.Z.)*

J.M. Sherrard Awards

Purpose: To encourage scholarly research and publication in the field of New Zealand regional history.

No. offered: One or more Awards biennially; the judges reserve the right to make no awards in years when there are no suitable applications.

Value: Approximately NZ$600.

Eligibility: Open to both amateur and professional historians. Titles are selected from the New Zealand *National Bibliography* and other New Zealand periodicals. The primary emphasis is placed on published research.
While personal applications are unnecessary, applications from individuals are considered.

Further information from:
Honorary Secretary
Historical Association (Canterbury)
c/o History Department
University of Canterbury
Private Bag, Christchurch
New Zealand

[911]

HISTORY OF SCIENCE SOCIETY *(U.S.A.)*

Pfizer Award: The Award of US$1,000 is offered annually to an American or Canadian author to recognize and reward distinguished writing (published articles, monographs and books) in the field of the history of science. *Closing date:* 1st May.

Henry Schuman Prize: The Prize of US$250 is offered annually to graduate or undergraduate students in any college, university or institute of technology for an essay on the history of science and its cultural influences. The paper should be approximately 5,000 words in length and thoroughly documented. Essays dealing with medical subjects are ineligible, but papers dealing with the relation between medicine and the natural sciences are acceptable. *Closing date:* 1st July.

Further information from:
History of Science Society
University of Pennsylvania
215 South 36th Street
Philadelphia, Pennsylvania 19104
U.S.A.

[912]

HODDER AND STOUGHTON *(London)*

Winifred Mary Stanford Prize: A Prize of £1,000 is given every two years for a book, published in English in the United Kingdom, which has been inspired in some way by the Christian faith and has been written by a man or women less than fifty years of age at the time of publication. Entries should be published between 1st January and 31st December of the two years for which the Prize is given, and require no specialized knowledge for their comprehension. The winning book will be selected primarily on its literary merit.

Closing date: 15th January.

Further information from:
Secretary, Stanford Prize
Hodder and Stoughton
47 Bedford Square
London
England WC1B 3DP

[913]

PAUL G. HOFFMAN AWARDS FUND

A number of Awards, valuing US$5,000 each, are made in recognition of significant achievement by an individual or group of individuals in the field of national and international development. Eligible recipients may be of any nationality and must be "development practitioners" with special attention paid to those who introduce innovative development projects or who build public understanding of development issues, and who have not already received major international recognition. Nominations may be submitted by anyone.

Further information from:
  Mr. Irving S. Friedman, Chairman
  Paul G. Hoffman Awards Fund
  860 U.N. Plaza, Apartment 7AW
  New York, New York 10017
  U.S.A.

[914]

HOOVER INSTITUTION (Stanford, California)
Stanford University

National Fellows Program

Approximately twelve Fellowships are awarded annually to allow particularly gifted younger scholars to spend one full year on unrestricted, creative research and writing at the Institution. The Fellowships afford scholars a unique opportunity to advance their professional careers by completing an original and significant research project in the form of a publishable manuscript. Subjects of research and writing may include one or more fields of study such as political science, economics, modern history, international relations, law and sociology. Research projects should deal with both current and historical issues in domestic and foreign affairs. Of particular interest are those proposals which consider important policy issues facing the United States today. It is expected that the Institution shall have the first opportunity to publish all manuscripts.

Eligibility: Based primarily on nomination and recommendation of leading scholars throughout the United States, as well as on submission of a carefully prepared research proposal. Candidates should be no more than forty years of age, hold a Ph.D. or its equivalent, and have approximately three or four years experience beyond the doctorate. Fellowships commence in September of each year.

Closing date: End of January of the year for which the Fellowship is desired.

Further information from:
  Executive Secretary
  National Fellows Program
  Hoover Institution
  Stanford University
  Stanford, California 94305
  U.S.A.

[915]

HORSERACE BETTING LEVY BOARD (U.K.)

Veterinary Research Training Scholarships

Subjects: Postgraduate training in any veterinary discipline.

No. offered: Usually four or five Scholarships annually at the discretion of the Board.

Value: £5,500 per annum, paid quarterly plus an allowance of £1,200 for necessary expenses connected with the award (accountable).

Tenable for one year at university veterinary schools; renewable for a maximum period of three years.

Eligibility: Open to suitably qualified graduates who are citizens of, and likely to remain resident in, the United Kingdom.

Closing date: 1st April.

Further information from:
  Horserace Betting Levy Board
  17-23 Southampton Row
  London
  England WC1B 5HH

[916]

HORTICULTURAL RESEARCH INSTITUTE *(Washington, D.C.)*

HRI Research Grants

Purpose: To support necessary research for the advancement of the nursery industry.

Subjects: Nursery industry, especially concerning woody landscape plants, their production, marketing, landscape applications, etc.

No. offered: Fifteen Grants annually.

Value: Five Grants of US$1,500 each, and ten Grants of US$1,000 each; paid in a lump sum.

Tenable at state/federal research laboratories, land-grant universities, forest research stations, botanical gardens and arboreta, etc., for one year. Grants are renewable annually by reapplication.

Eligibility: Open to any researcher submitting an appropriate project which the Institute feels is deserving of support.

Closing date: 1st May.

Further information from:
Horticultural Research Institute
230 Southern Building
Washington, D.C. 20005
U.S.A.

[917]

HOSPITAL FOR SICK CHILDREN FOUNDATION *(Toronto)*

Scholarships

Subject: Perinatal research.

No. offered: One or more Fellowships annually.

Value: Scholars with M.D. degrees receive Can$25,000 per annum and Ph.D. Scholars receive Can$20,000 per annum, with annual 10% increments. Research initiation costs of up to Can$20,000 are also provided. The Scholarships may not be held with other awards but income from medical fees and some teaching is generally permitted.

Tenable at the University of Toronto/Hospital for Sick Children for three years; renewable for a further two years.

Eligibility: Open to persons with an M.D. or Ph.D. degree who have a demonstrable capacity for independent perinatal research and adequate research experience.

Closing date: 1st February.

Further information from:
Chairperson
Scholarship Selection Committee
Hospital for Sick Children Foundation
555 University Avenue
Toronto, Ontario
Canada M5G 1X8

[918]

HOSPITAL FOR SICK CHILDREN FOUNDATION *(Toronto)*

Fellowships

Subjects: Pediatric medicine, including nutrition, infectious diseases, mental retardation, environmental health, and clinical pharmacology.

Value: Can$23,000 per annum and return economy air fare to place of tenure.

Tenable in any agreed institution outside Canada for one or two years.

Eligibility: Open to Canadian citizens or landed immigrants who are of outstanding academic achievement and can provide evidence of aptitude for teaching, research and administration.
Candidates should be nominated by the head of department in which they are employed or in which they will be employed upon completion of the Fellowship.

Note: Nominating institutions must agree to re-employment of Fellow upon return and to continue or establish a program in the field concerned.
Processsing of applications normally takes three months.

Further information from:
Fellowship Program
Hospital for Sick Children Foundation
555 University Avenue
Toronto, Ontario
Canada M5G 1X8

[919]

HOUBLON-NORMAN FUND *(U.K.)*

Fellowships, Grants

Purpose: To promote research into the working interaction and function of financial and business institutions in Great Britain and elsewhere, and the economic conditions affecting them.

No. offered: Approximately ten awards annually.

Value: Grants usually cover cost of travel, computing and miscellaneous research expenditure, and may also cover some maintenance expenses, except to individuals holding a university appointment. The value of a Fellowship depends on the grantee's circumstances, and will be of such amount as seems necessary for undertaking the work.

Tenable normally for one year, with the possibility of extension to a maximum of two years.

Eligibility: Open to those normally resident in the United Kingdom who can provide evidence of their capacity to undertake the proposed research. Candidates need not be university graduates, but awards are not normally made to assist work for a first degree, nor the first year of postgraduate research.

Note: Grants are made to help finance specific research projects, and are normally awarded to individuals working on their own or as part of a team. Fellowships are only awarded in exceptional cases, to senior research workers of outstanding experience.

Closing dates: Grants—1st March; Fellowships—as advertised in the press.

Further information from:
Secretary
Houblon-Norman Fund
c/o Bank of England
Threadneedle Street
London
England EC2R 8AH

[920]

HOUGHTON MIFFLIN COMPANY *(U.S.A.)*

Literary Fellowship

Purpose: To help authors who are at the beginning of their careers to complete literary projects in fiction and non-fiction.

Value: US$10,000 (US$2,500 outright, US$7,500 advance against royalties).

Eligibility: A finished manuscript, as well as work in progress, will be eligible for an award. Candidates must submit double-spaced, typewritten manuscripts in English (at least 50 pages of the actual project); an informal description of the theme and intention of the project; a brief biography; and a completed application form available from the address below.
Whether or not candidates receive an award, all manuscripts will be considered for publication on terms to be arranged.

Further information from:
Houghton Mifflin Literary Fellowships
Houghton Mifflin Company
2 Park Street
Boston, Massachusetts 02107
U.S.A.

[921]

GEORGE A. AND ELIZA GARDNER HOWARD FOUNDATION *(U.S.A.)*

Howard Foundation Fellowships

Purpose: To assist individuals in the middle stages of their careers.

Subjects: Literature and languages; social sciences and history; fine, applied and performing arts. Not available for work leading to any academic degree.

Value: US$5,000 and US$12,000 per annum.

Tenable anywhere in the world for one year.

Eligibility: Open to men and women of any nationality, who should normally be between 30 and 40 years of age. Preference will be given to those candidates who, regardless of their country of citizenship, are professionally based in the United States either by affiliation with an institution or by residence. Applications are accepted only upon nomination by the candidate's institution or by a person prominent in the prospective candidate's institution or by a person prominent in the prospective candidate's field.

Closing dates: 1st November for nominations; 10th December for completed applications.

Note: Fellowships will be announced by 15th April, for commencement of tenure 1st July.

Further information from:
Ernest S. Frerichs, Secretary
Howard Foundation
Box 1867, Brown University
Providence, Rhode Island 02912
U.S.A.

[922]

A.W. HOWARD MEMORIAL TRUST, INC. *(Australia)*

Research Fellowship and Study Awards

Subjects: Research and investigation in the fields of natural and social sciences (including economics) relating to pastures and to their development, management and utilisation.

Purpose: To assist Fellows to attend overseas conferences, to help finance study tours, or to be used as study awards.

Value: Varies.

Tenable at approved research institutes in Australia or abroad.

Eligibility: Open to any individual able to promote research and investigation relevant to pastures in Australia. Candidates must be engaged in aspects of pasture research and have resided continuously in Australia for three years preceding the closing date for applications, and must agree to return to Australia on completion of the Fellowship.

Further information from:
Chairman
A.W. Howard Memorial Trust, Inc.
c/o Department of Agriculture
Grenfell Street
Adelaide, South Australia
Australia 5000

[923]

S.S. HUEBNER FOUNDATION FOR INSURANCE EDUCATION *(U.S.A.)*

Predoctoral Fellowships

Purpose: To increase the supply of qualified teachers of insurance.

Subjects: Insurance: study towards Ph.D. degree in business and applied economics.

Value: Full tuition and fees at the Wharton School of the University of Pennsylvania plus a monthly living stipend, totalling approximately US$13,000 per year.

Tenable at the University of Pennsylvania.

Eligibility: Open to citizens of the United States and Canada, who hold a bachelor's degree from an accredited United States or Canadian university or college. Candidates are required to certify that it is their intention to follow an insurance teaching career and that they will major in risk and insurance for a graduate degree.

Note: Candidates must take the Admission Test for Graduate Study in Business. For information concerning these examinations, candidates should write directly to the *Educational Testing Service, 20 Nassau Street, Princeton, New Jersey 08540.*

Closing date: 15th February.

Further information from:
Dan M. McGill, Executive Director
S.S. Huebner Foundation for Insurance Education
3620 Locust Walk
Philadelphia, Pennsylvania 19104
U.S.A.

[924]

S.S. HUEBNER FOUNDATION FOR INSURANCE EDUCATION *(U.S.A.)*

Postdoctoral Fellowships

Purpose: To increase the supply of qualified teachers of insurance.

Subjects: Insurance and risk.

Value: By individual assessment.

Tenable at the University of Pennsylvania for one year.

Eligibility: Open to citizens of the United States and Canada who hold a Ph.D. or other terminal degree from an accredited university, and intend to follow an insurance teaching career.

Closing date: 15th February.

Further information from:
 Dan M. McGill, Executive Director
 S.S. Huebner Foundation for Insurance Education
 3620 Locust Walk
 Philadelphia, Pennsylvania 19104
 U.S.A.

[925]

HUGHES AIRCRAFT COMPANY *(U.S.A.)*

Master's, Engineer, and Doctoral Fellowships

Purpose: To provide the opportunity to scientists and engineers to gain professional work experience while studying toward a graduate degree.

Subjects: Electrical, electronic, mechanical, aerospace and systems engineering; physics; applied mathematics; computer science.

No. offered: Approximately 100 Fellowships annually.

Value: A regular professional salary for work performed for the Company, and an educational stipend of up to US$5,000 per academic year depending ypon the type of Fellowship (work-study or full-study), the degree program (master's, engineer or doctoral). Additional educational and other expenses are also included.

Tenable at any appropriate graduate school, usually near a Company facility, for one year. Renewable for one or more additional years.

Eligibility: Open to United States citizens who can secure admission to an appropriate graduate school without condition, and have the ability to succeed in the chosen field. Candidates for a Master's Fellowship require a bachelor of science degree in an appropriate field; candidates for either an Engineer Fellowship or Doctoral Fellowship require a master's degree or equivalent in an appropriate field.

Note: Work-study Fellows carry half of a full academic load and work 20 to 32 hours per week during the academic year. Full-study Fellows carry a full academic load and work not more than one-fifth of a regular work week. All Fellows normally work full-time at Hughes during the summer while on the program with the full salary and all employee benefits.

Closing date: 1st February for engineer and Doctoral Fellowships, and six months prior to commencing academic work for the Master's Fellowship.

Further information from:
 Hughes Aircraft Company
 Corporate Fellowship Office
 Culver City, California 90230
 U.S.A.

[926]

HUMAN SCIENCES RESEARCH COUNCIL *(South Africa)*

Bursaries for Honours Degree Study in South Africa

Subjects: Human sciences.

Value: R600.

Tenable at a South African university for one year.

Eligibility: Open to South African citizens with at least 65% pass in the bachelor degree examination or in the subject in which they wish to specialize and wish to study full-time at a South African university for a bachelor honours degree or the equivalent advanced course in the field of human sciences.

Note: A Bursar must pass the honours degree examination within the prescribed time for which the Bursary is awarded, otherwise the Bursary must be refunded or the course repeated and successfully completed at the expense of the Bursar.

Closing date: 15th January.

Further information from:
President
Human Sciences Research Council
Private Bag X41
Pretoria 0001
South Africa

[927]

HUMAN SCIENCES RESEARCH COUNCIL
(South Africa)

Bursaries for Master's and Doctor's Degrees in South Africa

Subjects: Human sciences.

Value: Master's—R800; Doctor's—R1,500 for the Bursary's support and tuition fees. Ad Hoc Grants may also be awarded to cover the costs of field work. See

Tenable at a South African University for one year; may be renewable by application for an additional year for the Doctor's degree.

Eligibility: Open to South African citizens who have passed their previous degree examination with at least 65% in the major subject in which they intend to specialize.

Note: Bursaries for part-time study are also available at the rate of R400 for a Master's degree and R600 for Doctor's degree. Bursaries in excess of R600 for a Doctor's degree may be available to part-time students in exceptional cases.

Applications should be submitted to the university on the prescribed form, which may be obtained by writing to the address below.

Closing dates: Master's—15th January; Doctor's—30th June; Ad Hoc Grants—30th June.

Further information from:
President
Human Sciences Research Council
Private Bag X41
Pretoria 0001
South Africa

[928]

HUMAN SCIENCES RESEARCH COUNCIL
(South Africa)

Bursaries for Post-Master's Degree Study and Training in Research Overseas

Subjects: Human sciences.

Value: In Great Britain and the continent of Europe—R2,000 and a travel grant of R500; in the United States, Canada, Australia and the Far East—R2,000 and a travel grant of R800. Pro-rated Bursaries may be considered for shorter periods of tenure, not less than six months.

Tenable at various universities in Great Britain, the continent of Europe, the United States, Canada, Australia and the Far East for eight months (one academic year) renewable in exceptional circumstances.

Eligibility: Open to South African citizens who hold a master's degree, are registered at a South African university, and require specialized training as research workers in a field for which there are no, or inadequate, training facilities in South Africa.

Note: A Bursar may register for a degree and use the results of his research for obtaining such a degree. The Bursary will be paid on production of proof that arrangements have been made for training at an approved institution.

Annual reports must be submitted through the person under whose guidance the candidate is training and who has previously been approved by the Council. The reports may be referred by the Council to experts in the field of training for an opinion.

On completion of their training, candidates must return to South Africa for at least two years.

Closing date: 30th June.

Further information from:
President
Human Sciences Research Council
Private Bag X41
Pretoria 0001
South Africa

[929]

HUMAN SCIENCES RESEARCH COUNCIL
(South Africa)

Grants for Senior Researchers

Subject: Human sciences: postgraduate research.

Value: Up to and including the following amounts: in South Africa—R3,000; in Great Britain and the continent of Europe—R3,000 and a travel grant of R500; in the United States and Canada—R3,000 and a travel grant of R800. A pro-rated Grant may be considered for shorter periods of not less than three months.

Tenable in South Africa, but the Council may at its discretion make exceptions in the case of applicants who can prove that they have already done outstanding work and would make better progress overseas. The Grants are awarded for periods of at least six months. It is not renewable and not awarded for the acquisition of a further degree.

Eligibility: Open to South African residents who are already in possession of a Doctor's degree, and proved their ability as research workers to the satisfaction of the Council.

Note: Where a university recommends a Grant for research overseas, special reasons for such recommendation should be given, and the university should be prepared to assume full responsibility for the necessary supervision and also to ensure that the rules of the Council are complied with.
Only applications from persons who have already undertaken research of a high standard and have fully exhausted the sources of research in a particular field in South Africa or wish to carry out investigations for which there are no, or inadequate, facilities in South Africa will be considered favourably.

Closing date: 30th June.

Further information from:
President
Human Sciences Research Council
Private Bag X41
Pretoria 0001
South Africa

[930]

HUMAN SCIENCES RESEARCH COUNCIL
(South Africa)

Ad Hoc Grants

Subject: Human sciences: research.

Value: Up to a maximum of R400 for a master's degree and R600 for a doctor's degree.

Tenable for up to two years.

Eligibility: Open to South African residents who can satisfy the Council that the research problem justifies research and the project is practicable; the methods to be used are scientific; and the expenses are justified and are in respect of the necessary costs of the investigation.

Note: Applications must be accompanied by a detailed budget.
Grants are made only for the actual expenses in connection with the investigation and not for support of the applicant himself; however subsistence expenses of up to R15 per day and travel expenses at the current public service rates may be eligible while the candidate is away from his usual place of residence in connection with his research.

Closing date: 30th June.

Further information from:
President
Human Sciences Research Council
Private Bag X41
Pretoria 0001
South Africa

[931]

HUMAN SCIENCES RESEARCH COUNCIL
(South Africa)

Grants for the Attendance of International Conferences

Applications are considered with due attention to the following: the possibility that a South African specialist in the particular field is already overseas and would be able to attend the conference; the status of the applicant in the particular field covered by the conference; the applicant will read a paper at the conference; the likelihood that research in South Africa will benefit through the participation of the applicant in the conference and that his position is such that the knowledge acquired will be easily disseminated on his return to South Africa.

The Council makes Grants not exceeding R900 for conferences in the United States, Canada, Australia and the Far East, and R600 for conferences in Europe and the British Isles. These amounts represent approximately 50 per cent of the normal total cost, and are provided only when the candidate's own institution contributes at least 30 per cent of the total costs involved. Grantees already abroad may receive 50 percent of the travelling expenses from his or her headquarters abroad to the conference centre, and a daily allowance of R30 per day with a maximum of ten days for the duration of the conference, provided that university or institution contributes 30 per cent of the total cost.

Preference will be given to applicants invited officially by the organisers of the conference, to personally read a paper or to make a contribution to the conference, and whose work in the relative field justifies this.

All applications should be accompanied by a complete list of the applicant's publications and a list of all conferences attended by him outside South Africa during the previous five years.

A report regarding attendance at the conference must be submitted to the Council who may consider it for publication in *Humanitas, Journal for Research in the Human Sciences*.

Note: Normally only one application for a particular conference will receive favourable consideration so as to ensure that available funds are distributed as widely as possible.

Closing date: Applications should be submitted three months before the conference date.

Further information from:
President
Human Sciences Research Council
Private Bag X41
Pretoria 0001
South Africa

[932]

HUMAN SCIENCES RESEARCH COUNCIL
(South Africa)

Publication Grants

Purpose: To publish work of outstanding quality in the field of human sciences which, owing to a limited sales potential or for other reasons, could not otherwise be published through the usual channels.

Value: Partial or full cost of publication up to R2,500.

Eligibility: Open to South African residents who can produce concisely and accurately presented work that is the result of original research, is of scientific value, and is in the main new material and not readily available to research workers. Short manuscripts which satisfy these requirements will receive priority.

Note: Applications for the publication of a Master's dissertation will not normally be considered. Publication of a Doctoral thesis will normally be considered if submitted in an adapted and abridged form suitable for a wise academic reading public.

The Council reserves the right to fix the publication price and to decide who the publisher will be. The Council will also recover the amount awarded from royalties after the author has recovered his own costs. Thereafter royalties will accrue to the Council in accordance with an agreement between the author and the publisher.

Two copies of the manuscript must be presented to the Council in an edited form.

The applicant must submit two quotations from well-known publishers with the conditions of publication, format, type of paper, cost of illustrations and labour, etc., the guarantee required by the publisher, and the proposed selling price.

Once notified that his or her application has been successful, the applicant must take steps to ensure, if possible, that publication takes place during the financial year in which the Grant is made.

Note: Further information may be obtained from the Registrars of any South African university, or by writing to the address below.

Further information from:
President
Human Sciences Research Council
Private Bag X41
Pretoria 0001
South Africa

[933]

HUMANE RESEARCH TRUST *(U.K.)*

Prize

A Prize of £1,000 is offered annually for the best scientific paper concerned with the advancement of research programmes in which the use of animals is replaced by other methods.

The Trust is a registered charity and welcomes donations. For further information, send a stamped, addressed envelope to:
R. MacAlastair Brown, Chairman
Humane Research Trust
Brook House, 29 Bramhall Lane South
Bramhall, Stockport, Cheshire
England SK7 2DN

[934]

HUMANITARIAN TRUST *(U.K.)*

Research Awards

Subject: Unrestricted; subject to the discretion of the Trustees.

No. offered: Varies according to availability of funds. Awards are offered twice yearly.

Value: Approximately £200-£300.

Tenable at any approved institution for one year; not renewable.

Eligibility: Open to persons already holding an original grant.

Note: Awards are not made for travel. They are intended only as supplementary assistance and are to be held concurrently with other awards. Applications are to be submitted by the host institution.

Further information from:
Secretary of Trustees
Humanitarian Trust
5 St. Helen's Place
Bishopsgate, London
England EC3A 6AV

[935]

VLACAV HUML INTERNATIONAL VIOLIN COMPETITION *(Zagreb)*

Prizes

Numerous Prizes and engagements are offered in the Competition which is held in Zagreb every four years (next in 1985). Violinists of any nationality who are between 16 and 30 years of age may apply.

Further information from:
Hrvatski glazbeni zavod
Gundulićeva 6
Zagreb
Yu 4100 Yugoslavia

[936]

HUNGARIAN CULTURAL FOUNDATION INC. *(U.S.A.)*

Scholarship

The Foundation occasionally awards Scholarships, of varying amounts, to promote research and publication in topics related to Hungarian culture. Candidates should furnish a curriculum vitae and description of the proposed project.

Further information from:
Hungarian Cultural Foundation
P.O. Box 364
Stone Mountain, Georgia 30086
U.S.A.

[937]

HUNGARIAN INSTITUTE FOR CULTURAL RELATIONS

Scholarships

Subjects: Unrestricted: postgraduate study and research in Hungary.

Value: Free accommodation and a monthly allowance to cover maintenance and personal expenses; also tuition and a grant towards the purchase of books. Generally, travel to and from Hungary is paid by the candidate's own government.

Tenable in Hungary for the duration of approved studies.

Eligibility: Open to suitable nationals of countries with which Hungary has a cultural agreement or an exchange programme—Argentina, Austria, Belgium, Bolivia, Bulgaria, Burma, Chile, People's Republic of China, Cuba, Czechoslovakia, Denmark, Ethiopia, Federal Republic of Germany, Finland, France, German Democratic Republic, Greece, India, Iran, Iraq, Italy, Japan, Democratic Republic of Korea, Mali, Mongolia, Norway, Peru, Poland, Romania, Spain, Sudan, Sweden, Syria, Tanzania, U.S.S.R., United Arab Republic, United Kingdom, United States, Socialist Republic of Vietnam and Yugoslavia. Some knowledge of Hungarian is necessary, depending on the programme followed.

Note: Candidates should apply to the appropriate scholarship agency or Hungarian diplomatic representative in their own country. United Kingdom—*British Council, 10 Spring Gardens, London SW1A 2BN*, before 26th February.

Address:
Hungarian Institute for Cultural Relations
Dorottya utca 8
Budapest V-1051
Hungary

[938]

HUNGARIAN RESEARCH CENTRE FOR WATER RESOURCES DEVELOPMENT

Scholarships for Courses

Courses: Hydrology; methods of ameliorating shortage of water resources.

No. offered: About ten Scholarships for each Course. One course is held each year.

Value: 3,000 forints per month, plus accommodation and travel allowances.

Tenable in Hungary for six months (February to July).

Eligibility: Priority is given to citizens of developing countries. Candidates should be no more than 40 years of age, should possess a bachelor's degree and have worked in the field of hydrology or in hydrology administration for at least two years. Instruction is in English.

Note: The Course is co-sponsored by Unesco, and assisted by FAO and WMO.

Closing date: 15th September.

Further information from:
Vizgazdálkodási Tudományos Kutató Központ
H-1453 Budapest p.f. 27
Hungary

[939]

HUNTINGTON LIBRARY AND ART GALLERY *(San Marino, California)*

Short-term Fellowships
Huntington Library-NEH Fellowships

Purpose: To enable outstanding scholars to carry out significant research in the collections of the Library and Gallery.

Subjects: English or American history or literature.

No. offered: Short-term Fellowships—approximately 30 annually; *Huntington Library-NEH Fellowships*—three or four annually.

Value: Short-term Fellowships—US$750 per month; *Huntington Library-NEH Fellowships*—adjusted to applicant's needs; usually one-half of the Fellow's current cash salary, not to exceed US$1,667 per month.

Tenable at the Huntington Library and Art Gallery for one to less than six months for *Short-term Fellowships* and for periods from six months to one year for *Huntington Library-NEH Fellowships*. Neither Fellowship may normally be renewed immediately.

Eligibility: Candidates should have demonstrated, to a degree commensurate with their age and experience, unusual abilities as scholars through publications of a high order of merit. Attention is paid to the value of the candidate's project and the degree to which the special strengths of the Library and Gallery will be used.

There are no citizenship restrictions for the *Short-term Fellowships; Huntington Library-NEH Fellows* must be U.S. citizens or U.S. residents for at least three years.

Note: Fellowships are not available for work towards doctoral dissertations.

Huntington Library-NEH Fellowships are funded by grants from the National Endowment for the Humanities.

Closing date: 31st December for commencement 1st June.

Further information from:
Martin Ridge, Coordinator of Research
Huntington Library and Art Gallery
San Marino, California 91108
U.S.A.

[940]

EDMUND NILES HUYCK PRESERVE, INC. BIOLOGICAL RESEARCH STATION
(U.S.A.)

Graduate and Post-graduate Grants

Purpose: To promote scientific research in the flora and fauna of Rensselaerville and vicinity.

Subjects: Any research involving the natural resources of the area.

No. offered: Varies.

Value: Up to US$2,000 plus laboratory space and lodging.

Tenable at the Preserve for variable amounts of time. Grants are renewable.

Eligibility: Awards are made without regard to sex, color, religion, ethnic origin or academic affiliation of the applicant. Support is based solely on the quality of the proposed research and its appropriateness to the natural resources and facilities of the preserve.

Closing date: 15th January.

Further information from:
Edmund Niles Huyck Preserve, Inc.
Post Office Box 77
Rensselaerville, New York 12147
U.S.A.

See *How to Use The Grants Register*, page ix

[941]

ICCROM-INTERNATIONAL CENTRE FOR THE STUDY OF THE PRESERVATION AND THE RESTORATION OF CULTURAL PROPERTY *(Rome)*

Scholarships for Courses

Subjects: (a) Architectural conservation (monuments and historic centres); (b) conservation of mural paintings; (c) scientific principles of conservation; (d) preventive conservation in museums.

Tenable at the Centre for (a) six months (January to June), (b) and (c) four months (February to June) and (d) eighteen days (generally starting the end of September).

Eligibility: Open to: (a) graduates in architecture, archaeology, urban design, civil engineering and art history with at least four years of professional experience; (b) candidates with a diploma from a restoration school or at least four years professional experience in conservation, who are aged between 25 and 40; and (c) graduates in humanities, scientists, curators, restorers; (d) curators, administrators, architects, librarians, and archivists in mid-career who have at least ten years professional experience.

Note: Although some scholarships are obtainable through ICCROM itself, candidates are encouraged to seek financial support from within their own countries or from the Italian Government through its embassy or consulate in the candidate's home country.

Closing dates: 15th February of the preceding year for (a), (b), and (c); 30th April of the same year for (d). United States citizens must apply to: *ICCROM Committee, c/o Executive Director, Advisory Council on Historic Preservation, Suite 430, 1522 K Street, N.W., Washington, D.C. 20005;* these applications must be returned to the Committee by 14th January.

Further information from:
ICCROM
13 Via di San Michele
00153 Rome
Italy

[942]

IMPERIAL CANCER RESEARCH FUND *(U.K.)*

Bursaries for Training in Research

Subjects: Cancer research fields, including cellular and molecular biology, endocrine chemistry and physiology, experimental pathology, immunology, pharmacology and virology: postgraduate training towards a Ph.D. degree.

No. offered: Up to twelve Bursaries annually.

Value: £4,140 per annum, plus additional allowances in some cases.

Tenable at the laboratories in Lincoln's Inn Fields or Mill Hill, London, for three years.

Eligibility: Open to British subjects, normally resident in the United Kingdom, who have, or are about to obtain, a first or upper second class degree in science, and are not over 25 years of age.

Further information from:
Director of Research
Imperial Cancer Research Fund
P.O. Box 123
Lincoln's Inn Fields
London
England WC2A 3PX

[943]

IMPERIAL CANCER RESEARCH FUND *(U.K.)*

Visiting Fellowships

One or two post-doctoral Fellowships in cancer research are given annually to applicants who are temporarily or permanently resident outside of the United Kingdom. The Fellowships will hold a value comparable with post-doctoral fellowships in the country of origin, and will be tenable at the Fund's laboratories for one year; not renewable. Fellowships will be advertised.

Further information from:
Director of Research
Imperial Cancer Research Fund
P.O. Box 123
Lincoln's Inn Fields
London
England WC2A 3PX

[944]

IMPERIAL COLLEGE OF SCIENCE AND TECHNOLOGY *(London)*

Bursaries

Concrete Structures Bursary: One Bursary annually at ten-twelfths value of a Research Council Studentship plus fees toward a Master of Science degree in concrete structures. The Bursary is tenable for one session at the College, and open to candidates having a good engineering degree. Applications may be obtained by writing to the address below. *Closing date:* 31st May.

Arthur William Groves Bursary: One Bursary annually at a monthly rate to be determined, for post-doctoral research in silicate mineralogy, geochemistry or petrology. The award is tenable at the College for one year, renewable for one additional year. Applications may be submitted at any time, and are available by writing to the address below.

Optics Bursary: One Bursary, every two years for study leading toward an M.Sc. degree in applied optics, is available to candidates having a good honours degree in physics or mathematics. Candidates must intend to work in British Industry upon completion of the M.Sc. degree. The award is tenable at the College for one year, not renewable. Applications may be obtained by writing to the address below. *Closing date:* 1st June.

Rees Jeffreys Road Fund Bursary: At least one Bursary annually toward an M.Sc. degree in transport is offered at the Department of Civil Engineering at the College for one year, not renewable. The award, paid monthly at Research Council Rates plus fees, is open to candidates from a range of disciplines related to transport, including town planners, civil engineers, architects, surveyors, and social scientists. Applications may be obtained by writing to the address below. *Closing date:* 15th May.

Rio Tinto-Zinc Advanced Course Bursary: One Bursary annually toward an M.Sc. degree in engineering rock mechanics, geophysics, mineral exploration, mineral process design, or mineral production management is offered at the College for one year, not renewable. The award will be paid monthly at Research Council rates, plus fees. Eligible candidates should have a first dgree in an appropriate subject. Applications may be obtained by writing to the address below. *Closing date:* 31st March.

Rio Tinto-Zinc Research Bursary: One Bursary annually is offered for research in some subject connected with the discovery, mining and beefication of minerals, i.e. applied geochemistry, geophysics, mineral exploration, mining geology, mining, mineral technology or extraction metallurgy. The Bursary, tenable for up to three years at the College, is paid monthly at Research Council rates plus fees. Candidates should have an honours degree in an appropriate subject. Applications may be obtained by writing to the address below. *Closing date:* 31st March.

Further information from:
Registrar
Imperial College of Science and Technology
London
England SW7 2AZ

[945]

IMPERIAL COLLEGE OF SCIENCE AND TECHNOLOGY *(London)*

Partial Scholarships

Metalliferous Mining Scholarships: One or more Scholarships are offered annually for research or an advanced course of study at the Mineral Resources Engineering Department of the College for one year, not renewable. The award's value is based on the financial need or the Scholar, but is not intended to cover all expenses. Candidates should have a good honours degree and at least two years experience in the mining industry, preferably overseas. Applications may be obtained by writing to the address below. *Closing date:* 31st August.

William Selkirk Scholarships: One or more Scholarships are offered annually for research of an advanced course of study at the Mineral Resources Engineering Department of the College for one year, may be renewable. All particulars are the same as above. *Closing date:* 31st August.

Further information from:
Registrar
Imperial College of Science and
 Technology
London
England SW7 2AZ

[946]

IMPERIAL OIL LIMITED *(Canada)*

Graduate Research Fellowships

Purpose: to recognize academic excellence and demonstrated aptitude of those best qualified to contribute to the advancement of knowledge in specialized doctoral fields of study.

No. offered: Three Fellowships for pure and applied natural and/or exact sciences and three Fellowships for humanities.

Value: Can$7,000 per annum.

Tenable at any recognized university (not necessarily in Canada), subject to approval of the Fellowship Selection Committee: for three years, subject to satisfactory progress towards a doctoral degree.

Eligibility: Open to Canadian citizens who are university graduates in the year of competition and who are supported by the faculty of the nominating university.

Note: There is no restriction on the number and value of other awards held by a Fellow, as long as he is able to accept at least 75% of the Graduate Research Fellowship, prior approval by the Committee on Higher Education is required before undertaking any part-time employment.

Closing date: 1st February.

Further information from:
Coordinator
Graduate Research Fellowships
Imperial Oil Limited
111 St. Clair Avenue West
Toronto, Ontario
Canada M5W 1K3

[947]

IMPERIAL OPTICAL COMPANY LTD. *(Canada)*

Percy Hermant Fellowships in Ophthalmology

No. offered: Two Fellowships annually to the unversities of Alberta (Edmonton), British Columbia (Vancouver), McGill (Montreal), Queen's University (Kingston), Montreal and Ottawa. One Fellowship annually to the universities of Dalhousie (Halifax), Saskatchewan (Saskatoon), Manitoba (Winnipeg), Western Ontario (London), Sherbrooke.

Value: Can$1,500.

Tenable at any of the above-listed universities for one year.

Eligibility: Open to medical graduates who can show that they plan to practise in the field of ophthalmology in Canada on completion of their training.

Note: Applications should be submitted to the head of the department of ophthalmology at the appropriate university.

Further information from:
Imperial Optical Company Ltd.
Hermant Building, 21 Dundas Square
Toronto, Ontario
Canada M5B 1B7

[948]

INDEPENDENT BROADCASTING AUTHORITY *(U.K.)*

IBA Fellowships/Grants

Purpose: To further the study of the relationship between education and broadcasting.

No. offered: Two or three Fellowships annually.

Value: Current salary and superannuation, plus certain expenses for recipients on secondment; negotiable amount in the form of a grant for other recipients, and in some cases a living allowance, are paid for the period of secondment, plus reimbursement for additional approved expenses.

Tenable at appropriate institutions in the United Kingdom for up to one year.

Eligibility: Open to experienced educationalists working in the United Kingdom.

Note: Applicants should make sure that secondment is available prior to submitting an application.

Further information from:
Independent Broadcasting Authority
70 Brompton Road
London
England SW3 1EY

[949]

INDIAN COUNCIL FOR CULTURAL RELATIONS

Jawaharlal Nehru Award for International Understanding

An annual Award of 100,000 rupees and a citation is given in recognition of outstanding contribution toward the promotion of international understanding, goodwill and friendship among peoples of the world. Awardees may be persons of any nationality, race, creed or sex. Candidates may be nominated for work achieved within five years immediately preceding the nomination, or for earlier work, the significance of which has only recently become apparent. Proposals may be submitted by leaders of international organizations and institutions, academicians, heads of Indian missions abroad, heads of learned societies and research institutions, or any other persons whom the jury feels to be competent to make nominations.

Not confirmed for 1983.

Further information from:
Jawarharlal Nehru Award
c/o Secretary
Indian Council for Cultural Relations
Azad Bhavan, Indraprastha Estate
New Delhi
India

[950]

INDIAN COUNCIL OF MEDICAL RESEARCH

Medical Research Prizes

The Council offers numerous awards, ranging in value from 500 rupees to 5,000 rupees each. Prizes are in the broad field of medical research and cover the following areas: internal medicine, community medicine, leprosy, eye diseases, cancer, nutrition, cardiovascular disease, microbiology, bio-medical science, and dermatology. Eligibility is open to Indian residents engaged in medical research in India. Nominations may be submitted by principals and officers of Indian medical colleges, research institutes, and universities.

Further information from:
Indian Council of Medical Research
P.O. Box 4508
Ansari Nagar
New Delhi 110016
India

[951]

INDIAN COUNCIL OF SOCIAL SCIENCE RESEARCH

Research Fellowships and Grants

The following annual awards are available for research to be carried out at approved institutions, usually in India. The awards are offered in all fields of the social sciences. Generally, awards may not be held concurrently with other awards or paid work, without prior consent of the Council. Application form may be obtained from the address below.

Fellowships: Awarded to relatively junior social scientists who have completed their Ph.D. or have done equivalent research work, and wish to work on approved research. The Fellowships cover current salaries of employed scholars and offer a consolidated amount to others. In addition, they carry an annual contingency grant of 5,000 rupees.

Doctoral Fellowships: Awarded to scholars who are registered candidates for a doctorate in any of the social sciences. The value of the fellowship is 600 rupees per month for the first two years and may be increased to 700 rupees per month for the subsequent period. A contingency grant of 3,000 rupees per year is also attached to the fellowship. College teachers and members of professional staff in research institutions below the age of 35 years may be given the benefit of salary protection. These fellowships are administered as follows—(1) Institutional Fellowships are awarded to young scholars preferably below the age of 30 years who are enrolled for research leading to a doctoral degree at any of the research institutions supported by the ICSSR; (2) Centrally Administered Fellowships are awarded directly by the ICSSR under its sponsored research programmes. These are available to students at any institution; (3) A certain number of fellowships are awarded to scholars from foreign countries, and especially neighbouring countries who are desirous of undertaking research in India. The awards range between 700 rupees and 1,500 rupees per month, depending on the present status of the scholars; those who are not employed are treated on an equal par with their counterparts in India; (4) *Short-term Doctoral* Fellowships, of up to 12 months, are given for field work or for completing writing work already undertaken. The value of the Fellowship is 700 rupees per month and carries a contingency grant not exceeding 3,000 rupees per year. A scholar selected under this scheme may also be considered for salary protection.

National Fellowships: Up to six Fellowships are given to eminent social scientists who have made outstanding contributions in their own areas of specialization. They are offered by the ICSSR at its own initiative and purely on the basis of merit irrespective of age and status of the scholar.

Senior Fellowships are awarded on request to senior social scientists who have made significant contributions to social science research. The awards cover existing salaries of employed scholars to enable them to take leave of absence and work full-time on a piece of research; a consolidated salary is offered to other scholars. In addition, the Fellowships carry an annual contingency grant of 10,000 rupees.

Contingency Grants of up to 5,000 rupees are awarded to doctoral students who are not in receipt of any fellowship or who receive a fellowship without an adequate contingency grant for meeting expenses on field work, computer fees, printing, purchase of books, etc.

Study Grants: Financial assistance is provided to cover travel and maintenance costs for scholar visiting libraries and other centres of documentation for collection of materials pertaining to their research.

Further information from:
 Member-Secretary
 Indian Council of Social Science
  Research
 IIPA Hostel, Indraprastha Estate
 Ring Road
 New Delhi 110001
 India

[952]

INDIAN HEALTH EMPLOYEES SCHOLARSHIP FUND *(U.S.A.)*

Scholarship Fund

Purpose: To educate American Indians in the health field.

Subjects: Various health professions.

No. offered: Varies annually, as funds allow.

Value: US$250 to US$1,200, according to need and availability of funds, to be paid in a lump sum.

Tenable at any accredited school of higher learning, renewable yearly.

Eligibility: Open to any American Indian with scholastic ability who needs assistance.

Note: Applicants do not need a certain blood quantum, but proof of Indian descent is necessary.

Closing dates: 1st January, June and October.

Further information from:
 Indian Health Employees Scholarship
  Fund
 Federal Building, Room 215
 Aberdeen, South Dakota 57401
 U.S.A.

[953]

INDIAN UNIVERSITY MUSEUM OF HISTORY, ANTHROPOLOGY, AND FOLKLORE *(Bloomington, Indiana)*

Graduate Assistantships

Purpose: To assist in the general operation of the museum and to supervise the museum students.

Subjects: Anthropology, history and folklore.

No. offered: Three and one-half Assistantships annually.

Value: US$2,600 annually plus full fee remission.

Tenable at the Museum for one year, renewable for an additional three years.

Eligibility: Candidates should be graduate students who can provide three letters of recommendation in their field of specialty. There are no restrictions in regard to age, sex, or residency.

Closing date: March.

Further information from:
 Student Building 209
 Indiana University
 Indiana University Museum
 Bloomington, Indiana 47401
 U.S.A.

[954]

INDO-U.S. SUBCOMMISSION OF EDUCATION AND CULTURE

Indo-American Fellowship Program for Advanced Research/Professional Development

Purpose: To support advanced research and professional development of U.S. scholars.

Subjects: Unrestricted for studies that may be carried out in India.

No. offered: Ten to twenty fellowships annually.

Value: Approximately US$1,200 to US$1,500 per month, paid in U.S. dollars and Indian rupees.

Tenable in India for two to ten months.

Eligibility: Open to U.S. citizens who have attained the doctorate or an equivalent professional status.

Closing date: 1st July.

Further information from:
 Council for International Exchange of
  Scholars
 11 Dupont Circle, N.W., Suite 300
 Washington, D.C. 20036
 U.S.A.

[955]

INDUSTRIAL RESEARCH/DEVELOPMENT *(Barrington, Illinois)*

Scientist of the Year Award

An Award of US$1,000 and a plaque is presented annually to a scientist for recognition of an outstanding body of work which has made a major contribution to the applied sciences. The recipient must deliver the annual Scientist of the Year Lecture on a specified date. Nominations may be made by anyone.

Not confirmed for 1983.

Further information from:
 Robert R. Jones, Editor
 Industrial Research/Development
 1301 South Grove Avenue
 Barrington, Illinois 60010
 U.S.A.

[956]

M.A. INGRAM TRUST *(Australia)*

Research Grants

A number of Grants are made, depending upon available funds, for research into the origin, habits, life, use and scientific benefits of indigenous (especially Victorian) mammals and birds, and to encourage their preservation. Any person whom the Trustees consider to be sufficiently qualified to undertake the proposed research, is eligible. Grants, tenable in Australia for one year and possibly renewed for an additional year, are paid in a lump sum and vary in value to a maximum of A$1,900.

Closing dates: 1st May and 1st November.

Further information from:
Trustees
M.A. Ingram Trust
c/o Mr. E.R. Allan
9 Mowbray Street
East Hawthorn, Victoria
Australia 3123

[957]

INNER LONDON EDUCATION AUTHORITY

Robert Blair Fellowships

Subjects: Applied science and technology.

No. offered: One Fellowship awarded every two or three years as finances permit.

Value: Up to £5,000, subject to United Kingdom income tax.

Tenable in the United States, or other countries abroad, for one year.

Eligibility: Open to British subjects who are resident in the United Kingdom and are not less than 21 years of age.

Note: Recipients will be required to undertake an advanced course of study or research as may be approved by the Authority.

Closing date: 1st January.

Further information from:
Education Officer (EO/FHE6/TF)
Inner London Education Authority
County Hall
London
England SE1 7PB

[958]

JOHN INNES FOUNDATION *(U.K.)*

John Innes Studentships

Purpose: To encourage postgraduate studies in biological research related to plants.

Subjects: Genetics, applied genetics, virology and ultrastructures of the cells of microorganisms and viruses.

No. offered: As available.

Value: Studentships are the equivalent of those offered by the Science and Engineering Research Council.

Tenable at the John Innes Institutes, for two years.

Eligibility: Applicants should hold an initial degree at a recognized university; they need not be citizens of the United Kingdom.

Note: Application should be by a letter enclosing full curriculum vitae and the names and addresses of at least two scientific referees.
The Institute is associated with the University of East Anglia and receives a Grant in Aid from the Agricultural Research Council.

Further information from:
Clerk to the Trustees
John Innes Foundation
Colney Lane
Norwich
England NR4 7UH

[959]

INSTITUT FRANCAIS DE WASHINGTON

Gilbert Chinard Research Grants

Purpose: To help candidates for the Ph.D. or young researchers to pursue or complete their research.

Subjects: French history and literature.

No. offered: Two or three Grants annually.

Value: US$750, paid in one lump sum.

Tenable in France for at least two months.

Eligibility: Open to U.S. citizens and permanent residents, who are Ph.D. candidates at the final stage of their dissertation, or who have held a Ph.D. degree for no longer than six years prior to 1st January of the year in which the Grant is sought. Candidates should be studying, teaching or doing postdoctoral research at an American university.

Note: Upon completion, the recipient of the Grant should submit a brief report to the Institute.

Closing date: 1st January.

Further information from:
 Edouard Morot-Sir, President
 Institut Français de Washington
 Dey Hall, University of North Carolina
 Chapel Hill, North Carolina 27514
 U.S.A.

[960]

INSTITUTE OF ACTUARIES *(U.K)*

Memorial Prize Fund: The Institute administers funds which give prizes for meritorious contributions to actuarial science, for special merit in passing Institute examinations, and for papers presented to the Institute.

Memorial Education and Research Fund: Assistance is available for: (a) the promotion for educational purposes of research in actuarial science and related subjects, and the publication of the results of such research; (b) the advancement of education in actuarial science and related subjects; and (c) study by actuaries or by persons intending to become actuaries at any educational establishment approved by the Institute or for the purpose of obtaining professional training.

Further information from:
 Secretary-General
 Institute of Actuaries
 Staple Inn Hall, High Holborn
 London
 England WC1V 7QJ

[961]

INSTITUTE FOR ADVANCED STUDIES IN THE HUMANITIES
University of Edinburgh

Visiting Research Fellowships

Purpose: To promote advanced research within the field of the humanities, and especially literature, language, linguistics, history, art, archaeology, and philosophy.

No. offered: Approximately fifteen Fellowships annually.

Value: Small stipends ofered to one or two candidates. Both stipendiary and honorary Fellows have the use of study-rooms in the Institute near the University Library and within easy reach of the National Library and Record Office.

Tenable at the Institute for periods from one to three months, and for up to one year.

Eligibility: Open to scholars of established reputation, and also to younger scholars holding a doctorate or offering equivalent evidence of aptitude for advanced study. Nationals of all countries may apply.

Closing date: 31st January.

Further information from:
 Director
 Institute for Advanced Studies in the
  Humanities
 17 Buccleuch Place
 Edinburgh
 Scotland EH8 9LN

[962]

INSTITUTE FOR ADVANCED STUDY
(Princeton, New Jersey)

General information: The Institute for Advanced Study is devoted to the encouragement, support and patronage of learning. To this end, it welcomes temporary members of high intellectual development.

It awards no degrees, and admits to membership only those who have already taken their highest degree.

In so far as it is possible, the Institute makes its facilities available to qualified members from all parts of the world.

The Institute maintains some of the facilities necessary for academic life, and relies heavily on a fortunate symbiosis with Princeton University, from which it is organically and administratively separate but with which it enjoys close academic and intellectual relations.

The academic work of the Institute is carried on in four schools—mathematics, natural sciences, historical studies, and social science.

Grants: About half of the members are supported by grants-in-aid from funds available to the schools, and supplementary specific purpose funds of the Institute; the other half are supported by the members' own institutions, by the United States and foreign governments and by private foundations.

Note: Admission to membership is by vote of the faculty concerned. Most memberships are by invitation, but some members are selected from the many applicants who write to the Institute outlining the state of their researches and their reason for desiring admission. The number of places is limited, and each year there are many more qualified applicants than can be invited.

Applications for membership may be made to the appropriate school preferably by 31st December of the preceding year for the school of mathematics, 15th December for the school of natural sciences, by 15th October of the preceding year for the school of historical studies and by 1st December for the school of social science.

Further information from:
Institute for Advanced Study
Princeton, New Jersey 08540
U.S.A.

[963]

INSTITUTE FOR AFRICAN MEDICINE AND EPIDEMIOLOGY *(Paris)*
Ministry of Foreign Affairs *(France)*

Scholarships

Purpose: To enable qualified doctors to obtain the diploma of higher studies in tropical medicine and epidemiology.

No. offered: 20 Scholarships annually.

Tenable for nine months at the Institute.

Eligibility: Open to foreign nationals who are qualified doctors of medicine or who hold an equivalent qualification from their country of origin, and to medical assistants.

Closing date: 1st September.

Further information from:
Mme. Fanton
Institute for African Medicine and Epidemiology
Hôpital Claude-Bernard
10 avenue de la Porte d'Aubervilliers
75019 Paris
France

[964]

INSTITUTE FOR AMERICAN UNIVERSITIES *(Aix-en-Provence, France)*

Awards

Approximately 20 Awards are offered annually to enable students, mostly nationals of the United States, to study for one year at the Institute's Centers in France (Aix-en-Provence, Avignon, Toulon), and in England (Canterbury). The subjects of the courses are European studies sociology, history, economics, politics, philosophy, arts, psychology), and French language and literature. Applicants should have completed two years of a university course of study. Instruction is given in both English and French.

Value: Between US$100 and US$500, to assist with tuition fees.

Not confirmed for 1983.

Further information from:
Institute for American Universities
27 place de l'Université
13625 Aix-en-Provence
France

[965]

INSTITUTE FOR BALKAN STUDIES *(Thessaloniki)*

Summer Scholarships

University students and graduates of Belgium, Bulgaria, Czechoslovakia, Denmark, Romania, and the United Kingdom are eligible for Scholarships to enable them to attend

courses on Greek language, history and culture at the International Summer School organized by the Institute for Balkan Studies in Thessaloniki. The Scholarships cover all expenses. Applications may be obtained through the Greek embassy in the candidate's home country.
British applicants should apply to:
Greek Embassy
1A Holland Park
London
England W11 3TP

[966]

INSTITUTE OF BUSINESS STUDIES
(Barcelona)

Scholarships

Course: Economics and business management: study for a master's degree.

Value: A monthly allowance of 30,000 pesetas, plus tuition fees and equipment expenses. Travel costs are not paid by the Institute.

Tenable at the Institute for two years.

Eligibility: Open to nationals of all countries who are between 23 and 30 years of age and have the ability to manage economic and business activities. Scholars must have a good knowledge of Spanish or English.

Not confirmed for 1983.

Further information from:
 Director of Admissions
 Institute of Business Studies
 avenida Pearson 21, Pedralbes
 Barcelona-17
 Spain

[967]

INSTITUTE OF CANCER RESEARCH
(U.K.)

Research Studentships

Subject: Cancer research.

Value: £2,770 per annum; amount reviewed annually.

Tenable at the Institute, for two or three years.

Eligibility: Open to science graduates wishing to undertake study leading normally to a Ph.D. degree.

Note: A limited number of Postdoctoral Fellowships are offered from time to time as vacancies occur.

Further information from:
 Secretary
 Institute of Cancer Research
 Royal Cancer Hospital
 34 Sumner Place
 London
 England SW7 3NU

[968]

INSTITUTE OF CANCER RESEARCH
(U.K.)

Royal Marsden Hospital Fellowships

Subject: Cancer research.

Value: £8,070 per annum.

Tenable at the Royal Marsden Hospital or the Institute of Cancer Research, for one to three years.

Eligibility: Open to graduates in medicine or surgery of an approved university or medical school.

Further information from:
 House Governor
 Royal Marsden Hospital
 Fulham Road
 London
 England SW3 6JJ

[969]

INSTITUTE OF CHARTERED SECRETARIES AND ADMINISTRATORS
(U.K.)

Postgraduate Exhibition

Purpose: To enable the holder to pursue full-time advanced studies of a postgraduate character in a subject within the general field of administration and management to be selected each year by the Council.

No. offered: One Exhibition annually, provided that suitable applications are received.

Value: £1,500 per annum.

Tenable at any university or polytechnic in the United Kingdom for one full academic year.

Note: The successful applicant will be required to make his own arrangements for acceptance by a university for postgraduate study or research if he has not already been granted admission. Applications should be supported by two referees, one of whom should be the head of the appropriate department.

Closing date: 30th April.

Further information from:
  Secretary
  Institute of Chartered Secretaries and
    Administrators
  16 Park Crescent
  London
  England W1N 4AH

[970]

INSTITUTE OF CHARTERED ACCOUNTANTS IN ENGLAND AND WALES

Research Grants

The work of the Research Sub-committee of the Institute's Technical and Research Committee is financed by various charitable trusts associated with the Institute. Enquiries from persons interested in undertaking research within the Sub-committee's programme should be made to:
  Secretary, Technical and Research
    Committee
  Institute of Chartered Accountants in
    England and Wales
  P.O. Box 433
  Chartered Accountants' Hall
  Moorgate Place
  London
  England EC2P 2BJ

[971]

INSTITUTE OF CONSTITUTIONAL AND PARLIAMENTARY STUDIES *(New Delhi)*

Parliamentary Fellowship Programme

Purpose: To provide young social scientists, university teachers, journalists, lawyers, parliamentary officials and others in public and private employment with opportunities for observing at first hand the operation of the democratic system in India and the role and relationship of the Indian Parliament vis-a-vis other organs of government and decision-making processes.

Subjects: The Programme enables participants to observe the Houses of Parliament, the State Legislatures, courts of law and government and other institutions at work, in addition to providing academic and research background in depth. Participants also have the opportunity of working with members of the Indian Parliament.

No. offered: Seven Fellowships annually (two for applicants from Bangladesh).

Value: 1,000 rupees per month. Travel expenses are not paid.

Tenable in New Delhi for six months; not renewable.

Eligibility: Open to foreign nationals who hold the following qualifications: social scientists—Ph.D. or master's degree in political science or sociology (preference is given to persons who intend to pursue a career in teaching); journalists and officials from legislature secretariats—bachelor's degree in political science or sociology, with at least three years' experience; lawyers—LL.B. or equivalent degree with either two years' professional experience or higher academic qualifications.

Note: Direct applications are not accepted. Candidates should submit their applications through the Indian diplomatic missions in their own countries.

Closing date: 30th September.

Further information from:
  Institute of Constitutional and
    Parliamentary Studies
  18 Vithalbhai Patel House
  Rafi Marg
  New Delhi-110001
  India

[972]

INSTITUTE OF COST AND MANAGEMENT ACCOUNTANTS *(U.K.)*

Grants in Aid of Research

To promote and develop the science of cost and management accountancy, the Institute offers small Grants in Aid (usually about £300 each) to senior investigators for costs related to research in the United Kingdom or overseas (for United Kingdom researchers) or solely in the United Kingdom (for others).

The Institute does not provide assistance for research leading to higher degrees.

Further information from:
Institute of Cost and Management
   Accountants
63 Portland Place
London
England W1N 4AB

[973]

INSTITUTE OF CURRENT WORLD AFFAIRS *(U.S.A.)*
Crane-Rogers Foundation

Fellowships: Two or three Fellowships are offered annually to individuals, usually in their twenties or early thirties, to enable them to gain experience overseas in international affairs. Fellowships are tenable for two to five years and provide a monthly stipend. It is hoped that Fellows' experience will enhance useful careers in academe, government, foundation administration, writing, corporate management, law, medicine, and other fields.

Overseas Journalism Fellowships Program: The Institute seeks to identify reporters, writers, and editors of great promise and give them two years of training in in-depth reportage of a particular area of the world.

Forest and Man Fellowships are offered to people with graduate degrees in forestry or forest-related specialties so that they may gain an understanding of forest-resource problems from the point of view of humans, including policy-makers, environmentalists, peasants, religious leaders, scientists, energy planners, and forest-product industrialists.

Note: In selecting Fellows the Institute takes into account the candidates previous experience, training, interest, self-discipline, writing ability, powers of analysis, language facility and other attributes. Candidates are invited to write to the Executive Director, explaining briefly the personal background and professional experience that would qualify them in the Institute's current areas of concern which are: South Korea and their future impact on East Asia and the World; contemporary issues and differences of the Eastern Mediterranean as seen from the point of view of a person with an education in the Classics; and East Germany—its future.

Further information from:
Institute of Current World Affairs
4 West Wheelock Street
Hanover, New Hampshire 03755
U.S.A.

[974]

INSTITUTE OF DEVELOPING ECONOMIES *(Tokyo)*

Visiting Research Fellowships

Purpose: To provide opportunities for the exchange of scholarly opinions, research and data and to study the experience of Japan in order to gain comparative insights into the process of development.

Subjects: Economic, political and social problems of the developing areas.

No. offered: Approximately seven Fellowships annually.

Value: 357,000 yen per month, plus return air fare.

Tenable for a maximum period of ten months at the Institute.

Eligibility: Open to specialists from universities, government or private institutions who are engaged in research on the problems of developing areas.

Note: The Institute may be able to accept a limited number of affiliated Fellows who are self-supporting or receiving assistance from other sources.

Closing dates: 31st May and 30th November.

Further information from:
International Exchanges Department
Institute of Developing Economies
42 Ichigaya-Honmura-cho
Shinjuku-ku
Tokyo 162
Japan

[975]

INSTITUTE OF EARLY AMERICAN HISTORY AND CULTURE *(Williamsburg, Virginia)*

Postdoctoral Fellowship

Subjects: Early American history and culture.

No. offered: One Fellowship annually.

Value: Beginning stipend US$12,000, plus a small house or housing allowance and travel funds for research; funds are also available for purchase of photographic copies of manuscript and printed sources.

Tenable for two years as a staff member of the Institute, holding the rank of Assistant Professor of History at the College of William and Mary.

Eligibility: Open to young scholars at an early stage in their careers who either hold doctoral degrees or are assured of completing the degree requirements by the beginning date of the Fellowship. Each candidate must be nominated by a graduate school professor and must have written a dissertation which shows potential as a significant contribution to scholarship. Candidates should be able to submit a significant portion of their dissertation with their application.

Note: Fellows are obliged to teach two three-hour courses at the College during term of Fellowship; the teaching schedule is usually arranged to allow a full year of 15 months of uninterrupted time for research and writing. The Institute holds first claim on publication of book manuscripts.

Closing date for letters of nomination is 15th November—candidates are then sent application forms. Appointments are usually made by February for Fellowship terms beginning in July.

Further information from:
Director
Institute of Early American History and Culture
Box 220
Williamsburg, Virginia 23187
U.S.A.

[976]

INSTITUTE OF EARLY AMERICAN HISTORY AND CULTURE *(Williamsburg, Virginia)*

Jamestown Prize

An annual Prize of US$1,500 is offered for the best book-length, scholarly manuscript on early American history or culture. The competition is open only to authors who have never previously published a book. Manuscripts may be submitted at any time.

Further information from:
Editor of Publications
Institute of Early American History and Culture
Box 220
Williamsburg, Virginia 23187
U.S.A.

[977]

INSTITUTE OF ELECTRICAL AND ELECTRONICS ENGINEERS, INC. *(U.S.A.)*

Charles LeGeyt Fortescue Fellowship

Subject: Electrical engineering.

No. offered: One Fellowship annually.

Value: US$8,500 per annum.

Tenable at an engineering school fo recognized standing in the United States or Canada, for one year of full-time graduate work.

Eligibility: Open to graduates in electrical engineering from an engineering college or university of recognized standing. Candidates need not be United States citizens. Preference will be given to candidates who are about to begin their first year of graduate work.

Closing date: 15th January.

Further information from:
Secretary
Charles LeGeyt Fortescue Fellowship
  Committee
Institute of Electrical and Electronics
  Engineers, Inc.
345 East 47th Street
New York, New York 10017
U.S.A.

[978]

INSTITUTE OF ELECTRICAL AND ELECTRONICS ENGINEERS, INC. *(U.S.A.)*

IEEE Prize Paper Awards

W.R.G. Baker Prize Award—awarded annually for an outstanding paper reporting original work in any of the *IEEE Transactions, Journals, Magazines,* or *Proceedings* issued between 1st January and 31st December. Certificate and US$1,000.

Donald G. Fink Prize Award—awarded annually for an outstanding survey, review or tutorial paper in any of the *IEEE Transactions, Journals, Magazines,* or *Proceedings* issued between 1st January and 31st December. Certificate and US$1,000.

Browder J. Thompson Memorial Prize Award—awarded annually for the best paper by author(s) under 30 years of age in any *IEEE* publication issued between 1st January and 31st December. Certificate and US$1,000.

Note: Nominations for IEEE Prize Paper Awards are due by 1st July. All individual members, societies or sections of the Institute are eligible to nominate candidates for Awards. Awards are not restricted to United States citizens.

Further information from:
Secretary, Awards Board
Institute of Electrical and Electronics
  Engineers, Inc.
345 East 47th Street
New York, New York 10017
U.S.A.

[979]

INSTITUTE OF ELECTRICAL AND ELECTRONICS ENGINEERS, INC. *(U.S.A.)*

IEEE (Annual) Field Awards

Cledo Brunetti Award—for outstanding contributions in the field of miniaturization in the electronic arts. Certificate and US$1,000.

Control Systems Science and Engineering Award—for meritorious achievement in contributions to theory, design, or technique, over an extended period of time, as evidenced by publications or patents in the area of control systems science and engineering. Certificate and US$1,000.

Harry Diamond Memorial Award—for outstanding technical contributions in the field of government service in any country, as evidenced by publication in professional society journals. Certificate and US$2,000.

William M. Habirshaw Award—awarded to an individual or group for outstanding contribution in the field of transmission and distribution of electrical power. Bronze medal, certificate and US$1,000.

IEEE Award in International Communication in Honor of Hernand and Sosthènes Behn—awarded to an individual or group for outstanding contribution in the field of international communication. Plaque, certificate and US$2,000.

Morris E. Leeds Award—awarded to an individual or group for outstanding contribution in the field of electrical measurement. Illuminated certificate and US$1,000.

Morris N. Liebmann Memorial Award—for an important contribution to emerging technologies within recent years. Certificate and US$2,000.

Jack A. Morton Award—is given to an individual or group for outstanding contributions in the field of solid-state devices. A bronze medal, certificate and US$2,000.

Frederik Philips Award—awarded to an individual or group for accomplishments in management of research and development resulting in effective innovation in the electrical and electronics industry. Gold medal, certificate and US$2,000.

Emanuel R. Piore Award—for outstanding achievement in the field of information processing, in relation to computer science, to an individual or team of two individuals. A bronze medal, certificate, US$2,000 and US$2,500 international travel grant.

David Sarnoff Award—for an outstanding contribution in the field of electronics. Gold medal, bronze replica, certificate and US$1,000.

Charles Proteus Steinmetz Award—for major contributions to the development of standards in the field of electrical and electronics engineering. Certificate and US$1,000.

Nikola Tesla Award—is offered to an individual or group for outstanding contributions in the field of generation and utilization of electric power. A plaque and US$1,000.

Vladimir K. Zworykin Prize Award—for an outstanding technical contribution in the field of electronic television. Certificate and US$1,000.

Note: All individual members, Groups, Societies or Sections of the Institute are eligible to nominate candidates for Awards. Nominations are due by 1st April. In general, the Awards mentioned above are not restricted to United States citizens.

The Institute also awards a *Medal of Honor* (gold medal, certificate and US$10,000), and the following major annual medals: *Alexander Graham Bell Medal; Edison Medal; Founders Medal; Lamme Medal; IEEE Education Medal; Simon Ramo Medal.*

Further information from:
Secretary, Awards Board
Institute of Electrical and Electronics Engineers, Inc.
345 East 47th Street
New York, New York 10017
U.S.A.

[980]

INSTITUTE OF ENERGY *(U.K.)*

R.H. Gummer Exhibition: The Exhibition is tenable annually at the Imperial College of Science and Technology in the University of London, by a student, whether at the undergraduate or postgraduate level, in the subject of fuel technology. The award has a value of £75. Conditions of the award are announced by the authorities at Imperial College in April. Applications should be made to the *Department Head, Chemical Engineering and Applied Chemistry, Imperial College, London SW7.*

Lubbock-Sambrook Award: A scroll together with a prize of about £50 will be awarded to the author of the best paper on the properties, preparation, handling, or utilization of liquid fuels, read at a meeting of or published by the Institute. The selection of the recipient will be made at the end of March each year from the author or authors of papers submitted during the preceding 12 months.

Bone-Wheeler Medal and Prize: A medal and cash prize of £50 will be awarded each year for the best paper published by the Institute on any subject within the purview of fuel technology, including the application of modern scientific techniques, by an author not over 33 years of age on 1st September in that year.

Thring Award: A money prize, awarded approximately every five years, is intended for an outstanding practical project by a student of energy management. Entry is by invitation only.

Foxwell Memorial Award: The Award, with a value of £100 per annum, is for the endowment of an Exhibition, and is tenable alternately at the Universities of Leeds and Sheffield to a student in energy engineering at either the undergraduate or postgraduate level in one of these universities.

Townend Medal and Prize: A medal together with a travel award up to £300 is offered bienially for an essay of 2,000 words with open title to any person working in the field of fuel technology who is under 30 years of age on 1st September in the year of the competition.

Roscoe Student Prize: One prize of £200 and one prize of £50 are presented annually to a student for a paper on a subject of interest to the Institute.

Further information from:
  Institute of Energy
  18 Devonshire Street
  London
  England W1N 2AU

[981]

INSTITUTE FOR EUROPEAN HISTORY
(Mainz)

Scholarships

Purpose: To assist Ph. D. candidates in their research in German archives or to give them the opportunity to prepare their dissertation for publication.

Subjects: History of the Reformation; modern European history.

No. offered: Ten Scholarships annually.

Value: DM13,680 to DM17,280 per annum.

Tenable at the Institute, for one year; renewable.

Eligibility: Open to students of the history of the Reformation or of modern European history who have finished or are about to complete their Ph.D. theses. There are no nationality restrictions.

Further information from:
  Institute for European History
  Alte Universitätsstrasse 19
  D-6500 Mainz
  West Germany

[982]

INSTITUTE FOR EUROPEAN HISTORY
(Mainz)

Research Scholarships

Purpose: To assist young Scholars preparing for an academic career.

Subjects: Modern European history, with special attention from the 17th century to the present; history of the Reformation, its causes and consequences.

No. offered: Ten Scholarships, granted as and when a Scholarship becomes vacant.

Value: DM17,280 per annum, plus a limited travel allowance for visiting archives, etc.

Tenable normally for one year at the Institute; renewable.

Eligibility: Open to young Scholars who have, essentially, completed graduate work, and wish to complete their dissertations at the Institute in order to prepare for an academic career.

Note: Applications should be accompanied by references from two university teachers. Residence in Mainz is obligatory (the Institute offers accommodation for DM150), except when travelling for research purposes; the duration of the Scholarship will be decided by the head of the department concerned. Applications for study of modern European history should be addressed to *Prof. K.O.v. Aretin, Department of World History;* applications for study of religious history should be addressed to *Prof. Peter Manns, Department of the History of Western Religion.*
  Applications are received at all times.

Further information from:
  Institute for European History
  Alte Universitätsstrasse 19
  D-6500 Mainz
  West Germany

[983]

INSTITUTE OF FOOD TECHNOLOGISTS
(U.S.A.)

Graduate Fellowships

Subjects: Food science and technology. Study should be directed to extending or improving knowledge in some phase of food conservation, food production or food processing, rather than related research in genetics, nutrition, etc.

No. offered: Approximately 26 Fellowships annually.

Value: Three at *US$6,000;* five at *US$2,000;* one at *US$2,500;* one at *US$2,000.*

Tenable at approved institutions in the United States or Canada; renewable annually by reapplication.

Eligibility: Open to final year students who

will be enrolled in graduate studies at the time the Fellowship becomes effective and to current graduates pursuing a course of studying leading to an M.S. and/or Ph.D. degree. Candidates must possess an above average interest in research together with demonstrated scientific aptitude.

Closing date: 1st February.

Further information from:
Scholarship Department
Institute of Food Technologists
221 North LaSalle Street, Suite 2120
Chicago, Illinois 60601
U.S.A.

[984]

INSTITUTE FOR HUMANE STUDIES
(Menlo Park, California)

Leander J. Monks Memorial Fund Award is offered annually in recognition of distinguished writing in the fields of jurisprudence and political philosophy. It is intended to further the understanding of law, in its broadcast sense, as related to the development of a free society. Authors and nominators of other's writings are invited to submit recently published articles and books as well as out-of-print classics. Subject matter should be of particular interest to members of the legal profession and be of sufficient breadth to interest scholars in related fields, such as economics and history. The Award of US$200 to the author and US$100 to the first nominator, may also include re-publication, if out of print, and selective distribution and promotion. Entries may be received at any time during the year for selection to be made in December. Entries may be held over for consideration in a subsequent year.

Further information from:
Institute for Humane Studies
1177 University Drive
Menlo Park, California 94025
U.S.A.

[985]

INSTITUTE FOR INDUSTRIAL RECONSTRUCTION *(Rome)*

Scholarships

Subjects: Aeronautical engineering, agro industry, air and sea, transport, banking, energy, informatics, infrastructures, iron and steel production, mechanical engineering, plant and machinery, shipbuilding, telecommunications, vocational training.

No. offered: Approximately 100 Scholarships.

Value: 550,000 lire per month, plus travel expenses and 560,000 lire to cover expenses involved in moving.

Tenable in Italy for five months (January-June).

Eligibility: Open to nationals of developing countries, who have had advanced technical training and experience in one of the above-mentioned fields, preferably in their own countries, as well as managerial experience. Candidates must have a knowledge of spoken and written Italian, French, English or Spanish. Instruction is given in Italian.

Closing date: 31st August.

Further information from:
I.R.I./Direzioe Estero Ufficio
Cooperazione Tecnica Internazionale
Via Liguria, 40
00187 Rome
Italy

[986]

INSTITUTE OF INTERNATIONAL EDUCATION *(U.S.A.)*

The Institute publicizes and conducts the competition and screening of applications for grants for study, research or professional training abroad, provided by the United States government, various foreign governments, educational institutions, foundations and private donors.

ITT International Fellowships: These Fellowships are to enable American university graduates to study abroad for one academic year and foreign graduate students to pursue master's degrees in the U.S. Twenty-five American and twenty-five foreign student awards of varying amounts are offered. Value for an American student depends on country of assignment; for foreign students in the U.S., value depends on academic institution attended. Fellowships are initially tenable to U.S. students for one academic year only, extension may be possible; to foreign students for one academic year initially, and may be extended up to a total of 21 months if needed to complete degree requirements. Closing date for Americans, 1st November of year preceding the Award; for foreign students, varies with individual country.

The United States Government Grants are provided as part of the educational and cultural exchange program administered by the International Communication Agency [q.v.] under the Fulbright-Hays Act. The majority of the Fulbright-Hays Grants are reserved for advanced students who, in most cases, will be engaged in research for their doctoral dissertation. Most of the grants will be awarded for programs of study or research that will require an academic year.

Fulbright-Hays Full Grants: These Grants provide roundtrip transportation, tuition, books and maintenance for one academic year.

Fullbright-Hays Partial Grants: These Grants provide a fixed sum payment in U.S. dollars, and may not, in themselves, be sufficient to meet all expenses incurred during the Grant period.

Fulbright-Hays Travel Grants: These Grants provide for roundtrip transportation to the country where the student will pursue his research program.

Teaching Opportunities: France—Teaching Assistantships in English: These are teaching positions in English conversation in secondary schools and teacher-training institutions.

Further information on teaching in elementary and secondary schools and for modern language and area studies training and research on both the pre- and postdoctoral level is available from: *US Department of Education, Office of International Education, Washington, D.C. 20202.*

Information on postdoctoral research assistance and university lecturing can be obtained from: *Council for International Exchange of Scholars (CIES), 11 Dupont Circle, Suite 300, Washington, D.C. 20036.*

Awards for nationals of developing countries offered under the United States Participant Training Program are administered by the Agency for International Development.

Further information from:
Institute of International Education
809 United Nations Plaza
New York, New York 10017
U.S.A.

[987]

INSTITUTE OF INTERNATIONAL SUMMER COURSES IN GERMAN LANGUAGE AND LITERATURE *(Salzburg)*

Scholarships

Courses: German language and literature; German in a special field.

No. offered: Approximately ten Scholarships annually.

Value: Approximately 5,000 Austrian schillings.

Tenable in Salzburg for three or four weeks in the summer; not renewable.

Eligibility: Open to persons of any nationality over 16 years of age.

Note: Candidates must attach a curriculum vitae and references to their application forms.

The Summer Courses are given in association with the University of Salzburg.

Not confirmed for 1983.

Further information from:
International Summer Courses in German Language and Literature
Franz-Josef-Strasse 19
A-5020 Salzburg
Austria

[988]

INSTITUTE OF MANAGEMENT SERVICES
(U.K.)

R.M. Currie Travelling Fellowship

Purpose: To enable the successful applicant to travel abroad for a period of up to eight weeks to progressive overseas countries, and examine in their industries and universities some of the recent developments in productivity improvement and management services.

No. offered: One Fellowship annually.

Value: Up to £1,500.

Eligibility: Open to British subjects who have been trained in the management services field, and are currently using that training in their employment.

Closing date: 1st March.

Further information from:
Secretary
R.M. Currie Travelling Fellowship Trustees
c/o Institute of Management Services
1 Cecil Court, London Road
Enfield, Middlesex
England EN2 6DD

[989]

INSTITUTE OF MICROBIOLOGY *(Prague)* CZECHOSLOVAK ACADEMY OF SCIENCES

Long-Term Postgraduate Training Course—Unesco

Purpose: To enable young scientists to obtain a more profound education and methodical preparation for a research career.

Subjects: Microbiology (physiology, biochemistry, ecology, immunology); virology (plant and animal); cell biology (ultrastructure, cytochemistry, transplantation, radiation effects); parasitology; medical physiology (neurophysiology, human adaptability, physiology of development); plant physiology, ecology and productivity studies in terrestrial and freshwater ecosystems.

No. offered: Ten awards annually.

Value: 1,600 Czechoslovak crowns per month. Participants from developing countries may be given travel expenses.

Tenable at institutes and laboratories of the Czechoslovak Academy of Sciences for one year.

Eligibility: Open to nationals of the developing countries who hold on M.Sc., Ph.D. or equivalent degree, and who have two or three years' practical experience in their field. Candidates should be not more than 35 years of age, and should possess a good knowledge of English.

Note: The Courses are given in cooperation with the Ministry of Education CSR, and are sponsored by Unesco.

Closing date: 30th April.

Further information from:
Unesco Course
Institute of Microbiology
Czechoslovak Academy of Sciences
Videnská 1083
142 20 Prague 4
Czechoslovakia

[990]

INSTITUTE OF NAVIGATION *(U.S.A.)*

Burka Award

To recognize outstanding achievement in contributing to the advancement of navigation and space guidance, the Institute annually offers the Burka Award (a certificate and honorarium of US$500) to the author of an article published in the Institute's journal, *Navigation*.
The other awards of the Institute have no monetary value.

Further information from:
Chairman, Awards Selection Committee
Institute of Navigation
815 15th Street, N.W., Suite 832
Washington, D.C. 20005
U.S.A.

[991]

INSTITUTE FOR NORTHERN STUDIES
University of Saskatchewan

Musk-Ox Scholarship
Institute Scholarships

Subjects: Problems pertaining to northern Canada, particularly northern Saskatchewan, the Northwest Territories and the Yukon: postgraduate study and research in any field of scholarly investigation.

No. offered: One Musk-Ox Scholarship and a number of Institute Scholarships annually.

Value: Musk-Ox Scholarship—Can$6,700 per annum; Institute Scholarships—Can$5,500 per annum.

Tenable at the Institute for one year; renewable to completion of degree or research.

Eligibility: Open to citizens of all countries who are admitted to a graduate program at the University of Saskatchewan.

Note: Studies and research work will be carried out under the supervision of a department at the University of Saskatchewan.
Through the Institute, *Faculty Grants* are available, with a maximum value of Can$1,500, the employment of student field assistants by a professor, for field expenses for a professor supervising a graduate student in the field, or for the the initiation of a research project which will eventually involve students.

Not confirmed for 1983.

Further information from:
Chairman, Scholarships and Faculty Grants Committee
Institute for Northern Studies
University of Saskatchewan
Saskatoon, Saskatchewan
Canada S7N 0W0

[992]

INSTITUTE OF ORTHOPAEDICS
(Oswestry, Shropshire)
Robert Jones and Agnes Hunt Orthopaedic Hospital

Fellowship in Paediatric Orthopaedic Surgery

Purpose: To give the opportunity of an introduction into paediatric medicine in its relation to orthopaedic surgery, and for instruction in the practice and principles of paediatric orthopaedic surgery.

No. offered: One Fellowship when the vacancy occurs.

Value: Salary of £7,100—£8,070.

Tenable in the Children's Unit of the Hospital for six months or one year.

Eligibility: Open to U.K. residents who are trainee orthopaedic specialists with experience in orthopaedic surgery, and to establish orthopaedic surgeons and medical practitioners from the Commonwealth and other countries, whose interest is to pursue study in paediatric or orthopaedic surgery, and who are suitably medically qualified.

Note: The successful Fellow is expected to contribute to the academic and research activities at the Hospital and to arrange educational seminars for other residents.
The Fellowship is tailored to suit the special needs of the candidate, depending upon his or her particular qualifications and experience. A proportion of research and service element of this commitment depends on each individual, his needs and the needs of the Department. The Fellow works under the direct supervision of the Director of the Children's Unit.

Further information from:
Gwyn A. Evans
Director, Children's Unit
Institute of Orthopaedics
Robert Jones and Agnes Hunt
 Orthopaedic Hospital
Oswestry, Shropshire
England SY10 7AG

[993]

INSTITUTE FOR PALESTINE STUDIES
(Beirut)

Grants and Fellowships are awarded by the Institute for study which deals with the Palestine problem or the Arab-Israeli conflict, and falls within the scope and interests of the Institute.

Open to postgraduate students preparing a dissertation or to writers completing a manuscript or compiling an original work.

The Institute issues invitations to persons from abroad who wish to come to Beirut and make use of the Institute library and other facilities for a set period of time. Guest's accommodations, while in Beirut, will be paid for by the Institute.

Conditions of all Grants and Fellowships are on an individual basis and are agreed upon between the Institute and the recipient.

Further information from:
Institute for Palestine Studies
Nsouli, Versun Street
Beirut
Lebanon

[994]

INSTITUTE OF PAPER CHEMISTRY
(Appleton, Wisconsin)

Fellowships

Purpose: To develop industrial scientists well versed in several disciplines within the physical sciences.

Subjects: Interdisciplinary program in natural sciences, involving work in organic and physical chemistry, chemical engineering, physics, biology, pulp and paper technology, and mathematics.

No. offered: 35 Fellowships annually.

Value: US$8,000 per calendar year, plus tuition.

Tenable at the Institute for up to 16 terms to pursue either an M.S. or Ph.D. degree program.

Eligibility: Open to first year graduate students of an accredited college or university who are United States or Canadian citizens. Applicants should have a bachelor's degree, ordinarily in chemistry or chemical engineering.

Closing date: 15th March.

Further information from:
Director of Admissions
Institute of Paper Chemistry
1043 East South River Street
P.O. Box 1039
Appleton, Wisconsin 54911
U.S.A.

[995]

INSTITUTE OF PETROLEUM AND GAS
(Ploiesti, Romania)

Scholarships for Courses

Courses: Petroleum refining and the petrochemical industry.

No. offered: About 15 places on each Course.

Value: Cost of tuition, lodging, medical expenses, and a monthly allowance of 800 lei to cover board and miscellaneous expenses.

Tenable at the Institute for eleven months (1st December to October)

Eligibility: Open to specialists in the fields of chemistry or the chemical industry who wish to become teachers or research workers in their own countries. The Course is primarily intended for nationals of developing countries. Candidates must be no more than 40 years of age and should have a good knowledge of English. Some knowledge of French or Spanish is also desirable.

Note: The Course is organized under the auspices of the Romanian Ministry of Education, the Romanian National Commission for Unesco, and Unesco.

Closing date: 15th September.

Further information from:
Institute of Petroleum and Gas
Bulevardul Bucuresti nr. 39
Oras Ploiesti-2000
Romania

[996]

INSTITUTE OF PHYSICS (U.K.)

Medals and Prizes

Bragg Medal and Prize: A bronze Medal and Prize of £150 is awarded in odd-numbered years for distinguished contributions to the teaching of physics.

Charles Chree Medal and Prize: A silver Medal, parchment certificate, and Prize of £150 is awarded in odd-numbered years for distinguished research in one or more of the following subjects: terrestrial magnetism, atmospheric electricity and related subjects, such as other aspects of geophysics comprising the earth, oceans, atmosphere and solar-terrestrial problems.

Charles Vernon Boys Prize: £150 is awarded annually for distinguished research in experimental physics. Work for which the Prize is made shall be either still in progress, or have been carried out within the ten year period preceding the date of the award. Candidates should normally be not more than thirty-five years of age in the year of the award.

Duddell Medal and Prize: A bronze Medal and Prize of £150 is awarded annually for a contribution to the advancement of knowledge by the invention or design of scientific instruments, or by the discovery of materials used in their construction or by outstanding work in the application of physics.

Glazebrook Medal and Prize: A silver gilt Medal and Prize of £250 is awarded annually for outstanding contributions in the organization, utilization or application of science.

Guthrie Medal and Prize: A silver gilt Medal and Prize of £250 is awarded annually to a physicist of international reputation for his contributions to physics.

Holweck Medal and Prize: A gold Medal and Prize of £150 is awarded in even-numbered years to a British physicist, and in odd-numbered years to a French physicist. It is given for distinguished work in experimental physics, or in theoretical physics if closely related to experimental work. Research should be either still in progress, or have been carried out within the ten year period preceding the date of the award. This Prize is given jointly with the French Physical Society.

Max Born Medal and Prize: A silver Medal, a certificate and a Prize of £150 is presented in even-numbered years in England to a German physicist, and in odd-numbered years in Germany to a British physicist, for outstanding contributions in the field of physics. This Prize is given jointly with the German Physical Society.

Maxwell Medal and Prize: A bronze Medal and Prize of £150 is awarded annually for outstanding contributions to theoretical physics made within the ten year period preceding the date of the award. Candidates should be no more than thirty-five years of age in the year of the award.

Rutherford Medal and Prize: A bronze Medal and Prize of £150 is awarded in even-numbered years for contributions to nuclear physics, elementary particle physics or nuclear technology.

Simon Memorial Prize: A parchment certificate and a Prize of £300 is awarded approximately every three years for distinguished work in experimental or theoretical low temperature physics.

Thomas Young Medal and Prize: A bronze Medal and Prize of £150 is awarded in odd-numbered years for distinguished work on optics principles other than those associated with the visible region of the spectrum. This includes work with infrared rays, ultraviolet rays, x-rays and radio physics, as well as some aspects of electron physics.

No. offered: Only members of the Institute and the Awards Committee may take nominations.

Further information from:
Institute of Physics
47 Belgrave Square
London
England SW1X 8QX

[997]

INSTITUTE FOR PORTUGUESE CULTURE AND LANGUAGE

The Institute provides the following awards

for the study of Portuguese culture, language and literature.

Scholarships for Annual Courses (eight months of study in the faculty of arts of the Universities of Lisbon or Coimbra) are offered to foreign students. Tuition is free and a monthly allowance of 16,000 escudos is awarded. A knowledge of Portuguese is essential. Applications should be submitted by 30th May.

Scholarships for Summer Courses (five weeks of study in the faculty of arts of the Universities of Lisbon or Coimbra) are offered to foreign students currently enrolled in a university or college and studying Portuguese. Tuition is free and an allowance of 16,000 escudos is awarded.

Research Grants of not less than 21,000 escudos per month are awarded to researchers and teachers of Portuguese language at foreign universities.

Artistic Project Grants with Portuguese cultural significance are awarded annually for work (up to a year) in Portugal. Recipients are provided with a monthly allowance of 16,000 escudos.

Grants-in-Aid are offered to support projects in Portuguese culture and language. This includes Grants for publication of appropriate works.

Further information from:
Dr. A. Pina e Silva
Institute for Portuguese Culture
and Language
Praca do Principe Real, 14-1°.
1200 Lisbon
Portugal

[998]

INSTITUTE OF PUBLIC ADMINISTRATION OF CANADA

Research Grants

Field of research: Projects should qualify as studies of public policy, of public sector management or of public organization in Canada. Multi-disciplinary projects are welcome. Topics of particular interest to the Institute at this time include governmental program evaluation, provincial governments and municipal administration.

The Research Grants are part of a broad range of research, seminar and publication activities of the Institute designed to enlarge the body of knowledge about public administration. They are expected to lead to additional contributions to the literature.

Value: No project will receive more than Can$8,000 in any fiscal year. As long as the Institute is notified accordingly, projects may receive funding from other sources.

In the case of research reports or manuscripts which are already completed the Institute will consider providing publication assistance Grants within the scope of this program.

Eligibility: Applicants should be either public servants or academics in the field of public administration in Canada. Any project which is being pursued to obtain a diploma or degree is not eligible.

Note: Applications should include detailed explanations as to the nature of the proposed research project, its duration, the various budget items, its relevance to the field of public administration and personal information on the researcher(s). For more detailed guidelines on project submission and for additional information about the Grants write to the Institute.

Closing date: Mid-December.

Further information from:
Institute of Public Administration
of Canada
897 Bay Street
Toronto, Ontario
Canada M5S 1Z7

[999]

INSTITUTE FOR RESEARCH IN THE HUMANITIES *(U.S.A.)*

Postdoctoral Fellowships

Purpose: To assist young scholars in developing research in the humanities.

Subjects: Cultural, institutional and intellectual history, including the history of art, music and science; philosophy, including the history of philosophy and systematic philosophy; and language and literature (critical and historical studies).

No. offered: Two.

Value: Approximately US$14,000.

Tenable for one academic year at the Institute.

Eligibility: Candidates should have a doctoral degree by the time of application and must intend to pursue research in Madison in some aspect of the humanities.

Note: The Institute is particularly anxious to assist young scholars who have research projects well advanced towards completion.

Copies of past publications may be submitted in support of an application, and will be returned after the Board of Selection has made its recommendations.

Closing date: 15th October.

Further information from:
Institute for Research in the Humanities
University of Wisconsin
Old Observatory
Madison, Wisconsin 53706
U.S.A.

[1000]

INSTITUTE OF SOCIETY, ETHICS AND THE LIFE SCIENCES *(Hastings-on-Hudson, New York)*

Fellowship Program

Purpose: To permit both older and younger researchers to prepare themselves systematically for future productive research on ethical problems arising from advances in medicine, biology, and the behavioral sciences.

Subjects: Ethics and life sciences.

No. offered: Three Fellowships annually.

Value: Average stipend is US$21,000, plus $1,000 for professional expenses. Stipends are expected to cover all costs, including transportation and housing.

Tenable for one year; at least nine months of which to be spent at the Hastings Center.

Eligibility: Candidates should be United States citizens who have an advanced doctoral or professional degree, or its equivalent, and can demonstrate previous experience and scholarly achievements in the field.

Note: Applicants are required to complete a formal application, appended with a detailed statement analyzing the candidate's past work, future aspirations in the field, and a proposal in the scope and nature of the proposed study.

It is not the Institute's purpose to provide support for a specific research project.

Closing date: 1st January.

Further information from:
Fellowship Program
The Hastings Center
Institute of Society, Ethics and the Life Sciences
360 Broadway
Hastings-on-Hudson, New York 10706
U.S.A.

[1001]

INSTITUTE OF SOUTHEAST ASIAN STUDIES *(Singapore)*

ISEAS Research Fellowship Programme

Purpose: To aid Fellows nearing completion of their research projects, who seek the appropriate facilities and necessary freedom from other responsibilities to complete the writing of their final reports or monographs/books.

Subjects: Unrestricted within the social sciences and humanities, with special emphasis on modern Southeast Asia. The research interests of the Institute itself are focused primarily on problems of development, modernization and social and political change.

No. offered: Usually three to four Fellowships annually, depending upon monies available and the quality of the applications received.

Value: Basic stipend is S$1,000 to S$2,500 per month, depending upon qualifications and experience. Adjustments in the stipend can be made for Fellows having other financial support or those requiring only partial assistance. In addition, Fellows will also receive a housing subsidy, medical care and travel expenses.

Tenable at the Institute for any length of time up to twelve months.

Eligibility: Open to Asians. Preference given to those who are nationals of Southeast Asian countries, and who hold a Ph.D. or other equivalent qualifications. Candidates should be able to complete their research projects during the stipulated period of the Fellowship.

Note: The Institute also offers a *Stiftung Volkswagenwerk Research Fellowship* in Southeast Asian Studies, which is instituted by the Volkswagen Foundation of the Federal Republic of Germany, and open to nationals or permanent residents of Southeast Asia. Further information may be obtained by writing to the Institute at the address below.

A *Fulbright-Hays Research Grant* is also tenable at the Institute on an annual basis, and open to American citizens with Ph.D. qualifications. Further information may be obtained by writing to the *Council of International Exchange of Scholars, 11 Dupont Circle, Suite 300, Washington, D.C. 20036.*

Closing date: 31st October.

Further information from:
 Executive Secretary
 Institute of Southeast Asian Studies
 Heng Mui Keng Terrace
 Pasir Panjang
 Singapore 0511

[1002]

INSTITUTE OF SOUTHEAST ASIAN STUDIES *(Singapore)*

ISEAS/ASEAN Economic Research Fellowship Programme

Purpose: Research projects within the broad areas of food, nutrition, energy, water resources, and rural development in the region.

Value: A stipend and housing subsidy of S$1,700 to S$3,500 per month. Actual amount depends on candidate's qualifications and experience. In addition, the Fellow receives travel, research and field-work allowances, as well as medical coverage.

Tenable at the ASEAN Economic Research Unit of the Institute for periods ranging from a few months to a maximum of one year.

Eligibility: Open to nationals and permanent residents of the ASEAN countries. Preference will be given to candidates with Ph.D. or equivalent professional qualifications, and who will be in a position to complete their proposed projects within the stipulated Fellowship period.

Note: Applications, giving full details, should be sent directly to the respective ASEAN National Secretariat in the candidate's own country.

Further information from:
 Executive Secretary
 Institute of Southeast Asian Studies
 Heng Mui Keng Terrace
 Pasir Panjang
 Singapore 0511

[1003]

INSTITUTE OF SOUTHEAST ASIAN STUDIES *(Singapore)*

Research Fellowships in ASEAN Affairs

Subjects: Any topic pertaining to developmental and associated problems of ASEAN, with special emphasis on publishable research.

No. offered: Two Fellowships.

Value: A stipend and housing subsidy totaling S$2,300 to S$3,000 per month, in accordance with Fellows qualifications and experience. In addition, the recipient also is awarded travel and research allowances, as well as free medical care.

Tenable at the Institute for any length of time up to a maximum of twelve months.

Eligibility: Open to nationals or permanent residents of ASEAN countries on a rotating basis. Preference will be given to candidates holding a Ph.D. or equivalent degree, or those with first-hand high-level experience in ASEAN affairs, and who are in a position to complete their proposed projects in the stipulated period of the Fellowship.

Note: All applications, giving full details, should be sent the respective ASEAN National Secretariat in the candidate's own country.

Further information from:
　Executive Secretary
　Institute of Southeast Asian Studies
　Heng Mui Keng Terrace
　Pasir Panjang
　Singapore 0511

[1004]

INSTITUTE OF SOUTHEAST ASIAN STUDIES *(Singapore)*

Research Fellowship in Australian/Southeast Asian Relations

Subjects: Any topic pertaining to Australian and Southeast Asia, or parts thereof. Specific interest in the following areas may be given preference: the economic, political, trade, social, and cultural dimensions of Australian-Southeast Asian relations.

No. offered: One Fellowship.

Value: A stipend and housing subsidy ranging from S$2,000 to S$3,500 per month, in accordance with the Fellow's qualifications and experience. In addition, travel, and research allowances, as well as free medical care will be provided.

Tenable at the Institute for one year, not renewable.

Eligibility: Open to nationals or permanent residents of Australia and Southeast Asia. Preference is given to candidates having Ph.D. or equivalent professional qualifications, or those with high-level experience in Australia/Southeast Asian affairs, and who are in a position to complete their proposed projects within the Fellowship period.

Closing date: 15th June.

Further information from:
　Executive Secretary
　Institute of Southeast Asian Studies
　Heng Mui Keng Terrace
　Pasir Panjang
　Singapore 0511

[1005]

INSTITUTE OF SPORTS MEDICINE *(U.K.)*

Research Award

Purpose: To encourage in-depth research in all aspects of sports medicine.

No. offered: One Award annually.

Value: Up to £500.

Eligibility: Open to United Kingdom residents medically qualified in the field of sports medicine.

Closing date: 1st February.

Further information from:
　Honorary Secretary
　Institute of Sports Medicine
　10 Nottingham Place
　London
　England W1M 4AX

[1006]

INSTITUTE FOR THE STUDY OF MAN IN AFRICA *(South Africa)*

Grants-in-Aid

Purpose: To assist young persons at the graduate and postgraduate level to engage in research relating to any aspect of man in Africa.

Subjects: Physical and social anthropology, archaeology, sociology, history, linguistics, literature.

No. offered: From two to five Grants annually.

Value: Between R100 and R250, paid in a lump sum or two installments.

Tenable in Africa, preferably southern Africa.

Note: After the recipient has done field work in his chosen subject, he may be asked to present his findings at one of the Institute's monthly meetings, or to submit a paper for publication.

Further information from:
  Secretary
  Institute for the Study of Man in Africa
  Room C24, Old Medical School
  Hospital Street
  University of the Witwatersrand
  Johannesburg 2001
  South Africa

[1007]

INSTITUTE FOR THE STUDY OF WORLD POLITICS *(U.S.A.)*

Fellowships

Purpose: To promote research on major international issues, such as arms control, economic development, human rights, resources and environmental problems.

Subjects: Sociology, economics, politics, history, law, and international relations.

No. offered and value: A varying number of Fellowships of variable amounts offered annually.

Tenable for three to nine months at U.S. universities.

Eligibility: Open to individuals of any nationality who are either predoctoral students in the later stages of Ph.D. work or college-level teachers or researchers, or persons with comparable qualifications.

Further information from:
  Institute for the Study of World Politics
  1995 Broadway, Sixth Floor
  New York, New York 10023
  U.S.A.

[1008]

INSTITUTION OF CIVIL ENGINEERS *(U.K.)*

Culmann Travelling Fellowship

Purpose: To enable a member or associate member of the Institution to make a study of the present trend of design and practice in the execution of engineering works of reinforced concrete and steelwork construction in Western Europe.

No. offered: One Fellowship every three years.

Value: £1,500 to cover all expenses.

Tenable in Western European countries for not less than four months.

Eligibility: Open to British subjects who are either members or associate members of the Institution, are not less than 25 or more than 34 years of age, and possess a working knowledge of the language of the country in which studies will be undertaken.

Associate members of the Institution must have taken a degree exempting them from, or must have passed parts I and II of the examinations conducted by the Council of Engineering Institutions.

Note: The Fellow must submit a report or thesis to the Institution on the results of his studies and investigations, in a form suitable for communication to the members, the sum of £50 from the Fellowship being withheld until the report is received. The details of the report or thesis must not be communicated previously to the technical press.

Closing date: 31st May.

Further information from:
  Secretary (CTF)
  Institution of Civil Engineers
  Telford House, P.O. Box 101
  26-34 Old Street
  London
  England EC1P 1JH

[1009]

INSTITUTION OF CIVIL ENGINEERS *(U.K.)*

Awards for Papers: Medals, Premiums and Prizes

Awards are given annually for papers published in *Proceedings* or in *Proceedings of Conferences*. Papers by corporate members of the Institution which have been read and discussed at a meeting of a local Association, and papers by associate or student members of the Institution which are to be read before a local association, are also eligible for consideration. Associate members' and students' papers must be sent to the Institution by the honorary secretary of the association concerned for registration before being read.

Further information from:
Secretary (Awards)
Institution of Civil Engineers
Telford House, P.O. Box 101
26-34 Old Street
London
England EC1P 1JH

[1010]

INSTITUTION OF CIVIL ENGINEERS *(U.K.)*

Institution Medal and Premium (Local Associations)

Each Local Association in Great Britain may submit one paper prepared by an associate member or student of the Institution, under 27 years of age on 31st October in the year of the competition, which is considered to be of sufficient merit. The method of selection is left entirely to the discretion of the Local Association committee.

The Medal and a Premium of £50 will be awarded annually in competition, for a paper of about 4,000 words, on engineering design, research or practice.

Further information from:
Secretary (Awards)
Institution of Civil Engineers
Telford House, P.O. Box 101
26-34 Old Street
London
England EC1P 1JH

[1011]

INSTITUTION OF ELECTRICAL ENGINEERS *(U.K.)*

Institution Scholarships

Subjects: Electrical or electronic engineering.

Tenable normally at approved universities or institutions of higher learning in the United Kingdom.

Eligibility: Open to postgraduate and undergraduate students who have received the necessary preliminary education and training and who are normally resident in the United Kingdom, or are pursuing an approved course of education in the United Kingdom. If a candidate is not already attending a university or other place of higher learning, he must have been offered a place at such an institution from the date on which he wishes the award to begin. For postgraduate awards a candidate should have been a member of the Institution for at least two years.

Note: Each candidate must be nominated by the head of an educational establishment or by a corporate member of the Institution.

Closing date: 1st May.

Further information from:
Qualifications Department
Institution of Electrical Engineers
2 Savoy Place
London WC2R OBL
England

[1012]

INSTITUTION OF ELECTRICAL ENGINEERS *(U.K.)*

Jubilee Scholarships

Purpose: To assist undergraduates to obtain professional qualifications in electrical or electronic engineering.

Value: £500 per year, payable in instalments commencing at the beginning of the course of instruction.

Tenable for three years at a university or other place of higher education in the United Kingdom.

Eligibility: Open to students who are normally resident in the United Kingdom, and who will commence their degree in the next academic session. A candidate must be nominated by the head of an education establishment or by a corporate member of the Institution.

Closing date: Applications must reach the Institution's Secretary no later than 1st May in the year in which the scholarship is needed.

Further information from:
  Secretary
  Qualifications Department
  Institution of Electrical Engineers
  2 Savoy Place
  London
  England WC2R OBL

[1013]

INSTITUTION OF ELECTRICAL ENGINEERS *(U.K.)*

Robinson Research Fellowship

Purpose: To enable research students to pursue original work in electrical or electronic engineering.

No. offered: One Fellowship every three years.

Value: £3,500 per annum, paid in instalments.

Tenable in the United Kingdom for a postgraduate course of study/research not exceeding three years.

Eligibility: Open to students who have fulfilled the educational requirements for election to the class of Members of the Institution and are normally resident in the United Kingdom. The candidate must be a member of the Institution in any class and have been such for not less than two years at the time the award is to commence. A candidate must be nominated by the professor or other person responsible for the course of advanced study or research, which should lead to a higher degree, in he wishes to engage.

Note: It is expected that the original work undertaken by the Fellow will be supervised and nominated by nominated persons in higher education. The student is required, from time to time, to submit reports of his work in such form as the Council may determine.

Closing date: 1st May in the year in which the Fellowship is to commence.

Further information from:
  Secretary
  Qualifications Department
  Institution of Electrical Engineers
  2 Savoy Place
  London
  England WC2R OBL

[1014]

INSTITUTION OF ELECTRICAL ENGINEERS *(U.K.)*

J.R. Beard Travelling Fund Grants

Purpose: To enable United Kingdom members of the Institution to travel overseas to study developments in electrical or electronics technology, or to present a paper in a country outside the United Kingdom.

No. offered: Two Grants annually.

Value: £150.

Closing dates: 1st March and 1st September.

Further information from:
  Secretary
  Qualifications Department
  Institution of Electrical Engineers
  2 Savoy Place
  London
  England WC2R OBL

[1015]

INSTITUTION OF ELECTRICAL ENGINEERS *(U.K.)*

I.E.E. and Hudswell Research Awards

Members of the Institution, in any class, are eligible for Research Awards of £100 each for research in universities and colleges in the United Kingdom. Six to ten Awards are made annually.

Closing date: 31st March.

Further information from:
  Secretary
  Qualifications Department
  Institution of Electrical Engineers
  2 Savoy Place
  London
  England WC2R OBL

[1016]

INSTITUTION OF ELECTRICAL ENGINEERS *(U.K.)*

I.E.E. Prizes

Prizes of £50 and a certificate are given annually to reward students who are already pursuing electrical or electronic engineering courses and have done outstandingly well. The Council decides from which university the candidates are to be selected and then invites the appropriate authority at each of these universities to nominate one candidate for a Prize. The Council places no restriction on the manner in which the awards are used, but intends that they may help the recipients in such matters as overseas travel or the purchase of books.

Further information from:
Secretary
Qualifications Department
Institution of Electrical Engineers
2 Savoy Place
London
England WC2R OBL

[1017]

INSTITUTION OF FIRE ENGINEERS *(U.K.)*

Commonwealth Fire Engineering Scholarships
United Kingdom Fire Engineering Scholarships

Purpose: To assist men and women in the profession of fire engineering, whether in firefighting, fire engineering, fire protection, or fire research, who wish to carry out research or further their studies in some particular aspect of the field.

No. offered: Three Commonwealth and three United Kingdom Scholarships annually.

Value: Approximately £300 each for the United Kingdom Scholarships; approximately £1,000 each for the Commonwealth Scholarships.

Tenable in the United Kingdom or immediately adjacent countries for about one month for the United Kingdom Scholarship; in any country of the Scholar's choice for one to two months for the Commonwealth Scholarship.

Eligibility: United Kingdom Scholarships are open to any candidates from the U.K.; Commonwealth Scholarships are open to any candidates from the Commonwealth countries.

Note: Selection for both scholarships will be made on the merit of the project and its relevance and value to firefighting, fire engineering, fire protection, or fire research.

Closing date: 30th August for Commonwealth Scholarships; 31st December for United Kingdom Scholarships.

Further information from:
General Secretary
Institution of Fire Engineers
148 New Walk
Leicester
England LEI 7QB

[1018]

INSTITUTION OF GAS ENGINEERS *(U.K.)*

Dempster Travelling Fellowship
W.H. Bennett Travelling Fellowship

Subjects: Technical developments of interest to the gas industry.

Value: By individual assessment.

Tenable in the United Kingdom or overseas for a period of time to be assessed.

Eligibility: Open to persons who hold a first degree or its equivalent and have experience in the gas industry. Exceptionally, candidates who are not at first degree level but who have appropriate industrial experience may be considered.
The Dempster Fellowship is available to candidates who are not more than 30 years of age, and the Bennett Fellowship to candidates who have between 25 and 35 years of age.

Note: When the Award becomes available it is advertised in the national and trade press.

Further information from:
Institution of Gas Engineers
17 Grosvenor Crescent
London
England SW1X 7ES

[1019]

INSTITUTION OF MECHANICAL ENGINEERS *(U.K.)*

Joseph Bramah Scholarship

Purpose: To encourage the study of hydraulic

mechanisms, particularly hydrostatic transmissions and servo mechanisms.

Value: By individual assessment.

Tenable at an approved centre or laboratory for one year, with the possibility of an extension to a maximum of two years. Shorter periods of study will also be considered.

Eligibility: Candidates must satisfy or be making adequate progress towards satisfying the academic requirements for graduate membership, and preferably have had two years acceptable professional training.

Note: A programme of proposed work must be submitted, together with an estimate of the cost of carrying it out, including personal expenses. Any other financial resources (apart from the private funds of the candidate) which are available or for which application has been made must be declared.

The application must be supported by the names and addresses of three referees.

At the completion of a Scholarship, or at the end of each twelve months, a report of work must be submitted. It is one of the major objectives of the Institution to publish new or original work. The Institution has the copyright in and the right publish any report made by a Scholar.

Closing date: 28th February (31st January for overseas candidates).

Further information from:
   Manager—QET Division
   Institution of Mechanical Engineers
   P.O. Box 23, Northgate Avenue
   Bury St. Edmunds, Suffolk
   England IP32 6BN

[1020]

INSTITUTION OF MECHANICAL ENGINEERS *(U.K.)*

Raymond Coleman Prescott Scholarship

Purpose: To enable Scholars to study for a first degree after having obtained an outstanding HNC or other technical or non-professional qualification; or to obtain special experience in the practice of mechanical engineering which might include a study period abroad; or to pursue advanced studies of a postgraduate character in mechanical engineering or related science; or to pursue an approved programme of research in mechanical engineering or related science.

No. offered: Usually one Scholarship annually.

Value: By individual assessment.

Tenable for one year, with the possibility of an extension. Applications for shorter periods will also be considered.

Eligibility: Open to persons who either hold an approved engineering qualification or have satisfied the Institution's requirements for student membership, and have had two years' acceptable professional training. Preference is given to members of the Institution.

Note: A programme of proposed work must be submitted, together with an estimate of the cost of carrying it out, including personal expenses. Any other financial resources (apart from private funds of the candidate) which are available or for which application has been made, must be stated. The application must be supported by the names and addresses of three referees.

At the completion of a Scholarship, or at the end of each twelve months, a report of work must be submitted. It is one of the major objectives of the Institution to publish new or original work. The Institution has the copyright in and the right to publish any report made by a Scholar.

Closing date: 28th February (31st January for overseas candidates).

Further information from:
   Manager—QET Division
   Institution of Mechanical Engineers
   P.O. Box 23, Northgate Avenue
   Bury St. Edmunds, Suffolk
   England IP32 6BN

[1021]

INSTITUTION OF MECHANICAL ENGINEERS *(U.K.)*

James Clayton Fellowships

Purpose: To enable Fellows to obtain special experience or training in practice beyond that of an apprentice, pupil or trainee in mechanical engineering, or to pursue advanced studies of a postgraduate nature in mechanical engineering or related science, or to pursue an approved programme of research in mechanical engineering or related science.

Value: By individual assessment.

Tenable for one or two years, with the possibility of an extension. Applications for shorter periods will be considered.

Eligibility: Open to persons not less than 23 years of age who hold an approved engineering degree or can satisfy the Institution's examination requirements for graduate membership by some other means. Candidates should preferably have had not less than two years acceptable practical training. Preference is given to members of the Institution in the graduate or member class.

Note: A programme must be submitted outlining the use to which the candidate will put the Fellowship, together with an estimate of the cost of carrying it out, including personal expenses. Any other financial resources (apart from private funds of the candidate) which are available or for which application has been made, must be stated.

At the completion of a Scholarship, or at the end of each twelve months, a report of work must be submitted. It is one of the major objectives of the Institution to publish new or original work. The Institution has the copyright in and the right to publish any report made by a Scholar.

Closing date: 28th February (31st January for overseas candidates).

Further information from:
Manager—QET Division
Institution of Mechanical Engineers
P.O. Box 23, Northgate Avenue
Bury St. Edmunds, Suffolk
England IP32 6BN

[1022]

INSTITUTION OF MECHANICAL ENGINEERS (U.K.)

Senior James Clayton Fellowship

Purpose: To encourage members of the Institution of greater experience and maturity to carry out essential study or research programmes.

Subjects: Within the Institution's fields of interest.

No. offered: One Fellowship annually.

Value: Assessed individually; normally payable in three installments, plus a contribution to expenses.

Tenable normally for one or two years.

Eligibility: Candidates must not be less than 23 years of age, and should preferably have qualified for graduate membership of the Institution and should have had appreciable experience relevant to the proposed project. Preference is given to candidates who are members of the Institution in the classes of graduate, member or fellow.

At the completion of a Scholarship, or at the end of each twelve months, a report of work must be submitted. It is one of the major objectives of the Institution to publish new or original work. The Institution has the copyright in and the right to publish any report made by a Scholar.

Closing date: 28th February (31st January for overseas candidates).

Further information from:
Manager—QET Division
Institution of Mechanical Engineers
P.O. Box 23, Northgate Avenue
Bury St. Edmunds, Suffolk
England IP32 6BN

[1023]

INSTITUTION OF MECHANICAL ENGINEERS (U.K.)

Manville Fellowship

Purpose: To enable Fellows to pursue advanced studies of a postgraduate nature or to undertake an approved programme of research in automobile engineering or related science, or to obtain special experience in automobile engineering which might include a tour of shorter duration than a year for the purpose of studying current practice at home and/or abroad.

No. offered: Usually one Fellowship annually.

Value: By individual assessment.

Tenable normally for one year. In exceptional circumstances, an extension of six to twelve months or more may be considered, provided satisfactory progress is made during the first year and a scheme of extended work proposed is approved.

Eligibility: Open to persons who hold an approved engineering degree, but those with HND or HNC in mechanical engineering will also be considered. Candidates should preferably have had not less than twelve months' acceptable training in automobile engineering. Preference is given to members of the Institution.

Note: A programme of proposed work must be submitted, together with an estimate of the cost of carrying it out, including personal expenses. Any other financial resources (apart from private funds of the candidate) which are available or for which application has been made, must be stated. The application must be supported by the names and addresses of three referees.

At the completion of a Fellowship, or at the end of each twelve months, a report of work must be submitted. It is one of the major objectives of the Institution to publish new or original work. The Institution will have the copyright in and the right to publish any report made by a Fellow.

Closing date: 28th February (31st January for overseas candidates).

Further information from:
Manager—QET Division
Institution of Mechanical Engineers
P.O. Box 23, Northgate Avenue
Bury St. Edmunds, Suffolk
England IP32 6BN

[1024]

INSTITUTION OF MINING ENGINEERS *(U.K.)*

Prizes and Scholarships

Maskell Peace Scholarship: Candidates who are under 25 years of age and recommended by the mining department of the college or school at which they are studying, are eligible for a grant of approximately £70 to be used to assist the Scholar in visiting mines overseas or in Great Britain.

Tom Seaman Travelling Scholarships: Two Scholarships are offered annually, one to a candidate under 30 years of age and one to a candidate over 30 years of age, to enable the Scholars to visit mines outside the United Kingdom, preferably in the United States, to study any aspect of the science and practice of coal mining management or any cognate fields. Applicants should be British citizens who have been trained as mining engineers. The value of these Scholarships are determined by individual assessment. Applications should be accompanied by a thesis of between 500 and 1,000 words which should include a statement of the operations or specific problems the applicant wishes to study, and an estimate of the intended duration of the visit.

Note: The Institution also offers a number of medals, prizes, and smaller cash awards. Further information on all awards may be obtained by writing to the address below.

Further information from:
Institution of Mining Engineers
Hobart House
Grosvenor Place
London
England SW1X 7AE

[1025]

INSTITUTION OF MINING AND METALLURGY *(U.K.)*

Stanley Elmore Fellowships

Subjects: Non-ferrous metallury or mineral processing: postdoctoral research.

Tenable at an approved United Kingdom university for two years, with possible renewal to a maximum of three years.

Eligibility: Open to persons who are fully qualified to undertake postdoctoral research.

Note: The number of awards offered and their value depends on funds available each year.

Closing date: 15th March.

Further information from:
 Secretary
 Institution of Mining and Metallurgy
 44 Portland Place
 London
 England W1N 4BR

[1026]

INSTITUTION OF MINING AND METALLURGY *(U.K.)*

Edgar Pam Fellowship

Subjects: Any aspect of the science or practice of mining or related subjects, e.g., economic geology, mineralogy, mineral processing, extractive metallurgy: advanced study or research.

No. offered: One Fellowship; awarded in even-numbered years.

Value: £1,200.

Tenable at approved universities in the United Kingdom for one year only.

Eligibility: Open to young graduates domiciled in Australia, Canada, New Zealand, South Africa, and the United Kingdom.

Closing date: 15th March.

Further information from:
 Secretary
 Institution of Mining and Metallurgy
 44 Portland Place
 London
 England W1N 4BR

[1027]

INSTITUTION OF MINING AND METALLURGY *(U.K.)*

Bosworth Smith Trust Fund Award

Subjects: Metal mining, non-ferrous extraction metallurgy, or mineral dressing: postgraduate research.

Tenable at an approved university in the United Kingdom for one year only.

Eligibility: Open to persons who possess a degree in a relevant subject.

Closing date: 15th March.

Note: The number of awards offered and the value depends on the funds available each year.

Further information from:
 Secretary
 Institution of Mining and Metallurgy
 44 Portland Place
 London
 England W1N 4BR

[1028]

INSTITUTION OF MINING AND METALLURGY *(U.K.)*

G. Vernon Hobson Bequest

Purpose: For the advancement of the teaching and practice of geology as applied to mining.

Tenable for one year only.

Eligibility: Open to members of university staffs in the United Kingdom.

Closing date: 15th March.

Note: The number of awards offered and the value depends on funds available each year.

Further information from:
 Secretary
 Institution of Mining and Metallurgy
 44 Portland Place
 London
 England W1N 4BR

[1029]

INSTITUTION OF NUCLEAR ENGINEERS *(U.K.)*

Pinkerton Award

£40 plus an illuminated certificate is offered annually for work in any peaceful aspect of nuclear technology. This Prize is open to full-time graduate students who are sponsored by the head of their department or supervisor. Candidates should be prepared to present their work at the Annual Conference of University Nuclear Engineering Educationalists.

Not confirmed for 1983.

Further information from:
 Institution of Nuclear Engineers
 1 Penerley Road
 London SE6
 England

[1030]

INSTITUTION OF PLANT ENGINEERS
(U.K.)

Alexander Duckham Memorial Awards: Corporate members of the Institution may submit papers containing between 3,000 and 5,000 words, on any subject within the field of plant or works engineering. Papers must not have been previously published in writing other than in the journal of the Institution.

Subject to the entries being of sufficient merit, a silver medal together with a cash prize of £150 and a bronze medal together with a cash prize of £75 are offered annually for the best two papers which contribute most to the advancement of plant engineering.

Licentiates and Students Prizes: Licentiates of the Institution may submit a paper of not more than 5,000 words, and Students of the Institution may submit a paper of no more than 3,000 words, on any subject within the field of plant or works engineering. Papers must not have been previously published.

Subject to the entries received being of sufficient merit an award of £75 is offered annually, in the case of both Licentiates and Students, for the best paper in competition.

Closing date: End of February.

Further information from:
 Institution of Plant Engineers
 138 Buckingham Palace Road
 London
 England SW1W 9SG

[1031]

INTER-AMERICAN FOUNDATION

Pre-Doctoral Fellowship Program

Purpose: To promote research on social change in Latin America and the Caribbean.

Subjects: Social sciences.

No. offered: 10-15 Fellowships annually.

Value: Varies; approximately US$550 per month.

Tenable in the Caribbean or Latin America for six months to two years.

Eligibility: Applicants should have a multidisciplinary background and be concerned with the processes of social change from a problem-oriented perspective. Written and verbal command of the language in the area of study is required. There are no restrictions in regard to age, sex or citizenship.

Note: Doctoral candidates should be enrolled in higher education institutions in the U.S. and have fulfilled all degree requirements other than the dissertation at the time of the Award.

Closing date: 5th December.

Further information from:
 Pre-doctoral Fellowship Program
 Inter-American Foundation
 1515 Wilson Boulevard
 Rosslyn, Virginia 22209
 U.S.A.

[1032]

INTER-AMERICAN PRESS ASSOCIATION
IAPA Scholarship Fund, Inc.

At least ten Scholarships of US$5,000 or more are awarded to residents of North America, Latin America and the West Indies, in an effort to help develop more rounded journalists through cultural exposure and study in a foreign country. Candidates should be between 21 and 35 years of age, have good command of the language of the country they intend to visit, and be either professional journalists with at least three years of experience, or graduates of a school of journalism. Latin American and West Indian candidates should apply for admission at a U.S. or Canadian university school of journalism, subject to the Fund's approval. These recipients must study at the school for one academic year. U.S. and Canadian candidates may select a Latin American country in which they wish to study and work, subject to the Fund's approval. These recipients must take a minimum of two university courses, participate in the Fund's Reporting Program, and undertake a major research project.

Note: The Fund also gives IAPA-Pedro Joaquin Chamorro Awards of US$500 and a scroll to Latin American journalists.

Closing date: 1st September.

Further information from:
IAPA Scholarship Fund, Inc.
2911 N.W. 39th Street
Miami, Florida 33142
U.S.A.

[1033]

INTERGOVERNMENTAL OCEANOGRAPHY COMMISSION

Scholarships

Subjects: Coastal zone and marine resource studies; also marine affairs.

Tenable for one year (renewable) at the School of Oceanography, Oregon State University, Corvallis, or at the University of Rhode Island, Kingston.

Eligibility: Open to suitably qualified and experienced nationals of member states of IOC.

Closing date: December.

Further information from:
Intergovernmental Oceanography Commission
1 rue Miollis
Paris
F-75015 France

[1034]

INTERNATIONAL AGENCY FOR RESEARCH ON CANCER

Fellowships for Research Training in Cancer

Purpose: To assist junior scientists who are actively engaged in research in medical or allied sciences, and wish to pursue a career in cancer research.

Subjects: Environmental carcinogenesis: biostatistics and epidemiology of cancer and all aspects of chemical and viral carcinogenesis.

No. offered: Approximately 15 Fellowships annually.

Value: Travel for the Fellow and his dependents, and stipends in accordance with United Nations scales. Travel for dependents accompanying a Fellow may be paid. Family allowances of US$400 for spouse and US$450 for each dependent child are paid annually.

Tenable in any country and institution where suitable research facilities and materials exist, for one year.

Eligibility: Open to persons who have had some postdoctoral experience in medicine or the natural sciences.

Closing date: 31st January.

Further information from:
Head, Research Training and Liaison Programme
International Agency for Research on Cancer
150 cours Albert Thomas
69372 Lyon Cedex 2
France

[1035]

INTERNATIONAL AGRICULTURAL CENTRE *(Wageningen, Netherlands)*

Fellowships

Purpose: To offer postgraduate specialization in agricultural sciences, through individual study programs, to nationals of industrial countries.

Subjects: All aspects of agricultural science.

Value: 540 Dutch florins per month, plus free board and lodging in IAC Building, insurance, a book allowance, allowance for study tours in the Netherlands. International travel costs from and to the country of origin are not paid.

Tenable in the Netherlands for six months; renewable for a further six months in some cases.

Eligibility: Open to postgraduates who have experience in the field of study.

Note: Applicants should be seconded by the candidate's employer and government. (For nationals of developing countries, similar fellowships are available through the Ministry of Foreign Affairs.

Further information can be obtained either from the Netherlands diplomatic or consular post in the applicant's country or directly from:
International Agricultural Centre
P.O. Box 88
6700 AB Wageningen
Netherlands

[1036]

INTERNATIONAL AMERICAN MUSIC COMPETITIONS

Purpose: To stimulate interest among performers, teachers and students in American recital music written since 1900.

Subjects: Violin—1983; piano—1984.

No. offered: Up to twelve prizes; one 1st, 2nd and 3rd prize, and up to nine semi-finalist prizes.

Value: 1st Prize—US$10,000, US$35,000 in career promotion funds, and limited recording contract, plus an additional Award of US$5,000 may be offered for a second year; 2nd Prize—US$5,000; 3rd Prize—US$3,000; Semi-finalist Prizes—up to nine cash Awards of US$1,500 each.

Eligibility: Musicians and singers of both sexes, of any age and nationality are eligible.

Note: The competition has three rounds: preliminary, semi-final and final. The location of regional preliminary competitions depends on the number of applicants received from such regions. Final competition is held at Carnegie Hall. Travel costs are the responsibility of the contestants. Semi-finalists and finalists are provided with accommodation and practice facilities in New York.

Note: The Competitors are sponsored by the Rockefeller Foundation and Carnegie Hall.

Further information from:
International American Music Competitions
Carnegie Hall
881 Seventh Avenue
New York, New York 10019
U.S.A.

[1037]

INTERNATIONAL ASSOCIATION FOR THE EXCHANGE OF STUDENTS FOR TECHNICAL EXPERIENCE

Purpose: To provide students at institutions of higher education with technical experience abroad relative to their studies in the broadest sense; and to promote international understanding and goodwill among the students of all nations.

Principles of the Exchange: Each member country (see list below) collects offers from industrial and other organisations for receiving students from abroad for a temporary training period, in close connection with the student's field, and as a supplement to the student's university or college education.

Technical experience, in the sense of the aims of the Association, does not mean experience restricted to technical study fields. It refers to experience through an on-the-job training to supplement university and college education in all relevant study fields.

Subjects: The majority of industrial offers are made to students of engineering and technology. However, students of science, agriculture (including forestry and similar fields), applied arts (such as architecture, industrial design), and also commerce, language and similar fields to a lesser extent may also take part in the Exchange.

Value: The offering companies or organisations are expected to grant to students a payment sufficient to enable them to cover their cost of living during the actual training period.

Receiving countries arrange for necessary permits, lodgings, and in many cases, for social and cultural programmes during or after the training period.

Students pay their own transporation expenses, sometimes taking advantage of travel facilities arranged through sending countries.

Tenable in any member country of IAESTE (see list below). The main aim of the Association is to exchange students during their long vacations, i.e., for 8 to 12 weeks. Bilateral arrangements can be made for longer training periods, i.e., between 3 and 12 months, which help to develop long-distance exchanges, or for training periods during other seasons of the year (normal season for period of training is June to October), for example, in exchange with countries of the southern hemisphere.

Eligibility: Open to bona fide students following courses at universities, institutes of technology and similar higher institutions in member countries of IAESTE.

Many countries also exchange students taking full-time courses at colleges or technical schools below university levels.

For various reasons, IAESTE cannot include persons who have left their universities or colleges, or have not started their studies at institutes of higher education.

Member countries of IAESTE (including both full and associate members)—Argentina, Australia, Austria, Belgium, Brazil, Canada, Columbia, Cyprus, Czechoslovakia, Denmark, Egypt, Finland, France, Germany, Ghana, Greece, Guyana, Iceland, India, Iraq, Ireland, Israel, Italy, Japan, Jordan, Korea, Lebanon, Libya, Luxembourg, Netherlands, Nigeria, Norway, Philippines, Poland, Portugal, South Africa, Spain, Sudan, Sweden, Switzerland, Syria, Thailand, Tunisia, Turkey, United Kingdom, United States, and Yugoslavia.

Note: Interested students should contact the national secretariats in the countries in which they are studying for further information:

Canada—*National Secretary, IAESTE Canada, Box 1473, Kingston, Ontario;* Ireland—*Hon. Secretary, IAESTE Ireland, Engineering School, Upper Merrion Street, Dublin 2;* South Africa—*National Secretary, IAESTE (South Africa), P.O. Box 61019, Marshalltown 2107, Johannesburg;* United Kingdom—*IAESTE (United Kingdom), c/o Central Bureau for Educational Visits and Exchanges, Seymour Mews House, Seymour Mews, London W1H 9PE;* United States—*IAESTE/US, Inc., 217 American City Building, Columbia, Maryland 21044.*

For address of national secretariats in other countries write to:
Mr. G. Anemoyannis
General Secretary
IAESTE
P.O. Box 3414
Kolonaki Post Office
Athens
Greece

[1038]

INTERNATIONAL ASSOCIATION OF FIRE CHIEFS FOUNDATION, INC.

Scholarships

A varying number of Scholarships, averaging US$250, are offered annually to aid in better fire service administration and to support training in this area.

Any member of the fire service who is a member of a state, county, provincial, municipal, community, industrial or federal fire department and who has demonstrated proficiency as a member, is eligible to apply for a Scholarship to a recognized institution of higher education of his or her choice. Applicants should have the approval of their department chief.

Further information from:
International Association of Fire Chiefs Foundation, Inc.
1329 18th Street, N.W.
Washington, D.C. 20036
U.S.A.

[1039]

INTERNATIONAL ASSOCIATION OF STUDENTS IN ECONOMICS AND MANAGEMENT

Reciprocal Exchange Programme—Traineeships

Purpose: To enable recipients to acquire practical experience with commercial concerns abroad as part of, or supplementary to, their academic study in economics and management fields.

No. offered: Over 5,000 Traineeships annually.

Value: Students are paid by the firms with which they work; in some cases the cost of travel is paid by the educational authorities in the student's country.

Tenable in the participating countries generally for eight to ten weeks between June and October.

Eligibility: Open to students of economics and commerce who are attending institutions of higher education in AIESEC member countries (Argentina, Australia, Austria, Belgium, Brazil, Canada, Chile, Colombia, Costa Rica, Czechoslovakia, Denmark, Ecuador, Egypt, Finland, France, West Germany, Ghana, Greece, Hong Kong, Hungary, Iceland, India, Ireland, Israel, Italy, Ivory Coast, Japan, Kenya, Republic of Korea, Liberia, Malaysia, Mexico, Netherlands, Nigeria, Norway, Panama, Peru, Philippines, Poland, Portugal, Puerto Rico, Sierra Leone, Singapore, Spain, South Africa, Sudan, Sweden, Switzerland, Taipei, Thailand, Togo, Tunisia, Turkey, United Kingdom, United States, Venezuela, Yugoslavia and Zimbabwe).

Note: Applications are made to the national AIESEC committee at the student's university, school or institute, in participating countries.

Further information from:
International AIESEC Secretariat
Avenue Adolphe Buyl, 123
B-1050 Brussels
Belgium

[1040]

INTERNATIONAL ASTRONOMICAL UNION

Travel Grants

Purpose: To enable astronomers to undertake research or study at observatories and universities abroad.

No. offered: Variable, according to funds available.

Value: Travel expenses only, as a rule.

Tenable at approved observatories for varying periods of time.

Eligibility: Open to persons of any nationality who have a university degree suitable for scientific work at an observatory, and can obtain permission for the visit from both the home and the host observatories.

Note: Full details of I.A.U. Grants are published in the Transactions and Information Bulletin of the Union available in observatory libraries.
Applicants should apply to *Prof. F.B. Wood, Department of Physics and Astronomy, University of Florida, Gainesville, Florida 32611, U.S.A.*

Address:
IAU-UAI Secretariat
61, avenue de l'Observatoire
75014 Paris
France

[1041]

INTERNATIONAL ATLANTIC SALMON FOUNDATION

Fellowships and Project Grants

Purpose: To encourage individuals seeking to assure the Atlantic salmon's future, through advanced training, or the development of new techniques or concepts.

Subjects: Atlantic salmon biology, management or related fields.

No. offered: One or two Fellowships annually.

Value: US$1,000 to US$3,000.

Tenable at any accredited university or research laboratory, or in an active management program, anywhere in the world where specialized information on Atlantic salmon is available.

Eligibility: Open to legal residents of the U.S. and Canada.

Note: The Foundation also makes available *Project Grants* to support a wide variety of endeavors in aid of the Atlantic salmon. Grants are made annually to candidates of any country, epsecially to candidates not eligible for funding through any other means. The value of these Grants are determined through individual assessment and are tenable anywhere for any length of time necessary to complete the project.
Application forms and further information may be obtained by writing to *International Atlantic Salmon Foundation, P.O. Box 429, St. Andrews, New Brunswick, Canada E0G 2X0,* or to:
International Atlantic Salmon Foundation
100 Park Avenue
New York, New York 10017
U.S.A.

[1042]

INTERNATIONAL ATOMIC ENERGY AGENCY

Fellowships are offered to nationals of developing member states of IAEA, to train in the field of nuclear energy for peaceful purposes. Training supported includes formal courses of study, guided research, technician training, or on-the-job training. Candidates should be university graduates or possess equivalent qualifications, except for those undertaking training at the technician level.

Special Grants for Established Scientists are offered to nationals of developing countries to enable them to broaden their qualifications, by making scientific visits (usually two months or less) to nuclear centres in more advanced countries.

Note: Approximately 450 Fellowships/Scientific Visits are offered each year. Stipends are within the range of those offered under the United Nations Development Programme.
Applications should be made through the appropriate ministry or National Atomic Energy Commission in candidates' own countries. All candidates must be nominated by their respective governments.

Address:
Head
Fellowships and Training Section
Division of Technical Assistance
International Atomic Energy Agency
P.O. Box 100
A-1400 Vienna
Austria

[1043]

INTERNATIONAL ATOMIC ENERGY AGENCY

Fellowships for IAEA Courses

Courses: Questions connected with the peaceful application of atomic energy in different fields. Subjects vary each year.

No. offered: Approximately 650 places on about 30 courses annually.

Value: Based on stipend rates of the United Nations Development Programme.

Tenable for periods from two weeks to three months. Locations vary each year.

Eligibility: Open to nationals of developing IAEA member countries, and in some cases, to FAO and WHO member states. Qualifications required depend on the Course to be taken, but generally, candidates should be university graduates; certain courses are open to candidates at a senior technician level. Instruction is mostly in English but some courses are also given in French, Spanish and Russian. Applications must be submitted through official channels.

Further information from:
Training Courses Section
Division of Technical Assistance
International Atomic Energy Agency
P.O. Box 100
A-1400 Vienna
Austria

[1044]

INTERNATIONAL BALLET COMPETITION
(Varna, Bulgaria)

The Competition is open to male and female dancers of all nationalities. It is divided into two classes for which separate prizes and titles are awarded: Class A (Seniors) is for dancers not over 28 years of age, and Class B (Juniors) is for dancers between 14 and 19 years of age to compete in Class A, provided permission to do so is granted by the International Jury. Where candidates choose to dance a pas de deux in one of the three stages of the Competition, competing couples may be formed from one and the same class or from two different classes.

Prizes are as follows: in Class A the major Prize is the *Grand Prix of the City of Varna*, consisting of 3,000 leva, a gold medal and a diploma; in addition there are two First Prizes (one for men, one for women) of 2,000 leva, a gold medal and a diploma; two Second Prizes of 1,500 leva, a silver medal and diploma; two Third Prizes of 1,000 leva, a bronze medal and a diploma; two Fourth Prizes of 700 leva, a bronze medal and a diploma; and two Fifth Prizes of 500 leva, a bronze medal and a diploma. In Class B the major Prize is the *Special Distinction of the Youth Organization of Varna*, consisting of 1,000 leva, a diploma and a medal; in addition there are two First Class Awards (one for boys, one for girls) of 800 leva, a diploma and a medal; two Second

Class Awards of 500 leva, a diploma and a medal; two Third Class Awards of 300 leva, a diploma and a medal. There are also a number of Special Awards and Token Awards of between 300 leva and 1,000 leva.

The organizing committee defrays all accommodation and subsistence expenses for competitors, their partners and pianists.

Further information from:
 Secretariat
 International Ballet Competition
 56 Alabine Street
 1040 Sofia
 Bulgaria

[1045]

INTERNATIONAL BALZAN FOUNDATION

Balzan Foundation Prize

The Foundation awards prizes of varying amounts annually, for the encouragement of humanitarian and cultural activities, without regard to nationality, race or religion. Prizes are given in the broad fields of the humanities and social sciences, natural and mathematical sciences and the creative arts.

Further information from:
 International Balzan Foundation
 Balzan Foundation Prize
 via Manzoni 38
 Milan
 Italy

[1046]

INTERNATIONAL BEETHOVEN PIANO COMPETITION *(Vienna)*

The next Competition will be held in May and June 1985. The contest is open to pianists of both sexes and any nationality. Prizes: 1st—60,000 Austrian schillings; 2nd—50,000 schillings; 3rd—40,000 schillings and three additional Prizes of 15,000 schillings each.

Closing date: 1st March 1981.

Further information from:
 Secretary General
 Mrs. Elga Ponzer
 International Beethoven Piano
  Competition
 Hochschule für Musik und darstellende
  Kunst
 Lothringerstrasse
 A-1037 Vienna
 Austria

[1047]

INTERNATIONAL BRAIN RESEARCH ORGANIZATION

IBRO/Unesco Travel Fellowships

Purpose: To stimulate and facilitate international interdisciplinary advanced research in brain sciences.

Subjects: Neuroanatomy, neurochemistry, neuroendocrinology, neuropharmacology, neurophysiology, behavioral sciences (specifically confined to the relationships of brain and behavior), neurocommunication and biophysics, and brain pathology.

No. offered: Approximately 32 Fellowships.

Value: Living expenses during tenure of Fellowship.

Tenable at the research laboratories of donor institutions in various countries. Fellows are usually expected to stay for one year.

Eligibility: Open to young scientists, especially from developing countries, wishing to acquire new techniques in a discipline other than their primary field of research. Candidates must have established competence in one of the subject areas listed above.

Note: The programme is essentially a means of providing grants to complement fellowships made available by a number of donor institutions (a list of which is available from IBRO). Before applying for these Fellowships, candidates should make arrangements for their work with the laboratory they wish to visit.

Further information from:
IBRO Fellowship Secretariat
c/o Professor D. Albe-Fessard
Université Pierre et Marie Curie
  Laboratoire de Physiologie des
  Centres Nerveux
4, Place Jussieu
75230 Paris Cedex 05
France

[1048]

INTERNATIONAL BUREAU OF WEIGHTS AND MEASURES *(Sèvres, France)*

Training Opportunities

Subject: Metrology; study of high precision standards of measurement.

Tenable at the Bureau for a period from a few days to several months according to the number of persons that can be accommodated.

Eligibility: Open to persons who possess at least a B.Sc. degree in the physical sciences and have a good knowledge of English or French. A candidate must show the possibility of exchange of profitable scientific information between himself and the physicists of the Bureau.

Note: Applications should be made through the agency of a laboratory or an official metrological service. The Bureau itself does not offer financial assistance.

Closing date: At least four months before the desired period of study.

Further information from:
International Bureau of Weights and
  Measures
Pavillon de Breteuil
F-92310 Sèvres
France

[1049]

INTERNATIONAL CENTRE FOR ADVANCED MEDITERRANEAN AGRONOMIC STUDIES

Postgraduate Scholarships *(Bari)*

Subject: Irrigation.

No. offered: Approximately 30 Scholarships annually.

Value: 420,000 lire per month living allowance; FF1,500 for tuition expenses.

Tenable at the Mediterranean Agronomic Institute, Bari, Italy, for nine months.

Eligibility: Open to graduates in agronomy or economics under 40 years of age. Preference is given to candidates from Mediterranean countries.

Note: Courses of a shorter duration, one to three months, are also organized each year with a more specialized purpose.

Closing date: 30th March.

Further information from:
International Centre for Advanced
  Mediterranean Agronomic Studies
11 rue Newton
75116 Paris
France

[1050]

INTERNATIONAL CENTRE FOR ADVANCED MEDITERRANEAN AGRONOMIC STUDIES

Postgraduate Scholarships *(Montpellier)*

Subjects: Economic development; forestry.

No. offered: Approximately 40 Scholarships annually.

Value: FF2,100 per month living allowance; FF1,500 for tuition expenses.

Tenable at the Mediterranean Agronomic Institute, Montpellier, France, for nine months.

Eligibility: Open to graduates in agronomy or economics under 40 years of age. Preference is given to candidates from Mediterranean countries.

Note: Courses of a shorter duration, one to three months, are also organized each year with a more specialized purpose.

Closing date: 30th March.

Further information from:
International Centre for Advanced
  Mediterranean Agronomic Studies
11 rue Newton
75116 Paris
France

[1051]

INTERNATIONAL CENTRE FOR ADVANCED MEDITERRANEAN AGRONOMIC STUDIES

Postgraduate Scholarships (*Saragossa*)

Subjects: Animal husbandry, agricultural planning and development.

No. offered: Approximately twenty Scholarships annually.

Value: 37,000 pesetas per month living allowance; FF1,500 per month for tuition fees.

Tenable at the Mediterranean Agronomic Institute, Saragossa, Spain, for nine months.

Eligibility: Open to graduates in agronomy or economics under 40 years of age. Preference is given to candidates from Mediterranean countries.

Note: Courses of a shorter duration, one to three months, are also organized each year with a more specialized purpose.
  The Saragossa Institute is financed by the Spanish government.

Closing date: 30th March.

Further information from:
International Centre for Advanced
  Mediterranean Agronomic Studies
11 rue Newton
75116 Paris
France

[1052]

INTERNATIONAL CENTRE FOR ADVANCED TECHNICAL AND VOCATIONAL TRAINING (*Turin*)
International Labour Organization

Course Scholarships

Subjects: Regularly scheduled courses in the fields of (a) management training, (b) trade union training, (c) educational technology, (d) industrial training.

Tenable at the Centre for varying periods from 2 to 24 weeks.

Eligibility: Open to managers, trade union officials, training officials and instructors of technicians from the industrial, commercial and agricultural sectors in developing countries, who possess the specific qualifications needed for each course, with regard to (a) present position, (b) years of experience, (c) formal education or equivalent, (d) age, and (e) language competence.

Note: Fellowships are financed through projects supported by the United Nations Development Programme and administered by its executing agency—the International Labor Organization [q.v.], through one of the other international or region funding bodies operating within the framework of international technical co-operation, and by direct governmental or private enterprise funding.
  Courses are held in French, English, Italian, Portugese, Spanish and Arabic.
  The Centre does not itself grant Fellowships.

Further information from:
International Centre for Advanced
  Technical and Vocational Training
201 Via Ventimiglia
I-10127 Turin
Italy

[1053]

INTERNATIONAL CENTRE FOR AGRICULTURAL EDUCATION
(*Bern*)

Full and Partial Fellowships for Courses

Course: Agriculture: professional training and education, including special seminars and visits.

Value: Full or partial support.

Tenable in Switzerland for four or five weeks (July to August) in even-numbered years.

Eligibility: Open to experienced teachers and administrators in the field of agriculture from any country.
Instruction is in English, French or German.

Closing date: 31st May.

Further information from:
Secretariat, Federal Office of Agriculture
International Centre for Agricultural
    Education
CH-3003 Bern
Switzerland

[1054]

INTERNATIONAL CENTRE OF HYDROLOGY "DINO TONINI"

Scholarships for International Postgraduate Course in Hydrology

Purpose: To enable civil engineering graduates who are specialized in hydrology to complete their training, particularly in hydrometeorology and the application of hydraulic construction techniques.

Value: Monthly living expenses allowance, round trip travel costs, tuition fees.

Tenable at the Centre for six months (January to July).

Eligibility: Open to civil engineers, particularly from developing countries, who are not over 35 years of age. Instruction is in English.

Note: The Course is organized by the Centre at the University of Padua under the auspices of the Italian National Research Council, the Italian Ministry of Foreign Affairs, and Unesco.

Closing date: Mid-October.

Further information from:
International Centre of Hydrology "Dino
    Tonini"
Via Loredan 20
35100 Padua
Italy

[1055]

INTERNATIONAL CENTRE OF STUDIES FOR THE DIFFUSION OF ITALIAN MUSIC *(Rome)*

Scholarships for Advanced Courses

Subjects: Performances, seminars and discussions with eminent musicians designed to contribute to the knowledge and the reevaluation of the musical heritage of Italy.

No. offered: 20 Scholarships annually.

Value: 100,000 lire.

Tenable in Venice for the annual summer courses, which last one month.

Eligibility: Open to musicians with a degree from a conservatory or academy of music who are under 35 years old. Awards are made on the basis of an audition.

Note: An admission fee of 15,000 lire and a contribution fee of 30,000 lire must be paid by all applicants.
Candidates should apply through the Italian diplomatic representative in their own country.

Not confirmed for 1983.

Further information from:
Segreteria dei Corsi
Centro Internazionale di Studi per la
    Divulgazione della Musica Italiana
Via del Babuino 135
Rome
Italy

[1056]

INTERNATIONAL CENTRE FOR THE STUDY OF MOSAICS *(Ravenna)*

Scholarships for Courses

Subject: Mosaics.

No. offered: Five Scholarships annually.

Value: 100,000 lire.

Tenable at the summer school of the Academy of Fine Arts at Lido Adriano, near Ravenna, for 15 days.

Eligibility: Open to students from any country. Individuals who make mosaics professionally, or who have obtained diplomas from institutes teaching mosaic work are ineligible.

Note: Scholarships will be made available to those applicants approved by their embassies, Italian cultural institutes abroad, universities, art and trade schools.

Closing date: 20th April.

Further information from:
International Centre for the Study of Mosaics
c/o Azienda Autonoma Soggiorno e Turismo
2 Via San Vitale
48100 Ravenna
Italy

[1057]

INTERNATIONAL CENTRE FOR THEORETICAL PHYSICS *(Trieste, Italy)*

Participation Grants in Seminars or Extended Courses

Subjects: Theoretical physics, including mathematical aspects.

No. offered: Varies from year to year.

Value: Approximately US$650 per month.

Tenable for three to twelve weeks; renewable.

Eligibility: Open to nationals of all member states of the International Atomic Energy Agency and Unesco; priority is given to nationals from developing countries.

Further information from:
International Centre for Theoretical Physics
Strada Costiera 11
34100 Trieste
Italy

[1058]

INTERNATIONAL CENTRE FOR TROPICAL AGRICULTURE *(Cali, Colombia)*

Training Scholarships

Subjects: Tropical agriculture, including studies concerning tropical pasture land and the production of legumes, rice, yucca, etc.

Value: Payment of tuition fees and travel, plus a monthly allowance of US$350 (single Scholars) or US$450 (married Scholars).

Tenable in the training programs of the Centre for the duration of the course.

Eligibility: Open to nationals of tropical zone developing countries with a good knowledge of English or Spanish. Candidates should possess, minimally, a degree in agronomy and be working in their countries in programs related to tropical agriculture.

Further information from:
International Centre for Tropical Agriculture
apartado aéreo 6713
Cali
Colombia

[1059]

INTERNATIONAL CHARLEMAGNE PRIZE OF THE CITY OF AACHEN *(West Germany)*

An annual Prize of DM5,000, an illuminated document and a medallion is awarded annually in recognition of the most notable achievement in the service of encouraging international understanding and cooperation in the European sphere. The recipient may be of any nationality, religion or race. The prize is awarded, usually on Ascension Day, in Aachen.

Further information from:
International Charlemagne Prize of the City of Aachen
Postfach 1210
5100 Aachen
West Germany

[1060]

INTERNATIONAL CHILDREN'S CENTRE
(Paris)

Course Awards

Subjects: Courses are given in the broad fields of family and community health; food, health and development; teaching/learning methodology; development of information.

No. offered: 15 to 25 Awards per Course.

Value: Tuition expenses, plus board and lodging costs. The participant must pay his own fares to and from Paris.

Tenable in Paris or countries other than France according to the particular course, for one to twelve weeks.

Eligibility: Awards are available to specialists and competent persons from approximately 30 countries: (1) for teaching staff; (2) for members of juvenile courts; (3) for pediatricians and public health doctors; (4) for health, social and administrative workers.

Note: Participants are elected by the Centre only when proposed by the relevant ministry of their government. The ministry should attest their qualifications and their knowledge of the French language, and also submit a detailed curriculum vitae from the candidate.

The Courses are paid for by the Centre whose budget is controlled by UNICEF and the French government. Several courses are also given each year in Latin America, Africa, Asia and the Middle East. The programme changes each year.

Further information from:
International Children's Centre
Château de Longchamp
Bois de Boulogne
75016 Paris
France

[1061]

INTERNATIONAL CIVIL AVIATION ORGANIZATION

Fellowships

Eligibility: Open to nationals of developing countries who are directly connected with the civil aviation activities of the country concerned, but are not necessarily government employees.

Awards may be made when the following conditions are met: (a) an individual must be officially nominated for a Fellowship by the agency in his home country authorized to sponsor candidates for Fellowships under the United Nations Development Program; (b) the Organization must be satisfied that the award of such a Fellowship is of benefit to the further development of civil aviation in the candidate's country rather than to him as an individual; (c) the government making the nomination must have made provision under the technical assistance country project in order that the funds may be made available to ICAO to finance the Fellowship applied for. Alternatively, the interested government may agree to finance the training of one or more of its nationals under Trust Fund arrangements with the Organization.

Note: Additional information about Fellowships in the field of civil aviation is available from the civil aviation authorities of most countries receiving aid under the United Nations Development Program.

Address:
International Civil Aviation Organization
Technical Assistance Bureau
Fellowships Section
1000 Sherbrooke Street West
Montreal, Quebec
Canada H3A 2R2

[1062]

INTERNATIONAL COLLEGE OF SURGEONS *(U.S.A. Branch)*

Scholarships

Postgraduate Scholarship Award: A number of annual Awards in the amount of US$1,000 are offered to enable medical doctors to pursue studies in general surgery or the surgical specialties in clinical work or research projects in the U.S. or abroad.

Open to U.S. citizens who are licensed to practice medicine in one of the states of America and have graduated from an accredited medical school within the past eight years.

Third Year Undergraduate Scholarship Award: A number of annual Awards in the amount of US$1,000 are offered to encourage qualified third year medical students to broaden their experience in the field of surgery through a period of approximately three months' study in a foreign country.

Open to U.S. citizens who are third year medical students in good standing of an accredited school of medicine, and are committed to a career in surgery or a surgical specialty.

Not confirmed for 1983.

Further information from:
International College of Surgeons
1516 North Lake Shore Drive
Chicago, Illinois 60610
U.S.A.

[1063]

INTERNATIONAL COMMUNICATION AGENCY *(U.S.A.)*

(a) Postdoctoral Research Scholarships
(b) Postdoctoral Lectureships

Value: A maintenance allowance and international travel expenses.

Tenable at colleges and universities in the United States for (a) three months to one academic year; (b) usually one academic year.

Eligibility: Postdoctoral Research Scholarships are open to nationals of countries and territories having United States diplomatic or consular posts, who have a doctoral degree or equivalent qualification.

Postdoctoral Lectureships are open to non-United States citizens (the list of countries varies from year to year). Preference is given to those persons who have not had extensive previous experience in the United States.

Note: Applications should be made to the binational educational commission or the United States embassy or consulate in the candidate's home country.

[1064]

INTERNATIONAL COMMUNICATION AGENCY *(U.S.A.)*

Fulbright-Hays Program

Subjects: Unrestricted.

Value: From travel expenses only to allowances for tuition and fees, books, room, board, and travel; in certain cases, expenses for an orientation and language course prior to the regular studies will be paid.

Tenable at colleges and universities in the United States for usually one academic year; renewable.

Eligibility: Open to nationals of countries (also overseas territories of these countries) and territories having United States diplomatic or consular posts. Candidates should have a working knowledge of English and have a bachelor's degree or its equivalent. Exceptionally, in the case of a person who has advanced as far as possible in his subject of study in his home country, a lesser qualification will be accepted.

Note: Applications should be made to the binational educational commission or the United States embassy or consulate in the individual's home country.

[1065]

INTERNATIONAL COMMUNICATION AGENCY *(U.S.A.)*

Awards for United States Citizens (Fulbright-Hays Program)

Qualified United States citizens may visit another country to *study* for a year at the graduate level at an institution of higher learning or on an approved project; *teach* for a year in an elementary or secondary school; *lecture* preferably for a year but at least for a semester in a college or university, or conduct seminars for shorter periods; *conduct advanced research* for a year or at least for six months at an institution of higher learning or on an approved subject project; *serve as a consultant* for a period of three to six months in a special field, or as a lecturer before general audiences on topics of current interest; or *participate in summer seminars* in foreign languages, social studies or education.

Cooperating agencies administering grant competitions under the Fulbright-Hays Program for United States citizens:

For predoctoral study or research—*Institute of International Education, 809 United Nations Plaza, New York, New York 10017.*

For teaching in elementary schools and for modern language and area studies training and research—*Department of Health, Educa-*

tion, and Welfare; Division of International Education; Teacher Exchange Section; Office of Education, Washington, D.C. 20202.

For postdoctoral research and university lecturing—*Council for International Exchange of Scholars*, 11 Dupont Circle, Washington, D.C. 20036.

In any given year, a United States candidate may apply either to the Institute of International Education or to the Council for International Exchange of Scholars, but not to both. However, he may apply to one of these agencies and also to the Department of Health, Education, and Welfare in the same year.

Further information from:

Director, Congressional and Public Liaison
International Communication Agency
1750 Pennsylvania Avenue, N.W.
Washington, D.C. 20547
U.S.A.

[1066]

INTERNATIONAL COMMUNICATION AGENCY *(U.S.A.)*

Awards for Non-United States Citizens (Fulbright-Hays Program)

Qualified foreign nationals may go the United States to *study*, usually at the graduate level, for one year at a college or university; *teach* for one year in an elementary or secondary school; *observe and study* teaching methods and school administration at the elementary and secondary school level, usually for a period of six months; *participate in seminars; lecture*, preferably for one year but at least for a semester at a college or university; *conduct postdoctoral research and postdoctoral lectureships* for three months to one year at an institution of higher learning; *participate* in individually arranged programs or group projects offering specialized study and opportunities to obtain practical professional experience; and *observe* the American scene and confer with professional colleagues during a visit of 30 to 60 days.

Note: Applications and enquiries should be made to the binational educational commission or the United States embassy or consulate in the applicant's home country.

[1067]

INTERNATIONAL COMMUNICATION AGENCY *(U.S.A.)*

Foreign Teachers Grants (Fulbright-Hays Program)

Purpose: To enable teachers from abroad to acquire valuable teaching experience by teaching in elementary and secondary schools in the United States.

Value: Grants cover transportation only. Other expenses are met by the salary from the United States host institution. Teachers from the United Kingdom receive their salaries from their home institutions, plus a supplemental grant from the British government.

Tenable in the United States for one academic year.

Eligibility: Open to non-United States citizens (the list of countries varies from year to year). Candidates must have had three continuous years of teaching experience and must indicate their intention of remaining in the field of education. Preference is given to candidates between 25 and 50 years of age.

Note: Applications and enquiries should be made to the binational educational commission or the United States embassy or consulate in the individual's home country.

[1068]

INTERNATIONAL COMMUNICATION AGENCY *(U.S.A.)*

Study and Research Grants (Fulbright-Hays Program)

Purpose: To increase mutual understanding between the people of the United States and the people of other countries by means of educational and cultural exchange.

Subjects: Study and research in all fields, as well as professional training in the creative and performing arts.

Value: To cover international transportation, language or orientation course (where appropriate), tuition, book, and maintenance allowances, and health and accident insurance. Some Grants, however, will consist of travel expenses only, supplementing maintenance and tuition scholarships which are granted to students by universities and other organizations.

An applicant who has received a doctoral degree since applying, or has been admitted to doctoral candidacy, having completed all requirements except the writing of the dissertation, may, upon arrival in certain countries, receive a higher stipend.

Tenable at institutions of higher learning abroad, for one academic year. A list of participating countries in a given year may be obtained from the address below.

Eligibility: Open to United States citizens who have a bachelor's degree or equivalent qualification. Candidates must have a high scholastic record, have an acceptable plan of study, demonstrate proficiency in the language of the host country, and be in good health. (In some cases special language training is provided as part of a Grant.) Preference is given to persons who have not had prior experience of, or opportunity for, extended foreign study, residence or travel.

Note: Applicants enrolled in a college or university should apply to the Fulbright Program Adviser on their campus. Applicants not enrolled in a college or university may apply directly to the address below. Applications should be requested at least 15 days prior to the closing date.

Closing date: 1st November.

Further information from:
Institute of International Education
809 United Nations Plaza
New York, New York 10017
U.S.A.

[1069]

INTERNATIONAL COMMUNICATION AGENCY *(U.S.A.)*

Postdoctoral Research Grants (Fulbright-Hays Program)

Purpose: To increase mutual understanding between the people of the United States and the people of other countries by enabling United States citizens to undertake postdoctoral research abroad.

Subjects: Unrestricted.

Value: To cover international transportation expenses for grantee, family living expenses, and possibly a small book and services allowance.

Tenable in colleges or universities abroad, usually for one academic year.

The list of countries varies from year to year.

Eligibility: Open to United States citizens who have a Ph.D. degree or equivalent qualifications, and have a good knowledge of the necessary language for the proposed research.

Closing date: Recommended before 1st July (12 to 18 months in advance), but subject to change.

Further information from:
Council for International Exchange of Scholars
11 Dupont Circle
Washington, D.C. 20036
U.S.A.

[1070]

INTERNATIONAL COMMUNICATION AGENCY *(U.S.A.)*

Lectureships (Fulbright-Hays Program)

Purpose: To increase mutual understanding between the people of the United States and the people of other countries by enabling college and university teachers from the United States to lecture in colleges and universities abroad for one year.

Value: To cover international transportation costs plus transportation for one dependent, living expenses, and possibly a small allowance for books and services. Grants may also include a U.S. dollar supplement.

Tenable in colleges and universities abroad, usually for one academic year.

Eligibility: Open to United States citizens who have college or university teaching experience at the level for which the application is made. Candidates are normally expected to lecture in English; however, in Latin America and in certain European countries ability to lecture in the language of the country is generally required for all fields except American literature and English language; in French-speaking African countries a working knowledge of French is essential.

Closing date: Recommended before 1st July (12 to 18 months in advance), but subject to change.

Further information from:
  Council for International Exchange of
    Scholars
  11 Dupont Circle
  Washington, D.C. 20036
  U.S.A.

[1071]

INTERNATIONAL COMMUNICATION AGENCY *(U.S.A.)*

International Educational Development Program (Fulbright-Hays Program)

Purpose: To enable teachers and school administrators from abroad to study and observe educational methods and school systems in the United States.

Subjects: Elementary, secondary and vocational teacher education, science education, English (as a foreign language), school administration and supervision, and American civilization.

Value: Travel expenses, maintenance allowance, tuition and books.

Tenable in the United States for approximately six months, unless on a short-term project or workshop (30- to 90-day projects in specialized fields of education; 40-day Puerto Rico workshop).

Eligibility: Open to nationals of countries and territories having United States diplomatic or consular posts, who have had three continuous years of teaching experience and intend to remain in the field of education. Candidates should have a good working knowledge of English, except in the case of short-term projects in specialized fields of education for English-speaking or non-English-speaking teachers, and the Puerto Rico workshop for Spanish-speaking Latin Americans with no knowledge of English. Candidates should be between 25 and 40 years of age.

Note: Applications should be made to the binational educational commission or the United States embassy or consulate in the candidate's own country.

[1072]

INTERNATIONAL COMMUNICATION AGENCY *(U.S.A.)*

Teachers Program (Fulbright-Hays Program)

Purpose: To increase mutual understanding between the people of the United States and the people of other countries by enabling United States teachers to teach for one academic year in elementary or secondary schools abroad, or to attend summer seminars.

Value: To cover international transporation expenses for all countries except the United Kingdom, Canada and Switzerland. Teachers continue to receive their salaries from their own schools in the United Kingdom, Canada and Germany. A maintenance allowance to cover major expenses is paid in the currency of the host country in Denmark, Switzerland and New Zealand. Transportation is not provided for dependents.

Tenable in elementary, secondary or post-secondary schools in Canada, Denmark, West Germany, New Zealand, Switzerland and the United Kingdom for one academic year.

Eligibility: Open to United States citizens who have a bachelor's or master's degree with three years' teaching experience, and are currently employed in an elementary, secondary or teacher-training school, college, junior college or university. Candidates should have a working knowledge of the language of the host country.

Note: These grants are awarded on a reciprocal or non-reciprocal basis depending on the particular program in the country concerned.

Closing date: 1st November.

Further information from:
  Teacher Exchange Section
  Division of International Education
  U.S. Office of Education
  Washington, D.C. 20202
  U.S.A.

[1073]

INTERNATIONAL COMMUNICATION AGENCY *(U.S.A.)*

International Visitors Program

Purpose: To increase mutual understanding between the people of the United States and the people of other countries by means of educational and cultural exchange. The following grants are awarded by invitation only, on a non-competitive basis, to persons recommended by the appropriate United States Foreign Service posts in their own countries. (Grants are available to nationals of most countries having United States diplomatic or consular posts).

Grants for Observation and Consultation in the United States are awarded to highly qualified persons from abroad, who are leaders in their particular fields. The Grant may include a per diem allowance, international travel expenses, and travel costs within the United States, as well as additional major allowance. They are tenable for approximately four to six weeks.

Grants for Specialized Programs are awarded to specialists from abroad so that they may obtain professional experience available in the United States in their particular field. The Grant includes a per diem allowance, international travel expenses, travel within the United States, as well as additional minor allowances, and is tenable for an average of three months, although shorter or longer programs are conducted. A working knowledge of English is required.

Grants for Educational Travel are awarded to university or college students, young professionals, or persons concerned with youth, to participate in educational travel visits to the United States, generally as members of a group, to observe campus activities, become familiar with United States cultural and educational institutions, and visit Americans in their homes. Grants are tenable for between 30 and 45 days.

Note: Enquiries should be made to the binational educational commission or the United States embassy or consulate in the home country.

[1074]

INTERNATIONAL COMPETITION FOR CHAMBER MUSIC ENSEMBLES *(Colmar, France)*

Prizes

Prizes ranging from 5,000 to 20,000 French francs are offered in the Competition held in Colmar each year in the spring. Types of competing ensembles vary from year to year. The age limit for participants is 35 years (or 140 years for the ensemble). Musicians of any nationality may apply. Applications should be submitted by mid-January.

Further information from:
International Competition for Chamber Music Ensembles
Office de tourisme
4, rue d'Unterlinded
F-68000 Colmar
France

[1075]

INTERNATIONAL COMPETITION FOR MUSICAL PERFORMERS *(Geneva)*

First Prizes of 6,000 or 5,000 Swiss francs and Second Prizes of 2,500 Swiss francs are offered in the annual Competition. Musical performers of any nationality, between 15 and 32 years of age, may apply. A prospectus in English, French, German and Italian is available on request. The competition is usually held in September and applications should be received by 1st June.

Further information from:
Secretariat
International Competition for Musical Performers
12, rue de l'Hôtel de Ville
CH-1204 Geneva
Switzerland

[1076]

INTERNATIONAL COMPETITION FOR OPERA AND BALLET COMPOSITION *(Geneva)*

A First Prize of 15,000 Swiss francs with the possibility of a stage production is offered whenever the Competition is held. Composers of any nationality may apply. The Competition is organized by the City of Geneva and the Director of Swiss Radio and Musical Broadcasting.

Further information from:
Secretariat
International Competition for Opera and Ballet Composition
Maison de la Radio
CH-1211 Geneva 8
Switzerland

[1077]

INTERNATIONAL COMPETITION FOR YOUNG CONDUCTORS *(Besançon, France)*

A major prize—the Lyre d'Or plaque together with the Emile Vuillermoz Prize, of FF10,000—and various other prizes, are offered in the annual Competition held in September.

Conductors of any nationality who are not more than 30 years of age in the year of the Competition may apply.

Closing date: 1st June.

Further information from:
Secretariat
Concourse International de Jeunes Chefs d'Orchestre
2D, rue Isenbart
25000 Besançon
France

[1078]

INTERNATIONAL COMPETITION FOR YOUNG MUSICIANS *(Belgrade)*

Prizes

Six Prizes are awarded in each category of the Competition. Young musicians of any nationality, under the age of 30 are eligible to enter. Categories: 1983—piano and string quartet; 1984—violoncello and composition (for chamber a cappela: 16 to 24 members); 1985—violian and vocal ensemble (chamber choir a cappela: 16 to 24 members).

Closing date: 1st July.

Further information from:
Secretariat
International Competition for Young Musicians
Terazije 26-11
11000 Belgrade
Yugoslavia

[1079]

INTERNATIONAL COMPETITION FOR YOUNG OPERA SINGERS *(Sofia)*

The Competition, which is open to male and female singers of all countries who are under 33 years of age, is held every four years (next Competition is June 1983). It is divided into three stages, the third stage involving the singing of a principal part in a regular performance of the Sofia National Opera. The supreme prize is the *Grand Prix de Sofia*: 4,000 leva, a gold medal, a gold ring and a diploma. The Competition is divided into two classes, for male singers and for female singers, and the prizes in each class are as follows: first prize—3,500 leva, a gold medal and a diploma; second prize—2,500 leva, a silver medal and a diploma; third prize—1,500 leva, a bronze medal and a diploma. In addition there are various token awards ranging from 300 to 500 leva, and all competitors who reach the third stage and are not among the major prizewinners or token award winners receive a prize of 200 leva and a certificate of participation.

The organizing committee defrays all accommodation and subsistence expenses for competitors and their accompanists.

Further information from:
Secretariat
International Competition for Young Opera Singers
56 Alabine Street
1040 Sofia
Bulgaria

[1080]

INTERNATIONAL CONFEDERATION OF SOCIETIES OF AUTHORS AND COMPOSERS

Law Prize

A Prize of up to FF30,000 is awarded to the author of a work, submitted in French or English, on one of the following subjects: Copyright and the public interest in the developing countries, influence of competition law on copyright, legal status of works created on commission or by a salaried author, collective administration of author's rights, or protection of works created by the use of computers. Authors of any nationality may submit their work which must be unpublished as of the date it is received by the Confederation.

Closing date: 30th June.

Further information from:
General Secretariat
International Confederation of Societies of Authors and Composers
11, rue Keppler
75116 Paris
France

[1081]

INTERNATIONAL CO-OPERATIVE ALLIANCE
Bonow Fund

Study Tour Grants

Purpose: To afford cooperators of developing countries the opportunity to visit cooperatives and other institutions in other developing countries.

Value: Up to £1,000 per Grant, to cover travel and living expenses.

Tenable in developing countries for 2 to 4 weeks.

Eligibility: Open to residents of developing countries. Candidates should generally be between 21 and 40 years of age, have not travelled outside their own country for a study tour in the previous two years, and should be members and/or employees of a cooperative society.

Note: Employers of Grant recipients must guarantee to continue payment of salary during period of the study tour. Recipients will be required to submit a report to the ICA no later than 45 days after completion of the tour.

Inquiries and application forms for persons from Malaysia, Korea, Philippines, India, Pakistan, Thailand, Indonesia, Bangladesh, Sri Lanka and Singapore should write to the *ICA Regional Office, Bonow House, 43 Friends Colony, P.O. Box 3312, New Delhi 110-014,* *India;* persons from Kenya, Tanzania, Uganda, Zambia and Mauritius should write to *ICA Regional Office, P.O. Box 946, Moshi, Tanzania*; interested persons from all other countries should contact the ICI Head Office at the address below.

Grants are awarded by the ICA Cooperative Development Committee which normally meets in February and October of each year.

Not confirmed for 1983.

Address:
International Co-Operative Alliance
11 Upper Grosvenor Street
London
England W1X 9PA

[1082]

INTERNATIONAL COPPER RESEARCH ASSOCIATION, INC.

INCRA Fellowships and Grants-in-Aid

The Association provides funds to institutions for the support of graduate students toward advanced degrees in the field of copper research. Awards are generally for one year, and are renewable until the student earns the degree, providing satisfactory progression of the work is maintained.

Further information from:
INCRA
708 Third Avenue
New York, New York 10017
U.S.A.

[1083]

INTERNATIONAL COUNCIL FOR PHILOSOPHY AND HUMANISTIC STUDIES

Subsidies

On the Council's recommendation Unesco may grant subsidies for two purposes: to cover expenses of meetings with scientific aims, and to cover expenses incurred by the preparation or printing of publications. It is essential that such projects are of a specifically international character, both by way of collaborators or participants and through the interest of the work under consideration, which must not be restricted to any geographical region. Requests are examined every two years at the time of the Council's General Assembly.

Note: All requests for subsidies must be introduced by one of the international scholarly organizations which are members of CIPSH.

Further information from:
Secretary-General
Maison de l'Unesco
1 rue Miollis
75732 Parid Cedex 15
France

[1084]

INTERNATIONAL DENTAL FEDERATION

International Miller Prize: Up to three Prizes, of a medal and diploma, are awarded every five years to candidates who have made the greatest contributions to dental research, clinical dentistry or academic dentistry, or are considered to have raised the status of the profession. Prizewinners, who are selected by an international jury, should be members of the dental profession and nominated by member associations of the Federation.

Georges Villain Prize: One Prize, of a bronze medal, is awarded every five years for outstanding contributions in the fields, alternately, of orthodontics or prosthodontics. Prizewinners, who are selected by an international jury, should be members of the dental profession and nominated by member associations of the Federation.

Jessen Fellowship in Children's Dentistry: One Fellowship, which consists of a travel grant of at least US$1,500, is awarded every five years to a dentist from a developing country. The purpose of the Fellowship is to assist developing countries to improve their dental health services for children by allowing the Fellow to visit another country (or countries) to study its children's dental services. The place and duration of the tenancy of the Fellowship is decided by the Fellow, the host country and the Federation. Candidates should be young members of the dental profession from developing countries. They must be nominated by a member association of the Federation, and the Fellow is then selected by an international jury.

Johnson & Johnson International Preventive Dentistry Awards: Three Awards of US$2,000 each, are offered every three years to dental personnel who have researched, developed and implemented preventive dentistry projects. One Award is given in each of the following categories: community programmes, professional education, and research. Members of the dental profession worldwide may apply.

Further information from:
Executive Director
International Dental Federation
64 Wimpole Street
London
England W1M 8AL

[1085]

INTERNATIONAL EXCHANGE OF YOUNG AGRICULTURISTS

Purpose: To help young farmers and horticulturists to make working visits abroad, to broaden their experience and gain practical knowledge of current husbandry methods.

Scope: Participants spend between three and twelve months on suitable holdings or farms in any of the participating countries (see below) and are paid wages, but participants have to meet traveling expenses.

For United Kingdom participants visiting Canada, the period of tenure is usually for six months, and for visits to the United States, Australia and New Zealand, the period is twelve months.

A group visit is arranged for Europeans in collaboration with the University of Minnesota, and entails eight to nine months' practical farm work on selected farms, followed by a three-month Short Course at the University's Institute of Agriculture. There is an optional six to nine months period during which participants can work anywhere in the United States. Candidates wishing to travel to the United States should apply by 25th October.

Eligibility: Requirements vary with each participating country. Candidates wishing to travel to the United Kingdom must be genuinely employed in agriculture or horticulture, have had at least two years' practical experience, and be between 18 and 26 years of age.

Participating countries: Austria, Belgium, Denmark, Finland, France, Federal Republic of Germany, Iceland, Netherlands, Norway, Poland, Sweden, Switzerland, United Kingdom, and to a limited extent, Australia, Canada, New Zealand, and the United States.

Note: Candidates should apply to the appropriate sponsoring authority in their own country.

United Kingdom address:
United Kingdom Sponsoring Authority for the International Exchange of Young Agriculturists
Agriculture House
London
England SW1X 7NJ

[1086]

INTERNATIONAL EYE FOUNDATION
(U.S.A.)

Fellowships

Purpose: To provide surgical experience while improving eye care in areas of need throughout the world.

Value: Normally a monthly stipend of US$750, plus housing and transportation.

Tenable in Brazil, El Salvador, Honduras, Dominican Republic, Haiti, Puerto Rico, Peru, Ethiopia, Kenya, Malawi, Pakistan and Indonesia, for three months to one year.

Eligibility: Open to suitably qualified persons who have completed their ophthalmology residency and are recommended by their professors. A knowledge of a foreign language is desirable.

Note: Fellowships are offered as vacancies occur. Most positions are filled through participating Eye Institutes who rotate their senior residents through IEF units abroad on a three or four month basis.
Reciprocal Fellowship arrangements are made for nationals in participating countries to study in the United States. Fellowships are usually awarded to persons who have made an outstanding contribution to ophthalmology in their own country who can benefit from further education in their area of specialization.

Further information from:
Society of Eye Surgeons
International Eye Foundation
7801 Norfolk Avenue
Bethesda, Maryland 20814
U.S.A.

[1087]

INTERNATIONAL FEDERATION OF LIBRARY ASSOCIATIONS AND INSTITUTIONS

Martinus Nijhoff Study Grant

Purpose: To afford a teacher of library science from a developing country the opportunity to study a specific subject matter in his field in one or more Western European countries.

Subject: Any branch of library science.

No. offered: One Grant, annually.

Value: 10,000 Dutch guilders, to cover costs of study, board and lodging, and surface study travel within Western Europe. In addition, economy-class air fare is provided between the Grantee's country and the Netherlands. Where there is a climatic difference between the recipient's home country and Europe, a clothing allowance of up to 1,000 Dutch guilders may be applied for.

Tenable in one or more countries in Western Europe for ten to fifteen consecutive weeks.

Eligibility: Candidates must be nationals of countries in which librarianship is in an early stage of development, and be either (a) employed in that country as a teacher at a school for library and/or information science, or at a comparable libarary training institute; or (b) employed outside the teaching field, but in a position to disseminate knowledge of the candidates region by way of lecturing, writing or in-service training. Applicants should be no more than forty years of age on 1st February of the year in which the award is made, and possess an adequate command, both written and verbal, of English, French, German or Dutch.

Note: Application forms, which may be obtained from the address below, must be accompanied by a "Statement of Intent". Actual study should commence within nine months after date on which the Grantee is informed of acceptance. No later than six months after completion of the program, a typewritten report of at least 4,000 words shall be submitted to the Federation.

Closing date: 1st February for applications. Grantees are informed of the Federation's decision in April.

Further information from:
International Federation of Library
  Associations and Institutions
P.O. Box 82128
2508 EC The Hague
Netherlands

[1088]

INTERNATIONAL FEDERATION OF MEDICAL STUDENTS ASSOCIATIONS

Medical Clerkships

Purpose: To provide the opportunity for students of clinical medicine to gain experience abroad during vacations, including attendance at international summer schools.

No. offered: As many as each country is able to supply.

Value: Usually cost of maintenance and tuition, pocket-money being provided in some countries by bilateral agreement.

Tenable in any of the 50 countries represented in the International Federation of Medical Students Associations with either full or corresponding member status.

Eligibility: Open to students of medicine from medical students organizations represented in the Federation. Any nationality and age is acceptable. Further qualifications may be required by the host country.

Note: Candidates should apply in the first instance to the medical student association in their own country, from whom they will receive an application form (for which a fee must be paid) to complete and submit to the association in the country of their choice.

Further information from:
International Federation of Medical
  Students Associations
Liechtensteinstrasse 13
A-1090 Vienna
Austria

[1089]

INTERNATIONAL FEDERATION OF UNIVERSITY WOMEN

Ida Smedley Maclean International Fellowship
A. Vibert Douglas International Fellowship
Queensland International Fellowship

Subjects: Humanities, social sciences, and natural sciences.

Value: Maclean Fellowship: 8,000 Swiss francs; Douglas Fellowship: Can$6,000; Queensland Fellowship: A$5,000.

Tenable in a country other than that in which the candidate was educated or habitually resides, for at least eight months.

Eligibility: Open to women graduates who are members of a national federation or association of university women affiliated to I.F.U.W. At least one year of graduate work must have been completed and candidates must be well started on a research programme.

Further information from:
International Federation of University
  Women
37 Quai Wilson
CH-1201 Geneva
Switzerland

[1090]

INTERNATIONAL FEDERATION OF UNIVERSITY WOMEN

Winifred Cullis Grants
Dorothy Leet Grants

Purpose: To carry out research, obtain specialised training essential to research, or training in new techniques in the humanities, social sciences and natural sciences.

Value: Varies, between 3,000 and 6,000 Swiss francs.

Tenable in any country other than that in which the candidate was educated or habitually resides, for two or three months.

Eligibility: Open to women graduates who are members of a national federation or association of university women affiliated to I.F.U.W. At least one year of graduate study must have been completed. Dorothy Leet Grants are reserved for candidates from developing countries.

Further information from:
International Federation of University Women
37 Quai Wilson
CH-1201 Geneva
Switzerland

[1091]

INTERNATIONAL HARP COMPETITION *(Jerusalem)*

Harpists of any nationality who are no more than 35 years of age may enter the Competition which is held every three years—it will next be held in September 1985.

Prizes: 1st—a grand concert harp from the House of Lyon & Healy, Chicago; 2nd—US$2,000; 3rd—US$1,500; 4th—US$1,000; 5th—US$750; 6th—US$500.

Note: Board and lodging is provided by the Competition Committee. There is a registration fee of US$100.

Closing date: 28th February of the Competition year.

Further information from:
Secretariat
International Harp Competition
P.O. Box 29334
Tel Aviv
Israel

[1092]

INTERNATIONAL HARPISCHORD COMPETITION *(Paris)*

Festival Estival de Paris

Candidates from all countries may enter the Competition, which is held every two years. The next Competition will be held n 1983. The set works include works by d'Anglebert, Han-del, Sweelinck, Scarlatti, Rameau, Baumgartner, L. Couperin, and J.S. Bach. The winner of the first prize will receive FF30,000 and concert engagements; the winner of the second prize will receive FF15,000; the two winners of the third prize and the winner of the Contemporary Music Prize will receive FF10,000 each. Competitors should be no more than 32 years of age.

Closing date: 1st July.

Further information from:
Festival Estival de Paris
Concours International de Clavecin
5, place des Ternes
F-75017 Paris
France

[1093]

INTERNATIONAL INSTITUTE OF ADMINISTRATIVE SCIENCES *(Brussels)*

The Institute receives and assists teachers, civil servants, research workers and others who wish to complete their training by advanced study and personal research in comparative administration. Monetary awards are not made by the Institute.

Further information from:
International Institute of Administrative Sciences
Rue de la Charité 25
B-1040 Brussels
Belgium

[1094]

INTERNATIONAL INSTITUTE FOR DEVELOPMENT, COOPERATION AND LABOUR STUDIES
Afro-Asian Institute—Histadrut Israel

International Study Grants and Scholarships

Courses: Development, cooperation, labour movement, trade unionism and related subjects.

No. offered: 220 Scholarships annually.

Value: US$3,000.

Tenable at the Institute for the duration of the various Courses. Three regular sessions are held each year: two in English (April-July,

August-November); and one in French (December-March). Special shorter Courses at Institute or abroad on request.

Eligibility: Open to nationals of countries in Africa, Asia, the Caribbean and Oceanic regions (elsewhere by special arrangement). All courses are open to both men and women. Applicants must have had considerable experience in development, cooperation or trade unionism, and must be sponsored by a labour organization, trade union, cooperative, institute of higher education, government or international organization.

Note: Candidates should apply through their labour or cooperative college, or through the Israeli diplomatic representative in their country.

Closing dates: 15th March and 15th July for Courses in English; 15th November for Course in French.

Address:
International Institute for Development, Cooperation and Labour Studies
7 Nehardea Street
P.O. Box 16201
Tel Aviv 64235
Israel

[1095]

INTERNATIONAL INSTITUTE FOR EDUCATIONAL PLANNING *(Paris)*

Visiting Fellows Programme

Purpose: To aid the career development of highly qualified persons who already hold responsible positions in teaching and research or in the practice of educational planning.

Value: The Institute is not able to provide fellowships or grants to cover the travel and maintenance of Fellows. Candidates from developing countries are advised to seek United Nations Technical Assistance Fellowships [q.v.] through their government, or fellowship aid directly from their government or from any foreign assistance agency or other appropriate source. Candidates from developed countries are advised to seek support from their government or from any appropriate public or private source.

Tenable at the Institute, usually for one to four months.

Eligibility: Priority is given to (a) well qualified persons who are pursuing or fitting themselves for careers as teachers, researchers or international expert advisers in educational planning; (b) senior planning experts of individual nations.

Candidates must have strong academic qualifications (ordinarily a university first degree or higher in a relevant field such as education, economics or another social science), and a substantial period of practical experience. They must be well recommended by their national authorities (in the case of senior civil servants) or by their University.

Note: Fellows are expected to have a previously acquired general acquaintance with educational planning. While at the Institute they can enrich this general knowledge, but their certain aim is to dig deeply into some particular aspect of special importance to their future work (a list of topics which can be chosen for study is available on request).

Further information from:
Visiting Fellows Programme
International Institute for Educational Planning
7-9 rue Eugène-Delacroix
75016 Paris
France

[1096]

INTERNATIONAL INSTITUTE FOR EDUCATIONAL PLANNING *(Paris)*

Advanced Training Programme for Educational Planning Specialists

Subjects: Theoretical and practical aspects of the planning, implementation and evaluation of educational development programmes.

Tenable at the Institute in Paris and within and outside France for the purpose of studying developments in educational planning related to important components of the training programme. The Programme usually lasts from 15th September to 31st May.

Eligibility: All applicants are required to meet the following conditions: (a) a university degree or its equivalent, with a strong academic record. Preference is given to candidates with graduate training in a field appropriate to educational planning and development; (b) at least two years of relevant professional experience in administrative research or teaching roles related to the problems of educational planning and development; (c) previous training in education planning. Preference is given to candidates who have undergone training at a Unesco Regional Education Office; (d) written and spoken fluency in either French or English; (e) candidates must supply the Institute with a written undertaking that they intend to pursue a career in educational planning or related fields upon the completion of the Programme; and (f) favourable references.

Note: The Institute is not in a position to offer fellowships covering travel and maintenance. Thus, a participant or his sponsor must meet these costs directly or, alternatively, secure a fellowship from some appropriate source. The Institute's admission decision is independent of a candidate's prospects for funding, but it will assist successful applicants in identifying possible sources of fellowship support.

In seeking highly-qualified candidates for its Training Programme, the Institute invites nominations from all the member states of Unesco.

Closing date: 31st March.

Further information from:
Advanced Training Programme
International Institute for Educational
 Planning
7-9 Rue Eugène-Delacroix
75016 Paris
France

[1097]

INTERNATIONAL INSTITUTE FOR GEOTHERMAL RESEARCH *(Pisa)*

Scholarships for Courses

Course: Geothermics.

No. offered: About fifteen places for each Course.

Value: 500,000 lire per month plus return travel costs.

Tenable at the Institute for ten months (February to December).

Eligibility: Open to geologists, geophysicists, and chemists who possess a university degree or the equivalent and wish to undertake advanced training in geothermics. The course is open in alternative years to all member countries of UNESCO (1984, 1986) and to citizens of the Latin-American countries only (1983, 1985). Instruction is accordingly in English or Spanish.

Note: The Course is organized by the Institute under the auspices of the Italian National Research Council, the Italian Ministry of Foreign Affairs, and Unesco.

Closing date: 31st August.

Further information from:
Instituto Internazionale per le Ricerche
 Geotermiche
Via del Buongusto 1
56100 Pisa
Italy

[1098]

INTERNATIONAL INSTITUTE FOR LABOUR STUDIES *(Geneva)*

Course Fellowships

Purpose: To provide leadership training for participants engaged in the formulation or implementation of labour and social policy and to increase their capacity for constructive decision-making.

No. offered: Approximately 27 Fellowships.

Value: Round trip air travel between Geneva and the country of residence plus basic living expenses in Geneva during the period of the course.

Tenable in Geneva for six or seven weeks; not renewable.

Eligibility: Open to nationals of all countries between the ages of 25 and 40 who hold a position of responsibility in the area of social policy. Applicants must be sponsored by governments, employers' organisations, trade unions or universities or other institutions specialising in labor matters. Knowledge of the working language of the course (French, English or Spanish on a rotation basis) is required.

Further information from:
Director
International Institute for Labour Studies
Case Postale 6
CH-1211 Geneva 22
Switzerland

[1099]

INTERNATIONAL INSTITUTE FOR POPULATION STUDIES *(Bombay)*

Fellowships for Courses

Subject: Demography/population studies.

No. offered: Approximately 15 Fellowships annually.

Value: A monthly stipend of 2800 rupees, plus 500 rupees per month for room and board, and return air fare.

Tenable for one year at the Institute; renewable.

Eligibility: Open to nationals of Asian and the Pacific countries who hold an appropriate graduate degree. Preference is given to candidates with training in demography, social science or statistics.

Note: Since the Fellowships are awarded by the United Nations, application should be made through the UN representative in the candidate's own country.

Closing date: May.

Further information from:
Dr. K. Srinivasan, Director
International Institute for Population Studies
Govandi Station Road, Deonar
Bombay-400088
India

[1100]

INTERNATIONAL INSTITUTE OF SEISMOLOGY AND EARTHQUAKE ENGINEERING *(Tsukuba, Japan)*

Scholarships for Courses

No. offered: 20-22 places on the Regular Course; four places on the Advanced Course.

Value: Cost of tuition, maintenance, etc.

Tenable at the Institute for the duration of the Course: one year for the Regular Course; three to six months for the Advanced Course.

Eligibility: Open to nationals of African, Asian, Latin American, and Middle Eastern countries who are between 25 and 35 years of age. Candidates for the Regular Course should have a bachelor's degree or equivalent; candidates for the Advanced Course should have a master's degree or equivalent and should wish to undertake mainly research work. Instruction is in English.

Not confirmed for 1983.

Further information from:
International Institute of Seismology and Earthquake Engineering
1, Tatehara, Ohomachi, Tsukuba-gun
Ibaraki Prefecture
Japan

[1101]

INTERNATIONAL INSTITUTE OF TROPICAL AGRICULTURE *(Ibadan, Nigeria)*

Research Scholarships—M.Sc. Degree
Research Fellowships—Ph.D. Degree

Purpose: To enable postgraduate degree candidates to conduct degree-related research in the humid tropics.

Subjects: Agricultural economics, agricultural engineering, agroclimatology, agronomy, biochemistry, crop cultivation, entomology, farm mechanization, nematology, plant breeding, plant pathology, plant physiology and soil microbiology sciences.

No. offered: Variable.

Value: US$6,000 per annum: includes board and lodging, laundry, limited local transportation, travel to and from the Institute, medical accident insurance and a monthly stipend of US$100 per month for personal expenses and all research costs.

Tenable at the Institute for six months to one year (Research Scholars) and one to two years (Research Fellows).

Eligibility: Candidates should be registered for a postgraduate degree at the university (generally a faculty of agriculture).

Note: Applications for admission to the Institute's training program may be submitted by individuals. However, it is expected that most Scholars and Fellows will be sponsored by institutions or organizations and government agencies. Applications must be supported by a letter from the candidate's adviser, and the candidate, adviser and university must agree to accept a scientist from the Institute as supervisor of research.

Further information from:
Training Office
International Institute of Tropical
  Agriculture
Oyo Road, PMB 5320
Ibadan
Nigeria

[1102]

INTERNATIONAL INSTITUTE OF TROPICAL AGRICULTURE *(Ibadan, Nigeria)*

Postdoctoral Fellowships

Purpose: To increase and strengthen the body of trained agricultural scientists available to work on problems of food crop production in the tropics.

Subjects: Agricultural economics, agricultual engineering, agroclimatology, agronomy, biochemistry, crop cultivation, entomology, farm mechanization, nematology, plant breeding, plant pathology, plant physiology and soil microbiology sciences.

No. offered: Thirty Fellowships annually.

Value: US$1,283.33 per month, travel from the Fellow's home to the Institute, use of a car, and subsidized housing.

Tenable for one year at the Institute; renewable for one further year.

Eligibility: Open to recent graduates with a Ph.D. degree or the equivalent.

Further information from:
Training Office
International Institute of Tropical
  Agriculture
Oyo Road, PMB 5320
Ibadan
Nigeria

[1103]

INTERNATIONAL LABORATORY FOR RESEARCH ON ANIMAL DISEASES *(Nairobi)*

Postdoctoral Fellowships and Visiting Scientists Programs

Subjects: Career and training opportunities in animal diseases and immunology, especially in the field of parasitic diseases in Africa, including trypanosomiasis and theileriasis.

Value: Varies. Normally established investigators concurrently hold sabbatical or other leave salary.

Tenable at ILRAD, normally for one year (for established investigators) or for two years (for recent recipients of doctoral degrees).

Eligibility: Open to suitably qualified recent or advanced researchers in the field of animal parasitic diseases in Africa.

Note: Senior Visiting Scientists often pursue their own research within ILRAD's framework; Fellows and younger Visitors are usually assigned to ILRAD projects.

Further information from:
Director
International Laboratory for Research on
  Animal Diseases
P.O. Box 30709
Nairobi
Kenya

[1104]

INTERNATIONAL LABOUR ORGANISATION
International Centre for Advanced Technical and Vocational Training *(Turin)*

ILO Fellowship Programme

General information: The ILO Fellowship Programme is part of a wider programme of technical cooperation for the economic and social progress of developing countries, which enables governments requesting this type of assistance to send selected individuals abroad to receive education or training at an international level in all fields within the competence of the ILO. It is a joint undertaking in which the ILO, the Fellow, his government and the host government assume definite responsibilities.

The ILO Fellowship Programme and Study Grants are managed on behalf of the ILO by the International Centre for Advanced Technical and Vocational Training. Most programmes are tailor-made to suit the specific training needs of the country, institution or private firm sponsoring the training. Group training schemes normally include sessions devoted to technicological upgrading and training methodology, complemented by practical study in specific undertakings at specialized trainers institutions. Individual programmes are also organized.

(a) *Fellowships* may be awarded either under the ILO Regular Programme or under the United Nations' Development Programme (see) or under multibilateral arrangements with a number of donor countries. In the majority of cases, Fellowships are part of national technical cooperation projects involving expert assistance, or are requested by governments within the overall framework of national long-term development plans.

As Fellowships are intended for advanced training abroad, candidates are required to have had practical experience in their subject of study. Their position, qualifications and experience should be such as to enable them to make effective use of the knowledge to be acquired abroad. They should enjoy good health and be proficient in language which can be used for the proposed studies.

The period of study is usually from three to six months. The choice of the host country or countries is determined by the availability of training facilities and the candidate's linguistic qualifications.

Fellowships provide the cost of international travel, a monthly subsistence allowance and tuition fees in addition to certain specified allowances towards travel within the host country or countries and purchase of publications.

(b) *Study Grants* are intended for participation in seminars, study tours and training courses organised by the ILO at the request of governments. They are usually arranged on a regional basis and intended to enable participants from a given group of countries with similar problems to discuss these problems under the guidance of international experts. Lectures and field visits are included.

Study Grants provide for the cost of travel to and from the host country and a subsistence allowance.

Note: Candidates for awards are nominated by national authorities who submit the applications. Requests from individuals are not entertained.

Further information from:
International Centre for Advanced Technical and Vocational Training
Fellowship Management Section
Via Ventimiglia 201
10127 Turin
Italy

[1105]

INTERNATIONAL LEAD ZINC RESEARCH ORGANIZATION, INC.

Postgraduate, Predoctoral, Postdoctoral, Research and Project Fellowships

Subjects: Zinc die casting; process improvement; finishing; cadmium; lead and zinc chemicals; paints and pigments; ceramics; batteries; cable sheathing; composites.

No. offered: Six to ten.

Value: Generally from US$8,000 to US$15,000 per annum, paid quarterly or full amount in advance.

Tenable at various universities for two to three years, renewable.

Eligibility: There are no other limitations except for academic qualifications in the chosen area.

Note: Fellowships are offered as vacancies occur, or as the opportunity arises.

Closing date: 1st June for Fellowships commencing the following year.

Further information from:
Dr. S.F. Radtke
International Lead Zinc Research Organization, Inc.
292 Madison Avenue
New York, New York 10017
U.S.A.

[1106]

INTERNATIONAL LEAGUE OF ANTIQUARIAN BOOKSELLERS

I.L.A.B. Prize for Bibliography

The triennial Prize of US$1,000 is given to the author of the best work published or unpublished, of learned bibliography or of research into the history of the book or of typography, and books of general interest on the subject. The competition is open, without restriction, but only entries submitted in accordance with these conditions are considered. Entries must be submitted in a language which is universally used. A work already published is eligible only if its publication occurred within the three years immediately preceding the closing date for submission, or if it has an imprint bearing a date within those three years. Entries in the form of a specialised catalogue of one or more books destined for sale are not eligible, nor periodicals or public library catalogues. Two copies of each work whether published or unpublished must be deposited at the office of the Secreary at the very latest sixteen months before date of award. The next award will be made in 1985.

Further information from:
Secretary, I.L.A.B. Prize
International League of Antiquarian Booksellers
Rathenaustr. 21
D-7000 Stuttgart 1
West Germany

[1107]

INTERNATIONAL MARITIME ORGANIZATION

Fellowships and Training Awards

Subjects: Naval architecture, shipbuilding, navigational aids, sea-keeping operations, port operations, marine engineering, marine electronics, marine surveying procedures, fire-fighting, oil pollution control.

Value: A monthly allowance based on stipend rates of the United Nations Development Programme.

Tenable for the duration of the approved studies in countries where suitable facilities exist (Fellowships).

Eligibility: Open to suitably qualified nationals of developing countries which are member states of the United Nations.

Note: Application should be made through the appropriate government department in the candidate's own country to the local resident representative of the United Nations Development Programme. Nomination forms are available from local United Nations offices.

Further information from:
International Maritime Organization
101-104 Piccadilly
London
England W1V 0AE

[1108]

INTERNATIONAL MONETARY FUND INSTITUTE *(Washington, D.C.)*

Training Courses

The Institute organizes a series of Courses each year for the benefit of officials from Fund member countries, especially developing ones, with a professional interest and some experience in the subject matter of the specific Course that they wish to follow. The aim of these Courses is to enable participants to discharge their responsibilities more effectively upon their return to their home countries, and to acquaint them with Fund procedures and policies.

Subject and duration of Courses: Financial analysis and policy—20 weeks; Techniques of Economic Analysis—8 weeks; Financial Programming and Policy—12 weeks; balance of payments methodology—8 weeks; public finance—10 weeks; Government Finance Statistics—8 weeks.

Value: To include travel costs to and from Washington, D.C., free housing accommodation, and a living allowance of US$25 per day.

Eligibility: Open to persons employed in ministries of finance or economy, central banks and similar public agencies of Fund member countries. Candidates must be sponsored by the senior official thereof, who must certify that the candidate, if accepted, will receive leave of absence with regular pay for the duration of the Course, and upon completion, will be employed in present position or in one of equal or greater responsibility.

Note: All Courses are given in English, French and Spanish, but not necessarily in all three languages every year.

Further information from:
Director
International Monetary Fund Institute
Washington, D.C. 20431
U.S.A.

[1109]

INTERNATIONAL MUSIC COMPETITION
(Athens)

Prizes

Various monetary Prizes are offered in the Competition which is held in Athens in March/April of odd-numbered years. Pianists and singers of any nationality are eligible to apply for the 1983 Competition (disciplines may vary in subsequent years). Male singers should be no more than 32 years of age; female singers and pianists should be no more than 30 years of age.

Further information from:
International Music Competition
Atheneum International Cultural Centre
36a Kefallinias Street
Athens 802
Greece

[1110]

INTERNATIONAL MUSIC COMPETITION
(Budapest)

A total amount of 100,000 forints is offered in each category of the Competition, held annually in September. Categories vary annually.

Closing date: 1st May.

Further information from:
Secretariat
International Music Competition
Vörösmarty tér 1
P.O.B. 80
H-1366 Budapest 5
Hungary

[1111]

INTERNATIONAL MUSIC COMPETITION OF THE BROADCASTING CORPORATIONS OF THE FEDERAL REPUBLIC OF GERMANY

Three Prizes per category are offered in the annual Competition held in Munich in September. The Prizes' value ranges from DM4,000 to DM18,000. Musicians of any nationality may apply. Solo instrumentalists should be aged between 17 and 30; vocalists between 20 and 30. Categories for 1983: piano, viola, horn, duo violin-piano, harp; for 1984: voice, violin, harpiscord, flute, duo cello-piano; for 1985: piano, violincello, organ, bassoon, percussion.

Note: There is an entry fee of DM50 for all competitors.

Closing date: 1st July.

Further information from:
Secretariat
International Music Competition
Rundfunkplatz 1
D-8000 Munich 2
West Germany

[1112]

INTERNATIONAL MUSIC COMPETITION
(Rio de Janeiro)
Sociedade Brasileira de Realizacões Artístico-Culturais

Singers of any nationality who are not more than 32 years of age may enter the Competition, held 10th June to 20th June in odd-numbered years at the Opera House and Concert Hall of Rio de Janeiro.

First prize—*US*$2,500; Second prize—*US*$2,000; Third and Fourth prizes—*US*$1,000 each. In addition, a Gold Medal is offered for the best interpretation of a work by Villa-Lobos. Winners are invited to perform in concerts in other cities of Brazil and abroad.

Closing date: 30th December of the year preceding the Competition.

Further information from:
International Music Competition
SBRAC
Avenida Franklin Roosevelt 23, Sala 310
Rio de Janeiro
Brazil

[1113]

INTERNATIONAL ORGANIZATION AGAINST TRACHOMA

Chibret Gold Medal

The Medal, worth FF8,000, is awarded annually at the International Congress of Ophthalmology to honor original work on conjunctive diseases, trachoma, and tropical and subtropical eye diseases. Entries should be written in French or English and should not exceed thirty typed pages.

Further information from:
Secretary
Ophthalmology Clinic
International Organization against
 Trachoma
H.I.A. Ste-Anne
83800 Toulon Naval
France

[1114]

INTERNATIONAL ORGANIZATION OF JOURNALISTS

The Organization annually offers three Prizes of US$500 each in three categories: (a) for professional activity which notably contributes, in the spirit of the United Nations Charter, to the maintenance of peace throughout the world and to the development of friendly relations among peoples; (b) for outstanding activity in the field of theory of the science of journalism; (c) for an important contribution to the development of cooperation and unity among journalists. Prizes are awarded each year to individuals or to editorial collectives.

Further information from:
General Secretariat
International Organization of Journalists
Parizska 9
10101 Prague
Czechoslovakia

[1115]

INTERNATIONAL P.E.N. SCOTTISH CENTRE

Frederick Niven Award

The Award of £100 is offered every third year to writers of Scottish birth who have written a novel published during the appropriate three year period. There are no restrictions as to age or sex. Previous award winners are ineligible. Entries for the next Award must be submitted by publishers by 31st July 1983.

Further information from:
Honorary Secretary
International P.E.N. Scottish Centre
18 Crown Terrace
Glasgow
Scotland G12 9ES

[1116]

INTERNATIONAL PRIZE FOR ARCHITECTURE
Belgian National Housing Institute

A Prize of 200,000 Belgian francs may be awarded for either a single family house or for an apartment building, taking into consideration the qualities presented by the design and which comply, notably, with present considerations concerning aesthetic appeal, disposition and equipment of the premises, acoustic and thermal insulation, choice and use of materials as well as cost price.

Another Prize of 200,000 Belgian francs may be awarded either for a complex of single-family houses, or a complex of apartment buildings, or for a mixed complex of single-family houses and apartment buildings, the conception of which is liable to bring about progress in rational use of land, the layout and aesthetics of the buildings, the layout of roads and pedestrian paths, private or community open spaces, playgrounds as well as other community facilities. The complex must both preserve the intimacy of the inhabitants' private life and favour the burgeoning and development of social relations among them.

Note: At their discretion, the Institute may award the Prizes' total of 400,000 Belgian francs in a different manner. In the first instance, interested architects should obtain

the description brochure and application information from:
Secretary General
Belgian National Housing Institute
International Prize for Architecture
Boulevard St.-Lazare 10
1030 Brussels
Belgium

[1117]

INTERNATIONAL READING ASSOCIATION

Annual Print Media Award: US$500 is presented annually in recognition of outstanding reporting in newspapers, magazines and wire services. Candidates must be professional journalists, and entries must have appeared during the calendar year for which the Award is made. Further information is available from *Dr. Donald Mass, Education Department, California Polytechnic State University, San Luis Obispo, California 93407. Closing date:* 15th January.

Albert J. Harris Award: A monetary Award of an unspecified amount is given annually for an outstanding contribution to the diagnosis and remediation of reading or learning disabilities. Publications which have appeared in a professional journal or monograph during the twelve month period beginning 1st June of the year prior to that for which the Award is given, are eligible. Seven copies of each publication should be submitted to *Dr. Jayne DeLawter, 6185 Orchard Station Road, Sebastopol, California 95472. Closing date:* 15th October.

IRA Children's Book Award: US$1,000 is given annually for a first or second book, either fiction or nonfiction, by an author of any nationality who shows unusual promise in the children's book field. Books submitted must be copyrighted during the calendar year for which the Award is made. This Award is sponsored by the *Institute for Reading Research*. Seven copies of each book should be submitted to *Mrs. Zena Sutherland, 1418 East 57th Street, Chicago, Illinois 60637. Closing date:* 1st December.

Institute for Reading Research Fellowship: US$1,000 is awarded annually to a young researcher outside the United States or Canada who has shown exceptional promise in reading research, and deserves encouragement to continue working in the field of reading. Awards are based on completed research which must not have been done at American or Canadian institutions. Application forms are available from *Dr. Hal Seaton, Reading Department, 309 Aderhold Building, University of Georgia, Athens, Georgia 30602. Closing date:* 15th October.

Nila Banton Smith Award: US$1,500 is presented annually to a classroom teacher or reading specialist who has made an outstanding contribution in helping students to become more proficient readers of content instructional materials. Applicants must be actively teaching students in the 1st to 12th grade range, and have demonstrated excellence at the classroom level in addition to either the building or district level. This Award is sponsored by *Prentice-Hall, Educational Book Division*. Nomination forms may be obtained from, and returned to *Dr. Margaret M. Griffin, Box 23029, TWU Station, Texas Woman's University, Denton, Texas 76204. Closing date:* 1st January.

Note: The IRA also makes several other awards which carry no monetary value.

Further information from:
International Reading Association
800 Barksdale Road
Newark, Delaware 19711
U.S.A.

[1118]

INTERNATIONAL RESEARCH AND EXCHANGES BOARD (U.S.A.)

Exchange Program with Eastern Europe: Bulgaria, Czechoslovakia, German Democratic Republic, Hungary, Poland, Romania, and Yugoslavia.

Purpose: To encourage the development of a scholarly interest among United States university professors and Ph.D. candidates in all disciplines, and especially in the contemporary and historical cultures in the exchange countries; to promote the interchange of ideas and experience between United States scholars and their overseas colleagues; and to provide opportunities for foreign scholars to receive training and to conduct research at academic institutions in the United States.

Value: The host country normally provides:

cost of instruction and research expenses, preliminary language training (except for German Democratic Republic), housing for participants and their families (except for Yugoslavia), medical and dental care for the participants (and in most cases for their families as well), a monthly stipend in the local currency, and a book and (in most cases), microfilm allowance.

IREX provides domestic and international transportation and an internal travel allowance for the participant; one-half of domestic and international transport costs for accompanying family members for participant stays of at least one semester, or for married graduate students a family allowance, determined by the number of dependents; for salaried participants, a partial stipend in lieu of salary less the value of housing and other benefits received from the host country (other than for visits taking place either primarily or entirely during June through August).

Tenable at institutions of higher learning in any of the above-named countries, for periods of at least two months (three months in Yugoslavia). Stays in the German Democratic Republic do not normally exceed six months.

Eligibility: Open to United States citizens who are affiliated full-time with a college, university or other educational institution in North America. Candidates must be faculty members or advanced doctoral candidates who will have completed all requirements for the Ph.D. degree except the thesis by the time of participation. All candidates will be expected to have mastery of the language of the host country sufficient for the purposes of their research and study.

Note: Exchange applicants are required, if eligible, to apply simultaneously for grants awarded under the Fulbright-Hays Act.

Participants may apply to more than one exchange program if their research so requires. Individuals wishing to divide their period between two or, in exceptional cases, more than two countries should indicate their intention on the application, available from the address below.

Closing date: 1st November.

Further information from:
International Research and Exchanges Board
655 Third Avenue
New York, New York 10017
U.S.A.

[1119]

INTERNATIONAL RESEARCH AND EXCHANGES BOARD *(U.S.A.)*

Exchange Program with the U.S.S.R.

Purpose: See preceding entry.

1. *Exchange with the U.S.S.R. Ministry of Higher and Specialized Secondary Education:* (a) exchange of graduate students and young faculty members (at least 40 United States participants annually); (b) exchange of senior research scholars (at least 10 United States participants annually); (c) summer exchange of language teachers (at least 35 United States teachers of Russian).

2. *American Council of Learned Societies—Soviet Academy of Sciences Exchange.* The agreement provides for 60 man-months of individual research each year, by senior American scholars in the humanities and social sciences. Visits are for a duration of two to ten months.

Value: The host country provides cost of instruction and research expenses (1c), housing for the participants (in all cases) and for accompanying family members (1c), medical care for the participants (1a,b,c), dental care for the participants (1a,b), a monthly or other allowance (in all cases), and internal travel directly related to research (2).

IREX provides domestic and international transportation (in all cases), one half domestic and international transportation for accompanying family members staying for at least one semester (1a), a small monthly maintenance allowance (1a), a stipend for married graduate students determined by the number of dependents (1a), a stipend for salaried participants in lieu of salary less the value of housing and other benefits received from the host country (1a,b), a stipend in lieu of salary less the value benefit from the host country (2). Stipends are adjusted to take into account such other resources as fellowships, etc.

Tenable at Institutions under the jurisdiction

of the Ministry, for one semester or an academic year (1a); for a period of between three to six months (1b); at Moscow State University for approximately eight weeks (1c); at Institutions under the jurisdiction of the Soviet Academy of Sciences for two to ten months (2).

Eligibility: See the general eligibility requirements in first IREX entry.

Special limitations: (1a) senior faculty, i.e., associate and full professors and those 40 years of age or over are not eligible; (1b) senior faculty status, i.e., associate or full professorship is preferred, though assistant professors may apply; (1c) full-time employment as a teacher of Russian language at the college or secondary school level (teaching assistants with equivalent experience at the college level who demonstrate special competence may apply); (2) senior scholar status and distinction in a discipline of the social sciences or humanities are required (in exceptional cases, applications from assistant professors will be accepted).

Note: Application forms are available from the address below.

Closing date: (1a) 1st November; (1b) 1st November; (1c) 15th January; (2) 1st November.

Further information from:
International Research and Exchanges Board
655 Third Avenue
New York, New York 10017
U.S.A.

[1120]

INTERNATIONAL RESEARCH AND EXCHANGES BOARD *(U.S.A.)*

Developmental Fellowships

Purpose: To provide linguistic preparation and area training in selected fields underrepresented in the Eastern Europe and Soviet Exchange Programs.

Subjects: Social sciences and humanities, especially archaeology, anthropology, business, economics, geography, demography, law, musicology, political science, psychology, and sociology for Disciplinary Fellowships; minority language training for Fellowships for the Study of Soviet Nationalities.

No. offered: Variable; limited.

Value: Applicants may apply for academic tuition; language training allowance for intensive summer work, academic year work, or tutoring; and stipend support. The extent of the award's value is determined by the selection committee.

Tenable for periods from three to fifteen months at appropriate study centers.

Eligibility: Open to United States citizens planning doctoral dissertations or research topics requiring access to materials available through exchange programs. Fellows are expected to apply to the appropriate IREX exchange program the following year.

Special limitations: Applicants for Disciplinary Fellowships should not already be in the field of Soviet and East European studies. Applicants for Fellowships for the Study of Soviet Nationalities should have strong preparation in Soviet area studies but need additional training in a minority language.

Note: Preliminary inquiries are advised.

Closing date: 15th March.

Further information from:
International Research and Exchanges Board
655 Third Avenue
New York, New York 10017
U.S.A.

[1121]

INTERNATIONAL RESEARCH AND EXCHANGES BOARD *(U.S.A.)*

Slavonic Studies Seminar Fellowships

Purpose: To enable scholars wishing to improve their knowledge of the Bulgarian language to attend the Slavonic Studies Seminar in Bulgaria.

No. offered: Up to ten Fellowships annually.

Value: Lodgings, tuition expenses and other local costs are covered by the Bulgarian State Committee for Science, Technical Progress.

IREX provides roundtrip transportation for the Scholar.

Tenable during August at Kliment Okhridski University, Sofia and at Kiril and Methodius Universities in Veleko Turnovo.

Eligibility: Open to United States citizens who should normally be full-time faculty or graduate student members of a North American university or college.

Closing date: 1st December.

Further information from:
International Research and Exchanges Board
655 Third Avenue
New York, New York 10017
U.S.A.

[1122]

INTERNATIONAL RESEARCH AND EXCHANGES BOARD *(U.S.A.)*

Grants for Collaborative Activities and New Exchanges

IREX makes a very limited number of grants to encourage the development of individual and institutional collaboration and exchange in the social sciences and humanities involving scholars from the United States, Eastern Europe, the U.S.S.R., as well as Albania, and Mongolia. Such undertakings as bilateral and multinational symposia, collaborative and parallel research, joint publications, exchanges of data, comparative surveys, and the like, as well as brief visits necessary in the planning of such projects, will be considered. Projects should involve sums of less than US$10,000 and no more than one year of financial support. Grants normally average less than US$2,000.

Note: Only proposals which give evidence of exceptional merit, feasibility, and substantial prior planning and consultation are considered. Grants are not available to support individual study, research, or attendance at scheduled scholarly conferences and meetings.
Recipients are responsible for all visa and travel arrangements.

Closing dates: 31st January; 30th April; 31st October. Decisions will be announced approximately one month after the respective deadlines.

Further information from:
Executive Director
International Research and Exchanges Board
655 Third Avenue
New York, New York 10017
U.S.A.

[1123]

INTERNATIONAL RESEARCH AND EXCHANGES BOARD *(U.S.A.)*

Travel Grants for Senior Scholars in the Social Sciences and Humanities

A very limited number of travel grants are made available to facilitate communication between prominent American scholars in the social sciences and humanities and their colleagues in the countries with which IREX conducts exchanges, as well as in Albania and Mongolia.

Value: Grants to American applicants will consist of round-trip economy air transportation only.

Tenable for short visits, normally less than two months, and not for individual research.

Eligibility: Applicants who have received a formal invitation from an appropriate institution in one of these countries, such as the Academy of Sciences or one of its institutes. Grants are intended for support of short visits (normally less than two months) for the purposes of consultation and/or lecturing.

Note: In order to encourage wider participation in East-West scholarly contacts, preference will normally be given to scholars outside the field of Soviet and East European studies.
Recipients are responsible for all visa travel arrangements.

Closing dates: 31st January; 30th April; 31st October. Decisions will be announced approximately one month after the respective deadlines.

Further information from:
　Executive Director
　International Research and Exchanges Board
　655 Third Avenue
　New York, New York 10017
　U.S.A.

[1124]

INTERNATIONAL RICE RESEARCH INSTITUTE *(Philippines)*

Scholarships, Fellowships and Course Trainees

Purpose: To enable young rice scientists from the developing countries to receive training in areas related to rice culture.

Subjects: Agronomy, plant breeding and genetics, soil chemistry, soil microbiology, plant pathology, entomology, plant physiology, biochemistry, cereal chemistry, agricultural engineering, agricultural economics, communication and extension, cropping systems, irrigation and water management and statistics.

No. offered: Approximately 126 research oriented Scholarships/Fellowships, and 96 formal training course Trainees annually.

Value: Awards cover round-trip economy air fare, pre- and post-departure expenses, shipping, a stipend, board and lodging, laundry service, medical and accident insurance, travel in the Philippines, books, and university fees where applicable, other training overhead costs.

Tenable at the Institute, Los Baños, Laguna, Philippines for periods ranging from six months to two years.

Eligibility: Open to persons possessing at least a B.S. degree (at least an M.S. degree for Fellowships and a Ph.D. degree for Postdoctoral Fellowships), who are staff members of a research or educational institution concerned with rice and rice based cropping systems. Candidates should be recommended by the institution or organization where they are employed and they must be assured a leave-of-absence from their employment during the period of training, and a position on their return, they should also be in excellent physical and mental health.

Note: While undergoing training, Scholarship holders may pursue graduate studies at the College of Agriculture, University of the Philippines at Los Baños.

Further information from:
　Director Research Training and Coordination
　International Rice Research Institute
　P.O. Box 933
　Manila
　Philippines

[1125]

INTERNATIONAL ROAD FEDERATION

Fellowships

Purpose: To promote the development of highways and highway transportation.

Value: US$4,000. This is applied towards the entire cost of a two week pre-academic program of seminars and observation, and partial costs of one academic year of graduate study. If, after the payment of tuition and fees, there remains a credit balance in the Fellowship, the excess will be transmitted to the award holder. Conversely, any debit must be covered by the Fellow from funds made available to him by his sponsor.

Tenable for one academic year (nine months) at a United States university and a pre-academic study tour (two weeks).

Eligibility: Open to graduate civil engineers, from outside the United States, preferably with some experience in a governmental agency, who possesses a good working knowledge of the English language.

Note: The Fellowship does not cover the cost of board and lodging or transportation expenses.
　Candidates should apply to their national Ministry of Public Works or appropriate equivalent, or to:
　International Road Federation
　1023 Washington Building
　Washington, D.C. 20005
　U.S.A.

[1126]

INTERNATIONAL SINGING COMPETITION
(s'Hertogenbosch, Netherlands)

A First Prize of 3,000 florins and Second Prize of 1,000 florins are offered for each voice category in the annual Competition which is usually held in August/September. Other prizes, varying from 1,000 florins to 3,000 florins are offered for outstanding interpretations of operatic arias, lieder and modern Dutch compositions. Vocalists of any nationality who are under 32 years of age may apply.

Closing date: 15th July.

Further information from:
Secretariat
International Singing Competition
P.B. 1225
5200 BG s'Hertogenbosch
Netherlands

[1127]

INTERNATIONAL SINGING COMPETITION *(Toulouse)*

Six Prizes of varying amounts are awarded in competition annually, to singers of opera, comic-opera, oratorios, songs and melodies. Prizes are as follows: Two First prizes of FF20,000 each; two Second prizes of FF7,500 eah; two Third prizes of FF4,000 each. The Competition, held for one week, usually in October, is open to singers of any nationality who are between the ages of 18 and 33.

Closing date: 15th September.

Further information from:
Gerald Van Ham
Concours International de Chant
Theatre du Capitole
Place du Capitole
31000 Toulouse
France

[1128]

INTERNATIONAL SOCIETY OF ARBORICULTURE

Grants

Purpose: To further research relating to arboriculture.

No. offered: One to ten Grants annually.

Value: Between US$500 and US$1,000.

Tenable for twelve months; renewable to a maximum of two years.

Eligibility: Open to qualified individuals in the United States and other countries who hold a B.Sc. degree and are planning to work at either the M.S. or Ph.D. degree level in the arboricultural research field.

Note: The prospective applicant's major professor at the institution where the applicant intends to work on an advanced degree should initiate the request for research project support.

Further information from:
Dr. Francis H. Holmes, Research
   Committee Chairman
International Society of Arboriculture
University of Massachusetts
Shade Tree Laboratories
Amherst, Massachusetts 01003
U.S.A.

[1129]

INTERNATIONAL SOCIETY FOR PHOTOGRAMMETRY

Otto von Gruber Award

The Award of 500 Dutch florins is presented every four years to promote the application of photogrammetric techniques. The recipient must have written an article of outstanding merit on the subjects of photogrammetry or photo-interpretation, be a graduate of a recognized university, in photogrammetry or photo-interpretation, have completed a post-doctoral course in either of these subjects, or be a graduate from the International Training Centre for Aerial Survey at Delft.

To further encourage the advancement of photogrammetry, the Society awards the *Brock Gold Medal* every four years for an outstanding landmark in the evolution of photogrammetry.

Each Award is presented at the Society's quadrennial Congress.

Further information from:
International Society for Photogrammetry
Dr. F.J. Doyle
U.S. Geological Survey 516
Reston, Virginia 22092
U.S.A.

[1130]

INTERNATIONAL STATISTICAL EDUCATION CENTRE *(Calcutta)*

Fellowships

Courses: Theoretical and applied statistics.

No. offered: Approximately 20 Fellowships annually.

Value: 10,000-12,000 Indian rupees. This excludes any transportation payments to and from India.

Tenable for the duration of the Regular Course (ten months) at the Indian Statistical Institute in Calcutta.

Eligibility: Open to nationals of Middle Eastern, South and South-East Asian, Far Eastern and African Commonwealth countries. Candidates should be officials with experience in statistical work, teachers and research workers in statistics, or officials in non-statistical fields who need to acquire a knowledge of statistics. Participants should preferably have a bachelor's degree with specialization in mathematics. All applicants must be sponsored by their governments.

Note: Instruction in English.
Fellowships are also awarded to a few trainees attending Special Courses on such subjects as sample surveys, economic statistics, econometrics, and economic planning, lasting three months to a year.
Fellowships are also available for three to six months for visiting senior statisticians. Applications should be made in duplicate.

Further information from:
Director, Permanent Office
International Statistical Education Centre
428 Prinses Beatrixlaan
Voorburg
Netherlands

[1131]

INTERNATIONAL STRING QUARTET COMPETITION *(Portsmouth, England)*

Prizes

Prizes are offered in the Competition which is held in Portsmouth from time to time. Prize amounts in 1982 were: 1st—£4,500; 2nd—£3,000; 3rd—£1,500; 4th—£1,200; 5th—£750; and special awards. The total ages of competing quartets may not exceed 120 years on 1st March of the year of the Competition.

Further information from:
Administrator
International String Quartet Competition
Civic Offices, Guildhall Square
Portsmouth
England P01 2AL

[1132]

INTERNATIONAL SUMMER SCHOOL
University of Oslo

Summer School Scholarships

Purpose: To impart knowledge about some aspects of Norwegian and Scandinavian civilization, comparatively presented, and to increase international understanding.

No. offered: 50 Scholarships under cultural agreements and 23 Scholarships for students from developing countries.

Subjects: General courses—Norwegian art, applied arts and crafts; Norwegian language; history, music and literature of Norway; Norwegian economics; politics and society; Norway and Scandinavia in international relations. Graduate courses—educational system of Norway; special education in Norway; Scandinavian education; physical education in Scandinavia; urban and regional planning in Norway; medical care and health services in Norway; Norwegian literature; peace research; energy planning and the environment.

Value: Normally covers all basic fees including tuition, room and board.

Tenable for six weeks in Oslo, from late June to early August.

Eligibility: Open to (1) students with good

academic records as evidenced by an official transcript (United States students should have completed their college sophomore year; non-United States students must present evidence of matriculation at a recognized university in their own country); (2) teachers with a good professional record as evidenced by a statement from the teacher's present supervisor, principal or headmaster; (3) members of graduate courses who have good professional records and/or other qualifications listed on the application form concerned.

Note: All lectures are given in English. Candidates should apply to the Norwegian embassy in their country. Prospective participants from the United States and Canada should make formal application for admission on special forms from *Oslo International Summer School, North American Admissions Office, c/o St. Olaf College, Northfield, Minnesota 55057, U.S.A.*

Closing date: 15th March.

Further information from:
International Summer School
University of Oslo
Box 10, Blindern
Oslo 3
Norway

[1133]

INTERNATIONAL TELECOMMUNICATION UNION

Fellowships

Fellowships are designed to (a) improve the specialized knowledge of the Fellow in the field of telecommunications—installation, operation, maintenance, administration, techniques, professional training, etc; (b) provide training at all levels; (c) enable qualified telecommunication officials to attend seminars dealing with very specialized telecommunication subjects.

No. offered: Approximately 500 Fellowships annually.

Value: To include cost of travel from country of origin to the country/countries of study and return; daily subsistence; allowances for the purchase of books; travel within the country/countries of study; insurance against illness and accident; and in some cases language training.

Tenable for up to twelve months; renewable at the request of the government concerned.

Eligibility: Open to nationals of member states of the United Nations and affiliated organizations who have been nominated by governments through resident representatives of the United Nations Development Programme. Candidates should possess a sound technical background. Fellows should work in the field in which they have been trained on return to their home country.

Note: Candidates should apply to the national authority in their own country, which coordinates technical cooperation programmes.

Fellows are expected to work in the field in which they have been trained on return to their home country.

Further information from:
Secretary-General
International Telecommunication Union
Palais des Nations
CH-1211 Geneva 20
Switzerland

[1134]

INTERNATIONAL TRAINING INSTITUTE
(Washington, D.C.)

Partial Tuition Scholarships for Seminars

Two Scholarships, each covering up to one-third cost of tuition, are given to foreign students for transition seminars held for four weeks in July, August and November/December. They consist of an introduction to and discussions of United States government, economy, education and social problems, and are primarily intended for students ready to enter higher education at the undergraduate or graduate level in the United States. Seminars are normally conducted in English, but can be given in French, German or Spanish upon the request of groups well in advance of arrival.

Further information from:
International Training Institute
Dupont Circle Building
1346 Connecticut Avenue, N.W.
Washington, D.C. 20036
U.S.A.

[1135]

INTERNATIONAL UNION AGAINST CANCER

American Cancer Society—Eleanor Roosevelt International Cancer Fellowships

Purpose: To enable experienced research workers from any country to work in collaboration with outstanding scientists in other countries.

Subjects: Within the fields of experimental or clinical aspects of cancer research.

No. offered: 12 Fellowships annually.

Value: An average of US$20,000, plus return economy air fares for the Fellow and accompanying dependents who join the Fellow for at least six months.

Tenable in any country, usually for one year, but for not less than six months; not renewable.

Eligibility: Open to senior postdoctoral investigators in medical or natural sciences, who have had at least seven years research experience after receiving the doctorate or equivalent degree, and who are capable of independent research. Applicants should have adequate knowledge of a language that will permit effective communication in the host institution, show evidence of acceptance at the host institution during the proposed dates, and furnish a written statement that they will return to their parent institute at the end of the Fellowship.

Note: The Felowship is not intended for brief visits to several institutions, nor to assist Fellows who wish to perfect their training in methods of cancer detection.
These Fellowships cannot run concurrently with awards granted by other agencies. Applications may be obtained by writing to the address below.

Closing date: 1st October for Fellowships commencing within the 12 months' period starting 1st May of the following year.

Further information from:
International Union Against Cancer
Rue du Conseil-Général, 3
1205 Geneva
Switzerland

[1136]

INTERNATIONAL UNION AGAINST CANCER

Cancer Research Campaign International Fellowships

Purpose: To enable investigators to work abroad to gain new experience in clinical or basic research in cancer, including investigators in the behavioral and social sciences related to cancer.

No. offered: Ten Fellowships annually.

Value: Approximately US$18,000 plus travel allowances for the Fellow and spouse who accompanies the Fellow for at least six months.

Tenable in an approved place outside the country where the Fellow resides, ordinarily for one year; under exceptional circumstances awards may range from six months to two years.

Eligibility: Candidates must have between two and ten years post-doctoral experience (Ph.D., M.D., D.V.M.) or equivalent; provide evidence of acceptance at the host institution for the proposed period; have a satisfactory command of the language commonly used at the host laboratory; and provide written assurance that they will return to the parent institution upon completion of the Fellowship.

Note: Fellowships are not granted to individuals who wish to perfect their training or for brief visits to several institutions.
Fellowships cannot run concurrently with awards granted by other agencies.

Closing date: 1st October for Fellowships comencing within the 12 months' period starting 1st May of the following year.

Further information from:
  International Union Against Cancer
  Rue du Conseil—General, 3
  1205 Geneva
  Switzerland

[1137]

INTERNATIONAL UNION AGAINST CANCER

Yamagiwa-Yoshida Memorial International Study Grants

Purpose: To encourage international collaboration by enabling investigators to gain experience in, or make comparative studies of, special techniques.

Subject: Clinical and biological aspects of cancer research.

No. offered: 12 Study Grants; offered twice a year.

Value: Approximately US$4,000 in the form of a per diem living allowance based on a scale established by the Union and related to the cost of living in the host country. A travel allowance is provided for the Grantee only. No allowances for dependents.

Tenable in any approved place outside the country in which the Grantee resides, for two to six weeks (under no circumstances longer than 90 days). Applicants are required to furnish a written statement of intention to return to the home institution on completion of tenure.

Eligibility: Open only to persons who are currently actively engaged in cancer research; candidates must hold scientific qualifications appropriate to the programme proposed; show evidence of acceptance at the host institution during the proposed dates, and furnish a written statement that they will return to their parent institution at the end of the Grant period. Adequate fluency in an appropriate language is required.

Note: Grants are not given for the purpose of visiting a number of institutions or solely for participation in congresses, conferences, symposia.
  Study Grants cannot run concurrently with awards granted by other agencies.

Closing dates: 30th June and 31st December of each year.

Further information from:
  International Union Against Cancer
  Rue du Conseil-General 3
  1205 Geneva
  Switzerland

[1138]

INTERNATIONAL UNION AGAINST CANCER

International Cancer Research Technology Transfer Project

Purpose: To promote direct and rapid transfer of information about new or improved techniques or methods between investigators of different countries.

Subjects: Basic, clinical or behavioral research relating to the further progress of cancer research.

No. offered: 113 Project Grants annually.

Value: Approximately US$2,000 in the form of a per diem living allowance based on a scale established by the Union and related to the cost of living in the host country. A travel allowance is provided for the Grantee only.

Tenable in any approved place outside the country in which the Grantee resides, for a maximum of 28 days.

Eligibility: Open to persons who are currently involved with cancer research, are at an early stage in their career, possess appropriate qualifications. Candidates must show evidence of being accepted by the host institution during the proposed time period and have an adequate facility with a language that will permit effective communication at the host institution.

Note: Applicants are required to furnish a written statement of intention to return to the home institution upon completion of tenure. Funds will not be provided for attending scientific meetings of a general nature, or for support of a series of lectures in one or more countries.

Project Grants cannot be held concurrently with awards granted by other agencies. United States Government employees of any agency are ineligible to receive ICRETT funds.

Closing date: Applications may be submitted at any time throughout the year; candidates will normally be notified within 40 days of receipt of application, which can be obtained by writing to the address below.

Further information from:
 International Union Against Cancer
 Rue du Conseil-General, 3
 1205 Geneva
 Switzerland

[1139]

INTERNATIONAL UNION OF FORESTRY RESEARCH ORGANIZATIONS

Scientific Acievement Awards

A limited number of Awards, consisting of a gold medal, a scroll and a cash honorarium, are formally presented at each IUFRO World Congress (next presentation in 1986) to recognize distinguised individual achievement in forestry research and products. Award recipients should be under 45 years of age at the time of presentation and their parent organizations should be members of the Union.

Closing date: March.

Further information from:
 International Union of Forestry Research
  Organizations
 Schönbrunn
 A-1131 Vienna
 Austria

[1140]

INTERNATIONAL UNION OF LOCAL AUTHORITIES

Course Fellowships

Purpose: To enable senior public officials, who are responsible for the formulation and implementation of new policy, to study ideas from other systems of local administration in order to compare techniques and approaches to similar problems.

Subjects: Comparative studies of various themes relevant to local administration.

No. offered: 25-50 Fellowships annually, provided by agencies mentioned in note below.

Value: Fellowships currently average 9,400 Dutch florins, cover the participation fee, board and lodging, travel within Europe in matters connected with the Course, and a book allowance. In addition, there may be a contribution to the travel costs incurred in attending the Course.

Tenable for the duration of a Course which lasts eight weeks. The Course normally starts and finishes in The Hague, Netherlands, with study visits totalling five weeks at two or three other European countries.

Eligibility: Open to senior officials (elected or appointed) responsible for the formulation of policy for local administration. Officials may be members of local authorities, or of central or state governments.

Note: Candidates should seek Fellowships assistance at the same time as applying to join a Course. Applications must be made by a candidate's own government through such agencies as: United Nations Development Programme; European Economic Community; Organisation for Economic Cooperation and Development; and the Netherlands Ministry of Foreign Affairs.

Closing date: Applications, which may be obtained from the address below, must be submitted to IULA at least two months before the start of a Course.

Further information from:
 Director of Training
 International Union of Local Authorities
 45 Wassenaarseweg
 The Hague 2596-CG
 Netherlands

[1141]

INTERNATIONAL UNION FOR THE SCIENTIFIC STUDY OF POPULATION

Grants for Demographers: The purpose of the Grants is to enable specialists in demography to attend population conferences organized by the Union. The Grants consist of partial or total payment of travel and per diem expenses for the duration of the conference, which occurs about every four years. Open to specialists in the scientific study of population playing an active role in the conference, and preferably members of the Union.

Grants for Junior Demographers: In an effort to promote participation of junior demographers in the activities of the Union, a full travel and per diem grant is awarded annually to enable the successful candidate to attend a seminar or conference organized or co-sponsored by the Union. Open to members and non-members who are less than 30 years of age and hold an M.A. or Ph.D. degree in demography. Applicants must be sponsored by two Unions members.

Further information from:
International Union for the Scientific
 Study of Population
rue des Augustins, 34
4000 Liège
Belgium

[1142]

INTERNATIONAL UNION OF STUDENTS

Scholarships

Subjects: Unrestricted.

No. offered: 120 to 150 Scholarships annually.

Value: To cover maintenance, tuition, pocket money and transportation to student's home on completion of study.

Tenable in universities in Bulgaria, Czechoslovakia, German Democratic Republic, Hungary, Poland, Finland, or U.S.S.R. for four to seven years. A year of language study is included.

Eligibility: Open to unmarried students from developing countries in Africa, Asia and South America, as well as students from Cyprus, who are under 25 years of age.

Closing date: 1st April.

Note: Application should be made through the national union of students in the candidate's country, which must be a member of the International Union of Students. No direct applications are accepted.

Further information from:
International Union of Students
17th November Street
11001 Prague 01
Czechoslovakia

[1143]

INTERNATIONAL UNION FOR VACUUM SCIENCE, TECHNIQUE AND APPLICATIONS

M.W. Welch Foundation Scholarship

Subject: Vacuum science, technique, and applications.

Value: Approximately US$7,000 per annum, payable in two instalments. In special cases, travel expenses may be paid.

Tenable at laboratories in Austria, Canada, France, Hungary, the Netherlands, United Kingdom, United States, and Federal Republic of Germany, or any country with suitable laboratory facilities, as chosen by the Fellow, for one academic year.

Eligibility: Open to nationals of all countries who are students or scientific research workers and have at least a bachelor's degree. Preference is given to persons with doctoral degrees.

Note: Applicants are urged to select laboratories in countries other than their own.

Closing date: 15th April.

Further information from:
International Union for Vacuum Science,
 Technique and Applications
c/o Dr. P. Hobson
Division of Radio and Electrical
 Engineering
National Research Council
Ottawa, Ontario
Canada K1A OR8

[1144]

INTERNATIONAL UNIVERSITY INSTITUTE *(Luxembourg)*

Grants for Advanced Summer Courses

Each summer, Courses are offered at three IUI Centres: International Centre for Comparative Law and Judicial Studies; International Centre for European Research and Studies; and International Centre for Political Economy. A number of Grants are available. Course candidates who wish to apply for a Grant should attach a recommendation from an academic authority or professional superior to their application for admission. Courses are given in English and French.

Further information from:
Secretariat
International University Institute
162a, avenue de la Faïencerie
Luxembourg

[1145]

IODE *(Canada)*

War Memorial Scholarships

Subjects: Any subject vital to the interests of the Commonwealth.

Value: Can$10,000 outside Canada; Can$5,500 in Canada. Second year awards—overseas Can$3,000; within Canada, Can$3,000.

Tenable at any university in the Commonwealth for one year, with the possibility of extension for a further year. Recipients applying for re-appointment will not be in competition with new applicants.

Eligibility: Open to Canadian citizens between 20 and 30 years of age, who are Canadian university graduates. Candidates must have been registered at a graduate school, and have undertaken postgraduate work.

Note: IODE expects recipients to work in Canada after completion of their studies.

Closing date: 1st December.

Applications should be sent to the IODE convenor in the province in which the candidate graduated, or to the address below.

Further information from:
IODE, National Chapter
40 Orchard View Boulevard, Suite 254
Toronto, Ontario
Canada M4R 1B9

[1146]

IOTA SIGMA PI

Agenes Fay Morgan Research Award

Purpose: To promote interest among young women in chemistry research.

Subjects: Chemistry or biochemistry.

No. offered: One Award every three years; next Award given in 1984.

Value: US$300, paid in a lump sum.

Eligibility: Open to women chemists or biochemists who are U.S. residents, and not over forty years of age at the time of nomination. Where achievement is of equal merit, preference will be given to the younger candidate.

Note: Nominations may be made by active chapters, members or groups of members of Iota Sigma Pi.

Closing date: 15th January of the year of the Award.

Further information from:
Sister Mary Rose Stockton, Chairperson
Agnes Fay Morgan Research Award
  Committee
Department of Chemistry
Marian College
3200 Cold Spring Road
Indianapolis, Indiana 46222
U.S.A.

[1147]

IOWA SCHOOL OF LETTERS AWARD FOR SHORT FICTION
University of Iowa

The annual competition for the Award is open to any writer who has not previously published a volume of prose fiction. Manuscripts must be collections of short stories of at least 150 typewritten pages. Stories previously published in periodicals are eligible for inclusion. Revised manuscripts which have been previously entered may be resubmitted. The winning author receives a cash award of US$1,000 plus publication of the winning manuscript.

Note: The Award is given in cooperation with the Iowa Arts Council, Writers Workshop, and University of Iowa Press. Manuscripts, accompanied by stamped, return packaging, should be submitted between 1st August and 30th September.

Further information from:
Iowa School of Letters Award for Short Fiction
Department of English
English-Philosophy Building
University of Iowa
Iowa City, Iowa 52242
U.S.A.

[1148]

IRISH ACADEMY OF LETTERS

Annual Award for Literature: The Academy gives an Award of £250 for a book or play published or presented during the year by a writer of Irish birth, or for distinguished writing during previous years. The Award is made solely at the discretion of the Academy and applications are not accepted.

Gregory Medal: The Academy awards the Medal from time to time (not more frequently than every three years) for outstanding and lengthy service to Irish literature.

Not confirmed since 1979.

Further information from:
Honorary Secretary
Irish Academy of Letters
16 Castlepark Road
Sandycove, Dun Laoghaire
County Dublin
Ireland

[1149]

IRISH AMERICAN CULTURAL INSTITUTE
(St. Paul, Minnesota)

Literary Awards

£5,000 is offered annually to stimulate literary and scholarly writing in both Irish and English languages in Ireland. Work submitted should be published or in proof sheets and must be original work and not a translation.

Further information from:
Irish American Cultural Institute
683 Osceola Avenue
St. Paul, Minnesota 55105
U.S.A.

[1150]

RICHARD D. IRWIN FOUNDATION
(U.S.A.)

Doctoral Fellowships

A limited number of Fellowships are offered to assist prospective teachers in the fields of business, economics and the social sciences, toward completion of their dissertations.

Fellowships vary in amount, and are expected to be in the range of US$1,500 to US$2,500, to be paid over a twelve month period unless the Fellow's need requires a different method of payment.

Candidates are limited to persons who have been admitted to candidacy for the doctoral degree, and have completed all work except writing the dissertation and passing final orals. Applicants must be enrolled in, or accepted to a school with an accredited doctoral program. For candidates just reaching the dissertation stage, the Foundation will give consideration to those who have made some progress on dissertations and who may need assistance to carry them through to completion. Preference is usually given to applicants whose contribution to teaching is to be made in the United States or Canada. Awards are not made for foreign travel or the purchase of equipment.

Candidates must be nominated by a dean of a school of business. Direct applications from candidates are not accepted.

Closing date: 15th February.

Further information from:
Richard D. Irwin Foundation
1818 Ridge Road
Homewood, Illinois 60430
U.S.A.

[1151]

ISRAEL MUSEUM *(Jerusalem)*

Joseph H. Hazen Art Essay Award for 20th Century Art Literature: US$1,000 is awarded annually for the best essay or article submitted by an Israeli resident. Non-renewable.

Closing date: 28th February.

Beatrice S. Kolliner Award for a Young Israeli Artist: US$2,000 is awarded annually to a young Israeli resident showing exceptional artistic talent. Non-renewable. *Closing date:* 28th February.

Percia Schimmel Award for Achievement in the Archaeological Research of Eretz Israel and the Lands of the Bible. US$6,000 is awarded annually for the achievement judged most worthy. Non-renewable. There are no residency requirements for this Award. *Closing date:* 28th February.

Enrique Kavlin Photography Grant: US$1,000 is awarded annually to an Israeli resident, for excellence in the field of photography in Israel. Non-renewable. *Closing date:* 28th February.

Sandberg Prize for Israel Art: US$6,000 is awarded annually to an Israeli artist, resident in Israel. Non-renewable. *Closing date:* 28th February.

Sandberg Prize for Research and Development: US$1,600 is awarded annually to an Israeli resident, to encourage excellence in design in Israel. Non-renewable. *Closing date:* 28th February.

Further information from:
 Department of Public Affairs
 Israel Museum
 Jerusalem
 Israel

[1152]

ITALIAN INSTITUTE (London)
MINISTRY OF FOREIGN AFFAIRS (Italy)

Italian Government Scholarships, Bursaries and Grants

Subjects: Unrestricted.

No. offered: 200 Awards annually.

Value: 330,000 lire per month. The Italian Government will arrange insurance coverage for the duration of the Award while the holder is in Italy.

Tenable at various centres throughout Italy, a list of which may be obtained by writing to the Institute at the address below. Long-term Scholarships and Grants are awarded for periods of 4 to 8 months; Summer Bursaries and Short-term Grants are awarded for periods of 2 to 3 months, and under special circumstances for 4 months.

Eligibility: Open to United Kingdom citizens. Candidates for Long-term Scholarships will be interviewed at the Italian Institute in both Italian and English. Preference will be given to scholars doing research on Italian history, literature, art and sciences; particularly favourable consideration will be given to students and graduates who intend to teach Italian in the United Kingdom.

Note: All fares and necessary enrolment fees, as well as accommodation, are the responsibility of the applicant.

Application forms for all awards are available from the Institute at the address below; a stamped addressed foolscap envelope must be sent. Completed forms are to be sent to the Institute: to the Scholarship Department (in triplicate) for Long-term Scholarships and Research Grants; to the Bursary Department (in duplicate) for Summer Bursaries and Short-term Grants.

Closing dates: 31st October, 30th November, for short-term awards; 15th January for long-term awards.

Further information from:
 Bursary Department
 Italian Institute
 39 Belgrave Square
 London
 England SW1X 8NX

[1153]

ITALIAN INSTITUTE (London)
MINISTRY OF FOREIGN AFFAIRS (Italy)

Scholarships

The Italian Miinistry of Foreign Affiars, through the Italian Institute in London, offers a number of awards for study or research in any subject to those who are from other Council of Europe member states, and to Italian citizens who are permanently resident abroad.

Scholarships carry a monthly stipend of 330,000 lire and cover insurance during the period of study. Travel expenses will also be paid for non-Italian Scholars. Non-Italian candidates must be 35 years of age or under, and preference will be shown to those having a good knowledge of Italian.

Closing dates: 15th January for Italian applicants; 28th February for others.

Further information from:
Italian Institute
39 Belgrave Square
London
England SW1X 8NX

[1154]

ITALIAN INSTITUTE FOR HISTORICAL STUDIES *(Naples)*

Federico Chabod Scholarship
Adolfo Omodeo Scholarship
Comune DI Napoli Scholarship

Purpose: To allow students to participate in life at the Institute while completing a personal research project in history with the assistance of its staff.

No. offered: Three Scholarships annually.

Value: 2,400,000 lire for each Scholarship.

Tenable at the Institute for eight months.

Eligibility: Open to nationals of all countries who possess a B.A. degree and are under 30 years of age.

Closing date: 15th October.

Further information from:
Italian Institute for Historical Studies
Via Benedetto Croce, 12
Naples 80134
Italy

[1155]

ITALIAN UNIVERSITY FOR FOREIGNERS *(Perguia)*

Scholarships

Subjects: Preparatory, intermediate and advanced courses in Italian language and culture (literature, history, art, philosophy). Advanced course in cultural studies; course in the history of art; course in Etruscology and Italian antiquities; course in contemporary Italian; course for teachers of Italian abroad.

No. offered: Approximately 700 Scholarships annually.

Value: From 175,000 to 275,000 lire per month.

Eligibility: Open to foreign students of all nationalities.

Note: Study Awards of 330,000 lire each are granted by the Italian Ministry of Foreign Affairs for one or more monthly periods of study at the University. Applications for these Awards should be made directly to the applicant's local Italian embassy or consulate, or to an Italian cultural institute.

Further information from:
Ufficio Borse di Studio
Università Italiana per Stranieri
Piazza Fortebraccio, Palazzo Gallenga
06100 Perugia
Italy

J

See *How to Use The Grants Register*, page ix

[1156]

JACKSON LABORATORY *(Bar Harbor, Maine)*

Postdoctoral Associateships

Purpose: Research training.

Subjects: Mammalian biological sciences, with an emphasis placed on mammalian genetics.

No. offered: Approximately seven new Awards annually.

Value: US$13,000 to US$15,000 per year, paid in monthly instalments.

Tenable at the Jackson Laboratory; Institutional Awards for one year and Training Grants offered by the U.S. National Institutes of Health for one to two years.

Eligibility: Open to recent recipients of a doctoral degree in medicine, veterinary medicine, or the biological sciences. There are no citizenship requirements for the Institutional Awards; candidates for the U.S. National Institutes of Health Training Grants should be U.S. citizens or have permanent resident visa status.

Note: Training Grants from the U.S. National Institutes of Health are restricted to mammalian genetics and reproductive biology; Institutional Awards are open in any field under investigation at the Laboratory.

Applications may be submitted at any time.

Further information from:
  Training Office
  Jackson Laboratory
  Bar Harbor, Maine 04609
  U.S.A.

[1157]

JACKSONVILLE UNIVERSITY PLAYWRITING COMPETITION *(U.S.A.)*
College of Fine Arts

Intended to encourage original writing for the stage, the Competition is held annually and is open to all playwrights regardless of age, sex, citizenship or nationality. The winner receives a prize of US$1,000 and premiere production of the winning play.

Only full-length and one-act scripts, originals and previously unproduced, will be accepted. Scripts may be submitted between 1st September and 1st January, and should be typewritten and firmly bound, and sent with a stamped, self-addressed envelope. Competitors may send not more than two scripts. In addition, competitors should include their telephone number, complete return address and an indication of employment or educational status.

Competitors are advised that the University cannot assume responsibilty for loss, damage to or return of the scripts.

Further information from:
  Davis Sikes, Director
  Playwriting Competition
  College of Fine Arts
  Jacksonville University
  Jacksonville, Florida 32211
  U.S.A.

[1158]

JACOB'S PILLOW DANCE FESTIVAL, INC. *(Becket, Massachusetts)*

Dance Scholarships

Value: Room, board and tuition, or tuition only. There is no travel allowance for foreign nationals.

Tenable at the Festival for twelve weeks.

Eligibility: Open to United States and foreign

nationals who are over 16 years of age and have experience in the field of dance.

Closing date: End of February.

Further information from:
 Director of School
 Jacob's Pillow Dance Festival, Inc.
 Box 287
 Lee, Massachusetts 01238
 U.S.A.

[1159]

CATHERINE AND LADY GRACE JAMES FOUNDATION *(Wales)*

D.J. James Pantyfedwen Scholarships and Fellowships

As part of the Foundation's charitable activities, it offers assistance in the form of grants, subscriptions, donations, etc., for the following purposes: (1) to assist and encourage the training of Welsh persons of any denomination who wish to become ministers of religion; (2) to maintain an annual D.J. James Lectureship on a religious subject to be given by a minister of religion (preferably Welsh); (3) to promote religion and education by encouraging the production of poetry, prose and other literary works of a religious or educational nature by Welsh writers; (4) to assist in the advancement, education, or training of sons Welsh ministers, schoolmasters and other Welsh persons; (5) to provide Fellowships and Scholarships for Welsh at all or any of the Universities of Wales, Oxford, Cambridge, London or other universities; (6) to establish Scholarships for Welsh students who require further training in music and drama; (7) to help Welsh medical students to proceed to Oxford or Cambridge for pre-clinical training and thereafter to return to the Welsh National School of Medicine; (8) to encourage among Welsh persons the study of, and training in, farming, agriculture, forestry and horticulture, by the provision of Scholarships, etc., particularly for Welsh members of Young Farmers Clubs.

Applications should be made on the appropriate forms.

Further information from:
 Secretary
 Catherine and Lady Grace James
  Foundation
 Pantyfedwen, 9 Market Street
 Aberystwyth, Dyfed
 Wales SY23 1DL

[1160]

JAPAN FOUNDATION

Professional Fellowships

Purpose: To assist scholars and other professionals abroad who are engaged in studies relating to Japanese culture and society by offering an opportunity to conduct their research in Japan.

Value: 240,000 to 300,000 yen per month, plus return air fare and a limited amount of allowances.

Tenable in Japan for four to twelve months (for long-term Fellowships) and for two to four months (for short-term Fellowships); not normally renewable.

Eligibility: Open to faculty members, writers, artists and other professionals who have substantial training and experience in some aspect of Japanese studies and who desire to carry out research in Japan, or who wish to upgrade their skills or add a new dimension to their professional capacities. Faculty members whose area of specialization is not Japanese studies but who wish to increase their professional competence in the Japanese field are also eligible. Specialists such as translators from Japanese into English, librarians concerned with the field of Japanese studies, or museum staff dealing with Japanese art objects may also apply.

Closing date: 1st December.

Address
 Japan Foundation
 Park Building
 3, Kioi-cho, Chiyoda-ku
 Tokyo 102
 Japan

[1161]

JAPAN FOUNDATION

Dissertation Fellowships

Purpose: To assist scholars abroad who are engaged in doctoral study in the social sciences and the humanities by offering an opportunity to conduct their dissertation research in Japan.

Value: 180,000 yen per month, plus return air fare and a limited amount of allowances.

Tenable in Japan for periods ranging from four to fourteen months; not normally renewable.

Eligibility: Applicants should have completed all requirements except the dissertation when they take up their Fellowship. The subject of the dissertation should be related in some substantial part to Japan. Proficiency in Japanese is desirable but not essential, except in cases where it is necessary to complete the project successfully. However, in the absence of ability in Japanese, some proficiency in English is necessary.

Note: Detailed information concerning application procedures may be obtained from the Foundation's overseas offices: Australia—*2nd Floor, Phoenix House, 88 Northbourne Avenue, Braddon, A.C.T. 2061;* United Kingdom—*35 Dover Street, London, W1X 3RA;* United States—*44th Floor, Citicorp Center, 153 East 53rd Street, New York, New York 10022, or, Suite 570, Watergate Office Building, 600 New Hampshire Avenue, N.W., Washington, D.C. 20037,* or from Japanese diplomatic missions abroad.

Closing date: 1st December.

Address
Japan Foundation
Park Building
3, Kioi-cho, Chiyoda-ku
Tokyo 102
Japan

[1162]

JAPAN FOUNDATION

Visiting Professorships

The Professorships are intended for Japanese professors in such fields as the social sciences, humanitites, education, law and business administration who are invited by one or more foreign institutions to teach, lecture or participate in collaborative research projects relating to Japan. The programme is also intended for artists-in-residence.

Recipients are provided with return economy class air fare from Tokyo, plus stipends and other allowances as stipulated by the Foundation's regulations. Visiting Professorships are tenable for periods ranging from three months to one year.

Note: Institutions making applications under the programme are requested to designate the specific individual who will be invited. They should also determine the interest and availability of the invitee in advance of the application.

Detailed information on application procedures may be obtained from the Foundation's overseas offices: Australia—*2nd Floor Phoenix House, 88 Northbourne Avenue, Braddon, A.C.T. 2601;* United Kingdom—*35 Dover Street, London W1X 3RA;* United States—*44th Floor, Citicorp Center, 153 East 53rd Street, New York, New York 10023, or, suite 570, Watergate Office Building, 600 New Hampshire Avenue, N.W., Washington, D.C. 20037.* Information may also be obtained through Japanese diplomatic missions abroad.

Closing date: 1st December.

Address:
Japan Foundation
Park Building
3, Kioi-cho, Chiyoda-ku
Tokyo 102
Japan

[1163]

JAPAN NEWSPAPER PUBLISHERS AND EDITORS ASSOCIATION

NSK-CAJ Fellowship Program

Subjects: News reporting journalism (courses and seminars).

No. offered: 3 Fellowships granted for each ASEAN country.

Value: To cover a per diem allowance, local transportation, books and materials, and other expenses.

Tenable in Japan for two months.

Eligibility: Open to working journalists of ASEAN countries (Indonesia, Malaysia, Philippines and Thailand), who are under 35 years of age, are employed by newspapers or news agency organizations, and have had a minimum of 5 years professional experience.

Note: Applications should be sent with the recommendation of a member organization of the Confederation of ASEAN Journalists organizations or institutions concerned.

Further information from:
Nihon Shinbun Kyokai
Japan Newspaper Publishers and Editors Association
Nippon Press Center Building
2-1, Uchisaiwaicho 2-chome
Chiyoda-ku
Tokyo 100
Japan

[1164]

JAPAN SOCIETY FOR THE PROMOTION OF SCIENCE

Short Term Research Fellowship Programme

Purpose: To promote international cooperation in scientific research in the fields of the humanities, social and natural sciences.

No. offered: 200 Fellowships annually.

Value: 18,000 yen per diem and tourist class air fare to and from Japan. No allowance is provided for accompanying dependents.

Tenable at host organizations (universities, colleges and other research institions) in Japan for one to four months.

Eligibility: Open to foreign senior scientists, university professors and people who are noted for their achievements and can contribute to the progress of science in Japan.

Applications must be presented by Japanese host scientists.

Further information from:
Head, Exchange of Persons Divison
Japan Society for the Promotion of Science
Yamato Building, 6th Floor
5-3-1 Kojimachi, Chiyoda-ku
Tokyo 102
Japan

[1165]

JAPAN SOCIETY FOR THE PROMOTION OF SCIENCE

Long Term Research Fellowship Programme

Purpose: To promote international cooperation in scientific research in the fields of humanities, social and natural sciences.

No. offered: 50 Fellowships annually.

Value: Approximately 270,000-300,000 yen per month for senior researchers and 240,000 yen per month for junior researchers, plus return air fare.

Tenable at univesities and research institutions in Japan for six to ten months in the case of senior researchers and for six to twelve months in the case of junior researchers.

Eligibility: The senior Programme is open to university professors, assistant professors and other persons of substantial professional experience. The junior Programme is open to postdoctoral researchers and other persons of comparable research experience who are at least 25 years of age.

Note: Applicants are invited to be considered for an award by Japanese scientists.

Further information from:
Head, Exchange of Persons Division
Japan Society for the Promotion of Science
Yamato Building, 6th Floor
5-3-1 Kojimachi, Chiyoda-ku
Tokyo 102
Japan

[1166]

JAPANESE NATIONAL COMMISSION FOR UNESCO

Fellowship Program

Purpose: To provide the opportunity to persons from member-states of Unesco in the region of Asia and Oceania to undertake study and research on activities in Japan in the fields of education, science, culture and communication within the scope of Unesco's competence, and thus to contribute to the promotion of Unesco activities in the region and the development of international understanding and cooperation as advocated by Unesco.

No. offered: Five Fellowships annually.

Value: A monthly stipend of 195,000 yen, local travel expenses, plus free interpretation services for study interviews for Fellows having no knowledge of Japanese.
   Travel expenses to and from Japan are borne by Commission.

Tenable in Japan for a maximum period of two months.

Eligibility: Open to staff members of the National Commissions for Unesco in Asia and Oceania, or those researchers from member-states of Unesco in those regions who can meet the following qualifications in the fields of education, science, culture or communication: (a) candidates must be university or college graduates or those who can be regarded by the Secretary-General to have qualifications and experience equal or superior to such graduates; (b) they must have had considerable experience in research, teaching, guidance or other practical activity, as specialists in their specialized fields; (c) they must have a good working knowledge of either Japanese or English; (d) they must be healthy enough to pursue their studies in Japan.

Note: Candidates must be recommended by the Secretary-General of the respective National Commission for Unesco. The letter of recommendation must contain an assurance that if the Fellowship is granted, the recipient will be engaged, upon his return home from Japan, in work related to the studies for which the Fellowship was awarded.
   Applications should be made, initially, to the National Commission for Unesco in the applicant's country, who in turn should forward applications to the Japanese National Commission for Unesco not later than 16th January.

Not confirmed for 1983.

For addresses of the National Commissions for Unesco in the Asian area, write to:
   Japanese National Commission for
      Unesco
   2-2 Kasumigaseki, 3-chome
   Chiyoda-ku
   Tokyo 100
   Japan

[1167]

JERUSALEM INTERNATIONAL BOOK FAIR

Jerusalem Prize

One Prize of US$3,000 and a citation is given in odd-numbered years to an author who has contributed to the world's understanding of "the freedom of the individual in society". The Competition is open to all authors, regardless of race, religion, nationality or place of residence. The recipient is the guest of the Fair, where his or her works are exhibited.

Closing date: Approximatley 18 months in advance of the Fair, usually held in April.

Further information from:
   Jerusalem Prize
   Jerusalem International Book Fair
   22 Jaffa Road
   Jerusalem 91000
   Israel

[1168]

LYNDON BAINES JOHNSON FOUNDATION (U.S.A.)

Moody Grant Awards

A limited number of Awards are made annually to defray living and travel expenses incurred through conducting research while at the Johnson Library. Awards are tenable for one year, beginning 1st September, and may not be renewed or extended. Value is calculated on the basis of US$40 per day plus actual travel costs, to be paid in full upon arrival at the Library.

There are no restrictions in regard to age, sex, academic background, citizenship or residency. It should be agreed that the product of the research, made possible through the Grant, will not be used for any political purposes. A copy of any publication, article or book resulting from this Grant will be presented to the Chief Archivist of the Library.

Funds are not awarded for reproduction expenses, secretarial or research assistance, etc. Prior to submitting a Grant proposal, applicants are recommended to write to the Chief Archivist, at the Foundation to obtain information on the materials available.

Further information from:
Executive Director
Lyndon Baines Johnson Foundation
2313 Red River
Austin, Texas 78705
U.S.A.

Note: Application forms may be obtained from the address below. All information submitted to the Council will become available for dissemination among educators throughout the United States.

Closing date: 15th July. Entries submitted to a state sponsored awards competition must be resubmitted to the Council by 1st September. Notification of Awards are made no later than 1st October.

Further information from:
Economic Education Awards Program
Joint Council on Economic Education
1212 Avenue of the Americas
New York, New York 10036
U.S.A.

[1169]

JOINT COUNCIL ON ECONOMIC EDUCATION

International Paper Company Foundation National Awards Program for the Teaching of Economics

Purpose: To stimulate improvements in economic education teaching, to encourage teachers to develop descriptions of their teaching methods, and to foster an invaluable exchange of teaching experiences by economic education teachers of all levels.

No. offered: 72 Awards, including honorable mentions, annually.

Value: A total of US$11,100 annually. In addition, each winner receives an inscribed plaque.

Eligibility: Open to all elementary and secondary school teachers in the United States. College and University teachers offering economics courses, or those including economics, are also eligible. Teaching programs must have been carried out during the twelve month period beginning 1st July of the year preceding that in which the Award is made.

[1170]

JOINT U.S.-SPANISH COMMITTEE FOR EDUCATIONAL AND CULTURAL AFFAIRS

Postdoctoral Fellowships for Research in Spain

Approximately twelve Fellowships are offered annually to U.S. citizens who hold a Ph.D. degree or equivalent qualifications, and are competent in oral and written Spanish. The Fellowships, tenable in Spain for four to ten months, are offered in the following areas: the arts, humanities, education law, communications, anthropology, economics, political science, psychology, and the social sciences. Support ranges from US$1,000 to US$1600 per month, determined by the number of dependents accompanying the Fellow, plus economy air travel for the Fellow, 50% air fare for one dependent (if funds permit), as well as, health and accident insurance for the Fellow.

Closing date: 1st April.

Further information from:
Council for International Exchange of Scholars
11 Dupont Circle, N.W., Suite 300
Washington, D.C. 20036
U.S.A.

[1171]

JOURNALISTS IN EUROPE
Centre de Formation et de Perfectionnement des Journalistes-International Department

Journalists in Europe Program
Individual Training Programs

Purpose: To enable journalists of all nationalities to acquire an in depth understanding of Europe.

No. offered: Thirty Journalists in Europe scholarships; a variable number of awards for individual training.

Value: Full cost of Program, including tuition, and a living allowance.

Tenable for eight months: in Paris (and travel throughout Europe) for the Journalists in Europe Program; in Paris or the provinces for individual training programs.

Eligibility: Journalists in Europe—candidates should be journalists of any nationality who are between twenty-five and thirty-five years of age, have a good knowledge of both English and French, and have a minimum of four years full-time professional experience. Candidates for individual training programs must be fluent in French, have a minimum of two years professional experience, and already hold another award through the French or their own government, or some international foundation, firm, or organization. There is no age limit for the individual training program.

Note: Individual training programs are tailored to the journalist's needs, and may be awarded for special training in radio, television, subediting, press management, etc.
Candidates not fluent in either of the required languages must take an intensive language course organized by the Centre de Formation et de Perfectionement des Journalists prior to the start of the programe.

Closing date: 15th February for Journalists in Europe Program beginning in October of the same year.

Further information from:
Centre de Formation et de Perfectionnement des Journalistes
International Department
33 rue de Louvre
75002 Paris
France

[1172]

ALFRED JURZYKOWSKI FOUNDATION, INC. *(U.S.A.)*

Awards

Approximately 10 Awards of US$5,000 each are presented annually in New York to scholars, writers and artists of Polish ethnic background—regardless of their places of residence or citizenship—for outstanding creative achievements in the sciences, humanities, medicine, creative writing, literary criticism, the theatre, fine arts and music (composition and performance), as well as for significant contributions to the advancement of Polish culture including an Award for the best translation of Polish literature into other languages, and for this the criterion of Polish background is not applicable.

Awards are also presented in Brazil to writers and scientists resident in or nationals of Brazil for outstanding creative achievements in their respective fields.

Candidates for Awards are submitted to the Board of Trustees by the Cultural Advisory Committee in New York, and by the Brazilian Academy of Letters and the Brazilian Academy of Medicine in Brazil. Applications from individuals are not accepted.

Note: The number and value of the Awards are determined every second year by the Board of Trustees.

Further information from:
Alfred Jurzykowski Foundation, Inc.
21 East 40th Street
New York, New York 10016
U.S.A.

[1173]

SIGRID JUSÉLIUS FOUNDATION *(Finland)*

Sigrid Jusélius Research Fellowship

Purpose: To support and promote medical research, independent of language and nationality, with the aim of combating diseases particularly fatal to mankind.

Subjects: Medical research, mainly in fields such as anatomy, bacteriology, biochemistry, medical chemistry, pathology, physiology, virology, etc.

No. offered: Approximately 100 Fellowships annually.

Value: Approximately 10,000 Finnish marks to 420,000 marks.

Tenable at Helsinki, Turku, Tampere, Kuopio, Jyväskylä, or Oulu universities in Finland for one year, renewable.

Eligibility: Open to graduates under 60 years of age. The Fellows are generally heads of medical departments in research institutes or groups and are usually Finnish nationals. However, the Fellowship is in principle international.

Note: A written undertaking must be given to submit an annual report.

Closing date: 15th November.

Further information from:
 Sigrid Jusélius Foundation
 Aleksanterinkatu 48 B
 00 100 Helsinki 10
 Finland

[1174]

JUVENILE DIABETES FOUNDATION
(U.S.A.)

Fellowships

Purpose: To attract qualified and promising scientists entering on their professional career, into fields of research which can reasonably be expected to bear directly on future discoveries of cause, treatment, cure and prevention of diabetes and its complications.

Value: A stipend of US$14,000 plus US$1,000 for each year of relevant postdoctoral experience. In addition, a US$3,000 research allowance is awarded to cover research support and fringe benefits. Payments are made quarterly.

Tenable at appropriate institutions for one year; Fellows may apply for a second year of funding.

Eligibility: By the beginning of the period of support, the applicant must have a doctoral degree, or the equivalent, from an accredited institution. Fellows may not simultaneously hold an internship or residency appointment. Each application should be sponsored by a scientist affiliated full-time with an accredited nonprofit institution, who agrees to supervise the Fellow's training. The institution must have adequate staff and facilities to support the proposed training.

Note: The Foundation also offers *Research Grants* which are intended to fit a variety of needs in scientific investigations related to diabetes. A Grant is generally made to cover the cost of such items as salaries for technical assistance, special equipment, animals, consumable supplies and other miscellaneous supplies required to conduct the proposed research. Grant funds are not awarded to discharge an institution's obligation for a tenure position, except under special circumstances.

New Grants are ordinarily made for a term of one year. Consideration will be given to extending Research Grants up to two years.

Further information from:
 Grants Administrator
 Juvenile Diabetes Foundation
 23 East 26th Street
 New York, New York 10010
 U.S.A.

[1175]

JUVENILE DIABETES FOUNDATION
(U.S.A.)

Career Development Award

Purpose: To provide the opportunity for promising young medical investigators with demonstrated aptitude in diabetes research, to develop into independent investigators. The Award, made to the institution, is designed to enable such individuals to investigate a well-defined problem with a sponsor competent to provide guidance in the chosen problem and to foster growth toward independent research.

It is anticipated that this Award may provide the transition between fellowship or traineeship experience and a career in independent investigation and that it will also provide future faculty for health professional institutions in the United States.

Value: Salary support not to exceed US$35,000 annually. The actual salary must be consistent with the established salary structure of the institution for persons or equivalent qualifications, experience and rank. Up to a total of US$5,000 annually is provided for necessary items such as supplies, equipment and travel.

Tenable at appropriate United States institutions for three years.

Eligibility: Candidates should have a doctoral degree or the equivalent from an accredited institution with four to seven years of total professional postdoctoral clinical and/or research experience by the projected start of the Award. It is expected that clinical candidates will have a minimum of two years of clinical experience and two years of research training; research candidates will have a minimum of four years of research training. In exceptional circumstances, individuals with less than four, and more than seven years of such experience may apply, but must justify those special circumstances (e.g., time in service). Individuals holding the academic position of associate professor or professor at the time of award are not eligible for this Award. Candidates should have broad training, should demonstrate individual competence in clinical and/or research activities, and should show research potential in the chosen area of interest. Candidates should provide evidence of a serious intent for an academic career related to that area.

The grantee institution must be a university, medical school, or comparable institution with strong, well-established research and training programs in the chosen area, adequate members of highly-trained faculty in clinical and basic departments relevant to the chosen area, and interest and capability to provide guidance to clinically trained individuals in the development of research independence.

Note: The clinical applicant is expected to spend a minimum of 75% of time in research. The research applicant is expected to spend 100% of time in research. An appropriate sponsor must assume responsibility and provide guidance for the research development in the chosen area.

Institutions may apply for awards in behalf of named individuals. It is not essential for the applicant institution to commit itself to eventual placement of the candidate on its permanent, full-time faculty, but it is expected that institutions will choose the candidate with criteria for that decision in mind. Evidence of the commitment of the institution to the candidate's research development must be provided.

Further information from:
Grants Administrator
Juvenile Diabetes Foundation
23 East 26th Street
New York, New York 10010
U.S.A.

[1176]

JWB JEWISH BOOK COUNCIL *(U.S.A)*

National Jewish Book Awards

Gerrard and Ella Berman Awards for a Book of Jewish History of US$500 is given annually to the author of a work dealing with the whole or some aspect of Jewish history, past or present, which combines scholarship and literary merit. Generally, the Award is given to the author of a book published during the preceding calendar year, but the judges may select an author for his cumulative contribution to Jewish history. Books to be considered must have been written originally in English, Hebrew or Yiddish, by citizens or residents of the United States or Canada. Books on the Holocaust and Israel are not eligible for this Award.

Frank and Ethel S. Cohen Award is given annually to the author of a published work dealing with some aspect of Jewish thought, past or present. The cast award is US$500. United States or Canadian citizens or residents may apply with appropriate books originally written in English and published during the calendar year preceding announcement of the Award.

William and Janice Epstein Award for Jewish Fiction: Cash award of US$500.

Leon Jolson Award is given annually to the author of a non-fiction book dealing with some aspect of the Nazi holocaust period, and is in the amount of US$500. United States or Canadian citizens or residents may apply with appropriate books published in English, Yiddish or Hebrew. One Award is given every three years for a book in one of the three languages. Submissions may be written in or translated into one of the three languages.

Morris J. Kaplun Award is awarded annually to the author of a non-fiction work dealing with the whole or some aspect of the State of Israel, and is in the amount of *US$500*. Generally, the Award is given to the author of a book published during the preceding calendar year, but the judges may select an author for his cumulative contribution on the subject. Works to be considered must have been written originally in English, Hebrew or Yiddish, by citizens or residents of the United States or Canada.

Workmen's Circle Award for Yiddish Literature of *US$500* is awarded annually for a book of literary merit in the Yiddish language. Works of fiction, poetry, essays and memoirs are eligible.

William (Zev) Frank Memorial Award: US$500 is given annually for a novel or a collection of short stories of Jewish interest.

Leon L. Gildesgame Award: US$500 is given annually to the author of a book of Jewish interest in art in all forms. Books published in the past two years are eligible.

Further information from:
 JWB Jewish Book Council
 15 East 26th Street
 New York, New York 10010
 U.S.A.

K

See *How to Use The Grants Register*, page ix

[1177]

KALINGA FOUNDATION TRUST

Kalinga Prize for the Popularization of Science

Purpose: To recognize outstanding public service in the interpretation of science and research to the public, by a writer, editor, speaker, or radio/television programme director.

No. offered: One Prize annually.

Value: The Prize of £1,000 will enable the recipient to travel to India where he will be the guest, for one month, of Mr. B. Patnaik and of the Trust. He will be given every facility to familiarize himself with Indian life and culture, to inspect Indian research and educational institutions, to study the development of Indian industry and economy and will be invited to visit Indian universities and to attend meetings of Indian scientific societies, particularly that of the Indian Science Congress Association.

Note: The Director-General of Unesco will annually invite one nomination of a candidate for the Prize from each of the existing national associations for the advancement of science (or equivalent), and one from each of the national associations of science writers in member-states. In countries where no such associations exist, candidatures are also receivable from the respective national commissions for Unesco. Applications from individuals are not accepted.

While in India, the recipient will be asked to deliver one or more formal addresses or to take part in informal discussions, with a view to giving an interpretation to India of recent progress in science or in the social, cultural and educational consequences of science. On his return to his own country, he will be expected to interpret India and Indian science by means of published articles, books, lectures or radio/television programmes.

Further information from:
Kalinga Foundation Trust
c/o Unesco
7, place de Fontenoy
75700 Paris
France

[1178]

KALTENBORN FOUNDATION *(U.S.A.)*

Grants

The Foundation annually offers three or four Grants of about US$1,500 each for scholarly studies in the field of communications. This includes a wide variety of projects concerned with television, radio, the press and magazines. In the recent past the Foundation has supported studies dealing with the effectiveness of medical information programs on television, problems involved in science news broadcasting, Spanish news programs, and Pentagon press secretaries and their role in the Vietnam war.

Further information from:
Trustee
Kaltenborn Foundation
349 Seaview Avenue
Palm Beach, Florida 33480
U.S.A.

[1179]

KAPPA TAU ALPHA *(U.S.A.)*

Frank Luther Mott-Kappa Tau Alpha Research Award in Journalism

An annual Award of US$300 plus a certificate is offered for a published book concerned with research in journalism. Qualified individuals may apply with an appropriate book published during the preceding year (i.e., carrying a 1982 copyright for the 1983 Award). Textbooks are not eligible for the Award. Application materials should be submitted before 1st February.

Further information from:
   Chief, Central Office
   Kappy Tau Alpha
   University of Missouri School of
      Journalism, Box 838
   Columbia, Missouri 65205
   U.S.A.

[1180]

HEINZ KARGER MEMORIAL FOUNDATION *(Switzerland)*

Heinz Karger Prize

An annual Prize of 7,000 Swiss francs is given to a scientist, medical doctor or Ph.D. of any nationality, for outstanding scientific work in the field of medical research. The subject of the competition, which changes each year, is announced worldwide in the Karger journals.

Papers should be submitted (by 28th February) in English, German or French, and should conform to regulations as set forth in *Rules for the Preparation of Manuscripts*. This booklet may be obtained free of charge from the address below, if the request is marked 'Competition'. Winning papers are published in English in one of the Karger journals.

Note: A special prize of 20,000 Swiss francs will be awarded in 1983 to commemorate the Foundation's 20th anniversary.

Further information from:
   S. Karger AG
   Heinz Karger Memorial Foundation
   Allschwilerstrasse 10
   4009 Basel
   Switzerland

[1181]

ROBERT F. KENNEDY MEMORIAL *(U.S.A.)*

Robert F. Kennedy Fellowships

Purpose: To encourage young people (those who are victims of poverty or discrimination and those more fortunate) to investigate, report and act on problems in their communities and schools.

Subjects: High school journalism, Indian education, street law programs, various community programs involving education.

No. offered: Approximately 20 Fellowships per annum.

Value: US$10,000 per annum.

Tenable in the United States for one year; community groups act as host for Fellows.

Eligibility: Open to United States citizens who have a project to present for review.

Further information from:
   Robert F. Kennedy Memorial
   1029 31st Street, N.W.
   Washington, D.C. 20007
   U.S.A.

[1182]

KENNEDY MEMORIAL FUND *(U.K.)*
Association of Commonwealth Universities

Kennedy Scholarships at Harvard University and Massachusetts Institute of Technology

Subjects: All fields of social science and political studies.

No. offered: Approximately 12 Scholarships annually.

Value: US$7,500 per annum (intended to cover support costs, special equipment, and cost of travel in the United States), plus tuition fees and travelling expenses to and from the United States. A further US$6,500 is paid if the Scholarship is renewed for a second year.

Tenable for one year at Harvard University, and the Massachusetts Institute of Technology at Cambridge; renewable, in special circumstances, for a second year.

Eligibility: Open to citizens of the United Kingdom under 26 years of age, ordinarily resident in the United Kingdom or having been wholly or mainly educated there. At time of application candidates must have spent at least two of the last four years at a university, university college or a polytechnic in the United Kingdom, and must have graduated before taking up their award in the following year. No application will be considered from persons already in the United States.

Note: Scholarships for the study of business administration and management will be granted only in exceptional circumstances, and candidates must have completed one year's employment in business or public service since graduation. An independent application to Harvard or M.I.T. is necessary as well as the taking of a test administered by the *Educational Testing Service, Box 966, Princeton, New Jersey 08540*, to whom application should be made at the earliest opportunity.

Recipients are not required to study for a degree in the United States but are encouraged to do so if they are eligible and able to complete the requirements for it.

Further information from:
Kennedy Memorial Fund (U.K.)
c/o Association of Commonwealth Universities
36 Gordon Square
London
England WC1H 0PF

[1183]

JOSEPH P. KENNEDY, JR. FOUNDATION
(U.S.A.)

Research Grants

The Foundation is willing to receive applications for research projects from senior scholars in the neurosciences, experimental psychology, special education, communications, demography, ethics and law. Applicants should submit the following: a brief description of the project; specific goals and the methodology of research; qualifications of the personnel involved; and a detailed budget stipulating allocation of funds and anticipated time period.

Additional material will be requested if the Foundation's Scientific Advisory Board finds the proposal eligible for possible funding.

Further information from:
Eunice Kennedy Shriver
Joseph P. Kennedy, Jr. Foundation
1701 K Street, N.W., Room 205
Washington, D.C. 20006
U.S.A.

[1184]

JOHN FITZGERALD KENNEDY SCHOOL OF GOVERNMENT
Harvard University

William Hodson Jr. Fellowship

Purpose: To train staff members of an international organization in the field of public administration.

No. offered: One Fellowship annually, provided funds are sufficient.

Value: Cost of tuition.

Tenable at the Kennedy School of Government, Harvard University, Cambridge, Massachusetts, for one academic year.

Eligibility: Open to staff members of United Nations organizations or some other public international organizations who are between 25 and 35 years of age. Candidates must have the equivalent of an American bachelor's degree and previous government service with plans to continue a career in government service.

Closing date: 15th March.

Further information from:
John Fitzgerald Kennedy School of Government
Harvard University
Littauer Center
Cambridge, Massachusetts 02138
U.S.A.

[1185]

KENYA PUBLISHERS ASSOCIATION

Kenyatta Prize for Literature

A Prize of 5,000 shillings is awarded annually to the author of the most outstanding work of literature, written in English or Swahili by a citizen of East Africa, and a Prize of 1,500 shillings is awarded annually for the best first work of literature written in English or Swahili. English or Swahili translations of books written in other languages are not acceptable. Publishers may submit up to four works (six copies of each work) by June of each year.

Further information from:
  Honorary Secretary
  Kenya Publishers Association
  P.O. Box 14681
  Nairobi
  Kenya

[1186]

KIDNEY FOUNDATION OF CANADA
(Montreal, Quebec)

The following programs are offered to fund research into the causes, prevention, and cure of kidney and urinary tract diseases.

National Fellowship Program: Five Fellowships, one of which is earmarked for the study of urology, are granted for a period of one year with the possibility of renewal for a second year. Payments are made in quarterly installments. *Closing date:* 1st October.

Summer Student Fellowship Program: 25 Fellowships are awarded for a period of 12 weeks. Payment is made in one lump sum. *Closing date:* 15th February.

National Research Grant Program: Can$550,000 are offered in Grants which are tenable for one or two years with the possibility of renewal for an additional year or two. Payments are made in quarterly installments. *Closing date:* 15th October.

Note: All programs are open to Canadian citizens only. Research awards are open to individuals holding staff appointments at Canadian universities or other recognized Canadian institutions. Preference will be given to nephrologists, urologists, transplantation surgeons or new investigators in these fields.

Further information from:
  Kidney Foundation of Canada
  1650 de Maisonneuve West, Suite 400
  Montreal, Quebec
  Canada H3H 2P3

[1187]

KINDERGARTEN UNION OF SOUTH AUSTRALIA

Jean Denton Memorial Fund—Postgraduate Scholarship

Purpose: To provide financial support to students who wish to increase their knowledge and qualifications in early childhood and related fields.

No. offered: Usually one Scholarship annually.

Value: No set monetary value. Scholarship is to cover cost of a one or two year course of postgraduate study.

Tenable for one or two years at an approved institution in Australia or abroad.

Eligibility: Open to permanent residents of Australia who are working in the field of early childhood or related disciplines, and possess some formal qualification in early childhood education.

Further information from:
  Executive Director
  Kindergarten Union of South Australia
  108 Kermode Street
  North Adelaide, S.A.
  Australia 5006

[1188]

KING ABDUL AZIZ RESEARCH CENTRE
(Riyadh)

King Abdul Aziz Prize

Purpose: To promote studies related to the history, geography, cultural and intellectual heritage of Saudi Arabia.

Value: Variable.

Venue: Riyadh, Naseria, Saudi Arabia.

Eligibility: Persons of any nationality may submit original and unpublished work.

Further information from:
  King Abdul Aziz Research Centre
  P.O. Box 2945
  Riyadh
  Saudi Arabia

[1189]

KING EDWARD VII BRITISH-GERMAN FOUNDATION

Scholarships

Subjects: Unrestricted.

No. offered: One or two Scholarships annually.

Value: DM700 per month, a book grant of DM150, exemption from tuition fees, plus travelling expenses between a Scholar's home in the United Kingdom and his place of study in Germany.

Tenable at a university or other institution of higher education in Germany, for ten months.

Eligibility: Open to persons of British nationality who are graduate members of British universities, and have a working knowledge of German.

Closing date: 20th January.

Further information from:
Secretary
King Edward VII British-German
  Foundation
18 Woodgrove Road
Henbury, Bristol
England BS10 7RE

[1190]

MARTIN LUTHER KING MEMORIAL PRIZE *(U.K.)*

A Prize of £100 is given annually for a literary work reflecting the ideals to which Dr. Martin Luther King dedicated his life. The work may be a novel, story, poem (exceeding 500 lines), essay, play, or a script for television, radio or a motion picture, first published or performed in the United Kingdom during the calendar year preceding the date of the award.

Three copies of the work, in published form, should be furnished to the adjudicators preferably at the time of publication or performance but in any case not later than 15th January of the year following publication or performance. Brief biographical details of the author should also be sent and, where necessary, information concerning publication or performance. Advance notice of a broadcast which the author wishes to be considered would be appreciated.

Further information may be obtained by sending a self addressed envelope to:
John Brunner
Martin Luther King Memorial Prize
c/o National Westminster Bank
7 Fore Street
Chard, Somerset
England TA20 1PJ

[1191]

MACKENZIE KING SCHOLARSHIP TRUST *(Canada)*

Mackenzie King Open Scholarship

Subjects: Unrestricted.

No. offered: One Scholarship annually.

Value: Can$7,000.

Tenable in Canada or elsewhere for one year of full-time postgraduate studies.

Eligibility: Open to graduates of any Canadian university. Applicants should be persons of unusual worth or promise. Awards are determined on the basis of academic achievement, personal qualities and demonstrated aptitudes. Consideration is also given to the applicant's proposed programme of postgraduate study.

Closing date: 15th February.

Further information from:
Awards Office
Room 50, General Services
  Administrative Building
University of British Columbia
Vancouver, B.C.
Canada V6T 1W5

[1192]

MACKENZIE KING SCHOLARSHIP TRUST *(Canada)*

Mackenzie King Travelling Scholarships

Purpose: To give Canadian students the opportunity to broaden their outlook and sympathies and contribute in some measure to the understanding of the problems and policies of other countries.

Subjects: International or industrial relations, including the international or industrial aspects of law, history, politics, and economics.

No. offered: Four or five Scholarships annually.

Value: Not less than Can$7,000 per annum.

Tenable at suitable insititutions either in the United States or the United Kingdom.

Eligibility: Open to graduates of any Canadian university who propose to engage, either in the United States or the United Kingdom, in postgraduate studies in the fields of International or Industrial Relations including the international or industrial aspects of law, history, politics, economics.

Closing date: 15th February.

Further information from:
Awards Office
Mackenzie King Travelling Scholarships
Room 50, General Services
   Administration Building
University of British Columbia
Vancouver, B.C.
Canada V6T 1W5

[1193]

KATE NEAL KINLEY MEMORIAL FELLOWSHIP COMMITTEE
University of Illinois *(Urbana-Champaign)*

Kate Neal Kinley Memorial Fellowship

Subjects: Art, music, architecture.

No. offered: One Fellowship annually.

Value: US$4,000.

Tenable in the United States or abroad for one academic year.

Eligibility: Open to graduates of the College of fine and Applied Arts of the University of Illinois at Urbana-Champaign or graduates of similar institutions of equal educational standing, whose principal or major studies have been in any branch of art, music, or in the design or history of architecture. Preference is given to applicants under twenty-five years of age.

Note: The Fellowship is awarded upon the basis of unusual promise in the fine arts as attested by: academic grades in major field of study as well as related cultural fields; quality of work submitted or performed; character, merit and suitability of the proposed program; personality, seriousness of purpose and moral character of applicant.

Closing date: 15th March.

Further information from:
Dean Jack H. McKenzie
Kate Neal Kinley Memorial Fellowship
   Committee
College of Fine and Applied Arts
110 Architecture Building
University of Illinois
608 East Lorado Taft Drive
Champaign, Illinois 61820
U.S.A.

[1194]

NORMAN KIRK MEMORIAL TRUST *(N.Z.)*

Overseas Grants

Grants to cover the costs of approved studies or training overseas when not available in the home country are offered to persons of any age from the South Pacific (Australia, Cook Islands, Fiji, Gilbert Islands, Nauru, New Hebrides, New Zealand, Niue, Papua New Guinea, Solomon Islands, Tokelau, Tonga, Tuvalu and Western Samoa).

Preference is given to applicants who are not able to acquire other grants or assistance.

Applications should be submitted by 24th July together with supporting documents from the candidate's educational institution or employer.

Further information from:
Secretary
Norman Kirk Memorial Trust
P.O. Box 12-376
Wellington
New Zealand

[1195]

KNIGHTS OF THE SOUTHERN CROSS *(Australia)*

Dr. Horace Nowland Travelling Scholarship

Purpose: To qualify the Scholar to serve Australia with distinction.

Subjects: Variable.

No. offered: One Scholarship annually.

Value: A$5,000 per annum.

Tenable outside Australia for two years.

Eligibility: Open to Australian lay Catholics who intend to pursue careers in Australia and who are graduates or undergraduates in their final year at an Australian university.

Not confirmed for 1983.

Further information from:
Administrator
Dr. Horace Nowland Travelling
  Scholarship
Knights of the Southern Cross
Box 184c, G.P.O.
Melbourne, Victoria
Australia 3001

[1196]

FRANK KNOX MEMORIAL FOUNDATION *(U.K.)*
Association of Commonwealth Universities

Frank Knox Fellowships at Harvard University

Subjects: Fellows will devote most of their time to study in one of the following faculties: arts and sciences (including engineering and medical sciences), business administration, design, divinity, education, law, public administration and public health. Harvard University will try to arrange a suitable course for each individual.

No. offered: Five Fellowships annually.

Value: US$5,000 plus tuition fees. Unmarried Fellows may be accommodated in one of the University dormitories or halls.

Tenable at Harvard University, Cambridge, Massachusetts, for one academic year; awards may be renewed for Fellows registered for a degree programme of more than one year's duration.

Eligibility: Open to citizens of the United Kingdom who are ordinarily resident there. At time of application candidates must have spent at least two of the last four years at a university, university college or polytechnic in the United Kingdom, and must graduate before taking up their award at Harvard. Fellowships are not awarded for postdoctoral study, and no application will be considered from persons already in the United States.

Note: Candidates must file an Admissions Application directly with the graduate school of their choice at an early date; admission to a school is a prior condition of the award of a Fellowship.

Candidates wishing to study business administration should apply by 5th February. They are required to take the Admissions Test for Graduate Study in Business in October or January and should apply to do so in writing to the *Educational Testing Service, Box 966, Princeton, New Jersey 08540.* Two and a half months notice is usually required. A period of full-time work since graduation is necessary prior to embarking on the M.B.A. programme.

Law School candidates should have completed four years of university education.

Travel grants are not awarded, however in cases of extreme hardship applications can be made to Harvard University for travel cost assistance.

Further information from:
Secretary General Frank Knox
  Fellowships
Association of Commonwealth
  Universities
36 Gordon Square
London
England WC1H 0PF

[1197]

KODAK LTD. *(U.K.)*

Kodak Photographic Bursaries

Purpose: To stimulate and to extend the uses of photography and to foster and broaden the undertaking of photographic studies.

Subjects: The subject matter of the project is open.

No. offered: Three or more Bursaries annually.

Value: Up to £3,500 each, which can include awards to individual young students attending a course of full-time study at a recognized school or college.

Tenable in the United Kingdom.

Eligibility: Open only to British subjects or permanent residents of the United Kingdom.

Closing date: Last day of February.

Further information from:
Administrator
Kodak Photographic Bursaries
Kodak Ltd.
P.O. Box 66
Kodak House, Station Road
Hemel Hempstead, Hertfordshire
England HP1 1JU

[1198]

KOSCIUSZKO FOUNDATION *(U.S.A.)*

Awards for Polish Studies in the United States

Scholarships and Grants: A limited number of Grants, usually in the amount of *US*$1,000, are offered as funds become available to American students of any ethnic background who are working towards a doctorate related to some aspect of Polish culture.

Doctoral Dissertation Award: The Foundation will award *US*$1,000 towards the publication of a revised doctoral dissertation which, in its opinion, has made the most significant contribution to the development of Polish studies in a given year. Candidates should contact the Foundation for full requirements prior to submitting manuscripts.

Note: Applications for these awards should be received by 15th January.
The Foundation also supports the development of Polish studies programs at American colleges and universities, especially those located in or near larger concentrations of Polish-Americans. Grants for this purpose are on a matching basis.

Further information from:
Grants Office
Kosciuszko Foundation
15 East 65th Street
New York, New York 10021
U.S.A.

[1199]

KOSCIUSZKO FOUNDATION *(U.S.A.)*

Grants and Programs for Americans to Study in Poland

Graduate and Postgraduate Study: Grants are given on an annual basis, to American and Canadian citizens of Polish descent, for one academic year (renewable for an additional year of study) at accredited institutions of higher learning in Poland. Grantees receive tuition and housing, plus an allowance for food and miscellaneous expenses. Priority is given to university faculty wishing to spend their sabbaticals in Poland, and they receive higher allowances than students. Priority is also given to doctoral candidates whose dissertations require continued study and research in Poland. Applicants should possess an excellent knowledge of Polish. *Closing date:* 15th January.

Note: The following programs are also sponsored by the Foundation: *Year Abroad at the University of Cracow*, Closing date—15th January; *Summer Sessions in Poland*, Closing date—1st February; *Medical Studies in Poland*.

Further information from:
Grants Office
Kosciuszko Foundation
15 East 65th Street
New York, New York 10021
U.S.A.

[1200]

KOSCIUSZKO FOUNDATION *(U.S.A.)*

Chopin Piano Scholarships: Three Scholarships are awarded annually on the basis of a national competition held at the Foundation House, commencing the first Monday in June. The competition is open to talented U.S. pianists of any ethnic background between 15 and 21 years of age at the commencement of the competition. A *US*$1,000 First Prize, *US*$500 Second Prize, and *US*$250 Third Prize are offered unless the judges decide otherwise. Prizes are awarded as Scholarships for further study at recognized music schools or with a private teacher. Application deadline is 1st March of the year of competition.

Marcella Sembrich Scholarship in Voice: Each year a Scholarship is awarded to encourage highly talented students of voice to study the works of Polish composers. The Scholarship is offered to citizens or legal residents of the United States regardless of ethnic background, who have demonstrated unusual musical ability, but who have not yet made extensive professional appearances. Applicants should be between the ages of 19 and 25. In addition to the application, a tape of at least 20 minutes in length including one or more songs or arias by a Polish composer should be submitted.

The Scholarship of approximately US$1,000 may be used to further study at a recognized school or with a private teacher. Application deadline is 1st March.

Michael Twarowski Scholarship of US$1,500 is awarded annually for piano or violin study for an American of Polish extraction.

Further information from:
Grants Office
Kosciuszko Foundation
15 East 65th Street
New York, New York 10021
U.S.A.

[1201]

KOSCIUSZKO FOUNDATION *(U.S.A.)*

Scholarships and Grants for Americans of Polish Background

Kazimiera Adrian-Adrianowska Scholarship of US$1,000 is awarded annually to assist a qualified Polish or Polish American student or scholar.

Harriet and Feliks Basista Scholarships provide assistance to citizens of the United States of America studying in the United States of America, or Poland, and citizens of Poland studying in the United States of America, provided such students are studying in the fields of the Polish language, Polish history or Polish literature, along with the arts and social or applied sciences.

Dr. Stanislas Chylinski Scholarship of US$1,000 is awarded annually to assist a qualified graduate student in the humanities and social sciences.

Dr. Stanislas Chylinski Grants-in-Aid: A number of scholarships and grants are made annually to students of Polish background, regardless of their field of study.

Alfred Jurzykowski Foundation Grants: A number of scholarships are offered to Americans of Polish background.

Dr. Casimir Victor Kierzkowski Memorial Scholarship is awarded annually in the amount of US$1,000 to assist a major in Polish studies—Polish history, language, literature and culture.

John E. Kierzkowski Scholarship of US$1,000 is awarded annually to assist a needy student in the field of journalism.

Stan Lesny Scholarships: Several Scholarships are awarded annually, with a stipend of from US$500 to US$1,000 each, for the study of engineering, mathematics, or the natural sciences, at selected American colleges, universities and schools of engineering.

Massachusetts Federation of Polish Women's Clubs Scholarship: Offered to a young woman of Polish background for the study of medicine. Preference is first given to children of the Federation's members, and then to residents of the state of Massachusetts.

Stephen P. Mizwa Memorial Scholarship of US$1,000 is awarded annually to a deserving graduate student in any field of study.

Dr. Stanislaw Mrozowski Scholarly Journal Fund: A number of grants are made to enable physicists in Poland to subscribe to membership in scientific societies within the United States.

Margaret M. Patterson Memorial Scholarship of US$1,000 is awarded annually to qualified students in the sciences, with priority given to those pursuing a career in engineering.

Wanda Roehr Fund: A number of small grants are awarded annually, primarily to Polish students and scholars to assist in short term cultural, scientific and educational projects.

Arthur and Genevieve Roth Scholarship of US$1,000 is awarded annually to assist qualified students in the field of business administration, banking and finance, with preference given to those attending the Arthur T. Roth School of Business Administration of Long Island University.

Albert Spiezny Journalism Scholarships: Two Scholarships of US$5,000 each toward tuition expenses at the Graduate School of Journalism of Columbia University in New York City. The Scholarships are awarded on a competitive basis to Americans of Polish extraction and to Poles who are American citizens. These Scholarships are connected with the possibility of apprentice editorship on the staff of

New Horizons magazine, an English-language monthly devoted to Polish and Polish-American affairs. In the event that no candidates are found who wish to study at Columbia, the Scholarship will be available for study at other schools of journalism in the United States.

Joseph Slotkowski Memorial Publication Fund: Grants are awarded to assist in the publication of works dealing with current problems relating to the Polish-American community.

Jerome and Mary Jane Straka Scholarship of US$1,000 is awarded annually to assist a qualified student in the sciences, with preference given to a student of chemistry.

William and Mildred Zelosky Grants: These Awards are offered to enable Americans to pursue graduate and postgraduate studies in Poland, and for Poles to study in the United States. Grants are usually for one academic year.

Michalina and Herman Zimber Scholarship Fund: Annual awards are offered for the benefit of financially needy American citizens of Polish descent for the study of professions such as medicine, law, engineering, arts and sciences and education at institutions of higher learning such as accredited colleges and universities.

Further information from:
Grants Office
Kosciuszko Foundation
15 East 65th Street
New York, New York 10021
U.S.A.

[1202]

ALFRIED KRUPP VON BOHLEN UND HALBACH FOUNDATION *(West Germany)*

Prize for Energy Research

One Prize of DM500,000 is awarded to recognize achievement in the development, promotion and application of research in the field of energy resources. An adjudicating committee selects candidates from among those nominated, and the Board of Trustees of the Foundation then makes the final decision as to the recipient.

Further information from:
Alfried Krupp von Bohlen und
Halbac-Stiftung
Hügel 15
4330 Essen-Bredeney
West Germany

[1203]

LADY DAVIS FELLOWSHIP TRUST
(Israel)

Graduate and Postdoctoral Fellowships; Visiting Professorships

Purpose: To advance the interests of international scholarship and Israeli higher education.

Subjects: Unrestricted.

No. offered: Varies annually.

Value: Awards are intended to defray transportation, tuition and maintenance expenses. Payments are made on a montly basis.

Tenable at the Hebrew University, Jerusalem or the Technion, Israel Institute of Technology, Haifa for one year; renewable.

Eligibility: There are no restrictions on age, sex, citizenship, or residency. Individuals are selected on the basis of demonstrated excellence in their studies, promise of distinction in chosen fields of specialization, as well as on qualities of mind, intellect and character, which would enable the recipient to benefit from the opportunity for study in Israel.

Note: Similar awards are available to promising students of the Hebrew University or the Technion to study or undertake research in outstanding institutions abroad.

Closing date: 1st December.

Further information from:
Lady Davis Fellowship Trust
P.O. Box 1255
Jerusalem 91000
Israel

L

See *How to Use The Grants Register*, page ix

[1204]

LADY TATA MEMORIAL TRUST *(U.K.)*

International Predoctoral Awards
International Postdoctoral Awards

Subjects: Leukaemia and malignant disease.

No. offered: A variable number of each Award, depending upon available funds.

Value: The value of each Award is appropriate to the age, seniority, and experience of the successful candidate and to the Institution in which the work is to be carried out. Candidates should enquire from the Institution concerned what stipend would be appropriate for them.

Tenable in any country for one year, renewable to a maximum of three years.

Eligibility: Open to nationals of any country who are science or medical graduates. Predoctoral candidates must have had some research experience and the proposed research should be "most likely to throw light on the nature of leukaemia in particular, or malignant disease in general."

Note: Predoctoral candidates must work under supervision in the laboratory of a recognized institution.

Closing date: 1st March.

Further information from:
　Secretary, Scientific Advisory Committee
　Lady Tata Memorial Trust
　MRC Leukaemia Unit
　　Royal Postgraduate Medical School
　　Ducane Road
　　London
　　England W12 0HS

[1205]

LAIDLAW FOUNDATION *(Canada)*

Fellowships

A small number of Fellowships are given each year to experienced practitioners in the social and behavioural sciences. Applications for formal degree or diploma studies are not accepted. University faculty members on sabbatical leave with partial salary are ineligible.

Note: At the time of going to press, the Fellowships were under review.

Further information from:
　Laidlaw Foundation
　Suite 203
　60 St. Clair Avenue East
　Toronto, Ontario
　Canada M4T 1N5

[1206]

LATIN AMERICAN CENTER FOR MONETARY STUDIES

Rodrigo Gomez Prize

Purpose: To encourage papers in fields of interest to central banks of Latin America.

Subjects: Monetary policies, central banking, and other financial matters at the regional and national level.

No. offered: One Prize annually.

Value: US$5,000, paid in a lump sum.

Eligibility: Open to citizens of Latin American and Caribbean countries, and of Spain. Papers must be submitted in Spanish, English, French or Portuguese.

Note: Prize winning paper will be published by the Center.

Closing date: 15th January of each year.

Further information from:
  Director
  Centro de Estudios Monetarios
    Latinoamericano
  Durango 54
  Delegacion Cuauhtemoc
  06700 Mexico, D.F.

[1207]

LATIN AMERICAN INSTITUTE FOR ECONOMIC AND SOCIAL PLANNING
(Santiago)
United Nations

Assitance for Courses

Courses: Basic training and specialization in economic and social planning.

No. offered: 30 places per Course.

Value: Tuition is free.

Tenable at the Institute for the duration of the Course: Basic Course—April to October; Social Course—May to July.

Eligibility: Open to university students and teachers and officials working in fields related to planning. Preference is given to candidates between 25 and 35 years of age from Latin American countries and the Caribbean. Participants must be nominated by their government. Instruction is in Spanish.

Note: Intensive Courses are also organized in Latin American countries requesting such Courses.

Closing date: 31st October for Basic Course; 31st January for Social Course.

Further information from:
  Training Program
  Latin American Institute for Economic
    and Social Planning
  Casilla 1567
  Santiago
  Chile

[1208]

LATIN AMERICAN SCHOLARSHIP PROGRAM OF AMERICAN UNIVERSITIES

LASPAU is an association of almost 400 institutions of higher learning in the United States, Latin Aemrica and the Caribbean, whose purpose is to strengthen university teaching, research and administration in the developing nations of Latin America and the Caribbean. Graduate scholarships are arranged for faculty members of these developing nations at U.S. institutions. Candidates must be nominated and sponsored by a participating Latin American or Caribbean university, and contract to return to a teaching or administrative position there, upon completion of the Scholarship. Funding is shared by the sponsoring institution and other national and international agencies with whom LASPAU enters into an agreement.

Further information from:
  LASPAU
  25 Mount Auburn Street, Room 302
  Cambridge, Massachusetts 02138
  U.S.A.

[1209]

LAW STUDENTS CIVIL RIGHTS RESEARCH COUNCIL *(U.S.A.)*

LSCRRC Summer Internship Grant

Purpose: To provide students with an opportunity to acquire legal skills; to provide needy communities and organizations with qualified, dedicated workers; and to motivate law students to practice people's law upon graduation.

Subjects: Internship in civil liberties, civil rights and public interest law.

No. offered: Approximately 200 Internships annually.

Value: US$1,500.

Tenable for ten weeks in various locations under various circumstances. Internships may be renewed for a second summer.

Eligibility: Open to any first or second year law student.

Closing date: 1st February.

Further information from:
  Law Students Civil Rights Research
    Council
  132 West 43rd Street, Third Floor
  New York, New York 10036
  U.S.A.

[1210]

D.H. LAWRENCE FELLOWSHIP
University of New Mexico *(Albuquerque)*

Purpose: To provide time and a good creative climate to aspiring and promising writers of fiction, poetry, and drama.

No. offered: One Fellowship annually.

Value: US$700 stipend, plus residence on the Lawrence Ranch, north of Taos, New Mexico.

Tenable at the Lawrence Ranch for three months.

Eligibility: Open to creative writers of all stages of experience and achievement.

Note: Applications should be by personal letter outlining the plan of work during the Fellowship. Applicants should also submit: a curriculum vitae; samples of work; and three supporting letters from others known in the writing field.

Closing date: 31st January.

Further information from:
  Chairman
  D.H. Lawrence Fellowship Committee
  Department of English
  Humanities Building 217
  University of New Mexico
  Albuquerque, New Mexico 87131
  U.S.A.

[1211]

LEAGUE FOR THE EXCHANGE OF COMMONWEALTH TEACHERS *(U.K.)*

Approximately 260 United Kingdom government Grants are available to teachers (in all types of schools—primary, secondary, special, technical colleges, colleges of education) from the United Kingdom who are accepted for exchange with teachers in Australia, the Bahamas, Barbados, Canada, Jamaica, Kenya (Nairobi), New Zealand, Singapore and Trinidad, and who are between 25 and 45 years of age and have not less than five years' teaching experience in the United Kingdom, with at least two years under the current employing authority. The Grants are tenable for one academic year and comprise a variable cost-of-living allowance, travel allowance and grants for dependent children, if accompanying their parents.

Further information from:
  League for the Exchange of
    Commonwealth Teachers
  Seymour Mews House, 2nd Floor Suite
  26-37 Seymour Mews
  London
  England W1H 9PE

[1212]

LEAGUE OF RED CROSS SOCIETIES

Study visits are offered to selected personnel, volunteer or paid, of national Red Cross or Red Crescent Societies for study concerning Red Cross or Red Crescent national and international organisations and/or services. Recipients visit national Red Cross or Red Crescent Societies and/or the International Institutions of the Red Cross in Geneva, namely the ICRC and the League of Red Cross Societies. Applications must be made through, and endorsed by the candidate's National Society. Recipients are expected to participate in the development of their National Society.

Further information from:
  League of Red Cross Societies
  P.O. Box 276
  CH-1211 Geneva 19
  Switzerland

[1213]

LEATHERSELLERS' COMPANY *(U.K.)*

Theological and Secular Exhibitions

The Company awards Theological and Secular Exhibitions tenable at English universities. Theological Exhibitions are limited to students who have been recommended for Holy Orders in the Church of England.

Detailed application forms should be returned no later than 31st January and 15th September of each year for Secular and Theological Exhibitions respectively.

Further information from:
  Clerk
  Leathersellers' Company
  15 St. Helen's Place
  London
  England EC3A 6DQ

[1214]

LEEDS INTERNATIONAL PIANOFORTE COMPETITION

In association with Harvey's of Bristol, up to 20 monetary prizes and a series of concert engagements are offered in the Competition, which is held every third year (next in 1984). Prizes offered: one of £2,000; one of £1,000; one of £500; three of £300; four of £150; ten of £75. Open to professional pianists of all nationalities who are under 30 years of age on 31st August in the year of the Competition.

Not confirmed for 1984.

Further information from:
  Honorary Administration
  Leeds International Pianoforte
    Competition
  Great George Street
  Leeds
  England LS1 3AE

[1215]

LEGACY CO-ORDINATING COUNCIL OF AUSTRALIA

Sir John Gellibrand Memorial Scholarship

Subjects: Unrestricted.

No. offered: One Scholarship biennially.

Value: A$5,500 per annum.

Tenable at an approved university or college of advanced education for two years, with the possibility of extension for a third year.

Eligibility: Open to Australian citizens who are children of deceased ex-servicemen. A candidate must be a member, ex-member, or eligible as a member of a Junior or Intermediate Legacy Club.

Note: Scholarships are awarded to residents of the various Australian states, in the following order: Tasmania, 1984; South Australia, 1986; Queensland, 1988; Western Australia, 1990; New South Wales, 1992; Victoria, 1994.

Further information from:
  Legacy Co-ordinating Council of Australia
  Box 368F
  G.P.O. Melbourne, Victoria
  Australia 3001

[1216]

LERICI FOUNDATION FOR ARCHAEOLOGICAL PROSPECTING *(Italy)*

Course Study Grants

The purpose of the Course is to give the participants an outline of the principles and use of the modern methods of archaeological prospecting. The Course is held during a two week period in April. Nine Grants are made available annually to foreign nationals from Europe, North Africa and the Near East. The Grants cover travelling and a contribution towards living expenses in Rome during the period of the Course in addition to the fee of the Course itself.

Further information from:
  Lerici Foundation for Archaeological
    Prospecting
  Via Vittorio Veneto 108
  00187 Rome
  Italy

[1217]

LEUKAEMIA RESEARCH FUND *(U.K.)*

Research Grants and Exchange Fellowship

Research Grants are offered for periods of up to three years for the support of research into leukaemia and related blood disease, and patient support. The Grants are tenable at approved hospitals and university medical centers in the United Kingdom. Applications are considered by the Fund's Medical and Scientific Advisory Panel three times a year. Recipients of Grants must submit a progress report each year, and applications for further support are dependent upon the results so reported.

An *Exchange Fellowship* is awarded annually

to graduates for the furtherance of research into leukaemia enabling the selected applicant to spend a year in France at a centre recommended by the French Institute of Health and Medical Research. A French Fellow is similarly received at a research institute in the United Kingdom.

Training Fellowships are also awarded within the United Kingdom to medical and science graduates.

Further information from:
Leukaemia Research Fund
43 Great Ormond Street
London WC1N 3JJ
England

[1218]

LEUKEMIA SOCIETY OF AMERICA, INC.

Scholarships

Purpose: To encourage continued investigation in the field, while assuring the investigator adequate income for a period of five years.

Value: US$25,000 per annum.

Tenable for five years; not renewable.

Eligibility: Applicants, who may be citizens of any country, should have demonstrated distinct ability in the investigation of leukemia and related disorders. Nominations should be made through the office of the dean or the chief administrative officer of the sponsoring institution.

Note: Only one Scholar will be appointed at any one department or program of an institution in any year.

Closing date: 1st September for commencement in July.

Further information from:
Vice-President for Medical and Scientific Affairs
Leukemia Society of America, Inc.
800 Second Avenue
New York, New York 10017
U.S.A.

[1219]

LEUKEMIA SOCIETY OF AMERICA, INC.

Fellowships

Purpose: To encourage promising younger investigators to embark on a academic career involving clinical or fundamental research in or related to leukemia.

Value: US$30,000.

Tenable for two years; not renewable, although application may be made for Special Fellowship status after at least one year of Fellowship.

Eligibility: Applicants, who may be citizens of any country, should show evidence of a particular interest in leukemia or related disorders. Nominations should be made through the office of the dean or the chief administrative officer of the sponsoring insitution.

Closing date: 1st September for commencement in July.

Further information from:
Vice-President for Medical and Scientific Affairs
Leukemia Society of America, Inc.
800 Second Avenue
New York, New York 10017
U.S.A.

[1220]

LEUKEMIA SOCIETY OF AMERICA, INC.

Special Fellowships

Purpose: To give support to a variety of individuals intermediate between the Fellow and Scholar programs.

Value: US$37,000.

Tenable for two years; not renewable, although application may be made for Scholarship status after at least one year of Special Fellowship.

Eligibility: Applicants, who may be citizens of any country, should have demonstrated ability in research and have become interested in working in the field of leukemia and related disorders. Nominations should be made through the office of the dean or the chief administrative officer of the sponsoring institution.

Note: Only one Special Fellow will be appointed at any one department or program of an institution in any year.

Closing date: 1st September for commencement in July.

Further information from:
Vice-President for Medical and Scientific Affairs
Leukemia Society of America, Inc.
800 Second Avenue
New York, New York 10017
U.S.A.

[1221]

LEVERHULME TRUST *(U.K.)*

General Information

The grants by the Leverhulme Trust are in two categories—awards to individuals on the recommendation of a Research Awards Advisory Committee [see following listings] which amount to about £350,000 per annum, and grants to institutions which amount to about £3,000,000 per annum.

Grants to institutions: Grants are made to institutions for short-term research projects, for educational innovations and under Trust-designed schemes of academic interchange between the U.K. and other countries. Support takes the form of research and teaching fellowships, studentships and the like; grants for endowments, buildings, equipment or general funds are excluded.

There are no limits to the fields of enquiry or the countries which are eligible but the Trustees' policy is generally to concentrate on business studies, industrial relations, economics, government, international relations, education, the humanities and the fine arts in the U.K. and underdeveloped countries of the Commonwealth. Institutions to be eligible must have charitable status.

Further information from:
Director
Leverhulme Trust
15-19 New Fetter Lane
London
England EC4A 1NR

[1222]

LEVERHULME TRUST
on recommendation of its
RESEARCH AWARDS ADVISORY COMMITTEE

Study Abroad Studentships

Subjects: Not students wishing only to improve knowledge of modern languages; otherwise unrestricted.

No. offered: A limited number.

Value: £3,600 per annum plus return air passage and other allowances at the discretion of the Committee.

Tenable at centres of learning in Europe or any other part of the world except the U.K. and the U.S.A., for one year or two years if circumstances warrant it.

Eligibility: At the time of application candidates must be first degree graduates of a U.K. university, holders of a CNAA degree or able to show evidence of equivalent education in the U.K. They must have been educated at a school or schools in the U.K. or other part of the Commonwealth. They must be normally resident in the U.K. and under the age of 30 on 1st October in the year of the award.

Closing date: Normally 5th January.

Further information from:
Secretary
Research Awards Advisory Committee
Leverhulme Trust
15-19 New Fetter Lane
London
England EC4A 1NR

[1223]

LEVERHULME TRUST
on recommendation of its
RESEARCH AWARDS ADVISORY COMMITTEE

Research Fellowships and Grants

Purpose: To assist senior persons pursuing investigations who are prevented by routine duties or other cause from undertaking or completing a research programme. They are not available as replacement for past support or to persons reading for higher degrees or equivalent awards.

Subjects: Unrestricted.

Value: By individual assessment, but not exceeding a total of £4,400.

Tenable in the U.K. or abroad for a minimum of three months to a maximum of two years.

Eligibility: Open to persons educated in the U.K. or in any other part of the Commonwealth who are normally resident in the U.K.

Closing date: Normally 1st December.

Further information from:
Secretary
Research Awards Advisory Committee
Leverhulme Trust
15-19 New Fetter Lane
London
England EC4A 1NR

[1224]

LEVERHULME TRUST
on recommendation of its
RESEARCH AWARDS ADVISORY COMMITTEE

Emeritus Fellowships

Purpose: To assist persons who have recently reached, or are about to reach, retirement age, who have held academic positions in universities or institutions of similar status in the U.K. and who have an established record of research. They are primarily designed to help in the completion of research already begun but persons with an established record of research who have retired early and wish to start new projects may also be considered.

Subjects: Unrestricted.

Value: By individual assessment, but not exceeding £3,300 per annum.

Tenable in the U.K. or abroad for one or two years.

Closing date: Normally 1st December.

Further information from:
Secretary
Research Awards Advisory Committee
Leverhulme Trust
15-19 New Fetter Lane
London
England EC4A 1NR

[1225]

LIFE INSURANCE MEDICAL RESEARCH FUND OF AUSTRALIA AND NEW ZEALAND

Postgraduate Scholarships

Support is available to Australian and New Zealand graduates, who are less than 35 years of age and are engaged in full-time supervised courses of advanced study and research in cardiovascular medicine, while enrolled as candidates for higher degrees.

Tenable at any approved university for one year, renewable for an additional two years. The level of support will not exceed that offered by the National Health and Medical Research Council of Australia.

Further information from:
Prof. M.G. Taylor, Medical Director
Life Insurance Medical Research Fund of Australia and New Zealand
Box 4134, G.P.O.
Sydney, N.S.W.
Australia 2001

[1226]

LIFE INSURANCE MEDICAL RESEARCH FUND OF AUSTRALIA AND NEW ZEALAND

Research Fellowships

Fellowships are available for scientific and medical research broadly related to cardiovascular function and disease.

Fellowships tenable in Australia and New Zealand are available to graduates who have shown promise of research ability. Normally, a successful candidate will have served a probationary period as a research assistant. A candidate with little or no research experience may be appointed as a research assistant to the nominated investigator under a Grant-in-Aid. Appointments will be made for one or two years in the first instance. The salary awarded will be in accordance with the current rates for research workers.

Fellowships tenable overseas are available to graduates with at least two years' experience and proven ability for research. Fellowships will be granted for a period of two or three years (the first, or first and second year must be spent abroad, and the final year in an approved insitution in Australia or New Zealand). The salary will vary according to experience and the country in which the work is to be done, but it will be at the level of a Senior Fellowship. In addition, travelling expenses will be provided for the Fellow and his family.

Note: Both Fellowships are open to persons possessing medical degrees or equivalent scientific training. In most cases, candidates should be under 35 years of age.

An applicant is expected to have made prior arrangements with the established investigator under whose supervision he hopes to work, and with the institution in which he proposes to work. He must supply an outline of the proposed research.

A Fellow is expected to devote his entire time to the approved project and is required to give a concise report of his activities and research progress at the end of each calendar year and a final report when his Fellowship terminates. Participation in teaching and attendance at advanced courses relevant to the research programme may be approved if they occupy only a limited portion of his time.

Closing date: 1st June.

Further information from:
Prof. M.G. Taylor, Medical Director
Life Insurance Medical Research Fund of
    Australia and New Zealand
Box 4134, G.P.O.
Sydney, N.S.W.
Australia 2001

[1227]

LIFE INSURANCE MEDICAL RESEARCH FUND OF AUSTRALIA AND NEW ZEALAND

S.A. Smith Visiting Fellowships

The Fund will consider nominations, from established research workers in Australia and New Zealand, of distinguished overseas persons in the field of cardiovascular function and disease for award of the Fellowship. Under the Fellowship, it is expected that the Fellow should work in the sponsoring institution for a period of not less than six months or more than one year. The value depends upon individual circumstances, but normally includes the fares for the Fellow, together with additional allowances. No Fellowship exceeds A$10,000, but, depending on funds available, more than one Fellowship may be awarded in any one year.

Nominations should be accompanied by a curriculum vitae of the person proposed, together with a list of his publications, and supported by referees' letter.

Closing date: 1st June.

Further information from:
Prof. M.G. Taylor, Medical Director
Life Insurance Medical Research Fund of
    Australia and New Zealand
Box 4134, G.P.O.
Sydney, N.S.W.
Australia 2001

[1228]

LIFE INSURANCE MEDICAL RESEARCH FUND OF AUSTRALIA AND NEW ZEALAND

Grants-in-Aid

Application may be made by a full-time responsible investigator, with the approval of the head of his department or institution, for financial support of a particular research programme which is related to cardiovascular function and disease. Grants will be made only to non-profit institutions in Australia and New Zealand which possess the requisite research facilities.

The Grant-in-Aid should, if possible, provide for the entire, rather than supplementary, financial needs of the project. It is realised that programmes usually extend over two or three years and requests should be made accordingly, unless the project is of a pilot nature or clearly will need aid for one year only. The Grant may include salaries for graduate research assistants, graduate or technical assistants, the cost of equipment, animals and special supplies. However, the salary of the investigator must be provided from other sources and must be reasonably assured for the duration of the proposed work.

Although strict adherence to the details of the programme and expenditure for which a Grant is approved is not required, the investigator should discuss any proposed major departure with the Medical Director. The investigator is required to give a concise report of research progress at the end of each calendar year and a final report when the Grant terminates.

Closing date: 1st June.

Further information from:
Prof. M.G. Taylor, Medical Director
Life Insurance Medical Research Fund of
   Australia and New Zealand
Box 4134, G.P.O.
Sydney, N.S.W.
Australia 2001

[1229]

LIFE UNDERWRITERS ASSOCIATION OF CANADA EDUCATIONAL FOUNDATION

Bursaries

Purpose: To encourage the study of the fundamentals and practice of life insurance.

No. offered: Four Bursaries annually.

Value: Can$750 per annum.

Tenable at any university or college affiliated with the Association of Universities and Colleges of Canada.

Eligibility: Open to full-time Canadian students entering the second or subsequent year of an undergraduate course containing at least 15 hours of lectures on the fundamentals and practice of life insurance. Candidates must have a satisfactory academic record and require financial aid.

Closing date: 1st June.

Further information from:
Life Underwriters Association of Canada
   Educational Foundation
41 Lesmill Road
Don Mills, Ontario
Canada M3B 2T3

[1230]

ELI LILLY AND COMPANY *(U.S.A.)*

Lilly International Fellowships

Subjects: Internal medicine and related fields, e.g. infectious diseases, diabetes and other metabolic disorders, gastroenterology, cardiovascular diseases, immunology, renal disorders, pulmonary diseases, and hematology. Consideration is also given to training in pediatrics, dermatology, pathology, public health, and tropical medicine.

No. offered: Between 3 and 5 Fellowships annually.

Value: Single—US$1,000 per month plus round trip economy airfare; married—US$1,200 per month plus round trip economy airfare for Fellow only.

Tenable in United States or Canadian medical centers for twelve months.

Eligibility: Open to physicians from selected countries other than the United States who are active participants in the work of their universities and hospitals. They should be between 26 and 40 years of age, have had several years' experience in medical practice, clinical research or medical teaching, and be proficient in English.

Note: The selection of candidates and the awarding of Fellowships is the responsibiligy of the appointed committees in the countries concerned.
Recipients must undertake to return and contribute to the advancement of medical education and research in their own countries.

Not confirmed for 1983.

Further information from:
Secretary
Lilly International Fellowship Committee
Eli Lilly and Company
Indianapolis, Indiana 46206
U.S.A.

[1231]

JAMES F. LINCOLN ARC WELDING FOUNDATION *(U.S.A.)*

Awards for Papers

The Award program is intended to stimulate innovation and the development of ideas for the use of arc welded design, engineering and fabrication in structures, machinery and manufactured products. Awards totalling US$50,000 are made for written entries describing how arc welding was used to conserve material, improve function or appearance, or reduce cost on specific structures, machines or products.

A total of 30 Awards are offered as follows: Three Gold Awards of *US*$5,000 each; three Silver Awards of *US*$3,000 each; three Bronze Awards of *US*$2,000 each; twenty Merit Awards of *US*$500 each.

The awards are open to residents of the United States (excluding government officials) who have made a contribution to the work described either in design, engineering, fabrication, manufacture or erection. Qualified persons may apply individually or in groups. *Closing date:* 31st January.

Student Engineering Design Competition: Awards totalling *US*$23,800 are made to recognize and reward student achievement in solving design, engineering or fabricating problems related to structures, machines, mechanical apparatus or their component parts. The Awards, which range from *US*$250 to *US*$1,250, are competed for by both undergraduates and graduates in two Divisions: Division I—Structural; Division II—Mechanical. The Competition is open to any student enrolled in an undergraduate or graduate engineering or technology course in any college or university in the United States. Students may participate either as individuals or as a group of not more than five members. *Closing date:* 1st July.

Further information from:
 Secretary
 James F. Lincoln Arc Welding
  Foundation
 P.O. Box 3035
 Cleveland, Ohio 44117
 U.S.A.

[1232]

LINGUISTIC SOCIETY OF AMERICA

Fellowships

Purpose: To give graduate and postgraduate students an opportunity for concentrated study in linguistics with professors from universities throughout the United States and from institutions in other countries.

No. offered: From 20 to 50 Fellowships annually, according to the availability of funds.

Value: Awards usually cover tuition and a contribution towards subsistence expenses.

Tenable for two months in the summer at the university which is co-sponsoring the Fellowship.

Eligibility: Applicants should have a recognized baccalaureate degree or at least first year graduate status.

Note: Awards will not be made for the study of a specific language except as part of a linguistics program.

Further information from:
 Linguistic Society of America
 3520 Prospect Street, N.W.
 Washington, D.C. 20007
 U.S.A.

[1233]

LINNEAN SOCIETY OF LONDON
Percy Sladen Memorial Fund

Grants

Grants, generally for sums of £100 to £500, are offered twice yearly for research or investigations in natural science, especially in the sciences of zoology, geology and anthropology, experimental physiology, pathology and therapeutics. Funds are not provided for undergraduate expeditions nor for major support for research towards a postgraduate qualification. Closing dates for application are 30th January and 30th September annually.

Further information from:
  Percy Sladen Memorial Fund
  Linnean Society of London
  Burlington House, Piccadilly
  London
  England W1V 01Q

[1234]

LISZT SOCIETY (*U.K.*)

Liszt Piano Competition

A First Prize of £500, paid in a lump sum, is offered to a pianist at the beginning of his or her career for excellence in the performance of music by Liszt. It is anticipated that future Competitions will be open to individuals of any nationality and of either sex. Pianists should be professionals, not over thirty years of age, and be able to submit references from eminent musicians. The Competition is held approximately every six or seven years (last awarded in 1976).

Further information from:
  Alan Paul
  Liszt Society Ltd.
  59 Leopold Road
  London SW19
  England

[1235]

GERALD LOEB AWARDS (*U.S.A.*)

The Awards are given annually, in four categories, to recognize writers who have made important contributions to public understanding of business, finance and the economy. Each Award winner receives US$1,000 and a plaque and attends the Awards ceremony, held alternately in New York City or Los Angeles, and Washington, D.C. The categories are: single article or series in a newspaper with circulation of 250,000 or more; single article or series in a newspaper with circulation of 250,000 or less; single article or series in a national magazine; editorial or commentary. Material for consideration must have been published in the United States during the 12-month period ending 31st December of the year preceding that of the Award.

Closing date: 30th January.

Further information from:
  Gerald Loeb Awards
  Graduate School of Management
    Room 4250-E
  UCLA
  405 Hilgard Avenue
  Los Angeles, California 90024
  U.S.A.

[1236]

LONDON CHAMBER OF COMMERCE AND INDUSTRY

Charles R.E. Bell Scholarships

Subjects: Commerce or foreign languages.

Value: By individual assessment, to a normal maximum of £1,000.

Tenable at approved centres in the United Kingdom or overseas, for one year.

Eligibility: Applicants should be domiciled in the United Kingdom, 18 years of age or over, and preferably graduates or professionally-qualified persons. They should be engaged in commerce (including the commercial functions of industry) or be teachers in commercial education, who intend to continue therein.

Note: Proposed work must be for the purpose of increasing the recipient's knowledge of commerce or a foreign language.

Closing date: 31st December.

Further information from:
  London Chamber of Commerce and
    Industry
  Commercial Education Scheme
  Marlowe House
  109 Station Road
  Sidcup, Kent
  England DA15 7BJ

[1237]

MARGUERITE LONG-JACQUES THIBAUD INTERNATIONAL COMPETITION FOR PIANO AND VIOLIN (*Paris*)

Violinists and pianists of any nationality, between 16 and 32 years of age, may enter the Competition which is held in June in odd-numbered years. The first prize for each branch is FF35,000. Board and lodging is organized by the Competition Committee to those who make the request; however, these expenses are the responsibility of the competitor. The closing date for entry is 15th March.

Further information from:
Secretariat
Marguerite Long-Jacques Thibaud International Competition for Piano and Violin
45 rue la Boétie
F-75008 Paris
France

[1238]

ROBERTO LONGHI FOUNDATION FOR THE STUDY OF THE HISTORY OF ART *(Italy)*

Fellowships

Subjects: Postgraduate research in the history of art.

Value: 300,000 lire per month (180,000 lire per month for residents of the city and provinces of Florence).

Tenable at the Longhi Institute, Florence for eight months, commencing in November. At the recommendation of the Scientific Committee, Fellowships for four months may be awarded.

Eligibility: Open to Italian citizens who possess a degree from an Italian university with a thesis in the history of art, and to non-Italian citizens who have fulfilled the preliminary requirements for a doctoral degree at an accredited university or similar institution. Candidates should be under 30 years of age on 30th April of the year of their application.

Note: Applications should include the following: (a) the candidate's biographical data; (b) a transcript of the candidate's undergraduate and graduate records; (c) a copy of the degree thesis (if available) and other published or unpublished original works; (d) a curriculum studiorum, indicating knowledge of foreign languages; (e) letters of reference from at least two persons of academic standing who are familiar with the candidate's work; (f) the subject of the proposed research; (g) two passport photographs.

Closing date: 30th April.

Further information from:
Secretariat
Roberto Longhi Foundation for the Study of the History of Art
Via Benedetto Fortini 30
Florence 50125
Italy

[1239]

LONGY SCHOOL OF MUSIC *(Cambridge, Massachusetts)*

Vocal, Instrumental and Composition Scholarships

Value: Full or partial tuition. Travel assistance is not provided.

Tenable at the School for one year; renewable up to four years.

Eligibility: Open to suitably qualified students from any country.

Closing date: 15th April.

Further information from:
Longy School of Music
1 Follen Street
Cambridge, Massachusetts 02138
U.S.A.

[1240]

GIOVANNI LORENZINI FOUNDATION *(Italy)*

Scholarships

To promote scientific research, mainly in the fields of medicine, pharmacology, chemistry and biology, the Foundation offers a limited number of Scholarships of approximately 5,000,000 lire. Eligibility is restricted to graduates and laboratory technicians who are Italian citizens.

Further information from:
Giovanni Lorenzini Foundation
via Monte Napoleone 23
20121 Milan
Italy

[1241]

LOUISIANA STATE UNIVERSITY PRESS

Jules F. Landry Award

One US$1,000 Award is given annually to the author of the best manuscript on Southern history, Southern biography or Southern literature. All manuscripts submitted in these fields will be considered without formal application. Authors need not have published previously with the Press.

Further information from:
Leslie E. Phillabaum, Director
Louisiana State University Press
Baton Rouge, Louisiana 70803
U.S.A.

[1242]

HENRY LUCE FOUNDATION, INC. *(U.S.A.)*

Scholarships Program

Purpose: To develop a new level of understanding of Asia among future leaders of American society.

Subjects: Unrestricted.

No. offered: 15 Scholarships annually.

Value: US$9,000 per annum, economy class air travel, and a cost-of-living adjustment where applicable. Married Scholars accompanied by their wife or husband receive an additional US$2,000. The Foundation also assumes the cost of basic travel and medical insurance.

Tenable for one year in Asian countries.

Eligibility: Open to citizens of the United States who are no more than 27 years of age and hold, or are about to receive, at least a bachelor's degree. Candidates should have a record of the highest academic achievement, outstanding leadership capability, and a clearly defined career interest in a specific field.

Note: While some Scholars may be attached to Asian Institutions in teaching or research capacities, none are formally enrolled as students in colleges or universities, and no academic credit is extended. The Asia Foundation, which administers all Asian aspects of the Program, arranges internships or job-placements for Scholars, which last for approximately ten months. It is to be hoped that each Scholar will be able to make a professional contribution to the host organization, but such a contribution is not essential.

Candidates may not apply directly to the Foundation. Any individual interested in seeking nomination should contact the faculty or administration member who is designated as Luce Scholars Program Liaison officer on his or her campus.

Note: The Program is under major review (Summer 1982).

Latest information from:
Luce Scholars Program
Henry Luce Foundation, Inc.
111 West 50th Street
New York, New York 10020
U.S.A.

[1243]

HENRY LUCE FOUNDATION, INC. *(U.S.A.)*

Henry R. Luce Professorship Program

The Foundation offers support for innovative programs in the humanities and social sciences at privately funded colleges and universities in the United States. It is designed to stimulate greater academic flexibility within these institutions by focusing in a new way on a subject previously fragmented, thus lowering artificial barriers that separate academic areas.

Each Professorship is funded for an initial five-year period. The amount of each grant covers the Luce Professor's salary, and certain additional expenses relating to the inauguration and operation of new programs. In some instances existing awards may be extended for a further three years. New Professorships are awarded only when one of the existing twelve terminates (one offered for 1982).

Note: The Program is under major review (Summer 1982).

Latest information from:
Henry R. Luce Professorship Program
Henry Luce Foundation, Inc.
111 West 50th Street
New York, New York 10020
U.S.A.

[1244]

LUNAR AND PLANETARY INSTITUTE
(Houston, Texas)

Visiting Fellowships

Purpose: To provide the opportunity for scientists to undertake lunar and planetary research at the Institute and in cooperation with the NASA Johnson Space Center.

No. offered: Varies.

Value: Negotiable on a no-profit/no-loss basis.

Tenable at Houston, preferably for periods ranging from one week to three months. Some Fellowships may be awarded for longer periods if the proposed research justifies doing so.

Eligibility: Applicants should be graduates, postdoctoral workers or experienced scientists who are capable of pursuing an active program in research related to lunar and planetary science.

Closing date: 1st April and 1st October.

Further information from:
Director
Lunar and Planetary Institute
3303 NASA Road 1
Houston, Texas 77058
U.S.A.

[1245]

LUTHERAN WORLD FEDERATION

International Scholarships and Exchange Program

Purpose: To strengthen the life, witness and world awareness of the churches by offering church groups, institutions and members opportunities for international education, training and study.

Subjects: Academic studies, primarily on the graduate level, both degree-oriented and non-degree-oriented, in theology and other disciplines, as well as interdisciplinary studies; vocationally- or professionally-oriented courses and degree programs, practice-oriented, short-term educational and training programs; workshops and seminars, programs of inter-cultural and interdisciplinary research in another culture.

No. offered: Approximately 100 awards annually.

Value: Variable; grant normally covers travel, tuition and fees, health and accident insurance, book allowance and an allowance for board, lodging and incidentals (according to the circumstances in the country of study).

Tenable abroad, usually for up to one year; Scholarships for long-term studies are renewable.

Eligibility: Open to applicants nominated and endorsed by a Lutheran church which is a member of, or in permanent relation to, the Lutheran World Federation. Each applicant's educational level must meet the academic requirements of the desired study program.

Note: Applications should be made through the candidate's home church or through the Federation's national committee in the candidate's country.

Closing date: 15th October.

Further information from:
Lutheran World Federation
Scholarship and Exchange Office
Route de Ferney 150
CH-1211 Geneva 20
Switzerland

[1246]

CECIL LYONS MEMORIAL FOUNDATION
South African Jewish Board of Deputies

Scholarships

The Foundation awards Scholarships for the following: (1) To assist members of the Jewish community in order to qualify for some field of Jewish communal service in South Africa; (2) to encourage studies and research in the history and sociology of the South African Jewish community; (3) to assist persons already in Jewish communal service who wish to undertake further studies in order to improve their qualifications; (4) to assist persons, irrespective of race or religion, undertaking studies which deal with inter-race and interfaith problems in South Africa, more particularly in so far as they relate to the Jewish community. In adjudicating applications for assistance for study abroad, the Committee takes into consideration whether facilities for such study already exist in local institutions in South Africa.

It is a condition of any grant in categories (1) and (3) that the holder, if studying abroad, must give an undertaking to return to serve the South African Jewish community for a specific period.

Closing date: 15th December.

Further information from:
Secretary
Cecil Lyons Memorial Foundation
P.O. Box 1180
Johannesburg
South Africa

M

See *How to Use The Grants Register*, page ix

[1247]

MACDOWELL COLONY *(Peterborough, New Hampshire)*

Residence Fellowships

The Colony offers established writers, painters, sculptors, printmakers, film makers and composers the opportunity to work under excellent conditions.

There are 30 studios available at the Colony in the summer and 16-24 in other seasons. Fellowships are available to cover partial or full residency fees.

Closing date: 15th of January, April, July and October for Fellowships to become tenable in summer, fall, winter and spring, respectively.

Further information from:
 Admissions Office
 Macdowell Colony
 100 High Street
 Peterborough, New Hampshire 03458
 U.S.A.

[1248]

ELLAINA MACNAMARA MEMORIAL SCHOLARSHIP *(U.K.)*

Subjects: Etruscan studies

Tenable at an appropriate centre for one year.

Value: Up to £1,400 per annum.

Eligibility: Open to students of any nationality who have had at least two years of postgraduate experience or who possess a qualification equivalent to a London D.Phil.

Note: Applications (typewritten) should be supported by details of experience and achievements, an outline of the proposed research, and the names of two sponsors. At the same time the sponsors should submit references on behalf of the applicant.

Closing date: 1st April.

Further information from:
 Ellaina Macnamara Memorial Scholarship
 31-34 Gordon Square
 London
 England WC1H 0PX

[1249]

MAMMAL RESEARCH INSTITUTE *(South Africa)*
University of Pretoria

Postgraduate Bursaries and Postdoctoral Fellowships

Purpose: To further research in the physiology, ecology and ethology of South African mammals.

No. offered: Variable.

Value: Bursaries—R2,500 to R5,000 per annum; Fellowships—from R4,000 per annum. A part or whole of running expenses may also be paid.

Tenable at the Institute for one year, renewable for up to three years (Bursaries), or for a second year (Fellowships).

Eligibility: Open to South African and foreign scientists and students holding an M.Sc. degree (Bursaries) or a doctoral degree (Fellowships).

Further information from:
 Director
 Mammal Research Institute
 University of Pretoria
 Pretoria 0002
 South Africa

[1250]

MANANAN FESTIVAL *(Port Erin, Isle of Man)*

Music Competitions

The Festival is held in summer each year and the following Competitions rotate triennially: *Maria Korchinska International Harp Competition* (1983); *Lionel Tertis International Viola Competition* (1984); and *International Double Bass Competition* (1985).

The Competitions are open to all musicians aged 35 or under and offer cash prizes totalling £3,000 or more. There is also a Wigmore Hall (London) recital for the winner, a broadcast and opportunites for performing a specially commissioned concerto with an orchestra in London.

Applications should be submitted by 1st March of the year in which the competition is held.

Note: Workshops are given at the Festival. These feature the world's leading virtuosi and new works are encouraged.

Further information from:
  Secretariat
  Mananan Festival
  Port Erin, Isle of Man
  Great Britain

[1251]

MANHATTAN SCHOOL OF MUSIC

Music Scholarships

Purpose: To recognize outstanding talent, achievements and performance.

Subject: Professional music study at the bachelor's or master's level.

No. offered: Approximately 250 Scholarships.

Value: Tuition expenses; Awards range from US$600 to full tuition costs, payable in equal installments by semester.

Tenable at the School for one academic year; renewable for a total of four years (undergraduates) or two years (graduates).

Eligibility: Open to United States and foreign nationals of college age. Candidates must demonstrate through performance that they have attained excellence in the field of music and have the capacity for further development.

Closing date: 1st March for current students; four weeks prior to scheduled audition date for prospective students.

Further information from:
  Financial Aid Office
  Manhattan School of Music
  120 Claremont Avenue
  New York, New York 10027
  U.S.A.

[1252]

THOMAS MANN PRIZE *Lübeck*

A Prize of DM10,000 is awarded every three years to "individuals who have distinguished themselves in literary or critical work in the spirit of humanity cultivated by Thomas Mann." Next Prize given in 1984.

Further information from:
  Thomas Mann Prize
  Der Senat der Hansestadt Lübeck
  Amt für Kultur, Rathaushof
  D 2400 Lübeck 1
  West Germany

[1253]

KATHERINE MANSFIELD MEMORIAL FELLOWSHIP *(N.Z.)*

Purpose: To give a New Zealand creative writer the opportunity to spend a period of time abroad to write and study.

No. offered: One Fellowship annually.

Value: NZ$5,000 plus travelling expenses.

Tenable in the South of France for six months.

Eligibility: Open to established writers normally resident in New Zealand.

Further information from:
  Secretary
  Katherine Mansfield Memorial Fellowship
  P.O. Box 10256
  Wellington
  New Zealand

[1254]

MAORI PURPOSES FUND BOARD *(New Zealand)*

Maori Writers Awards

Two Awards in the amount of NZ$1,000 each, are offered annually to foster creative writing in the English and Maori languages. The Awards, one in English and one in Maori, are offered to any person of Maori descent and are tenable in New Zealand. Awards are not renewable. University theses are not acceptable.

Further information from:
  Secretary
  Maori Purposes Fund Board
  c/o Department of Maori Affairs
  Private Bag
  Wellington
  New Zealand

[1255]

MARCH OF DIMES BIRTH DEFECTS FOUNDATION *(U.S.A.)*

The Foundation offers a number of research programs and research grants, all with the ultimate aim of the prevention of birth defects. The Foundation defines birth defects as an abnormality of structure, function or metabolism, whether genetically determined or as a result of environmental interference during embryonic or fetal life. A congenital defect may cause disease from the time of conception through birth or later in life. The research interests of the Foundation include the broader aspects of pregnancy outcome, i.e., factors underlying the birth and survival of a normal infant; the cognitive development of low birthweight infants; as well as the structure and function of chromosomes, their subunits, genes, supporting structures and the like. Amount of support available varies, depending upon the number of awards and the grant or program. A maximum grant of US$25,000 per year is available for the *Basil O'Connor Starter Research Grant Program* and for the *Social and Behavioral Sciences Research Program.*

Further information from:
  Grants Administration
  March of Dimes Birth Defects Foundation
  1275 Mamaroneck Avenue
  White Plains, New York 10605
  U.S.A.

[1256]

MARGARINE INSTITUTE FOR HEALTH NUTRITION

Heinrich Wieland Prize

Purpose: To promote research.

Subjects: The chemistry, biochemistry and physiology of fats and lipids, as well as their clinical importance and significance in the physiology of nutrition.

No. offered: One Prize annually.

Value: DM20,000 paid in a lump sum.

Eligibility: Open to authors of any nationality, submitting a scientific treatise, either unpublished or published during the calendar year preceding that in which the Prize is made, written in German, English or French.

Note: Papers having received other prizes are not eligible. Entries made in English or French must be accompanied by a summary in German or English, outlining the main results and the experimental method, as well as providing bibliographic details.

Closing date: 1st March.

Further information from:
  Heinrich Wieland Prize
  Professor Alfons Fricker
  Ringelberghohl 12
  7500 Karlsruhe 41
  West Germany

[1257]

JOHN AND MARY R. MARKLE FOUNDATION *(U.S.A.)*

The purpose of the Foundation's program is the improvement of all media including services growing out of new technologies for the processing and transfer of information. These goals are supported through a wide range of efforts, including research on the role of mass communications in society, analysis of issues of public policy and public interest, projects that improve the performance of professionals involved in the mass communication services, and activities which enrich the quality of media.

Grant proposals may be submitted in an informal letter and include the following: the purpose for which aid is sought, resources needed, personnel involved, and a description of methods to be used in completing the project, Grants are awarded in March, June and November.

Further information from:
John and Mary R. Markle Foundation
50 Rockefeller Plaza
New York, New York 10020
U.S.A.

[1258]

MARSDEN FOUNDATION (U.S.A.)

Grants

The Foundation makes Grants (1) to individuals of exceptional promise who have demonstrated a persistent concern for self-understanding and for greater meaning and usefulness in life, and (2) to universities and other organizations in the United States seeking funds for original research or exceptional approaches to education. Value of the Grants is usually between US$1,000 and US$3,000.

There are no rigid geographic requirements in relation to the Grant and no restrictions as regards race, religion, nationality, sex or age within the adult years. The Foundation's chief interests are in interdisciplinary and integrative approaches to comparative religion and philosophy, oriental and native traditions, advanced studies in inner growth, and related aspects of other fields. Grants made for academic studies or projects are usually limited to the graduate or post-graduate levels. The Foundation is especially interested in applicants who have promising insights beyond or apart from the academic sphere.

There is no fixed closing date for applications. Applicants should send a preliminary letter briefly stating their aims and qualifications and giving a summary of the work for which funds are requested. If found appropriate, the Foundation will send application forms and request other material to aid their evaluation of the application.

Further information from:
Elizabeth M. Bonbright, M.D.
Director, Marsden Foundation
P.O. Box 569
F.D.R. Station
New York, New York 10150
U.S.A.

[1259]

MARSHALL AID COMMEMORATION COMMISSION (U.K.)
Association of Commonwealth Universities

Marshall Scholarships

Subjects: Unrestricted.

No. offered: Up to 30 Scholarships annually.

Value: Tuition fees, residence and related costs.

Tenable at universities in the United Kingdom for two academic years, with possible extension for a third year.

Eligibility: Open to United States citizens, under 26 years of age, who have graduated with a minimum grade point average of 3.7, or A- from an accredited United States college at the time of taking up the Scholarship. Recipients are required to take a degree at their British university. Preference is given to candidates who combine high academic ability with the capacity to play an active part in the United Kingdom university to which they go.

Note: Information and application forms may be obtained from the following British Consulates-General: Mid-Eastern Region: *British Embassy, 3100 Massachusetts Ave., N.W., Washington, D.C. 20008*; Mid-Western Region: *33 North Dearborn Street, Chicago, Illinois 60602*; North-Eastern Region: *4740 Prudential Tower, Prudential Center, Boston, Massachusetts 02199;* Pacific Region: *Equitable Building, 120 Montgomery Street, San Francisco, California 94104*; Southern Region: *Suite 912, 225 Peachtree Street, N.E., Atlanta, Georgia 30303.*

Address:
British Embassy (Cultural Department)
3100 Massachusetts Avenue, N.W.
Washington, D.C. 20008
U.S.A.

[1260]

MARTEN BEQUEST *(Australia)*
Permanent Trust Company Ltd.

Travelling Scholarships

Categories: Prose, poetry, acting, singing, music, ballet, architecture, sculpture, and painting.

No. offered: One Scholarship in each of three of the categories each year.

Value: A$2,900 per annum, to augment the Scholar's own resources.

Tenable within or outside Australia for two years.

Eligibility: Open to Australians between the ages of 21 and 35 who are pursuing studies or training in the arts and who are adjudged to be of outstanding ability and promise in their field.

Closing date: 31st December.

Further information from:
Marie Carre, Assistant Trust Officer
Marten Bequest
Permanent Trust Company Ltd.
G.P.O. Box 4270
Sydney, N.S.W.
Australia 2001

[1261]

MARTIN MUSICAL SCHOLARSHIP FUND
New Philharmonia Orchestra of London

Martin Musical Scholarships

Purpose: To assist outstanding musical talent.

Value: Awards payable from 1st April, renewable by further audition. Awards may be made for tuition fees and for subsistence grants.

Tenable in England and Europe for two years.

Eligibility: Open to individual practising musicians as well as students no more than 25 years of age who are preparing to be solo or instrumental performers. Preference is given of the United Kingdom. Selection of candidates is by audition.

Closing date: Application forms should be submitted by autumn. Preliminary auditions are held in October/November; final auditions are held the following March/April.

Further information from:
Martin Musical Scholarship Fund
12 de Walden Court
85 New Cavendish Street
London
England W1M 7RA

[1262]

PAUL MARTINI FOUNDATION *(Mainz)*

Paul Martini Prize

Purpose: To help promote the development of scientific methods of evaluation.

Subjects: Clinical pharmacology and therapeutics.

No. offered: One Prize annually.

Value: DM20,000.

Eligibility: Open to authors of any nationality who submit an appropriate paper which is self-contained and not more than two years old if published. Entries should be in German or English.

Closing date: April of each year.

Further information from:
Paul Martini Foundation
Medizinisch-Pharmazeutische
  Studien-gesellschaft e.V.
Bilhildisstrasse 2
65 Mainz
West Germany

[1263]

MASSEY-FERGUSON (UK) LIMITED

Massey-Ferguson National Award for Services to United Kingdom Agriculture

Purpose: To encourage and reward contributions towards the advancement of agriculture in the United Kingdom.

No. offered: One Award annually.

Value: £1,000, paid in a lump sum, plus a medallion.

Eligibility: Open to (a) persons normally resident in the United Kingdom who, at the time of the development of the contribution, derived a substantial part of his or her livelihood through farming in the U.K., or (b) any person who, at the time of the development of the contribution, was undertaking the activity by reason of membership, paid or unpaid, of any organization, official or unofficial, having as its prime objective the furtherance of United Kingdom agriculture or a significant aspect thereof. Contributions developed through a commercial organization, by persons either employed or retained, are ineligible.

Further information from:
Mr. A.F. Dawe
Director of Public Affairs U.K.
Massey-Ferguson (U.K.) Limited
P.O. Box 62
Banner Lane
Coventry
England CV4 9GF

[1264]

MATERNITY CENTER ASSOCIATION (U.S.A.)

Hazel Corbin Assistance Fund Grants

Purpose: To prepare nurses for nurse-midwifery, and to provide refresher courses for nurse-midwives out of practice.

Subjects: Nurse-midwifery, including maternal and child health, family planning and philosophy of midwifery in the United States.

Value: According to individual circumstances.

Tenable in the United States.

Eligibility: Open to registered nurses who seek to prepare for nurse-midwifery certification in the United States, to nurse-midwives in the United States who were trained in other countries, and to American nurse-midwives who are not currently working or who have turned to other nursing duties. Students in any of these categories must have a licence to practice nursing in a state of the United States, and must already have been accepted in an approved nurse-midwifery basic or refresher program at a United States school. Preference is given to students who intend to practice nurse-midwifery in the United States for at least a year after completion of the program.

Further information from:
Hazel Corbin Assistance Fund
Maternity Center Association
48 East 92nd Street
New York, New York 10028
U.S.A.

[1265]

CATHERINE McCAIG'S TRUST (U.K.)

McCaig Postgraduate Scholarships

Subjects: Celtic studies

No. offered: Varying number of Scholarships annually.

Value: Variable; usually £450 per annum.

Tenable for one year at any Scottish university with an M.A. programme which includes Gaelic among its course subjects.

Eligibility: Open to M.A. students of any Scottish university who have studied Gaelic among their course subjects.

Closing date: First week in May.

Further information from:
W. Hume, Clerk to the Governors
Catherine McCaig's Trust
8 Buchanan Street
Glasgow
Scotland G1 3LL

[1266]

WILLIAM McCUNN'S TRUST *(Scotland)*

Medical Research Scholarships

Purpose: To enable graduates in medicine to take a course of original research.

Subjects: Research in any of the following: medicine, including psychiatry; surgery; medical and surgical paediatrics and child health; pathology, including pathological chemistry; bacteriology, including virology; therapeutics, including pharmacology; obstetrics and gynaecology; hygiene and public health; radiology and electronics; physiology and physiological chemistry.

No. offered: Varies according to the number of application and the amount of funds available.

Value: £1,000.

Tenable at home or abroad for one year; renewable at the discretion of the Trustees.

Eligibility: Open to graduates in medicine of one of the Scottish universities, namely Edinburgh, Glasgow, Aberdeen, St. Andrews, Dundee.

Note: Nominations must be made on an application form obtainable from the Trust.

Closing date: 1st June.

Further information from:
William McCunn's Trust
c/o Mitchells Johnston, Hill and Hoggan, Solicitors
160 West George Street
Glasgow
Scotland G2 2JB

[1267]

WILLIAM McCUNN'S TRUST *(Scotland)*

Travelling Scholarships

Purpose: To enable graduates in medicine to pursue further studies abroad.

No. offered: Varies according to the number of applications and the amount of funds available.

Value: Approximately £100.

Tenable at home or abroad for a period of less than one year, the duration being decided by the Trustees after consideration of an approved itinerary.

Eligibility: Open to graduates in medicine of one of the Scottish universities, namely Edinburgh, Glasgow, Aberdeen, St. Andrews, Dundee.

Note: Nominations must be made on an application form obtainable from the Trust.

Closing date: 1st June.

Further information from:
William McCunn's Trust
c/o Mitchells Johnston, Hill and Hoggan, Solicitors
160 West George Street
Glasgow
Scotland G2 2JB

[1268]

McGRAW-HILL BOOK COMPANY *(U.S.A.)*
Gregg Division

John Robert Gregg Award in Business Education is given annually for a contribution by a person or persons to the field of business education sustained during two previous calendar years. The Award consists of US$1,000 and a citation.

Robert E. Slaughter Research Awards in Business, Distributive and Office Education are given annually in the amount of US$1,000 to up to three recipients to stimulate, encourage and reward outstanding contributions to the advancement of business, distributive and office education through research. Awards for research studies may be (but are not limited to) doctoral dissertations, master's theses and independent research. Completion of the study must be made during the twelve months prior to 1st June of the year in which the Award is made. Members of the Research Award Committee and employees of McGraw-Hill are not eligible.

Closing date: 1st June.

Further information from:
Annette Imperati, Research Assistant
McGraw-Hill Book Company
Gregg Divison
1221 Avenue of the Americas
New York, New York 10020
U.S.A.

[1269]

MEAT INDUSTRIES RESEARCH INSTITUTE OF NEW ZEALAND

Meat Industries Research Fellowship

Subjects: Research in an appropriate field of study, which may include a variety of disciplines in the sciences and social sciences.

No. offered: One Fellowship annually.

Value: NZ$4,020 per annum, plus fees up to NZ$250.

Tenable at the University of Waikato, Hamilton, for up to three years.

Eligibility: Open to graduates of any university in New Zealand.

Closing date: 1st November.

Further information from:
Registrar
University of Waikato
Private Bag
Hamilton
New Zealand

[1270]

MEAT AND LIVESTOCK COMMISSION
(U.K.)

MLC Postgraduate Scholarship

Subjects: Those related to the meat and livestock industry, such as: animal production, economics, marketing and meat technology including processing, statistics, and veterinary medicine.

No. offered: Varies as vacancies occur and funding becomes available.

Value: £2,820, paid monthly plus contributions to experimental expenses and university fees. Supplementary allowances are also available for dependants, postgraduate experience or older students.

Tenable at approved universities or research institutes in Great Britain, for one to three years.

Eligibility: Open to citizens and residents of Great Britain, who have, or are expected to obtain, at least a second class honours degree in the above subjects, and who are likely to make a contribution towards the improvement of the British meat, beef cattle, pig and sheep industries.

Note: Support for specific research projects of the same nature are also awarded under similar guidelines as the above Scholarships.

Closing date: 1st March.

Further information from:
Director of Research and
    Veterinary Services
Meat and Livestock Commission
P.O. Box 44
Queensway House
Bletchley, Milton Keynes
England MK2 2EF

[1271]

MEDICAL MISSIONARY ASSOCIATION
(U.K.)

Awards

Purpose: To enable students with no alternative source of support to qualify as doctors in preparation for a career in overseas missionary service.

Value: Variable, depending on available funds and the merits of individual applications.

Tenable normally at a United Kingdom medical school for the pre-clinical portion of study only; possibility of renewal annually.

Eligibility: Open to nationals of various countries who have gained admission to a United Kingdom medical school. Each application is judged on its own merits, but preference is given to Protestant Christians who have been offered a place in one of the London medical schools.

Closing date: At least six months prior to commencement of proposed course.

Note: Grants are also made to postgraduate missionary doctors on leave in the United Kingdom and who are returning abroad, to do postraduate studies to further their career, and small grants are also made to fully registered doctors to work in a mission or church-related hospital abroad for one year under the "Oyster" scheme.

Further information from:
Secretary
Medical Missionary Society
6 Canonbury Place
London
England N1 2NJ

[1272]

MEDICAL RESEARCH COUNCIL *(U.K.)*

Advanced Course Studentships

Purpose: To enable graduates to take an approved postgraduate course of instruction in a science relevant to medicine.

Value: To include a tax free maintenance grant depending on location and nature of living accommodation, compulsory university and college fees, certain travel expenses, additional allowances for dependents in certain circumstances and allowances for older students and those with approved experience.

Tenable in a recognized institution in the United Kingdom for a period corresponding to the duration of the course.

Eligibility: Candidates should have recently graduated with a good honours degree and be planning to take up a research or academic career in the biomedical field in the United Kingdom. Support is confined to candidates who have been ordinarily resident in the United Kingdom throughout the period of 3 years immediately preceding the application date.

Note: Candidates must be sponsored by the head of the department in which they intend to receive training. Awards are made only in respect of full-time courses.
Applications for a quota of awards should reach the Council by the middle of November.

Further information from:
Training Awards Group
Medical Research Council
20 Park Crescent
London
England W1N 4AL

[1273]

MEDICAL RESEARCH COUNCIL *(U.K.)*

Research Studentships

Purpose: To enable individuals of special promise to receive whole-time training in research methods in the biomedical field under suitable direction in recognised institutions.

Value: To include a tax-free maintenance grant depending on location and nature of accommodation, compulsory university and college fees, plus additional allowances for dependents in certain circumstances and allowances for older students and those with approved experience. In addition, a support grant is paid to the university as a contribution towards the incidental departmental costs incurred in the student's training.

Tenable in a recognised institution in the United Kingdom for one year; renewable to a maximum of three years.

Eligibility: Candidates should have recently graduated with a good honours degree and should intend to take up a research or academic career in the biomedical field in the United Kingdom.
Support is confined to candidates who have been ordinarily resident in the United Kingdom throughout the period of 3 years immediately preceding the application date.

Note: Applications must be made by heads of departments on behalf of candidate. Applications for a quota of awards should be submitted by departments by the middle of November.

Further information from:
Training Awards Group
Medical Research Council
20 Park Crescent
London
England W1N 4AL

[1274]

MEDICAL RESEARCH COUNCIL (U.K.)

Training Fellowships

Purpose: To enable medical and dental graduates, at any stage of their careers, up to and including senior registrar, lecturer or equivalent levels, and science graduates with postgraduate experience up to lecturer or equivalent level, to gain specialised experience in research in the biomedical field in the United Kingdom.

Value: Stipends are calculated in relation to the basic salary point currently being received either on NHS clinical or non-clinical academic salary scales or their equivalents. Course or examination fees are not reimbursed by the Council except when a Fellowship is awarded only for attendance at an M.Sc. course. A support grant is paid to the university as a contribution towards the incidental departmental costs incurred in the Fellow's training, with the exception of a Fellow who is undertaking a formal course.

Tenable at a suitable university department or similar institution in the United Kingdom for from six months to three years. Tenure for longer periods may be considered only in special circumstances. The attention of applicants is also called to the possibility of spending at least part of the period of the award at the Clinical Research Centre, the National Institute for Medical Research or another Medical Research Council establishment.

Eligibility: Open to persons ordinarily resident in the United Kingdom throughout the 3 years immediately preceding the application date, who intend to pursue, in the United Kingdom, careers at least partly devoted to biomedical research. Candidates should be (1) medical graduates from post-registration to senior registrar or equivalent grade; (2) dental graduates with at least one year's postgraduate experience acceptable to the Council; (3) science graduates with Ph.D. or D.Phil. degrees (candidates yet to receive their degrees may apply). Science graduates with an M.Sc. by course work plus a further period of acceptable postgraduate work (normally not less than three years) may be considered in exceptional cases.

Note: Applications must be supported by the head of the department or establishment in which the candidate is currently working. Candidates should make their own arrangements for acceptance in the host institution. A report is required on completion of the Fellowship, and acknowledgement of the award should be made in any publication.

Closing date: 28th February.

Further information from:
Training Awards Group
Medical Research Council
20 Park Crescent
London
England W1N 4AL

[1275]

MEDICAL RESEARCH COUNCIL (U.K.)

Travelling Fellowships

The following Fellowships are available for award by the Council;

(a) Medical Research Council Travelling Fellowships (a variable number each year)

(b) Alexander Pigott Wernher Memorial Trust Fellowships in opthalmology and otology (two Fellowships annually)

(c) Dorothy Temple Cross Research Fellowship in lung diseases (one Fellowships annually)

(d) French Exchange Fellowships (four Fellowships annually).

The following Fellowships are available for nomination by the Council:

(a) US National Institutes of Health International Research Fellowships (up to six candidates nominated annually).

(b) Lilly International Fellowship Program (one candidate nominated annually).

Value: Stipends are based on the appropriate U.K. University or National Health Service basic salary level, and will include a cost of living allowance, depending on the centre chosen and the Fellow's marital status, and also a contribution to actual rent payments. Stipends remain fixed for the duration of the Fellowship. Travel expenses are paid for the Fellow and spouse and/or children when the award is for one year or more. An internal travel allowance is paid for the Fellow only. Fellows on paid leave will receive allowances only. In the case of the US National Institutes of Health International Research Fellowships and the Lilly International Research Fellowship Program, the stipends and allowances are set by the bodies concerned.

Tenable at any recognised research centre abroad, normally for three months to one year but, exceptionally, applications for a maximum period of two years will be considered.

Eligibility: Open to persons ordinarily resident in the United Kingdom throughout the 3 years immediately preceding the application date, who propose to take up a clinical, academic or research appointment on their return. The Alexander Pigott Wernher Memorial Trust Fellowships are also open to Commonwealth candidates who wish to work in the United Kingdom. Candidates should be either: (1) medically or dentally qualified and presently holding appointments of status comparable with that of NHS registrar or senior registrar; (2) scientifically qualified with a Ph.D. degree or expecting to receive a Ph.D./D.Phil. degree before taking up the award; (3) more senior workers who wish to spend a collaborative period overseas while on paid sabbatical leave.

Note: Applicants should make the necessary provisional arrangements with the intended host institution prior to submitting an application. On the conclusion of awards, all Fellows must submit a short report on their activities to the Council, together with details of the appointment to be taken up on return to the United Kingdom.

Closing date: 30th September of year preceding that of the award; 28th February for nomination to U.S. National Institutes of Health.

Further information from:
  Training Awards Group
  Medical Research Council
  20 Park Crescent
  London
  England W1N 4AL

[1276]

MEDICAL RESEARCH COUNCIL OF CANADA

Studentships

Subjects: Predoctoral (M.Sc. or Ph.D.) training in research in the health sciences.

No. offered: Approximately 120 new Studentships annually.

Value: Can$8,900 per annum, plus a travel grant in appropriate cases.

Tenable for one year in Canadian schools of medicine, dentistry, or pharmacy, or under certain circumstances in Canadian schools of nursing, physical education, psychology and optometry; renewable up to four times. Awards may be held outside Canada in exceptional circumstances, provided that the candidate is a Canadian citizen or landed immigrant.

Eligibility: Applicants (a) should have a high academic standing; (b) must have, or be about to receive, an honours B.Sc. degree; or must have completed, or expect to complete, sufficient academic work so that they will be admitted in full standing to graduate school by the time the award is to take effect; or must already be engaged in an M.Sc. or Ph.D. program. These awards are designed primarily for Canadian citizens or landed immigrants; a limited number of awards may also be made to individuals who are neither Canadian citizens nor landed immigrants and who intend to proceed towards an M.Sc. or Ph.D. degree in the health sciences at a Canadian university.

Closing date: 1st December and 1st April.

Application forms may be obtained from the dean of medicine, dentistry, or pharmacy at any Canadian university, or from:
  Awards Office
  Medical Research Council of Canada
  Ottawa, Ontario
  Canada K1A 0W9

[1277]

MEDICAL RESEARCH COUNCIL OF CANADA

Scholarships

Purpose: To provide support for the investigator who has recently completed his training and shows promise of ability to initiate and carry out independent research in the health sciences. This will afford what will usually be the first opportunity for an investigator to develop and demonstrate such ability, unhampered by the necessity of carrying out the heavy teaching duties often expected of a regular member of the university staff.

Value: Salary is dependent on recipient's qualifications and experience, and may be supplemented from university funds and personal earnings. An outright research grant of Can$10,000 is provided in the first year to those individuals who are not already established at the university at which they will hold their appointment.

Tenable for five years in Canadian schools of medicine, dentistry, pharmacy, or veterinary medicine, or associated institutions.

Eligibility: Candidates must hold an M.D., D.D.S., D.V.M., or Ph.D. degree. They must have shown promise of attaining competence as an independent investigator, and should under normal circumstances not be registered for a higher degree at the time of application nor undertake such studies during the period of their appointment.

Closing date: 1st November.

Note: Applications must be made by the president of the university on the recommendation of the head of the department and the dean concerned. The university must undertake to provide adequate accommodation and research facilities and to administer the award in accordance with the terms laid down by the Council.

Application forms may be obtained from the dean of medicine, dentistry, pharmacy, or veterinary medicine at any Canadian university, or from:
Awards Office
Medical Research Council of Canada
Ottawa, Ontario
Canada K1A 0W9

[1278]

MEDICAL RESEARCH COUNCIL OF CANADA

Fellowships

Subjects: Full-time training in research in the health sciences.

No. offered: Approximately 150 new Fellowships annually.

Value: Can$17,000 to Can$27,500 per annum, depending upon previous training and experience, plus a research allowance of Can$1,000 and a travel grant in appropriate cases.

Tenable for one year, generally in health science faculties at universities or affiliated institutions in Canada or, under appropriate circumstances, outside Canada; renewable on approval.

Eligibility: Candidates must have an M.D., D.D.S., D.V.M., or Ph.D. degree. Ph.D. degree holders are eligible to receive support only during the first three years of postdoctoral research training, and may not receive an award for tenure in the same department in which they received their predoctoral training. This program is designed primarily for Canadian citizens or landed immigrants to Canada; a limited number of awards may also be made to exceptional candidates from abroad who wish to continue their research training in Canada.

Both academic standing and evidence of ability in research will be taken into account when applications are considered. Although most Fellowships will be awarded without respect to the fields in which the applicants propose to take their training, a limited number will be provided in competition after assessment of both the scientific and academic merit of the applications and the relevance of the proposed training to the special goals of the Council's training program. When Fellowships are awarded in the latter category, due account will be taken of research training proposed in the following areas: anaesthesiology, behavioral sciences, biological engineering, dental sciences, drug toxicology, environmental pollution, infectious diseases, medical bacteriology, medical genetics, neuropathology, obstetrics, ophthalmology, otolaryngology, population control, radiology, rehabilitation medicine, and surgery.

Closing date: 1st September, 1st December, and 1st April.

Application forms may be obtained from the dean of medicine, dentistry, pharmacy, or veterinary medicine at any Canadian university, or from:
Awards Office
Medical Research Council of Canada
Ottawa, Ontario
Canada K1A 0W9

[1279]

MEDICAL RESEARCH COUNCIL OF CANADA

Centennial Fellowships

Purpose: To enable young men and women of special academic distinction to broaden their fields of interest and thus equip themselves for independent research in clinical investigation and interdisciplinary research in the health sciences.

No. offered: Up to ten Fellowships annually.

Value: Can$23,500 to Can$28,500 per annum, plus a research allowance of up to Can$3,000 and a travel grant in appropriate cases.

Tenable for up to three years at universities and affiliated institutions in Canada or abroad.

Eligibility: Candidates must be citizens or residents of Canada. These awards are open both (a) to those with an M.D., D.D.S., or D.V.M. degree who have had at least four years of postgraduate experience and have completed a year of special work (either clinical or research) in their proposed field of study, which, as a rule, should be such as would normally lead to a Ph.D. degree, and (b) to those with a Ph.D. degree who have had at least two years of postdoctoral research experience by the time they plan to take up the award.

Closing date: 1st December.

Application forms may be obtained from the dean of medicine, dentistry, pharmacy, or veterinary medicine at any Canadian university, or from:
Awards Office
Medical Research Council of Canada
Ottawa, Ontario
Canada K1A 0W9

[1280]

MEDICAL RESEARCH COUNCIL OF CANADA

Research Professorships

Purpose: To provide an opportunity for a limited number of faculty members to spend a year of full-time research in their laboratories free of their ordinary teaching and administrative responsibilities. The awards are intended for those investigators whose research has reached a point at which special benefits can be expected from a period of intensive work.

Value: Salary is dependent on the recipient's qualifications and experience, and may be supplemented from university funds.

Tenable for one year only.

Eligibility: Applicants must be members of a health science faculty at a Canadian university engaged on a research program of high promise.

Closing date: 1st November.

Applications must be made by the dean of the sponsoring health science faculty in Canada to:
Awards Office
Medical Research Council of Canada
Ottawa, Ontario
Canada K1A 0W9

[1281]

MEDICAL RESEARCH COUNCIL OF CANADA

Grants-in-Aid of Research

Purpose: To assist in defraying the normal costs of research in the health sciences (with the exception of health care research) proposed by investigators holding or otherwise enjoying the privileges of staff appointments at Canadian universities or other recognized Canadian institutions.

Operating Grants: For the purchase and maintenance of experimental animals. expendable materials and supplies, small items of equipment and the payment of assistants. A certain proportion of the Grant may be used for travel, including attendance at scientific meetings. These Grants are not intended to cover the entire costs of the research, since space and certain basic facilities at the institution are considered a prerequisite to an application for a Grant. Operating Grants may also be made in block form to a group of investigators.

Term Grants provide financial support on a term basis to scientists with well-developed programs which have reached a relatively stable level of expenditure. They are tenable for a period of three or five years.

Continuing Grants offer continuing support for periods of one to two years for research projects growing or changing materially from year to year and for which the long-term budget is difficult to estimate.

New Grants, tenable for periods of up to two years, provide support for new projects for an initial period sufficient to enable the Grantee to carry out his research for at least twelve months and to permit his writing a progress report with his request for renewal.

Grants for one year only are available to provide support for projects which can be completed within a twelve-month period or which warrant an award for a limited period only.

Major Equipment Grants: For the purchase of unites of special equipment costing Can$10,000 or more. Application of Grants for computer hardware may be provided also in certain cases.

Equipment Maintenance Grants to cover the cost of maintaining major items of research equipment, generally items used by a number of investigators in a department are available.

Closing date: 1st November for all Grants-in-Aid.

Further information from:
Director, Grants Program
Medical Research Council of Canada
Ottawa, Ontario
Canada K1A 0W9

[1282]

MEDICAL RESEARCH COUNCIL OF CANADA

Special Programs

Medical Research Groups: To provide support to groups of two or more accomplished investigators over a period of years in what appear to be especially productive areas. The support provides, when necessary, the salaries of investigators and also covers the salaries of professional assistants, graduate students, technicians and other personnel as well as the cost of supplies and minor equipment. Consultation with the Council President is advised in planning for an application. Applications should be made by the president or principal of the university on the recommendation of the dean of the faculty.

Development Grants: Designed to assist in the recruitment or establishment of highly qualified new faculty members with a major interest in research in designated Canadian schools of medicine, dentistry, and pharmacy where research activity is thought to be inadequate from the stand-point of the contribution it should make to professional education and health care. Support for operating funds and/or equipment may be provided for periods of up to three years; support for investigators' salaries is provided for a period of five years, renewable once. Applications should be made by the dean of the school, and are accepted at any time.

Subject Research Development Grants: Designed to increase the potential of existing teams of researchers by adding to the number of senior investigators working in subject areas of particular interest to the Council, or to assist in the establishment of major investigators in the health professional schools in which there has been little research in the subject area. Support may be provided for major equipment, operating funds for approximately three years, research assistant and trainee stipends, and salary support for the principal investigator(s) for three to five years, depending on seniority. Grants are awarded only in those situations where there is a definite university intention to establish and maintain a new research program in the subject concerned. At present, this program applies only to research in perinatology. Grants are not renewable, but support beyond the initial period may be sought through other Council programs. Consultation with the Council President is advised in planning for an application.

Program Grants: To facilitate the further growth in Canada of team research in the health sciences, by providing support for research programs involving closely integrated research activities carried out by two or more investigators at the same or different institutions. Grants may be awarded for up to three years and may be renewed.

Support of Symposia and Workshops: To provide a contribution towards the cost of travel of invited participants or towards the administrative costs connected with the organization of workshops and some symposia. The complete costs of such symposia will not be paid, nor will the printing of the proceedings be subsidized.

Travel Grants: To enable an investigator to visit a specified laboratory for the purpose of furthering his research. Applications should be submitted in the form of a letter to the Council before 15th January, 15th April, and 1st October for consideration in February, June, and November.

Visiting Professorships: To encourage collaboration and exchange of information among Canadian investigators and to strengthen graduate training programs in research. Funds are available to enable distinguished Canadian scientists to spend from one to seven days at a university in Canada other than their own. Faculties of pharmacy and dentistry may request support of visits by outstanding non-Canadian scientists.

Visiting Scientists Grants: To enable investigators to spend some time in pursuit of their research endeavours in laboratories other than their own. Scientists from abroad who are invited to engage in research in a Canadian university for periods of between 3 and 24 months and Canadian scientists who, for the advancement of their research, wish to work in another laboratory in Canada or abroad for periods of between 3 and 12 months, are eligible. Scientists from abroad will be provided with an honorarium of not more than Can18,000 per annum depending upon their qualifications and experience, plus a travel grant. They may also apply for a research allowance pro-rated at Can5,000 per annum. Canadian scientists will be provided with a travel grant and, in certain cases, a research allowance pro-rated at Can5,000 per annum. Applications may be made by the president or dean of medicine, dentistry or pharmacy of the host university no later than 1st December. Application forms may be obtained from the dean of medicine, dentistry or pharmacy at any Canadian university, or from:
Awards Office
Medical Research Council of Canada
Ottawa, Ontario
Canada K1A 0W9

[1283]

MEDICAL RESEARCH COUNCIL OF IRELAND

Fellowships; Training Grants; Grants-in-Aid; Student Grants; Postgraduate Student Scholarships; Summer Research Projects

The general purpose of the Council is to organise, carry out, promote and assist research in any or all branches of medicine and in any or all sciences or allied subjects.

Eligibility: The general academic requirement for the awarding of any Grant is the possession of a medical or science degree. There are no requirements regarding citizenship or age. However, Grants in general are normally available only to workers carrying out research in Ireland, and Training Grants are confined to recent graduates who are working towards a higher degree.

Note: The Council is the Irish nominating body for Fellowships offered under the United States Public Health Service International Postdoctoral Research Fellowship Program.

Further information from:
Secretary
Medical Research Council of Ireland
9 Clyde Road
Dublin 4
Ireland

[1284]

MEDICAL RESEARCH COUNCIL OF NEW ZEALAND

Fellowships

Training Fellowships are intended for those

who are considered well qualified to undertake research training in medicine, dentistry and immediately related biological sciences. From time to time the Council may assist the development of certain research fields by offering Fellowships for award in these fields. However, more usually the topic of research is given less emphasis than the ability and potential of the individual.

This training must be taken in New Zealand. Application must be made to the Council by the head of the university or hospital department in which the Fellow will be accommodated.

Training Fellowships are renewable on the basis of an annual report from the Fellow and his supervisor, and the maximum duration of tenure is three years.

The value of Fellowships is fixed for each individual, but is usually equivalent to current rates for graduates of the same level in the university, hospital or other host institution.

Fellows may undertake teaching or clinical duties relevant to their research and may study for approved higher qualifications.

Applications must reach the Council by 1st April or 1st October in each year and Fellowships must normally be taken up within twelve months of the date of award.

Postgraduate Scholarships are intended to provide personal support for selected graduate students whose programme of research for a higher degree is in a biomedical field approved by the Council. They are intended especially for graduate research workers in appropriate fields who are contemplating a career in medical research and who do not qualify for other tyes of award offered by the Council. Graduate students are eligible to apply for these Scholarships if they are enrolled in an approved course leading to a higher degree (usually a Ph.D. degree, although applications will be considered from postgraduate scholars in other categories) at a New Zealand university and if they propose to carry out research in a biomedical field in fulfilment of the requirements of this course. Scholarships are tenable initially for a period of two and a half years of full-time study with the possibility of a six months extension. Permission to teach up to six hours per week, or to hold any other scholarship grants, must be granted by the Council. Application must be made to the Council through the head of the department in which the Scholar will be accommodated; applications are called for biannually by advertisement in the *New Zealand Medical Journal* with normal closing date of 1st April and 1st October.

Postdoctoral Fellowships are intended for the support of graduates who have recently completed a degree at doctoral level. Their purpose is to provide interim support for recently trained research workers in biomedical fields of relevance to the Council in order to allow them opportunity to gain further experience in their chosen field and to make known the quality of their work to the scientific community. Fellowships are tenable within New Zealand universities, hospitals, or other suitable research institutions for an initial period of twelve months, renewable for another twelve months. Candidates should normally be less than 35 years of age, should have or be about to receive a Ph.D. degree or its equivalent, and will be judged on academic standing and research capabilities. Awards will be comparable in value to similar awards offered by New Zealand universities, and may include an allowance for payment of special fees, for travel to one scientific meeting in Australasia, and for reasonable working expenses of the research. In the case of Postdoctoral Fellows appointed from overseas, financial assistance for travel to New Zealand may be given. Applications are called for bi-annually by advertisement in the *New Zealand Medical Journal* with closing dates of 1st April and 1st October.

Overseas Research Fellowships are available for the support of research workers from New Zealand, in various categories and at different levels of seniority, whose intended programme of research in another country is considered likely to bring eventual benefit to the health sciences in New Zealand. The award includes a return economy class air fare, plus living and other expenses, for a period of up to two years, to be determined individually. The majority of these Fellowships will be awarded to professional research scientists, but applications will also be accepted from senior technical and paramedical staff currently engaged in active medical research programmes in New Zealand. In making such awards the Council takes account of such factors as academic background; research training; relevant experience and productivity; importance of the research field; necessity for overseas travel and its relevance to proposed programme on return to New Zealand; suitability of proposed programme, overseas sponsor and institution; previous travel grants; confidential opinions from referees in New Zealand. Applications should be submitted to the Council either through the head of the applicant's department or the head of his institution; they are called for bi-annually by advertisement in the *New Zealand Medical Journal* with closing dates of 1st April and 1st October.

Senior Fellowships are intended to support trained investigators who have shown ability to initiate and carry out independent research. Candidates must have completed at least three years of research training and should have completed a postgraduate degree, e.g. M.D. or Ph.D.

Senior Fellowships are tenable only in approved institutions within New Zealand, for an initial period of three years, with the possibility of renewal for up to five years.

The initial salary depends on qualification and experience, but is usually comparable with the level of lecturer or senior lecturer in the university. In the case of Senior Fellows appointed from overseas, the Council may offer financial assistance towards the cost of travel to New Zealand.

Applications are called by notice in the *New Zealand Medical Journal*, with closing dates of 1st April and 1st October each year.

Career Fellowships are intended for individuals of outstanding ability who wish to make a full-time career of medical research.

Such awards are made only in response to an approach from the vice-chancellor of the university concerned, and the salary is equivalent to that of senior lecturer, associate professor, or, exceptionally, professor on the relevant university scale.

Visiting Fellowships are occasionally offered by the Council to bring to New Zealand distinguished workers who have shown ability in subject of special relevance to New Zealand. These Fellowships are tenable in one of the Council's units, in a university or in the research laboratory of a hospital, and support is offered for a period of up to two years.

The salary and allowances for Visiting Fellowships are fixed individually.

Further information from:
Secretary, Awards Committee
Medical Research Council of New Zealand
P.O. Box 5541
Wellesley Street
Auckland
New Zealand

[1285]

MEDICAL RESEARCH COUNCIL OF NEW ZEALAND

Project and Programme Grants: The Council awards Grants for approved research by investigators who are employed by other bodies in New Zealand, usually a university or hospital. Grants may be made to individuals with a clearly defined research project requiring support for a limited period (Project Grants), or to groups of investigators working on some aspect of a broader research field which justifies more prolonged support (Programme Grants). Normal closing dates are 1st February and 1st August of each year.

Research Units: The Council maintains a small number of Research Units (teams of investigators led by a scientist of proven ability, working with wide terms of reference in a particular field) undertaking long-term research in special fields. The Units have been established when research has been justified on a larger scale than could be supported in a university department, or when there has been no appropriate department in which such research might be accommodated. Units function in a close relationship with university departments.

Further information from:
Secretary
Medical Research Council of New Zealand
P.O. Box 5541
Wellesley Street
Auckland
New Zealand

[1286]

MEDICAL RESEARCH FOUNDATION OF BOSTON, INC.

Grants-in-Aid

Grants in varying amounts are provided for research and advanced study in medical and biological fields by individuals who hold the doctorate in one of those fields and are associated with United States institutions equipped to support the proposed research, or who have been accepted for advanced research training.

Further information from:
Medical Research Foundation of Boston
127 Bay State Road
Boston, Massachusetts 02215
U.S.A.

[1287]

MEDIEVAL ACADEMY OF AMERICA

Prizes

John Nicholas Brown Prize: US$500 is awarded annually to a North American resident for a first book or monograph on a medieval subject. Works must have been published three years before the competition. Authors should submit three copies along with a statement that the book is their first published in the medieval field. *Closing date:* 1st November of each year.

Elliot Prize: US$300 is offered annually to a North American resident for a first article on a medieval topic. Articles must be no less than five pages in length, and have been published in a journal two years before the competition. Authors should submit three copies along with a statement that the article is their first published in the medieval field. *Closing date:* 1st November of each year.

Note: The Academy also offers the Haskins Medal, for which no monetary award is made.

Further information from:
Medieval Academy of America
1430 Massachusetts Avenue
Cambridge, Massachusetts 02138
U.S.A.

[1288]

MELCHER BOOK AWARD *(Boston, Massachusetts)*

An annual Award of US$1,000 and a certificate is given for a book in any form (fiction, non-fiction, drama, poetry), written in the tradition of free inquiry, which has made the most significant contribution to religious liberalism. The book must have been published in America during the year prior to the Award year. Any author is eligible. Publishers only may submit works. The judges make special requests for books they wish to see, and authors and publishers should enquire by letter before sending a book.

Further information from:
Melcher Book Award
25 Beacon Street
Boston, Massachusetts 02108
U.S.A.

[1289]

MELLOR FELLOWSHIP/RESEARCH SCHOLARSHIP
University of the Witwatersrand
(Johannesburg)

Subjects: Biochemistry or biophysics.

Value: An average annual amount of approximately R3,000.

Tenable at the University of the Witwatersrand.

Eligibility: Open to graduates of any South African university who are postdoctoral research workers or higher degree candidates of particular merit.

Closing date: 7th March.

Further information from:
Secretary
Faculty of Science
University of the Witwatersrand
1 Jan Smuts Avenue
Johannesburg 2001
South Africa

[1290]

MEMORIAL FOUNDATION FOR JEWISH CULTURE *(U.S.A.)*

Scholarships for Post-Rabbinical Students

A number of Scholarships are awarded to assist in training of future Jewish religious scholars and leaders, and to help newly ordained rabbis obtain advanced training for careers as head of Yeshivot, as Dayanim and in other leadership positions. Any recently ordained rabbi engaged in full-time studies at a

Yeshiva, Kollel or rabbinical seminary is eligible to apply.

Not confirmed for 1983.

Further information from:
Memorial Foundation for Jewish Culture
15 East 26th Street
New York, New York 10010
U.S.A.

[1291]

MEMORIAL FOUNDATION FOR JEWISH CULTURE *(U.S.A.)*

International Scholarship Program for Community Service

Purpose: To assist well-qualified individuals for career training.

Subjects: The rabbinate, Jewish education, communal service or religious functionaries (e.g. shohatim, mohalim).

Value: Variable, depending on the country in which the recipient is trained and other considerations.

Tenable in diaspora Jewish communities in need of such personnel, excluding the U.S. Scholarships are for one year, renewable.

Eligibility: Open to any individual, regardless of country of origin, who is presently receiving, or plans to undertake training in his chosen field in a recognized yeshiva, teacher training seminary, school of social work, university or other educational institution.

Note: The recipient must commit himself to serve in a community of need. He should also be knowledgeable in the language and culture of that country or be prepared to learn it.

Not confirmed for 1983.

Further information from:
Memorial Foundation for Jewish Culture
15 East 26th Street
New York, New York 10010
U.S.A.

[1292]

MEMORIAL FOUNDATION FOR JEWISH CULTURE *(U.S.A.)*

International Doctoral Scholarships

Purpose: To assist in the training of future Jewish scholars for careers in Jewish scholarship and research, and to enable religious, educational and other Jewish communal workers to obtain advanced training for leadership positions.

Value: Variable, depending on the country where study is undertaken; usually between US$500 and US$1,200 per annum.

Tenable at a recognized university for one academic year; in exceptional cases, renewable for an additional year.

Eligibility: Open to graduate students of all nationalities who are specializing in a Jewish field and are officially enrolled or registered in a doctoral program at a recognized university.

Not confirmed for 1983.

Further information from:
Memorial Foundation for Jewish Culture
15 East 26th Street
New York, New York 10010
U.S.A.

[1293]

MEMORIAL FOUNDATION FOR JEWISH CULTURE *(U.S.A.)*

International Fellowships in Jewish Studies

Purpose: To assist well-qualified individuals to carry out independent scholarly, literary or artistic projects in a field of Jewish specialization which will make a significant contribution to the understanding, preservation, enhancement or transmission of Jewish culture.

Value: Variable, depending on the country in which the project is undertaken; usually between US$1,000 and US$1,500.

Tenable for one academic year; in exceptional cases, renewable for an additional year.

Eligibility: Open to recognized and/or qualified scholars, researchers or artists of any nationality who possess the knowledge and experience to formulate and implement a project in a field of Jewish specialization.

Not confirmed for 1983.

Further information from:
   Memorial Foundation for Jewish Culture
   15 East 26th Street
   New York, New York 10010
   U.S.A.

[1294]

MEMORIAL FOUNDATION FOR JEWISH CULTURE *(U.S.A.)*

Institutional Support Programs

Grants for Jewish Research and Publication: Grants are awarded to the following: to universities and recognized scholarly bodies for research and publication in Jewish fields; to universities and Jewish educational organizations for the preparation of textbooks and educational literature for children and youth; and to university student groups for national and international publications and activities related to Jewish culture.

Support for Jewish Education of University and College Students: The Foundation provides grants to bolster Jewish educational programs for university and college students, and to help universities to establish departments of Jewish studies. Grants are awarded on the understanding that the recipient institution will assume responsibility for the program following the initial limited period of Foundation support.

Grants for Special Projects: In order to ensure scholarly documentation of holocaust experience during World War II, Grants are given to aid scholarly publications and the development of teaching materials and other activities intended to document and commemorate the event.

Not confirmed for 1983.

Further information from:
   Memorial Foundation for Jewish Culture
   15 East 26th Street
   New York, New York 10010
   U.S.A.

[1295]

MENDELSSOHN SCHOLARSHIP FOUNDATION *(U.K.)*

Mendelssohn Scholarship

Purpose: To enable postgraduate students to pursue their study of musical composition either in the United Kingdom or abroad.

No. offered: One Scholarship in even-numbered years.

Value: £2,000.

Tenable in the United Kingdom or abroad.

Eligibility: Open to music students of any nationality under the age of 30 who are resident in the United Kingdom or any part of Ireland.

Note: Candidates compete for the Scholarship by submitting up to three compositions, which are assessed by independent judges.
  In the event of a tie between two competitors, the Performing Right Society offers the *PRS/Mendelssohn Scholarship* of the same value and conditions as that given by the Foundation.
  There is a small entrance fee for the competition.

Closing date: Varies, but is usually in the second half of March of the year of the Scholarship.

Further information from:
   Honorary Secretary
   Mendelssohn Scholarship Foundation
   14 Bedford Square
   London
   England WC1B 3JG

[1296]

MENNINGER FOUNDATION *(Topeka)*

Postdoctoral Fellowships in Clinical Psychology

Purpose: Training to develop the individual clinician as a responsible and respected member of a clinical team.

Subjects: Psychotherapy, psychodiagnosis and research.

Value: A minimum stipend for new Ph.D.'s of US$12,000.

Tenable for two years at the Foundation in Topeka.

Eligibility: Open to U.S. citizens who have a Ph.D. in clinical psychology with a minimum of one year of supervised clinical experience.

Closing date: 31st January for program to begin the following September.

Further information from:
William H. Smith, Ph.D., Director
Clinical Psychology Training Program
Menninger Foundation
Box 829
Topeka, Kansas 66601
U.S.A.

[1297]

MENTAL HEALTH FOUNDATION *(U.K.)*

Fellowships

Subjects: Psychiatry and all sciences basic to it, including psychology and sociology.

No. offered: Up to five Fellowships annually.

Value: The salaries offered will be in the range registrar to senior registrar or lecturer to senior lecturer according to seniority and experience.

Tenable in the United Kingdom for three years with the possibility of extension to a maximum of five years in exceptional circumstances.

Eligibility: Open to medical or science (including psychology and sociology) graduates who wish to pursue full-time research work bearing on problems of mental health whether in clinical psychiatry or in one of its supporting sciences. Awards are mainly intended for United Kingdom residents, although candidates may apply from abroad if they understand that, if shortlisted, they must pay their own travel expenses to and from an interview in London.

Note: Fellowships are for full-time research only, not education involving research.

Closing date: 1st March.

Further information from:
Honorary Secretary, Research Committee
Mental Health Foundation
8 Hallam Street
London
England W1N 6DH

[1298]

MENTAL HEALTH FOUNDATION *(U.K.)*

Grants in Aid of Travel during medical students' elective periods: Each year an unlimited number of awards, valued at up to £200 for each student, are given to each medical school in the United Kingdom for support of student electives in psychiatry. Individual students should apply to the deans of their medical schools.

Grants for Research Assistance and Expenses: Grants of varying amounts are available to doctors and scientists with research experience for periods of from one to five years. Grants should be in the fields of psychiatry and all sciences basic to it, including psychology and sociology. Applications may be submitted before 1st of March and September of each year.

Essay Prize for Medical Students: Essay topics are decided annually and details are sent to all medical schools in the United Kingdom in early summer. The Awards for the best submitted essays are as follows: One Gold Prize of £500; one Silver Prize of £250; a number of Bronze Prizes of £100 each, depending upon the merit of the entries. *Closing date:* 31st December.

Further information from:
Honorary Secretary, Research Committee
Mental Health Foundation
8 Hallam Street
London
England W1N 6DH

[1299]

MENUHIN PRIZE FOR YOUNG COMPOSERS *(U.K.)*

The competition for the Menuhin Prize is held every three years to promote musical composition and to give assistance to young composers. The Prize consists of a substantial financial award plus arrangements for the winning work to receive a public performance in London. Composition requirements vary from one competition to the next, but work submitted must not have been previously published or performed. Open to residents of the United Kingdom under 30 years of age.

The Prize is offered by the City of Westminster Arts Council.

Further information from:
Honorary Secretary
Menuhin Prize Management Committee
Marylebone Library
Marylebone Road
London
England NW1 5PS

[1300]

MERCK COMPANY FOUNDATION *(U.S.A.)*

Merck Sharpe & Dohme International Fellowships in Clinical Pharmacology

Subjects: Clinical pharmacology: training.

No. offered: Up to five Fellowships annually.

Value: US$18,300 per year plus travel and tuition allowances.

Tenable at recognized training centers in the United States for periods of up to two years.

Eligibility: Open to physicians of countries other than the United States who are licensed to practice in the country of residence, are eligible for certification by the Educational Council for Foreign Medical Graduates, and who plan to return to the country of residence and contribute to the advancement of clinical pharmacology in that country through teaching and research as a full-time career. Preference will be given to candidates who have also completed at least one year's internship and two years' residency, or some other combination of training experience adding up to three years postgraduate research experience. The ability to write and speak English fluently is most important.

Note: It is essential that candidates are accepted for training by a sponsor at an appropriate educational institution in the United States, and that they obtain certificates from the Educational Council for Foreign Graduates before taking up their Fellowship. It is equally essential that candidates are guaranteed a position in clinical pharmacology after completion of their training, by a sponsor in their own countries.

Closing date: 1st July, but may vary.

Further information from:
Merck Company Foundation
P.O. Box 2000
Rahway, New Jersey 07065
U.S.A.

[1301]

METEOROLOGICAL SERVICE OF ISRAEL

Study Fellowships in Agricultural Meterology

Purpose: To enable graduate students, preferably those from developing countries, to specialize in agricultural meteorology.

No. offered: Between 10 and 15 Fellowships annually.

Value: Fellowships comprise a lump sum to cover all local expenses, plus tuition. Travel to and from Israel is not included.

Tenable for two and one-half to three and one-half months at the Meteorological Service of Israel, Bet Dagan.

Eligibility: Open to foreign nationals who hold a bachelor's degree in agriculture, geography or meteorology and have at least one years' practical experience. Preference is given to graduates from developing countries.

Note: Applications may be obtained from the Israeli Embassy in the candidates' own country.

Closing date: 15th October.

Further information from:
Director
Meteorological Service of Israel
P.O. Box 25
Bet Dagan 50250
Israel

[1302]

METROPOLITAN MUSEUM OF ART *(New York City)*

Fellowships

Classical Fellowship: Awarded annually to an outstanding graduate student who has been admitted to the Ph.D. program of a university in the U.S., and who has submitted the outline of a thesis dealing with Greek and Roman Art which has already been accepted by the applicant's thesis advisor at the time the Fellowship is applied for. Preference is given to an applicant who, in the opinion of the Grants Committee, will profit most from utilizing the Museum's various resources.

Chester Dale Fellowships: Painters, sculptors, art historians and art critics whose fields are related to the fine arts of the western world, and who are preferably American citizens under 40 years of age, are eligible for these independent study or research Fellowships. Grants are usually tenable for periods ranging from three months to one year.

John J. McCloy Fellowships in Art: Two Awards are offered to curators of American museums for up to six weeks of travel in Germany. The Fellowships are intended for study, research, travel, and cultural exchange with German colleagues.

Andrew W. Mellon Fellowships: Awarded to promising young scholars with commendable research projects related to the Museum's collections, as well as for the support of distinguished visiting scholars from the United States and abroad, who can serve students as teachers and advisors, and make their own expertise available in cataloguing and refining the collections. Applicants should have received the doctorate or have completed substantial work toward it. Tenable for one year. Fellows are expected to spend most of their tenure at the Metropolitan Museum.

Andrew W. Mellon Fellowship in the Conservation of Paintings: One Fellowship is awarded annually to a United States citizen who has reached an advanced level of training in the conservation of paintings, and has some years of practical experience. The Fellowship is tenable for two consecutive years. The Fellow will be expected to work during those academic years at the Paintings Conservation Department of the Metropolitan, and study in Europe during the summer months.

J. Clawson Mills Scholarship: Open to scholars interested in pursuing research projects in any branch of the fine arts related to the Museum's collections. Grants are generally reserved for mature scholars of demonstrated ability. Tenable for one year with possible renewal for second year.

NS Fellowship for Mediterranean Art and Archaeology: Awarded annually to an outstanding graduate student who has been admitted to the Ph.D. program of a university within the U.S. and who has submitted the outline of a thesis dealing with Ancient Near Eastern art and archaeology or with Greek and Roman art. Preference will be given to the applicant who, in the opinion of the Grants Committee, would profit most from utilizing the Museum's various resources.

Theodore Rousseau Fellowships: Awarded annually for the purpose of training students, who plan to enter museums as curators of painting, by enabling them to undertake related study in Europe.

Note: Fellowships generally cannot be given for projects proposing that an exhibition be organized and presented within the Fellowship period. The total number of Fellowships awarded depends on available funds; stipends may vary in amount depending on particular circumstances. Announcement of awards is made 1st March.

Closing date: 9th January.

Further information from:
  Secretary of the Grants Committee
  Metropolitan Museum of Art
  Fifth Avenue and 82nd Street
  New York, New York 10028
  U.S.A.

[1303]

METROPOLITAN OPERA NATIONAL COUNCIL *(U.S.A.)*

Awards and Scholarships

The Council offers various Awards and Scholarships through national and regional levels of vocal competition to assist young singers in furthering their musical studies toward an ultimate operatic career.

In addition, local Awards are donated by various individuals and sponsoring organizations in many districts and regions. Yearly Awards and Scholarships total approximately US$106,000.

The use of funds is limited to expenses incurred for educational purposes, and specifically, to training and perfecting the singer's voice, style, acting and languages. Nationals of all countries may apply for the Awards and Scholarships but they must be resident in the United States, Canada, Australia or Puerto Rico during the competition.

Further information from:
Metropolitan Opera National Council
Regional Auditions
Lincoln Center
New York, New York 10023
U.S.A.

[1304]

MEXICAN AMERICAN LEGAL DEFENSE AND EDUCATIONAL FUND

Educational Assistance

Purpose: To provide financial assistance to economically disadvantaged Hispanic law students.

Subjects: Law.

No. offered: One Scholarship annually.

Value: US$1,000, paid in two equal installments. The scholarship Awards are not renewable, but may be reapplied for each year.

Tenable for one year at any accredited law school.

Eligibility: Open to Hispanic, full-time law students in need of financial support. Candidates must submit the following: a letter from a member of the Hispanic community attesting to the applicant's standing and involvement in the Hispanic community, a letter or acceptance from a law school, a letter of recommendation from a college, university or law school official, a financial need statement from the applicant's law school, an LSDAS report, copies of financial statement demonstrating indebtness, and a one-page essay detailing his or her reasons for studying law, professional objectives, and plans upon completion of legal training.

Note: The Fund also provides financial assistance on an annual basis by means of twenty scholarship loans.

Applications may be obtained from the Fund.

Closing date: 31st July.

Further information from:
Mexican American Legal Defense and Educational Fund
Educational Programs Department
28 Geary Street, 6th Floor
San Francisco, California 94108
U.S.A.

[1305]

MIGRAINE TRUST (U.K.)

Research Fellowships and Grants-in-Aid

Subject: The diagnosis, alleviation and cure of migraine.

Tenable at approved universities or research institutions, for an unspecified duration.

Note: Grants are awarded on merit and not according to predetermined criteria. Awards may be given to individuals of any nationality or to institutions, as Fellowships or as Grants-in-Aid of research projects.

Further information from:
Director
Migraine Trust
45 Great Ormond Street
London
England WC1N 3HD

[1306]

MILBANK MEMORIAL FUND (U.S.A.)

Milbank Scholar Program

Purpose: The Program is intended to assist selected clinical departments in academic settings to develop a capability in epidemiology and an understanding of the implications of this discipline for clinical practice. A basic component is clinicians trained in epidemiology; it is such individuals, in the persons of the Scholars, that the Program will bring to clinical departments of medicine, obstetrics and gynecology, pediatrics, psychiatry and surgery.

No. offered: Five awards annually.

Value: An annual stipend of US$26,000 and an allowance of US$1,300 per child per year for up to two dependent children during the first two years. For the last three years, Scholars receive an annual payment of US$30,000 towards salary. The Fund pays for transportation to and from the United Kingdom for the Scholar and family, and for tuition fees while there.

Tenable for five years. The first year is spent at the London School of Hygiene and Tropical Medicine where the Scholar is enrolled in the graduate program in epidemiology. The Scholar, during the second year of the fellowship, joins a clinical epidemiology unit of a teaching hospital in the United Kingdom. Upon completion of these two years of study and training, the Scholar returns to his or her American school for the last three years of the Program. Here, while participating in the regular departmental activities, the Scholar is expected to develop research and teaching projects designed to introduce and apply epidemiologic concepts and methods to problems of clinical medicine.

Eligibility: A nomination may be made only by the heads of the departments of medicine, obstetrics and gynecology, pediatrics, psychiatry, or surgery within United States medical schools. The candidate may come from any of the subspecialty units within these departments.

Only one nomination may be made by a department head, but each of the five eligible departments within a medical school may nominate a candidate.

The candidate must have completed clinical training and be Board-eligible or certified by July, and be a member of the nominating department with training status or faculty rank. Individuals at a more advanced stage are not to be excluded by this minimum requirement.

The candidate should be selected by the department head from among past and present members of the house staffs and fellowship programs or from among regular members of the department.

Closing date: 25th September.

Further information from:
Richard V. Kasius
Milbank Memorial Fund
1 East 75th Street
New York, New York 10021
U.S.A.

[1307]

MILK MARKETING BOARD *(England and Wales)*

Studentships in Agricultural Economics

Purpose: To increase the supply of professional agricultural economists in the United Kingdom.

No. offered: Variable.

Value: £4,260; to be reviewed periodically.

Tenable normally at a British university for one year but extendable on recommendation from the university for a longer period.

Eligibility: Candidates must be graduates of British universities who have obtained first or upper second class honours in their first degrees. Preference is given to those who have already studied economics, business studies, social studies or agriculture. Applications are also considered from candidates who will graduate during the current academic year and awards are dependent on examination performance.

Note: No conditions are attached to the Studentships regarding subsequent employment.

Closing date: 31st January.

Further information from:
Secretary
Awards in Agricultural Economics
Milk Marketing Board
Thames Ditton, Surrey
England KT7 0EL

[1308]

MINISTRY OF AGRICULTURE, FISHERIES AND FOOD *(U.K.)*

Postgraduate Agricultural Studentships

Subjects: Crop and animal production; horticulture; farm management; agricultural economics; agricultural and horticultural marketing and rural estate management; agricultural statistics; agricultural and dairy engineering, farm mechanisation and building; agricultural science and agricultural extension—formal courses or research training.

No. offered: Approximately 70 Studentships are allocated on a quota system to universities.

Value: To cover compulsory fees, and, in certain circumstances, travelling expenses and dependents' allowance, as well as maintenance allowance of up to £2,770 per annum (London area) and £2,245 per annum (elsewhere) for students living in college, hostel or lodgings, and up to £1,640 per annum (London or elsewhere) for students living at home. In the case of married students, the maintenance grant is subject to a spouse's contribution.

Tenable at universities and colleges in the United Kingdom for up to two years, with the possibility of extension for a third year for research training. Applicants should enquire at the institution where they wish to undertake postgraduate study about the possibility of being nominated. Studentships are not tenable at research institutes grant-aided by the Agricultural Research Council.

Eligibility: Open to British subjects (including Commonwealth citizens) who are normally resident in England or Wales. Studentships are also open to children of EEC nationals who are or have been working in the United Kingdom, and who are themselves resident in England or Wales at the time of application. Most candidates are required to have a good honours degree from a university in the United Kingdom. The degree held should be appropriate to the subject of study. Normally candidates should be under 27 years of age on 1st October of the year of application.

Note: The Ministry considers applications in agricultural science which relate to the more applied aspects of the subject. Applicants wishing to undertake postgraduate study in less applied aspects of agricultural science should apply to the *Science Research Council, P.O. Box 18, Swindon SN1 5BW.*

Candidates normally resident in Scotland or Northern Ireland should apply to the *Department of Agriculture and Fisheries for Scotland, Chesser House, Gorgie Road, Edinburgh EH11 3AW,* or the *Department of Agriculture,*

Northern Ireland, Dundonald House, Upper Newtownards Road, Belfast BT4 3SB.

Closing date: 1st August for England and Wales.

Further information from:
 Ministry of Agriculture, Fisheries and
  Food (R116)
 Great Westminster House
 Horseferry Road
 London
 England SW1P 2AE

[1309]

MINISTRY OF AGRICULTURE AND NATURAL RESOURCES *(Cyprus)*
Cyprus Forestry College

Scholarships

Purpose: To enable Scholars to acquire sufficient academic and practical training in forestry, especially as practised under Mediterranean and semi-arid conditions.

No. offered: Seven Scholarships awarded every other year: five Scholarships are allocated to Commonwealth citizens, one Scholarship to an African Zimbabwe national, and one to a citizen of a non-self-governing territory.

Value: Scholarships comprise tuition, books and instruments, board and lodging, and free medical attention. In addition a subsistence allowance is paid daily during vacations, when Scholars are not provided with free board and lodging.

Tenable for one academic year (covering Part I of the course) at the Cyprus Forestry College; renewable for a further ten months (covering Part II of the course).

Eligibility: Open to Commonwealth citizens, African Zimbabwe nationals and Citizens of non-self-governing territories who are between 18 and 30 years of age, have completed their secondary education and possess a working knowledge of English and a good knowledge of mathematics. In addition, they should have had some practical experience of forestry.

Note: Applications must be accompanied by a recommendation from a sponsoring authority in the candidate's own country.

An estimated amount of C£35 per month is

required as pocket money, and the provision of this amount is the responsibility of the Scholar or the sponsoring authority.

Occasionally Scholarships in addition to those noted above are awarded to citizens of other countries at the discretion of the Government of Cyprus.

Closing date: 31st July.

Further information from:
Director, Department of Forests
Ministry of Agriculture and Natural Resources
Nicosia
Cyprus

[1310]

MINISTRY OF COLLEGES AND UNIVERSITIES *(Ontario)*

Ontario Graduate Scholarship Program

Purpose: To encourage excellence in graduate studies.

Subjects: Unrestricted.

No. offered: 1,000: 40 to Scholars nominatd by Ontario universities; 960 to Scholars nominated by a selection board appointed by the Ministry.

Value: Can$1,900 per term. Students are responsible for the payment of their fees.

Tenable for two or three consecutive terms of full-time graduate study at a Canadian university; students must re-apply each year, and may receive a maximum of four awards.

Eligibility: Open to Canadian, preferably Ontario, residents with first class standing in most courses, enrolled in a graduate program leading to a master's or doctoral degree. (Up to 10% of the awards may be allocated to landed immigrants).

Note: Students may hold another award up to Can$2,500 and/or may accept research assistantships or a part-time teaching or demonstrating appointment, providing that the total amount paid to the Scholar within the period of the award shall not interfere with their status as full-time graduate students. The total time spent by the student in connection with such an appointment, including preparation, marking examinations, etc., must not exceed an average of ten hours per week.

Scholars to be nominated by the Selection Board must apply to the graduate school of the university on the prescribed form.

Closing dates: 2nd November for applications; 1st December for supporting documentation.

Further information from:
Students Awards Branch
Ministry of Colleges and Universities
8th Floor, Mowat Block
Queen's Park
Toronto, Ontario
Canada M7A 2B4

[1311]

MINISTRY OF CULTURE AND EDUCATION *(Iceland)*

Scholarships

Subjects: Icelandic language, literature and history.

No. offered: Approximately 12 Scholarships annually.

Value: 25,000 kronur, plus free tuition.

Tenable at the University of Iceland, Reykjavik, for seven months.

Eligibility: Open to students from all countries. One Scholarship is awarded to a student of Icelandic origin from Canada or the United States. Some knowledge of Icelandic is essential. Beneficiary countries are decided each year by the Ministry.

Note: Candidates should apply to the relevant government department in their own country. United States candidates should apply to the *Institute of International Education, 809 United Nations Plaza, New York, New York 10017.*

Address:
Ministry of Culture and Education
Hverfisgata 6
101 Reykjavik
Iceland

[1312]

MINISTRY OF DEFENCE *(U.K.)*

Senior and Principal Research Fellowships

Subjects: In-depth investigation within the science field and relating to the current programmes of the Ministry's Research and Development Establishments (advertised when opportunities occur).

Value: Senior—£6,263 to £7,712 per annum; Principal—£8,608 to £11,350 per annum. (Under review).

Tenable at a Research and Development Establishment for three years (Senior), or for one to three years with the possibility of an extension (Principal).

Eligibility: Senior Fellowships are open to persons who are, and always have been, British subjects and who have a minimum of three years' research experience. Principal Fellowships are open to British subjects who were born in the Commonwealth of parents also born in the Commonwealth and who are leading investigators in their field.

Further information from:
 Procurement Executive
 Ministry of Defence
 Room 310, Savoy Hill House
 London
 England WC2R 0BX

[1313]

MINISTRY OF EDUCATION *(Colombia)*
ICETEX

Graduate Exchange Scholarships

Subjects: Graduate studies offered by the Colombian universities.

No. offered: Approximately 50 Scholarships annually.

Value: 15,000 Colombian pesos per month for board and lodging, plus a book allowance of 10,000 pesos per annum, and 10,000 pesos upon arrival to assist with accommodation costs. Recipients also receive free tuition, medical insurance and one-way travel expenses.

Tenable at universities or higher education establishments in Colombia for twelve months; renewable for up to twelve additional months.

Eligibility: Open to nationals of any country who possess a bachelor's degree.

Note: Applications must be presented to the embassies or consulates of Colombia abroad.

Further information from:
 ICETEX
 Apartado Aéreo No. 5735
 Bogotá, D.E.
 Colombia

[1314]

MINISTRY OF EDUCATION
(Czechoslovakia)

Czechoslovak Government Scholarships

Subjects: Unrestricted.

Value: Variable, depending upon level of studies, plus tuition, medical fees and return travel. Undergraduate Scholars may also receive an allowance for books and clothing.

Tenable at universities or other institutions in Czechoslovakia for the duration of the approved study.

Eligibility: Citizens of most countries may study in Czechoslovakia but Scholarships are generally offered to students from developing countries and to other countries have a Scholarship exchange scheme with Czechoslovakia. Candidates should have either completed their secondary education and be between 17 and 27 years of age, or have completed their higher education and have at least three years of practical experience in their field of study. A good working knowledge of a universal language is essential.

Note: Candidates should apply through the foreign scholarship agency in their own country or through their local Czechoslovakian diplomatic mission.
 British students may apply under a British-Czechoslovakia Exchange Agreement for postgraduate or research Scholarships in Czechoslovakia. Applications should be sent to the *British Council, 10 Spring Gardens, London SW1A 2BN*.

Address:
Ministry of Education
Prague
Czechoslovakia

[1315]

MINISTRY OF EDUCATION *(Ecuador)*

Exchange Scholarships

Subjects: Any university studies.

No. offered: Two Scholarships annually.

Value: Cost of board, lodging and registration fees.

Tenable in Ecuador for the duration of the approved study.

Eligibility: Open to nationals of the United States who possess a university degree or equivalent qualification.

Note: Candidates should confirm details with the *Institute of International Education, 809 United Nations Plaza, New York, New York 10017.*

Address:
Ministry of Education
Quito
Ecuador

[1316]

MINISTRY OF EDUCATION *(Finland)*

Reciprocal Scholarship Programme

The Finnish Government gives a number of Scholarships annually for graduate and postgraduate studies in Finland. Awards are made on an exchange basis to nationals of Australia, Austria, Belgium, Bulgaria, Canada, China, Cuba, Czechoslovakia, Denmark, Federal Republic of Germany, France, German Democratic Republic, Greece, Hungary, Iceland, India, Iraq, Ireland, Israel, Italy, Japan, Mexico, Mongolia, Netherlands, Norway, Poland, Portugal, Romania, Spain, Sweden, Switzerland, Turkey, U.S.S.R., United States, United Kingdom, and Yugoslavia.

Candidates should have passed a final examination at a university or institution of higher education in their home country and must have a working knowledge of Finnish, Swedish, English or German. Scholarships are tenable for three to nine months, and provide a monthly allowance of 1,000 to 1,300 Finnish marks, free tuition and approved travel within Finland. Lodging in Helsinki is available at the Ministry of Education's student dormitories. Applications should be made on the special application forms through the appropriate government department in the candidate's own country, before 31st March.

U.S. citizens should see *Note* in next entry.

Address:
Ministry of Education
Department for International Relations
Scholarship Centre
Vuorikatu 5 B 18
SF-00100 Helsinki 10
Finland

[1317]

MINISTRY OF EDUCATION *(Finland)*

Finnish Language and National Subjects Programme

A number of Scholarships are given for postgraduate study in Finnish language and M.S. level study of other national subjects such as history, archaeology, folklore, literature and politics, etc. Scholarships are tenable for three to four months, and provide a monthly allowance of 1,300 Finnish marks plus free tuition and approved travel within Finland. Lodging in Helsinki is available at the Ministry of Education's student dormitories. Application should be made on the special application form through the Finnish diplomatic mission in the candidate's own country, before 31st March.

Note: Applicants from the United States should write to *The Institute of International Education, Division of Study Abroad Programs, 809 United Nations Plaza, New York, N.Y. 10017* for additional information regarding awards for U.S. citizens.

Address:
Ministry of Education
Department for International Relations
Scholarship Centre
Vuorikatu 5 B 18
SF-00100 Helsinki 10
Finland

[1318]

MINISTRY OF EDUCATION *(Finland)*

Specialists Programme

A number of Scholarships are given to nationals of all countries for research and specialization at a postdoctoral level, or equivalent, intended for discussion and making contacts with specialists in the candidate's own field and for becoming acquainted with the Finnish educational, scientific or cultural systems. Awards are tenable for one to five months. The Programme provides for a monthly allowance of 1,600 Finnish marks plus free tuition and approved travel within Finland. Lodging in Helsinki is available at the Ministry of Education's student dormitories. Applications should be made on the special application form through the Finnish diplomatic mission in the applicant's own country or through the Ministry of Education, and may be sent at any time.

U.S. citizens should see *Note* in preceding entry.

Address:
Ministry of Education
Department for International Relations
Scholarship Centre
Vuorikatu 5 B 18
SF-00100 Helsinki 10
Finland

[1319]

MINISTRY OF EDUCATION *(Greece)*
Greek State Scholarships Foundation

Scholarships

Subjects: Suitable studies include archaeology, classical and Byzantine history, modern Balkan history, folklore, sociological research, fine arts and any other field taught in the Greek institutions of higher education.

Value: 12,000 drachmas per month, plus 5,000 drachmas on arrival for accommodation fees, plus tuition fees, free emergency medical care, and return fare only.

Tenable at any university or institution of higher education in Greece, usually for ten months.

Eligibility: Open to nationals of Argentina, Belgium, Bulgaria, Chile, China, Czechoslovakia, Denmark, Egypt, Ethiopia, France, Federal Republic of Germany, Hungary, India, Iran, Israel, Italy, South Korea, Lebanon, Malta, Netherlands, Pakistan, Poland, Romania, Spain, Syria, Turkey, the United Kingdom and Yugoslavia. Preference is given to graduates.

Note: United Kingdom graduates should obtain further information and application forms from the *Greek Embassy, 1A Holland Park, London W11 3TP.*

Address:
Greek State Scholarships Foundation (IKY)
14 Lysicratus Street
GR 119 Athens
Greece

[1320]

MINISTRY OF EDUCATION *(Guatemala)*

Exchange Scholarships

Subjects: Any university studies.

No. offered: Two Scholarships annually.

Value: US$100 per month plus registration fees.

Tenable in Guatemala for the duration of the approved study.

Eligibility: Open to U.S. citizens.

Note: Candidates should confirm details with the *Institute of International Education, 809 United Nations Plaza, New York, New York 10017.*

Address:
Ministry of Public Education
Palacio Nacional
Guatemala

[1321]

MINISTRY OF EDUCATION *(Honduras)*

Exchange Scholarships

Subjects: Any university studies.

No. offered: Two Scholarships annually.

Value: US$100 per month.

Tenable in Honduras for the duration of the approved studies.

Eligibility: Open to nationals of the United States who have a bachelor's degree and wish to study in Honduras.

Note: Candidates should confirm details with the *Institute of International Education, 809 United Nations Plaza, New York, New York 10017.*

Address:
   Ministry of Education
   Palacio Nacional
   Tegucigalpa
   Honduras

[1322]

MINISTRY OF EDUCATION *(Jamaica)*
Commonwealth Scholarship and Fellowship Plan—in Jamaica

Jamaican Award

Purpose: To provide opportunities for Commonwealth students normally resident in other countries to pursue advanced courses of study in the West Indies.

Subjects: Postgraduate work in agriculture, the arts, law, engineering, natural sciences, medicine, social sciences and education.

No. offered: One Scholarship annually.

Value: J$4,000 (postgraduate) and J$2,700 (undergraduate) and maintenance allowance, J$250 allowance for books and apparatus, J$100 for approved travel in connection with the course of study, J$150 clothing allowance for Scholars from temperate countries, plus approved tuition, laboratory and examination fees and round-trip transportation fares. Married male Scholars accompanied by their wives receive a marriage allowance of J$800, provided the Scholar was married at the time of application and the wife is not a Scholarship holder herself or in paid employment, plus one-half return passage for the Scholar's wife when the duration of the Scholar's course of study is more than one academic year.

Tenable at any campus of the University of the West Indies.

Eligibility: Open to Commonwealth citizens or British protected persons resident in countries of the Commonwealth other than Jamaica who are college or university graduates or holders of equivalent qualifications. Scholars should not have reached their 35th birthday by 1st October of the award year. In special circumstances, applications may be accepted from candidates who exceed the age limit. Candidates are required to submit a medical certificate.

Closing date: 31st December.

Further information from:
   Ministry of Education
   Scholarships Section
   2 National Heroes Circle, Room 402
   Kingston N4
   Jamaica

[1323]

MINISTRY OF EDUCATION *(Japan)*

Japanese Government Scholarships

Subjects: Humanities, natural sciences, social sciences and Japanese language.

No. offered: Approximately 400 Scholarships annually.

Value: A monthly maintenance allowance of 159,000 yen, plus tuition fees etc.; also a lump sum of 25,000 yen on arrival and up to 43,000 yen for travel in Japan.

Tenable at a Japanese university usually for two years.

Eligibility: Open to nationals from countries having educational exchange agreements with Japan. Graduates should be under 35 years of age. Preference is given to persons with a good knowledge of Japanese; those with no knowledge of Japanese take a Japanese language course lasting from 12 to 18 months at a government-designated language school.

Note: Applicants from the United Kingdom should apply through the *Japan Information Centre, 9 Grosvenor Square, London W1X 9LB.* Other applicants should contact the Japanese diplomatic mission in their own country.

Address:
Ministry of Education
Student Exchange Division
2-2 Kasumigaseki 3-chome
Chiyoda-ku
Tokyo
Japan

[1324]

MINISTRY OF EDUCATION *(Korea)*

Scholarships

Purpose: To enable foreign graduates to undertake advanced studies at colleges and universities in Korea.

No. offered: Approximately sixty Scholarships annually.

Value: A stipend of 250,000 won per month for the duration of the Scholarship, tuition, allowance for books and stationery, economy class air travel for the Scholar to and from Korea, travel expenses for field study, personal accident insurance, and a settling-in allowance of 60,000 won upon arrival. All expenses for dependents must be borne by the Scholar.

Tenable for one year (Scholars following non-degree research courses or auditing courses), two years (Scholars following courses leading to a master's degree) and three years (Scholars following courses leading to a doctor's degree) at a college or university in Korea; under certain conditions, renewable for a further year; six months to one year of Korean language training prior to the above mentioned courses for those who are required to take it.

Eligibility: Open to citizens of various foreign countries who are under 35 years of age as of the date application is made and who have graduated or are about to graduate from an accredited college or university. Candidates are required to be proficient in the Korean language or must take the language training.

Note: Preliminary selection of candidates is the responsibility of the Korean diplomatic missions overseas, following recommendation of candidates by the government in that country.

Closing date: At least three months prior to the commencement of the proposed course.

Further information from:
Overseas Students Division
Ministry of Education
Seoul
Korea

[1325]

MINISTRY OF EDUCATION *(Mexico)*

Scholarships for Foreign Students

Subjects: Humanities, particularly education.

No. offered: Depends on the cultural agreement between Mexico and the foreign country concerned.

Value: 6,000 pesos per month.

Tenable in Mexico for one year; renewals will be considered on merit.

Eligibility: Open to postgraduate students from any country who meet all the qualification requirements of the Mexican institution at which they wish to study.

Note: Candidates should apply through the agency in their own country which administers scholarship exchange programs. Direct applications are not considered.

Address:
Direccion General de Relaciones
    Internacionales
Secreteria de Educacion Publica
Brasil 31, Oficina 330
Mexico 06020, D.F.

[1326]

MINISTRY OF EDUCATION *(Mexico)*

Colegio de Mexico Scholarship

Subjects: Mexican history, Spanish linguistics, Latin American literature, international relations (Latin American), demography, economics, sociology and urbanization.

No. offered: One Scholarship annually.

Value: A monthly allowance of 4,500 pesos and exemption from tuition fees. Scholars are required to pay their own travelling expenses.

Tenable at the Colegio de Mexico for ten months, commencing in September.

Eligibility: Open to United Kingdom citizens. Scholars must have graduate status by the time of taking up the award. A working knowledge of Spanish is essential.

Note: Candidates should apply to the *Mexican Embassy, 8 Halkin Street, London SW1* by 2nd December.

Address:
El Colegio de México
Camino al Ajusco No. 20
México 20, D.F.

[1327]

MINISTRY OF EDUCATION *(Morocco)*

Study, Research and Exchange Scholarships

Subjects: Any university or technical studies.

No. offered: Variable.

Value: A monthly allowance which varies according to level of study.

Tenable in Morocco for the duration of the studies.

Eligibility: Open to nationals of countries having cultural agreements with Morocco. Candidates must hold a bachelor's degree and be at least 17 years of age.

Note: Applications should be made in the first place to the Moroccan diplomatic mission in the candidate's own country.

Closing date: 31st August.

Address:
Ministry of Education
Victory Plaza
Rabat
Morocco

[1328]

MINISTRY OF EDUCATION *(Pakistan)*

**Cultural Scholarship Scheme:
Scholarships and Research Fellowships**

Subjects: Medicine, dentistry, engineering, science and arts.

No. offered: 70 awards annually.

Value: Scholarships—between 350 and 425 rupees per month (depending on whether the course is for an intermediate diploma or a degree), plus equipment allowance if applicable of 250 or 300 rupees per annum and annual study tour allowance of 250 rupees; Fellowships—550 rupees per month, plus 300 rupees for annual study tour allowance and 300 rupees for equipment if applicable.

Tenable at universities and affiliated colleges in Pakistan, until completion of course provided that progress is satisfactory.

Eligibility: Open to nationals of all countries. Candidates should possess the required academic qualifications in their field of study. A sufficient knowledge of English is required and, preferably, some knowledge of Urdu.

Note: Applications must be made by 31st July through Pakistan embassies in the applicants' own countries.

Address:
Ministry of Education and Provincial
  Coordination
Islamabad
Pakistan

[1329]

MINISTRY OF EDUCATION *(Romania)*

Grants for Foreign Students

Subjects: Most fields of study: academic work, research or training.

Tenable at Romanian universities or institutions of higher education and research for one academic year. Some Grants are renewable for up to six years.

Eligibility: Open to nationals of countries with

which Romania has cultural agreements (includes the U.K. and the U.S.A.).

Candidates must have a university degree, a working knowledge of either German, English, Spanish, French or Russian, and should be between 17 and 30 years of age. Doctoral candidates should be no more than 40 years of age.

Note: Applications should be made to the following addresses: United Kingdom—*British Council, 10 Spring Gardens, London SW1A 2BN*; United States—*Institute of International Education, 809 United Nations Plaza, New York, New York 10017*. Other candidates should apply to their national agency for foreign government awards.

Address:
Foreign Students Department
Ministry of Education
Spiru Haret Street, 12
Bucharest 70738
Romania

[1330]

MINISTRY OF EDUCATION *(Syria)*

Scholarships

Subjects: Science, literature, medicine.

No. offered: 800 to 1,000 Scholarships annually.

Value: A monthly maintenance allowance, plus tuition and medical assistance.

Tenable at certain universities in Syria for one year; renewable.

Eligibility: Open to nationals of African and Arab countries, and of countries maintaining friendly relations with Syria.

Note: Candidates are advised to obtain further information from the Syrian diplomatic representative in their own country before making application.

Address:
Ministry of Education
Foreign Student's Section
Damascus
Syria

[1331]

MINISTRY OF EDUCATION *(Taiwan)*

Foreign Student Scholarships

Subjects: Chinese culture.

Value: A monthly allowance for students from countries which have cultural conventions with Taiwan. All scholars receive free tuition and accommodation.

Tenable in Taiwan for one year; renewable up to total of four years (undergraduate) and two years (graduate).

Eligibility: Open to university graduates and undergraduates from most countries and have a genuine interest in Chinese culture and a working knowledge of Chinese.

Note: Candidates should apply to the Taiwan diplomatic representative in their own country. Australians should apply to the *Department of Education, P.O. Box 826, Woden, A.C.T. 2606.*

Not confirmed for 1983.

Address:
Ministry of Education
Taipei
Taiwan

[1332]

MINISTRY OF EDUCATION *(Thailand)*

Scholarships

Purpose: To enable students from foreign countries to attend schools and universities in Thailand; specifically, Chulalongkorn University, Mahidol University (University of Medical Sciences), Kasetsart University, University of Fine Arts, Thammasat and Sri-nakharinwirot Universities, and Silpakorn University (University of Fine Arts).

Subject: Chulalongkorn University in any field offered by the faculties of arts, commerce and accountancy, communication arts, economics, education, engineering, law, political science, science, architecture, pharmacy, dentistry, medicine, veterinary science Mahidol University in the fields of medicine and dentistry, pharmacy, public health, tropical medicine, nursing and midwifery, and medical technology; Kasetsart University in the fields of agriculture, forestry, fisheries and veterinary science, cooperative sciences and economics, and irrigation engineering; Silpakorn University in the fields of painting and sculpture, Thai architecture, decorative art and archaeology; Thammasat University in the fields of law, economics, commerce, political science, public administration and social administration, and Sri-nakharinwirot University in the fields of elementary education, secondary education, vocational education, educational administration and physical education.

No. offered: Four Scholarships annually.

Value: 15,000 bahts per annum.

Tenable for one to six years, depending upon the Fellow's choice of subject.

Eligibility: Open to citizens of Australia, Malaysia, France, India, Indonesia, Japan, New Zealand, the Philippines, Pakistan, Republic of Korea, Sri Lanka, United Kingdom, United States, and Singapore. Candidates must not be more than 30 years of age and must have attained at least a standard equivalent to grade 12 in Thailand. An adequate knowledge of Thai and English is required; instruction of the Thai language will be furnished when necessary.

Note: The government institutions in the candidate's own country conducts a preliminary screening of candidates in cooperation with its Unesco National Commission or other appropriate organizations. The recipient government nominates two suitable applicants for each award to the Thailand National Commission for Unesco through the Thai Ministry of Foreign Affairs.

Closing date: 1st March.

Further information from:
  Secretary-General, Thailand National Commission for Unesco
  Ministry of Education
  Bangkok
  Thailand

[1333]

MINISTRY OF EDUCATION *(Thailand)*

Fellowships

Purpose: To enable students from foreign countries to conduct research work in Thailand at the following institutions: Chulalongkorn University, Mahidol University of Medical Sciences, Kasetsart University, University of Fine Arts, Thammasat University, Sri-nakharinwirot University, and the Behavioral Science Research Institute.

Subjects: Chulalongkorn University: any field offered by the faculties of arts, architecture, commerce and accountancy, communication arts, dentistry, economics, education, engineering, law, medicine, pharmacy, political science, science and veterinary science; Mahidol University: any field offered by the faculties of medicine, dentistry, pharmacy, public health, medical technology, medical sciences, and tropical medicine, science, nursing, environment and resources studies, institute for population and social research, and the institute of nutrition; Kasetsart University: in the fields of agriculture, agricultural education and economics, forestry, sciences and economics, fisheries, veterinary science, applied radiation and isotopes, environmental science, education and home economics. Silpakorn University: in the fields of painting and sculpture, Thai architecture, decorative art and archeology; Thammasat University: in the fields of law, economics, commerce and accountancy, political science, public administration and social administration; Sri-nakharinwirot University: in the fields of education, educational research and administration, psychology, natural and social sciences, behavioral sciences; and at the Behavioral Science Research Institute: in the field of child development or psychology.

No. offered: Six Fellowships annually.

Value: 20,000 bahts per annum.

Tenable at the specified institutions for one year.

Eligibility: Open to nationals of all Unesco member countries with a scholarly or professional status in their given fields. Candidates for Fellowships at the University of Fine Arts must have recommendations from recognized art institutes in their native countries; all other candidates must hold a bachelor's degree.

Note: The government institution in the candidate's own country conducts a preliminary screening of candidates in cooperation with its Unesco National Commission or other appropriate organizations. The recipient government nominates two suitable applicants for each award to the Thailand National Commission for Unesco through the Thai Ministry of Foreign Affairs

Closing date: 1st March.

Further information from:
Secretary-General, Thailand National Commission for Unesco
Ministry of Education
Bangkok
Thailand

[1334]

MINISTRY OF EDUCATION *(Turkey)*

Study, Doctoral and Research Scholarships

Subjects: Unrestricted; preference is given, however, to studies in Turkish language and civilization, history, geography, fine arts and agriculture.

Value: Study Scholarships—T£16,000 per month, plus tuition and medical care; Doctoral Scholarships—T£18,000 per month, plus tuition and medical care; Research Scholarships—T£20,000 per month, plus tuition and medical care.

Tenable at universities in Turkey. Duration varies: Study Scholarships—until end of course, including a preparatory course in the Turkish language; Doctoral Scholarships—until doctorate is obtained, including preparatory course in Turkish; Research Scholarships—for eight months, renewable.

Eligibility: Open to nationals of countries with which Turkey has cultural agreements, who can fulfill the following requirements: Study Scholarships—candidates should possess a certificate of secondary education and be under 25 years of age; Doctoral Scholarships—candidates should possess a degree and be under 30 years of age; Research Scholarships—candidates should possess a degree and be under 35 years of age.

Note: The Turkish government also offers *Summer Course Scholarships* (July to September) on Turkish language and culture at the University of Istanbul. Scholars receive a monthly allowance of T£16,000 for both undergraduates and graduates. Candidates should be under 35 years of age.

Candidates for all Turkish scholarships should apply to the international scholarship agency in their own country. United States—*Institute of International Education, 809 United Nations Plaza, New York, New York 10017;* United Kingdom—*Cultural Attaché, Turkish Embassy, Camelot House, 76 Brompton Road, London SW3.*

Address:
Director General
External Relations Department
Ministry of Education
Ankara
Turkey

[1335]

MINISTRY OF EDUCATION *(Venezuela)*

Exchange Scholarships

Subjects: Any university studies.

No. offered: Two Scholarships annually.

Value: US$200 per month.

Tenable in Venezuela for one year.

Eligibility: Open to nationals of the United States who have a bachelor's degree.

Note: Candidates should confirm details with the *Institute of International Education, 809 United Nations Plaza, New York, New York 10017.*

Address:
Scholarships Department
Ministry of Education
esquina El Conde
Caracas
Venezuela

[1336]

MINISTRY OF EDUCATION AND CULTURE *(Bolivia)*

Exchange Scholarships

Subjects: Archaeology, cosmic physics, ethnography, folklore, etc.

No. offered: Two Scholarships annually.

Value: Cost of board and lodging and registration fees.

Tenable in Bolivia for the duration of the approved studies.

Eligibility: Open to nationals of the United States who possess a bachelor's degree.

Note: Candidates should confirm details with the *Institute of International Education, 809 United Nations Plaza, New York, New York 10017.*

Address:
 Director
 Department of International Relations
 Ministry of Education
 La Paz
 Bolivia

[1337]

MINISTRY OF EDUCATION AND CULTURE *(India)*

General Cultural Scholarship scheme

Purpose: To enable foreign students to undertake higher education studies or practical training in India in the following fields: arts and humanities (including anthropology, civilization and culture; music, dance and drama); law and jurisprudence; international relations; education and teacher training; architecture and engineering technology; medicine (including public health, tropical medicine, nursing, pharmacy, hygiene, dentistry, optometry and osteopathy); social work; community and rural development; journalism; broadcasting techniques; archives; library science; home science; statistics; commerce; business administration; industrial management.

No. offered: 180 Scholarships (postgraduate and undergraduate) annually.

Value: A monthly allowance of 600 rupees (postgraduates) and 500 rupees (undergraduates), plus tuition, equipment, books, and miscellaneous fees. Approved study travel to introductory course and rail fare up to a maximum of 500 rupees are also allowed for journeys undertaken during the vacation. Travel costs to and from India for students from non-self-governing territories and partial travel costs for needy students from other countries are paid on the recommendation of the Indian diplomatic mission in the candidate's country.

Tenable at approved institutions in India for periods of time determined by the requirements of study.

Eligibility: Open to nationals of various African, Asian and other countries (including several Commonwealth countries). Candidates for postgraduate courses must possess a bachelor's degree and should preferably be between 20 and 25 years of age. Candidates for undergraduate courses should be between 17 and 22 years of age and have passed the Senior Cambridge Matriculation examination, or its equivalent. Preference is given to candidates wishing to take a course for which facilities are not available in their own country.

Note: Under intergovernmental programmes, etc., the Indian government also offers awards to students from numerous other countries.
 Candidates for all Indian government awards should apply to the Indian diplomatic representatives in their own country.

Address:
 External Scholarship Division
 Department of Education
 Ministry of Education and Culture
 Shastri Bhavan
 New Delhi
 India

[1338]

MINISTRY OF EDUCATION AND CULTURE *(India)*

Commonwealth Scholarships and Fellowships

Purpose: To enable Commonwealth citizens to undertake postgraduate studies research in India. Under special circumstances, a few awards may be made for undergraduate or other courses, facilities for which are not available in the nominating country. The awards are provided by the Indian government and fall within the framework of the Commonwealth Scholarship and Fellowship Plan.

No. offered: 50 awards annually.

Value: A maintenance allowance of 600 rupees per month for postgradute studies research and 500 rupees per month for undergraduate studies, plus cost of tuition, travel cost to and from India and back to his country, approved study-related tours, medical expenses, participating in holiday and youth camps, up to 400 rupees for books and equipment, and 200 rupees for clothing.

Tenable at recognised universities or institutions of higher learning in India for two years.

Eligibility: Open to citizens of Commonwealth countries who are graduates under 35 years of age.

Note: Applications should be submitted through the appropriate agency in the candidate's country.

Address:
External Scholarship Division
Department of Education
Ministry of Education and Culture
Shastri Bhavan
New Delhi
India

[1339]

MINISTRY OF EDUCATION AND CULTURE *(India)*

Commonwealth Senior Visiting Fellowships

Purpose: To enable Fellows to study and observe in India in an educational field and administration of their choice. The Fellowships are provided by the Indian government and all within the framework of the Commonwealth Scholarship and Fellowship Plan.

No. offered: Three Fellowships annually.

Value: A maintenance allowance of 150 rupees per day. Return tourist air fares, travel within India, and free medical and hospital facilities are also provided.

Eligibility: Open to senior educators (professors and senior headmasters) and senior educational administrators from Commonwealth countries.

Candidates are nominated by their governments, and the final selection is made by the Indian Government.

Address:
External Scholarship Division
Department of Education
Ministry of Education and Culture
Shastri Bhavan
New Delhi
India

[1340]

MINISTRY OF EDUCATION AND CULTURE *(India)*

Training Bursaries

No. offered: Ten Bursaries annually.

Value: A maintenance allowance of 500 rupees per month, tuition and examination fees, an allowance for books and equipment, medical expenses, approved study tours and/or stay at holiday or youth welfare camps, and an outfit allowance. Travel costs are not paid by the Indian government, but may be provided by the candidate's own government or other agency.

Tenable at central training institutes in India for twelve months.

Eligibility: Open to citizens from developing countries of the Commonwealth who are between 18 and 40 years of age. Candidates must have reached matriculation standard and have a good knowledge of the chosen trade. Preference is given to those possessing a diploma or employed as instructors or supervisors. Knowledge of English is essential.

Closing date: February.

Note: The Bursaries are offered under the Commonwealth Education Cooperation Plan. Candidates should apply through the relevant government department in their own country.

Address:
External Scholarship Division
Department of Education
Ministry of Education and Culture
Shastri Bhavan
New Delhi 1
India

[1341]

MINISTRY OF EDUCATION AND SCIENCES *(Netherlands)*

Scholarships

Subjects: Unrestricted.

Value: 1,050 Dutch florins per month, plus tuition.

Tenable at universities and institutions of higher education in the Netherlands for variable lengths of time.

Eligibility: Open to nationals of most countries who possess a university degree or have completed several years of higher studies. Applicants should have a working knowledge of French or German but preferably English.

Note: Further information and application forms may be obtained from the proper education authority in the applicant's home country after 15th December of each year.

Further information from:
Ministry of Education and Sciences
Nieuwe Uitleg 1
The Hague 2514 BP
Netherlands

[1342]

MINISTRY OF FOREIGN AFFAIRS *(Brazil)*

Brazilian Government Scholarships

Subjects: Unrestricted.

Value: Equivalent of US$150 per month in cruzeiros, plus tuition and travel to and from Brazil.

Tenable at any Brazilian university or institution of higher education and research for one year.

Eligibility: Open to foreign nationals who hold a degree or equivalent qualification. Candidates wishing to study the plastic arts, music or the visual arts may not be required to possess a degree. A good knowledge of Portuguese is essential.

Note: Candidates should apply to the Brazilian embassy in their own country.

Not confirmed for 1983.

Address:
Department of Culture
Ministry of Foreign Affairs
Esplanada dos Ministérios
Brasilia, D.F.
Brazil

[1343]

MINISTRY OF FOREIGN AFFAIRS *(Czechoslovakia)*

Czechoslovak Government Exchange Scholarships

Subjects: Unrestricted.

No. offered: Approximately 350 Scholarships annually.

Value: Allowances for room, board, and other personal expenses.

Tenable at universities in Czechoslovakia for ten months or for shorter periods of not less than two months.

Eligibility: Open to nationals of various countries, including Ireland and the United Kingdom. Candidates must possess a university degree or equivalent qualification and should have had three years of practical experience in their field of study. A good working knowledge of a universal language is essential.

Note: United Kingdom candidates should apply to the *Higher Education Department, British Council, 10 Spring Gardens, London SW1A 2BN,* and Irish candidates to *Scholarships Exchange Board, 80 St. Stephen's Green, Dublin 2.*

Address:
Ministry of Foreign Affairs
Prague
Czechoslovakia

[1344]

MINISTRY FOR FOREIGN AFFAIRS
(Finland)
Department for International Development Cooperation

Finnish Government Scholarships

Purpose: To provide technical assistance to developing countries.

Subjects: Postgraduate study in fields which are important to the social and economic development of the applicant's country.

Value: The Department will pay a monthly allowance of 1,750 Finnish marks, medical expenses, insurance, travel costs within Finland (agreed upon in advance) and will make individual arrangements in each case with regard to travel costs to and from the applicant's home country.

Tenable in Finland for one year; renewable.

Eligibility: Priority is given to students from countries receiving development aid from Finland. They should be sponsored or recommended by the government of their own country. Applicants must give evidence of academic or professional competence with appropriate certificates or diplomas.

Note: The Scholar must undertake to return to his native country at the end of the Scholarship period. All agreements for payment of homeward travel costs become void if the holder does not return within three months of expiration of the Scholarship.

Further information from:
Department for International
 Development Cooperation
Ministry for Foreign Affairs
Erottajankatu 19B
00130 Helsinki 13
Finland

[1345]

MINISTRY OF FOREIGN AFFAIRS
(France)

Scholarships

Subjects: Postgraduate research.

No. offered: Approximately 8,500 Scholarships annually.

Value: FF1,500 per month (more for certain studies) plus tuition and an eventual accommodation allowance.

Tenable at universities and other institutions in France for the duration of studies, usually one to three years.

Eligibility: Open to nationals of all countries, with the exception of French-speaking African countries. Candidates should possess the appropriate qualifications, and a sufficient knowledge of French to enable them to follow courses in that language.

Application addresses: Australia—*Department of Education, P.O. Box 826, Woden, A.C.T. 2606;* Canada—*Association of Universities and Colleges of Canada, 151 Slater Street, Ottawa, Ontario K1P 5N1;* United Kingdom—*Cultural Attaché, French Embassy, 22 Wilton Crescent, London SW1X 8SB* or (for candidates in science, technology or medicine)—*Scientific Counsellor, French Embassy, Silver City House, 62 Brompton Road, London SW3 1BW;* United States—*Institute of International Education, 809 United Nations Plaza, New York, New York 10017.* Candidates from Commonwealth and other countries should apply to the French embassies in their own countries.

Candidates attached to universities should forward their applications through the head of the department in which they are working.

Not confirmed for 1983.

Address:
Ministry of Foreign Affairs
37 quai d'Orsay
75007 Paris
France

[1346]

MINISTRY OF FOREIGN AFFAIRS (Israel)

Scholarships

Subjects: A wide programme of seminars, workshops, study and training courses, postgraduate research, etc.

Value: Maintenance and tuition allowances, plus a small allowance for personal expenses.

Tenable in Israel for several weeks (seminars and accelerated courses) to several years (long-term study programmes).

Eligibility: Open primarily to trainees from developing countries who have a working knowledge of English, French or Spanish.
Scholarships are also awarded to nationals of non-self-governing territories under the United Nations Programme.

Note: Applications, supported by Government request, must be made to the nearest Israeli diplomatic or consular representative.

Address:
International Cooperation Division
Ministry of Foreign Affairs
Hakirya
Jerusalem
Israel

[1347]

MINISTRY OF FOREIGN AFFAIRS (Italy)

Italian Government Scholarships and Grants

Subjects: Postgraduate scholarships in any field; Grants for study and research in the arts, music and Italian language.

Value: 330,000 lire per month. Transportation costs to and from Italy are paid for nationals of developing countries for tenure of eight months or more.

Tenable in Italy for a minimum of one month (short-term language courses) to a maximum of twelve months.
Long-term Scholarship applicants must generally attend an intensive Italian language course (one or two months) before starting their studies.
Scholarships can be renewed if the student's results are satisfactory.

Eligibility: For postgraduate studies candidates must possess at least a master's degree; musicians and artists must pass an admission examination. To attend university courses, possession of a high-school diploma is necessary.

Note: Applications should be sent to the Italian diplomatic representative in the candidate's own country.

Address:
Ministry of Foreign Affairs
Piazzale della Farnesian
00100 Rome
Italy

[1348]

MINISTRY OF FOREIGN AFFAIRS (Netherlands)

Netherlands Fellowship Programme for Development Cooperation

Subjects: International Courses (more than 70) in: hydraulic engineering; hydrology; sanitary engineering; environmental science and technology; port management; natural resources survey; integrated surveys; urban surveys; photogrammetry; aerial photography and navigation; mineral exploration; cartography; electronic engineering; telecommunications (telephone switching, H.F. communication, transission); health development; soil science and water management; land drainage; rural extension; plant breeding; plant protection; potato production; vegetable growing; dairy cattle husbandry; poultry or pig husbandry; tropical animal production; farm mechanization; agricultural teacher training; labor studies; women's studies; European integration; public administration; law; local government; socio-economic planning; regional development planning; project analysis; international and national development and economics; development administration; statistics and national accounting; industrialization; industrial relations; industrial management; regional industrial management; housing; planning and building; radio and television program production.

No. offered: Approximately 1,000 Fellowships annually.

Value: 1,635 Dutch florins for the first month, 1,275 florins for the following months; a book allowance; and travel costs relating to studies within the Netherlands. For Programmes of three months and more the Netherlands government may pay for the outward and/or homeward journey from or to the Fellow's home country.

Tenable in the Netherlands for the duration of the course, with the possibility of a short extension.

Eligibility: Open to nationals of developing countries who are employed in a developing country. Candidates must be in good health and have sufficient training and experience in the particular field of study which will enable them to benefit from advanced study and observation in the Netherlands. Nearly all international courses are at postgraduate level. Candidates should have a good knowledge of English.

Note: Application forms and additional information can be obtained from the office of the Netherlands diplomatic representative in or designated for the candidate's home country.

On completion of their studies, Fellows must return to their home country to continue work in their profession.

Address:
Section for Training in the Netherlands
Ministry of Foreign Affairs
Muzenstraat 30
2511 VW The Hague
Netherlands

[1349]

MINISTRY OF FOREIGN AFFAIRS *(N.Z.)*

Bilateral Aid Programme Scholarships

Subjects: Undergraduate and postgraduate study in fields related to the economic development of the candidate's own country.

No. offered: Variable: a quota of awards is allocated to recipient countries each year.

Value: A tax-free stipend of NZ$3,952 per annum, plus tuition, economy class air fares to and from New Zealand, and an establishment grant of NZ$400. There is no allowance for married Scholars.

Tenable at universities in New Zealand for a length of time requested by the nominating government; renewable in certain circumstances.

Eligibility: Open to nationals of developing countries receiving aid under the New Zealand Bilateral Aid Programme. Candidates should hold qualifications required by the receiving university for admission to the proposed course. Candidates for undergraduate awards must have their university entrance qualifications approved by the New Zealand Overseas Students Admissions Committee.

Note: Recipients of awards must undertake to return to their own countries upon completion of their course.

Applications must be made to the government department in the candidate's own country which is responsible for selection of students and trainees for scholarships to study overseas.

Address:
Ministry of Foreign Affairs
Private Bag
Wellington 1
New Zealand

[1350]

MINISTRY OF FOREIGN AFFAIRS *(N.Z.)*

Special Commonwealth African Assistance Plan Scholarships

Subjects: Undergraduate and postgraduate study in fields related to the economic development of the candidate's own country.

No. offered: Variable; a quota of awards is allocated to recipient countries each year.

Value: A tax-free stipend of NZ$3,952 per annum, plus tuition, economy class air fares to and from New Zealand, and an establishment grant of NZ$400. There is no allowance for married Scholars.

Tenable at universities in New Zealand for a length of time requested by the nominating government; renewable in special circumstances.

Eligibility: Open to nationals of developing countries receiving aid under the New Zealand Bilateral Aid Programme. Candidates should hold qualifications required by the receiving university for admission to the proposed course. Candidates for undergraduate Scholarships must have their university entrance qualifications approved by the New Zealand Overseas Students Admissions Committee.

Note: Recipients of awards must undertake to return to their own countries upon completion of their course.

Applications must be made to the government department in the candidate's own country which is responsible for selection of students and trainees for Scholarships to study overseas.

Address:
Ministry of Foreign Affairs
Private Bag
Wellington 1
New Zealand

[1351]

MINISTRY OF FOREIGN AFFAIRS
(Norway)

Norwegian Scholarships for Foreigners

Subjects: Preference is given to Norwegian language and literature, history, folklore, law, natural history (flora, fauna, geology), geography and economic life.

No. offered: Approximately 600 man-months annually.

Value: 2,500 Norwegian kroner per month.

Tenable at suitable institutions in Norway normally for a full academic year (September 1st to June 1st).

Eligibility: Open to university students and graduates from Austria, Belgium, Bulgaria, China, Czechoslovakia, Egypt, France, German Democratic Republic, West Germany, Greece, India, Ireland, Israel, Italy, Mexico, Netherlands, Poland, Portugal, Spain, Switzerland, Turkey, U.S.S.R., United Kingdom, and Yugoslavia.

Candidates must be 30-35 years of age and should have a good command of a Scandinavian language or English.

Note: Applicants from Ireland should apply to the Norwegian embassy in Dublin; applicants from the United Kingdom should apply to the *British Council, 10 Spring Gardens, London SW1A 2BN.*

Applicants from other countries should apply to their own country's foreign scholarships agency, or to the Norwegian diplomatic representative in their own country.

Address:
Ministry of Foreign Affairs
Scholarship Section
7 juni-plassen 1
Oslo-Dep. 1
Norway

[1352]

MINISTRY OF FOREIGN AFFAIRS
(Singapore)

Scholarships and Postgraduate Scholarships

Purpose: To provide educational opportunities to nationals of member countries of the Colombo Plan with the aim of raising the standard of living and social well-being of these countries through technical assistance.

Subjects: Various professional and technical fields.

Value: S$500 per month living allowance and S$160 per annum book and equipment allowance for Scholarships; S$700 per month living allowance and S$200 book and equipment allowance for Postgraduate Scholarships. Both awards cover full tuition, registration and examination fees.

Tenable in Singapore for periods of 1 to 4 years for Scholarships and up to 2 years for Postgraduate Scholarships.

Eligibility: Open to suitably qualified nationals of member countries of the Colombo Plan who have a working knowledge of the English language.

Note: Candidates should apply to the government agency administering Colombo Plan awards in their own country.

Further information from:
Ministry of Foreign Affairs
City Hall
St. Andrew's Road
Singapore 0617

[1353]

MINISTRY OF FOREIGN AFFAIRS
(Singapore)

Junior and Senior Fellowships

Purpose: To provide educational opportunities to nationals of member countries of the Colombo Plan with the aim of raising the standard of living and social well-being of these countries through technical assistance.

Subjects: Various professional and technical fields.

Value: S$600 per month living allowance for Junior Fellows; S$700 per month living allowance for Senior Fellows.

Tenable in Singapore for: Junior Fellowships—up to 1 year; Senior Fellowships—up to 6 months.

Eligibility: Open to suitably qualified nationals of member countries of the Colombo Plan who have a working knowledge of the English language.

Note: Candidates should apply to the government agency administering Colombo Plan [q.v.] awards in their own country.

Further information from:
Ministry of Foreign Affairs
City Hall
St. Andrew's Road
Singapore 0617

[1354]

MINISTRY OF FOREIGN AFFAIRS *(Spain)*

Scholarships

Subjects: Unrestricted.

Value: A monthly allowance of 25,000 pesetas, an installation grant, free university registration, medical care and life insurance.

Tenable at universities and institutions of higher education and research in Spain, for nine months.

Eligibility: Open to graduates of all nationalities, but preference is given to students from countries maintaining diplomatic relations with Spain.

Note: Candidates should apply to their own country's foreign scholarships agency or to the Spanish diplomatic representative in their own country.

Address
Department of Cultural Relations
Ministry of Foreign Affairs
Plaza de la Provincia I
Madrid
Spain

[1355]

MINISTRY OF FOREIGN RELATIONS
(Chile)
Chilean Commission for Intellectual Cooperation

Exchange Scholarships

Subjects: Any university studies.

No. offered: Two Scholarships annually.

Value: A monthly allowance plus expenses. Cost of travel is provided by the United States government.

Tenable at any Chilean university or other institution of higher education, for nine months.

Eligibility: Open to United States nationals who wish to study in Chile.

Note: Candidates should apply to the *Institute of International Education, 809 United Nations Plaza, New York, New York 10017.*

Not confirmed for 1983.

Address
Chilean Commission for Intellectual
 Cooperation
Ministry of Foreign Relations
Palacio de la Moneda
Santiago
Chile

[1356]

MINISTRY OF FOREIGN RELATIONS
(Mexico)

Lincoln-Juárez Scholarships

Subjects: Advanced technical education, and specialist training.

Value: 4,500 pesos per month, registration and other school fees, examination and medical insurance fees, and an annual book subsidy of 1,000 pesos.

Tenable at Mexican universities or institutions of advanced education or training for one year; renewable.

Eligibility: Open to nationals of countries having reciprocal educational and cultural agreements with Mexico. Candidates should be no more than 35 years of age and be following, or have followed, a course of technical or advanced studies at university standard. They must be able to speak and write Spanish fluently, and should submit letters of recommendation from their teachers and educational institution. On completion of studies, Scholars are expected to return to their own countries.

Further information from:
Ministry of Foreign Relations
Dirección General de Asuntos Culturales
avenida Ricardo Flores Magón 1
México 3, D.F.

[1357]

MINISTRY OF FOREIGN RELATIONS
(Paraguay)

Exchange Scholarships

Subjects: Any university studies.

No. offered: Two Scholarships annually.

Value: Cost of board and lodging, and registration fees.

Tenable in Paraguay for the duration of approved studies.

Eligibility: Open to nationals of the United States who have a bachelor's degree and wish to study in Paraguay.

Note: Candidates should confirm details with the *Institute of International Education, 809 United Nations Plaza, New York, New York 10017.*

Address
Ministry of Foreign Relations
Asunción
Paraguay

[1358]

MINISTRY OF HEALTH AND SOCIAL WELFARE *(Poland)*

Scholarships

Subjects: Health and social welfare.

Value: Either 2,250 zlotys per month (undergraduates) or up to 4,200 per month (graduates) plus tuition, medical expenses and free accommodation in a student hostel.

Tenable in Poland for the duration of the approved study.

Eligibility: Open to nationals of all countries who possess the appropriate qualifications and have a good knowledge of Polish; candidates without such knowledge must complete a one-year course in Polish either at Lodz or Cracow.

Note: Information on application procedure may be obtained from the diplomatic representative of Poland in the candidate's own country or from the Ministry.

Address
Ministry of Health and Social Welfare
Warsaw
Poland

[1359]

MINISTRY OF HIGHER EDUCATION *(Cuba)*

Exchange Scholarships

Subjects: Various university studies.

Value: Allowances for maintenance, free modation, books, medical assistance, laundry, and an annual clothing allowance.

Tenable at universities or higher education establishments in Cuba for the duration of approved studies.

Eligibility: Scholarships are open to nationals of African, Asian and Latin American countries, and to foreign nationals of countries having cultural exchange agreements with Cuba, who wish to use facilities available at Cuban higher education centers.

Candidates should have good graduate qualifications in appropriate subjects.

Note: Candidates should apply to their government representatives or the Cuban diplomatic representative in their own country.

Closing date: March.

Address
Department of International Relations
Ministry of Higher Education
Cave 23 y F.—Vedado
Havana
Cuba

[1360]

MINISTRY OF NATIONAL EDUCATION AND CULTURE *(Belgium)*
Department of International Cultural Relations

Scholarships

Subjects: Unrestricted: postgraduate study and/or research.

No. offered: Approximately 200 Scholarships annually.

Value: 14,000 to 17,000 Belgian francs per month. Tuition fees and return travel costs are occasionally available.

Tenable at universities and other institutions of higher education in Belgium for generally between eight and twelve months.

Eligibility: Open to nationals of Algeria, Argentina, Australia, Austria, Brazil, Bulgaria, Canada, Czechoslovakia, Denmark, France, West Germany, Greece, Hungary, Iran, Israel, Italy, Luxembourg, Mexico, Morocco, Netherlands, Norway, Pakistan, Poland, Portugal, Romania, Senegal, South Africa, Spain, Tunisia, Turkey, United Kingdom, United States, U.S.S.R., Venezuela and Yugoslavia. Candidates must have a working knowledge of either French or Dutch.

Note: Further information and application forms may be obtained through the Belgian embassy in the candidate's own country.

Address
Ministry of National Education and Culture
Department of International Cultural Relations
158 avenue de Cortenberg
1040 Brussels
Belgium

[1361]

MINISTRY OF OVERSEAS DEVELOPMENT *(U.K.)*

Studentships, Fellowships and Awards

(a) *Natural Resources Postgraduate Studentships* are awarded to British nationals who have a good honours degree and are resident in the U.K. These Studentships are normally tenable in Africa (for one or two years) and are for studies concerning the utilisation of natural resources such as agricultural land, forests and fisheries, and for study of veterinary medicine.

(b) *Commonwealth Tropical Medicine Research Studentships* are awarded to Commonwealth citizens and British protected persons resident in tropical Commonwealth countries. Candidates should be no more than 35 years of age and should normally be in the early postgraduate stage of their careers and possess a fair command of English. These Studentships are tenable at U.K. institutions for one (or possibly two) years.

(c) *Commonwealth Tropical Medicine Research Fellowships:* General conditions are similar to the Tropical Medicine Research Studentships except that preference is usually given to candidates between 30 and 40 years of age. Fellows are usually research workers who have already obtained postgraduate qualifications and who require further study or research in the field.

(d) *Technical Cooperation Training Awards* include those formerly administered by the Commonwealth Education Fellowship Scheme. The Awards are tenable in the U.K.

for periods from three months to three years. Subjects, all within the field of technical cooperation, vary according to the intergovernment scheme involved. The Awards are intended for citizens of developing countries and are not open to direct application. Those interested should contact the agency in their own country, responsible for intergovernment awards schemes, or the British government representatives in their country.

(e) *Education Development Awards* are awarded to British citizens with five or more years of overseas experience in educational fields. Specific areas of study include administration, planning, teacher training, technical education, curriculum planning, and non-formal education and communication in the field of social education. The Awards are tenable in any agreed institution for periods from six months to two years. An interview in London is required. Travel expenses to the U.K. will not be paid, but an allowance is made for travel within the U.K. Award holders are expected to take up an appropriate appointment in education in a developing country or with suitable organisations involved in overseas education.

Note: For more detailed information on the Ministry's programmes, candidates should apply to the administering authorities in their own countries. United Kingdom candidates should write to:
Ministry of Overseas Development
Eland House, Stag Place
London
England SW1E 5DH

[1362]

MINISTRY OF SCIENCE, HIGHER EDUCATION AND TECHNOLOGY *(Poland)*

Scholarships and Exchange Scholarships

Subjects: Advanced or postgraduate study in any subject.

Value: A monthly maintenance allowance of between 2,400 and 5,000 zlotys, free tuition, plus accommodation, medical care, cost of travel within Poland during the course of study, and free access to libraries, laboratories and archives. Scholars are expected to pay their own fare to and from Poland.

Tenable at universities and similar institutions in Poland.

Eligibility: Scholarships—open to suitably qualified nationals of any country; Exchange Scholarships—open to suitably qualified nationals from countries operating exchange schemes with Poland.

Note: Candidates for Exchange Scholarships should apply to the appropriate authority in their own country. Candidates for Scholarships should apply to the Polish diplomatic representative in their own country or to their national agency responsible for foreign scholarship programs.

Address
Ministry of Science, Higher Education
 and Technology
6—8 Miodowa Street
00-251 Warsaw
Poland

[1363]

MINISTRY OF SCIENCE, HIGHER EDUCATION AND TECHNOLOGY *(Poland)*

Poland-Unesco Scholarships

20 Scholarships are awarded annually to nationals of member states of Unesco for study in the humanities, social sciences, physical and natural sciences, engineering, astronomy, physics and mathematics. The value of the Scholarships is 3,500 zlotys per month, plus an accommodation allowance, medical care, cost of travel within Poland during the course of study, and free access to libraries, laboratories and archives.

In addition, 50 Scholarship-months are offered to nationals of developing member states of Unesco for scientific study and research in Poland. The value of these is the same as the Scholarships above.

Candidates should apply through their National Commission for Unesco.

Address
Ministry of Science, Higher Education
 and Technology
6—8 Miodowa Street
00-251 Warsaw
Poland

[1364]

MINISTRY OF SCIENCE AND RESEARCH
(Austria)

Art Scholarships

No. offered: Approximately 35 full Scholarships annually.

Value: 5,000 Austrian schillings per month for students and 5,500 schillings for postgraduates, plus exemption from tuition fees.

Tenable at Austrian academies of art generally for nine months, but exceptionally for longer periods.

Eligibility: Open to nationals of all countries whose prior training conforms to the requirements set by the particular academy of art concerned. Candidates should be between the ages of 19 and 35 years, and have studied for at least two years at a college of art. Proof of adequate knowledge of the German language must be furnished.

Closing date: March.

Further information from:
Ministry of Science and Research
Minoritenplatz 5
1014 Vienna 1
Austria

[1365]

MINISTRY OF SCIENCE AND RESEARCH
(Austria)

Exchange Scholarships

Subjects: Unrestricted.

No. offered: A total of about 120 Scholarships annually, including: United Kingdom—10; South Africa—2; Ireland—1; United States—3. The Ministry also offers one-month Exchange Grants for the summer only (United Kingdom—7).

Value: 5,000 Austrian schillings per month (undergraduates) and 5,500 schillings per month (graduates), plus an initial and book allowance of 1,000 schillings per term.
Allowances for fees, clothing and accomodations are not provided.
Summer Grants—7,500 schillings plus fees.

Tenable in Austria at institutions of higher learning, including art academies, for 9 months.

Eligibility: Open to nationals of Belgium, Bulgaria, China, Colombia, Czechoslovakia, Denmark, East Germany, Egypt, Finland, France, West Germany, Hungary, India, Ireland, Italy, Japan, Luxembourg, Mexico, Netherlands, Norway, Poland, Portugal, Romania, South Africa, Spain, Sweden, Switzerland, Turkey, United Kingdom, United States, U.S.S.R., Venezuela and Yugoslovia. Candidates must have a good working knowledge of German, should be between 20 and 35 years of age and have completed at least four semesters of university study.

Note: Applications must be addressed to the competent national authority in the student's home country, or to the Austrian cultural institutes and Austrian diplomatic missions, respectively. Candidates in the United Kingdom should apply to *Austrian Institute, 28 Rutland Gate, London SW7 1PQ.*

For additional information on Exchange Scholarships and other opportunities for study in Austria, the following brochures may be obtained from the *Austrian Foreign Student Service, Universität, 1010 Vienna 1, Austria:* (a) Scholarships for Foreign Students at Austrian Universities, (b) Study in Austria, (c) Information, (d) German Language Courses.

Closing date: February.

Address
Ministry of Science and Research
Minoritenplatz 5
1014 Vienna 1
Austria

[1366]

MINISTRY OF SCIENCE AND RESEARCH
(Austria)

Postgraduate Scholarships

Subjects: Any field except art.

Value: 5,000 Austrian schillings per month (undergraduates) and 5,500 schillings per month (graduates).

Tenable in Austria for one academic year.

Eligibility: Open to nationals of all countries in which Austria has diplomatic representatives.

Candidates should be between 20 and 35 years of age, and must have successfully completed at least six semesters of university study.

Note: Applications should be made to the office of the Austrian diplomatic representative in the candidate's own country.

United Kingdom applicants—*Austrian Institute, 28 Rutland Gate, London SW7 1PQ,* by 25th February; Australian applicants—*Department of Education, P.O. Box 826, Woden, A.C.T. 2606.*

Address
Ministry of Science and Research
Minoritenplatz 5
1014 Vienna 1
Austria

[1367]

MINISTRY OF SCIENCE AND RESEARCH *(Austria)*

Technical Assistance Scholarships

Subjects: Specialized study or research in any field except art.

Value: 5,500 Austrian schillings per month, plus 1,000 schillings at the beginning of each semester for the purchase of books, etc. Scholars from tropical and sub-tropical countries receive a clothing allowance of 500 schillings at the beginning of the winter semester.

Tenable at Austrian universities and other institutions of higher learning for nine months.

Eligibility: Open to nationals of developing countries who hold a bachelor's degree, are between 20 and 35 years of age, and have a working knowledge of the German language.

Note: Application should be made to the Austrian diplomatic representative in the candidate's own country.

For further information on Postgraduate scholarships and other opportunities for study in Austria, the following brochures may be obtained from the *Austrian Foreign Student Service, Universität, 1010 Vienna 1, Austria:* (a) Scholarships for Foreign Students at Austrian Universities, (b) Study in Austria, (c) Information, (d) German Language Courses.

Address
Ministry of Science and Research
Minoritenplatz 5
1014 Vienna 1
Austria

[1368]

MINISTRY OF STATE *(Monaco)*

Postgraduate Scholarships

Subjects: Botany and anthropology.

No. offered: Two Scholarships annually.

Value: FF1,500 per month.

Tenable in Monaco at the Botanical Gardens or at the Museum of Prehistoric Anthropology for two weeks.

Eligibility: Open to nationals of all countries qho hold at least a B.Sc. degree or equivalent qualification.

Closing date: 1st July.

Further information from:
Ministère d'Etat
Place de la Visitation
Monaco-Ville

[1369]

MINNA-JAMES-HEINEMAN FOUNDATION *(West Germany)*

Research Grants and Doctoral Fellowships

Grants to Scientists of all nationalities are awarded annually to enable them to carry out research in foreign countries, thereby serving scientific knowledge and international cooperation. Emphasis is placed on natural sciences. A Grant is given for a period of not more than one year, with maximally DM1,500 to DM2,000 monthly and, if needed, travel costs for the applicant only.

Doctoral Fellowships of DM800 monthly are awarded to doctoral candidates of all nationalities whose performances are above average and from whom the obtaining of a doctoral degree can be expected during the period of the Fellowship (up to one year).

Natural sciences applicants intending to pursue a career in academic teaching are shown preference.

Dannie Heineman Prize of DM30,000 is conferred biennially by the Academy of Sciences at Göttingen for an outstanding work in the natural sciences. Applications are not accepted.

Note: Only a small number of Doctoral Fellowships are granted directly by the Foundation. Most are conferred at the suggestion of certain universities and institutions under existing agreements.

Closing date: Applications must reach the Foundation by 1st February, and awards are allocated in the spring.

Further information from:
 Minna-James-Heineman Stiftung
 Am Hofen Ufer 6
 D-3000 Hannover 1
 West Germany

[1370]

MISSIONARY MART *(U.K.)*

Grants

The aim of the organization is to help further the spread of Christianity throughout the world. Funds totalling approximately £30,000 per annum are available to support missionaries and missionary societies working overseas.

Further information from:
 B.E. Chapman, Honorary Treasurer
 Missionary Mart
 99 Woodmansterne Road
 Carshalton Beeches, Surrey
 England SM5 4EG

[1371]

MARK MITCHELL RESEARCH FOUNDATION

Applications are invited for funding of scientific research and advancement of education in South Australia. The Foundation is particularly interested in the promotion of research in the natural history of South Australia. The duration, value and number of awards made are at the discretion of the Trustee.

Further information from:
 Mark Mitchell Research Foundation
 c/o Elder's Trustee and Executor Co.
 27-39 Currie Street
 Adelaide, S.A.
 Australia 5001

[1372]

MITTAG-LEFFLER FOUNDATION OF THE SWEDISH ACADEMY OF SCIENCES

Stipends and Grants

The Foundation offers a few Stipends and Grants annually for studies and research in mathematics at the Mittag-Leffler Institute. The fields of research in mathematics vary, certain areas being emphasized in different years. The Stipend provides a contribution to travelling and living expenses, and is tenable at the Institute for one year, with the possibility of renewal. Open to persons holding a doctoral degree in mathematics.

Further information from:
 Mittag-Leffler Foundation
  Swedish Academy of Sciences
 Auravägen 17
 S-182 62 Djursholm
 Sweden

[1373]

MODERN LANGUAGE ASSOCIATION OF AMERICA

James Russell Lowell Prize: One Prize of US$1,000 and a certificate is awarded annually to a member of the Association who has published an outstanding literary or linguistic study, a critical edition of an important work, or a critical biography. Nominations may be made by publisher or author. *Closing date:* 31st January.

Howard R. Marraro Prize: One Prize of US$750 and a certificate is awarded every two years to the author of a distinguished scholarly study of book or essay length on any phase of Italian literature or comparative literature involving Italian. The recipient must be a member of the Association who has published works in this field. Nominations may made by publisher or author. *Closing date:* 31st May.

Kenneth W. Mildenberger Medal: One Prize of US$500, a medal and a year's membership is awarded annually for an outstanding research publication in the field of teaching languages and literatures other than English and American. Nominations must be made by Association members. *Closing date:* 1st March.

William Riley Parker Prize: One Prize of US$500 and a certificate is awarded annually to recognize outstanding achievement in literary or linguistic research. The award is given for the most outstanding article in *Publications of the Modern Language Association of America (PMLA)* for the academic year. No nominations are accepted.

Mina P. Shaughnessy Medal: One Prize of US$500, a medal, and a year's membership is awarded annually for an outstanding research publication in the field of teaching English language and literature. Nominations must be made by Association members. *Closing date:* 1st March.

Further information from:
  Modern Language Association of
    America
  62 Fifth Avenue
  New York, New York 10011
  U.S.A.

[1374]

MOFOLO-PLOMER PRIZE

A Prize of R1,000 is awarded for an unpublished novel or volume of short stories, having a minimum of 30,000 words. Applicants may be writers who are resident in southern Africa, or southern Africans who are currently living abroad. There is no age limitation for the Prize, and young writers who are not yet established are encouraged to apply.

Closing date: 31st May.

Further information from:
  Mofolo-Plomer Prize Committee
  Ravan Press
  P.O. Box 31134
  Braamfontein 2017
  South Africa

[1375]

MONEY FOR WOMEN FUND, INC. *(U.S.A.)*

Grants to Individual Artists

10 to 20 Grants of between US$200 and US$500 each are offered annually to feminist artists who seek to achieve greater development in the arts and whose projects shed light upon the condition of women. There are two Grant periods each year—the fall and the spring.

Further information may be obtained by sending a stamped, addressed envelope to:
  Money for Women Fund
  207 Coastal Highway
  St. Augustine, Florida 32084
  U.S.A.

[1376]

ANNA MONIKA FOUNDATION
(West Germany)

Prizes

Three Prizes of US$15,000, US$5,000 and US$2,500 are offered in odd-numbered years for research papers, written in German, French or English, which contribute to the investigation of the physical substrate and functional disturbances of endogenous depressions. Preference is given to studies of a biochemical, histological, neuropathological, psychopharmacological, psychiatric or psychosomatic nature. The research should be carried out in close cooperation with a psychiatric clinic, a university institute or equivalent scientific institution. So far as possible the paper should give information about recent advances in knowledge that would be helpful in promoting treatment and would open up new paths of progress. Entries should be submitted by the end of September in even-numbered years.

Further information from:
  Prof. Dr. P. Kielholz
  Director of the Psychiatric Clinic of the
    University of Basel
  Wilhelm-Klein-Strasse 27
  Basel
  Switzerland

[1377]

MONTREAL INTERNATIONAL MUSIC COMPETITION

The Competition is held in June on a four-year rotating schedule, stressing in turn violin (1983), piano (1984), and voice (1985). There will be no Competition in 1986. Muisicians of any nationality who are between 16 and 35 years of age may compete, and should apply by 1st March. First prize is *Can*$10,000; second, *Can*$5,000; third, *Can*$2,500; fourth, *Can*$1,500; fifth, *Can*$1,000; and four prizes of *Can*$500 each.

Further information from:
Montreal International Music Competition
106 Dulwich Avenue
St. Lambert, Quebec
Canada J4P 2Y7

[1378]

MONTREAL NEUROLOGICAL INSTITUTE
McGill University

Izaak Walton Killam Scholarship

Subjects: Research and study in neurology, neurosurgery and related basic disciplines.

No. offered: Approximately five Scholarships annually; new awards made as vacancies occur.

Value: Up to *Can*$15,000 per annum, paid in monthly installments.

Tenable at the Institute for two years; renewable on the basis of actual scientific contributions and the need for continued support.

Eligibility: Open to Canadian citizens and landed immigrants who are medically qualified and/or hold a Ph.D. degree in an appropriate field.

Closing date: 1st March.

Further information from:
Director
Montreal Neurological Institute
3801 University Street
Montreal, Quebec
Canada H3A 2B4

[1379]

MONTREUX-VEVEY MUSIC FESTIVAL
(Switzerland)

Clara Haskil Competition

One Prize of 10,000 Swiss francs is offered to a pianist of any nationality who is of either sex and no more than 32 years of age. The Competition is held in odd-numbered years, usually during the last week of August. There is an entry fee of 250 Swiss francs.

Closing date: 1st July of the Competition year.

Further information from:
Clara Haskil Competition
Montreux-Vevey Music Festival
Case Postale 124
1820 Montreux
Switzerland

[1380]

JOHN MOTLEY MOREHEAD FOUNDATION
University of North Carolina *(Chapel Hill)*

Morehead Fellowships

Purpose: To finance the recipient through a program of study leading to the master's degree in business, J.D., M.D., Ph.D., or M.S. in dentistry.

Subjects: Any area of study catered for by the Graduate School, the Graduate School of Business Studies, the Law School, and the Medical School at the University of North Carolina, or the advanced education program of the School of Dentistry.

Value: Announced annually by each school.

Tenable at the University of North Carolina, Chapel Hill: Graduate School—three years; Medical School—four years; Law School—three years; Graduate School of Business Studies—two years; School of Dentistry—two years.

Eligibility: The following attributes are taken into consideration in the selection of candidates: moral force of character; scholastic ability and attainments; motivation towards the chosen field, and promise of distinction in that field. Each eligible school nominates candidates to compete for the Fellowships. Foreign nationals who are eligible to apply for admission to the appropriate school may be nominated by the School for a Fellowship, in the same way as United States citizens.

Further information from:
James H. Wright, Assistant
John Motley Morehead Foundation
P.O. Box 348
Chapel Hill, North Carolina 27514
U.S.A.

[1381]

VIANNA DA MOTTA INTERNATIONAL COMPETITION *(Lisbon)*

A First Prize of US$4,000 is given to a pianist of any nationality. Musicians wishing to enter the Competition held in June, should be between the ages of 16 and 30.

Note: The Competition was not held in 1981 or 1982.

Further information from:
Secretary
Vianna da Motta International Competition
Edificio Castil-Fraccâo H-11⁰
Rua Castilho 39
Lisbon 1
Portugal

[1382]

MOUNT CARMEL INTERNATIONAL TRAINING CENTRE FOR COMMUNITY SERVICES *(Haifa)*

Assistance for Courses

Purpose: To assist developing countries to promote community services.

Course: Rural community development, including nutrition; kindergarten teaching and supervision; out-of-school education and training programmes for youth; home industry and cooperative marketing. Courses (which are given in English or Spanish) include lectures, discussion groups, study tours and field work.

No. offered: 20 places on each Course.

Value: Tuition, lodging and board, plus a monthly pocket money allowance, are covered by international fellowships. Application should be made through the Israeli diplomatic or consular representative in the country concerned, or directly to the MCTC.

Tenable at the Centre for the duration of the Course (three to eight months).

Eligibility: Open mainly to women aged 25-40 from developing countries. Male students are accepted for relevant courses. Participants must have completed at least twelve years of schooling, have undergone relevant professional training, and have work experience. A good knowledge of the language in which the course will be given is essential.

Note: For admission to the Course, candidates should apply to the Israeli diplomatic representative in their country three months prior to commencement of the Course (April and August).

Not confirmed for 1983.

Address:
Mount Carmel International Training Centre for Community Services
12 David Pinsky Street, P.O. Box 6111
Haifa
Israel

[1383]

MOZART MEMORIAL PRIZE *(London)*

Instrumentalists and singers under the age of 30, of any nationality, normally resident or studying in the U.K. may take part in a competition (held in even-numbered years) for performances of Mozart. Prizes range from £250 to £1,000.

Further information from:
Administrator
11a Queens Road
London
England SW19 8NG

[1384]

MULTIPLE SCLEROSIS SOCIETY OF CANADA

Awards

The purpose of the Society's Award program is to stimulate and support research in multiple sclerosis and allied diseases. Applications are therefore welcomed from researchers working in Canada or intending to return to Canada upon completion of training in another country.

Research Grants are provided for projects that will be conducted in, or under the auspices of, an approved institution. The request for funding may cover a period of one or two years. If further funding is requested, re-application in full must be made. A report of work accomplished and relevant published papers must be submitted upon terminaton of the Grant, application for renewal, or specific request by the Society.

Research Studentships are for qualified persons holding a degree other than an M.D. or Ph.D., who require further training in a specialized area related to research in multiple sclerosis. Studentships may be considered for training towards a doctorate degree. Awards are for a maximum period of four years, but may be extended under unusual circumstances. Students must re-apply annually. Studentships are held in a recognized institution and applicants must be responsible to an appropriate authority in the proposed field of study. Salary scales are equivalent to those suggested by the Medical Research Council for Studentships, plus 10%.

Postdoctoral Fellowships are for qualified persons who hold an M.D. or Ph.D. degree, and intend to continue in research work relevant to multiple sclerosis. Grants are for one year but are annually renewable for up to three years, subject to evidence of satisfactory progress. In exceptional circumstances Fellowships may be extended. Awards must be held at recognized institutions which deal with problems relevant to multiple sclerosis and applicants must be responsible to an appropriate authority in the proposed field of study. Salary scales and transportation allowances are equivalent to those suggested by the Medical Research Council for Fellowships, plus 10%.

Career Development Awards are sponsored by the Society for individuals holding a doctoral degree. Applicants should be capable of carrying out independent research and should intend to work full-time at a Canadian School of medicine on research relevant to multiple sclerosis. Awards are normally made for three years with limited renewal permitted in exceptional circumstances. Salary scales are the same as those defined for Medical Research Council Scholarships.

Closing dates: 1st April (for commencement on 1st October of same year) or 1st October (for commencement on 1st April of following year).

Further information from:
Chairman, Medical Advisory Board
Multiple Sclerosis Society of Canada
130 Bloor Street West
Suite 700
Toronto, Ontario
Canada M5S 1N5

[1385]

MULTIPLE SCLEROSIS SOCIETY OF GREAT BRITAIN AND NORTHERN IRELAND

Research Grants

Purpose: To promote medical research into the cause and cure of multiple sclerosis.

Value: Research Grants may be awarded in the form of Fellowships, to provide remuneration for research workers; they may also be awarded for the provision of scientific assistance in connection with some particular aspect of research by a qualified doctor or graduate scientist, to meet the entire or part cost of technical laboratory assistance, clerical assistance, apparatus and materials, and also to meet the cost of travel in connection with attendance at regional or international conferences.

Tenable in suitable institutions, normally in the United Kingdom, for a period of three years.

Eligibility: Open to nationals of all countries.

Note: Applications should, where applicable, be sponsored by the head of the hospital department or laboratory in which the work is to be carried out.
The Society's committee normally meets in the spring and the autumn for consideration of applications.

Further information from:
General Secretary
Multiple Sclerosis Society
286 Munster Road
London
England SW6 6BE

[1386]

GILBERT MURRAY TRUST *(U.K.)*

Junior Awards

Subjects: International affairs or international law.

No. offered: Six or more Awards annually.

Value: £150.

Tenable outside the United Kingdom.

Eligibility: Open to persons of any nationality who are not more than 25 years of age and are undergraduate or postgraduate students at a university or similar institution in the United Kingdom. Candidates should be taking or should have taken part in a course on international affairs or international law.

Note: The Award is to be used for studies abroad related to the activities of the United Nations or its agencies.
 A letter of application should include a full curriculum vitae, details of intentions with regard to future career and full particulars of the purpose for which the Award would be used, and be accompanied by a supporting testimonial from a person capable of judging the candidate's ability to use the Award profitably.

Closing date: 1st May.

Further information from:
N.S. Marsh, Q.C., Honorary Secretary
Gilbert Murray International Affairs
 Committee
13 North Side, Clapham Common
London
England SW4 ORF

[1387]

GILBERT MURRAY TRUST *(U.K.)*

Senior Awards

Purpose: To assist an individual who undertakes to produce a substantial study of international affairs or international law, and who requires financial aid for expenses, e.g., foreign travel connected with the study.

No. offered: One Award in odd-numbered years.

Value: £500.

Eligibility: Open to persons of any nationality: they need not be resident in the United Kingdom. The award is given to the most suitable applicant whose qualifications fall within one or more of the following categories: (a) the performance of either voluntary or professional work promoting a fuller understanding of the United Nations, in circumstances in which the Award would enable the recipient to continue and develop such work; (b) the carrying out by a person in public life of a mission or study journey in connection with the United Nations, its associated agencies or activities generally; (c) the preparation of a work in the field of international relations with particular reference to the United Nations, where the Award might be used to meet the cost of journeys and other outgoings incidental to the task.

Note: A letter of application should include a full curriculum vitae and two supporting testimonials from persons capable of judging the candidate's ability to use the Award profitably.

Closing date: 1st May.

Further information from:
N.S. Marsh, Q.C., Honorary Secretary
Gilbert Murray International Affairs
 Committee
13 North Side, Clapham Common
London
England SW4 ORF

[1388]

MUSCULAR DYSTROPHY ASSOCIATION *(U.S.A.)*

Postdoctoral Fellowships

Purpose: To provide research opportunities for young and senior scientists, in order to add to current knowledge about the muscular dystrophies, amyotrophic lateral sclerosis, peroneal muscular atrophy, the various progressive spinal muscular atrophies, myositis, Friedreich's ataxia, myasthenia gravis and related neuromuscular diseases. The ultimate goal is to find the cause and cure or effective treatment of these diseases through applied and basic research in molecular biology, anatomy, pathology, physiology, biochemistry, biophysics, genetics, pharmacology, etc. Considerable relevance is required in the nature of the research program sponsored.

No. offered: An unspecified number of annual Fellowships to young scientists; a limited number of annual Fellowships to senior scientists.

Value: To include a base annual stipend of US$14,500 for personal support (not for the maintenance of the research program). An additional US$1,000 per year is added to the base stipend for each year of postdoctoral training up to a maximum of US$18,500. In addition, a departmental allowance of US$1,000 will be awarded to the institution in which the Fellow will work.

Tenable at a qualified institution for one year; renewable for a maximum of two additional years. Senior Fellowships are for one year only.

Eligibility: Open to persons in the United States or abroad who possess an M.D., Ph.D., D.Sc. or equivalent degree. Candidates should have negotiated successfully for permission to conduct the research under the direction of a qualified senior investigator at an institution at which adequate research facilities suited to the proposed research program are available.

Closing dates: 31st December for commencement 1st July; 30th June for commencement 1st January.

Further information from:
Research Department
Muscular Dystrophy Association
810 Seventh Avenue
New York, New York 10019
U.S.A.

[1389]

MUSCULAR DYSTROPHY ASSOCIATION *(U.S.A.)*

Grants-in-Aid

Purpose: To provide research programs which will add to current knowledge about muscular dystrophies, amyotrophic lateral sclerosis, peroneal muscular atrophy, the various progressive spinal muscular atrophies, myositis, Friedreich's ataxia, myasthenia gravis and related neuromuscular diseases. The ultimate goal is to find the cause and cure or effective treatment of these diseases through applied and basic research in molecular biology, anatomy, pathology, physiology, biochemistry, biophysics, genetics, pharmacology, etc. Considerable relevance is required in the nature of the research program sponsored.

Value: To cover the costs of hiring collaborating investigators and technicians, fringe benefits, supplies and equipment, travel, and other miscellaneous expenses; plus overheads of up to 8% of the total amount of the Grant awarded. The chief investigator may not receive a salary, stipend, or fringe benefits under an M.D.A.A. Grant. Payments are annual.

Tenable for one year at suitable institutions in the United States or abroad which possess adequate research facilities; renewable.

Eligibility: Open to staff members of research institutions in the United States or abroad who possess an M.D., Ph.D., D.Sc. or equivalent degree, and are qualified to conduct and supervise programs of original research.

Closing dates: 30th June for commencement 1st January; 31st December for commencement 1st July.

Further information from:
Research Department
Muscular Dystrophy Association
810 Seventh Avenue
New York, New York 10019
U.S.A.

[1390]

MUSCULAR DYSTROPHY GROUP OF GREAT BRITAIN

Research Grants

Purpose: To support research into neuromuscular function in health and in disease, with particular reference to muscular dystrophy and related disorders.

No. offered: Varies, according to funds available.

Value: Variable, according to nature of research and qualifications and experience of applicant.

Tenable in universities, hospitals and other research institutions in the United Kingdom; normally for three years.

Eligibility: Open to persons currently resident in the United Kingdom. Grants are made to candidates with appropriate qualifications and experience.

Further information from:
Muscular Dystrophy Group of Great Britain
Nattrass House
35 Macaulay Road
London SW4
England

[1391]

MUSEUM OF SCIENCE *(Boston)*

Bradford Washburn Award

An Award of US$5,000 and a gold medal is presented annually to an individual of any nationality, for an outstanding contribution toward public understanding and appreciation of science in its nature and importance in everyday life. The Award is intended to honor a writer or lecturer of national or international influence, and is not meant to reward specific research, technical accomplishment or teaching. On occasion, the Award may be given for a contribution of an exceptional nature within New England. Presentation is made at the annual dinner in autumn.

Further information from:
Museum of Science
Science Park
Boston, Massachusetts 02114
U.S.A.

[1392]

MUSIC ACADEMY OF THE WEST *(Santa Barbara, California)*

Instrumental and Vocal Scholarships

Value: Up to US$700.

Tenable at the Academy for an eight-week summer session; renewable.

Eligibility: Open to United States and foreign nationals who are advanced music students.

Closing date: 21st March.

Further information from:
Music Academy of the West
1070 Fairway Road
Santa Barbara, California 93108
U.S.A.

[1393]

MUSIC AND ARTS INSTITUTE OF SAN FRANCISCO, INC.
College of Music, Drama and Opera

The following awards are open to music students of any nationality who are suitably qualified and wish to study at the Institute.

Outstanding Performers Partial Scholarships: Annual Scholarships of US$500 are awarded to assist in graduate or undergraduate studies. Extensive previous study and performance experience are prerequisites. Auditions are scheduled upon application.

San Francisco Boys Guild Scholarship: An annual Scholarship of US$500 is awarded to an outstanding performer to assist in attending a full-time college program leading to a bachelor of music degree.

Teaching Fellowships: A variable number of Fellowships are awarded as vacancies occur to students engaged in postgraduate studies in music. The Fellowships provide tuition and subsistence.

Partial Tuition Awards: Ten Awards of US$100 are made each semester to provide funding for students who need financial assistance to attend a full-time college program leading to a bachelor of music degree; renewable upon confirmation of continuing need for assistance and satisfactory progress.

Not confirmed for 1983.

Further information from:
  Office of Admissions
  Music and Arts Institute of San
    Francisco, Inc.
  College of Music, Drama and Opera
  2622 Jackson Street
  San Francisco, California 94115
  U.S.A.

[1394]

MYASTHENIA GRAVIS FOUNDATION, INC. *(U.S.A.)*

Doctor Kermit E. Osserman Postdoctoral Fellowship

Subjects: Research in myasthenia gravis and related conditions.

No. offered: One Fellowship annually.

Value: A stipend of US$20,000, paid quarterly, plus up to US$10,000 for support services.

Tenable at a United States university or medical research institution for one year; not renewable.

Eligibility: Open to candidates who possess a Ph.D. or M.D. There are no restrictions as to age, sex, citizenship or residency.

Note: Applications should be in the form of a letter and should include the following information: (1) personal data, education and reason for application; (2) curriculum vitae; (3) proposed program of research and the names of two sponsors able to provide references; (4) letters of recommendation from the two sponsors outlining the proposed program and guaranteeing acceptance of the candidate.

Closing date: 31st December.

Further information from:
  Executive Director
  Myasthenia Gravis Foundation, Inc.
  15 East 26th Street
  New York, New York 10010
  U.S.A.

[1395]

MYASTHENIA GRAVIS FOUNDATION, INC. *(U.S.A.)*

Doctor Henry R. Viets Medical Student Research Fellowships

Subject: Research in myasthenia gravis and related fields.

No. offered: Ten Fellowships annually.

Value: US$1,500 in a lump sum.

Tenable for one year at a recognized United States medical school; not renewable.

Eligibility: Open to medical students attending recognized United States medical schools. There are no restrictions as to age, sex, citizenship or residency.

Note: Applications should be made in the form of a letter, and should include the following information: (1) personal data, education and reason for application; (2) proposed program of study and name of sponsor; (3) a letter of recommendation from the sponsor outlining the proposed program and guaranteeing acceptance of the candidate.

Closing date: 1st May.

Further information from:
  Executive Director
  Myasthenia Gravis Foundation, Inc.
  15 East 26th Street
  New York, New York 10010
  U.S.A.

[1396]

MYCOLOGICAL SOCIETY OF AMERICA

Graduate Fellowship

Subject: Research in mycology.

No. offered: Two Fellowships annually.

Value: US$1,000 each.

Tenable at the Fellow's institution for one year (September-June); not renewable.

Eligibility: Open to graduates who are candidates for the Ph.D. degree in the field of mycology and are in residence at a university in the United States or Canada.

Note: The Fellowship is intended as a supplementary grant for an outstanding candidate and is awarded in addition to any fellowship, scholarship or assistantship support from other sources. The Fellowship may be used by the recipient to further his graduate studies in any way.

Closing date: 1st April.

Further information from:
Roger D. Goos, Secretary-Treasurer
Mycological Society of America
c/o Department of Botany
University of Rhode Island
Kingston, Rhode Island 02881
U.S.A.

N

See *How to Use The Grants Register*, page ix

[1397]

N.Z. FOREST PRODUCTS LTD.

David Henry Scholarships

Purpose: The advancement of education and knowledge in the academic and practical fields of forest establishment, forest maintenance and utilisation, forest maintenance and utilisation, ancillary and related services.

No. offered: At least one Scholarship annually.

Value: Normally NZ$4,000 per annum (reviewed annually), although applicants may be required to meet a reasonable proportion of their expenses either from their own resources, or from salary or allowances payable by their employers. Only in exceptional circumstances will the Board meet all expenses.

Tenable in New Zealand or overseas for a period specified by the Board of Selection.

Eligibility: Open to persons normally resident in New Zealand who possess the necessary qualifications to undertake the proposed study topic.

Note: Equal importance will be accorded to research work, theory, administration and practical skills when making the award.
  Recipients are required to return to New Zealand after termination of the Scholarship and resume previous or similar employment for at least two years.

Closing date: 30th April.

Further information from:
  Trustee, David Henry Scholarship Fund
  N.Z. Forest Products Ltd.
  Private Bag
  Auckland 1
  New Zealand

[1398]

N.Z. FOREST PRODUCTS LTD.

Selwyn J. Robinson Scholarships

Purpose: Study and/or research relating to new and/or improved production and quality of pulp and paper manufactured or likely to be manufactured in New Zealand.

No. offered: At least one Scholarship annually.

Value: Total amount of NZ$10,000 is available annually. Individual Scholarships are determined in regard to projected costs likely to be incurred.

Tenable in New Zealand or overseas for a period to be specified by the selection board.

Eligibility: Open to any individual currently residing in New Zealand.

Note: The selection board may specify the research, study or other investigation which the Scholar is to undertake.
  The Scholar will be required to remain in or return to New Zealand for a minimum of two years upon completion of the Scholarship.

Closing date: 1st December.

Further information from:
  Manager
  Executive Development and Salaries
    Administration
  N.Z. Forest Products Ltd.
  Private Bag
  Auckland 1
  New Zealand

[1399]

GEORGE JEAN NATHAN AWARD FOR DRAMATIC CRITICISM

The annual Award of US$5,000 is offered annually to the American who has written "the best piece of drama criticism during the theatrical year, whether it is an article, an essay, treatise or book." Selection of the winner is made by the heads of the English departments of Cornell, Princeton and Yale universities.

Any author or publisher may submit entries and the Selection Committee makes every effort to review all publications in which eligible work may appear.

Further information from:
George Jean Nathan Award
Manufacturers Hanover Trust
600 Fifth Avenue
New York, New York 10020
U.S.A.

[1400]

NATIONAL ACADEMY OF DESIGN

Edwin Austin Abbey Memorial Scholarship

Purpose: To provide the means for advanced study of mural painting, both in the United States and abroad.

No. offered: One Scholarship awarded biennially.

Value: US$6,000, paid in equal quarterly installments.

Tenable anywhere in the U.S. or abroad for one year; renewable for an additional year of study.

Eligibility: Open to U.S. citizens who have completed their regular art studies, are not more than 35 years of age, and have worked for at least 4 years at recognized art schools or their equivalent.

Note: Scholarships are made in odd-numbered years. Requests for applications are kept on file until applications become available.

Further information from:
Abbey Memorial Scholarship Fund
   for Mural Painting in the U.S.A.
1083 Fifth Avenue
New York, New York 10028
U.S.A.

[1401]

NATIONAL ACADEMY OF SCIENCES
(U.S.A.)

Exchange Programs with the USSR and Eastern Europe

Purpose: To provide opportunities for scientists to lecture and/or conduct research.

Subjects: Natural, mathematical, non-patient-oriented medical, engineering and quantitatively oriented behavioral sciences.

No. offered: Varies annually.

Value: Grants cover round-trip air fare, living costs, reimbursement for loss of salary of up to US$1,400 per month, and other miscellaneous costs.

Tenable in the institutes of the Academies of Sciences of the USSR, Bulgaria, Czechoslovakia, the German Democratic Republic, Hungary, Poland, Romania and Yugoslavia, for up to twelve months (minimum one month).

Eligibility: Open to United States citizens with a Ph.D. or equivalent qualification.

Note: Application forms and inquiries for information are available up to 1st March.

Closing date: 17th March (post-dated) for receipt no later than 20th March.

Further information from:
Section on USSR and Eastern Europe
Commission on International Relations
National Academy of Sciences
2101 Constitution Avenue
Washington, D.C. 20418
U.S.A.

[1402]

NATIONAL AGRICULTURAL INSTITUTE
(Paris)

Grants

Grants are offered annually, to nationals of countries with whom France has close cultural relations, for the study of biology as applied to agronomic science, physics and chemistry as applied to agronomic science and techniques of agriculture and food, economics and social science, and development of natural environment. It is also possible to study for the doctorate in engineering. Students must be certified by a faculty of agriculture. Grants are administered by French embassies in the various countries.

Further information from:
Institut national agronomique
  Paris-Grignon
16 rue Claude-Bernard
75231 Paris Cedex 05
France

[1403]

NATIONAL ASSOCIATION OF BROADCASTERS *(U.S.A.)*

Grants for Research in Broadcasting

Purpose: To stimulate interest in broadcasting research and to expand existing knowledge of the role and function of broadcasting.

Subjects: The social, cultural, political and economic aspects of American commercial broadcasting. Proposals may pertain to either basic or applied problems. Research designs concerned with radio are particularly encouraged.

No. offered: Ten Grants annually.

Value: To a maximum of US$1,400 each.

Eligibility: Open to all academic personnel working in the several disciplines that relate to the social, cultural, political and economic aspects of broadcasting. Graduate students and senior undergraduates are particularly invited to submit proposals.

Closing date: 1st January.

Further information from:
Dr. W. Lawrence Patrick
Senior Vice President for Research
National Association of Broadcasters
1771 N Street, N.W.
Washington, D.C. 20036
U.S.A.

[1404]

NATIONAL ASSOCIATION OF PURCHASING MANAGEMENT, INC. *(U.S.A.)*

Doctoral Fellowships

Purpose: To provide financial assistance to qualified students desiring to do advanced study and research in preparation for careers in purchasing and materials management or university teaching in the field; and to encourage research.

No. offered: A limited number of Fellowships annually.

Value: Varies annually.

Eligibility: Open to United States citizens who are in attendance at, or accepted for admission to, a university in the United States offering a Ph.D. or equivalent degree in the field of purchasing, materials management, economics, marketing, management or business administration. Applicants should have completed at least two full years of graduate study by the time the Fellowship becomes effective. Preference will be given to candidates who have completed all or substantially all of the required course work for doctoral degrees.

Note: Upon successful completion of the research, the Association will be interested in the publication of material from the study.
  Individual applications are not accepted. Nominations are invited from departments of economics, management, marketing and business administration at universities in the United States offering a doctoral degree in appropriate fields.

Closing date: 1st February.

Further information from:
Doctoral Research Grant Selection
  Committee
National Association of Purchasing
  Management, Inc.
Professional Activities
11 Park Place
New York, New York 10007
U.S.A.

[1405]

NATIONAL ASSOCIATION OF REALTORS
American Land Title Association

Real Estate Journalism Achievement Competition

Purpose: To recognize excellence in the field of real estate reporting and writing.

No. offered: One Award in magazine writing and three in newspaper reporting annually.

Value: First Prize of US$1,000 plus air fare and lodging for recipient to attend the awards presentation in Anaheim, California. Plaques are awarded to runners-up.

Eligibility: Open to real estate, business or financial writers, reporters or editors submitting an article or series of articles published during the twelve month period ending in September of the competition year.

Note: A series of articles submitted as a single entry must be identified as a series in the first article.
Applications may be obtained from the address below after 1st June of the year of competition.

Not confirmed for 1983.

Further information from:
Ginny Hulterstrum
National Association of Realtors
430 North Michigan Avenue
Chicago, Illinois 60611
U.S.A.

[1406]

NATIONAL AUTONOMOUS UNIVERSITY OF MEXICO

Scholarships

Subjects: Any university studies.

Value: A monthly allowance (United Kingdom Scholars receive 7,000 pesos) plus free tuition. Scholars are expected to pay their own travel expenses. Supplementation from other sources is necessary.

Tenable at the National Autonomous University of Mexico, Mexico City for ten months (commencing October or November) with the possibility of renewal in some cases.

Eligibility: Open to nationals of all countries. Scholars must have graduate status by the time of taking up the award. A working knowledge of Spanish is essential.

Note: Candidates should initiate applications through their own university. United Kingdom candidates should apply to the *Mexican Embassy, 8 Halkin Street, London SW1* by 2nd December.

Address:
Universidad Nacional Autónoma
 de México
Dirección General de Intercambio
 Académico
Edificio de Postgrado, 2o. piso
04510 Delegación Coyoacán
México D.F.

[1407]

NATIONAL BOARD FOR SCIENCE AND TECHNOLOGY *(Ireland)*

Research Grants

Purpose: To promote high quality basic or applied research projects. Consideration is given to projects with regard to national development programs; the development in Ireland of important sciences and technologies; the promotion of inter-disciplinary and inter-institutional activities; the development of international collaboration, and especially, improved access to relevant knowledge or facilities.

Subjects: All branches of science. Medical and dental projects of a clinical nature are not eligible.

No. offered: Varies annually, depending upon available funds.

Value: Varies according to project needs, and may cover costs of salaries, equipment, materials and travel.

Tenable in most cases for three years at any third level educational institution in Ireland.

Eligibility: A project must have scientific or technical merit and measure up to reputable international standards. Special consideration will be given to projects submitted by new researchers.

Note: Applications are invited in February/March.

Further information from:
National Board for Science and Technology
Shelbourne House, Shelbourne Road
Dublin 4
Ireland

[1408]

NATIONAL BOARD FOR SCIENCE AND TECHNOLOGY *(Ireland)*

Petroleum Technology Scholarships

Purpose: To enable Irish scientists and technologists to undertake training in the area of petroleum-related technologies.

Subjects: Petroleum exploration studies, petroleum engineering, applied geophysics, and offshore structures.

No. offered: Varies; offered annually.

Value: Quarterly payments to cover tuition, living and travel expenses during period of training.

Value: at designated centres in Ireland and the United Kingdom.

Eligibility: Open to Irish nationals who are less than 30 years of age on 1st September of the year of application, hold a university second class honours grade 1 degree or equivalent qualification in a scientific or engineering discipline. A grade 2 degree with relevant working experience will also be acceptable at certain centres.

Note: The Board offers these Scholarships on behalf of the Department of Industry and Energy.

Closing date: April/May of each year.

Further information from:
National Board for Science and Technology
Shelbourne House, Shelbourne Road
Dublin 4
Ireland

[1409]

NATIONAL BOARD FOR SCIENCE AND TECHNOLOGY *(Ireland)*

National Centre of Scientific Research *(France)*

Exchange Awards

Purpose: To contribute to the development and intensification of scientific cooperation between France and Ireland by enabling Irish research workers to spend short periods in France in order to share in scientific research in laboratories, libraries, and/or research institutes.

Subjects: All branches of science and the humanities, with priority given to the areas of marine biology and aquaculture, chemistry of natural products, mineral resources, linguistics, mathematics, solid-state physics and devices, and energy sources.

No. offered: Variable according to funds available; offered annually.

Value: Travel and subsistence for period of visit.

Tenable for varying periods of time in universities and research institutes in France.

Eligibility: The candidature of the scientists sharing in these exchanges must be submitted for prior approval by the host organisation.

Note: Similar awards are available to French research workers wishing to spend time in Irish universities or research institutes; French candidates should apply to the *Centre national de la recherche scientifique, 15 quai Anatole-France, 75700 Paris, France.*

Applications are invited in November/December of each year, for Exchange Visits the following year. Applications and further information may be obtained by writing to the *Royal Irish Academy, 19 Dawson Street, Dublin 2, Ireland,* or to:

National Board for Science and Technology
Shelbourne House, Shelbourne Road
Dublin 4
Ireland

[1410]

NATIONAL BOOK LEAGUE *(U.K.)*

Booker Prize for Fiction: A Prize of £10,000 is offered annually for a full-length novel published in the United Kingdom during the year of the award. The entry should have been published in English and written by a citizen of the Commonwealth, Ireland or South Africa. Up to four books may be submitted by any one publisher in a given year.

Commonwealth Poetry Prize: One Prize of £500 is awarded annually for a first book of poetry in English by an author from a Commonwealth country other than Britain. Entries should be submitted by the publisher to the *Librarian, Commonwealth Institute, Kensington High Street, London W8 6NQ.* Seven copies of each entry are required. *Closing date:* 30th June.

Thomas Cook Travel Book Awards: One annual Award of £1,500 for the best travel book, and one annual Award of £500 for the best guide book. Books must be published during the twelve month period ending 1st October.

Christopher Ewart-Biggs Memorial Prize: An annual Prize of £1,500 is awarded to the writer of any nationality, whose work contributes most to peace and understanding in Ireland, to closer ties between the peoples of Britain and Ireland, or to co-operation between the partners of the European Community. Entries should be published during the twelve months ending on 31st May of the year of the presentation. *Closing date:* 1st July.

David Higham Prize for Fiction: A Prize of £500 is offered annually for any first novel or book of short stories. The work should be written in English by a citizen of th Commonwealth, Ireland or South Africa, and should be published or about to be published in the year the award is given. *Closing date:* 1st July.

Jewish Chronicle/Harold H. Wingate Awards: Two Awards of £1,000 each are offered annually for the fiction and non-fiction books which best stimulate an interest in, and an awareness of, themes of Jewish interest. Eligible books should first be published in English in the United Kingdom during the twelve months ending on 31st March of the year of the presentation. Books should have been written by authors who are normally resident in Britain or the British Commonwealth, Israel or South Africa.

MIND Book of the Year/Allen Lane Award: One Award of £1,000 is offered annually for a work of fiction or non-fiction which best furthers public understanding of mental illness. Books must be published in the year for which the Award is made.

Odd Fellows (Manchester Unity) Social Concern Annual Book Awards: Two Prizes of £500 each are awarded annually for the books or pamphlets, of not less than 10,000 words, that provide the most stimulating impetus for the improvement in living conditions within the fields of social concern (to be specified each year). Entries should have been first published in English during the twelve months, ending on 31st July, of the year of the presentation.

George Orwell Memorial Prize: One Prize of £750 is awarded annually for an article or series of articles commenting on current cultural, social or political issues published in a journal or pamphlet in the United Kingdom during the year preceding the Prize.

John Llewelyn Rhys Memorial Prize: An annual Prize of £300 is offered for a memorable literary work of any kind by a Commonwealth writer who is under thirty years of age at the time of publication. Eligible books should have been published in the year previous to that of the Award, and should be in English.

Sinclair Prize for Fiction: One annual Prize of £5,000 is given for an unpublished novel of great literary merit having political or social significance. Sinclair-Browne Ltd. retains first publishing rights of the winning novels. *Closing date:* 30th June.

The Universe/Catholic Newspaper Literary Prize: One Prize of £500 is awarded annually for the novel which best supports and defends Christian values. Any novel written in English and published in Great Britain or Ireland between 1st February of the preceding year and 31st March of the award year is eligible.

Francis Williams Prize: An Award of £500 is offered every five years (next in 1987) for any book published in Great Britain in which illustration is a major element, including newly illustrated editions of the classics. Books of a purely technical nature and photographs are not eligible.

Note: Entries for all of the above Prizes and Awards, with the exception of the *Sinclair Prize,* may be submitted by their publisher only.

Further information from:
National Book League
Book House
45 East Hill
London
England SW18 2QZ

[1411]

NATIONAL CANCER ASSOCATION OF SOUTH AFRICA

Assistantships

Subjects: Demographical, statistical, clinical, pathological, chemical, etc., aspects of the cancer problem, particularly those aspects which have a South African significance and can be investigated locally.

Value: Bursaries—R2,000—R7,000; Skilled Laboratory and other Assistantships—R2,500-R6,500; General Laboratory and other Assistantships—R1,000—R3,000; Unskilled Laboratory and other Assistantships—R1,000R2,500. These salaries are inclusive of cost-of-living allowances and are determined in accordance with the salary structure of the institution where assistants are to be employed. The above are not necessarily maximum salaries offered.

Tenable in suitably equipped laboratories at recognised universities, medical schools, hospitals and research institutions in South Africa, and also occasionally overseas, for twelve months; renewable upon application.

Eligibility: Open to persons of proven research standing who have adequate time for research and who need technical or specialised help to carry out their research. As a general rule, applicants should be resident in South Africa.

Note: All correspondence and enquiries, as well as applications, should be submitted through a sponsor (executive head of the institution at which the research will be undertaken) if possible. Applications made directly to the Association by individuals will be considered only in exceptional circumstances, e.g., appointments of skilled and unskilled laboratory technicians will be made by the university or institution concerned, on behalf of the officer to whom a grant has been made. The conditions attached to such appointments will conform reasonably closely to similar appointments on the staff of the university or institution as regards to status, salary and conditions of service.

Closing date: 31st March.

Further information from:
National Cancer Association of South Africa
P.O. Box 2000
Johannesburg
South Africa

[1412]

NATIONAL CANCER ASSOCIATION OF SOUTH AFRICA

Bursaries and Fellowships

Subjects: Demographical, statistical, clinical, pathological, chemical, etc., aspects of the cancer problem, particularly those aspects which have a South African significance and can be investigated locally.

Value: Fellowships—R3,500-R10,00; Bursaries—R2,000-R7,000.

Tenable in suitably equipped laboratories at recognised universities, medical schools, hospitals and research institutions in South Africa as well as overseas, for twelve months; renewable upon application.

Eligibility: Open to medical graduates, biochemists, graduates in social science, etc., who are in full-time employment (not in private practice) and can show distinct evidence of a capacity for original research or (in the case of B.Sc. graduates) have won distinction during their undergraduate studies. As a general rule, candidates should be resident in South Africa.

Note: All correspondence and enquiries, as well as applications, should be submitted through a sponsor (executive head of the applicant's institution) if possible. Applications made directly to the Association by individuals will be considered only in exceptional circumstances.

Holders of research grants overseas will be required to sign an undertaking that they will return to South Africa to work in the same research field for a minimum period of three years. Awards may be made to cover travel expenses from and to South Africa.

Closing date: 31st March.

Further information from:
National Cancer Association of South Africa
P.O. Box 200
Johannesburg
South Africa

[1413]

NATIONAL CANCER ASSOCIATION OF SOUTH AFRICA

Grants

Grants for running expenses may be awarded to research workers for unskilled laboratory or other assistants and laboratory materials required for the conduct of the proposed research project.

Grants for printing and/or publication may be awarded for the publication of the results of all types of research which fall within the Association's scope, whether these results have been achieved through its assistance or not. The Association may also support publication, in suitable form, of monographs of outstanding merit. Grants for publication will be made only for publication in approved scientific journals.

Grants for major or specialised equipment may be awarded, in appropriate circumstances; however all major equipment will remain the property of the Association.

Note: For specific details of the types of research which fall within the Association's scope, eligibility requirements for research officers, and additional information regarding application, etc.

The Association also offers support to certain foreign medical scientists in the cancer field whom it invites to visit South Africa to participate in scientific meetings and congresses, or for particular purposes as the need may arise.

Further information from:
National Cancer Association of South Africa
P.O. Box 2000
Johannesburg
South Africa

[1414]

NATIONAL CANCER ASSOCIATION OF SOUTH AFRICA

Travel and Susistence (Study) Grants

Purpose: To assist workers in the cancer field in improving their academic and/or technical qualifications and experience, for the furtherance of cancer research and education, and for the improvement of diagnostic and/or treatment services to cancer patients in South Africa.

Travel Grants are awarded to suitable applicants to enable them to attend national or international conferences in the cancer field.

Study Grants are awarded to suitable applicants who, by study at specialized centres, will be able to increase their knowledge in the cancer field with a view to its subsequent application in South Africa.

Value: Not to exceed 50% of the minimum costs (on condition that the applicant, through his own institution or by other means, pays the balance of the minimum costs). Minimum costs are calculated on the basis of an economy class air fare to the furthest point of travel with such deviations as may be approved by the Association, plus a subsistence allowance appropriate to the geographical area concerned.

Eligibility: Open to suitably qualified workers in some aspect of the cancer field who are in full-time employment.

Note: Grantees are required to return to South Africa within a period of six months after expiration of the period for which the Grant was awarded (an extension will be considered on application) and to continue for a period of two years in the service in which they were employed at the time of the award.

Grants may not be used for the purpose of studying for or obtaining degrees or diplomas.

Closing date: 31st January and 31st July of each year.

Further information from:
National Cancer Association of South Africa
P.O. Box 2000
Johannesburg
South Africa

[1415]

NATIONAL CANCER ASSOCIATION OF SOUTH AFRICA
Cancer Research Campaign *(U.K.)*

Lady Cade Memorial Fellowship

Subjects: Research into the causation, diagnosis and/or treatment of cancer.

No. offered: One Fellowship every five years (last award given 1980-81).

Value: R22,000 plus return economy air fare to the United Kingdom for the Fellow and his family.

Tenable in the United Kingdom for a minimum of one year and a maximum of three.

Eligibility: Open to medical graduates of senior status who are resident in South Africa, or South African nationals who are domiciled in the British Commonwealth, or in some cases elsewhere. Preference is given to those holding senior posts at universities or other institutions to which the Fellows will be expected to return upon termination of the Fellowship.

Note: South Africans in the U.K. may apply through *Cancer Research Campaign, 2 Carlton House Terrace, London SW1Y 5AR.*

Closing date: Approximately six months prior to commencement of the Fellowship.

Further information from:
National Cancer Association of South Africa
P.O. Box 2000
Johannesburg
South Africa

[1416]

NATIONAL CANCER INSTITUTE OF CANADA

Research Studentships

Purpose: To provide training in cancer research for outstanding candidates who plan a career in cancer research in Canada.

No. offered: Up to ten new Studentships annually.

Value: Minimum of Can$8,900 per annum.

Tenable for one year at institutions in Canada recognized by the Institute; renewable on the basis of progress reports submitted by the Student and the comments of the supervisor.

Eligibility: Open to applicants who are resident in Canada at the time of application. Preference is given to those who submit evidence of previous research experience.

Note: For further details and conditions of Research Studentships, consult the manual *Support for Research and Training*, which is available from the Institute.

Closing date: 15th November.

Further information from:
National Cancer Institute of Canada
130 Bloor Street West, Suite 1001
Toronto, Ontario
Canada M5S 2V7

[1417]

NATIONAL CANCER INSTITUTE OF CANADA

Research Fellowships

Purpose: Research Fellowships are designed for persons who plan a career in cancer research in Canada.

Value: Minimum of Can$17,000 per annum, subject to annual review. A Fellow may apply for a transportation grant to and from the laboratory where his training will take place, and if married, an amount to assist in the expense of moving his family.

Tenable at a university laboratory or teaching hospital approved by the Institute, in Canada or abroad for one year; renewable. Applications for support for training abroad, however, will, except in unusual circumstances, only be accepted from applicants who have already received prior training under Institute auspices. Fellowships will commence as soon as practicable after 1st April.

Eligibility: Open to Canadian citizens or residents who have graduated from universities approved by the Institute.

Candidates must be accepted for postdoctoral training or research towards a Ph.D. degree in a university laboratory or teaching hospital approved by the Institute, and be engaged in the field of cancer research.

Note: Research Fellowships are not awarded for the purpose of providing practical clinical training.

For further details and conditions of Research Fellowships, consult the manual *Support for Research and Training*, which is available from the Institute.

Closing date: 15th November.

Further information from:
National Cancer Institute of Canada
130 Bloor Street West, Suite 1001
Toronto, Ontario
Canada M5S 2V7

[1418]

NATIONAL CANCER INSTITUTE OF CANADA

Research Fellowship in Clinical Oncology

Purpose: To provide specialized training in the research aspects of the broad field of clinical oncology (including epidemiology, medical statistics, clinical trials and biomedical research).

Value: Minimum of *Can*$23,000 (subject to periodic review), economy air fare for the Fellow, spouse and children to take up the appointment, and up to *Can*$500 to support travel for the Fellow to an appropriate Clinical Research Conference.

Tenable for one year in Canada and for a second year outside of Canada; a third year of support may be granted in unusual circumstances.

Eligibility: Applicants should be Canadian citizens or residents at the time of application who have successfully completed all the requirements (or will have successfully completed all the requirements prior to receiving the award) for Fellowship of the Royal College of Physicians and Surgeons of Canada. Candidates should plan to embark on a career in academic medicine in Canada.

Note: Fellows may supplement their award through clinical service at the host institution provided the work is directly related to the career plans of the Fellow, it does not adversely affect the quality or quantity of research training that the Fellow may reasonably be expected to receive, and that the total amount of external support does not exceed twenty-five per cent of the value of the Fellowship.

Closing date: 15th April for commencement 1st January of the following year; 15th November for commencement 1st July of the following year.

Further information from:
National Cancer Institute of Canada
130 Bloor Street West, Suite 1001
Toronto, Ontario
Canada M5S 2V7

[1419]

NATIONAL CANCER INSTITUTE OF CANADA

Career Appointments

Application for any career appointment is made by the university or institution in which the candidate will conduct his research; the institution concerned must be prepared to provide suitable space and research facilities.

Research Associate of the National Cancer Institute of Canada: The Institute offers funds to Canadian universities for the payment of salaries of senior career scientists in cancer research who have demonstrated their ability to plan, develop and execute significant research programmes. The initial appointment is for three years, and is tenable in any Canadian university.

The university concerned must undertake to appoint the Research Associate to appropriate academic rank within the university and to provide a salary in accordance with the salary levels of university staff members holding appointments of equivalent seniority.

Candidates must hold a doctorate in medicine or related science, should normally be under 40 years of age, and must state their intention to remain in Canada.

Clinical Research Associate: The Institute offers funds to Canadian universities for the payment of salaries of clinicians who are career investigators of outstanding ability and training, and who have demonstrated major interest in clinical cancer research. The appointment is tenable in the faculty of medicine of any Canadian university for an initial period of three years.

The university must undertake to appoint the Clinical Research Associate to appropriate academic rank within the university, and provide a salary in accordance with the experience and demonstrated ability of the appointee.

Candidates must hold a degree in medicine, hold an appointment in a clinical department in an approved institution, should normally be under 40 years of age, and must state their intention to remain in Canada.

Research Scholar: Scholarships are designed to develop the abilities and research potential of trained investigators interested in careers in cancer research, and will enable candidates to work full-time on the research project without involvement in major teaching responsibilites. The initial appointment will be for a period of three years, and the initial salary will depend on the experience and competence of the individual.

Candidates must hold a doctorate in medicine or in related science, should have completed three years of postdoctoral training in research, should normally be under 40 years of age, and must state their intention to remain in Canada.

Clinical Trials Scholar: The Institute offers funds to Canadian universities for the payment in part of salaries of clinicians who have completed their clincial training in medical, radiation, or surgical oncology, and who have a major interest in promoting cancer research through the clinical trials mechanism.

The univesity must undertake to appoint the Clinical Trials Scholar to an appropriate academic rank within the university. The initial contribution to the salary of a Scholar is in accordance with a scale fixed by the Institute, taking into account the experience and ability of the Scholar.

Scholarships are tenable at a faculty of medicine of any Canadian university for three years; renewable, subject to review.

Candidates must hold a degree in medicine, have completed their clinical training, hold an appointment in a clinical department of an approved institution, show outstanding competency in the field of study, should normally be under 40 years of age, and must state their intention to remain in Canada.

Note: Research Associates, Clinical Research Associates and Research Scholars should apply to the Institute for funds to carry out the research under the regulations set forth in Research Grants to Individuals.

Closing date: 15th November for all career appointments.

Address:
National Cancer Institute of Canada
130 Bloor Street West, Suite 1001
Toronto, Ontario
Canada M5S 2V7

[1420]

NATIONAL CANCER INSTITUTE OF CANADA

Research Grants to Individuals

Subjects: To cover the purchase and maintenance of animals, expendable supplies, minor items of equipment, and payment of graduate students, postdoctoral fellows, and technical and research assistants, but not personal support for the Grantee.

Tenable at Canadian universities or other institutions for two years in the first instance; renewable for periods of one, two or three years.

Eligibility: Open to persons with research experience and competence, holding appointments at Canadian universities or other institutions.

Note: Grants will be awarded to projects deemed worthy of support, provided that the basic equipment and research facilities are available in the institution concerned and that it will provide the necessary administrative services.

Grants are made only with the consent and knowledge of the administrative head of the institution at which they are to be held, and applications must be countersigned accordingly.

The Institute also makes available to individuals engaged in studies related to cancer research, grants for purchase of permanent equipment, including specialized major equipment.

For further information and conditions of application, consult the manual *Support for Research and Training*, which is available from the Institute.

Closing date: 15th November.

Further information from:
National Cancer Institute of Canada
130 Bloor Street West, Suite 1001
Toronto, Ontario
Canada M5S 2V7

[1421]

NATIONAL CANCER INSTITUTE OF CANADA

Desmond Magner Awards

Eight Awards are made annually to Canadian pathology residents for study and diagnosis of up to one month at the Canadian Tumour Reference Centre in Ottawa. Candidates should have completed at least one year of training in surgical pathology. The value of the Awards is based on thirty days support at a rate to be authorized by the Institute, plus return economy fare to Ottawa. An additional annual Award is available to an individual who is not in need of travel or subsistence support. Awardees are encouraged to undertake small research projects. Those interested in applying should submit the following to the address below: curriculum vitae; supporting letter from the applicant's training program director; list of dates during the coming year that the applicant would be available; a statement of interests and requirements in relation to tumour pathology.

Further information from:
Dr. W.T.E. McCaughey, Director
Canadian Tumour Reference Centre
Clinical Studies Unit Building
Ottawa Civic Hospital
60 Ruskin Avenue
Ottawa, Ontario
Canada K1Y 4M9

[1422]

NATIONAL CENTER FOR ATMOSPHERIC RESEARCH *(Boulder, Colorado)*

Graduate Assistantships

Purpose: To aid cooperative research between the Center and academic institutions by providing support of M.S. and Ph.D. thesis work carried out in association with research programs at the Center.

Subjects: The broad field of atmospheric sciences, including: atmospheric dynamics, climate, cloud physics, atmospheric chemistry and radiation, upper atmospheric solar and space physics, and oceanography.

No. offered: Varies; Assistantships are awarded as vacancies occur.

Value: US$8,813 annually for Graduate Assistants who have passed their comprehensive examination, and US$8,202 for those who have not passed the examination; payments are made biweekly. Graduate Assistants are on a regular half-time appointment at the Center and are entitled to all benefits in proportion to the appointment. In addition, travel expenses for two trips per year to the student's home institution or to appropriate scientific conferences may be paid if funds are available. The university scientist is expected to seek partial support in the form of tuition waivers.

Tenable at the Center for up to two years for a Ph.D. thesis and one year for an M.S. thesis. Eligiblity for continuation is reviewed annually and renewed at that time.

Eligibility: Open to graduate students who state their intentions of working on an M.S. or Ph.D. thesis in cooperation with a Center's program, and are from a university program having common interests with the Center's project, facility, or research group concerned. Students must be able to be in residence at the

Center for the thesis work, except when research requires residence elsewhere.

Note: Awards are made on the basis of proposals submitted jointly by a university scientist and a Center scientist, and are evaluated quarterly on 1st March, June, September and December of each year. Arrangements are to be made by the student applicant, and the Center scientist should be a member of the student's thesis committee.

Funding is not available for equipment grants or field projects.

Students holding additional fellowships or awards will receive the difference up to the salary offered by the Center.

The Center is sponsored by the National Science Foundation.

Further information from:
National Center for Atmospheric Research
P.O. Box 3000
Boulder, Colorado 80307
U.S.A.

[1423]

NATIONAL CENTER FOR ATMOSPHERIC RESEARCH *(Boulder, Colorado)*

Postdoctoral Appointments in the Advanced Study Program

Purpose: To enrich research and teaching in the atmospheric sciences by bringing in the field of highly qualified Ph.D. physicists, astrophysicists, chemists, applied mathematicians and engineers, and to enhance the capability of recent Ph.D. scientists already involved in atmospheric research to pursue their work and to develop expertise in new areas.

Subjects: Atmospheric sciences, including the following: climate, large-scale dynamics, mesoscale meterorology, oceanography, geophysical fluid dynamics, severe storms, atmospheric chemistry, atmospheric physics, solar physics, and environmental and societal impact assessment.

No. offered: Approximately 8 Appointments annually.

Value: Minimum of US$19,000 per annum (for recent Ph.D.s); Appointees with more than one year's experience receive a stipend of US$19,000 per annum. All Appointees receive noncontributory life and health insurance. Travel expenses to NCAR are reimbursed for the Appointee and family. Faculty applicants will be paid on the basis of "no loss, no gain"; however the Appointee is expected to arrange for partial support from the home institution or from other grants.

Tenable at the National Center for Atmospheric Research, Boulder, Colorado. The Appointments are for up to one year; an additional year of support may be applied for.

Eligibility: Open to persons who have recently received their Ph.D., and to scientists with no more than four years' experience since receiving their Ph.D. Foreign nationals may apply; NCAR is an equal opportunity employer with an affirmative action program.

Closing date: 15th January for Appointments commencing in the summer or early autumn.

Note: The Center is sponsored by the National Science Foundation.

Further information from:
Betty Wilson, Administrator
National Center for Atmospheric Research
P.O. Box 3000
Boulder, Colorado 80307
U.S.A.

[1424]

NATIONAL CENTRE FOR SCIENTIFIC RESEARCH *(France)*

Research Fellowships and Short-Term Bursaries: Exchange Schemes

Subjects: All fields of scientific research.

Value: A montly allowance; second class return travel for Research Fellows only.

Tenable at research institutions in France for periods of one month to one year.

Eligibility: Open to nationals of countries with whom the Centre has concluded exchange agreements. Candidates should have at least one year's postgraduate research experience at a university or research institution and possess a working knowledge of French.

Note: Applications (which should incude a letter of acceptance from the institution where the proposed research is to be carried out) may be made in the first instance to the appropriate organization in the candidate's own country. Canada—*National Research Council, Ottawa, Ontario K1A 0R6;* Ireland—*National Board of Science and Technology, Shelbourne House, Shelbourne Road, Dublin 4;* United Kingdom—*British Council, 10 Spring Gardens, London SW1A 2BN;* United States—*National Science Foundation, 1800 G Street N.W., Washington, D.C. 20550.*

The Centre also operates exchange schemes with Algeria, Belgium, China, Cuba, Czechoslovakia, Egypt, Federal Republic of Germany, Finland, Hungary, India, Israel, Italy, Japan, Korea, Mexico, Netherlands, Poland, Romania, Spain, Sweden, Tunisia, U.S.S.R., and Yugoslavia.

Address:
Centre nationale de la recherche scientifique
15 quai Anatole-France
75700 Paris
France

[1425]

NATIONAL CONSUMER AFFAIRS INTERNSHIP PROGRAM

Purpose: To provide graduate students with an opportunity to supplement their academic training by working in consumer affairs offices in government, industry and non-profit associations.

Subjects: Consumer affairs.

No. offered: Thirty Interships in each of three classes are given annually.

Value: US$125 per week for the duration of the Program, plus a relocation allowance of US$200 and round-trip transportation between the recipient's college and work location.

Tenable for thirteen weeks at a participating consumer affairs organization in the United States.

Eligibility: Open to all interested graduate students of U.S. colleges and universities regardless of age or sex. The Program is interdisciplinary and open to all majors. Candidates must be nominated by a faculty advisor who is willing and able to act as advisor, arrange for internship credit, and participate in the preinternship conference.

Note: Both Interns and faculty advisors are reimbursed for travel and accommodation expenses incurred. Faculty advisors will receive US$200 for their services.

Closing dates: Class 1-31 December for Program to begin the following January: Class 2-20th April for Program to begin the following May; Class 3-31st July for Program to begin the following August.

Further information from:
National Consumer Affairs Internship Program
P.O. Box 40445
Tucson, Arizona 85717
U.S.A.

[1426]

NATIONAL COUCIL FOR THE CARE OF CRIPPLES IN SOUTH AFRICA

Travelling Scholarships

Scholarships are offered from time to time to South African personnel working in fields related and of benefit to the care of cripples and the rehabilitiation of crippled persons. The amount of each award and the duration of tenure are variable, depending upon the merit of individual applications.

Further information from:
H.J.C. Parker, Director
National Council for the Care of Cripples in South Africa
P.O. Box 10173
Johannesburg 2000
South Africa

[1427]

NATIONAL COUNCIL OF COMMERCIAL PLANT BREEDERS

Genetics and Plant Breeding Awards

An annual Award of US$1,000 and a suitably engraved plaque is given in recognition of outstanding basic contribution to the advancement of plant breeding and genetics. Nominations may be anyone and will be considered for up to three years. *Closing date:* 15th March of the Award year.

Further information from:
Robert Falasca, Secretary
National Council of Commerical Plant Breeders
Executive Building, Suite 964
1030 15th Street, N.W.
Washington, D.C. 20005
U.S.A.

[1428]

NATIONAL COUNCIL OF TEACHERS OF ENGLISH RESEARCH FOUNDATION *(U.S.A.)*

Research Grants-in-Aid

Purpose: To encourage research, experimentation and investigation in the teaching of English at any level of instruction.

Value: Primary support is not available for travel costs or salary subsidies unless cooperating agencies are willing to bear the greater part of such costs.

Eligibility: Open to qualified researchers (individuals or groups).

Note: When submitting proposals, applicants should define their purpose clearly and limit the project so that it can be completed in a reasonable time. Applicants should also show that they have already explored the question and related research. As well, a valid method of analyzing data should be included. Studies designed to include only the accumulation of data by questionnaires are not approved.

Closing date: 15th February.

Further information from:
Executive Secretary
Natiuonal Council of Teachers of English
1111 Kenyon Road
Urbana, Illinois 61801
U.S.A.

[1429]

NATIONAL DAIRY COUNCIL *(U.S.A.)*

National Research Grants-in-Aid

Purpose: To encourage investigations directed toward evaluating the total nutritional value of milk and dairy foods in the human diet as related to their proper role in improving growth and development and maintaining good health. Support is given to facilitate research already in progress, to provide assistance in undertaking a research effort, or to develop a new approach to an existing situation in nutrition research.

Subjects: Various aspects of the need for, or utilization of, the proteins, fats, carbohydrates, minerals or vitamins found in or added to milk or milk products, or of some human disease or disturbance suggested as being related to or alleviated by the consumption of dairy foods.

Value: Average approximately US$20,000 per annum, paid quarterly. Funds are not available for alteration of facilities or purchase of permanent equipment.

Tenable for one year initially, with the possibility of renewal for additional years necessary to complete a project.

Eligibility: Open to qualified investigators associated with accredited institutions of higher learning in the United States who hold a Ph.D., M.D., D.D.S., D.V.M., or equivalent degree.

Note: Six copies of a preliminary letter of intent should be submitted to the Director of Nutrition Research, containing a brief curiculum vitae, a title for the project, a brief statement of proposed objectives, experimental procedures, estimated total budget and time requirements, and significance of proposed research to the dairy industry. The Advisory Committee may then request a formal application.

Closing date: 1st May, for support to commence 1st January of the following year.

Further information from:
Director of Nutrition Research
National Dairy Council
6300 North River Road
Rosemont, Illinois 60018
U.S.A.

[1430]

NATIONAL DESIGN COUNCIL
Department of Industry, Trade and Commerce (*Canada*)

"Design Canada" Scholarships

Purpose: (a) industrial design, graphic design, interior design, furniture design, industrial pottery, textile design, etc.; (b) special courses towards master's degrees, or the equivalent, with the aim of teaching design.

Value: Variable; a lump sum dependent on cost of tuition, materials, travel and living in country of study.

Tenable at Canadian and foreign schools of design of high standing, for one year; renewable for up to three years.

Eligibility: Open to Canadian citizens or landed immigrants with at least one year's residence in Canada who intend to continue in the field of design in Canada upon completion of their studies. Candidates' academic qualifications should be as follows: (a) graduate designers who wish to continue their studies towards a master's degree or equivalent; (b) non-graduate designers with demonstrated ability; (c) outstanding students who have completed a post-secondary design program in a recognized school and wish to continue their studies on an advanced level; or (d) mid-career designers and professionals in related design fields who wish to pursue specialized studies with a view to teaching design.

Note: Scholarships are awarded by an independent jury, with decisions based on (a) merit of applicant's previous achievements, (b) academic level and planned program of study, (c) choice of school, and (d) potential impact of study on the quality of design or design education in Canada.

Closing date: 30th April.

Further information from:
Registrar
"Design Canada" Scholarships
Department of Industry, Trade and Commerce
Ottawa, Ontario
Canada K1A 0H5

[1431]

NATIONAL EASTER SEAL SOCIETY
(*U.S.A.*)

Alpha Chi Omega National Women's Fraternity

Supplemental Aid Scholarships

Purpose: To provide financial aid to master's degree candidates accepted in accredited programs in the field of speech pathology and audiology.

Value: Not to exceed US$750.

Eligibility: Open to United States citizens who intend to work in the career field in the United States for at least one year upon completion of the master's program. Consideration is given to scholastic achievement, financial need, references, and letters of application.

Note: The Scholarship program is conducted on a rotating regional basis. Details of the rotation may be obtained from the Society at the address below.
Interested persons accepted in an accredited program in a participating region should contact their department Chairman to determine their eligibility. If nominated, they will be instructed on the application procedures.

Closing date: 1st May.

Further information from:
Scholarship Coordinator
National Easter Seal Society
2023 West Ogden Avenue
Chicago, Illinois 60612
U.S.A.

[1432]

NATIONAL EDUCATION ASSOCIATION
(*U.S.A.*)

William G. Carr Scholarship

Purpose: To develop leadership in the teaching profession, to promote international education, and to strengthen independent professional organizations.

No. offered: Two Scholarships annually.

Value: US$2,500 each.

Tenable for one year; not renewable.

Eligibility: Awards are made to applicants who qualify as one of the following: (a) a graduate student in the United States studying international or comparative education, or a teacher from the United States or another country interested in aiding and studying teachers' associations in other countries, or (b) an officer or a staff member of a local or state professional organization in the United States, to pursue or complete graduate education designed to improve some aspect of professional association work.

Closing date: 1st February.

Further information from:
William G. Carr Scholarship Committee
National Education Association
1201 Sixteenth Street, N.W.
Washington, D.C. 20036
U.S.A.

[1433]

NATIONAL ELECTRICAL ENGINEERING RESEARCH INSTITUTE
South African Council for Scientific and Industrial Research

Contract Appointments

Subjects: Electrical engineering (semiconductor technology, IC design, design methods, signal processing, computer technology, digital communication, lightning research, high voltage and insulation, system disturbances, power control, industrial automation, development and construction, measurements and testing, maintenance services, calibration services).

Value: R8,370 per annum or higher, according to qualifications and experience, plus transportation costs.

Tenable in Pretoria for at least three years.

Eligibility: Open to persons of any nationality who have a B.Sc., M.Sc., Ph.D. or their equivalent in electrical engineering.

Note: Conditions of service are supplied to suitable applicants on request.

Further information from:
Director
National Electrical Engineering Research Institute
P.O. Box 395
Pretoria 0001
South Africa

[1434]

NATIONAL EMPLOYMENT ACCIDENT INSURANCE INSTITUTE OF ITALY

Buccheri La Ferla International Prizes

Three Prizes are awarded in even-numbered years to research workers of any nationality for effective and original contribution toward the development of labour medicine, legal and insurance medicine, and traumatology. The Prizes, of equal amounts, are paid in a lump sum and constitute at least 60% of the accrued interest over a period of two years, from a legacy left to the Institute. *Closing date*: 31st March of even-numbered years for Prizes to be awarded no later than 31st December.

Further information from:
INAIL
Buccheri La Ferla International Prizes Secretariat
14 Via Aniene
Rome
Italy

[1435]

NATIONAL ENDOWMENT FOR THE ARTS *(U.S.A.)*

Fellowships to Individuals

The National Endowment for the Arts is an agency of the Federal Government which makes Grants both to organizations and individuals concerned with the arts throughout the United States. Its major goals are to foster excellence in American arts, to help create a climate in which the arts can flourish, to preserve the American cultural heritage in all its diversity, and to make the arts available to the widest possible public.

The Endowment provides financial assistance to individuals through non-matching Fellowships. These are awarded to artists of exceptional talent for the advancement of their work and careers. Fellowships are usually given to citizens or permanent residents of the United States.

Note: For more detailed information inquiries should be made to:
National Endowment for the Arts
2401 E Street, N.W.
Washington, D.C. 20506
U.S.A.

[1436]

NATIONAL ENDOWMENT FOR THE HUMANITIES *(U.S.A.)*

Division of Fellowships and Seminars—Program

The Endowment supports a variety of activities in the humanities, especially through grants in response to open application. The following are descriptions of annual NEH Programs which offer grants to individuals. Eligible candidates are United States citizens and nationals, and foreign nationals who have lived in the United States or its territories for at least three years at the time of application. The number of Fellowships offered and value for each award will be determined in accordance to the Endowment's fiscal budget which may vary conciderably from year to year. A fuller description of individual Endowment Programs is available by writing to the address below.

Fellowships for Independent Study and Research: Open to scholars, teachers and other humanists, on a full-time basis. *Closing date:* 1st June.

Fellowships for College Teachers: Open to teachers in two-, four-, and five-year colleges and universities which do not have means to support advanced study and research to undertake programs of general study, studies related to their courses, or research projects. *Closing date:* 1st June.

Fellowships in the Humanities for Journalists: For full-time journalists to spend an academic year at the University of Michigan or Stanford University. Applicants should apply directly to the Fellowship Institution. *Closing date:* 1st March.

Summer Stipends: Open to college and university teachers and other humanists to provide support for two consecutive months of full-time independent study and research. Teachers must be nominated by their institution. Others may apply directly to the Division at the address below. *Closing date:* 5th October.

Summer Seminars for College Teachers—Participants: Open to teachers at undergraduate two-year colleges for participation in eight-week summer seminars directed by distinguished scholars at institutions with libraries suitable for advanced study. *Closing date:* 1st April.

Summer Seminars for Professional-School Teachers: Open to teachers in law schools, medical shcools and other schools of health care for participation in four- to six-week summer seminars directed by distinguished humanists. *Closing date:* 1st March.

Further information from:
Division of Fellowships and Seminars Programs
c/o Office of Public Affairs
National Endowment for the Humanities
Mail Stop 351
806 15th Street, N.W.
Washington, D.C. 20506
U.S.A.

[1437]

NATIONAL ENDOWMENT FOR THE HUMANITIES *(U.S.A.)*

Division of Research Programs

The Endowment supports a variety of activities in the humanities; especially through grants in response to open application. The following are descriptions of annual NEH Programs which offer grants to individuals. Eligible candidates are United States citizens and nationals, and foreign nationals who have lived in the United States or its territories for at least three years at the time of application. The number of awards offered and their value will be determined in accordance to the Endowment's fiscal budget which may vary considerably from year to year. A fuller description of individual Endowment Programs is available by writing to NEH.

General Research Program—Support is for projects in all fields of the humanities and aspects of the social sciences that explore a problem through original research and creative thought. Awards are made in the following three areas:

Basic Research: Supports research projects, often longer-term and collaborative, in all fields of the humanities, including archaeology. *Closing dates:* 15th October for archaeological projects; 1st April for all others.

Research Conferences: Support meetings of scholars whose purpose is to discuss and advance research in a particular topic or field. *Closing dates:* 15th February; 15th September; 15th November.

State, Local and Regional Studies: Support research that fosters the understanding of the history and culture of regions and communites. *Closing dates:* 1st March; 1st September.

Research Materials Program—Support is provided for preparation of reference works considered of highest importance for the advancement of research in the humanities and for the general dissemination of knowledge throughout the country. Awards are made in the following three areas:

Editions: Grants support the preparation of editions of documents and works from all fields in the humanities. *Closing date:* 1st Ocotober.

Research Tools and Reference Works: Grants support to creation of research tools such as dictionaries, encyclopedias, atlases, catalogues raisonnes, linguistic grammars, decriptive catalogues, and data bases. *Closing date:* 1st October.

Translations: Support of the creation of annotated translations into English of primary and secondary documents and works significant to the humanities. *Closing date:* 1st July.

Research Resources Program—Grants are given for projects to place hitherto unavailable materials in public repositories; to facilitate access by preparing catalogues, inventories, registers, guides, bibliographies, and other finding aids; and to impove the ways in which librarians, archivists, and others care for and make available the research materials entrusted to them. *Closing date:* 1st June.

Further information from:
Division of Research Programs
c/o Office of Public Affairs
National Endowment for the Humanities
Mail Stop 351
806 15th Street, N.W.
Washington, D.C. 20506
U.S.A.

[1438]

NATIONAL ENDOWMENT FOR THE HUMANITIES *(U.S.A.)*

Office of Planning and Policy Assessment

The following grants are eligible to United States citizens and nationals, and foreign nationals who have lived in the United States for at least three years at the time of application. The number of awards offered and their value will be determined in accordance to the Endowment's fiscal budget which may vary considerably from year to year.

Planning and Assessment Studies Program: Awards support studies and experiments designed to collect and analyze data—including information about financial, material, and human resources—which help assess the condition of important sectors in the humanities. Explorations of significant trends or emerging issues in the humanities are also encouraged, along with the design, testing, and implementation of analytical tools for evaluation and policy analysis. *Closing date:* 1st February; 1st August.

Note: The Division of Special Programs offers support for humanities projects with concrete end products initiated, developed, and conducted by young people themselves, including educational projects, research in the humanities, media presentations and community programs. No thesis work or foreign travel projects are eligible. *Closing date:* 15th October for initial application.

Further information from:
Office of Public Affairs
National Endowment for the Humanities
Mail Stop 351
806 15th Street, N.W.
Washington, D.C. 20506
U.S.A.

[1439]

NATIONAL FEDERATION OF MUSIC SOCIETIES *(U.K.)*

Award for Young Concert Artists

The Federation offers an Award each autumn to young concert artists who are British subjects and are normally resident in the United Kingdom. The upper age limit is 26 for instrumentalists and 28 for singers. The Award offers engagements with affiliated societies, to all the finalists (normally 4) pro rata, according to their final placing. In addition the winner receives a small monetary prize, a sum to commission a new work and a recital at the Wigmore Hall, London. Future competitions are as follows: 1982—men's voices; 1983—pianos; 1984—strings; 1985—women's voices; 1986—wind instruments; 1987—men's voices.

Application forms are available from the Federation in May. Two testimonials are required.

Further information from:
National Federation of Music Societies
Francis House
Francis Street
London
England SW1P 1DE

[1440]

NATIONAL FEDERATION OF STATE POETRY SOCIETIES *(U.S.A.)*

The Federation, comprised of official state poetry societies throughout the U.S., offers approximately 50 contests annually for the promotion of excellence in writing poetry. Grand prizes vary from contest to contest, and range from US$25 to US$1,000. Eligibility also varies, depending upon the state society sponsoring the award. In general, contests are either open to anyone without restriction or are open to all members of any official state society. A brochure describing the contests may be obtained by sending a self-addressed, stamped envelope to the address below. *Closing date:* 15th March for all contests.

Further information from:
Alice Briley, Strophes Editor
National Federation of State Poetry Societies
1121 Major Avenue, N.W.
Albuquerque, New Mexico 87107
U.S.A.

[1441]

NATIONAL FELLOWSHIP FUND *(U.S.A.)*

Granduate Fellowships for Black Americans

Purpose: To provide qualified black personnel for careers in higher education in the U.S.

Subjects: Doctoral study in the basic biological and physical sciences, the basic social sciences and the humanities.

No. offered: Varies according to the rate of attrition of funds and number of completions of programs by earlier awardees.

Value: A basic stipend of US$350 per month plus a book allowance of up to US$300, full tuition and fees, and an allowance of US$50 per month for dependent spouse and US$50 per month for each dependent child.

Tenable at any U.S. graduate school of the Fellow's choice, for ten or twelve months; renewable.

Eligibility: Open to black Americans who are U.S. citizens and have completed at least the equivalent of three academic years of full-time graduate study; are currently engaged in or can give evidence of intent to enter into a career of higher education in the U.S.; and who are currently enrolled in or plan to enter a U.S. graduate school offering the doctoral degree in their field of interest in the summer session or fall term of the Fellowship year.

Note: Candidates are required to include with their applications a copy of their Graduate Record Examination scores on the Aptitude and Advanced Tests. If these tests have not been taken the applicant should arrange to take them at the earliest possible date through the *Educational Testing Service, Post Office Box 955, Princeton, New Jersey 08540.* Scores should be sent by them directly to the Fund, Code Number R5487-4-00. Holders of a first post-bacalaureate professional degree should submit scores (verbal, quantitative and total) from the professional school admission test.

Fellows are required to submit an annual progress report, an official transcript, and an evaluation of academic progress by his or her major professor or faculty advisor.

Closing date: 5th January, for filing applications. Application forms may be requested until 23rd December.

Not confirmed for 1983.

Further information from:
Graduate Fellowships for Black Americans
National Fellowship Fund
795 Peachtree Street, N.E., Suite 484
Atlanta, Georgia 30308
U.S.A.

[1442]

NATIONAL FELLOWSHIP FUND *(U.S.A.)*

Middle East and Africa Field Research Fellowship Program for Black Americans

Purpose: To provide opportunities for extended dissertation research in the overseas setting.

Subject: Field research.

Value: A maximum of US$10,000 to cover transportation costs, maintenance, and certain project related expenses. Payment is made in quarterly instalments in amounts designated by the Fellow.

Tenable for field research in Africa or the Middle East, for nine to twelve months.

Eligibility: Open to black Americans at the dissertation-year level. Candidates are required to provide evidence that they will have completed all course work, passed all qualifing examinations, passed all language requirements, and have been formally admitted to candidacy for the doctoral degree by July or September of the grant period.

Note: The proposal submitted as part of the application, should have been approved by the candidate's faculty advisor as a dissertation topic.
Applications are reviewed by a panel of Africanists from various academic settings. Semi-finalists are invited to Atlanta for a personal interview. The basic criteria for selection is academic quality and the applicant's ability to carry out the stated research successfully within a twelve-month period.
Fellows are required to submit quarterly progress reports. After the initial payment, stipends are withheld until reports are received.

Closing date: 5th January, for filing applictions. Application forms may be requested until 23rd December.

Not confirmed for 1983.

Further information from:
Middle East and Africa Field Research Fellowship Program for Black Americans
National Fellowship Fund
795 Peachtree Street, N.E., Suite 484
Atlanta, Georgia 30308
U.S.A.

[1443]

NATIONAL 4-H COUNCIL *(U.S.A.)*

International 4-H Youth Exchange: Professional Rural Youth Leader Exchange

Purpose: To provide opportunities for young people to live with host families in other countries and to work in rural youth programs and undertake personal studies.

Value: Maintenance and round-trip transportation for United States citizens, and maintenance and transportation within the United States for foreign citizens.

Tenable in the United States (for foreign citizens) and in the countries listed below (for United States citizens), for three to six months.

Eligibility: Open to United States citizens, and to citizens of Antigua, Australia, Barbados, Belgium, Botswana, Brazil, Canada, Republic of China, Costa Rica, Denmark, Egypt, Finland, France, Federal Republic of Germany, Greece, India, Italy, Jamaica, Japan, Kenya, Republic of Korea, Luxembourg, Nepal, Netherlands, New Zealand, Norway, Paraguay, Philippines, Poland, St. Kitts, Spain, Sri Lanka, Swaziland, Sweden, Switzerland, Thailand, Trinidad and Tobago, United Kingdom, and Zambia.
Candidates should be single and between 19 and 25 years of age.

Note: United States candidates should apply through their County or State Extension 4-H Office, or to the address below. Foreign candidates should write to the address below for information concerning the cooperating agency in their own country.

Address:
International Programs
National 4-H Council
7100 Connecticut Avenue
Chevy Chase, Maryland 20815
U.S.A.

[1444]

NATIONAL FUND FOR THE ARTS
(Argentina)

Scholarship for British Subjects

Suspended Spring 1982

[1445]

NATIONAL FUND FOR MEDICAL EDUCATION *(U.S.A.)*

Fellowships in Medical Education

Purpose: To enhance the knowledge and skills of young postdoctoral students who plan careers in academic medicine.

Subjects: Supervised study or investigation in any related area of medical education.

No. offered: Varies, annually.

Value: Stipends of up to US$20,000 are paid directly to the sponsoring institution in quarterly installments. the amount, to be determined in consultation with the dean of the sponsoring institution, is to cover, as nearly as possible, the salary ordinarily paid to a full-time member of the faculty at the same level.

Tenable at appropriate institutions throughout the U.S. and abroad for one year; renewable only in exceptional cases.

Eligibility: Candidates should be young postdoctoral students who have completed their residency or other formal training and plan to make their careers in academic medicine. Evidence that the Fellow will be working under the direction of a person or persons having extensive knowledge and experience in the chosen field of study must be documented.

Note: Applications, along with a letter of endorsement, should be submitted through the dean or chief executive officer of the institution at which the candidate wishes to study. In addition, a letter from the sponsor should also be included.

It is intended that this Fellowship will be the recipient's principal source of support.

Applicants who are unsure as to whether their plans are appropriate are advised to consult the Fund prior to submitting an application.

Closing date: 1st November for Fellowships to commence 1st July of the following year.

Further information from:
National Fund for Medical Education
999 Asylum Avenue
Hartford, Connecticut 06105
U.S.A.

[1446]

NATIONAL FUND FOR MEDICAL EDUCATION *(U.S.A.)*

SmithKline Foundation Fellowship Program of Creative Learning Opportunities for Medical Students

This Program provides opportunities for medical and osteopathic students to initiate and carry through creative projects that will give them learning experiences not ordinarily encountered in the usual course of their education. Few guidelines are imposed on the nature or scope of the project, except that it must lead to an impoved understanding of clinical medicine and/or the delivery of health care. The number and value of Fellowships vary annually.

Further information from:
National Fund for Medical Education
999 Asylum Avenue
Hartford, Connecticut 06105
U.S.A.

[1447]

NATIONAL FUND FOR RESEARCH INTO CRIPPLING DISEASES *(U.K.)*
Action Research for the Crippled Child

Research Grants

Purpose: To support basic and clinical research projects: by direct grant and through the establishment of professional departments or research units; the award of research fellowships; the erection of buildings; and the provision of research equipment. Travel grants are occasionally given for attendance at conferences likely to be of benefit to an existing grant holder. Competitive research training fellowships are awarded annually to further the training in research methods of young medical and non-medical graduates and others with appropriate qualifications.

Subjects: Medical research into all aspects of crippling, regardless of cause. Current emphasis is on prevention, especially in the child, but ways of alleviating the effects of an existing handicap in all age groups are included.

Value: Variable.

Tenable at any approved institution.

Eligibility: Open to scientists in the United Kingdom. Applications from younger investigators must be supported by heads of department.

Further information from:
Director, National Fund for Research into Crippling Diseases
Vincent House, 1 Springfield Road
Horsham, Sussex
England RH12 2PN

[1448]

NATIONAL GALLERY OF ART
(Washington)

Center for Advanced Study in the Visual Arts

Predoctoral Fellowship Program

Application for the following Fellowships is open to Ph.D. candidates in any field of art history who have finished all of their course work and have devoted at least one full year's research to their proposed dissertation topic.

Chester Dale Fellowships: Four Fellowships: Four Fellowships of US$9,000 each are offered for one year, and are usually intended for the advancement or completion of the doctoral dissertation, either in America or abroad. The Dale Fellowships may be used entirely at one place of research or for travel, or for a combination of the two; they carry no stipulation for the candidate's residence as a Fellow at the National Gallery, although such a use for them is possible. Not renewable.

David E. Finley Fellowship: One Fellowship of US$9,000 per annum is available for three years and is intended usually as a two-year European sojourn for travel and research on a dissertation topic already well advanced, plus a supplementary period to be spent as a research fellow in residence at the National Gallery. A primary requirement for the award of this Fellowship is that the candidate have a real interest in museum work, which could be developed during his travel to visit major European collections as well as during his eight months at the Gallery in Washington; there is, however, no requirement as to the candidate's subsequent choice of a career. The Finley Fellowship is not renewable, but its terms and especially its tenure are somewhat flexible with each award.

Samuel H. Kress Fellowships: Two research Fellowships of US$9,000 each are offered for two years, and are to be held in residence either entirely or partly at the Center in Washington, D.C. Kress Fellows are expected to give approximately half their time to Gallery research projects assigned for training purposes, and they are free to devote an equal amount of time to their own work, either in Washington, elsewhere in the United States, or abroad. Not renewable.

Robert H. and Clarice Smith Fellowship: One Fellowship of US$9,000 is offered for one year for productive scholarly work in Dutch or Flemish art history, and is intended for the advancement or completion of a doctoral dissertation, or of a book, in either field. The candidate may use the grant to study either in the United States or abroad; there are no residence requirements at the National Gallery, although the candidate may be based in Washington if he desires. In rare cases warranted by the special requirements of a recipient's work, the Smith Fellowship may sometimes be renewed for a second year.

Note: Applications may only be made through the chairman of graduate departments of art history who act as sponsors for the candidate.

Closing date: 30 November for all Fellowships; tenure to commence 1st September of the following year.

Further information from:
Dr. Douglas Lewis, Fellowship Office
National Gallery of Art, C.A.S.V.A.
Washington, D.C. 20565
U.S.A.

[1449]

NATIONAL GALLERY OF ART
(Washington)

Center for Advanced Study in the Visual Arts

Senior Fellowships; Visiting Senior Fellowships; Associate Appointments

Subjects: History, theory and criticism of the visual arts of any geographical area and of any period.

No. offered: Varies.

Value: Senior Fellows receive a monthly stipend and additional allowances for research materials, travel and housing. Visiting Senior Fellows receive support on an individual basis, according to need. Both are provided with a study and subsidized luncheon privileges. Associates are provided with a study, but must obtain funding elsewhere.

Tenable at the Center: for a single academic term, one full academic year, or in exceptional cases for two academic years. In addition, Visiting Senior Fellows may receive tenure for short-term study of up to a maximum of sixty days. Fellowships are not renewable.

Eligibility: Open to scholars of any nationality who holds a doctoral or equivalent degree in one of the visual arts, or in a tangential discipline whose work examines physical objects or has implication for the analysis and criticism of physical form.

Note: Resources represented by the collections of the Gallery, the Library, and the Photographic Archives, as well as the Library of Congress and other specialized research libraries and collection in Washington, D.C. will be available to Senior Fellows.

Associates may not hold teaching or any other professional obligations while in residence at the Center.

Application forms may be requested from the address below.

Closing date: 31st October for Senior Fellowships and Associates; 31st March, August and October for Visiting Senior Fellowships and Associates desiring appointments for less than one academic term.

Further information from:
National Gallery of Art
Center for Advanced Study in the Visual Arts
Washington, D.C. 20565
U.S.A.

[1450]

NATIONAL GEOGRAPHIC SOCIETY
(U.S.A.)

Research Grants

Purpose: To support research projects relevant to the field of geography all over the world.

Subjects: Grants are given for basic research in the sciences pertinent to geography. These sciences include, but are not limited to, projects in geography, anthropology, archaeology, astronomy, general biology, botany, ecology, ethnology, geology, glaciology, marine biology, mineralogy, oceanography, paleontology, and zoology (including its many branches such as entomology, ornithology, mammalogy, primatology, and ethology).

Support may also be provided for projects in the above fields that depend on exploration.

Value: Grants may vary in amount, depending upon the need and nature of the project. Normally, awards range from a few hundred dollars to a few thousand. Very occasionally a Grant for as much as US$100,000 has been made. The Society's annual budget for research approximately US$2,500,000.

Tenable for one year. Where a project requires two or more years the investigator may apply again after submitting a report on the use made of the Grant in the first year.

Eligibility: Open to investigators of any nationality who hold earned doctor's degrees and are associated with institutions of higher leaning or other scientific and educational non-profit organizations, such as museums. Occasionally Grants are awarded to exceptionally well-qualified graduate students or scientific workers who do not have research degrees or who are not associated with a university but who do have full qualifications for research on a scientific project of significance.

Note: The investigator in writing for request forms should state the nature of his program briefly.

Closing date: Applications may be submitted at any time. The Committee meets approximately ten times annually to consider applications.

Further information from:
Edwin W. Snider, Secretary
Committee for Research and Exploration
National Geographic Society
17th and M Streets, N.W.
Washington, D.C. 20036
U.S.A.

[1451]

NATIONAL HEALTH AND MEDICAL RESEARCH COUNCIL *(Australia)*

Medical and Dental Postgraduate Research Scholarships

Subjects: Medicine and dentistry: training in research, including studies for higher degrees.

No. offered: Approximately 60 Scholarships annually.

Value: Stipends vary, and are in the range of A$10,145 to A$11,598.

Tenable in Australia for one year, renewable for one or more years, subject to suitable progress reports.

Eligibility: Open to medical or dental graduates of Australian universities. Candidates are expected to have made prior arrangements with the heads of the departments or institutions in which they propose to study.

Not confirmed for 1983.

Further information from:
Secretary
National Health and Medical Research Council
P.O. Box 100
Woden, A.C.T.
Australia 2606

[1452]

NATIONAL HEALTH AND MEDICAL RESEARCH COUNCIL *(Australia)*

C.J. Martin Travelling Fellowships

Subjects: Medical, dental or related fields of research: specific work projects overseas under nominated advisors.

No. offered: Approximately three Fellowships annually.

Value: Stipends range from A$16,291 to A$21,401, plus return tourist air fare for the Fellow and his dependents if they return to Australia within one month of completion of the Fellowship. In addition, an annual travel allowance of A$300 and living allowance of A$200 are provided as well as an annual family allowance of A$600 for the Fellow's wife and A$300 for each dependent child (United Kingdom and Europe) or A$800 for the Fellow's wife and A$500 for each dependent child. A rent allowance of A$200 per month is also applicable in North America.

Tenable normally for three years, of which the first two are to be spent overseas and the third in Australia.

Eligibility: Open to persons who are preferably less than 35 years of age, and who have had more than five years of postdoctoral experience in medical, dental or related fields of research in Australia. Fellowships are normally awarded to workers intending to follow a research career in Australia.

Note: Annual reports are expected, as well as a report on the intended program for the following year. A full report of the work undertaken during the tenure of the Fellowship must be submitted to the Council within three months after completion of the Fellowship.

Not confirmed for 1983.

Further information from:
Secretary
National Health and Medical Research Council
P.O. Box 100
Woden, A.C.T.
Australia 2606

[1453]

NATIONAL HEALTH AND MEDICAL RESEARCH COUNCIL *(Australia)*

Public Health Travelling Fellowships

Subjects: Public health; postgraduate study abroad related to the candidate's work and speciality.

No. offered: Approximately four Fellowships annually.

Value: Not to exceed A$10,000 for a Fellowship of twelve months.

Tenable outside Australia for a study tour period not exceeding twelve months.

Eligibility: Open to all graduates and qualified para-medical and nursing personnel working and experienced in the field of public health in Australia.

Note: The granting of a Fellowship is conditional upon the employing authority maintaining the recipient's salary, allowances, and service benefits for the duration of the Fellowship.

A report of the study tour must be submitted to the Council within three months of returning to Australia.

Not confirmed for 1983.

Further information from:
Secretary
National Health and Medical Research Council
P.O. Box 100
Woden, A.C.T.
Australia 2606

[1454]

NATIONAL HEALTH AND MEDICAL RESEARCH COUNCIL *(Australia)*

Research Fellowships in Applied Health Sciences

Purpose: To assist appropriately qualified younger persons, within a definite period of time, to acquire research skills through study and observation, in approved research and teaching institutions both in Australia and overseas.

Subjects: Training in research methods and their application to medicine; training in scientific research methods, including those of the social and behavioral sciences which can be applied to clinical or community medicine. These areas might include research into allergic diseases, biostatistics, clinical aspects of surgery, dermatology, economics and evaluation of health care or health services, epidemiology, family studies, genetics, human nutrition, and psychiatry.

No. offered: At the Council's discretion.

Value: Within the range of A$15,000 to A$21,000. Return economy air fare for the Fellow and his dependants for travel to overseas centres. In addition, Fellows will receive a travel allowance of A$300 per annum and a cost of living allowance of A$200 per annum. Family allownces are as follows: Fellowships in Europe and the United Kingdom—$600 per annum for spouse and A$300 per annum for each dependant child; Fellowships in the United States and Canada—A$800 per annum for spouse and A$500 for each dependant child. A$200 per month rent allowance may be where applicable. All Fellows may receive an additional allowance equivalent to compulsory fees for laboratory services upon the approval of the Chairman of the Council.

Tenable in institutions approved by the Council, such as teaching hospitals, universities and research institutions, for a period of up to three years, of which the first two may be spent overseas and the third in Australia. Fellowships must be taken up not later than 31st March of the year following the award.

Eligibility: Open to graduates in all relevant fields. In considering applications the Council places emphasis on the applied value of the proposed research training and preference is given to persons who already have research experience and are seeking advanced study not available in Australia.

Note: A Fellow must submit to the Council an annual report on the research work done during the year.

Not confirmed for 1983.

Further information from:
Secretary
National Health and Medical Research
    Council
P.O. Box 100
Woden, A.C.T.
Australia 2606

[1455]

NATIONAL HEALTH AND MEDICAL RESEARCH COUNCIL *(Australia)*

Research Project Grants

Grants are made to an institution for the support of a scientific investigation in any field of medicine or dentistry in Australia which is proposed by a staff member of that institution; the investigation having objectives of mutual interest to the Council, the recipient institution, and the investigator. Research Project Grants so supported vary from small, short-term, single objective studies, to very large programme projects devoted to a major medical or health problem.

Note: The number of awards and amount of each award depends on the availability of funds, but on average new and renewed awards total approximately A$7,500,000 per annum for the support of approximately 450 medical research projects at Australian universities, research institutes and hospitals.
The Grants may provide salaries for research workers and assistants, equipment, supplies, maintenance and other specific expenses.

Not confirmed for 1983.

Further information from:
Secretary
National Health and Medical Research
    Council
P.O. Box 100
Woden, A.C.T.
Australia 2606

[1456]

NATIONAL HEART FOUNDATION OF AUSTRALIA

Warren McDonald International Fellowship

Purpose: To add a special viewpoint or skill not available in Australia to an active Australian research group.

Subjects: Relating to the cardiovascular field.

Value: Up to A$30,995 per annum (as of 1981), plus allowances for travel and dependents. The Foundation also makes a grant of up to A$1,000 to cover departmental expenses.

Tenable in Australian universities, hospitals or reserach institutions for one year.

Eligibility: Open to senior research workers of proven ability in the cardiovascular field, whose normal employment is outside Australia.

Note: Candidates must be nominated by the head of the host department or institution and may not apply directly to the Foundation.

Closing date: 31st May.

Further information from:
Director
National Heart Foundation of Australia
P.O. Box 2
Woden, A.C.T.
Australia 2606

[1457]

NATIONAL HEART FOUNDATION OF AUSTRALIA

Overseas Clinical Fellowships

Purpose: To provide opportunities for advanced clincial training in cardiovascular medicine and surgery.

Value: In the United Kingdom—£7,600 per annum, plus dependants' allowances £600 per annum (spouse) and £300 per annum (child). In the United States—US$16,000 per annum, plus dependants' allowances of US$1,200 per annum (spouse) and US$600 per annum (child).
All stated amounts are as of 1981.

Tenable at approved institutions outside Australia for one year.

Eligibility: Open to persons whose usual residence is in Australia and who have had appropriate experience and possess qualifications suitable for advanced clinical training in cardiovascular medicine and surgery.

Note: Candidates must make their own arrangements with the Institution concerned for acceptance and the provision of a suitable programme of training.

Closing date: 31st May.

Further information from:
Director
National Heart Foundation of Australia
P.O. Box 2
Woden, A.C.T.
Australia 2606

[1458]

NATIONAL HEART FOUNDATION OF AUSTRALIA

Research Fellowships

Subjects: Clinical or basic medical sciences related to cardiovascular problems.

Value: Ranges between US$19,821 and US$26,036 (as of 1981).

Tenable at approved institutions in Australia for one or two years, with the possibility of extension to a maximum of five years.

Eligibility: Open to graduates whose usual residence is in Australia and who have shown promise of capacity for research.

Closing date: 31st May.

Further information from:
Director
National Heart Foundation of Australia
P.O. Box 2
Woden, A.C.T.
Australia 2606

[1459]

NATIONAL HEART FOUNDATION OF AUSTRALIA

Overseas Research Fellowships

Subjects: Clinical or basic medical sciences related to cardiovascular problems.

Value: In the United Kingdom—£7,600 per annum, plus allowances for travel and dependents at the rate of £600 per annum (spouse) and £300 per annum (child). In the United States—US$16,000 per annum, plus allowances for travel and dependents at the rate of US$1,200 per annum (spouse) and US$600 per annum (child).

Tenable for two years, the first year at suitable institutions overseas, the second at an approved institution in Australia.

Eligibility: Open to persons normally resident in Australia with at least two years postgraduate experience and significant achievement in research.

Note: Fellowships are awarded on the understanding that the Fellow will return to Australia to continue his career upon completion of the Fellowship.

Closing date: 31st May.

Further information from:
Director
National Heart Foundation of Australia
P.O. Box 2
Woden, A.C.T.
Australia 2606

[1460]

NATIONAL HEART FOUNDATION OF AUSTRALIA

Senior Research Fellowships

Subjects: Clinical or basic medical sciences related to cardiovascular problems.

Tenable at approved institutions in Australia for three years, with the possibility of extension to a maximum of five years.

Eligibility: Open to graduates with substantial experience and proven ability in research, whose usual residence is in Australia.

Note: Grants-in-Aid for medical research and research training are available to non-profit institutions in Australia. Grants may cover: (a) salaries for full-time or part-time research personnel other than the responsible investigator; (b) the cost of scientific apparatus; and (c) running expenses such as chemicals, glassware, animals and other necessary specified items.

Closing date: 31st May.

Further information from:
Director
National Heart Foundation of Australia
P.O. Box 2
Woden, A.C.T.
Australia 2606

[1461]

NATIONAL HEART FOUNDATION OF NEW ZEALAND

Fellowships, Project Grants, Travel Grants and Grants-in-Aid

Subjects: Any aspect of cariovascular disease including research, rehabilitation and education.

Tenable in New Zealand, but Travel Grants and Clinical Training Fellowships may be held abroad.

Eligibility: Normally only New Zealand graduates are eligible.

Note: The number and monetary value of awards varies according to determination of the Scientific Committee and within an annual budget. Candidates should apply to the Foundation for the publication "A Guide to Applicants for Research and Other Grants."

Closing date: Project Grants and Fellowships-1st April, 1st September; Travel Grants and Grants-in-Aid—1st February, 1st April, 1st September

Further information from:
Medical Director
National Heart Foundation of New Zealand
Princess Margaret Hospital
Christchurch 2
New Zealand

[1462]

NATIONAL HEMOPHILIA FOUNDATION
(U.S.A.)

Judith Graham Pool Postgraduate Research Fellowships in Hemophilia

Purpose: To support post-graduate studies by young investigators in clinical and/or basic science aimed at furthering understanding, or improving management, of the hemophilias and von Willebrand's Disease.

Subjects: Hemophilia-related research.

No. offered: Varies annually.

Value: Up to US$15,000 per annum, including up to 10% institutional sharing. In addition, up to US$500 is given for domestic travel. Payments are made directly to the sponsoring institution.

Tenable for one year at appropriate sponsoring institutions throughout the United States. Fellowships may be renewed for a second year of research if merited.

Eligibility: Open to U.S. citizens who are postgraduates and currently engaged in, or intend to pursue research related to hemophilia. Preference will be given to investigators whose proposals aim to further the understanding of, or improve the management of the hemophilias. Preference will also be shown to candidates having prior experience in the area of their proposal.

Note: This program is not intended for established investigators.

Closing date: 15th December, for notification by 15th February.

Further information from:
National Hemophilia Foundation
19 West 34th Street, Room 1204
New York, New York 10001
U.S.A.

[1463]

NATIONAL HISTORICAL SOCIETY
(U.S.A.)

NHS Book Prize

An annual Prize of US$1,000 is offered to a new author, for a book concerned with some aspect of the American experience. To be eligible, the work must be the author's first published book and be published during the calendar year preceding that in which the award is given. Entries should be non-fiction, and may include biographies and general histories, as well as books dealing with the nation's past from its beginnings to recent times (no manuscripts, theses, or dissertations are eligible). Submissions of three copies can be made by authors or publishers. *Closing date:* 31st May.

Bell I. Wiley Prize: A biennial Prize of US$1,000 if offered for a distinguished work in the field of the civil war and reconstruction. Submissions must be original non-fiction books, published in the preceding two years (no theses, manuscripts, or dissertations are eligible). Three copies must be submitted by either the authors themselves or their publishers. *Closing date:* 1st March.

Note: Books qualifying for both Prizes may be submitted for both.

Further information from:
National Historical Society
2245 Kohn Road
Harrisburg, Pennsylvania 17110
U.S.A.

[1464]

NATIONAL HOME FASHIONS LEAGUE, INC. *(U.S.A.)*

Design Fellowships

Purpose: To encourage arts, crafts and design students to design for the interior furnishings industry and to bring their work to its attention.

No. offered: One national award annually, and several local chapter awards.

Value: National award of US$2,000; chapter awards vary from US$50 to US$500.

Eligibility: Open to any student enrolled as a second, third or fourth year undergraduate or graduate student of a state accredited college or university, or a second year student of a two-year college.

Note: The winning entry from each chapter is judged by a national jury.
Award recipients are requested to be present at the Annual Conference for presentation. All expenses are paid by the NHFL.

Closing dates: Chapter advise applicants of deadline dates.

Further information from:
National Home Fashions League, Inc.
Design Fellowship Program
P.O. Box 58945
Dallas, Texas 75258
U.S.A.

[1465]

NATIONAL INSTITUTE FOR ARCHITECTURAL EDUCATION *(U.S.A.)*

William Van Alen Architect Memorial Fellowship

Purpose: For further study, either towards an advanced degree or a research project of some architectural nature, or for travel and study in countries other than one's country of origin.

No. offered: Eight awards annually.

Value: First prize—US$12,000; second prize—US$5,000; third prize—US$2,500; five honorable mention prizes of US$200 each.

Tenable for travel and/or study for twelve months (first prize); for six months (second prize); for two months (third prize).

Eligibility: Open to any student enrolled in an architectural or engineering school, or equivalent thereof, full or part time, working towards a professional degree.

Note: The Fellowship is awarded on the basis of designs submitted by the candidates. The nature of the design project is specified each year by the institute.

Closing date: 1st June.

Further information from:
National Institute for Architectural Education
139 East 52nd Street
New York, New York 10022
U.S.A.

[1466]

NATIONAL INSTITUTE FOR ARCHITECTURAL EDUCATION *(U.S.A.)*

Lloyd Warren Fellowship

Purpose: For further study, either towards an advanced degree or a research project of some architectural nature, or for travel and study in countries other than one's country of origin.

No. offered: Three Fellowships annually.

Value: First prize—US$12,000; second prize—US$6,000; third prize—US$3,500.

Tenable for travel and/or study outside the United States for twelve months, six months, and three months, respectively.

Eligibility: Candidates must have, or anticipate receiving their architectural degrees from a United States school of architecture during a three and one-half year period, ending in December of the year in which the Fellowship is awarded.

Note: The Fellowship is awarded on the basis of designs submitted by candidates. The nature of the design project is specified each year by the Institute.
In addition, the *Albert A. Arbeit Memorial Prize* of US$100 will be awarded for an outstanding presentation.

Closing date: 1st June.

Further information from:
National Institute for Architectural Education
139 Each 52nd Street
New York, New York 10022
U.S.A.

[1467]

NATIONAL INSTITUTE OF CARDIOLOGY IGNACIO CHÁVEZ *(Mexico City)*

Fellowships

Each year the Institute offers a total of 50 Fellowships in the field of cardiology: twelve Fellowships, tenable for two years, are awarded to cardiological residents; three Fellowships, tenable for three years, to surgical residents; one Fellowship in anatomopathology, tenable for two years; four Fellowships in anesthesiology, tenable for one year; one Fellowship for a nephrological resident, tenable for two years; and 30 Fellowships for full-time voluntary assistants, tenable for at least one year.
Resident Fellows receive a monthly salary of at least US$600 during the first year of tenure, plus board, lodging and uniforms. Voluntary assistants receive only medical education and are required to support themselves through grants from other sources.
Candidates, who may be nationals of any country, should be under 35 years of age and have had two or three years of internal medical experience in a high-level hospital.
Residents and full-time voluntary assistants may begin their Fellowships 1st March. Voluntary assistants may also being on 1st September.

Further information from:
Jefe de la División de Enseñanza
Instituto Nacional de Cardiologia Ignacio Chávez
Juan Badiano 1, Tlalpan 14080
Mexico, D.F.

[1468]

NATIONAL INSTITUTE FOR THE FOODSERVICE INDUSTRY *(U.S.A.)*

Golden Plate Scholarships: Approximately 100 Awards of US$600 each are given annually to students enrolled or about to enroll in a full-time acedmic program in hotel/restaurant management, dietetics, and other foodservice related curricula. Programs must lead to a baccalaureate, associate or graduate degree. Scholarships are for one acadmeic year; renewable. *Closing date:* 1st April.

NIFI-Heinz Graduate Degree Fellowships: One Fellowship of US$2,000, one Fellowship of U.S.$1,200, and five Fellowships of U.S.$1,000 each are awarded awarded annually on a competitive basis . Open to teachers or administrators undertaking an academic program leading to a master's or doctor's degree to improve skills in teaching foodservice courses or administering foodservice career education. Programs should be on a full-time or substantial part-time basis. *Closing date:* 1st April.

NIFI-Heinz Scholarships: Seven *Senior College Awards* of US$2,600 each, tenable for full-time study over a two year period, and three *Junior/Community College Awards* of U.S.$1,900 each, tenable over a two year period, are awarded to students of food service management. Scholarships are judged on the basis of motivation toward an industry career, academic records, and financial need. *Closing date:* 1st April.

NRA/NIFI Teacher Work-Study Grants: Thirty Grants of US$1,500 each are awarded annually on a competitive basis to teachers and administrators who wish to obtain work experience in the foodservice industry. Applicants should be undertaking work experience programs to improve their qualifications for teaching foodservice courses. *Closing date:* 1st November.

Note: Application forms are available after 1st September.

Further information from:
National Institute for the Foodservice Industry
20 North Wacker Drive, Suite 2620
Chicago, Illinois 60606
U.S.A.

[1469]

NATIONAL INSTITUTE OF HEALTH
(Rome)

Fellowships

Purpose: To provide the opportunity for postgraduate research and study.

Subjects: Epidemiology and biostatistics, bacterial and viral diseases, non-infectious pathology, parasitology, veterinary medicine, cell biology and immunology, biomedical technology, pharmacology, drug chemistry, foods, toxicology, environmental hygiene, radiation, and occupational hygiene.

No. offered: Varies annually.

Value: 350,000 lire, paid monthly.

Tenable at the Instituto Superiore di Sanità, Rome, for six to ten months.

Eligibility: Open to university graduates from all countries who have already had some research experience.

Note: Competition announcement for the Fellowships are published annually in *Gazzetta Ufficiale della Reupbblica Italiana*, available through all Italian Embassies.

Further information from:
Instituto Superiore di Sanità
Viale Regina Elena, 299
00161 Rome
Italy

[1470]

NATIONAL INSTITUTE ON MENTAL RETARDATION *(Canada)*

Awards for Graduate Students

Purpose: To provide support to promising graduate students who wish to involve themselves in the field of mental retardation.

Subjects: Tenable in a wide area of study, including sociology, psychology, education, physical education, etc. Students in medical schools, law schools, business administration and other disciplines unrelated to mental retardation who have an interest in applying their professional training to the field are encouraged to apply.

Value: Can$1,500 per annum.

Tenable at a recognized Canadian university for one year.

Eligibility: Open to Canadian citizens or landed immigrants who have been accepted into a full-time graduate program at a Canadian university. Applicants must be recommended by the Provincial Association for the Mentally Retarded in their province. Candidates must state their intention to pursue a career in their selected field in Canada.

Note: Applicants may apply directly to their Provincial Association for the Mentally Retarded or through their Local Association. Provincial Associations must send their recommendations to the Institute no later than 30 May. Applications are accepted directly from students or from the faculty on the student's behalf.

Closing date: 15th February.

Further information from:
Secretary, Awards Committee
National Institute on Mental Retardation
Kinsmen NIMR Building
York University Campus
4700 Keele Street
Downsview, Ontario
Canada M3J 1P3

[1471]

NATIONAL INSTITUTE ON MENTAL RETARDATION *(Canada)*

Research Grants

Purpose: To provide support to promising students in a doctoral program doing research in the field of mental retardation.

Subjects: Tenable in a wide area of study relating to human services and mental retardation, including sociology, psychology, education, physical education, etc.

Value: Up to Can$8,000 per annum.

Tenable at a recognized Canadian university.

Eligibility: Open to Canadian citizens or landed immigrants who have been accepted into a full-time graduate program at a Canadian university. Candidates must have definate research projects supported by an academic advisor.

Note: Applications are accepted directly from the student or from the faculty on the student's behalf.

Closing date: 30th April.

Further information from:
Secretary, Awards Committee
National Institute on Mental Retardation
Kinsmen NIMR Building
York University Campus
4700 Keele Street
Downsview, Ontario
Canada M3J 1P3

[1472]

NATIONAL INSTITUTE FOR METALLURGY *(South Africa)*

Bursaries for Postgraduate Study

Subjects: Chemical engineering, electrical engineering (light current and electronics), chemistry (with the emphasis on inorganic, organic, physical, or analytical chemistry), metallurgy (extraction and physical), mineralogy, geology, or physics.

Value: Postgraduate—(Scheme A) an initial value of between R7,650 and R10,440 per annum, depending on academic qualifications and appropriate postgraduate experience—(Contract Researcher Scheme) an initial value of $6,210 per annum, depending on academic qualifications and appropriate postgraduate experience. Annual increments are given in both postgraduate schemes.

Tenable at any South African university, unless research facilities are not available, for up to two years for an M.Sc. degree and up to two and one-half years for a Ph.D. degree (postgraduate).

Eligibility: Postgraduate—open to graduates of any nationality who possess an appropriate four-year degree or higher qualification. A knowledge of English is essential.

Further information from:
Head of Personnel
National Institute for Metallurgy
Private Bag X3015
Randburg 2125
South Africa

[1473]

NATIONAL INSTITUTE OF NEUROLOGICAL AND COMMUNICATIVE DISORDERS AND STROKE *(U.S.A.)*
National Institutes of Health

Research Project Grants

Subjects: Normal and pathological aspects of the neurological and communicative sciences and of the special senses such as taste, smell, touch, etc.

No. offered: 300 Grants annually.

Value: Average about US$75,000 per project per annum; payments are made quarterly.

Tenable at any university or non-profit research institution. Grants are usually made for three to five years and are renewable indefinitely on a competitive basis.

Eligibility: Candidates, of any nationality, must submit applications through a university or other non-profit research institution. The application is reviewed by a committee of experts and, if approved, it is given a numerical rating on scientific merit. Awards are made based on scientific merit to the extent that funds are available.

Further information from:
  Extramural Activities Program
  National Institute of Neurological and Communicative Disorders and Stroke
  National Institutes of Health
  Bethesda, Maryland 20205
  U.S.A.

[1474]

NATIONAL INSTITUTE OF NUCLEAR SCIENCE AND TECHNOLOGY *(France)*

Postgraduate Courses: Grants

Subjects: Analytical chemistry, data processing, metallurgy, reactor physics, mechanics of structure, production economics.

No. offered: Three Grants annually.

Value: FF3,00 per month.

Tenable at the National Institute of Nuclear Science and Technology (Centre For Nuclear Studies of Saclay), Gif-sur-Yvette, for nine months (October-June).

Eligibility: Open to persons from member countries of Unesco with a qualification equivalent to the French M.Sc. degree. Instruction is given in French.

Note: These Grants are awarded by the French Atomic Energy Commission in collaboration with Unesco and the French National Commission for Unesco. Application must be made through the French embassies of member countries of Unesco. Candidates should contact the embassy's counsellor for cultural and technical cooperation Grants.

Closing date: 15th April.

Further information from:
  Institut national des sciences et techniques nucléaires
  Cen-saclay
  91191 Gif s/ Yvette Cedex
  France

[1475]

NATIONAL JEWISH WELFARE BOARD *(U.S.A.)*

National Scholarships

Subjects: Health and physical education.

No. offered: Variable.

Eligibility: Open to United States and Canadian citizens who hold a B.A. degree in health and physical education and plan to acquire a master's degree.
Recipients must make a commitment to accept employment in any Jewish Welfare Board-affiliated Jewish community center or YM-YWHA for a period of two years following completion of their Master's degree studies.

Closing date: 1st February.

Further information from:
  Scholarship Department
  JWB
  15 East 26th Street
  New York, New York 10010
  U.S.A.

[1476]

NATIONAL JEWISH WELFARE BOARD *(U.S.A.)*

National Scholarships

Purpose: To enable students of social work to concentrate their studies in the social group work method in preparation for practice in a Jewish community center or YM-YWHA.

Value: US$3,000 annually.

Tenable for one year; renewable for a further year, subject to satisfactory progress.

Eligibility: Open to United States and Canadian citizens who have a B.A. degree. Scholarships and Fellowships are granted on the basis of achievement and leadership potential.

Note: Recipients must make a commitment to accept employment in any Jewish Welfare Board-affiliated Jewish community center or YM-YWHA in North America for a period of two years following completion of their studies.

Information regarding Local Scholarships can be obtained from:
Scholarship Department
JWB
15 East 26th Street
New York, New York 10010
U.S.A.

[1477]

NATIONAL KIDNEY FOUNDATION
(U.S.A.)

Postdoctoral Fellowships

Subjects: Research and training in the field of kidney function and disease.

No. offered: Approximately 40 Fellowships annually.

Value: US$13,500 per annum.

Tenable for one year; renewable for a second year.

Eligibility: Open to qualified investigators of any nationality who are interested in a career in kidney research, and will not have had more than one year of research training at the time the award is activated.

Note: Applications should be made in the form of a proposal (15 copies required) which should contain the following: (a) a curriculum vitae and list of publications of the principal investigators and other professional personnel involved; (b) a concise description of the proposed research (including aims, significance, methodolgoy and relevant research); (c) a list of other current and pending financial support.

Closing date: 1st October.

Further information from:
Research and Fellowship Grants Committee
National Kidney Foundation
2 Park Avenue
New York, New York 10016
U.S.A.

[1478]

NATIONAL KIDNEY FOUNDATION OF SOUTH AFRICA

Charlotte Roberts Trust Kidney Research Award

The Award of R2,000 is intended to sponsor a suitable person on a short-term overseas visit devoted to research or study in the field of kidney disease. Suitably qualified medical practitioners registered in South Africa may apply. In determining the Award, the value of the proposed research project to kidney research in South Africa is taken into consideration. The Award will not be disbursed until the Foundation is satisfied that the successful applicant has been accepted by an appropriate research institute or university department, and the recipient must undertake to return to South Africa on the termination of the project.

Applications should be admitted by the end of March and should include: (a) summary of the proposed study; (b) evidence of suitability to undertake the research programme; (c) names and addresses of two referees.

Further information from:
Honorary Secretary
National Kidney Foundation of South Africa
P.O. Box 5706
Johannesburg 2000
South Africa

[1479]

NATIONAL LEUKEMIA ASSOCIATION
(U.S.A.)

Research Grants and Fellowships

Subjects: Leukemia: studies that will contribute to a better understanding of pathophysiology and treatment.

No. offered: Six new awards annually

Tenable in the United States for two years, subject to approval of a progress report submitted at the end of the first year.

Value: Up to US$20,000 per annum payable in a lump sum. Institutional and overhead charges must be paid out of this funding.

Eligibility: Open to suitably qualified researchers who will undertake their work in the United States.

Closing date: 30th September.

Further information from:
National Leukemia Association, Inc.
Lower Concourse, Roosevelt Field
Garden City, New York 11530
U.S.A.

[1480]

NATIONAL MEDICAL FELLOWSHIPS, INC. *(U.S.A.)*

Financial Assistance Program for Minority Groups

Purpose: To provide financial assistance to minorities currently under-represented in the medical profession to attend medical school for first or second year study, leading to an M.D. degree.

No. offered: Approximately 1,000 awards annually.

Eligibility: Open to United States citizens who are members of the following minority groups: American Blacks, Mexican Americans, Puerto Ricans, and American Indians. Candidates must have been admitted to a United States medical school and must be in need of financial assistance. Awards are given only to students in the first and second years of medical school.

Note: Because of NMF's limited resources, the grants are not large enough to meet the student's total financial need. All applicants should apply through the financial aid office of the medical school for additional support.

Closing dates: 15th August, except in cases of late acceptance to medical school; 15th March for application for second year study.

Further information from:
Scholarship Department
National Medical Fellowships, Inc.
250 West 57th Street
New York, New York 10019
U.S.A.

[1481]

NATIONAL MENTAL HEALTH ASSOCIATION, INC. *(U.S.A.)*

Clifford W. Beers Award

An annual Award of US$500 is given for a major contribution on a nationwide scale, aimed at helping those suffering from mental or emotional disorders, and aiding in the general education of the public regarding the positive aspects of mental health. This effort must be made by a past or present recipient of mental health services, and should include the stating of a position, not necessarily popular, and a commitment involving a readiness to incur risk to career, finances, and public acceptance.

Not confirmed for 1983.

Further information from:
National Mental Health Association, Inc.
1800 North Kent Street
Arlington, Virginia 22209
U.S.A.

[1482]

NATIONAL MULTIPLE SCLEROSIS SOCIETY *(U.S.A.)*

Junior Faculty Awards

Purpose: Awards are offered to highly qualified candidates, who have concluded their research training and have begun academic careers as independent investigators in an area of the neurosciences related to multiple sclerosis.

No. offered: A limited number of Awards, annually.

Value: Up to US$25,000 towards salary and US$25,000 towards research in the first year, and up to US$35,000 towards salary and US$35,000 towards research in the final year. Fringe benefits will be paid by the Society at the rate current in the sponsoring institution, on that part of the salary contributed by the Society. The institution itself is expected to contribute at least 25 per cent of the total salary of the candidate.

Tenable at an approved university, professional school or research institute for five years, not renewable.

Eligibility: Candidates must hold a doctoral degree and have had sufficient research training at the pre- or postdoctoral levels to be capable of independent research. Individuals who have already carried out independent research for more than five years are ineligible.

Note: The candidate will not be an employee of the Society, but rather of the institution. It is expected that the institution will develop plans for continuing the candidate's appointment and for continued salary support beyond the five-year period of the award.

Fellows may not supplement their salary through private practice or consultation, nor accept another concurrent award.

The grantee institution holds title to all equipment purchased with award funds.

Closing date: 15th January for awards to become effective 1st July or 1st September.

Further information from:
National Multiple Sclerosis Society
Research Programs Department
205 East 42nd Street
New York, New York 10017
U.S.A.

[1483]

NATIONAL MULTIPLE SCLEROSIS SOCIETY *(U.S.A.)*

Postdoctoral Fellowships

Subject: Training in research applicable to multiple sclerosis.

Value: Stipend varies according to professional status, previous training, experience, accomplishments in research, and to the payscale of the institution in which the training is provided. It is expected that the stipend requested will provide the applicant's total remuneration. Fellowships are not available to supplement otherwise inadequate salaries.

Tenable at institutions of the candidate's choice for any requisite period of time for the training proposed, but seldom for more than two years.

Awards for a term in excess of one year will be terminated automatically unless an acceptable report of progress and recommendation for continuation are received separately from both the trainee and his mentor within 90 days after each twelve-month period of the grant.

Eligibility: Open to unusually promising recipients of M.D. and/or Ph.D. degrees. The program of training to be supported by the grant must materially enhance the likelihood of the trainee performing meaningful and independent research on multiple sclerosis, and obtaining a suitable position which will enable him to do so. Foreign nationals are welcome to apply.

Besides its attention to younger researchers, the Society will also consider applications from established investigators who seek support to obtain specialized training in some field in which they are not expert, when such training will materially enhance their capacity to conduct more meaningful research on multiple sclerosis.

Note: These Fellowships are awarded to support training in research and are not awarded to support clinical training directed towards the completion of internship and/or specialty board certification. Similarly, they cannot be used to provide support for individuals whose primary responsibility is teaching and/or service, although Fellows are encouraged to spend a reasonable amount of their time (up to 10%) in teaching.

Fellows are not considered as employees of the Society but rather of the institution where the training is provided; and the Fellowship is to be administered in accordance with the prevailing policies of the sponsoring institution.

It is the responsibility of the applicant to make all arrangements for his training with the mentor and institution of his choice. No Postdoctoral Fellowship may be held concurrently with any other fellowship or employment.

Closing date: 15th January for grants to become effective 1st July.

Further information from:
National Multiple Sclerosis Society
Research Programs Department
205 East 42nd Street
New York, New York 10017
U.S.A.

[1484]

NATIONAL MULTIPLE SCLEROSIS SOCIETY *(U.S.A.)*

Research Grants

Purpose: To stimulate, coordinate, and support research, fundamental or applied, clinical or non-clinical in nature, aimed at elucidating the cause, prevention, alleviation and cure of multiple sclerosis.

Value: Funds may be used to pay in whole or in part the salaries of associate professional personnel, technical assistants and other non-professional personnel in proportion to their time spent directly on the project. Salaries are in accordance with the prevailing policies of the grantee institution. If requested, other expenses, such as travel costs and fringe benefits, may also be paid.

Tenable Grants are awarded to an institution to support the research of the principal investigator, for periods of up to five years.

Eligibility: Open to suitably qualified investigators.

Note: Scientific equipment and supplies bought with Grant funds become the property of the grantee institution. Regular progress reports are required, and appropriate publication is expected.

Closing dates: 15th January and 15th July for Grants to become effectve 1st July or 1st January respectively.

Further information from:
National Multiple Sclerosis Society
Research Programs Department
205 East 42nd Street
New York, New York 10017
U.S.A.

[1485]

NATIONAL MUSEUM OF MAN *(Ottawa)*

Financial support by means of service contracts is available to professional scholars for research in Canadian studies. Preference is given to research in archaeology, ethnology, ethnolinguistics, folk culture and social, economic and military history.

Further information from:
Directorate
National Museum of Man
Metcalfe and McLeod Streets
Ottawa, Ontario
Canada K1A OM8

[1486]

NATIONAL OPERA INSTITUTE *(U.S.A.)*

Apprenticeships in Opera Administration and Production: Approximately 10 grants are given annually to provide one-to-one training of young professionals with an experienced administrator. Work opportunities will involve such fields as stage direction, design, administration and coaching. Apprenticeships are tenable for periods of four months to one year, with a monthly stipend of US$750.

Assistance to Young Opera Singer: Approximately 10 grants are given annually to provide financial assistance to young professional opera singers for specific purposes necessary for the advancement of their careers. Assistance of up to US$5,000 per annum is given only where financial need is demonstrated.

Note: Extensive guidelines exist for both awards.

Further information from:
National Opera Institute
John F. Kennedy Center
Washington, D.C. 20566
U.S.A.

[1487]

NATIONAL ORCHESTRAL ASSOCIATION *(U.S.A.)*

Fellowships

Purpose: To prepare instrumental musicians for positions in symphony orchestras.

Subjects: Intensive training in orchestral repertoire; sight-reading and performance, including symphonic, ballet and opera literature, as well as a study of contemporary music and accompanying techniques.

No. offered: Approximately 100 fellowships annually; approximately 30 to 40 new awards are offered annually, depending upon vacancies.

Value: US$1,050 to US$1,750, depending on year, position and advancement, paid monthly for a seven-month orchestral season (October to May).

Tenable in New York City for training in the orchestra of the National Orchestral Association. Fellowships may be renewed for up to three years, which is the extent of the training period.

Eligibility: Based on auditions given each fall for current openings. Fellows are accepted on musical and technical competence. There are no restrictions in regard to race, color, or national origin.

Closing date: 10th September.

Further information from:
National Orchestral Association
111 West 57th Street
Suite 1400
New York, New York 10019
U.S.A.

[1488]

NATIONAL OSTEOPATHIC FOUNDATION *(U.S.A.)*

Mead Johnson Awards for Graduate Training

Purpose: To provide financial assistance to osteopathic graduates toward the completion of a year of full-time residency in training.

Subjects: Residency training in any American Osteopathic Association approved specialty.

No. offered: 14 Awards annually.

Value: US$1,500, paid in quarterly installments.

Tenable in any osteopathic hospital approved for training.

Eligibility: Applicants must have graduates from an osteopathic college not more than four years prior to date of application.

Note: Arrangement for graduate training should be made through the Director of Medical Education at the hospital where the training is to take place.

Not confirmed for 1983.

Further information from:
National Osteopathic Foundation
212 East Ohio Street
Chicago, Illinois 60611
U.S.A.

[1489]

NATIONAL RADIO ASTRONOMY OBSERVATORY *(U.S.A.)*.

Postdoctoral Research Associateships

Purpose: To provide outstanding opportunities to qualified young Ph.Ds who wish to devote full time to research.

Areas of present interest include: theoretical and observational studies of discrete radio sources, galaxies, the interstellar medium, planets; millimeter wave instrumentation and research; interferometry, aperture, synthesis, large antenna arrays; radio astronomy instrumentation (parametric amplifiers, radiometer systems, cryogenics); data processing, information theory, computer system applications, digitial and online techniques.

Research Associates may formulate and carry out investigations either independently or in collaboration with others. Publication of results is encouraged.

Value: US$17,500 per year plus liberal vacation allowance, authorized travel expenses, moving allowance, etc.

Tenable at the Observatory's centers (Charlottesville, Virginia—headquarters; Green Bank, West Virginia; Sororro, New Mexico) for two years; renewable for a further year.

Eligibility: Open to astronomers, physicists, electrical engineers and computer specialists who have already received a Ph.D. degree.

The initial letter should include a statement of the individual's research interests together with his own appraisal of his qualifications for carrying out research, and the names of at least three references who have been asked to write on behalf of the applicant.

Note: Appointments normally commence in September or October.

Special facilities including a 300-foot diameter radio telescope, a 140-foot fully-steerable telescope, a 36-foot millimeter-wave telescope, a 27-element variable baseline very large array interferometer, various computers including IBM 360/65, Dec 10, Dec 11/70, Vax and Mod Comp, a wide variety of radiometer systems and well-equipped electronics laboratories, as well as skilled technical supporting staffs, are available to Associates.

Closing date: 15th January.

Further information from:
Director
National Radio Astronomy Observatory
Edgemont Road
Charlottesville, Virginia 22901
U.S.A.

[1490]

NATIONAL REHABILITATION COUNSELING ASSOCIATION *(U.S.A.)*

NRCA Counselor-of-the-Year Award: One Award of a National Trophy is presented annually to recognize devoted professional rehabilitation counselors whose outstanding accomplishments are recognized by their peer professionals, supervisors and community. Candidates must be United States citizens employed full-time in counseling and assisting handicapped persons. Candidates are considered without regard to place of employment or professional memberships. On 31st December of each year Counselors are selected on the state level, on 31st January regional winners are chosen, and the national winner is selected on 28th February. The Award is presented at the annual meeting of the Association.

NRCA-AMVETS Auxiliary Scholarships of US$1,000, US$500 and two of US$100 are awarded annually to students enrolled full time in graduate rehabilitation counseling programs. They are open to United States citizens enrolled in graduate programs at universities and colleges offering a master's degree with a major in rehabilitation counseling. Applicants must submit a paper of not more than 1,500 words dealing with the topic, "What is one crucial need in rehabilitation, possible solutions, and your opinion of the 'best solution'?"

Not confirmed for 1983.

Further information from:
National Rehabilitation Counseling
 Association
1522 K Street, N.W.
Washington, D.C. 20005
U.S.A.

[1491]

NATIONAL RESEARCH ADVISORY COUNCIL *(N.Z.)*

Postdoctoral Research Fellowships

Purpose: To enable young scientists from varied backgrounds to work on problems of particular interest to New Zealand.

Subjects: Any subject area catered for by the scientific branches of New Zealand government departments.

No. offered: Up to six Fellowships annually.

Value: NZ$23,520 per annum, adjustable upwards, plus air travel grants to and from New Zealand for the Fellow and his dependents, and travel expenses incurred in connection with the research.

Tenable at any scientific branch of New Zealand government departments for two to three years; may be extended under certain conditions.

Eligibility: Open to graduates possessing a Ph.D. or equivalent degrees, and with some research experience since graduation. A good working knowledge of English is required.

Note: See next entry for application addresses.

Closing date: 1st September.

Address:
Executive Director
National Research Advisory Council
P.O. Box 12240
Wellington
New Zealand

[1492]

NATIONAL RESEARCH ADVISORY COUNCIL *(N.Z.)*

Senior Research Fellowships

Purpose: To enable distinguished overseas scientists to work in some field of particular interest to New Zealand.

Subjects: Any subject area catered for by the scientific branches of New Zealand government departments.

No. offered: Up to six Fellowships annually.

Value: NZ$30,525—NZ$41,566 per annum, adjustable upwards, plus air travel grants to and from New Zealand for the Fellow and spouse and travel expenses incurred in connection with the research.

Tenable at any scientific branches of New Zealand government departments for nine months to one year.

Eligibility: Open to graduates with a Ph.D. or high qualification, and to those who have a distinguished record of scientific research. Awards are intended for research workers who have had professional experience and have published original material. A good working knowledge of English is required.

Application forms may be obtained from: Canada—*New Zealand High Commission, Suite 804, Commonwealth Building, 77 Metcalfe Street, Ottawa K1P 5L6*; New Zealand—*Executive Director, National Research Advisory Council, P.O. Box 12240, Wellington*; United Kingdom—*Senior Scientific Adviser, New Zealand High Commission, New Zealand House, Haymarket, London SW1Y 4TQ*; United States—*New Zealand Embassy, 19 Observatory Circle, N.W., Washington, D.C. 20008*; Australia—*New Zealand High Commission, Commonwealth Avenue, Canberra A.C.T. 2600*; Japan—*New Zealand Embassy, 20—40 Kamiyama-cho, Shibuya-ku, Tokyo 150*, as well as from the Council.

Closing date: 1st September.

Address:
Executive Director
National Research Advisory Council
P.O. Box 12240
Wellington
New Zealand

[1493]

NATIONAL RESEARCH COUNCIL *(U.S.A.)*

National Academy of Sciences
National Academy of Engineering
Institute of Medicine

Research Associateships

Purpose: To provide opportunities for basic and applied research free from administrative duties, in cooperation with selected federal laboratories in the United States, to postdoctoral and in some programs senior postdoctoral scientists and engineers of unusual ability and promise.

Subjects: Chemistry; engineering; physics; mathematics; atmospheric, earth, environmental, life and space sciences.

No. offered: Approximately 250 Awards annually.

Value: Stipends, paid monthly, range from US$22,400 per annum upwards. Stipends are subject to income tax. Grants are also provided for family relocation and limited professional travel during tenure.

Tenable for one year at various Federal laboratories throughout the United States, with the possibility of renewal for a second year.

Eligibility: Open to scientists and engineers who have received the doctorate and, in most cases, to foreign nationals who have demonstrated superior ability for creative research. Senior awards are for candidates with at least five years of postdoctoral experience.

Closing dates: 15th January. Additional limited reviews are held in June and October with their respective closing dates of 15th April and 15th August.

Further information from:
  Associateship Office (JH 610-D5)
  National Research Council
  2101 Constitution Avenue, N.W.
  Washington, D.C. 20418
  U.S.A.

[1494]

NATIONAL RESEARCH INSTITUTE FOR MATHEMATICAL SCIENCES *(South Africa)*
Council for Scientific and Industrial Research

Contract and Permanent Appointments

Subjects: Mathematical sciences (mathematics, applied mathematics, mathematical statistics, computer science, and operations research): postgraduate and postdoctoral research.

Value: Up to R22,650 per year, according to qualifications and experience, plus transport costs.

Tenable in Pretoria, South Africa, for at least two years.

Eligibility: Appointments are open to persons who hold an M.Sc. or Ph.D. degree of their equivalent in mathematics, applied mathematics, mathematical statistics, or computer science.

Further information from:
  Director
  National Research Institute for
    Mathematical Sciences
  P.O. Box 395
  Pretoria 0001
  South Africa

[1495]

NATIONAL RETINITIS PIGMENTOSA FOUNDATION, INC. *(U.S.A)*

Research Grants

Subjects: A wide range of basic and clinical research which may improve understanding of retinitis pigmentosa or other retinal degenerative processes.

Value: Varies according to nature of the proposal, qualifications, etc.

Tenable at any agreed institution for one to three years.

Eligibility: Open to experienced and established investigators in the field.

Closing date: 1st April annually.

Further information from:
  Executive Director
  National Retinitis Pigmentosa Foundation,
    Inc.
  Rolling Park Building
  8331 Mindale Circle
  Baltimore, Maryland 21207
  U.S.A.

[1496]

NATIONAL SCHOOL OF ADMINISTRATION *(Paris)*

Specialist Course: Grants

Study programme: Comparative civil law, economics, etc., with seminars in current affairs. The programme is organized for international groups.

Value: To cover the cost of tuition.

Tenable at the School (for theoretical studies) and in various French government administrative offices, either in Paris or in the provinces (for practical studies). The programme includes nine months of theoretical study and three months of practical study.

Eligibility: Open to civil servants who are nominated by their governments. Candidates must have a university degree or equivalent qualification and an excellent knowledge of French language.

Note: Applications must be made through the appropriate government agency in the candidate's own country.

Address:
  Ecole nationale d'administration
  Service des étrangers
  13 rue de l'Université
  75007 Paris
  France

[1497-1498]

NATIONAL SCIENCE FOUNDATION
(U.S.A.)

Programs in Biological, Behavioral and Social Sciences
Programs in Mathematical and Physical Sciences

The majority of support offered for the following programs is made available for basic research, although work of a more applied nature may also be funded. Individual projects are supported for periods of up to 60 months (generally 24 to 36 months), with annual increments contingent upon availability of the funds and satisfactory progress of the research. The most frequent recipients of these grants are academic institutions and non-profit research institutions. Awards, under special circumstances, may be awarded to other types of institutions as well as individuals (preliminary inquiries should be made to the cognizant program officer at the address below). Support may be given for work involving a single scientist or for projects covering the activities of a number of researchers. Projects are not necessarily confined to a single discipline.

[1497]

Programs in Biological, Behavioral and Social Sciences support individual research projects designed to strengthen scientific understanding of biological and social phenomena. Projects may range from the fundamental molecules of living organisms to the complex interactions of human beings and societal organizations. The basic areas of research supported by this division are: physiology, cellular and molecular biology, environmental biology, behavioral and neural sciences, social and economic sciences, and information science and technology.

[1498]

Programs in Mathematical and Physical Sciences supported by this division aim toward the development of a fundamental understanding of the physical laws of nature. The basic areas of research funded are: materials research, chemistry, mathematical sciences, computer research and physics.

Proposals may be submitted at any time during the year, and applicants should allow approximately six to nine months for consideration. Those projects needing support in a particular fiscal year (ending 30th September) should be submitted no later than January of the year concerned. The Foundation's brochure *Grants for Scientific Research* (NSF78-41) should be consulted prior to submitting applications. Requests for additional information should be directed to the appropriate division director.

Address:
National Science Foundation
Washington, D.C. 20550
U.S.A.

[1499-1502]

NATIONAL SCIENCE FOUNDATION
(U.S.A.)

Engineering Programs

There are four major Program areas:

[1499]

Division of Electrical, Computer, and Systems Engineering: This Division seeks to stimulate exploration of fundamental engineering principles applicable to man-made electrical devices and systems. Emphasis is upon innovative investigations that exhibit a potential for high technical impact. Specific areas of research include: automation, bioengineering, and sensing systems; electrical and optical communications; computer engineering; quantum electronics, waves and beams; solid-state microstructures engineering; systems theory and operations research; and science and technology to aid the handicapped.

[1500]

Division of Chemical and Process Engineering: Focus is on the design, optimization, and operation of a wide range of processes in the chemical, petroleum/petrochemical, food, biochemical/pharmaceutical, mineral, and allied industries. The Division supports research that lays the foundation for technological innovation. Specific areas of research include: kinetics, catalysis and reaction engineering; chemical and biochemical processes; engineering energetics; thermodynamics and transport phenomena; particulate and multiphase processes; separation processes; minerals and primary materials processing; and renewable materials engineering.

[1501]

Division of Civil and Environmental Engineering: The Division deals with (1) extending our understanding of the basic behavior of natural and man-made physical structures and systems from both the elemental and macroscopic viewpoints, and (2) studying the effects of human activities on the natural environment. Hence, one objective of these programs is to increase understanding of how to provide an efficient, satisfactory, and economically built environment. A second objective is to study the phenomena involved in earthquake hazards and to learn ways to mitigate these hazards. Specific areas of research include: geotechnical engineering; structural mechanics; water resources and environmental engineering; and earthquake hazards mitigation.

[1502]

Division of Mechanical Engineering and Applied Mechanics: The purpose of this Division is to develop a better understanding of the physical processes associated with power developed by various machines and engines, and to focus that understanding on key issues in industrial productivity. Problems related to U.S. industrial productivity and the competitiveness of U.S. industry in the world market are of particular concern, and the research seeks to increase knowledge to promote efficiency and the most effective use of materials and processes in industrial production. Specific areas of research include: solid mechanics; fluid mechanics; heat transfer; mechanical systems; production research; and technology innovation projects.

Eligibility: The most frequent recipients of support for research are academic institutions and nonprofit research institutions, although awards are occasionally made to profitmaking organizations, individuals, and state, local, and federal government agencies.

Most awards result from unsolicited research proposals, which should be prepared according to the guidelines set forth in *Grants for Scientific Research* (NSF 78-41).

Note: Unsolicited proposals may be submitted at any time. Proposals received too late for consideration in a particular fiscal year (ending September 30) are considered in the following year. If a specific start date for the project is important, the circumstances should be clearly explained and at least six-months lead time allowed for review and processing.

Inquiries should be sent to the Directorate for Engineering or to the Appropriate Engineering Division.

Address:
Directorate for Engineering
National Science Foundation
Washington, D.C. 20550
U.S.A.

[1503]

NATIONAL SCIENCE FOUNDATION *(U.S.A.)*

Engineering Research Initiation Grants

Purpose: To initiate and support basic and applied research programs to strengthen research potential in engineering and to apprise the impact of engineering research upon industrial development and the national welfare.

Subjects: Any area normally supported by the Directorate for Engineering [see preceding entry].

Eligibility: This program is directed toward full-time engineering faculty members who have had no substantial research support. Applicants are encouraged to submit proposals in areas which will expand their research capabilities beyond the research done for the doctoral degree.

Note: Grants are awarded on a comparative basis. Additional information is available upon request from the Engineering Communications Program, NSF.

Address:
Directorate for Engineering
National Science Foundation
Washington, D.C. 20550
U.S.A.

[1504]

NATIONAL SCIENCE FOUNDATION
(U.S.A.)

Engineering Specialized Research Equipment Grants

NSF provides funds for research equipment as part of regular research grants, and it also makes separate awards exclusively for specialized research equipment. The objective of a grant for research equipment is to improve the quality or broaden the scope of the research to be conducted at the proposing institution. Important considerations in making such awards are the quality and importance of the research for which the equipment is to be used; the appropriateness of the equipment and its expected contribution to the research; the qualifications and past record of the Principal Investigator and associated staff; and provisions for essential supporting facilities and maintenance of the proposed equipment. Other considerations are the likelihood that the equipment will be useful for several different research projects and that the proposing institution considers the equipment important enough to make a reasonable contribution of its own funds toward the projected purchase. Additional information on these grants is available on request.

Eligibility: Awards for equipment requested as part of a research proposal will be made in accordance with the guidelines in the NSF booklet *Grants for Scientific Research* (NSF 78-81).
Proposals for research equipment exclusively, and those which do not request funds for faculty, graduate students, or other staff, may be initiated by individual researchers, research groups, engineering departments, or engineering colleges.

Note: Proposals may be submitted at any time.
The brochure, *Engineering Specialized Research Equipment Grants* (NSF 81-31) is available on request.

Further information from:
Engineering Communications Program
Directorate for Engineering
National Science Foundation
Washington, D.C. 20550
U.S.A.

[1505-1510]

NATIONAL SCIENCE FOUNDATION
(U.S.A.)

[1505]

Astronomy Project Supporting Programs provide a broad base of support for fundamental research directed at understanding the states of matter and physical processes in the solar system, our Milky Way galaxy and the larger universe. All qualified scientists are eligible to submit proposals which are accepted throughout the year. Approximately 7 months should be allowed for reviewing and processing a formal proposal.

NSF-Supported Astronomy Research Centers and Observatories

[1506]

National Astronomy and Ionosphere Center [NAIC] near Arecibo, Puerto Rico is an independent National Research Center for the conduct of radio astronomy, radar astronomy, and aeronomy. The Observatory is managed and operated by Cornell University under contract with the Foundation.
The primary instrument at NAIC is a 305-meter diameter fixed spherical radio/radar telescope which is the world's largest single radio reflector. A second observing site, located 9.6 kilometers from the main site, has a 30.5-meter steerable parabolic antenna paired with the main antenna to provide an effective interferometric S-band radar mapping system.
NAIC facilities and instrumentation are available on a competitive basis to qualified scientists from all over the world, subject to priorities based on the scientific merit of the proposed research, the capability of the instruments to carry out the proposed observations, and the availability of telescope time.
Additional information is available from the *Director, National Astronomy and Ionosphere Center, Cornell University, Ithaca, New York 14853.*

[1507]

Kitt Peak National Observatory [KPNO] is an independent National Research Center that makes available optical telescopes, observing equipment and research support services to qualified scientists.
Headquarters of KPNO is in Tucson, Ariz-

ona; observing facilities are located at an elevation of 6,893 feet on Kitt Peak, 54 miles southwest of Tucson.

Major astronomical instruments at Kitt Peak consist of a 4.0-meter Mayall telescope and the largest solar research instrument, the 1.5-meter McMath solar telescope. In addition to the 11, other telescopes atop Kitt Peak are those of the Universities of Arizona and Michigan, and Case Western Reserve University. KPNO has a staff of resident scientists, engineers and technicians.

KPNO makes observing time on each instrument available for the use of visiting scientists. All qualified United States scientists and, on occasion, foreign visitors may use the instruments, subject to priorities based on the scientific merit of the proposed research, the capability of the instruments to do the work, and the available time.

Additional information is available from the *Director, Kitt Peak National Observatory, P.O. Box 26732, Tucson, Arizona 85726.*

[1508]

Cerro Tololo Inter-American Observatory [CTIO] is an astronomical research center whose optical telescopes and related facilities are available to all qualified scientists from the United States, Chile, and elsewhere in Latin America. CTIO provides astronomers with the opportunity to observe those parts of the Southern Hemisphere skies which are not visible or not adequately observable from the United States, using telescopes made available by the federal government and other organisations.

The Observatory is located on a 7,240-foot mountain in the foothills of the Andes Mountains 289 miles north of Santiago.

Major astronomical instruments at Cerro Tololo include a 4.0-meter near twin to the Kitt Peak telescope, a 1.5-meter, a 1.0-meter on loan from Yale University, a 91-centimeter, a 61/91-centimeter Schmidt on loan from the University of Michigan, a 61-centimeter originally established jointly with the Lowell Observatory, and two 41-centimeter telescopes. Cerro Tololo has a small permanent staff of research scientists, engineers and technicians.

Most of the observing time at Cerro Tololo is used by visiting astronomers. Qualified scientists may use the instruments subject to priorities based on the scientific merit of the proposed research, the capability of the instruments to do the work proposed, and the available time.

Additional information is available from the CTIO Liaison Officer at Kitt Peak National Observatory [see preceding section].

[1509]

National Radio Astronomy Observatory

[NRAO] is an independent National Research Center which makes radio astronomy facilities available to qualified scientists. The NRAO staff assists visiting scientists with the large radio antennas, receivers and other equipment needed to detect, measure, and identify radio waves from outer space.

Headquarters for NRAO is in Charlottesville, Virginia; observing facilities are located at Green Bank, West Virginia, Kitt Peak near Tucson, and 50 miles west of Socorro, New Mexico.

Major research facilities at NRAO include a 141-foot precision surface, fully steerable radio telescope and a 300-foot radio telescope steerable in declination (latitude) only. A four-element interferometer, formerly supported by NRAO, will remain operational through a cooperative agreement with the U.S. Naval Observatory. A 36-foot radio telescope operating at millimeter wavelengths is located at the Kitt Peak National Observatory in Arizona. The Very Large Array [VLA] near Socorro, New Mexico is currently in partial operation and provides observational detail on faint radio sources never before possible. NRAO has a staff of resident scientists, engineers, and technicians.

NRAO makes observing time on each instrument available for the use of visiting scientists. All qualified United States scientists and, on occasion, foreign visitors may use the instruments, subject to priorities based on the scientific merit of the proposed research, the capability of the instruments to do the work proposed, and the time available.

Additional information is available from the *Director, National Radio Astronomy Observatory, Charlottesville, Virginia 22901.* [Also see separate entry for NRAO.]

[1510]

Sacramento Peak Observatory [SPO] is located at an elevation of 9,240 feet in south-central New Mexico. The Observatory facilities are used for studies in the fields of solar physics, solar-terrestrial relationships, and related disciplines. Principal instruments include a 109-

meter high solar vacuum tower telescope with an echele spectrograph, digital diode array and tunable filters, and an 8-meter spar in the Big Dome complex equipped with a 40-centimeter aperture coronagraph, a magnetograph, and a polarimeter. A permanent staff of scientists, engineers, and technicians is available to assist visiting investigators with their own observing programs.

All qualified U.S. scientists and, on occasion, foreign visitors have access to SPO facilities on a competitive basis, subject to priorities based on the scientific merit of the proposed research, the capability of the instruments to do the work proposed, and the time available.

Additional information is available from the *Director, Sacramento Peak Observatory, Sunspot, New Mexico 88349*.

Further information on NSF Astronomy Project Support Programs and on the Centers and Observatories may be obtained from:
Division of Astronomical Science
Astronomy Research Section
National Science Foundation
Washington, D.C. 20550
U.S.A.

[1511-1512]

NATIONAL SCIENCE FOUNDATION
(U.S.A.)

[1511]

Atmospheric Project Support Programs are designed to continue to build a base of fundamental knowledge of the atmospheres of the earth, other planets, and the sun. Specific objectives are to develop the scientific basis for understanding the dynamic and physical behavior of climate and weather on all scales and for understanding the natural global cycles of gases and particulates in the earth's atmosphere; to improve understanding of the composition, energetics, and particularly the dynamcis of the coupled upper atmospheric system; and to improve our knowledge of the sun and neighboring planets, especially as they relate to the earth's upper atmosphere and space environment. All qualified scientists are eligible to submit proposals which are accepted throughout the year. Approximately 6 to 9 months should be allowed for review and processing of a formal proposal.

[1512]

National Center for Atmospheric Research [NCAR] and the *National Scientific Balloon Facility* [NSBF] are independent research centers. NCAR serves as a focal point for an expanding national research effort in the atmospheric sciences and offers support services, fellowships, and research facilities to qualified scientists working in the field of atmospheric research. NSBF provides the scientific community with ballooning support for high altitude experiments and conducts research and developmental programs towards the advancement of scientific ballooning technology.

Headquarters and major laboratories of NCAR are located in Boulder, Colorado. NSBF headquarters is located in Palestine, Texas. Research activities and operations are worldwide.

NCAR research programs include investigation of the earth's upper atmosphere, of the physics of the sun, and of the regions between the sun and earth.

In addition to conducting its own research programs, NCAR participates in a number of atmospheric research efforts conducted by government agencies, university scientists, and research groups on a national or international scale. Approximately 600 scientists, engineers, technicians, and support personnel comprise the NCAR staff.

NSBF provides support for U.S. and foreign investigators conducting a broad spectrum of experiments in the fields of cosmic rays, X-rays, infrared astronomy, particles and fields in the magnetosphere, etc. Approximately 50 engineers, technicians, and support personnel comprise the NSBF staff.

Visiting scientists study and conduct research at NCAR under fellowships and research programs. NCAR and NSBF facilities are available to qualified scientists, subject to scheduling feasibility. Additional information is available from the *Director, National Center for Atmospheric Research, P.O. Box 1470, Boulder, Colorado 80302* [Also see separate entry for NCAR.]

Further information on Atmospheric Project Support Programs may also be obtained from:
Division of Atmospheric Sciences
National Science Foundation
Washington, D.C. 20550
U.S.A.

[1513]

NATIONAL SCIENCE FOUNDATION

Earth Sciences Project Support Programs are concerned primarily with the geological geophysical, geochemical, and petrological constitution of the Earth's crust. The objective is to provide a basic knowledge of the structure and composition of rocks that comprise the Earth's crust and the processes that form and modify these rocks. Research also focuses on applying the theory of plate tectonics to the study of the origin and evaluation of continents. All qualified scientists may submit proposals, which are accepted throughout the year. Approximately 6 months should be allowed for review and processing of a formal proposal.

The Division of Earth Sciences also sponsors the *Ocean Sediment Coring Program* for the purposes of obtaining geological samples from the floor of the deep ocean basin by means of rotary drilling and coring in the sediments and the underlying crystalline rocks. Portions of the core samples are made available to qualified scientists for individual research projects.

Further information from:
Division of Earth Science
National Science Foundation
Washington, D.C. 20550
U.S.A.

[1514]

NATIONAL SCIENCE FOUNDATION
(U.S.A.)

Ocean Sciences Research Programs: fund a broad range of research projects dealing with the physical, chemical, geological and biological processes in the ocean. Large and small grants of several months' to several years' duration are awarded to highly qualified research scientists. Grants are awarded on the basis of a competitive peer review of unsolicited research proposals. These proposals may by submitted throughout the year. Approximately 6 months are required for review and processing of a formal proposal.

Note: The NSF Oceanographic Facilities Support Program supports construction, modification, conversion, purchase, and operation of oceanographic facilities that lend themselves to shared usage. Details are available from the Oceanographic Facilities Support Section of the Division.

Further information from:
Divsion of Ocean Sciences
National Science Foundation
Washington, D.C. 20550
U.S.A.

[1515]

NATIONAL SCIENCE FOUNDATION
(U.S.A.)

Polar Programs

U.S. Antarctic Research: The NSF awards grants or contracts for research in and around Antarctica and for antarctic research at home institutions.

U.S. academic institutions and academically related nonprofit organizations may submit proposals for grants or contracts for research project support. Industry and other local, state, and federal agencies are also eligible for support.

Arctic Research: The NSF supports both individual research and large multidisciplinary projects. Institutions and agencies eligible for the U.S. Antarctic Research Programs are eligible for this Program.

Note: Individuals may make proposals for polar research through their institutions.

An annual brochure further describes the Programs. An investigator should obtain the brochure and a proposal preparation kit from the Division before writing a proposal.

Address:
Division of Polar Programs
National Science Foundation
Washington, D.C. 20550
U.S.A.

[1516]

NATIONAL SCIENCE FOUNDATION
(U.S.A.)

Bilateral Cooperative Science Activities

The Programs focus on: (1) industrial countries of Western Europe, East Asia and Oceania; (2) China, the Soviet Union, and other countries of Eastern Europe; and (3) countries that are industrially underdeveloped and poor in natural resources.

Common features: The programs are designed to support the work of U.S. scientists cooperating with scientists of other coounntries in research and related activities. The programs have the following general goals: to stimulate scientific progress by bringing U.S. scientists and engineers together with counterparts from other countries or traditions but with similar scientific interests; to enchance scientific knowledge in priority areas of mutual interest; to provide opportunities for U.S. scientists to participate in projects aimed at improving scientific infrastructure in developing countries; to assist U.S. and foreign scientists in efforts to share access to important or unique research facilities; to share in the allocation of personnel and work; and to improve mutual understanding with other nations and cultures.

Types of activities: The following may receive support: (1) cooperative research projects which are jointly designed and jointly conducted by principal investigators from the U.S. and the foreign country; (2) research oriented seminars (or workshops), which are meetings of small groups of researchers from the U.S. and from the foreign country, to exchange information, review the current status of a specific field of science or engineering, and plan cooperative research; (3) scientific visits for planning cooperative activities or for research.

Eligibility: Eligible areas of research and research-related activities vary somewhat according to the program priorities of the participating countries.

U.S. universities and colleges, professional societies, research institutes, and individual scientists and agencies affiliated with such organizations may apply for support. Principal investigators/project directors should be U.S. scientists with professional experience equivalent to at least five years of postdoctoral scientific work.

Deadlines: Some programs have deadlines for receipt of applications at NSF; where deadlines are not stated, proposals may be submitted at any time. Processing time for proposals for cooperative research, seminars, and long-term scientific visits averages 7 months, but seminar organizers often need to submit their proposals up to 12 months in advance for planning purposes. Proposals for short-term scientific visits (visits of a month or so) should be received at NSF at least 4 months before desired departure date.

Note: U.S. scientists may obtain further information about any international program, including program announcements (i.e., guidelines for the preparation of proposals), by writing to the Division of International Programs.

The United States has Cooperative Science Programs with the following countries: Argentina, Australia, Belgium, Brazil, Bulgaria, China, France, Federal Republic of Germany, Greece, Hungary, India, Italy, Japan, Republic of Korea, Mexico, New Zealand, Pakistan, Romania, Switzerland, the U.S.S.R. and Venezuela.

Additionally projects are supported in Africa, Latin America, South Asia and Southeast Asia.

Further information from:
Division of International Programs
National Science Foundation
Washington, D.C. 20550
U.S.A.

[1517]

NATIONAL SCIENCE FOUNDATION
(U.S.A.)

Science in Developing Countries Program

The SDC Program is primarily directed toward improving the scientific infrastructure of developing countries.

Types of Projects: The following categories of awards are made to U.S. institutions which sponsor SDC projects:

Research Participating Grants to support (a) the participation of U.S. scientists or engineers in a research project in an eligible developing country, (b) the participation by scientists or engineers from an eligible developing country in an appropriate U.S.-based research project, or (c) a combination of these. This program provides only supplemental costs related to collaboration; primary costs of the project are not provided.

Conference Grants to support these national, regional, and international activities: (a) seminars that are research oriented and focused on developing-country problems; (b) workshops concerned with the planning and initiation of cooperative research activities; or (c) colloquia at which U.S. and counterpart scientists or engineers who are involved with state-of-the-art research explore the application of science and technology to development problems.

Dissertation Improvement Grants for the incremental support of developing-country graduate students who are enrolled at U.S. universities and qualified to undertake a dissertation research project. Such costs as those for field equipment and supplies, and for travel to and from research sites, are covered. No stipend, tuition, fees, or indirect costs are provided. Only projects related to a developing-country problem and approved by a U.S. research advisor are considered for support.

Further information from:
SDC Program
Division of International Programs
National Science Foundation
Washington, D.C. 20550
U.S.A.

[1518]

NATIONAL SCIENCE FOUNDATION
(U.S.A.)

International Travel Grant Program

Organizations may apply for travel grants to cover the cost of a group of U.S. scientists participating in a single scientific meeting or more than one group of travelers participating in several selected meetings. Individual applications will be considered only if the applicant has been invited to (1) present a paper at a plenary or symposium (or equivalent) session of an international scientific meeting; (2) organize such a session at an international scientific meeting; or (3) participate in a NATO Advanced Study Institute (and was recommended for travel by the institute director). A prospective participant in a NATO Advanced Study Institute should write directly to the NATO institute director expressing interest in both admission and travel support.

Further information from:
International Travel Grant Program
National Science Foundation
Washington, D.C. 20550
U.S.A.

[1519]

NATIONAL SCIENCE FOUNDATION
(U.S.A.)

Science and Engineering Education Programs

At press time, the status of these Programs was not known, pending congressional action on NSF's budget.

Latest information from:
Directorate for Science and Engineering Education
National Science Foundation
Washington, D.C. 20550
U.S.A.

[1520]

NATIONAL SCIENCE FOUNDATION
(U.S.A.)

Doctoral Dissertation Research Improvement Grants

Dissertation awards are made to allow doctoral candidates opportunities for greater creativity in the gathering and analysis of data than would otherwise be possible. The Grants are intended to cover research-related expenses, including field equipment and supplies as well as travel to and from research sites. These Grants do not include stipends, nor do they cover everyday personal expenses. The Grantee is free to receive concurrent support from other sources.

Proposals are judged on the basis of scientific content, importance and originality. The candidate must be able to show that receipt of the award will improve the quality of research.

These Grants are only available in the social and behavioral sciences and certain biological, earth, atmospheric and ocean sciences. Awards are not made in the mathematical or physical sciences, engineering, physiology, or cellular and molecular biology. Doctoral students wishing to apply should contact the particular division of the Foundation in which the Grant is sought.

Address:
National Science Foundation
Washington, D.C. 20550
U.S.A.

[1521]

NATIONAL SCIENCE FOUNDATION
(U.S.A.)

NATO Postdoctoral Fellowships in Science

Approximately 50 Fellowships are made to U.S. citizens for full-time postdoctoral study of science in countries that are members of NATO (other than the U.S.) or in countries which cooperate with NATO. Candidates should have received their doctorates within 5 years prior to the date of application. Fellowships consist of US$1,500 per month for six to twelve months. Normally, the Fellow is provided with some dependents' allowances, according to her/her status as of the award date, and to aid in defraying the costs of travel.
Closing date: 9th November, for awards to be announced in late February of the following year. A detailed program description and guidelines for preparation of applications are contained in the brochure *NATO Postdoctoral Fellowships in Science* (SE82-17), available from:
    Division of Scientific Personnel
      Improvement
    NATO Postdoctoral Program
    National Science Foundation
    Washington, D.C. 20550
    U.S.A.

[1522]

NATIONAL SCIENCE TEACHERS ASSOCIATION *(Washington, D.C.)*

AGA-NSTA Science Teaching Achievement Recognition (STAR) Awards are given annually for papers which deal with a novel idea or approach aimed at future progress and improvement in science education at the elementary and/or secondary (pre-college) levels. All members of the science teaching profession are eligible. This Awards Program is sponsored by the American Gas Association.

Gustav Ohaus Awards for Innovation in Elementary and Secondary Science Teaching are given annually to educators submitting papers concerned with substantial improvement in the effectiveness of science education. Areas of possible interest may include, but are not confined to, curricula, instructional methods, organization and administrative patterns, new approaches to laboratory activities, etc. This Awards Program is sponsored by the Ohaus Scale Corporation.

Gustav Ohaus Awards for Innovations in College Science Teaching are given annually to teachers of undergraduate science for papers expressing their ideas of how science teaching can be made more effective. This Program is aimed at the development of new designs for course and curricula, new instructional material, new organizational and administrative patterns, new approaches to laboratory activities, and other innovative revisions, as related to the teaching of science for non-science majors in junior colleges and the lower division of four-year institutions. This Awards Program is sponsored by the Ohaus Scale Corporation.

Value: Each program offers awards in the amounts of US$1,000, US$750, US$500 and US$250. In addition, winners wil receive medallions. Presentation of awards will take place at the annual national convention of the National Science Teachers Association.

Note: All submitted papers will be considered for publication and cannot be returned. Entrants may not submit the same paper for dual consideration in other NSTA award programs. Awardees become automatically ineligible for participation in any of the awards programs for the following two years.

Closing date: 1st December of the year preceding that for which the awards are given.

Further information from:
    National Science Teachers Association
    1742 Connecticut Avenue, N.W.
    Washington, D.C. 20009
    U.S.A.

[1523]

NATIONAL SOCIETY TO PREVENT BLINDNESS *(U.S.A.)*

Grants-in-Aid

The Society annually offers Grants-in-Aid to provide prompt support to small feasibility studies in areas which can lead to major advances in prevention of blindness.
    Grants are for one year.

Value: US$10,000 maximum for a one-year period, payable to the appropriate institution.

Tenable anywhere in the U.S. Awards are made throughout the year and applications may be submitted at any time.

Note: Applicants are not eligible to receive Grants for two different projects during the same period, nor if they are receiving support for the project from another source.

Applications should be accompanied by a letter from the candidate's scientific supervisor, detailing the facilities and equipment available and the competencies of the investigator to carry out the proposed study.

Recipients must submit two progress reports annually and a financial statement on expenditure of the funds.

Further information from:
National Society to Prevent Blindness
79 Madison Avenue
New York, New York 10016
U.S.A.

[1524]

NATIONAL SOCIETY OF PROFESSIONAL ENGINEERS *(Washington, D.C.)*

Engineering Journalism Awards

Three cash Prizes of US$500, US$300 and US$200 are presented annually to reporters making the most significant contributions toward public knowledge and understanding of the role of engineering in modern life. Articles, or series of articles, should deal specifically with professional engineering. The competition is open to any journalist working for a recognized daily, semi-weekly, or weekly newspaper or general interest magazine in the United States. Entries must be published during the calendar year for which the Awards are made.

Closing date: 15th December.

Further information from:
Director of Public Relations
National Society of Professional
  Engineers
2029 K Street, N.W.
Washington, D.C. 20006
U.S.A.

[1525]

NATIONAL SPACE CLUB *(Washington, D.C.)*

Dr. Robert H. Goddard Scholarship

One Scholarship of US$2,000 is awarded annually to a U.S. citizen, at or above the junior year of study at an accredited university, who has the intention of pursuing undergraduate or graduate study in science or engineering during the interval of the award. It is hoped that the Scholarship will stimulate the interest of talented students in space research and exploration, and therefore help to promote the advancement of scientific knowledge.

Selection is based upon official school transcripts, faculty letters of recommendation, accomplishments demonstrating personal qualities of creativity and leadership, and scholsatic plans leading to future participation in some phase of the aerospace sciences and technology. Personal need is considered, but not as a primary criteria. A recipient may be eligible to apply for a second year of support if the circumstances and accomplishments are warranted.

Applications providing the above mentioned information should be submitted to the address below.

Not confirmed for 1983.

Further information from:
Mr. James M. Murray
National Space Club
1629 K Street, N.W., Suite 700
Washington, D.C. 20006
U.S.A.

[1526]

NATIONAL SPELEOLOGICAL SOCIETY *(U.S.A.)*

Ralph W. Stone Graduate Research Award

Subjects: Speleology and related studies: research; applicable to work on thesis or dissertation for M.Sc. or Ph.D. degree.

No. offered: One Award annually.

Value: US$500.

Tenable anywhere that research can be carried out.

Eligibility: Open to duly registered graduate students of any nationality who are members of the Society.

Closing date: 1st May.

Further information from:
Ralph W. Stone Research Award Committee
Mail Stop 239-12
NASA-Ames Research Center
Moffett Field, California 94035
U.S.A.

[1527]

NATIONAL TRUST FOR HISTORIC PRESERVATION *(U.S.A.)*

Community Preservation Workshop Scholarships: 30 tuition Scholarships of approximately US$1,000 are awarded each year to individuals in either staff or volunteer positions working at a government preservation agency, community preservation group or a preservation oriented historical society to attend the Conference which is held in two different locations each year. The week-long Conference is devoted to the broad range of problems and solutions encountered by persons working for community preservation organizations. *Closing date:* two months before start of Conference.

Williamsburg Seminar Scholarships: Eighteen tuition Scholarships are given annually to enable younger professionals in the field of administration of historical agencies the opportunity to attend the summer seminar at Colonial Williamsburg. The Seminars deal with various aspects of historical preservation and agency administration, and last four weeks. Open to United States citizens who are younger professional historical administrators with experience in American history, American studies, American art and architectural history and other allied fields. *Closing date:* March.

Further information from:
Office of Preservation Services
National Trust for Historic Preservation
1785 Massachusetts Avenue, N.W.
Washington, D.C. 20036
U.S.A.

[1528]

NATIONAL TURKEY FEDERATION *(U.S.A.)*

Research Award

The Award of US$1,000 and an appropriately inscribed plaque is offered in even-numbered years, for research conductd in the United States during the five-year period immediately preceding the year in which the presentation is made. Research may be in any of the related fields of study, including economics, food technology, genetics, merchandising, pathology, physiology and nutrition.

Further information from:
National Turkey Federation
Reston International Center, Suite 302
Reston, Virginia 22091
U.S.A.

[1529]

NATIONAL UNION OF STUDENTS *(U.K.)*

Gisbert and Treasy Kapp Travelling Scholarships

Subjects: Unrestricted; preference, however, will be given to students of engineering with particular reference to electrical and electrochemical engineering.

No. offered: Several Scholarships annually.

Tenable during any part of the summer vacation for travel abroad.

Eligibility: Open to undergraduate or postgraduate students who have been in attendance at a United Kingdom university for two or more years.

Note: Candidates must be nominated by the representative student bodies of university unions or junior common rooms.

Closing date: 31st March.

Further information from:
Educational and Welfare Department
National Union of Students
3 Endsleigh Street
London
England WC1H ODU

[1530]

NATIONAL UNION OF STUDENTS (U.K.)

Mrs. T.M. Kapp Will Trust Grant

Purpose: To assist a student from India or a Far Eastern country who is studying at any university or university college in the United Kingdom and is in need of financial assistance.

No. offered: One or two Grants annually.

Value: £30 to £50.

Closing date: 31st October.

Note: The award is made by the Public Trustee on the recommendation of the Secretary of NUS.

Further information from:
 National Union of Students
 3 Endsleigh Street
 London
 England WC1H ODU

[1531]

NATIONAL UNION OF STUDENTS (U.K.)

Charitable Trust Fund

Five or six awards ranging from between £30 to £50 are offered to students who are members of the Union who are in unexpected financial difficulty during the last year of their course and who would otherwise have to abandon their studies.

Further information from:
 Education and Welfare Department
 National Union of Students
 3 Endsleigh Street
 London
 England WC1H ODU

[1532]

NATIONAL UNION OF TEACHERS (U.K.)

Page Scholarships

Subjects: Study of any particular aspect of the American education system.

No. offered: Two Scholarships annually.

Value: £400 with complete hospitality in the United States provided by the English-Speaking Union of the United States.

Tenable in the United States for one month.

Eligibility: Open to members of the National Union of Teachers or affiliated organizations who are between 25 and 55 years of age.

Note: Recipients are required to report on their visit to teacher groups, educational meetings, etc., on their return home.

Closing date: 30th November.

Further information from:
 National Union of Teachers
 Hamilton House, Mabledon Place
 London
 England WC1H 9BD

[1533]

NATIONAL UNIVERSITY OF SINGAPORE

ASEAN Postgraduate Scholarships

Subjects: Non-research postgraduate studies in medicine and engineering.

No. offered: Two Scholarships annually.

Value: A stipend of S$1,000 per month plus tuition, health insurance, examination and other approved fees. In addition, cost of travel expenses to and from Singapore and a book allowance are provided.

Tenable at the University of Singapore.

Eligibility: Candidates must be nationals of member-countries of the Associaton of South-East Asian Nations (Indonesia, Malaysia, Philippines and Thailand) who have a good degree, outstanding academic merit, good character, personality and leadership qualities.
 Awards are subject to candidates' admission to the University of Singapore.

Further information from:
 Registrar
 University of Singapore
 Kent Ridge
 Singapore 0511

[1534]

NATIONAL UNIVERSITY OF SINGAPORE

Research Scholarships

Subjects: Postgraduate studies in all fields, towards a research degree and submission of a thesis.

No. offered: Approximately twenty Scholarships annually.

Value: Between S$800 and S$1,100 per month. No travel or additional expenses are reimbursed.

Tenable for one year at the National University of Singapore; may be renewed for up to two additional years.

Eligibility: Open to any university graduate having an outstanding academic record, who has applied to and been accepted as a higher degree student at the National University of Singapore.

Closing date: April and October of each year.

Further information from:
 Registrar
 National University of Singapore
 Kent Ridge
 Singapore 0511

[1535]

NATIONAL VEGETABLE RESEARCH STATION *(Warwick, U.K.)*

Agricultural Research Council Research Scholarship

Purpose: To enable the Scholar to pursue further studies and obtain training in one of the following lines of research at the Station: plant breeding, social science, biochemistry, plant physiology, entomology, plant pathology, ecology and control of weeds, and statistics.

Value: £2,245 per annum, plus university fees for a higher degree.

Tenable at the Station for three years.

Eligibility: Open to United Kingdom honours graduates and to those who are shortly to graduate.

Closing date: 28th February for commencement in October.

Further information from:
 Secretary
 National Vegetable Research Station
 Wellesbourne, Warwick
 England CV35 9EF

[1536]

NATIONAL WILDLIFE FEDERATION *(U.S.A.)*

Environmental Conservation Fellowships

Purpose: To encourage advanced study in fields relating to wildlife, natural resource management and protection of environmental quality.

Subjects: Wildlife management and conservation; ecosystem analysis and modeling for natural resource management, range management, forestry, water resources planning and management; energy conservation and conservation education, marine resources, economics of resource conservation, pollution control and abatement, soil conservation, park administration and management, outdoor recreation, public relations and journalism (with conservation emphasis).

No. offered: Varies annually.

Value: Up to US$4,000 per annum, payable in two installments.

Tenable in the United States or abroad, for one academic year (nine months); renewable.

Eligibility: Open to citizens of the United States, Canada and Mexico who have been accepted as candidates for a graduate or law degree at an accredited college or university.

Note: Mid-year and final reports from students and faculty advisers are required. NWF and the American Petroleum Institute will jointly fund studies involving conservation and petroleum.

Closing date: 31st December.

Further information from:
    Executive Vice President
    National Wildlife Federation
    1412 16th Street, N.W.
    Washington, D.C. 20036
    U.S.A.

[1537]

NATURAL ENVIRONMENT RESEARCH COUNCIL *(U.K.)*

Advanced Course Studentships

Purpose: To provide for the maintenance of well-qualified graduates taking recognized advanced courses of instruction to prepare students for employment.

Subjects: See

Value: £1,640 to £2,770 per annum, paid quarterly in advance, plus fees and other allowances as appropriate (subject to annual review).

Tenable at United Kingdom universities, colleges and government establishments, normally for one year on postgraduate courses recognized by the Council.

Eligibility: Candidates should have been ordinarily resident in Great Britain for at least three years immediately preceding the date of application for an NERC Studentship, and have a first or second class honours degree, or the equivalent, in science and technology.

Note: Applications should be made to the institution where the Studentship will be held, preferably early in the year in which the Studentship is required.
Full information about NERC awards is contained in a booklet available from:
    University Support Section
    Natural Environment Research Council
    Polaris House, North Star Avenue
    Swindon, Wiltshire
    England SN2 1EU

[1538]

NATURAL ENVIRONMENT RESEARCH COUNCIL *(U.K.)*

Industrial Studentships

Purpose: To encourage the further training of scientists in industry.

Subjects: Any field of the natural environmental sciences having industrial applications.

No. offered: A limited number of Studentships annually.

Value: Variable; applicants should have the support of their firm during tenure of the award.

Tenable at an appropriate institution acceptable to the Council for three years.

Eligibility: Candidates should have been ordinarily resident in Great Britain for at least three years immediately preceding the date of application, be between 26 and 35 years of age, and have at least three years of professional experience in industry at postgraduate level. Applicants should normally possess a first or upper second class honours degree or an equivalent qualification. Exceptionally, a candidate not so qualified, but with proof of outstanding ability in an industrial environment, will be considered on his merits. Importance is attached to the employer's report on an applicant's work in industry. Students are expected to return to industry after completing their training.

Note: Applications to the Council should be made by 31st July.

Further information from:
    University Support Section
    Natural Environment Research Council
    Polaris House, North Star Avenue
    Swindon, Wiltshire
    England SN2 1EU

[1539]

NATURAL ENVIRONMENT RESEARCH COUNCIL *(U.K.)*

Co-operative Awards in Sciences of the Environment (CASE Studentships)

Purpose: To ensure that a number of postgraduate students receive a broad training of relevance to, and in collaboration with, industry who will play an active part in their supervision.

Subjects: See

Value: £1,640 to £2,770 per annum, paid quarterly in advance, plus fees and other allowances as appropriate (subject to annual review).

Tenable at United Kingdom universities and at non-academic institutions for up to three years. At least three months must be spent with the non-academic institution during the training period.

Eligibility: Candidates should have been ordinarily resident in Great Britain for at least three years immediately preceding the date of application, and have a first or upper second class honours degree, or the equivalent, in an appropriate branch of science or technology. It is preferred that applicants be less than 27 years of age.

Note: Applications should be made through the institution where the Studentship will be held.

Further information from:
University Support Section
Natural Environment Research Council
Polaris House, North Star Avenue
Swindon, Wiltshire
England SN2 1EU

[1540]

NATURAL ENVIRONMENT RESEARCH COUNCIL *(U.K.)*

Research Studentships

Purpose: To provide for the maintenance of well-qualified graduates while being trained in the environmental sciences, the methods of research.

Subjects: (a) The solid earth, its physical properties and mineral resources (geology, geophysics, geochemistry and physiography); (b) the inland waters and their living resources (hydrology, freshwater biology, ecology and fisheries); (c) the terrestrial plant and animal communities (ecology, forestry, conservation and other scientific aspects of land use); (d) the seas and oceans, their behaviour and their living and mineral resources (oceanography, marine biology and ecology, and fisheries); and (e) the atmosphere (some aspects of meteorology).

Value: £1,640 to £2,770 per annum, paid quarterly in advance, plus fees and other allowances as appropriate (subject to annual review).

Tenable at United Kingdom universities, colleges and government establishments normally for two to three years.

Eligibility: Candidates should have been ordinarily resident in Great Britain for at least three years immediately preceding the date of application for an NERC Studentship, and preferably under 27 years of age, and have a first or upper second class honours degree, or the equivalent, in an appropriate branch of science or technology.

Note: Applications should be made to the institution where the Studentship will be held, preferably early in the year in which the Studentship is required.

Full information about NERC awards is contained in a booklet available from:
University Support Section
Natural Environment Research Council
Polaris House, North Star Avenue
Swindon, Wiltshire
England SN2 1EU

[1541]

NATURAL ENVIRONMENT RESEARCH COUNCIL *(U.K.)*

Research Fellowships

Purpose: To assist promising young research workers.

Subjects: See preceding entry.

Value: United Kingdom university non-clinical academic scale for lecturers.

Tenable at universities, colleges or other acceptable institutions in the United Kingdom, normally for two years.

Eligibility: Candidates should have been ordinarily resident in Great Britain for at least three years immediately preceding the date of application for an NERC Fellowship, and preferably between 24 and 27 years of age, hold a Ph.D., and have a marked aptitude for original and independent research in science.

Note: Applicants should approach the institution concerned for tenure of award in the first instance.

Full information about NERC awards is contained in a booklet available from the Council.

Closing date: 31st January.

Further information from:
University Support Section
Natural Environment Research Council
Polaris House, North Star Avenue
Swindon, Wiltshire
England SN2 1EU

[1542]

NATURAL ENVIRONMENT RESEARCH COUNCIL *(U.K.)*

Research Grants

Purpose: To provide assistance for research workers wishing to initiate and develop their own ideas and projects relating to man's natural environment and its resources.

Subjects: Physical and biological sciences.

Value: Salaries for scientific, laboratory, technical or other assistants; costs of scientific apparatus, materials and services necessary to the research. Related travel expenses are also included.

Tenable at universities, polytechnics, technical colleges and similar institutions suitable for the research. Grants are normally for three years with the possibility of extension.

Eligibility: Applicants should normally be research workers, ordinarily resident in Great Britain, and be members of the staff of suitable institutions within the United Kingdom.

Note: Awards are formally made to the institution involved, rather than the individual applicant.
Full information about NERC awards is contained in a booklet available from the Council.

Closing date: 1st July and 1st December.

Further information from:
University Support Section
Natural Environment Research Council
Polaris House, North Star Avenue
Swindon, Wiltshire
England SN2 1EU

[1543]

NATURAL SCIENCES AND ENGINEERING RESEARCH COUNCIL *(Canada)*

1967 Science Scholarships

Purpose: To stimulate exchanges of students between different cultural and geographical regions of Canada.

Subjects: Science and engineering.

No. offered: 50 Scholarships annually.

Value: Can$14,000 plus travel expenses.

Tenable in Canadian universities for 36 months; renewable for a further twelve months.

Eligibility: Open to outstanding Canadian students in their final year of an honours course or in the qualifying year after graduation from a general course in science or engineering, who are interested in studying for a Ph.D. at a Canadian university.

Note: Candidates must first be invited by their university to submit an application.

Closing date: 1st December.

Further information from:
Scholarships Officer
Natural Sciences and Engineering
  Research Council
Ottawa, Ontario
Canada K1A OR6

[1544]

NATURAL SCIENCES AND ENGINEERING RESEARCH COUNCIL *(Canada)*

Postgraduate Scholarships

Subjects: Agriculture, astronomy, biology, chemistry, forestry, oceanography, physics, geology, physical geography, mathematics, engineering, experimental psychology.

Value: Can$9,350 per annum, plus a travel grant, if required.

Tenable at Canadian universities for up to four years.

Eligibility: Open to Canadian citizens or landed immigrants who have been accepted for the upcoming year as fully qualified candidates by a graduate school for a program of postgraduate studies and research leading to an advanced degree. Landed immigrants must, at the time of application, be residing in Canada.

Closing date: 1st December.

Further information from:
Scholarships Officer
Natural Sciences and Engineering
  Research Council
Ottawa, Ontario
Canada K1A OR6

[1545]

NATURAL SCIENCES AND ENGINEERING RESEARCH COUNCIL
(Canada)

Postgraduate Scholarships in Science Librarianship and Documentation

Purpose: To assist science or engineering graduates in obtaining advanced degrees in the fields of science librarianship and documentation.

Value: Can$9,350 per annum, plus travel.

Tenable at Canadian universities that have a recognized school of library science and documentation, for twelve months; renewable once.

Eligibility: Open to Canadian citizens or landed immigrants who have, or expect to receive, a degree in science or engineering, and who have been accepted by a recognized school of library science or documentation.

Closing date: 1st December.

Further information from:
Scholarships Officer
Natural Sciences and Engineering
  Research Council
Ottawa, Ontario
Canada K1A OR6

[1546]

NATURAL SCIENCES AND ENGINEERING RESEARCH COUNCIL
(Canada)

E.W.R. Steacie Memorial Fellowship

Purpose: To permit promising and outstanding young scientists to devote an entire year to their research activities.

Subjects: Science and engineering.

Value: Equal to the recipient's normal university salary.

Tenable at Canadian universities for a period of up to two years.

Eligibility: Open to scientists of any nationality or citizenship who have obtained a doctorate within the last twelve years and hold an academic appointment in a Canadian university.

Note: Applicants may not apply on their own initiative, but must be nominated by heads of departments in Canadian universities.

Closing date: (for nominations) 1st September for awards to be announced in December.

Further information from:
Programs Branch
Natural Sciences and Engineering
  Research Council
Ottawa, Ontario
Canada K1A OR6

[1547]

NATURAL SCIENCES AND ENGINEERING RESEARCH COUNCIL
(Canada)

Postdoctoral Fellowships

Purpose: To provide persons who have recently completed a doctorate to add to their experience through specialized training.

Subjects: Natural sciences and engineering.

Value: Can$18,700 per annum, plus a travel allowance.

Tenable at a university of the Fellow's choice for one year, renewable for an additional year.

Eligibility: Open to Canadian citizens or landed immigrants residing in Canada, who have recently received a Ph.D. from a Canadian university.

Closing date: 1st December; awards announced in late March.

Further information from:
  Scholarships Officer
  Natural Sciences and Engineering
    Research Council
  Ottawa, Ontario
  Canada K1A OR6

[1548]

NATURAL SCIENCES AND ENGINEERING RESEARCH COUNCIL
(Canada)

Senior Industrial Fellowships

Purpose: To increase collaboration between Canadian universities and industry by enabling faculty members to spend a minimum of one year in an industrial environment in Canada.

Subjects: Science, engineering.

Value: The NSERC will contribute towards the Fellow's salary and provide a travel grant where necessary. The salary component of the NSERC award will be payable to the university and will supplement the university's salary contribution so as to ensure that the Fellow receives, in total, an amount equal to his normal salary.

Tenable with industrial organizations in Canada and with certain quasi-industrial federal corporations and provincial utilities, for one year or more.

Eligibility: Open to staff members of Canadian universities who are eligible to apply for NSERC grants.

Note: No restrictions will be placed on the kind of work to be carried out during tenure of a Fellowship.
  Applications may be submitted at any time.

Further information from:
  Programs Branch
  Natural Sciences and Engineering
    Research Council
  Ottawa, Ontario
  Canada K1A OR6

[1549]

NATURAL SCIENCES AND ENGINEERING RESEARCH COUNCIL
(Canada)

Industrial Research Fellowships

Purpose: To encourage highly qualified scientists and engineers to seek careers in Canadian industry.

Subjects: Science and engineering.

Value: A maximum of Can22,000 per annum towards the gross salary which is set up by the sponsoring company, plus travel costs.

Tenable in industrial organizations in Canada for three years; renewable for two additional years.

Eligibility: Open to Canadian citizens or landed immigrants who have recently completed a doctorate degree, and who are seeking employment in industry in Canada for the first time.

Further information from:
  Scholarships Officer
  Natural Sciences and Engineering
    Research Council
  Ottawa, Ontario
  Canada K1A OR6

[1550]

NATURAL SCIENCES AND ENGINEERING RESEARCH COUNCIL
(Canada)

University Research Fellowships

Purpose: To expand the career opportunities in research for a select number of promising scientists and engineers.

Subjects: Natural sciences and engineering.

Value: Can25,850 per year for the three years; renewable for an additional two years.

Tenable at Canadian universities.

Eligibility: Open to Canadian citizens and landed immigrants who hold a doctoral degree and have had experience equal to that normally required by the university for appointment to the rank of assistant professor. Preference is given to applicants having no more than five years experience.

Closing date: 1st November.

Further information from:
  Scholarships Officer
  Natural Sciences and Engineering
    Research Council
  Ottawa, Ontario
  Canada K1A OR6

[1551]

NATURAL SCIENCES AND ENGINEERING RESEARCH COUNCIL
(Canada)

NATO Postdoctoral Fellowships

These Fellowships are designed to stimulate the international exchange of graduate students in the pure and applied sciences between member-countries of NATO, and are similar in every respect to the Council's Postdoctoral Fellowships [q.v.], and are tenable in any NATO country [see NATO Research Fellowships].

Applications received for NATO Postdoctoral Fellowships will be automatically considered for the equivalent NSERC award.

Further information from:
  Scholarships Officer
  Natural Sciences and Engineering
    Research Council
  Ottawa, Ontario
  Canada K1A OR6

[1552]

NATURAL SCIENCES AND ENGINEERING RESEARCH COUNCIL
(Canada)

Visiting Fellowships in Canadian Government Laboratories

Visiting Fellowships are awarded annually to afford promising scientists the opportunity to work with well-established groups or leaders in their fields and to foster close relationships between Canadian government laboratories, universities and research institutions.

Fellowships of *Can*$22,068 per annum plus a travel allowance are tenable for one year and may be renewed for an additional year upon consideration.

Applicants should have obtained, no more than five years prior to the time of application, either a doctorate from a recognized university or a master's degree with a demonstrated capability for conducting successful independent research.

Closing date: 15th January for awards to be announced by 1st April.

Further information from:
  Scholarships Officer
  Natural Sciences and Engineering
    Research Council
  Ottawa, Ontario
  Canada K1A OR6

[1553]

NATURAL SCIENCES AND ENGINEERING RESEARCH COUNCIL
(Canada)

Grants

Purpose: To support and encourage research for the creation of new knowledge in the natural sciences and engineering, and to promote and support the development of selected fields of research which are of regional and national importance.

Subjects: Agriculture, astronomy, biology, chemistry, computing and information science, engineering, food science, forestry, physical geography, geology, geophysics, mathematics, metallurgy, meteorology, oceanography and limnology, physics, experimental psychology, space research, statistics and interdisciplinary research.

Operating Grants are awarded on any annual of three-year basis to individual researchers or groups of researchers at Canadian universities as contributions towards the normal operating costs of their projects—employing assistants, purchasing minor equipment, materials and supplies, defraying costs of computing services, field trips and other limited travel.

Travel Grants awarded to assist established scientists who wish to spend at least three months at a laboratory other than their own.

Equipment Grants are provided to assist in the purchase of special research equipment or installations.

General Research Grants for promoting scientific research are made by the Council to executive heads of Canadian universities; these funds are disbursed by the university president.

Strategic Grants are operating or equipment grants to individuals and groups to encourage researchers in Canadian universities to make a greater contribution toward the solution of problems of Canadian concern. Applicants should be eligible to apply for an NSERC operating grant and undertake research projects in biotechnology, communications, energy, environmental toxicology, food/agriculture, or oceans.

PRAI (Project Research Applicable in Industry) Grants are awarded to capitalize on advances in universdity research showing potential for eventual commercial exploitation in Canada by providing financial support for the further development of such advances in university laboratories to the point at which they can be transferred to industry.

The Council also awards *Publication Grants*, supporting the publication of original research periodicals, and occasionally books, and *Conference Grants* to support both national and international scientific and technical conferences.

Eligibility: Open to academic staff members of Canadian universities.

Closing date: 1st November.

Further information from:
Programs Branch
Natural Sciences and Engineering Research Council
Ottawa, Ontario
Canada K1A OR6

[1554]

NATURAL SCIENCES AND ENGINEERING RESEARCH COUNCIL
(Canada)

International Collaborative Research Grants

Purpose: To provide financial asssistance to Canadian scientists and engineers engaging in a collaborative research project with co-workers in a foreign country.

Subjects: Natural sciences and engineering.

No. offered: A small number of Grants are awarded twice yearly.

Value: Economy return air fare to foreign host institution plus a possible living allowance.

Tenable at research institutions outside Canada.

Eligibility: Open to academic staff members of Canadian universities.

Note: Candidates should intend to return to Canada following completion of the award.

Closing dates: 15th March; 15th October.

Further information from:
Awards Oficer (International Relations)
Natural Sciences and Engineering Research Council
Ottawa, Ontario
Canada K1A OR6

[1555]

NATURAL SCIENCES AND ENGINEERING RESEARCH COUNCIL
(Canada)

Scientific Exchange Programs

The Council maintains programs of scientific exchange with: the Conselho Nacional de Desenvolvimento Cientifico e Technologico of Brazil; the Czechoslovak Academy of Sciences; France as part of the Cultural Exchange Agreement—specifically, the Centre National de la Recherche Scientifique; and the Japan Society for th Promotion of Science and the State Committee for Science and Technical Progress (Bulgaria.

Under these Programs, arrangements are made

to send Canadian scientists on short-term and long-term visits to one of the above countries and to receive scientists from those countries for similar visits in Canada.

The Council also participates with the Canadian International Development Agency in a Research Associates Program for scientists from developing countries (see).

Further information from:
  Awards Officer (International Relations)
  Natural Sciences and Engineering Research
    Council
  Ottawa, Ontario
  Canada K1A OR6

[1556]

FRIEDRICH NAUMANN FOUNDATION
(West Germany)

Scholarships

Purpose: To aid qualified students and graduates who see themselves related to liberal philosophies.

No. offered: Varies annually.

Tenable in West Germany for the duration of studies (two years for graduates).

Eligibility: Open to German and foreign students and graduates.

Closing dates: 30th June and 30th November.

Further information from:
  Friedrich-Naumann Foundation
  Referat Studienförderung
  D5270 Gummersbach 31
  West Germany

[1557]

WALTER W. NAUMBURG FOUNDATION

International Violin Competition

A number of cash awards plus orchestra appearances and two recitals at Alice Tully Hall, Lincoln Center, New York, are given to competitors of any nationality who are between the age of 17 and 30.

Not confirmed for 1983.

Further information from:
  Walter W. Naumburg Foundation
  144 West 66th Street
  New York, New York 10023
  U.S.A.

[1558]

MARIO NEGRI INSTITUTE OF PHARMACOLOGICAL RESEARCH *(Milan)*

Johananoff International Fellowship

Purpose: To enable a distinguished scientist to spend his/her sabbatical year reading, thinking and writing on a chosen topic of his/her specific competence.

Subject: Advanced biomedical studies.

No. offered: One Fellowship annually.

Value: US$25,000, paid monthly.

Tenable at the Institute for one year.

Eligibility: Open to non-Italian scientists who are internationally renowned for outstanding contributions to cancer chemotherapy and/or immunology, cardiovascular pharmacology, neuropsychopharmacology or drug metabolism. Only scientists from academic institutions, non-profit organizations or governmental agencies will be considered. Preference will be given to mid-career scientists, 35 to 50 years of age.

Note: There are no objections to the Fellow receiving his regular stipend or any other support.

Closing date: Varies annually.

Further information from:
  Mario Negri Institute for Pharmacological
    Research
  Via Eritrea 62
  20157 Milan
  Italy

[1559]

MARIO NEGRI INSTITUTE OF PHARMACOLOGICAL RESEARCH *(Milan)*

Postdoctoral Training Fellowships

Subjects: Cancer chemotherapy, neuropsychopharmacology, cardiovascular pharmacology.

No. offered: Approximately 100 Fellowshps, usually offered as a vacancy occurs, but some are offered annually.

Value: At least 300,000 lire per month.

Tenable at the Institute generally for one year; renewable.

Eligibility: Open to graduates wth degrees in appropriate subjects who have had at least two years of laboratory experience.

Note: Applications are received at any time.

Further information from:
 Professor A. Leonardi
 Mario Negri Institute of Pharmacological Research
 Via Eritrea 62
 20157 Milan
 Italy

[1560]

NETHERLANDS—SOUTH AFRICA ASSOCIATION

Study Fund

Nationals of South Africa of all races who are undertaking postgraduate study in the Netherlands may qualify for funds from the government of the Netherlands for up to one year of support.
 Candidates should be no more than 28 years of age and should have been registered students at a university for at least three years.

Further information from:
 Netherlands—South Africa Association
 P.O. Box 1219
 Pretoria 001
 South Africa

[1561]

NEW DANCE GROUP STUDIO, INC.
(New York City)

Scholarships

Purpose: To train and develop professional performers.

Subjects: Dance: modern, ballet, ethnic and jazz.

No. offered: Approximately 15 Scholarships.

Value: Full or partial tuition.

Tenable at the Studio for one year; renewable.

Eligibility: Open to United States and foreign adult dancers. Candidates should be able to demonstrate ability as potential dancers and/or dance teachers.

Not confirmed for 1983.

Further information from:
 New Dance Group Studio, Inc.
 254 West 47th Street
 New York, New York 10036
 U.S.A.

[1562]

NEW ENGLAND THEATRE CONFERENCE
(U.S.A.)

John Gassner Memorial Playwriting Award

The annual competition is open to all playwrights in the United States who wish to submit a play which is both commercially unpublished and unproduced, and has a running time of no more than one hour. Two cash Awards are presented: First Prize of US$200; Second Prize of US$100. Both winning plays are given stage readings at a "NETC New Scripts Showcase." *Closing date:* 15th April.

Further information from:
 John Gassner Memorial Playwriting Award
 New England Theatre Conference
 50 Exchange Street
 Waltham, Massachusetts 02154
 U.S.A.

[1563]

NEW MEDICAL JOURNALS LTD. *(U.K.)*

John Rowan Wilson Award

The Award, of £500 and a silver trophy, is given annually (a) to the writer who has done most to promote wit, style and lucidity in the treatment of medical subjects, or (b) for the best piece of writing, not necessarily on a medical subject, by a writer who is also a qualified doctor.

The judges consider work published from October one year to October the next. An announcement of the Award is published in October in the journal *World Medicine*, and anyone may submit nominations. Nominations should be received not later than one month after the appearance of the announcement.

Not confirmed for 1983.

Address
'World Medicine'
New Medical Journals Ltd.
Clareville House
26/27 Oxendon Street
London
England SW1Y 4EL

[1564]

NEW ORLEANS BAPTIST THEOLOGICAL SEMINARY

Performance Awards

No. offered: Up to ten Awards annually.

Value: Approximately US$120.

Tenable at the Division of Church Music Ministries, New Orleans Baptist Theological Seminary for study leading to the master of church music degree.

Eligibility: Open to non-United States citizens who hold a bachelor of music degree or equivalent and are at least 21 years of age.
Candidates must be committed to the Christian ministry as a vocation.

Closing date: 1st July.

Further information from:
Chairman
Division of Church Music Ministries
New Orleans Baptist Theological Seminary
3939 Gentily Boulevard
New Orleans, Louisiana 70126
U.S.A.

[1565]

NEW SCHOOL FOR MUSIC STUDY, INC.
(Princeton, New Jersey)

Internships in Piano Pedagogy

No. offered: Two Internships annually.

Value: US$2,200 to US$4,500.

Tenable at the School, for one year; renewable.

Eligibility: Open to United States or foreign colege graduates with a major in piano or equivalent qualifications, or with piano teaching experience. Candidates must be fluent in spoken and written English.

Closing date: 15th March.

Further information from:
Registrar
New School for Music Study, Inc.
Box 407
Princeton, New Jersey 08540
U.S.A.

[1566]

NEW SOUTH WALES STATE CANCER COUNCIL

Clinical Fellowships

Subjects: Clinical aspects of cancer.

No. offered: Variable number of Fellowships annually.

Value: Fellowships held in Australia will be on the scale of the National Health and Medical Research Council awards. Fellowships held abroad wil carry a personal allowance of up to A$6,000 is held in the United Kingdom and A$8,000 in the United States. In addition, up to A$1,000 will be paid for dependents, plus return air fare of a Fellow's wife.

Tenable at any approved institution in Australia or overseas, for a maximum of one year.

Eligibility: Open to suitable medical practitioners with permanent residency in New South Wales.

Note: The Fellow is required to return to New South Wales after the Fellowship is terminated.

Closing date: 30th June.

Further information from:
Director
Committee in Medicine
Coppleson Institute
University of Sydney
Sydney, N.S.W.
Australia 2006

[1567]

NEW SOUTH WALES STATE CANCER COUNCIL

Travel Grants-in-Aid

Subjects: Clinical investigation and treatment of cancer.

Value: Up to a maximum of A$1,500.

Tenable for three to four months.

Eligibility: Open to graduates in medicine and/or science engaged in the clinical investigation and treatment of cancer, who are practising in New South Wales and who hold teaching or approved hospital appointments.

Note: Applicants should indicate in what way the award is likely to advance or improve the knowledge, diagnosis, management or treatment of cancer in New South Wales and the way in which in any knowledge gained would be disseminated.

Closing date: 30th June.

Further information from:
Director
Postgraduate Committee in Medicine
Medical Institute
Coppleson Institute
University of Sydney
Sydney, N.S.W.
Australia 2006

[1568]

NEW YORK ACADEMY OF SCIENCE

Annual Children's Science Book Award Program

Purpose: To encourage the writing and publishing of high quality science books for children, especially those which might lead young children toward careers in science.

Subjects: General books for children in the basic sciences, anthropology, folklore, customs of foreign countries, human nature and sociology.

Value: US$500 each.

Eligibility: Open to authors/illustrators of general trade books for children in the following categories: (a) for children under ten years of age, and (b) for children betwen the ages of ten and sixteen. Books submitted must be published during the period of 1st December and 30th November preceding the year in which the Award is given. Award presentation is made in New York in March.

Closing date: 30th November for receipt of manuscripts.

Further information from:
Ann E. Collins, Public Relations Director
New York Academy of Sciences
2 East 63rd Street
New York, New York 10021
U.S.A.

[1569]

NEW YORK CIVIL LIBERTIES UNION

Florina V. Lasker Award

An annual Award of US$1,000 is given to honor the individual, organization or group which has displayed consistent and outstanding courage and integrity in defense of civil liberties, and in so doing, has made a constructive and significant contribution to them, whether in the performance of duty or that above and beyond its requirements. Nominations are invited from both civil liberties union members and the general public.

Further information from:
Gara LaMarche
New York Civil Liberties Union
84 Fifth Avenue
New York, New York 10011
U.S.A.

[1570]

NEW YORK STATE HISTORICAL ASSOCIATION

Cooperstown Graduate Program Fellowships

Subjects: Museology and historical studies.

Value: Up to US$2,400: partial support for a full-time graduate student.

Tenable in connnection with New York State University at Oneonta, in Cooperstown, New York for eleven months.

Eligibility: Open to United States citizens who possess a bachelor of arts degree or equivalent qualification. Candidates should have had at least a year's experience in the musuem field, be proficient in English and have a background in American studies.

Note: Candidates should apply at the same time for admission to the program and for a Fellowship (awarded on the basis of past performance, potential as a professional in the field, and need).

Closing date: 1st February.

Further information from:
Cooperstown Graduate Program Fellowships
New York State Historical Association
Cooperstown, New York 13326
U.S.A.

[1571]

NEW ZEALAND COMMONWEALTH SCHOLARSHIPS AND FELLOWSHIPS COMMITTEE

Commonwealth Scholarships

Purpose: To enable persons of high intellectual promise to study in New Zealand in the expectation that they will make a significant contribution to life in their own countries on their return. The Scholarships are provided by the New Zealand government and fall within the framework of the Commonwealth Scholarship and Fellowship Plan [q.v.].

No. offered: Approximately fifteen Scholarships anually.

Value: NZ$387 per month plus travel and allowances.

Tenable in New Zealand for up to three years.

Eligibility: Open to graduates from a Commonwealth country who are between 22 and 28 years of age, exceptionally up to 35.

Note: Nominations should be sent to the appropriate agency in the home country and must reach New Zealand by 31st July.

Further information from:
New Zealand Commonwealth Scholarships
 and Fellowships Committee
c/o University Grants Committee
P.O. Box 12348
Wellington North
New Zealand

[1572]

NEW ZEALAND COMMONWEALTH SCHOLARSHIPS AND FELLOWSHIPS COMMITTEE

Commonwealth Administrative Fellowships

Purpose: To enable administrators from Commonwealth countries to observe administrative systems in New Zealand. The Fellowships are provided by the New Zealand government and fall within the framework of the Commonwealth Scholarship and Fellowship Plan [q.v.].

Subjects: Administration in government departments or universities.

Value: A maintenance allowance of NZ$50 per diem and tourist air fares to and from New Zealand. Fellowships are not subject to New Zealand income tax.

Tenable in New Zealand for up to three months; not renewable.

Note: Awards are made by direct invitation.

Address
New Zealand Commonwealth Scholarships
 and Fellowships Committee
c/o University Grants Committee
P.O. Box 12348
Wellington North
New Zealand

[1573]

MEW ZEALAND COMMONWEALTH SCHOLARSHIPS AND FELLOWSHIPS COMMITTEE

Commonwealth Prestige Fellowships

Purpose: To enable distinguished scholars to visit New Zealand to undertake a programme of lectures, seminars and discussions with university staff and research students and visit state organizations and research establishments. The Fellowships are provided by the New Zealand government and fall within the framework of the Commonwealth Scholarship and Fellowship Plan [q.v.].

Subjects: Unrestricted.

No. offered: Up to three Fellowships annually.

Value: A maintenance allowance of NZ$70 per diem, plus economy air fare to and from New Zealand and travel within New Zealand. The Fellowships are not subject to New Zealand income tax.

Tenable in New Zealand for periods from six weeks to three months; not renewable. Visits to each university last up to two weeks, but longer visits to particular universities may be arranged. The Fellowships may be held concurrently with other awards.

Eligibility: Open to eminent scholars from Commonwealth countries other than New Zealand.

Note: Fellowships are offered by direct invitation only. Applications are not accepted.

Further information from:
New Zealand Commonwealth Scholarships
  and Fellowships Committee
c/o University Grants Committee
P.O. Box 12348
Wellington North
New Zealand

[1574]

NEW ZEALAND COUNCIL FOR EDUCATIONAL RESEARCH

J.R. McKenzie Senior Fellowship in Educational Research

Subjects: Educational research; preference may be given to projects in the areas of early childhood education, test developments, Maori schooling, and curriculum evaluation of vocational and professional education.

No. offered: One Fellowship every two years.

Value: NZ$14,500 payable on a monthly basis.

Tenable at the Council or at some other agreed New Zealand location for six to twelve months. All Fellows are expected to spend some time at the Council.

Eligibility: It is expected that applicants will be university graduates of good standing, preferably with master's degrees or better, and distinction as a teacher or administrator will be a primary consideration. Preference will be given to applicants who are able to provide evidence of literary scholarship, outstanding service in schools, colleges or universities and an easily identifiable interest in educational policies or practices. The Fellowship is not offered to advance or complete individual's academic qualifications and professional certificates.

Further information from:
Director
New Zealand Council for Educational
  Research
P.O. Box 3237
Wellington
New Zealand

[1575]

NEW ZEALAND FEDERATION OF UNIVERSITY WOMEN

Postgraduate Felowships

Subjects: Unrestricted: research.

No. offered: Two Fellowships annually.

Value: NZ$4,000 per annum, plus overseas

travel and other allowances at the Federation's discretion.

Tenable at any recognised university or research institution in any country (under conditions to be approved by the Trust Board) for one year.

Eligibility: Open to female graduates of a New Zealand university, or female graduates of other universities who have resided in New Zealand for at least five years prior to application. Candidates must be members of the New Zealand Federation of University Women, of at least two months' standing.

Note: Recipients must submit to the Federation a full report of research carried out during the tenure of the Fellowship.

Closing date: 31st July.

Further information from:
Secretary-Treasurer
New Zealand Federation of University Women
P.O. Box 2006 Wellington
New Zealand

[1576]

NEW ZEALAND INSTITUTE OF INTERNATIONAL AFFAIRS

The Institute occasionally makes Grants to finance research activities in the area of international affairs.

Further information from:
New Zealand Institute of International Affairs
P.O. Box 19-102
Wellington 2
New Zealand

[1577]

NEW ZEALAND LIBRARY ASSOCIATION

Russell Clark Award of NZ$50 and a medal is offered annually for the most distinguished illustrations for a children's book. The illustrator must be a citizen or resident of New Zealand. Books may be nominated by the judges or submitted for consideration.

Esther Glen Award of NZ$50 and a medal is offered annually to the author of the book which is considered to be the most distinguished contribution to literature for children, by an author who is a citizen or resident of New Zealand. Books may be nominated by the judges or submitted by authors.

John Harris Award of NZ$50 and a diploma is offered each year for published works in the bibliographical, critical, historical or administrative fields which are contributions to New Zealand librarianship. Works to be considered must have been published within the last three years and should be submitted by 1st July.

Further information from:
Executive Officer
New Zealand Library Association
P.O. Box 12.212
Wellington North
New Zealand

[1578]

NEW ZEALAND SOCIETY OF ACCOUNTANTS

Peter Barr Research Fellowship

No. offered: One Fellowship in even-numbered years.

Value: Up to NZ5,000.

Tenable in New Zealand or overseas.

Eligibility: Open to members of the Society wishing to extend their knowledge of developments in their profession. Preference is given to members of some years' standing.

Note: The Fellowship may also be used to finance the visit of a leading overseas member of the accounting profession to give a series of lectures in New Zealand.

Closing date: 30th September in the year of the award.

Further information from:
Executive Director
New Zealand Society of Accountants
P.O. Box 11342
Wellington
New Zealand

[1579]

NEW ZEALAND WOOL BOARD

F.R. Callaghan Wool Awards

Purpose: To enable personnel to undertake projects, research programmes, travel or education which will be of benefit to the New Zealand wool industry.

Subjects: Unrestricted—relevant to New Zealand wool.

No. offered: Variable.

Value: Variable; a total sum of NZ$5,000 is offered annually.

Tenable anywhere for a year or more.

Eligibility: Open to persons currently working within the wool industry, or intending to take up employment in the industry, or wishing to undertake a project of importance to the industry.

Note: Recipients must undertake to provide a written report on completion of tenure.

Awards are advertised in New Zealand newspapers, universities, trade associations and government departments annually in July/August.

Closing date: 30th September.

Further information from:
Secretary
New Zealand Wool Board
Private Bag
Wellington, C.1
New Zealand

[1580]

NEWBERRY LIBRARY (Chicago)
Center for the History of the American Indian

Francis C. Allen Fellowships are available to women of Indian heritage who are pursuing an academic program at any stage beyond the undergraduate degree. Candidates may be working in any graduate or pre-professional field, but the particular purpose of the Fellowship is to encourage study in the humanities and social sciences. Length of term may vary from one month to a year; stipend varies according to need. Fellows are expected to spend a significant amount of their Fellowship term in residence at the Center for the History of the American Indian. Applicants will be evaluated according to their academic goal, demonstrated potential for accomplishment, and financial need. Applications are due 1st February.

Exxon Education Foundation Fellowships: One six-month Fellowship with stipend of US$8,500, and up to ten shorter-term Fellowships (for periods not longer than three months) with stipends of US$600 per month, for work in residence at the Newberry. Applicants must be post-doctoral scholars at early statges in their professional careers whose work gives clear promise of productivity and whose careers would be significantly enhanced by their residence at the Newberry. Applications will be accepted for study in any field appropriate to the Newberry's collections. Completed applications are due 1st March.

D'Arcy McNickle Memorial Fellowships: Awarded to Indian applicants, primarily for work in residence at the Newberry Library. The length of stay and value of this Fellowship vary according to individual circumstances. Fellowships are designed to be used by academic students, adults who can spare only short periods of time from community commitments, tribal historians, and librarians and archivists of tribal cultural centers. Further information and application forms are available from the Library.

Pre-doctoral Fellowship: One Fellowship of US$7,500 for an eleven month appointment, plus US1,500 to be contributed by the Fellow's own institution, or two Fellowships for six months each of US$3,750, plus US$750 to be contributed by the Fellow's own institution are available annually to candidates who have completed all requirements for the doctorate, except the dissertation. *Closing date:* 1st April.

Intermediate Fellowships: Fellowships of four, six and eleven months each are available annually to young scholars at the postdoctoral level, or to individuals who have virtually completed doctoral dissertations, with or without academic appointments. Awards are designed for promising young historians just beginning their careers for scholars in other disciplines wishing to develop competence in American Indian history. Stipends are US$13,000 maximum for eleven month's residency, plus a contribution by the Fellow's own institution, if any, at the rate of US$2,000 to match the maximum eleven month stipend. *Closing date:* 1st February.

Further information from:
Committee on Awards
Newberry Library
60 West Walton Street
Chicago, Illinois 60610
U.S.A.

[1581]

NEWBERRY LIBRARY *(Chicago)*

Short-Term Resident Fellowships for Individual Research in any field appropriate to the Library's collections are available to applicants of any nationality. Candidates should have a Ph.D. degree or have completed all requirements for the degree except the dissertation. Preference is given to those who particularly need the facilities of the Library and live outside Chicago. The Fellowships of US$600 per month are tenable at the Library for up to three months. *Closing date:* 1st March and 15th October.

Resident Fellowships for Unaffiliated Scholars are awarded for work on a specific research project in any field appropriate to the Library's collections. Eligible scholars are those who are not employed professionally as such, who have a Ph.D., and who propose to use the Newberry as a scholarly base (at least 6 to 8 hours per week in residence and full participation in the intellectual life of the Newberry). Stipends of US$250 or US$500 per calendar quarter, depending upon needs, may be renewed quarterly for up to one year. After one year, Fellowship status may be renewed annually, but without stipend. *Closing dates:* 1st March and 15th October.

Further information from:
Committee on Awards
Newberry Library
60 West Walton Street
Chicago, Illinois 60610
U.S.A.

[1582]

NEWBERRY LIBRARY *(Chicago)*

Newberry Library Program in the Humanities of the Associated Colleges of the Midwest and the Great Lakes Colleges Association: Two Fellowships annually, one for eleven months and one for six months, are available to faculty members of the ACM/GLCA. Fellows share teaching responsibilities and continue their own research. In addition, the eleven-month Fellow serves as Program Director for the year. Stipends are approximately US$1,300 per month (depending on salary), plus partial housing subsidy. *Closing date:* 15th February.

Note: Candidates for ACM/GLCA Fellowships should contact *Elizabeth Hayford, 18 South Michigan Avenue, Suite 1010, Chicago, Illinois 60603.*

Hermon Dunlap Smith Center for the History of Cartography offers Fellowships for research in the history of cartography of US$600 per month for periods not exceeding three months. Candidates may be of any nationality and applications may be submitted at any time.

Further information from:
Committee on Awards
Newberry Library
60 West Walton Street
Chicago, Illinois 60610
U.S.A.

[1583]

NEWBERRY LIBRARY *(Chicago)*
National Endowment for the Humanities

Postdoctoral Fellowships

Purpose: To encourage scholarly research in any field appropriate to the Library's collections, and to deepen and enrich the opportunities for serious intellectual exchange through the active participation of Fellows in the Library community.

No. offered: Variable, depending upon available funds.

Value: Up to US$20,000 (for eleven months' residency).

Tenable at the Library for periods of from six to eleven months.

Eligibility: Open to United States citizens or nationals and foreign nationals living in the U.S. for at least three years who are established scholars at the postdoctoral level or its equivalent.

Note: Fellowships may be combined with sabbatical or other stipendiary support.

Also see National Endowment for the Humanities.

Closing date: 15th January.

Further information from:
Committee on Awards
Newberry Library
60 West Walton Street
Chicago, Illinois 60610
U.S.A.

[1584]

NEWBERRY LIBRARY *(Chicago)*
Center for Renaissance Studies

Seminar and Summer Institute Fellowships

Ten Fellowships are available for post-doctoral scholars participating in a summer Institute on the reading, describing, citing and editing of French 16th- to 18th-century manuscripts and printed sources. Scholarships are for eight weeks and carry a stipend of US$2,500. *Closing date:* 1st March.

Note: The Center also aawards Fellowships of US$2,000 to faculty members and graduate students of member institutions of the Center to participate in seminars either at the Newberry Library or at the Folger Institute of Renaissance and Eighteenth-Century Studies. Further information on these Fellowships is available from the applicant's faculty representative or from the Center.

Further information from:
Committee on Awards
Newberry Library
60 West Walton Street
Chicago, Illinois 60610
U.S.A.

[1585]

NEWBERRY LIBRARY *(Chicago)*

Monticello College Foundation Fellowship for Women

Purpose: To offer the opportunity to young women to undertake work in residence at the Library, and to significantly enhance their careers through research and writing.

Subjects: Open to study in any field appropriate to the Newberry's collections.

Value: US$7,500.

Tenable at the Library for six months.

Eligibility: Open to women who hold at least a Ph.D.

Note: The Award is designed especially for younger women whose work gives clear promise of scholarly productivity. Preference is given to the applicant whose proposed study is concerned with the study of women.

Closing date: 1st March.

Further information from:
Committee on Awards
Newberry Library
60 West Walton Street
Chicago, Illinois 60610
U.S.A.

[1586]

NEWBERRY LIBRARY *(Chicago)*
National Research Council *(U.S.A.)*

Ford Foundation Postdoctoral Minorities Fellowships

Stipends of US$13,000, US$18,000, and US$25,000 are available through the National Research Council to postdoctoral applicants who are Black Americans, Mexican Americans, Puerto Ricans and American Indians. The Fellowships for research at the Library are tenable for twelve months and stipends vary in accordance to the number of years beyond the doctorate. In addition, the successful applicant is eligible for up to US$5,000 from the Library to cover specific research costs such as travel, duplication and typing.

Note: Further information can be obtained from the *National Research Council, 2101 Constitution Avenue, Washington, D.C. 20418*

Completed applications should be forwarded to the Library by 1st February.

Address
Committee on Awards
Newberry Library
60 West Walton Street
Chicago, Illinois 60610
U.S.A.

[1587]

NEWBERRY LIBRARY *(Chicago)*

Newberry Library-British Academy Fellowship for Study in the U.K.

Subjects: Humanities.

No. offered: One Fellowship annually.

Value: A stipend of £12 per diem while the Fellow is in the United Kingdom. The Fellow's home institution is expected to continue to pay his salary.

Tenable in the United Kingdom for three months.

Eligibility: Preference is given to established scholars on the staffs of universities, museums or libraries.

Closing date: 1st March.

Further information from:
  Committee on Awards
  Newberry Library
  60 West Walton Street
  Chicago, Illinois 60610
  U.S.A.

[1588]

NEWCOMEN SOCIETY OF NORTH AMERICA

The Society maintains a program of 17 Awards and one Grant, for work in various fields. The Grant consists of an annual Postdocatoral Fellowship at Harvard University in the amount of US$18,000 tenable for one year, for the purpose of reesearch and study in the field of business history. The *Thomas Newcomen Award in Business History* of US$1,000 and an inscribed scroll is awarded in cooperation with the Harvard Graduate School of Business Administration for the best book on the history of business published during a three-year period. Two *Newcomen Awards in Business History* are offered annually for articles publshed in *Business History Review*. First Prize of US$300 and an inscribed scroll is given for the best article published in the *Review*; Second Prize of US$150 and an inscribed scroll is given for the best article published in the *Review* by an author no more than 35 years of age who has not published a book. The *Newcomen Gold Medal in Steam* is awarded every three years, in cooperation with the Franklin Institute, to an individual who has made an outstanding contribution in the field of steam and steam utilization.

Newcomen Awards in Material History of US$250 and a scroll are awarded to students submitting winning theses in material or industrial history. Awards are presented annually at twelve selected United States universities. The *Newcomen Award for Notable Proficiency in Mathematics, Physics and Chemistry* of US$250 and an inscribed scroll is presented annually at Drexel University.

Further information from:
  Newcomen Society of North America
  P.O. Box 113
  Downington, Pennsylvania 19335
  U.S.A.

[1589]

NEWSPAPER FUND, INC. *(U.S.A.)*

Teacher Fellowship Program

Purpose: To provide journalism education to those teachers who have been placed in the position of teaching journalism and advising student publications, but have had no formal journalism education themselves.

Subjects: Basic journalism courses, including reporting, layout and design, and newspaper publication workshops.

No. offered: Fifty Fellowships annually.

Value: US$350, to be used as tuition costs.

Tenable at a department of journalism in a college or university in the United States, as approved by the Fund.

Eligibility: Open to high school journalism teachers and publications advisors with little or no previous journalism background.

Closing date: 1st April.

Further information from:
  Newspaper Fund
  P.O. Box 300
  Princeton, New Jersey 08540
  U.S.A.

[1590]

NEWSPAPER GUILD *(U.S.A.)*

Heywood Broun Award

An annual Award of US$1,000 and a Guild Citation is offered in recognition of individual journalistic achievement, particularly that which helps right a wrong or correct an injustice. The competition is open to professional journalists who are employees in the Guild's jurisdiction on newspapers, news, and wire services, news magazines, and radio and television stations in the United States, Canada and Puerto Rico, whether they are members of the Guild or not. Team entries are not excluded; however first consideration will be given behalf of individuals and teams of no more than two persons. Managerial or other employees, freelancers, and publications or entries by entire staffs are ineligible. Entries may be submitted by anyone, on their own or another's behalf. Work for which the Award is sought must be done or completed during the calendar year preceding that of the closing date. All entries must be received no later than 15th January.

Further information from:
Broun Award Committee
Newspaper Guild
1125 Fifteenth Street, N.W.
Washington, D.C. 20005
U.S.A.

[1591]

NIEMAN FOUNDATION FOR JOURNALISM *(U.S.A.)*
Harvard University

Lucius W. Nieman Fellowships for Journalists

Purpose: To provide a mid-career opportunity for journalists (including news photographers) to study and broaden their intellectual horizons.

No. offered: Approximately twelve Fellowships annually.

Value: A weekly stipend, plus tuition charges.

Tenable at Harvard University, Cambridge, Massachusetts, for one academic year.

Eligibility: Open to United States citizens who have had at least three years' media experience (most have had between five and ten). Candidates must secure consent from employers for leave of absence, and must agree to return to their organization at the end of the academic year. No professional writing is allowed during the period of the Fellowship. Journalists who work full-time for newspapers, magazines of general interest, press services, television or radio are eligible.

Note: All departments of Harvard University are open to Nieman Fellows, who may select their own studies and pursue them through courses or in more informal ways—usually in public affairs (history, government, economics, sociology, foreign area studies) or such fields as science, labor, education, law and literature.

Fellows are not candidates for degrees and receive no formal credit for studies; they are therefore free of the usual degree requirements.

Each year the program includes between three and seven additional Nieman Fellows from foreign countries. These journalists must meet the same requirements as the American journalists but their stipends and tuition ordinarily must be obtained from sources other than the Foundation. Prospective foreign applicants should obtain application forms from the Foundation and then seek funding from a sponsoring agency in their region or nation.

Closing date: 1st February.

Further information from:
Nieman Foundation for Journalism
1 Francis Avenue
Cambridge, Massachusetts 02138
U.S.A.

[1592]

NOBEL FOUNDATION *(Sweden)*

Nobel Prizes

The Foundation exists to award five Prizes annually to those who "have conferred the greatest benefits on mankind" in the fields of physics, chemistry, physiology or medicine, literature and peace.

The prizes are adjudicated as follows: physics and chemistry—Royal Swedish Academy of Sciences; physiology or medicine—Nobel Assembly of Karolinska Institutet, Stockholm;

literature—Swedish Academy, Stockholm; peace—Norwegian Nobel Committee.

No account is taken of nationality, race, religion or ideology.

The Foundation cannot accept personal applications. The awarding institutions invite every year a certain number of statutorily competent persons to make proposals of candidates for the Prizes. Closing date is 1st February, and Prizes are announced in October or November.

The Nobel Foundation also administers a Prize in economic sciences offered by the Bank of Sweden in memory of Alfred Nobel. This Prize is adjudicated by the Royal Swedish Academy of Sciences according to rules corresponding to the ones governing the Nobel Prizes.

Further information from:
Nobel Foundation
Sturegatan 14
S-114 36 Stockholm
Sweden

[1593]

NORTH ATLANTIC TREATY ORGANIZATION

NATO Research Fellowships

Purpose: To promote study and research leading to publication on aspects of the North Atlantic Alliance.

Value: 130,000 Belgian francs, or the equivalent in the currency of any other member-state plus authorized travel expenses.

Tenable in one or more member-countries of NATO.

Eligibility: Open to citizens of any NATO member-state who are university graduates of established reputation.

Candidates will be selected on the basis of their special aptitude and experience for carrying through a major project of research. In making this selection such factors as academic qualifications, professional experience and publications will be taken into account.

NATO member-states—Belgium, Canada, Denmark, France, West Germany, Greece, Iceland, Italy, Luxembourg, Netherlands, Norway, Portugal, Turkey, United Kingdom, United States.

Note: Fellows are required to submit to NATO before the expiraton of their grant a final report in English or French on their studies. All studies are considered for publication, and manuscripts should be submitted in duplicate to NATO. Fellows are required to acknowledge the fact that their research was made possible through a NATO award.

Further details may be obtained from the national authority in the relevant NATO member-country: Canada—*Awards Committee, Royal Society of Canada, 344 Wellington Street, Ottawa, Ontario K1A ON4*; United Kingdom—*Director, Higher Education Department British Council, 10 Spring Gardens, London SW1A 2BN*; United States—*Council on International Exchange of Scholars, Suite 300, 11 Dupont Circle, N.W., Washington, D.C. 20036.*

Headquarters:
Information Service
North Atlantic Treaty Organization
B-1110 Brussels
Belgium

[1594]

NORTH ATLANTIC TREATY ORGANIZATION

NATO Science Fellowships

Purpose: To enable scientists and engineers to further their training, and to engage in research at laboratories in other NATO member countries.

Subjects: Basic, applied and engineering sciences.

No. offered: About 850 Fellowships annually.

Tenable in member countries of NATO for a few months to three years; renewable in some countries.

Eligibility: Open to citizens of NATO member-countries [see listing under NATO Research Fellowships] at the postgraduate or postdoctoral level.

Selection is based on the scientific quality of applicants and the proposed studies.

Note: For further details of support provided, eligibility and method of application, applicants should consult the national programme administrator in the relevant NATO member-country: Canada—*Dr. G. Julien, Directeur général, Conseil de recherches en sciences naturelles et en génie, Ottawa, Ontario K1A OR6*; United Kingdom—*Miss J. Melville, Science Research Council, P.O. Box 18, Swindon, Wiltshire SN2 1ET*; United States—*Dr. Lewis A. Gist, Division Director, Science Personnel Improvement, Higher Education in Science, National Science Foundation, 1800 G Street, N.W., Washington, D.C. 20550*.

Headquarters:
Scientific Affairs Division
North Atlantic Treaty Organization
B-1110 Brussels
Belgium

[1595]

NORTH ATLANTIC TREATY ORGANIZATION

Research Grants

Purpose: NATO Grants assist specific projects which rely mainly on national funding and where the international collaboration being promoted entails costs that are not met from other sources. The projects supported are carried out as joint efforts between teams in university, government and other institutes involved in scientific research, including industrial laboratories. Support provided includes travel and living expenses for the investigators to work in each other's institutions abroad; 85% of total awards are used for this purpose. Running expenses to allow flexibility in carrying out the project, such as consumables required for effective collaboration, can also be covered. Most fields of science are eligible though support is not given to projects in areas where other international funding agencies are already active. Although emphasis is given to fundamental aspects rather than to technological development, projects with promising applications are also funded. Theoreticians and experimentalists are involved in most projects; a sizeable amount of the research is of an interdisciplinary nature.

Value & Duration: Grants awarded are on average US$5000 for an initial period of one year. Upon demonstration of significant progress a Grant can be renewed, but projects are supported for a limited period and after two to four years they are expected to have reached a conclusion.

Restrictions: No financial support can be provided for scientists while on sabbatical or other extended leave abroad; no financial support can be provided to allow attendance at conferences or seminars; scientists working in non-member countries are not eligible for support irrespective of nationality; scientists working in member countries are eligible for support irrespective of nationality; projects which are a direct result or a continuation of postdoctoral research done abroad are not encouraged; a Research Grant cannot be awarded to a researcher already supported under this programme, and applicants who are involved in a previous grant must ensure that it is formally closed (by provision of a final report, inlcuding reprints and a financial statement) before making any new application.

Closing dates: 31st March, 15th April and 30th November.

Further information from:
Scientific Affairs Division
Research Grants Programme
North Atlantic Treaty Organization
B-1110 Brussels
Belgium

[1596]

NORTH ATLANTIC TREATY ORGANIZATION
Committee on the Challenges of Modern Society [CCMS]

Fellowship Programme

Purpose: To stimulate serious study of public policy as related to the natural and social environment; to help scholars and public officials increase their skills and knowledge in the field; and to contribute to training promising individuals for national and international positions in fields involving formulation of public policy with respect to problems of modern society. Priority is given to proposals which are related to current CCMS pilot studies.

Value: Variable. Not normaly exceeding 300,000 Belgian francs, paid in two equal installments in the currency of the member countries as required.

Tenable in NATO countries for periods from six to twelve months; not renewable.

Eligibility: Open to citizens of NATO member-countries [see NATO Research Fellowships] who must generally hold a degree equivalent to the first university-level degree (normally, graduate work would be expected for qualification).

Candidates should have demonstrated research interest and/or experience in subject areas related to one of the on-going CCMS pilot projects.

Note: For applications and further information, candidates should write to the national authority in the relevant NATO member-country: Canada—*CCMS Fellowship Programme, Finance and Planning Service, International Programmes Branch, Environment Canada, Ottawa, Ontario K1A OH3*; United Kingdom—*CCMS Coordinator for U.K. Room A3 10, Romney House, Marsham Street, London SW1*; United States—*CCMS Coordinator for U.S.A., Room 819—West Tower, Environmental Protection Agency, 401 M Street, S.W., Washington, D.C. 20460*.

Closing date: 31st March.

Address:
Scientific Affairs Division
CCMS Secretariat
North Atlantic Treaty Organization
B-1110 Brussels
Belgium

[1597]

NORTH ATLANTIC TREATY ORGANIZATION

Science Committee Special Programmes

The NATO Science Committee has identified specialised scientific areas as deserving particular encouragement or preferential support for limited periods. A variety of mechanisms are employed to stimulate greater international collaboration—e.g., grants supporting study abroad or collaborative research, personnel exchanges, and conferences and workshops. The following four areas are being promoted in this way: eco-sciences, human factors, marine sciences and materials science.

Support for projects in these areas is available to scientists who are citizens of NATO member-countries [see NATO Research Fellowships].

Further information from:
Scientific Affairs Division
North Atlantic Treaty Organization
B-1110 Brussels
Belgium

[1598]

NORTH ATLANTIC TREATY ORGANIZATION

Advanced Institutes and Workshops Programme

The purpose of the Programme is to contribute to the dissemination of advanced knowledge, to favour the establishment of personal, cultural and professional contacts among scientists from different countries and different research sectors (university, government, industry), to make an assessment of the state-of-the-art in a given subject, and to recommend future research directions. With these objectives in mind, two specific types of interactive meeting are supported:

An *Advanced Study Institute* (ASI) is primarily a high-level teaching activity at which a carefully defined subject is presented in a systematic and coherently-structured programme to meetings of between 60 and 100 persons from various countries, and of about two weeks' duration. The subject is treated in considerable depth by lecturers eminent in their field and normally of international standing; the subject is presented to other scientists who will already have specialised in the field or possess an advanced general background. An ASI is aimed at an audience of approximately postdoctoral level this does not, however, necessarily exclude (post)graduate students and may well include senior scientists of high qualifications and notable achievement in the subject of the Institute or related fields. For ASIs financial support of approximately US$30,000 is provided to cover the major part of travel and living expenses for lecturers and to contribute to these expenses for students from NATO countries who are unable to find sufficient support from elsewhere. The NATO grant often represents only part sponsorship of the Institute, and additional funds may be obtained from other sources.

An *Advanced Research Workshop* (ARW) is a meeting of one week's duration or less at which a limited number of scientific leaders and experts from various countries, from different scientific fields and different sectors, come together for a short period to achieve one or more of the following general objectives: (a) to exchange thoughts at the boundaries of knowledge or at the frontiers of different fields; (b) to review and critically assess the state-of-the-art; (c) to make recommendations for future research directions; (d) to formulate plans for large international scientific experiments. An ARW, as any working meeting, should also have well-defined specific objectives. Such workshops are not tutorial in character. Each participant is, therefore, expected to play an active role in the meeting and to contribute to the discussions and preparation of reports as appropriate. Attendance at an ARW is between 30 and 50 persons. The level of funding for ARWs is fixed on a case-by-case basis, taking into account the objective, the number of participants and the duration of the meeting, together with the work involved in preparing the output. Direct organizational expenses are covered, and a contribution may be made to the travel and living expenses of participants, depending on the degree of their involvement.

Note: In principle ASIs and ARWs are supported in almost all scientific fields, with preference given to those involving scientists from different disciplines and different research sectors. However, some subjects, such as space sciences, nuclear energy and clinical medicine, do not generally qualify for support since they receive considerable support from other sources. Where appropriate, for both ASIs and ARWs participation from industrial, academic and governmental research sectors is encouraged, with the aim of achieving the optimum blend of expertise and a variety of complementary yet diverse viewpoints.

Scientists and engineers working permanently in NATO member countries are eligible to apply for financial support to direct a NATO meeting.

Closing dates: 15th January, 15th May and 15th September of the year preceding the proposed meeting.

Further information from:
Scientific Affairs Division
North Atlantic Treaty Organization
B-1110 Brussels
Belgium

[1599]

NORTH-RHINE/WESTPHALIAN MINISTRY OF EDUCATION
Heinrich Hertz Foundation

Scholarships

Purpose: To promote the sciences through the international exchange of university teachers and young scientists.

Value: Dependent upon individual needs.

Tenable in North-Rhine/Westphalia for non-German citizens, and outside the area for German citizens.

Eligibility: Open to university teachers and young scientists. Non-German citizens should have a working knowledge of German, and German citizens a working knowledge of the language of the host country.

Note: Applications should be submitted through a university teacher working in North-Rhine/Westphalia, and include a curriculum vitae, examination record, two references, and full description of the planned project with a timetable.

Further information from:
Minister für Wissenschaft und Forschung
Heinrich-Hertz-Stiftung
Völklinger Strasse 49
4000 Düsseldorf
West Germany

[1600]

NORTHWEST COLLEGE AND UNIVERSITY ASSOCIATION FOR SCIENCE *(U.S.A.)*
U.S. Department of Energy

Faculty Appointment Program: To provide an opportunity for university faculty members to participate in research activities at various Department of Energy sites, a number of Appointments are available to U.S. citizens who are employed by U.S. educational institutions.

Appointments are for a period of two months to one year in duration, and are salaried at US$1,750 per month or the appointee's certified university salary, whichever is less. A relocation allowance of US$75 per month plus round-trip transportation charges may be made.

All applications are considered without reference to sex, race, creed, color or national origin. Selection is based upon the educational and scientific qualifications of the applicant, the nature of the proposed research, the extent that it would be enhanced if conducted at a DOE site and the ultimate benefit to the home institution.

Faculty Appointments are contingent upon the granting of necessary security clearance and the availability of funds. Applicants on sabbatical leave are eligible for an Appointment. Application forms may be obtained by writing to the address below. *Closing date:* 10th January.

Laboratory Graduate Program: An unspecified number of qualified graduate students, primarily those working toward the doctoral degree in a scientific field, are offered the opportunity to perform the major portion of their dissertational or thesis research using laboratory facilities available at the project site. Initial appointments are for three months to one academic/calendar year and are renewable for an additional year. The annual basic stipend for twelve months is US$7,800. An allowance for round-trip travel is also provided. Candidates should be U.S. citizens who are registered at U.S. universities.

Applications are considered without reference to sex, race, creed, color or national origin. Selection is based largely on the extent to which the proposed research would be enhanced if conducted at a DOE facility. Awards are made contingent upon the granting of necessary security clearance and availability of funds.

Applications are to be made by the graduate dean on behalf of the candidate and should be filed at least four months in advance of the date the candidate wishes to begin the proposed research. Applications may be received at any time or by 10th January for a summer appointment.

Further information from:
Northwest College and University Association for Science
100 Sprout Road
Richland, Washington 99352
U.S.A.

[1601]

NORWEGIAN AGENCY FOR INTERNATIONAL DEVELOPMENT

Fellowships for NORAD Courses

Courses: Professional shipping (Oslo); ship and offshore structure inspection (Oslo); pulp and paper technology (Trondheim); hydro-power development (Trondheim); electric power distribution systems (Trondheim); nutrition (Bergen); fishing and fish technology (Trondheim); petroleum prospecting and reservoir evaluation (Trondheim); oceanography for marine civil engineering (Trondheim); animal husbandry (As); soil science (As).

Value: Tuition fees, living expenses and round-trip fare.

Tenable for the duration of the Courses at the centres listed above.

Eligibility: Applicants should be nationals of developing countries, aged between 25 and 35 years, and highly qualified in their respective fields. They must have a good working knowledge of English, Fellowships are awarded only to candidates nominated by their governments, and Fellows must agree to return to the home country upon termination of the Fellowship to take up their duties again.

Note: Applications in duplicate, with transcripts of examination records, certificates and recommendations, should be forwarded to the nearest Norwegian embassy or consulate for transmission to NORAD.

Closing date: 31st December.

Further information from:
Norwegian Agency for International Development
P.O. Box 8142 Dep
Oslo 1
Norway

[1602]

NORWEGIAN COLLEGE OF AGRICULTURE *(As-NLH)*

Exchange Scholarships

Exchange Scholarships are open to agricultural students from Denmark, Finland, Hungary, Poland, Sweden, Switzerland and the United Kingdom, and are tenable at the College for two weeks. The Scholarships cover tuition and lodging. Scholars from Hungary and Poland also receive pocket money. For the one place annually available to them, United Kingdom candidates should apply through the *Student Exchange Committee, Faculty of Agriculture, University of Nottingham, Sutton Bonington, Loughborough, Leicestershire.*

Further information from:
 Agriculture Students Exchange
  Committee
 Boks 208
 1432 As-NLH
 Norway

[1603]

NORWEGIAN RESEARCH COUNCIL FOR SCIENCE AND THE HUMANITIES

Postgraduate and Senior Research Fellowships

Subjects: Basic research in the humanities, social sciences, medical sciences and natural sciences.

Value: From 100,000 Norwegian kroner per year and higher, depending upon qualifications and experience.

Tenable for one year at a Norwegian research institution; renewable for a period of up to three years.

Eligibility: Open to suitably qualified foreign nationals who intend to pursue a programme of research of interest to a Norwegian research institution.

Note: Application to the Council should be made on the candidate's behalf by a Norwegian research institution willing to accept the candidate for the proposed programme of research. Personal applications are not accepted.

Closing date: 15th May.

Further information from:
 Norwegian Research Council for Science
  and the Humanities
 Munthes Gate 29
 Oslo 2
 Norway

[1604]

NORWICH JUBILEE ESPERANTO FOUNDATION *(U.K.)*

Grants-in-Aid

Purpose: To encourage the thorough study of Esperanto by enabling young students to travel abroad, and to promote research into the teaching of Esperanto.

No. offered: According to available funds.

Value: Normally between £50 and £150; maximum £350.

Tenable in a country other than that of the recipient for a period of one week to several months.

Eligibility: Open to citizens of any country who are not more than 25 years old, require financial assistance and have a high standard of competence in Esperanto. An efficiency test will be given. There are no set academic or age requirements for research Grants.

Note: Candidates may obtain further information from *British Esperanto Association, 140 Holland Park Avenue, London W11 4UF,* or from:
 Norwich Jubilee Esperanto Foundation
 237 Two Trees Lane
 Denton, Manchester
 England M34 1QL

[1605]

NUFFIELD FOUNDATION *(U.K.)*

Social Science Research Fellowships

Purpose: To enable teachers in universities and polytechnics in the United Kingdom to pursue their research interest on a full-time basis.

Subjects: Social sciences and social studies.

Value: According to individual projects.

Tenable in social science departments of United Kingdom universities or polytechnics for three months to two years.

Eligibility: Open to social scientists with some research experience.

Closing date: 31st December.

Further information from:
Nuffield Foundation
Nuffield Lodge, Regent's Park
London
England NW1 4RS

[1606]

NUFFIELD FOUNDATION *(U.K.)*

Science Research Fellowships

Purpose: To enable young university scientists to pursue full-time research.

Subjects: Natural and applied sciences, excluding mathematics.

Value: To cover replacement teaching for the period of the Fellowship, plus research expenses.

Tenable in the United Kingdom for one year.

Eligibility: Open to science lecturers holding posts in United Kingdom universities and polytechnics who are less than forty years of age.

Closing date: Mid-October.

Further information from:
Nuffield Foundation
Nuffield Lodge, Regent's Park
London
England NW1 4RS

[1607]

NUFFIELD FOUNDATION *(U.K.)*

Elizabeth Nuffield Educational Fund

Purpose: To provide assistance to women students whose educational needs cannot be met from other sources.

Subjects: Courses of study or training leading to careers of service.

Value: By individual assessment.

Tenable at universities, colleges and other educational institutions in the United Kingdom.

Eligibility: Preference is given to candidates who are working for a first degree or other similar intial qualifications.

Candidates must intend to live and work permanently in the United Kingdom.

Note: Applications must be supported by a university, college or other educational institution.

Further information from:
Secretary
Elizabeth Nuffield Educational Fund
Nuffield Foundation
Nuffield Lodge, Regent's Park
London
England NW1 4RS

[1608]

NURSES' EDUCATIONAL FUNDS, INC. *(U.S.A.)*

Fellowships and Scholarships

Purpose: To provide the opportunity to registered nurses who seek to qualify through advanced study for positions in administration, supervision, education, clinical specialization and research.

Value: Between US$1,000 and US$3,000.

Tenable for at least one academic year in any college or university offering programs in nursing accredited by the NLN.

Eligibility: Open to United States citizens or persons who have officially declared the intention of becoming United States citizens. Preference is given to full-time students.

Note: Completed applications must be accompanied by transcripts of academic records, references, proof of membership in the American Nurses Association, and proof of admission to a program of nursing education accredited by the National League for Nursing. Application forms are available from Nurses' Educational Funds, Inc. at any time.

Fellowships and Scholarships administered by the NEF include those donated by: *American Journal of Nursing Company, Mead Johnson, E.R. Squibb and Sons, C.V. Mosby Company, W.B. Saunders Company, Nurses' Scholarship and Fellowship Fund, National Student Nurses' Association, Edith M. Pritchard Award, Isabel Hampton Robb Award, Leisel M. Hiemenz Award, Blanche Urey*

Award, Bernard J. Springer Award, Isabel McIsaac Award, Lucy C. Perry Award.

Applicants are advised to apply to the school of nursing of their choice concerning fellowships and scholarships available there.

Closing date: 15th January preceding the academic year for which funds are sought.

Further information from:
Nurses' Educational Funds, Inc.
555 West 57th Street
New York, New York 10019
U.S.A.

O

See *How to Use The Grants Register*, page ix

[1609]

OCEANOGRAPHIC MUSEUM *(Monaco)*

Research Grants

Subjects: Biological or physical oceanography.

No. offered: Two or three Grants per annum.

Value: Variable; a total of FF15,000 is available for grants annually.

Tenable for a minimum of one month; non-renewable.

Eligibility: Open to qualified oceanographers from all countries who hold at least a B.Sc. or equivalent qualification and are not less than 25 years of age.

Closing date: 1st April.

Further information from:
Directeur
Musée océanographique
MC Monaco-Ville

[1610]

GEORGE OLMSTED FOUNDATION *(U.S.A.)*

Olmsted Scholar Program

The Program offers each year educational grants for two years of study in a foreign university to two outstanding officers from each of the three United States service academies and one outstanding officer from each military department who has earned a regular commission through other officer training programs. Study must be in a foreign language. Social and political sciences and international affairs are the preferred subject areas, but another choice by the Scholar is not precluded.

The Program also provides for assistance in obtaining an advanced degree at the conclusion of the overseas study, if approved by the Scholar's service. This study can take place at any accredited university in the United States approved by the Department of Defense for attendance by military officers immediately following the overseas study, or later if this is more convenient.

A descriptive brochure on the Program is available from:
Executive Vice President
George Olmsted Foundation
1515 North Courthouse Road
Arlington, Virginia 22201
U.S.A.

[1611]

EUGENE O'NEILL MEMORIAL THEATER CENTER *(Waterford, Connecticut)*

National Playwrights Conference

Sixteen playwrights are chosen annually to participate in the Conference by working on their plays together with other talented professional theater and media artists. Stipends of US$200 plus room and board for the month of the Conference, held in July-August, are awarded.

Playwrights, who are United States citizens or permanent residents may submit one script of an original play for the theater and/or original scripted work for television. All submissions must be previously unproduced works. All plays selected, both theater and media, are eligible for the ABC Theater Award, consisting of a US$10,000 cash grant and first option to negotiate for television rights by ABC television.

Manuscripts are accepted from 15th September to 1st December.

Further information from:
Eugene O'Neill Memorial Theater Center
Suite 601, 1860 Broadway
New York, New York 10023
U.S.A.

[1612]

EUGENE O'NEILL MEMORIAL THEATER CENTER *(Waterford, Connecticut)*

O'Neill Composer/Librettist Conference

The Conference, aimed toward the development of talented composers and librettists in the field of lyric theater, is held at the Center each summer. Lyric theater is understood to include opera, musical plays or any comparable work. Adaptations are acceptable.

Those chosen will have the opportunity to develop their work, while in residence at the Center, with a group of professional singers and artistic staff. One work will be developed for television and the others for stage.

Participating composers and librettists will receive a stipend of *US*$250 plus room and board, as well as transportation to the Conference.

All submitted works should be complete or near completion, and must be original, previously unproduced, and not currently under option. Further information may be obtained from *Marilyn Glassman, O'Neill Theater Center, 305 Great Neck Road, Waterford, Connecticut 06385*. Applications are accepted between 15th September and 30th November. Notification will be made in December.

Address:
Eugene O'Neill Memorial Theater Center
Suite 601, 1860 Broadway
New York, New York 10023
U.S.A.

[1613]

ONTARIO INSTITUTE FOR STUDIES IN EDUCATION

Graduate Assistantships

Purpose: To enable candidates of any nationality to enter the programs of the Institute's various departments for work toward a master's or doctoral degree.

Subjects: Curriculum, educational planning, history and philosophy of education, sociology in education, applied psychology, higher education, special education, educational measurement and evaluation, computer applications, and educational administration.

No. offered: Approximately 350 Assistantships annually (including those offered to Canadian citizens and landed immigrants).

Value: Up to *Can*$5,500 (in 1981) for one academic year (eight months), plus up to *Can*$2,750 for the summer period.

Eligibility: Open to persons who are suitably qualified for the graduate program concerned.

Closing date: 1st February.

Further information from:
Admissions, Office of the Coordinator
of Graduate Studies
Ontario Institute for Studies in Education
252 Bloor Street West
Toronto, Ontario
Canada M5S 1V6

[1614]

ERNST OPPENHEIMER MEMORIAL TRUST *(South Africa)*

University Travelling Fellowships

Purpose: To enable selected members of staff of Southern African universities to travel overseas in order to undertake a year of advanced study and research.

Value: R4,000.

Eligibility: Southern African universities may submit the names of not more than two candidates, on order of merit. In selecting Fellows, consideration will be given to the value of the work proposed (its implication for education as a whole and its application to the university concerned), the effectiveness and practicability of the programme, and the credentials of the applicant, including the ability to profit from the study.

Closing date: Universities should submit nominations by 30th September.

Note: Further information is available from Southern African universities.

[1615]

ORDER OF THE ALHAMBRA *(U.S.A.)*

Scholarships

Purpose: To assist teachers of retarded persons, and those preparing to teach who wish to undertake special studies to qualify them for teaching the mentally, physically and emotionally handicapped child.

Value: US$200 each.

Tenable at any accredited public or private university or college offering bona fide courses in special education. Scholarships may be renewed annually without stipulation as to the lenth of time to be spent in pursuing training.

Eligibility: Open to postgraduates and to those entering their third year of college. Applicants should be able to give evidence of earning at least three credit hours during any specified semester, and should obtain a letter of endorsement from the college or university authority.

Further information from:
Order of the Alhambra
4200 Leeds Avenue
Baltimore, Maryland 21229
U.S.A.

[1616]

ORENTREICH FOUNDATION FOR THE ADVANCEMENT OF SCIENCE, INC. *(U.S.A.)*

Research Grants

Purpose: To promote research in dermatology and aging.

Subjects: Acne and hirsutism, alopecia areata, plasmapheresis and steroid hormones in foods.

No. offered: Approximately five Grants annually.

Value: Between US$5,000 and US$10,000, paid in a lump sum.

Eligibility: Open to suitably qualified persons engaged in research at accredited universities and research institutions in the United States.

Further information from:
Orentreich Foundation for the
Advancement of Science, Inc.
910 Fifth Avenue
New York, New York 10021
U.S.A.

[1617]

ORGANIZATIONS OF AMERICAN HISTORIANS

The Organization gives five Awards each year and a sixth and seventh Award every two years to encourage scholarly writing in the field of American history.

Ray Allen Billington Award of US$500 and a medal will be awarded every two years for the best book on American frontier history.

Binkley—Stephenson Award is given annually to an author of any nationality who has written the best scholarly article published in the *Journal of American History* during the preceding year. The Award is US$500.

Merle Curti Award of US$500 and a medal is awarded annually, alternating between a book in American intellectual history and one in social history published during the preceding two years. *Closing date:* 1st October.

Richard W. Leopold Prize of an unstated value is given every two years for the best book on foreign policy, military affairs, historical activities of the federal government, or biography by a government historian.

Louis Pelzer Memorial Award is given annually to a graduate student of any nationality for the best essay in American history submitted to the committee. The value of the award is US$500, a medal and publication of the essay in the *Journal of American History*. *Closing date:* 1st January.

Charles Thomson Prize of US$250 plus publication in *Prologue*, is given annually to the author of a previously unpublished essay to encourage archival research. This Prize is cosponsored by the National Archives.

Frederick Jackson Turner Award is given annually to the author of a book-length manuscript on American history who has not previously published such a study. A university press committed to the publication of the work must submit the manuscript by 1st September. An Award of US$500, a certificate and a medal is presented to the author. The university press that publishes the manuscript receives a subsidy of US$3,000 to be used for the publication of another manuscript on American history.

Further information from:
Organization of American Historians
Indiana University
112 North Bryan Street
Bloomington, Indiana 47401
U.S.A.

[1618]

ORGANIZATION OF AMERICAN STATES

OAS Fellowships

Subjects: Except for medical sciences, the subjects are unrestricted: advanced study, training or research.

No. offered: Approximately 300 Fellowships annually.

Value: By individual assessment to cover registration and tuition fees, study material, subsistence and travel expenses.

Tenable in any OAS member-country other than the recipient's own, for not less than three months and not more than two years.

Eligibility: Open to citizens of OAS member-countries who hold a university degree. In addition, candidates must have sufficient knowledge of the language of the country in which they wish to study, be in good health, present proof that they have been accepted by the institution in which they wish to study or that they will have access to the facilities needed for research and agree to return to their own country at the end of the Fellowship. For advanced study or training Fellowships, an applicant is required to submit a detailed plan of study; for research Fellowships, an applicant must submit a detailed plan of his proposed research.

Note: The member-countries of OAS are Argentina, Barbados, Bolivia, Brazil, Chile, Colombia, Costa Rica, Dominican Republic, Ecuador, El Salvador, Grenada, Guatemala, Haiti, Honduras, Jamaica, Mexico, Nicaragua, Panama, Paraguay, Peru, Saint Lucia, Suriname, Trinidad and Tobago, the United States, Uruguay and Venezuela.

Closing dates: Selection is made in June to commence in September, and in November to commence in January. Applications should be completed by 30th April and 31st August.

Further information from:
Office of Fellowships and Training
Secretariat for Development Cooperation
Organization of American States
19th and Constitution Avenue, N.W.
Washington, D.C. 20006
U.S.A.

[1619]

ORIENTAL CERAMIC SOCIETY *(U.K.)*

George De Menasce Memorial Trust Bursary

A Bursary, usually £500, is offered from time to time to promote research in some aspect of oriental art. The recipient is required to write a paper on the research undertaken. Applicants are required to complete a form giving complete academic qualifications. Research connected with a Ph.D. degree is normally not considered adequate for the Bursary.

Further information from:
Secretary
Oriental Ceramic Society
31B Torrington Square
London
England WC1E 7JL

[1620]

PALOMA O'SHEA INTERNATIONAL PIANO COMPETITION *(Santander, Spain)*

The Competition, held annually in late July/early August in Santander, is open to pianists of any nationality who are between the ages of 16 and 32. The following Prizes are offered:

Great International Prize: First place—1,000,000 pesetas, a gold medal, recitals in Spain, and in Warsaw, Bordeaux and Bratislava, also one in Portugal and a U.S. tour, and a recording; Second place—500,000 pesetas, a silver medal and concerts in Spain; Third place—300,000 pesetas, a silver medal and concerts in Spain;

Fourth place—150,000 pesetas and a bronze medal; Fifth place—100,000 pesetas.

Best Performance Prize of Contemporaneous Music: This award, sponsored by the Gulbenkian Foundation, consists of 150,000 pesetas.

Prize for Best Interpretation of Contemporary Music: 100,000 pesetas.

Travel Grants and other awards are also offered.

Note: There is a nonrefundable registration fee of 2,000 pesetas. Registration forms are available upon request.

Closing date: 20th March for registration.

Further information from:
    Secretary
    Paloma O'Shea International Piano
        Competiton
    Hernán Cortés 3
    Santander
    Spain

[1621]

OVERSEAS ACADEMY OF SCIENCES
(France)

Georges Bruel Prize of FF200 is given annually to an author for writings concerned with the geography, economic history and cultural/ethnic studies of central Africa.

Eugene Etienne Prize of FF200 is given annually for individual or collective social or scientific works in the field of health, particularly in Africa.

Further information from:
    Académie des Sciences d'Outre-Mer
    15, rue la Pérouse
    Paris
    France

[1622]

OVERSEAS DEVELOPMENT ADMINISTRATION *(U.K.)*

Postgraduate Training Award Scheme

Purpose: To provide developing countries with experts and other skilled manpower to assist these countries in making the fullest use of their natural resources, and to build up the supply of young people in Great Britain who will be qualified, after their Studentships and some years of experience, to fill more senior overseas posts.

Subjects: Agriculture, agronomy, botany, cooperatives plant pathology, plant breeding, agricultural chemistry, agricultural economics, agricultural biometrics, agricultural engineering, soil science, fisheries, forestry, land tenure, veterinary surgery, highway engineering, water engineering, physical planning, human nutrition, education.

No. offered: Approximately 40 Awards annually.

Value: Students will receive the appropriate rates payable to graduates on first appointment to the Home Civil Service under the Ministry of Agriculture, Fisheries and Food—between £5,447 and £7,999 per annum; paid monthly.
    A foreign service allowance calculated on the Student's basic allowance, is payable during the period of any overseas study or attachment, and on outfit allowance also may be payable to Students going overseas. In addition to these direct payments, tuition fees, the cost of study projects not covered by fees, and the travel and overseas medical expenses of Students will be paid.

Tenable for the first year at a university in Britain for academic training usually leading to a master's degree; for the second year, practical training is most often provided overseas in a government department or other suitable organization.
    Studentships are given for either academic or practical training, or a combination of the two, depending upon the subject and needs of the Student.

Eligibility: Open to citizens of the United Kingdom who are normally resident there and have, or are about to obtain, their first degree or other qualification as required for the particular subject of study.

Note: Following training, Students are required to take up, for at least one tour of service (betwen two and three years), any overseas vacancies, if such vacancies exist, which the Administration has on its books and considers suitable for them.

Closing date: 31st January in the year the award is required.

Further information from:
Appointments Officer (PTAS)
Overseas Development Administration
Room AH364
Abercrombie House
Eaglesham Road
East Kilbride
Glasgow
Scotland G75 8EA

[1623]

OVERSEAS DEVELOPMENT ADMINISTRATION *(U.K.)*

Regional Technical Cooperation Training Programmes

Purpose: Awards are intended for postgraduate or practical studies which will assist in the social or economic development of developing countries.

Value: To cover the cost of travel to and from the United Kingdom, tuition fees, a monthly allowance sufficient to meet all day-to-day living expenses, and, in appropriate cases, book and warm clothing allowances.

Tenable in the United Kingdom for a minimum of three months to a maximum of three years, and in certain third-world countries.

Eligibility: Open to nationals of developing countries participating in United Kingdom technical cooperation arrangements, who are suitably qualified to undertake the proposed training course.

Note: Candidates for either of these training schemes should apply to the central external aid authority of their own government, which in turn may forward nominations to either the British Council Representative or the British Embassy or High Commission in the country concerned. Applications directly from individuals cannot be considered.

Address:
Overseas Development Administration
Eland House, Stag Place
London
England SW1E 5DH

[1624]

OVERSEAS DEVELOPMENT ADMINISTRATION *(U.K.)*

Commonwealth Tropical Medicine Research Studentships

Purpose: To increase research potential in tropical Commonwealth countries by providing further training and study in tropical medicine and related subjects such as nutrition, entomology and virology at universities and research centres in the United Kingdom (Studentships are not intended as a means of obtaining postgraduate qualifications).

Value: £269 per month plus return economy air fare. A marriage allowance of £135 per month is paid for a dependent spouse and £17, £14 and £11 per month, respectively, for the first three children under 16 accompanying the Student. Allowances are also paid for certain travel within the United Kingdom, books, laboratory fees, and, where applicable, clothing.

Tenable normally for one year at an approved institution.

Eligibility: Open to Commonwealth and British-protected students in the early postgraduate stages who are permanently resident in tropical Commonwealth countries, have research promise and wish to further their career prospects with a period of research training in Britain.

Note: Students are required to sign an undertaking to return to their own country on expiry of the Studentship. Applications should be sponsored by the appropriate governmental authority medical school or other appropriate institution. Particulars may be obtained from the British High Commission or the British Council office in the candidate's own country.

Further information from:
Room A418, Health and Natural
  Resources Department
Overseas Development Administration
Eland House, Stag Place
London
England SW1E 5DH

[1625]

OVERSEAS DEVELOPMENT ADMINISTRATION *(U.K.)*

Commonwealth Tropical Medicine Research Fellowships

Purpose: To increase research potential in tropical Commonwealth countries by providing further training and study in tropical medicine and related subjects such as nutrition, entomology and virology at universities and research centres in the United Kingdom.

Value: £385 per month plus return economy air fare. A marriage allowance of £135 per month is paid for a dependent spouse and £17, £14 and £11 per month, respectively, for the first three children under 16 accompanying the Fellow. Allowances are also paid for certain travel within the United Kingdom, books, laboratory fees, and, where applicable, clothing.

Tenable normally for one year at an approved institution.

Eligibility: Open to Commonwealth and British-protected research workers permanently resident in tropical Commonwealth countries, who have obtained postgraduate qualifications and can give evidence of good health and competence in English. Fellowships are not open to those normally resident in the United Kingdom.

Note: Fellows are required to sign an undertaking to return to their own country on expiry of the Fellowship. Applications should be sponsored by the appropriate governmental authority medical school or other appropriate institution. Particulars can be obtained from the British High Commission or the British Council office in the candidate's own country.

Further information from:
 Room A418, Health and Natural
  Resources Department
 Overseas Development Administration
 Eland House, Stag Place
 London
 England SW1E 5DH

[1626]

OVERSEAS DEVELOPMENT ADMINISTRATION *(U.K.)*

Commonwealth Tropical Medicine Senior Research Fellowships

Purpose: To enable senior established research workers from Commonwealth countries to acquaint themselves with current British practices in their own specialty.

Subjects: Tropical medicine and related fields.

Value: £36 per diem, tax-free, and return tourist air fare.

Tenable for three months at a university or appropriate research center in the United Kingdom.

Eligibility: Open to Commonwealth citizens or British-protected persons normally resident in tropical Commonwealth countries outside the United Kingdom. Candidates will generally be heads of departments or research team leaders, and should be competent in English.

Note: Fellows are required to sign an undertaking to return to their own country on expiry of the Fellowship. Applications should be sponsored by the appropriate governmental authority in the candidate's country (usually Department of Health), or by a university medical school or other appropriate institution. Particulars may be obtained from the British High Commission or the British Council office in the candidate's own country.

Further information from:
 Room A418, Health and Natural
  Resources Department
 Overseas Development Administration
 Eland House, Stag Place
 London
 England SW1E 5DH

[1627]

OVERSEAS DEVELOPMENT INSTITUTE *(U.K.)*

ODI Fellowships

Purpose: To give young development economists practical training and experience by providing them with the opportunity to work in economic and development planning ministries, or in planning units of other ministries, or with development corporations, etc., in developing countries.

Subjects: Economics or an allied field.

No. offered: Approximately twelve Fellowships annually.

Value: Approximately £6,000 per annum on average. Salary and gratuity from the employing organisation is supplemented by the institute.

Tenable in certain countries in East, Central or Southern Africa and the Caribbean for two years; not renewable, but Fellows may negotiate to continue under direct contract terms if they and the governments concerned wish them to remain for a further period.

Eligibility: Open to graduates of British universities; preference is given to British nationals. A good degree in economics or an allied field, with specialization in papers of particular relevance to the type of assignments likely to be undertaken is required; some knowledge of statistics is an advantage. Persons in their final year of studying for a first degree are eligible, subject to their obtaining a good degree. There is no fixed age limit, but Fellows are usually between 21 and 25 years of age.

Note: The Fellows become temporary civil servants of the governments concerned, and carry out such assignments as assisting in the preparation of a development plan, undertaking a manpower survey, recommending priorities for the allocation of development funds, and project appraisal and evaluation in a variety of sections.

Application forms are available from the address below and from appointment boards of British universities. Those selected normally take up Fellowships in August or September.

Closing date: Second Friday in November.

Further information from:
 Administrative Department
 Overseas Development Institute
 10-11 Percy Street
 London
 England W1P OJB

[1628]

OVERSEAS DEVELOPMENT INSTITUTE *(U.K.)*

Overseas Social Science Research Fellowships

Purpose: To enable British social scientists to carry out research in developing countries at institutions associated with the Research Fellowship Scheme.

Subjects: Empirical research useful for policy-making in subjects regarded as important by the receiving institution and government.

No. offered: Usually two or three Fellowships per annum, as vacancies occur.

Tenable at certain institutions in East Africa and the Caribbean for two years. Shorter or longer appointments may be possible.

Eligibility: Open to British nationals. Postgraduate qualifications and research records are normally required. Specific requirements may vary according to individual posts.

Note: Vacancies are advertised as they occur, and when additional information relevant to individual posts can be made available.

Further information from:
 Administrative Department
 Overseas Development Institute
 10-11 Percy Street
 London
 England W1P OJB

[1629]

OXFORD REGIONAL HOSPITAL BOARD
Medical Research Council *(U.K.)*
Oxford University

Fellowship in Clinical Psychopharmacology

Purpose: To offer training in some basic aspects of neuropharmacology relevant to a research project in clinical psychopharmacology.

Value: Remuneration appropriate to seniority. The salary will not be greater than that equivalent to a National Health Service senior registrar.

Tenable within the University Department and MRC Unit of Clinical Pharmacology, Oxford in close association with the University Department of Psychiatry. Normally the Fellowship is not offered for more than three years.

Eligibility: Open to young psychiatrists who require training in clinical and basic psychopharmacology. The Fellow is expected to take a higher degree during the tenure.

Further information from:
  MRC Clinical Pharmacology Unit
  University Department of Clinical
    Pharmacology
  Radcliffe Infirmary, Woodstock Road
  Oxford
  England OX2 6HE

P

See *How to Use The Grants Register*, page ix

[1630]

P.E.N. AMERICAN CENTER *(New York City)*

Ernest Hemingway Foundation Award: One Award of *US$6,000* is annually offered for the best novel or collection of short stories in the English language which is the first published work of fiction by an American author. Only books published in the United States are eligible for consideration. "Mysteries" or "westerns" will not be included unless their genre is deemed secondary to their overall literary purpose and literary quality. *Closing date:* 31st December.

P.E.N./Faulkner Award for Fiction of *US$2,000* is awarded annually to recognize the most distinguished work of fiction by an American author which has been published during the calendar year preceding that for which the Award is made. Entries may be novels or short story collections. Juvenile titles are not accepted. Publishers, authors and their agents should submit four copies of book titles, or preferable, one copy and one set of bound galleys to *P.E.N./Faulkner Award for Fiction, P.E.N. South, P.O. Box 3787, Charlottesville, Virginia 22903*. Further information may be requested from the address below. *Closing date:* 31st December.

P.E.N. Fund for Writers is available to help established United States writers through a financial emergency. Several grants with a maximum of *US$500* are given annually.

American-Scandinavian Foundation/P.E.N. Translation Prizes of *US$500* each plus publication are awarded for translations of poetry and fiction into English, by Danish, Finnish, Icelandic, Norwegian or Swedish authors born after 1880. Further information may be obtained from *Kathleen Madden, American-Scandinavian Foundation, 127 East 73rd Street, New York, New York 10021*, or from the P.E.N. Center. *Closing date:* 15th February.

Calouste Gulbenkian-P.E.N. Translation Prize: US$500 is awarded in odd-numbered years for a distinguished translation from the Portugese into English.

P.E.N. Translation Prize: US$1,000 is given annually for the best translation from any language into English published in the United States in the award year. Technical, scientific or reference works are not eligible. *Closing date:* 31st December.

Further information from:
P.E.N. American Center
47 Fifth Avenue
New York, New York 10003
U.S.A.

[1631]

P.E.N. INTERNATIONAL NEW ZEALAND CENTRE

First Book of Prose Award: One Award of NZ$600 is given annually for the most meritorious first book in the field of imaginative prose written by a New Zealand citizen.

First Book of Poetry Award: One Award of NZ$600 is given annually for the best first book of poetry written by a New Zealand citizen.

Not confirmed for 1983.

Further information from:
P.E.N. International New Zealand Centre
P.O. Box 2283
Wellington
New Zealand

[1632]

P.E.N. INTERNATIONAL—ZIMBABWE CENTRE

Longman Zimbabwe Literary Award

Three Awards, each consisting of Z$200 and a trophy, are given annually for a published work in English, Shona and Sindebele. Entries, which are judged on literary merit and popular appeal, may be in the following categories: books, series of articles, collections of poetry, broadcast radio scripts, published or performed plays, and creative writings. Individual works submitted, should be published between 1st January and 31st March of the following year; a series or number of works may be published over a greater length of time. Eligibility is restricted to those who are Zimbabwean by birth, are resident in or have a long association with Zimbabwe. *Closing date:* 31st March.

Further information from:
Awards Secretary
P.E.N. International—Zimbabwe Centre
P.O. Box 1900
Salisbury
Zimbabwe

[1633]

P.E.O. SISTERHOOD *(U.S.A., Canada)*

P.E.O. International Peace Scholarships

Subjects: Unrestricted, excepting medicine, dentistry and research.

No. offered: Approximately 100 Scholarships annually.

Value: Up to a maximum of US$2,400 depending on individual circumstances.

Tenable at approved universities and colleges in the United States and Canada for one year, with the possibility of renewal.

Eligibility: Open to women from any country, other than the United States and Canada, who have obtained admission to an approved university or college, for full-time graduate study leading towards a doctoral degree.
Applicants must have completed their master's degree program prior to application. Candidates who have enrolled at Cottey Junior College, Nevada, Missouri, which is owned and operated by the P.E.O. Sisterhood, as well as doctoral students applying for the first time and working only on their dissertation, are not eligible.

Note: Candidates must have a nonacademic sponsor who is a resident of the United States or Canada, and must sign a witnessed statement that they will return to their own countries immediately upon completion of the educational program.

Scholarships are awarded as grants-in-aid and as such may not necessarily cover all personal and academic expenses. Because of this, candidates must show proof of other resources.

Closing dates: Requests for applications are accepted between 1st October and 15th January of the following year.

Further information from:
P.E.O. International Peace Scholarship Fund
P.E.O. Executive Office
3700 Grand Avenue
Des Moines, Iowa 50312
U.S.A.

[1634]

NICOLO PAGANINI INTERNATIONAL VIOLIN COMPETITION *(Genoa)*

The Competition is held from late September to early October each year. Violinists of any nationality who are under 35 years of age may apply. The closing date for entry is 15th July. Prizes: 1st (Paganini Prize)—7,000,000 lire (indivisible); 2nd—2,000,000 lire; 3rd—1,000,000 lire; 4th—700,000 lire; 5th—500,000 lire; 6th—300,000 lire.

Further information from:
Secretariat
Nicolo Paganini International Violin Competition
Palazzo Tursi, Via Garibaldi 9
I-16100 Genoa
Italy

[1635]

PALESTINE EXPLORATION FUND *(U.K.)*

Grants

Research and/or Excavation Grants in Palestine are available annually. Applications should be received before the end of January and are considered on their merits by the Executive Committee, which would hope to make its decision in early March.

Further information from:
Secretary
Palestine Exploration Fund
2 Hinde Mews, Marylebone Lane
London
England W1M 5RH

[1636]

PAN AMERICAN HEALTH ORGANIZATION
Pan American Sanitary Bureau

Fellowships

Purpose: To promote improved standards of teaching and training in the health, medical and related professions which will assist in the strengthening of national health services.

Subjects: Public health, medical education and related fields.

Value: To cover the cost of transportation, tuition and maintenance.

Tenable outside the country of origin, usually in Latin America, for normally between two and twelve months.

Eligibility: Open to nationals of member-states of the Pan American Health Organization, i.e., all countries in the Americas, who are public health workers in all fields, especially deans or faculty members of schools of public health, medicine, dentistry, engineering, veterinary medicine and nursing. Candidates should not normally be over 55 years of age.
Pan American Health Organization Fellowships follow the same regulations as those of the World Health Organization [q.v.].

Note: Applications must be made to the health administration department in the candidate's own country.

Address:
Pan American Sanitary Bureau
525 23rd Street, N.W.
Washington, D.C. 20037
U.S.A.

[1637]

PARALYZED VETERANS OF AMERICA TECHNOLOGY AND RESEARCH FOUNDATION

Research Grants and Fellowships

Subject: Spinal cord injury. Special consideration is given to proposals which benefit the severely disabled. Priority areas include: basic spinal cord regeneration; applied research in interdisciplinary medical, psychological and behavioral specialties; and technological and assistive devices.

Value: Varies according to nature of the project.

Tenable for one year; renewable for a further two years in some instances.

Eligibility: Open to suitably qualified individuals who are seeking funds to develop a project in the field of spinal cord injury.

Note: A brochure, "Guidelines and Procedures for Grant Request," is available from the Foundation.

Closing dates: 1st January; 1st July.

Further information from:
Research Director
Paralyzed Veterans of America
Technology and Research Foundation
4350 East-West Highway, Suite 900
Washington, D.C. 20014
U.S.A.

[1638]

PARAPSYCHOLOGY FOUNDATON
(U.S.A.)

Research Grants

The Foundation awards a varying number of Grants at unspecified times for scientific investigation of the paranormal, i.e., extrasensory perception, psychokinesis, precognition and related phenomena. The amount of each Grant varies and each Grant is tenable at an agreed place for the duration of the proposed project. Open to established paranormal investigators.

Further information from:
Parapsychology Foundation
228 East 71st Street
New York, New York 10021
U.S.A.

[1639]

PARENTERAL DRUG ASSOCIATION FOUNDATION FOR PHARMACEUTICAL SCIENCES, INC.

Awards and Grants Program

Research Achievement Award: US$3,000 and a plaque is presented every three years (next awarded in 1985) in recognition of an individual's overall contributions to the advancement of science and technology in parenteral medications. An additional award of up to US$1,000 will be given to cover travel expenses to the annual meeting. Fields of discipline for which the Award is made are pharmaceutics, microbiology, biology, clinical medicine, quality control, manufacturing, engineering or other appropriate disciplines related to sterile medications. Nominations should be addressed to the President of the Foundation at the address below. *Closing date:* 15th August.

Schaufus Parenteral Technology Award: US$2,000 and a plaque, as well as up to US$1,000 for travel costs to the annual meeting, are given each year for the best publication emanating from academia, government or industry in the area of parenteral and/or related sciences and technology published during the previous year, worldwide. Fields of research and technology include pharmaceutics, microbiology, biology, clinical medicine, quality control, manufacturing, engineering and other appropriate disciplines related to sterile medication. Candidates may be of any nationality. Nominations may be made by anyone. *Closing date:* 15th August.

Student Research Award: Graduate or undergraduate students are eligible for this Award, offered for the best unpublished manuscript based on original laboratory research in any of the following fields: pharmaceutics, physical pharmacy, biology, analytical chemistry, pharmaceutical chemistry, microbiology, parenteral manufacturing, pharmacology, quality control, engineering or other related disciplines relevant to parenterals and other sterile pharamceuticals. The Award consists of US$1,000, a plaque and travel and lodging expenses of up to US$1,000 for the recipient to attend the annual meeting. In addition, US$1,000 is given to the college, and up to US$1,000 for the sponsoring professor to attend the annual meeting. Eligible students must have been enrolled in an accredited college or university during the 12 month period prior to submission of the manuscript. *Closing date:* 15th August.

Dr. William S. Bucke Grant: One Grant of US$20,000 is given annually for the best research proposal submitted in the area of parenteral nutrition. Fields of research include pharmaceutics, quality control, biochemistry, medicine, nutrition, pharmacology or other appropriate disciplines. The Grant stipend must be used in direct support of the research proposal, and may be extended upon the approval of a resubmitted proposal. *Closing date:* 15th August.

Grants for Stimulation of Research: Two Grants of up to US$10,000 each are awarded to stimulate research in parenteral technology and related disciplines, including pharmaceutics, microbiology, biology, medicinal chemistry, clinical medicine, quality control, clinical pharmacology, manufacturing and engineering. Grants may be extended for a maximum of one additional year of research. *Closing date:* 15th August.

Further information from:
Soloman C. Pflag, Executive Director
Parenteral Drug Association Foundation for Pharmaceutical Sciences, Inc.
P.O. Box 242
Garden City, New York 11530
U.S.A.

[1640]

PARIS INTERNATIONAL SINGING COMPETITION

Singers from any country may apply to take part in the biennial Competition offered in even numbered years. Competitors should be no more than 32 years of age for women, and 34 years of age for men. The total prize fund is FF112,000, with a Grand Prize of FF30,000. Competitors are provided with free accommodation. Winners are offered important singing engagements. *Closing date:* 1st April.

Further information from:
  Concours International de Chant de Paris
  14 Bis, Avenue du Président Wilson
  75116 Paris
  France

[1641]

PARIS REVIEW *(U.S.A.)*

Aga Khan Prize for Fiction: One Prize of US$500 is awarded annually for the best short fiction submitted. Besides the cash award, the winning story is published in the *Paris Review*. All short fiction is eligible if not previously published. Stories should be submitted between 1st May and 1st June. Final selection is made by 1st September.

Bernard F. Conners Prize for Poetry: One Prize of US$1,000 is awarded annually for the best unpublished poem over 300 lines submitted between 1st April and 1st May. Translations are acceptable and should be accompanied by a copy of the original text. The winning poem will be published in the *Paris Review*.

Further information from:
  Paris Review, Editorial Office
  541 East 72nd Street
  New York, New York 10021
  U.S.A.

[1642]

PARKINSON'S DISEASE SOCIETY *(U.K.)*

Research Fellowships

Fellowships are awarded from time to time to young people for postgraduate research in the field of Parkinson's disease. Applications should be supported by the head of the applicant's university department or hospital department, under whose direction the Fellow usually works. The Society reimburses quarterly the hospital or university for the salary and other expenses of the Fellow. The Research Fellowship is tenable for one year, renewable for a maximum of three years. Work must be undertaken in the United Kingdom. Indication of availability of funds is normally published in *BMJ*, *Lancet* and *Nature*.

Further information from:
  Executive Director
  Parkinson's Disease Society
  81 Queens Road
  London
  England SW19 8NR

[1643]

PASTEUR INSTITUTE *(Tunis)*

Charles Nicolle Scholarships

Subjects: Areas related to human or animal pathology or other areas of biology.

No. offered: Two Scholarships annually.

Value: 2,000 Tunisian dinars per annum.

Tenable in Tunisia for ten to twelve months; renewable once.

Eligibility: Open to nationals of all countries with suitable scientific qualifications.

Note: Candidates should submit to the Committee President a request describing the proposed project, together with a detailed curriculum vitae, indicating in full their scientific qualifications and credentials.

Closing date: 1st April.

Further information from:
  Monsieur le Président du Comité des
    Bourses Charles Nicolle
  Institut Pasteur
  13 place Pasteur
  Tunis
  Tunisia

[1644]

TONY PATIÑO FELLOWSHIP
Hastings College of the Law *(San Francisco)*

Purpose: To provide financial assistance to worthy candidates of demonstrated need, who would otherwise be unable to pursue their studies, or would be caused hardship by so doing.

Subject: Law.

No. offered: Currently 4 Fellowships annually. This number may be increased in the near future.

Value: US$5,000 per year provided for educational and living expenses. Additional support is given to Fellows with children aged 6 months to 3 years. This is made possible through the *Antenor Patiño, Jr. Endowment Fund.*

Tenable for one year to Hastings College of the Law, University of California at San Francisco. The Fellowship is renewable on an annual basis and continuation is determined in accordance with academic and personal performance, as well as extra-curricular commitment to human services.

Eligibility: Open to students accepted by Hastings College of the Law who show qualities of leadership, have exemplary academic and personal records, a history of involvement and concern for the betterment of people and government at the community, state, national and/or international levels, and have financial need.

Note: Supportive data will be required to verify conditions of eligibility. Application forms are available.

Further information from:
Tony Patiño Fellowship (Room 1-M)
Hastings College of the Law
University of California
198 McAllister Street
San Francisco, California 94102
U.S.A.

[1645]

ALICIA PATTERSON FOUNDATION
(U.S.A.)

Fellowships

Purpose: To give journalists the opportunity to pursue independent projects of significant interest.

No. offered: Three to five Fellowships annually.

Value: Fellows (and family, if any) receive monthly stipends sufficient to maintan themselves in reasonable comfort and health.

Tenable for one year; not renewable.

Eligibility: Open to print journalists who are United States citizens, with at least five years' professional experience.

Note: Fellows are required to write articles based on their projects for the *APF Reporter.*

Closing date: 1st October; application forms are available after 1st June.

Further information from:
Alicia Patterson Foundation
122 East 42nd Street
New York, New York 10017
U.S.A.

[1646]

PEABODY CONSERVATORY OF MUSIC
(Baltimore, Maryland)

Music Scholarships and Teaching Assistantships

Purpose: To make possible the further musical training of highly talented students.

Subjects: Performance, accompanying, composing, conducting (choral or instrumental emphasis), music education, music history and literature, piano pedagogy, harpischord.

Value: Scholarships vary according to talent and need; Assistantships cover full tuition—US$4,950.

Tenable at the Conservatory for one to two years; renewable.

Eligibility: Scholarships are awarded solely by audition to applicants intending to study full-time at the Conservatory. Assistantship candidates must, in addition, have prior teaching experience or exhibit teaching potential.

Closing date: 15th January.

Further information from:
Director of Admissions
Peabody Conservatory of Music
1 East Mount Vernon Place
Baltimore, Maryland 21202
U.S.A.

[1647]

PENNSYLVANIA ACADEMY OF THE FINE ARTS *(Philadelphia)*

Foreign Student Scholarships

Subjects: Painting, sculpture, graphic arts and printmaking.

No. offered: Varies annually.

Value: Cost of tuition. Travel expenses are not paid.

Tenable at the Academy for one year; renewable. Students who qualify by reason of financial need and demonstrated talent may compete in the spring of each school year for tuition scholarships.

Eligibility: Open to non-United States arts students applying from outside the U.S.

Note: Scholars are responsible for all other expenses related to study and are required to furnish proof of support.
Scholarships are also offered to United States citizens, but only when they are present undergraduate students of the Academy.

Closing date: 15th March.

Further information from:
Admissions Office
Pennsylvania Academy of the Fine Arts
Broad and Cherry Streets
Philadelphia, Pennsylvania 19102
U.S.A.

[1648]

PEOPLE'S REPUBLIC OF CHINA

Exchange Scholarships

Subjects: Chinese language, with history, literature or philosophy as possible extra options. Other options which may be available are archaeology and economics.

Value: Return fares between London and Peking may be paid by the British Council. The People's Republic of China offers a monthly stipend to cover living expenses and accommodation. The scholars should have additional finance of approximately £250 to £300 for travel within China.

Tenable at universities in China for one academic year.

Eligibility: Open to graduate citizens of the United Kingdom specialising in Chinese studies and having a working knowledge of P'ut'ung hua.

Note: A few places may be made available for research workers as Senior Advanced Scholars. These candidates will spend approximately three months in the People's Republic of China and should already have a good knowledge of Chinese. Scholars will not be expected to follow a university course and should be able to begin their research upon arrival.

Closing date: January.

Further information from:
Overseas Educational Appointments Department
British Council
10 Spring Gardens
London
England SW1A 2BN

[1649]

PERROTT-WARWICK STUDENTSHIP IN PSYCHICAL RESEARCH *(U.K.)*

The Studentship is offered annually to a United Kingdom resident who is at least 21 years of age. Value of the award depends upon candidate's age, qualifications and circumstances; for graduate students it is generally equivalent to what would be received on a Research Council grant. The Student is required to devote the whole, or a very substantial part, of the tenure period to investigating some problems on psychical research. The Studentship is tenable for one year in the first instance, but may be renewed.
Applications should outline the research project envisaged, specifying where the work is to be done, and include a statement of qualifications and experience together with the names of two referees. Four copies of the application should be submitted.

Further information from:
Prof. D.J. West
32 Fen Road
Milton, Cambridge
England CB4 4AD

[1650]

PETROLEUM RESEARCH FUND
American Chemical Society

Grants

Grants are intended to assist advanced scientific education and fundamental research in the petroleum field, and are applicable to any field of pure science which may afford a basis for subsequent research directly connected with the petroleum field.

Grants are offered to: academic institutions for regularly appointed faculty scientists to assist advanced education and fundamental research; selected staff members of undergradute departments for research designed to stimulate student interest in graduate study and improve the qualifications of the Grantee; young faculty members with a Ph.D. degree who are within their first three years of appointment as regular faculty members of colleges and universities in the United States.

The value of Grants is variable to a maximum of US$45,000 for a three year period.

Further information from:
Program Administrator
Petroleum Research Fund
American Chemical Society
1155 16th Street, N.W.
Washington, D.C. 20036
U.S.A.

[1651]

PFIZER COMPANY LTD. *(Canada)*

The Pfizer Company offers several awards for advanced studies in pharmacy at universities in Canada.

Pfizer Canada Bursary in Pharmacy is granted to a deserving student who is entering the final year of the undergraduate program.

Pfizer Fellowships: One Fellowship is offered annually, tenable at the University of Toronto. Apply to *Secretary, Faculty of Pharmacy, University of Toronto, Toronto 5, Ontario.*

One Fellowship is offered annually, tenable at the University of British Columbia. Apply to *Dean Walter H. Gage, University of British Columbia, Vancouver 8.*

Pfizer Research Fellowship: One Fellowship is offered annually, tenable at the University of Alberta. Apply to *Mr. R.B. Wishart, University of Alberta, Edmonton.*

Further information from:
Pfizer Company Ltd.
P.O. Box 800
Pointe Claire-Dorval, Quebec
Canada H9R 4V2

[1652]

PHARMACEUTICAL MANUFACTURERS ASSOCIATION FOUNDATION, INC.
(U.S.A.)

Medical Student Research Fellowship in Pharmacology-Clinical Pharmacology

Value: US$6,000 for stipend support.

Tenable for up to one year full-time in a specific research effort within a pharmacology or clinical pharmacology unit, within the student's own school or at another institution.

Eligibility: Candidates must be enrolled in a United States medical school, have finished at least one year of the school curriculum and must demonstrate a strong interest in a research and teaching career in pharmacology-clinical pharmacology. Candidates must be sponsored by an organization with a demonstrated commitment to training in the fields of pharmacology-clinical pharmacology.

Note: Requests for the Fellowship must be submitted by the appropriate representative of the school or university in which research will be undertaken, indicating a proposed project in full detail and a full description of the candidate.

Closing date: 15th January.

Further information from:
Pharmaceutical Manufacturers Association Foundation, Inc.
1155 Fifteenth Street, N.W.
Washington, D.C. 20005
U.S.A.

[1653]

PHARMACEUTICAL MANUFACTURERS ASSOCIATION FOUNDATION, INC.
(U.S.A.)

Fellowships for Careers in Clinical Pharmacology

Purpose: Postdoctoral support of physicians, dentists and veterinarians presently engaged in or having just completed clinical training who are interested in devoting one or two years to intensive study in the general field of pharmacology in preparation for a career in clinical pharmacology. The emphasis is on training in the field—the program is not a clinical residency program and patient care is not a primary objective of the Fellowship.

Value: Varies according to the stipend requested by the sponsoring university, supplementary support available, etc. The award is intended only as a stipend, and aims to be within existing stipend levels for equivalent postdoctoral fellows. No other subsidies for travel, tuition, etc., are given.

Tenable at a U.S. clinical or pre-clinical department in a university for up to two years. The second year is contingent on a satisfactory performance during the first year.

Eligibility: Candidates must have doctoral degrees or the equivalent, must be sponsored by a university, must have completed at least one year of clinical training at the residency level and indicate a strong determination for a career in clinical pharmacology.

Note: Applications for an award, sponsoring a specificaly designated candidate, must be submitted by the sponsoring unit, through its appropriate representative. Applications, in the form of letters, should describe the proposed specific plan for the candidate's training in the general field of pharmacology; they must be accompanied by candidate's statement and curriculum vitae, reprints of publications, and appropriate references.

Closing date: 1st October.

Further information from:
Pharmaceutical Manufacturers Association Foundation, Inc.
1155 Fifteenth Street, N.W.
Washington, D.C. 20005
U.S.A.

[1654]

PHARMACEUTICAL MANUFACTURERS ASSOCIATION FOUNDATION, INC.
(U.S.A.)

Fellowship Awards in Pharmacology-Morphology

Purpose: To encourage activities in the interdisciplinary area of pharmacology-morphology, aimed at relating drug action with drug-induced morphologic changes. Studies should (a) advance understanding of drug action through discovery of specifically related cellular and tissue changes; and (b) concurrently, uncover associations between normal and abnormal function in particular tissue and cellular structures.

Value: Variable, according to stipend requested by university, at normal level of postdoctoral fellowships in that university, and other funds available to supplement it. The award is intended solely as a stipend, and no other subsidies, such as research costs, travel, tuition, etc., are provided.

Tenable for two years within the sponsoring university.

Eligibility: The candidate must be sponsored by an appropriate department and should indicate a strong determination to continue research in pharmacology-morphology. He must be qualified (with a doctoral degree or equivalent) either in a morphologic specialty or in pharmacology, with training, not necessarily formal, in the complementary discipline.

Note: Applications for a Fellowship award, sponsoring a specifically designated candidate, must be submitted by the university where the research is to be carried out. Applications, in letter form, should include a full research and training plan, description of facilities, curriculum vitae of candidate, reprints of publications, and letters of recommendation.

Closing date: 15th January.

Further information from:
　Pharmaceutical Manufacturers Association
　　Foundation, Inc.
　1155 Fifteen Street, N.W.
　Washington, D.C. 20005
　U.S.A.

[1655]

PHARMACEUTICAL MANUFACTURERS ASSOCIATION FOUNDATION, INC.
(U.S.A.)

Fellowships for Advanced Predoctoral Training in Pharmacology-Toxicology

Purpose: To assist in the predoctoral training of promising students during their thesis research.

Value: US$5,040 a year, paid in montly installments of US$420, plus tuition. In addition, US$500 per year will be provided for incidentals directly associated with the thesis research preparation (e.g. secretarial help, artwork, books, travel, etc.)

Tenable for one to two years at a U.S. school of medicine, pharmacy, dentistry, or veterinary medicine.

Eligibility: Candidates must be sponsored by the school or university at which the research is to be conducted. Applicants should be full-time, in-residence Ph.D. candidates in the fields of pharmacology of toxicology who are enrolled in a U.S. school of medicine, pharmacy, dentistry or veterinary medicine. Students should have begun their thesis research by the time the Fellowship becomes active.

Note: Awards are made to the university on behalf of the Fellow. The application should be submitted by the appropriate representative of the school to the Foundation on the applicant's behalf.
　The program is designed for candidates who expect to complete the requirements for the Ph.D. in two years or less from the time the Fellowship begins.

Closing date: 15th September.

Further information from:
　Pharmaceutical Manufacturers Association
　　Foundation, Inc.
　1155 Fifteenth Street, N.W.
　Washington, D.C. 20005
　U.S.A.

[1656]

PHARMACEUTICAL MANUFACTURERS ASSOCIATION FOUNDATION, INC.
(U.S.A.)

Research Starter Grants in Pharmacology, Clinical Pharmacology, Drug Toxicology

Purpose: To offer financial support to the beginning investigator in pharmacology, clinical pharmacology or drug toxicology: research projects.

Value: US$6,500 per year for direct use in research. The funds may not be used for salary support; no more than US$500 a year may be used for travel to professional meetings by the applicant; no indirect costs are provided to the institution.

Tenable for two years, with the second year of support contingent upon a continuing need for the funds.

Eligibility: Applicants must be sponsored by a school or university. Awards are open to those holding the academic rank of assistant professor and investigators at the doctoral level with equivalent positions who are attempting to establish their independent research careers. Applicants will be judged on the scientific worthiness of the proposed research and on the degree of need.

Note: This program is viewed as primarily directed towards assisting the individual, through the vehicle of a specific research proposal. However, application must be made through the appropriate representative of the university involved, submitting the applicant's statement of his proposed research plan, reprints of publications, curriculum vitae and appropriate letters of support.
　These Grants are not offered to augment an ongoing research effort. Research projects which extend or develop the proprietary value of specific drug products are not acceptable, although this does not preclude research in which specific drug products are used to test hypotheses which have a general applicability.

Closing date: 1st September.

Further information from:
Pharmaceutical Manufacturers Association Foundation, Inc.
1155 Fifteenth Street, N.W.
Washington, D.C. 20005
U.S.A.

[1657]

PHARMACEUTICAL MANUFACTURERS ASSOCIATION FOUNDATION, INC.
(U.S.A.)

Faculty Development Awards in Pharmacology

Purpose: To strengthen basic pharmacology by first helping to maintain the present academic capability and ultimately to expand this by broadening the faculty base: support to selected junior faculty.

Value: Variable up to US$25,000 for salary and fringe benefits proposed by the sponsoring university.

Tenable in a U.S. medical or pharmacy school, or university for a two-year period of training, involving research, some teaching and administration or other duties.

Eligibility: Candidates must be sponsored by an appropriate institution, must have a doctoral degree, and should hold academic rank up to and including assistant professor or be investigators at the doctoral level with equivalent positions. Individuals seeking postdoctoral fellowship support should not apply, since the program is designed for those beyond this stage of career development. However, individuals in a fellowship program scheduled tp conclude by the activation date of the Award under this program may apply.

Note: Applications for awards, sponsoring specifically designated candidates, should be submitted in letter form by the appropriate representative of the school or university. Applications must include detailed plans for the candidate's activities, a complete curriculum vitae, reprints of publications, and appropriate references.

Closing date: 15th September.

Further information from:
Pharmaceutical Manufacturers Association Foundation, Inc.
1155 Fifteenth Street, N.W.
Washington, D.C. 20005
U.S.A.

[1658]

PHARMACEUTICAL MANUFACTURERS ASSOCIATION FOUNDATION, INC.
(U.S.A.)

Faculty Development Awards in Clinical Pharmacology

Purpose: To help meet some of the manpower needs in the field of clinical pharmacology by supporting the development of the research potential of clinical pharmacologists during the years immediately following their formal training programs.

Value: Variable; salary support for a full-time junior faculty member at the existing salary level of the university concerned up to US$30,000 per year. Fringe benefits are included.

Tenable at a United States medical school for two years; possible renewal for a third year.

Eligibility: Candidates must be sponsored by medical schools in which the junior faculty position is or will be established. Preferably they should have at least one year's clinical training at the residency level and two years' experience in a research training program related to clinical pharmacology; they should indicate a strong determination for a full-time career in clinical pharmacology, either in a medical school or related institution, or in the pharmaceutical industry.

Note: Applications for an award, sponsoring a specifically designated candidate, must be submitted by a medical school or university through its appropriate representative. Applications, in the form of letters, should describe the proposed position—training, research, teaching and other duties (keeping in mind that the award has as its primary focus the extension of the candidate's research skills); they must be accompanied by candidate's statement and a curriculum vitae, reprints of publications, and appropriate references.

Closing date: 1st October.

Further information from:
Pharmaceutical Manufacturers Association Foundation, Inc.
1155 Fifteenth Street, N.W.
Washington, D.C. 20005
U.S.A.

[1659]

PHARMACEUTICAL SOCIETY OF GREAT BRITAIN

Leverhulme Scholarships

Purpose: To provide the means for full-time studies or research in the field of pharmaceutical sciences.

No. offered: Two Scholarships annually.

Value: £2,770 for students attending establishments within the City of London and the Metropolitan Police District; £2,245 for students attending any other establishment. Payment is made in equal monthly installments. The school of pharmacy at which the research is carried out receives a fee to cover the Scholar's tuition.

Tenable for one year at any school of pharmacy or other establishment in Great Britain.

Eligibility: Open to pharmacists or persons holding a degree in pharmacy approved for the purpose of registration in Great Britain by the Council of the Pharmaceutical Society.

Note: Applications should be submitted on behalf of the candidate, by the head of the school of pharmacy, or in the case of some other establishment, by the supervisor, who should be a pharmacist registered in Great Britain.
The Awardee may not teach or engage in any other form of employment for more than six hours in a week, and any remuneration in excess of £735 will be taken into account when making the Award.

Closing date: 1st August. Awards are made the second week in August and tenure may commence immediately.

Further information from:
Pharmaceutical Society of Great Britain
1 Lambeth High Street
London
England SE1 7JN

[1660]

PHARMACEUTICAL SOCIETY OF GREAT BRITAIN

Victor Reed Scholarships

Purpose: To provide for postgraduate studies or training in research in the pharmaceutical sciences on a full-time basis.

No. offered: Two Scholarships annually.

Value: £2,770 for students attending establishments within the City of London and the Metropolitan Police District; £2,245 for students attending any other establishment. Payment is made in equal monthly instalments. The school of pharmacy at which the research is to be carried out receives a fee to cover the Scholar's tuition.

Tenable at any school of pharmacy or other establishment in Great Britain.

Eligibility: Open to candidates who have been awarded the Pharmaceutical Chemists' Qualifying Diploma or a degree in pharmacy approved for the purposes of registration in Great Britain by the Council of the Pharmaceutical Society.

Note: Applications should be submitted on behalf of the candidate by the head of the school of pharmacy, or in the case of some other establishment, by the supervisor, who should be a pharmacist registered in Great Britain.
The Awardee may not teach or engage in any other form of employment for more than six hours in a week, and any remuneration in excess of £735 will be taken into account when making the Award.

Closing date: 1st August. Awards are made the second week in August and tenure may commence immediately.

Further information from:
Pharmaceutical Society of Great Britain
1 Lambeth High Street
London
England SE1 7JN

[1661]

PHARMACEUTICAL SOCIETY OF GREAT BRITAIN

Research Awards

Purpose: To allow students of pharmaceutical sciences to take up research on a full-time basis.

No. offered: Varies annually.

Value: £2,770 for students attending establisments within the City of London and the Metropolitan Police District; £2,245 for students attending any other establishment. Payment is made in equal monthly installments. The school of pharmacy at which the research is carried out receives a fee to cover tuition of the student undertaking the research.

Tenable at any school of pharmacy in Great Britain for one year.

Eligibility: Open to pharmaceutical chemists or, except for the *Lewis Edwards Memorial Scholarship*, graduates in pharmacy of a university approved by the Council of the Society.

Note: Applications for the awards should be made on behalf of the candidate by the head of the school of pharmacy at which the research is to be undertaken.
The Awardee may not teach or engage in any other form of employment for more than six hours in a week, and any remuneration in excess of £735 will be taken into account when making the Award.
The Society's Research Awards are named as follows: *Jacob Bell Memorial Scholarship and F.C.J. Bird Award; Burroughs Scholarship; Lewis Edwards Memorial Scholarship; Rammel Studentship; Ransom Fellowship; Redwood Scholarship.*

Closing date: 1st August. Awards are made the second week in August, and tenure may commence immediately.

Further information from:
Pharmaceutical Society of Great Britain
1 Lambeth High Street
London
England SE1 7JN

[1662]

PHARMACEUTICAL SOCIETY OF SOUTH AFRICA
Foundation for Pharmaceutical Education

Awards

Purpose: To enable South Africans of all races to undertake postgraduate study for additional qualifications and research projects in pharmaceutical fields.

No. offered: Approximately 15 new or renewed Awards annually.

Value: R500 to R2,000 per annum, normally paid in a lump sum.

Tenable at South African institutions or occasionally elsewhere, for one year; renewable.

Eligibility: Open to all South African citizens who have a basic South African academic qualification registered by the South African Pharmacy Board.

Closing date: 30th September of year preceding year for which Award is required.

Further information from:
Secretary
Foundation for Pharmaceutical Education
Pharmaceutical Society of South Africa
P.O. Box 31360
Braamfontein 2017
South Africa

[1663]

PHARMACOLOGICAL SOCIETY OF CANADA

Upjohn Award in Pharmacology

Purpose: To stimulate and recognize research in Canada, which has made significant contributions toward the advancement and extension of knowledge in the fields of pharmacology and toxicology.

No. offered: One Award annually.

Value: Can$1,000, an engraved plaque and up to *Can*$500 in expenses for travel to the Society's annual meeting.

Eligibility: Open to Canadian scientists for

work primarily done in Canada. Society members may nominate candidates of either sex from academic institutions, foundations, governmental, industrial and research organizations, etc. The Award is given on the basis of published reprints or manuscripts ready for publication, on either a specific piece of research or on a large body of pharmacological research done over a period of many years. In addition, a two-page summary is required.

Note: Winners must present an oration covering their major contributions.

Further information from:
Pharmacological Society of Canada
c/o Radan Capek, M.D., Ph.D.
Department of Pharmacology and Therapeutics
McGill University
3655 Drummond Street
Montreal, Quebec
Canada H3G 1Y6

[1664]

PHI BETA KAPPA (U.S.A.)

Ralph Waldo Emerson Award of US$2,500 is given annually for the best study contributing to historical, philosophical or religious interpretations of the human condition, published in the United States between 1st June and 31st May of the Award year.

Christian Gauss Award of US$2,500 is given annually for an outstanding book of literary scholarship or criticism published in the United States between 1st June and 31st May of the Award year.

Science Award of Us$2,500 is given annually for an outstanding book of science or interpretation of science written by a scientist and published in the United States between 1st June and 31st May of the award year.

Note: Works are submitted by publishers for consideration for these Awards.

Further information from:
Phi Beta Kappa
1811 Q Street, N.W.
Washington, D.C. 20009
U.S.A.

[1665]

PHI BETA KAPPA (U.S.A.)

Mary Isabel Sibley Fellowship

Subjects: French language and literature (even-numbered years); Greek language, literature, history, and archaeology (odd-numbered years).

No. offered: One Fellowship annually.

Value: US$7,000.

Tenable for one year.

Eligibility: Open to single women between 25 and 35 years of age who hold a doctoral degree or have fulfilled all the requirements for a doctorate except the dissertation. The Fellowship is not restricted to members of Phi Beta Kappa nor to United States citizens.

Closing date: 15th January.

Further information from:
Mary Isabel Sibley Fellowship Committee
Phi Beta Kappa
1811 Q Street, N.W.
Washington, D.C. 20009
U.S.A.

[1666]

PHI CHI THETA FOUNDATION (U.S.A.)

Scholarships

Purpose: To support the higher education of women in economics and business administration.

No. offered and value: Dependent upon available funds.

Tenable for one year; not renewable, but recipients may re-apply.

Eligibility: Open to women of at least high freshman standing who are currently enrolled in a full time program leading to a bachelor's, or master's or doctorate degree in economics or business administration at a college or university approved by the Foundation in the United States or Canada. Foreign nationals will only be considered after a semester of work in economics or business administration in a United States or Canadian university.

Note: Application forms are available January through 1st April from the presidents of chapters of Phi Chi Theta Fraternity and from the deans of the schools of business administration or economics where those chapters exist, or from the address below.

Not confirmed for 1983.

Further information from:
Mrs. Jessie M. Erickson
Executive Director
Phi Chi Theta Foundation
718 Judah Street
San Francisco, California 94122
U.S.A.

[1667]

PHILIPS INTERNATIONAL INSTITUTE OF TECHNOLOGICAL STUDIES *(Eindhoven, Netherlands)*

Scholarships

Subjects: Electronics engineering.

No. offered: 25-30 Scholarships annually.

Value: Cost of living allowance of 1,100 Dutch florins per month; return travel; winter clothing allowance of 350 florins; and a book allowance of 550 florins.

Tenable at the Institute, for one year for the diploma course and the electronics design engineering course, and for 17 months for the master of electronics engineering course.

Eligibility: Open to graduates aged between 20 and 30 who hold at least an upper second class honours degree in engineering sciences. Applicants of any nationality will be considered, but preference is given to individuals from developing countries. A good working knowledge of English is essential.

Note: The Institute is aided by the Government of the Netherlands which finances a number of Scholarships, and by the Netherlands Universities Foundation for International Cooperation which accepts responsibility for awarding master's degrees.

Information about these awards can be obtained from offices of the Philips organization in any country as well as from the Institute.

Closing date: 1st September.

Further information from:
Philips International Institute of
 Technological Studies
Vestdijk 2d
Eindhoven
Netherlands

[1668]

PHYSIOLOGICAL SOCIETY *(U.K.)*

Dale Fund Travel Grants

The purpose of the Travel Grant is to assist persons engaged in physiological research in the United Kingdom in making short-term visits to pursue their research or research training in other centres. In addition to covering travel expenses the Grants may include a contribution toward subsistence; the total value of each Grant will not exceed £160.

Grants are open to both members and non-members of the Society who are engaged in physiological research.

Further information from:
Professor R.J. Linden
Department of Cardiovascular Studies
University of Leeds
Leeds
England LS2 9JT

[1669]

PIRA *(U.K.)*

Research Fellowships and Investigatorships

PIRA occasionally offers support to investigators to undertake research at the PIRA Laboratories in areas of current relevance to PIRA's programmes, which are concerned with the paper and board, printing and packaging industries. The research period may take the form of a Research Fellowship, or it may be a less-formal arrangement comprising partial support of use of facilities only, while on secondment.

In certain cases, researchers may register for a higher degree of a cooperating university.

Further information from:
  Director
  PIRA
  Randalls Road
  Leatherhead, Surrey
  England KT22 7RU

[1670]

PITT RIVERS MUSEUM
University of Oxford

Swan Fund Award

The Museum sponsors research on the small peoples of Africa (e.g. Bushmen and Pygmies) and their prehistorical antecedents.

Awards, of varying amounts, are normally tenable in Africa. There are no eligibility stipulations.

Further information from:
  Curator
  Pitt Rivers Museum
  Parks Road
  Oxford
  England OX1 3PP

[1671]

MAX PLANCK SOCIETY FOR THE ADVANCEMENT OF SCIENCE (F.D.R.)

Fellowships

Subjects: Fields of basic science: research work.

Value: Group 1—up to DM2,100 per month Group 2—up to DM2,400 per month; Group 3—up to DM2,900 per month. The final amount is determined by the Institute's Director. Scientists completing their doctoral thesis receive DM1,000 per month, those of them having a graduate degree equivalent to the German university degree and having done research work for at least two years receive up to DM1,300 per month.

Tenable at the Max Planck Institutes in Germany, usually for one or two years.

Eligibility: Open to foreign scientists whose proposed research plans are of interest to the institutes to which they are applying. Group 1—for scientists with a doctoral degree who have done research work for at least two years; Group 2—for sceintists with a doctoral degree who have done research work for at least five years; Group 3—for internationally recognized scientists with outstanding scientific accomplishments who have at least the status of an associate professor, assistant professor or the like. The Institutes may also admit scientists who are completing their doctoral thesis.

Note: Applications should be submitted directly to the appropriate Institute. A full list of the Max Planck Institutes may be obtained from:
  Max Planck Society for the Advancement of Science
  P.O. Box 647
  8000 Munich 1
  West Germany

[1672]

PLAYBOY MAGAZINE *(Chicago)*

Editorial Awards

A number of Awards are presented annually in recognition of the best judged works appearing in *Playboy Magazine* during the calendar year. The Awards, each consisting of US$1,000 and a medallion, are given in the fields of writing, photography and art.

Further information from:
  Playboy Magazine
  Playboy Building
  919 North Michigan Avenue
  Chicago, Illinois 60611
  U.S.A.

[1673]

POETRY MAGAZINE *(Chicago)*

Poetry Magazine Awards are made annually and are restricted to poets whose work has appeared in *Poetry Magazine* during the previous year. The Awards consist of the *Frederick Bock Prize* of US$300, the *Levinson Prize* of US$500, the English-Speaking Union Prize of US$1,000 and four smaller prizes, each of no less than US$100.

Further information from:
  Poetry Magazine
  601 South Morgan Street
  P.O. Box 4348
  Chicago, Illinois 60680
  U.S.A.

[1674]

POETRY SOCIETY (U.K.)

Alice Hunt Bartlett Prize: The Prize of £500 is offered annualy to provide recognition and encouragement to poets of all nationalities. It is awarded to the most outstanding new collection of poetry by a young or emerging poet. If, in the opinion of the adjudicators, there is no such poet who merits the Prize, and established poet will be considered. Poetry collections should contain not less than 20 poems or 400 lines. Collections should be submitted before 31st December.

In the event of poems being translated into the English language, the original poet must be alive and the Prize will be divided equally between him and the translator.

Arnold Vincent Bowen Prize: The Prize of £10 is offered annually for the best single lyric poem in open competition. Competitors may submit only one poem of not more than 30 lines. Longer poems cannot be considered. A nom-de-plume must be adopted and the name and address of the sender should be given in a sealed envelope bearing the pseudonyum. Entries should be submitted by 28th February. Poems cannot be returned so copies should be kept. The winning poem will be published in the *Newsletter*.

Further information from:
Poetry Society
21 Earls Court Square
London
England SW5 9BY

[1675]

POETRY SOCIETY OF AMERICA

Awards, Grants-in-Aid and Prizes

Barber Memorial Award of US$200 is given annually for a poem of exceptional merit or character of any length, style or theme; *Witter Bynner Poetry Translation Prize* of US$1,000 is given annually for a volume of poetry translated into English, and published during the prior two-year period in the United States; *Witter Bynner Poetry Translation Grant-in-Aid* of US$1,000 is awarded for a book-in-progress; *Melville Cane Award* of US$500 is given annually, in even-numbered years for a published book on poetry, poetry critcism, or the biography of a poet, and in odd-numbered years for a published book of poems; *Gustav Davidson Memorial Award* of US$500 is given annually for a sonnet or sonnet sequence not to exceed three sonnets; *Mary Carolyn Davies Award* of US$250 is given annually for a poem that may be set to music; *Alice Fay di Castagnola Award* of US$2,000 is given annually for a work-in-progress which may be either poetry or about poetry; *Gertrude B. Claytor Memorial Award* of US$250 is given annually for a poem on the American scene or character; *Emily Dickinson Award* of US$100 is given annually for a poem inspired by Emily Dickinson, though not necessarily in imitation of her style; *Consuelo Ford Memorial Award* of US$250 is given annually for a lyric poem; *Cecil Hemley Award* of US$300 is given annually for a lyric poem on a philosophical theme: *Alfred Kreymborg Memorial Award* of US$100 is given annually for a poem worthy of the name; *Elias Liebermann Student Poetry Award* of US$100 is given annually for the best poem by a high school or preparatory school student in the United States; *John Masefield Memorial Award* of US$500 is given annually for a narrative poem in English which is not more than 200 lines; *Lucille Medwick Memorial Award* of US$500, is given annually for a poem of humanitarian meaning; *PSA Gold Medal* is given occasionally for achievement in poetry; *Shelley Memorial Award* of about US$1,750 is given annually to a living American poet, on the basis of merit and need (no manuscripts accepted); *Celia B. Wagner Memorial Award* of US$250 is given annually for a poem worthy of the tradition of the art, in any style, in any length; *William Carlos Williams Award* for a book being published for the first time, and by a small press, non-profit press or university press. Translations or adaptations are not eligible. Manuscripts are to be submitted by the publisher. Manuscripts submitted by the author will not be accepted.

Closing dates: 30th May for the *William Carlos Williams Award*; 30th August for the *Witter Bynner Poetry Translation Prize* and *Grant-in-Aid;* 1st September for the *Consuelo Ford Memorial Award;* 15th December for the *Gertrude B. Claytor Memorial Award*; 31st December for all other awards.

Note: Members of the Society are eligible for all awards; non-members for only the *Bynner Prize* and *Grant-in-Aid*, and the *Williams, Masefield, Shelley, Cane, Liebermann* and *Wagner Awards.*

Further information from:
  Poetry Society of America
  National Arts Club
  15 Gramercy Park
  New York, New York 10003
  U.S.A.

[1676]

POLISH CULTURE INSTITUTE *(U.K.)*

Postgraduate Scholarships

Purpose: For study in all disciplines in universities and other institutions of higher educaton and research in Poland.

Subjects: Unrestricted; and especially in Polish philology, Slavonic languages, and the history and geography of Poland.

No. offered: 26 Scholarships annually.

Value: A monthly stipend of 3,200 zloty plus free accommodation in student hostels or an additional allowance of 2,000 zloty for accommodation found privately, free medical care and exemption from tuition fees.
  Scholarships holders are required to pay their own fares to and from the place of study in Poland.

Tenable for periods up to twelve months in Poland. Preference is given to those wishing to study for periods of more than six months.

Eligibility: Open to United Kingdom citizens who have a university degree or equivalent qualification. Priority is given to candidates who hold an honours degree and have some experience of research, laboratory techniques or teaching since graduation.

Closing date: 7th December.

Note: Application forms are obtainable from any British Council office in the United Kingdom, by sending a stamped, addressed, foolscap envelope. Completed forms should be submitted in duplicate to *Scholarship Department, British Council, 10 Spring Gardens, London SW1A 2BN.*
  One *Chopin Fellowship* of 3,500 zloty, on similar terms as the above listed Scholarships, may be offered to the best of the music candidates recommended for a Polish Government scholarship. All music candidates are expected to attend an audition. Further details are available at the time of application. *Closing date:* 7th December.

Short-Term Bursaries: Thirty months of Bursaries for periods of up to three months each are offered to candidates under similar terms as above. Applicants should have some postgraduate research or lecturing experience. Preference is given to those undertaking doctoral or postdoctoral work. Polish authorities pay for necessary travel expenses within Poland from one academic centre to another. Bursaries cannot normally be taken up during the university summer vacation from 1st July to 3oth September. *Closing date:* varies annually.

Further information from:
  Polish Culture Institute
  36 Portland Place
  London
  England W1N 3AG

[1677]

PONTIFICAL INSTITUTE OF MEDIAEVAL STUDIES *(Canada)*

Awards by the Council of the Institute: A varying number of bursaries and Scholarships are made annually to second and third year junior associates engaged in mediaeval studies at the Institute. A select number of grants are made to first year junior associates engaged in mediaeval studies at the Institute. The value of these awards vary, depending upon available funds. These Awards are tenable for one year. *Closing date:* 31st March.

Michaelmas Conference Research Associateships: Two Associaeships are awarded annually and are tenable for one year at the Institute. The value of the Associateships vary, depending upon available funds. Open to postdoctoral students of mediaeval studies. Candidates must apply personally and directly to the Secretary. *Closing date:* 31st October.

Further information from:
  Secretary
  Pontifical Institute Mediaeval Studies
  59 Queen's Park Crescent East
  Toronto, Ontario
  Canada M5S 2C4

[1678]

POPULATION COUNCIL (U.S.A.)

Social Science Fellowships

Subjects: Population studies narrowly defined (including demography and biostatistics) or in combination with a social science discipline, such as economics, sociology, anthropology, political science or public administration.

Value: Stipends are based on the particular type of fellowship held and the place of study. In addition, travel, tuition and incidental expenses are paid by the Council.

Tenable at research and training institutions at any geographic location, which have a strong program in population studies.

Eligibility: Open to (1) persons who have made considerable progress toward a Ph.D. or an equivalent degree specializing in population studies; (2) persons having completed a Ph.D. or equivalent degree and wishing to undertake postdoctoral training/research, specializing in population studies; and (3) persons with professional experience in the field of population studies who wish to undertake mid-career training.

Note: Fellows are chosen on their potential contribution to the field of population study in scientific and policy-making careers. Strong preference is given to applicants from developing countries who have a firm commitment to return to their home countries upon completion of their study.
   Application forms may be obtained from the Council.

Further information from:
Fellowship Secretary
Population Council
1 Dag Hammarskjold Plaza
New York, New York 10017
U.S.A.

[1679]

POPULATION COUNCIL (U.S.A.)

Biomedical Fellowships

Subjects: Biomedical related to reproductive biology.

Value: US$13,000 per annum for candidates having just completed a doctoral degree. Increments are commensurate with experience.

Tenable at the Council's Center for Biomedical Research for two years, providing the Fellow and preceptor agree on the second year.

Eligibility: Open to individuals of all nationalities who have successfully completed an advanced degree, M.D., Ph.D., or the equivalent.

Note: Applications, which may be obtained from the address below, may be made in anticipation of receiving the doctoral degree. Fellowships, however, will not be presented until after the degree has been granted.

Further information from:
Fellowship Secretary
Population Council
Rockefeller University
66th Street and York Avenue
New York, New York 10021
U.S.A.

[1680]

POTATO MARKETING BOARD (U.K.)

Postgraduate Studentships

Purpose: To enable British postgraduate students, permanently resident in Great Britain, to undertake specialised research likely to be of value to the potato industry in the United Kingdom.

Subjects: Production and marketing of potatoes to meet consumer requirements, the physiology and biochemistry of the tuber in relation to resistance to damage and improved quality, and the reduction of wastage during harvesting and handling.

No. offered: Approximately four Studentships annually.

Value: £2,420 per annum plus fees.

Tenable at selected universities and research institutions in the United Kingdom for a maximum period of three years.

Eligibility: Open to British graduates who hold a first or upper second class honours degree in pure or applied science.

Closing date: 1st March.

Further information from:
Information Officer
Potato Marketing Board
50 Hans Crescent
London
England SW1X ONB

[1681]

POTATO MARKETING BOARD *(U.K.)*

Research Grants

Purpose: To aid special projects or new developments considered likely to be of direct practical value to a large section of the potato industry in a relatively short period of time.

Subjects: Preference is given to research into ways of increasing the efficiency of economic production and utilisation of the crop, particularly the reduction of mechanical damage and the attendant wastage.

No. offered: Approximately three to five Grants annually.

Value: Covers employment of assistants specially needed for the purposes of the research; their travel expenses; apparatus not normally provided in a well-equipped laboratory; materials and service needed for the research on a scale which the institution is unable to supply; and other research and development purposes if the Board so decides.

Tenable at suitable universities and research institutions in the United Kingdom, normally for a maximum period of three years; subject to annual review.

Eligibility: Grants will normally be made to the investigator's university or institution, and will require the institution to accept all the normal duties and responsibilities of employer including those relating to national insurance and income tax, in relation to any person whose services are provided by means of a Grant.

Closing date: 1st March.

Further information from:
Information Officer
Potato Marketing Board
50 Hans Crescent
London
England SW1X ONB

[1682]

POTATO MARKETING BOARD *(U.K.)*

James E. Rennie Awards

Two or three Awards are given annually to assist persons within the industry to improve, by means of study tours abroad, their knowledge of the potato industry of the visited country and a foreign language. Open to British nationals or persons resident in the United Kingdom for at least three years who are over 23 years of age and are actively engaged in the potato industry, either in the production of the crop or the marketing of potatoes or potato products. Persons employed in an advisory or education capacity in the industry and employees of the Potato Marketing Board are also eligible. *Closing date:* 20th November.

Further information from:
Information Officer
Potato Marketing Board
50 Hans Crescent
London
England SW1X ONB

[1683]

POYNTER FUND *(U.S.A.)*

Scholarships

Subjects: Newspaper career field, including news writing, editing and administration; business and administration of circulation and station management; sales, art, layout, promotion and broadcast production; mechanical production and research.

No. offered: Varying number of Scholarships annually.

Value: Up to US$2,000 per annum.

Tenable at any United States college or university with a journalism program, for one year; renewable.

Eligibility: Open to United States citizens with outstanding potential for successful careers in the fields of journalism and broacasting.

Note: Scholars are expected to work in some field of journalism, broadcasting or newspaper work for at least three years following completion of their education. Any Scholar failing to do so is required to pay back the full amount of his scholarship at 5% interest within five years after graduation.

In addition, the Poynter Fund may award Fellowships of US$1,000 or more each year. Fellowships must be used for graduate study or travel which will further a newspaper or broadcasting career.

Closing date: 1st July.

Further information from:
Poynter Fund
Personnel Department
Times Publishing Co.
P.O. Box 1121
St. Petersburg, Florida 33731
U.S.A.

[1684]

PRAEMIUM ERASMIANUM FOUNDATION
(Netherlands)

Erasmus Prize

Purpose: To confer awards upon individuals or institutions who have made important contributions in European cultural, social or social-scientific spheres.

No. offered: One or two Prizes annually.

Value: 100,000 Dutch guilders.

Eligibility: Open to persons (and institutions) who have benefited the development of European culture in the fields of humanities or the arts. There are no restrictions as to age, sex or citizenship.

Note: A portion of the Prize is to be used for a project of European scope, preferably focused on the younger generation.

Further information from:
Praemium Erasmianum Foundation
Jan van Goyenkade 5
1075 HN Amsterdam
Netherlands

[1685]

PRAGUE SPRING INTERNATIONAL MUSIC COMPETITION

Musicians of any nationality who are not more than 30 years of age may enter the Competition which is held in May each year. The Competition categories, precise qualifications and prizes vary from year to year; in 1982 the Competition was for horn, trumpet and trombone: 1st prize—10,000 Czechoslovak crowns; 2nd prize—7,000 crowns; two 3rd prizes of 4,000 crowns each. Other money prizes are also awarded. There is an application fee of 100 crowns.

The 1983 Competition is for organ and string quartet performances.

Further information from:
Secretariat
Prague Spring International Music Festival
House of Artists, Alšovo nábrezí 12
CS-110 00 Praha 1
Czechoslovakia

[1686]

PREHISTORIC SOCIETY *(U.K.)*

Research Fund Grant

Purpose: To further research in prehistoric archaeology by excavation or other means.

Value: At the discretion of the Society.

Tenable for one year only, but re-applications are considered.

Eligibility: Open to all members of the Society. The Society may make specific conditions relating to individual applications.

Note: Awards are made on the understanding that a detailed report will be made to the Society as to how the Grant was spent. Applications should include the names of two references.

Closing date: 31st March.

Further information from:
 Honorary Secretary
 Prehistoric Society
 Department of Archaeology
 University of Reading
 Reading
 England RG6 2AA

[1687]

PREMIO CITTA DI TRIESTE INTERNATIONAL COMPETITION FOR SYMPHONIC COMPOSITION

A first prize of 3,000,000 lire and public performance of the work, a second prize of 1,000,000 lire and a third prize of 500,000 lire are offered in this annual Competition for an orchestral composition which is ten minutes or more in length and has previously never been performed or published. Composers of any age and from any country may apply.
Closing date: 10th October.

Further information from:
 "Premio Musicale Citta di Trieste"
 Palazzo Municipale
 Piazza dell'Unità d'Italia 4
 I-34121 Trieste
 Italy

[1688]

PRESIDENT STEYN—GEDENKFONDSBEURSTRUST *(South Africa)*

Bursary

Subjects: Home management, mothercraft and domestic science.

Value: R600 per annum in South Africa; R100 per annum overseas.

Tenable at any university in South Africa or overseas for three years; may be extended for a further year in special cases or may be awarded for a shorter period.

Eligibility: Open to South African woman students who either hold a B.Sc. degree or diploma in domestic science or equivalent qualifications.

Further information from:
 Secretary
 President Steyn-Gedenkfondsbeurstrust
 P.O. Box 1234
 Bloemfontein
 South Africa

[1689]

BERNARD PRICE INSTITUTE OF GEOPHYSICAL RESEARCH *(Johannesburg)* University of the Witwatersrand— Department of Geophysics

Mones Michaels Scholarships

Purpose: To further formal studies or research in geophysics. Scholars may read a one-year honours degree course in geophysics, or undertake research for an M.Sc. or Ph.D. degree.

Subjects: Gravity, geomagnetism, rock mechanics, seismology, isotope geophysics and geochronology.

No. offered: A few Scholarships annually.

Value: Dependent upon the degree read by the candidate.

Tenable at the University of the Witwatersrand.

Further information from:
 Director
 Bernard Price Institute of Geophysical Research
 University of the Witwatersrand
 1 Jan Smuts Avenue
 Johannesburg 2001
 South Africa

[1690]

PRINCE PIERRE OF MONACO MUSICAL COMPOSITION PRIZE

Various monetary prizes amounting to FF30,000 are offered in the Competition held in April each year. The Competition is for orchestral compositions: the categories vary annually. Nationals of any country may apply; there are no age restrictions. Works must be unpublished and not previously performed in public. Manuscripts should be submitted by 1st April.

Further information from:
General Secretariat
Prince Pierre of Monaco Musical Composition Prize
Palais princier
Monaco

[1691]

PRINCETON UNIVERSITY *(New Jersey)*

Jane Eliza Procter Visiting Fellowships

Subjects: Liberal arts and sciences, excluding professional, technical or commercial subjects: advanced study and investigation.

No. offered: Two Fellowships annually.

Value: Approximately US$4,500 per annum, plus tuition fees.

Tenable at Princeton University, Princeton, New Jersey, for one year.

Eligibility: Open to United Kingdom or Commonwealth citizens. Fellows must hold a first class honours B.A. degree from a United Kingdom university and be able to prove "exceptional scholarly power." Preference is given to candidates who would be in their second or third year of postgraduate research when, if elected, they take up tenure of the award.

Closing date: Late November.

Further information from:
Registrar
Procter Visiting Fellowships
University Registry, The Old Schools
Cambridge
England CB2 1TN

[1692]

PRINT CLUB *(Philadelphia)*

Awards

A variable number of awards, whose total value is not less than US$8,000 in any given year, are presented annually in competition to participating artists for excellence in printmaking and photography. A number of awards are purchases for the permanent collection maintained at the Philadelphia Museum of Art.

Entrants must be Club members; however membership is open to the public on an annual basis.

The competition is held each fall.

Further information from:
Print Club
1614 Latimer Street
Philadelphia, Pennsylvania 19103
U.S.A.

[1693]

PROVINCE OF ONTARIO

Queen Elizabeth II Ontario Scholarships

Purpose: To assist exceptional candidates preparing to write their Ph.D. thesis.

Subjects: Humanities, social sciences and mathematics.

No. offered: Normally five Scholarships annually.

Value: Varies; a minimum of Can$10,000 plus Can$500 for expenses; paid in four installments.

Tenable at Ontario universities for one year, not renewable.

Eligibility: Open to Canadian citizens and landed immigrants, preferably from Ontario, who express a commitment to a career in his or her chosen field of study. Candidates should have a high scholastic record and are expected to be in the final year of their thesis research and writing during tenure of the award.

Note: A Scholar may not receive income from any other major academic award concurrently with the Scholarship. The candidate must be willing to appear for a personal interview with the selection committee at the expense of the Scholarship fund.

Candidates must be sponsored by the dean of graduate studies of their university, from whom application forms may be obtained and to whom they must be returned with supporting documents. All approved applications will then be forwarded by the dean to the chairman of the Selection Committee before 1st December of the year prior to the beginning of tenure.

Further information from:
Dr. H.H. Yates, Executive
  Vice Chairman, OCGS
Queen Elizabeth II Ontario Scholarships
130 St. George Street
Suite 8039
Toronto, Ontario
Canada M5S 2T4

[1694]

PULITZER PRIZES
Columbia University *(New York City)*

The following Prizes are made by the Trustees of Columbia University on the recommendation of the Pulitzer Prize Board.

Prizes in Journalism: The following awards are made annually, based on material appearing in a United States newspaper published daily, on Sunday or at least once a week; for an example of meritorious public service by a newspaper through the use of its journalistic resources—a gold medal. A prize of US$1,000 is awarded in each of the following categories: general or spot news reporting; investigative or other specialized reporting; reporting on national affairs; reporting on international affairs; editorial writing; cartoon work; spot news; photography; feature photography; commentary; criticism; and feature writing.

Prizes in Letters: The following awards in the amount of US$1,000 each, are made annually for works, published during the year, by American authors: for fiction published in book form; for a play; for a book on American history; for a biography or autobiography; for a volume of verse; and for a book of nonfiction.

Prize in Music: An annual award of US$1,000 is made for musical composition by an American, in the larger forms, including chamber, orchestral, choral, opera, song, dance, or other forms of musical theatre. The composition must have had its first American performance during the year.

Note: Competition for journalism prizes is restricted to work done during the calendar year, ending 31st December; competition for drama prizes is restricted to work done during a twelve month period from 1st April to 31st March of the subsequent year; competition for music is restricted to works performed between 15th March of one year and 14th March of the next.

Closing dates: 1st February for journalism prizes; 1st November for prizes in letters; 1st March for music prizes.

Further information from:
Secretary of the Board
Pulitzer Prizes
702 Journalism
Columbia University
New York, New York 10027
U.S.A.

[1695]

PULP AND PAPER RESEARCH INSTITUTE OF CANADA

Harold Hibbett Memorial Fellowship: One Fellowship of Can$17,200 plus travel assistance is awarded annually for research in organic chemistry, with application to Institute activities. Tenable at the Institute (McGill University) for one year. Open to persons holding a Ph.D. degree in chemistry, physics or equivalent from approved universities.

The following awards (totaling at least Can$9,350 per annum) are available for graduate students in chemistry, chemical engineering or mechanical engineering who are conducting their thesis research at the Institute: *Otto Maass Memorial Fellowship; S.G. Mason Fellowship; F.L. Mitchell Fellowship; C.B. Purves Memorial Fellowship; Carl A. Winkler Memorial Fellowship; and the Pulp and Paper Research Institute Studentships.*

Further information from:
Chairman, Education Committee
Pulp and Paper Research Institute of
  Canada, Department of Chemistry
Pulp and Paper Building
McGill University
3420 University Street
Montreal, Quebec
Canada H3A 2A7

Q

See *How to Use The Grants Register*, page ix

[1696]

QUAID-I-AZAM ACADEMY *(Karachi)*

Academic and Literary Prizes: Seven Prizes of 10,000 rupees each are given triennially for works of academic and literary merit, based upon research on Quaid-i-Azam or on any aspect of the Pakistan movement, including earlier movements in modern Indo-Muslim history. The Prizes, open to Pakistani nationals and foreign scholars, are designated as follows: one Prize for a work published in Urdu, the national language of Pakistan, one Prize for a work published in each of the five regional languages of Pakistan, and one Prize for a work published in any foreign language.

Human Rights International Prize: An annual Prize of 500,000 rupees and a citation is given for outstanding contributions to the protection and promotion of human rights. Individuals of any nationality, race, creed or sex are eligible. Nominations are invited from all competent persons.

Further information from:
Quaid-i-Azam Academy
297 M.A. Jinnah Road
Karachi 5
Pakistan

[1697]

QUEEN ELISABETH INTERNATIONAL MUSIC COMPETITION *(Brussels)*

The Competition, which is divided into three categories, will be held in the following years: piano—1983; violin—1985; composition—1986. Each category will be held thereafter every fourth year.

All categories are open to performers of any nationality, between the ages of 17 and 31. The Competitions for piano and violin each have three stages of increasing difficulty. The twelve participants in the second stage who have not been retained for the final stage are each given 15,000 Belgian francs.

First prize for the piano and violin Competitions is 300,000 Belgian francs, second prize—200,000 Belgian francs, third prize—175,000 Belgian francs, plus nine additional prizes. First prize for the composition Competition is 150,000 Belgian francs.

Further information from:
Secretariat du Concours Musical
International Reine Elisabeth
Rue Baron Horta, 11
B-1000 Brussels
Belgium

[1698]

QUEEN ELIZABETH HOUSE *(Oxford)*

Visiting Fellowships

Purpose: To enable senior government administrators (and occasionally other persons of similar standing) from developing countries to conduct personal research and study at the University of Oxford.

Subjects: Those relevant to the Fellow's normal duties; for example aid and trade, agricultural economics, development planning, economic development, education, theory and practice of government, politics and law, manpower planning, scientific subjects, statistics and urbanisation.

No. offered: Up to 20 Fellowships at any given time.

Value: Cost of return passage to Oxford, single residential accommodation at Queen Elizabeth House, tuition fees and a daily allowance.

Tenable at Queen Elizabeth House for one to three terms, generally commencing in October.

Eligibility: Open to senior government administrators (and occasionally other persons of similar standing) from developing countries who have considerable experience and are nominated by their government for a British Technical Cooperation Training Programme Award. Nominees should preferably be between 35 and 45 years of age. A high standard of competence in English is required.

Note: Applications are mainly by government nomination. Enquiries should be made to a British diplomatic mission or to the British Council representative in the applicant's own country.

Applications (directed to the address below) from candidates having alternate sources of finance are welcomed.

The Fellowships are sponsored by the Overseas Development Administration in conjunction with the University of Oxford and Queen Elizabeth House.

Closing date: Six months before commencement of tenure.

Address:
Queen Elizabeth House
21 St. Giles
Oxford
England OX1 3LA

[1699]

QUEEN ELIZABETH II ARTS COUNCIL OF NEW ZEALAND

Grants to Individuals

Purpose: To assist artists in all fields to develop their talents and skills, particularly in relation to the development of the arts in New Zealand.

Subjects: Music, ballet, dance, drama, visual arts, film and video, and traditional Maori and South Pacific arts.

Value: Dependent upon requirements and funds available.

Tenable for periods of study in New Zealand or abroad, for up to one year, with possibility of extension in certain cases.

Eligibility: Open to persons domiciled in New Zealand and New Zealand citizens temporarily domiciled abroad.

Further information from:
Queen Elizabeth II Arts Council of New Zealand
P.O. Box 6040
Te Aro, Wellington
New Zealand

[1700]

QUEEN MARIE-JOSÉ PRIZE FOR MUSICAL COMPOSITION *(Geneva)*

A Prize of 10,000 Swiss francs is offered in even-numbered years to composers of all nationalities and of any age, for a musical composition; subject and form are prescribed in advance by the Committee. All works submitted must be previously unpublished and submitted in manuscript form, together with a tape recording. The award-winning work remains its author's exclusive property, but is performed as part of the Merlinge concerts. *Closing date:* 31st May.

Further information from:
Secretariat
Prix de Composition Musicale Reine Marie-Jose
Merlinge
1249 GY/Geneva
Switzerland

[1701]

QUOTA INTERNATIONAL, INC. *(U.S.A.)*

Fellowship Fund

The Fund has been created to provide financial assistance for the education of deaf or hearing impaired students, or to hearing students who are preparing to work with hearing and speech handicapped people to help improve and develop their skills.

Grants, in the form of Scholarships to undergraduates and Fellowships to graduates, are available to students of any nationality and are tenable at any accredited college or university.

Not confirmed for 1983.

Further information from:
Quota International, Inc.
Suite 908
1828 L Street, N.W.
Washington, D.C. 20036
U.S.A.

R

See *How to Use The Grants Register*, page ix

[1702]

RADIO RESEARCH BOARD *(Australia)*

Fellowship in Telecommunications and Radio Science

Purpose: To encourage young research workers in the area of telecommunications and radio science by providing opportunities for them to work in situations which widen their experience. The agreed area of research is determined by the negotiation between the prospective Fellow and the Board but the Board is open to consider any proposal in the broad field of telecommunications and radio science.

No. offered: One Fellowship annually.

Value: Currently A$20,762 per annum (increased to A$22,304 per annum for Fellows aged 28 or over); reviewed periodically. Fellows are self-employed with the host institution administering the Fellowship and paying the stipend. There is an allowance of A$500 per annum for Fellow's dependent spouse and A$200 per annum for each dependent child under the age of 16. The Fellowship also covers "superannuation-type" payments, appropriate insurance and necessary travel expenses. Host institutions may be paid an allowance towards the cost of supporting the Fellow.

Tenable for two years at an Australian university, approved research institute or industrial laboratory as determined by negotiation between the prospective Fellow and the Board.

Eligibility: Open to young scientists and engineers of exceptional promise and proven merit holding a Ph.D. or equivalent qualification in a pertinent discipline. Although there are no restrictions as to nationality, it is hoped that Fellows will remain in Australia for several years after completion of the Fellowship. Applicants should be 30 years of age or less.

Note: Stipends are subject to Australian income tax laws.

Closing date: Mid-November; Fellowships to be announced by the end of the year.

Further information from:
Secretary
Radio Research Board
P.O. Box 225
Dickson, A.C.T.
Australia 2602

[1703]

RALSTON PURINA COMPANY *(U.S.A.)*

Research Fellowships in Animal Science

Purpose: To assist in the training of exceptional personnel for leadership in the science of livestock and poultry production.

No. offered: Six Fellowships annually.

Value: Variable.

Tenable at any U.S. agricultural college, including approved Canadian colleges, for one year; renewable for up to two years.

Eligibility: Open to persons qualified for graduate study in any U.S. agricultural college or approved Canadian college.

Further information from:
Ralston Purina Research Fellowship Committee
c/o Mr. George H. Kyd
Checkerboard Square
St. Louis, Missouri 63188
U.S.A.

[1704]

RALSTON PURINA COMPANY *(U.S.A.)*

Research Fellowships in Food Science

Purpose: To assist in the training of qualified personnel for future leadership in the field of food science.

No. offered: Six Fellowships annually.

Value: Variable.

Tenable in an M.S. or Ph.D. program at an institution with faculty in specific departments of food science or food technology for one year; renewable twice for a total tenure not to exceed three years.

Eligibility: Open to individuals who have pursued satisfactory undergraduate programs with a food science orientation.

Note: The Ralston Purina Company also offers *Undergraduate Scholarships* in agriculture and a *Matching Gifts Program* for support of institutions of higher education.

Further information from:
Ralston Purina Food Science Graduate
   Fellowship Committee
c/o Mr. George H. Kyd
Checkerboard Square
St. Louis, Missouri 63188
U.S.A.

[1705]

RAMSAY MEMORIAL FELLOWSHIPS TRUST *(U.K.)*

British (General) Fellowship

Subject: Chemistry; postdoctoral research.

No. offered: Normally one Fellowship annually.

Value: Normally equivalent to the lower part of the Lecturer scale for United Kingdom universities, plus superannuation benefits and a maximum of £100 for research expenses.

Tenable normally at a university, university college or other place of higher education in the United Kingdom or, exceptionally, elsewhere, for two years.

Eligibility: Usually open to British or Commonwealth citizens who have had training in research methods as evidenced by the possession of a Ph.D., or its equivalent, preferably from a British university, or similar institution, and who can demonstrate their capacity for original research in chemical science.

Note: Recipients are encouraged to undertake a small amount of teaching work, not exceeding three hours per week.

Closing date: 3rd December of year preceding award.

Further information from:
Joint Honorary Secretaries
Ramsay Memorial Fellowships Trust
University College London
Gower Street
London
England WC1E 6BT

[1706]

RAMSAY MEMORIAL FELLOWSHIPS TRUST *(U.K.)*

Glasgow Fellowship

Subject: Chemistry.

No. offered: Normally one Fellowship annually.

Value: Normally equivalent to the lower part of the Lecturer scale for United Kingdom universities plus superannuation benefits and a maximum of £100 for research expenses. The stipend is paid monthly.

Tenable at a university, university college or other place of higher education in the United Kingdom, or exceptionally elsewhere, for two years.

Eligibility: Open to British or Commonwealth citizens who have had training in research methods as evidenced by the possession of Ph.D. or its equivalent, preferably from a British university or similar institution, and who can demonstrate their capacity for original research in chemical science. Applicants should either intend to do their postdoctoral work at Glasgow or Strathclyde University, or have been educated at Glasgow or Strathclyde University.

Note: Recipients are encouraged to undertake a small amount of teaching work, not exceeding three hours per week.

Closing date: 3rd December of year preceding award.

Further information from:
  Joint Honorary Secretaries
  Ramsay Memorial Fellowships Trust
  University College London
  Gower Street
  London
  England WC1E 6BT

[1707]

RCA CORPORATION *(U.S.A.)*

RCA Fellowships and Scholarships

Subjects: Electronics, electrical engineering, physics, journalism, engineering physics, telecommunications, industrial relations, marketing, business and procurement/materials management.

No. offered: Eight Fellowships annually, plus a number of Scholarships.

Value: Fellowships—U.S.$4,000 per annum plus fees and an unrestricted departmental grant. An additional summer grant of U.S.$1,000 may be made. Scholarships—U.S.$1,000 each.

Tenable at universities designated by RCA, for one year; Fellows may be reappointed.

Eligibility: Open to United States citizens who are selected by appropriate officials of United States universities designated by RCA.

Note: RCA also sponsors: three *Scholarships in Electrical Engineering*, awarded to women engineers through a program administered by the Society of Women Engineers; fellowships to women in engineering and business through the American Association of University Women; *Minority Introduction to Engineering Summer Programs* are sponsored by RCA at several universities, and are administered by the Accreditation Board for Engineering and Technology; RCA supports scholarships in engineering for minorities through the National Action Council for Minorities in Engineering; a similar program for minorities in accounting through the American Institute of Certified Public Accountants; a special *RCA-NBC Scholarship* at the Center for New York City Affairs of the New School for Social Research; Hispanic scholarships through LULAC and the National Hispanic Scholarship Fund; four *U.S.$1,500 RCA Dual Degree Program Fellowships* at Atlanta University Center/Georgia Institute of Technology; and a number of *NBC Fellowships* awarded to members of minority groups seeking graduate degrees in several disciplines related to broadcasting. Fellows receive full tuition, a living stipend and summer employment.

Further information from:
  Educational Aid Committee
  RCA Corporation
  Building 202-2
  Cherry Hill, New Jersey 08358
  U.S.A.

[1708]

A.H. AND A.W. REED LTD. *(New Zealand)*

A.W. Reed Memorial Book Award

The Award of NZ$5,000 is offered annually to a New Zealand citizen or permanent resident for a work of non-fiction. Manuscripts should be submitted by the end of each year.

Further information from:
  A.H. and A.W. Reed Ltd.
  P.O. Box 14029
  Wellington 3
  New Zealand

[1709]

REGIONAL INSTITUTE FOR POPULATION STUDIES *(Accra)*

United Nations Fellowships

Purpose: To enable Fellows to obtain advanced training through study or research, leading to a graduate diploma, a master of arts or Ph.D. degree.

Subject: Population studies.

No. offered: 45 Fellowships annually.

Value: ₡1,200 for the first month and ₡981 for each subsequent month, plus costs for books, minor equipment and production of dissertations and theses.

Tenable at the Regional Institute at the University of Ghana for one year; renewable.

Eligibility: Open to Africans, nominated by their governments, who are capable of pursuing a course of study or research using English as a medium of expression. Candidates should have a good degree for the graduate diploma; a graduate diploma in population studies or equivalent qualification for the master of arts degree; and a master's degree in population studies or equivalent qualification for the Ph.D. degree.

Note: Application forms are obtainable at any United Nations Development Office in the capital city of all African countries, through which all applications should be routed.

Closing date: May or June.

Further information from:
 Director
 Regional Institute for Population Studies
 P.O. Box 96
 Legon, Accra
 Ghana

[1710]

REID TRUST *(U.K.)*

Purpose: To promote the higher education of women.

Subjects: Non-vocational studies.

Value: By individual assessment; rarely exceeds £150.

Tenable at a United Kingdom university for one year; renewable for one or two years.

Eligibility: Open to women who are residents of the United Kingdom and are over 25 years of age who hold the minimum qualification of an upper-second class degree.

Note: Candidates should satisfy the Trustees that any additional funds required for the course can be obtained from other sources. The Trustees rarely make awards toward the cost of second first-degree studies.

Not confirmed for 1983.

Further information from:
 C.R. Goymer
 Secretary to the Trustees
 Reid Trust
 c/o Department of Teaching Studies
 Polytechnic of North London
 Prince of Wales Road
 London NW5
 England

[1711]

RELIGIOUS ARTS GUILD *(U.S.A.)*

Pauly D'Orlando Memorial Art Scholarship: Approximately U.S.$700 is awarded annually to a student of art, for further art studies at an accredited school. Candidates may be anyone who is a member in good standing for at least one year prior to application, or sponsored by a member of a Unitarian Universalist Society. *Closing date:* 1st November.

Dorothy Rosenberg Annual Poetry Award: For the poem best dealing with "the human spirit." Two Awards are given annually: First Prize, U.S.$50; Second Prize, U.S.$25. The Competition is open to anyone, without restrictions. *Closing date:* 31st March.

Try Works Prize: One Prize of U.S.$100 is given annually for a worship service celebrating a great occasion in the lives of persons in order that it is shared within a religious community. The Competition is open to anyone, without restrictions. *Closing date:* 15th February.

Note: Interested persons should send a self-addressed stamped envelope to the Guild.

Further information from:
 B. Hutchins
 Religious Arts Guild
 25 Beacon
 Boston, Massachusetts 02108
 U.S.A.

[1712]

RESEARCH CORPORATION *(U.S.A.)*

Cottrell College Science Program Grants: 50 to 100 awards of U.S.$3,000 to U.S.$25,000 or more are given annually throughout the year, for basic research in the natural sciences. Grants are usually tenable for periods of up to three years, and occasionally may be renewed.

The Program is open to academic scientists at private, predominantly undergraduate institutions in the United States and Canada. There are no restrictions with regard to age, rank, length of service, or previous or current research activities. Applications are judged primarily on the scientific originality and significance of the research proposed, and on the demonstrated competence or promise of creativity of the principal investigator.

Cottrell Research Program Grants: 150 to 200 awards of U.S.$3,000 to U.S.$25,000 are given annually throughout the year, for basic research in the physical sciences. Grants are usually tenable for any period of time, but periodic reports are required. The Program is open to all academic scientists at private and public universities in the United States and Canada, especially faculty members early in their professional careers, or established investigators undertaking particularly speculative research. Scientific significance is the prime criterion in the evaluation of research proposals.

Note: Applicants for both Programs should consult published guidelines and describe the proposed research in a letter to the Grants Program. Application forms will be provided if it appears that a research proposal falls under program guidelines.

Further information from:
 Grants Program
 Research Corporation
 405 Lexington Avenue
 New York, New York 10017
 U.S.A.

[1713]

RESEARCH INSTITUTE FOR MANAGEMENT SCIENCE *(Delft, Netherlands)*

Postgraduate Award

Purpose: To develop managerial skills in business and regional development executives of developing countries by enabling them to attend programmes of the Institute.

Subjects: General management and business policy, marketing, production, finance, extension work, consultancy, regional development.

Value: Tuition payment of 9,700 Dutch florins per course, a book allowance of 550 Dutch florins per course, 1,250 Dutch florins per month for board and lodging, 350 Dutch florins for insurance, and up to 1,775 Dutch florins for travel expenses.

Tenable at the Institute for 22 weeks for all programmes except the consultancy programme which runs for 13 weeks.

Eligibility: Open to graduates from developing countries who hold a bachelor's or master's degree, are less than 40 years old, have a good knowledge of English, and a minimum of two years' actual business experience in a relevant field.

Further information from:
 Dean of Studies
 Research Institute for Management
  Science
 P.O. Box 143
 Mijnbouwplein 11
 2600 AC Delft
 Netherlands

[1714]

RESEARCH INSTITUTE FOR MANAGEMENT SCIENCE *(Delft, Netherlands)*

Fellowships

Subjects: Executive development programmes in several areas of functional management (business policy, marketing, production, finance), extension work, consultancy and regional development.

Tenable at the Institute, usually for 22 weeks.

Eligibility: Open to graduates from developing countries who hold a bachelor's or master's degree. Candidates should have a good knowledge of English and should have had a minimum of two years' professional experience in the related fields of study.

Note: Fellowships are awarded by the Ministry of Foreign Affairs, International Technical Assistance Department on application through the Royal Netherlands Embassy in the candidate's country. Fellowships may also be awarded by the executing agencies of the United Nations.

The Program is open to academic scientists at private, predominantly undergraduate institutions in the United States and Canada. There are no restrictions with regard to age, rank, length of service, or previous or current research activities. Applications are judged primarily on the scientific originality and significance of the research proposed, and on the demonstrated competence or promise of creativity of the principal investigator.

Cottrell Research Program Grants: 150 to 200 awards of U.S.$3,000 to U.S.$25,000 are given annually throughout the year, for basic research in the physical sciences. Grants are usually tenable for any period of time, but periodic reports are required. The Program is open to all academic scientists at private and public universities in the United States and Canada, especially faculty members early in their professional careers, or established investigators undertaking particularly speculative research. Scientific significance is the prime criterion in the evaluation of research proposals.

Note: Applicants for both Programs should consult published guidelines and describe the proposed research in a letter to the Grants Program. Application forms will be provided if it appears that a research proposal falls under program guidelines.

Further information from:
Grants Program
Research Corporation
405 Lexington Avenue
New York, New York 10017
U.S.A.

[1713]

RESEARCH INSTITUTE FOR MANAGEMENT SCIENCE *(Delft, Netherlands)*

Postgraduate Award

Purpose: To develop managerial skills in business and regional development executives of developing countries by enabling them to attend programmes of the Institute.

Subjects: General management and business policy, marketing, production, finance, extension work, consultancy, regional development.

Value: Tuition payment of 9,700 Dutch florins per course, a book allowance of 550 Dutch florins per course, 1,250 Dutch florins per month for board and lodging, 350 Dutch florins for insurance, and up to 1,775 Dutch florins for travel expenses.

Tenable at the Institute for 22 weeks for all programmes except the consultancy programme which runs for 13 weeks.

Eligibility: Open to graduates from developing countries who hold a bachelor's or master's degree, are less than 40 years old, have a good knowledge of English, and a minimum of two years' actual business experience in a relevant field.

Further information from:
Dean of Studies
Research Institute for Management Science
P.O. Box 143
Mijnbouwplein 11
2600 AC Delft
Netherlands

[1714]

RESEARCH INSTITUTE FOR MANAGEMENT SCIENCE *(Delft, Netherlands)*

Fellowships

Subjects: Executive development programmes in several areas of functional management (business policy, marketing, production, finance), extension work, consultancy and regional development.

Tenable at the Institute, usually for 22 weeks.

Eligibility: Open to graduates from developing countries who hold a bachelor's or master's degree. Candidates should have a good knowledge of English and should have had a minimum of two years' professional experience in the related fields of study.

Note: Fellowships are awarded by the Ministry of Foreign Affairs, International Technical Assistance Department on application through the Royal Netherlands Embassy in the candidate's country. Fellowships may also be awarded by the executing agencies of the United Nations.

Grants provide chiefly for salaries of research assistants, research materials, and necessary travel within Australia. Grants may also be made to facilitate discussion of topics relevant to the Australian economy and, under special circumstances, to assist visits to Australia by distinguished economists. Applicants should be members of a recognised organisation and should forward applications through its administrative head, the vice chancellor in the case of a university. *Closing date:* 30th June.

Rural Credits Development Fund Grants are offered annually for research, development and extension projects directed towards the promotion of primary production in Australia, and having an applied benefit for primary industry, preferably within a few years. Primary industry includes agriculture and pastoral activities, fishing and forestry. Applications should be forwarded through the administrative head of the research organization. *Closing date:* 15th April.

Further information from:
Secretary Reserve Bank of Australia
Box 3947 G.P.O.
Sydney, N.S.W.
Australia 2001

[1719]

RHODE ISLAND MEDICAL SOCIETY

Fiske Fund Prize Dissertation

Prizes are offered annually to promote study and interest in various aspects of medicine.
There are no special terms of eligibility, and Prizes range from U.S.$200 to U.S.$1,000, depending on the subject. The contest is open from 1st June to 15th December.

Further information from:
Secretary
Fiske Fund
Rhode Island Medical Society
106 Francis Street
Providence, Rhode Island 02903
U.S.A.

[1720]

RHODE ISLAND SCHOOL OF DESIGN
(Providence)

Assistantships

Subjects: Ceramics, glass, industrial design, jewelry/metalsmithing, painting, photography, sculpture, teacher education, wood furniture design.

No. offered: 25 full Assistantships annually; often awarded as half Assistantships.

Value: Full Assistantship—full tuition and fees; half Assistantship—half tuition and fees. Supplies and living expenses are not included.

Tenable at the School.

Eligibility: Open to nationals of any country who are approved for admission to the graduate division; criteria for selection include teaching ability and experience, quality of arts work submitted, and financial need. Usually Assistantships are reserved for second year graduate students, but frequent exceptions are made.

Note: Candidates must apply for admission and indicate on the application form that an Assistantship is being sought.

Further information from:
Graduate Admissions
Rhode Island School of Design
2 College Street
Providence, Rhode Island 02903
U.S.A.

[1721]

RHODES TRUST *(U.K.)*

Rhodes Scholarships

Courses: Subject to the consent of his or her college, a Scholar may read for the Oxford B.A. degree in any of the final honours schools, or, with the consent of the college and the relevant faculty, the Scholar may be admitted, if qualified by previous training, to read for a higher degree such as the M.Litt., B.C.L., M.Phil., M.Sc. or D.Phil.

Value: The stipend consists of a direct payment to the Scholar's college of approved fees, plus a maintenance allowance of £3,000 per annum which is paid directly to the Scholar. Cost of travel to and from Oxford is (within limits) borne by the Trust.

Tenable at the University of Oxford, for two years in the first instance; renewable for a third year in certain cases.

Eligibility: Open to nationals of Australia (7), Bermuda (1), British Caribbean (1), Canada (11), India (2), Jamaica (1), Malaysia (1), New Zealand (2), Nigeria (1), Pakistan (1), South Africa (9), the United States (32), West Germany (2), Zambia (2) and Zimbabwe (2). Candidates should be between 19 and 25 years of age and should have been domiciled in the relevant country for at least five years. By the time of applicaton, candidates should have at least junior standing or equivalent at a recognized degree-granting university or college.

Note: After a candidate's election to a Scholarship, the Rhodes Scholarship authorities in Oxford seek a place for him or her, following his or her preference insofar as that is possible. Since Oxford colleges make their own admissions, there is no guarantee of a place, and the award of the Scholarship is not confirmed until the Scholar-elect has been accepted by a college for admission.

Tenure of other awards in conjunction with Rhodes Scholarships is not permitted without prior consultation with the Secretary of the Trust. Scholars forfeit the award if they marry before the end of their first year at Oxford.

Candidates should apply in the first instance to their home university or education authority.

Closing date: Between June and November, varying with each country.

Address:
Secretary
Rhodes Trustees
Rhodes House, South Parks Road
Oxford
England OX1 3RG

[1722]

MARY ROBERTS RINEHART FOUNDATION *(U.S.A.)*

Grants-In-Aid

The Foundation awards Grants-in-Aid of up to US$500 each to writers of creative ability who would otherwise lack financial means to finish their work. They are intended to encourage worthy contributions to the fields of biography, autobiography, fiction, history, poetry and drama. Preference is given to new and relatively unknown writers, without regard to citizenship, sex, color or creed. Application must be made on official application forms.

Further information from:
Mary Roberts Rinehart Foundation
516 Fifth Avenue, Room 504
New York, New York 10036
U.S.A.

[1723]

ROADS AND TRANSPORATION ASSOCIATION OF CANADA

RTAC Scholarships

Subjects: Highway sciences—highway engineering, transport economics, administration, etc.

No. offered: Five Scholarships annually.

Value: One Scholarship of *Can*$2,500 and four of *Can*$3,000.

Tenable at universities in Canada or the United States for one year.

Eligibility: Open to Canadian citizens and landed immigrants who hold university degrees and are acceptable to the university at which they plan to carry out postgraduate studies in the transportation field.

Note: Scholarships currently offered are the *Allied Chemical, Canadian Salt, Chris Fisher (ARMCO), De Leuw Cather,* and *Motor Vehicle Manufacturers' Association Scholarships.*

Closing date: 1st March.

Further information from:
Roads and Transportation Association of Canada
1765 St-Laurent Boulevard
Ottawa, Ontario
Canada K1G 3V4

[1724]

ROCHE RESEARCH FOUNDATION FOR SCIENTIFIC EXCHANGE AND BIOMEDICAL COLLABORATION WITH SWITZERLAND

Fellowships

Purpose: To enable scientists and clinicians from foreign countries to work for several months as guests of Swiss academic institutions; to promote communication of experiences with new methods and thereby gain scientific insight into the conditions of the sick and the treatment of diseases; and to promote active cooperation in research projects requiring the participation of specialists.

Eligibility: Open to advances and qualified basic or clinical scientists, regardless of citizenship, who are under 40 years of age. Exceptionally, Fellowships are offered to scientists over 40. Applications must be made by the head of the Swiss host institution or working group.

Closing date: 1st March; 1st September.

Further information from:
Roche Research Foundation
F. Hofmann-La Roche and C., Ltd.
CH-4002 Basel
Switzerland

[1725]

ROCKEFELLER FOUNDATION *(U.S.A.)*

Humanities Fellowships

Purpose: To support the production of works of humanistic scholarship intended to illuminate and assess the values of contemporary civilization. The focus is on the contemporary experience and its dilemmas as well as on long-range, perennial and universal human concerns in a world context.

Subjects: Support is given to applicants with proposals in the traditional areas of the humanities (broadly defined as the branches of knowledge concerned with the human experience), but proposals in fields not generally considered as humanities are also encouraged so long as their humanistic implications and methodology are clear. In all instances applicants must demonstrate the broad implications of their project for a deeper understanding of contemporary values.

Value: Generally between US$10,000 and US$15,000, and, in most cases, not more than US$20,000. Grants may cover the cost of salary, travel, secretarial or research support, or research materials.

Tenable for one year, and for a minimum of six months.

Eligibility: Open to mature scholars and humanists of any nationality, as well as to younger persons of high creative potential. Applicants with interdisciplinary skills and interests are favored, as are projects that show promise of transdisciplinary significance. Applicants need not necessarily have an institutional affiliation.

Note: Fellowships are not awarded for the completion of graduate or professional studies, nor can proposals for the writing of poetry or fiction be entertained.

Closing date: 1st October for first-stage applications.

Further information from:
Humanities Fellowships
Rockefeller Foundation
1133 Avenue of the Americas
New York, New York 10036
U.S.A.

[1726]

ROCKEFELLER FOUNDATION

International Relations Fellowships

Purpose: Career development of young scholars and professionals anywhere in the world, and the generation of published policy-relevant analyses on important international relations problems.

Subjects: Long-range goals and interests facing governments in the areas of international security and economic cooperation. Two broad issues are: (a) How might threats to peace arising from the intersection of local tensions and the competition for security or influence between the United States and the Soviet Union be reduced? (b) How can political and institutional obstacles to sound management of economic relations among countries be overcome?

No. offered: Approximately 10 Fellowships annually.

Value: Varies.

Tenable at any institution chosen by the Fellow for a one- to two-year period. A significant portion of the Fellow's research must be carried out at one or more foreign countries. The Foundation will assist each Fellowship winner in planning overseas research and arranging for appropriate institutional affiliations.

Eligibility: Open to young men and women who have completed their undergraduate and postgraduate academic or professional training and have several years of work experience. Applicants should be between 25 and 35 years of age (under unusual circumstances, up to age 40). Young people pursuing careers in academics, business, law, journalism, science, engineering, or public service are encouraged to apply. The Foundation particularly seeks applications from women, members of minorities, people from developing countries and others for whom access to international fellowships has been limited.

Note: Research proposals should focus on specific contemporary or anticipated problems within one of the subject areas mentioned. Proposed research should be policy-oriented, designed to contribute to the development and evaluation of alternative courses of action or institutional arrangements to deal with the problem to be studied.

Closing date: 1st November.

Further information from:
International Relations Fellowships
Rockefeller Foundation
1133 Avenue of the Americas
New York, New York 10036
U.S.A.

[1727]

ROOTHBERT FUND, INC. *(U.S.A.)*

Scholarships and Educational Aid Awards

Purpose: To help young people who are primarily motivated by spiritual values and who are in need of financial aid to further their education.

Subjects: Unrestricted, but preference is given to those who are considering teaching as a vocation.

Value: Grants average US$1,000; they are dependent on individual need and circumstances and are meant to be supplementary.

Tenable in the United States for one academic year at an accredited college or university. Renewals are considered in the light of achievements during the previous year.

Eligibility: Open to all in the United States who can satisfy fairly high scholastic requirements.

Closing date: 1st March each year.

Further information from:
Secretary
Roothbert Fund, Inc.
815 2nd Avenue, Room 516
New York, New York 10017
U.S.A.

[1728]

ROTARY FOUNDATION

Graduate Fellowships for International Understanding

Purpose: To further international understanding by enabling recipients to undertake one year of study in a country other than that in which they normally reside.

Subjects: Unrestricted.

No. offered: Up to 1,000 Fellowships annually (about 40 from Great Britain and Ireland).

Value: To cover the cost of travel to and from place of study, tuition and registration fees, books and study materials, room, board and incidental living costs, and a limited allowance for travel within the country of study. An allowance may also be made for intensive language training in the country of study.

Tenable for one academic year in any country in which there are Rotary Clubs, but other than that country in which the recipient normally resides.

Eligibility: Open to citizens of countries in which there are Rotary Clubs. Candidates should be able to demonstrate high scholastic ability, qualities of leadership and maturity, and possess the ability to speak in public.

Closing date: 1st March of the calendar year preceding that in which the award will be tenable.

Note: Candidates should have an adequate knowledge of the language of the country of study, and must not be studying in that country at the time of application. Recipients must undertake to visit and address Rotary Clubs upon return.

Applications should be sent to the Rotary Club nearest the candidate's permanent residence.

Further information is available from *Rotary International, Sheen Lane House, London SW14 8AF,* or from:
Rotary Foundation
1600 Ridge Avenue
Evanston, Illinois 60201
U.S.A.

[1729]

ROTCH TRAVELING SCHOLARSHIP
(U.S.A.)

Purpose: To provide the opportunity for advanced and mature study of architecture in foreign countries.

No. offered: One or two Scholarships annually.

Value: U.S.$13,000 stipend, paid in a lump sum, plus U.S.$1,000, to be paid at the completion of the Fellowship.

Tenable for study and travel outside the U.S. for a period of eight months.

Eligibility: Applicants should be U.S. citizens who are under 35 years of age on 10th March of the year of competition; have a degree from an accredited school of architecture plus one full year of professional experience in an architectural office in Massachusetts; or have received a degree from an accredited Massachusetts school of architecture and have one full year of professional experience in an architectural office not necessarily in Massachusetts.

Note: The Scholar is selected through a two-stage design competition and personal interviews. The one year of professional experience required should be completed prior to the beginning of the preliminary competition.

Fellows are required to return to the U.S. after the duration of the Fellowship and submit a report of their travels.

Closing date: 8th January, for application requests.

Further information from:
Norman C. Fletcher, Secretary
Rotch Traveling Scholarship
46 Brattle Street
Cambridge, Massachusetts 02138
U.S.A.

[1730]

ROTHMANS OF PALL MALL (AUSTRALIA) LTD.

Fellowships

Purpose: To assist in the development of postgraduate studies in Australian universities.

Subjects: Unrestricted.

No. offered: About four Fellowships annually.

Value: Up to A$16,000 per annum plus fees and expenses.

Tenable at any Australian university or approved institution for one year. Fellowships are awarded in the first instance for one year and may be renewed for a second year and in exceptional cases for a third year.

Eligibility: Open to men and women of any nationality who have at least three years' postgraduate research experience, and are less than 28 years of age. Candidates must complete five application forms and referees' reports are obtained.

Note: No Fellowships will be awarded to an applicant who is proceeding on sabbatical, study or other leave (including leave without pay), or to a permanent member of academic staff.

Closing date: About second Friday in July.

Further information from:
 Mr. H. McCredie, Secretary
 Rothmans University Endowment Fund
 c/o University of Sydney
 Sydney, N.S.W.
 Australia 2006

[1731]

ROYAL ACADEMY OF DRAMATIC ART *(London)*

Amanda Steel Scholarship

No. offered: One Scholarship every two and a quarter years.

Value: Remission of fees.

Tenable at the Academy for two and a quarter years.

Eligibility: Open to United States nationals who are at least 17 years of age.

Further information from:
 Royal Academy of Dramatic Art
 62 Gower Street
 London
 England WC1E 6ED

[1732]

ROYAL AERONAUTICAL SOCIETY *(U.K.)*

Edward Busk Studentship in Aeronautics

Subjects: Aeronautics: stability, meteorology and gust research, aeronautical instruments, bomb sights and appliances, the calculations and mathematical problems relating to these subjects, and, generally, any scientific work in connection with any branch or trade which conduces to progress in, or the use of, flying.

No. offered: One Studentship annually.

Value: £100 per annum.

Tenable in approved United Kingdom or foreign establishments for one year, with possibility of extension for a further year.

Eligibility: Open to citizens of the United Kingdom or the Commonwealth who are under 25 years of age.

Note: The Studentship is to enable the recipient to engage in research or the preparation of research, and may in certain cases be augmented by a grant from the Society's education funds.

Closing date: 1st June.

Further information from:
 Secretary
 Royal Aeronautical Society
 4 Hamilton Place
 London
 England W1V 0BQ

[1733]

ROYAL AERONAUTICAL SOCIETY *(U.K.)*

Charter Scholarship

Subject: Aeronautics.

No. offered: One Scholarship annually.

Value: £100 per annum.

Tenable in approved United Kingdom or foreign establishments for one year, with possibility of extension for a further year.

Eligibility: Open to United Kingdom or Commonwealth citizens wishing to undertake advanced studies and/or research.

Note: The Scholarship may be augmented by a grant from the Society's education funds when necessary.

Closing date: 1st June.

Further information from:
 Secretary
 Royal Aeronautical Society
 4 Hamilton Place
 London
 England W1V 0BQ

[1734]

ROYAL AERONAUTICAL SOCIETY *(U.K.)*

Robert Blackburn Memorial Trust Open Scholarship

Purpose: To encourage promising young persons to broaden their education and experience with further study or employment in the aircraft industry. Special consideration will be given to applicants who propose to travel abroad in connection with such study or employment.

No. offered: One Scholarship annually.

Value: Up to £6,000 per annum.

Eligibility: Open to candidates with reasonable educational qualifications who have attained positions of responsibility within the aircraft industry or major supporting companies (air-frame or power plant) or, alteratively, a higher qualification by further study; normally, applicants will be under 30 years of age.

Closing date: 1st June.

Further information from:
Secretary
Royal Aeronautical Society
4 Hamilton Place
London
England W1V 0BQ

[1735]

ROYAL AERONAUTICAL SOCIETY (U.K.)

Geoffrey de Havilland Memorial Scholarship

Purpose: To enable research workers to undertake advanced study in the field in which they are engaged.

Subject: Aeronautics.

No. offered: One Scholarship annually.

Value: £100 per annum.

Tenable in approved United Kingdom and foreign establishments for one year, with possibility of extension for a further year.

Eligibility: Open to United Kingdom and Commonwealth citizens who are graduates, or have reached graduate standard, and are already engaged in either theoretical or practical aeronautical research.

Note: The Scholarship may be augmented by a grant from the Society's education funds when necessary.

Closing date: 1st June.

Further information from:
Secretary
Royal Aeronautical Society
4 Hamilton Place
London
England W1V 0BQ

[1736]

ROYAL AERONAUTICAL SOCIETY (U.K.)

Handley Page Award

Subject: Aeronautics, with special reference to safety and reliability in air transportation.

No. offered: Usually one Award annually.

Value: Approximately £2,700 to be awarded in whole or in part to an individual or group.

Tenable preferably with the British Commonwealth, for one year.

Eligibility: Open to citizens of the British Commonwealth who are suitably qualified to undertake the proposed work.

Note: The Award is for original work leading to advancement and progress in the art and science of aeronautics, with special reference to the practical application of a device, or the long-term implications of a new concept, directed towards the safety of those who work with or travel in aircraft.

Closing date: 31st May.

Further information from:
Secretary
Royal Aeronautical Society
4 Hamilton Place
London
England W1V 0BQ

[1737]

ROYAL AERONAUTICAL SOCIETY (U.K.)

Letitia Eadon Memorial Award

Purpose: To broaden the experience of a promising young Society member by assisting him to attend an international aeronautics conference.

No. offered: One Award annually.

Value: Approximately £200.

Eligibility: Open to British subjects, resident in the United Kingdom, who are under 28 years of age, members of the Royal Aeronautical Society, and show qualities of leadership and technical promise in aeronautics.

Closing date: 31st December.

Further information from:
Secretary
Royal Aeronautical Society
4 Hamilton Place
London
England W1V OBQ

[1738]

ROYAL ANTHROPOLOGICAL INSTITUTE
(U.K.)

Emslie Horniman Anthropological Scholarship

Subject: Anthropology.

No. offered: Variable, depending on available funds and number and calibre of applicants.

Value: Depends on available funds.

Tenable for a fieldwork project approved by the Trustees.

Eligibility: Open to citizens of the United Kingdom, Commonwealth or Eire who are university graduates or who can satisfy the Trustees of their suitability for the study proposed. Preference is given to applicants whose proposals include fieldwork outside the United Kingdom.
Graduates who already hold a doctorate in anthropology are not eligible.

Note: Support is not granted for university courses, or for expeditions (unless the applicant has the required qualifications).
Application forms may be obtained by writing to the address below.

Closing date: 31st March, for payment on 1st October.

Further information from:
Honorary Secretary to the Trustees
Emslie Horniman Anthropological
   Scholarship Fund
Royal Anthropological Institute
56 Queen Anne Street
London
England W1M 9LA

[1739]

ROYAL ANTHROPOLOGICAL INSTITUTE
(U.K.)

Ruggles-Gates Grant for Research in Biological Anthropology

Up to £200 annually is available for one or two Grants to be made for research projects in biological anthropology. The Grants, which are open to postgraduates of any nationality, must be able to satisfy the Institute of their own merit and that of the research project. The awards are tenable at any accredited institution offering approved research facilities or in a fieldwork project approved by the Trustees. *Closing date:* 31st March.

Further information from:
Honorary Secretary, Ruggles-Gates Fund
Royal Anthropological Institute
56 Queen Anne Street
London
England W1M 9LA

[1740]

ROYAL ANTHROPOLOGICAL INSTITUTE
(U.K.)

Wellcome Medal for Research in Anthropology as Applied to Medical Problems: One award of £200 and a bronze medal is given in even-numbered years to recognize distinguished publications in medical anthropology. Candidates may apply or be nominated. There are no restriction regarding nationality. Preference is given to the relatively young candidate. *Closing date:* 1st December on odd-numbered years.

Curl Essay Prize: One Prize of £250 is given annually for the best essay of not more than 10,000 words "relating to the results or analysis of anthropological work." Candidates may be of any nationality. Winning essays are normally published by the Institute. Entries, to be submitted in triplicate, cannot be returned to the authors. *Closing date:* 30th September.

Further information from:
Secretary to the Director
Royal Anthropological Institute
56 Queen Anne Street
London
England W1M 9LA

[1741]

ROYAL AUSTRALASIAN COLLEGE OF RADIOLOGISTS

Baker Fellowship: This Fellowship is intended to promote the study and advancement of diagnostic radiology and radiation oncology. It is awarded to an Australian or New Zealand member of the College of less than five years standing, to assist in travelling expenses in visiting centres in the northern hemisphere. A report to Council is expected on the Fellow's return, and he or she must remain resident in Australasia for two years thereafter.

Baker Professorship: The Baker Professorship is intended to promote the study and advancement of diagnostic radiology and radiation oncology. It covers total expenses for one month, usually leading to attendance at the Annual Meeting of the College.

It is expected that the Professor visit most branches of the College in Australia and New Zealand and will have some recreation leave. The Professorship is open to radiologists of senior standing everywhere, but a good command of the English language is essential. The award is made by invitation.

Rohan William Travelling Professorship: Sponsorship of the Professorship rotates between the Royal Australasian College of Radiologists and the Royal College of Radiologists on an annual basis and is open only to radiologists of senior standing resident in Australasia or the United Kingdom. This professorship is intended to promote study in the advancement of diagnostic radiology and radiation oncology. It covers travelling expenses for one month, usually leading up to the Annual Meeting of the relevant College. United Kingdom candidates should apply to the *Honorary Secretary, Royal College of Radiologists, 38 Portland Place, London W1N 3DG.*

Rouse Travelling Fellowship: The Fellowship is intended to promote the study and advancement of diagnostic radiology and radiation oncology. It covers the travelling expenses of the Fellow and spouse for one month, often with attendance at the Annual Meeting of the College. A few days recreation leave is expected. The Fellowship alternates yearly between Australia and New Zealand and is open only to radiologists of senior standing resident in those countries.

Further information from:
Honorary Secretary
Royal Australasian College of Radiologists
37 Lower Fort Street
Millers Point, N.S.W.
Australia 2000

[1742]

ROYAL AUSTRALIAN CHEMICAL INSTITUTE

Masson Memorial Scholarship

Subjects: Chemistry or its branches, e.g. biochemistry and chemical engineering.

No. offered: One Scholarship annually.

Value: A$300.

Tenable at an Australian tertiary educational institution for one year.

Eligibility: Open to members and student members of the Institute. Candidates must have attained the minimum academic requirements for eventual corporate membership of the Institute, i.e., a B.Sc. degree or equivalent qualification in chemistry or its branches.

Closing date: 20th January.

Further information from:
Executive Secretary
Royal Australian Chemical Institute
Clunies Ross House, 191 Royal Parade
Parkville, Victoria
Australia 3052

[1743]

ROYAL AUSTRALIAN COLLEGE OF GENERAL PRACTITIONERS

Francis Hardey Faulding Memorial Research Fellowship

Purpose: To promote the advancement of the efficiency and efficacy of general practitioners in the diagnosis, treatment and prevention of disease.

Subjects: Research relevant to the field of general practice. Within this field, no limitation of topics will be imposed. Research of an educational nature conducted by general practitioners which can benefit the continuing education of general practitioners comes within the scope of the Fellowship.
The Fellowship is awarded only for a completed thesis on some aspect of general practice.

No. offered: One Fellowship annually.

Value: A$2,500.

Tenable in Australia; not renewable.

Eligibility: Open to general practitioners registered in Australia and actively engaged in practice.

Note: A *Francis Hardey Faulding Memorial Research Grant* of A$1,000 is awarded annually to the candidate whose thesis, while failing to receive the Fellowship, is yet considered to be of sufficient merit that, with further work, it can become of Fellowship standard.

Closing date: 28th February.

Further information from:
 Chairman, Research Committee
 Royal Australian College of General Practitioners
 15 Gover Street
 North Adelaide, South Australia
 Australia 5006

[1744]

ROYAL AUSTRALIAN COLLEGE OF OPHTHALMOLOGISTS

Travelling Fellowship

Subject: Ophthalmology.

No. offered: One Fellowship as vacancy occurs.

Value: A$2,000.

Tenable outside Australia for one year.

Eligibility: Open to ophthalmologists in private practice.

Further information from:
 RACO Travelling Fellowship
 Director
 Postgraduate Committee in Medicine
 Coppleson Institute
 University of Sydney
 Sydney, N.S.W.
 Australia 2006

[1745]

ROYAL AUSTRALIAN INSTITUTE OF ARCHITECTS

RAIA/Sisalation Scholarship

Purpose: To enable the successful candidate to travel and to study the practice of architecture and the building industry, and to obtain training and experience in the duties of an executive architect for the better management and organisation of building projects.

No. offered: One Scholarship annually.

Value: A$5,000 per annum.

Eligibility: Open to graduates of one of the schools of architecture in Australia, recognised by the Institute, who are under 40 years of age, associates or student-members of the Institute, and have had not less than two years' experience.
In very exceptional circumstances, the above eligibility requirements may be disregarded.

Note: Candidates must prepare and submit a proposed literary, including studies to be undertaken, and, if successful, must commence travel or studies within six months of acceptance.
Following completion of the Scholarships, recipients must prepare and submit a full report to the Institute, deliver a series of not less than three lectures, and remain in Australia for a period of not less than one year.

Closing date: March.

Further information from:
   Royal Australian Institute of Architects
   2a Mugga Way
   Red Hill, A.C.T.
   Australia 2603

[1746]
ROYAL AUSTRALIAN INSTITUTE OF ARCHITECTS

RAIA Caroma Doulton Research Grant

Subjects: The use of the Grant is entirely at the discretion of the Institute, but generally the emphasis will be on research into improving the understanding and relationship between the architectural profession and the building industry.

No. offered: One Grant annually.

Value: A$2,000 per annum.

Closing date: September.

Further information from:
   Royal Australian Institute of Architects
   2a Mugga Way
   Red Hill, A.C.T.
   Australia 2603

[1747]
ROYAL CHILDREN'S HOSPITAL RESEARCH FOUNDATION *(Melbourne)*

Lady Latham Trainee Research Fellowship

Purpose: To enable a medical or science graduate to work on a defined project in paediatrics or paediatric surgery (including studies for higher degrees) under the direct supervision of a senior research worker.

Subjects: Major current fields of interest are endocrinology, gastroenterology, genetics, haematology, immunology, orthopaedic surgery and thoracic medicine. Opportunities also exist in other areas of paediatrics and paediatric surgery.

No. offered: One Fellowship annually.

Value: Stipend is determined according to qualifications and experience and whether postgraduate studies are to be pursued. It can vary widely but will be based on either stipends usually awarded to postgraduate students by other Australian institutes and granting bodies or the research salaries of the N.H. & M.R.C.

Tenable at the Royal Children's Hospital, Parkville, Melbourne, for one year; possibility of renewal for one further year.

Eligibility: Open to medical or science graduates. Applicants are expected to have completed their basic training (FRACP part 1, FRACS part 1, Bachelor of Science honours degree) but previous experience in the chosen field of investigation is not necessary.

Closing date: 31st July.

Further information from:
   Chief Executive Officer
   Royal Children's Hospital
   Flemington Road, Parkville
   Melbourne, Victoria
   Australia 3052

[1748]
ROYAL CHILDREN'S HOSPITAL RESEARCH FOUNDATION *(Melbourne)*

Trainee Research Fellowship for Medical Graduates

Purpose: To enable a medical graduate to work on a defined project in paediatrics or paediatric surgery (including studies for higher degrees) under the direct supervision of a senior research worker.

Subjects: Major current fields of interest are endocrinology, gastroenterology, genetics, haematology, immunology, orthopaedic surgery and thoracic medicine. Opportunities also exist in other areas of paediatrics and paediatric surgery.

No. offered: One Fellowship annually.

Value: Stipend is determined according to qualifications and experience and whether postgraduate studies are to be pursued. It can vary widely but will be based on either stipends usually awarded to postgraduate students by other Australian institutes and granting bodies or the research salaries of the N.H. & M.R.C.

Tenable at the Royal Children's Hospital, Parkville, Melbourne, for one year; possibility of renewal for one further year.

Eligibility: Open to medical graduates. Applicants are expected to have completed their basic training (FRACP part 1, FRACS part 1) but previous experience in the chosen field of investigation is not necessary.

Closing date: 31st July.

Further information from:
Chief Executive Officer
Royal Children's Hospital
Flemington Road, Parkville
Melbourne, Victoria
Australia 3052

[1749]

ROYAL COLLEGE OF OBSTETRICIANS AND GYNAECOLOGISTS *(U.K.)*

Unless otherwise specified, Awards are offered annually in the field of obstetrics and gynaecology to qualified candidates from all countries.

Florence and William Blair Memorial Fellowship: An Award of up to £10,000 is offered for one year initially but may be renewed annually in certain cases.

Eden Fellowship in Obstetrics and Gynaecology: A Fellowship of up to £2,000 is available to medical graduates of not less than two years' standing from any approved university in the United Kingdom or the Commonwealth. The Fellowship will enable the holder to visit, for a specified period of time, another department or other departments of obstetrics and gynaecology or of closely related disciplines where he or she may gain additional knowledge and experience in the pursuit of a specific research project in which he or she is currently engaged. Applications must be accompanied by a brief curriculum vitae and details of the original work proposed and the departments in which it will be undertaken.

Edgar Research Fellowship: A maximum of £10,000 is awarded for the purpose of research into obstetric and gynaecological conditions. In making the award the Council of the College will bear in mind the original intention of the Fellowship, which was to encourage research into chorion carcinoma or other forms of malignant disease. Where applications of equal merit are received, priority will be given to the project most closely related to this condition. Candidates should be of high academic standing and are required to submit a report on the work carried out as soon as the tenure of the Fellowship is completed.

Edgar Gentilli Prize: One Prize of £100 is offered in recognition of original work on the cause, nature, recognition and treatment of any form of cancer of the female genital tract, including chorion carcinoma. Candidates should submit the results of their researches in the form of an essay or article, written in English, and not previously published; it is a condition of the award that the successful essay shall remain the property of the College.

Harold Malkin Prize: £25 is awarded to the candidate for, or holder of, membership of the College who, in the opinion of the assessors, undertakes the best original work whilst holding a registrar or senior registrar post in a hospital in the United Kingdom or the Republic of Ireland. The record of the work can be submitted by way of an original manuscript or by means of a reprint of a published article. If joint authorship is involved all authors must satisfy the conditions pertaining to membership or potential membership of the College. Reprints or manuscripts submitted to the College should be accompanied by an attested statement about the post held by the candidate whilst undertaking the research.

William Blair-Bell Memorial Lectureships in Obstetrics and Gynaecology: Two lectures, each with an honorarium of £100, will be delivered annually by Members of the College and Fellows of not more than two years' standing. Material submitted for the award must contain some original unpublished work and should be in obstetrics or gynaecology, or a closely related subject. In applying, candidates shoud note that the whole lecture should be submitted and should be suitable for presentation in 45 minutes.

Note: In addition to these awards, grants are offered for any research of direct or indirect relevance to obstetrics and gynaecology; these are open to all.

Closing date: 30th January.

Further information from:
  Secretary
  Birthright Royal College of Obstetricians and Gynaecologists
  27 Sussex Place, Regent's Park
  London
  England NW1 4SP

[1750]

ROYAL COLLEGE OF PHYSICIANS *(U.K.)*

Will Edmonds Research Fellowships for research in diseases that are usually treated at a general hospital (excluding tropical and rare diseases) is open to suitably qualified candidates, and is tenable in hospitals in the metropolitan area of London for a maximum of three years.

Saltwell Research Fellowships for the study of cancer, rheumatism, malaria, etc., are open to qualified candidates of any nationality, and are tenable in the United Kingdom for one year, and renewable to three years.

Watson Smith Trust Memorial Fellowships for medical research are open to suitably qualified candidates of any nationality, and are tenable in the United Kingdom for one year, and renewable for up to three years.

T.K. Stubbins Fellowship for study of medicine, is open to suitably qualified candidates and is tenable at the Royal College of Physicians, London, for one year, and renewable for up to three years.

Joseph Senior White Fellowship for scientific research solely with a view to the discovery of means to alleviate human suffering by the prevention and cure of disease, is open to suitably qualified candidates and is tenable at the Royal College of Physicians, London, for a maximum of three years.

Note: Vacancies for Fellowships are advertised in the medical press. Persons are requested to apply *only* when such advertisements appear.

Address:
  Royal College of Physicians
  11 St. Andrew's Place, Regent's Park
  London
  England NW1 4LE

[1751]

ROYAL COLLEGE OF PHYSICIANS OF EDINBURGH

Hill Pattison-Struthers Bursary

A Bursary of £100 is awarded annually to any candidate attending a course in internal medicine organised by the Edinburgh Postgraduate Board for Medicine. Applicants should submit details of their age, marital status, children, career and an indication of their plans for their future career after they have attended the course. They should also give the names of two referees, not necessarily medically qualified, to whom application can be made. It would be of help to the selection committee if applicants also offered details of any financial hardship caused by attendance at the course.

Further information from:
  Secretary
  Royal College of Physicians of Edinburgh
  9 Queen Street
  Edinburgh
  Scotland EH2 1JQ

[1752]

ROYAL COLLEGE OF PHYSICIANS OF EDINBURGH

Derrick Dunlop Travelling Fellowship

Purpose: To encourage studies in therapeutics and the contribution of the pharmaceutical industry to therapy.

Subjects: Therapeutics, pharmacology, the regulation of the pharmaceutical industry, national differences in therapy or similar topics.

No. offered: One Fellowship annually.

Value: £5,000.

Tenable at centres in the United Kingdom or abroad for up to two years.

Eligibility: Open to members of the Royal Colleges of Physicians in the United Kingdom and in Ireland.

Note: This Fellowship was endowed by the Winthrop Foundation.

Further information from:
  Secretary
  Royal College of Physicians of Edinburgh
  9 Queen Street
  Edinburgh
  Scotland EH2 1JQ

[1753]

ROYAL COLLEGE OF PHYSICIANS AND SURGEONS OF CANADA

Continuing Medical Education Fellowships

Purpose: To enable the recipient to study in recognized centres which have developed expertise in continuing medical education. The study program must be designed to allow the recipient to gain experience in the use or application of new knowledge or techniques in the continuing medical education field. The program should contain elements which will enable the recipient to evaluate specialist CME needs, design appropriate programs using the latest in adult education techniques and to assess the content and outcome of programs as to their effectiveness.

No. offered: Up to three Fellowships annually.

Value: Can$1,500 per month.

Tenable for six to twelve months.

Eligibility: Open to fellows of the College who reside in Canada.
  Applicants need not be in university centres. The applicant must be sponsored by an established department of continuing medical education in a university, major institution, or recognized association or organization.
  Selection will be based upon an overall assessment of the merit of the application, including the purpose and objectives of the travel and its benefits both to the individual and the institution or community which he/she represents, the availability of funds for the type of project envisaged, and financial need of the applicant.

Note: Prior to departure, Fellows must submit evidence of their acceptance for training by the heads of the centres to be visited.
  At the conclusion of tenure, a short report should be submitted to the College.

Ideally the recipient, upon return, would work closely with established departments of continuing medical education in universities, major institutions or in the community as a resource and planning person.

Closing date: 30th September.

Further information from:
  Committee on Awards
  Royal College of Physicians and Surgeons of Canada
  74 Stanley
  Ottawa, Ontario
  Canada K1M 1P4

[1754]

ROYAL COLLEGE OF PHYSICIANS AND SURGEONS OF CANADA

Detweiler Travel Fellowships

Purpose: To improve the quality of medical and surgical practise in Canada. The Fellowships enable the recipients to visit medical centres in Canada or abroad, to study or gain experience in the use or application of new knowledge or techniques in their fields. Study may be directed towards acquiring knowledge or experience for direct application to clinical practise or to the further pursuit of a fundamental or clinical research problem.

Value: Can$1,000 per month.

Tenable for six to twelve months.

Eligibility: Open to fellows of the College. Applicants need not be in university centres and additional consideration will be given to those engaged in practise.
  Selection is based on an overall assessment of the merit of the application, incuding the purpose and objectives of the travel and its benefits, the availability of funds for the type of project envisaged, and financial need of the applicant.

Note: Prior to departure, Fellows must submit evidence of their acceptance for training by the heads of the departments to be visited.
  At the conclusion of tenure, a short report should be submitted to the College.

Closing date: 30th September.

Further information from:
Committee on Awards
Royal College of Physicians and Surgeons of Canada
74 Stanley
Ottawa, Ontario
Canada K1M 1P4

[1755]

ROYAL COLLEGE OF PHYSICIANS AND SURGEONS OF CANADA

Walter C. MacKenzie-Ethicon Travel Fellowship

Purpose: To allow a practicing surgeon to visit one or more centres for surgical research or clinical surgical training.

No. offered: One Fellowship annually.

Value: Can$12,000 for travel and maintenance expenses.

Tenable at approved centres for one year.

Eligibility: Open to practicing surgeons in Canada who are Fellows of the Division of Surgery of the College.

Closing date: 30th September.

Further information from:
Committee on Awards
Royal College of Physicians and Surgeons of Canada
74 Stanley
Ottawa, Ontario
Canada K1M 1P4

[1756]

ROYAL COLLEGE OF PHYSICIANS AND SURGEONS OF CANADA

Annual Medal Awards

Purpose: To provide national recognition for original work by young clinicians and investigators.

Subjects: Any original work in the field of clinical investigation, or in the basic sciences relating to medicine or surgery.

No. offered: One Award in medicine and one in surgery each year.

Value: Bronze Medal and Can$500 in each instance.

Eligibility: Open to graduates in medicine who are Canadian citizens; and to graduates in medicine of any nationality whose nomination is based on work done in Canada; and to Fellows and Certified Specialists of the College. Applicants should not have reached 45 years of age before 31st December of the year in which the submission is made.

Note: Applications must be accompanied by an abstract of the author's work and a complete manuscript of approximately 20 to 30 pages in length, submitted in triplicate. Where the applicant is not a Fellow, his application must be sponsored by a Fellow of the College.

Closing date: 1st March.

Further information from:
Secretary
Royal College of Physicians and Surgeons of Canada
74 Stanley
Ottawa, Ontario
Canada K1M 1P4

[1757]

ROYAL COLLEGE OF RADIOLOGISTS
(U.K.)

Reginald G. Reid Memorial Fellowship in the amount of £250 (taxable) is offered annually to a diagnostic radiologist, under the age of 35, to visit departments in the United Kingdom or abroad for a period of not less than three weeks to learn a new technique or to study a specific problem related to his own work, including teaching or research. Closing date is usually early February.

Graham-Hodgson Scholarship of £170 is offered in even-numbered years to a consultant radiologist who is a Fellow of the College in clinical practice in the United Kingdom, to assist with expenses incurred in visiting a centre in his own country or abroad to study a new technique or to further a research project. *Closing date:* Early February.

Kodak Scholarship of £3,000 (taxable) is offered annually to senior registrars, or those of equivalent status, in diagnostic radiology holding an appointment in the United Kingdom. Candidates should submit details of their proposed study project and the centre, either in the United Kingdom or overseas, they wish to visit. Scholarships are for a minimum of three months' duration. *Closing date:* Early February.

Not confirmed for 1983.

Further information from:
Examinations Secretary
Royal College of Radiologists
38 Portland Place
London
England W1N 3DG

[1758]

ROYAL COLLEGE OF SURGEONS OF ENGLAND

Mackenzie Mackinnon Streatfeild Research Fellowship

Subject: Scientific medical investigation.

Tenable for a maximum of three years; no restriction on place of tenure. Fellowships may be held part time.

Eligibility: Open to persons with a suitable degree or medical qualification.

Note: Applications should be submitted through a medical school.

Not confirmed for 1983.

Address:
Secretary
Royal College of Surgeons of England
35-43 Lincoln's Inn Fields
London
England WC2A 3PN

[1759]

ROYAL COLLEGE OF SURGEONS OF ENGLAND

Norman Capener Travelling Fellowship

Purpose: To provide travel expenses to and from the United Kingdom for the study of orthopaedic surgery and surgery of the hand.

No. offered: One Fellowship biennially (first award in 1981).

Value: Varies according to travel costs; paid in one lump sum.

Eligibility: Open to medical practitioners. Preference is given to candidates enrolled for, or having recently completed, advanced training in orthopaedic surgery or an appropriate course.

Not confirmed for 1983.

Further information from:
Secretary
Royal College of Surgeons of England
35-43 Lincoln's Inn Fields
London
England WC2A 3PN

[1760]

ROYAL COLLEGE OF SURGEONS OF ENGLAND
Faculty of Dental Surgery

Quintin Hogg/Florence Mills Research Fellowship in Dental Science

Subjects: Research relevant to dental science under the direction of the Nuffield Professor of Dental Science.

No. offered: As vacancies occur.

Value: Variable.

Tenable at the Department of Dental Science, Royal College of Surgeons of England; renewable annually to a maximum of three years.

Eligibility: Open to candidates who possess a dental or medical qualification or a degree in a cognate science.

Not confirmed for 1983.

Further information from:
Nuffield Professor of Dental Science
Royal College of Surgeons of England
35-43 Lincoln's Inn Fields
London
England WC2A 3PN

[1761]

ROYAL COLLEGE OF SURGEONS OF ENGLAND
Royal College of Physicians of London

Sir Ratanji Dalal Research Scholarship

Subjects: Tropical medicine or tropical surgery.

Value: Not more than £5,500 per annum.

Tenable for a maximum of three years; no restriction on place of tenure.

Eligibility: Open to British Commonwealth registered medical practitioners.

Not confirmed for 1983.

Further information from:
  Secretary
  Royal College of Surgeons of England
  35-43 Lincoln's Inn Fields
  London
  England WC2A 3PN

[1762]

ROYAL COLLEGE OF SURGEONS OF ENGLAND
Royal College of Physicians of London

Travenol Travelling Fellowships

Purpose: To acquire special knowledge of nutrition in in-patient care.

No. offered: One or more Fellowships annually.

Value: £1,500 per annum.

Eligibility: Open to surgeons, physicians and anesthetists.

Not confirmed for 1983.

Further information from:
  Secretary
  Royal College of Surgeons of England
  35-43 Lincoln's Inn Fields
  London
  England WC2A 3PN

[1763]

ROYAL COLLEGE OF SURGEONS OF ENGLAND

Lister Award in Ophthalmology

Purpose: The Award is available for travel of unspecified duration.

Eligibility: Open to British ophthalmologists on the nomination of Moorfields Eye Hospital, London.

Note: Applications should be submitted through *Moorfields Eye Hospital, City Road, London EC1V 2PD*.

Not confirmed for 1983.

Address:
  Secretary
  Royal College of Surgeons of England
  35-43 Lincoln's Inn Fields
  London
  England WC2A 3PN

[1764]

ROYAL COLLEGE OF SURGEONS OF ENGLAND
British Association of Plastic Surgeons

Hayward Foundation Grant

Plastic surgery trainees, senior registrars and consultants of less than five years' standing are eligible for travel grants for the study of new techniques abroad. Applications for assistance should be sent to the address below, and should contain the various details of the purpose and a costing for the intended travel. Grant requests may be submitted at any time and are considered at the Association's regular meetings.

Not confirmed for 1983.

Further information from:
  British Association of Plastic Surgeons
  Royal College of Surgeons of England
  35-43 Lincoln's Inn Fields
  London
  England WC2A 3PN

[1765]

ROYAL COLLEGE OF VETERINARY SURGEONS *(U.K.)*

Miss Aleen Cust Research Fellowship
Sir Frederick Smith Research Fellowship

Subjects: Any branch of veterinary science: research or preparation of such research.

No. offered: One Fellowship as vacancy occurs.

Value: £1,000 per annum plus £200 per annum research expenses.

Tenable at institutions approved by the College for a maximum of three years.

Eligibility: Open to Members of the Royal College of Veterinary Surgeons who have had some postgraduate experience. Applicants for the Miss Aleen Cust Research Fellowship should have been born in England, Ireland, Scotland or Wales. In the case of deciding between two candidates of equal merit, preference will be given to women.

Further information from:
Registrar
Royal College of Veterinary Surgeons
32 Belgrave Square
London
England SW1X 8QP

[1766]

ROYAL COLLEGE OF VETERINARY SURGEONS *(U.K.)*

P.D.S.A. Small Animal Postgraduate Scholarship

Subject: Disease in small animals: research.

No. offered: One Scholarship, as and when vacant.

Value: £5,000 per annum with up to £250 per annum for expenses.

Tenable at approved universities, research institutes or other centres in the United Kingdom for one year, with possibility of renewal up to a maximum of three years.

Eligibility: Open to Fellows or Members of the College who are citizens of the United Kingdom and colonies, of any Commonwealth country or of the Irish Republic.

Note: The Scholarship will be advertised as and when it becomes vacant.

Further information from:
Secretary
Royal College of Veterinary Surgeons
  Trust Fund
32 Belgrave Square
London
England SW1X 8QP

[1767]

ROYAL COMMISSION FOR THE EXHIBITION OF 1851 *(U.K.)*

Science Research Scholarships for Overseas Universities

Subjects: Pure or applied physical or biological science, or engineering.

No. offered: Ten Scholarships annually.

Value: £3,300 per annum plus additional allowance for university or college fees.

Tenable at a university institution in the United Kingdom, for two years; renewable in certain cases for a third year.

Eligibility: Open to citizens of Commonwealth countries (excluding the United Kingdom), South Africa, Pakistan or Ireland, who are under 26 years of age and can give evidence of their capacity for research. A candidate must have been a student in a university or equivalent institution for a period of not less than three years, and must have spent one full academic year at the institution by which he is recommended.

Note: Recommendations on behalf of candidates are only acceptable from universities outside the United Kingdom.
Applications must be made through the candidate's university.

Closing date: 21st March.

Further information from:
  Secretary
  Royal Commission for the Exhibition of 1851
  1 Lowther Gardens, Exhibition Road
  London
  England SW7 2AA

[1768]

ROYAL COMMISSION FOR THE EXHIBITION OF 1851 *(U.K.)*

1851 Research Fellowships

Subjects: Pure or applied physical or biological sciences, or engineering.

No. offered: Four Fellowships annually.

Value: £5,750 to £6,325 per annum, plus discretionary additional allowances for university fees and research expenses.

Tenable at any approved institution for two years.

Eligibility: Open to citizens of the United Kingdom, the Commonwealth, South Africa, Pakistan and Ireland. Candidates should generally be under 30 years of age, should hold a Ph.D. degree or equivalent, and should be able to demonstrate exceptional promise and proven capacity for original work.

Note: Recommendations on behalf of candidates will be accepted only from United Kingdom universities, for whose students the awards are primarily intended. A candidate may be recommended through the executive authority of an institution other than that at which he graduated.

Closing date: 1st May.

Further information from:
  Secretary
  Royal Commission for the Exhibition of 1851
  1 Lowther Gardens, Exhibition Road
  London
  England SW7 2AA

[1769]

ROYAL COMMONWEALTH SOCIETY FOR THE BLIND

Scholarships

Subjects: Teaching of blind children; training of blind adults; resettlement and/or placement of trained blind adults; general welfare of the blind; advanced ophthalmic training for qualified doctors.

Value: Variable, depending on individual requirements. Scholarships are awarded to cover tuition fees, accommodation, travel for purposes connected with the course being followed, equipment, books and incidental expenses incurred during the course. Scholarships do not cover pocket money, clothing expenses or return travel expenses.

Tenable at approved institutions in the United Kingdom and abroad for the duration of the course being followed.

Eligibility: Open to suitably qualified nationals of overseas developing countries of the Commonwealth following courses in the United Kingdom or elsewhere.

Note: Candidates must be nominated by the affiliated organisation in the country of origin and supported by the appropriate department of their national government.

Further information from:
  Deputy Director
  Royal Commonwealth Society for the Blind, Scholarship Fund
  Commonwealth House, Heath Road
  Haywards Heath, Sussex
  England RH16 3AZ

[1770]

ROYAL DUTCH/SHELL GROUP OF OIL COMPANIES

Shell Scholarship in Geophysics

No. offered: One Scholarship annually.

Value: £2,590 per annum, plus fees.

Tenable at the University of Cambridge for two years; renewable for a third year subject to satisfactory progress.

Eligibility: Open to men or women of any nationality who are under the age of 27 on 1st October in the year of the award, and who hold, or expect to hold, a university degree.

Note: An elected Scholar will be required to pursue a course of training in research in geophysics at the University of Cambridge and must be, or must become, registered as a research student. Applications for the Scholarship should be accompanied by a statement of the candidate's academic career, his or her date of birth, and the names of two referees.

Closing date: 1st April.

Further information from:
Secretary
Department of Geophysics
Madingley Rise, Madingley Road
Cambridge
England CB3 OEZ

[1771]

ROYAL GEOGRAPHICAL SOCIETY *(U.K.)*
Commonwealth Foundation
Commonwealth Geographical Bureau

Bursaries Scheme

Bursaries are awarded to provide the means by which geographers of proven ability (usually at the postgraduate level) from Commonwealth countries, may increasee their competence by working with geographers of a Commonwealth country other than their own. The awards are intended for research, the learning of new techniques, or other valid study in the field of applied geography. Study towards higher degrees or diplomas are specifically excluded from the purposes of this scheme.

Bursaries cover travel costs and a maintenance allowance, averaging £100 per month, depending on the applicant's circumstances and the cost of living in the country of tenure. No provisions are made for families of recipients.

It is expected that award holders occupy permanent salaried positions to which they will return upon completion of their study. Further information and applications are available from the address below. *Closing dates:* 15th March and September of each year.

Address:
Director
Royal Geographic Society
Kensington Gore
London
England SW7 2AR

[1772]

ROYAL HISTORICAL SOCIETY *(U.K.)*

David Berry Prize

In order to encourage research into Scottish history a money prize is offered every three years (next in 1982) for an essay, between 6,000 and 10,000 words long excluding footnotes and appendices, on an aspect of Scottish history within the reigns of James I to James VI inclusive. Subjects should be approved by the Council of the Society. Essays submitted must be the result of genuine research and should not previously have been published or awarded any other prize. Nationals of any country may submit work, but the essay must be written in English.

Note: The Society also awards annually the *Alexander Prize* (a silver medal) for an essay on any historical subject.

Further information from:
Executive Secretary
Royal Historical Society
University College London
Gower Street
London
England WC1E 6BT

[1773]

ROYAL INSTITUTE OF BRITISH ARCHITECTS

Research Awards

Subjects: Those fields which are relevant to the contemporary or historical study of architecture, architectural education or practice, planning or building.

The Research Awards can be made for: (a) the financing of secondments of teachers and practising architects with some research interest and experience to established research centres for periods of from three to twelve months at current research salary level; (b) the extension of research activities of members of staff in schools of architecture and practising architects (the aim is to cover expenses rather than to augment salaries or compensate for possible loss of earnings); (c) group research projects in schools of architecture; and (d) travel or secretarial expenses essential to a programme of research and its completion for publication (candidates under this category will be required to demonstrate that no other assistance is available).

Value: To be determined by the estimated requirements of each project; applications for up to £5,000 will be considered, although a number of smaller Awards will be made.

Eligibility: Open to individual architects or groups and in certain circumstances non-architects. Overseas applicants are considered provided their research project is of more than local interest.

Note: Projects must normally be supervised and supported by a school of architecture or research institution, and results of research should be presented in publishable form.

Closing date: January.

Further information from:
RIBA Research Awards
Research and Statistics Office
Royal Institute of British Architects
66 Portland Place
London
England W1N 4AD

[1774]

ROYAL INSTITUTE OF PUBLIC ADMINISTRATION *(U.K.)*

Haldane Essay Competition

An annual award of £100 and a silver medal is given for significant and original contribution toward the study of public administration practice and history in Commonwealth countries. Additional awards of up to £50 may also be given for chosen essays.

Essays may be submitted by any member, past or present, of the public services throughout the Commonwealth, and should be between 7,500 and 12,500 words. Winning essays may be published in the Institute's journal, *Public Administration. Closing date:* 31st October of each year.

Further information from:
Director-General
Royal Institute of Public Administration
Haldane Essay Competition
3 Birdcage Walk
London
England SW1H 9JJ

[1775]

ROYAL INSTITUTION *(U.K.)*

Dewar Research Fellowship

Subjects: Independent research related to chemical and physical sciences.

The Fellowship is offered at infrequent intervals and is tenable for an indefinite period. The Fellowship, valued at £400 per annum, will be advertised in publications such as *Nature* and *The Times* when it becomes available, and candidates are kindly requested to apply for further details *only* at that time.

Further information from:
Royal Institution
21 Albermarle Street
London
England W1X 4BS

[1776]

ROYAL INSTITUTION OF CHARTERED SURVEYORS *(U.K.)*

RICS Education Trust Award

Subjects: All areas of surveying—building surveying, general practice (valuation and land management), land agency and agriculture, land surveying, minerals surveying, planning and development, and quantity surveying.

Value: Normally £100 to £500.

Eligibility: Open to chartered surveyors or others carrying out research studies in relevant subjects.

Further information from:
Secretary for Education and Membership
Royal Institution of Chartered Surveyors
12 Great George Street
Parliament Square
London
England SW1P 3AD

[1777]

ROYAL INSTITUTION OF NAVAL ARCHITECTS *(U.K.)*

Sir William White Postgraduate Scholarship in Naval Architecture

Subjects: Research into problems connected with the design and construction of ships and their machinery, or a postgraduate course of study relevant to ship technology.

No. offered: One Scholarship from time to time as a vacancy occurs.

Value: £1,250 per annum.

Tenable at an approved university, college or research establishment for two years.

Eligibility: Open to British subjects, under 30 years of age, who have graduated in naval architecture or marine engineering, and have at some time been employed in shipbuilding or marine engineering.

Further information from:
Royal Institution of Naval Architects
10 Upper Belgrave Street
London
England SW1X 8BQ

[1778]

ROYAL INSTITUTION OF NAVAL ARCHITECTS *(U.K.)*

Froude Research Scholarship in Naval Architecture

Subjects: Naval architecture: research in hydrodynamic problems connected with ships. A detailed list of subjects in this field is available from the Institution.

No. offered: One Scholarship from time to time as a vacancy occurs.

Value: £1,250 per annum.

Tenable for two years, with possibility of renewal for a third year. Recipients are required to undertake part of their research work at the National Maritime Institute, Feltham, Middlesex.

Eligibility: Open to British subjects under 30 years of age who have shown unusual promise in the study of naval architecture.

Candidates should be associate members or students of the Institution and be recommended by the appropriate head of department of the university from which they graduated.

Further information from:
Royal Institution of Naval Architects
10 Upper Belgrave Street
London
England SW1X 8BQ

[1779]

ROYAL IRISH ACADEMY

Visiting Fellowships and Grants

The Academy awards, on behalf of the Irish government, Senior Visiting Fellowships for scientific research (other than in social sciences, dentistry and theoretical and clinical medicine). It participates in the Royal Society European Scheme in pure and applied science, in the Polish Academy Exchange Scheme in science and the humanities, and in the Austrian Academy Exchange Scheme in science and linguistics. Small Grants for work in the field of natural science and archaeology are available annually from the academy's own funds.

Further information from:
Secretary
Royal Irish Academy
19 Dawson Street
Dublin 2
Ireland

[1780]

ROYAL NATIONAL EISTEDDFOD OF WALES

Prizes

The National Eisteddfod is held annually during the first week of August at a location which changes from year to year. Prizes are offered in drama, poetry and literature written in the Welsh language, and in vocal and instrumental music, art, crafts, photography and architecture.

Note: A special award of £1,800 is given annually for vocal music.

Further information from:
   Director
   Royal National Eisteddfod of Wales
   10 Park Grove
   Cardiff
   Wales CW1 3BN

[1781]

ROYAL NETHERLANDS ACADEMY OF ARTS AND SCIENCES

Van't Hoff Fund Grants

Grants of DFL3,000 each are available annually for research in pure and applied chemistry. The Grants are tenable in the Netherlands, and are open to nationals of all countries. *Closing date:* 31st December.

Further information from:
   Royal Netherlands Academy of Arts and Sciences
   P.O. Box 19121
   1000 GC Amsterdam
   Netherlands

[1782]

ROYAL NORWEGIAN COUNCIL FOR SCIENTIFIC AND INDUSTRIAL RESEARCH

Postdoctorate Fellowships

Subjects: Science and engineering.

No. offered: 20 Fellowships annually.

Value: 60,000 Norwegian kroner for single Fellows, 76,000 Norwegian kroner for married Fellows, and 4,000 kroner for each dependent child. Additional allowances are available to cover transportation from European countries.

Tenable in Norway for one year; renewable.

Eligibility: Open to nationals of all countries who are under 35 years of age, and have at least the equivalent of a British or American Ph.D. degree in science or engineering.

Closing date: 1st December.

Further information from:
   Royal Norwegian Council for Scientific and Industrial Research
   Sognsveien 72
   P.O. Box 70, Tasen
   Oslo 8
   Norway

[1783]

ROYAL OVER-SEAS LEAGUE *(U.K.)*

The League sponsors a festival in the early spring of each year in order to offer help, encouragement and a platform to young musicians. The festival competition is open to artists from the Commonwealth overseas, including former Commonwealth countries and the United Kingdom. The upper age limit is 25 for instrumentalists and 28 for singers. The main Prizes of the Festival include the *Barclays Bank International Award* of £1,000; £100 each for best singer, pianist, string and woodwind player, for the most outstanding musician of the Festival; other Prizes are as follows: the *Society of Women Musicians Award* for the best woman competitor of £200; *Australian Musical Overseas Scholarship* for Australian pianists of £500; the *Miller Ensemble Prize* of £300; the *Stella Murray Memorial Prize for New Zealanders* of £150; *Liza Fuchsova Memorial Prize for a Chamber Music Pianist* of £60; the *Eric Rice Memorial Prize for Accompanists* of £50; *Ivor Walsworth Memorial Prize for a Violinist* of £100. In addition, the *Society of Women Musicians Gold Medal*, which entitles the winner to a shared recital in the Purcell Room, is awarded to the best competitor in the festival, and Prizes are awarded to all finalists.

The League also arranged an annual art exhibition in the autumn, open to artists of all ages from the Commonwealth overseas, including former Commonwealth countries and the United Kingdom. Prizes of £500 and over are awarded for the best works by artists under the age of 35; one Prize of £150 is awarded to an artist over the age of 35.

Further information from:
   Music and Art Department
   Royal Over-seas League
   Over-Seas House, Park Place
   St. James's Street
   London
   England SW1A 1LR

[1784]

ROYAL PHILHARMONIC SOCIETY (U.K.)

Kathleen Ferrier Memorial Scholarship and Decca-Kathleen Ferrier Prize: Awards to the value of £3,000 are offered in April each year. The competition is open to singers of either sex who are British born, or holders of British, Commonwealth or Republic of Ireland passports, are between 21 and 26 years of age on the day of the Finals, and who are sponsored by two musicians of repute. The closing date for application is 28th February.

Julius Isserlis Scholarship: Awards of £5,000 per annum, tenable for two years, are made for musical study abroad. Open to United Kingdom residents of any nationality who are between the ages of 15 and 20 years of age, and 15 and 22 years of age in the case of singers. Closing date: 1st May.

Further information from:
Administrative Secretary
Royal Philharmonic Society
10 Stratford Place
London
England W1N 9AE

[1785]

ROYAL SCOTTISH ACADEMY OF PAINTING, SCULPTURE AND ARCHITECTURE

Annual Student Competition: Awards and Prizes

The Academy annually holds a Competition for students of painting, sculpture and architecture as a result of which the following are some of the Awards and Prizes: *Royal Scottish Academy Awards* of £400 each in painting, sculpture and architecture; *Carnegie Travelling Scholarship* of £175; *Adam Bruce Thomson* Award of approximately £100 (given in alternate years); *Chalmers Bursary* of £50; *Stuart Prize* of £30; and the *Chalmers-Jervise Prize* of £10.

All eligible candidates must be resident in Scotland. Painting and sculpture students should be in their penultimate, final or postgraduate years of study at a college or art in Scotland; others, not being students or graduates of such a college, may submit work to the Competition provided they are proposed and seconded by painter or sculptor members of the Academy. Applicants should submit two works. Architecture students should be in their final year and present work normally related to the requirements of the R.I.B.A. Part II syllabus.

Closing date: February.

Further information from:
Royal Scottish Academy of Painting,
Sculpture and Architecture
Princes Street
Edinburgh
Scotland EH2 2EL

[1786]

ROYAL SCOTTISH ACADEMY OF PAINTING, SCULPTURE AND ARCHITECTURE

Annual Exhibition: Awards and Prizes

The Academy sponsors an Annual Exhibition of painting (oil, water-colour, pastel, black and white), sculpture, architectural drawings and photographs. As a result of this Exhibition, the following are some of the Awards and Prizes:

Guthrie Award of £500 for the most outstanding work by a young Scottish artist.

Ireland Alloys Award: £250 for an outstanding new work in stainless steel, nickel alloys or titanium.

Latimer Awards: Two Prizes of £150 each to artists under the age of 33.

William J. Macaulay Award: £150 for the most distinguished work exhibited within the galleries during the course of the year.

John Thomson Award: £100 to a promising young artist.

Benno Schotz Prize of £30 to sculptors under the age of 33 and resident in Scotland.

Keith Prize of £15 for work by a student.

Ottillie Helen Wallace Scholarship Fund Prize of £30 for work by a woman sculptor.

Meyer Oppenheim Prize of £100 to painters or sculptors under the age of 28.

Academy Medal for Architecture: Gold Medal for outstanding work, preferably drawing, done by a younger architect.

Further information from:
   Royal Scottish Academy of Painting,
      Sculpture and Architecture
   Princes Street
   Edinburgh
   Scotland EH2 2EL

[1787-1796]

ROYAL SOCIETY *(U.K.)*

N.B.: The following awards are offered as vacancies occur. When an award becomes available, it is advertised in the usual scientific journals such as *Nature*. Candidates are kindly requested to apply only when such a public avertisement has appeared.

Not confirmed for 1983.

[1787]
Armourers and Brasiers' Research Fellowship: One offered every two to five years for research in metallurgy or the kindred sciences connected with base metals and alloys and preferably those used in connection with the ancient crafts of the Armourers and Brasiers' Company. The Fellowship is tenable at approved institutions for two years (renewable up to a maximum of three or five years), and is open to persons of any nationality who are suitably experienced in independent research. Value—£7,011 to £8,481 per annum.

[1788]
Henry Head Research Fellowship: One offered about every five years (next award in 1983) for research in neurology. The Fellowship is tenable at approved institutions for up to a maximum of five years, and is open to persons of any nationality who are suitably experienced in independent research. Value— £7,011 to £8,481 per annum.

[1789]
Mr. and Mrs. John Jaffé Donation Research Fellowships: One or more offered from time to time for original research in practical sciences (e.g., chemistry, physics, medicine) and the application of scientific discoveries to industry. The Fellowships are tenable at approved institutions for periods from two to five years, and are open to persons of any nationality who are suitably experienced in independent research. Awards may not be made to Nobel Prize winners. Value—usually between £7,011 to £8,481 per annum or £4,998 to £6,438 per annum.

[1790]
Alan Johnston, Lawrence and Moseley Research Fellowship: One Fellowship is offered every two to five years for research into the causes of disease in men and animals and conditions of healthy life, development and inheritance, with a view to the prevention and relief of human suffering and promotion of racial health. The Fellowship is tenable at approved institutions for two years (renewable to a maximum of five years), and is open to persons of any nationality who are suitably experienced in independent research. Value—£7,011 to £8,481 per annum.

[1791]
Horace Le Marquand and Dudley Bigg Research Fellowship: One offered from time to time (last awarded in 1978) to "further the application of physiological principles to medicine, or such other research of a biological nature, in relation to the problems of health or disease." The Fellowship is tenable at approved institutions for two years (renewable up to a maximum of five years), and is open to persons of any nationality who are suitably qualified university graduates with two or three years of research experience. Candidates need not have a doctoral degree. Value—£4,998 to £6,438.

[1792]
Locke Research Fellowship: One offered every one to five years (next award in 1984) for research in the fields of experimental physiology and pharmacology. The Fellowship is tenable at approved institutions for up to a maximum of five years, and is open to persons of any nationality who are experienced in independent research. Value—£7,011 to £8,481 per annum.

[1793]
Rosenheim Research Fellowship: One offered from time to time for research in biochemistry of plants and the simpler forms of life. The Fellowship is tenable in any appropriate university department or research institution in Great Britain, subject to the approval of the Council of the Royal Society, for two years in the first instance (renewable for a further one or exceptionally three years). Nationals of any country who are suitably experienced in inde-

pendent research may apply. Value—£4,998 to £6,438 per annum.

[1794]
Warren Research Fellowships: Offered from time to time (last awarded in 1977) for research in metallurgy, engineering, physics or chemistry. The Fellowships are tenable at such place as is prescribed by the Warren Committee, for four years; renewable for a further period of four years and then possibly extendable until the Fellow reaches 65 years of age. Persons who can demonstrate ability for independent research may apply. Value—£7,011 to £8,481 per annum.

[1795]
Foulerton Gift Research Fellowship: One offered from time to time (last awarded in 1976) for medical research—"the improvement of disease and the relief of human suffering." The Fellowship is tenable at approved institutions for two years (renewable up to a maximum for four years), and is open to United Kingdom citizens, under 35 years of age, who are suitably experienced in independent research and whose father and paternal grandfather were also of British nationality. Value—£4,998 to £6,438 per annum.

[1796]
Stothert Research Fellowship: One offered every four years (last awarded in 1978) for research in the field of medicine, including the sciences on which medical knowledge is based, particularly with a view to increasing knowledge useful to the investigation or treatment of disease and relief of suffering in human beings and animals. The Fellowships are tenable at approved institutions for two years (renewable up to a maximum of four years), and are open to United Kingdom citizens who are suitably experienced in independent research. Value—£4,998 to £6,438 per annum.

Address:
Executive Secretary
Royal Society
6 Carlton House Terrace
London
England SW1Y 5AG

[1797]

ROYAL SOCIETY *(U.K.)*

Pickering Research Fellowship

Subjects: Chemistry (especially physical and inorganic) or botany.

Value: £4,998 to £6,438 per annum.

Tenable at any university or other research institution, subject to the approval of the Council of the Royal Society, for two years in the first instance; renewable up to a total tenure of three or, exceptionally, five years.

Eligibility: Open to persons of any nationality who are suitably experienced in independent research.

Note: When a vacancy occurs, these Fellowships will be advertised in *Nature* and other scientific journals. Candidates are kindly requested to apply only when such a public advertisement has appeared.

Not confirmed for 1983.

Further information from:
Executive Secretary
Royal Society
6 Carlton House Terrace
London
England SW1Y 5AG

[1798]

ROYAL SOCIETY *(U.K.)*

Bruno Mendel Fellowship

Subject: Medicine: experimental research.

No. offered: One or more Fellowships annually.

Value: Usually up to £5,000 per annum, depending on qualifications and place and duration of visit.

Tenable for up to three years at universities or medical research centres or medical schools by candidates normally resident in the United Kingdom, the Netherlands, or Israel.

Eligibility: Open to suitably qualified postgraduate candidates.

Not confirmed for 1983.

Further information from:
  Executive Secretary
  Royal Society
  6 Carlton House Terrace
  London
  England SW1Y 5AG

[1799]

ROYAL SOCIETY *(U.K.)*

John Murray Travelling Studentship

Subjects: Oceanography and limnology.

No. offered: One or more Studentships annually.

Value: By individual assessment, up to £2,000.

Tenable for period of one year or less; possibly extendable to two years.

Eligibility: Open to postgraduate students who are citizens of the United Kingdom and are under 35 years of age.

Not confirmed for 1983.

Further information from:
  Executive Secretary
  Royal Society
  6 Carlton House Terrace
  London
  England SW1Y 5AG

[1800]

ROYAL SOCIETY *(U.K.)*

Florey Fellowship

Subjects: Biomedical research, including mammalian physiology, biochemistry, pathology, pharmacology and related subjects.

No. offered: One Fellowship every other year.

Value: £8,000 per annum, plus superannuation benefits, family allowances and return fares to Australia.

Tenable at any university, medical school or other research institution in Australia, for two years; not normally renewable.

Eligibility: Open to persons who are normally resident in the United Kingdom, and are under 30 years of age on the closing date for applications.

Note: When a vacancy occurs, this Fellowship will be advertised in *Nature* and other scientific journals. Candidates are kindly requested to apply only when such a public advertisement has appeared.

Not confirmed for 1983.

Further information from:
  Executive Secretary
  Royal Society
  6 Carlton House Terrace
  London
  England SW1Y 5AG

[1801]

ROYAL SOCIETY *(U.K.)*

Travel Grants for Fellows and Non-Fellows

Purpose: To assist with the travelling expenses of non-governmental scientists of Ph.D. status, who are normally resident in the United Kingdom, making short visits abroad for the purpose of consultation or to learn new techniques or to attend scientific meetings directly related to their own research.

Closing dates: Grants are allocated four times a year, and applications, on forms obtainable from the Executive Secretary, should be submitted not later than 1st March, 1st June, 1st October or 1st December.

Not confirmed for 1983.

Further information from:
  Executive Secretary
  Royal Society
  6 Carlton House Terrace
  London
  England SW1Y 5AG

[1802]

ROYAL SOCIETY *(U.K.)*

R.W. Paul Instrument Fund Grants

Purpose: For the design, construction and maintenance of novel, unusual or much improved types of physical instruments and apparatus for investigations in pure or applied physical science, particularly in cases where a relatively large expenditure may be justified on experimental apparatus.

Eligibility: Open to British subjects who are working in Great Britain and whose qualifications in physical research are supported by the signed recommendation of one of the following persons: (a) President of the Royal Society (if a physicist) or alternatively, the Secretary of the Royal Society dealing with physical subjects); (b) President of the Institute of Physics; (c) President of the Institution of Electrical Engineers.

Note: Applications may be submitted by any worker or group of workers in Great Britain. Grants, however, may not be used to relieve expenditure in any establishment controlled by the government, or to relieve any university or other educational establishment of its normal financial obligations.

Not confirmed for 1983.

Further information from:
 Executive Secretary
 Royal Society
 6 Carlton House Terrace
 London
 England SW1Y 5AG

[1803]

ROYAL SOCIETY *(U.K.)*

Overseas Visiting Professorships

Purpose: To enable British senior scientists to participate in higher education in developing countries of the Commonwealth as visiting professors to universities and other scientific institutions.

Subjects: Natural sciences and technology. The work programme will vary in each case but would probably include lecturing, taking seminars, helping with research, advising on organization, etc.

No. offered: Five Visiting Professorships annually.

Value: The Society provides first class return air fares for the professor and his wife, an honorarium of £1,000 and an outfit allowance of up to £60. Board and lodging to an appropriate standard and travel within the country concerned connected with the work programme are the responsibility of the host institution.

Tenable at universities and other scientific institutions overseas for a minimum of four months usually over a university session, but preferably for a longer period of up to an academic year.

Note: The Overseas Visiting Professorships Committee asks the overseas universities selected to nominate fields in which visitors would be particularly welcome. Appropriate persons are then sought from within the Fellowship of the Royal Society or, if no Fellows are available, from outside the Fellowship.

The procedure for making appointments allows for overseas universities taking the initiative asking for Visiting Professorships and for particular incumbents, and does not debar individual scientists asking the Society to consider proposing them as Visiting Professors, particularly to scientific establishments with which they already have connections.

Not confirmed for 1983.

Address:
 Executive Secretary
 Royal Society
 6 Carlton House Terrace
 London
 England SW1Y 5AG

[1804]

ROYAL SOCIETY *(U.K.)*

Rutherford Scholarship

Subjects: Experimental research in any branch of the natural sciences, with preference to experimental physics.

No. offered: One Scholarship annually.

Value: £2,250 per annum (under review) if held in the United Kingdom, plus travel allowance, university fees, research expenses, etc.

Tenable for three years in some part of the British Commonwealth other than that in which the candidate graduated. In special circumstances, the award may be held in a foreign country.

Eligibility: Open to United Kingdom or Commonwealth university graduates who are under 26 years of age and have not previously held a senior research award.

Note: Candidates living outside the United Kingdom should apply through their universities to the Royal Commission for the Exhibition of 1851 [q.v.] on the appropriate application form.

Not confirmed for 1983.

Further information from:
  Executive Secretary
  Royal Society
  6 Carlton House Terrace
  London
  England SW1Y 5AG

Eligibility: Open to scientists of postdoctoral level who are nationals of, and are working in, a Commonwealth country. Applicants should have a permanent post to which they will return at the conclusion of the visit and a continuing salary for the period.

Note: Bursars will not be permitted to prepare specifically for, or to take examinations for, higher degrees or diplomas.

Not confirmed for 1983.

Further information from:
  Executive Secretary
  Royal Society
  6 Carlton House Terrace
  London
  England SW1Y 5AG

[1805]

ROYAL SOCIETY *(U.K.)*

Royal Society and Commonwealth Foundation Bursaries
Royal Society and Nuffield Foundation Commonwealth Bursaries

Purpose: To increase the competence of scientists of proven ability by enabling them to pursue research, learn techniques or follow other forms of study in natural sciences and technology to working with scientists of a Commonwealth country other than their own.

Subjects: National sciences and technology. (Royal Society Commonwealth Foundation Bursaries only—mainly in agriculture, forestry, fisheries and the development of natural resources.)

No. offered: Approximately 25 Bursaries annually.

Value: By individual assessment, to include a maintenance allowance of up to £258 per month and travel allowance.
  Bursaries are not intended to provide any salary as such nor will any provision be made for a Bursar's wife or family.

Tenable overseas in a Commonwealth country where either the physical or personal environment is peculiarly favourable, for periods of usually six to twelve months.

[1806]

ROYAL SOCIETY *(U.K.)*

European Science Exchange Programme: Fellowships and Study Visits

Purpose: To establish closer contacts between laboratories working in the natural sciences in the United Kingdom and the following European countries—Austria, Belgium, Denmark, Finland, France, Federal Republic of Germany, Greece, Ireland, Italy, the Netherlands, Norway, Portugal, Spain, Sweden and Switzerland.

Fellowships: These may be held by a United Kingdom scientist in any of the other countries listed above or by scientists from those countries in the United Kingdom for visits of six to twelve months.

Study Visits: Awards will be made to United Kingdom research scientists (senior and junior) for periods of three weeks to three months, to be spent in laboratories in Western Europe, and may be used for acquiring new techniques, for consultations with scientific colleagues, or for carrying out research.
  The amount of the awards will be assessed on the cost of travel and a maintenance allowance.

Not confirmed for 1983.

Further information from:
  Executive Secretary
  Royal Society
  6 Carlton House Terrace
  London
  England SW1Y 5AG

[1807]

ROYAL SOCIETY *(U.K.)*

East European Science Exchange Programme

Purpose: To establish closer contacts between laboratories working in the natural sciences in the United Kingdom and the following European countries: Bulgaria, Czechoslovakia, German Democratic Republic, Hungary, Poland, Romania, the U.S.S.R. and Yugoslavia.

Value: The sending institution pays the return fare between capitals for its visitors; the receiving side arranges and pays for local accommodation and travel. No specific provision is made for dependents.

Tenable for periods from two weeks to ten months.

Note: Applicants for visits to East Europe should be holders of United Kingdom passports and resident in the United Kingdom. Applications may be made to the Royal Society at any time of the year. Selected candidates will be proposed to the Academy of Sciences of the country concerned not later than three months before the date on which the candidate is prepared to commence the visit. A similar procedure applies in reverse to prospective visitors to the United Kingdom from East Europe.

Not confirmed for 1983.

Further information from:
  Executive Secretary
  Royal Society
  6 Carlton House Terrace
  London
  England SW1Y 5AG

[1808]

ROYAL SOCIETY *(U.K.)*
Academy of Scientific Research and Technology *(Cairo)*

Egyptian Scientific Exchange Programme: Study Visits and Fellowships

Purpose: To promote Anglo-Egyptian scientific interchange.

Subjects: Natural sciences and technology.

Value: The sending institution pays the return fare between capitals for its visitors; the receiving side arranges and pays for local accommodation and travel.

Tenable Study Visits—short periods of not less than three weeks; Fellowships—longer periods of not less than four months.

Eligibility: Open to British and Egyptian scientists working in their respective countries who wish to undertake research in a laboratory in the other country. Applicants should normally have several years' postdoctoral experience.

Note: While the sending institution usually nominates recipients, the application procedure allows host institutions to take the initiative and request visitors either by name or by field of specialization.

Not confirmed for 1983.

Further information from:
  Executive Secretary
  Royal Society
  6 Carlton House Terrace
  London
  England SW1Y 5AG

[1809]

ROYAL SOCIETY *(U.K.)*
Israel Academy of Sciences and Humanities

Scientific Exchange Programme

Purpose: To further relations between research scientists and scientific institutions in the United Kingdom and Israel.

Postdoctoral Fellowships: Fellowships will include a salary payment and travelling expenses.

Preference will be given to applications for a full academic year. Applications for periods of six months or more will also be considered.

Short visits by Senior and Junior Scientists: Study visits are to be used for acquiring new techniques, for consultations with scientific colleagues, or for carrying out research.

The awards will be made to United Kingdom and Israeli junior and senior scientists for periods of between one week and six months. The value of the awards will be assessed on the cost of travel and a maintenance allowance for the period of the visit.

Not confirmed for 1983.

Further information from:
 Executive Secretary
 Royal Society
 6 Carlton House Terrace
 London
 England SW1Y 5AG

[1810]

ROYAL SOCIETY *(U.K.)*

Japan Programme: Fellowships and Study Visits

Purpose: To establish closer contacts between laboratories working in the natural and applied sciences and technology in the United Kingdom and Japan.

Value: Fellowships—return fares for scientist and accompanying dependents and a maintenance and marriage allowance (where applicable); Study Visits—return fare for scientist only plus a maintenance allowance.

Tenure: Fellowships—for periods of six months to two years; Study Visits—for periods of two weeks to three months.

Eligibility: Open to British and Japanese scientists working in their respective countries who wish to do research in a laboratory in the other country.

Note: Japanese candidates should apply to the *Japan Society for the Promotion of Science, 5-3-1 Kojimachi, Chiyoda-ku, Tokyo 102.*

Not confirmed for 1983.

Further information from:
 Executive Secretary
 Royal Society
 6 Carlton House Terrace
 London
 England SW1Y 5AG

[1811]

ROYAL SOCIETY *(U.K.)*

Latin American Science Exchange Programme

Purpose: To establish closer contacts between laboratories working in the natural and applied sciences and technology in the United Kingdom and Latin America.

Value: The sending institution pays the return fare between capitals of its visitors; the receiving side arranges and pays for local accommodation and travel.

Tenure: Study Visits—short periods of not less than three weeks, usually with the aim of visiting a number of laboratories in the host country; Fellowships—for longer periods of not less than four months, to carry out research projects predominantly in one laboratory.

Eligibility: Open to British and Latin American scientists of postdoctorate or similar level, particularly for visits to and from Argentina, Brazil, Chile, Mexico, Peru or Venezuela, where special arrangements have been agreed upon between the Royal Society and the corresponding organizations for exchange visits. Prospective visitors from these countries should contact these organizations rather than the Royal Society.

Not confirmed for 1983.

Further information from:
 Executive Secretary
 Royal Society
 6 Carlton House Terrace
 London
 England SW1Y 5AG

[1812]

ROYAL SOCIETY OF ARTS *(U.K.)*

Travel Bursaries for Students of Industrial Design

Purpose: To enable students of industrial design to undertake research or study abroad, or to undertake periods of attachment in the industry.

No. offered: Variable.

Value: Between £250 and £2,000 each.

Tenable in countries other than the United Kingdom. Periods of attachment are with companies within the United Kingdom.

Eligibility: Open to students who have studied for at least one term at a recognised college of design within the United Kingdom.

Further information from:
 Assistant Secretary, Design
 Royal Society of Arts
 8 John Adam Street, Adelphi
 London
 England WC2N 6EZ

[1813]

ROYAL SOCIETY OF ARTS *(U.K.)*

Travel Scholarships for Young Professional Singers and Instrumentalists

Purpose: To enable young professional singers and instrumentalists to undertake further study abroad.

No. offered: Variable.

Value: Between £500 and £2,000 each.

Tenable in countries other than the United Kingdom.

Eligibility: Open to citizens of the United Kingdom and Commonwealth who are accredited by a recognised college of music.

Further information from:
 Secretary
 Royal Society of Arts
 8 John Adam Street, Adelphi
 London
 England WC2N 6EZ

[1814]

ROYAL SOCIETY OF CANADA

Sir Arthur Sims Scholarship

Subjects: Humanities, social sciences or natural sciences.

No. offered: One Scholarship as funds are available.

Value: £650 per annum.

Tenable at approved institutions in the United Kingdom for two years, with possibility of extension for a further year.

Eligibility: Open to persons who have completed one year of postgraduate study and display outstanding merit and promise in their field of study. They must be British subjects who are graduates of Canadian universities.

Closing date: 15th February.

Address:
 Royal Society of Canada
 344 Wellington Street
 Ottawa, Ontario
 Canada K1A ON4

[1815]

ROYAL SOCIETY OF CANADA

Bancroft Award: A scroll and Can$1,000 are given every second year for publication, instruction and research in the geological and geophysical sciences that have conspicuously contributed to public understanding and appreciation of the subject.

Chauveau Medal: A silver Medal and Can$1,000 are awarded every second year for a distinguished contribution to knowledge in the humanities other than Canadian literature and history.

Thomas W. Eadie Medal: A silver Medal and Can$1,000 are awarded annually in recognition of major contributions to any field through engineering or applied science.

Flavelle Medal: A Medal and *Can*$1,000 are given evry second year for an outstanding contribution to biological science during the preceding ten years or for significant additions to a previous outstanding contribution to biological science.

Jason A. Hannah Medal: A bronze Medal and *Can*$1,000 is awarded annually for an important Canadian publication, made within the past ten years, on the history of medicine.

Innis-Gerin Medal: A bronze Medal and *Can*$1,000 are given every second year for a distinguished and sustained contribution to the literature of the social sciences including human geography and social psychology.

McLaughlin Medal: A medal and *Can*$1,000 is awarded annually for important research in any branch of medical science.

Lorne Pierce Medal: A Medal and *Can*$1,000 are awarded every second year for an achievement of special significance and conspicuous merit in imaginative or critical literature written in French or English. Preference is given to critical literature dealing with Canadian subjects.

Henry Marshall Tory Medal: A Medal and *Can*$1,000 are awarded every second year for outstanding research in a branch of astronomy, chemistry, mathematics, physics or an allied science carried out mainly in the eight years preceding the date of the award.

Miller Medal: A Medal and *Can*$1,000 are awarded every second year for outstanding research in any branch of the earth sciences.

Tyrrell Medal: A Medal and *Can*$1,000 are given from time to time, for outstanding work in the history of Canada.

Further information from:
 Royal Society of Canada
 344 Wellington Street
 Ottawa, Ontario
 Canada K1A ON4

[1816]

ROYAL SOCIETY OF CHEMISTRY *(U.K.)*

Awards

A number of awards consisting of a Bronze medal and £100 each are offered in various areas of Chemistry. The awards are open to any qualified person of either sex who is a British or British Commonwealth citizen, or is normally domiciled in the British Isles. There are no age restrictions, however it is the intention of the Society to make awards to persons at mid-career. Equal consideration will be given to those candidates who have made a fundamental contribution to their subject, and to those whose work has been directed to its application. Subject areas will be interpreted in the broadest manner. Awards are made in respect to all of the candidate's work, with particular attention being paid to recent work. *Closing date:* 30th November of the year of the award for applications and nominations.

Research Fund Awards: A limited number of Awards in the amount of £200 each, are made annually to members of the Society for research in chemistry and chemical education. Preference is given to those working institutions with limited resources and to members supporting their own research. Applications from candidates working in United Kingdom universities will not normally be entertained. Grants are usually awarded to the same applicant for more than three consecutive years. *Closing date:* 1st November.

Note: A number of Lectureships and Medals are also offered by the Society.

Further information from:
 Mrs. E.S. Wellingham
 Royal Society of Chemistry
 Burlington House
 London
 England W1V 0BN

[1817]

ROYAL SOCIETY OF CHEMISTRY *(U.K.)*

Medals and Prizes

Beilby Medal and Prize: One award consisting of £250 and a Silver Gilt Medal is given annually to a younger British investigator (usually under forty years of age), in recognition of independent original work of exceptional merit which has been carried out continuously over a period of years. The investigation should be in the development and application of scientific principles concerning chemical engineering, fuel technology or metallurgy in their modern interpretations. This Prize is awarded jointly with the Society of Chemical Industry *(U.K.)* and the Metals Society *(U.K.)*. *Closing date:* 31st December of the year following that for which the Prize is given.

Corday-Morgan Medal and Prize: Three awards, consisting of a Silver Medal and 250 guineas each, are given annually for work in different branches of Chemistry. Awards are made to chemists of British nationality of either sex who are less than 37 years of age as of 31st December in the awarding year, for the most meritorious contributions to experimental chemistry published during the award year and in the immediately preceeding five years. *Closing date:* 31st December of the year following that for which the Prize is given.

Harrison Memorial Prize: One award consisting of a bronze plaque and 100 guineas is given annually to natural-born British subject of either sex who is less than thirty years of age by 1st December of the year of the award, for the most meritorious and promising original investigations in chemistry whose results have been published in scientific periodicals. Investigation should have been carried out during the five years ending 1st December of the award year. *Closing date:* 31st December of the award year.

Meldola Medal and Prize: The Medal and £100 is awarded annually to a British subject under 30 years of age as of 31st December of the award year, for the most promise as indicated by the candidate's published chemical work. There are no restrictions placed upon the kind of chemical work or the place in which it is conducted. This award is a gift of the Society of Maccabaeans. *Closing date:* 31st December of the award year.

Further information from:
 Secretary (Scientific)
 Royal Society of Chemistry
 Burlington House
 London
 England W1V 0BN

[1818]

ROYAL SOCIETY OF EDINBURGH

Robert Cormack Bequest Fellowships

Purpose: To further study and research in astronomy or related subjects.

Value: About £2,500 per annum, payable quarterly in advance, plus fees.

Tenable for three years subject to annual review. Scottish graduates—no geographical restriction; all other graduates—study must be undertaken in Scotland (foreign nationals may apply under these conditions).

Eligibility: Open to persons with an appropriate university honours degree or its equivalent.

Note: Next awarded in 1984. Applications should be made in writing, with names of two referees, detailing the applicant's undergraduate record, research to be undertaken and institution at which it will be carried through.

Further information from:
 Executive Secretary
 Royal Society of Edinburgh
 22 George Street
 Edinburgh
 Scotland EH2 2PQ

[1819]

ROYAL SOCIETY OF EDINBURGH

John Moyes Lessells Fellowships

Purpose: To enable engineers of promise to study some aspect of their profession outside Scotland.

Subjects: Engineering—mechanical, electrical, civil and chemical (in that order of preference).

No. offered: Varies—as vacancies occur.

Value: An amount fixed individually according to circumstances; payable quarterly in advance. Additional research or travel expenditure may be sanctioned.

Tenable outside Scotland initially for one calendar year, but shorter periods, or extension for a second year may be considered.

Eligibility: Open to honours graduates in engineering from Scottish universities.

Note: Applications should detail in writing the undergraduate and postgraduate record of the applicant, the research/study to be undertaken, and should include the names of two referees. It is advantageous to begin preliminary negotiations with the department/institution where the research/study will be undertaken.

Acceptance of a Fellowship implies willingness to spend at least two years in the United Kingdom following tenure.

Further information from:
Executive Secretary
Royal Society of Edinburgh
22 George Street
Edinburgh
Scotland EH2 2PQ

[1820]

ROYAL SOCIETY OF EDINBURGH

Research Fellowships

Subjects: Unrestricted. A proportion of the Fellowships are awarded in fields likely to enhance the development of industry and encourage better uses of resources in Scotland.

Value: Annual stipends are within the scales for research and analagous staff, grades 1A-2, in universities (£6,070 to £12,680) with annual increments and superannuation benefits. Expenses to a maximum of £500 per annum for travel and attendance at meetings or incidentals may be reimbursed. No support payments are available to the institution but Fellows may seek support for their researches from other sources.

Tenable for up to three years of full time research at any university, college of technology, central institution, research institution or industrial laboratory in Scotland approved for the purpose by the Council of the Society.

Eligibility: Open to persons of postdoctoral or equivalent standing who plan to undertake a research project at a Scottish institution.

Note: Fellows may not hold other paid appointments without the express permission of the Council, but teaching or seminar work appropriate to their special knowledge may be acceptable.

Application forms are available from the Executive Secretary and should be returned by 31st March. Candidates should negotiate directly with the proposed host institution.

The Fellowships are offered with the support of the Scottish Education Department.

Further information from:
Executive Secretary
Royal Society of Edinburgh
22 George Street
Edinburgh
Scotland EH2 2PQ

[1821]

ROYAL SOCIETY OF LITERATURE *(U.K.)*

Royal Society of Literature Award: The Award is given for a book published in the current year in the English language. Preference is given to those publications which are less likely to command big sales and the Committee is especially interested in the work of younger authors who are not yet widely recognized. One, two or three prizes may be given, although no Award may be made if no work of sufficient merit is submitted.

Winifred Holtby Memorial Prize: The Prize is given for the best regional novel of the year written in the English language by an author of British or Irish nationality, or by a citizen of the Commonwealth.

Note: The Society cannot accept entries from authors themselves.

Further information from:
Secretary
Royal Society of Literature
1 Hyde Park Gardens
London
England W2 2LT

[1822]

ROYAL SOCIETY OF MEDICINE *(U.K.)*

William Gibson Research Scholarship for Medical Women: The Scholarship of £400 per annum is open to women who are United Kingdom citizens with appropriate medical qualifications, to enable them to undertake research into an aspect of medicine, either in the United Kingdom or abroad. The Scholarship is tenable for two years with the possibility of extension for a third year.

Nichols Fellowship: The Fellowship of £200 is open to suitably qualified United Kingdom citizens to enable them to study obstetrics and gynaecology in the United Kingdom or abroad. The Fellowship is tenable for two years.

Ophthalmology Prize of £50 is open to ophthalmologists in the British Isles of any nationality who have not attained an official consultant appointment, nor undertaken professional clinical work or equivalent responsibility for any substantial period before or during the execution of original work.

Travelling Fellowships in Ophthalmology of varying amounts are awarded to British ophthalmologists travelling abroad or to foreign ophthalmologists visiting the British Isles.

Registrar's Prize (Anaesthetics): One Prize of £100 is offered annually for a paper on a subject connected with anaesthesia. Medical practitioners of senior registrar or registrar status holding an appointment in anaesthesia in a department or hospital or in the armed forces of the Commonwealth, South Africa, or Ireland may apply. The closing date for submission of papers is 1st January.

Dowling Endowment: A travel grant is awarded to a British dermatologist whenever funds are available, to allow him to travel in the United Kingdom or abroad with the intention of furthering the study of dermatology.

Further information from:
   Sections Officer
   Royal Society of Medicine
   1 Wimpole Street
   London
   England W1M 8AE

[1823]

ROYAL SOCIETY OF NEW ZEALAND

Captain James Cook Fellowship

Purpose: To perpetuate Captain Cook's spirit of scientific enquiry and exploration in New Zealand and the Southwest Pacific.

Subjects: Anthropology, biology, geography, geology, geophysics, history, medicine and oceanography.

No. offered: One Fellowship every two years.

Value: Salary equivalent to the maximum for an associate professor in New Zealand universities, payable monthly. A travel grant given to overseas Fellows which covers economy air fare to and from New Zealand for Fellow and dependent family.

Tenable at a New Zealand university or research institution for two years; possible extension for a third year.

Eligibility: Open to persons of senior status with a good working knowledge of English, who have published results of original research. No restrictions as to nationality, age or sex. Fellows must meet the requirements of the New Zealand Immigration Authorities.

Note: Next Fellowship will be awarded in 1984.

Closing date: 31st May.

Further information from:
   Executive Officer
   Royal Society of New Zealand
   P.O. Box 12249
   Wellington
   New Zealand

[1824]

ROYAL TELEVISION SOCIETY
Radio Rentals Ltd.

John Logie Baird Travelling Scholarship

Subjects: Scientific aspects of electronic engineering, television or allied technology.

No. offered: One Scholarship annually.

Value: £1,000.

Tenable outside the United Kingdom for an investigation period of six to eight weeks.

Eligibility: Open to postgraduate students between 21 and 30 years of age who are currently attending a United Kingdom educational establishment.

Note: Candidates must submit a proposed investigation or study programme, and if awarded a Scholarship are expected to write a paper on their research for publication by the Society.

Closing date: 26th March.

Further information from:
Secretary
Royal Television Society
Tavistock House East
Tavistock Square
London
England WC1H 9HR

[1825]

ROYAL TOWN PLANNING INSTITUTE *(U.K.)*

George Pepler International Award

Subjects: Town and country planning, or some particular aspect of planning, theory and practice.

No. offered: One Award annually.

Value: Up to £450.

Tenable in any country other than that in which the applicant resides, for a period not exceeding six months. Ideally, to be undertaken during a vacation extending over two or three weeks.

Eligibility: Open to persons not more than 30 years of age who wish to visit Great Britain, or, being resident in Great Britain, desire to travel to another country.

Note: Each applicant is required to submit a statement showing the nature of the study that he proposed to undertake, together with an itinerary and such other information as the Council may require.
At the conclusion of the visit, the recipient must submit a report on the visit for publication in the Institute's journal.

Closing date: 31st January.

Further information from:
Secretary-General
Royal Town Planning Institute
26 Portland Place
London
England W1N 4BE

[1826]

ROYAL VICTORIAN EYE AND EAR HOSPITAL *(East Melbourne)*

Fellowship in Ophthalmology

Purpose: To further the training of a young specialist in ophthalmology.

No. offered: Two Fellowships annually.

Value: A$591 per week.

Tenable at Melbourne for one year. Fellows may be re-appointed on application for a further year.

Eligibility: Open to men and women under forty years of age who have postgraduate qualifications in ophthalmology.

Closing date: End of October.

Further information from:
Medical Director
Royal Victorian Eye and Ear Hospital
126 Victoria Parade
East Melbourne, Victoria
Australia 3002

[1827]

ARTHUR RUBINSTEIN INTERNATIONAL PIANO MASTER COMPETITION *(Israel)*

Pianists of any nationality between the ages of 18 and 32 are eligible for the Competition. It is comprised of three stages for which a programme of 16 pieces must be chosen and prepared from a repertoire of pre-classical to contemporary composers. Prizes: 1st Group, three prizes of US$5,000, US$4,000 and US$3,000 and gold medals; 2nd Group, three Prizes of US$1,000 and silver medals; and the 3rd Group, six Prizes of US$500 and bronze medals. In addition, various recording and concert engagements are offered. Closing date for applications is 1st November.

Further information from:
Secretariat
Arthur Rubinstein International Piano
  Master Competition
Shalom Tower
P.O. Box 29404
Tel Aviv
Israel

[1828]

RUI FOUNDATION *(Italy)*

Scholarships

Subjects: All university studies.

No. offered: About ten Scholarships annually.

Value: US$110 per month plus maintenance and tuition.

Tenable at the Universities of Bari, Bologna, Catania, Milan, Naples, Palermo, Rome or Verona for ten months; renewable to end of studies.

Eligibility: Open to nationals of all countries, particularly developing countries. Candidates should be between 17 and 26 years of age.

Further information from:
Fondazione Rui
Via Crescenzio 16
00193 Rome
Italy

[1829]

DAMON RUNYON-WALTER WINCHELL CANCER FUND *(U.S.A.)*

Human Cancer-Directed Fellowship Grant

Purpose: To advance cancer research through supporting the development of the most promising young investigators in human cancer research.

Subjects: Areas relevant to original clinical or basic human cancer-related research, including diagnostic and preventive care.

Value: Up to US$15,000 for the first year, and US$16,500 for the second year. A fixed sum of US$1,500 will be paid to the laboratory in which the Fellow is working, to be used at the discretion of the Sponsor for expenses incurred by the Fellow, such as travel to attend scientific meetings, health insurance and supplies. This may not be used for institutional overhead.

Tenable at an approved institution under a Sponsor, for one year, renewable for up to two additional years. United States citizens may train outside the U.S.; foreign scientists may train within the U.S. only.

Eligibility: Open to individuals of any nationality nearing completion of their clinical training programs, or those who have finished their training not more than two years prior to application. Doctors of Philosophy not holding an M.D. degree will be considered as long as the proposed research deals with human cancer.

Closing dates: 15th March, 15th August, and 15th December for consideration in June, November, and March respectively.

Further information from:
Research Department
Damon Runyon-Walter Winchell Cancer Fund
33 West 56th Street
New York, New York 10019
U.S.A.

[1830]

DAMON RUNYON-WALTER WINCHELL CANCER FUND *(U.S.A.)*

Postdoctoral Fellowships in Cancer Research

Purpose: To augment the training of a scientist who has demonstrated the motivation and potential to conduct original research under the supervision of a Sponsor, thus equipping the Fellow to become an independent investigator.

Subjects: All theoretical and experimental biology areas relevant to cancer and cancer research.

No. offered: Variable, depending on available funds and the number of suitable applicants.

Value: US$15,500 stipend for the first year. A stipend of US$16,500 is awarded for the second Fellowship year. The amount of the Fellowship is paid monthly to the sponsoring institution for the support of the Fellow. In addition US$1,500 is awarded annually to the sponsor laboratory to be used, at its discretion, for expenses incurred by the Fellow, such as health insurance, travel to scientific meetings or supplies. These funds may not be used for institutional overhead.

Tenable for a minimum of one year, with possibility of renewal for a further year. Citizens of the United States may elect to train abroad, but foreign candidates must train at institutions in the United States.

Eligibility: Open to individuals of any nationality who work in universities, hospitals, and research institutions, and who will have had no more than one year of postdoctoral fellowship or equivalent experience prior to taking up the Fellowship. M.D.'s who have completed their residency not more than two years prior to the decision date of the Fellowship are also eligible.

Closing dates: 15th August, 15th December and 15th March, for decisions in November, March and June, respectively.

Further information from:
  Research Department
  Damon Runyon-Walter Winchell Cancer Fund
  33 West 56th Street
  New York, New York 10019
  U.S.A.

[1831]

RUPERT FOUNDATION *(U.K.)*

International Young Conductors Award

Purpose: To give promising young conductors the opportunity to work with the BBC Symphony Orchestra and to conduct it in public.

No. offered: Varies.

Value: A total sum of £7,500 will be allocated at the discretion of the adjudicating panel to a maximum of three competitors.

Tenable for one year in the United Kingdom, during which time the winners will be considered to undertake a variety of work with the BBC's regional symphony orchestras as well as with the BBC Symphony Orchestra.

Eligibility: Open to men and women of all nationalities up to the age of 28 who have had practical experience of conducting on a regular basis with either professional orchestras or amateur bodies of reasonable standing.

Further information from:
  Rupert Foundation
  P.O. Box 120
  Aylesbury, Buckinghamshire
  England HP21 8SZ

S

See *How to Use The Grants Register*, page ix

[1833]

S.A. NATURE FOUNDATION (*Southern Africa*)

Grants

The Foundation makes Grants available to organizations and individuals for deserving nature conservation projects.

Applicants should submit a comprehensive description of the proposed project and a fully detailed budget. Indications should be given as to what funds are or will be available for the same project from other sources. In the case of applications by individuals, a competent institution or organization must accept administrative and technical responsibility for the project. Applicants are requested to submit a short précis of their project in no more than 150 words, black and white photographs, colour slides, and any other visual material such as maps, drawings, posters, prospectuses, etc.

Projects extending over a number of years are normally reviewed annually.

Further information from:
S.A. Nature Foundation
P.O. Box 456
Stellenbosch
South Africa 7600

[1834]

SAINT ANDREW'S SOCIETY OF THE STATE OF NEW YORK

Scholarships

Subjects: Unrestricted.

No. offered: Varies annually (two Scholarships awarded in 1982/83 academic year).

Value: US$4,000 plus tuition fees up to a maximum of US$6,000.

Tenable at any United States university for one year.

Eligibility: Open to men and women who have a Scotish background by way of residence or education, who graduate in the year of candidacy or have graduated in the previous year from a Scottish university or from Oxford or Cambridge.

Note: Recipients are expected to spend one or two months travelling in the United States at the conclusion of the Scholarship, before returning to Scotland.

Candidates from Scottish universities should submit their applications to their home institution; candidates from Oxford and Cambridge should submit their applications to the address below.

Closing date: 18th January.

Further information from:
Selection Committee
Saint Andrew's Society of the State of New York
c/o The Royal Bank of Scotland Ltd.
42 St. Andrew Square
Edinburgh
Scotland EH2 2YE

[1835]

ST. REGIS PAPER COMPANY (*U.S.A.*)

Graduate Fellowship

Subject: Forestry.

No. offered: One Fellowship annually.

Value: US$5,000 per annum.

Tenable at a suitable institution of the recipient's choice.

Eligibility: Open to qualified graduates from recognized colleges and universities in the United States or Canada who have completed one year's study in forestry at the graduate level by July of the year of application. The Fellowship is conditional upon matriculation for an advanced forestry degree at the master's or doctorate level.

Note: Applications should be secured through the head of the candidate's own school.

Closing date: 1st March.

Further information from:
St. Regis Paper Company
Chairman and C.E.O.'s Office
150 East 42nd Street
New York, New York 10017
U.S.A.

[1836]

SAN FRANCISCO CONSERVATORY OF MUSIC

Performance Scholarships in Music

Value: US$300 to US$4,600.

Tenable at the Conservatory for one year; renewable.

Eligibility: Open to United States and foreign nationals who will be attending the Conservatory on a full time basis. Candidates must have had considerable experience in musical performance.

Closing date: 1st April.

Further information from:
Office of Student Services
San Francisco Conservatory of Music
1201 Ortega Street
San Francisco, California 94122
U.S.A.

[1837]

LEOPOLD SCHEPP FOUNDATION
(U.S.A.)

Graduate Scholarships

Purpose: To assist young people who have insufficient means to obtain or complete their formal education.

Subjects: Unrestricted. Studies are favored which, in the opinion of the Foundation, show promise to future usefulness to society.

Value: Based on financial need. Scholars are expected to apply to all federal and state student aid programs available to them. The number of eligible applicants greatly exceeds the number of awards available.

Tenable at accredited colleges and universities in the United States.

Eligibility: Open to students in the United States who have high scholastic grades and are under 40 years of age.

Note: No aid was available for graduate study in 1982-83.

The Foundation also grants annually, a small number of Fellowships for independent study and research, usually beyond the doctoral level, upon recommendation from a recognized institution. These Fellowships, to encourage research of a character to improve the general welfare of mankind, have limited funds, and those interested should first seek other funding before applying to the Foundation.

Further information from:
Secretary
Leopold Schepp Foundation
106 East 35th Street
New York, New York 10016
U.S.A.

[1838]

SCHOLARSHIP EXCHANGE BOARD
Department of Foreign Affairs *(Ireland)*

Grants to Irish Citizens

A number of annual awards are made to Irish citizens to enable them to travel to the United States for study and research. Grantees are required to return to Ireland upon the completion of the award.

Further information from:
An Bord Schláireachtaí Cómalairte
72-76 St. Stephen's Green
Dublin 2
Ireland

[1839]

SCHOLARSHIP EXCHANGE BOARD
Department of Foreign Affairs *(Ireland)*

Grants to United States Citizens

A number of annual awards are made to United States lecturers or researchers who wish to spend an academic year in Ireland. The value of each award for the academic year of 1982-83 was £10,640. Interested candidates should contact the *Council for International Exchange of Scholars, Suite 300, 11 Dupont Circle, Washington, D.C. 20036, U.S.A.* for further information.

Address:
An Bord Scoláireachtaí Cómalairte
72-76 St. Stephen's Green
Dublin 2
Ireland

[1840]

ROBERT SCHUMANN INTERNATIONAL COMPETITION FOR PIANISTS AND SINGERS *(Zwickau)*

The Competition is held in Zwickau from time to time and is open to nationals of all countries. The eighth competition was held in June 1981. Pianists must be no older than 25 and singers no older than 30. Prizes are awarded in three categories: pianists, male singers and female singers. First prize in each category is 7,000 marks and a gold medal; seven lesser prizes are awarded to pianists, and five lesser prizes in each of the other categories.

Further information from:
Robert Schumann International
 Competition for Pianists and Singers
95 Zwickau, Münzstrasse 12
German Democratic Republic

[1841]

SCIENCE AND ENGINEERING RESEARCH COUNCIL *(U.K.)*

General Information

The Science and Engineering Research Council (SERC) makes its awards in science and technology *outside* the fields of: (a) agriculture (including horticulture), agricultural economics, agricultural engineering, and the more applied aspects of agricultural science; (b) natural environment sciences, which may be defined broadly as geology and geophysics (including seismology and geomagnetism), meteorology, hydrology, oceanography, marine and fresh-water biology, and terrestrial ecology; (c) medicine; (d) social science, except for awards made by the Joint SERC/SRCC Committee, and including those aspects of psychology which are closely related to fundamental biology and to the engineering and biological aspects of ergonomics and cybernetics.

Address:
Science and Engineering Research Council
Secretary's Department (PTSS)
Polaris House
North Star Avenue
Swindon, Wiltshire
England SN2 1ET

[1842]

SCIENCE AND ENGINEERING RESEARCH COUNCIL *(U.K.)*

Research and Advanced Course Studentships

Subjects: Science and technology. Applications are also considered for awards in certain courses of business and industrial administration or management, and from those candidates with some industrial experience who wish to be trained in the investigation of problems of industrial productivity and organisation.

Value: £2,270 for students in London; £2,245 for students elsewhere; £1,650 for students living at home (1981-82 rates). Values are reviewed annually. In addition, allowances for dependents and experience are payable under certain conditions. Approved tuition fees are paid directly to the institution.

Tenable wholly or partly at home or abroad at universities, polytechnics, technical schools, research laboratories, or other suitable institutions sponsoring the candidate's application. Research Studentships are normally tenable for up to three years; Advanced Course Studentships, for one year.

Eligibility: Open to persons who: (a) have been ordinarily resident in the United Kingdom for a period of three years immediately preceding the date of application; (b) hold a good honours degree from a British university (i.e., for a Research Studentship, first or upper second class honours; for an Advanced Course Studentship, first or second class honours) or alternatively a qualification or combination of qualifications and experience acceptable to the Council as demonstrating equivalent ability; (c) are normally under 30 years of age; and

(d) are recommended by the authorities of the institution of tenure (and also of graduation if this is not the same) as being likely to benefit substantially from full-time postgraduate training.

Note: The Council allocates its awards on a "quota" basis through the heads of department where the awards are to be held. Direct applications are not accepted from individual students. Heads of departments should apply to the Council each year for allocations of new awards to be held in their schools from the following autumn.

Applications on behalf of students from the following locations should be directed to the addresses below: Isle of Man—*Isle of Man Education Authority, Strand Street, Douglas*; Channel Islands—*Jersey Education Committee, St. Helier,* or *Guernsey Education Council, St. Peter Port*; Northern Ireland—*Department of Education of the Government of Northern Ireland, Rathgael House, Ballo Road, Bangor, County Down.*

Full information concerning SERC Studentships is given in the booklet of *SERC Postgraduate Studentships,* available at academic institutions or from the Council.

Closing dates: Advanced Course Studentships—31st October; Research Studentships—31st December; nominations of individual students—31st July except where otherwise stated.

Further information from:
Science and Engineering Research Council
Secretary's Department (PTSS)
Polaris House
North Star Avenue
Swindon, Wiltshire
England SN2 1ET

[1843]

SCIENCE AND ENGINEERING RESEARCH COUNCIL *(U.K.)*

Studentships Tenable Outside the United Kingdom

The Council encourages some recipients of *Research and Advanced Course Studentships* to spend all or part of their training outside the United Kingdom, and in conjunction with NATO, offers a limited number of Studentships to be held outside the United Kingdom.

Applications should be made through the department head as early as possible and in any case not later than 31st January.

Further information from:
Science and Engineering Research Council
Secretary's Department (PTSS)
Polaris House
North Star Avenue
Swindon, Wiltshire
England SN2 1ET

[1844]

SCIENCE AND ENGINEERING RESEARCH COUNCIL *(U.K.)*

Research Studentships for Former Part-time Students

These awards enable suitable part-time students to undertake up to one year of full-time training. The Studentships will be part of the *Instant Awards* scheme, as it is expected that most part-time students will be in employment and will need to seek awards early in the season.

Candidates should satisfy all SERC regulations governing eligibility for *Research Studentships*, and should normally have completed four years of relevant part-time study.

Studentships are awarded on a first come, first served basis. As the number of available awards is small, candidates are advised to apply early.

Closing date: 31st May.

Further information from:
Science and Engineering Research Council
Secretary's Department (PTSS)
Polaris House
North Star Avenue
Swindon, Wiltshire
England SN2 1ET

[1845]

SCIENCE AND ENGINEERING RESEARCH COUNCIL *(U.K.)*

Royal Society/SERC Industrial Fellowships

Purpose: To enhance communication between those in industry and those in institutions of higher learning to the benefit of United Kingdom firms or higher education institutions or both. To this end the scheme aims to provide opportunities for academic scientists, mathematicians and engineers to hold a job in an industrial environment and undertake a project at any stage in the chain from fundamental science to industrial innovation, and conversely, for industrial scientists, mathematicians and engineers to undertake research or course-development work in a university or poly-technic.

Subjects: Science and technology and their application.

Tenable normally for periods of six months to two years within the United Kingdom, although proposals to hold Fellowships overseas will be considered.

Eligibility: Open to individuals ordinarily resident in the United Kingdom, Channel Islands or the Isle of Man. Candidates should be of Ph.D. status or the equivalent, normally holding a tenured post in a university or polytechnic as a scientist, mathematician or engineer in industry or industrial research organizations. Candidates should preferably be between thirty and forty-five years of age. Additional consideration may be shown applicants who have already had previous contact with or interest in the opposite sector of employment.

Closing dates: 31st March and 31st October.

Further information from:
Science and Engineering Research Council
Secretary's Department (Fellowships Section)
Polaris House
North Star Avenue
Swindon, Wiltshire
England SN2 1ET

[1846]

SCIENCE AND ENGINEERING RESEARCH COUNCIL *(U.K.)*

Industrial Visiting Fellowships

Purpose: To allow suitably experienced individuals to spend periods in advanced industrial firms or research and development organisations in foreign countries.

Subjects: Advanced industrial techniques and innovations which meet modern industrial and commercial requirements.

Value: Salary, plus travel and overseas allowances.

Tenable overseas for six months to three years; shorter periods can be arranged.

Eligibility: No specific academic qualifications are required. Awards will be made on the basis of the applicant's experience and ability and on the benefit that will accrue him, his firm and the country. Preference is given to candidates aged between 25 and 35 who are employed in industry, commerce, local government or institutions of higher learning.

Note: Applications must be supported by the candidate's employer. Fellows must undertake to return to the United Kingdom upon completion of their studies to prepare a report for publication, be available for one year of consultation and to lecture on the information gained.

Further information from:
Science and Engineering Research Council
Secretary's Department (Fellowships Section)
Polaris House
North Star Avenue
Swindon, Wiltshire
England SN2 1ET

[1847]

SCIENCE AND ENGINEERING RESEARCH COUNCIL *(U.K.)*

Whitworth Foundation Fellowships and Exhibitions

Purpose: To encourage the promotion of engineering and mechanical industry in the United Kingdom.

Fellowships not exceeding £15,000 per annum are offered to candidates of high calibre to carry out approved projects in specific engineering topics of the candidate's choice. Applicants must be British subjets or Commonwealth citizens who are ordinarily resident in the United Kingdom. The scope and range of topics is not limited and may include study, teaching, research or a survey or appraisal from a wide field of engineering, including such associated skills as technical marketing, production management and economics as well as the normal technical aspects. The awards are normally made for one year and travelling expenses are paid where appropriate.

Exhibitions, the value of which may not normally exceed £7,500 per annum inclusive of allowances, are offered for projects of research or study in engineering or its teaching. Candidates should hold acceptable engineering qualifications and be practising engineers.

Closing date: 31st January for both.

Further information from:
Science and Engineering Research Council
Secretary's Department (Fellowships Section)
Polaris House
North Star Avenue
Swindon, Wiltshire
England SN2 1ET

[1848]

SCIENCE AND ENGINEERING RESEARCH COUNCIL *(U.K.)*

Postdoctoral Research Fellowships

Purpose: (a) To enable outstanding young British research workers to devote the whole of their time to original and independent research; (b) to enable outstanding candidates residing overseas, including practising engineers with considerable experience, to hold awards in the United Kingdom as part of the process of re-establishing themselves in the United Kingdom; (c) in the case of United Kingdom fellows under the NATO scheme, to stimulate the exchange of postdoctoral fellows between NATO countries.

Subjects: Science and technology; NATO awards—all fields including agricultural, natural, environmental, medical and social sciences.

No. offered: 75 Fellowships annually.

Value: Awards are made on the first seven points of the University Lecturer scale.

Tenable at any institution acceptable to the Council. Candidates from overseas will normally be expected to take up their Fellowships in the United Kingdom.

Eligibility: Open to young research workers of outstanding merit who have recently completed their postgraduate education to the level of the Ph.D. or its equivalent. Candidates must have ordinarily been resident in the United Kingdom, Channel Islands or the Isle of Man for a period of three years immediately preceding the date of application, be under 30 years of age and strongly recommended by the head of the department in which they have been working.

Closing dates: For awards tenable in Europe only—by 12th January and 10th May to the *Royal Society, 6 Carlton House Terrace, London SW1Y 5AG*; for awards tenable in the United Kingdom or abroad (excluding Europe)—by 31st January.

Note: Full information regarding SERC Fellowships is given in the booklet *SERC Fellowships* available at academic institutions or from:
Science and Engineering Research Council
Secretary's Department (Fellowships Section)
Polaris House
North Star Avenue
Swindon, Wiltshire
England SN2 1ET

[1849]

SCIENCE AND ENGINEERING RESEARCH COUNCIL *(U.K.)*

Senior Fellowships

Purpose: To enable a small number of outstanding scientists at the peak of their capabilities to devote themselves full-time to research and scholarships free of the restrictions imposed by their normal employment.

Subjects: Science and technology.

No. offered: Normally one or two per year.

Value: The Council will pay the salary, superannuation contributions and national insurance as if the Fellow were continuing in his normal employment at his home institution.

Tenable at any institution which has a firm working link with a university or polytechnic in the United Kingdom, for up to five years.

Eligibility: Open to scientists who are already established in their careers, having proved their exceptional research and interpretation ability. Applicants must be members of permanent staff of British universities, technical colleges or similar institutions. Home institutions are required to reinstate Fellows upon termination of their studies.

Note: Fellowships are not intended to replace sabbatical leave.

Closing date: 30th November.

Further information from:
  Science and Engineering Research Council
  Secretary's Department (Fellowships Section)
  Polaris House
  North Star Avenue
  Swindon, Wiltshire
  England SN2 1ET

[1850]

SCIENCE AND ENGINEERING RESEARCH COUNCIL (U.K.)

Senior Visiting Fellowships

Purpose: To enable a senior scientist of distinction from a recognized centre to visit a host institution and give full-time advice and assistance in the field of research in which he is eminent; introducing new techniques and new developments which may advance research work in the proposer's institution in the United Kingdom; or in connection with specific research projects supported by the Council.

Subjects: See *Research Grants.*

Value: Salary, plus travel expenses to and from the United Kingdom for the Fellow.

Tenable at an approved institution in the United Kingdom normally for three months; may be extended for up to one year.

Note: Awards are made by invitation only at the request of the host institution.
  Fellowships may be held concurrently with other awards or income, but value may be reduced accordingly.

Closing dates: 1st April, 15th September, 15th December for receipt of application from the host institution.

Further information from:
  Science and Engineering Research Council
  Research Grants Liaison Section
  Polaris House
  North Star Avenue
  Swindon, Wiltshire
  England SN2 1ET

[1851]

SCIENCE AND ENGINEERING RESEARCH COUNCIL (U.K.)

Advanced Fellowships

Purpose: To support for up to five years a small number of outstanding research workers who are well qualified for academic careers but who do not hold tenured posts at the time of application.

Subjects: Science and technology.

Value: Awards are made on the first twelve points of the University Lecturer scale.

Tenable at any academic institution in the United Kingdom.

Eligibility: Open to research workers (normally to those between the ages of 26 and 35 years) who have been ordinarily resident in the United Kingdom, the Channel Islands or the Isle of Man for a period of three years immediately preceding the date of application. Candidates must hold a Ph.D. or be of equivalent standing in their profession and have at least two years of research experience at postdoctoral level when the application is made.

Closing date: 30th September.

Further information from:
  Science and Engineering Research Council
  Secretary's Department (Fellowships Section)
  Polaris House
  North Star Avenue
  Swindon, Wiltshire
  England SN2 1ET

[1852]

SCIENCE AND ENGINEERING RESEARCH COUNCIL *(U.K.)*

Instant Awards

These Awards are intended for those individuals in employment wishing to return to university with a *Research or Advanced Course Studentship*.

The scheme provides an early decision on applications so that candidates may make early arrangements with employers, etc.

Applicants should be currently employed and have completed one year of full-time, relevant employment by the date of application.

Note: A limited number of Research and Advanced Course Studentships are reserved for these candidates, and are awarded on a "first come, first served" basis. Candidates should apply early in the calendar year (no later than 31st May) in which they wish to commence their postgraduate studies. All applications should be submitted through the institution in which the candidate proposes to work by the head of the department or research school.

Further information from:
Science and Engineering Research Council
Secretary's Department (PTSS)
Polaris House
North Star Avenue
Swindon, Wiltshire
England SN2 1ET

[1853]

SCIENCE AND ENGINEERING RESEARCH COUNCIL *(U.K.)*

CASE Awards (Co-operative Awards in Science and Engineering)

These awards are open to students eligible for SERC *Research Studentships*. They are intended to encourage collaboration between academic institutions and outside bodies (i.e., industry and the public sector). They also provide an opportunity for graduates to broaden their research training by gaining first-hand experience of work outside the academic environment. Students are allowed to receive a payment from the co-operating body and may participate in patent agreements together with the academic supervisor and the co-operating body. The student normally spends at least one month per year working at the premises of the co-operating body during the (maximum) three year Award.

Note: The basis of the CASE scheme is a research project, jointly set up between an academic department and a collaborating body, approved by SERC for the tenure of these Awards. Lists of approved projects are distributed to institutions early in the year in which they are available. Applications for CASE Studentships should be submitted through academic supervisors of approved projects.

The *Research Council Co-operative Awards (RCCA)* is a similar scheme which allows for participation of institutes of other Research Councils in the United Kingdom.

Further information from:
Science and Engineering Research Council
Secretary's Department (PTSS)
Polaris House
North Star Avenue
Swindon, Wiltshire
England SN2 1ET

[1854]

SCIENCE AND ENGINEERING RESEARCH COUNCIL *(U.K.)*

Appeals Awards

On 1st August each year, any *Research and Advanced Course Studentships* for which no suitable candidates have been nominated are taken back and re-allocated to form an "Appeals" Award pool. It is anticipated that the demand will always exceed the supply and that applications under this scheme will be competitive.

The criteria to be applied to candidates for an Appeals Award are determined by the SERC each year and may change from year to year. Applications must be made through the department head of an institution and must reach SERC by 31st July.

Appeals Awards may be sought from SERC for suitable candidates unprovided for, either by SERC or by other awards.

Note: Candidates who were unsuccessful in a bid for an Award under the *Instant* scheme may be recommended at the "Appeals" stage.

Applications are dealt with as quickly as possible after 1st August.

Further information from:
Science and Engineering Research Council
Secretary's Department (PTSS)
Polaris House
North Star Avenue
Swindon, Wiltshire
England SN2 1ET

[1855]

SCIENCE AND ENGINEERING RESEARCH COUNCIL (U.K.)

Research Grants

Subjects: Branches of science and technology, including astronomy, biology, chemistry, mathematics, nuclear physics, other physics, space sciences and the sciences between and adjoining these (for example: biochemistry, fundamental psychology and behavioral sciences, statistics, operational research, cybernetics and ergonomics), engineering (including aeronautical, chemical, civil, electrical, mechanical, marine and transport, and manufacturing systems), and computing, energy systems, metallurgial, polymer and materials science.

Value: To finance the employment of scientific, laboratory, technical or other assistants, and the purchase of scientific apparatus, materials and services, including travel, necessary and additional to that already available for the research.

Research Grants may include support for visits of up to several months to centres of excellence, overseas and in the United Kingdom, to study new techniques and research developments that may advance research works in specialized scientific fields.

Tenable at suitable institutions in the United Kingdom, normally for one to three years. Under special circumstances longer term financial support may be provided.

Eligibility: Applicants should normally be salaried members of the staff of United Kingdom universities, polytechnics, colleges and similar institutions.

Closing dates: 15th December, 1st April and 15th September.

Note: Full information regarding SERC Research Grants is given in the booklet *SERC Research Grants*, available at academic institutions, or from:
Science and Engineering Research Council
Research Grants Liaison Section
Polaris House
North Star Avenue
Swindon, Wiltshire
England SN2 1ET

[1856]

SCIENCE AND ENGINEERING RESEARCH COUNCIL (U.K.)

European Short-Visit Grants

Purpose: To encourage the development of European collaborative research projects.

Subjects: Science and technology.

Value: Return travel to a European institution and subsistence expenses necessarily incurred for the purposes of the visit.

Tenable at an appropriate institution in Europe for up to twenty-one days.

Eligibility: Open to research workers in the United Kingdom universities, technical colleges or similar institutions.

Note: Applications are accepted throughout the year.

Further information from:
Science and Engineering Research Council
International Section
Secretary's Department (PTSS)
Polaris House
North Star Avenue
Swindon, Wiltshire
England SN2 1ET

[1857]

SCIENCE AND ENGINEERING RESEARCH COUNCIL (U.K.)

Special Training Programmes and Special Schemes

In continuing to develop its effort to build up

an adequate base of university engineering research and training to meet the needs of industry and commerce, the Council offers a limited number of Studentships for special training programmes, and encourages the take-up of Studentships in special areas for further information on SRC's *Research and Advanced Course Studentships*).

The **Special Training Programmes** are:

(i) *Engineering Mathematics Scheme:* The Scheme is aimed to encourage more mathematics graduates to take up their postgraduate training in engineering departments, and to foster collaboration between engineering and mathematics departments. These awards are offered to mathematics departments separately from the normal Studentship quotas, and may be held either on an advanced course or for research training, subject to normal SERC eligibility requirements. In addition, candidates must hold a degree in mathematics or mainly mathematics. Heads of mathematics departments should apply by 31st October (Advanced Course) and 31st December (Research). An allocation of awards is then made to that department, and individual applications should subsequently be made on each student's behalf by the engineering department in which the award is to be held. The individual application should be made in the normal way but must be clearly marked as being for an Engineering Mathematics Studentship, and reach SERC by 31st July.

(ii) *Joint SERC/SSRC Committee:* The Council encourages postgraduate training aimed at providing a broad-band training fitted to the requirements of industry, and in conjunction with the Social Science Research Council, operates a Joint Committee to deal with postgraduate training which integrates science/technology with a social science discipline. To encourage this type of training, the Committee makes available a number of Research and Advanced Course Studentships. The Studentships are administered under SERC regulations and applications should be submitted through the heads of departments of research schools where the awards are to be held in the normal way.

(iii) *Polytechnics Pool:* This scheme is implemented by the awarding of ordinary Research or Advanced Course Studentships and comprises a number of studentships specifically for polytechnics. Applications should be directed to the Polytechnics Pool, and should reach the SERC by 31st July.

The **Special Areas** are:

(i) energy; (ii) manufacturing technology; (iii) marine technology; (iv) polymer engineering; (v) biotechnology; and (vi) "teaching company" scheme (programmes are directed by the staff of engineering companies in collaboration with university or polytechnic departments).

Further information from:
Science and Engineering Research Council
Secretary's Department (PTSS)
Polaris House
North Star Avenue
Swindon, Wiltshire
England SN2 1ET

[1858]

SCIENCE AND TECHNOLOGY AGENCY
(Japan)

Japanese Government Research Awards for Foreign Specialists

Purpose: To promote international scientific cooperation through enabling specialists of foreign countries to perform research in government laboratories in Japan.

Subjects: Natural and applied science and technology.

Value: To cover living expenses (13,000 yen per diem) plus travel expenses to and from Japan.

Tenable in various government laboratories in Japan, for approximately seven months.

Eligibility: Open to citizens of foreign countries who are government personnel or of similar status and will continue to do so during the tenure of the Award, and have been engaged in scientific and technical research for more than three years after graduating from university. Candidates should be in good health and have a fair knowledge of English or Japanese.

Note: Applications should be submitted through the appropriate host Japanese Government research institute. In Australia directly to the Japanese Embassy: *Embassy of Japan, 112 Empire Circuit, Yarralumla, Canberra, A.C.T. 2600.*

Closing date: December.

Address:
International Affairs Division, Promotion Bureau
Science and Technology Agency
2-2-1 Kasumigaseki, Chiyoda-ku
Tokyo 100
Japan

[1859]

SCOTTISH ARTS COUNCIL

The Council forms a part of the Arts Council of Great Britain [q.v.] and is empowered to give financial assistance to artistic organisations or organisations involved in the arts, provided these are independent and non-profit making. The Council also gives some direct help to individuals. Priority is given to professional work.

Examples of Assistance to Individuals

Art

Bursaries; Awards; Travel Studio Bursaries; Commissions and Assisted Purchases Fund; Fellowships, Residencies and other posts for professional artists; Purchases for SAC Collection; Travel Grants/International Exchanges; Bursaries for Art Critics and Writers on the Visual Arts; Major Exhibition Awards; Lecture Scheme and Artists in Schools; and Workshop and Artists Studio Provision.

Drama

Grants for: the training of assistant artistic directors; the development of acting skills; the study of mime overseas; the commissioning through theatre organisations of new plays; and Travel Grants.

Music

Music and Dance Awards: Grants, through organisations, to enable the commission of original works; Grants to enable the provision of performing material by composers based in Scotland; and Grants towards the cost of recordings.

Literature

Bursaries: Travel and Research Grants; Writers Fellowships; International Writers Fellowships; and Book Awards.

Film

Grants are available for the development and production of small scale professionally made fictional, documentary and animation films.

Training

A limited number of Bursaries are available to enable the training of arts administrators.

Further information from:
Information Officer
Scottish Arts Council
19 Charlotte Square
Edinburgh
Scotland EH2 4DF

[1860]

SCOTTISH EDUCATION DEPARTMENT

Scottish Studentship Scheme

The Department offers up to 65 Studentships each year for advanced postgraduate study in arts subjects to students who are ordinarily resident in Scotland. These awards correspond to those made by the Department of Education and Science under the State Studentship Scheme and the same requirements as to age, academic qualifications and United Kingdom residence apply; they are also of the same annual value.

Scottish Studentships are tenable for one year only, and Major Scottish Studentships are tenable for up to three years according to the approved programme of postgraduate study. Only in exceptional circumstances will Studentships be offered for study at universities outside the British Isles.

Applications for all Studentships must be submitted to the Department through universities. The closing date for receipt of applications is 1st May of the year in respect of which application is made.

Address:
Secretary, Awards Branch
Scottish Education Department
Clifton Terrace
Edinburgh
Scotland EH12 5DT

[1861]

SCOTTISH EDUCATION DEPARTMENT

Students' Allowances Scheme

The Department offers Students' Allowances to eligible students who are following short postgraduate courses of a professional or vocational nature—e.g., courses of teacher training for graduates, and postgraduate training courses which lead to diplomas and certificates in librarianship, social work, youth leadership and management. Allowances are granted to students who are ordinarily resident in Scotland, and they are at the same rates and conditions as the awards for undergraduate students. The number of allowances available is limited; therefore candidates will be in competition for these awards.

Candidates are advised to see the pamphlet *Guide to Students' Allowances*, published by the Department.

Address:
Secretary, Awards Branch
Scottish Education Department
Clifton Terrace
Edinburgh
Scotland EH12 5DT

[1862]

SCOTTISH EDUCATION DEPARTMENT

Adult Education Allowances

Grants are available to individuals at least 20 years of age and ordinarily resident in Scotland who are, or will be, attending full-time courses of liberal adult education at the following establishments: Newbattle Abbey College, Dalkeith; Ruskin College, Oxford; Plater College, Oxford; Fircroft Residential College, Birmingham; Northern College, Barnsley; Hillcroft College, Surbiton; Coleg Harlech, Wales; and Cooperative College, Loughborough. Grants will be paid at the same rates and conditions applicable under the Students' Allowances Scheme for courses lasting at least one academic year.

Candidates are advised to read the pamphlet *Guide to Students' Allowances*, published by the Department.

Address:
Secretary, Awards Branch
Scottish Education Department
Clifton Terrace
Edinburgh
Scotland EH12 5DT

[1863]

SCOTTISH NATIONAL ORCHESTRA SOCIETY

Ian Whyte Award

The triennial Award of £500 and a guarantee of several performances, is offered to a British composer of not more than 34 years of age, for a work for full symphony orchestra, not exceeding 30 minutes, which has not been previously published or performed. Entries should be submitted to the jury under a pseudonym, by 1st February. The next Award will be in 1984.

Further information from:
General Administrator
Scottish National Orchestra
3 La Belle Place
Glasgow
Scotland G37 L1A

[1864]

SCOTTISH OPERA ENDOWMENT TRUST

John Noble Bursary for Singers

Applications for audition are invited from singers, of either sex, who were born or trained in Scotland. There is no age limit. Applicants will be requested to give details of age, training and experience and should be able to give the names of two referees prominent in the operatic world. The amount of the Bursary is reviewed annually.

The Bursary is non-competitive and will be awarded to the most deserving singer or singers. Applicants should set out on the application form the purpose to which they would put such a Bursary.

Preliminary auditions take place in February of each year with final auditions in March.

Further information from:
 Scottish Opera
 John Noble Bursary
 39 Elmbank Crescent
 Glasgow
 Scotland G2 4PT

[1865]

SCOTTISH UNIVERSITIES

Stevenson Exchange Scholarships

Subjects: Any university studies.

No. offered: 25 to 30 Scholarships annually.

Value: Variable; normally between £250 and £350, depending upon country in which the award is held. Recipients are required to meet their own travelling expenses.

Tenable at any university in France, Federal Republic of Germany or Spain for one academic year. Recipients must secure enrollment at the university of their choice.

Eligibility: Open to graduates and undergraduates of Scottish universities who are under 25 years of age (in special cases, candidates up to 35 years of age are considered).

Note: At the discretion of the Executive Committee, the Scholarships may be held with other awards or assistantships.

Candidates should apply to the registrar or secretary of their Scottish university by 28th February.

Further information from:
 Dr. Morven J. Easton
 Administrative Assistant
 University of Glasgow
 Glasgow
 Scotland G12 8QQ

[1866]

SCRIPPS-HOWARD FOUNDATION
(U.S.A.)

Through the Foundation, awards are made from the *Roy W. Howard-Margaret Rohe Howard Fund*, to encourage talented young men and women to prepare for careers in journalism and the allied arts. Individual scholarships to graduate and undergraduate students are awarded in varying amounts of up to US$2,000.

Ellen Browning Scripps Fellowships: Ten annual Fellowships are given to men and women now working in the journalism profession who wish to increase their knowledge in any field through graduate studies at any recognized university. *Closing date:* 15th April.

Roy W. Howard Public Service Awards: Two Awards of US$2,500 and a bronze plaque are given annually to a newspaper and to a radio or TV station in the United States or its territories, judged to be outstanding in their public service efforts during the previous year. Cash prizes are to be distributed to those individuals most responsible for the achievement. Three runner-up prizes of US$1,000 will also be awarded. *Closing dates:* 1st March for newspaper entries; 1st February for broadcast entries.

Edward J. Meeman Conservation Awards: Five prizes are awarded annually in recognition of outstanding work in the cause of conservation published in newspapers. One first prize of US$2,500 and a bronze plaque is given. For papers with circulation of less than 100,000—prizes of US$2,000 and US$1,000; for papers with circulation of more than 100,000—prizes of US$2,000 and US$1,000. Open to any newspaperman or woman in the U.S. and its territories. *Closing date:* 15th February.

Ernie Pyle Memorial Awards are given annually to any newspaperman or woman in the U.S. or its territories whose work during the year prior to that of the contest most nearly exemplifies the style and craftsmanship of Ernie Pyle. First prize of US$1,000 and a bronze plaque; second prize of US$500. *Closing date:* 15th January.

Edward Willis Scripps First Amendment Award is awarded annually to a newspaper in the U.S. or its territories, which has performed the most outstanding service in the cause of the First Amendment guarantee of a free press. A cash award of US$2,500 is distributed to those individuals most responsible for the achievement. *Closing date:* 1st February.

Walker Stone Awards for Editorial Writing are given annually to recognize outstanding achievement in the field of editorial writing. Open to any newspaperman or woman in the

U.S. and its territories. First prize of US$1,000 and a bronze plaque; second prize of US$500.
Closing date: 1st February.

Special Grants: The Foundation funds selected special projects related to journalism and journalism education, including but not limited to seminars, minority students programs and internship programs. Complete details of the program to be considered must be made no later than 15th April.

Note: For additional information concerning awards and Special Grants, contact the Foundation at 1,100 Central Trust Tower, Cincinnati, Ohio 45202. For additional information concerning Scholarships, contact the Foundation at the address below.

Address:
Scripps-Howard Foundation
200 Park Avenue, Room 4310
New York, New York 10166
U.S.A.

[1867]

SERGEL DRAMA PRIZE
University of Chicago Theatre

To encourage the writing of new American plays, Prizes of US$1,500, US$750, and US$500 are offered in even-numbered years for the winning plays submitted in the competition.

The competition is open to anyone except previous winners. Only original plays are considered. Dramatizations, adaptations, and translations are not eligible.

Closing date: 1st June.

Further information from:
Sergel Drama Prize
University of Chicago
Court Theatre
5706 South University Avenue
Chicago, Illinois 60637
U.S.A.

[1868]

SETTLEMENT STUDY CENTRE *(Rehovot)*

Assistance for Postgraduate Courses

Courses: Three Courses annually: Two on integrated rural regional development, and one on comprehensive regional development planning—both with special emphasis on rural development and problems of socio-economic conditions in developing countries.

No. offered: Approximately 30 Fellowships for each course.

Value: Covers course and return air fare to Israel plus airfare to location of Project Exercize.

Tenable for the initial five months at the Centre, then for three months in a specific region of a developing country.

Eligibility: Open to graduates from developing countries with a B.A. or equivalent degree in economics, sociology, agriculture or architecture and at last three years' experience in a governmental or public services or in a comparable professional position related to regional planning. Participants must be sponsored by their local government.

Note: The language of instruction for African and Asian participants is English, and Spanish for Latin American participants.
Fellowships are granted by national or international institutions or agencies.

Further information from:
Settlement Study Centre
P.O. Box 2355
Rehovot
Israel

[1869]

SHASTRI INDO-CANADIAN INSTITUTE
(Canada)

Junior and Senior Fellowships

Purpose: To permit Fellows to pursue research in India.

Subjects: The humanities and social sciences.

No. offered: Variable.

Value: 60,000 rupees per annum or the difference between leave and regular salary, whichever is less, for unmarried Senior Fellows; 24,000 rupees for unmarried Junior Fellows, annually. Certain adjustments are made for up to three dependents. Round-trip economy air fare to India for the applicant only is also provided.

Tenable in India: for three to twelve months—renewable—Senior Fellowships; for periods up to, or exceeding one year—Junior Fellowships.

Eligibility: Fellowships are open to Canadian citizens and landed immigrants.

Note: Junior Fellowships may be used for students pursuing an M.A., M.Phil., or Ph.D. at Indian institutions, or to fulfill partial postgraduate degree requirements. Applicants for both Junior and Senior Fellowships will be expected to give all reasonable assurance that they intend to return to Canada upon completion of research.

Fellows are required to submit to the Institute copies of all written materials and dissertations deriving from their Fellowships research.

The Institute also provides *Language Training Grants* to Canadian citizens and landed immigrants who are qualified and have obtained some prior language training. These Grants, carrying similar value as regular Junior and Senior Fellowships, are tenable at Indian institutions approved by the Indian Government for periods not normally less than one year.

All awards are made in Indian rupees and can be used only in India.

Closing date: 10th October.

Further information from:
 Executive Director
 Shastri Indo-Canadian Institute
 University of Calgary
 2500 University Drive, N.W.
 Calgary, Alberta
 Canada T2N 1N4

[1870]

SHASTRI INDO-CANADIAN INSTITUTE
(Canada)

Faculty Training Grant
Performing Arts Fellowship

Faculty Training Grants: A small number of Grants are offered to Canadian citizens or landed immigrants who are senior scholars in the fields of social science and the humanities, and who have had little or no previous involvement with Indian studies (or who wish to change their disciplinary focus within Indian studies) but wish to develop an expertise in one of the areas normally supported by the Institute. The Grants of 60,000 rupees (for an unmarried scholar) for one year or the difference between leave and regular salary, whichever is less, are tenable in India. *Closing date:* 10th October.

Performing Arts Fellowships: A small number of Fellowships are awarded to Canadian citizens and landed immigrants who are established or junior artists wishing to study some aspect of Indian dance or music in association with an individual in India who is recognized by the appropriate Indian authorities as a competent teacher and skilled performer. The value of these Fellowships are at the same rate as Junior and Senior Fellowships. Awards are tenable for one year, renewable. *Closing date:* 10th October.

Further information from:
 Executive Director
 Shastri Indo-Canadian Institute
 University of Calgary
 2500 University Drive, N.W.
 Calgary, Alberta
 Canada T2N 1N4

[1871]

SHELL COMPANY OF AUSTRALIA LTD.

Shell Postgraduate Arts Scholarship

Purpose: To provide Australian graduates with the opportunity for study in the U.K. leading to a higher degree.

Subjects: Arts, commerce, economics, law.

No. offered: One Scholarship annually.

Value: Adequate funds to meet living costs, university tuition and materials and other university charges. Return economy air fare to Australia is provided if return is within a year of completion of the Scholarship.

Tenable at a university in the United Kingdom for two years with the possibility of renewal for a third year.

Eligibility: Open to Australian citizens who have been domiciled in Australia for the last five years, are under 25 years of age, and have obtained an honours degree from an Australian university in one of the above mentioned subjects by 31st January of the Scholarship year, or alternatively, have proceeded to a master's degree.

The selectors, while giving first consideration to intellectual attainment, will take account of an individual's breadth of vision, qualities of leadership and interest in other people and their problems as evidence that a candidate may ultimately have an important contribution to make outside the purely academic field.

Note: Applications should be made to the personnel manager of the Shell Company of Australia Ltd. in the capital city of the state in which the applicant resides. Application forms may be obtained through these personnel managers or through university registrars.

Closing date: Mid-September for decision to be reached in December. The Scholarship becomes tenable in October of the following year.

Address:
Shell Company of Australia Ltd.
155 William Street
Melbourne, Victoria
Australia 3001

[1872]

SHELL COMPANY OF AUSTRALIA LTD.

Shell Postgraduate Scholarship in Science/Engineering

Purpose: To provide Australian graduates with the opportunity for study in the U.K. leading to a higher degree.

Subjects: Science (including applied science) and engineering.

No. offered: One Scholarship annually.

Value: Adequate funds to meet living costs, university tuition and materials and other university charges. Return economy air fare to Australia is provided if return is within a year of completion of the Scholarship.

Tenable at a university in the United Kingdom for two years, with the possibility of renewal for a third year.

Eligibility: Open to Australian citizens who have been domiciled in Australia for the last five years, are under 25 years of age, and have obtained an honours degree in science (including applied science) or engineering from an Australian university by 31st January of the Scholarship year, or alternatively have proceeded to a master's degree.

The selectors, while giving first consideration to intellectual attainment, will take account of an individual's breadth of vision, qualities of leadership and interest in other people and their problems as evidence that a candidate may ultimately have an important contribution to make outside the field of academic or applied research.

Note: Applications should be made to the personnel manager of the Shell Company of Australia Ltd. in the capital city of the state in which the applicant resides. Application forms may be obtained through these personnel managers or through university registrars.

Closing date: Mid-September for decision to be reached in December. The Scholarship becomes tenable in October of the following year.

Address:
Shell Company of Australia Ltd.
155 William Street
Melbourne, Victoria
Australia 3001

[1873]

SHELL INTERNATIONAL PETROLEUM COMPANY LTD.

Studentships (Engineering)

Subjects: Mechanical, civil, structural or offshore engineering.

No. offered: Four Studentships annually.

Value: £2,590 (£3,115 for London) per annum, plus approved fees.

Tenable at any university in the United Kingdom or Ireland, for one year.

Eligibility: Open to citizens of the United Kingdom, honours graduates in mechanical, civil or structural engineering who wish to take an M.Sc. in a branch of one or other of these subjects. It is hoped that successful candidates will be interested in following a career in the exploration or oil production side of the petroleum industry.

Closing date: 1st April.

Further information from:
PNEL/22
Shell Centre
London
England SE1 7NA

[1874]

SHELL INTERNATIONAL PETROLEUM COMPANY LTD.

Studentships (Petroleum Geology or Engineering)

Subjects: Petroleum geology, petroleum reservoir engineering.

No. offered: Four Studentships annually.

Value: £2,590 (£3,115 for London) per annum, plus approved fees.

Tenable at any university in the United Kingdom or Ireland which offers postgraduate courses in any of the above mentioned subjects, for one year.

Eligibility: Open to citizens of the United Kingdom who are honours graduates in physics, mathematics or geology. It is hoped that successful candidates will be interested in following a career in the exploration and oil production side of the petroleum industry.

Closing date: April.

Further information from:
PNEL/22
Shell Centre
London
England SE1 7NA

[1875]

SHELL INTERNATIONAL PETROLEUM COMPANY LTD.

Studentships (Geology or Geophysics)

No. offered: Two Studentships annually.

Value: £2,590 (£3,115 for London) per annum, plus approved fees.

Tenable at any university department of geology or geophysics in the United Kingdom or Ireland, for a maximum of three years.

Eligibility: Open to citizens of the United Kingdom with an honours first degree in geology, physics or mathematics, who intend joining the exploration side of the petroleum industry but before doing so wish to take a Ph.D. in a suitable geological or geophysical topic.

Closing date: April.

Further information from:
PNEL/22
Shell Centre
London
England SE1 7NA

[1876]

SHELL INTERNATIONAL PETROLEUM COMPANY LTD.
Imperial College of Science and Technology *(London)*

Shell Scholarship in Geophysics or Geology

No. offered: One Scholarship annually.

Value: In accordance with the Research Council rates, paid monthly, plus fees.

Tenable at the Imperial College of Science and Technology, London, for one, two or three years.

Eligibility: Open to United Kingdom citizens who hold an honours degree in geology, preferably with mathematics and/or physics, or an honours degree in physics.

Closing date: 15th April.

Further information from:
Registrar
Imperial College of Science and
  Technology
London
England SW7 2AZ

[1877]

SHELL INTERNATIONAL PETROLEUM COMPANY LTD.

Shell Postgraduate Scholarship in Geophysics *(Cambridge)*

No. offered: One Postgraduate Scholarship annually.

Value: £2,590 per annum, plus approved fees.

Tenable at the University of Cambridge for three years.

Eligibility: Open to nationals of any country, under 27 years of age, holding a degree in mathematics, physics or geology.

Closing date: 1st April.

Further information from:
Head of Bullard Laboratories
Department of Earth Sciences
University of Cambridge
Madingley Rise, Madingley Road
Cambridge
England CB3 0EZ

[1878]

SHELL—LONDON SYMPHONY ORCHESTRA MUSIC SCHOLARSHIP

The Scholarship of £3,000 is offered annually as first prize in a music competition. Auditions are held early in the year. The 1982 competition was for strings.

Particulars of future competitions may be obtained from:
Shell—LSO Music Scholarship
Regent Arcade House
19-25 Argyll Street
London
England W1V 2LN

[1879]

SHORT SUMMER COURSES IN SCANDINAVIA FOR INTERNATIONAL UNDERSTANDING

Partial or Full Scholarships for Summer Courses

Ten-day Courses, with 35-50 participants of all age groups from many countries, are arranged annually in July and August in Denmark, Norway and Sweden. Through lectures, excursions, informal discussions and study-groups the Courses aim to create good fellowship and greater awareness of some important social and cultural issues in the world today. Instruction is in English.

Scholarships are sometimes available to cover half tuition fees, and under certain circumstances students from the developing countries may receive free tuition. Travel grants are not available.

Not confirmed for 1983.

Further information from:
Short Summer Courses in Scandinavia
  for International Understanding
Mr. K.E. Ødegå
Follo Folk High School
1540 Vestby
Norway

[1880]

JEAN SIBELIUS INTERNATIONAL VIOLIN COMPETITION *(Helsinki)*

Violinists of any nationality, born between 1952 and 1969 inclusive, may apply to participate in the Competition which is held every five years (next in 1985). Prizes for the 4th Competition, held in 1980, were as follows: 1st—US$5,000; 2nd—US$4,000; 3rd—US$3,000; 4th—US$2,000; 5th—US$1,000; 6th—US$700; 7th—US$500; 8th—US$400. In addition, a further prize of US$1,000 for the best performance of the Sibelius Violin Concerto is given by the Finnish Broadcasting Company.

Closing date: 15th August, 1985.

Further information from:
Jean Sibelius International Violin
  Competition
P. Rautatiekatu 9
SF-00100 Helsinki 10
Finland

[1881]

SIGMA ALPHA IOTA PHILANTHROPIES, INC.

Inter-American Music Awards

One Award for a musical composition is given every three years (next awarded in 1984), to a composer of any age from North, Central or South America. The Prize consists of US$500, publication and first performance of the work, plus transportation for the winner to the National Convention where the first performance of the work will take place. All submitted works must be unpublished and have not been performed publicly. Candidates may submit as many works as they wish; however there is a US$10 entry fee for each work.

Closing date: 15th March, for announcement to be made in August of the following year.

Further information from:
Euginie Dengel, Director
Inter-American Music Awards
Sigma Alpha Iota Philanthropies, Inc.
165 West 82nd Street
New York, New York 10024
U.S.A.

[1882]

SIGMA XI, THE SCIENTIFIC RESEARCH SOCIETY

Grants-In—Aid of Research

Subjects: Any field of scientific investigation.

Value: By individual assessment up to a maximum of US$1,000. No part of the Grant may be used for the payment of indirect costs to the institution involved—all of the funds must be expended directly in support of the proposed investigation. All equipment purchased remains the property of the institution. No salary or tuition support is given, nor are grants normally made for pulication expenses, travel to meetings, or usual and routine institutional obligations.

Eligibility: Open to nationals of any country who are adequately qualified research workers with a clearly outlined program of scientific investigation.

Closing dates: 1st February, 1st May, 1st November.

Further information from:
Committee on Grants-in-Aid of Research
Sigma XI Headquarters
345 Whitney Avenue
New Haven, Connecticut 06511
U.S.A.

[1883]

SINFONIA FOUNDATION (U.S.A.)

Research Assistance Grants

Subjects: American music or music education.

Value: According to need and the nature of the request. Usual maximum US$1,000.

Eligibility: Open to applicants of all nationalities who show evidence of previous successful writing and scholarly research (publication, M.A. thesis, Ph.D. dissertation, etc.) or to those who show evidence of unusual knowledge or competence in the field to be researched.

Closing date: 1st March.

Further information from:
Grant Committee
Sinfonia Foundation
10600 Old State Road
Evansville, Indiana 47711
U.S.A.

[1884]

SINO-BRITISH FELLOWSHIP TRUST

Fellowships

Purpose: To enable Fellows of Chinese origin to study in the U.K. and to enable British Fellows to study in the Far East.

Subjects: Advanced studies (not necessarily leading to a formal qualification) in art, architecture, music, law, sciences, textile engineering, medicine and nursing, religious education, and social welfare.

Value: Tuition fees, maintenance and a personal allowance are paid, plus return travel expenses. There are no allowances for dependants.

Tenable at institutions in the U.K. (for Fellows of Chinese origin) or in the Far East (for U.K. Fellows) for one year. The Trust arranges the place of study.

Eligibility: Open to persons of Chinese origin and to U.K. citizens. Candidates should have held a responsible position in a relevant field. Preference is given to those who have not previously studied abroad and who are over 27 years of age.

Note: Fellows are expected to return to their home country on completion of the Fellowship and to put into practice the knowledge and experienced gained.
 The Fellowships are not awarded to those wishing to extend their studies in the U.K.
 Hong Kong citizens may obtain particulars from the *British Council, Easey Commercial Building, 20th Floor, 253-265 Hennessey Road, Wanchai, Hong Kong*; Singaporeans may contact the *British Council, Singapore Rubber House, Collyer Quay, Singapore 1.*

British Address:
 Dr. E. Moore, Honorary Secretary
 Sino-British Fellowship Trust Committee
 23 Bede House, Manor Fields
 London
 England SW15 3LT

[1885]

SIR ERNEST CASSELL EDUCATIONAL TRUST *(U.K.)*

Mountbatten Memorial Grants to Commonwealth Students

Purpose: To assist overseas students who are in the final year of their course of study and are in unexpected financial difficulties.

Subjects: Unrestricted; but special consideration is given to students enrolled in advanced courses in nursing and public health, medicine, engineering, etc.

Value: Up to £300.

Eligibility: Open to British Commonwealth citizens from overseas who are pursuing a course of study at undergraduate or postgraduate level at universities or other recognised institutions of higher education in the United Kingdom.

Note: Applicants should contact their university or college student welfare officer for further information.

Address:
 Sir Ernest Cassel Educational Trust
 21 Hassocks Road
 Hurstpierpoint, Sussex
 England BN6 9QH

[1886]

SIR ERNEST CASSEL EDUCATIONAL TRUST *(U.K.)*

Overseas Research Grants

Subjects: Language, literature or civilisation of any country.

Value: Between £100 and £200 per annum (and more in some circumstances) towards the expenses of approved research abroad.

Eligibility: Open to the more junior teaching members of faculties of universities and other places of higher education in Great Britain and Northern Ireland, regardless of country of birth.

Note: Applications must be supported by a senior colleague.
 Applicants should contact their university or college student welfare officer for further information.

Closing date: 15th March.

Address:
 Sir Ernest Cassel Educational Trust
 21 Hassocks Road
 Hurstpierpoint, Sussex
 England BN6 9QH

[1887]

SIR HERBERT SCHLINK MEMORIAL TRUST FUND *(Australia)*

Fellowships

Subjects: Biology, cytology, therapy, statistical evaluation of aetiology and therapy relating to cancer of women.

No. offered: Variable number of Fellowships annually, depending upon number of suitable applicants.

Value: Variable, depending upon individual project.

Tenable at universities, hospitals and research institutions in Australia and overseas; duration of Fellowship is variable and renewable.

Eligibility: Open to men and women holding a medical degree or a position in a paramedical organisation inquiring into cancer of women. Applications should be supported by university departments, medical schools, hospitals cancer institutions, the Royal College of Obstetrics and Gynaecology or any other approved scientific body.

Note: The Trust Fund also provides *Grants-in-Aid* and *Travelling Professorships*, with guidelines similar to those of the Fellowships.

Further information from:
Honorary Secretary
Sir Herbert Schlink Memorial Trust Fund
c/o Royal Prince Alfred Hospital Medical Centre
100 Carillon Avenue, Newton
Sydney, N.S.W.
Australia 2042

[1888]

SIR JAMES CAIRD'S TRAVELLING SCHOLARSHIPS TRUST *(Scotland)*

Scholarships

The Trust grants Scholarships to mature candidates who wish to carry out research with an industrial application, at a university situated at a considerable distance from their present location. The value is from £1,000 to £1,500 per year, at the discretion of the Trustees. It may be held for one to two years. Applicants should be Scottish nationals who are members of staff of a Scottish university or college. The Scholarships will not normally be given to candidates who are eligible for Science Research Council (*U.K.*) Grants.

Further information from:
Secretary
Sir James Caird's Travelling Scholarships Trust
136 Nethergate
Dundee
Scotland DD1 4PA

[1889]

SIR JAMES CAIRD'S TRAVELLING SCHOLARSHIPS TRUST *(Scotland)*

Travelling Scholarships

The Trust grants Travelling Scholarships in three categories: (a) to enable members of staff of Scottish universities to travel abroad on study visits. Applications will also be considered from postdoctoral research fellows and postdoctoral research assistants who are making a substantial contribution to teaching in their university. The Trust usually augments salaries being paid by the university or college so that travel can be undertaken; (b) to allow graduates from industry to travel abroad on study visits. These Awards do not substitute for Science Research Council (*U.K.*) Industrial Fellowships, for which the applicant might be eligible; (c) to enable graduates who have completed their university careers to travel abroad to further their suitability to take up a job in industry.

Further information from:
Secretary
Sir James Caird's Travelling Scholarships Trust
136 Nethergate
Dundee
Scotland DD1 4PA

[1890]

SIR JAMES CAIRD'S TRAVELLING SCHOLARSHIPS TRUST *(Scotland)*

Travelling Scholarships in Music

Value: By individual assessment.

Tenable at an approved institution for one year, renewable to a maximum of three years.

Eligibility: Open to Scottish nationals who can provide evidence of exceptional musical ability.

Note: Candidates must submit an outline of the work they would like to undertake, stating where and with whom they would like to study.

Closing date: 15th February.

Further information from:
  Secretary
  Sir James Caird's Travelling Scholarships
    Trust
  136 Nethergate
  Dundee
  Scotland DD1 4PA

Further information from:
  Ronald Groves, M.A., Secretary
  Sir Richard Stapley Educational Trust
  1 York Street
  London
  England W1H 1PZ

[1891]

SIR JAMES CAIRD'S TRAVELLING SCHOLARSHIPS TRUST *(Scotland)*

Wiseman Prize

A Prize of £200 is offered to the applicant appearing before the Advisory Committee in Music who, in their opinion, gives the best musical performance each year.

The Prize is awarded in addition to any scholarship or grant which the applicant may be awarded by the Trustees.

Candidates must be of Scottish nationality.

Further information from:
  Secretary
  Sir James Caird's Travelling Scholarships
    Trust
  136 Nethergate
  Dundee
  Scotland DD1 4PA

[1892]

SIR RICHARD STAPLEY EDUCATIONAL TRUST *(U.K.)*

Awards

Purpose: To make available small amounts to supplement other scholarships or grants for students in degree courses.

Subjects: Unrestricted.

Value: By individual assessment: usually between £75 and £100 per annum.

Eligibility: Open to graduates and non-graduates who can produce evidence that they are satisfactorily pursuing a course of study. Candidates must have been ordinarily resident in the United Kingdom for at least three years.

[1893]

ALFRED P. SLOAN FOUNDATION *(U.S.A.)*

Research Fellowships

Purpose: To provide especially promising young scientists with flexible research support at an early stage of their academic careers.

Subjects: Physics, chemistry, mathematics, economics, neuroscience and certain interdisciplinary fields such as geochemistry and astrophysics.

No. offered: Approximately 88 Fellowships annually.

Value: Approximately US$25,000 payable in two annual payments.

Tenable for two years in recognized colleges and universities in the United States and Canada; not renewable.

Eligibility: Open to young (under 32 years of age) regular members of a college or university in the United States or Canada, holding a Ph.D. degree in one of the above subjects. In neuroscience, postdoctoral Fellows with at least one year's postdoctoral experience, who are not regular faculty members, are also eligible for consideration.

Closing date: 15th September.

Further information from:
  Program Administrator
  Sloan Fellowships for Basic Research
  Alfred P. Sloan Foundation
  630 Fifth Avenue
  New York, New York 10111
  U.S.A.

[1894]

SLOCUM-LUNZ FOUNDATION, INC.
(U.S.A.)

Scholarships and Grants

The Foundation provides Scholarships and Grants of varying amounts to be used in the support of scholars and educational institutions in the fields of marine biology and related natural sciences. Priority is given to candidates for the doctoral degree who plan to work in South Carolina at the completion of their education; applications from beginning graduate students and advanced undergraduates are also considered. Academic work does not have to be performed in South Carolina.

Applications should include a completed application form or letter describing the applicant's educational accomplishments and plans, level of scholarship funding requested and justification, two or more letters of recommendation or names and addresses of two or more references familiar with the applicant's educational achievements, and a recent transcript. Also required is a letter confirming the student's acceptance or enrollment in an accredited academic program. Applications may be submitted at any time during the year.

Further information from:
Slocum-Lunz Foundation, Inc.
c/o Dr. Paul A. Sandifer, Chairman
Scholarships and Grants Committee
Marine Resources Research Institute
P.O. Box 12559
Charleston, South Carolina 29412
U.S.A.

[1895]

SMALL INDUSTRY EXTENSION TRAINING INSTITUTE *(Hyderabad, India)*

Course Fellowships

Purpose: To assist in the promotion and modernisation of small industries by undertaking training, research and consultancy activities in the four related fields of small industry development, extension, information and management.

Courses: (1) Training Methods and Skills—for persons who are already engaged in training programmes in institutions offering training in management, technical skills, administration and development. Duration: eight weeks. (2) Information storage and retrieval systems—open to personnel working with information in industrial organisations and the staff of documentation centres. Duration: ten weeks. (3) Small industry management consultancy—open to graduates with at least two years' service in a development agency rendering assistance, advice or training to small industry. Duration: twelve weeks. (4) Small industry promotion in developing economies—open to persons with a few years' experience in policy making or programme inplementation. Duration: twelve weeks. (5) Small industry financing—open to people with experience of financial institutions or development corporations. Duration: eight weeks. (6) Techno-Managerial Programme for Biscuit and Bakery Industry—open to persons working in biscuit and bakery units, prospective entrepreneurs who intend to start a business, lecturers, craft teachers, and promotion officers of banks and extension departments. Duration: eight weeks. (7) Planning and Promotion of Agro-Industries—open to officers of development agencies concerned with promotion of small industries and agro-industries. Duration: eight weeks.

Value: To cover Course fees, return air fare and living allowance.

Note: Fellowships are awarded under the Technical Cooperation Scheme of the Colombo Plan, Special Commonwealth African Assistance Plan, Afro-Asian Rural Reconstruction Organisation and the Commonwealth Fund for Technical Cooperation by United Nations agencies and various other organisations.

Not all Courses are offered every year. The Institute may be contacted in January regarding Courses to be offered during that year.

Further information from:
Principal Director
Small Industry Extension Training
  Institute
Yousufguda
Hyderabad 500 045
India

[1896]

STANLEY SMITH HORTICULTURAL TRUST *(U.K.)*

The Trust invites applications for awards to institutions and individuals in the field of horticulture, but not for academic or diploma courses. All projects are judged entirely on merit, and there are no eligiblity requirements.

Further information from:
Director
Stanley Smith Horticultural Trust
Belhaven House
Dunbar, East Lothian
Scotland EH42 1NS

[1897]

SMITH AND NEPHEW FOUNDATION *(U.K.)*

Research Fellowships

Subjects: Surgery, internal medicine.

No. offered: Variable.

Value: £10,000 each award.

Tenable in the United Kingdom for one year.

Eligibility: Open to citizens of any country between 25 and 35 years of age who hold a medical qualification registrable in the United Kingdom and who have had two years' general clinical experience.
Normally, candidates should have held a residential hospital appointment in general medicine or surgery.

Note: Recipients must return to their own country within one year of completing their studies.
Conditions of Fellowships may change from year to year. Individuals are urged to contact the address below for further information.

Closing date: 31st January.

Further information from:
Secretary to the Trustees
Smith and Nephew Foundation
2 Temple Place, Victoria Embankment
London
England WC2R 3BP

[1898]

W.H. SMITH AND SON, LTD. *(U.K.)*

Annual Literary Award

The Award of £2,500 is awarded to a United Kingdom or Commonwealth author whose book, written in English and published in the United Kingdom within twelve months ending 31st December preceding the date of the Award, in the opinion of the judges makes the most outstanding contribution to English literature. Authors and publishers may not submit works for consideration.

Further information from:
W.H. Smith and Son, Ltd.
Strand House
10 New Fetter Lane
London
England EC4A 1AD

[1899]

SMITHSONIAN INSTITUTION *(Washington, D.C.)*

Daniel and Florence Guggenheim Fellowship

Purpose: To promote graduate research in the fields of technology transfer, planetary exploration, or the history of aviation.

No. offered: One Fellowship annually.

Value: Predoctoral, US$9,000; Postdoctoral, US$17,000.

Tenable at the National Air and Space Museum, Washington, D.C., for a one year residential appointment.

Eligibility: Open to suitably qualified graduate students.

Note: Candidates should submit a one page resumé stating academic background and qualifications, and a research proposal which defines: the objectives of the research; procedures to be used; why the research should be conducted at the National Air and Space Museum; anticipated benefits to the individuals and the academic community; and methods for dissemination of findings.

Closing date: 15th January for appointments to begin 1st May or after.

Further information from:
Office of Fellowships and Grants
L'Enfant Plaza, Room 3300
Smithsonian Institution
Washington, D.C. 20560
U.S.A.

[1900]

SMITHSONIAN INSTITUTION *(Washington, D.C.)*

Smithsonian Predoctoral Fellowships

Subjects: American history and material culture; anthropology; biological sciences; earth sciences; history of art; history of science and technology; history of Africa art and culture.

No. offered: Approximately 22 Fellowships annually.

Value: US$9,000 per annum, plus research and other allowances. Stipends are paid monthly.

Tenable at Smithsonian Institution facilities for periods of six months to one year.

Eligibility: Open to students of any nationality who are recommended to conduct research by universities where they have substantially completed formal course requirements for the doctorate or its equivalent. Satisfactory completion of the research is expected to result in the award of that degree. A working knowledge of English is required.

Note: Projects proposed will be approved in advance by a Smithsonian staff member who will serve as the appointee's advisor. Projects must be related to the research and interests of the Institution's professional staff.

Closing date: 15th January, for commencement in the following academic year.

Further information from:
Office of Fellowships and Grants
L'Enfant Plaza, Room 3300
Smithsonian Institution
Washington, D.C. 20560
U.S.A.

[1901]

SMITHSONIAN INSTITUTION *(Washington, D.C.)*

Smithsonian Postdoctoral Fellowships

Purpose: To offer apointments to those who wish to pursue postdoctoral research training at the Smithsonian Institution in collaboration with a member of the professional staff of the Institution.

Subjects: American history and material culture; history of science and technology; history of art; anthropology; biological sciences; earth sciences.

No. offered: Approximately 22 Fellowships annually.

Value: US$17,000 per annum, plus research and other allowances. Stipends are paid monthly.

Tenable at Smithsonian Institution facilities, including museums on the Mall and elsewhere in Washington, D.C., at its Astrophysical Observatory in Cambridge, Massachusetts, and at its Tropical Research Institute, Panama; normally for a period of six months to one year. Requests for renewal are considered in competition with new applications.

Eligibility: Open to candidates of any nationality who possess a Ph.D. or equivalent degree. Preference is given to those who have received the degree within five years preceding commencement of tenure at the Institution. A working knowledge of English is required.

Closing date: 15th January.

Further information from:
Office of Fellowships and Grants
L'Enfant Plaza, Room 3300
Smithsonian Institution
Washington, D.C. 20560
U.S.A.

[1902]

SMITHSONIAN INSTITUTION *(Washington, D.C.)*

Eppley Smithsonian Fellowship

Purpose: To support independent postdoctoral research.

Subjects: Solar radiation measurement, conversion of solar radiation to other usable forms of energy, and the effects of solar radiation on the biosphere. Research proposals may be in basic or applied areas.

No. offered: One Fellowship as a vacancy occurs.

Value: US$17,000 and allowances for travel and research-related expenses to a postdoctoral investigator, or up to US$16,500 for a senior scholar.

Tenable at the Smithsonian Radiation Biology Laboratory in Rockville, Maryland for the duration of the approved research.

Eligibility: Open to qualified postdoctoral investigators who are within five years of the degree, or to visiting scholars on sabbatical leave seeking to conduct specific research and use specialized equipment and facilities at the laboratory.

Note: The research is performed in association with the Smithsonian's staff, using its laboratories and other facilities.

Closing date: 15th January.

Further information from:
Office of Fellowships and Grants
L'Enfant Plaza, Room 3300
Smithsonian Institution
Washington, D.C. 20560
U.S.A.

[1903]

SMITHSONIAN INSTITUTION *(Washington, D.C.)*

Short-Term Visits: Financial support in small amounts is available to students and scholars seeking access to Smithsonian facilities and staff members for a short period of time, but not less than one week.

Fellowship in Materials Science: One Fellowship is available annually for research on problems in the application of techniques of the physical sciences to problems in art history, anthropology, archaeology and the history of technology. Applicants should have a doctorate in an appropriate discipline, or a degree or certificate of advanced training in the conservation of artifacts and art objects. *Closing date:* 15th January.

Fellowships for Field Study: Occasionally the Institution offers Fellowships for biological research in connection with Smithsonian-sponsored field projects abroad. Open to investigators who are engaged in dissertation research or who have recently completed the Ph.D. There are no closing dates for this Fellowship.

Postdoctoral Fellowships at the Smithsonian Astrophysical Observatory are made in various fields of astrophysics and astronomy, including atomic and molecular physics, geo-astronomy, high-energy astrophysics, optical and infrared astronomy, planetary sciences, radio astronomy, solar and stellar physics, and theoretical astrophysics. *Closing date:* 1st February.

Applicants are asked to correspond directly with the *Chairman of the Postdoctoral Committee, Smithsonian Astrophysical Observatory, 60 Garden Street, Cambridge, Massachusetts 02138.*

Visiting Research Student Appointments are offered to graduates and undergraduates for study and research under the guidance of Smithsonian staff members. Fellowships for students engaged in formal university training at the graduate level are valued at US$1,500 for a ten-week appointment. Appointments are offered in the fields of research pursued at the Smithsonian, including history, art and science. Fellows should expect to spend their entire tenure in residence at the Smithsonian. *Closing date:* 15th January.

Appointments for Visiting Scientists and Scholars: Support for investigators wishing to undertake longer-term research projects of a few months to a year is occasionally offered by individual bureaus of the Institution. Candidates carry out their projects at the Smithsonian, and usually hold a Ph.D. degree or equivalent and are in mid-career.

In addition to the awards listed in there entries, the Institution welcomes qualified visitors for study and training in a wide variety of fields in its museums, field stations, laboratories and bureaus. Individuals are encouraged to inquire directly to the individual museums and research organizations, or to the address below. Applicants should state their academic status, degree held or expected, and specific field of interest.

Further information from:
Office of Fellowships and Grants
L'Enfant Plaza, Room 3300
Smithsonian Institution
Washington, D.C. 20560
U.S.A.

[1904]

CONN SMYTHE RESEARCH FOUNDATION FOR CRIPPLED CHILDREN
(Canada)

Research Grants

Purpose: To encourage research in any area relating to the etiology, epidemiology, prevention, treatment, habilitation and rehabilitation of crippling conditions in children.

No. offered: No fixed number of Grants.

Value: Depends upon acceptance of budget submitted with the application.

Tenable for one year. Continuation of projects beyond one year will be conditional on the calibre of work and the merit of the project, in relation to other candidates. In special circumstances applications may be made for periods up to three years.

Note: Personnel support is also awarded in the form of Training Grants, Studentships and Fellowships.

Closing date: 15th July and 15th November.

Further information from:
Conn Smythe Research Foundation for Crippled Children
350 Rumsey Road
Toronto, Ontario
Canada M4G 1R8

[1905]

SOCIAL SCIENCE RESEARCH COUNCIL
(U.K.)

General Information: The subjects within the scope of the Social Science Research Council (SSRC) are: accountancy; area studies; criminology; economics; economic and social history; economic and social statistics; including demography; education; ethnology; history of science and science policy; human geography; international relations, management and industrial relations; planning; political science; psychology; social anthropology; socio-legal studies, sociology and social administration; aspects of linguistics and computing applied to the social sciences.

SSRC awards are open to graduates from all disciplines.

Full information can be obtained from the Council's handbook which is published annually in January.

Further information from:
Postgraduate Training Division
Social Science Research Council
1 Temple Avenue
London
England EC4Y OBD

[1906]

SOCIAL SCIENCE RESEARCH COUNCIL
(U.K.)

Bursaries

Purpose: To provide funds for postgraduate students on full-time vocational courses leading to a diploma in management and industrial relations.

Value: To include a maintenance grant (lodging rate £1,825 in London area, £1,535 elsewhere; home rate £1,180 or £630), approved fees, and dependents' allowances in appropriate cases. The maximum value may be reduced by a parental and a student contribution, but not normally below the minimum rate of £410 per annum.

Secondment terms may be arranged in approved cases.

Tenable at universities and colleges of further education.

Eligibility: Open to persons who hold a degree

or an acceptable equivalent qualification. Candidates, either of their parents or their spouse must have been ordinarily resident in England or Wales for at least three years immediately preceding the start of postgraduate study. Periods of temporary residence or study abroad will not be regarded as interrupting residence in England or Wales.

Note: Students who are ordinarily resident in Scotland, Northern Ireland, the Isle of Man, or the Channel Islands are not eligible for SSRC Bursaries. They should apply instead as follows: Scotland—*Scottish Education Department, Awards Branch, 2 South Charlotte Street, Edinburgh EH2 4AP;* Northern Ireland—*Ministry of Education, Rathgael House, Balloo Road, Bangor, County Down;* Isle of Man—*Isle of Man Education Authority, Strand Street, Douglas;* Jersey—*Jersey Education Committee, St. Helier;* Guernsey—*Guernsey Education Council, St. Peter Port.*

Candidates must apply to a department for a course which has been recognised by SSRC to be considered for nomination for an award. Details of these courses are contained in the free booklet *SSRC Bursary Scheme*.

Closing date: 1st July for all courses.

Address:
Social Science Research Council
1 Temple Avenue
London
England EC4Y OBD

[1907]

SOCIAL SCIENCE RESEARCH COUNCIL *(U.K.)*

Studentships

Purpose: To enable young graduates and others suitably qualified to spend a period of full-time postgraduate training.

Subjects: Social sciences.

Value: To include a maintenance allowance (£2,770 or £2,245 per annum for student in lodging and halls of residence or college; £1,370 per annum for students at home), approved fees, dependents' allowances and other allowances in appropriate cases. The maximum allowance may be reduced by a spouse contribution.

Tenable at universities, university colleges, polytechnics and other institutions acceptable to the Council for one or two years (for advanced courses), and two or three years (for research).

Eligibility: Candidates must satisfy the following conditions: (a) either they or either of their parents or their spouse must have been ordinarily resident in Great Britain for at least three years immediately preceding the start of postgraduate studies. If neither parent has been so resident the three-year qualifying period must exclude any period of full-time education. Periods of temporary residence or study abroad will not be regarded as interrupting residence in Great Britain; (b) they must hold a good honours degree (normally first or upper second class honours or equivalent in undivided second class honours) or an acceptable alternative qualification; (c) they must be nominated for an award by the authority of the university or college at which the award is to be held.

Quota Awards: Students may ask the head of the department in which the proposed course or research is to be undertaken, to be considered for a nomination for an award. Places may be offered after quota allocations to the university concerned are made in April, and may be conditional if students have not as yet obtained their degree.

Pool-awards: distributed by means of a competition, are also available and are additional to those distributed in the form of quotas.

Student Choice Awards: in certain subjects (currently economic and social history, political science, area studies, social anthropology and human geography) research training awards are distributed by means of a national competition. Additional details are available from proposed places of study.

Class Awards: involve a specified period of research with a collaborating body in the public or private sector. Additional information available from the address below.

Note: Applications can only be made through a nominating department recognized by the Council.

Closing date: 1st August for nomination of

students for both Quota and Pool-awards; 1st May for Student Choice Awards.

Address:
Postgraduate Training Division
Social Science Research Council
1 Temple Avenue
London
England EC4Y OBD

[1908]

SOCIAL SCIENCE RESEARCH COUNCIL
(U.K.)

Linked Studentships

These awards are intended to provide students with the opportunity to attain higher degrees while linked to an ongoing research project (not necessarily funded by the Council) which provides stimulus, guidance and data. The link is intended to be fairly loose. Those students receiving aid would not be regarded as research assistants. Eligibility and additional information are the same as those outlined for normal Studentships, however different closing dates may apply.

Address:
Postgraduate Training Division
Social Science Research Council
1 Temple Avenue
London
England EC4Y 0BD

[1909]

SOCIAL SCIENCE RESEARCH COUNCIL
(U.K.)

Secondment Studentships

Purpose: To enable young social scientists employed in a professional capacity in industry, commerce or other employment, and whose employers are prepared to release them on secondment, to undertake a period of full-time postgraduate training.

Subjects: Social sciences.

Value: As for other SSRC Studentships, except that no deduction will be made in respect of the income from the employer's contribution provided that the student's total remuneration from the Council and his employer is not greater than the salary he would receive from his employment.

Tenable at institutions approved by the Council for one or two years. Two-year research awards may be extended for a third year.

Eligibility: In addition to meeting the normal requirements for studentships, a candidate for a Secondment Studentship must (a) have had at least one year of postgraduate experience in an appropriate professional capacity in industry, commerce or other employment for which the proposed training will be valuable immediately before commencing the postgraduate training, and (b) have obtained the consent of his employer to release him on secondment for the required period and to supplement his award.

Employers are required to supplement the SSRC award so that take-home pay is as if on full salary.

Note: There is no separate allocation for Secondment Studentships. Students should apply for one in the same way as for an ordinary Studentship.

Closing date: 1st August.

Address:
Postgraduate Training Division
Social Science Research Council
1 Temple Avenue
London
England EC4Y 0BD

[1910]

SOCIAL SCIENCE RESEARCH COUNCIL
(U.K.)

Research Grant Scheme

Purpose: To provide initial support for new ideas and projects, particularly those which make a new contribution to theory or method, or which have important applications. Research should be of general significance and interest, and relevant to an audience wider than that of the sponsoring institution.

Subjects: Within the fields of accountancy, criminology, demography, economics, economic and social history, education, human geography history of science and science policy, industrial relations, international relations, management, planning, political science, public administration, psychology, sociology, social anthropology, socio-legal studies, social administration, and aspects of linguistics, computing and statistics related to the social sciences.

Value: No specified limit. Claims are normally submitted quarterly in arrears.

Tenable in the United Kingdom, normally for periods up to five years.

Eligibility: Grants are made to United Kingdom universities, colleges or established research institutions, and not to the individual applicants. Applicants should normally be salaried members of United Kingdom universities, colleges or established research institutions, or should have been ordinarily resident in the United Kingdom for at least three years immediately prior to submitting an application or would have been so resident had they or their spouse not been employed temporarily abroad. The applicant should normally be the person undertaking responsibility for directing the research as well as being actively involved in carrying it through. Applicants for personal research Grants should have already made a considerable contribution to their subject. Further conditions are supplied on request.

Note: The SSRC is also prepared to support research programmes. A programme is conceived as being wider in scope than a project, usually involving a longer time period than a project, and consisting of several inter-related projects which may be undertaken consecutively or simultaneously.

Closing date: Applications for amounts less than £20,000 may be submitted at any time. The closing dates for applications for personal research grants of between £20,000 and £100,000 are 15th January and 15th August; those for programmes and projects over £100,000 are 1st May and 15th October.

Further information from:
  Research Grant Division
  Social Science Research Council
  1 Temple Avenue
  London
  England EC4Y 0BD

[1911]

SOCIAL SCIENCE RESEARCH COUNCIL (U.K.)

Personal Research Grants

Purpose: To enable established staff of senior standing in United Kingdom universities, polytechnics and colleges of further education, particularly but not exclusively those oriented towards theoretical advances, to work full-time for a fixed period on research on a specified topic, freed from their normal duties.

Subjects: Social sciences.

No. offered: Varies.

Value: Recipient's salary (including superannuation, pension, National Insurance and any due salary increment) and support costs up to a total of £750 for a period of less than one year, or £1,000 per annum to cover part-time secretarial assistance, travel and subsistence expenses.

Tenable normally in the recipient's own institution for a minimum of 3 months to a maximum of 5 years.

Eligibility: Open to established staff of senior standing and with considerable research experience, in United Kingdom institutions whose department head and chief administrative authority provide assurance of the applicant's released time and replacement on a temporary basis, to be financed by the institution.

Note: Grants are made to United Kingdom universities, and are not paid to individual award holders.
  The Grants are meant to facilitate a net gain in time available for research work, and are thus intended to be a supplement to, not a substitute for, other research arrangements.
  Holders of awards of more than 18 months' duration may make a subsequent and separate application for assistance under the Research Grant Scheme [see preceding entry].

Closing date: 15th January and 15th August.

Further information from:
  Social Science Research Council
  1 Temple Avenue
  London
  England EC4Y 0BD

[1912]

SOCIAL SCIENCE RESEARCH COUNCIL
(U.S.A.)

Fellowships for Doctoral Research in Employment and Training

The Program supports dissertation research of graduate students who attend accredited United States institutions, and have completed all requirements for the doctoral degree except for the dissertation, or will have met these requirements before the award becomes effective. Dissertation topics must relate to problems of employment and training in the United States.

The awards are made to the institutions for the Fellow's use for a period not to exceed one year. Funds cover stipends, dependents allowances, clerical assistance, materials and supplies, computer time, travel, and communication costs. The maximum award to an individual is *U.S.*$10,000. In addition, the academic institution may receive both indirect costs and an allowance for tuition and fees not to exceed *U.S.*$2,500.

Applications should be submitted to the Council by a university in the name of the candidate, and must include a written recommendation from the candidate's doctoral advisor. This program is supported by the United States Department of Labor.

Closing date: 1st March; 1st June; 1st September; and 1st December.

Address:
Director, Program in Employment and Training
Social Science Research Council
1755 Massachusetts Avenue, N.W.,
  Suite 410
Washington, D.C. 20036
U.S.A.

[1913-1917]

SOCIAL SCIENCE RESEARCH COUNCIL
(U.S.A.)

Fellowships for International Doctoral Research

Fellowships are offered for doctoral dissertation research in the social sciences and the humanities to be carried out in Africa, Asia, Latin America and the Caribbean, the Near and Middle East or Western Europe. Applicants must have completed all requirements for a Ph.D. degree except the dissertation by the time the award is activated. Support is also given in Asia for the advanced research of students in professional schools where the doctoral degree is not generally offered. There are no age or citizenship restrictions for students enrolled in full-time study at universities in the United States or Canada.

Fellowships support 9 to 18 concsecutive months of field research in the relevant area. Awards normally include maintenance stipends, transportation expenses and health insurance for the Fellow and financial dependents, a research allowance and limited assistance towards tuition costs. Applicants may request up to six months of support for specialized preparatory training in disciplinary, language or methodological skills essential to the successful undertaking of the dissertation research, and up to six months limited support for writing the dissertation upon return to the home university. Support is not provided for the completion of normal predissertation requirements for the Ph.D. degree.

The total period of support for preparatory training, field research and dissertation write-up normally cannot exceed 24 months. Fellows must plan to work in the geographic area that constitutes the major focus of their research. They are usually expected to become affiliated with a university, research institute or other appropriate institution in the country where they will be conducting their research.

Funds for the international programs are provided by the National Endowment for the Humanities and the Ford Foundation. The Council sponsors all awards, either independently, or jointly with the American Council of Learned Societies.

Closing date: 2nd November.

[1913]
Fellowships for Research in Africa: Support is offered for doctoral dissertation research in the social sciences and humanities in Africa south of the Sahara. Particular attention is given to proposals for research in disciplines which have been underrepresented in African studies, such as sociology and economics. Students with interdisciplinary training, who show competence in the secondary disciplines related to their research, are given special consideration. All full-time students enrolled in doctoral programs in the United States or Canada, as well as citizens or permanent resi-

dents of the United States or Canada enrolled in full-time doctoral programs abroad may apply.

[1914]
Fellowships for Research in Asia: Fellowships are available for doctoral dissertation research in East, South and Southeast Asia in the social sciences and the humanities to be carried out in one or more countries of Asia, except India and Pakistan (those wishing to carry out research in these countries should contact the *American Institute of Indian Studies, Foster Hall, University of Chicago, 1130 East 59th Street, Chicago, Illinois 60639,* or the *American Institute of Pakistan Studies, 138 Tolentine Hall, Villanova University, Villanova, Pennsylvania 19085*). Applications for support of research on India or Pakistan to be conducted *outside* of these countries will be accepted if carried out in conjunction with research of at least nine months duration within either of these countries, funded by another organization. Applications are also accepted to support the advanced research of students in schools where the doctorate degree is not usually offered, such as schools of law, architecture or urban/regional planning. There are no citizenship requirements, however applicants must be enrolled in full-time graduate study at a university in the United States or Canada. The total period of support cannot exceed 24 months.

[1915]
Fellowships for Research in Latin America and the Caribbean: Fellowships are offered for doctoral dissertation research and special preparatory training in the social sciences and the humanities on topics related to aspects of cultural, economic, political, social and scientific development in Latin America or the Caribbean. The program particularly seeks to encourage research in disciplines in which few applications have been received in the past, such as art history, demography and population studies, drama, economics and literature. Similarly, proposals are encouraged for research on geographical areas which have received limited research attention, such as Cuba, other Caribbean countries and Central America. Consideration will be given to comparative projects involving Latin America or the Caribbean and other areas of the world. Fellows are required to affiliate themselves with a university, research institute or other appropriate institution in the country where they will be conducting research. These Fellowships are additionally funded by a grant from the Andrew W. Mellon Foundation.

[1916]
Fellowships for Research in the Near and Middle East: Fellowships are available to all full-time students enrolled in doctoral programs in the United States or Canada for research projects covering an area that includes North Africa, the Middle East, Turkey, Iran and Afghanistan for the period of time since the beginning of Islam. Citizens and permanent residents of the United States and Canada who are enrolled for full-time study in doctoral programs abroad are also eligible. All applicants must plan to spend at least nine months conducting research in one or more countries of the area.

[1917]
Fellowships for Research in Western Europe: Fellowships are offered for doctoral dissertation research in Western Europe and for special preparatory training of scholars in the social sciences and the humanities who are concerned with contemporary European affairs. Preference is given to research in disciplines in which relatively less attention has been devoted to Western Europe, such as economics, sociology, anthropology and social psychology. The program also promotes research on problems of public policy common to Western Europe and North America, particularly urban and regional problems, as well as research on relatively neglected geographical areas of Europe including the Low Countries, Portugal, Spain, Switzerland and Scandinavia. Proposals for comparative research involving Europe and North America may also be considered. All full-time students enrolled in doctoral programs in the United States or Canada are eligible to apply. Citizens and permanent residents of the United States and Canada who are enrolled in full-time study in doctoral programs abroad are also eligible.

Further information from:
  Fellowships and Grants
  Social Science Research Council
  605 Third Avenue
  New York, New York 10016
  U.S.A.

[1918-1926]

SOCIAL SCIENCE RESEARCH COUNCIL
(U.S.A.)

Postdoctoral Grants for Research—Area Studies

Grants for research on foreign areas are offered to scholars whose competence for research in the social sciences or humanities in relation to those areas has been demonstrated by their previous work and who hold a Ph.D. degree. These programs are designed to support research in one country, comparative research between countries in an area and comparative research between areas. Grants are not for training and are not available to candidates for academic degrees; they may be used for travel and research expenses and for maintenance. Awards are normally made for periods of three months to one year; however budgetary limitations may make it impossible to provide full maintenance for the duration of the Grant. Grants may be held concurrently with awards from other organizations and applicants are urged to seek additional sourses of funding. *Closing date:* 1st December for all programs.

[1918]
Grants for Research on Africa: Grants of up to U.S.$12,000 are offered to citizens and permanent residents of the United States and Canada whose competence for research on Africa has been demonstrated, and who intend to make continuing contributions to the field of African studies. Grants are offered for both field research, involving the gathering of original data, as well as for comparative, non-field theoretical research which goes beyond the analysis of previously gathered African materials. If travel to Africa is planned, applicants should arrange for affiliation with an African university or research institute. Collaborative research with African scholars is encouraged.

[1919]
Grants for Research on Contemporary and Republican China: Grants are offered to citizens or permanent residents of the United States or Canada who hold a Ph.D. degree, or its equivalent, for research in North America or abroad on post-imperial China, including studies in which 20th century China is viewed in historical perspective. [Grants for research concerned exclusively with pre-1911 China are offered by the American Council of Learned Societies, q.v.]. Applications are invited from scholars in every discipline of the social sciences and the humanities and from scholars engaged in cross-disciplinary projects. The applicant's salary will be taken into account in determining the amount of the Grant; maximum value is U.S.$25,000. Grants for research in the People's Republic of China are also awarded by the *Committee on Scholarly Communication with the People's Republic of China, 2101 Constitution Avenue, Washington, D.C. 20418.*

[1920]
Grants for Research on Japan: Grants of up to U.S.$25,000 are offered to citizens and permanent residents of the United States and Canada for research in the social sciences and humanities relating to Japan, to be conducted in North America or abroad. Particular interest is shown to disciplines in which less attention has been devoted to Japan, such as architecture, economics, law, psychology, regional planning, and sociology. Grants may be made for joint research projects by two or more eligible scholars, and by eligible scholars who are collaborating with Japanese scholars having other support. This Grant is also supported by the Japan-United States Friendship Commission.

[1921]
Grants for Research on Korea: Grants normally not exceeding U.S.$15,000, are offered to citizens and permanent residents of the United States or Canada. Scholars of all disciplines within the social sciences, the humanities may apply for research relating to North and South Korea, to be undertaken in North America or abroad. Applications for comparative research are strongly encouraged.

[1922]
Grants for Research on Latin America and the Caribbean Area: Grants are offered to social scientists and humanists of any country for research related to cultural, economic, political, social, or scientific development in Latin America or the Caribbean area, including research relevant to more than one area or country or involving a Latin and a non-Latin country. Latin American scholars may present proposals for research in their own country or abroad. There are no citizenship requirements. Applicants ordinarily should have a basic academic degree, acceptable for a university career or other professional appointment; Canadian and United States scholars must hold a Ph.D. degree at the time of application.

Support is available for two to twelve month periods, non-renewable; and usually involve the commitment of all or most of the scholar's time. Grants vary in amount according to need. Applicants should not expect to receive full funding if the cost of their project exceeds U.S.$12,500, nor should they anticipate full salary replacement. Travel expenses for dependents may be funded only for field stays of six months or more. Applicants desiring to improve their competence in language, research methodology, etc., may request funds for preparatory short-term study. These Grants are not offered for writing dissertations, nor to support an institute's research program. This Grant is additionally supported by the Andrew W. Mellon Foundation.

Latin American and the Caribbean International Collaborative Research Grants: Grants are offered jointly to two scholars of approximately equal scholarly maturity in the social sciences or the humanities who wish to collaborate on a project dealing with 19th or 20th century Latin American or Caribbean cultures, societies or institutions. One of the collaborators must be a Latin American or Caribbean scholar; the other must be working in another country within or outside Latin America or the Caribbean. Citizens of the same country are eligible to apply in collaboration only if they are working in different countries.

[1923]
Grants for Research on the Near and Middle East: Grants are offered to citizens and permanent residents of the United States or Canada who have demonstrated competence for research on this area, defined to include North Africa, the Middle East, Turkey, Iran, and Afghanistan, and to cover the time period since the beginning of Islam. The maximum Grant will normally be no more than U.S.$10,000 and may provide for partial maintenance, travel, and research expenses.

[1924]
Near and Middle East Fellowships for Advanced Training for Research on Law and Social Structure: Citizens and permanent residents of the countries of North Africa and the Middle East who have earned the law degree or the Ph.D. or its equivalent in a social science or law are eligible for advanced training for research on law as it related to social structure in these countries. Training, for periods of nine to twelve months will be provided at selected American universities. Support will cover up to U.S.$20,000 for transportation, tuition and living expenses. Interested persons should write to the Council (attention: Law Training Fellowship Program). Competency in written and spoken English is essential. This Program is made through a grant from the United States Agency for International Development.

[1925]
Grants for Research on South Asia: Grants are offered to social scientists and humanists who have demonstrated scholarly expertise on Bangladesh, India, Nepal, Pakistan and Sri Lanka. Applicants must be citizens or permanent residents of the United States or Canada. Applications are welcome for research on all aspects of the societies and cultures of historical and contemporary South Asia. Applicants whose normal place of work is isolated from research materials at major centers of South Asian studies or important research collections may include in their proposals requests for support at such locations. Grants may be used for travel (support for travel to or research within India and Pakistan are not covered by these Grants; funds for this purpose are available from *American Institute of Indian Studies, Foster Hall, University of Chicago, 1130 East 59th Street, Chicago, Illinois 60637;* or the *American Institute of Pakistan Studies, 138 Tolentine Hall, Villanova University, Villanova, Pennsylvania 19085*), research expenses, maintenance and to supplement sabbatical salaries or awards from other sources. Two types of Grants are offered: a relatively small number of awards of up to U.S.$15,000, and a larger number of awards at up to U.S.$5,000. Awards periods may range from two to twelve months.

[1926]
Grants for Research on Southeast Asia: Grants are offered for social scientists and humanists of any nationality, holding a Ph.D. degree or having equivalent research experience, to conduct research on Brunei, Burma, Indonesia, Kampuchea, Laos, Malaysia, the Philippines, Singapore, Thailand, and Vietnam. Comparative research between countries in the area is also encouraged.

Applications are welcome for research on all aspects of the societies and cultures of historical and contemporary Southeast Asia. Research may be carried out in Southeast Asia, at major collections of Southeast Asian materials, or at any other appropriate locale. Scholars whose normal place of work is isolated from major centers for Southeast Asian research may include in their proposals requests for support at such centers. Collaboration and team research projects among scholars of different disciplines, nationalities, or levels of seniority are encouraged.

Grants are available for any period up to 12 months but will not ordinarily exceed U.S.$14,000 per individual. They may be used for travel, research expenses, and maintenance if necessary, and to supplement sabbatical salaries or awards from other sources. Maintenance and travel of dependents may also be included if full-time research will be conducted outside the grantee's home country for more than six months. Funds are limited and all applicants are encouraged to seek other sources of support as well.

Note: The Social Science Research Council sponsors all awards, either independently, or jointly with the American Council of Learned Societies.

Further information from:
Fellowships and Grants
Social Science Research Council
605 Third Avenue
New York, New York 10016
U.S.A.

[1927]

SOCIAL SCIENCE RESEARCH COUNCIL
(U.S.A.)

Fulbright Grants for Research on Economic Policy Coordination Among Industrial Countries.

Grants are offered to American, Western European and Israeli scholars whose research projects promise to increase understanding of the opportunities and constraints that condition economic policy coordination among the advanced industrial countries. Topics of interest include international economic policies and trends, international and regional institutions such as those within the European Economic Community, and the major policy-making institutions and actors in each country as they affect international policy coordination. The study of economic and social policy and of international policy coordination is encouraged within a broad interdisciplinary framework.

Candidates should generally be university-based scholars (including doctoral candidates), but they may come from any academic profession or field. American recipients must carry out most of their research in Western Europe or Israel; European and Israeli recipients must carry out most of their research in the United States. All recipients are expected to devote full-time to their projects during the period of support.

Grants are for two to six months, and include a monthly maintenance allowance of up to U.S.$2,400 for senior scholars with accompanying dependents, and support for travel. Scholars will be responsible for their own housing, benefits, and all other direct and indirect expenses. Program funds are provided by the United States International Communications Agency and by various binational Fulbright Commission.

American applicants should write directly to the Council at the address below. European and Israeli candidates may write to the Council or to the binational educational commission in their country. *Closing date:* 15th January.

Address:
Social Science Research Council
SSRC-Fulbright Research Grants
605 Third Avenue
New York, New York 10158
U.S.A.

[1928]

SOCIAL SCIENCES AND HUMANITIES RESEARCH COUNCIL OF CANADA

Special M.A. Scholarships and The Queen's Fellowships

Special M.A. Scholarships: Approximately 100 awards are available to Canadian students of exceptional promise for studies at Canadian universities.

Queen's Fellowships: Three Special M.A. Scholarship candidates are selected for these Fellowships.

Value: Can$8,760 plus a travel allowance for the award holder only. The Queen's Fellowships also include tuition fees.

Tenable for one year; not renewable.

Eligibility: Open to Canadian citizens who at the time of application: are in the final year of an honours B.A. program or its equivalent at a

Canadian university, or hold a B.A. honours degree or its equivalent from a Canadian university, and have not yet started a master's program; have first class standing in their present or previous course of studies; and intend to pursue full-time graduate studies at a Canadian university for a master's degree.

Note: All candidates must first be nominated by a faculty member of a Canadian university.

Closing date: 15th November for nomination letters; 15th December for applications.

Further information from:
Fellowships Division
Social Sciences and Humanities
 Research Council of Canada
P.O. Box 1610
Ottawa, Ontario
Canada K1P 6G4

[1929]

SOCIAL SCIENCES AND HUMANITIES RESEARCH COUNCIL OF CANADA

Leave Fellowships

Subjects: Social sciences and humanities.

Value: Up to Can$10,000 for full professors; up to Can$9,000 for associate professors; and up to Can$7,000 for assistant professors and others. Under certain conditions, travel allowances for the award holder and dependents and up to Can$2,500 may also be granted for research expenses.

Tenable for a full twelve months or for a shorter period of not less than six months in Canada or elsewhere.

Eligibility: Open to Canadian citizens and permanent residents who are university scholars who, while on leave of absence, will be engaged in some form of creative research and will have held full-time teaching and/or research appointments at Canadian universities for at least five of the preceding six years or will be returning to such an appointment after a period in an administrative position.

Note: Up to two of the qualifying years may be counted for time spent in public service with the Government of Canada or provincial and municipal governments, or with their respective departments, agencies, boards or commissions. Canadian citizens may count appointments at universities abroad. Canadian citizens need not be on the faculty of a university at the time they apply, but all applicants must have a firm commitment of a Canadian university appointment on completion of their leave. When applying it is not necessary for the candidate to know whether he will obtain leave of absence. Leave Fellowships are not for work undertaken as part of the applicant's formal program of studies leading to a degree; registration in a degree course is permitted only when such enrolment is necessary to accomplish the proposed program of work.

Closing date: 1st October.

Further information from:
Fellowships Division
Social Sciences and Humanities
 Research Council of Canada
P.O. Box 1610
Ottawa, Ontario
Canada K1P 6G4

[1930]

SOCIAL SCIENCES AND HUMANITIES RESEARCH COUNCIL OF CANADA

Doctoral Fellowships

Subjects: Social sciences and humanities

No. offered: Approximately 1,200 Fellowships annually.

Value: Up to Can$8,760 for one year. for the award holder and his dependents will be paid. A thesis allowance of up to Can$500 for typing, copying and binding of final version of the thesis plus an allowance for travel necessary to defend it may also be granted.

Tenable for a full twelve months, or for a shorter period of not less than four months in Canada or elsewhere under certain conditions; renewable.

Eligibility: Open to persons who, by the time of taking up the Fellowship, will have completed one year of graduate study or all the requirements for the master's degree beyond the Honours B.A. or its equivalent, and will be registered in a program of studies leading to the Ph.D. or its equivalent.

Fellowships for tenure in Canadian universities are available to Canadian citizens and nationals of other countries who have obtained permanent resident status. Fellowships for tenure in universities abroad are available to Canadian citizens and, under the following conditions, to nationals of other countries; they must have obtained permanent resident status; at the time of application they must have held full-time appointments for two years as members of faculty in a Canadian university; and they must produce satisfactory evidence that they will be returning to a Canadian academic appointment on completion of their Fellowship.

Closing date: Completed application forms must reach the Council by 15th November; renewal applications must reach the Council by 15th January.

Further information from:
Fellowships Division
Social Sciences and Humanities
 Research Council of Canada
P.O. Box 1610
Ottawa, Ontario
Canada K1P 6G4

[1931]

SOCIAL SCIENCES AND HUMANITIES RESEARCH COUNCIL OF CANADA

General Research Grants

Grants are available to Canadian universities to enable them to meet certain requirements of their teaching staff, such as cost of travel to conferences and small research expenses.

Grants will be made on a formula basis according to the number of full-time faculty members in the humanities and social sciences.

Closing date: 1st January.

Further information from:
Fellowships Division
Social Sciences and Humanities
 Research Council of Canada
P.O. Box 1610
Ottawa, Ontario
Canada K1P 6G4

[1932]

SOCIAL SCIENCES AND HUMANITIES RESEARCH COUNCIL OF CANADA

Research Grants

Subjects: Advanced research in the social sciences and humanities.

Value: Research Grants are intended to defray actual costs (subject to some limitation as to rates) attributable to a project. No provision is made for income for the principal investigators nor for the overhead costs of universities.

Place and duration of tenure is dependent upon the nature of the research.

Eligibility: Open to career scholars in Canadian universities, and in certain cases researchers who are not actually employed by a university but who may qualify if their applications meet the same standards of judgment and scholarly merit.

Note: Research Grants are given only in support of free research initiated by the applicants who must apply on their own behalf. Contractual or commissioned research does not qualify for support, and Grants are not given for work undertaken as part of the applicant's formal program of studies leading to a degree. Requests for less than *Can*$2,500 should be addressed to "General Research Program."

Closing date: Applications should be submitted for 15th May or 15th October.

Further information from:
Fellowships Division
Social Sciences and Humanities
 Research Council of Canada
P.O. Box 1610
Ottawa, Ontario
Canada K1P 6G4

[1933]

SOCIAL SCIENCES AND HUMANITIES RESEARCH COUNCIL OF CANADA
Office of International Relations

Grants to Facilitate International Collaborative Research

Purpose: To support (a) small seminars, workshops or colloquia organized jointly by Canadian and foreign scholars to plan, coordinate or evaluate cooperation on specific research topics or themes; and (b) consultations between Canadian and foreign scholars on joint or parallel research projects.

Value: (a) Economy air fares for participation plus a subsistence allowance of *Can*$50 per day. In addition, limited administration costs will be provided. (b) Economy air fares for participation plus a subsistence allowance of *Can*$50 per day. Limited funds for other expenses occasioned by the collaboration may be provided.

Eligibility: Open to Canadian citizens who are private scholars or on the faculty of a Canadian post-secondary institution. Individuals and established Canadian scholarly societies or institutions may apply for seminar support.

Note: Any support offered must be met with reciprocal support from the foreign participant. Direct research project costs are not covered.

Closing date: 1st January and September.

Further information from:
 Fellowships Division
 Social Sciences and Humanities
  Research Council of Canada
 P.O. Box 1610
 Ottawa, Ontario
 Canada K1P 6G4

[1934]

SOCIAL SCIENCES AND HUMANITIES RESEARCH COUNCIL OF CANADA
Office of International Relations

International Scholarly Exchanges

In addition to its regular programmes, the Council administers and promotes international scholarly exchanges in the humanities and social sciences through special exchange programmes.
 Agreements for the exchange of scholars have been made with research institutes and academies in China, France, Hungary, Japan and the Soviet Union.

Further information from:
 Fellowships Division
 Office of International Relations
 Social Sciences and Humanities
  Research Council of Canada
 P.O. Box 1610
 Ottawa, Ontario
 Canada K1P 6G4

[1935]

SOCIAL SCIENCES AND HUMANITIES RESEARCH COUNCIL OF CANADA
Office of International Relations

Travel Grants for International Representation provide assistance to Canadian scholars who hold high executive office or key ad hoc positions in international scholarly organizations for travel to management and policy meetings. Grants cover return economy air fare and *Can*$50 per day subsistence allowance. Both university and private scholars who are Canadian citizens are eligible. *Closing date:* 1st March, July and November.

Travel Grants for International Scholarly Conferences assist both private and university scholars who are Canadian citizens, to participate in scholarly exchange at important international meetings held outside Canada. Grants cover return economy air fare plus *Can*$50 per day subsistence allowance. *Closing date:* 1st March, July and November.

Further information from:
 Office of International Relations
 Social Sciences and Humanities
  Research Council of Canada
 P.O. Box 1610
 Ottawa, Ontario
 Canada K1P 6G4

[1936]

SOCIAL SCIENCES AND HUMANITIES RESEARCH COUNCIL OF CANADA

Aid to Scholarly Publication, Travel and Conference Grants

Learned Journals: The Council makes sustaining grants on an annual basis to learned journals in the field of the humanities and the social sciences which are published and edited in Canada and have a regular schedule of publication. *Closing date:* 30th June of the year preceding that in which the Grant is awarded.

Scholarly Manuscripts: The Council assists the publication of book-length manuscripts of advanced scholarly research which make an original contribution to knowledge, through block grants to the Canadian Federation for the Humanities and the Social Science Federation of Canada. Further information can be obtained from these organizations at *151 Slater Street, Ottawa, Ontario K1P 5H3.*

Travel to Learned Societies: The Council will assist attendance at annual meetings of Canadian learned societies by means of block grants to the Canadian Federation for the Humanities and the Social Science Federation of Canada as well as through grants made directly to various of the societies. Further information can be obtained from these organizations at *151 Slater Street, Ottawa, Ontario K1P 5H3,* or from Council staff.

Conference Grants: The Council will promote scholarly conferences for the exchange and discussion of research findings in the humanities and social sciences. Grants, to be used for travel and subsistence costs, will not generally exceed *Can*$5,000 and the Council's contribution to the cost of subsistence (including meals and lodging) will not exceed *Can*$50 per day for an invited participant.

Further information from:
 Research Communications Division
 Social Sciences and Humanities
   Research Council of Canada
 P.O. Box 1610
 Ottawa, Ontario
 Canada K1P 6G4

[1937]

SOCIETY OF AMERICAN HISTORIANS, INC.

Allan Nevin Prize of U.S.$1,000 and publication is given for the best Ph.D. dissertation in American history accepted by an American university. Each department may nominate one candidate. *Closing date:* 31st December.

Francis Parkman Prize of U.S.$500 and a bronze medal is offered annually for the best book on American history or biography during the year prior to that in which the award is made. Nominations are made by the publishers. *Closing date:* 31st December.

Further information from:
 Society of American Historians, Inc.
 610 Fayerweather Hall
 Columbia University
 New York, New York 10027
 U.S.A.

[1938]

SOCIETY FOR ANIMAL RIGHTS, INC.
(U.S.A.)

Animal Rights Writing Award

One Award of U.S.$300 is given annually to the author of the best published article or book in the field of animal rights.

Further information from:
 Helen Jones, Chairman
 Reviewing Committee
 Animal Rights Writing Award
 Society for Animal Rights, Inc.
 421 South State Street
 Clarks Summit, Pennsylvania 18411
 U.S.A.

[1939]

SOCIETY OF ANTIQUARIES OF LONDON

William Lambarde Memorial Fund Travelling Scholarships: £100 to £300 are offered triennally to promote studies in archaeology and other antiquarian subjects. The awards are next offered in 1985. *Closing date:* 31st December.

Tessa and Mortimer Wheeler Memorial Fund Grants: A number of awards are offered annually to assist students of archaeology in taking part in excavation and field work. Applications may be obtained from the Society. *Closing date:* 31st January.
 The Society's Research Fund also makes a number of annual Grants in support of archaeological and documentary research *Closing date:* 31st December.

Further information from:
 General Secretary
 Society of Antiquaries of London
 Burlington House, Piccadilly
 London
 England W1V 0HS

[1940]

SOCIETY OF APOTHECARIES OF LONDON

Gilison Scholarship in Pathology

Purpose: To encourage original research.

Subjects: Any branch of pathology.

No. offered: One Scholarship every third year.

Value: £1,200 Payments are made twice annually for the duration of the Scholarship.

Tenable for three years, renewable for a second term of three years.

Eligibility: Open to candidates under thirty-five years of age who are either Licentiates or Freemen of the Society, or who obtain the Licence or the Freedom within six months of election of the Scholarship.

Note: Candidates should submit two testimonials and present evidence of their attainments and capabilities as shown by any papers already published, and/or by a detailed record of any pathological work already done. Candidates should also be undertaken and where it is to be carried out. Preference is given to the candidate who is engaged in the teaching of medical science or in its research.

Scholars are required to submit an interim report at the end of the first six months of tenure, and a complete report one month prior to the end of the third year. Any published results should also be submitted to the Society.

Closing date: 1st December.

Further information from:
Society of Apothecaries of London
Black Friars Lane
London
England EC4V 6EJ

[1941]

SOCIETY FOR APPLIED SPECTROSCOPY *(U.S.A.)*

William F. Meggers Award of U.S.$300 and a certificate is given annually to the author of an outstanding paper which has appeared during the preceding year in *Applied Spectroscopy.*

Lester W. Strock Award of U.S.$500 and a medal is given annually for the most outstanding paper in the field of analytical atomic spectroscopy published during the period from July to June preceding the year of the Award. The publication should concern the earth sciences (with special reference to geochemistry and archeology), life sciences (with special reference to agronomy), and stellar and cosmic sciences. This Award is sponsored by the New England Section of the Society.

Further information from:
Society for Applied Spectroscopy
Donna L. Welch, Executive Secretary
P.O. Box 1438
Frederick, Maryland 21701
U.S.A.

[1942]

SOCIETY OF AUTHORS *(U.K.)*

The Society offers four competitive Awards to British citizens:

Eric Gregory Trust Fund Awards are offered annually for the encouragement of young poets.

Candidate must submit a published or unpublished volume of belles-lettres, poetry (not more than 30 poems) or drama-poems. Applicants must be British subjects by birth but not nationals of "Eire or any of the British Dominions or Colonies"; ordinarily resident in the United Kingdom and less than 30 years of age on 31st March in the year of the Award.

The sum paid out in Awards varies from year to year, but in a recent year there were eight awards amounting to a total of £7,000. *Closing date:* 31st October.

Somerset Maugham Awards are given annually on the strength of the promise of a published work. Poetry, fiction, criticism, biography, history, philosophy, belles-lettres and travel books are all eligible for the Awards. Dramatic works are not eligible.

The value of each Award is approximately £500. The winners are required to use the money for a period or periods of foreign travel. Applicants must be British subjects by birth but not nationals of "Eire or any of the British Dominions"; ordinarily resident in the United Kingdom and Northern Ireland and under the age of 35. *Closing date:* 31st December.

Margaret Rhondda Award is given triennially to assist and support a woman journalist. It is to be used towards the expenses of a research project in journalism, and will not exceed £300. Applicants should be British or Commonwealth citizens ordinarily resident in the United Kingdom. *Closing date:* 31st December.

Tom-Gallon Trust Awards are offered in even-numbered years to fiction writers of limited means who have had at least one short story accepted for publication. Preference is given for work of a traditional rather than of an experimental character. Awards amount to about £100 a year for two years. *Closing date:* Mid-September.

Note: The Society also presents the *Cholmondeley Award for Poets* and the *Hawthornden Prize* which are non-competitive awards based on the strength of already-published work. Submissions for these awards are not sought.

Further information from:
 Secretary for Awards
 Society of Authors
 84 Drayton Gardens
 London
 England SW10 9SD

[1943]

SOCIETY OF AUTOMOTIVE ENGINEERS—AUSTRALASIA

J.E. Batchelor Award is given annually for an outstanding paper presented to any division or group of the Society. The Award of A$150 is open to any person who is resident in Australia, New Zealand or territories administered by the governments of Australia or New Zealand. Only *Rodda Award* recipients are ineligible. *Closing date:* 31st December for nominations.

Gas Turbine Award of a medal and certificate is given annually to a person who has made an outstanding original contribution to gas turbine technology within Australia or New Zealand. Any resident of Australia, New Zealand or territories administered by the governments of those countries is eligible. *Closing date:* 31st December.

Hartnett Award is given annually for an outstanding original contribution to automotive or aeronautical engineering knowledge or practice, in any branch of the profession, or within the scope of activities or interests of the Society. Any person who is a resident of Australia, New Zealand or territories administered by the governments of Australia or New Zealand is eligible for consideration. *Closing date:* 31st December.

O'Shannessy Award of A$100 is given annually for an outstanding paper delivered to any division or group of the Society or published in the journal by any person who is a resident of Australia, New Zealand or territories administered by the governments of Australia or New Zealand. *Rodda Award* and *J.E. Batchelor Award* winners are ineligible. Nominees must be less than 30 years of age. *Closing date:* 31st December.

Rodda Award of A$500 is given annually to a member of any grade in the Society who has submitted an outstanding written paper concerned with the original work and ideas in the fields of design, development, research or management relevant to the automotive industry. Division or independent group committees may nominate candidates before 31st December in any year.

Further information from:
 Society of Automotive
  Engineers-Australasia
 191 Royal Parade
 Parkville, Victoria
 Australia 3052

[1944]

SOCIETY OF AUTOMOTIVE ENGINEERS, INC. *(U.S.A.)*

Russell S. Springer Award of U.S.$150 is made annually to the youngest member of the Society whose paper, presented before an SAE Section, is published in SAE literature in the year of the Award. Entrants should be no more than 36 years of age.

Note: The Society also makes the following Awards and Medals, which have no monetary value: *Vincent Bendix Automotive Electronics Engineering Award; Edward N. Cole Automotive Engineering Innovation Award; Arch T. Colwell Merit Award: Arch T. Colwell Cooperative Engineering Medal; Horning Memorial Award; Ralph H. Isbrandt Automotive Safety Engineering Award; Manly Memorial Medal; Wright Brothers Medal;* and the *Franklin W. Kolk Air Transporation Progress Award.*

Further information from:
Society of Automotive Engineers, Inc.
400 Commonwealth Drive
Warrendale, Pennsylvania 15096
U.S.A.

[1945]

SOCIETY OF COMPANY AND COMMERCIAL ACCOUNTANTS *(U.K.)*

Annual Textbook Award

The £250 Award is given annually to the author of the most outstanding students' textbook published in the following fields: bookkeeping, business economics, commercial law, accounting, internal auditing, industry and finance, company law, business taxation, cost and management accounting, and business administration. There are no restrictions as to age, sex, citizenship, residency, or academic requirements. Presentations are also made to the publishers of the Award-winning book.

Further information from:
Society of Company and Commercial
Accountants
40 Tyndalls Park Road
Clifton, Bristol
England BS8 1PL

[1946]

SOCIETY OF COSMETIC CHEMISTS *(U.S.A.)*

Awards

Chapter Award: U.S.$250 and a scroll are presented annually to the author of the best technical or scientific paper delivered at a Chapter meeting during a calendar year.

Literature Award: U.S.$2,000 and a scroll are presented annually to the author of a scientific paper in basic research which is judged to be an outstanding contribution to cosmetic science and technology.

Medal Award: The Society's highest award is presented annually to an individual for accomplishments in actively supporting the best interests of the cosmetics industry through technical contributions.

Society Awards: A number of Awards of U.S.$1,000 and U.S.$2,000 and a few honorable mention Awards of U.S.$500 are given annually to recognize scientific achievements and outstanding contributions to research in fields particularly pertinent to the cosmetic and toiletries industry.

Society Fellowship Awards: Up to two Fellowships in the amount of U.S.$10,000 each are given annually to the awardee and his or her academic institution for a meritorious research proposal related to cosmetic science.

Society Frontiers of Science Lecture: U.S.$2,000 is given annually to invite scientists of international renown to present the results of their latest research at the Society's annual scientific meeting. This Award is sponsored by the Miranol Chemical Company, Inc.

Society Student Research Awards: Up to three graduate or undergraduate awards, each in the amount of U.S.$1,000 and a scroll, are presented annually for the most meritorious unpublished manuscripts based on original scientific research in disciplines relevant to cosmetic science.

Further information from:
Society of Cosmetic Chemists
Suite 1701, 1995 Broadway
New York, New York 10023
U.S.A.

[1947]

SOCIETY OF EXPLORATION GEOPHYSICISTS FOUNDATION *(U.S.A.)*

SEG Scholarships

Subjects: Geophysics and related earth sciences.

No. offered: Approximately 100 to 110 awards annually, depending upon the funds available.

Value: Usually between U.S.$750 and U.S.$1,500 per academic year.

Tenable at any college in the United States offering a course of study in geophysics, for one academic year; renewable.

Eligibility: Open to citizens of any country who are students at the high school, undergraduate or graduate level, with above-average grades and aptitude for physics, mathematics, and geology.

Note: Recipients must intend to pursue a college course directed towards a career in geophysics, or related career approved by the Society.

Closing date: 1st March of the award year.

Further information from:
Society of Exploration Geophysicists
  Foundation
Box 3098
Tulsa, Oklahoma 74101
U.S.A.

[1948]

SOCIETY OF THE FRIENDLY SONS OF ST. PATRICK OF PHILADELPHIA

Scholarships for Graduate Irish Students

Subjects: Unrestricted; study toward a master's or doctorate degree.

No. offered: One Scholarship offered every two years.

Value: Cost of tuition, plus living expenses.

Tenable at a university in the Philadelphia area for two years; renewable for a third year at the option of the Society.

Eligibility: Open to Irish men and women who are graduates of Irish universities or colleges who wish to pursue studies in the Philadelphia area toward a master's or doctorate degree.

Note: The Scholar is selected by Irish universities and a U.S. government representative in Ireland. College seniors should apply to the university they are attending in Ireland.

Further information from:
Society of the Friendly Sons
  of St. Patrick of Philadelphia
506 Bailey Building
1218 Chestnut Street
Philadelphia, Pennsylvania 19107
U.S.A.

[1949]

SOCIETY FOR HISTORIANS OF AMERICAN FOREIGN RELATIONS

Stuart L. Bernath Book Prize: U.S.$500 is awarded annually to recognize and encourage distinguished research and writing in any aspect of American foreign relations. The submitted work should be the author's first or second book. *Closing date:* 1st February.

Stuart L. Bernath Scholarly Article Award: U.S.$200 is awarded annually for the best submitted article in the field of diplomatic relations. Eligible scholars should be less than 35 years of age, or be within 5 years of receiving the Ph.D. degree at the time of publication. *Closing date:* 1st February.

Further information from:
  Gary R. Hess, National Office
  Society for Historians of American
    Foreign Relations
  Bowling Green State University
  Department of History
  Bowling Green, Ohio 43403
  U.S.A.

[1950]

SOCIETY FOR THE HISTORY OF TECHNOLOGY *(U.S.A.)*

Dexter Prize: U.S.$1,000 and a plaque are given annually to the author of a book on the history of technology published during the three years preceding the award. Both authors and publishers may submit books, written in any language, for consideration.

Joan Cahalin Robinson Prize: One Prize of U.S.$150 is given annually for the best paper presented at the Society's annual meeting, by a person under 30 years of age. Papers are to be submitted one full month prior to the meeting.

Abbott Payson Usher Prize: U.S.$250 and a certificate are given annually for an article or publication published by the Society in the three years before the award is given.

Further information from:
  Carroll Pursell
  Department of History
  University of California at Santa Barbara
  Santa Barbara, California 93106
  U.S.A.

[1951]

SOCIETY FOR ITALIAN HISTORICAL STUDIES *(U.S.A.)*
American Historical Association

Prize

The Society, affiliated with the American Historical Association, offers a Prize of *U.S.*$200 for the best unpublished study in the history of Italy, of article or dissertation length. Since the object of the award is to encourage fresh interest in Italian history, the Prize is offered for a first or second study in the field by a scholar under 35 years of age. Scholars and students regularly resident in the United States or Canada are eligible.

A double-spaced typescript or photocopy should be submitted in triplicate. The name and address of the author, brief vita, a short statement of interests, and the date of completion of the manuscript should be enclosed. Acceptance of a study for publication during the period of judging will not debar it from consideration.

Manuscripts should be received by 1st September. The winning entry will be announced in December.

Further information from:
  Prof. Alan J. Reinerman
  Executive Secretary-Treasurer
  Society for Italian Historical Studies
  c/o Department of History
  Boston College
  Chestnut Hill, Massachusetts 02167
  U.S.A.

[1952]

SOCIETY OF MEDICAL FRIENDS OF WINE

Wine Research Award

One Award of *U.S.*$1,000 is given every two years for an original published contribution or contributions of conspicuous value in identifying substances in wine, or in ascertaining the effects of components of wine on living cells, tissues or organs, or in indicating effective clinical applications of wine in the treatment or prevention of disease.

Further information from:
  Society of Medical Friends of Wine
  P.O. Box 218
  Sausalito, California 94965
  U.S.A.

[1953]

SOCIETY OF NAVAL ARCHITECTS AND MARINE ENGINEERS *(U.S.A.)*

Graduate Scholarships

Purpose: To encourage young men and women to enter the field of naval architecture and marine engineering.

Subjects: Awards are primarily for advanced study in naval architecture and marine engineering, but not necessarily limited to those subjects.

No. offered: Approximately five Scholarships annually.

Value: Variable; usually covers tuition costs at the selected school.

Tenable for one year; not renewable.

Eligibility: Applicants should be citizens of the United States or Canada who are college graduates of a recognized technical institution.

Note: The Society also awards some Scholarships of *U.S.*$1,000 for undergraduates.

Closing date: 1st February.

Further information from:
  Robert G. Mende
  Secretary and Executive Director
  Society of Naval Architects and Marine Engineers
  One World Trade Center
  Suite 1369
  New York, New York 10048
  U.S.A.

[1954]

SOCIETY OF PHOTO-OPTICAL INSTRUMENTATION ENGINEERS *(U.S.A.)*

George W. Goddard Award: U.S.$100 and a plaque are given annually to an individual for recognition of exceptional work in the field of photo-optical instrumentation technology. Preference is given to application work which has reached a successful completion within five years of the date of the Award.

Alan Gordon Memorial Award: U.S.$100 and a plaque are given annually to a worker, who, through his application of photo-optical instrumentation, has contributed substantially to the status of the discipline.

Rudolf Kingslake Medal and Prize: U.S.$1,000 and a silver-plated bronze medal are awarded annually in recognition of the most noteworthy original paper to appear in the Society's journal, *Optical Engineering*, on the theoretical or experimental aspects of optical engineering. All papers published in the journal are automatically considered for the Prize. Submissions are invited from all qualified professional engineers, scientists and technical practitioners having an appropriate interest in the field of optical engineering.

Note: The Society also awards other medals and prizes which are open to Society members only, or have no monetary value.

Not confirmed for 1983.

Further information from:
Society of Photo-Optical Instrumentation Engineers
P.O. Box 10
Bellingham, Washington 98225
U.S.A.

[1955]

SOCIETY OF PLASTICS ENGINEERS, INC. *(U.S.A.)*

International Awards

The following Awards are offered annually, and each consists of U.S.$1,000, a medal or plaque and a travel allowance to the Society's technical conference, where the presentation will be held. The Awards are open to individuals of any nationality, and candidates do not need to be members of the Society. Nominations can be made by both members and non-members.

International Award: Given for fundamental and outstanding contribution to plastics science engineering. The recipient of this Award will be expected to deliver a lecture at the Society's technical conference. *Closing date:* 1st November.

SPE Awards for Research, Education, Engineering/Technology and Business Management: Four Awards, one in each area, are given for fundamental and outstanding contributions to the related fields. *Closing date:* 1st November.

SPE Awards for Unique and Useful Plastic Products: Two Awards, one for a consumer product and one for an industrial product, are given to the designers or creators of products judged on the following criteria: uniqueness in the use of plastics; manner in which plastics contribute to making the products possible; usefulness of the products to their intended ultimate consumer; and creativity shown in using plastics to solve a design problem. The products must be commercially available at the time of nomination. *Closing date:* 1st December.

Further information from:
Chairman, Awards Committee
Society of Plastics Engineers, Inc.
Fairfield Drive
Brookfield Center, Connecticut 16805
U.S.A.

[1956]

SOCIETY FOR THE PROTECTION OF ANCIENT BUILDINGS *(U.K.)*

Plunket Memorial Scholarships

Subject: Architecture—construction, treatment and repair of old buildings. Among items covered in the first six months are: repairs to timber, stone and brick; roof structure and claddings; thatching; leadwork and lead casting; selection of stone; quarrying; bell hanging; inspection and recording of failures; building adaptations; and evidence-giving at public inquiries. The remaining three months are spent in detailed study of the history and culture of the English country house.

No. offered: Three Scholarships annually.

Value: £2,250, paid in monthly instalments.

Tenable for nine months (April through December). Study involves travel throughout England.

Eligibility: Open to those who have passed the Royal Institute of British Architects' Part II examinations or who have equivalent qualifications. Individuals with degrees in structural engineering, building surveying or closely related fields may also apply.

Closing date: 31st December annually.

Further information from:
Society for the Protection of
  Ancient Buildings
55 Great Ormond Street
London
England WC1N 3JA

[1957]

SOCIETY FOR THE PSYCHOLOGICAL STUDY OF SOCIAL ISSUES *(U.S.A.)*

Gordon Allport Intergroup Relations Prize of US$250 is given annually for the best submitted paper or article of the year on intergroup relations. Originality, whether theoretical or empirical, will be given special consideration. The area of research includes age, sex, race, and social-economic status. Entries may be submitted by either Society members or non-members; graduate students are especially urged to compete. Papers should be published during the current year or be unpublished manuscripts. In the latter case, the winning paper will be published in the *Journal of Social Issues*. Entries should be submitted in triplicate to the address below. *Closing date:* 1st December.

Social Issues Dissertation Awards of US$1,200 (first prize) and US$500 (second prize) are given annually for the best submitted doctoral dissertation in psychology or social science with psychological subject matter. The competition is open to all persons who have had their dissertation approved during the twelve month period beginning 1st March of the year prior to that in which the awards are made. Selection is based upon scientific excellence and potential application to social problems.

Applicants should submit four anonymous copies of their dissertation abstract; one copy of the abstract with identification, including name, address, telephone, school, and dissertation title; and a certificate by the dissertation advisor stating date that it has been accepted to: *Norbert L. Kerr, Ph.D., Department of Psychology, Snyder Hall, Michigan State University, East Lansign, Michigan 48823*.

Further information from:
Society for the Psychological Study of
  Social Issues
Central Office
P.O. Box 1248
Ann Arbor, Michigan 48106
U.S.A.

[1958]

SOCIETY FOR THE STUDY OF SOCIAL PROBLEMS

C. Wright Mills Award

An annual Award of US$500 is given to an author for a book, selected as best exemplifying social science scholarship. The books nominated must be published during the year preceding that in which the Award is made.

Closing date: 15th April for presentation to be made in August.

Further information from:
Society for the Study of Social Problems
208 Rockwell Hall
State University College at Buffalo
1300 Elmwood Avenue
Buffalo, New York 14222
U.S.A.

[1959]

FREDERICK SODDY TRUST *(U.K.)*

Grants

The Trust awards up to eight Grants per year of £100 to £250 each to groups studying the whole life of a particular area in Great Britain or elsewhere. Preference is given to students of the sociological sciences and particularly to younger men and women, both teachers and students.

Further information from:
 Chairman
 Federick Soddy Trust
 9 The Drive
 Hove, Sussex
 England BN3 3JS

[1960]

SOROPTIMIST INTERNATIONAL OF GREAT BRITAIN AND IRELAND

Golden Jubilee Fellowship

Purpose: To assist women who wish to advance their education in their particular field.

Subjects: Unrestricted.

No. offered: Usually four or five Fellowships annually, depending upon available funds.

Value: £150 to £350, based on individual needs. Awards are paid in a lump sum at the beginning of the academic year.

Tenable in any country where there is a member club. Fellowships are for one year, not renewable, though Fellows may reapply.

Eligibility: Open to women who are resident in any country where there is a member club. There are no restrictions as to age or academic qualifications. Each case is considered on its individual merits.

Note: There are member clubs in the following countries: Australia; Barbados; Fiji, Grenada; Hong Kong; India; Republic of Ireland; Jamaica; New Zealand; Pakistan; South Africa; Sri Lanka; Thailand; Trinidad; United Kingdom; and Zimbabwe.

Closing date: 31st March.

Further information from:
 Soroptimist International of Great Britain and Ireland
 63 Bayswater Road
 London
 England W2 3PJ

[1961]

SOUTH AFRICAN ASSOCIATION OF UNIVERSITY WOMEN

Students' Aid Fund

Subjects: Unrestricted.

No. offered: As many Grants as funds allow.

Value: R100 per annum.

Tenable at any university in South Africa; renewable.

Eligibility: Open to South African women of all races who have completed at least one year at a university and are in need in assistance.

Closing date: 15th January.

Further information from:
 Fellowships Secretary
 South African Association of University Women
 P.O. Box 342
 6140-Grahamstown
 South Africa

[1962]

SOUTH AFRICAN ASSOCIATION OF UNIVERSITY WOMEN

S.A.A.U.W. International Fellowship

Subjects: Unrestricted; postgraduate research.

No. offered: One Fellowship, when advertised.

Value: R1,000.

Tenable in South Africa, for not less than six months.

Eligibility: Open to members of the International Federation of University Women.

Closing date: 31st August.

Further information from:
 Fellowships Secretary
 South African Association of University Women
 P.O. Box 342
 6140-Grahamstown
 South Africa

[1963]

SOUTH AFRICAN ASSOCIATION OF UNIVERSITY WOMEN

Edna Machanick Award

Subjects: Unrestricted.

No. offered: 3 or 4 Awards annually.

Value: R250 per annum.

Tenable at any institution of tertiary education.

Eligibility: Open to South African women of all races in need of financial assistance to complete their studies toward qualification at the tertiary education level.

Closing date: 15th January.

Further information from:
    Fellowships Secretary
    South African Association of University Women
    P.O. Box 342
    6140-Grahamstown
    South Africa

[1964]

SOUTH AFRICAN ASSOCIATION OF UNIVERSITY WOMEN

Isie Smuts Research Award

Subjects: Unrestricted: research.

No. offered: Awarded annually.

Value: R250.

Tenable in South Africa.

Eligibility: Open to members of the South African Association of University Women.

Closing date: 15th June.

Further information from:
    Fellowships Secretary
    South African Association of University Women
    P.O. Box 342
    6140-Grahamstown
    South Africa

[1965]

SOUTH AFRICAN ASSOCIATION OF UNIVERSITY WOMEN

Bertha Stoneman Memorial Award for Botanical Research

No. offered: Awarded annually.

Value: R250.

Tenable in South Africa.

Eligibility: Open to members of the South African Association of University Women.

Closing date: 15th June.

Further information from:
    Fellowships Secretary
    South African Association of University Women
    P.O. Box 342
    6140-Grahamstown
    South Africa

[1966]

SOUTH AFRICAN ATOMIC ENERGY BOARD

Bursaries

Subjects: Engineering; physics; chemistry; biochemistry; geology; metallurgy; material science; microbiology.

No. offered: Varies annually, subject to need and available funds.

Value: Bursaries cover hostel and tuition fees, plus an allowance for books and pocket-money.

Tenable at South African universities for pre-graduate studies; any where for post-graduate studies. Bursaries are renewable for the duration of the course for which the award is made.

Eligibility: Open to South African citizens and residents who have obtained a four-year degree with above average academic achievements.

Note: Application forms are available by writing to the address below.
    There are no deadlines for application,

however candidates are urged to apply early in the year.

Further information from:
  Personnel Officer
  South African Atomic Energy Board
  Private Bag X256
  Pretoria 0001
  South Africa

[1967]

SOUTH AFRICAN-AUSTRIAN SCHOLARSHIP EXCHANGE PROGRAMME

Scholarships

Subjects: Unrestricted.

No. offered: Two Scholarships annually.

Value: R303 to R393 per month.

Tenable at any appropriate institution in Austria for one academic year.

Eligibility: Open to South African graduates with a B.A. from a South African university.

Note: Knowledge of German is required.

Closing date: 1st February.

Further information from:
  Secretary
  Austrian Embassy
  Box 851
  Pretoria
  South Africa

[1968]

SOUTH AFRICAN BUREAU OF RACIAL AFFAIRS

SABRA Bursaries

Four R100 Bursaries are offered annually for training in development strategy in the fields of social science and law. They are tenable in Afrikaans universities in South Africa, and open to undergraduates who have participated in the Bureau's youth programme.

Closing date: 31st January.

Further information from:
  Director
  South African Bureau of Racial Affairs
  P.O. Box 2768
  Pretoria 0001
  South Africa

[1969]

SOUTH AFRICAN COUNCIL FOR ENGLISH EDUCATION

In-Service Bursaries

Purpose: To assist teachers in service who wish to improve their qualifications.

Value: Dependent upon type of course taken but varying between R200 and R600.

Tenable at any English-medium university or training college in South Africa.

Eligibility: Open to South African teachers in English-medium primary and high schools and lecturers in English-medium training colleges.

Note: Recipients are required to sign an undertaking to teach for not less than one year in South African schools for every R200 received.

Closing date: 15th September in the year preceding that for which the Bursary is required.

Further information from:
  Director of Bursaries
  South African Council for English
    Education
  P.O. Box 660
  Pretoria 0001
  South Africa

[1970]

SOUTH AFRICAN-FRENCH SCHOLARSHIP EXCHANGE PROGRAMME

Scholarships

Subjects: Unrestricted.

Value: R270 per month.

Tenable at any university or academic institution in France for eight months.

Eligibility: Open to South African nationals under 30 years of age who have a B.A. degree from a South African university.

Note: A fair knowledge of French is desirable.

Further information from:
French Embassy
Cultural Section
P.O. Boz 29086
Sunnyside, 0132 Pretoria
South Africa

[1971]

SOUTH AFRICAN INSTITUTE OF RACE RELATIONS, INC.
Harvard-South Africa Fellowship Programme

Subjects: Business and financial management; public administration; secondary education; divinity; law; public health.

No. offered: Three Fellowships annually.

Value: Fellowships cover full board, tuition and travel expenses.

Tenable at Harvard University, Cambridge, Massachusetts for one year.

Eligibility: Open to all South Africans having a bachelor's degree or several years experience in the field of study.

Note: The Institute also offers the *Donald Molteno Award* of R750 for students who are working toward a master's or doctoral degree at any South African university, and whose theses are concerned with constitutional law or history or with race relations.

Further information from:
South African Institute of
   Race Relations, Inc.
68 De Korte Street
Johannesburg 2000
South Africa

[1972]

SOUTH AFRICAN INSTITUTION OF MECHANICAL ENGINEERS
Postgraduate Scholarship

Purpose: To assist in the postgraduate training of engineers so as to prepare them to take a leading part in the future industrial development of South Africa.

No. offered: One Scholarship annually.

Value: Up to R4,000; payments are made in periodic instalments conditional upon satisfactory academic progress.

Tenable for one year of full-time study at an approved university or institution.

Eligibility: Open to South African citizens who are university graduates in engineering and have had some experience in industry since obtaining the degree. Awards are conditional on admittance to the proposed course of study.

Note: A Scholar must undertake to remain for at least two years in suitable employment in industry or research, or in an educational organization in South Africa, upon completion of studies.

Closing date: 15th November.

Further information from:
Secretary
South African Institution of Mechanical
   Engineers
P.O. Box 61019
Marshalltown, 2107 Transvaal
South Africa

[1973]

SOUTH AFRICAN MEDICAL RESEARCH COUNCIL
Scholarships for Study in South Africa

Purpose: To assist students who have obtained a degree and who wish to obtain an advanced degree in one of the medical sciences.

Subjects: Physiology, biochemistry, pharmacology, anatomy, veterinary science, genetics, immunology, biophysics, bioengineering, microbiology, dentistry, biostatistics, nursing dietetics.

Value: As determined by the Council from time to time.

Tenable in South Africa.

Eligibility: Open to candidates in the faculties of medicine, dentistry, veterinary science, and engineering who hold a B.Sc. or B.Sc. honours degree. Applicants should be citizens of South Africa or domiciled in South Africa.

Further information from:
South African Medical Research Council
P.O. Box 70
Tygerberg 7505
South Africa

[1974]

SOUTH AFRICAN MEDICAL RESEARCH COUNCIL

Scholarships for Research and Study Overseas

Purpose: To support research in medical and related sciences where facilities are not available or are inadequate in South Africa.

Value: As determined by the Council from time to time.

Tenable in approved institutions in Europe, the United Kingdom, North America and Canada for a maximum of two years.

Eligibility: Open to South African scientists under 50 years of age holding at least a master's degree.

Note: Holders of M.R.C. grants must sign an undertaking that they will return to South Africa for at least three years for every year of support or for five years for two years of support.

Further information from:
South African Medical Research Council
P.O. Box 70
Tygerberg 7505
South Africa

[1975]

SOUTH AFRICAN MEDICAL RESEARCH COUNCIL

Miscellaneous Scholarships

Scholarships, each totalling up to R200 a year, may be granted to undergraduate students for the purpose of conducting an individual research project under the supervision of an approved department head or recognized researcher.

Funds are provided for the support of distinguished scientists from abroad to visit local researchers for a maximum period up to one year. Applications for this support must be made by the local scientist.

Should the funds be available, the Council will provide Scholarships tenable for a single year, to a suitable candidate who has just completed his internship. A candidate should show promise in a field of research and will have to undertake a year's training and work within an established research environment within South Africa. The value will be the equivalent of the salary of a senior house physician.

Further information from:
South African Medical Research Council
P.O. Box 70
Tygerberg 7505
South Africa

[1976]

SOUTH AFRICAN NATIONAL COUNCIL FOR THE AGED

Zerilda Steyn Memorial Trust Bursary

Purpose: To advance postgraduate research in the field of the needs and care of the aged in South Africa and Namibia.

No. offered: Several grants are made annually for a variety of small and large projects.

Value: R1,000 per annum.

Tenable in South Africa or Namibia for one year; renewable only in exceptional cases.

Eligibility: Open to researchers in all disciplines caring for the aged.

Closing date: 15th August.

Further information from:
Director
South African National Council for the Aged
P.O. Box 2335
Cape Town 8000
South Africa

[1977]

SOUTH AFRICAN NURSING ASSOCIATION

Bursaries, Scholarships and Grants

The Association administers the following Bursaries, Scholarships and Grants, available to members in good standing of the Association who hold the required registered nursing qualifications: *Commercial Exchange of South Africa Bursaries; Laura Niven Scholarship; South African Military Nursing Services Scholarship; E.B. Winter Scholarship; B.G. Alexander Scholarship; H.C. Horwood Memorial Scholarship; Mary Greta Borcherds Travel Grant; Constance Anne Nothard Research Grant; Dr. P.A. Hendriks Scholarship.*

Further information from:
South African Nursing Association
Private Bag X105
Pretoria 0001
South Africa

[1978]

SOUTH AFRICAN RESERVE BANK

Bursaries

Subjects: Economic, money and banking.

No. offered: Three Bursaries annully.

Value: R1,500 per annum.

Tenable at any university in South Africa for two years.

Eligibility: Open to South Africans who have obtained at least 70% in economics in the final year of the bachelor's degree and who are full-time students at residential universities in South Africa.

Note: Award holders must offer their services to the Bank for a period of time which at least equals that of their support.

Closing date: 31st January.

Further information from:
Secretary
South African Reserve Bank
P.O. Box 427
Pretoria 0001
South Africa

[1979]

SOUTH AFRICAN SOCIETY OF MUSIC TEACHERS

Ellie Marx Memorial Scholarships

Purpose: To promote and encourage study of the performance of stringed musical instruments, and in particular that of the violin, and to assist promising students in the performance of such instruments.

No. offered: Two Scholarships may be held at any given time.

Value: R500 per annum. May be varied at the discretion of the committee.

Tenable at approved institutions or with an approved teacher, outside South Africa, for three years.

Eligibility: Open to young students at institutions in South Africa with exceptional ability, who show promise of becoming outstanding solo performers.

Note: Applications should be made by a teacher on behalf of a student.

Further information from:
National Secretary
South African Society of Music Teachers
P.O. Box 5318
Walmer 6065
South Africa

[1980]

SOUTH AUSTRALIAN GOVERNMENT

Fellowships In Transport Research: One Fellowship of up to A$25,000 per annum is awarded annually for the general purpose of promoting interest in transport in South Australia. Tenable for up to two years at Flinders University of South Australia, the University of Adelaide or the South Australian Institute of Technology. Open to persons holding at least a master's degree who are engaged in some aspect of transportation research. *Closing date:* 30th September.

Research Scholarships for Postgraduate Studies in Transport: Up to three Scholarships of A$4,620 each per annum, paid monthly, are awarded annually for the general purpose of promoting interest in transport in South Australia. Tenable for up to three years at Flinders University of South Australia, the Univesity of Adelaide, or the South Australian Institute of Technology. Open to Australian citizens or permanent residents under 35 years of age, holding an upper second class honours degree or its equivalent. *Closing date:* 31st October.

Further information from:
Secretary
Transport Scholarships Committee
Department of Transport
G.P.O. Box 1599
Adelaide, South Australia
Australia 5001

[1981]

SOUTHEAST ASIAN MINISTERS OF EDUCATION ORGANIZATION

SEAMEO Scholarships

Purpose: To develop and up-grade the professional competence of nationals of member-countries.

Studies: Professional training. Courses depend on offers or requests by member-countries. Most of the programme activities are implemented through SEAMEO's regional centres/projects: Regional Centre for Tropical Biology, Bogor, Indonesia; Regional Centre for Educational Innovation and Technology, Quezon City, the Philippines; Regional Centre for Education in Science and Mathematics, Penang, Malaysia; Regional Language Centre, Singapore; Regional Centre for Graduate Study and Research in Agriculture, Los Baños, the Philippines; Project for Tropical Medicine and Public Health (national centres in Indonesia, Malaysia, the Philippines and Thailand, with headquarters in Bangkok, Thailand); SEAMEO Project in Archaeology and Fine Arts (coordinating unit at the SEAMEO Secretariat, Bangkok, and national centres in Thailand, the Philippines, and Indonesia); and SEAMEO non-formal Education Programme administered by the SEAMEO Secretariat, Bangkok.

Value: Varies according to requirements and courses offered. Usually, allowances are made for tuition, food, accommodation, books and supplies, out-of-pocket allowances, international and domestic travel, and research and thesis support.

Tenable at SEAMEO Regional Centres, listed above.

Eligibility: Candidates must be nominated by the Ministry of Education of the member-country and obtain subsequent acceptance by the SEAMEO Centre or Project.

Further information may be obtained from the Regional Centre/Project, or from:
Director
Southeast Asian Ministers of Education
  Secretariat
Darakarn Building, 920 Sukhumvit Road
Bangkok 11
Thailand

[1982]

SOUTHERN AFRICAN MUSIC RIGHTS ORGANIZATION, LTD.

SAMRO Overseas Scholarship for Southern African Composers of R2,500 per annum, usually for two years, is awarded in June of every third year. Nationals of the Republic of South Africa, Bophutatswana, Botswana, Ciskei, Lesotho, Namibia, Swaziland, Transkei and Venda may apply. Full details of requirements compositions to be submitted are available on request.

SAMRO Scholarship for Performing Artists is similar in detail to the Scholarship for Composers. Full details of requirements and tape recordings to be submitted are available on request.

SAMRO Southern African Bursaries: Ten bursaries of R1,000 each are awarded annually for the study of music at any institution of higher education within SAMRO's territory as described above. Nationals of any country within that territory may apply.

Further information from:
  Gideon Roos, Managing Director
  Southern African Music Rights
    Organization, Ltd.
  P.O. Box 9292
  Johannesburg
  2000 South Africa

[1983]

SOUTHERN ARTS ASSOCIATION *(U.K.)*

Composer-in-Residence Scholarship

Purpose: To provide a measure of financial stability for a young composer at the beginning of his or her career, and through this, to encourage interest in contemporary music in the region covered by the Association, i.e., the counties of Berkshire, Hampshire, Bournemouth/Poole area of Dorset, Isle of Wight, Oxfordshire, West Sussex and Wiltshire.

No. offered: One Scholarship every two or three years. Next Scholarship offered in 1984.

Value: Subject to constant review. The Composer will receive commissions in addition to basic salary.

Tenable for two years with possibility of extension for a third year. The Composer is required to reside for the Scholarship period within the region.

Eligibility: Open to all composers, regardless of age, sex, citizenship or residency. Selection is based on submitted scores and followed up by an interview.

Note: It is intended that the Composer act as a catalyst, giving others insight into his or her own way of composing, and transmitting the excitement of exploring the new rather than following tradition. The Composer will be required to work with performers based in the region, who will be encouraged to commission his works; he may also give lectures, lead discussion, give recitals, or promote and publicise concerts of contemporary music. Should the Composer wish, he or she may become attached to one of the region's arts centers.

Further information from:
  Music Officer
  Southern Arts Association
  19 Southgate Street
  Winchester, Hampshire
  England SO23 9EB

[1984]

SOUTHERN HISTORICAL ASSOCIATION *(U.S.A.)*

Francis Butler Simkins Award: A certificate and cash prize of US$200 are offered in odd-numbered years for a first book by an author or authors in the field of southern history published during the preceding two years.

Charles S. Snyder Award: The Award of US$500 is given in even-numbered years to an author of an outstanding book on southern history published during the preceding two years. Publishers should submit books.

Further information from:
  Bennett H. Wall, Secretary-Treasurer
  Southern Historical Association
  University of Georgia
  Athens, Georgia 30602
  U.S.A.

[1985]

SOUTHWEST REVIEW *(U.S.A.)*

John H. McGinnis Memorial Award

The Award of US$1,000 is offered annually to the author of the best judged story or non-fiction article appearing in the *Southwest Review* during the previous two years. Awards for fiction and non-fiction are given in alternating years and winners are announced in the winter issue.

Further information from:
  Southwest Review
  Southern Methodist University
  Dallas, Texas 75275
  U.S.A.

[1986]

SOVIET GOVERNMENT AWARDS

Subjects: Within the fields of social and human sciences, science and technology, fine arts and crafts, performing arts, education, and technical or vocational/professional studies or training.

No. offered: Approximately 25,000 Awards annually through the Soviet government and various Soviet institutions/organizations (see Note section).

Value: A monthly allowance of 80 to 150 roubles (in 1980), depending upon the level of study, plus free tuition, medical care, and a book allowance. Travel costs to and from the U.S.S.R. are paid by the Soviet government and/or by agencies in the student's home country or international organizations. Asian, African and Latin American students receive a warm clothing allowance. Low-cost hostel accommodation is available. The host institution may meet the cost of certain holiday arrangements.

Tenable at specialized secondary education establishments, specialized institutes, universities or other institutions of higher education in the U.S.S.R.

Duration: Three to four years for specialized secondary education; five to six years for undergraduate courses; three to four years for postgraduate courses; one or two years for advanced training or refresher courses.

Eligibility: Open to nationals of all countries. Requirements: (a) for training in industry, education, culture and health services: candidates should have a general school education equivalent to the Soviet eight-year school system; (b) for undergraduate courses: candidates should have completed a secondary school education, and be between 17 and 35 years of age; (c) for postgraduate courses: candidates should possess a suitable bachelor's degree, and be no more than 35 years of age; (d) for advanced training or refresher courses: candidates should have completed higher specialized education, and may be of any age.

Qualifications conferred: On successful completion of studies: (1) students at specialized secondary educational establishments qualify as technicians and receive a diploma; (2) graduates receive a diploma in their field of specialization (equivalent to a master's degree); (3) graduates who have presented the equivalent of a doctoral thesis receive a Candidate of Science degree.

Note: Foreign students are given further instruction in the Russian language in preparatory departments set up at various institutions. The preparatory departments also run preliminary courses, usually of one year's duration, for students whose national educational system varies substantially from the Russian system.

In most cases, application for admission to Soviet educational institutions should be submitted through the candidate's government to the Soviet diplomatic representative in the country concerned.

Most Soviet awards for foreign nationals are offered through the Ministry of Higher and Specialized Education in Moscow. The Ministry also operates awards under programmes of the United Nations, United Nations Economic Commission for Asia and the Far East, Unesco, International Union of Students and various exchange agreements. Many of the international awards schemes are for students from developing countries. Details of the Exchange Studentships for United Kingdom students offered under the Anglo-Soviet Cultural Agreement are given in entry 219.

Other Soviet organizations/institutions offering awards to foreign nationals include the following (all in Moscow): (i) *All-Union Central Council of Trade Unions*—Scholarships for students from developing countries; (ii) *Centrosoyus (Central Alliance of Consumer Societies of the U.S.S.R.);* (iii) *Patrice Lumumba Friendship University*—Scholarships in agriculture, economics and law, engineering, history and philology, medicine, and in natural physical and mathematical sciences, for students from developing countries; (iv) *Soviet Afro-Asian Solidarity Committee*—Scholarships for nationals of African and Asian countries; (v) *Societ Women's Committee*—Scholarships for African women; (vi) *U.S.S.R. Committee of Youth Organizations*—Scholarships for young people from developing countries; (vii) *Union of Soviet Societies for Friendship and Cultural Relations with Foreign Countries*—Travel Scholarships for students from developing countries.

Further information is available from the agency in candidate's own country which administers bilateral agreements and international exchanges (British Council, U.S. Institute of International Education, Association of Universities and Colleges of Canada, etc.). Candidates may also obtain information through many of the Soviet diplomatic missions.

[1987]

SPALDING TRUSTS *(U.K.)*

Grants-in-Aid of Research

Subjects: Study of world religions other than that of the award holder.

Value: Very limited amounts of the form of small travel Grants and subsistence allowances.

Tenable for short periods of time, usually but not invariably in the United Kingdom.

Eligibility: Open to undergraduates, postgraduates or academics of established reputation who are engaged in the study of a world religion or religions.

Note: Further information is available from *Spalding Trusts, 4 Park Town, Oxford OX2 6SH* or from:
General Secretary, Spalding Trusts
Orchard House
Steeple Langford
Salisbury, Wiltshire
England SP3 4NQ

[1988]

SPASTICS SOCIETY *(U.K.)*

Grants are awarded within the United Kingdom to experienced researchers for projects of a medical or social nature which have direct relevance to cerebral palsy or the problems and needs of cerebral palsied people. Travel grants up to a maximum of £200 are also awarded on the same criteria.

Further information from:
Spastics Society
12 Park Crescent
London
England W1N 4EQ

[1989]

SPECIAL LIBRARIES ASSOCIATION *(U.S.A.)*

Scholarships

Purpose: To train men and women in the theory and practice of library science, emphasizing special libraries which provide research and information services within business, industry or government.

No offered: Varies; one or two offered in 1982.

Value: Varies; US$5,000 in 1982.

Tenable for one academic year of graduate study, or an alternative plan of study acceptable to the Committee, at a recognized school of library or information science in the United States or Canada.

Eligibility: Open to college graduates working in a special library or with experience in a special library, and to recent college graduates wishing to enter special librarianship. Applicants must be citizens of the United States or Canada.

Note: Special librarians are trained both in library and information science in the fundamentals of a particular subject field, such as social sciences, economics, fine arts, engineering, sciences.

Closing date: 15th January.

Further information from:
Scholarship Committee
Special Libraries Association
235 Park Avenue South
New York, New York 10003
U.S.A.

[1990]

SPECIAL LIBRARIES ASSOCIATION *(U.S.A.)*

Plenum Scholarship

Purpose: To enable the recipient to study for a doctoral degree in library or information science (preferably special librarianship).

Value: US$1,000.

Tenable for one academic year at a recognized school of library or information science in the U.S. or Canada.

Eligibility: Open to Ph.D. candidates with an interest in special librarianship. Applicants should be citizens of the United States or Canada whose dissertation topics have been approved.

Closing date: 15th January.

Further information from:
Plenus Scholarship Committee
Special Libraries Association
235 Park Avenue South
New York, New York 10003
U.S.A.

[1991]

SPECIAL LIBRARIES ASSOCIATION
(U.S.A.)

Positive Action Program for Minority Groups—Stipend Program

Purpose: To train minority group members in the theory and practice of library science, emphasizing special libraries which provide research and information services within business, industry or government.

Subjects: Library and information sciences.

No. offered: Varies; up to three offered in 1982.

Value: Varies; US$2,000 in 1982.

Tenable for one semester or one-quarter of graduate study leading to a master's degree in library or information science.

Eligibility: Open to minority group members who are college graduates, college seniors or matriculated graduate library school students with an interest in special librarianship. Applicants must be citizens of the United States or Canada.

Closing date: 1st March.

Further information from:
Stipend Program
Special Libraries Association
235 Park Avenue South
New York, New York 10003
U.S.A.

[1992]

SPENCER FOUNDATION *(U.S.A.)*

Grants

The Foundation places special emphasis on the support of research in the behavioral sciences which extends or modifies understanding of the processes of education. The Grants are designed to encourage young behavioral scientists to engage in research on educational processes by providing support for their research activities. Grants, ranging from US$500 to US$1,000,000, are paid to institutions, not to the individuals undertaking the research. There are no established time limits for research. Before making detailed proposals, interested individuals and institutions should obtain further information from:
Vice President and Secretary
Spencer Foundation
875 North Michigan Avenue
Chicago, Illinois 60611
U.S.A.

[1993]

LOUIS SPOHR INTERNATIONAL VIOLIN COMPETITION *(Freiburg)*

A First prize of DM10,000, a Second Prize of DM6,000, and other monetary prizes are offered in the Competition which is held in Freiburg periodically. Violinists of any nationality who are not more than 32 years of age may apply.

Further information from:
Secretariat
Internationaler Violinwettbewerb
 Louis Spohr
Burgunderstrasse 4
D-7800 Freiburg
West Germany

[1994]

E.R. SQUIBB AND SONS LTD. *(U.K.)*

Grants

Funds are offered for research which falls within the interests of the company, including cardiovascular disease, anti-fungal drugs, fungal diseases, antibiotic research, schizophrenia, and aspects of dermatology. Grants are tenable at any approved institution; duration of research is not predetermined. Grants are open to nationals of all countries, however they are mostly taken up by researchers already working in the United Kingdom, where the proposed work must be carried out.

Further information from:
  Medical Director
  E.R. Squibb and Sons Ltd.
  Squibb House
  141/149 Staines Road
  Hounslow
  England TW3 3JA

[1995]

JOHN F. AND ANNA LEE STACEY SCHOLARSHIP FUND *(U.S.A.)*

Scholarships

One or more Scholarships of variable amounts totalling approximately US$4,000 are offered annually to students of painting and drawing who are skilled in and devoted to the classical or conservative tradition of western culture.

U.S. citizens between the ages of 18 and 35, although the age limit may be extended in exceptional cases, at the discretion of the selection committee.

Closing date: 1st November.

Further information from:
  John F. and Anna Lee Stacey
    Scholarship Fund
  P.O. Box 2
  Quemado, New Mexico 87829
  U.S.A.

[1996]

STANDING CONFERENCE OF MINISTERS OF EDUCATION AND CULTURAL AFFAIRS OF THE LAENDER *(West Germany)*

Educational Exchange Service

Foreign Language Assistant Exchange Scheme

The Scheme is open to young teachers and university students of German from all countries, for service as foreign language assistants in secondary schools in the Federal Republic of Germany. Candidates should be under 30 years of age and possess a bachelor's degree from a United States university or have studied for two years at a European university. Assistants receive a maintenance allowance for the academic year of DM900 per month; possibility of renewal for one year.

Candidates should apply to the Cultural Attaché at the embassy or consulate of the Federal Republic of Germany in their own country. United Kingdom candidates apply to the *Central Bureau for Educational Visits and Exchanges, Seymour Mews House, Seymour Mews, London W1H 9PE;* Scottish candidates to the *Central Bureau for Educational Visits and Exchanges, 3 Bruntsfield Crescent, Edinburgh EH10 4HD.*

Closing date: 1st February.

Address:
  Educational Exchange Service
  Standing Conference of Ministers of
    Education and Cultural Affairs
  Postfach 2240
  Nassestrasse 8
  5300 Bonn 1
  West Germany

[1997]

STATE AGRONOMICAL SCIENCES FACULTY *(Belgium)*

Scholarships

Subjects: Agronomic sciences: study towards a diploma of the Faculty.

No. offered: One Scholarship annually.

Value: 120,000 Belgian francs.

Tenable at the Faculty for one year; renewable.

Eligibility: Open to nationals of developing countries. Candidates must have a suitable qualification in agriculture, chemistry or industrial agriculture.

Closing date: 1st May.

Further information from:
  State Agronomical Sciences Faculty
  5800 Gembloux
  Belgium

[1998]

STATE COUNCIL OF THE REPUBLIC AND CANTON OF NEUCHÂTEL
(Switzerland)

Scholarships

The Council offers one Scholarship for advanced studies at the University of Neuchâtel, to a member of a British university or college. Applicants should be of British nationality and have a sound knowledge of French. Students of medicine, art or architecture are ineligible. Preference will be given to graduates or to candidates intending to graduate this year. The Scholarship consists of an allowance payable in ten monthly instalments, and an exemption from lecture fees.

Closing date: March.

Further information from:
Swiss Embassy
16 Montagu Place
London
England W1H 2BQ

[1999]

STATE EDUCATION DEPARTMENT *(New York)*

Herbert H. Lehman Graduate Fellowships

Purpose: To provide financial aid to students wishing to enter into a full-time graduate program leading towards a master's or doctoral degree.

Subjects: Social sciences, public affairs or international affairs. Education, social work, law, and other professional studies are not approved subjects for these awards.

No. offered: Thirty Fellowships annually.

Value: US$4,000 for the first year of study and US$5,000 per year thereafter.

Tenable at an approved college in New York State for up to four years.

Eligibility: Candidates should be legal residents of the U.S. (holders of non-immigrant visas do not qualify) for at least one year prior to the effective date of the Fellowship, have received a baccalaureate degree no later than the effective date of the Fellowship and have not yet entered upon any graduate study, part- or full-time, prior to the final date of application.

Note: Interested students should apply in September, or early in their final year of preprofessional or undergraduate study. As application dates and eligibility requirements are subject to change, it is advised that interested individuals contact the address below for an offical application containing a full statement of regulations currently in effect.

Candidates are responsible for having their application and all necessary transcripts, GRE test scores, etc., forwarded to the address below prior to the appropriate deadline.

Further information from:
Herbert H. Lehman Graduate Fellowships
State Education Department
Bureau of Higher and Professional
 Educational Testing
Albany, New York 12230
U.S.A.

[2000]

STATE FARM COMPANIES FOUNDATION
(U.S.A.)

Doctoral Dissertation Award

Purpose: To stimulate research and development of new knowledge in the insurance industry and to increase the number of qualified teachers of insurance in the colleges and universities of the United States.

No. offered: One Award annually.

Value: US$7,500 to the recipient and an additional US$2,500 to the college or university where the student is working towards his or her degree, provided the money is used in support of insurance education.

Tenable at appropriate institutions; not renewable.

Eligibility: Open to students who are United States citizens and have completed a major portion of their doctoral program and are majoring in insurance or a related field of study. Preference will be given to candidates below the age of 35 whose contributions are expected to be made primarily in the United

States. Applicants must be nominated by the director of the doctoral program.

Note: Direct applications from candidates are not considered. Application forms are available to institutions in January.

Closing date for application: 31st March.

Further information from:
State Farm Companies Foundation
One State Farm Plaza
Bloomington, Illinois 61701
U.S.A.

[2001]

STATE HISTORICAL SOCIETY OF WISCONSIN

Alice E. Smith Fellowship

Purpose: To encourage and support research in the field of American history by women.

No. offered: One Fellowship annually.

Value: US$600, paid in one lump sum.

Tenable for one year; generally not renewable.

Eligibility: Open to women undertaking research in American history, with preference given to those applicants doing graduate research in the history of Wisconsin or the Middle West.

Note: Applicants should write to the address below, describing the project in some detail. Letters of application should be approximately two typewritten pages in length.

Closing date: 15th July.

Further information from:
William F. Thompson
Director of Research
State Historical Society of Wisconsin
816 State Street
Madison, Wisconsin 53706
U.S.A.

[2002]

STATE LIBRARY OF NEW SOUTH WALES
(Australia)

C.H. Currey Memorial Fellowship

Three Fellowships are given annually in the amount of A$2,000 each to promote the writing of Australian history from original sources. *Closing date:* 1st October.

Further information from:
State Librarian
State Library of New South Wales
Macquarie Street
Sydney, New South Wales
Australia 2000

[2003]

STATE SERVICES COMMISSION *(N.Z.)*

Supplemental Awards

Purpose: To provide Supplemental Awards to New Zealand public servants who have already accepted scholarships, travel grants, etc., offered by other agencies.

Value: Covers leave on full or proportionate pay. The amount depends on the value of the primary award, the marital status of the officer, and the usefulness to the Service of the study undertaken. Total payments may not exceed the salary and allowances of a New Zealand officer of comparable grade serving abroad.

Tenable in New Zealand or abroad. Duration is tied to that of the primary award but may be extended at the discretion of the Commission.

Eligibility: Open to New Zealand public servants of more than average ability, whose proposed studies will be useful to the Service. Recipient must agree to return to the Service for a set period after tenure of the Award.

Note: Candidates should apply through the department for which they work.

Address:
Secretary
State Services Commission
Private Bag
Wellington
New Zealand

[2004]

STATIONERS' AND NEWSPAPER MAKERS' COMPANY (U.K.)

Stationers' Company Travelling Scholarship

Purpose: To enable the Scholar to study new techniques and management methods in printing, or in one of the associated trades of the guild, i.e., those trades directly concerned with the business of a stationer, printer, publisher, bookbinder, papermaker, paper merchant, and the press.

No. offered: One Scholarship every other year.

Value: Up to £600.

Tenable in the United Kingdom or abroad; usually for periods of between one and three months.

Eligibility: Open to young executives or management trainees in the printing industry, or one of the associated trades of the guild, in the United Kingdom. Candidates must be British nationals between 18 and 35 years of age.

Note: Preference will be given to the son of a freeman of the Stationers' Company, or to a past student of the Stationers' School, or to a past apprentice bound at Stationers' Hall.

Closing date: Mid-December.

Further information from:
 Clerk
 Stationers' Company
 Stationers' Hall, Ludgate Hill
 London EC4M 7DD
 England

[2005]

STATIONERS' AND NEWSPAPER MAKERS' COMPANY (U.K.)

Francis Mathew Travelling Scholarship

Purpose: To enable the Scholar to study existing and new methods of printing, publishing or paper-making, and the conditions and circumstances of the printing, publishing, and paper industry in the United Kingdom or elsewhere.

No. offered: One Scholarship annually.

Value: Up to £600.

Tenable in the United Kingdom and abroad usually for periods of between one and three months.

Eligibility: Open to young executives and management trainees of the printing, publishing, or paper industry in the United Kingom. Candidates must be British nationals between 18 and 35 years of age.

Closing date: Mid-December.

Further information from:
 Clerk
 Stationers' Company
 Stationers' Hall, Ludgate Hill
 London
 England EC4M 7DD

[2006]

TAYLOR STATTEN MEMORIAL FUND (Canada)

Fellowships

Subjects: Any professional field or career related to youth services.

No. offered: One Fellowship annually.

Value: Can$1,500 per annum.

Tenable at any appropriate university for one year.

Eligibility: Open to graduates who are under 25 years of age and are enrolled in an appropriate course in a Canadian university. Candidates should have a high academic standing with previous experience in the youth field.

Closing date: 1st March.

Further information from:
 Office of Student Awards
 Room 107, Simcoe Hall
 University of Toronto
 Toronto, Ontario
 Canada M5S 1A1

[2007]

STEEL AND ENGINEERING INDUSTRIES FEDERATION OF SOUTH AFRICA

SEIFSA Postgraduate Overseas Research Scholarship

Purpose: To enable the holder to undertake research work which must be original and preferably applicable to the metal industries.

Subjects: Chemical, civil, electrical or mechanical engineering; materials science; metallurgy; administration and/or management.

No. offered: One Scholarship annually.

Value: R8,000 per annum plus travel fare.

Tenable at an approved university or institution outside South Africa for two years; may be extended under special circumstances.

Eligibility: Open to South African citizens domiciled in South Africa or South-West Africa who have obtained at least a bachelor's degree in one of the subjects listed. The recipient will be expected to study for a master's or doctor's degree or appropriate equivalent.
At the time of application, a candidate need not necessarily be a student at university, but may be in employment in the metal industries.

Closing date: 31st March.

Further information from:
 Head, Education and Training Division
 Steel and Engineering Industries
  Federation of South Africa
 P.O. Box 1338
 Johannesburg 2000
 South Africa

[2008]

STROUD FESTIVAL INTERNATIONAL COMPOSERS COMPETITION *(U.K.)*

£600 is available for distribution at the discretion of the adjudicators for up to three prizes for a composition of a specific nature, individually prescribed for each year's Competition. Composers of any nationlity who are under 40 years of age on 30th April in the year of the Competition may apply. Compositions which have been publicly performed are not eligible. The adjudicators select the best three entries for performance by professional players at a concert in Stroud during the Festival.
Closing date: 28th February.

Further information from:
 Secretary
 Stroud Festival International Composers
  Competition
 Lenton, Houndscroft
 Stroud, Gloucestershire
 England GL5 5DG

[2009]

STUDY FUND FOR SOUTH AFRICAN STUDENTS *(Netherlands)*

Bursaries

Subjects: Unrestricted.

No. offered: Approximately two Bursaries annually.

Value: 950 Dutch florins per month for board and lodging; a book allowance of 300 Dutch florins; 120 Dutch florins for study tours in the Netherlands; free tuition and refunds for any urgent medical expenses.

Tenable at a Dutch university for one year; not renewable.

Eligibility: Open to South African nationals who possess a degree from any university in South Africa.

Note: No provisions are made toward maintenance of dependants.
Further information may be obtained by writing to the *Secretary, Genootskap Nederland—Zuid-Afrika, P.O. Box 1219, Pretoria 0001, South Africa.*

Closing date: 31st March.

Further information from:
 Secretary
 Study Fund for South African Students
 Keizersgracht 141
 1015 CK Amsterdam
 Netherlands

[2010]

WALTER C. SUMNER FOUNDATION
(Canada)

Fellowships

Subjects: Chemistry, physics and electronics.

No. offered: Approximately six Fellowships annually.

Value: Can$4,000 to Can$5,000 per annum.

Tenable for one year at the following Canadian universities: Dalhousie, McGill, Queen's, Saskatchewan, Toronto and British Columbia. Fellowships are renewable.

Eligibility: Open to Canadian citizens who reside in Canada and hold a degree from a Canadian university other than the one at which the Fellowship will be taken up. Applicants holding only the bachelor's degree are required to have had at least two years' experience in either teaching or industry in their chosen field of study.

Closing date: 15th March.

Further information from:
Walter C. Sumner Foundation
P.O. Box 2187
Halifax, Nova Scotia
Canada

[2011]

SIMONE SUTER SCHOOL OF DANCE
(Lausanne)

Dance Fellowships

No. offered: Two Fellowships annually.

Value: 5,280 Swiss francs.

Tenable in Switzerland for one academic year (September to July).

Eligibility: Open to nationals of all countries who are between 15 and 22 years of age. Candidates should have been engaged in serious study of dance for at least five years.

Note: Two *Bursaries for International Summer Courses,* valued at approximately 350 Swiss francs each, are also available annually for study at the School during the courses in and relating to dance held there each July. Conditions are the same as for the Fellowships and are renewable.

Not confirmed for 1983.

Further information from:
Simone Suter School of Dance
Caroline 7
CH-1003 Lausanne
Switzerland

[2012]

SWANN FOUNDATION FOR CARICATURE AND CARTOON *(U.S.A.)*

Fellowships and Grants-In-Aid

The Foundation makes available an annual Fellowship of US$7,250 (plus US$1,000 for travel expenses) to a Ph.D. candidate working in the field of cartoon and caricature. These are primarily in the history of art, and there is a preference for research into American satiric art. The Foundation also makes a limited number of Grants-in-Aid to individuals doing work consistent with the purposes of the Foundation. The Foundation exists to foster activities leading to an enhanced appreciation of the artistic qualities of cartoon and caricature drawings. It does not award grants in support of an artist's individual work, but it does support publications, research, exhibitions, films, oral history, and related scholarly work in the field. Applicants for Fellowships may obtain application forms from the office of the Foundation. Applicants for Grants-in-Aid should write to the Foundation providing a full statement of the project for which assistance is required, a full budget (including matching support from other grants or institutions), and a statement of personal qualifications. Foundation applications are due mid-February each year.

Further information from:
Henry J. Goldschmidt, President
Swann Foundation for Caricature
  and Cartoon
655 Madison Avenue
New York, New York 10021
U.S.A.

[2013]

SWEDISH CANCER SOCIETY

Research Support

The Society provides funds on a large scale for various aspects of cancer research, mainly in the following fields: biochemistry, virology, immunology, cell biology and pathology. For the improvement of methods of examination and treatment, grants have been provided for surgery, radiotherapy, radiophysics, endocrinology, chemotherapy, interferon research and other fields. Funds may also be provided for the purchase of equipment, consumables, travel expenses and salaries for scientific and technical assistants as well as for the scientists themselves.

Most grants are awarded for one year and are renewable by reapplication. Values per award vary considerably. There are six three-year research appointments, renewable for an additional three years, to enable scientists who lack fixed appointments to continue their research. There are also clinical research stipends which make it possible for a research worker to take a leave of absence from his daily public health duties and devote his full time to research. Many research projects sponsored by the Society are long-range and may involve funding for up to ten years.

Candidates may be of any nationality—research is to be carried out in Sweden. Support is also available to Swedish researchers for work to be carried out in countries other than Sweden.

Closing dates: 1st February and 1st October.

Further information from:
Swedish Cancer Society
Sturegatan 14
S-114 36 Stockholm
Sweden

[2014]

SWEDISH INSTITUTE

Bilateral Scholarships

Subjects: Unrestricted.

No. offered: 60 Awards annually.

Value: 2,600 Swedish kronor per month. No travel grants are offered.

Tenable in Sweden for periods ranging from four to eight months.

Eligibility: Open to nationals of Austria, Belgium, Bulgaria, Canada, China, Czechoslovakia, Denmark, Finland, France, Federal Republic of Germany, Hungary, Iceland, Italy, Japan, Netherlands, Poland, Switzerland, U.S.S.R., United Kingdom, and Yugoslavia.

Note: Applications should be submitted in the autumn preceding the Scholarship year through the authorities in the applicant's home country. A good knowledge of Swedish and/or English is required.

Further information from:
Swedish Institute
P.O. Box 7434
S-103 91 Stockholm
Sweden

[2015]

SWEDISH INSTITUTE

Council of Europe Higher Education Scholarships

The Institute awards ten Scholarships annually to citizens of member-states of the Council for Cultural Co-operation of the Council of Europe. Scholarships are for study in any subject and are at a value of 2,600 Swedish kronor per month, tenable for nine months. No travel grants are provided. Candidates should have completed a first degree course at university and have a good knowledge of Swedish and/or English.

Closing date: 15th January.

Further information from:
Swedish Institute
P.O. Box 7434
S-103 91 Stockholm
Sweden

[2016]

SWEDISH INSTITUTE

Guest Scholarships

Purpose: To aid foreign students who wish to complete an education already begun, to enter into a programme of further education or research, or to take certain special courses of training or study which can be completed within three years.

Subjects: Restricted to areas in which Sweden can offer scientific, scholarly or other special advantages.

Value: 2,600 Swedish kroner per month. No travel grants are offered.

Tenable in Sweden for up to three years.

Eligibility: Open to people from any part of the world are unable to obtain financial aid from their own country for studies in Sweden and who do not intend to settle permanently in Sweden.

Note: Prior to application, an eligibility test is administered to each candidate who must supply the following information: (a) name, (b) nationality, (c) education background including degree, if any, and/or work experience, (d) knowledge of languages and, (e) statement of purpose for training, study or research indicating clearly the reason for selecting Sweden as the place of study.
A good knowledge of the Swedish and/or English language is required.

Closing date: 1st December.

Further information from:
Swedish Institute
P.O. Box 7434
S-103 91 Stockholm
Sweden

[2017]

SWEDISH INSTITUTE

Fellowship for Strindberg Research

A Fellowship consisting of free accommodation in Stockholm is available to a scholar from abroad engaged in research on Strindberg. The Fellowship period will normally be not less than one month. Applications stating name, age, academic qualifications and a detailed statement of the proposed research must be submitted by 1st May.

Address:
Swedish Institute
P.O. Box 7434
S-103 91 Stockholm
Sweden

[2018]

SWEDISH NATIONAL ASSOCIATION AGAINST HEART AND CHEST DISEASES

Scholarships

Subjects: Cardiology, pneumology; research.

No. offered: Two Scholarships annaully in cardiology; two Scholarships annually in pneumology.

Value: 36,000 Swedish honor.

Tenable at a Swedish hospital or medical institution for one year; not renewable.

Eligibility: Open to non-Swedish cardiologists or pneumologists under 45 years of age, who have proven ability for research, are engaged in actual research in the field, and are interested in studying a special problem in Sweden.

Note: Applications for the two cardiological Scholarships and one of the pneumological Scholarships should be made to the *Office of Research Promotion and Development, World Health Organization, 1211 Geneva 27, Switzerland.* Applications for the other pneumological Scholarship should be sent to the *International Union against Tuberculosis, 3 rue George Ville, 75116 Paris, France.*
Applications must be endorsed by the candidate's institute or clinic, which should ensure a post and research facilities for the recipient after tenure of the award.

Address:
Swedish National Association against
  Heart and Chest Diseases
Kungsgatan 54
S-111 35 Stockholm
Sweden

[2019]

SWEDISH NATURAL SCIENCE RESEARCH COUNCIL

Swedish Government Grants

A limited number of Grants are offered to foreign scientists for visits to Swedish research institutes to study natural sciences including mathematics. These Grants are primarily connected to special research programmes. Usualy, foreign scientists should be nominated by a leading Swedish scientist. Direct applications are rarely considered. The Council also offers research, travel and publication Grants to Swedish nationals.

Further information from:
Swedish Natural Science Research
 Council (NFR)
P.O. Box 6711
S-Stockholm 113 85
Sweden

[2020]

SWISS ACADEMY OF MEDICAL SCIENCES

Robert Bing Prize

One Prize of approximately 40,000 Swiss francs is awarded every two years in recognition of outstanding work contributing towards the diagnosis, treatment and cure of neurological diseases. Candidates may submit applications themselves, or be nominated by their professor or institute director. The Prize is considered on the basis of submitted papers. Applicants must also supply a curriculum vitae, description of the research work, and a list of publications. *Closing date:* Usually November of the year preceding that in which the award is given.

Further information from:
Professor J. Girard, Secretary-General
Swiss Academy of Medical Sciences
Petersplatz 13
4000 Basel
Switzerland

[2021]

SWISS FEDERAL INSTITUTE OF TECHNOLOGY *(Zurich)*

Exchange Scholarships

Subjects: Architecture, engineering, chemistry, physics, mathematics, natural sciences, pharmacy, agricultural and forestry.

No. offered: 20 Scholarships anually.

Value: 800-950 Swiss francs per month, plus tuition.

Tenable at the Institute, for one academic year (October-July).

Eligibility: Open primarily but not exclusively to nationals of Canada, France, West Germany, Italy, Japan, Poland, Spain, the United Kingdom, and the United States. Candidates should be between 22 and 30 years of age, have had at least four years of university study, and have a good knowledge of German.

Note: Applications should be made to the following addresses:
Canada—*Dean of Inter-Faculty Affairs, University of British Columbia, Vancouver 8, British Columbia; Office of the Rector, Laval University, Quebec City, Quebec; Acting Dean of Graduate Studies, University of New Brunswick, Frederiction, New Brunswick.*
Federal Republic of Germany—*German Academic Exchange Service, Kennedyallee 50, D-53 Bonn-Bad Godesberg 1.*
France—*Ministère des affaires étrangères, Direction générale des affaires culturelles, 23, rue La Pérouse, F-75016, Paris.*
Italy—*Ministerio degli Affari Esteri, Direzione Generale delle Relazioni Culturali, piazza Firenze 27, Rome.*
Japan—*Tokyo Institute of Technology, Dean of Students, Ookayama, Meguro-ku, Tokyo; Kyoto University, Department for General Studies, Sakyo, Kyoto.*
Poland—*Institute of Technology, Warsaw.*
Spain—*Consejo Superior de Investigaciones Cinetificas, Serrano 117, Madrid-6.*
United Kingdom—*Registrar, Imperial College of Science and Technology, Prince Consort Road, London SW7 2BD.*
United States—*Institute of International Education, 809 United Nations Plaza, New York, New York 10017.*

Closing date: 31st March.

Further information from:
Eidgenössische Technische Hochschule
Rektorat/Austauschdienst
ETH-Zentrum
CH-8092 Zurich
Switzerland

[2022]

SYDNEY INTERNATIONAL PIANO COMPETITION

Prizes amounting to A$25,000 are offered in the Competition which is held from time to time in Sydney. Pianists of any nationality, who are not more than 30 years of age may apply.

Further information from:
  Sydney International Piano Competition
  Conservatorium of Music
  Maquarie Street
  Sydney, N.S.W.
  Australia 2000

[2023]

SYFRETS TRUST COMPANY LTD. *(South Africa)*

Winifred Wilson Bursary

Purpose: To foster the study and preservation of the English language and literature in the Republic of South Africa.

Subjects: English.

No. offered: Varies; offered annually at the discretion of the Trustees.

Value: Varies; a lump sum is given at the discretion of the Trustees.

Tenable at universities within the Republic or elsewhere; renewable for the duration of the course.

Eligibility: Open to South African citizens who have completed at least one year's full-time study in English at a South African university and intend to major in English, or hold a B.A. degree of a South African university in which they have completed three courses in English.

Closing date: 5th December.

Further information from:
  ·Trustees
  Winifred Wilson Bursary Fund
  Syfrets Trust Company Ltd.
  24 Wale Street
  P.O. Box 206
  Cape Town 8000
  South Africa

[2024]

SYFRETS TRUST COMPANY LTD. *(South Africa)*

Cecil John Adams Memorial Trust Travelling Fellowships

Subjects: Medicine or medical science: advanced study and research.

No. offered: Two Fellowships annually.

Value: R5,000 per annum.

Tenable in aproved institutions outside South Africa for one year.

Eligibility: Open to South African citizens who are graduates of South African universities in medicine or medical science. Candidates must have resided in South Africa for three years prior to application, and must undertake to return to South Africa at the end of the Fellowship tenure.

Note: Fellows may not hold a remunerative appointment during tenure of the Fellowship unless remuneration is refunded to the Trust.

Closing date: 31st August.

Further information from:
  Trustees
  Cecil John Adams Memorial Travelling Fellowships
  Syfrets Trust Company Ltd.
  24 Wale Street
  P.O. Box 206
  Cape Town 8000
  South Africa

[2025]

DAVID SYME AND COMPANY LTD. *(Melbourne)*

'The Age' Australian Book of the Year Award

Two prizes of A$2,000 each are given annually for a work of imaginative writing, and for a non-fiction work. The winning entries will be of outstanding literary merit and the best published during the award year. Authors must be Australian, either by birth or naturalization. Entries may be submitted by the publishers only.

Closing date: 31st October.

Further information from:
 Literary Editor, The Age
 250 Spencer Street
 Melbourne, Victoria
 Australia 3000

T

See *How to Use The Grants Register*, page ix

[2026]

ROBERT A. TAFT INSTITUTE OF GOVERNMENT *(U.S.A.)*

Taft Seminar for Teachers

Approximately 1,200 Fellowships are awarded annually to elementary and secondary school teachers, librarians and administrators who are actively involved in teaching social studies, government, politics and related subjects. The Fellowships are distributed between 35 to 40 universities and colleges in the United States, and provide teachers with techniques for improved teaching in the areas of American government, the two-party system, the role of political parties, and the responsibility of the individual citizen. Fellowships are usually tenable for 2 to 3 weeks and cover tuition, materials, texts, housing and meals for the duration of the seminar. Graduate credit is awarded for the seminar, but the amount varies upon the sponsoring university.

Further information from:
Marilyn Chelstrom, President
Robert A. Taft Institute of Government
420 Lexington Avenue
New York, New York 10017
U.S.A.

[2027]

LAWSON TAIT MEDICAL AND SCIENTIFIC RESEARCH TRUST *(U.K.)*

The Trust encourages and supports medical and scientific research and learning by awarding prizes and making grants for work which does not involve experimental animals. Applications for Grants-in-Aid are considered at bi-monthly meetings of the Trustees.

Further information from:
Lawson Tait Medical and Scientific
  Research Trust
Brook House
Bramhall Lane South
Bramhall, Cheshire
England SK7 2DN

[2028]

AMAURY TALBOT FUND *(U.K.)*

Amaury Talbot Prize

An annual Prize is given for the most valuable book, article or other published work of an anthropological nature, relating to any area of Africa. Preference will, however, be given first to Nigeria and then to any other region of West Africa or West Africa in general. The value of the Prize varies, but has averaged approximately £200. There are no restrictions on eligibility. Two copies of the publication should be submitted. Entries will not be returned to candidates, but will be at the disposal of the judges. *Closing date:* 31st January, for works published in the preceding calendar year.

Further information from:
Amaury Talbot Fund
c/o Trustees of the Fund
Barclays Bank Trust Company Ltd.
Central Administration Trustee Office
  (61/888)
Radbroke Hall
Knutsford, Cheshire
England WA16 9EU

[2029]

TAU BETA PI ASSOCIATION, INC. *(U.S.A.)*

Tau Beta Pi Fellowships

Purpose: To enable recipients to contribute to the engineering profession by studying at a graduate school.

No. offered: Eighteen Fellowships annually.

Value: US$4,500 per year paid in monthly instalments.

Tenable at any graduate school for one year; not renewable.

Eligibility: Applicants must be members of

Tau Beta Pi and submit letters of recommendation from two faculty members.

Note: Applicants should notify the Director of Fellowships if awards or help from any other sources are received.

Closing date: 15th February.

Further information from:
Tau Beta Pi Association, Inc.
Box 8840 University Station
Knoxville, Tennessee 37916
U.S.A.

[2030]

MURIEL TAYLOR SCHOLARSHIP FUND *(U.K.)*

Muriel Taylor Prize

One Prize of £1,000 is offered in competition each May for advanced cello study. Applicants may be of any nationality, and should be between 17 and 23 years of age on 31st March of the year of competition. A written letter of recommendation from the applicant's most recent teacher plus a £5 entry fee should be enclosed with the entry form. The Competition takes place in London. *Closing date:* 31st March. Entry form and syllabus are available from:
Mrs. Faith Deller, O.B.E.
Honorary Competition Secretary
Muriel Taylor Scholarship Fund
Copsley Court, Outwood
Redhill, Surrey
England RH1 5PP

[2031]

TCHAIKOVSKY INTERNATIONAL MUSIC COMPETITION *(Moscow)*

The last Competition held was in 1982. Categories for this contest were piano; violin; violin-cello; and singing. The Competition is open to both men and women of any nationality. Pianists, violinists and violin-cellists must be between 16 and 30 years of age. Singers must be between 18 and 32 years of age. Prizes total 53,000 roubles. Eight Prizes for each for category: piano, violin and violin-cello; six Prizes each for male and female singers. Information for future Competitions is available from:

Organizing Committee
Internatinal Tchaikovsky Competition
15 Neglinnaya Street
Moscow
U.S.S.R.

[2032]

TECHNICAL ASSOCIATION OF THE GRAPHIC ARTS *(U.S.A.)*

Graphic Arts Fellowships

Purpose: To encourage individuals to enter the printing and publishing industry.

Subjects: Engineering, chemistry, physics, mathematics, design, industrial education, or business technology (i.e., systems analysis, operations research and marketing research).

No. offered: Between one and five Fellowships annually.

Value: US$1,000 to US$3,000 per annum.

Tenable at United States universities and graduate schools for one year; renewable.

Eligibility: Open to graduate students with not less than one year of study remaining, or students qualifying for the bachelor's degree and for graduate study.

Closing date: 1st February.

Further information from:
Graphic Arts Fellowships
Technical Association of the Graphic Arts
4615 Forbes Avenue
Pittsburgh, Pennsylvania 15213
U.S.A.

[2033]

TEXTILE INSTITUTE *(U.K.)*

Scholarships

Purpose: To enable candidates (including holders of an approved non-textile or professional qualification) to study full-time (a) on courses leading directly to Associateship of the Textile Institute or, (b) for a degree in textile subjects that grants exemption from the Textile Institute examinations.

No. offered: Variable number of Scholarships annually.

Value: Maximum of £750 per annum.

Eligibility: Open to persons of any nationality who are living or studying in the British Isles. All candidates must undertake to be employed in and for the benefit of the British textile industry, and are expected to qualify and apply for Associateship of the Textile Institute.

Note: Applications for a *Postgraduate Grant* will be considered only from candidates nominated by their university. All other candidates must be recommended by their headmaster, principal, head of department or employer. *Complementary Awards* to supplement local authority maintenance grants are also offered.

Closing date: Last Friday of July.

Further information from:
Chief Education Officer
Textile Institute
10 Blackfriars Street
Manchester
England M3 5DR

[2034]

MAGGIE TEYTE PRIZE *(U.K.)*

A Prize of £100 is awarded annually to "preserve the traditions of classical singing." The contest is open to female singers under the age of 30. Closing date for applications is March/April.

Further information from:
Felicity Guinness
Maggie Teyte Prize
9 St. Alban's Grove
London
England W8 5PN

[2035]

THEATRE AMERICANA

Ruth Martin and C. Brooks Fry Award

An annual US$500 Award is given to the author of the best full-length play (90 to 120 minutes). Unknown playwrights of any nationality may submit works for consideration. American citizens may submit scripts on any subject, but foreign playwrights may only send works which are about the American scene. Entries must be original plays which have not been professionally produced; adaptations are ineligible. The winning play will be produced by the Theatre.

Not confirmed for 1983.

Further information from:
Theatre Americana
Box 245
Altadena, California 91104
U.S.A.

[2036]

THOMAS MEMORIAL FUND *(South Africa)*

Scholarship

Subject: Engineering.

Value: Normally not exceeding R750 per annum, based upon tuition and laboratory fees and an allowance for books.

Tenable at the Massachusetts Institute of Technology, Cambridge, for one academic year; renewable.

Eligibility: Open to graduates in engineering from South African universities, who propose to undertake a postgraduate course at the Massachusetts Institute of Technology.

Note: The Scholarship may be held in conjunction with a postgraduate scholarship or other award, subject to the consent of the body granting such awards.

Not confirmed for 1983.

Further information from:
Thomas Memorial Fund
c/o Mr. Cilliers
Bowman, Gilfillan & Blacklock
P.O. Box 1397
Johannesburg 2000
South Africa

[2037]

THOMSON FOUNDATION *(U.K.)*

Fellowships

Purpose: To provide advanced training for

journalists and television engineers from overseas.

No. offered: Up to 24 journalism and 44 television Fellowships annually.

Value: £2,500 each, for both journalism and television Fellowships.

Tenable at the Editorial Study Centre, near London, or at the Thomson Foundation Television College, Glasgow, for three months. Shorter courses are sometimes arranged on request.

Eligibility: Open to citizens of third world nations who are over 21 years of age and are sponsored by their employing newspaper or television organization. Applicants must have a good working knowledge of the English language and must undertake to return to their home country on completion of their training.

Note: In-country television production courses and editorial courses in journalism can be arranged.

Additional information can be obtained from the local British Council representative.

Further information from:
Thomson Foundation
16th Floor, International Press Centre
76 Shoe Lane
London
England EC4 3JB

[2038]

THOURON—UNIVERSITY OF PENNSYLVANIA FUND FOR BRITISH AMERICAN STUDENT EXCHANGE

Thouron Awards

Purpose: To promote better understanding between the people of the United Kingdom and the United States.

Subjects: Unrestricted.

No. offered: Approximately ten Awards annually.

Value: US$650 per month, plus tuition and fees of US$6,700 per annum.

Tenable at the University of Pennsylvania, Philadelphia, for up to three years.

Eligibility: Open to graduate United Kingdom citizens who are single and not more than 28 years of age. Postdoctoral candidates are ineligible unless their proposed study is in a field different from that in which they undertook their previous postgraduate study. No application will be considered from a student already in the United States.

Note: American citizens interested in studying in Britain should write to the University of Pennsylvania for further details.

Closing date: 8th November.

Further information from:
Registrar
Thouron Awards
University of Glasgow
Glasgow
Scotland G12 8QQ

[2039]

THRASHER RESEARCH FUND *(U.S.A.)*

Project Grants

Subjects: Research into children's diseases. Priority areas are health information and technology transfer, health promotion and disease prevention, infectious diseases, and nutrition. General biomedical and other child health concerns, while not of primary interest, continue to be considered. Lower priority is given to basic laboratory research and animal studies.

Value: From US$2,000 to US$30,000 annually, depending on the project to be undertaken.

Tenable at major research institutions and appropriate organizations for up to three years. There are no geographical limitations.

Eligibility: Open to promising young researchers and to established research scientists who wish to undertake a project within the Fund's area of concern. Non profit institutions may also apply.

Note: The Fund's Annual Report provides details of policy guidelines, application procedures, and review process.

Further information from:
 Executive Director
 Thrasher Research Fund
 7th Floor, East North Temple
 Salt Lake City, Utah 84150
 U.S.A.

[2040]

LOUIS COMFORT TIFFANY FOUNDATION *(Great Neck, New York)*

Tiffany Award in Painting and Sculpture

Twenty Awards of US$5,000 each are given biennially for excellence in painting and sculpture. Open to United States residents.

Closing date: 1st September 1983 for next Award.

Further information from:
 Louis Comfort Tiffany Foundation
 P.O. Box 1088
 Great Neck, New York 11023
 U.S.A.

[2041]

TIMES EDUCATIONAL SUPPLEMENT *(U.K.)*

Information Book Awards

Two Awards of £150 each are offered annually to the authors of the best children's information books. The Junior Award is for books for children up to the age of nine, and the Senior Award is for books for children between 10 and 16 years of age. To be eligible, books must have been published for the first time either in Great Britain or the Commonwealth between 1st September of the previous year and 31st August of the award year. The Judges reserve the right to make a further £150 Award to the Illustrator in each case.

Closing date: 31st August.

Further information from:
 Literary Editor
 Times Educational Supplement
 P.O. Box 7
 New Printing House Square
 Grays Inn Road
 London
 England WC1X 8EZ

[2042]

TINKER FOUNDATION *(U.S.A.)*

Postdoctoral Fellowship Program

Purpose: To further understanding among the peoples of the U.S., Latin America, Spain and Portugal by providing professionals interested in Ibero-American studies with an opportunity to do research in the social sciences, marine sciences, and internatinal relations which will have significant theoretical implications within or between disciplines or for public policy.

Scope: The research project must be carried out independently; it may not be used primarily for training or retraining purposes or for work in direct continuation of a candidate's dissertation.

No. offered: A maximum of eight annually.

Value: Annual stipend of US$18,000 payable in two instalments upon request, and up to US$2,000 travel expenses for the Fellow. No allowances are made for additional costs.

Tenable at suitable institutions for one year, renewable for a second year. United States citizens and others with a Ph.D. from a U.S. university may hold the Fellowship in a country of their choice justified by their research project; non-United States citizens who do not hold a U.S. doctorate may hold the Fellowships at a United States institution only.

Eligibility: Open to scholars and researchers who have completed their doctoral studies no less than three years, but no more than ten years prior to the time of application. Citizens and permanent residents of the United States, Canada, Spain, Portugal and the Latin American countries are eligible.

Note: Candidates should submit three copies of a typed letter of application in English, a curriculum vitae, a full description of their research project, and a bibliography covering related research. the application should be accompanied by letters of acceptance from the respective department chairman of the institution of affiliation and the selected senior consultant who may represent a second discipline. Each applicant must arrange for one letter of reference to be sent directly to the Foundation by 1st February of the year in which the Fellowship is sought. There are no formal application forms, however instructions describing the standard presentation format are available on request from the address below.

Closing date: 15th January of the year in which the Fellowship will be held.

Further information from:
Tinker Foundation
645 Madison Avenue
New York, New York 10022
U.S.A.

[2043]

TOKYO INSTITUTE OF TECHNOLOGY
Japanese National Commission for Unesco

Scholarships: International Postgraduate Courses

Purpose: To provide young scientists from the developing countries with a more advanced education as well as a methodical preparation for their own research or education activities.

Subjects: Chemistry and chemical engineering.

No. offered: 14 Scholarships annually.

Value: 207,000 yen per month, air transportation to and from Japan, and 30,000 yen on arrival.

Tenable at the Institute for twelve months (October-September); not renewable.

Eligibility: Open to candidates under 35 years of age, who are nationals of developing countries which are member-nations of Unesco, who are university graduates in chemistry or chemical engineering, and have had at least one year's experience in teaching or research at universities or educational and scientific institutions. Candidates must be proficient in English.

Note: The participants of the Course receive no degree since Unesco postgraduate courses are not regular university courses but special courses designed for short-term intensive training.

Closing date: 10th June.

Further information from:
Office of the Unesco Course
Tokyo Institute of Technology
12 0-okayama, 2-chome
Meguro-ku
Tokyo
Japan

[2044]

TOTAL SOUTH AFRICA (PTY) LTD.

Frost Combating Bursary

Subjects: Agricultural meteorolgy—frost combating.

No. offered: One Bursary annually.

Value: R500 per annum.

Tenable at the University of the Orange Free State, Bloemfontein.

Eligibility: Open to postgraduates. In the event of suitable postgraduate students not being available, the Bursary Committee may consider advanced undergraduated students.

Further information from:
Frost Combating Bursary
Academic Registrar
University of Orange Free State
P.O. Box 339
Bloemfontein 9300
South Africa

[2045]

TOULON MUSIC FESTIVAL

International Competition: Prizes

A First Prize of 12,000 French francs, Second Prize of 8,000 francs, and Third Prize of 5,000 francs are offered in the Competition of the annual Toulon Music Festival. Subjects vary from year to year (basoon in 1982).

Further information from:
Concours International
Festival de Musique de Toulon
Palais de la Bourse
Avenue Jean-Moulin
F-83000 Toulon
France

[2046]

TRANS-ATLANTIC ASSOCIATION

A number of annual Grants are awarded for proposed projects dealing with the furtherance of research on Antarctic regions, publication of results, cost of travel to Antarctica, attendance at international meetings, etc. Applicants should be over 21 years of age, have appropriate academic qualifications, and be a citizen of Australia, Britain, New Zealand, or South Africa. New Zealand applicants should contact *A.J. Heine, Secretary, New Zealand Advisory Committee, Department of Scientific and Industrial Research, Physics and Engineering Laboratory, Private Bag, Lower Hutt, New Zealand.* All other applicants should write to the address below.

Closing date: End of January of each year.

Further information from:
Secretary
Trans-Atlantic Association
c/o British Antarctic Survey
High Cross
Madingley Road
Cambridge
England CG3 OET

[2047]

TRANSLATORS ASSOCIATION *(U.K.)*

John Florio Prize of £500 is given annually for the best translation into English of a twentieth century Italian work of literary merit and general interest published by a British publisher during the preceding year. The Prize is sponsored by the Italian Institute and the British Italian Society.

Scott-Moncrieff Prize of £1,000 is given annually for the best translation of a French twentieth century work of literary merit and general interest published in the United Kingdom by a British publisher. The Prize is sponsored by the Society of Authors, assisted by the French Government, the Arts Council and British publishers.

Schlegel-Tieck Prize of £1,800 is established under the auspices of the Society of Authors incorporating the Translators Association with financial support from the Government of the Federal Republic of Germany, the German Publishers' Association, the Arts Council of Great Britain and British publishers. It is awarded annually for the best translation published in the United Kingdom by a British publisher. Only translations of Germany twentieth century works of literary merit and general interest are considered.

Note: Books may only be submitted by publishers.

Closing date: 31st December.

Further information from:
Translators Association
84 Drayton Gardens
London
England SW10 9SD

[2048]

TRANSPORT UNIVERSITY PROGRAMS
(Canada)

Fellowships

Purpose: To support and encourage transportation studies at Canadian universities, so as to ensure an adequate flow of graduate students to meet the demands of the Canadian transportation private and public sectors and universities.

No. offered: 35 to 40 Fellowships annually.

Value: Can$9,000 per annum for Special Assistantship candidates; *Can*$9,500 per annum for master's candidates; *Can*$10,000 per annum for Ph.D. candidates.

Tenable at Canadian universities for one year (master's) and for three years, renewable (Ph.D.).

Eligibility: Open to Canadian citizens or landed immigrants.

Closing date: 12th January.

Further information from:
M.A. Parnes
Chief, University Programs
Transport University Programs
Strategic Policy Branch
Transport Canada
Tower C
Place de Ville
Ottawa, Ontario
Canada K1A ON5

[2049]

HARRY S. TRUMAN LIBRARY INSTITUTE *(U.S.A.)*

(a) Tom L. Evans Research Grant
(b) Institute Grants
(c) Senior Research Fellowships

Purpose: To promote research on topics related to the career and administration of Harry S. Truman.

No. offered: (a) One Grant annually; (b) a limited number of Grants annually; (c) one Fellowship every two years.

Value: (a) US$10,000; (b) up to US$1,000 each; (c) US$20,000.

Eligibility: (a) Open to American postdoctoral scholars; (b) open to American doctoral candidates and to postdoctoral scholars; (c) open to individuals of any age or nationality who have a record of distinguished scholarship and publications.

Applicants should be competent researchers with viable topics for which the pertinent materials are available at the Library.

Closing dates: (a) 1st February; (b) 1st February and 1st October; (c) 1st April.

Note: The Institute also awards the *Harry S. Truman Book Award* of US$5,000 for the best book on the period of the presidency of Harry S. Truman. The book should deal with some aspect of the social and political development of the United States, primarily between 12th April, 1945 and 20th January, 1953, or should be directly associated with the public career of Harry S. Truman. The award covers a calendar biennium ending 31st December.

Closing date: 20th January of the award year.

Further information from:
Secretary, Truman Library Institute
Independence, Missouri 64050
U.S.A.

[2050]

TRUST FUND FOR MEDICAL RESEARCH IN THE WEST AFRICAN STATES WITHIN THE COMMONWEALTH

Medical Research Fellowships

Purpose: To enable West African graduates to train in medical research in the U.K. (usually in Oxford) and to enable U.K. medical researchers to visit institutions in West Africa.

Value: Each Fellowship is assessed individually.

Tenable for one year.

Eligibility: Open to West African and U.K. graduates who are suitably qualified for the proposed programme.

Note: Fellowships are not awarded for study toward a higher degree, but Fellows already working for a research degree are not precluded.
Awards are made from time to time when funds permit.

Further information from:
Secretary
Trust Fund for Medical Research in West African States Within the Commonwealth
Nuffield Department of Surgery
John Radcliffe Hospital
Headington, Oxford
England

[2051]

TWENTY-SEVEN FOUNDATION *(U.K.)*

Awards

Graduates of United Kingdom universities who possess an honours degree in history may apply for: (i) a subsidy towards the costs of publishing a book or article in the field of history, incorporating an academic thesis or other scholarly work, already accepted by a reputable publisher or learned journal, or (ii) to pay for special expenses incurred in the completion of advanced historical work (except theses for higher degrees) such as the cost of relevant books, photographic reproduction of material, typing, fares and subsistence during visits to libraries or record repositories.

Applicants should not ask for more than their minimum requirements for the year concerned. Individual Awards range between £50 and £1,000.

Applications, on regulation forms, giving age, academic record, present occupation, particulars of the purpose for which an award is sought and the names and addresses of two referees, should be sent not later than 1st March to:

Secretary
Twenty-Seven Foundation Awards
c/o The Institute of Historical Research
University of London, Senate House
London
England WC1E 7HU

U

See *How to Use The Grants Register*, page ix

[2052]

U.S. DEPARTMENT OF COMMERCE
NATIONAL BUREAU OF STANDARDS
in association with National Research Council, National Academy of Sciences, and National Academy of Engineering

NRC/NBS Postdoctoral Research Associateships

Purpose: To provide postdoctoral scientists and engineers of unusual ability and promise with opportunities for research on problems of their own choice, and to contribute to the general research effort of the Federal laboratories.

Subjects: Basic physical, chemical and engineering sciences, applied technology, computer sciences.

No. offered: Approximately 24 Associateships annually.

Value: A salary of US$20,611 per annum; paid bi-weekly.

Tenable for one year at the National Bureau of Standards, Washington, D.C., and Boulder, Colorado; renewable for a further year.

Eligibility: Open to United States citizens who hold the Ph.D., Sc.D. or other research doctoral degree. Except in unusual circumstances, it is expected that the applicant will have received his doctorate not earlier than five years prior to submitting his application.

Not confirmed for 1983

Further information from:
Robb Thomson
National Measurement Laboratory
National Bureau of Standards
Washington, D.C. 20234
U.S.A.

[2053]

U.S. DEPARTMENT OF DEFENSE
Air Force Office of Scientific Research

Grants and Contracts

Purpose: To stimulte high quality scientific research on problems of Air Force interest.

Subjects: Sciences of direct interest to strengthening Air Force operating capabilities: chemical sciences, mathematical and information sciences, electronics and solid state sciences, aerospace sciences, life sciences, general physics, geophysics, and atmospheric sciences.

No. offered: Current research program consists of about 700 individual work efforts.

Tenable at colleges and universities, and industrial or non-profit research laboratories.

Eligibility: AFOSR principal investigators are predominantly at the postdoctoral level. Awards are not restricted by citizenship.

Note: Prior to formal submission of a proposal, investigators should obtain the following publication from the address below: *Proposer's Guide to the AFOSR Research Program.*

Further information from:
Air Force Office of Scientific Research (PK)
Bolling Air Force Base
Washington, D.C. 20332
U.S.A.

[2054]

U.S. DEPARTMENT OF DEFENSE
Office of Naval Research

Contracts

Purpose: To support scientific research and exploratory development providing the Navy and Marine Corps with new and improved technological approaches to the performance of its mission.

Subjects: Areas related to Navy interests, such as: the earth (including geography and geophysics); engineering; materials (including metallurgy and chemistry); atmospheric, physical, nuclear, operations, mathematical, information, biological, medical and psychological sciences or related inter-disciplinary fields.

Eligibility: Open to qualified scientists, as well as non-profit and profit-making institutions, organizations or industrial establishments. Contracts are generally awarded on the basis of unsolicited proposals. There are no citizenship restrictions.

Further information from:
Office of Naval Research
800 North Quincy Street
Arlington, Virginia 22217
U.S.A.

[2055]

U.S. DEPARTMENT OF EDUCATION
Office of Educational Research and Improvement

National Institute of Education— Office of Public Affairs

The National Institute of Education was created by Congress in 1972 as the primary Federal agency for educational research and development. Its purpose is to promote educational equity and to improve the quality of educational practice. To this end, the Institute supports research development and dissemination activities that will help individuals realize their full potential through education, regardless of race, sex, age, economic status, ethnic origin, or handicapping condition. To achieve its goals, NIE has organized its work around the following three broad program areas:

Teaching and Learning supports research on literacy, teaching, the process of learning, evaluation of teaching and its improvement, etc. The program is concerned with education at all levels in both formal and informal settings, and sponsors the National Assessment of Education Progress. Some specific units within the program are: learning and development; reading and language; teaching and instruction; education in home, community and work; testing, assessment and evaluation.

Educational Policy and Organization supports research to improve educational policy-making, promote more effective management and governance of educational institutions, and increase the general understanding of educational finance issues. Some specific units within the program are: law and public management; educational finance; educational organizations and local communities.

Dissemination and Improvement of Practice seeks to ensure that the results of educational research and development are made available in usable form to those who need them. Specific units within the program are: information resources; regional programs; research and educational practice. The program also operates NIE's Educational Research Library, supports the Educational Resources Information Center (ERIC), and funds the R&D Exchange. A major emphasis is placed on minorities and women, and their participation in educational research.

Note: Further information regarding the above Programs may be obtained by writing to the address below.

Unsolicited proposals are accepted from individuals and groups throughout the year.

Requests for Proposals (RFP) are formal procurement actions which announce NIE's intent to issue a contract to carry out specific tasks. Brief synopses of all RFPs are published in the *Commerce Business Daily*, along with information on how to obtain a complete copy of the RFP.

Grants Competitions generally call for research proposals in one or more specific areas of interest. The areas covered by a particular competition, as well as application procedures, eligibility requirements and deadlines, are announced in the *Federal Register*.

Address:
National Institute of Education
Office of Public Affairs, Stop 12 11
Washington, D.C. 20208
U.S.A.

[2056]

U.S. DEPARTMENT OF HEALTH AND HUMAN SERVICES
Administration on Aging
Office of Human Development Services

The Administration on Aging is the focal point within the Federal Government to improve the life circumstances of older persons. The Administration promotes changes to ensure that older Americans have equal access to the opportunities and privileges accorded to others, as well as promoting the development of comprehensive and coordinated community-based services with particular emphasis on those services to sustain the most vulnerable older persons in their own homes or in the least restrictive setting.

Research, demonstration and training projects which build and disseminate this vital knowledge are supported by the Administration. The primary objectives are research to improve our understanding of the needs and conditions of older persons; to identify research needs which address public and private policies that have significant impact on the lives of the elderly; and research on policy and program issues related to the development and implemenation of comprehensive and coordinated community-based service systems.

Detailed information regarding individual grants and programs, their eligibility requirements and value, may be obtained by writing to:

Administration on Aging
Office of Human Development Services
Washington, D.C. 20201
U.S.A.

[2057]

U.S. DEPARTMENT OF HEALTH AND HUMAN SERVICES
Public Health Service

The Public Health Service is a complex organization comprised of six major agencies and the Office of the Assistant Secretary for Health, each of which has several divisions of its own. Assistance is made annually through these various agencies and their smaller components, in the form of project awards and grants. The booklet *Profiles of Financial Assistance Programs*, provides general descriptions of the various programs, agency by agency, and *Financial Assistance Process* provides more definitive information. Both booklets are available from the Public Health Service at the address below. Organizations and individuals may also contact the various administrations, institutes, offices or centers for information regarding their programs and grants.

The following is a brief description of the basic function of each of the major agencies:

Alcohol, Drug Abuse, and Mental Health Administration: Formed in 1973, this administration is comprised of the three Institutes of Health and their individual divisions. The primary objective of this Administration deals with the sociomedical problems of alcohol and drug abuse, as well as mental illness.

Center for Disease Control: The Center leads the national attack on communicable and vector-borne diseases and works to control many other non-infectious conditions.

Food and Drug Administration: This Administration acts as the nation's first consumer protection agency.

Health Resources Administration: Formed in 1973, along with the Alcohol, Drug Abuse, and Mental Health Administration, it is responsible for health planning, manpower training, and research and evaluation of health resources and needs.

Health Services Administration: The main objective of this agency is to improve the delivery of health services to the American people.

National Institutes of Health: The Institutes conduct and support basic research, research training, and biomedical communications.

Office of the Assistant Secretary for Health: This Office, in addition to providing overall program direction and management support to the six PHS agencies, also administers several health programs such as the Health Maintenance Organizations Program, the Adolescent Pregnancy Prevention and Services Program, the Health Services Research, Development, and Demonstration Program, and the Health Care Technology Research Program.

Address:
U.S. Department of Health
and Human Services
Public Health Service
5600 Fishers Lane
Rockville, Maryland 20857
U.S.A.

[2058]

U.S. DEPARTMENT OF THE INTERIOR
Bureau of Indian Affairs

Higher Education Grants Program

Purpose: To encourage qualified American Indian students to seek higher education.

Subjects: Unrestricted.

No. offered: Approximately 17,000 Scholarships annually, depending upon funds available.

Value: Payments range from US$200 to US$7,500, with the average award of US$1,575. Scholarships may be renewed by written request, usually for up to 5 years.

Eligibility: Open to United States citizens who possess one-fourth or more degree American Indian, Eskimo or Aleut blood and have membership in a tribal group served by the Bureau of Indian Affairs. Financial need and scholarships are factors of consideration, as well as enrollment or acceptance at a nationally accredited college or university.

Note: The Scholarships are primarily, but not necessarily, for undergraduates.
Application should be made through the agency or area office serving the applicant's tribe.

Closing date: 1st June.

Further information from:
U.S. Department of the Interior
Bureau of Indian Affairs
Office of Indian Education
Higher Education Grants Program
1951 Constitution Avenue, N.W.
Washington, D.C. 20245
U.S.A.

[2059]

U.S. DEPARTMENT OF JUSTICE
National Institute of Justice

Graduate Research Fellowship Program

A limited number of Fellowships are awarded to doctoral candidates through sponsoring universities, to support students engaged in the research and writing of a doctoral dissertation in the area of criminal justice. Applicants must have completed all degree requirements except for the research, writing and defense of the dissertation or internship prior to awarding of the grant.

Fellowships are tenable for periods not exceeding one year at fully accredited sponsoring institutions. The value of each award shall not exceed US$11,000 and may include the following types of support: fellow's stipend, allowances for certain dependents, major project costs, and certain university fees.

Note: All awards are subject to yearly appropriations, and therefore criteria and levels of support may vary from year to year.

Closing date: 31st October and 1st March.

Further information from:
Annesley K. Schmidt, Project Monitor
Graduate Research Fellowship Program
National Institute of Justice
633 Indiana Avenue, N.W.
Washington, D.C. 20531
U.S.A.

[2060]

U.S. DEPARTMENT OF JUSTICE
National Institute of Justice

Visiting Fellowship Program

Purpose: To provide creative criminal justice professional and research personnel with the opportunity to conduct worthwhile research projects in their areas of interest and expertise; to contribute to the state of knowledge in the field of criminal justice through support of innovative research.

Subjects: The specific and study design within the field of criminal justice are chosen by the Fellow, subject to approval by the Institute.

No. offered: Up to 5 Fellowships annually.

Value: An annual stipend, plus transportation expenses and funds for research and clerical assistance. Stipends for Fellows are determined on an individual basis depending on, at the time of the award, previous training and experience and such other factors as current salary and expected concurrent sabbatical salary; they will not exceed US$47,500 per annum. No separate allowance is provided for dependents or the applicant's current employer. Funds for research and clerical assistance do not exceed US$15,000 per annum.

Tenable at the Institute for periods of from three to fifteen months.

Eligibility: Open to criminal justice professionals and scholars seeking support for research projects focusing on problems related to law enforcement and criminal justice. Applicants are evaluated on the basis of the relevance of their project topic, the quality and feasibility of their project design in terms of training and past experience and productivity.

Note: All awards are subject to yearly appropriations, and therefore criteria and levels of support may vary.

Further information from:
Director, Visiting Fellowship Program
National Institute of Justice
U.S. Department of Justice
Washington, D.C. 20531
U.S.A.

[2061]

U.S. DEPARTMENT OF JUSTICE
National Institute of Justice

Research, Program Development, and Evaluation Grants

Grants are awarded to encourage and support research, program development, and evaluation in order to improve and strengthen all activities pertaining to crime prevention and enforcement of the criminal law within the United States and its protectorates.

The Institute publishes a *Program Plan* which lists priority areas of interest and outlines programs proposed for each fiscal year.

The Institute is authorized to make Grants, to enter into contracts with public agencies, institutions of higher education, private organizations, and individuals. Whenever feasible, as a condition of approval of a Grant or contract, the Institute requires that the recipient contribute money, facilities, or services to carry out the purposes for which the Grant or contract is sought.

Note: All awards are subject to yearly appropriations, and therefore criteria and levels of support may vary.

Further information from:
National Institute of Justice
U.S. Department of Justice
Washington, D.C. 20531
U.S.A.

[2062]

U.S. DEPARTMENT OF JUSTICE
National Institute for Juvenile Justice and Delinquency Prevention

Research, Evaluation, Training and Program Development Project Grants

Grants are awarded to encourage, conduct and support research and evaluation of research to gain new knowledge, and aid program development in the area of juvenile delinquency and juvenile justice. The Institute also provides assistance through the awarding of grants and contracts for training juvenile justice personnel and to support efforts to disseminate information on all aspects of juvenile delinquency.

Solicitations for grant applications, accepted from public and private agencies and organizations, institutions of higher learning, and individuals, are announced in the *Federal Register*.

Further information from:
Office of Juvenile Justice and
  Delinquency Prevention
National Institute for Juvenile Justice
U.S. Department of Justice
633 Indiana Avenue, N.W.
Washington, D.C. 20531
U.S.A.

[2063]

U.S. INTERNATIONAL DEVELOPMENT COOPERATION AGENCY
Agency for International Development [AID]

Participant Training Program

The Agency for International Development assists developing countries in their long-range programs of nation-building. The Agency's programs are directed toward the developing countries of Latin America, Africa, the Near East, South Asia and the Far East.

Organized under the Office of International Training, the Participant Training Program is designed to help meet the specialized manpower needs of developing countries.

Most participants are trained in the United States for a specific requirement of an agreed United States/host country project; however, some are trained in other countries, usually in their own region.

Objectives: To help developing nations in their efforts to promote economic and social progress: (1) by improving their human resources through academic studies, on-the-job training, special programs, and observational visits in the United States and other countries; (2) by providing leadership training as a major tool in preparing foreign nationals to perform key roles in their countries' development programs; (3) by encouraging the development of institutions by foreign nationals who, once trained, establish training centers in their home countries, thus multiplying the impact of their AID sponsored training; (4) by providing foreign nationals an opportunity to observe the democratic process in the political, social, and economic life of the United States.

Types of training: Academic training—more than a third of the participants are placed in universities and colleges throughout the United States for academic training. Of these, 75% are in graduate programs. On-the-job Training—designed to give actual work experience such as in a laboratory, a factory, or an office. The duration of such training may range from a few weeks to one or more years. Special Training—normally a combination of classroom and field training tailored to meet specific objectives of multinational groups. Observation Training—usually short in duration. This training is arranged for top management, labor officials, and government administrators—people who can profit most from personal observation.

Major fields of training: Agriculture; education; health; public administration; industry and mining; labor; transportation; atomic energy; community development; housing; communications; population/family planning.

No. offered: Each year about 3,000 new trainees arrive in the United States to join in programs. Approximately 4,500 participants are sponsored annually by AID to receive their instruction outside both the United States and their own countries.

Eligibility: The participant is chosen jointly by his own government and the AID host country mission. The candidate may be selected from government, industry, or any other sector of the economy, or the academic sector. It is essential that the tasks for which the participant is to be trained have a high priority in his country's economic and social development plans. The AID country program must confirm the need by the recipient country for the desired skills.

The participant must: (a) undertake training in a field needed to meet critical human resource requirements of the joint AID/host country program; (b) have experience in the field in which he is to be trained; (c) have completed all relevant training available in his home country; (d) have demonstrated an aptitude for training; (e) have good health and sufficient knowledge of the English language; (f) pledge to return to his homeland and serve his country in its development program.

Further information from the offices of the AID program in the candidate's own country.

Address:
Agency for International Development
Office of International Training
Washington, D.C. 20523
U.S.A.

[2064]

ULISSE *(Italy)*

European Cortina Ulisse Prize

One Prize of 2,000,000 lire is awarded from time to time for a work of popular science, in the belief that culture should be a common instrument of civilization and not the privilege of a few. Works published in a language other than English, French, German, Italian or Spanish must be accompanied by a translation into one of these languages. If the winning publication is by a non-Italian, it will be translated and published by an Italian publisher.

Further information from:
Ulisse
Rivista di Cultura Internazionale
11 Via Po
00 198 Rome
Italy

[2065]

UNION OF JEWISH WOMEN OF SOUTH AFRICA

Toni Saphra Bursary

Purpose: To support a course of advanced study which will fit the recipient more adequately to render some form of social service to the South African community.

Subjects: Related to the social work, psychological and human sciences fields.

No. offered: One Bursary annually.

Value: R1,000.

Tenable at any South African university for one year; renewable.

Eligibility: Open to South African women, regardless of race, colour, or creed, who hold a university degree or professional qualification.

Note: The recipient must make her own arrangements for admission to the university where she wishes to study.

Closing date: 1st December.

Further information from:
Bursary Officer
Union of Jewish Women of South Africa
Headquarters
P.O. Box 3622
Johannesburg 2000
South Africa

[2066]

UNION THEOLOGICAL SEMINARY *(New York City)*

Ecumenical Fellowships for Students from Other Countries

Subject: Theology.

No. offered: Five Fellowships annually.

Value: US$5,500, to be applied towards tuition, dormitory fees, meals, and other expenses.

Tenable at the Seminary, for one academic year, not renewable.

Eligibility: Open to persons of any nationality who are college or university graduates and have already completed a course of theological study, can demonstrate a capacity for leadership, the ability to benefit from one year of advanced theological study, and the potential for exercising increasing responsibility and influence in the church in their own countries.

Note: Fellowships have been designated in the following manner: one for a Scottish student, one for a student from England, one for a student from the European continent, and two for students from Africa, Asia, Oceania or Latin America.
Fellows are normally expected to complete the S.T.M. degree during their academic year at the Seminary.

Closing date: 1st February.

Further information from:
Academic Office
Union Theological Seminary
Broadway at 120th Street
New York, New York 10027
U.S.A.

[2067]

UNITARIAN UNIVERSALIST ASSOCIATION *(U.S.A.)*

Financial aid is available to students preparing for the Unitarian Universalist ministry who have completed the first year of their theological program at the graduate level and who have registered their intentions with the Unitarian Universalist Association.

Further information from:
Department of Ministerial Education
Unitarian Universalist Association
25 Beacon Street
Boston, Massachusetts 02108
U.S.A.

[2068]

UNITED CEREBRAL PALSY RESEARCH AND EDUCATIONAL FOUNDATION, INC.
(U.S.A.)

Clinical Fellowships are awarded to persons who have completed, or are near completion of, their basic professional training. Their purpose is to provide interested professionals with an opportunity to obtain further training and experience in the area of cerebral palsy and other developmental disabilities. Application is made by a senior level preceptor, who will be responsible for supervising the Fellow's training program. Fellows are expected to spend at least half of their time with children and adults who have cerebral palsy. Awards are made for a twelve-month period and may be renewed. Currently, the maximum amount of the Fellowship is US$12,500 per annum. No allowance is made for overheads or dependents.

UCP-J. William Hillman Graduate Student Fellowship Program in Cerebral Palsy is designed to interest the graduate student in the biomedical sciences in the problems of multidiscipline diagnosis and periodic evaluation of persons with developmental disability, and to involve the student in the problems of management of these persons. Any graduate student who is enrolled in a graduate program in one of the biomedical sciences in a state university or equivalent institution in the United States or Canada is eligible to apply. The stipend is US$300 per month payable directly to the student. On request, a sum up to US$100 will be made available to each Fellow for travel to other institutions of higher learning wherein his Fellowship program would be carried out. The minimum term of the Fellowship is two months and the maximum four months when students have consecutive free time for full-time study. It is anticipated that Fellows would spend their summers or elective quarters during the appropriate academic year working in an out-patient cerebral palsy or child development clinic, in an in-patient cerebral palsy or child development clinic, in an in-patient cerebral palsy facility connected with the university, in a rehabilitation facility where integrated services are offered by medical and related personnel or in a laboratory where basic biological physical or medical science studies are being conducted related to neuromuscular disabilities. Application forms are available from the address below.

UCP-J. William Hillman Medical Student Fellowships in Cerebral Palsy are intended for medical students who have completed their first year in an approved medical school in the United States or Canada. The terms of the program are identical to the Hillman Graduate Student Fellowship Program.

Research Grants are awarded for research in areas which have direct relevance to the prevention and management of cerebral palsy. With the full recognition that most areas of research in the central nervous system have potential relevance, the Foundation does not require that research proposals define clear and direct relevance. Currently, high priorities have been assigned to the areas of prevention of prematurity and improved management of the premature and full-term newborn as it relates to the prevention of neurologic disability. However, serious consideration is given to any research proposal designed to either prevent cerebral palsy or improve treatment and management of cerebral palsy and similar disabilities. Research Grants are awarded for a period not to exceed three years and may be renewed for up to an additional two years. The amount of the Grant may be within a range of US$2,500 to US$75,000 annually. Grant funds may include an indirect cost not in excess of 15% of each budgetary item, except that none is allowed on equipment. Grant funds may not include travel to conferences outside the continental United States and Canada. Details of application procedure are available from the address below.

Further information from:
United Cerebral Palsy Research and Educational Foundation, Inc.
66 East 34th Street
New York, New York 10016
U.S.A.

[2069]

UNITED DAUGHTERS OF THE CONFEDERACY *(U.S.A.)*

Mrs. Simon Baruch University Award

Purpose: To encourage research in southern history and to assist scholars in the publication of their theses, dissertations and other writings on the Confederate period.

Subjects: Southern United States history in or near the period of the Confederacy or bearing upon the causes that led to secession and the war between the states. The life of an individual, a policy or a phase of life may be eligible.

No. offered: One Award in even-numbered years.

Value: US$2,000 to aid in defraying the costs of publication.

Eligibility: Open to individuals who have graduates with an advanced degree from a United States university or college within the previous 15 years, or whose thesis or dissertation has been accepted by such institutions as part of graduation requirements. Book length manuscripts should contain at least 75,000 words; monographs, from 25,000 to 50,000 words.

Closing date: 1st May of the award year.

Further information from:
Chairman of the Committee
Mrs. Simon Baruch University Award
United Daughters of the Confederacy
328 North Boulevard
Richmond, Virginia 23220
U.S.A.

[2070]

UNITED METHODIST CHURCH *(U.S.A.)*

Bishop James C. Baker Graduate Awards

Subject: Advanced study for professional leaders in Wesley Foundations and similar campus ministries.

Value: All or part of the total US$5,000 annually set aside for Awards.

Tenable at universities in the United States for one year.

Eligibility: Open to United States citizens with an M.Div. degree or its equivalent, who have been members of the United Methodist Church or the Methodist Church for at least five years, and have had three or more years of professional experience in campus ministry or a similar ministry.

Note: Support for graduates is also offered by the Church through the following awards: *E. Craig Brandenburg Graduate Awards* are available to older persons who desire to make a positive contribution to society and who have special needs due to a change of vocation, interrupted study, or continuing education. Awards range in value from US$500 to US$2,000; *Reverend Charles W. Tadlock Scholarships* of US$500 to US$1,000 are offered to persons preparing for the parish ministry and studying in a school accredited by the American Association of Theological Schools and approved by the United Methodist University Senate.

Further information from:
Office of Loans and Scholarships
Board of Higher Education and Ministry
P.O. Box 871
Nashville, Tennessee 37202
U.S.A.

[2071]

UNITED METHODIST CHURCH *(U.S.A.)*

John Q. Schisler Graduate Awards

Subject: Preparation for professional leadership in local church Christian education.

No. offered: Several Awards annually.

Value: Variable; a total of US$10,000 is available for award annually.

Tenable in universities and schools approved by the University Senate of the United Methodist Church, for one year.

Eligibility: Open to United States citizens who have been members of the United Methodist Church for three years and are bona fide degree candidates preparing to be directors of Christian education. Awards are granted on the basis of academic standing, leadership ability, promise of usefulness, churchmanship, character and need.

Closing date: 1st February.

Address:
John Q. Schisler Award Committee
Office of Loans and Scholarships
Board of Higher Education and Ministry
P.O. Box 871
Nashville, Tennessee 37202
U.S.A.

[2072]

UNITED NATIONS
Department of Technical Cooperation for Development

Fellowships and Awards

Purpose: To enable persons who are already or are soon to be entrusted with functions important for the development of their countries, to broaden their professional knowledge and operational experience by acquainting themselves with more advanced methods and techniques.
A particular training programme may include attendance at an academic institution where a Fellow may take examinations and prepare a thesis or dissertation; however, the main purpose of every Fellowship is to enable the Fellow to derive from his training an increased ability to solve concrete problems when he returns to his home country.

Subjects: The broad and general field of economic and social development.
In addition, Awards are also available in the fields of narcotics control and human rights.

Value: To include a monthly stipend based on the cost of living (fixed by the United Nations Development Programme), tuition, book allowance and travel costs to the country of study as established in agreement with recipient governments.

No. offered: Approximately 1,800 individual awards and approximately 800 awards for participants in workshops and seminars.

Tenable in countries where special facilities exist for the higher training or advanced study of a kind which will benefit the country of the Fellow on his return home. Individual Fellowships are tenable for three to twelve months.

Awards for participation in seminars and workshops are tenable for two to three weeks.

Eligibility: Open primarily to nationals of developing countries upon specific request of the government concerned.

Note: Programmes for study are also offered in academic institutions and special courses; group, in-plant, in-service training; and programmes of practical observation, and seminars. In the training programmes established on the regional level, the Fellowships are available through the Economic Commission for Asia and the Far East, Bangkok (Thailand), Economic Commission for Europe, Geneva (Switzerland), Economic Commission for Latin America, Santiago (Chile), Economic Commission for Africa, Addis Ababa (Ethiopia), and the United Nations Economic and Social Office in Beirut (Lebanon).

Applications: Candidates must apply to the relevant government department in their own countries.

Address:
Fellowships Section
Department of Technical Cooperation for Development
United Nations
New York, New York 10017
U.S.A.

[2073]

UNITED NATIONS
Educational and Training Programme for Southern Africans—Department of Technical Cooperation for Development

Scholarships

Subjects: Unrestricted; but especially education, science, social sciences, medicine and related services, agriculture, engineering and other technical fields of study: higher-level secondary, vocational or university study.

Value: Costs of maintenance, tuition and books. Partial awards cover tuition only.

Tenable outside South Africa and Namibia for the duration of the approved study. Priority is given to training in Africa.

Eligibility: Open to South Africans and Namibians.

Further information from:
Fellowships Section
Department of Technical Cooperation for Development
United Nations
New York, New York 10017
U.S.A.

[2074]

UNITED NATIONS
Office of Public Information

Graduate Student Intern Programme

Subjects: Principles, purpose and activities of the United Nations and its related agencies: intensive study.

No. offered: Up to 100 Internships.

Value: There are no fees for studies. No stipend is paid by the United Nations. Recipients and/or sponsoring institutions are responsible for travel and accommodation.

Tenable (a) at the United Nations European Office, Geneva for three weeks in July; (b) at the United Nations Headquarters in New York for four weeks in June/July.

Eligibility: Open to graduate students from member-states of the United Nations. Candidates should be outstanding graduates specializing in subjects relevant to the United Nations fields of work. Interns in Geneva must have a good knowledge of English or French, and those in New York must have a good knowledge of English.

Note: Candidates should apply through their own college, university or United Nations permanent mission. Nominations should be addressed to *United Nations European Office Information Service, Palais des Nations, 1211 Geneva 20, Switzerland*, or to:
Coordinator
Office of Public Information
United Nations
New York, New York 10017
U.S.A.

[2075]

UNITED NATIONS ECONOMIC COMMISSION FOR AFRICA

Expanded Training and Fellowship Programme for Africa

Purpose: To assist ECA member-states in securing training and fellowship opportunities for the training of their nationals operating in public and private sectors in priority fields of social and economic development.

Subjects: Agriculture, education, economics, public administration, business administration, management, medicine, engineering, sciences, technology, and a variety of tailor-made individual course programmes.

No. offered and Value: Variable annually, according to established practice of donor governments and organizations, and available funds. Awards may or may not include travel expenses.

Tenable normally at training institutions in the donor country (African or non-African) for periods ranging from one month to seven years, depending on the programme. Some Fellowships are "third country" Fellowships for training, usually in a developing country (African or non-African).

Eligibility: Open to nationals of ECA memberstates who must be nominated by their governments. Undergraduate awards candidates should have qualifications equivalent to the baccalaureate, higher school certificate or general certificate of education (GCE) advanced level; graduate candidates should hold an honours or a general degree from recognized universities; candidates for non-degree programmes should have appropriate vocational or professional qualifications and some years of practical experience.

Closing date: Usually the end of April.

Further information may be obtained from the Training Administrator in the candidate's home country, or from:

Chief
Public Administration, Management and Manpower Division
United Nations Economic Commission for Africa
P.O. Box 3001
Addis Ababa
Ethiopia

[2076]

UNITED NATIONS ECONOMIC AND SOCIAL COMMISSION FOR ASIA AND THE PACIFIC *(Bangkok)*

ESCAP Fellowship Programme

USSR Fellowships: 10 Higher Education Fellowships are offered by the Soviet Government to nationals of developing countries in Asia and the Pacific. Awards cover all expenses for the full duration of the academic programme in all higher education areas, including board and lodging, tuition, textbooks, medical and dental care, research, recreational and sports facilities. In addition, an appropriate monthly stipend will be provided for personal expenses. Recipients must provide their own transporation to Moscow; however return travel expenses will be provided by the Soviet Government upon successful completion of the studies undertaken. Selection for these Fellowships is made by ESCAP.

Further information from:
United Nations Economic and Social Commission for Asia and the Pacific
Technical Co-operation Division
United Nations Building
Rajadamnern Avenue
Bangkok 2
Thailand

[2077]

UNITED NATIONS EDUCATIONAL, SCIENTIFIC AND CULTURAL ORGANIZATION

Unesco Fellowships

Purpose: To enable persons well established in their careers to gain international experience through study, training or observation abroad: individual Fellowships are given, as well as Fellowships for participation in group training schemes. Most awards are related not only to the needs of the individual Fellow, but also to his participation in specific national or international projects after the completion of the Fellowship. A large proportion of these projects is related to the promotion of economic and social development.

Only in exceptional cases are awards made for participation in courses leading to a specific degree in higher education.

Subjects: Education, natural sciences and technology, social sciences, culture and communication.

Value: Usually a monthly allowance to cover board, lodging and incidental expenses, based on United Nations stipend scales; round-trip international travel; travel within countries of study; tuition fees; book allowance. The rate varies with the cost of living, the Fellow's status (i.e. resident or travel), and the donations by member-states.

Tenable in one or more member-states of Unesco usually for periods of between three and nine months. (Fellowships donated by member-states and sponsored by Unesco are tenable only in the donor country.)

Eligibility: Open to nationals of all member-states and associate members of Unesco, unless otherwise restricted as in the case of Participation Programme and United Nations Development Programme (UNDP) Fellowships, to member-states which have signed agreements with Unesco.

Note: Applications must be made to the National Commissions for Unesco or other body established for cooperation with Unesco (usually located in ministries of education or ministries of foreign affairs) in the candidate's own country, which in turn submit nominations to the Unesco Secretariat. Direct applications by individuals cannot be considered.

Fellowships are financed from Unesco's regular budget (including Programme of Participation in the Activities of Member-States), United Nations Development Programme, Funds-in-Trust, United Nations Children's Fund, or from donations from member-states for Fellowships sponsored by Unesco.

Fellowships under the Regular Programmes are announced to member-states in open competition. The Participation Programme Fellowships (offered within the Regular Programme) are requested at the beginning of every biennium. A date limit is set for the reception of the requests. Fellowship applications in fields of Unesco competence and financed by the UNDP are passed on to Unesco by the UNDP resident representatives in their respective countries. Once approved, Unesco administers these Fellowships.

Address:
Unesco—attention CPX/FEL
7 Place de Fontenoy
75700 Paris
France

[2078]

UNITED NATIONS EDUCATIONAL, SCIENTIFIC AND CULTURAL ORGANIZATION

Unesco-Sponsored Fellowships and Regional Courses

Subjects: Unesco fields of interest—education (educational administration including educational planning, theories of child learning, vocational guidance, physical education, education for physically handicapped children, audio-visual education; sciences and techniques of rural, agricultural and forest development; mathematics, etc.); science (oceanography-hydrology; engineering; hydraulic construction and works; drilling and extraction, petroleum technology and petro-chemistry, etc.); social sciences, humanities and culture, language and literature, art and history; preservation and presentation of monuments and sites; social and economic sciences; public administration, etc.; communication (journalism, etc.).

Value: Sponsored Fellowships: the amount of the Fellowship and various benefits vary according to the sponsoring governments; Regional Fellowships: the amount is based on United Nations Development Programme stipend rates or ad hoc rates.

Eligibility: Open to nationals of Unesco member-states. All candidates must be officially nominated by their governments. The qualifications required vary according to the level of studies to be pursued. Usually candidates should be at the postgraduate level in their field of interest.

Further information from:
Unesco—attention CPX/FEL
7 Place de Fontenoy
75700 Paris
France

[2079]

UNITED NATIONS EDUCATIONAL, SCIENTIFIC AND CULTURAL ORGANIZATION

Unesco Travel Grants: Study Tours for Leaders in Workers' and Co-operative Education

Purpose: To enable leaders in workers' and co-operative education to undertake study programmes abroad in adult education, with a view to (i) improving education for workers in their own country and (ii) encouraging the participation of their organizations in the activities of Unesco.

Value: To cover the travel costs only. Other costs are borne by the sponsoring organization or by the Grantees themselves.

Tenable in Unesco member-states for the duration of the study programme. Next offered for 1984-85.

Eligibility: Open to nationals of member-states of Unesco who are engaged in the education of workers within a workers' organization (trade union, relevant co-operative or workers' educational association) or an adult education association.

Note: Applications are invited from workers' organizations and relevant co-operatives through the National Commission for Unesco or appropriate government department in the country concerned. Closing date is fixed by the Unesco Secretariat for each biennium, usually April-May of the first year of the biennium concerned. Direct applications from individuals cannot be considered by the Unesco Secretariat.

Address:
Unesco
ED/Adult Education Section
7 Place de Fontenoy
75700 Paris
France

[2080]

UNITED NATIONS EDUCATIONAL, SCIENTIFIC AND CULTURAL ORGANIZATION

Unesco Travel Grants for Youth and Student Leaders

Purpose: To enable leaders of youth and student organizations to undertake study programmes abroad, in order to exchange ideas and experience with youth organizations and services of different countries.

Tenable for the duration of the study programme in any of the member-states of Unesco.

Eligibility: Open to nationals of member-states of Unesco who are active youth leaders.

Note: Applications are invited from (i) selected international non-governmental organizations having consultative status with Unesco and from (ii) national youth organizations or services not affiliated to organizations in (i) above, provided the projects are supported by the Unesco National Commission (or corresponding governmental authority) of their country. Closing date is fixed by the Unesco Secretariat which informs the above-mentioned organizations. Direct applications from individuals cannot be considered by the Unesco Secretariat.

Address:
 Unesco—attention CPX/FEL
 7 Place de Fontenoy
 75700 Paris
 France

[2081]

UNITED NATIONS EDUCATIONAL, SCIENTIFIC AND CULTURAL ORGANIZATION

Unesco Professor Exchange Programme

Purpose: To enable staff of university departments of engineering in developing countries to visit similar departments in neighbouring countries and given seminars in their own speciality, compare curricula, study laboratory facilities, etc.

Value: To cover economy class air fare, and a subsistence allowance.

Tenable for three to six weeks in a country adjacent to the candidate's own country.

Note: Candidates are nominated by either their own universities, or by the receiving institutions, but only after the terms of the exchange have been arranged between the two.

Further information from:
 Engineering Education Section
 Division of Technological Education and
  Research
 Unesco
 7 Place de Fontenoy
 75700 Paris
 France

[2082]

UNITED NATIONS HIGH COMMISSIONER FOR REFUGEES

Assistance for Refugees

The function of the United Nations High Commissioner for Refugees (UNHCR) is to provide international protection to refugees and to seek permanent solutions to their problems, mainly through the facilitation of voluntary repatriation, resettlement in another country, or local settlement in the country of asylum. Under its general programmes, UNHCR provides assistance in the education of refugees at the primary and lower secondary levels and at vocational training schools.

Educational assistance at the post-primary level is also provided, mainly through a special Refugee Education Account. Through this Account, grants are provided to enable refugees to follow secondary courses of an academic, technical or vocational nature. In a limited number of cases, scholarships are also made available for university education.

Under an agreement with the United Nations Educational and Training Programme for Southern Africa (UNETPSA), defining the spheres of competence of the two organizations in respect of educational assistance to refugees from South Africa, UNHCR provides such refugees with assistance up to and including the lower secondary level; assistance beyond this level is provided by UNETPSA.

Further information from:
United Nations High Commissioner for Refugees
Palais des Nations
CH-1211 Geneva 10
Switzerland

Address:
United Nations Industrial Development Organization, Training Section
P.O. Box 300
A 1400 Vienna
Austria

[2083]

UNITED NATIONS INDUSTRIAL DEVELOPMENT ORGANIZATION

UNIDO Fellowships in Connection with Technical Assistance for Developing Countries

Purpose: To enable candidates on postgraduate level from developing countries to train in countries where special facilities exist for industrial and managerial training which will benefit their home countries.

Subjects: Industrial development planning and programming, industrial financing, industrial technologies, industrial institutions, industrial administration, industrial legislation, industrial information, small-scale industry, industrial management and industrial training.

No. offered: Approximately 1,000 Fellowships for individual and 1,300 in group training programmes.

Value: Subsistence allowance according to established United Nations rules, plus travel expenses, tuition, book allowance.

Tenable in any country for several weeks to several months. The awards are intended for training in industry, institutions and government or semi-government bodies dealing with industrial development, etc.

Eligibility: Open to nationals of developing countries upon specific request of the government concerned. Candidates should have a university degree or equivalent and practical experience in the chosen field of study.

Note: Applications can only be made by a candidate's government through the resident representative of the United Nations Development Programme to UNIDO.

Not confirmed for 1983.

[2084]

UNITED NATIONS INSTITUTE FOR TRAINING AND RESEARCH

UNITAR Training Courses and Seminars; Fellowships; Internships

Purpose: To enable international officials, foreign service officers and other officials working or interested in international relations, mainly from developing countries, to participate in Seminars and Training Courses, and to assist them in gaining knowledge and understanding which will be of benefit to them in their positions.

The following is a list of some of the Seminars and Training Courses organized by UNITAR. This is not exhaustive and should be used only as a guide to the types of activities organized annually by UNITAR.

General Seminars on the United Nations and Multilateral Diplomacy are held every year for younger members of Permanent Missions and of the U.N. Secretariat. The lectures and seminars are on specific topics falling within a general subject area.

Courses on the Workings of International Organizations. A specialized and intensive annual programme for members of Permanent Missions and the U.N. Secretariat.

Course on General Assembly Procedures is held at the commencement of the General Assembly sessions in September each year and is meant for new members of permanent missions and delegates to the General Assembly. The seminars at the course are led by experienced diplomats and international officials.

UN/UNITAR Annual Fellowship Programme in International Law is intended to enable middle-grade government officials and young university teachers of international law, primarily from developing countries, to acquire additional knowledge of international law and of the legal work of the United Nations and its associated bodies. The Programme consists of lectures and seminars in Geneva or at The Hague, followed by a period of practical training at UNITAR, at the United Nations Office of Legal Affairs, or at one of the legal departments of an associated agency. Applicants must be sponsored by their governments. About 20 Fellowships are awarded each year. Travel costs and stipends of participants are paid from UNITAR or United Nations funds.

Regional Training and Refresher Courses in International Law are held annually in an African, Asian or Latin American country. Their object is to provide government legal officers and university teachers of international law with an opportunity of updating their knowledge of the subject. The travel costs of one participant from each country in the region are met from United Nations funds.

UNITAR Officer Attachment Programme. Under this programme, UNITAR accepts a limited number of graduate students with an outstanding academic record in such fields as international relations, law, government and economic and social sciences, as research Interns. The object of the Internships, which vary in duration, is to enable the Interns to carry out research under a supervisor designated by UNITAR. UNITAR does not pay any stipend, travel costs or living expenses to persons accepted under this programme.

In-Service Training Fellowships. This is another class of Internship under which the persons selected are assigned to specific research projects and are paid a small stipend. They are very limited in number.

Further information from:
United Nations Institute for Training and Research
801 United Nations Plaza
New York, New York 10017
U.S.A.

[2085]

UNITED STATES-ARGENTINA EDUCATIONAL EXCHANGE COMMISSION

Exchange Scholarships

Subjects: Any university studies.

Value: A maintenance allowance, and cost of necessary travel.

Tenable at universities and higher educational establishments in Argentina for the duration of the approved studies.

Eligibility: Open to American graduates who wish to complete their studies or research in Argentina.

Note: Candidates should apply through the Institute of International Education [q.v.].

Not confirmed for 1983.

Address:
U.S.-Argentina Educational
  Exchange Commission
Juez Tedín 2716
1425 Buenos Aires
Argentina

[2086]

UNITED STATES FOUNDATION *(France)*

Harriet Hale Woolley Scholarships

Subjects: Music and art.

No. offered: Four to six Scholarships annually.

Value: US$3,800 per annum; an additional US$800 to pianists for the rental of a piano.

Tenable at the Foundation, for one academic year (1st October to 30th June).

Eligibility: Open to single United States citizens, between 21 and 34 years of age, who have a bachelor's degree in arts, fine arts or music, or can show evidence of equivalent training.

Note: Recipients must live at the Foundation and take an active part in the organization of its cultural program.
Applicants should send seven international postal coupons with letters of inquiry.

Closing date: 31st January.

Further information from:
  Ronald Frazee, Director
  Foundation des États-Unis
  15 boulevard Jourdan
  75690 Paris Cedex 14
  France

[2087]

UNITED STATES INDUSTRIAL COUNCIL EDUCATION FOUNDATION

Editorial Writers Awards Competition: Five cash Awards, ranging from US$100 to US$500 each, and an honorable mention prize of US$50, are given annually for those editorials which best interpret the spirit and goals of the American free enterprise system, and which describe and analyze the achievements of it. Individuals may submit as many entries as they wish. Editorials must have been published in a daily or weekly newspaper, or broadcast on a television or radio station in the United States during the calendar year for which the Awards are made. Editorials should be submitted to the address below no later than 31st January of the following year, for decision to be reached by 30th April.

Editorial Cartoon 'Dragonslayer' Contest: Five cash Awards, ranging from US$100 to US$500 each, and an honorable mention prize of US$50, are given annually for the best editorial cartoons attacking government intervention, bureaucratic harassment, inflation, unfair union demands and practices, unreasonable criticism from consumer and environmental groups, etc. Cartoonists may send as many entries as they wish. Cartoons, which must be published during the Awards year, should be submitted to the address below no later than 31st January of the following year. Decisions will be reached by 30th April.

Further information from:
  Editorial Awards Competitions
  United States Industrial Council
    Education Foundation
  306 Gay Street, Room 303
  Nashville, Tennessee 37201
  U.S.A.

[2088]

UNITED STATES-ISRAEL BINATIONAL SCIENCE FOUNDATION

BSF Cooperative Research Project Grants

Purpose: To promote and support cooperation between the United States and Israel in scientific and technological research.

Subjects: Basic and applied research in health sciences, natural and mathematical sciences, atmospheric and earth sciences, oceanography and limnology, materials research, energy, environmental research, biomedical engineering, economics, sociology, anthropology and social and developmental psychology.

No. offered: Varies according to funds available.

Value: Varies, depending upon direct costs of the approved research. Payments are made in Israeli currency in three annual instalments. Grants do not cover salaries of principal investigators.

Tenable at non-profit research organizations in Israel, for up to three years, dependent on acceptable annual science and fiscal reports.

Eligibility: Open to United States and Israeli resident scientists who submit applications through non-profit research organizations with legal status such as universities, government research institutions and hospitals. Only programs involving close cooperation between United States and Israeli scientists are eligible. Graduate students may not apply. Proposals are supported in order of scientific merit, collaborative arrangements, and mutual United States-Israeli government interest.

Note: United States candidates may obtain further information from the *Division of International Programs, National Science Foundation, Washington, D.C. 20550.*

Closing date: 1st December for decision in July of the following year.

Address:
  United States-Israel Binational Science
    Foundation
  P.O. Box 7677
  Jerusalem
  Israel

[2089]

UNIVERSAL ESPERANTO ASSOCIATION
(Rotterdam)

Awards

Purpose: To train young volunteer workers for the advancement of the international language.

Subject: The language and literature of Esperanto.

No. offered: Two or three Awards annually.

Value: A monthly stipend of 500 Dutch florins, plus travel, insurance, and other expenses.

Tenable at the Head Office of the Association in Rotterdam, or at the Association's Graphical Centre in Antwerp, for up to one year; non-renewable.

Eligibility: Open to individuals of all nations who are between the ages of 18 and 29 years. Previous fluent knowledge of Esperanto, both written and spoken, is an essential qualification.

Further information from:
Universal Esperanto Association
Nieuwe Binneweg 176
3015 BJ Rotterdam
Netherlands

[2090]

UNIVERSAL POSTAL UNION

Fellowships

Approximately 400 Fellowships are offered annually under the United Nations Development Programme, the Special Fund of the Universal Postal Union and its Regular Budget to postal staff from the developing countries. Applications must be made by the postal authorities themselves, and not by the individual. Scholarships are in the field of postal service only.

Further information from:
Universal Postal Union
CH-3000 Berne 15
Switzerland

[2091]

UNIVERSITIES FEDERATION FOR ANIMAL WELFARE *(U.K.)*

Postgraduate Award Scheme

Subjects: Care, management and control of farm, laboratory or wild animals including companion animals—not necessarily by means of a formal course of training.

No. offered: One Award annually.

Value: £1,000.

Tenable in the United Kingdom for the duration of the approved course or project.

Eligibility: Open to students, preferably under 30 years of age, from any country who possess a degree in the biological, pharmaceutical, veterinary or medical sciences or other relevant qualification. Applicants should be proficient in written and spoken English.

Closing date: 30th August each year.

Further information from:
Secretary
Universities Federation for Animal Welfare
8 Hamilton Close
South Mimms, Potters Bar
Hertfordshire
England EN6 3QD

[2092]

UNIVERSITIES FIELD STAFF INTERNATIONAL-INSTITUTE OF WORLD AFFAIRS

Summer Seminar Scholarship for International Relations

Purpose: To enable exceptional graduates and postgraduates to participate in a seminar on contemporary issues.

Subjects: International relations—specific topics vary.

No. offered: Varies annually.

Value: Varies, according to individual need.

Tenable for four weeks.

Eligibility: Open to persons who have completed the requirements for a bachelor's degree, graduates and postgraduates. There are no restrictions in regard to age, sex, citizenship or residency.

Note: Travel expenses are not covered by the Institute.

Closing date: 15th May.

Further information from:
UFSI-IWA Summer Seminar
P.O. Box 150
Hanover, New Hampshire 03755
U.S.A.

[2093]

UNIVERSITY ASSISTANCE FUND
(Netherlands)

Scholarships

Subjects: Unrestricted.

Value: 780 Dutch florins per month; Scholarships cover living expenses, tuition, books, etc., and transportation when necessary.

Tenable at universities or institutions of intermediate and advanced vocational training in the Netherlands.

Eligibility: Open to suitably qualified refugees and other students who have been forced to cease their studies in their own countries and are resident in the Netherlands.

Further information from:
University Assistance Fund
F.C. Donderstraat 16
Utrecht
Netherlands

[2094]

UNIVERSITY OF CAPE TOWN
(South Africa)

Unless otherwise stated, the following awards are offered to suitably qualified graduates, regardless of age, sex or citizenship, for postgraduate study and research at the University of Cape Town.

J.W. Duncan Baxter Scholarships: A number of renewable Scholarships of approximately R2,000 per year are available for research in the medical and related sciences. Preference is given for research in relation to cancer. *Closing date:* 30th September.

Forman Awards: One or two Awards of up to R2,000 each are given annually to promote or assist the study of medicine and/or medical research. The Awards are tenable for one year; not renewable. *Closing date:* 30th September.

J.W. Jagger Scholarship: Several Scholarships are offered annually for two years' postgraduate study of at least the Master's level, in any discipline. Each Scholar receives approximately R2,500 per annum plus travel expenses. Only male graduates from Great Britain are eligible, and preference is given to candidates wishing to take up permanent residence in South Africa. *Closing date:* 30th September.

Wilfred Kramer Law Grants: Renewable Grants of variable value are offered to suitably qualified overseas students for postgraduate study in the Faculty of Law. *Closing date:* 31st October.

Overseas Students' Scholarships: To enable graduates from universities outside South Africa to study for a higher degree in a discipline offered at the University of Cape Town. Several Scholarships of not less than R2,500 are offered annually, and are renewable subject to satisfactory progress. *Closing date:* 30th September.

Smuts Memorial Fellowship: To enable a suitably qualified person to undertake study and research, by preference, in the systematics and geographical distribution of South African flora, one Fellowship of R2,000 is offered as a vacancy occurs. The Scholarship is tenable at the National Botanic Gardens, South Africa and the University of Cape Town for two years; renewable for a further year. Preference is given to graduates of the University of Cape Town and citizens of Cape Town. *Closing date:* As advertised in *Nature*.

UCT Post-doctoral Fellowships: Up to three Fellowships of R17,500 and a travel grant each are offered annually for one year of post-doctoral study and research in any discipline offered at the University of Cape Town. Fellowships are not renewable. *Closing date:* as advertised in *Nature*. *Science* and the *Times Higher Education Supplement*.

UCT Post-graduate Research Scholarships: A number of Scholarships are offered annually for approved courses of study in any discipline. The Scholarships are offered for one year and are renewable. Values (as of 1981) are R1,800 for Honours. R2,250 for Masters and R4,000 for Doctoral levels of study. Values are reviewed annually. *Closing date:* 31st October.

Further information from:
 Registrar
 University of Cape Town
 Private Bag
 Rondebosch 7700
 South Africa

[2095]

UNIVERSITY CENTER FOR COOPERATIVES
University of Wisconsin *(Madison)*

Seminar Scholarships

Seminar: Cooperative education and management—the organization and operation of cooperatives in developing countries. The program includes training in cooperative principles, structure and organization, finance, marketing, management, education, and public relations.

Value: A few partial Scholarships are occasionally offered by Cooperative Education and Training, Inc., to participants from developing countries who have most of their funding from other sources.

Tenable at the Center for 16 weeks, commencing in August.

Eligibility: Open to suitably qualified persons from, or who plan to work in, developing countries of Africa, Asia and Latin America.

Closing date: Six weeks prior to commencement of the Seminar. Applicants requiring Scholarships should make enquiries well in advance.

Further information from:
 University Center for Cooperatives
 University of Wisconsin
 610 Langdon Street
 Madison, Wisconsin 53706
 U.S.A.

[2096]

UNIVERSITY OF EAST ANGLIA *(Norwich)*
Eastern Arts Association

Eastern Arts Fellowship

The Fellowship of £2,000 and free accommodation is offered annually to enable a creative writer to work in a university atmosphere on a reciprocal basis. The Fellowship is tenable for the spring or summer terms at the University of East Anglia.

Closing date: 1st October.

Further information from:
 Establishment Officer
 University of East Anglia
 University Plain
 Norwich
 England NR4 7TJ

[2097]

UNIVERSITY GRANTS COMMITTEE *(N.Z.)*

Postgraduate Scholarships

Subjects: Unrestricted.

Value: NZ$4,020 per annum.

Tenable in New Zealand, for two years, with the possibility of extension.

Eligibility: Open to first class honours graduates who are proceeding directly towards a doctoral degree.

Note: At the time of going to press, the Scholarships were under review.

Closing date: 1st October.

Further information from:
 Secretary
 University Grants Committee
 Box 12348
 Wellington North
 New Zealand

[2098]

UNIVERSITY GRANTS COMMITTEE *(N.Z.)*

BP Postgraduate Scholarship for Study in New Zealand

Subjects: Agriculture, arts, commerce, engineering, law or science.

Value: NZ$1,000 per annum.

Tenable at any university in New Zealand, as a supplement to a postgraduate scholarship.

Eligibility: Open to British subjects who have lived in New Zealand for four years preceding the date of application, and who have been awarded a U.G.C. Postgraduate Scholarship tenable in New Zealand.

Closing date: 1st October.

Further information from:
 Secretary
 University Grants Committee
 Box 12348
 Wellington North
 New Zealand

[2099]

UNIVERSITY GRANTS COMMITTEE *(N.Z.)*

Internal Affairs Wildlife Scholarship

Subject: Ornithology, or, exceptionally, study involving some animal (preferably vertebrate) other than a bird.

Value: NZ$4,020 per annum plus fees, etc.

Tenable at a university institution in New Zealand which offers Ph.D. courses, for two years.

Eligibility: Open to British subjects resident in New Zealand who are eligible to proceed to a Ph.D. degree at a New Zealand university.

Closing date: 1st October.

Further information from:
 Secretary
 University Grants Committee
 Box 12348
 Wellington North
 New Zealand

[2100]

UNIVERSITY GRANTS COMMITTEE *(N.Z.)*

Gordon Watson Scholarship

Subjects: International relationships or social and economic conditions outside New Zealand.

No. offered: One Scholarship biennially.

Value: At least NZ$2,800 per annum.

Tenable at a university or universities in the United Kingdom, Europe, Asia or America, for two years.

Eligibility: Candidates must hold an honours degree, or a degree in theology from a university in New Zealand, and must undertake to return to New Zealand after the Scholarship period of not less than two years.

Closing date: 1st October in even-numbered years.

Further information from:
 Secretary
 University Grants Committee
 Box 12348
 Wellington North
 New Zealand

[2101]

UNIVERSITY GRANTS COMMITTEE *(N.Z.)*

L.B. Wood Travelling Scholarship

Subjects: Unrestricted.

No. offered: One Scholarship annually.

Value: NZ$1,000 per annum, as a supplement to another postgraduate scholarship.

Tenable for up to three years at a university or institution of university rank in Great Britain.

Eligibility: Open to all graduates from any faculty of any university in New Zealand, provided that application is made within three years from the date of graduation.

Closing date: 1st October.

Further information from:
  Secretary
  University Grants Committee
  Box 12348
  Wellington North
  New Zealand

[2102]

UNIVERSITY GRANTS COMMITTEE *(N.Z.)*

Claude McCarthy Fellowships

Purpose: To enable graduates to undertake original work or research in any aspect of the fields of literature, science, or medicine.

No. offered: Varies, depending upon available funds.

Value: Varies, according to seniority, marital status, country of residence during tenure, and the nature of the project itself. Assistance for expenses incurred in travel, employment of technical staff, special equipment, etc., may be provided.

Tenable in New Zealand or abroad, normally for not more than one year.

Eligibility: Open to any graduate of a New Zealand university.

Closing date: 1st August.

Further information from:
  Secretary
  University Grants Committee
  Box 12348
  Wellington North
  New Zealand

[2103]

UNIVERSITY GRANTS COMMITTEE *(N.Z.)*

Sir Walter Mulholland Fellowship

Subjects: Advanced studies or research in the field of processing and marketing of primary produce (economics, biochemistry, microbiology, engineering, food technology, etc.).

No. offered: One Fellowship.

Value: NZ$4,600 per annum, plus travel and other allowances.

Tenable at institutions in New Zealand or overseas for up to three years.

Eligibility: Candidates should hold or be completing an honours degree in physics, chemistry, biology, economics, mathematics, agriculture, engineering, home science or food technology from a New Zealand university.

Note: Details of conditions of the Fellowships may be obtained from the address below.
  Funds are provided by the New Zealand Meat Producers Board.

Closing date: 1st October.

Further information from:
  Secretary
  University Grants Committee
  Box 12348
  Wellington North
  New Zealand

[2104]

UNIVERSITY GRANTS COMMITTEE *(N.Z.)*

Shirtcliffe Fellowship

Purpose: To provide further aid for holders of U.G.C. Postgraduate Scholarships.

Subjects: Arts, science, law, commerce or agriculture.

Value: NZ$1,000 as a supplement to the postgraduate scholarship emolument.

Tenable at a suitable educational institution in New Zealand or a commonwealth country overseas for such period as the Fellow holds the postgraduate scholarship.

Eligibility: Open to graduates of New Zealand universities who have been awarded a U.G.C. Postgraduate Scholarship.

Further information from:
  Secretary
  University Grants Committee
  Box 12348
  Wellington North
  New Zealand

[2105]

UNIVERSITY OF KANSAS MEDICAL CENTER

Logan Clendening Travelling Fellowship

Subject: History of medicine.

Value: US$1,000.

Tenable anywhere for three months in the summer.

Eligibility: Open to United States and Canadian citizens who are medical students or university students accepted by a recognized medical or osteopathic school in the United States or Canada.

Not confirmed for 1983.

Further information from:
 Chairman
 Department of the History of Medicine
 University of Kansas Medical Center
 Kansas City, Kansas 66103
 U.S.A.

[2106]

UNIVERSITY OF LONDON

Rogers Prize

The Rogers Prize of £25 is offered from time to time and is open to all persons whose names appear on the Medical Register of the United Kingdom. The Prize is awarded for an essay or dissertation on a medical or surgical subject which is named by the University at least twelve months before the last date of entry for the Prize.

Before submitting essays or dissertations, candidates should obtain the latest details from:
 Rogers Prize
 Academic Department
 Scholarships Section
 University of London
 Senate House
 London
 England WC1E 7HU

[2107]

UNIVERSITY OF MARYLAND INTERNATIONAL PIANO FESTIVAL AND COMPETITION

Main prizes of US$5,000, US$3,000, US$1,500 and US$1,000 are offered annually. Pianists between the ages of 16 and 32 years may apply. Enrollment deadline is 1st April. The Competition is held in July. Orchestral and recital engagements are arranged for the First Prize winner.

Further information from:
 International Piano Festival
  and Competition
 University of Maryland
 College Park, Maryland 20742
 U.S.A.

[2108]

UNIVERSITY OF MELBOURNE

Research Fellowships: Several Fellowships are awarded twice each year for full-time research in all departments of the University. The awards are tenable for one year, with the possibility of extension for an additional 6 or 12 months. Fellows receive return economy air-fare to Melbourne, and a stipend of between A$17,083 to A19,570 (Research Fellow Grade 1) or A$19,821 to A$26,037 (Research Fellow Grade 2). Open to young scholars from Australia or overseas having a Ph.D. or at least equivalent postgraduate research experience. This degree or experience should have been attained within the five year period preceding application. Candidates should be no more than 35 years of age. *Closing date:* 31st January and July of each year. Further information is available from the Secretary, Office of Research and Graduate Studies, at the address below.

Grants-in-Aid: Awarded twice each year in all departments of the University to enable academics on sabbatical or other types of leave to conduct full-time research at the University of Melbourne, preferably for a period of not less than six months. The amount of support varies upon individual circumstances. Maximum Grants, including travel, are A$7,500 (under review). Interested persons should contact the chairman of the department they wish to visit, at the address below. *Closing dates:* 31st January and July of each year.

Postgraduate Scholarships: A$4,500 per annum, payable monthly, an establishment allowance of up to A$75, and if eligible, a dependent's allowance of A$2,000 per annum for spouse and A$500 per annum for child, are awarded for graduate research at the University. The Scholarships are tenable, at the Master's level, usually for up to one year, with the possibility of extension for an additional 6 or 12 months, and at the Ph.D. level for up to three years, with the possibility of extension for an additional 6 or 12 months. The Scholarships are open to candidates from Australia and foreign countries. Additional information may be obtained from the Office of Research and Graduate Studies, at the address below. *Closing date:* 31st October of each year.

Address:
University of Melbourne
Parkville, Victoria
Australia 3052

[2109]

UNIVERSITY FOR MINING AND METALLURGY *(Leoben, Austria)*

Postgraduate Scholarship

Purpose: To provide specialized training to graduates in the mining sciences and in the geosciences who are from developing countries.

Subjects: All aspects of mineral prospection and exploration.

No. offered: A limited number of Scholarships annually.

Value: 5,500 schillings per month, plus one clothing allowance of 2,500 schillings. The Austrian Government provides all tuition, travel expenses during field work and excursions within Austria, as well as free health and accident insurance.

Tenable in Leoben for five months.

Eligibility: Open to candidates from developing countries who are between the ages of 25 and 35 and have an adequate knowledge of English and all basic subjects necessary for participation in an advanced course of study.

Note: Dependents are not permitted to accompany Scholars. Transportation to and from the country of origin is the responsibility of the Scholar; however a contribution to these costs usually is provided by a grant from Unesco, and paid after arrival in Leoben.

Applications should be returned to the Austrian Diplomatic Mission, via the appropriate government authority, in the candidate's own country. Applications may be obtained by writing to the address below.

Closing date: 31st October.

Further information from:
University for Mining and Metallurgy
A-8700 Leoben
Austria

[2110]

UNIVERSITY OF OTAGO *(Dunedin, N.Z.)*

The following Fellowships are offered annually, subject to funds being available, to persons normally resident in New Zealand. Applicants need not possess any degree or diploma, nor need they belong to any artistic/professional organization; but they should be able to demonstrate that they will be likely to benefit from holding the Fellowship. The Fellowships are tenable at the University of Otago for one year and may be renewed for a further year. Subject to sufficient income in the Fellowships' fund, the annual value is not less than the minimum salary for a full-time university lecturer, and is payable in twelve monthly instalments. Closing date for application is 10th August.

Robert Burns Fellowship: Offered to encourage and promote imaginative New Zealand literature and to associate writers thereof with the University. Applicants are required to submit details of works published and contemplated. Between candidates of comparable merit, preference is given to those under 40 years of age. Except in special circumstances, the Fellowship is not awarded to a person who is a full-time teacher at a university.

Frances Hodgkins Fellowship: Offered to aid and encourage painters and sculptors in the practice of their art, to associate them with the life of the University, and at the same time to foster an interest in the arts within the University. Candidates should be able to demonstrate that they have executed sufficient work to show their talent, and are serious artists who will diligently practise, improve and develop their talent. Between candidates of comparable merit, preference is given to those under 40 years of age. Except in special circumstances, no full-time teacher in an art school is eligible.

Mozart Fellowship: Offered to aid and encourage composers of music in the practice and advancement of their art, to associate them with the life of the University, and at the same time to foster an interest in contemporary music within the University and community. The Fellowship is open to persons over 27 years of age, who, in the opinion of the Selection Committee, have shown themselves to be composers of talent and serious intention. Under some circumstances, the Fellowship may be awarded to an overseas composer.

Further information from:
Registrar
University of Otago
P.O. Box 56
Dunedin
New Zealand

[2111]

UNIVERSITY OF TASMANIA *(Australia)*

Estelle Marguerite Taylor Postgraduate Scholarship: One award, when funding permits, of A$4,300 per annum, a dependents' allowance and other expenses, is given for study or research in any subject. The Scholarship is tenable at the University of Tasmania for up to three years, and may be extended for an additional year. Candidates of all nationalities are eligible. *Closing date:* 31st October.

Merle Weaver Postgraduate Scholarship: One award, when funding permits, of A$4,200 per annum, a dependents' allowance and other expenses, is given to women graduates from South East Asia and the Pacific region for study or research in any subject. The Scholarship is tenable at the University of Tasmania for up to three years, and may be extended for an additional year. *Closing date:* 31st October.

University Postgraduate Coursework Scholarships: Approximately five awards, as funding permits, are offered annually for course work leading to a Master's degree in clinical psychology, environmental studies, special education, transport economics and education, fine arts, music and welfare law. Each Scholarship is tenable at the University of Tasmania for up to two years and provides for A$4,300 per annum, dependents' allowance and other expenses. Awards are not renewable. Canidates of any nationality with at least an upper second class honours degree or its equivalent, and some employment experience are eligible. *Closing date:* 30th September.

University Postgraduate Research Scholarships: Five to ten Scholarships, as funding permits, are offered annually for study or research in any subject, leading to a higher degree. Awards in the amount of A$4,300 per annum, dependents' allowance and other expenses are tenable at the University of Tasmania initially for one year; may be renewed for an additional year (Master's degree). Occasionally Ph.D. awards may be extended for further periods. Candidates of all nationalities who have at least an upper second class honours degree or its equivalent are eligible. Final year undergraduate students may apply. *Closing date:* 31st October.

Note: Non-Australian Scholars are not subject to university tuition fees, Australian income tax or Australian visa charges.

Further information from:
Registrar
University of Tasmania
G.P.O. Box 252C
Hobart, Tasmania
Australia 7001

[2112]

UNIVERSITY OF TENNESSEE PRESS
Southern Anthropological Society
(U.S.A.)

James Mooney Award

The Award of US$1,000, plus publication of the winning manuscript, is offered annually to encourage distinguished writing in anthropology (including ethnography, linguistics, archaeology, physical anthropology, history, folklore, sociology, and other related disciplines).

Students of the cultures and societies of the New World may submit manuscripts which should be in English, typed and approximately 100,000 words in length. Authors are encouraged to illustrate their manuscripts with maps, charts and photographs. Unrevised theses and dissertations are not eligible.

No substantial part of the manuscripts may

have been published previously, be under consideration from another publisher, or be under submission for any other award.

Each manuscript should be accompanied by a letter describing in 250 words or less, the subject, scope, significance and length of the manuscript.

Closing date: 31st December.

Further information from:
Harriet J. Kupferer
James Mooney Award
Department of Anthropology
University of North Carolina
Greensboro, North Carolina 27405
U.S.A.

[2113]

UNIVERSITY OF THE WITWATERSRAND
(Johannesburg)

The following awards are offered annually by the University of the Witwatersrand to distinguished graduates of approved universities in South Africa. All are tenable at the University for one year of full-time study, and renewable for additional periods of study. *Closing date:* 31st December for all awards.

Herbert Ainsworth Scholarship: One Scholarship of R1,000 per annum for study towards an honours degree in modern history.

E.P. Bradlow Scholarship: One Scholarship of R1,250 per annum, paid in four equal installments, for postgraduate study towards a Ph.D. Preference is given to applicants studying business administration.

Henry Bradlow Scholarship: One Scholarship of R,1250 per annum, paid in four equal installments, for postgraduate study towards a master's or Ph.D. Preference is given to applicants studying dentistry.

Carnovski Postgraduate Scholarship: One Scholarship of R600 per annum, paid in four equal installments, for honours degree study in African studies, i.e. Bantu languages, social anthropology and African government.

G.A. Denny Postgraduate Research Scholarship: One Scholarship of R800 per annum, paid in four equal installments for study in the broad field of social relations, including civics, municipal administration, and race relations.

Freda Lawenski Scholarship Fund Grants: Approximately 10 Grants, ranging in value from R500 to a maximum of R2,000 per annum, are awarded in all fields of study offered at the University of the Witwatersrand.

John Lemmer/Bradlow Scholarship: One Scholarship of R2,500 per annum, paid in four equal installments, is awarded for postgraduate master's or Ph.D. study. Preference is given to applicants studying dental research.

Mones Michaels Bursary: One Bursary of up to R1,000 per annum, paid in four equal installments, is awarded for postgraduate degree study or research in geophysics.

Bernard Price Scholarships in Power Engineering: Two Scholarships of up to R2,000 per annum, paid in four equal installments, are given for study and research in the field of electrical engineering.

Raikes Scholarship: Five Scholarships of R600 each per annum are awarded for study towards an honours degree in the arts or sciences.

J. Arthur Reavell Foundation Scholarships: Two Scholarships of up to R1,000 per annum, paid in four equal installments, are awarded for postgraduate study in the field of chemical engineering.

Adolph Wagner Scholarships: Two Scholarships of up to R1,000 per annum, paid in four equal installments, are awarded for postgraduate research in engineering. Preference will be given to applicants studying mining engineering.

Further information from:
Bursaries Officer
University of the Witwatersrand
1 Jan Smuts Avenue
Johannesburg 2001
South Africa

[2114]

UNIVERSITY WOMEN'S ASSOCIATION OF DELHI
Indian Federation of University Women's Associations

Sarojini Naidu Memorial Scholarship

Purpose: To promote the exchange of scholars between India and other countries; to foster better international understanding; to promote studies on Indian culture and other areas.

Courses of study: Arts and humanities—language studies, history and cultural history, psychology, economics, philosophy, sociology, political science; basic and applied sciences—home science (child development, nutrition and home management); professional courses—teacher education, business administration, library science, office management, journalism, social work; research, field work, and postgraduate diploma—international studies and international relations, community development and rural uplift, anthropology, culture and civilization, music, dance and drama, psychiatry.

No. offered: One Scholarship annually.

Value: 600 rupees per month.

Tenable at institutions in Delhi for six to twelve months with possibility of an extension.

Eligibility: Open to women students of any country who qualify for study or research work at the postgraduate level in an appropriate subject. Candidates should be first class graduates of recognized universities, should be not more than 45 years of age, and must be members of the Federation of University Women's Associations in their own countries. The Scholarship is not given for study towards a master's degree.

Not confirmed for 1983.

Further information from:
The Convenor (Scholarships)
University Women's Association of Delhi
15/90 Connaught Circus
New Delhi-110001
India

[2115]

UNIVERSITY WOMEN'S ASSOCIATION OF NAGPUR
Indian Federation of University Women's Associations

Scholarships

Purpose: To enable a foreign student to undertake a course of study in India.

Subjects: Natural sciences, medical sciences, social sciences, humanities, engineering and home science.

No. offered: One Scholarship annually.

Value: 250 rupees per month.

Tenable at Nagpur University, India for two academic years.

Eligibility: Open to women graduates of any nationality who are members of the International Federation of University Women and hold a bachelor's degree from a recognised university. Candidates must gain admission to the appropriate faculty at Nagpur University

Closing date: September.

Note: Applicants should send biographical data and academic records.

Further information from:
University Women's Association of Nagpur
c/o Mrs. I. Kelkar
240 Shankarnagar
Nagpur 440010
India

[2116]

PHILIP USHER MEMORIAL FUND *(U.K.)*

Philip Usher Memorial Scholarship

Subjects: Life, worship, history, theology, art or archaeology of the Orthodox Church.

No. offered: One Scholarship annually.

Value: Approximately £1,200 paid in one lump sum.

Tenable at Orthodox Churches in Greece,

Lebanon, Romania, Yugoslavia and the U.S.S.R., for not less than six or more than eighteen months.

Eligibility: Open to ordained ministers and accepted ordinands of the Church of England, Church of Ireland, Church in Wales, Episcopal Church in Scotland, or Episcopal Church in Jerusalem and the Middle East. Candidates under 35 years of age are given preference.

Closing date: 31st January.

Further information from:
 Honorary Secretary
 Philip Usher Memorial Fund
 Palace Court, 222 Lambeth Road
 London
 England SE1 7LB

V

See *How to Use The Grants Register*, page ix

[2117]

VAN CLIBURN FOUNDATION, INC. *(Fort Worth, Texas)*

International Quadrennial Piano Competition

This International Competition is held every four years with the purpose of building the careers of extraordinarily gifted young pianists who are ready to commit themselves to the life of a concert artist with a major career. The next Competition will be held in May, 1985. The Prizes are as follows: Grand Prize—US$12,000 plus a 2 year concert tour of the United States and Europe; Silver Medalist—US$8,000 and a concert tour; Bronze Medalist—US$5,000 and a concert tour; 4th Prize—US$3,000; 5th Prize—US$2,000; 6th Prize—US$1,000. The Competition is open to pianists of any nationality who are between the ages of 18 and 30 years. Repertoire requirements are available from the address below.

Closing date: 1st January of the year of Competition.

Further information from:
Van Cliburn Foundation, Inc.
3505 West Lancaster
Forth Worth, Texas 76107
U.S.A.

[2118]

VAN DEN BERGHS & JURGENS LTD. *(U.K.)*

Nutrition Awards

A First Prize of £1,000, Second Prize of £500, and Third Prize of £250 are offered annually to encourage the search for new solutions to human nutrition problems and to stimulate public discussion and awareness.

Citizens and residents of the United Kingdom, and citizens of the United Kingdom working in EEC member countries may apply.

Manuscripts should be typewritten in English and should not exceed 5,000 words. Entries should be based on original, reasoned or critical attempts to deal in depth with the subject and its relevance to the United Kingdom, in the form of either research findings, commentary or essay. Prize winning papers will be published in the book series *Getting the Most Out of Food*, and will become the property of Van den Berghs & Jurgens Ltd., which will also hold the copyright. *Closing date:* 31st October.

Further information from:
Nutrition Education Service
Van den Berghs & Jurgens Ltd.
Sussex House
Burgess Hill, Sussex
England RH15 9AW

[2119]

VAN DEN BERGHS & JURGENS LTD. *(U.K.)*

Nutrition Reporting Award

An Award of £1,000 is offered annually to recognize journalists and writers whose work has contributed to a better understanding of some aspect, or aspects, of human nutrition.

Journalists and writers employed by, or contributing to, newspapers, journals, radio or television in the United Kingdom may apply.

Entries should have been published or broadcast within the United Kingdom during the year of the Award.

Entries should not exceed 2,500 words. Newspaper and journal entries should be cuttings annotated with the name of the publication and publication date. Radio and television productions should be submitted as scripts annotated with programme and transmission details. Entries from freelance writers should include the endorsement of the editor or producer of the publication or broadcast programme concerned.

Closing date: 15th January.

Further information from:
  Nutrition Education Service
  Van den Berghs & Jurgens Ltd.
  Sussex House
  Burgess Hill, West Sussex
  England RH15 9AW

[2120]

TIBOR VARGA FESTIVAL *(Sion, Switzerland)*

International Competition for Violinists

Eight Prizes, totalling 15,500 Swiss francs are offered annually in competition for interpretive performance. Applicants may be of any nationality and should be between the ages of 15 and 35 years of age. Participants will compete at Sion during August. Prize-winners are obliged to remain in Sion for the awards presentation at the end of the competition. They will also be expected to perform in the presentation concert. The First Prize winner will be presented as soloist with a symphony orchestra at the international music Festival Tibor Varga. There is an application fee of 70 Swiss francs.

Closing date: 30th June.

Further information from:
  International Competition
  Tibor Varga Festival
  P.O. Box 3374
  CH-1951 Sion
  Switzerland

[2121]

CHARLES VEILLON FOUNDATION

European Essay Prize

10,000 Swiss francs are offered annually to a European author for a constructive critique of contemporary social problems. The essay must be written in a major European language and published in the award year.

Not confirmed for 1983.

Further information from:
  Charles Veillon Foundation
  Route de Crissier
  1030 Bussigny, Lausanne
  Switzerland

[2122]

VERGILIAN SOCIETY, INC. *(U.S.A.)*

Scholarships

Purpose: To promote effective teaching of Latin literature, history and life.

Subjects: Classical civilization as revealed by archaeology, art, and literature in Greece and especially Italy. Scholars study under the guidance of professors at the Classical Summer School operated by the Society in Italy and elsewhere.

No. offered: Variable number of Scholarships annually.

Value: From US$100 to US$500 according to need. The money is applied to tuition charges, and any surplus is given to the recipient in one sum.

Tenable at the Society's summer program at the Villa Vergiliana in Cumae, near Naples, and in conjunction with one of the Society's other study program.

Eligibility: Open to United States and Canadian citizens who are graduate students or teachers interested in classical civilization. Preference is given to high school teachers.

Closing date: Applications with supporting papers should be received by 15th February.

Further information from:
  Robert J. Rowland, Jr.
  Executive Secretary
  149 A&S UMC
  Columbia, Missouri 65211
  U.S.A.

[2123]

VETERANS ADMINISTRATION *(U.S.A.)*

Assistance Programs

The Veterans Administration has four programs of educational assistance:

(1) Education and training for post-Korean conflict veterans and serving persons.

(2) Vocational rehabilitation for veterans with

a service-connected disability for which compensation can be paid.

(3) Education assistance for children, spouses, and surviving spouses of veterans whose deaths or permanent total disabilities were service-connected and the spouses and children of servicepersons missing in action or forcibly detained.

(4) Contributory educational assistance program for post-Vietnam era veterans.

Subjects: (1) Unrestricted; (2) unrestricted—dependent upon a vocational rehabilitation plan worked out with V.A. counseling; (3) unrestricted; (4) unrestricted.

Value: (1) Educational assistance allowance based at the rate at which studies are pursued, and in the case of veterans, based on the number of dependents, for up to 45 months, depending upon length of service; (2) educational assistance for up to four years, and sometimes more, to include subsistence allowance, tuition, books and fees; (3) educational assistance for up to 45 months; (4) monthly payments based on the number of months a participant contributed (or for 36 months, whichever is less). Participants' contributions are matched by the VA on a 2 to 1 basis. The Department of Defense may also contribute.

Tenable at any approved institution in the United States. Eligible persons may pursue a program of education outside the United States at an approved educational institution of higher learning excepting vocational rehabilitation program participants who, generally, may not attend insitutions outside the United States or its territories.

Eligibility: (1) Open to honorably discharged veterans who served and servicepersons currently serving on active duty for more than 180 days, any part of which occurred after 31st January 1955. Also eligible are persons who enlisted in military service prior to 1st January, 1977, and who subsequently entered on active duty during 1977. Persons remain eligible until ten years after release (or until 31st December 1989, which comes first). (2) Open to honorably discharged veterans with compensable service-connected disabilities which the VA determines constitute a basis for rehabilitation services; eligibility for the seriously disabled can go back as far as World War II, but in general eligibility lasts twelve years from the date of separation. (3) Open to surviving spouses of deceased veterans, spouses of living veterans and children of veterans between 18 and 26 years of age when death or permanent disability was the result of service in the Armed Forces after 28th April, 1898. Spouses and children of servicepersons missing in action or held as prisoners of war are also eligible. For spouses and surviving spouses the period of eligibility generally extends to 30th November 1978 or ten years from the date of the serviceperson's death or total disability (whichever date is or was later). (4) Open to veterans who entered military service on or after 1st January, 1977 and who served on active duty for at least 180 consecutive days, commencing on or after 1st January, 1977, and were released or discharged from service for reasons other than dishonorable, or who were released or discharged from active duty after that date for a service-connected disability. Persons in this category must have contributed to the fund while they were in the service.

Note: Applicants are advised to obtain *Federal Benefits for Veterans and Dependents* (VA IS-1 Fact Sheet, U.S. Government Printing Office). Further information and application forms should be obtained from: VA offices, active duty stations and American embassies in other countries and forms should be submitted to the nearest VA office or embassy when completed.

Headquarters address:
   Veterans Administration
   Central Office
   Department of Veterans Benefits
   Washington, D.C. 20420
   U.S.A.

[2124]

VICTORIA LAW FOUNDATION *(Australia)*

Grants and Awards

The Foundation offers support for research relating to law reform in Victoria, the promotion of legal education in Victoria, the investigation of proposals for improvement of the administration of law in Victoria, and for law libraries in Victoria.

There are no formal terms of eligibility; every application is treated on its merits. Duration of Awards varies with the project.

Research projects may be undertaken either within or outside Victoria.

Enquiries are examined at an informal level in the first instance by Foundation staff, who advise in relation to the nature of a formal application.

Further information from:
Executive Director
Victoria Law Foundation
160 Queen Street
Melbourne, Victoria
Australia 3000

[2125]

VICTORIAN ORDER OF NURSES FOR CANADA

VON Bursary Assistance

A limited number of Bursaries are available to help nurses obtain their master's or post-master's degree in an approved area of study. Bursaries are paid in the amount of up to *Can*$9,000 for two years of study.

Recipients are required, upon completion of the degree, to accept an appointment with the Order, or a local branch of it, for a period of at least one year for each year of financial support.

Further information from:
Ada E. McEwen, National Director
Victorian Order of Nurses for Canada
5 Blackburn Avenue
Ottawa, Ontario
Canada K1N 8A2

[2126]

VICTORIAN OVERSEAS FOUNDATION
(Australia)

Scholarships

Purpose: To enable skilled tradesmen to proceed overseas to gain further experience in their trades and to study overseas methods and equipment.

No. offered: Eight Scholarships annually.

Value: Cost of passage to the overseas country and return to Australia.

Tenable in appropriate countries for up to two years.

Eligibility: Open to Australian citizens between 21 and 25 years of age, who have completed their apprenticeship indentures and have passed the prescribed course at a technical college or school.

Note: Scholars must: (a) undertake to take up the training arranged in the country to which they will go; (b) provide evidence of their intention to return to Australia on completion of the Scholarships; (c) take up the Scholarship within twelve months of the date of the award.

Closing date: 31st May.

Further information from:
Secretary
Victorian Overseas Foundation
P.O. Box 21
Hawthorn, Victoria
Australia 3122

[2127]

VIENNA INTERNATIONAL COMPETITION FOR COMPOSITION

A First Prize of 100,000 schillings, Second Prize of 75,000 schillings and a Third Prize of 50,000 schillings are offered in the Competition which is held from time to time. Composers of any nationality who are not more than 40 years of age may apply.

Further information from:
Österreichischer Komponistenbund
Baumannstrasse 8-10
A-1030 Vienna
Austria

[2128]

VILLE DE TOULOUSE INTERNATIONAL SINGING COMPETITION

Prizes in the amount of 63,000 French francs are offered in the annual Competition which is held in Toulouse in October. Singers of any nationality who are between the ages of 18 and 33 may enter. Applications should be made by 15th September.

Further information from:
Secretariat
Concours International de Chant
  de la Ville Toulouse
Théâtre du Capitole
F-31000 Toulouse
France

[2129]

G.P. VIOTTI INTERNATIONAL MUSIC COMPETITION *(Vercelli, Italy)*

Prizes totalling 8,000,000 lire are offered in the Competition which is held annually from October to December. Categories for 1982 will be: singing; piano; piano duets, and composition. There are no age limits for composers but pianists and singers should be under 34 years of age.

Further information from:
G.B. Viotti International Music
  Competition
Società del Quartetto
Casella postale 127
1-13100 Vercelli
Italy

[2130]

VIRGINIA CENTER FOR THE CREATIVE ARTS *(U.S.A.)*

Fellowships

Purpose: To provide writers, painters, sculptors, composers and photographers with the proper environment for creative work for extended periods of time.

No. offered: 24 Fellowships are available simultaneously. Approximately 200 Fellowships are offered during the course of a year.

Value: Subsidized residency at the Center. No cash stipends or travel allowances are provided.

Tenable at the Center for one to three months each year; renewable.

Eligibility: Open to artists with professional competence and promise, regardless of age, sex, citizenship or academic background.

Further information from:
William Smart, Director
Virginia Center for the Creative Arts
Sweet Briar, Virginia 24595
U.S.A.

[2131]

VIRGINIA QUARTERLY REVIEW *(U.S.A.)*

Emily Clark Balch Prize Contests

To stimulate appreciation and creation of American literature, Prizes of US$500 are offered annually to Americans for short stories and poetry.

Prize-winning stories and poems are selected at the end of the calendar year from those published in the manazine that year. Short stories should be within the range of 3,000 to 7,000 words; poems of great length cannot be considered.

Further information from:
Emily Clark Balch Prize Contests
Virginia Quarterly Review
One West Range
Charlottesville, Virginia 22903
U.S.A.

[2132]

VISNEWS LTD. *(U.K.)*

Fellowships in International Television Journalism

Subjects: Latest techniques in television news-gathering and transmission.

No. offered: Up to three Fellowships annually.

Value: Approximately £3,400, to include cost of travel, subsistence, accommodation and training.

Tenable in England, Europe, the United States or Canada.

Eligibility: Open to citizens (25 to 35 years of age) of developing countries where there is a national or regional television system.

Note: Application forms, available from Visnews Ltd., should be accompanied by a 2000-word report or equivalent audio or video tape or film on "the development of television news in my country."

Further information from:
   Secretary of the Trustees
   Visnews Fellowships
   Visnews Ltd.
   Cumberland Avenue
   London
   England NW10 7EH

[2133]

VISUAL RESEARCH TRUST *(U.K.)*

Grants-In-Aid

Purpose: To encourage the development of promising research schemes for projects designed to advance an understanding of the eye and vision, including research into abnormal ocular conditions and improved clinical methods of ophthalmic investigation.

No. offered: Approximately four Grants-in-Aid annually.

Value: A maximum of £1,000 to help defray the cost of equipment and supplies required for the project. Recipients may supplement a Grant with funds from other sources.

Tenable at any approved United Kingdom institution or venue offering facilities suitable to the research project. Grants may be renewed if research progress is favorable and if funds are available.

Eligibility: Open to anyone within the United Kingdom whose background and interests are likely to contribute to the project undertaken.

Note: When working from an institution it is the responsibility of the candidate to make appropriate arrangements with that institution. The Grantee must submit to the Committee a brief report or summary of the work done not more than two months after completion of the proposed programme of work. Appropriate acknowledgment to the Grantor should be given in all relevant publications.

Further information from:
   Honorary Secretary
   Visual Research Trust
   179 West Geogre Street
   Glasgow
   Scotland G2 2LQ

[2134]

VOCI VERDIANE INTERNATIONAL COMPETITION *(Milan)*

Prizes amounting to about 8,000,000 lire and a study scholarship of 2,500,000 lire are offered in the annual Competition for singing (music of Verdi) in June. Winners perform in a concert at the Piccola Scala in Milan. Singers of any nationality who are not more than 35 years of age may apply.

Further information from:
   Concorso Internazionale per
      "Voci Verdiane"
   c/o Famiglia Artistica Milanese
   16 Corso Porta Vitoria
   I-20122 Milan
   Italy

[2135]

ALEXANDER VON HUMBOLDT FOUNDATION *(West Germany)*

Purpose: To provide opportunities for young, highly qualified scholars from abroad to carry out research projects of their own choice in Germany.

Subjects: Unrestricted: postdoctoral academic research.

No. offered: Approximately 450 Research Fellowships annually.

Value: DM2,100 to DM2,900 plus travel allowance for research Fellow only, and dependents' allowance.

Tenable at universities or research institutions in the Federal Republic of Germany and in West Berlin for six to twelve months, with the possibility of extension up to a total of 24 months.

Eligibility: Open to persons of any nationality other than German, between 25 and 40 years of age, who have obtained a Ph.D. degree or equivalent, have had some experience in advanced research at a university or independent research at a university or independent research institute and possess sufficient knowledge of German to carry out their proposed research project (German language courses at the Goethe Institute for two to four months, may be available prior to commencement of the Research Fellowship). For candidates in the sciences, good knowledge of English is regarded as sufficient. Candidates should already have established relations with a German research institute where the project can be realized.

Note: Application may be forwarded directly to the Foundation or through diplomatic or consular offices of the Federal Republic of Germany in the candidates' respective countries. United Kingdom applicants may apply to the *German Academic Exchange Service, 11-15 Arlington Street, London SW1 1RD*. Candidates must submit a detailed research plan in German or English. Applications may be submitted at any time. Selection meetings take place in March, July and November.

Address:
Alexander von Humboldt-Stiftung
Bad Godesberg
Jean-Paul-Str. 12
D-5300 Bonn 2
West Germany

[2136]

VON KARMAN INSTITUTE FOR FLUID DYNAMICS *(Rhode-Saint-Genèse, Belgium)*

VKI Diploma Course Scholarships

Scholarships covering living expenses (15,000 Belgian francs monthly) are offered to engineers, physicists and mathematicians so that they may attend a nine-month postgraduate diploma course in fluid dynamics with specialization in turbomachinery, aeronautics, environmental fluid dynamics, or computational techniques. The Course is open to nationals of NATO countries who have an engineering degree and a M.Sc. degree or equivalent; the Institute also accepts candidates for doctoral and postdoctoral programmes. Instruction is in English and French.

The Institute also organizes short Courses of one week's duration for members of industrial, research, and university establishments.

Further information from:
Von Karman Institute for Fluid Dynamics
Chaussée de Waterloo 72
B-1640 Rhode-Saint-Genèse
Belgium

W

See *How to Use The Grants Register*, page ix

[2137]

WARNER-LAMBERT CANADA, INC.

Parke-Davis Pharmacy Research Award Fellowship

Subject: Can$2,000 annually. At the discretion of the college, part of the funds may be used for special equipment and supplies.

Tenable at recognized Canadian colleges of pharmacy for one year with the possibility of renewal.

Eligibility: Open to pharmacy graduates of recognized Canadian colleges of pharmacy.

Note: Applications should be made through the dean of the college of pharmacy concerned, who should endorse the applicant, the applicant's qualifications and the purpose for which the funds are to be used.

Further information from:
Community Services Supervisor
Warner-Lambert Canada, Inc.
2200 Eglinton Avenue East
Scarborough, Ontario
Canada M1K 5C9

[2138]

CHARLES WARREN CENTER FOR STUDIES IN AMERICAN HISTORY—HARVARD UNIVERSITY
(Cambridge, Massachusetts)

Research Fellowships

Purpose: To free the grantee from teaching and other academic responsibilities to enable him or her to pursue his proposed plan of research in American history.

No. offered: 3 to 5 Fellowships annually.

Value: Up to a maximum of US$15,000. Amount varies according to individual circumstances. Payments are made monthly.

Tenable at Cambridge for one year; not renewable.

Eligibility: Open to anyone who has obtained a Ph.D. degree; however, non-U.S. citizens will only be eligible for the Fellowship without a stipend.

Note: Individuals who have obtained additional funding elsewhere are encouraged to apply.

The Center also offers Fellowships to junior and permanent members of the Harvard faculty, and to scholars from other countries who will return to their own countries after one year, to teach.

Applications for support for the completion of a dissertation are not considered.

Closing date: 15th January.

Further information from:
Director, Charles Warren Center
Robinson Hall 118
Harvard University
Cambridge, Massachusetts 02138
U.S.A.

[2139]

EARL WARREN LEGAL TRAINING PROGRAM *(U.S.A.)*

Earl Warren Law Scholarship

Purpose: To increase the number of Black lawyers in the United States, and thereby provide a pool of Black legal talent to give sympathetic leadership to the unresolved and continuing problems involving the protection of human rights.

Value: Approximately US$1,000, payable in the fall.

Scholarships are provided for students who are U.S. citizens and have been accepted at an accredited law school in the United States for a three-year course of full-time study. Preferred consideration is given to applicants in need and under 35 years of age and those who plan to practice where there is a dearth of Black lawyers. 50 to 70 Scholarships are awarded annually, depending on available funds.

Closing date: 15th March.

Further information from:
Earl Warren Legal Training Program
Suite 2030, 10 Columbus Circle
New York, New York 10019
U.S.A.

[2140]

WASHINGTON JOURNALISM CENTER

Stokes Award

US$1,000 and a citation are awarded annually for the best reporting, analysis or comment in a daily newspaper on energy, the environment, conservation or other natural resource issues. The submitted work must have been published in a daily newspaper in the United States or Canada between 1st January and 31st December of the year of the Award. Entries should be accompanied by a letter summarizing the work, and may be submitted by anyone, on their own or on another's behalf. No more than ten examples of a person's writings are accepted.

Closing date: 1st February of the year following that for which the Award is made.

Further information from:
Stokes Award
Washington Journalism Center
2401 Virginia Avenue, N.W.
Washington, D.C. 20037
U.S.A.

[2141]

WALTER RESEARCH FOUNDATION OF AUSTRALIA

Research Grants

Grants are made available at Australian universities annually for the initiation, promotion and furtherance of scientific and technological research into all aspects of the efficient use of water.

Closing date: 1st September.

Further information from:
Secretary
Water Research Foundation of Australia
P.O. Box 47
Kingsford, N.S.W.
Australia 2032

[2142]

WATTIE INDUSTRIES LTD. *(N.Z.)*

James Wattie Award for the New Zealand Book of the Year: Three Awards, totalling NZ$10,000, are offered annually for literary works undertaken by New Zealand writers and published in New Zealand. All entries must have been published between 31st July and the closing date of 30th June.

James Wattie Visiting Professorship is given annually to afford the New Zealand medical profession the opportunity of meeting an overseas specialist and hearing his lectures. The Visiting Professorship covers travelling and living expenses, plus a small fee. The recipient is required to conduct a lecture and visiting tour of New Zealand for one month, and specifically to give a lecture to the medical profession of Hawkes Bay in Napier.

Further information from:
Wattie Industries Ltd.
Private Bag
Hastings
New Zealand

[2143]

WEIZMANN INSTITUTE OF SCIENCE
(Rehovot, Israel)

Postdoctoral Fellowships

Subjects: Life science (biology, biochemistry, biophysics); chemistry (physical, theoretical, organic, geological and biological); physics (theoretical, experimental, applied); mathematics (pure, applied); computer science; science teaching (chemistry, mathematics, physics).

Value: The Fellowships provide a 12-month stipend (with possible renewal for a second year), a small relocation allowance and a one-way air ticket. Round-trip airfare is provided if the Fellowship is extended for a second year.
    The annual stipend is adjusted periodically.

Tenable at the Feinberg Graduate School of the Weizmann Institute for one year; renewable for a second year.

Eligibility: Open to nationals from all countries who possess a Ph.D. degree or have equivalent research experience.

Closing dates: 15th May for commencement 1st October; 15th November for commencement 1st April.

Further information from:
Fellowships Program
Feinberg Graduate School
Weizmann Institute of Science
P.O. Box 26
Rehovot
76100 Israel

[2144]

ROB AND BESSIE WELDER WILDLIFE FOUNDATION *(Sinton, Texas)*

Rob and Bessie Welder Wildlife Foundation Fellowship
Winnie Smith Fellowship

To provide support of graduate student research and education programs in wildlife ecology and management, twenty awards of up to US$10,000 each are in force at any given time. The amounts vary according to individual need and are generally tenable for the duration of a graduate degree program. Candidates must be United States citizens or aliens registered in a U.S. university for a graduate degree. Priority is given to students who wish to work at the Welder Foundation Refuge or in the Coastal Bend Region of Texas.

Closing date: Usually mid-April for Fellowships to begin in September of the same year.

Further information from:
Dr. James G. Teer, Director
Rob and Bessie Welder Wildlife
  Foundation
P.O. Drawer 1400
Sinton, Texas 78387
U.S.A.

[2145]

WELLCOME TRUST *(U.K.)*

Senior Research Fellowships in Clinical Science are offered to ensure that workers of high promise as clinical investigators are not deprived of the opportunity to continue to develop their research because of the lack of an academic vacancy at the appropriate time. Medically qualified graduates working in any university department on a subject directly related to a clinical problem are eligible.

Direct personal applications by candidates are not considered. The heads of appropriate university departments are invited to put forward nominations for these awards which are advertised in January each year.

Research Fellowships in Surgery are offered to give research training to young surgeons who may wish to take up an academic career. The Fellowships are tenable in Great Britain only. Candidates must be medical graduates of British universities and under the age of 35. These Fellowships are advertised annually in June.

Professors of surgery are invited to nominate candidates. Direct personal application by candidates is not considered.

Research Fellowships in Pathology are offered to provide time for research for medical graduates of British universities who intend to make an academic career in pathology, histopathology, chemical pathology, microbiology, haematology or immunology. These Fellowships are tenable in Great Britain only in university departments of pathology. Departmental heads are invited to nominate candidates for these Fellowships which are advertised annually in June. Direct personal application by candidates is not considered.

Interdisciplinary Linked Fellowships in Universities are offered to provide an opportunity for basic scientists to work on medical problems with clinical research workers who would value the association. Fellows remain members of the basic science departments.

Further information about Linked Fellowship awards may be obtained from the Grants Section.

Research Leave Fellowships are offered to relieve university staff from teaching and administrative duties so that they can undertake an uninterrupted period of full-time research.

The Trust provides for the cost of a temporary replacement for the university staff member. Applicants are required to show that they are actively engaged in research which is being hampered in its development by lack of time. They will be expected to remain in the department during the tenure of the Fellowship. The proposal must be sponsored by the head of department.

Travelling Research Fellowships to Europe are offered to encourage postdoctoral and medical British graduates to undertake research in countries in Western and Eastern Europe. They are normally tenable for one year. Special Fellowships are available for Denmark, Norway, Sweden, Finland and Hungary. These Fellowships are advertised in October each year.

Further information from:
Grants Section
Wellcome Trust
1 Park Square West
London
England NW1 4LJ

[2146]

WELLCOME TRUST *(U.K.)*

Research Grants

The Trustees provide Grants to research workers in universities, research institutes and hospitals in the U.K. or developing countries for the expenses of their investigations in human and veterinary medicine, as well as related fields of experimental science. Such Grants may include provision for the payment of scientific or technical assistance.

Further information from:
Grants Section
Wellcome Trust
1 Park Square West
London
England NW1 4LJ

[2147]

WELLCOME TRUST *(U.K.)*

Special Travel Grant Scheme

To provide the opportunity for research workers in human and veterinary medicine, and related fields of experimental science, to visit other countries to exchange views and work with colleagues having similar research interests, special cooperative arrangements have been made between the United Kingdom and Ireland, and the following countries: Australia, Canada, New Zealand, South Africa, and the United States. These travel Grants may last for up to three months.

Applicants from the United Kingdom and Ireland may write to the address below for further information: Australian candidates should write to (medical researchers) *The Clive and Vera Ramaciotti Foundations, Sydney*, or, (veterinary research workers) *Post Graduate Foundation in Veterinary Science, University of Sydney;* New Zealand candidates may write to *Medical Research Council of New Zealand, Dunedin;* Canadian veterinary research workers may write to *The Registrar, University of Saskatchewan,* or *The Dean, Ontario Veterinary College, University of Guelph;* South African candidates may write to *Stella and Paul Lowenstein Charitable and Educational Trust, Johannesburg;* U.S. applicants may write to *The Burroughs Wellcome Fund, Research Triangle Park, North Carolina.*

Address:
Grants Section
Wellcome Trust
1 Park Square West
London
England NW1 4LJ

[2148]

WELSH ARTS COUNCIL

The Council is a constituent part of the Arts Council of Great Britain and in the main, operates on similar lines.

Awards for Advanced Study in Music: A limited number of Awards are annually available to provide opportunities for advanced study in Britain and abroad. These Awards are open to singers, instrumentalists and composers under 30 years of age on 30th March in the year of application, who were born and educated in Wales, or who are living or working in Wales.

Commissions to Composers: The Council will respond to applications from organizations or musicians who are able to guarantee the first performance of a new work. The Council will provide a grant to cover the cost of the commission fee. The commissions will be offered to composers born in Wales, living in Wales, or of Welsh parentage, to write works to be first performed in Wales, or elsewhere. Commission will also be offered to composers of any nationality, providing the first performance will be given in Wales. Further information for both music awards programs from the *Music Director, Welsh Arts Council, 9 Museum Place, Cardiff CF1 3NX*.

Bursaries to Writers: Bursaries of up to £5,000 for twelve months, £2,500 for six months and £1,250 for three months (subject to review) are annually offered to writers who must normally have been permanently resident in Wales for at least one year prior to the application date and should intend to remain in Wales during the period of tenure. Applicants must be authors of published work preferably in one of the following categories: poetry, the novel, the short story, literary criticism or history, the essay, biography and autobiography. Bursaries will be awarded mostly to prosewriters but poets may also apply for assistance, usually for periods of up to six months. Further information from the Literature Director at the address below. Playwrights should write to the Director of Drama for a copy of the *New Writing Scheme* which enumerates the types of awards available to playwrights who are commissioned by theatre companies.

Gregynog Fellowship: This annual appointment is supported by the Council and University of Wales. Applications are invited from practising artists, writers, composers and musicians to enable them to take up residence at Gregynog Hall in order to work and conduct tutorials for the University.

Grants to Theatre Artists: A variety of small awards are available to theatre artists, including dancers, for the purpose of in-service training. A limited number of bursaries for trainee directors and designers are also available. Additional information may be obtained from the Drama Director at the address below.

Young Artist Grants: Up to £400 (subject to review) are available to artists between the ages of twenty and thirty for expenses including the purchase of materials and exhibition costs.

Special Project Grants: Up to £2,000 (subject to review) are offered to assist with major developments in artists' work.

Applicants for the above *Young Artist* and *Special Project Grants* must be living and/or working in Wales for at least nine months of the year, and have previously sent information to the Welsh Arts Council for its Artists Register. Additional information may be obtained from the *Arts Department, ORIEL, 53 Charles Street, Cardiff CF1 4ED*.

Grants for Training in Arts' Administration: A limited number of bursaries are available in arts administration to allow appropriate candidates to follow particular courses of study. Further information may be obtained from the address below.

Grants to Film Makers: In Wales, the Welsh Arts Council provides financial support both for professionally made documentary films on art subjects and for film makers and video makers whose projects explore and investigate the nature of the medium. Such financial support is in general in the form of grant-aid and rarely, if ever, includes direct payment to the film maker. Additional information is available from the Film Department of the Council at the address below.

Crafts, Special Project Grants: Craft societies, organizations and individuals are eligible to apply for granting of projects specifically related to Wales. Interested parties may contact the *Craft Department, Welsh Arts Council, ORIEL, 53 Charles Street, Cardiff CF1 4ED.*

Further information from:
  Director, Welsh Arts Council
  9 Museum Place
  Cardiff Wales CF1 3NX

[2149]

WENNER-GREN FOUNDATION FOR ANTHROPOLOGICAL RESEARCH, INC.
(U.S.A.)

Sphere of interest: All branches of anthropology and related disciplines pertaining to the sciences of man. Projects supported use cross-cultural, historical, biological, and linguistic approaches toward understanding man's origins, development and variation. Special consideration is given to projects combining and integrating two or more subfields of anthropology or related disciplines, particularly with reference to theoretical or methodological issues.

Regular Grants-in-Aid: The majority of the Foundation's research grants fall into this category. They are normally for up to US$5,000 and cover various research expenses contemplated by the applicant.

Senior Research Scholar Grants-in-Aid: A limited number of Grants of up to US$10,000 are available to senior scholars with established research and publication records for the purpose of carrying out longer or more costly pieces or research than that normally contemplated under the Regular Grant-in-Aid program.

Further information from:
   Wenner-Gren Foundation
   1865 Broadway
   New York, New York 10023
   U.S.A.

[2150]

WENNER-GREN FOUNDATION FOR ANTHROPOLOGICAL RESEARCH, INC.
(U.S.A.)

Postdoctoral Fellowships: A limited number of Fellowships up to US$15,000 are available to young Ph.D.'s of any nationality for the purpose of research or study in a field or fields related to anthropology.

Richard Carley Hunt Memorial Postdoctoral Fellowships: These have a maximum stipend of US$4,000, are non-renewable, and are usually to aid completion of specific studies or preparation of field materials by younger scholars of any nationality.

Developing Country Fellowships: A limited number of Fellowships for younger scholars from the Third World of up to US$12,500 are offered to provide additional or specialized training unavailable in the home country. The Foundation considers proposals to attend any institution in the world where appropriate training can be made available.

Note: See *Sphere of interest* information in preceding entry.

Further information from:
   Wenner-Gren Foundation
   1865 Broadway
   New York, New York 10023
   U.S.A.

[2151]

WEST AFRICAN HEALTH COMMUNITY

Fellowships

Purpose: To promote health manpower development programmes in West African countries.

Subjects: Internal medicine; community health; psychiatry; pathological sciences; paediatrics; surgery; ear, nose and throat; obstetrics; gynaecology; radiology; radiotherapy; dentistry; ophthalmology; and anaesthesiology.

No. offered: Ten Fellowships annually.

Value: N300 per month plus tuition fees, approved textbooks up to a maximum of N200, costs of examination and re-examination fees, student union fees, and approved equipment up to 50% of cost.

Tenable for courses, ranging in duration from two to four years in: Ghana—Ghana Medical School, Accra; Nigeria—Colleges of Medicine at Lagos, Zaria, Benin City, Ibadan, Enugu, Ife, Ilorin, and Jos.

Eligibility: Open to West Africans without discrimination as to age or sex, who possess the pre-entry requirements stated by the West African College of Physicians or Surgeons.

Note: Countries submit nominations for the particular courses in the areas of their needs. The West African Health Community solicits places for the nominees in institutions, mainly in Nigeria and Ghana.
   Some institutions may not provide hotel accommodation.

Closing date: Usually between March and April.

Further information from:
West African Health Community
  Secretariat
P.M.B. 2023
Yaba, Lagos
Nigeria

[2152]

WEST AUSTRALIAN PETROLEUM PTY. LTD.
WESTERN AUSTRALIAN WILDLIFE AUTHORITY

Barrow Island Research Grant

Purpose: To obtain published biological data about Barrow Island of value in one or more of the following areas: rehabilitation and preservation programme on the island; management of the island's flora and fauna to insure their persistence; biological survey of the island's flora and fauna and their relationship with the mainland. (Barrow Island lies off the northwest coast of Australia and is a "Class A" nature reserve. It is about 233 square kilometers and harbours a diverse flora and fauna, some species being unique to the island or rare elsewhere).

No. offered: One Grant is offered annually.

Value: Time on the Island is at no cost; travel expenses between Barrow Island and Perth are also paid.

Tenable on Barrow Island for up to four weeks.

Eligibility: Open to Australian residents who are considered suitably qualified but who do not necessarily possess formal academic qualifications. Applicants should be experienced and recognised workers in their nominated field of study.

Closing date: 31st October annually.

Further information from:
  Managing Director
  West Australian Petroleum Pty. Ltd.
  Box X1580 G.P.O.
  Perth, W.A.
  Australia 6001

[2153]

WESTERN HISTORY ASSOCIATION
(U.S.A.)

Ray A. Billington Award: US$300 to the author and US$100 to the winning publication, are given annually for a best article on western history published in a regular periodical (other than the Association's own publication) during the 12 month period ending 1st July of the Award year. Articles must deal with a topic relating to the North American West, including Mexico, Canada and Alaska. Nominations may be made by the editor of submitting publications. *Closing date:* 31st July.

Oscar O. Winther Award: US$200 is awarded annually to the author of the best article appearing each calendar year in the *Western Historical Quarterly.*

Further information from:
  Western History Association
  William D. Rowley, Executive Secretary
  Department of History
  University of Nevada
  Reno, Nevada 89557
  U.S.A.

[2154]

WGN CONTINENTAL BROADCASTING COMPANY *(Chicago)*
WGN-Illinois Opera Guild

Auditions of the Air

This competition is held every two years for the advancement of professional and non-professional singers who have completed, or are engaged in completing, a suitable musical education for the operatic stage. First Prize of US$5,000 and featured soloist appearance at Chicago's Grant Park Summer Concerts; Second Prize of US$2,000; and two honorable mention Prizes of US$500 each. Contestants must be United States citizens who are between the ages of 20 and 33, and have not made an operatic debut in a leading role with a major operatic company. Both men and women are eligible.

Closing date: 1st October in even-numbered years.

Further information from:
Dick Jones
Opera Guild Auditions Board
WGN Continental Broadcasting Company
2501 Bradley Place
Chicago, Illinois 60618
U.S.A.

[2155]

WILLIAM ALLEN WHITE FOUNDATION
(Lawrence, Kansas)

National Award of Journalistic Merit

An annual Award of US$500 and a gold medallion are given annually in February, to recognize journalistic effort which exemplifies service both to the profession and to the community. A letter of recommendation is all that is necessary for nominating a candidate.

Further information from:
Del Brinkman, Director
William Allen White Foundation
University of Kansas
Lawrence, Kansas 66045
U.S.A.

[2156]

WHITE HOUSE FELLOWSHIPS *(U.S.A.)*

White House Fellowship Program

Purpose: To provide gifted and highly motivated Americans with some first-hand experience in the process of governing the nation and a sense of personal involvement in the leadership of the society.

White House Fellows will perform high level work within the executive branch of the United States Federal Government, and, in addition to their daily tasks, participate in an educational program, meeting as a group with high-level officials for off-the-record discussions.

No. offered: Between 14 and 20 Fellowships annually.

Value: A government salary of up to U.S.$49,700, based on previous education, experience and earnings. Fringe benefits from previous employers may be continued, but no other outside renumeration is permitted.

Tenable: The Program begins 1st September each year and concludes 31st August of the following year.

Eligibility: Open to United States citizens from all occupations who are in the early stages of their chosen career. Fellows will have demonstrated exceptional ability, marked leadership qualities, unusual promise of future development, high moral character, and tangible expression of concern about the problems facing American society.

No employees of the Federal Government are eligible for the program, except military career personnel of the United States Armed Services.

Note: White House Fellows are full-time Schedule A employees of the Federal Government, working in a Cabinet level agency, in the Executive Office of the President, or with the Vice President.

Individuals may apply by submitting an official application.

Applications are invited each year in August when the Program is announced.

Further information from:
Director
President's Commission on White House
    Fellowships
712 Jackson Place, N.W.
Washington, D.C. 20503
U.S.A.

[2157]

HELEN HAY WHITNEY FOUNDATION, INC. *(U.S.A.)*

Research Fellowships

Subjects: Early postdoctoral training in basic biomedical research.

No. offered: 17 to 18 new Fellowships annually.

Value: US$15,000 per annum.

In addition, an annual contribution of US$1,000 is made to the laboratory to help defray expenses, as well as the expense of travel for both the Fellow and his family.

Tenable at any educational institution or scientific laboratory for three years. Non-U.S. citizens must train within the U.S.

Eligibility: Open to qualified persons, generally less than 35 years of age who are resident in North America, hold an M.D., Ph.D., or equivalent qualification, are fluent in both oral and written English and who are seriously considering a career in biological or medical research, relating in some way to the purpose of the Foundation. Candidates should have not more than one year of postdoctoral laboratory experience at the time of application. Exceptions may be made for those with less than two years' experience who plan continued training in another research area under a new mentor. Such Awards would be limited to two years.

Note: The allowance toward expenses is non-accountable and its use is wholly at the discretion of the Fellow's supervisor.

A Fellowship to a non-United States citizen is tenable only in the United States; however the Foundation assumes no responsibility for securing the training location. The Foundation hopes that Fellows will continue a career in basic biomedical research.

Closing date: 15th August. Fellowships commence the following July.

Further information from:
Administrative Director
Helen Hay Whitney Foundation, Inc.
450 East 63rd Street
New York, New York 10021
U.S.A.

[2158]

JOHN HAY WHITNEY FOUNDATION
(U.S.A.)

The mission of the Foundation is to help achieve social and economic justice for all Americans; to this end it supports individuals who propose projects with the following characteristics:

The beneficiaries of the project are (a) minority groups in areas where economic and social conditions are particularly difficult; (b) women who have been denied equal participation and equal opportunity; and (c) the poor (priority over projects serving moderate-income people).

The project is community based (this usually precludes regional, state and national efforts), community initiated (by people directly affected by the problem or issue), and community governed.

The project leaders are indigenous to the community or have demonstrated a continuing commitment to it, exhibit leadership capabilities or potential, and stand to be directly affected by the outcome of the proposed work.

In addition to addressing the needs and problems of local people, projects should have potential for broader implication in terms of policy, model-building, or enterprise development. If the project is concerned with policy change or formulation, then the proposed policies advocated should have a meaningful bearing on alternative local, state or national policies. If the project is a model, then it should promise an improvement upon what has already been done and should be oriented to building a constructive alternative to existing institutions. If the project is enterprise development, then it should be oriented toward changing the structure and exercise of authority in the allocation and exchange of scarce resources in the local economy.

The Foundation also looks for: (a) projects unlikely to receive assistance from elsewhere; (b) projects in early, formative stages of development; and (c) projects which can benefit from the Foundation's technical assistance and consulting capacity.

Grants: In addition to the Foundation's program of support to individuals, some modest grants are made each year to organizations which provide important supportive services (training, technical assistance, networking, etc.) to community based efforts directed toward achieving social and economic justice.

Further information from:
John Hay Whitney Foundation
111 West 50th Street
New York, New York 10020
U.S.A.

[2159]

HENRYK WIENIAWSKI INTERNATIONAL COMPETITIONS *(Poznan, Poland)*

Violinmakers Competition: The Competition is held every five years (next in 1986), and is open to violinmakers of any nationality, irrespective of age, who have never won a previous Competition. Instruments being submitted must be handmade not earlier than 1981, have never won a prize, and be the property of the participating violinmaker. All instruments must reach Poznan two months before the beginning of the Competition.

Violin Playing Competition: The Competition will next be held in 1986 and is open to players of any nationality who are under 30 years of age.

Composers Competition will next be held in 1985.

Note: At the time of going to press, prize amounts were not known.

Further information from:
Secretariat
Henryk Wieniawski International
  Competitions
Ul. Swietoslawska 7
61-840 Poznan
Poland

[2160]

WILDLIFE MANAGEMENT INSTITUTE *(U.S.A.)*

Fellowships, Scholarships, Grants-in-Aid

Purpose: To provide training for specialists in wildlife ecology, management and related biological fields; and to assist with graduate projects that will develop essential information in those fields.

Subjects: Life history and ecology of individual wildlife species and biotic communites; special consideration will be given to graduate level research into human behavior, economic, social and political science areas as they relate to wildlife.

No. offered: Between six and fifteen awards annually.

Value: Awards vary in amount depending upon the needs and the nature of the request. Normally, however, awards do not exceed US$3,000 per annum.

Tenable for one calendar year, with the possibility of renewal up to a total of three years.

Eligibility: Open to qualified graduate students with demonstrated ability to conduct independent research.

Note: No official application forms are issued.

Candidates should apply through the head of department where their research is to be conducted.

Closing date: 31st October.

Further information from:
  Dr. L.R. Jahn, Vice-President
  Wildlife Management Institute
  1000 Vermont Avenue, N.W.
  709 Wire Building
  Washington, D.C. 20005
  U.S.A.

[2161]

VERNON WILLEY TRUST *(N.Z.)*

Scholarships

Purpose: To aid, by opportunity of further study or practical experience, the general development and improvement of the sheep and wool industry. Special interest is shown to manufacturing aspects.

No. offered: One Scholarship annually.

Value: NZ$500 per year, plus round-trip travel expenses for the Scholar between his home and the approved institution.

Tenable at an institution (academic, commercial or otherwise) approved by the Advisory Committee for the duration of the course.

Eligibility: Open to New Zealanders who are between the ages of 19 and 27, hold the endorsed School Certificate, university entrance or equivalent qualification, and have shown outstanding merit and promise in the positions held in the wool handling or manufacturing industry.

Note: Applicants should have their employers supply a statement directly to the South British Guardian Trust conveying approval of the application and noting the financial support which they are prepared to grant if the applicant should be successful in gaining the Scholarship.
  At the end of each year's tenure, recipients should furnish a report of their work, as testified to by the head of the institution at which they are working.

Closing date: 31st October.

Further information from:
South British Guardian Trust Co. Ltd.
Vernon Willey Trust Scholarship
P.O. Box 1354
Christchurch
New Zealand

[2162]

WOODROW WILSON INTERNATIONAL CENTER FOR SCHOLARS *(Washington, D.C.)*
Smithsonian Institution

Fellowships

Purpose: To provide scholars the opportunity to work on outstanding project proposals covering the entire range of the humanities and social sciences, with priority given to proposals which promise to make a major contribution to man's understanding of the human condition, or which attempt broad synthesis involving different fields or different cultures.

Subjects: The Center's *residential* Fellowships are awarded in one broadly defined program: History, Culture and Society; five more specifically focused programs are: American Society and Politics Program, Kennan Institute for Advanced Russian Studies Program, Latin American Program, East Asia Program and the International Security Studies Program.

No. offered: Up to 45 Fellowships annually.

Value: A stipend and certain travel expenses.

Tenable at the Center, for four to twelve months.

Eligibility: Open to established scholars at the postdoctoral level and also to people with careers in government, journalism, diplomacy, international organizations and law. Approximately two-thirds of the Fellowships are awarded to scholars from the United States and one-third to scholars from other countries.

Closing date: 1st October.

Further information from:
Assistant Director for Fellowships
Woodrow Wilson International Center for Scholars
Smithsonian Institution Building
Washington, D.C. 20560
U.S.A.

[2163]

WOODROW WILSON NATIONAL FELLOWSHIP FOUNDATION *(U.S.A.)*

Research Grants in Women's Studies

Purpose: To assist men and women writing doctoral dissertations in the field of research concerning the history, education, psychology, etc. of women.

No. offered: Fifteen Grants annually.

Value: Grants average US$1,000.

Tenable for one year.

Eligibility: Open to doctoral candidates at American universities who have completed all requirements except the dissertation.

Note: The Foundation also offers the *Administrative Internship Program* which is conducted by selection from American Graduate Schools of Business.

Closing date: 1st November.

Further information from:
Secretary
Woodrow Wilson National Fellowship Foundation
Box 642
Princeton, New Jersey 08540
U.S.A.

[2164]

WILSON ORNITHOLOGICAL SOCIETY *(U.S.A.)*

Louis Agassiz Fuertes and Margaret Morse Nice Awards

One Nice Award and one Fuertes Award at least of US$100 each, is given annually to encourage and stimulate research in any aspect of ornithology by young amateurs and students. Each proposal is considered primarily on the basis of possible contribution to ornithological knowledge.

Recipients of the Fuertes Award need not be associated with any academic institution. Nice Awards are limited to applicants who are not associated with a college or university, being intended for the encouragement of the independent researcher without access to funds and facilities generally available at the college. High school students are also eligible.

It is hoped, though not required, that Awardees submit their manuscripts to the editor of *The Wilson Bulletin* for consideration.

Closing date: 1st March.

Further information from:
 Carl D. Marti
 Department of Zoology
 Weber State College
 Ogden, Utah 84408
 U.S.A.

[2165]

WILSON ORNITHOLOGICAL SOCIETY *(U.S.A.)*

Paul A. Stewart Awards

Annual Awards in the amount of US$200 each are given to support research in ornithology, especially studies of bird movements based on banding and analyses of recoveries and returns, and investigations pertaining to economic ornithology. Awards are equally available to students, amateurs and professionals.

Closing date: 1st March.

Further information from:
 Carl D. Marti
 Department of Zoology
 Weber State College
 Ogden, Utah 84408
 U.S.A.

[2166]

WOLFSON FOUNDATION *(U.K.)*

Wolfson Literary Awards for History

A First Prize of £7,000 and a Second Prize of £5,000 are given annually to promote and encourage the standards of excellence in history writing.

Applications are not accepted.

Further information from:
 Wolfson Foundation
 P.O. Box 1BZ
 University House
 251-256 Tottenham Court Road
 London
 England W1A 1BZ

[2167]

WOMEN'S MEDICAL ASSOCIATION OF THE CITY OF NEW YORK

Mary Putnam Jacobi Fellowships

Subjects: Medical research, clinical investigation, or postgraduate study in a special field of medicine.

No. offered: One or more Fellowships every two years.

Value: The amount available is about US$2,000, all of which may be awarded to one applicant or may be divided between several applicants as the committee determines.

Tenable at any approved institution, usually for one year.

Eligibility: Open to graduate women physicians.

Note: Applications must be accompanied by: transcripts of college and medical school records; personal letters of recommendation from at least two physicians under whom the applicant has studied; a statement from the applicant describing the problem she proposes to investigate or the special study she plans to undertake; a statement from the person under whom she proposes to study regarding his interest in her subject; a recent photograph; and, if foreign-born, a certificate of proficiency in English or in the language of the country in which the Fellowship will be used.

Closing date: 1st March in odd-numbered years.

Further information from:
  Anne Moore, M.D., Chairman
  Mary Putnam Jacobi Fellowship
    Committee
  Women's Medical Association of the City
    of New York
  1300 York Avenue, Room K-200
  New York, New York 10021
  U.S.A.

[2168]

WOMEN'S NATIONAL FARM AND GARDEN ASSOCIATION, INC. *(U.S.A.)*

Sarah B. Tyson Fellowship

Several awards of US$500 each are presented annually to graduate students in the fields of agriculture, floriculture, landscape gardening, conservation and allied subjects. Fellows must be resident in the United States. Preference is given to women applicants.

Closing date: March of each year.

Further information from:
  Mrs. Elmer Braun, Tyson Fellowship
    Chairperson
  Women's National Farm and Garden
    Association, Inc.
  13 Davis Drive
  Saginaw, Michigan 48602
  U.S.A.

[2169]

AUDREY WOOD PLAYWRITING COMPETITION
American University *(Washington, D.C.)*

US$500 and the production of the winning play are awarded annually to the author of the best submitted original unproduced manuscript of any length. Competitors may not submit more than one entry in any given year.

Closing date: 15th May.

Further information from:
  Professor Kenneth Baker
  Audrey Wood Playwriting Competition
  Department of Performing Arts
  American University
  Washington, D.C. 20016
  U.S.A.

[2170]

WOODS HOLE OCEANOGRAPHIC INSTITUTION *(Massachusetts)*

Summer Student Fellowships

Purpose: To acquaint advanced undergraduates and students commencing graduate work with ocean studies and with the opportunities available to them in the various disciplines involved in oceanography.

Subject: Any of the fields of science or engineering.

No. offered: About 20 Fellowships annually.

Value: US$20,000, plus travel allowance.

Tenable at Woods Hole for a minimum of twelve weeks.

Eligibility: Open to United States citizens and foreigners who are at least through their junior year of undergraduate study. Candidates must be students of good standing in an acceptable college or university.

Note: Fellows are selected on a competitive basis, and assigned to a sponsor who will help the student select and pursue a research problem that can provide meaningful results in one summer's work.

Closing date: 1st March, for notification by 15th April.

Further information from:
  Fellowship Committee
  Education Office, Clark Laboratory
  Woods Hole Oceanographic Institution
  Woods Hole, Massachusetts 02543
  U.S.A.

[2171]

WOODS HOLE OCEANOGRAPHIC INSTITUTION *(Massachusetts)*

Postdoctoral Awards in Marine Policy and Ocean Management

Scope of research: Not rigidly defined; novel proposals in such fields as political science, international affairs, decision theory, economics, diplomacy management, geography, law, engineering and anthropology will be considered. Award recipients in the program have pursued such studies as the implications of oil exploration along the northeastern coast of the United States, problems of international law created by new developments in aquaculture and fish farming, economic benefits of some oceanographic research, a perceptual study of New England fishermen, and oceanic waste disposal.

Value: A stipend of US$20,000 per annum (partially non-taxable). In addition, modest research and travel expenses are available.

Tenable at Woods Hole, normally for one year beginning in June or September. Depending upon the nature and scope of the recipient's research effort, the renewal of the Award for a second year may be considered.

Eligibility: Open to scholars and practitioners from relevant fields in the social sciences and management who are interested in applying their disciplinary training and experience to investigations which require a significant component of marine research. Applicants must have completed their doctorate degree or possess equivalent professional qualifications through career experience.

Note: In adition to their major research effort, Awardees are expected to participate in Woods Hole seminars and study groups and to work with various members of the scientific and technical staff on problems of mutual interest. Workshops and conferences involving senior policy makers and academicians are planned from time to time as part of the Program.

Closing date: 1st March, for notification in April.

Further information from:
Dean of Graduate Studies
Education Office, Clark Laboratory
Woods Hole Oceanographic Institution
Woods Hole, Massachusetts 02543
U.S.A.

[2172]

WOODS HOLE OCEANOGRAPHIC INSTITUTION *(Massachusetts)*

Postdoctoral Awards in Ocean Science and Engineering

Purpose: To acquaint new and recent recipients of Ph.D. degrees in the physical and biological sciences with the field of oceanography and to stimulate an interest in applying their skills towards a better understanding of the oceans. For recent recipients of Ph.D. degrees in oceanography, the Award tenure provides the individual with an opportunity to broaden his experiences in oceanographic research before making a commitment to a more permanent position.

No. offered: Six to eight Awards annually.

Value: US$20,000 per annum (partially non-taxable, plus limited additional support for equipment, supplies and travel.

Tenable at Woods Hole for one year.

Eligibility: Open to United States citizens and foreign nationals who have completed all requirements for the Ph.D. degree in biology, chemistry, geology, geophysics, physics, oceanography, meteorology, ocean engineering, or mathematics.

Note: Award holders work in the laboratory, and under the general supervision of an appropriate member of the staff, but are expected to work independently on research problems of their own choice.

Closing date: 1st February, for notification in March.

Further information from:
Fellowship Committee
Education Office, Clark Laboratory
Woods Hole Oceanographic Institution
Woods Hole, Massachusetts 02543
U.S.A.

[2173]

WORLD ALLIANCE OF YOUNG MEN'S CHRISTIAN ASSOCIATIONS

Certain national YMCA centers organize various educational activities including short-term study courses at home or abroad and leadership training schemes. Candidates must be members of their national YMCA.

Further information is available from: Headquarters—*John R. Mott House, 37 Quai Wilson, CH-1201 Geneva, Switzerland;* Australia—*196 Albert Road, South Melbourne, Victoria 3205;* Canada—*2160 Yonge Street, Toronto, Ontario M4S 2A9;* United Kingdom—*640 Forest Road, London, E17 3DZ.*

Not confirmed for 1983.

U.S. Address:
World Alliance of YMCA
291 Broadway
New York, New York 10007
U.S.A.

[2174]

WORLD COUNCIL OF MANAGEMENT

Prize Paper Contest for Young Executives

The Contest is held once every three years, at the Triennial International Management Congress, in order to encourage original thought and research in the field of scientific management all over the world. The Contest is open to young executives up to 35 years of age. Original papers having topicality and importance to the management field may be submitted.

Further information from:
Dr. Müllers
CIOS Secretary
RKW—Rationalisierungs Kuratorium
 der Deutschen Wirtschaft e.V.
P.O. Box 5867
6236 Eschborn
West Germany

[2175]

WORLD FEDERATION FOR MENTAL HEALTH

Grove School Fellowship

Purpose: To provide theoretical and practical experience in the field of special education to enable teachers to work with emotionally disturbed and/or learning disabled children.

No. offered: Two Fellowships annually.

Value: Stipend of US$2,500, full tuition, room and board, plus round-trip transportation from and to the Fellow's home country.

Tenable at Southern Connecticut State College for 14 months; not renewable.

Eligibility: Open to candidates who hold a bachelor's degree from an accredited college or university.

Note: Candidates should submit transcripts of all undergraduate records directly from their college or university and three letters of reference attesting to their academic ability and/or teaching experience.

Fellows reside at the Grove School, Madison, Connecticut during their tenure.

Applications should be addressed to *Grove School Fellowship, World Federation for Mental Health, Health Sciences Centre Hospital, 2255 Westbrook Crescent, University of British Columbia, Vancouver, British Columbia V6T 1W5, Canada.*

Closing date: 1st April.

Further information from:
Grove School Fellowship
c/o Resident Director
175 Copse Road
Box 646
Madison, Connecticut 06443
U.S.A.

[2176]

WORLD HEALTH ORGANIZATION

WHO Fellowships and Training Programme

Purpose: To promote the international exchange of scientific knowledge and techniques relating to health, for the purpose of improving standards of teaching and training in the health, medical and related fields; and to strengthen national health services.

Value: To cover the cost of travel, maintenance, tuition fees and other expenses in special cases.

Tenable (a) academic study of 9 to 24 months duration (exceptionally for longer periods); (b) individual and group study visits not resulting in any academic qualification, the majority lasting one to four months; (c) attendance at short courses lasting approximately ten days to three months.

Eligibility: Open to nationals of member-states and associate members of WHO and to nationals of trust and other territories for whose international relations WHO member-states are responsible, or which are administered by international authorities established by the United Nations—(a) who are, or will be, engaged in medical or health work in their national health organization, and whose applications are supported by their national health administration (ministry of health or equivalent authority); (b) for whom the national health administration is prepared to certify that, if a Fellowship is granted, full use will be made of the Fellow in the field covered by the Fellowship; (c) who have not less than two years' experience in the subject they wish to study; (d) who have exhausted the opportunities available in their own countries for studying that subject; (e) who submit subjects of study which are directly connected with the country's own health programmes; (f) who undertake to place their services at the disposal of their national health organization for at least three years immediately following their Fellowship, etc. Preference is given to applicants for training which is necessary for carrying out a governmental health project assisted by WHO.

Awards may exceptionally be made to persons without medical or allied qualifications.

Note: Candidates should apply through the national health administration in their own countries. An information booklet describing the Fellowship programme in detail may be obtained from:

World Health Organization
1211 Geneva 27
Switzerland

[2177]

WORLD LITERATURE TODAY *(U.S.A.)*

Neustadt-International Prize for Literature

The Prize consisting of US$25,000, a silver eagle feather and a certificate is given biennially for distinguished and continuing artistic achievement in the fields of poetry, drama or fiction. An international jury of eleven is appointed for each successive award by the editor in consultation with the President of the University of Oklahoma and the editorial board. Each member of the jury may present one candidate or his choice. Representative selections of a candidate's work must be available to the jury in either French or English. The University of Oklahoma Press will seriously consider the publication of a book by or on the recipient. Interested authors should note that direct applications cannot be considered.

Further information from:
World Literature Today
630 Parrington Oval, Room 110
University of Oklahoma
Norman, Oklahoma 73019
U.S.A.

[2178]

WORLD METEOROLOGICAL ORGANIZATION

WMO Fellowships

Approximately 400 WMO Fellows receive training each year under the United Nations Development Programme, the WMO Voluntary Cooperation Programme and other WMO schemes. Fellowships are for study or training in meteorology and operational hydrology at universities or meteorological training institutes in countries where facilities are available.

Candidates should be nationals of countries which are members of the United Nations or one of its affiliated organizations, and the qualifications required will depend on the needs of the candidate's home country.

Individual applications are not accepted. Fellowships are awarded only at the request of the candidate's government.

Value: Based on stipend rates of the United Nations Development Programme, plus fees and travel.

Address:
World Meteorological Organization
Case postale No. 5
1211 Geneva 20
Switzerland

[2179]

WORLD PATHOLOGY FOUNDATION

Gordon Signy Foreign Fellowship in Pathology

One or more annual awards of US$2,000 are given to provide a young pathologist with the means to travel to another country in order to acquire skills which will be advantageous upon his or her return home. Young pathologists of any nationality, who are completing, or have recently completed training in pathology, are eligible.

Further information from:
Dr. Hermann Lommel, Secretary
World Pathology Foundation
Postfach 10-08-44
5090 Leverkusen
West Germany

[2180]

WORLD PRESS INSTITUTE *(U.S.A.)*

Fellowships

Purpose: To set out the history, present realities, and future directions of the American people for journalists from other nations so that they may return home with the personal knowledge and experience to report and interpret United States affairs more accurately and with deeper understanding.

Scope: Participation in a specialized American studies program—American history, government, social and religious institutions, economics, literature, culture, communications media and extensive travel.

No. offered: Twelve Fellowships annually to journalists from twelve different countries.

Value: During the eight month period of study and travel in the United States, the Institute pays for travel costs, tuition, books, room and board and a partial salary. Return air fare is included.

Eligibility: Open to full-time professional journalists with a minimum of three years' experience. They should be fluent in English and be between the ages of 25 and 35 years. Americans are not eligible.

Further information from:
Executive Director
World Press Institute
Macalester College
1600 Grand Avenue
St. Paul, Minnesota 55105
U.S.A.

[2181]

WORLD REHABILITATION FUND, INC. *(U.S.A.)*

Rehabilitation Study Visits

Subjects: International innovations in rehabilitation.

No. offered: Ten Study Visits annually.

Value: Travel and per diem not to exceed US$5,000.

Tenable at approved rehabilitation centers outside the United States, for four to six week visits.

Eligibility: Open to American experts in rehabilitation who have a relevant study-visit plan and a meaningful plan for utilizing the experience when back in the United States.

Note: Applications may be submitted at any time.

Further information from:
Diane E. Woods, Project Director
World Rehabilitation Fund, Inc.
400 East 34th Street
New York, New York 10016
U.S.A.

[2182]

WORLD UNIVERSITY SERVICE *(U.K.)*

The U.K. section of the World University Service offers assistance through scholarship programs to refugee students and academics from Chile, Ethiopia and a small number of Southern Africans and Kurds. Individuals meeting the criteria of the WUS small grants scheme are also eligible to receive assistance in continuing their studies.

Further information from:
　World University Service (U.K.)
　20/21 Compton Terrace
　London
　England N1 2UN

[2183]

WORLD WILDLIFE FUND

WWF Grants

The WWF provides Grants for projects dealing with the conservation of nature. WWF gives preference to practical conservation activities in the field based on previous evaluation and recommendations by other institutions or by WWF/IUCN (International Union for Conservation of Nature and Natural Resources) personnel.

Most projects financed by WWF are initiated within the WWF/IUCN operations, in line with agreed priorities.

In urgent cases research projects are supported if they help to identify the conservation needs for a species and/or environment and/or if they lead to conservation action which will help to improve the status of a species or of an endangered habitat. Research which is not linked with important problems and which is not set up to stimulate conservation action is not supported.

Most support is given to projects which are designed to achieve a specified conservation goal. All projects are screened by the IUCN's international scientific and technical network of advisors. Applications may be submitted at any time.

Further information from:
　Conservation Officer
　World Wildlife Fund
　Avenue du Mont-Blanc
　CH-1196 Gland
　Switzerland

[2184]

WORLD WILDLIFE FUND AUSTRALIA

Grants

Grants ranging between A$5,000 and A$20,000 are offered to support research which is directly related to the protection of endangered Australian species and ecosystems, or which will lead to an increased awareness of the need for wildlife conservation within Australia.

Further information from:
　Director
　World Wildlife Fund Australia
　St. Martin's Tower, Level 17
　31 Market Street
　Sydney, N.S.W.
　Australia 2000

[2185]

WORLD WILDLIFE FUND—U.S.

J. Paul Getty Wildlife Conservation Prize

An annual Prize of US$50,000 is awarded for outstanding achievement in wildlife and habitat conservation of international significance. Both individuals and organizations from anywhere in the world are eligible for the award, which may be judged from a number of criteria, including conservation of rare or endangered species and their habitats, conservation of ecosystems, the increase in public awareness of the importance of the natural world, establishment of conservation legislation, or the foundation of an organization of unusual importance to wildlife conservation.

Further information from:
　World Wildlife Fund—U.S.
　1601 Connecticut Avenue, N.W.
　Washington, D.C. 20009
　U.S.A.

[2186]

WORLD YOUNG WOMEN'S CHRISTIAN ASSOCIATION

YWCA Training Scholarships and Opportunities

Subjects: Areas related to YWCA community service.

Tenable for an agreed period of time in countries where there is a YWCA. There are no set regulations; opportunities are arranged to suit the needs of the particular YWCA and the trainee herself.

Eligibility: Members, leaders and staff of YWCA's should apply for training opportunities through the YWCA in their own country.

Note: Further information may be obtained from national YWCA offices, or from:
World Young Women's Christian Association
37 Quai Wilson
CH-1201 Geneva
Switzerland

[2187]

WORLD ZIONIST ORGANIZATION—AMERICAN SECTION, INC.

Hayim Greenberg Partial Scholarship Award

Purpose: The two major goals of the Hayim Greenberg College in Jerusalem, where the Partial Scholarships are tenable, are (a) to prepare a selected group of promising young students to become teachers in Jewish Schools in the Diaspora and (b) to provide an opportunity for a year or two of intensive study of Judaica and Hebraica for Jewish-youth who are potential Jewish community leaders, rabbis and communal workers.

Value: Partial Scholarships are applied to tuition, room and board.

Tenable at the Hayim Greenberg College for one year.

Eligibility: Open to American and Canadian students, between 18 and 25 years of age, who are interested in spending a year in Israel to study Judaica and Hebraica. Applicants must be prepared to pay their own travel to Israel.

Note: Candidates who do not possess an acceptable Hebrew language background will receive preliminary intensive language instruction.

Closing date: 30th July.

Further information from:
Department of Education and Culture
World Zionist Organization—American Section, Inc.
515 Park Avenue
New York, New York 10022
U.S.A.

[2188]

WORSHIPFUL COMPANY OF MUSICIANS
(U.K.)

Allcard Grants: A limited number of Grants not exceeding £500 are offered to individuals undertaking advanced training as performers (at home or abroad) or significant projects of a special nature (e.g., in the field of musicological research). The Grants are not available for courses leading either to a first degree at a university or to a diploma at a college of music, and only in exceptional cases will assistance towards the cost of a fourth or fifth year at a college of music be considered.

W.T. Best Memorial Scholarship: The Scholarship of £1,000 per annum is awarded to an advanced student of the organ. It is tenable for a maximum of three years. Nominations must be made by any one of the following: professors of music at Oxford, Cambridge or London Universities; directors, Royal College of Music, and Royal College of Organists; principals, Royal Academy of Music, Guildhall School of Music and Drama, Royal Northern College of Music, and Royal Scottish Academy of Music and Drama; directors, Edinburgh, Cardiff and Belfast Universities.

John Clementi Collard Fellowship: The Fellowship of £2,000 per annum is awarded from time to time (about every three years; next in 1983) to a professional musician of standing and experience who shows excellence in one or more of the higher branches of musical activity, i.e., composition, research, and performance (including conducting). Nominations should be made by one of the following: professors of music at Oxford, Cambridge or London Universities; principal, Royal Academy of Music; director, Royal College of Music.

Maisie Lewis Young Artists Fund: The Fund assists young instrumentalists (including organists) and singers of outstanding ability who wish to acquire experience on the professional soloist concert platform. The upper age limit is normally 28 years.

Note: No application in respect of the Collard Fellowship or Best Scholarship should be made to the Worshipful Company of Musicians direct.

Further information from:
  Clerk
  Worshipful Company of Musicians
  4 St. Paul's Churchyard
  London
  England EC4M 8BA

[2189]

WRITER'S DIGEST *(U.S.A.)*

Creative Writing Contest

Prizes are given annually in three categories—short story (2,000 words), article (2,500 words), and poetry (16 lines or less). Entries must be original and unpublished. Prizes awarded to 301 winners include cash, electric typewriters and awards. Contestants may submit one piece of work in each category. Authors of any nationality may enter but works must be written in English. Manuscripts will not be returned and each entry must be made on an official entry form.

Closing date: 1st June.

Further information from:
  Writer's Digest
  9933 Alliance Road
  Cincinnati, Ohio 45242
  U.S.A.

[2190]

HELENE WURLITZER FOUNDATION OF NEW MEXICO

Residence Program

Residences are individual, furnished, combined studio-living spaces located in Taos, New Mexico. These are offered rent-free and utilities-free to persons engaged in creative, not interpretive, fields in all media, after submission of examples of work, references, outline of project, requested time and length of stay. The Residencies are awarded for varying periods of time, normally three months. They are awarded regardless of age, sex, religion, or ethnic origin. No monetary grants or stipends for living expenses or supplies are offered. All work submitted in support of the application should be accompanied by a self-addressed, stamped envelope.

Further information from:
  Henry A. Sauerwein, Jr.
  Executive Director
  Helene Wurlitzer Foundation of New Mexico
  Box 545
  Taos, New Mexico 87571
  U.S.A.

X Y Z

See *How to Use The Grants Register*, page ix

[2191]

XEROX CANADA INC.

Fellowships

Purpose: To assist in developing faculties in Canadian business schools, and highly qualified personnel for Canadian business.

Subject: Business administration.

No. offered: 28 Fellowships annually.

Value: Doctoral—*Can*$5,000; Master's—*Can*$2,000; Undergraduate—*Can*$1,000. The money is given to the university and may be used to assist more than one student.

Tenable for the final year of a course, as follows: Doctoral—Universities of British Columbia, Western Ontario, Toronto, York, Queen's University, Simon Fraser University and Laval University; Master's—Universities of Alberta, Ottawa, Sherbrooke, Saskatchewan, Windsor, and Manitoba, École des Hautes Études Commerciales, and Dalhousie, McMaster, St. Mary's, Queens, and McGill Universities; Undergraduate—Universities of Prince Edward Island, Western Ontario, Calgary, New Brunswick and Québec, Carleton University, Memorial University of Newfoundland, Lakehead University and Ryerson Polytechnical Institute.

Eligibility: Open to Canadian citizens or students with landed immigrant status. As the Fellowships are administered by the individual universities, they are awarded in accordance with their regular award procedures on the basis of academic achievement and need.

Note: An additional doctoral Fellowship is offered at Guelph University in the field of water quality.
Candidates should apply to the relevant university for all information concerning the Fellowships, and applications must be made direct to the university.

Address:
Xerox Canada Inc.
703 Don Mills Road
Don Mills, Ontario
Canada M3C 1S2

[2192]

YADDO *(Saratoga Springs, New York)*

Yaddo offers hospitality, temporary residence and proper working conditions at a country estate to writers, visual artists, sculptors and composers who have already published, exhibited, or had performed work of high artistic merit.
Only those who have already reached a high level of professional achievement may apply. There are no restrictions regarding nationality but the admissions procedures make the English language a necessity.

Closing date: 15th January.

Address:
Yaddo
Box 395
Saratoga Springs, New York 12866
U.S.A.

[2193]

YALE CENTER FOR BRITISH ART *(U.S.A.)*

Resident Fellowship Program

These Fellowships, covering travel and lodging expenses, are awarded annually to enable advanced scholars in the U.S. and from abroad to study the Center's holdings of British paintings, drawings, prints, and rare books, dating from the late 15th to mid-19th centuries, and to make use of the Center's research facilities (photograph archive and art reference library).

Closing date: 1st November.

Further information from:
    Director
    Yale Center for British Art
    Box 2120 Yale Station
    New Haven, Connecticut 06520
    U.S.A.

[2194]

YALE UNIVERSITY PRESS *(New Haven, Connecticut)*

Yale Series of Younger Poets

American poets under 40 years of age who have not previously had a volume of verse published may submit poetry manuscripts of 48 to 64 pages. The prize is book publication at the usual royalty rates. Manuscripts are accepted only during the month of February of each year. There is an entry fee of US$5.00.

Further information from:
    Editor, Yale Series of Younger Poets
    Yale University Press
    92A Yale Station
    New Haven, Connecticut 06520
    U.S.A.

[2195]

YIVO INSTITUTE FOR JEWISH RESEARCH *(New York City)*
Max Weinreich Center for Advanced Jewish Studies

Fellowships, Tuition Scholarships, and Travel Stipends

Purpose: Fellowships—to enable qualified candidates for graduate degrees and postdoctoral students to pursue advanced studies in the Center's fields of interest through a coordinated program between the Center and the student's university; Tuition Scholarships—to facilitate participation in the Center's inter-university graduate seminars; Travel Stipends—to make it possible for students outside the New York Metropolitan area to participate in the seminars.

Subjects: Jewish life and culture in Eastern and East-Central Europe; the destruction of European Jewry by the Nazis; the period of Jewish mass settlement in the United States; Yiddish language, literature and folklore.

Value: Fellowships—up to US$3,000 per annum; Tuition Scholarships and Travel Stipends—are required.

Eligibility: Open to qualified candidates for advanced degrees at recognized universities in the United States and to postdoctoral students in the United States.

Not confirmed for 1983.

Further information from:
    YIVO Institute for Jewish Research
    1048 Fifth Avenue
    New York, New York 10028
    U.S.A.

[2196]

YIVO INSTITUTE FOR JEWISH RESEARCH *(New York City)*

Scholarships

Purpose: To facilitate participation in the Uriel Weinreich Yiddish Language, Literature and Culture Program which is sponsored in the summer session by Columbia University in cooperation with YIVO.

Value: Cost of tuition.

Eligibility: Open to graduate and undergraduate students in the United States.

Not confirmed for 1983.

Further information from:
    YIVO Institute for Jewish Research
    1048 Fifth Avenue
    New York, New York 10028
    U.S.A.

[2197]

YIVO INSTITUTE FOR JEWISH RESEARCH *(New York City)*

Seltzer-Brodsky Research Prize

The Prize of US$500 is offered annually for an essay or research paper related to the American Jewish community. Graduate students in the United States with advanced knowledge in the Jewish field may apply.

Not confirmed for 1983.

Further information from:
YIVO Institute for Jewish Research
1048 Fifth Avenue
New York, New York 10028
U.S.A.

[2198]

YORKSHIRE POST *(U.K.)*

The following awards are offered to encourage the writing and publishing of worthwhile literature. Entries are not accepted direct from authors. Publishers may submit a maximum of three fiction and three non-fiction entries each.

Book of the Year: A first prize of at least £400 and a second prize of £250 are offered annually. If the panel of judges' choice for the first prize falls upon a work of fiction then the second prize will go to a non-fiction work and vice versa. The books must have been published (or due for publication) in the year for which the awards are being made, and may not be translations, re-issues, or of a strictly scientific or professional nature. Entries should be submitted by mid-November for presentations in the following April.

Best First Work by a New Author: A Prize of £350 and a runner-up prize of £200 are offered annually to the authors of the books selected by the panel. The same conditions apply as for the Book of the Year. Entries should be submitted in late January for announcements in April.

Art and Music Awards: An art prize of £350 and a music prize of £350 are offered annually to authors whose work, in the opinion of the panel, has made the greatest contribution to the understanding of art or music.

Note: Books submitted must have been published in the United Kingdom but authors need not be British, nor residents.

Closing date: 31st December of award year.

Further information from:
E. Malcolm Slingsby
Yorkshire Post Book Awards
P.O. Box 168
Wellington Street
Leeds
England LS1 1RF

[2199]

YOUNG CONCERT ARTISTS, INC. *(U.S.A.)*

Young Concert Artists International Auditions are held annually in New York for young solo performers and string quartets from all over the world. Winners become members of YCA's roster, and receive all management services and materials free. Young Concert Artists are eligible to receive the awards described below. Artists may either perform in the preliminary auditions in New York, or submit a tape recording. The semi-final and final auditions must be performed in person in New York, and each year a jury of musicians selects those artists deemed to possess extraordinary gifts and ready to begin important careers. Young Concert Artists presents the winners in New York recitals, and books recital and orchestral appearances throughout the United States until commercial management is ready to take over.

Philip M. Faucett Prize is awarded biennially to an outstanding artist on the YCA roster on the basis of superior career achievement, by an anonymous panel of distinguished professionals in the music field.

Kathleen Ferrier Memorial Prize is awarded annually to underwrite opportunities to promote the careers of young singers who have won the annual *YCA International Auditions*.

Mortimer Levitt Career Development Awards for Women Artists are offered to those of exceptional talent, who are or have been on the Young Concert Artists' roster. The annual Awards are given to sponsor a wide range of opportunities including travel for auditions, subsidy of recordings, concert presentations, underwriting of special promotion and publicity materials, etc.
Priority is given to female pianists who are currently on the Young Concert Artists' roster.

Michaels Award is given biennially or less often, at the discretion of the award panel. The recipients are artists launched on professional careers by Young Concert Artists, whose degree of success in professional engagements over a period of several seasons is exceptional. The Award consists of a recital at Alice Tully Hall, Lincoln Center, New York, plus engagements as soloist with major symphony orchestras throughout the country.

Further information from:
  Susan Wadsworth, Director
  Young Concert Artists, Inc.
  65 East 55th Street
  New York, New York 10022
  U.S.A.

[2200]

YOUNG MUSICIANS FOUNDATION
(U.S.A.)

Debut Competition

The Competition is open to residents of the United States who will not have reached their 22nd birthday by June 30th of the year in which they compete, and who are not yet under professional management. First Prizes of US$2,500, Second Prizes of US$1,000, and Third Prizes of US$500 are offered in three categories—cello, violin and piano. The *Lynn & Stanley Beyer Debut Competition Award* of US$5,000 is presented at the discretion of the judges.

Semi-final auditions are held in April in Los Angeles and New York; final auditions are in June in Los Angeles. Applications are due 1st March. Prior to application candidates should write for the Debut Competition brochure.

Further information from:
  Debut Competition
  Young Musicians Foundation
  914 South Robertson Boulevard
  Los Angeles, California 90035
  U.S.A.

[2201]

YOUTH AND MUSIC OF GERMANY

International Summer Courses

Subjects: Opera, chamber music and orchestra.

No. offered: Approximately 50 awards annually.

Value: DM500 to cover tuition and/or lodging and board.

Tenable at the Schloss Weikersheim, Würtemberg, from July to September.

Eligibility: Open to students of music and young musicians between 16 and 30 years of age.

Closing date: 31st May.

Note: Applications should include a supporting letter of reference.

Further information from:
  General Secretary
  Youth and Music of Germany
  Markplatz 12
  D-6992 Weikersheim Tauber
  West Germany

[2202]

YWCA OF AUSTRALIA

Georgina Sweet Scholarship

Purpose: To enable the holder to pursue a course of study in any subject at a university or other tertiary educational institution.

Value: A$600 per annum paid in two installments.

Tenable in Australia for one year. If the Scholarship is awarded to a student during the first year of a two or three year course, she may renew the Scholarship for a second and third year, subject to satisfactory results.

Eligibility: Open to Australian women of all ages. Applicants must be willing to work for the YWCA of Australia for at least one year after completion of studies, or alternatively, refund a part of the Scholarship.

Note: Application forms are available, and when completed, should be returned with a fee of A$1.00.

Not confirmed for 1983.

Further information from:
  National Executive Director
  YWCA of Australia
  68 Powlett Street
  East Melbourne, Victoria
  Australia 3002

[2203]

YWCA OF AUSTRALIA

C.I. and F.W. Wood Scholarship

Purpose: To assist with the educational expenses of a member of one of the Aboriginal peoples of Australia or its Territories.

Value: A$700 per annum, paid in two installments.

Tenable in Australia for one year only.

Eligibility: Open to Aboriginal women of any age.

Note: Application forms are available, and when completed, should be returned with a fee of A$1.00.

Not confirmed for 1983.

Further information from:
National Executive Director
YWCA of Australia
68 Powlett Street
East Melbourne, Victoria
Australia 3002

[2204]

ZAHEER SCIENCE FOUNDATION *(India)*

Awards

A limited number of Awards are offered to research workers from the developing countries in the following subjects: science policy and planning; science and technology for peace and socio-economic development; working conditions of scientists and technologists; the role of the scientific community in society; and scientific temper.

Recipients may work at any Indian university or research institute for one year. Value depends on the individual circumstances of the Award; payments are made monthly.

Applicants should have high academic qualifications and research experience, and may apply directly to the Foundation or be nominated by recognised professionals. Applications are accepted at any time.

Assistance may be provided through scholarships, fellowships and grants, including research projects, advanced training and exchange of workers from the developing countries.

Further information from:
Secretary
Zaheer Science Foundation
CSIR Building
Rafi Marg, New Delhi-110001
India

[2205]

ZONTA INTERNATIONAL *(U.S.A.)*

Amelia Earhart Fellowship Award

Purpose: To encourage and assist women in graduate study and research in aerospace-related sciences and engineering.

No. offered: Variable. Depends upon the number of qualified candidates.

Value: US$5,000 per annum.

Tenable at a suitable graduate school, for one year; applicants may reapply for an additional grant.

Eligibility: Open to women who hold a bachelor's degree or the equivalent, in a science preparatory for graduate study in aerospace-related sciences and engineering. Applicants should show proof of acceptance in a full-time graduate program at an accredited institution and show evidence of exceptional ability and commendable character. There are no age or citizenship requirements.

Closing date: 1st January.

Further information from:
Zonta International
35 East Wacker Drive
Chicago, Illinois 60601
U.S.A.

INDEX OF AWARDS AND AWARDING BODIES

This index contains (i) the names or organizations and agencies (with locations in parentheses) that offer or administer funds and (ii) awards with distinctive names. Organizations and awards named after individuals are filed under the surname (last name). Names usually appearing before the surname are listed in parentheses.

Numbers listed refer to the code numbers which appear at the head of each entry in the main text.

Aachen International Charlemagne Prize: 1059
Abagnale (Roy M.) Fellowship: 567
Abbe (Cleveland) Award: 138
Abbey (Edwin Austin) Scholarship Fund: 1400
Abbey Major Scholarship: 427
ABC Award: 1611
Abel (John J.) Award: 194
Abrams (Charles) Scholarship: 156
Academic Links with China Scheme: 397
Academic Links with Eastern Europe Scheme: 396
Academic Links and Interchange Scheme: 395
Academy of American Poets, Inc.: 1, 2
Academy of Arts (Czechoslovakia): 3
Academy of Motion Picture Arts and Sciences (USA): 4
Academy of Natural Sciences of Philadelphia: 5
Academy of Sciences (Gottingen, West Germany): 1369
Academy of Sciences of the USSR (Moscow): 6
Academy of Scientific Research and Technology (Cairo): 7, 1808
Academy of the Social Sciences in Australia: 312
Ackerley (Joe) Prize: 763
ACTIM: 16
Action Research for the Crippled Child (UK): 1447
ACUM Ltd. (Tel-Aviv): 8
Adams (Clay) Grant: 191
Adams (Cecil John) Trust (South Africa): 2024
Adams (Herbert Baxter) Prize: 105
Adenauer (Konrad) Foundation (West Germany): 9
Administration on Aging (USA): 2056
Adrian-Adrianowska (Kazimiera) Scholarship: 1201
AECI Ltd. (South Africa): 10
AFGRAD: 11
African-American Institute (New York City): 11
African Institute for Economic Development and Planning (Dakar): 12
African Studies Association (USA): 13
African Training and Research Centre in Administration for Development (Tangier): 14
Afro-Asian Institute—Histadrut Israel: 1094
Afro-Asian Institute in Vienna: 15
Afro-Asian Rural Reconstruction Organization: 1895
Aga Khan Prize: 1641
Age, (The) Award (Australia): 2025
Agency for International Development (USA): 1924, 2063
Agency for Technical, Industrial and Economic Cooperation (France): 16
Agricultural Development Council, Inc. (USA): 17
Agricultural Institute (Ireland): 18
Agricultural Institute of Canada: 19, 587
Agricultural Research Council (UK): 20-22, 1535
Agricultural Research Council of Norway: 23, 24
Agricura Ltd. (South Africa): 25
AID: *See* Agency for International Development (USA)
Ainsworth (Herbert) Scholarship: 2113
Air Chief Marshal The Lord Dowding Fund for Humane Research (UK): 26
Air Force Office of Scientific Research (USA): 2053
Albee (Edward F.) Foundation, Inc. (USA): 27
Albright Institute (Jerusalem): 173
Albright (William Foxwell) Fellowship: 172
Alcan Fellowships: 34
Alcohol, Drug Abuse, and Mental Health Administration (USA): 2057
ALCS: 397
ALEES: 396
Alexander Prize: 1772
Alexander (B.G.) Scholarship: 1977
Alfred Hospital (Melbourne): 28, 29
ALIS: 395
All Saints Educational Trust (UK): 30
Allcard Grants: 2188
Allegheny International (USA): 31
Allen (Edward B.) Award: 99
Allen (Francis C.) Fellowships: 1580
Allied Artists of America, Inc.: 32

Allied Chemical Scholarships: 1723
Allport (Gordon) Prize: 1957
Alpha Chi Omega National Women's Fraternity (USA): 1431
Alpha Chi Sigma Fraternity: 120
Alsberg-Schoch Lectureship: 55
Altrusa International Foundation, Inc. (USA): 33
Aluminium Company of Canada, Ltd.: 34
Amalgamated Dental Company Scholarships: 399
America-Israel Cultural Foundation: 35
American Academy for Cerebral Palsy and Developmental Medicine: 36
American Academy of Facial Plastic and Reconstructive Surgery: 37
American Academy of Family Physicians: 38
American Academy and Institute of Arts and Letters: 39
American Academy of Neurological Surgery: 40
American Academy of Pediatrics: 41-43
American Academy of Periodontology: 44
American Academy in Rome: 45
American Accordion Musiciological Society: 46
American Accounting Association: 47
American Agricultural Economics Association: 48
American Antiquarian Society: 49-52
American Assembly of Collegiate Schools of Business: 53
American Association for the Advancement of Science: 54
American Association of Cereal Chemists: 55
American Association of Law Libraries: 56
American Association of Obstetricians and Gynecologists Foundation, Inc.: 57
American Association of Petroleum Geologists: 58
American Association of Physics Teachers: 59
American Association for Public Opinion Research: 60
American Association for the Study of Headache: 61
American Association of University Women: 62, 1707
American Automatic Control Council: 63
American Bar Foundation: 64
American Broadcasting Corporation: 1611
American Cancer Society, Inc.: 65, 66, 1135
American Catholic Historical Association: 67
American Chemical Society: 154, 1650
American College of Chest Physicians: 68
American College of Hospital Administrators: 69
American College of Physicians: 70, 71
American College of Psychiatrists: 72

American College Testing Program: 90
American College Theatre Festival: 73
American College of Veterinary Pathologists: 74
American Congress of Rehabilitation Medicine: 75
American Congress on Surveying and Mapping: 76
American Conservatory of Music: 77
American Council on Education: 78
American Council of Learned Societies: 79-85, 1119, 1913-1926
American Council of Life Insurance: 108
American Crystallographic Associations: 86
American Diabetes Association, Inc: 87
American Dietetic Association: 88, 89
American Educational Research Association: 90
American Federation of Labor and Congress of Industrial Organizations: 91
American Film Festival: 749
American Film Institute: 92
American Foundation for Pharmaceutical Education: 93
American Friends of the Hebrew University: 94
American Fund for Dental Health: 95-98
American Gas Association: 1522
American Geriatrics Society, Inc.: 99
American Heart Association, Inc.: 100-104
American Heart Association, New York State, Affiliate, Inc.: 104
American Historical Association: 105-107, 1951
American Historical Association—Pacific Coast Branch: 106
American Home Economics Association Foundation: 108-111
American Hospital Association: 117
American Indian Scholarships, Inc.: 112
American Institute of Aeronautics and Astronautics: 113
American Institute of Architects: 114-117
American Institute of Baking: 118
American Institute of Certified Public Accountants: 119, 1707
American Institute of Chemical Engineers: 120
American Institute for Economic Research (Great Barrington, Mass.): 121
American Institute for Exploration: 122
American Institute of Indian Studies: 123
American Institute of Nutrition: 124
American Institute of Physics: 125, 126
American Institute of Real Estate Appraisers: 127
American Institute of Steel Construction, Inc.: 128, 129
American-Italian Historical Association (USA):

American Journal of Nursing Company: 1608
American Land Title Association: 1405
American Library Association: 131, 132
American Lung Association: 133-136
American Mathematical Society: 137
American Meteorological Society: 138
American Museum of Natural History: 139-141
American Musicological Society, Inc.: 142
American Nuclear Society: 143
American Numismatic Society: 144, 145
American Nurses' Foundation, Inc.: 146
American Occupational Therapy Foundation, Inc.: 147
American Oil Chemists' Society: 148
American Oriental Society: 149, 150
American Osteopathic Association: 151
American Otological Society: 152
American Petroleum Institute: 1536
American Philosophical Society: 153
American Physical Society: 154
American Physical Therapy Association: 155
American Planning Association: 156
American Podiatry Association: 157
American Political Science Association: 158-161
American Production and Inventory Control Society, Inc.: 162, 163
American Psychiatric Association: 164
American Psychological Association: 165
American Research Institute in Turkey, Inc.: 166
American Risk and Insurance Association, Inc.: 167
American-Scandinavian Foundation: 168, 169, 1630
American School of Classical Studies at Athens: 170, 171
American Schools of Oriental Research: 172-174
American Society of Agricultural Engineers: 175
American Society of Anesthesiologists: 176
American Society of Church History: 177
American Society of Civil Engineers: 178-181
American Society of Clinical Pathologists: 182
American Society of Composers, Authors and Publishers: 183
American Society for Eighteenth-Century Studies: 184
American Society for Engineering Education: 185
American Society of Enologists: 186
American Society of Heating, Refrigerating and Air Conditioning Engineers, Inc.: 187
American Society of Hospital Pharmacists Research and Education Foundation: 188, 189
American Society of Mechanical Engineers: 190
American Society for Medical Technology Education and Research Fund, Inc.: 191-193
American Society for Pharmacology and Experimental Therapeutics, Inc.: 194
American Society of Photogrammetry: 195-197
American Society of Plant Physiologists: 198
American Society of Plastic and Reconstructive Surgeons, Inc.: 199
American Society for Psychical Research, Inc.: 200
American Sociological Association: 201, 202
American Technion Society (New York City): 203
American Telephone & Telegraph Co.: 4
American University (Washington, D.C.): 2169
American Urological Association: 204
American Water Works Association: 205
Ames Company: 193
Amity Institute (USA): 206
Ammann (O.H.) Fellowship: 178
AMOCO (UK) Exploration Company: 207
Amy (Harold) Award: 513
Andersen (Arthur) and Company Foundation (USA): 208
Anderson (Emily) Prize: 814
Anderson (Troyer Steele) Prize: 105
Anglican Studentships: 375
Anglo-Austrian Music Society: 209
Anglo-Danish Society: 210, 211
Anglo-German Foundation for the Study of Industiral Society: 212
Anglo-Israel Association: 213
Anglo-Jewish Association: 214
Anglo-Soviet Cultural Agreement: 215
Anglo-Spanish Cultural Foundation: 216
Angus and Robertson Publishers (Australia): 217
Animal Health Trust (UK): 218, 219
Ainsfield-Wolf Award (USA): 220
Annual Simulation Symposium: 221
Anthony (Hattie Margaret) Fellowship: 110
Anti-Cancer Council of Victoria (Australia): 222
Anti-Cancer Foundation of the Unversities of South Australia: 223
Antigua Government: 597
ANZAC Fellowships: 668, 689
AOPA Air Safety Foundation (USA): 224
Apex Foundation for Research into Mental Retardation Ltd. (Australia): 225
Apex Trust for Autism (Australia): 226
Arbeit (Albert A.) Prize: 1466
Architects Registration Council of the United

Kingdom: 227
Architectural Association (UK): 228
Arctic Institute of North America: 229, 230
Argentinian Government: 2085
Arlen (Stephen) Fund (UK): 231
Armourers and Brasiers' Fellowship: 1787
Armstrong (Kenneth) Fellowship: 546
Art Gallery of New South Wales: 232
Arthritis Care (UK): 233
Arthritis Foundation-National Office (USA): 234-236
Arthritis and Rheumatism Council for Research (UK): 237-239
Arthritis Society (Canada): 240-243
Arts Council (Ireland): 244
Arts Council of Great Britain: 245, 246, 2047, 2148
Arts Council of Northern Ireland: 247
Asahi Shimbun Publishing Company (Japan): 248
ASCAP: 183
ASEAN Awards: 1002, 1003, 1533
Asia Foundation: 160, 249, 1242
Asian Cultural Council (USA): 250
Asian Institute of Technology (Bangkok): 251
Aspen Institute for Humanistic Studies: 252
Assistant Masters and Mistresses Association (UK): 253
Associated Board of the Royal Schools of Music (UK): 254
Associated Colleges of the Midwest: 1582
Association of African Universities: 255-257
Association of American Geographers: 258
Association of Anaesthetists of Great Britain and Ireland: 259
Association of British Theatre Technicians: 245
Association of Commonwealth Universities: 260, 587, 1182, 1196, 1259
Association for Computing Machinery (New York City): 261
Association of Engineers and Architects in Israel: 262
Association of Environmental Engineering Professors: 263
Association of Official Analytical Chemists (USA): 264
Association for Research in Vision and Ophthalmology, Inc. (USA): 810
Association for Retarded Citizens (USA): 265
Association of Rhodes Scholars in Australia: 266
Association of South African Quantity Surveyors: 634
Association of Southeast Asian Institutes of Higher Learning: 267, 268
Association of Universities and Colleges of Canada: 269-295

Asthma & Allergy Foundation of America: 296
Asthma Foundation of Victoria (Australia): 297, 298
Asthma Research Council (UK): 299
Astronomical Society of the Pacific (San Francisco): 300
Astronomical Society of Southern Africa: 301
Astwood (Edwin B.) Award: 759
Atlantic Monthly (Boston, Mass.): 302
Atlantic Salmon Trust, Ltd. (UK): 303
Atomic Energy Research Establishment, Harwell (UK): 305
Atwood (Wallace W.) Fund: 258
Auckland Medical Research Foundation (NZ): 305, 306
Australia/China Student Exchange Scheme: 307
Australia Council-Literature Board: 308
Australia/Japan Business Co-operation Committee: 309
Australia-Japan Foundation (Sydney): 310
Australian Academy of the Humanities (Canberra): 311, 312
Australian Academy of Science: 313
Australian-American Educational Foundation: 314-316
Australian-Asian Universities' Cooperation Scheme: 343
Australian Broadcasting Commission: 317
Australian Cancer Society: 318
Australian College of Paediatrics: 319
Australian Conservation Foundation, Inc.: 320
Australian Early Childhood Association, Inc.: 321
Australian Entomological Society, Inc.: 322
Australian-European Awards Program: 664
Australian Federation of University Women: 323-326
Australian Film Institute: 327
Australian Forestry Council: 704
Australian Government: 307-309, 314-316, 578, 597, 598, 662, 664-671, 686, 689, 699, 700, 704-712, 715, 1451-1455
Australian Institute of Aboriginal Studies (Canberra City): 328
Australian Institute of International Affairs: 329
Australian Institute of Nuclear Science and Engineering: 330-332
Australian Institute of Urban Studies: 333
Australian Kidney Foundation: 334
Australian Meat Research Committee: 335, 336
Australian Music Foundation in London: 337
Australian National University: 338, 339
Australian Parliament: 340
Australian Postgraduate Federation in Medi-

cine: 341
Australian Tobacco Research Foundation: 342
Australian Vice-Chancellors' Committee: 343
Australian War Memorial: 344
Australian Water Resources Council: 700
Australian Wool Corporation: 345
Austrian Academy of Sciences: 346
Austrian Federal Economic Chamber: 347
Austrian Government: 346, 1364-1367, 1967, 2109
Austrian Institute (New York City): 348
Auxiliary to the American Osteopathic Association: 349
Aviation/Space Writers Association (USA): 350
Ayerst Award: 463, 759
Aziz (King Abdul) Prize: 1188

Bach (Johann Sebastian) International Competition: 351
Back Pain Association, Ltd. (UK): 352
Bage (Freda) Scholarship: 324
Bagehot (Walter) Fellowship: 579
Bahamas Government: 597
Baird (John Logie) Scholarship: 1824
Baker (Bishop James C.) Awards: 2070
Baker Fellowship: 1741
Baker (E.A.) Foundation for Prevention of Blindness: 502
Baker Harris Saunders Prize: 814
Baker Professorship: 1741
Baker (W.R.G.) Prize: 978
Balch (Emily Clark) Prize: 2131
Balint Orban Prize: 44
Ball (Robert S.) Award: 350
Balzan Foundation Prize: 1045
Bancroft Award: 1815
Bancroft Prizes (USA): 353
Bangladesh Government: 597
Bank of Ireland: 354
Bank of New Zealand: 355, 356
Bank of Sweden: 357, 1592
Baptist Union of Great Britain and Ireland: 358
Barbados Government: 597
Barber (Gordon) Award: 1675
Barclay Prize: 411
Barclays Bank International Award: 1783
Bark Award: 820
Barker (Aubrey) Awards: 586
Barley Industry Research Council (Australia): 359
Barr (Peter) Fellowship: 1578
Barrow Island Research Grant: 2152
Bartlett (Alice Hunt) Prize: 1674
Barton (George A.) Fellowship: 172
Baruch (Bernard M.) Award: 75
Baruch (Mrs. Simon) Award: 2069

Basedow Prizes: 855
Basista (Harriet and Feliks) Scholarships: 1201
Bass Charrington Award: 247
Batchelor (J.E.) Award: 1943
Bausch and Lomb Award: 196
Baxter (J.W. Duncan) Scholarships: 2094
Beard (J.R.) Grants: 1014
Beare (John and Arthur) Prize: 814
Bech (Joseph) Prize: 795
Beckmann (Max) Scholarships: 436
Beer (George Louis) Prize: 105
Beers (Clifford W.) Award: 1481
Beethoven International Piano Competition (Vienna): 1046
Behn (Hernand and Sosthènes) Award: 979
Beilby Prize: 1817
Beit Memorial Fellowships (UK): 360
Beit Trust (Zimbabwe): 361
Belgian American Educational Foundation, Inc.: 362
Belgian Government: 278, 574, 1360, 1997
Belgian National Housing Institutes: 1116
Belgian Royal Society of Numismatics: 363
Belize Government: 597
Bell Laboratories (USA): 154
Bell (Alexander Graham) Medal: 979
Bell (Charles R.E.) Scholarships: 1236
Bell (Jacob) Scholarship: 1661
Bell (Robert) Scholarship: 544
Bendix (Vincent) Award: 185, 1944
Bennett (Viscount) Fellowship: 461
Bennett (W.H.) Fellowship: 1018
Berkshire Conference of Women Historians: 364
Berkshire Music Center (Lenox, Mass.): 365
Berman (Gerrard and Ella) Award: 1176
Bermuda Government: 597
Bernath (Stuart L.) Awards: 1949
Berry (David) Prize: 1772
Best (W.T.) Scholarship: 2188
Beta Phi Mu Award: 132
Bevan (Aneurin) Memorial Foundation (UK): 366
Beveridge (Albert J.) Award: 105
Beyer (Lynn and Stanley) Award: 2200
Billington (Ray Allen) Award: 1617, 2153
Bing (Robert) Fund: 2020
Bingham (Worth) Memorial Fund (Washington, D.C.): 367
Binkley-Stephenson Award: 1617
Binnie (Ruth) Scholarship: 488
Biochemical Society (UK): 368, 369
Biological Research Station (Rensselaerville, N.Y.): 940
Bio-Serv Award: 124
Bird (F.C.J.) Award: 1661
Birla (R.D.) Smarak Kosh (India): 370
Bishop James C. Baker Awards: 2070

Black (James Tait) Memorial Prizes (UK): 371
Blackall Machine Tool and Gage Award: 190
Blackburn (Robert) Trust: 1734
Blackwell's Bookshop (Oxford, UK): 372, 373
Blair Awards: 465
Blair (Florence and William) Fellowship: 1749
Blair (Robert) Fellowships: 957
Blair-Bell (William) Lectureships: 1749
Blanch (Vicẽnte Canada) Fellowships: 216
Blegen (Theodore C.) Award: 819
B'nai B'rith International: 374
Board for Mission and Unity of the General Synod of the Church of England: 375
Bôcher Prize: 137
Boehringer Mannheim Awards: 368
Boise Foundation (UK): 376
Bolivian Government: 1336
Bollingen Prize in Poetry of the Yale University Library (New Haven, Conn.): 377
Bologna Center of the Johns Hopkins University: 378
Bolton (Herbert E.) Prize: 605
Bolus Medal: 383
Bombay Hospital Trust: 370
Bone-Wheeler Medal and Prize: 980
Boni (Albert) Fellowship: 49
Bonner (Tom W.) Prize: 154
Bonow Fund: 1081
Booker Prize: 1410
Booksellers Association of Great Britain and Ireland: 379
Borcherds (Mary Greta) Grant: 1977
Borden Award: 108, 124, 820
Born (Max) Medal and Prize: 996
Bosanquet (Theodora) Bursary Fund (UK): 380
Boston Globe (USA): 381
Botanical Society of America, Inc.: 382
Botanical Society of South Africa: 383
Botswana Government: 597
Bouwcentrum International Education (Rotterdam): 384
Bouwhis (Rev. Andrew L.) Scholarship: 531
Bowen (Arnold Vincent) Prize: 1674
Boys (Charles Vernon) Prize: 996
BP Scholarship: 2098
Brackenbury Award: 417
Bradford Chamber of Commerce, Inc. (UK): 385
Bradlow (E.P.) Scholarship: 2113
Bradlow (Henry) Scholarship: 2113
Bragg Prize: 996
Bramah (Joseph) Scholarship: 1019
Brandeis University Creative Arts Awards (Waltham, Mass.): 386
Brandenburg (E. Craig) Awards: 2070
Brazilian Government: 1342
Bread Loaf Writers' Conference (Middlebury, Vt.: 387
Brewer Prize: 177
British Academy: 388-391, 1587
British Archaeological Association: 392
British Association of Plastic Surgeons: 1764
British Council: 393-398
British Council of Churches: 557
British Dental Association: 399, 400
British Diabetic Association: 401
British Digestive Foundation: 402
British Electric Traction Company: 544
British Esperanto Association: 1604
British Federation of University Women, Ltd.: 403
British Gas Corporation: 207, 404
British Government: see United Kingdom Government
British Heart Foundation: 103, 405
British Institute of Archaeology at Ankara: 406, 407
British Institute in Eastern Africa: 408
British Institute in Paris: 409
British Institute of Persian Studies: 410
British Institute of Radiology: 411
British Institution Fund: 412
British-Italian Society: 2047
British Leather Manufacturers' Research Association: 413
British Leprosy Relief Association: 414
British Library: 415
British Medical Association: 416, 417
British Medical Students' Trust: 418
British Orthopaedic Association: 419
British Paediatric Association: 420
British Ports Association: 544
British Press Awards: 421
British Reserve Insurance Co.: 814
British School of Archaeology in Iraq: 422
British School of Archaeology in Jerusalem: 423, 424
British School at Rome: 425-427
British Small Animal Veterinary Association: 428
British Travel Educational Trust: 429
British Universities Summer Schools Joint Committee: 430
British Veterinary Association: 431
British Virgin Islands Government: 597
Brittain (Harry) Fellowships: 591
Broadcast Music, Inc. (USA): 432
Brock Gold Medal: 1129
Brodie (Bernard B.) Award: 194
Broida (Herbert P.) Prize: 154
Bronfman (Samuel) Foundation (Canada): 433
Brookhaven National Laboratory (USA): 434
Brookings Institution (USA): 435
Brooklyn Museum Art School (New York

City): 436
Brooks (Charles Franklin) Award: 138
Broome Agency, Inc. (Sarasota, Fla.): 437
Broun (Haywood) Award: 1590
Browaldh (Tore) Foundation for Social Science Research and Education (Stockholm): 438
Brower (A. Blaine) Scholarships: 71
Brown (Emil) Fund (Los Angeles, Calif.): 439
Brown (John Nicholas) Prize: 1287
Bruce (Catherine Wolfe) Medal: 300
Brucebo Scholarship: 509
Bruel (Georges) Prize: 1621
Brunei Government: 597
Brunetti (Cledo) Award: 979
Buccheri La Ferla Prizes: 1434
Bucke (Dr. William S.) Grant: 1639
Buckley (Oliver E.) Prize: 154
Buell Award: 742
Bulgarian Government: 440
Bulgarian Institute for Foreign Students: 440
Bulova (Arde) Fellowship: 441
Bunting (Mary Ingraham) Institute (Cambridge, Mass.): 442, 443
Bureau of Indian Affairs (USA): 2058
Burka Award: 990
Burmese Government: 578
Burns (Robert) Fellowship: 2110
Burroughs Scholarship: 1661
Burroughs Wellcome Fellowship: 74
Burroughs Wellcome Fund (USA): 176, 444
Bush Foundation (USA): 445, 446
Business and Professional Women's Foundation (USA): 447-449
Busk (Edward) Studentship: 1732
Busoni (F.) International Piano Competition: 450
Butler (Sally) Scholarships: 448
Buxtehude Prize (Lübeck): 451
Byas (Hugh Fulton) Memorial Foundation (USA): 452
Bynner (Witter) Awards: 1675

Cabot (Maria Moors) Prizes (USA): 580
Cade (Lady) Fellowship: 1415
CADESS Trust: 269
CAFRAD: 14
Caird's (Sir James) Travelling Scholarships Trust (Scotland): 1888-1891
Caldecott Medal: 132
California College of Arts and Crafts (Oakland): 453
Callaghan (F.R.) Awards: 1579
Cambridge University: 1877
Campbell (Francis J.) Citation: 132
Canada Council: 454-456
Canada Department of Agriculture: 457
Canada Mortgage and Housing Corporation: 458

Canadian Agricultural Economics Society: 459
Canadian Authors Association: 460
Canadian Bar Association: 461, 462
Canadian Biochemical Society: 463
Canadian Booksellers Association: 464
Canadian Cancer Society: 465, 466
Canadian Commonwealth Scholarship and Fellowship Committee: 467-469
Canadian Cystic Fibrosis Foundation: 470-474
Canadian Dental Research Foundation: 475
Canadian Federation for the Humanities: 476
Canadian Federation of University Women: 477, 831
Canadian Friends of the Hebrew University: 479
Canadian Fund for Dental Education: 480
Canadian Government: 271, 279-295, 454, 457, 467-469, 491-493, 515, 516, 578, 597, 682, 683, 688, 693-698, 702, 703, 713, 714, 892, 1276-1282, 1430, 1543-1555, 1928-1936, 2048
Canadian Heart Foundation: 481-485
Canadian Home Economics Association: 486-489
Canadian Institute of Mining and Metallurgy: 490
Canadian International Development Agency: 19, 491-493, 601
Canadian Library Association: 494
Canadian Life and Health Insurance Association: 495
Canadian Liver Foundation: 496-498
Canadian Lung Association: 499, 500
Canadian Medical Association: 501
Canadian National Institute for the Blind: 502
Canadian National Sportsmen's Fund: 503, 504
Canadian Nurses' Foundation: 505
Canadian Osteopathic Educational Trust Fund: 506
Canadian Pharmaceutical Association: 507
Canadian Political Science Association: 508
Canadian Salt Scholarships: 1723
Canadian-Scandinavian Foundation: 509
Canadian Society of Biblical Studies: 510
Canadian Society for Clinical Investigation: 511
Canadian Society of Exploration Geophysicists: 512
Canadian Society of Laboratory Technologists: 513
Canadian Steel Construction Council: 514
Canadian Wildlife Service: 515, 516
Canal Association (UK): 544
Canals (Maria) International Music Competition (Barcelona): 517
Cancer Research Campaign (UK): 518, 1136
Cancer Research Society, Inc. (Canada): 519
Cancer Society of New Zealand: 520

Cane (Melville) Award: 1675
Capener (Norman) Fellowship: 1759
Captain James Cook Fellowship: 1823
Cardiac Society of Australia and New Zealand: 521
Carley-Canoyer-Cutler Fellowship: 111
Carlson (Chester F.) Award: 185
Carnation Company Award: 486
Carnegie Foundation (Netherlands): 522
Carnegie Fund for Authors (USA): 523
Carnegie Hall (New York City): 1036
Carnegie Institution of Washington: 524
Carnegie Scholarship: 1785
Carnegie Trust for the Universities of Scotland: 525, 526
Carnovski Scholarship: 2113
Caroma Doulton Grant: 1746
Carr (William G.) Scholarship: 1432
Carver Research Foundation (USA): 527
Casagrande (Alessandro) International Piano Competition (Terni, Italy): 528
CASE Awards: 1853
CASE Studentships: 1539
Casella (Alfredo) International Competition of the Music Academy of Naples: 529
Cassel (Sir Ernest) Educational Trust (UK): 1885, 1886
Castagnola (Alice Fay di) Award: 1675
Cather (De Leeuw) Scholarships: 1723
Catholic Library Association (USA): 530, 531
Catholic Newspaper Prize: 1410
Catholic Women's League of Austria: 532, 533
Cattell (James McKeen) Fund (USA): 534
Cayley Scholarships: 865
Cayman Islands Government: 597
Celanese Corporation of America: 120
Center for Advanced Study in the Behavioral Sciences (Stanford, Calif.): 535
Center for Advanced Study in the Visual Arts: 1448, 1449
Center for Disease Control (USA): 2057
Center for Field Research (Belmont, Mass.): 536
Center for Hellenic Studies (Washington, D.C.): 537
Center for Reformation Research (St. Louis, Mo.): 538
Center for Theoretical Studies (Coral Gables, Fla.): 539
Central Association of Obstetricians and Gynecologists (USA): 540
Central Neuropsychiatric Association (Cleveland, Ohio): 541
Central News Agency, Ltd. (South Africa): 542
Centre de Formation et de Perfectionnement des Journalistes: 1171
Centre for Intergroup Studies (Cape Town): 543
CERN: 787-789
Cerro Tololo Inter-American Observatory (Chile): 1508
Chabod (Federico) Scholarship: 1154
Chalmers Bursary: 1785
Chalmers-Jervise Prize: 1785
Chamberlain (Sir William) Awards: 544
Chamorro (Pedro Joaquin) Awards: 1032
Chapman Fellowship: 139
Charlemagne Prize (Aachen): 1059
Chartered Institute of Transport (UK): 544
Chartres Prize: 868
Chateaubriand Bursaries: 834
Chautauqua Institution (New York): 545
Chautauqua Scholarships: 765
Chauveau Medal: 1815
Chávez (Ignacio)/National Institute of Cardiology (Mexico City): 1467
Chemical Institute of Canada: 546
Chemical Manufacturers Association (USA): 547
Chest, Heart and Stroke Association (UK): 548
Chibret Medal: 1113
Chibret Laboratories (Clermont-Ferrand, France): 549
Chigiana Musical Academy (Siena): 550
Child Accident Prevention Foundation of Australia: 551
Children's Book Circle (UK): 552
Children's Medical Research Foundation (Australia): 553
Childs (James B.) Award: 132
Childs (Jane Coffin) Memorial Fund for Medical Research (USA): 554
Chilean Commission for Intellectual Cooperation: 1355
Chilean Government: 1355
Chinard (Gilbert) Grants: 959
Chinese Academy: 312
Chinese Culture University (Taipei): 555
Chinese Government (People's Republic): 279, 307, 1648
Cholmondeley Award: 1942
Chopin Fellowship: 1676
Chopin (Frederic) International Piano Competition (Warsaw): 556
Chopin Scholarship: 1200
Choysa Bursary: 692
Chree (Charles) Prize: 996
Christian Aid (UK): 557
Church (Edwin F.) Medal: 190
Churchill (Winston) Fellowships: 769
Churchill (Winston) Foundation of the United States: 558
Churchill (Winston) Memorial Trust (Australia): 559
Churchill (Winston) Memorial Trust (NZ):

Churchill (Winston) Memorial Trust (UK): 561
Chylinski (Dr. Stanislas) Scholarship: 1201
Ciba-Geigy Corporation: 759
Ciba-Geigy Fellowship Trust (UK): 562
CIDA: 19, 491-493, 601
City Arts Trust (London): 814
City of London Festival: 814
City of Montevideo International Piano Competition: 563
City of New York: 564
City of Sydney Cultural Council: 565, 566
City of Toronto Book Award: 612
City of Westminster Arts Council (London): 1299
Civitan International Foundation (USA): 567, 568
Clairol Loving Care Scholarships: 449
Clark (John William) Award: 417
Clark (Russell) Award: 1577
Clarke (Mary A.) Scholarship: 489
Clayton (James) Fellowships: 1021, 1022
Claytor (Gertrude B.) Award: 1675
Clements Memorial Prize (UK): 569
Clendening (Logan) Fellowship: 2105
Cleveland Competition: 740
Cleveland Foundation (USA): 220
Cleveland Institute of Music (USA): 570
Cleveland (Newcomb) Prize: 54
Clifford (James L.) Prize: 184
Clift (David H.) Scholarship: 131
Cline (Howard F.) Prize: 605
Clinical Research Institute of Montreal: 571
Clothing and Footwear Institute (UK): 572
Clothworkers' Company (UK): 573
Cohen (Frank and Ethel S.) Award: 1176
Cole (Arthur H.) Grants: 585
Cole (Edward N.) Award: 1944
Cole (Frank Nelson) Prizes: 137
Colegio de Mexico: 1326
Collard (John Clementi) Fellowship: 2188
College of Europe (Bruges): 574
College of Music, Drama and Opera (San Francisco): 1393
College Placement Services, Inc. (USA): 575
Collins (Joseph) Foundation (USA): 576
Collins Publishers (UK): 579
Colombian Government: 1313
Colombo Plan: 493, 578, 1352, 1353, 1895
Columbia University (New York City): 353, 579, 580, 723, 875, 1694, 2196
Colwell (Arch T.) Awards: 1944
COMLA: 590
Commission for Administration (South Africa): 581
Commission on Adult Jewish Education: 374
Commission of the European Communities: 582, 583
Commission for Racial Equality (UK): 584
Committee on the Challenges of Modern Society: 1596
Committee on Research in Economic History (USA): 585
Commonwealth Africa Assistance Program: 493
Commonwealth Association of Surveying and Land Economy (UK): 586
Commonwealth Caribbean Assistance Program: 493
Commonwealth Education Cooperation Plan: 1340
Commonwealth Foundation (UK): 19, 587, 601, 1771, 1805
Commonwealth Fund (New York): 588, 589
Commonwealth Fund for Technical Cooperation: 1895
Commonwealth Geographical Bureau (UK): 1771
Commonwealth Library Association: 590
Commonwealth Poetry Prize: 1410
Commonwealth Press Union (UK): 587, 591
Commonwealth Scholarship Commission in the United Kingdom: 592-596
Commonwealth Scholarship and Fellowship Plan: 467-469, 592-597, 669-671, 803, 1322, 1338, 1339, 1571-1573
Commonwealth Scientific and Industrial Research Organization (Australia): 598
Commonwealth Secretariat (London): 599
Commonwealth Veterinary Interchange Fund: 601
Commonwealth Youth Programme (UK): 600
Composers, Authors and Publishers Association of Canada, Ltd.: 602
Compton (Arthur Holly) Award: 143
Compton (Karl Taylor) Medal: 125
Comune Di Napoli Scholarship: 1154
Concert Artists Guild, Inc. (USA): 603
Confederation of ASEAN Journalists: 1163
Confederation of British Industry: 604
Conference on Latin American History (USA): 605
Congressional Fellowships (USA): 158
Conners (Bernard F.) Prize: 1641
CONOCO Inc. (USA): 606
Conservation and Research Foundation, Inc. (USA): 607
Consortium for Graduate Study in Management (USA): 608
Control Systems Award: 979
Cook (James) Scholarship: 372
Cook (Captain James) Fellowships: 1823
Cook (Thomas) Awards: 1410
Cooper (Duff) Memorial Trust Fund (UK): 609

Cooperstown Fellowships: 1570
Copeman Fellowship: 237
Corbin (Hazel) Fund: 1264
Corday-Morgan Prize: 1817
Corey (Albert B.) Prize: 105
Cormack (Robert) Fellowships: 1818
Corn Industries Research Foundation (USA): 610
Corn Refineries Association, Inc. (USA): 610
Coro Foundation (USA): 611
Corporation of the City of Toronto (Canada): 612
Cortina Ulisse Prize: 2064
Cotton (Dr. M. Aylwin) Foundation (Italy): 720
Cottrell Grant Programs: 1712
Council for British Archaeology: 613
Council for Cultural Cooperation (Europe): 614, 615
Council of Egg Marketing Authorities (Australia): 708
Council of Europe: 614-619, 1153, 2015
Council on Foreign Relations, Inc. (USA): 620
Council for International Exchange of Scholars (USA): 621, 622, 1069, 1070
Council of International Programs for Youth Leaders and Social Workers, Inc. (USA): 623
Council on Legal Education Opportunity (USA): 624
Council for Opportunity in Graduate Management Education (USA): 625
Council for Scientific and Industrial Research (South Africa): 626-634
Council on Social Work Education (USA): 635
Council for Tobacco Research—USA: 636
Countess of Munster Musical Trust (UK): 637
Covello (Leonard) Award: 130
Cranbrook Academy of Art (Bloomfield Hills, Mich.): 638
Crane-Rogers Foundation (USA): 973
Crawshay (Rose Mary) Prizes: 391
C.R.B. Fellowships: 362
Creasy (William N.) Professorships: 444
Creswick (Alice) Scholarship: 321
Criminology Research Council (Australia): 639
Crombie Scholarship (UK): 640
Cross (Dorothy Temple) Fellowship: 1275
Crouch (Derek) Fellowship: 402
Crouch (George E.) Foundation (USA): 154
Cuban Government: 1359
Cullis (Winifred) Grants: 1090
Culmann Fellowship: 1008
Curci (Alberto) Foundation (Italy): 641
Curl Prize: 1740
Currey (C.H.) Fellowship: 2002
Currie (R.M.) Fellowship: 988

Curti (Merle) Award: 1617
Curtis Institute of Music (Philadelphia, Pa.): 642
Cussins (M.) Fellowship: 402
Cust (Miss Aleen) Fellowship: 1765
Cyprus Forestry College: 1309
Cyprus Government: 597, 1309
Cystic Fibrosis Foundation (USA): 643-645
Cystic Fibrosis Research Trust (UK): 646
Czechoslovak Academy of Sciences: 989
Czechoslovak Government: 989, 1314, 1343

DAAD (West Germany): 283, 852, 853
Dade Scholarships: 192
Dafoe (J.W.) Foundation (Canada): 494, 647
Dairy Education Scheme (Australia): 648
Dairy and Food Industries Supply Association, Inc. (USA): 175
Dairying Research Committee (Australia): 648
Dalal (Sir Ratanji) Scholarship: 1761
Dale (Chester) Fellowships: 1302, 1448
Dale Fund Grants: 1668
Dallas Morning News (USA): 649
Dallas Theater Center (Tex.): 650
Dalzell-Ward (Dr. A.J.) Fellowship: 891
Damian (Father) Foundation (Belgium): 800
Damrosche Scholarships: 815
Danish Government: 280, 651-652
Danish Ministry of Education: 651
Danish Research Councils: 652
Darbarker Award: 382
Darmstadt International Music Institute (West Germany): 653
Dartmouth Medal: 132
Dartmouth Street Trust (UK): 654
Dautrebande (Lucien) Foundation: 823
David Library of the American Revolution: 73
Davidson (Gustav) Award: 1675
Davies (Mary Carolyn) Award: 1675
Davis (Henry and Lily) Fund: 246
Davis (Shelby Cullom) Center for Historical Studies (Princeton, N.J.): 655
Davis (Lady) Fellowship Trust (Israel): 1203
Davisson-Germer Prize: 154
Day (Richard Hopper) Medal: 5
Day Lewis (C.) Fellowships: 871
De Menasce (George) Trust: 1619
Dealy (G.B.) Awards: 649
Dean (Stanley R.) Award: 72
DeBakey Medical Foundation (USA): 656
Debs (Eugene V.) Foundation (USA): 657
Decca-Kathleen Ferrier Prize: 1784
Deedes (Wyndham) Scholarships: 213
DeKnight (Freda A.) Fellowship: 110
del Duca Foundation: *see* Duca Foundation
Delmas (Gladys Krieble) Foundation (USA): 658
Delta Kappa Gamma Society International

(USA): 659
Dempster Fellowship: 1018
Denny (G.A.) Scholarship: 2113
Denoyer (L.P.)/O.E. Geppert Fund: 258
Dental Association of South Africa: 660, 661
Denton (Jean) Fund: 1187
Department of Aboriginal Affairs (Australia): 662
Department of Agriculture (New South Wales): 799
Department of Agriculture and Fisheries for Scotland: 663
Department of Education (Australia): 664-671
Department of Education (India): 1337-1340
Department of Education (Ireland): 672, 673
Department of Education (Northern Ireland): 674
Department of Education and Science (England and Wales): 675-681
Department of Energy, Mines and Resources (Canada): 682
Department of the Environment (Canada): 683
Department of External Affairs (Canada): 279, 454, 1934
Department of Fisheries and Forestry (Ireland): 684, 685
Department of Foreign Affairs (Australia): 686
Department of Foreign Affairs (Ireland): 1838, 1839
Department of Health and Social Services (Northern Ireland): 687
Department of Indian Affairs (Canada): 688, 694
Department of Industry, Commerce and Energy (Ireland): 1408
Department of Industry, Trade and Commerce (Canada): 1430
Department of Internal Affairs (New Zealand): 689-692, 2099
Department of International Cultural Relations (Belgium): 1360
Department of International Development Cooperation (Finland): 1344
Department of Justice (Canada): 693-697
Department of Labour (Canada): 698
Department of National Defence (Canada): 270, 271
Department of National Development and Energy (Australia): 699, 700
Department of National Education (South Africa): 701
Department of National Health and Welfare (Canada): 702, 703
Department of Primary Industry (Australia): 704-708
Department of Science and Technology (Australia): 709-712
Department of the Secretary of State (Canada): 713, 714
Department of Social Security (Australia): 715
Design Canada Scholarships: 1430
Design and Industries Association Trust (UK): 716
Detweiler Fellowships: 1754
Deutscher (Isaac) Memorial Prize (UK): 717
Dewar Fellowship: 1775
Dexter Prize: 1950
Diamond (Harry) Award: 979
Dickinson (Emily) Award: 1675
Difco Scholarship: 192
Dinerman (Helen S.) Fund: 60
Dio Fund: 246
Distilled Spirits Council of the United States, Inc.: 718
Dr. A.J. Dalzell-Ward Fellowship: 981
Dr. Casimir Victor Kierzkowski Scholarship: 1201
Dr. Courtney W. Shropshire Grants: 568
Dr. Dorothy Jordan Lloyd Trust: 413
Dr. Hadwen Trust for Humane Research (UK): 719
Dr. H.P. Heineken Award: 895
Dr. Henry R. Viets Medical Student Research Fellowships: 1395
Dr. Kermit E. Osserman Fellowship: 1394
Dr. M. Aylwin Cotton Foundation (Italy): 720
Dr. P.A. Hendriks Scholarship: 1977
Dr. Robert H. Goddard Scholarship: 1525
Dr. Stanislaw Mrozowski Fund: 1201
Dr. William S. Bucke Grant: 1639
Dr. Williams's Trust (UK): 721
Doherty (Henry L. and Grace) Charitable Foundation, Inc. (USA): 722
Dominica Government: 597
D'Orlando (Pauly) Scholarship: 1711
Doubleday and Company, Inc. (USA): 723
Douglas (A. Vibert) Fellowship: 1089
Dow Award: 185
Dowling Endowment: 1822
Downs (Robert B.) Award (USA): 724
Dragonslayer Contest: 2087
Dreyfus (Camille and Henry) Foundation, Inc. (USA): 725
Drummond Trust (UK): 726
Dublin Institute for Advanced Studies: 727-729
Duca (Simone and Cino del) Foundation: 730, 731
Duckham (Alexander) Awards: 1030
Duddell Medal and Prize: 996
Duff-Rinfret Scholarship (Canada): 697
Dumbarton Oaks: Trustees for Harvard University (USA): 732
Dunlop (Derrick) Fellowship: 1752

Dunlop (Florence S.) Memorial Fellowship Fund (Canada): 733
Dunning (John H.) Prize: 105
Dyason Bequest: 232
Dybwad (Rosemary F.) Awards: 265
Dye (Marie) Fellowship: 110
Dyer (A.J.) Observatory (Nashville, Tenn.): 734
Dyslexia Research Foundation, Inc. (Australia): 735

Eadie (Thomas W.) Medal: 1815
Eadon (Letitia) Award: 1737
Earhart (Amelia) Fellowship: 2205
Earhart Foundation (USA): 736
East Malling Research Station (UK): 737
East-West Center (Honolulu): 738
Eastern Arts Association (Norwich): 2096
Eastman Dental Center (Rochester, N.Y.): 739
Eastman School of Music (Rochester, N.Y.): 740
Eaton (Max A.) Prize: 138
Ebert (Friedrich) Foundation (West Germany): 741
ECFMG: 748
Eckman Award: 63
Ecological Society of America: 742
Economic Commission: *see* United Nations Economic Commission
Economic Development Institute (Washington, D.C.): 743
Economic History Association (USA): 585
Economic and Social Commission for Asia and the Pacific (Bangkok): *see* United Nations
Economic and Social Research Institute (Dublin): 744
Ecuadorian Government: 1315
Ecumenical Scholarships Programme (West Germany): 745
Eden Fellowship: 1749
Edgar Fellowship: 1749
Edison Medal: 979
Edmonds (Will) Fellowship: 1750
Education Council of the Graphic Arts Industry (USA): 746, 747
Educational Commission for Foreign Medical Graduates (USA): 748
Educational Film Library Association (USA): 749
Educational Opportunities Council (South Africa): 750
Educational Policy Fellowship Program (USA): 751
Edwards (Lewis) Scholarship: 1661
Eggs Authority (UK): 752
1851 Fellowships: 1768
1820 Settlers National Monument Foundation (South Africa): 753
Einstein (Alfred) Award: 142
Eisenhower Exchange Fellowships, Inc. (USA): 754
Eisteddfod (Wales): 1780
Eldredge (Marie H.) Award: 164
Electrical Women's Round Table, Inc. (USA): 755
Eleutherian Mills-Hagley Foundation (USA): 756, 757
Elida-Gibbs Fellowship: 660
Elliot (F.J.) Award: 513
Elliot Prize: 1287
Elmore (Stanley) Fellowships: 1025
Elmslie Scholarships: 828
Elvehjem (Conrad A.) Award: 124
Emanuel (Bessy) Educational Trust (UK): 758
EMBO: 786
Emergency Planning Canada Fellowship: 272
Emerson (Ralph Waldo) Award: 1664
Endocrine Society (USA): 759
Engineering Foundation (USA): 760
Engineering Science, Inc.: 263
English Academy of Southern Africa: 761
English-American Institute (Austria): 762
English Centre of International P.E.N.: 763
English-Speaking Union of the Commonwealth (UK): 253, 764-766
English-Speaking Union Ltd. (New South Wales Branch): 767
English-Speaking Union Ltd. (Victoria Branch, Australia): 768
English-Speaking Union of the United States: 769, 1673
ENI: Enrico Mattei Institute (Milan): 770
Environment Canada: 515, 516
Environmental Protection Agency (USA): 771-774
Epilepsy Foundation of America: 776-778
Epinal International Piano Competition (France): 775
Episcopal Church Foundation (USA): 779
Eppley Smithsonian Fellowship: 1902
Epstein (William and Janice) Award: 1176
Erasmus Prize: 1684
ESCAP: 2076
Esmond Scholarship: 409
Eternit International Prize for Architecture: 780
Ethicon Fellowship: 1755
Etienne (Eugene) Prize: 1621
European Association for the Study of Diabetes: 781
European Centre (Nancy, France): 782
European College Foundation (Hamburg): 783
European Cultural Foundation (Amsterdam): 784

European Economic Community: 792
European Institute for Business Administration (Fontainebleau): 785
European Molecular Biology Organisation: 786
European Organisation for Nuclear Research: 787-789
European Parliament: 790
European Space Agency: 791
European University Institute (Florence): 792
Ewart-Biggs (Christopher) Prize: 1410
Excerpta Medica Foundation (Netherlands): 793
Experiment in International Living (USA): 794
Exxon Educational Foundation Fellowships: 1580
Exxon International, Inc.: 120
Exxon Research and Engineering Company: 120

F.V.S. Foundation (West Germany): 795
Faber & Faber Ltd. (UK): 796
Facts on File Award: 132
Fairbank (John K.) Prize: 105
Fankuchen Award: 86
FAO: 797, 816-818
FAO International Food Technology Training Centre (Mysore, India): 797
Farjeon (Eleanor) Award: 552
Farm Foundation (USA): 798
Farrar (L.S.) Scholarship: 400
Farrer Memorial Trust (New South Wales): 799
Father Damian Foundation for the Campaign Against Leprosy (Belgium): 800
Father James B. Macelwane Awards: 138
Faucett (Philip M.) Prize: 2199
Faulding (Francis Hardy) Fellowship: 1743
Faulkner Award: 1630
Faxon (Frederick W.) Scholarship: 131
Federal Administration for International Scientific, Educational, Cultural and Technical Cooperation (Yugoslavia): 801
Federal Commission for Scholarships for Foreign Students (Switzerland): 802
Federal Ministry of Education (Nigeria): 803
Fedmech Foundation for Advanced Education and Research: 804
Fellowship of Engineering (UK): 805
Feng Chia College of Engineering and Business (Taichung, Taiwan): 806
Ferrier (Kathleen) Scholarship: 1784, 2199
Fight for Sight, Inc. (USA): 807-810
Fiji Government: 597
Fine Arts Work Center in Provincetown, Inc. (USA): 811
Finet (Paul) Foundation (Luxembourg): 812

Fink (Donald G.) Prize: 978
Finley (David E.) Fellowships: 1448
Finnish Federation of University Women: 813
Finnish Government: 281, 1316-1318, 1344
Fisher (Chris) Scholarships: 1723
Fiske Fund: 1719
Flavelle Medal: 1815
Flesch (Carl) International Violin Competition (UK): 814
Florey Fellowship: 338, 1800
Florio (John) Prize: 2047
Fontainebleau Fine Arts and Music Schools Association, Inc. (USA): 815
Food and Agriculture Organization of the United Nations: 816-818
Food and Drug Administration (USA): 2057
FOPERDA (Belgium): 800
Ford (Consuelo) Award: 1675
Ford Foundation: 750, 1586, 1913-1917
Ford Motor Company: 154
Forest History Society (USA): 819
Forst Products Research Society (USA): 820
Forman Awards: 2094
Forrest (Lena Lake) Fellowship: 447
Fortescue (Charles LeGeyt) Fellowship: 977
Foulerton Gift Fellowship: 1795
Foundation for Chiropractic Education and Research (USA): 821
Foundation for Microbiology (USA): 822
Foundation for Physiopathology-Lucien Dautrebande: 823
Foundation for Public Relations Research and Education (USA): 824, 825
Foxwell Award: 980
Frank (William Zev) Award: 1176
Franklin (Miles) Literary Award: 826
Free Church Federal Council (UK): 827, 828
Freedoms Foundation at Valley Forge (USA): 829
Freeman Fellowship: 179
Freeman Scholarship: 190
French-American Foundation: 830
French Association of University Women: 831
French Atomic Energy Commission: 1474
French Colonial Historical Society: 832
French (R.T.) Company (Rochester, N.Y.): 833
French Embassy in the United States: 834
French Foundation for Medical Research: 835
French Government: 282, 834, 963, 1345, 1409, 1424, 1474, 1970
French Petroleum Institute: 836
French Physical Society: 996
Freund (Clement J.) Award: 185
Frew (Geoffrey) Fellowship: 313
Friday Morning Music Club Foundation, Inc. (USA): 837
Friends of American Writers: 838

Frost (Robert) Prize: 814
Froude Scholarship: 1778
Fry (C. Brooks and Ruth Martin) Award: 2035
Fuchsova (Liza) Prize: 1783
Fuertes (Louis Agassiz) and Margaret Morse Nice Awards: 2164
Fulbright Program: 1927
Fulbright-Hays Program: 314-316, 621, 622, 986, 1001, 1064-1072
Fuller (Anna) Fund (USA): 839
Fund for Environmental Studies (West Germany): 840
Fund for Investigative Journalism, Inc. (USA): 841
Fund for Theological Education, Inc. (USA): 842-844

Gairdner Foundation (Canada): 845
Gambia Government: 597
Gassner (John) Award: 1562
GATT: 848
Gauss (Christian) Award: 1664
Gay News (UK): 846
Geach (Portia) Memorial Fund: 847
Gellibrand (Sir John) Scholarship: 1215
General Agreement on Tariffs and Trade: 848
General Electric Foundation: 154
General Diagnostics: 193
General Mills Foundation (USA): 42
General Semantics Foundation: 849
General Synod of the Church of England: 375
Gentilli (Edgar) Prize: 1749
Geological Society of America: 850
Georgia Library Association (USA): 851
German Academic Exchange Service: 283, 852, 853
German Marshall Fund of the United States: 854
German Physical Society: 996
German Publishers' Association: 2047
German Society of Endocrinology: 855
Germanistic Society of America: 856
Gershoy (Leo) Award: 105
Getty (J. Paul) Prize: 2185
Ghana Government: 597
Gibraltar Government: 597
Gibson Fund: 258
Gibson (Robert) Methodist Trust Board (NZ): 857
Gibson (William) Scholarship: 1822
Gilchrist Educational Trust (UK): 858
Gildesgame (Leon L.) Award: 1176
Giles (Louise) Scholarship: 131
Gillespie (William Honyman) Scholarship Trust (Scotland): 859
Gillette Company (UK): 860
Gillson Scholarship: 1940
Gilman Award: 194

Gilmore (Jean) Bursary: 325
Glasgow Bursary: 721
Glasgow Fellowship: 1706
Glasstone (Samuel) Award: 143
Glazebrook Prize: 996
Glen (Esther) Award: 1577
Gloeckner (Fred C.) Foundation: 861
Goddard (George W.) Award: 1954
Goddard (Dr. Robert H.) Scholarship: 1525
Goethe Institute (Munich): 862
Goethe Prize: 795
Gold (Harry) Award: 194
Golden Jubilee Fellowship: 1960
Golden Plate Award: 1468
Goldsmiths' Company (UK): 863
Gomez (Rodrigo) Prize: 1206
Goodman and Gilman Award: 194
Gordon (Alan) Award: 195, 1954
Gottlieb (Adolph and Esther) Foundation (USA): 864
Gottschalk (Louis) Prize: 184
Gough (Michael) Prize: 407
Gould League of New South Wales: 865
Government of Ontario: 1310
Governor General's Awards (Canada): 454
Gowrie Scholarship Trust Fund (Australia): 866
Graduate Institute of International Studies (Geneva): 867
Graham-Hodgson Scholarship: 1757
Grand Prix de Chartres International Organ Contest: 868
Grant (Eugene L.) Award: 185
Grass Foundation (USA): 869, 870
Great Lakes Colleges Association (USA): 1582
Greater London Arts Association: 871
Greek Government: 872, 965, 1319
Greek State Scholarships Foundation: 872, 1319
Greenberg (Hayim) College (Jerusalem): 2187
Greenshields (Elizabeth T.) Memorial Foundation (Canada): 873
Gregg (John Robert) Award: 1268
Gregory Medal: 1148
Gregory (Eric) Awards: 1942
Gregynog Fellowship: 2148
Grenada Government: 597
Grierson (John) Award: 749
Griffith (George C.) Scholarships: 71
Grolier Foundation Award: 132
Grove School Fellowship: 2175
Gruber (Otto von) Award: 1129
Guardian (UK): 874
Guatemala Government: 1320
Guggenheim (Daniel and Florence) Foundation (USA): 875, 876, 1899
Guggenheim (Harry Frank) Foundation (USA): 877

Guggenheim (John Simon) Memorial Foundation (USA): 878, 879
Guilday (Peter) Prize: 67
Gulbenkian (Calouste) Foundation (Portugal): 880
Gulbenkian (Calouste) Prize: 1630
Gulbenkian Rome Scholarship: 427
Gulf Canada Ltd.: 273
Gummer (R.H.) Exhibition: 980
Gunton (T.P.) Award: 417
Guthrie Award: 1786
Guthrie Prize: 996
Gutmacher (Manfred S.) Award: 164
Guyana Government: 597

Habirshaw (William M.) Award: 979
Hackney (Louise Wallace) Scholarship: 150
Hadwen (Dr.) Trust for Humane Research (UK): 719
Hagley Foundation (USA): 756, 757
Hague Academy of International Law: 881
Halbach Foundation (West Germany): 1202
Haldane Competition: 1774
Hales (Stephen) Award: 198
Hall (R.T.) Prize: 521
Hallmark Foundation (USA): 746
Hamilton (James A.) Award: 69
Hammarskjold (Dag) Foundation (Sweden): 882
Hammerschlag (Alice Berger) Trust Award: 247
Hancock (John) Mutual Life Insurance Company (USA): 883
Handley Page Award: 1736
Hanks (Howard H.), Jr. Scholarship: 138
Hansberry (Lorraine) Award: 73
Hanseatic Goethe Prize: 795
Hanson (Norman) Awards: 634
Haring (Clarence H.) Prize: 105, 605
Harkness Fellowships: 588
Harman (Katherine Bishop) Award: 417
Harman (Nathaniel Bishop) Award: 417
Harris (Albert J.) Award: 1117
Harris (John) Award: 1577
Harrison Prize: 1817
Hartford Jewish Community Center (Conn.): 884
Hartford Public Library (Conn.): 885
Hartnett Award: 1943
Harvard-South Africa Fellowships: 1971
Harvard University (Cambridge, Mass.): 274, 339, 732, 1182, 1184, 1196, 1591, 2138
Harvard University Press (Cambridge, Mass.): 886
Harvey Prize: 203
Harvey's of Bristol: 1214
Haskil (Clara) Competition: 1379
Hastings (Sir Charles) Award: 417

Hastings Center (Hastings-on-Hudson, N.Y.): 1000
Hastings College of the Law (San Francisco): 1644
Havilland (Geoffrey de) Scholarship: 1735
Haven (Samuel Foster) Fellowships: 50
Hawthornden Prize: 887, 1942
Hawthorne (Charles Oliver) Award: 417
Hayden Award: 5
Haystack Mountain School of Crafts (Deer Isle, Maine): 888
Hayward Foundation: 1151, 1764
Head (Henry) Fellowship: 1788
Health Education Council (UK): 889-891
Health Resources Administration (USA): 2057
Health Services Administration (USA): 2057
Health and Welfare Canada: 892
Hebrew University of Jerusalem: 479, 893, 894
Heerbrugg (Wild) Fellowship: 76, 197
Heineken (Dr. H.P.) Award: 895
Heineken Foundation (Netherlands): 895
Heineman (Dannie N.) Prize: 125, 154, 1369
Heinz Fellowships: 420, 1468
Heinz-Schwarzkopf-Foundation Young Europe (West Germany): 896
Heiser Fellowship Program (New York City): 897-899
Hellaby (Rose) Medical Scholarships Trust (NZ): 900
Hemingway (Ernest) Foundation (USA): 1630
Hemley (Cecil) Award: 1675
Henderson Award: 99
Henderson (William Ramsay) Trust (UK): 901
Hendriks (Dr. P.A.) Scholarship: 1977
Henry (Charles and Julia) Fund (UK): 902
Henry (Charles and Julia) Fund (USA): 903
Henry (David) Scholarships: 1397
Herder Prize: 795
Hermant (Percy) Fellowships: 947
Herskovits Award: 13
Hertz (Heinrich) Foundation (West Germany): 1599
Hess (Henry) Award: 190
Hess (Myra) Trust (UK): 904
Hewins (Caroline M.) Scholarship: 885
Heydenrych (B.G.) Trust Fund (South Africa): 905, 906
Hewlett-Packard Company: 185
Hiatt (Frances) Fellowship: 51
Hibbett (Harold) Fellowship: 1695
Hibbs (Samuel G.) Award: 164
Hiemens (Leisel M.) Award: 1608
Higgins (T.R.) Award: 129
Higham (David) Prize: 1410
Higher Council for Scientific Research (Spain): 907
Hill Pattison-Struthers Bursary: 1751
Hillenbrand Fellowship: 96

Hillman (J. William) Fellowships: 2068
Hillman (Sidney) Foundation, Inc. (USA): 908
Hinrichsen Foundation (UK): 909
Hirsh (Jacob) Fellowship: 171
Historical Association (Christchurch, NZ): 910
History of Science Society (USA): 911
Hobson (G. Vernon) Bequest: 1028
Hodder and Stoughton: 912
Hodgkins (Frances) Fellowship: 2110
Hodgson (Robert H.) Grant: 258
Hodson (William, Jr.) Fellowship: 1184
Hoffman (Paul G.) Awards Fund: 913
Hoffmann-La Roche, Inc.: 194
Hogg (Quintin)/Florence Mills Fellowship: 1760
Holden (David) Award: 421
Holt (Geoffrey) Award: 417
Holtby (Winifred) Prize: 1821
Holweck Medal and Prize: 996
Honduras Government: 1321
Hong Kong Government: 597
Hooper (Grace Murray) Award: 261
Hoover Institution (Stanford, Conn.): 914
Horn Book Awards: 381
Horne (Walter Jobson) Prize: 416
Horniman (Emslie) Scholarship: 1738
Horning Award: 1944
Horserace Betting Levy Board (UK): 915
Horticultural Research Institute: 916
Horwood (H.C.) Scholarship: 1977
Hospital for Sick Children Foundation (Toronto): 917, 918
Houblon-Norman Fund (UK): 919
Houghton Mifflin Company (USA): 920
Howard (George A. and Eliza Gardner) Foundation (USA): 921
Howard (Margaret Rohe) Fund: 1866
Howard (Roy W.) Awards: 1866
Howard (A.W.) Memorial Trust, Inc. (Australia): 922
Hubbard Scholarship: 851
Hudswell Awards: 1015
Huebner (S.S.) Foundation for Insurance Education (USA): 923, 924
Hughes Aircraft Company (USA): 925
Human Sciences Research Council (South Africa): 926-932
Humane Research Trust (UK): 933
Humanitarian Trust (UK): 934
Humboldt (Alexander von) Foundation (West Germany): 2135
Huml (Vlacav) International Violin Competition (Zagreb): 935
Hungarian Cultural Foundation, Inc. (USA): 936
Hungarian Government: 284
Hungarian Institute for Cultural Relations: 937
Hungarian Research Centre for Water Resources Development: 938
Hunt (Richard Carley) Fellowships: 2150
Hunt (Thomas) Grant: 402
Huntington Library and Art Gallery (San Marino, Calif.): 939
Hurst Grant: 402
Hutton (Dorothy S.) Scholarship: 71
Huyck (Edmond Miles) Preserve, Inc. (Rensselaerville, N.Y.): 940

ICCROM-International Centre for the Study of the Preservation and the Restoration of Cultural Property (Rome): 941
Icelandic Government: 1311
ICETEX: 1313
ICI New Zealand Ltd.: 692
ILEA: 957
Illinois Opera Guild: 2154
Immroth (John Philip) Award: 132
Imperial Cancer Research Fund (UK): 942, 943
Imperial College (London): 944, 945, 1876
Imperial Oil Ltd. (Canada): 946, 947
Imperial Order Daughters of the Empire (Canada): 1145
Independent Broadcasting Authority (UK): 948
Indian Council for Cultural Relations: 949
Indian Council of Medical Research: 950
Indian Council of Social Science Research: 951
Indian Federation of University Women's Associations: 2114, 2115
Indian Government: 366, 578, 597, 795, 949-951, 954, 1337-1340
Indian Health Employees Scholarship Fund (USA): 952
Indiana University Museum of History, Anthropology and Folklore (Bloomington): 953
Indo-U.S. Subcommission on Education and Culture: 954
Indonesian Government: 578
Industrial Research/Development (Barrington, Ill.): 955
Ingram (M.A.) Trust (Australia): 956
Inner London Education Authority: 957
Innes (John) Foundation (UK): 958
Innis-Gerin Medal: 1815
INSEAD: 785
Insole Award: 417
Institut Français de Washington: 959
Institute of Actuaries (UK): 960
Institute for Advanced Studies in the Humanities (Edinburgh): 961
Institute for Advanced Study (Princeton, N.J.): 962
Institute for African Medicine and Epidemi-

ology (Paris): 963
Institute for American Universities (Aix-en-Provence, France): 964
Institute of Arts & Letters (USA): 39
Institute for Balkan Studies (Thessaloniki): 965
Institute of Business Studies (Barcelona): 966
Institute of Cancer Research (UK): 967, 968
Institute of Chartered Accountants in England and Wales: 970
Institute of Chartered Secretaries and Administrators (UK): 969
Institute of Constitutional & Parliamentary Studies (New Delhi): 971
Institute of Cost and Management Accountants (UK): 972
Institute of Current World Affairs (USA): 973
Institute of Developing Economies (Tokyo): 974
Institute of Early American History and Culture (Williamsburg, Va.): 975, 976
Institute for Educational Leadership (USA): 751
Institute of Electrical and Electronics Engineers, Inc. (USA): 977-979
Institute of Energy (UK): 980
Institute for European History (Mainz): 981, 982
Institute of Food Technologists (USA): 983
Institute for Humane Studies: 984
Institute for Industrial Reconstruction (Rome): 985
Institute of International Education (USA): 160, 986, 1068
Institute of International Summer Courses in German Language and Literature (Salzburg): 987
Institute of Jewish Studies (Jerusalem): 894
Institute of Limnology (Austria): 346
Institute of Management Services (UK): 988
Institute of Medicine (USA): 1493
Institute of Microbiology (Prague): 989
Institute of Navigation (USA): 990
Institute for Northern Studies (Saskatchewan): 991
Institute of Orthopaedics (Oswestry, Shropshire): 992
Institute for Palestine Studies (Beirut): 993
Institute of Paper Chemistry (Appleton, Wis.): 994
Institute of Petroleum & Gas (Ploiesti, Romania): 995
Institute of Physics (UK): 996
Institute for Portuguese Culture and Language: 997
Institute of Public Administration of Canada: 998
Institute for Reading Research: 1117

Institute for Research in the Humanities (USA): 999
Institute of Society, Ethics and the Life Sciences (Hastings-on-Hudson, N.Y.): 1000
Institute of South African Architects: 634
Institute of Southeast Asian Studies (Singapore): 1001-1004
Institute for the Sponsorship of Talented Students (West Germany): 9
Institute of Sports Medicine (UK): 1005
Institute for the Study of Man in Africa (South Africa): 1006
Institute for the Study of World Politics (USA): 1007
Institute of Civil Engineers (UK): 1008-1010
Institute of Electrical Engineers (UK): 1011-1016
Institute of Fire Engineers (UK): 1017
Institute of Gas Engineers (UK): 1018
Institute of Mechanical Engineers (UK): 1019-1023
Institute of Mining Engineers (UK): 1024-1028
Institute of Nuclear Engineers (UK): 1029
Institute of Plant Engineers (UK): 1030
Inter-American Foundation: 1031
Inter-American Press Association: 1032
Intergovernmental Oceanography Commission: 1033
Inter-University Council for Higher Education Overseas (UK): 398
International Agency for Research on Cancer: 1034
International Agricultural Centre (Wageningen, Netherlands): 1035
International American Music Competitions: 1036
International Association for the Exchange of Students for Technical Experience: 1037
International Association of Fire Chiefs Foundation, Inc.: 1038
International Association of Students in Economics and Management: 1039
International Astronomical Union: 1040
International Atlantic Salmon Foundation: 1041
International Atomic Energy Agency: 1042, 1043
International Ballet Competition (Varna, Bulgaria): 1044
International Balzan Foundation: 1045
International Beethoven Piano Competition (Vienna): 1046
International Brain Research Organization: 1047
International Bureau of Weights and Measures (Sevres, France): 1048
International Business Machines Corporation: 154
International Centre for Advanced Mediter-

ranean Agronomic Studies: 1049-1051
International Centre for Advanced Technical and Vocational Training (Turin): 1052
International Centre for Agricultural Education (Bern): 1053
International Centre for Comparative Law and Judicial Studies (Luxembourg): 1144
International Centre for European Research and Studies (Luxembourg): 1144
International Centre of Hydrology 'Dino Tonini' (Padua): 1054
International Centre for Political Economy (Luxembourg): 1144
International Centre of Studies for the Diffusion of Italian Music (Rome): 1055
International Centre for the Study of Mosaic (Ravenna): 1056
International Centre for the Study of the Preservation and the Restoration of Cultural Property (Rome): 941
International Centre for Theoretical Physics (Trieste, Italy): 1057
International Centre for Tropical Agriculture (Cali, Colombia): 1058
International Charlemagne Prize of the City of Aachen (West Germany): 1059
International Children's Centre (Paris): 1060
International Civil Aviation Organization: 1061
International College of Surgeons (USA Branch): 1062
International Communication Agency (USA): 160, 621, 1063-1073, 1927
International Competition for Chamber Music Ensembles (Colmar, France): 1074
International Competition for Musical Performers (Geneva): 1075
International Competition for Opera and Ballet Composition (Geneva): 1076
International Competition for Young Conductors (Besançon, France): 1077
International Competition for Young Musicians (Belgrade): 1078
International Competition for Young Opera Singers (Sofia): 1079
International Confederation of Societies of Authors and Composers: 1080
International Co-operative Alliance: 1081
International Copper Research Association, Inc.: 1082
International Council for Philosophy and Humanistic Studies: 1083
International Dental Federation: 1084
International Double Bass Competition: 1250
International Exchange of Scholars (USA): 1839
International Exchange of Young Agriculturists: 1085
International Eye Foundation (USA): 1086

International Federation of Library Associations and Institutions: 1087
International Federation of Medical Students Associations: 1088
International Federation of University Women: 813, 1089, 1090
International Geological Congress: 6
International Harp Competition (Jerusalem): 1091
International Harpsichord Competition (Paris): 1092
International Institute of Administrative Sciences (Brussels): 1093
International Institute for Development, Cooperation and Labour Studies (Tel Aviv): 1094
International Institute for Educational Planning (Paris): 1095, 1096
International Institute for Geothermal Research (Pisa): 1097
International Institute for Labour Studies (Geneva): 1098
International Institute for Population Studies (Bombay): 1099
International Institute of Seismology and Earthquake Engineering (Tsukuba, Japan): 1100
International Institute of Tropical Agriculture (Ibadan): 1101, 1102
International Laboratory for Research on Animal Diseases (Nairobi): 1103
International Labour Organization: 1052, 1104
International Lead Zinc Research Organization, Inc.: 1105
International League Against Epilepsy: 194
International League of Antiquarian Booksellers: 1106
International Maritime Organization: 1107
International Monetary Fund Institute (Washington, D.C.): 1108
International Music Competition (Athens): 1109
International Music Competition (Budapest): 1110
International Music Competition of the Broadcasting Corporations of the Federal Republic of Germany: 1111
International Music Competitions (Rio de Janeiro): 1112
International Organization Against Trachoma: 1113
International Organization of Journalists: 1114
International P.E.N.: 763
International P.E.N. Scottish Centre: 1115
International Paper Company Foundation: 1169
International Prize for Architecture: 1116
International Reading Association: 1117
International Research and Exchanges Board

(USA): 1118-1123
International Rice Research Institute (Philippines): 1124
International Road Federation: 1125
International Singing Competition (s'Hertogenbosch, Netherlands): 1126
International Singing Competition (Toulouse): 1127
International Society of Aboriculture: 1128
International Society for Photogrammetry: 1129
International Statistical Education Centre (Calcutta): 1130
International String Quartet Competition (Portsmouth, England): 1131
International Summer School (Oslo): 1132
International Telecommunication Union: 1133
International Training Institute (Washington, D.C.): 1134
International Union Against Cancer: 1135-1138
International Union of Architects: 780
International Union for Conservation of Nature and Natural Resources: 2183
International Union of Forestry Research Organizations: 1139
International Union of Local Authorities: 1140
International Union for the Scientific Study of Population: 1141
International Union of Students: 1142
International Union for Vacuum Science, Technique and Applications: 1143
International University Institute (Luxembourg): 1144
IODE (Canada): 1145
Iota Sigma Pi: 1146
Iowa School of Letters Award for Short Fiction: 1147
Ireland Alloys Award: 1786
IREX: 1118-1123
Irish Academy: 1779
Irish Academy of Letters: 1148
Irish American Cultural Institute (St. Paul, Minn.): 1149
Irish Government: 672, 673, 684, 685, 1283, 1407-1409, 1779, 1838, 1839
Irwin (Richard D.) Foundation (USA): 1150
Isakon (Frank) Prize: 154
Isbrandt (Ralph H.) Award: 1944
ISEAS: 1001-1004
Israel Academy of Sciences and Humanities: 1809
Israel Institute of Technology, Inc. (Haifa): 203
Israel Museum (Jerusalem): 1151
Israeli Government: 1151, 1301, 1346, 2088
Isserlis (Julius) Scholarship: 1784
Italian Government: 550, 941, 1152, 1153, 1347

Italian Institute (London): 1152, 1153, 2047
Italian Institute for Historical Studies (Naples): 1154
Italian University for Foreigners (Perugia): 1155
Ittleson (Blanch F.) Award: 164

Jackson Laboratory (Bar Harbor, Maine): 1156
Jacksonville University (College of Fine Arts) Playwriting Competition (USA): 1157
Jacobi (Mary Putnam) Fellowships: 2167
Jacob's Pillow Dance Festival, Inc. (Lee, Mass.): 1158
Jaffe (Mr. and Mrs. John) Fellowships: 1789
Jagger (J.W.) Scholarship: 2094
Jamaican Government: 597, 1322
James (D.J.) Awards: 1159
James (T.V.) Fellowship: 416
James (Catherine and Lady Grace) Foundation (Wales): 1159
Jameson (J. Franklin) Fellowship: 107
Jamestown Prize: 976
Japan Foundation: 1160-1162
Japan Newspaper Publishers and Editors Association: 1163
Japan Society for the Promotion of Science: 1164, 1165, 1810
Japan-U.S. Friendship Commission: 1920
Japanese Government: 309, 578, 1166, 1323, 1858
Japanese National Commission for Unesco: 1166, 2043
Jerusalem International Book Fair: 1167
Jerusalem Prize: 1167
Jerusalem Scholarship: 424
Jervise Prize: 1785
Jessen Fellowship: 1084
Jewish Chronicle (UK): 1410
Jobst (Conrad) Foundation: 75
Johananoff International Fellowship: 1558
Johns Hopkins University (Bologna Center): 378
Johnson (Mead) Awards: 38, 41, 124, 1488, 1608
Johnson (Lyndon Baines) Foundation (USA): 1168
Johnson and Johnson Awards: 1084
Johnson Library (Austin, Tex.): 1168
Johnston (Alan), Lawrence and Moseley Fellowship: 1790
Joint Council on Economic Education: 1169
Joint U.S.-Spanish Committee for Educational and Cultural Affairs: 1170
Jolson (Leon) Award: 1176
Jones (Robert) and Agnes Hunt Orthopaedic Hospital (Oswestry, Shropshire): 992
Jones (Robert) Prize Essay: 419

Journal of Risk and Insurance Awards: 167
Journalists in Europe: 1171
Jubilee Scholarships: 1102
Jurzykowski (Alfred) Foundation, Inc. (USA): 1172, 1201
Jusélius (Sigrid) Foundation (Finland): 1173
Juvenile Diabetes Foundation (USA): 1174, 1175
JWB Jewish Book Council (USA): 1176

Kalinga Foundation Trust (India): 1177
Kaltenborn Foundation (USA): 1178
Kaplun (Morris J.) Award: 1176
Kapp (Gisbert and Treasy) Scholarships: 1529
Kapp (Mrs. T.M.) Will Trust: 1530
Kappa Omicron Phi Fellowship: 110
Kappa Tau Alpha (USA): 1179
Karger (Dr. Heinz) Memorial Foundation (Switzerland): 1180
Karolinska Institutet (Stockholm): 1592
Kavlin (Enrique) Grant: 1151
Keith Prize: 1786
Kennedy (John F.) Center for the Performing Arts (Washington, D.C.): 73
Kennedy (Joseph P., Jr.) Foundation (USA): 1183
Kennedy (Robert F.) Memorial (USA): 1181
Kennedy Memorial Fund (UK): 1182
Kennedy (John Fitzgerald) School of Government (Cambridge, Mass.): 1184
Kent Incorporated Society for Promoting Experiments in Horticulture (East Malling): 737
Kenya Publishers Association: 1185
Kenya Government: 597
Kenyatta Prize: 1185
Kettering (Charles F.) Award: 198
Keuffel and Esser Fellowship: 76
Kidney Foundation of Canada (Montreal): 1186
Kiene (Julia) Fellowship: 755
Kierzkowski (Dr. Casimir Victor) Scholarship: 1201
Kierzkowski (John E.) Scholarship: 1201
Killam (Izaak Walton) Scholarships: 454, 1378
Kindergarten Union of South Australia: 1187
King Abdul Aziz Research Centre: 1188
King Edward VII British-German Foundation: 1189
King (Martin Luther) Memorial Prize (UK): 1190
King (Mackenzie) Scholarship Trust (Canada): 1191, 1192
Kinkeldey (Otto) Award: 142

Kinley (Kate Neal) Memorial Fellowship Committee (Urbana-Champaign): 1193
Kiribati Government: 597
Kirk (Norman) Memorial Trust (NZ): 1194
Kishida Award: 175
Kitt Peak National Observatory (Tucson, Ariz.): 1507
Kittrell (Flemmie P.) Fellowship: 111
Klumpe-Roberts (Dorothea) Award: 300
Klumpke Scholarship: 815
Knights of the Southern Cross (Australia): 1195
Knott (W.E.C.) Fellowship: 402
Knox (Frank) Fellowships: 274
Knox (Frank) Memorial Foundation (UK): 1196
Koch (Fred Conrad) Award: 759
Kodak Ltd. (UK): 1197, 1757
Kolk (Franklin W.) Award: 1944
Kolliner (Beatrice S.) Award: 1151
Koontz (Louis Knott) Award: 106
Korchinska (Maria) International Harp Competition: 1250
Korean Government: 1324
Kosciuszko Foundation (USA): 1198-1201
Krafts, Inc.: 108
Kramer (Wilfred) Grants: 2095
Kranichsteiner Prize: 653
Kress (Samuel H.) Fellowships: 1448
Kreymborg (Alfred) Award: 1675
Krupp Von Bohlen (Alfried) und Halbach Foundation (West Germany): 1202
Kulp (Clarence A.) Award: 167

La Ferla (Buccheri) Prize: 1434
Lady Cade Fellowship: 1415
Lady Davis Fellowship Trust (Israel): 1203
Lady Latham Fellowship: 1747
Lady Tata Memorial Trust (UK): 1204
Laidlaw Foundation (Canada): 1205
Lambarde (William) Fund (London): 1939
Lambert (Nancy Stirling) Scholarship: 373
Lamme Medal: 979
Lamont Poetry Selection: 2
Landau (Tobias) Fellowships: 893
Landis (James N.) Award: 190
Landon (Harold Morton) Award: 2
Landry (Jules F.) Award: 1241
Lane (Allen) Award: 1410
Langmuir (Irving) Prize: 154
Larson (Gustus L.) Award: 190
Lasker (Florina V.) Award: 1569
Latham (Lady) Fellowship: 1747
Latimer Awards: 1786
Latin American Center for Monetary Studies: 1206
Latin American Institute for Economic and Social Planning (Santiago): 1207

Latin American Scholarship Program of American Universities: 1208
Law Students Civil Rights Research Council (USA): 1209
Lawenski (Freda) Grants: 2113
Lawrence (D.H.) Fellowship (Albuquerque): 1210
Lawrence Fellowship: 401
Le Caine (Hugh) Award: 602
Le Marquand (Horace) and Dudley Bigg Fellowship: 1791
League for the Exchange of Commonwealth Teachers (UK): 1211
League of Red Cross Societies: 1212
Lear (Norman) Award: 73
Leathersellers' Company (UK): 1213
Lederle Award: 124
Leeds (Morris E.) Award: 979
Leeds International Pianoforte Competition: 1214
Leet (Dorothy) Grants: 1090
Legacy Coordinating Council of Australia: 1215
Lehman (Herbert H.) Fellowship: 1999
Leidy Medal: 5
Lemberg (Rudi) Fellowships: 313
Lemmer (John) Scholarship: 2113
Lemmer/Bradlow Scholarship: 2113
Leopold (Richard W.) Prize: 1617
LEPRA (UK): 414
Lerici Foundation for Archaeological Prospecting (Italy): 1216
Lerner—Gray Fund: 140
Lesny (Stan) Scholarships: 1201
Lesotho Government: 597
Lessells (John Moyes) Fellowships: 1819
Leukaemia Research Fund (UK): 1217
Leukemia Society of America, Inc.: 1218-1220
Lever Brothers Limited (Canada): 275
Leverhulme Scholarships: 1659
Leverhulme Trust (UK): 1221-1224
Levinson Prize: 1673
Levitt (Mortimer) Awards: 2199
Lewis (Maisie) Fund: 2188
Lewis (Warren K.) Award: 120
Licette (Miriam) Scholarship: 246
Lieberman (Elias) Award: 1675
Liebmann (Morris N.) Award: 979
Life Insurance Medical Research Fund of Australia and New Zealand: 1225-1228
Life Underwriters Association of Canada Educational Foundation: 1229
Lilly (Eli) and Company (USA): 194, 401, 1230
Lilly International Fellowships: 1275
Lincoln (James F.) Arc Welding Foundation (USA): 1231
Lincoln-Juárez Scholarships: 1356
Lindabury (Virginia A.) Scholarship: 505

Lindemann Trust Fellowships: 764
Linguistic Society of America: 1232
Linnean Society of London: 1233
Lippincott (Joseph) Award: 132
Lister Award: 1763
Liszt Society (UK): 1234
Litty (Mary) Fellowships: 776
Lloyd (Dr. Dorothy Jordan) Trust: 413
Lloyds Bank Prize: 814
Locke Fellowship: 1792
Loeb (Gerald) Awards (USA): 1235
London Chamber of Commerce and Industry: 1236
London Symphony Orchestra: 1878
London Transport Award: 544
Long (Marguerite)-Jacques Thibaud International Competition for Piano and Violin (Paris): 1237
Longhi (Roberto) Foundation for the Study of the History of Art (Italy): 1238
Longman Zimbabwe Award: 1632
Longy School of Music (Cambridge, Mass.): 1239
Lorenzini (Giovanni) Foundation (Italy): 1240
Louisiana State University Press: 1241
Low (William St. Clair) Award: 602
Lowell (James Russell) Prize: 1373
Lubbock-Sambrook Award: 980
Luce (Henry) Foundation, Inc. (USA): 1242, 1243
Lumumba (Patrice) Friendship University (USSR): 1986
Lunar and Planetary Institute (Houston, Tex.): 1244
Lutheran World Federation: 1245
Lyons (Cecil) Memorial Foundation (South Africa): 1246

Maass (Otto) Fellowships: 1695
Macaulay (William J.) Award: 1786
Macaulay Fellowship: 244
MacDowell Colony (Peterborough, N.H.): 1247
Macelwane (Father James B.) Awards: 138
Machanick (Edna) Award: 1963
MacKenzie (Walter C.)-Ethicon Fellowship: 1755
MacLaggan (Katherine E.) Fellowship: 505
Maclean (Ida Smedley) Fellowship: 1089
MacMillan (Sir Ernest) Award: 602
Macnamara (Ellaina) Memorial Scholarship (UK): 1248
MacRobert Award: 805
Magner (Desmond) Awards: 1421
Malawi Government: 597
Malaysian Government: 578
Malkin (Harold) Prize: 1749
Maltese Government: 597

Mammal Research Institute (South Africa): 1249
Mananan Festival (Isle of Man): 1250
Manhattan School of Music: 1251
Manley Medal: 1944
Mann (Margaret) Citation: 132
Mann (Thomas) Prize (Lubeck): 1252
Mansfield (Katherine) Award: 356
Mansfield (Katherine) Fellowship (NZ): 1253
Mansfield (Katherine)-Menton Prize: 763
Manville Fellowship: 1023
Maori Purposes Fund Board (NZ): 1254
March of Dimes Birth Defect Foundation (USA): 1255
Marconi Fellowship: 252
Margarine Institute for Health Nutrition: 1256
Marius-Tausk Award: 855
Markland Fellowship: 402
Markle (John and Mary) Foundation (USA): 1257
Markwardt (L.J.) Award: 820
Marraro (Howard R.) Prize: 67, 105, 1373
Marsden Foundation (USA): 1258
Marshall Aid Commemoration Commission (UK): 1259
Marshall (George C.) Fellowships: 169
Marshall Fund of the United States: 854
Marten Bequest (Australia): 1260
Martin (Allie Beth) Award: 132
Martin (C.J.) Fellowships: 1452
Martin (Eleanor Jean) Award: 505
Martin Musical Scholarship Fund (UK): 1261
Martin (Ruth) and C. Brooks Fry Award: 2035
Martini (Paul) Foundation (Frankfurt): 1262
Marx (Ellie) Scholarship Fund (South Africa): 1979
Masefield (John) Award: 1675
Maskell Peace Scholarship: 1024
Mason (S.G.) Fellowship: 1695
Massachusetts Federation of Polish Women's Clubs: 1201
Massachusetts Institute of Technology (Boston): 1182
Massey-Ferguson (UK) Limited: 1263
Masson Scholarship: 1742
Maternity Center Association (USA): 1264
Mathew (Francis) Scholarship: 2005
Mattei (Enrico) Institute (Milan): 770
Maugham (Somerset) Awards: 1942
Mauritius Government: 597
Maverick (Edward) Scholarship: 815
Maxwell Prize: 996
Maxwell (James Clerk) Prize: 154
Mayer (Andre) FAO Fellowships: 817
Mayer (Cecile Lehman) Awards: 68
Mayo Graduate School (Rochester, Minn.): 341
Mays (Benjamin E.) Fellowships: 842

McArthur (Helen) Fellowship: 505
McCaig's (Catherine) Trust (UK): 1265
McCarthy (Claude) Fellowships: 2102
McCloy (John J.) Fellowships: 1302
McClure (Madeline Gegenheimer) Fellowship: 746
McCunn's (William) Trust (Scotland): 1266, 1267
McDonald (Warren) Fellowship: 1456
McEachern Awards: 466
McGavin (Agnes Purcell) Award: 164
McGill University (Montreal): 1378
McGinnis (John H.) Award: 1985
McGraw (Curtis W.) Award: 185
McGraw (James H.) Award: 185
McGraw-Hill Book Company (USA): 185, 1268
McIntyre Award: 301
McIsaac (Isabel) Award: 1608
McKenzie (J.R.) Fellowship: 1574
McLaughlin Medal: 1815
McMillan Scholarship Program: 155
McNaughton (Ella H.) Fellowship: 110
McNickle (D'Arcy) Fellowship: 1580
McWilliams (Margaret) Fellowship: 477
Meat Industries Research Institute of New Zealand: 1269
Meat and Livestock Commission (UK): 1270
Medical Missionary Association (UK): 1271
Medical Research Council (UK): 1272-1275, 1629
Medical Research Council of Canada: 1276-1282
Medical Research Council of Ireland: 1283
Medical Research Council of New Zealand: 1284, 1285
Medical Research Foundation of Boston, Inc.: 1286
Medieval Academy of America: 1287
Medwick (Lucille) Award: 1675
Meeman (Edward J.) Awards: 1866
Meggers (William F.) Award: 1941
Meisinger Award: 138
Melcher Book Award (Boston, Mass.): 1288
Melcher (Frederic G.) Scholarship: 131
Melchett Award: 716
Meldola Medal: 1817
Mellon Fellowships: 80
Mellon (Andrew W.) Foundation: 80, 1302, 1915, 1922
Mellor Fellowship/Research Scholarship (Johannesburg): 1289
Melville Medal: 190
Melville (Stanley) Award: 411
Memorial Foundation for Jewish Culture (USA): 1290-1294
Mendel Award: 124
Mendel (Bruno) Fellowship: 1798

Mendelsohn Scholarship Foundation (UK): 1295
Menninger Foundation (Topeka, Kans.): 541, 1296
Mental Health Foundation (UK): 1297, 1298
Menton Prize: 763
Menuhin Prize for Young Composers (UK): 1299
Menzies (Robert Gordon) Scholarship: 339
Merck Company Foundation (USA): 1300
Merck Sharp and Dohme Fellowships: 1300
Merryfield (Fred) Award: 185
Metals Society (UK): 1817
Metcalf (Vicky) Award: 460
Meteorological Service of Israel: 1301
Metropolitan Museum of Art (New York City): 1303
Metropolitan Opera National Council (USA): 1303
Mexican American Legal Defense and Education Fund: 1304
Mexican Government: 285, 1325, 1326, 1356, 1406
Meyer Foundation: 311
Meyer (Adolf) Lectureship: 164
Michaelmas Conference, Pontifical Institute (Canada): 1677
Michaels Award: 1689, 2199
Michaels (Mones) Scholarships: 2113
Middlemore Award: 417
Middleton-Shaw (J.C.) Fellowship: 661
Migraine Trust (UK): 1305
Milbank Memorial Fund: 1306
Milburn (C.H.) Award: 417
Mildenberger (Kenneth W.) Medal: 1373
Milk Marketing Board (England and Wales): 1307
Miller (Banner I.) Award: 138
Miller Medal: 1815
Miller Prize: 1084, 1783
Millikan Award: 59
Mills (C. Wright) Award: 1958
Mills (Florence) Fellowship: 1760
Mills (J. Clawson) Scholarships: 1302
Mills (Mark) Award: 143
Ministry of Agriculture, Fisheries and Food (UK): 1308
Ministry of Agriculture and Natural Resources (Cyprus): 1309
Ministry of Colleges and Universities (Ontario): 1310
Ministry of Culture and Education (Iceland): 1311
Ministry of Defence (UK): 1312
Ministry of Education (Colombia): 1313
Ministry of Education (Czechoslovakia): 1314
Ministry of Education (Ecuador): 1315
Ministry of Education (Finland): 1316-1318

Ministry of Education (Greece): 1319
Ministry of Education (Guatemala): 1320
Ministry of Education (Honduras): 1321
Ministry of Education (Jamaica): 1322
Ministry of Education (Japan): 1323
Ministry of Education (Korea): 1324
Ministry of Education (Mexico): 285, 1325, 1326
Ministry of Education (Morocco): 1327
Ministry of Education (Pakistan): 1328
Ministry of Education (Romania): 995, 1329
Ministry of Education (Syria): 1330
Ministry of Education (Taiwan): 1331
Ministry of Education (Thailand): 1332, 1333
Ministry of Education (Turkey): 1334
Ministry of Education (Venezuela): 1335
Ministry of Education and Culture (Bolivia): 1336
Ministry of Education and Culture (India): 1337-1340
Ministry of Education and Sciences (Netherlands): 1341
Ministry of Foreign Affairs (Brazil): 1342
Ministry of Foreign Affairs (Czechoslovakia): 1343
Ministry of Foreign Affairs (Finland): 1344
Ministry of Foreign Affairs (France): 963, 1345
Ministry of Foreign Affairs (Israel): 1346
Ministry of Foreign Affairs (Italy): 1097, 1152, 1153, 1347
Ministry of Foreign Affairs (Netherlands): 1348
Ministry of Foreign Affairs (NZ): 1349, 1350
Ministry of Foreign Affairs (Norway): 1351
Ministry of Foreign Affairs (Singapore): 1352, 1353
Ministry of Foreign Affairs (Spain): 1354
Ministry of Foreign Relations (Chile): 1355
Ministry of Foreign Relations (Mexico): 1356
Ministry of Health and Social Welfare (Poland): 1358
Ministry of Higher Education (Cuba): 1359
Ministry of Higher and Specialized Education (USSR): 1119
Ministry of National Education and Culture (Belgium): 1360
Ministry of Overseas Development (UK): 1361
Ministry of Science, Higher Education and Technology (Poland): 1362, 1363
Ministry of Science and Research (Austria): 1364-1367
Ministry of State (Monaco): 1368
Minkowski Prize: 781
Minna-James-Heinemann Foundation (West Germany): 1369
Miranol Chemical Company, Inc. (USA): 1946
Miss Aleen Cust Fellowship: 1765

Missionary Mart (UK): 1370
Mitchell (F.L.) Fellowship: 1695
Mitchell (Mark) Research Foundation: 1371
Mittag-Leffler Foundation of the Swedish Academy of Sciences: 1372
Mizwa (Stephen P.) Scholarship: 1201
Modern Language Association of America: 1373
Mofolo-Plomer Prize: 1374
Molson Prizes: 454
Molteno (Donald) Award: 1971
Monaco Government: 1368
Money for Women, Inc. (USA): 1375
Monika (Anna) Foundation (West Germany): 1376
Monks (Leader J.) Award: 984
Montaigne Prize: 795
Montevideo Competition: 563
Monticello College Foundation: 1585
Montreal International Music Competition: 1377
Montreal Neurological Institute: 1378
Montreux-Vevy Music Festival (Switzerland): 1379
Montserrat Government: 597
Moody Grant: 1168
Mooney (James) Award: 2112
Moorfields Eye Hospital (London): 1763
Morehead (John Motley) Foundation (USA): 1380
Morgan (Agnes Fay) Award: 1146
Morgan Prize: 1817
Morison (R.S.) Fellowships: 870
Moroccan Government: 1327
Morse (Robert T.) Award: 164
Morton (Jack A.) Award: 979
Mosby (C.V.) Co. (USA): 1608
Motor Vehicle Manufacturers' Association (Canada): 1723
Mott (Frank Luther) Award: 1179
Motta (Vianna da) International Competition (Lisbon): 1381
Mount Carmel International Training Centre for Community Services (Haifa): 1382
Mountbatten Grants: 1885
Mozart Fellowship: 2110
Mozart Memorial Prize (London): 1383
Mr. and Mrs. John Jaffe Fellowships: 1789
Mrozowski (Dr. Stanislaw) Fund: 1201
Mrs. Simon Baruch Award: 2069
Mrs. T.M. Kapp Will Trust: 1530
Mudge (Isidore C.) Citation: 132
Mulholland (Sir Walter) Fellowships: 2103
Multiple Sclerosis Society of Canada: 1384
Multiple Sclerosis Society of Great Britain and Northern Ireland: 1385
Murray (Stella) Prize: 1783
Murray (John) Studentship: 1799

Murray (Gilbert) Trust (UK): 1386, 1387
Murray-Green Award: 91
Muscular Dystrophy Association (USA): 1388, 1389
Muscular Dystrophy Group of Great Britain: 1390
Museum of Science (Boston, Mass.): 1391
Music Academy of Naples: 529
Music Academy of the West (Santa Barbara, Calif.): 1392
Music and Arts Institute of San Francisco, Inc.: 1393
Musk-Ox Scholarship: 991
Myasthenia Gravis Foundation, Inc. (USA): 1394, 1395
Mycological Society of America: 1396

N.Z. Forest Products Ltd.: 1397, 1398
Nagpur University: 2115
Naidu (Sarojini) Scholarship: 2114
Nalco Awards: 263
NASA Johnson Space Center (Houston): 1244
Nathan (George Jean) Award for Dramatic Criticism: 1399
Nathan Scholarship: 409
National Academy of Design: 1400
National Academy of Engineering (USA): 1493, 2052
National Academy of Sciences (USA): 1401, 1493, 2052
National Agricultural Institute (Paris): 1402
National Association of Broadcasters (USA): 1403
National Association of Purchasing Management, Inc. (USA): 1404
National Association of Realtors: 1405
National Astronomy and Ionosphere Center (Arecibo, Puerto Rico): 1506
National Autonomous University of Mexico: 1406
National Board for Science and Technology (Ireland): 1407-1409
National Book League (UK): 1410
National Broadcasting Corporation: 1707
National Bureau of Standards (USA): 2052
National Cancer Association of South Africa: 1411-1415
National Cancer Institute of Canada: 1416-1421
National Center for Atmospheric Research (Boulder, Colo.): 1422, 1423, 1512
National Centre of Scientific Research (France): 1409, 1424
National Consumer Affairs Internship Program: 1425
National Council for the Care of Cripples in South Africa: 1426
National Council of Commercial Plant

Breeders: 1427
National Council of Teachers of English Research Foundation (USA): 1428
National Dairy Council (USA): 1429
National Design Council (Canada): 1430
National Development Fund for the Building Industry (South Africa): 634
National Easter Seal Society (USA): 1431
National Education Association (USA): 1432
National Electrical Engineering Research Institute (South Africa): 1433
National Employment Accident Insurance Institute of Italy: 1434
National Endowment for the Arts (USA): 1435
National Endowment for the Humanities (USA): 52, 174, 939, 1436-1438, 1583, 1913-1917
National Energy Office (Australia): 699
National Federation of Music Societies (UK): 1439
National Federation of State Poetry Societies (USA): 1440
National Fellowship Fund (USA): 1441, 1442
National 4-H Council (USA): 1443
National Fund for the Arts (Argentina): 1444
National Fund for Medical Education: 1445, 1446
National Fund for Research into Crippling Diseases (UK): 1447
National Gallery of Art (Washington, D.C.): 1448, 1449
National Geographic Society (USA): 1450
National Health and Medical Research Council (Australia): 1451-1455
National Heart Foundation of Australia: 1456-1460
National Heart Foundation of New Zealand: 1461
National Hemophilia Foundation (USA): 1462
National Hispanic Scholarship Fund: 1707
National Historical Society (USA): 1463
National Home Fashions League, Inc. (USA): 1464
National Institute for Architectural Education (USA): 1465, 1466
National Institute of Cardiology/Ignacio Chavez (Mexico City): 1467
National Institute of Education (USA): 2055
National Institute for the Food Service Industry (USA): 1468
National Institute of Health (Rome): 1469
National Institute of Justice (USA): 2059-2061
National Institute for Juvenile Justice and Delinquency Prevention (USA): 2062
National Institute of Mental Retardation (Canada): 1470, 1471
National Institute for Metallurgy (South Africa): 1472

National Institute of Neurological and Communicative Disorders and Stroke (USA): 1473
National Institute of Nuclear Science and Technology (France): 1474
National Institutes of Health (USA): 1156, 1275, 1473, 2057
National Jewish Book Awards (USA): 1176
National Jewish Welfare Board (USA): 1475, 1476
National Kidney Foundation (USA): 1477
National Kidney Foundation of South Africa: 1478
National Leukemia Association (USA): 1479
National Medical Fellowships, Inc. (USA): 1480
National Mental Health Association, Inc. (USA): 1481
National Multiple Sclerosis Society (USA): 1482-1484
National Museum of Man (Ottawa): 1485
National Opera Institute (USA): 1486
National Orchestral Association (USA): 1487
National Osteopathic College Scholarships: 349
National Osteopathic Foundation (USA): 1488
National Playwrights Conference (USA): 1611
National Porketts Fellowship: 110
National Radio Astronomy Observatory (Charlottesville, Va.): 1489, 1509
National Rehabilitation Counseling Association (USA): 1490
National Research Advisory Council (NZ): 1491, 1492
National Research Council (Canada): 457
National Research Council (USA): 1493, 1586, 2052
National Research Institute for Mathematical Sciences (South Africa): 1494
National Retinitis Pigmentosa Foundation, Inc. (USA): 1495
National School of Administration (Paris): 1496
National Science Foundation (USA): 1422, 1423, 1497-1519, 2088
National Science Teachers Association (Washington, D.C.): 1522
National Scientific Balloon Facility (Palestine, Tex.): 1512
National Society to Prevent Blindness (USA): 1523
National Society of Professional Engineers (Washington, D.C.): 1524
National Space Club (Washington, D.C.): 1525
National Speleological Society (USA): 1526
National Student Nurses' Association (USA): 1608

National Trust for Historic Preservation (USA): 1527
National Turkey Federation (USA): 1528
National Union of Students (UK): 1529-1531
National Union of Teachers (UK): 1532
National University of Singapore: 1533, 1534
National Vegetable Research Station (Warwick, UK): 1535
National Wildlife Federation (USA): 1536
NATO: 1521, 1551, 1593-1598, 1843, 1848
Natural Environment Research Council (UK): 1537-1542
Natural Sciences and Engineering Research Council (Canada): 1543-1555
Naumann (Friedrich) Foundation (West Germany): 1556
Naumburg (Elsie Binger) Fellowship: 139
Naumburg (Walter M.) Foundation: 1557
Nauru Government: 597
Negri (Mario) Institute of Pharmacological Research (Milan): 1558, 1559
Nehru (Jawaharlal) Award: 949
Neill (Agnes Campbell) Award: 505
Nestlé Paediatric Fellowships: 319
Netherlands Government: 286, 287, 1341, 1348, 1560
Netherlands-South Africa Association: 1560
Neuchatel State Council (Switzerland): 1998
Neustadt Prize: 2177
Nevin (Allan) Prize: 1937
New Dance Group Studio, Inc. (New York City): 1561
New England Theatre Conference (USA): 1562
New Medical Journals Ltd. (UK): 1563
New Orleans Baptist Theological Seminary: 1564
New Philharmonica Orchestra of London: 1261
New School for Music Study, Inc. (Princeton, N.J.): 1565
New South Wales State Cancer Council: 1566, 1567
New South Wales State Council: 2002
New York Academy of Science: 1568
New York Civil Liberties Union: 1569
New York State Education Department: 1999
New York State Historical Association: 1570
New Zealand Academy of Fine Arts: 355
New Zealand Book Awards: 691
New Zealand Commonwealth Scholarships and Fellowships Committee: 1571-1573
New Zealand Council for Educational Research: 1574
New Zealand Federation of University Women: 1575
New Zealand Government: 578, 597, 668, 689-692, 1284, 1285, 1349, 1350, 1491, 1492, 1571-1573, 1699, 2003, 2097-2104
New Zealand Institute of International Affairs: 1576
New Zealand Library Association, Inc.: 1577
New Zealand Literary Fund: 690-692
New Zealand Society of Accountants: 1578
New Zealand Women Writers' Society: 356
New Zealand Wool Board: 1579
Newberry (John) Medal: 132
Newberry Library (Chicago): 1580-1587
Newcomb Cleveland Prize: 54
Newcomen Society of North America: 1588
Newspaper Fund, Inc. (USA): 1589
Newspaper Guild: 1590
Nice (Margaret Morse) Awards: 2164
Nichols Fellowship: 1822
Nichols Institute (USA): 759
Nicolle (Charles) Scholarships: 1643
Nieman Foundation for Journalism (USA): 1591
Nigerian Government: 597, 803
Nijhoff (Martinus) Grant: 1087
1967 Science Scholarships: 1543
Niven (Frederick) Prize: 1115
Niven (Laura) Scholarship: 1977
Nobel Foundation (Sweden): 1592
Noble (John) Bursary: 1864
North Atlantic Treaty Organization: 1521, 1551, 1593-1598, 1843, 1848
North Rhine/Westphalian Ministry of Education: 1599
Northwest College and University Association for Science (USA): 1600
Norwegian Agency for International Development: 1601
Norwegian College of Agriculture (As-NLH): 1602
Norwegian Government: 288, 1351, 1601, 1603
Norwegian Nobel Committee: 1592
Norwegian Research Council for Science and the Humanities: 1603
Norwich Jubilee Esperanto Foundation (UK): 1604
Nothard (Constance Anne) Grant: 1977
Nuffield Foundation (UK): 1605-1607, 1805
Nuffield Grants: 276
Nuffield (Elizabeth) Fund: 1607
Nurses' Educational Funds, Inc. (USA): 1608
Nystrom (Warren) Fund: 258

Oberly (Eunice Rockwell) Award: 132
O'Brian (Ruth) Grant: 108
Oceanographic Museum (Monaco): 1609
O'Connor (Basil) Program: 1255
Odd Fellows (Manchester Unity) Award: 1410
Odlum (Doris) Award: 417
Oersted Award: 59
Office of Human Development Services (USA):

2056
Office of International Relations (Canada): 1933-1935
Office of Naval Research (USA): 154, 2054
Office of Public Information: See United Nations Office of Public Information
Ogilvie Flour Mills (Canada): 546
Ohaus (Gustav) Awards: 1522
Ohaus Scale Corporation (USA): 1522
Old Guard Prize: 190
Old Mutual 1820 Settlers Scholarship: 753
Olmsted (George) Foundation (USA): 1610
Olofson (Shirley) Award: 131
Omodeo (Adolfo) Scholarship: 1154
O'Neill (Eugene) Memorial Theater Center (Waterford, Conn.): 1611, 1612
Ontario Government: See Government of Ontario
Ontario Heart Foundation
Ontario Institute for Studies in Education: 1613
Ontario Veterinary College: 587
Oppenheim (Meyer) Prize: 1786
Oppenheimer (Ernst) Award: 759
Oppenheimer (Ernst) Memorial Trust (South Africa): 1614
Oppenheimer (Frank) Award: 185
Oppenheimer (J. Robert) Prize: 539
Orban (Balint) Prize: 44
Order of the Alhambra (USA): 1615
Orentreich Foundation for the Advancement of Science, Inc. (USA): 1616
Organization of American Historians: 1617
Organization of American States: 1618
Oriental Ceramic Society (UK): 1619
Ortho Diagnostics Scholarship: 192
Orville (Howard T.) Scholarship: 138
Orwell (George) Prize: 1410
Osborn (Earl D.) Award: 350
Osborne Award: 124
O'Shannessy Award: 1943
O'Shea (Paloma) International Competition (Santander, Spain): 1620
Osler Scholarship: 501
Osserman (Dr. Kermit E.) Fellowship: 1394
Overseas Academy of Science (France): 1621
Overseas Development Administration (UK): 1622-1626, 1698
Overseas Development Institute (UK): 1627, 1628
Oxford Regional Hospital Board (UK): 1629
Oxford University: 1629

P.E.N. American Center (New York City): 1630
P.E.N. International New Zealand Centre: 1631
P.E.N. International—Zimbabwe Centre: 1632

P.E.O. Sisterhood (USA): 1633
Pacific Historical Review: 106
Paganini (Nicolo) International Violin Competition (Genoa): 1634
Page Scholarships: 766, 1532
Page (Walter Hines) Scholarships: 253
Pakistani Government: 578, 1328
Palache Scholarships: 815
Palestine Exploration Fund (UK): 1635
Pam (Edgar) Fellowship: 1026
Pan American Health Organization: 1636
Pan-American Sanitary Bureau: 1636
Pantyfedwen Awards: 1159
Papua New Guinea Government: 597
Paraguayan Government: 1357
Paralyzed Veterans of America, Inc.: 1637
Parapsychology Foundation (USA): 1638
Parenteral Drug Association, Inc. (Philadelphia): 1639
Paris International Singing Competition: 1640
Paris Review (USA): 1641
Parke-Davis Fellowship: 2137
Parker (Ethel L.) Fellowship: 109
Parker (William Riley) Prize: 1373
Parkinson's Disease Society (UK): 1642
Parkman (Francis) Prize: 1937
Pasteur Institute (Tunis): 1643
Patiño (Tony) Fellowship: 1644
Paton Prize: 827
Patterson (A.L.) Award: 86
Patterson (Alicia) Foundation (USA): 1645
Patterson (Margaret M.) Scholarship: 1201
Paul (R.W.) Grants: 1802
Peabody Conservatory of Music (Baltimore, Md.): 1646
Pelton (Jeanette Siron) Award: 382, 607
Pelzer (Louis) Award: 1617
Pennsylvania Academy of Fine Arts (Philadelphia): 1647
Penrose Grants: 850
People's Republic of China: 1648
Pepler (George) Award: 1825
Performing Rights Society (UK): 1295
Permanent Trustee Co. Ltd. (Australia): 1260
Perrott-Warwick Studentship in Psychical Research (UK): 1649
Perry (Lucy C.) Award: 1608
Petroleum Research Fund (USA): 1650
Pfister (Oskar) Award: 164
Pfizer Award: 911
Pfizer Company Ltd. (Canada): 1651
Phalin (Howard V.) Scholarship: 494
Pharmaceutical Manufacturers Association Foundation, Inc. (USA): 1652-1658
Pharmaceutical Society of Great Britain: 1659-1661
Pharmaceutical Society of South Africa: 1662
Pharmacological Society of Canada: 1663

Phi Beta Kappa (USA): 1664, 1665
Phi Chi Theta Foundation (USA): 1666
Philippine Government: 578
Philips (Frederik) Award: 979
Philips International Institute of Technological Studies (Eindhoven, Netherlands): 1667
Philp (Margaret Dale) Award: 477
Physiological Society (UK): 1668
Pi Tau Sigma Gold Medal: 190
Pickering Fellowship: 1797
Pierce (Lorne) Medal: 1815
Piercy (Esther J.) Citation: 132
Pinkerton Award: 1029
Piore (Emanuel R.) Award: 979
Piper (Marion K.) Fellowship: 109
PIRA (UK): 1669
Pitt Rivers Museum (Oxford): 1670
Planck (Max) Society for the Advancement of Science (West Germany): 1671
Playboy Magazine: 1672
Plenum Scholarship: 1990
Plunket Scholarships: 1956
Plyer (Earle K.) Prize: 154
Poetry Magazine (Chicago): 1673
Poetry Society (UK): 1674
Poetry Society of America: 1675
Polish Culture Institute (UK): 1676
Polish Government: 289, 1358, 1362, 1363
Pontifical Institute of Mediaeval Studies (Canada): 1677
Pool (Judith Graham) Fellowships: 1462
Population Council (USA): 1678, 1679
Portugese Government: 290, 997
Potato Marketing Board (UK): 1680-1682
Pothecary (Walter) Scholarship: 573
Pott (Anthony) Award: 228
Potter (James M.) Medal: 190
Poynter Fund (USA): 1683
Praemium Erasmianum Foundation (Netherlands): 1684
Prague Spring International Music Competition: 1685
Prehistoric Society (UK): 1686
Premio Citta di Trieste International Competition for Symphonic Composition: 1687
Prentice-Hall Publishing Company (USA): 59, 1117
Prescott (Raymond Coleman) Scholarship: 1020
President Steyn-Gedenkfondsbeurstrust (South Africa): 1688
Price (Arnan) Award: 262
Price (Bernard) Institute of Geophysical Research (Johannesburg): 1689
Price (Bernard) Scholarships: 2113
Prince Pierre of Monaco Prize for Musical Composition: 1690
Princeton University (N.J.): 722, 876, 1691

Pringle (Thomas) Award: 761
Print Club (Philadelphia): 1692
Pritchard (Edith M.) Award: 1608
Proctor (Jane Eliza) Fellowships: 1691
Province of Ontario: 1693
Public Health Service (USA): 2057
Puech Milhaud (M.L.) Award: 831
Pulitzer Prizes (USA): 1694
Pulp and Paper Research Institute of Canada: 1695
Purves (C.B.) Fellowship: 1695
Putnam (Herbert W.) Award: 131
Pye (Ernie) Awards: 1866

Quaid-i-Azam Academy (Karachi): 1696
Queen Elisabeth International Music Competition (Brussels): 1697
Queen Elizabeth House (Oxford): 1698
Queen Elizabeth II Arts Council of New Zealand: 1699
Queen Elizabeth II Fellowships (Australia): 710
Queen Elizabeth II Ontario Scholarships: 1693
Queen Marie-José Prize for Musical Composition (Geneva): 1700
Queen's Fellowship (Canada): 1928
Queen's Fellowships (Australia): 711
Queensland Association of University Women: 324
Quinn Scholarship: 409
Quota International, Inc. (USA): 1701

Radcliffe College (Cambridge, Mass.): 442, 443
Radell (Inez Eleanor) Fellowship: 110
Radiation Industry Award: 143
Radio Corporation of America: 1707
Radio Rentals Ltd. (UK): 1824
Radio Research Board (Australia): 1702
Raikes Scholarship (South Africa): 2113
Raise/Printing Industries Association (Southern California): 746
Ralston Purina Company (USA): 1703, 1704
Rammell Studentships: 1661
Ramsay Memorial Fellowships Trust (UK): 1705, 1706
Ransom Fellowship: 1661
Ray (Isaac) Award: 164
RCA (USA): 1707
Reavell (J. Arthur) Scholarships: 2113
Rechter (Zeev) Award: 262
Redwood Scholarship: 1661
Reed (A.H. and A.W.) Ltd. (NZ): 1708
Reed (A.W.) Award: 1708
Reed (Victor) Scholarships: 1660
Rees Jeffreys Road Fund: 944
Regional Institute for Population Studies (Accra): 1709

Reid Fellowship: 1757
Reid Trust (UK): 1710
Religious Arts Guild (USA): 1711
Rennie (James E.) Awards: 1682
Rentokil Foundation Scholarships: 211
Research Corporation (USA): 1712
Research Institute for Management Science (Delft, Netherlands): 1713, 1714
Research Institute for the Study of Man: 1715
Reserve Bank of Australia: 1716-1718
Rev. Andrew L. Bouwhuis Scholarship: 531
Rev. Charles W. Tadlock Scholarship: 2070
Reynolds (R.J.) Fellowships: 53
Rhode Island Medical Society (Providence): 1719
Rhode Island School of Design (Providence): 1720
Rhodes Trust (UK): 1721
Rhondda (Margaret) Award: 1942
Rhys (John Llewelyn) Prize: 1410
Rice (Eric) Prize: 1783
Richards (Charles Russ) Award: 190
Richards (Ellen H.) Fellowship: 110
Richepin (Eliane) Association: 563
Richmond (Rebecca) Scholarships: 765
Richtmyer Award: 59
Rinehart (Mary Roberts) Foundation (USA): 1722
Rio Tinto Zinc Bursaries: 944
Road Haulage Association (UK): 544
Roads and Transportation Association of Canada: 1723
Robb (Isabel Hampton) Award: 1608
Roberts (Charlotte) Trust: 1478
Robertson (Finlay) Prize: 814
Robertson (James A.) Prize: 605
Robin Hood Multifoods Award: 487
Robinson Fellowship: 1013
Robinson (Joan Cahalin) Prize: 1950
Robinson (Selwyn J.) Scholarships: 1398
Roche Research Foundation for Scientific Exchange and Biomedical Collaboration with Switzerland: 1724
Rockefeller Foundation (USA): 1036, 1725, 1726
Rodda Award: 1943
Rodgers (Richard) Award: 39
Roe (Ralph Coats) Award: 185
Roe (Ralph Coats) Medal: 190
Roehr (Wanda) Fund: 1201
Rogers Prize: 2106
Rohan (William) Professorship: 1741
Romanian Government: 995, 1329
Rome Prize Fellowships: 45
Rome Scholarships: 427
Rontgen Prize: 411
Roothbert Fund, Inc. (USA): 1727
Roosevelt (Eleanor) Fellowships: 1135
Roosevelt (Theodore) Memorial Fund: 141
Roscoe Prize: 980
Rosenberg (Dorothy) Award: 1711
Rosenheim Fellowship: 1793
Rossby (Carl-Gustaf) Medal: 138
Rotary Foundation: 1728
Rotch Traveling Scholarship (USA): 1729
Roth (Arthur and Genevieve) Scholarship: 1201
Rothmans of Pall Mall (Australia) Ltd.: 1730
Rouse Fellowship: 1741
Rousseau (Theodore) Fellowships: 1302
Rowe (John R.) Award: 132
Roxon (Lillian) Grant: 298
Royal Academy of Arts (UK): 412
Royal Academy of Dramatic Art (London): 1731
Royal Aeronautical Society (UK): 1732-1737
Royal Alexandra Hospital for Children (N.S.W.): 553
Royal Anthropological Institute (UK): 1738-1740
Royal Australasian College of Radiologists: 1741
Royal Australian Chemical Institute: 1742
Royal Australian College of General Practitioners: 1743
Royal Australian College of Ophthalmologists: 1744
Royal Australian Institute of Architects: 1745, 1746
Royal Children's Hospital Research Foundation (Melbourne): 1747, 1748
Royal College of Obstetricians and Gynaecologists (UK): 1749
Royal College of Physicians (UK): 1750
Royal College of Physicians of Edinburgh: 1751, 1752
Royal College of Physicians of London: 1761, 1762
Royal College of Physicians and Surgeons of Canada: 1753-1756
Royal College of Radiologists (UK): 1741, 1757
Royal College of Surgeons (UK): 419
Royal College of Surgeons of England: 1758-1764
Royal College of Veterinary Surgeons (UK): 1765, 1766
Royal Commission for the Exhibition of 1851 (UK): 1767, 1768
Royal Commonwealth Society for the Blind: 1769
Royal Dutch/Shell Group of Oil Companies: 1770
Royal Geographical Society (UK): 587, 1771
Royal Historical Society (UK): 1772
Royal Institute of British Architects: 1773

Royal Institute of Public Administration (UK): 1774
Royal Institution (UK): 1775
Royal Institution of Chartered Surveyors (UK): 1776
Royal Institution of Naval Architects (UK): 1777, 1778
Royal Irish Academy: 1779
Royal Marsden Hospital (London): 968
Royal National Eisteddfod of Wales: 1780
Royal Netherlands Academy of Arts and Sciences: 1781
Royal Norwegian Council for Scientific and Industrial Research: 1782
Royal Overseas League (UK): 1783
Royal Philharmonic Society (UK): 814, 1784
Royal Scottish Academy of Painting, Sculpture and Architecture: 1785, 1786
Royal Society (UK): 587, 1787-1811, 1845
Royal Society of Arts (UK): 572, 1812, 1813
Royal Society of Canada: 1814, 1815
Royal Society of Chemistry: 1816, 1817
Royal Society of Edinburgh: 1818-1820
Royal Society of Literature (UK): 1821
Royal Society of Medicine (UK): 1822
Royal Society of New Zealand: 1823
Royal Swedish Academy of Sciences: 1592
Royal Television Society: 1824
Royal Town Planning Institute (UK): 1825
Royal Victorian Eye and Ear Hospital (East Melbourne): 1826
Rubinstein (Arthur) International Piano Master Competition (Israel): 1827
Ruggles-Gates Fund: 1739
Rui Foundation (Italy): 1828
Runyon (Damon)—Walter Winchell Cancer Fund (USA): 1829, 1830
Rupert Foundation (UK): 1831
Rush (Benjamin) Lectureship: 164
Russell (George) AE Fund: 354
Russia: See Soviet Government
Rutherford Prize: 996
Rutherford Scholarships: 1804

S.A. Nature Foundation (Southern Africa): 1833
SABRA Bursaries: 1968
Sacramento Peak Observatory (Sunspot, New Mexico): 1510
Saint Andrew's Society of the State of New York: 1834
St. Christopher Government: 597
St. Helena Government: 597
Saint-John Perse Fellowships: 830
St. Laurent (Louis S.) Fellowship: 462
St. Regis Paper Company (USA): 1835
St. Vincent & the Grenadines Government: 597

Saltwell Fellowships: 1750
SAMRO Scholarships: 1982
San Francisco Boys Guild: 1393
San Francisco Conservatory of Music: 1836
Sandberg Prizes: 1151
Saphra (Toni) Bursary: 2065
Sarnoff (David) Award: 979
Saunders (W.B.) Co. (USA): 1608
Scandinavian Airlines Systems: 509
Schaff (Philip) Prize: 177
Schaufus Award: 1639
Scheick (William H.) Fellowship: 115
Schepp (Leopold) Foundation (USA): 1837
Schering Fellowship: 511
Schimmel (Percia) Award: 1151
Schisler (John Q.) Awards: 2071
Schlegel-Tieck Prize: 2047
Schliemann (Heinrich) Fellowship: 170
Schlink (Sir Herbert) Memorial Trust Fund (Australia): 1887
Schoch Lectureship: 55
Schoeller-Junkmann Prizes: 855
Scholarship Exchange Board (Ireland): 1838, 1839
Schotz (Benno) Prize: 1786
Schreiner (Olive) Prize: 761
Schuck Award: 63
Schumacher (Fritz) Prize: 795
Schuman (Henry) Prize: 911
Schuman (Robert) Prize: 795
Schuman (Robert) Scholarships: 790
Schumann (Robert) International Competition for Pianists and Singers: 1840
Schuyler (Robert Livingston) Prize: 105
Science and Engineering Research Council (UK): 1841-1857
Science and Technology Agency (Japan): 1858
Scientific Products Foundation: 193
Scientist of the Year Award: 955
Scott-Moncrieff Prize: 2047
Scottish Arts Council: 371, 1859
Scottish Education Department: 1820, 1860-1862
Scottish National Orchestra Society: 1863
Scottish Opera Endowment Trust: 1864
Scottish Universities: 1865
Scribner's Sons (Charles) Award: 131
Scripps (Edward Willis) Award: 1866
Scripps (Ellen Browning) Fellowships: 1866
Scripps-Howard Foundation (USA): 1866
Seagram Awads: 433
Seaman (Tom) Scholarships: 1024
SEAMEO Scholarships: 1981
Second Half Century Award: 138
SEIFSA Scholarship: 2007
Selby Fellowship: 313
Selkirk (William) Scholarships: 945
Seltzer-Brodsky Prize: 2197

Sembrich (Marcella) Scholarship: 1200
Sergel Drama Prize (USA): 1867
Settlement Study Centre (Rehovot): 1868
Seychelles Government: 597
Seymour (Thomas Day) Fellowship: 170
Shakespeare Prize: 795
Shareet Scholarships: 35
Shastri Indo-Canadian Institute (Canada): 1869, 1870
Shaughnessy (Mina P.) Medal: 1373
Shaw (Ralph R.) Award: 132
Shea (John Gilmary) Prize: 67
Sheard-Sanford Award: 182
Shell Company of Australia Ltd.: 1871, 1872
Shell International Petroleum Company Ltd.: 1873-1877
Shell—London Symphony Orchestra Music Scholarship: 1878
Shell Scholarship: 1770
Shelley Award: 1675
Sherrard (J.M.) Awards: 910
Shirtcliffe Fellowship: 2104
Short Summer Courses in Scandinavia for International Understanding: 1879
Shropshire (Dr. Courtney W.) Grants: 568
Shull (Charles Albert) Award: 198
Shuster (Benjamin) Award: 37
Sibelius (Jean) International Violin Competition (Helsinki): 1880
Sibley (Mary Isabel) Fellowship: 1665
Sierra Leone Government: 597
Sigma Alpha Iota Philanthropies, Inc.: 1881
Sigma Xi Scientific Research Society: 1882
Signy (Gordon) Fellowships: 2179
Simkins (Francis Butler) Award: 1984
Simon Prize: 996
Sims (Sir Arthur) Scholarship (Canada): 1814
Sinclair-Browne Ltd. (UK): 1410
Sinfonia Foundation (USA): 1883
Singaporean Government: 578, 597, 1352, 1533
Sino-British Fellowship Trust: 1884
Sir Arthur Sims Scholarship (Canada): 1814
Sir Charles Hastings Award: 417
Sir Ernest Cassel Educational Trust (UK): 1885, 1886
Sir Ernest MacMillan Award: 602
Sir Frederick Smith and Miss Aleen Cust Fellowship: 1765
Sir Herbert Schlink Memorial Trust Fund (Australia): 1887
Sir James Caird's Travelling Scholarships Trust (Scotland): 1888-1891
Sir John Gellibrand Scholarship: 1215
Sir Ratanji Dalal Scholarship: 1761
Sir Richard Stapley Educational Trust (UK): 1892
Sir Walter Mulholland Fellowships: 2103
Sir William Chamberlain Awards: 544
Sir William White Scholarship: 1777
Sisalation Scholarships: 1745
Skelly (William J.) Kinsmen Award: 471
Sladen (Percy) Memorial Fund: 1233
Slaughter (Robert E.) Award: 1268
Sloan (Alfred P.) Foundation (USA): 1893
Slocum-Lunz Foundation, Inc. (USA): 1894
Slotkowski (Joseph) Publication Fund: 1201
Small Industry Extension Training Institute (Hyderabad, India): 1895
Smith (Alice E.) Fellowship: 2001
Smith (Bosworth) Trust Fund (UK): 1027
Smith (Hermon Dunlap) Center (Chicago): 1582
Smith (J. Waldo) Fellowship: 180
Smith and Nephew Foundation (UK): 1897
Smith (Nila Banton) Award: 1117
Smith (Robert H. & Clarice) Fellowship: 1448
Smith (S.A.) Fellowships: 1227
Smith (Sir Frederick) and Miss Aleen Cust Fellowship: 1765
Smith (Stanley) Horticultural Trust (UK): 1896
Smith (W.H.) Prize: 814
Smith (W.H.) & Son, Ltd. (UK): 1897
Smith (Watson) Trust: 1750
Smith (Winnie) Fellowship: 2144
SmithKline Foundation: 1446
Smithson (Robert) Scholarships: 436
Smithsonian Institution (Washington, D.C.): 1899-1903, 2162
Smuts (Isie) Award: 1964
Smuts Fellowship: 2094
Smythe (Conn) Research Foundation for Crippled Children (Canada): 1904
Snydor (Charles S.) Award: 1984
Social Science Research Council (UK): 1857, 1905-1911
Social Science Research Council (USA): 80, 84, 1912-1927
Social Sciences and Humanities Research Council of Canada: 1928-1936
Society of American Historians, Inc.: 1937
Society for Animal Rights, Inc. (USA): 1938
Society of Antiquaries of London: 1939
Society of Apothecaries of London: 1940
Society for Applied Spectroscopy (USA): 1941
Society of Authors (UK): 1942, 2047
Society of Automotive Engineers—Australasia: 1943
Society of Automotive Engineers, Inc. (USA): 1944
Society of Chemical Industry (UK): 1817
Society of Company and Commercial Accountants (UK): 1945
Society of Cosmetic Chemists (USA): 1946
Society of Exploration Geophysicists Foundation (USA): 1946
Society of the Friendly Sons of St. Patrick of

Philadelphia: 1948
Society for Historians of American Foreign Relations: 1949
Society for the History of Technology (USA): 1950
Society for Italian Historical Studies (USA): 1951
Society of Maccabaeans (UK): 1817
Society of Medical Friends of Wine: 1952
Society of Naval Architects and Marine Engineers (USA): 1953
Society of Photo-Optical Instrumentation Engineers (USA): 1954
Society of Plastics Engineers, Inc. (USA): 1955
Society for the Protection of Ancient Buildings (UK): 1956
Society for the Psychological Study of Social Issues (USA): 1957
Society for the Study of Social Problems: 1958
Society of Women Engineers: 1707
Society of Women Musicians (UK): 1783
Soddy (Frederick) Trust (UK): 1959
Sollmann (Torald) Award: 194
Solomon Islands Government: 597
Soroptimist International of Great Britain and Ireland: 1960
South African Association of University Women: 1961-1965
South African Atomic Energy Board: 1966
South African-Austrian Scholarship Exchange Programme: 1967
South African Bureau of Racial Affairs: 1968
South African Council for English Education: 1969
South African Council for Scientific and Industrial Research: 1433, 1494
South African-French Scholarship Exchange Programme: 1970
South African Government: 626-634, 701, 926-932, 1433, 1494, 1966-1970, 1973-1975
South African Institute of Race Relations: 1971
South African Institution of Mechanical Engineers: 1972
South African Jewish Board of Deputies: 1246
South African Medical Research Council: 1973-75
South African Military Nursing Services: 1977
South African Nursing Association: 1977
South African Reserve Bank: 1978
South African Society of Music Teachers: 1979
South Australian Government: 1980
South Place Concerts Society (UK): 569
Southeast Asian Ministers of Education Organization: 1981
Southern Africa Music Rights Organization, Ltd.: 1982
Southern Anthropological Society (USA): 2112
Southern Arts Association (UK): 1983

Southern Historical Association (USA): 1984
Southwest Review (USA): 1985
Soviet Academy of Sciences: 1119
Soviet Government: 6, 215, 294, 1119, 1986, 2076
Spalding Trusts (UK): 1987
Spanish Government: 291, 1170, 1354
Spann (Bryant) Prize: 657
Spastics Society (UK): 1988
Speak (John) Trust Scholarships: 385
Special Commonwealth African Assistance Plan: 1350, 1895
Special Libraries Association (USA): 1989-1991
Spencer Foundation (USA): 1992
Speniarov (L.A.) Prizes: 6
Spiezny (Albert) Scholarships: 1201
Spohr (Louis) International Violin Competition (Freiburg): 1993
Springer (Bernard H.) Award: 1608
Springer (Russell S.) Award: 1944
Spurrier (Henry) Awards: 544
Squibb (E.R.) and Sons: 1608, 1994
Sri Lanka Government: 578, 597
Stacey (John F. and Anna Lee) Scholarship Fund (USA): 1995
Standing Conference of Ministers of Education and Cultural Affairs of the Laender (West Germany): 1996
Stanford University (Conn.): 914, 1436
Stapley (Sir Richard) Educational Trust (UK): 1892
State Agronomical Sciences Faculty (Belgium): 1997
State Council of the Republic and Canton of Neuchâtel (Switzerland): 1998
State Education Department (New York): 1999
State Farm Companies Foundation (USA): 2000
State Historical Society of Wisconsin: 2001
State Library of New South Wales: 2002
State Services Commission (NZ): 2003
Stationers' and Newspaper Makers' Company (UK): 2004, 2005
Statten (Taylor) Memorial Fund (Canada): 2006
Steacie (E.W.R.) Fellowship: 1546
Steel and Engineering Industries Federation of South Africa: 2007
Steel (Amanda) Scholarship: 1731
Steele (LeRoy P.) Prizes: 137
Steele-Bodger (Harry) Scholarship: 431
Steffens Prize: 795
Stein (Freiherr vom) Prize: 795
Steinmetz (Charles Proteus) Award: 979
Stengel (Alfred) Scholarship: 71
Stevenson Scholarships: 1865

Stewart (Paul A.) Awards: 2165
Stewart Prize: 416
Steyn (Zerilda) Bursary: 1976
Stokes Award: 2140
Stone (Ralph W.) Award: 1526
Stoneman (Bertha) Award: 1965
Stothert Fellowship: 1796
Straka (Jerome and Mary) Scholarship: 1201
Streatfeild (Mackenzie Mackinnon) Fellowship: 1758
Strebig (James J.) Award: 350
Strindberg Fellowship: 2017
Strock (Lester W.) Award: 1941
Stroud Festival International Composers Competition (UK): 2008
Stuart Prize: 1785
Stubbins (T.K.) Fellowship: 1750
Study Fund for South-African Students (Netherlands): 2009
Stuyvesant (Peter) Cultural Foundation: 556
Suggia (Guilhermina) Gift: 246
Sumner (Walter C.) Foundation (Canada): 2010
'Sun' Aria Contest: 565
Sunkist Growers Competition: 89
Suter (Simone) School of Dance (Lausanne): 2011
Sverdrup Medal: 138
Swan Fund Award: 1670
Swann Foundation for Caricature and Cartoon (USA): 2012
Swaziland Government: 597
Swedish Academy: 1592
Swedish Academy of Sciences: 1372
Swedish Cancer Society: 2013
Swedish Government: 2015-2017, 2019
Swedish Institute: 2014-2017
Swedish Institute (Canada): 509
Swedish National Association against Heart and Chest Diseases: 2018
Swedish Natural Science Research Council: 2019
Sweet (Georgina) Fellowship: 323
Sweet (Georgina) Scholarship: 2202
Swiss Academy of Medical Sciences: 2020
Swiss Federal Institute of Technology (Zurich): 2021
Swiss Government: 292, 802, 2021
Sydney International Piano Competition: 2022
Syfrets Trust Company Ltd. (South Africa): 2023, 2024
Syme (David) and Company Ltd. (Melbourne): 2025
Syrian Government: 1330

Tadlock (Rev. Charles W.) Scholarship: 2070
Taft (Robert A.) Institute of Government (USA): 2026

Tait (Lawson) Medical and Scientific Research Trust (UK): 2027
Taiwan Government: 555, 1331
Talbot (Amaury) Fund (UK): 2028
Tanzania Government: 597
Tastemaker Award: 833
Tata (Lady) Memorial Trust (UK): 1204
Tate (John T.) Medal: 125
Tau Beta Pi Association, Inc. (USA): 2029
Tauber (Richard) Prize: 209
Taylor (Deems) Award: 183
Taylor (Estelle Marguerite) Scholarship: 2111
Taylor (Muriel) Scholarship Fund: 2030
Taylor (Reginald) Prize: 392
Tchaikovsky International Piano Competition (Moscow): 2031
Technical Association of the Graphic Arts (USA): 2032
Technion-Israel Institute of Technology, Inc. (Haifa): 203
Teleglobe Canada Fellowship: 277
Terman (Frederick Emmons) Award: 185
Tertis (Lionel) International Viola Competition: 1250
Tesla (Nikola) Award: 979
Textile Institute (UK): 2033
Textronix Foundation (USA): 185
Teyte (Maggie) Prize (UK): 2034
Thai Government: 293, 578
Thailand Fellowships: 293, 1332, 1333
Thank-Offering to Britain Fellowship: 389
Theatre Americana: 2035
Thew (H.E.) Fund: 246
Thewlis (Malford W.) Award: 99
Thibaud/Long Competition (Paris): 1237
Thomas (Julius A.) Fellowships: 575
Thomas Memorial Fund (South Africa): 2036
Thompson (Willard O.) Award: 71, 99
Thompson (Browder J.) Prize: 978
Thomson (Adam Bruce) Award: 1785
Thomson Foundation (UK): 2037
Thomson (Charles) Prize: 1617
Thouron-University of Pennsylvania Fund for British American Student Exchange: 2038
Thrasher Research Fund (USA): 2039
3M Company (USA): 185, 746
Thring Award: 980
Tiffany (Louis Comfort) Foundation (Great Neck, N.Y.): 2040
Times Educational Supplement (UK): 2041
Tinker Foundation (USA): 2042
Tobenkian (Paul) Award: 580
Tocqueville Grants: 830
Tokyo Institute of Technology: 2043
Tom-Gallon Awards: 1942
Tomkinson (Helen) Award: 417
Tonino (Dino) International Centre for Hydrology: 1054

Toonder (Marten) Awards: 244
Toronto (City of) Book Award: 612
Tory (Henry Marshall) Medal: 1815
Total South Africa (Pty.) Ltd.: 2044
Toulon Music Festival: 2045
Toulouse Competition: 2128
Townend Medal and Prize: 980
Trans-Antarctic Association: 2046
Translators Association (UK): 2047
Transport University Programs (Canada): 2048
Travenol Fellowship: 1762
Tresley (Ira J.) Award: 37
Trieste International Competition: 1687
Trinidad and Tobago Government: 597
Trinity University (Dallas, Tex.): 650
Troup (Robert) Prize: 886
Trudeau (Edward Livingston) Fellowships: 135
Truman (Harry S.) Library Institute (USA): 2049
Trumpler (Robert J.) Award: 300
Trust Fund for Medical Research in the West African States within the Commonwealth: 2050
Turing (A.M.) Award: 261
Turkish Government: 1334
Turner (Frederick Jackson) Award: 1617
Tuskegee Institute (Alabama): 527
Tuvalu Government: 597
Twarowski (Michael) Scholarship: 1200
Twenty-Seven Foundation (UK): 2051
Tyrrell Medal: 1815
Tyson (Sarah B.) Fellowship: 2168

U.S. Department of Commerce: 2052
U.S. Department of Defense: 154, 2053, 2054, 2123
U.S. Department of Education: 2055
U.S. Department of Energy: 1600
U.S. Department of Health and Human Services: 2056, 2057
U.S. Department of the Interior: 2058
U.S. Department of Justice: 2059-2062
U.S. Department of Labor: 1912
U.S. Department of State: 986
U.S. Government: See United States Government
U.S. International Development Cooperation Agency: 2063
U.S. National Institutes of Health: See National Institute of Health
U.S.S.R. Government: See Soviet Government
Uganda Government: 597
UK Government: See United Kingdom Government
Ulisse (Italy): 2064
UN: See United Nations
Unesco: 293, 989, 995, 1047, 1083, 1097, 1166, 1177, 1332, 1333, 1363, 1474, 2043, 2077-2081, 2109
UNICEF: 1060
UNIDO: 2083
Unilever European Fellowships: 369
Union of Jewish Women of South Africa: 2065
Union Theological Seminary (New York City): 2066
UNITAR: 2084
Unitarian Universalist Association (USA): 2067
United Cerebral Palsy Research and Educational Foundation, Inc. (USA): 2068
United Daughters of the Confederacy (USA): 2069
United Kingdom Government: 215, 245, 246, 393-398, 440, 578, 592-597, 663, 674-681, 687, 1272-1275, 1308, 1312, 1361, 1622-1626, 1820, 1841-1857, 1859-1862, 1905-1911
United Methodist Church (USA): 2070, 2071
United Nations: 816-818, 1207, 1709, 1895, 2072-2084
United Nations Department of Technical Cooperation for Development: 2072, 2073
United Nations Economic Commission for Africa (Addis Ababa): 2072, 2075
United Nations Economic Commission for Europe (Geneva): 2072
United Nations Economic Commission for Latin America (Santiago): 2072
United Nations Economic and Social Commission for Asia and the Pacific (Bangkok): 2072, 2076
United Nations Economic and Social Office (Beirut): 2072
United Nations Education, Scientific and Cultural Organization: See Unesco
United Nations Educational and Training Programme for Southern Africans: 2073
United Nations High Commission for Refugees: 2082
United Nations Industrial Development Organization: 2083
United Nations Institute for Training and Research: 2084
United Nations Office of Public Information: 2074
United States-Argentina Educational Exchange Commission: 2085
United States Foundation (France): 2086
United States Government: 154, 160, 314-316, 578, 620-622, 771-774, 954, 986, 1063-1073, 1118-1123, 1156, 1170, 1436-1438, 1448, 1473, 1493, 1497-1521, 1537-1542, 1600, 1912-1927, 2052-2063, 2088, 2123, 2156
United States Industrial Council Education Foundation: 2087
United States-Israel Binational Science Foundation: 2088

United States Steel Foundation: 126
Universal Esperanto Association (Rotterdam): 2089
Universal Postal Union: 2090
Universe Prize: 1410
Universities Federation for Animal Welfare (UK): 2091
Universities Field-Staff International Institute of World Affairs: 2092
University Assistance Fund (Netherlands): 2093
University of California (San Francisco): 1644
University of Cape Town: 543, 2094
University Center for Cooperatives (Madison, Wis.): 2095
University of Chicago Theatre: 1867
University College London: 726
University of Delaware (Newark): 756
University of East Anglia (Norwich): 2096
University of Edinburgh: 371, 961
University Grants Committee (NZ): 2097-2104
University of Illinois (Urbana/Champaign): 724, 1193
University of Iowa (Iowa City): 1147
University of Kansas Medical Center (Kansas City): 2105
University of London: 889, 2106
University of Manchester: 890
University of Maryland International Piano Festival and Competition (College Park): 2107
University of Melbourne: 2108
University of Miami: 539
University of Michigan: 1436
University for Mining and Metallurgy (Leoben, Austria): 2109
University of Minnesota: 69
University of Nancy: 782
University of New Mexico (Albuquerque): 1210
University of North Carolina (Chapel Hill): 1380
University of Oslo: 1132
University of Otago (Dunedin, NZ): 2110
University of Oxford: 1670, 1698
University of Pennsylvania (Philadelphia): 2038
University of Pretoria: 1249
University of Salzburg: 987
University of Saskatchewan: 991
University of Tasmania: 2111
University of Tennessee Press (Knoxville): 2112
University of Toronto: 917, 918
University of Vienna: 762
University of Wisconsin (Madison): 2095
University of the Witwatersrand (Johannesburg): 1289, 1689, 2113
University Women's Association of Delhi: 2114

University Women's Association of Nagpur: 2115
Upjohn Award: 1663
Urey (Blanche) Award: 1608
Usher (Abbott Payson) Prize: 1950
Usher (Philip) Memorial Fund (UK): 2116

Van Alen (William) Award: 1465
Van Cliburn Foundation, Inc. (Fort Worth, Tex.): 2117
Van den Berghs & Jurgens Ltd. (UK): 2118, 2119
Vanderbilt University (Nashville, Tenn.): 734
Van 't Hoff Fund: 1781
Vanuata Government: 597
Varga (Tibor) Festival (Sion, Switzerland): 2120
Veblen (Oswald) Prize: 137
Veillon (Charles) Foundation: 2121
Venezuelan Government: 1335
Ventris (Michael) Award: 228
Vergilian Society, Inc. (USA): 2122
Vestermark (Seymour) Lectureship: 164
Veterans Administration (USA): 2123
Victoria Law Foundation (Australia): 2124
Victorian Order of Nurses for Canada: 2125
Victorian Overseas Foundation (Australia): 2126
Vienna International Competition for Composition: 2127
Viets (Dr. Henry R.) Fellowships: 1395
Villain (Georges) Prize: 1084
Ville de Toulouse International Singing Competition: 2128
Viotti (G.B.) International Music Competition (Vercelli, Italy): 2129
Virginia Center for the Creative Arts (USA): 2130
Virginia Quarterly Review (USA): 2131
Viscount Bennett Fellowship: 461
Visnews Ltd. (UK): 2132
Visual Research Trust (UK): 2133
Visser (Martha) Scholarship: 1201
Voci Verdiane International Competition (Milan): 2134
Volkswagen Foundation (West Germany): 1001
von Humboldt (Alexander) Foundation (West Germany): 2135
Von Karman Institute for Fluid Dynamics (Rhode-Saint Genese, Belgium): 2136

Wagner (Adolph) Scholarships: 2113
Wagner (Celia B.) Award: 1675
Wallace (Ottillie Helen) Scholarship: 1786
Wallander (John) Foundation for Social Science Research (Stockholm): 438
Wallant (Edward Lewis) Award: 884
Walsh (Edith) Award: 417

Walsworth (Ivor) Prize: 1783
Warburg (Moritz and Charlotte) Prizes: 894
Waring (Amelie) Fellowship: 402
Warner-Lambert Canada, Inc.: 2137
Warner (Worcester Reed) Medal: 190
Warren (Bertram E.) Award: 86
Warren (Charles) Center for Studies in American History (Cambridge, Mass.): 2138
Warren (Earl) Legal Training Program, Inc. (USA): 2139
Warren Fellowships: 1794
Warren (Lloyd) Fellowship: 1466
Washburn (Bradford) Award: 1391
Washington International Competition: 837
Washington Journalism Center: 2140
Wateler Peace Prize: 522
Water Research Foundation of Australia: 2141
Watland (Gerald) Scholarship: 815
Watson (Gordon) Scholarship: 2100
Wattie Industries, Ltd. (NZ): 2142
Wattie (James) Awards: 2142
Watumull Prize: 105
Weaver (Merle) Scholarship: 2111
Weicker (Theodore) Award: 194
Weinreich (Max) Center for Advanced Jewish Studies (New York City): 2195
Weinreich (Uriel) Program, Columbia University (New York City): 2196
Weizmann Institute of Science (Rehovot, Israel): 2143
Welch (M.W.) Foundation: 1143
Welder (Rob and Bessie) Wildlife Foundation (Sinton, Tex.): 2144
Weldon (Sylvia) Scholarship: 509
Wellcome Medal: 1740
Wellcome Trust (UK): 2145-2147
Welsh Arts Council: 2148
Wenner-Gren Foundation for Anthropological Research, Inc. (USA): 2149, 2150
Wernher (Alexander Pigott) Fellowships: 1275
West German Government: 852, 853, 1996
West African Health Community: 2151
West Australian Petroleum Pty. Ld.: 2152
Western Australian Wildlife Authority: 2152
Western History Association (USA): 2153
Western Publishing Company (USA): 746
Western Samoa Government: 597
Westinghouse Awards: 54
Weyerhaeuser (Frederick K.) Award: 819
WGN Continental Broadcasting Company (Chicago): 2154
Wheat Industry Research Council (Australia): 359
Wheeler (James R.) Fellowship: 170
Wheeler (Tessa and Mortimer) Grants: 1939
Whitbread & Company Ltd. (UK): 379
White House Fellowships (USA): 2156
White (John W.) Fellowship: 170

White (Joseph Senior) Fellowship: 1750
White (Sir William) Scholarship: 1777
White (William Allen) Foundation (Lawrence, Kans.): 2155
Whitman (Walt) Award: 2
Whitney (Helen Hay) Foundation, Inc. (USA): 2157
Whitney (John Hay) Foundation (USA): 2158
Whittaker (Hermon) Bursaries: 401
Whitworth Foundation (UK): 1847
Whyte (Ian) Award: 1863
Wieland (Heinrich) Prize: 1256
Wieniawski (Henryk) International Competition (Poznań): 2159
Wightman Award: 845
Wilder (Laura Ingalls) Medal: 132
Wildlife Management Institute (USA): 2160
Wiley (Bell I.) Prize: 1463
Wiley (Harvey W.) Award: 264
Wilhelm (R.H.) Award: 120
Willey (Vernon) Trust (NZ): 2161
Williams (D. Elizabeth) Fellowship: 109
Williams (Francis) Prize: 1410
Williams (Robert H.) Award: 759
Williams (William Carlos) Award: 1675
Williamsburg Seminar Scholarships: 1527
Williams's (Dr.) Trust (UK): 721
Williston (Arthur L.) Medal: 190
Wilson (Alice E.) Grants: 477
Wilson (Edward) Fellowship: 28
Wilson (H.W.) Awards: 494
Wilson (John Rowan) Award: 1563
Wilson Ornithological Society (USA): 2164, 2165
Wilson (Thomas J.) Prize: 886
Wilson (Winifred) Bursary: 2023
Wilson (Woodrow) Foundation (USA): 161
Wilson (Woodrow) International Center for Scholars (Washington, D.C.): 2162
Winchell (Walter) Cancer Fund (USA): 1829, 1830
Wingate (Harold H.) Awards: 1410
Winkler (Carl A.) Fellowship: 1695
Winter (E.B.) Scholarship: 1977
Winther (Oscar O.) Award: 2153
Winthrop Foundation: 1752
Wisconsin State Historical Society: 2001
Wiseman Prize: 1891
Wolff (Harold G.), M.D. Award: 61
Wolfson Fellowships: 389
Wolfson Foundation (UK): 2166
Women's Medical Association of the City of New York: 2167
Women's National Farm and Garden Association, Inc. (USA): 2168
Wood (Audrey) Playwriting Competition: 2169
Wood (C.I. and F.W.) Scholarship: 2203
Wood (L.B.) Scholarship: 2101

Woods Hole Oceanographic Institution (Woods Hole, Mass.): 2170-2172
Wooldridge Farm Fellowships: 218
Woolley (Harriet Hale) Scholarships: 2086
Workmen's Circle Award: 1176
World Alliance of Young Men's Christian Associations: 2173
World Bank: 743
World Book Scholarships: 494
World Council of Management: 2174
World Federation for Mental Health: 2175
World Health Organization: 2176
World Literature Today (USA): 2177
World Meteorological Organization: 2178
World Pathology Foundation: 2179
World Press Institute (USA): 2180
World Rehabilitation Fund: 2181
World University Service (UK): 2182
World Wildlife Fund: 2183
World Wildlife Fund Australia: 2184
World Wildlife Fund—U.S.: 2185
World Young Women's Christian Association: 2186
World Zionist Organization—American Section, Inc.: 2187
Worldbook-Childcraft Award: 530
Worshipful Company of Musicians (UK): 814, 2188
Worthington (Henry R.) Award: 190
Woursell Stipend: 762
Wright Brothers Medal: 1944
Wright (Elizur) Award: 167
Wright (Gerald) Scholarship: 753
Writer's Digest (USA): 2189
Wurlitzer (Helene) Foundation of New Mexico: 2190

Xerox Canada, Inc.: 2191
Xerox Corporation (USA): 746

Yaddo (Saratoga Springs, N.Y.): 2192
Yale Center for British Art (New Haven, Conn.): 2193
Yale University Press (New Haven, Conn.): 377, 2194
Yamagiwa-Yoshida Grants: 1137
Yivo Institute for Jewish Research (USA): 2195-2197
YMCA: 2173
Yorkshire Post (UK): 2198
Young Concert Artists, Inc. (USA): 2199
Young Musicians Foundation (USA): 2200
Young (Thomas) Medal and Prize: 996
Youth and Music of Germany: 2201
Yugoslav Government: 295, 801
YWCA: 2186
YWCA of Australia: 2202, 2203

Zahasky (Mary C.) Awards: 88
Zambia Government: 597
Zaheer Science Foundation (India): 2204
Zelosky (William and Mildred) Grants: 1201
Zimbabwe Government: 597
Zimber (Michalina and Herman) Scholarship: 1201
Zochonis (C.P.) Fellowship: 402
Zonta International (USA): 2205
Zworykin (Vladimir K.) Award: 979

BIBLIOGRAPHY

The following publications may also be of interest to those seeking financial support for their studies:

International

Study Abroad XXII, 1981-82, 1982-83. 1980. Lists international scholarships and courses from United Nations organizations, intergovernmental programmes, international non-governmental organizations, as well as some of the major scholarships and courses offered by national organizations, universities, etc. Available from Unesco offices or government booksellers.

World Dictionary of Awards and Prizes. 1979. A guide to awards, prizes, medals and lectureships worldwide. *Europa Publications, 18 Bedford Square, London WC1B 3JN.*

The Commonwealth

Awards for Commonwealth University Academic Staff 1981-83. 1980. Lists fellowships, visiting professorships, etc. open to university staff in a Commonwealth country who wish to carry out research, make study visits, or teach for a while in another Commonwealth country. *Association of Commonwealth Universities, 36 Gordon Square, London WC1H OPF.*

Scholarships Guide for Commonwealth Postgraduate Students 1980-82. 1979. Lists scholarships and other awards for postgraduate students wishing to continue their university studies in a Commonwealth country other than their own. *Association of Commonwealth Universities, 36 Gordon Square, London WC1H OPF.*

Australia

Awards for Postgraduate Study in Australia (Handbook of Grants 1). 4th ed., 1979. Lists fellowships and scholarships tenable at universities in Australia. Published in association with the Australian Vice-Chancellors' Committee and the Australia Conference of Principals of Colleges of Advanced Education by the *Graduate Careers Council of Australia, P.O. Box 28, Parkville, Victoria 3052.*

Awards for Postgraduate Study Overseas (Handbook of Grants 2). 4th ed., 1979. Lists scholarships, fellowships and grants for study leave open to Australians for study overseas. Published in association with the Australian Vice-Chancellors' Committee and the Australian Conference of Principals of Colleges of Advanced Education by the *Graduate Careers Council of Australia, P.O. Box 28, Parkville, Victoria 3052.*

Grants for University Research in Australia (Handbook of Grants 3). 3rd ed., 1981. Lists research and project grants, and grants-in-aid tenable at Australian universities and research institutions. Published in association with the Australian Vice-Chancellors' Committee by the *Graduate Careers Council of Australia, P.O. Box 28, Parkville, Victoria 3052.*

South Africa

Awards Available for Post-Graduate Study in the Republic of South Africa and Overseas. Lists many awards tenable at universities. *Human Sciences Research Council, Private Bag 41, Pretoria.*

United Kingdom

Scholarships Abroad. September annually. Lists awards offered to British students by overseas agencies, which are administered in the UK by the British Council. *British Council, 10 Spring Gardens, London SW1A 2BN.*

United States

Foundation Grants to Individuals. 2nd ed., 1979. Lists awards and loans available from many US foundations. *Foundation Center, 888 7th Ave., New York, NY 10019.*

Fulbright Grants and other grants for graduate study abroad 1982-83. Identifies awards for US nationals under Fulbright-Hays Act and other US-foreign programs. *Institute of International Education, 809 United Nations Plaza, New York, NY 10017.*

GPSR Compliance
The European Union's (EU) General Product Safety Regulation (GPSR) is a set of rules that requires consumer products to be safe and our obligations to ensure this.

If you have any concerns about our products, you can contact us on

ProductSafety@springernature.com

In case Publisher is established outside the EU, the EU authorized representative is:

Springer Nature Customer Service Center GmbH
Europaplatz 3
69115 Heidelberg, Germany

www.ingramcontent.com/pod-product-compliance
Ingram Content Group UK Ltd.
Pitfield, Milton Keynes, MK11 3LW, UK
UKHW022229230426

12048UKWH00016BA/1151